Lecture Notes in Computer Science 4393

Commenced Publication in 1973
Founding and Former Series Editors:
Gerhard Goos, Juris Hartmanis, and Jan van Leeuwen

T0189700

Wolfgang Thomas   Pascal Weil (Eds.)

STACS 2007

24th Annual Symposium
on Theoretical Aspects of Computer Science
Aachen, Germany, February 22-24, 2007
Proceedings

 Springer

Volume Editors

Wolfgang Thomas
RWTH Aachen
Lehrstuhl Informatik 7
52056 Aachen, Germany
E-mail: thomas@informatik.rwth-aachen.de

Pascal Weil
Laboratoire Bordelais de Recherche en Informatique
Université de Bordeaux
33405 Talence Cedex, France
E-mail: pascal.weil@labri.fr

Library of Congress Control Number: 2007920489

CR Subject Classification (1998): F, E.1, I.3.5, G.2

LNCS Sublibrary: SL 1 – Theoretical Computer Science and General Issues

ISSN   0302-9743
ISBN-10   3-540-70917-7 Springer Berlin Heidelberg New York
ISBN-13   978-3-540-70917-6 Springer Berlin Heidelberg New York

Springer is a part of Springer Science+Business Media

springer.com

© Springer-Verlag Berlin Heidelberg 2007
Printed in Germany

Typesetting: Camera-ready by author, data conversion by Scientific Publishing Services, Chennai, India
Printed on acid-free paper   SPIN: 12020942   06/3142   5 4 3 2 1 0

Preface

The Symposium on Theoretical Aspects of Computer Science (STACS) is alternately held in France and in Germany. The conference of February 22-24, 2007, held at Aachen was the 24th in this series. Previous meetings took place in Paris (1984), Saarbrücken (1985), Orsay (1986), Passau (1987), Bordeaux (1988), Paderborn (1989), Rouen (1990), Hamburg (1991), Cachan (1992), Würzburg (1993), Caen (1994), München (1995), Grenoble (1996), Lübeck (1997), Paris (1998), Trier (1999), Lille (2000), Dresden (2001), Antibes (2002), Berlin (2003), Montpellier (2004), Stuttgart (2005), and Marseille (2006).

The interest in STACS has been increasing continuously in recent years. The STACS 2007 call for papers led to approximately 400 submissions from all over the world. We had a two-day physical meeting for the Program Committee at Aachen in November 2006 where all members of the committee were present. We would like to thank the Program Committee and all external referees for the valuable work they put into the reviewing process. Each submission was assigned to at least three Program Committee members, hence each member was in charge of about 70 papers. Only 56 papers (i.e., less than 15 % of the submissions) could be accepted, as we wanted to keep the conference in its standard format with only two parallel sessions.

We would like to thank the three invited speakers, S. Abiteboul, M.Y. Vardi and D. Wagner, for their contributions to the proceedings.

STACS 2007 received funds from Deutsche Forschungsgemeinschaft (DFG), Gesellschaft für Informatik (GI), and RWTH Aachen University; we thank them for their support.

Special thanks are due to A. Voronkov for his EasyChair software (www.easychair.org) and for his support in running it, as well as to A. Carayol for his intensive work in preparing the camera-ready copy of this proceedings volume.

December 2006

Wolfgang Thomas
Pascal Weil

Organization

STACS 2007 was organized by the Chair of Computer Science 7 (Logic and Theory of Discrete Systems) of RWTH Aachen University under the auspices of the Special Interest Groups for Theoretical Computer Science of the Gesellschaft für Informatik (GI).

Program Committee

Eugene Asarin (Université Paris 7)
Cristina Bazgan (Université Paris Dauphine)
Marie-Pierre Béal (Université de Marne-la-Vallée)
Gerth Brodal (Aarhus Universitet)
Henning Fernau (Universität Tübingen)
Rudolf Fleischer (Fudan University, Shanghai)
Ricard Gavaldà (Universitat Politècnica de Catalunya)
Joachim Giesen (Max-Planck-Institut für Informatik, Saarbrücken)
Edith Hemaspaandra (Rochester Institute of Technology)
Martin Hofmann (Universität München)
Sophie Laplante (Université Paris 11)
Rajeev Raman (University of Leicester)
R. Ramanujam (Institute of Mathematical Sciences, Chennai)
Christian Scheideler (Technische Universität München)
Anand Srivastav (Universität Kiel)
Wolfgang Thomas (RWTH, Aachen), Co-chair
Pascal Weil (Université Bordeaux 1), Co-chair

Organizing Committee

Erich Grädel
Christof Löding
Peter Rossmanith
Wolfgang Thomas (Chair)
Berthold Vöcking

Referees

Scott Aaronson	Luca Aceto	Pavan Aduri
Slim Abdennadher	Jiri Adámek	Klaus Aehlig
Parosh Abdulla	Ben Adida	Hassene Aissi
Andreas Abel	Bharat Adsul	Deepak Ajwani

Ali Akhavi
Julien Allali
Eric Allender
Jan Altenbernd
Ernst Althaus
Carme Àlvarez
Roberto Amadio
Klaus Ambos-Spies
Christoph Ambühl
Ola Angelsmark
Marcella Anselmo
Pavlos Antoniou
Luis Antunes
V. Arvind
Albert Atserias
Yossi Azar
Christine Bachoc
Maria-Florina Balcan
Andreas Baltz
Evripidis Bampis
Nikhil Bansal
Jeremy Barbay
David A. Barrington
Rana Barua
A. Baskar
Frédérique Bassino
Surender Baswana
Michael Bauland
Paul Beame
Danièle Beauquier
Veronica Becher
Nicolas Bedon
Rene Beier
Pascal Berthomé
Valérie Berthé
Dietmar Berwanger
Ivona Bezakova
Nicole Bidoit
Francine Blanchet-Sadri
Andreas Blass
Guillaume Blin
Johannes Blömer
Henrik Blunck
Luc Boasson
Hans L. Bodlaender

Prosenjit Bose
Ahmed Bouajjani
Felix Brandt
Franck van Breugel
Véronique Bruyère
Francois Bry
Anne Brüggemann-Klein
Kevin Buchin
Harry Buhrman
Costas Busch
Thierry Cachat
Luís Caires
Arnaud Carayol
Arturo Carpi
Olivier Carton
John Case
Jorge Castro
Didier Caucal
Frédéric Cazals
Julien Cervelle
Kevin Chang
Krishnendu Chatterjee
Arkadev Chattopadhyay
Kaustuv Chaudhuri
Frédéric Chazal
Otfried Cheong
Andrea Clementi
Thomas Colcombet
Richard Cole
Hubert Comon-Lundh
Matthew Cook
Colin Cooper
Graham Cormode
José Correa
Bruno Courcelle
Maxime Crochemore
Victor Dalmau
Peter Damaschke
Carsten Damm
Samir Datta
Anuj Dawar
Wolfgang Degen
Charles Delorme
Marc Demange
Frank Drewes

Gérard Duchamp
Philippe Duchon
Vida Dujmović
Arnaud Durand
Jérôme Durand-Lose
Christoph Dürr
Cynthia Dwork
John Eblen
Michael Eckert
Thomas Eiter
Leah Epstein
Thomas Erlebach
Zoltán Ésik
Juan Luis Esteban
Rolf Fagerberg
Piotr Faliszewski
Lene Favrholdt
Uriel Feige
Michael Fellows
Jiří Fiala
Marcelo Fiore
Francesca Fiorenzi
Felix Fischer
Stephan Flake
Jörg Flum
Fedor Fomin
Lance Fortnow
Jean-Claude Fournier
Pierre Fraigniaud
John Franco
Gudmund S. Frandsen
Tom Friedetzky
Matteo Frigo
Stanley P. Y. Fung
Stefan Funke
Kim Gabarró
Anna Gal
Bernd Gärtner
Sumit Ganguly
Raúl García-Patrón
Gemma C. Garriga
William Gasarch
Leszek Gasieniec
Joachim von zur Gathen
Cyril Gavoille

Markus Geyer
Dora Giammarresi
Jürgen Giesl
Robert Gilman
Michael Gnewuch
Mordecai Golin
Carla P. Gomes
Martin C. Golumbic
Teofilo Gonzalez
Rajeev Goré
Daniel Gottesman
Laurent Gourvès
Sathish Govindarajan
Maria Gradinariu
Serge Grigorieff
Dmitry Grigoriev
Martin Grohe
Roberto Grossi
Hermann Gruber
Jakob Grue Simonsen
Peter Grünwald
Erich Grädel
Allan G. Jørgensen
Joachim Gudmundsson
Irène Guessarian
Stefan Gulan
Jiong Guo
Michel Habib
Torben Hagerup
Vesa Halava
Magnús Halldórsson
Sariel Har-Peled
Tero Harju
Paul Harrenstein
Edmund Harriss
Aram Harrow
Refael Hassin
Peter Hauck
Mathias Hauptmann
Herman Haverkort
Nils Hebbinghaus
Pavol Hell
Sébastien Hémon
Danny Hermelin
Ulrich Hertrampf

John Hitchcock
Florent Hivert
Petr Hliněný
Michael Hoffmann
Markus Holzer
Christopher Homan
Hendrik Jan Hoogeboom
Peter Høyer
Juraj Hromkovič
Falk Hüffner
Mathilde Hurand
Thore Husfeldt
David Ilcinkas
Costas Iliopoulos
Neil Immerman
Nicole Immorlica
Robert Irving
Kazuo Iwama
Riko Jacob
Robert Jaeschke
Klaus Jansen
Inuka Jayasekara
Emmanuel Jeandel
Mark Jerrum
Jan Johannsen
Vincent Jost
Ari Juels
Valentine Kabanets
Yuri Kalnishkan
Haim Kaplan
Marc Kaplan
Christos Kapoutsis
Juhani Karhumäki
Jarkko Kari
Wong Karianto
Marek Karpinski
Irit Katriel
Jonathan Katz
Michael Kaufmann
Dimitris Kavvadias
Julia Kempe
Iordanis Kerenidis
Delia Kesner
Daniel Keysers
Daniel Kirsten

Hartmut Klauck
Lasse Kliemann
Ton Kloks
Alexander Knapp
Christian Knauer
Timo Koetzing
Pascal Koiran
Arist Kojevnikov
Guy Kortsarz
Sven Kosub
Yiannis Koutis
Dan Král
Andreas Krebs
Martin Kreuzer
Danny Krizanc
Oliver Kullmann
Amit Kumar
K. Narayan Kumar
Clemens Kupke
Petr Kůrka
Piyush Kurur
Martin Kutrib
Ralf Küsters
Ugo dal Lago
Yassine Lakhnech
Gadi Landau
Martin Lange
Mike Langston
Lawrence L. Larmore
Benoit Larose
Sören Laue
Emmanuelle Lebhar
James R. Lee
Troy Lee
Hans Leiß
Hao Li
Yuri Lifshits
René Lindloh
Kamal Lodaya
Christof Löding
Markus Lohrey
Satya Lokam
Sylvain Lombardy
María López-Valdés
Antoni Lozano

Hsueh-I Lu
Joan Lucas
Gábor Lugosi
Ulrike von Luxburg
Alejandro Maass
P. Madhusudan
Frédéric Magniez
Meena Mahajan
Ali Ridha Mahjoub
J.A. Makowsky
Elitza Maneva
Sabrina Mantaci
Giovanni Manzini
Maurice Margenstern
Stuart Margolis
Conrado Martínez
Jiří Matoušek
E. Mayordomo Cámara
Catherine McCartin
Pierre McKenzie
Klaus Meer
Mark Mercer
Carlo Mereghetti
Wolfgang Merkle
Filippo Mignosi
Peter Bro Miltersen
Dieter Mitsche
Michael Mitzenmacher
Samuel E. Moelius III
Daniel Mölle
Manal Mohamed
Jérôme Monnot
Fabien de Montgolfier
Christopher Moore
G. Moreno Socías
Philippe Moser
Marcin Mucha
Markus Müller-Olm
Madhavan Mukund
Jochen Mundinger
Anca Muscholl
Veli Mäkinen
Norbert Müller
Stefan Näher
Assaf Naor

Rouven Naujoks
Gonzalo Navarro
Ashwin Nayak
Ralph Neininger
Jean Néraud
Uwe Nestmann
François Nicolas
Rolf Niedermeier
Jesper Buus Nielsen
Johan Nilsson
Noam Nisan
Nicolas Nisse
Damian Niwinski
Ilia Nouretdinov
Johannes Nowak
Elzbieta Nowicka
Yahav Nussbaum
Mitsunori Ogihara
Hans Jürgen Ohlbach
Martin Olsen
Ralf Osbild
Friedrich Otto
Joel Ouaknine
Sang-il Oum
Eric Pacuit
Paritosh K. Pandya
Rafael Pass
Dirk Pattinson
Christophe Paul
Gheorghe Pãun
Christian N. S. Pedersen
Andrzej Pelc
David Peleg
Paolo Penna
Giuseppe Persiano
Jean-Éric Pin
Nadia Pisanti
Greg Plaxton
Bruno Poizat
Sanjiva Prasad
Roberto De Prisco
Andrzej Proskurowski
Bartosz Przydatek
Evangelia Pyrga
Xavier Pérez

Yuri Rabinovich
J. Radhakrishnan
Tomasz Radzik
Stanislaw Radziszowski
Mathieu Raffinot
Daniel Raible
Jean-Francois Raskin
Dror Rawitz
Ran Raz
Alexander Razborov
Andreas Razen
Jan Reimann
Klaus Reinhardt
Steffen Reith
Antonio Restivo
Eric Rivals
Mike Robson
Martin Rötteler
Dana Ron
Michel de Rougemont
Frances A. Rosamond
Adi Rosén
Dominique Rossin
Günter Rote
Jörg Rothe
Salvador Roura
Bimal Roy
Paul Ruet
Irena Rusu
Mugizi R. Rwebangira
Ashish Sabharwal
Michael Sagraloff
Jacques Sakarovitch
Kai T. Salomaa
Peter Sanders
Volkmar Sauerland
Dietmar Saupe
Saket Saurabh
Francesco Scarcello
Nicolas Schabanel
Marcus Schaefer
Sebastian Schaffert
Christian Schaffner
Dominik Scheder
Ingo Schiermeyer

Stefan Schimanski
Ilka Schnoor
Ulrich Schöpp
Eva Schuberth
Jennifer Seberry
Detlef Seese
Helmut Seidl
Pranab Sen
Olivier Serre
Hadas Shachnai
Qiaosheng Shi
David B. Shmoys
Amin Shokrollahi
R. K. Shyamasundar
Sunil Simon
G. Sivakumar
S. Sivaramakrishnan
Robert Špalek
Bettina Speckmann
Joel Spencer
Jerry Spinrad
Jiri Srba
Aravind Srinivasan
Ludwig Staiger
Ian Stark
Elias C. Stavropoulos
Daniel Stefankovic
Ulrike Stege
Angelika Steger
Jochen J. Steil
Frank Stephan
Howard Straubing
Volker Strumpen

Aaron Stump
C. R. Subramanian
Karol Suchan
Jan Šupol
S. P. Suresh
Maxim Sviridenko
Tibor Szabó
Stefan Szeider
Géraud Sénizergues
Christino Tamon
Till Tantau
Véronique Terrier
Pascal Tesson
Guillaume Theyssier
Thomas Thierauf
Mikkel Thorup
Sophie Tison
Arnaud Tisseran
Ioan Todinca
Jacobo Torán
Patrick Traxler
Denis Trystram
Christian Urban
Mario Valencia-Pabon
Leslie Valiant
Gabriel Valiente
Kasturi Varadarajan
Vinodchandran Variyam
Yde Venema
V. Venkateswaran
Juan Vera
Éric Colin de Verdière
Nikolai Vereshchagin

Elias Vicari
Adrien Vieilleribière
Tiziano Villa
Berthold Vöcking
Roland Vollmar
Heribert Vollmer
Tjark Vredeveld
Imrich Vrťo
Uli Wagner
Charles Wallace
Guilin Wang
Rolf Wanka
John Watrous
Ingmar Weber
Sebastian Wernicke
Sören Werth
Matthias Westermann
Thomas Wilke
Andreas Winter
Ronald de Wolf
Prudence Wong
Thomas Worsch
Qin Xin
Boting Yang
Neal Young
Sheng Yu
Bruno Zanuttini
Marcin Zawada
Qing Zhang
Wiesław Zielonka
Michal Ziv
Philipp Zumstein

Table of Contents

Session 5A

Session 5B

Session 6A

Session 6B

Session 7A

Session 11B

A Calculus and Algebra
for Distributed Data Management*

Serge Abiteboul

INRIA-Futurs, Orsay & Univ. Paris 11
`firstname.lastname@inria.fr`

Abstract. The sharing of content by communities of users (e.g., scientists) in a P2P context remains cumbersome. We argue that main reasons for this is the lack of calculus and algebra for distributed data management. We present the ActiveXML language that extends the XML language with features to handle distribution. More precisely, ActiveXML documents are XML documents with a special syntax for specifying the embedding of Web service calls, e.g. XML queries such as XQueries. We also present ActiveXML algebra that extends ActiveXML notably with explicit control of data exchanges. ActiveXML algebra allows describing query plans, and exchanging them between peers.

1 Introduction

The field of distributed data management [17] has centered for many years around the relational model. More recently, the Web has made the world wide and intranet publication of data much simpler, by relying on HTML, Web browsers, plain-text search engines and query forms. The situation has also dramatically improved with the introduction of XML [22] and Web services [25]. Together, these two standards provide an infrastructure for distributed computing at large, independent of any platform, system or programming language, i.e., the appropriate framework for distributed management of information. However, the sharing of content by communities of users (e.g., scientists) in a P2P context remains cumbersome. We argue that main reasons for this is the lack of calculus and algebra for distributed data management and propose such languages based on Web standards, namely XML and Web services.

In [8], we propose the *data ring* that can be seen as a network analogue of a database or a content warehouse. The vision is to build a P2P middleware system that can be used by a community of non-experts, such as scientists, to build content sharing communities in a declarative fashion. Essentially, a peer joins a data ring by specifying which data (or services in general) are to be shared, without having to specify a schema for the data, load it in a store, create any indices on it, or specify anything complex regarding its distribution. The data ring enables users to perform declarative queries over the aggregated

---

* This work has been partially supported by the ANR Project WebContent and the EC project Edos [13] on the development and distribution of open source software.

W. Thomas and P. Weil (Eds.): STACS 2007, LNCS 4393, pp. 1–11, 2007.

data, and becomes responsible for reorganizing the physical storage of data and for controlling its distribution. Thus a primary focus of the data ring is *simplicity of use*. To achieve these goals, we identified a number of challenges:

Self-administration. Since the users of the data ring are non-expert, the deployment of the ring and its administration should be almost effort-less. This means that a number of tasks such as the selection of access structures (indices) or the gathering of the statistics to be used by optimizers have to be fully automatic.

File management. Since a large part of the data is going to reside in file systems, we need very efficient processing and *optimization* of queries over files, including for instance the automatic selection of specific access structures over file collections.

Query language. To facilitate the exploitation of the ring by non-experts, the interfaces have to be mostly graphical and require the minimum expertise. They therefore must be based on declarative languages (calculus) in the style of relational calculus, rather than on languages such as Java or Ajax that require programming skills.

Query optimization. Query optimization has, by nature, to be distributed and peers should be able to exchange query plans. This motivates adopting an algebra for describing distributed query plans interleaving query optimization, query evaluation, and possibly, error recovery and transaction processing.

We present ActiveXML, a declarative framework that harnesses XML and Web services for the integration and management of distributed data. An ActiveXML document is an XML document where some of the data is given explicitly, while other portions are given only intensionally by means of embedded calls to Web services, typically XML queries. By calling the services, one can obtain up-to-date information. In particular, ActiveXML provides control over the activation of service calls both from the client side (pull) or from the server side (push).

It should be noted that the idea of mixing data and code is not new, e.g., stored procedures in relational systems [19], method calls in object-oriented databases [10], and queries in scripting languages such as PHP. The novelty is that since both XML and Web services are standards, ActiveXML documents can be universally understood, and therefore can be universally *exchanged*.

We also present the ActiveXML algebra that extends ActiveXML in two main directions: (i) with generic services that can be supported by several peers (e.g., query services), (ii) with explicit control of the evaluation of ActiveXML documents (eval operator) and of data exchange (send and receive operators). The algebra can be used to describe query (evaluation) plans. Using rewrite rules, query plans may be optimized in a standard way. More fundamentally, the query plans are distributed and can be exchanged between peers. Thus the tasks of query evaluation and optimization can be distributed among the peers of the network.

The ActiveXML project has been going on for several years. A system is now available as open source [9]. In [16], a technique to decide whether or not calls should be activated based on typing is introduced. The general problem has deep connections with tree automata [12] and alternating automata, i.e., automata alternating between universal and existential states [18]. Optimization issues in the context of ActiveXML are presented in [2]. In [5], a framework for managing distribution and replication in the context of ActiveXML is considered. Foundations of ActiveXML are studied in [3]. A preliminary version of the algebra appeared in [7].

We conclude this introduction by a brief discussion of XML and Web services.

```
<directory>
  <movies>
    <director>Hitchcock</director>
    <sc service="movies@allocine.com" >Hitchcock</sc>
    <movie> <title>Vertigo</title>
      <actor>J. Stewart</actor> <actor>K. Novak</actor>
      <reviews> <sc service="reviews@cine.com" >Vertigo</sc></reviews>
    </movie>
    <movie> <title>Psycho</title>
      <actor>N. Bates</actor>
      <reviews> <sc service="reviews@cine.com" >Psycho</sc></reviews>
    </movie>
  </movies>
</directory>
```

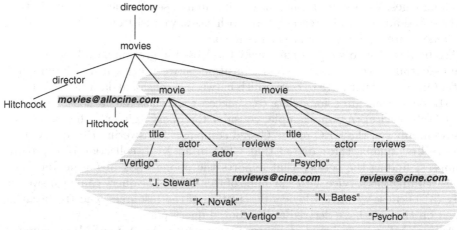

Fig. 1. An ActiveXML document and its tree representation

XML and Web services. XML is a semistructured data exchange format [4] promoted by the Word-Wide-Web Consortium and widely adopted by industry. An XML document can be viewed as a labeled, unranked, ordered tree, as seen in the example[1] of Figure 1 (ignoring the grey area for now). Unlike HTML, XML does not provide any information about the document presentation. This is typically provided externally using a CSS or XSL style-sheet. XML documents may be typed, e.g., using XML Schema [23], and may be queried using query languages such as XPath or XQuery [24]. Web services consist of an array of emerging standards. For instance, to find a desired service, one can query a UDDI [21] directory. To understand how to interact with the service, one relies on WSDL [26], something like Corba's IDL. One can then access the service using SOAP [20], an XML-based lightweight protocol for the exchange of information.

The article is organized as follows. The calculus is discussed in Section 2 and the algebra in Section 3. The last section is a conclusion.

2   A Stream Calculus: ActiveXML

In this section, we briefly describe ActiveXML. Details may be found from [9] as well as papers on ActiveXML and the open-source code of an ActiveXML peer.

The success of the relational model essentially comes from the combination of a declarative language (relational calculus), an equivalent relational algebra, and optimization techniques based on rewrite rules. There have been a number of extensions such as object databases, but the classical pattern (calculus, algebra, rewrite rules) proved its robustness. It should also be adopted in the data ring context. However, the situation is essentially different (distributed vs. centralized, semi-structured vs. very structured) so requires a complete overhauling of the languages. We present a calculus for distributed semi-structured data in this section and an algebra in Section 3. In both cases, we insist on the features that we believe are fundamental for such languages.

We believe that to support effectively the loose integration paradigm of data, one essential aspect is the seamless transition between explicit and intentional data. One should not have to distinguish between extensional data (e.g., XML or HTML pages) and intensional data (e.g., access to a relational database provided by a Web service). As an example, consider the query "give me the name and phone number of the CEO of the Gismo company". Answering this query may require first finding the name of that CEO in an XML collection of company synopses, finding the service that exports the phone book of Gismo Inc, and finally calling this service with the name of this CEO. The query can be answered only (a) because we have a logical description of the resources, and (b) because based on that, we have derived a distributed query plan.

ActiveXML was designed to capture such issues. An ActiveXML document is an XML document where certain elements denote embedded calls to Web

---

[1] We will see in the next section that this XML document is also an ActiveXML document.

services. For instance, the company synopsis may contain the CEO phone number as a Web service call. The service calls embedded in the document provide intensional data in the sense of deductive databases [6]. Now suppose that the phone number of the CEO changes, then the second time we call the service, the result changes. So, the home page of the company that includes this service call changes. Thus the embedding of service calls is also capturing active data in the sense of active databases [11].

Note that the use of intensional information is quite standard on the Web, e.g. in PHP-mySQL. It is also common in databases, see object or deductive databases. The main novelty is that the intensional data is provided by a Web service. Thus the corresponding service calls may be activated by any peer and do not have to be evaluated prior to sending the document.

In what sense can this be viewed as a calculus for distributed semi-structured data? First, we rely on some calculus for *local* semi-structured data. From a practical viewpoint, we can use the standard declarative language, XQuery. But one could use any calculus over XML as well. ActiveXML provides the support for handling distribution. The interaction with local queries is achieved by using query services. In some sense, the resulting language may be viewed as a deductive database language such as datalog [6] with XQuery playing the role of the single datalog rule and with ActiveXML acting as the "glue" between the rules, i.e., as the datalog program. Negation may be handled in any standard way [6]. Clearly, distribution introduces new issues with respect to evaluation and optimization, notably the detection of termination [1].

Henceforth, we assume that every peer exports its resources in the form of ActiveXML documents or Web services. The logical layer thus consists of a set of ActiveXML documents and services and their owning peers. The external layer will be dealing with the semantics (e.g., ontologies), but this aspect will be ignored here. A computation will consist in local processing and exchanging such documents.

ActiveXML is an XML dialect, as illustrated by the document in Figure 1. (Note that the syntax is simplified in the example for purposes of presentation.) The **sc** elements are used to denote embedded service calls. Here, reviews are obtained from cine.com, and information about more Hitchcock movies may be obtained from allocine.com. The data obtained by a call to a Web service may be viewed as intensional, as it is not originally present. It may also be viewed as dynamic, since the same service call possibly returns different data when called at different times. When a service call is activated, the data returned is inserted in the document that contains the call. Therefore, documents evolve in time as a consequence of call activations. Of particular importance is thus the decision to activate a particular service call.

Two aspects are essential to the framework and motivate basing it on XML streams (as in ActiveXML) and not simply on XML documents:

Push vs. Pull. In pull mode, a query-service is called to obtain information. But we are often interested on the Web in query subscription. The result of a subscription is typically a stream of answers, e.g., notifications of certain events of interest. A company synopsis may include such a service to, for instance, obtain the news of the company. Such a subscription feature is also essential for supporting a number of functionalities ranging from P2P monitoring, to synchronization and reconciliation of replicas, or gathering statistics.

Recursion. The embedded service calls may be seen as views in the spirit of those found at the core of deductive databases. In classical deductive databases, recursion comes from data relationships and recursive queries such as *ancestor*. In our setting, recursion kicks in similarly and also from the XPATH // primitive. But more fundamentally, recursion comes from the graph nature of the Web: site1 calls site2 that calls site3 that calls site1, etc. Indeed, the use of recursive query processing techniques in P2P contexts has been recently highlighted in several works in topics as different as message rooting on the Web [15] and error diagnosis in telecom networks [1]. Now, recursive query processing clearly requires the use of streams.

The basis of a theory proposed in [3,1] makes two fundamental simplifying assumptions:

set-oriented. The ordering in XML is a real cause of difficulty. We assume that the documents are labeled, unranked, *unordered* trees.

Query-services. If the services are black boxes, there is little reasoning one can do about particular computations. We assume that the queries are defined logically (e.g., by conjunctions of tree pattern queries over the documents.)

Since documents contain intensional data (views), this result in a setting quite close to deductive databases. In [3], positive results are exhibited for limited query languages. They are obtained by combining techniques from deductive databases (such as Query-sub-Query) and from tree automata.

3   A Stream Algebra

Besides the logical level, our thesis is that a language in the style of ActiveXML should also serve as the basis for the physical model. In particular, the use of streams is unavoidable: see trivially, how answers are returned by Google or try to send 100K in a standard Web service without obtaining a *timeout*. As shown in a recent work [7], distributed query evaluation and optimization can be naturally captured using ActiveXML algebraic expressions, based on the exchange of distributed query execution plans. The expressions include standard algebraic XML operations and send/receive operators, all over XML streams. Note that these may be seen as particular workflow descriptions, very particular ones of a strong database flavor. Thus, we propose that the physical model be based on a the ActiveXML algebra [7].

The algebraic evaluation of queries is performed by collaborating query processors installed on different peers exchanging ActiveXML data in a streaming manner. Query optimization is performed also in a distributed manner by algebraic query rewriting. Standard distributed query optimization techniques can all be described using the proposed framework and simple rewrite rules in the language.

The ActiveXML algebra is an extension of the ActiveXML language with two main features: (i) generic data and services and (ii) a more explicit control of execution (e.g., eval) and distribution (send/receive). *Generic* data and services are data and services available on several sites, an essential feature to capture replication and the fact that a query service may be evaluated by any peer with query processing facilities (see [5]). We also provide the capability to explicitly control the shipping of data and queries, an essential feature to specify the delegation of computations (see [1]).

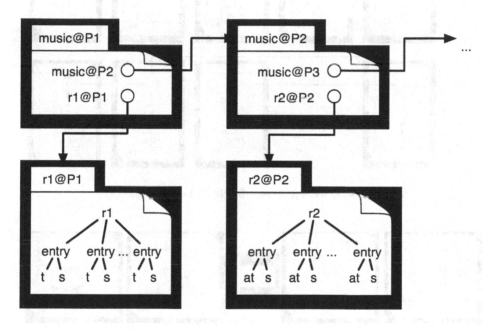

Fig. 2. A graphical representation of ActiveXML data

An example will best illustrate this principle. Consider the data described in Figure 2. We use here a visual representation of ActiveXML documents. Peer $p1$ and $p2$ have their own collections of music with metadata described in relations $r1, r2$, respectively. Peer $p1$ knows about s(ingers) and t(itles), whereas $p2$ knows about s(ingers) and a(lbum) t(itles). Peer $p1$ also knows that $p2$ has some music; $p2$ knows that $p3$ (not shown here) has some; $p3$ knows $p4$, etc. The metadata of $p3, p4, p5$ are organized as that of $p1$. The actual texts underneath the tags s, t, at are not shown. Now suppose that $p1$ wants to get the titles of songs by Carla Bruni. Figure 3 shows three different query plans. Each box describes some peer computation. Query Plan (a) is the one that would result from an evaluation

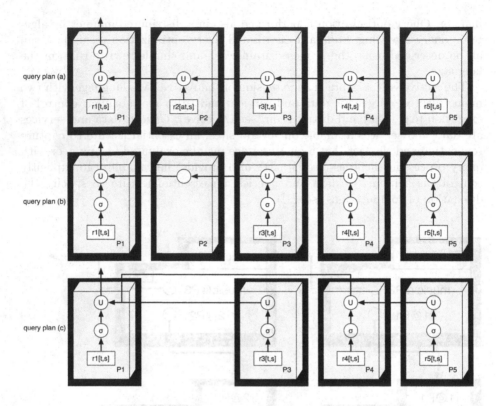

Fig. 3. Three equivalent distributed query plans

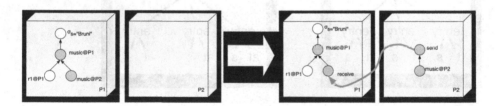

Fig. 4. An algebraic rewriting

of the query without optimization, i.e., from applying the pure semantics of ActiveXML. Query plan (b) results from pushing selections, while Query plan (c) is obtained by also optimizing data transfers (cutting some middle persons in data transmissions). One (particularly interesting) rewrite rule is illustrated in Figure 4. Consider only the shaded nodes. To perform the evaluation, an external service call is replaced by a receive node and remotely a computation is activated. It is requested that its result be sent to the location of the receive node. The communication is asynchronous.

We can make the following observations:

1. Peers 1 and 2 can already be producing answers, while Peer 3 is still optimizing the request it receives, while Peer 5 is still not even aware of the query. This is illustrating the need for streaming, Peer 2 can send answers to Peer 1 before obtaining the entire data she has to transmit.
2. Each peer separately receives a request and is fully in charge of evaluating it. (Some optimization guidelines may be provided as well.) For instance Peer 2 receives a query where she cannot really contribute and may decide to cut herself out of it to ask Peer 3 to evaluate its part and send the result directly to Peer 1.
3. We assumed so far that the peer cooperate to evaluate a query. Think now that the goal is to support a subscription. Then the same plans apply. Suppose a new song of Carla Bruni is entered in Site 3. Then it is sent to Site 1 (with Query Plan (c)), then produced as a new answer unless this title has already been produced.

In all cases, a query (subscription) for the songs of Carla Bruni (at the logical layer) is translated to a distributed plan (at the physical layer). Observe that the physical plan is essentially a workflow of Web services (i.e., an ActiveXML document), where the services encapsulate the different plan operators and the respective locations encode the distribution of computation and the flow of data. The main idea therefore is that the complete plan itself (or a portion of it), along with its current state of execution, can be described as an ActiveXML document, which in turn can be exchanged between peers in order to support query optimization and error recovery in a distributed fashion.

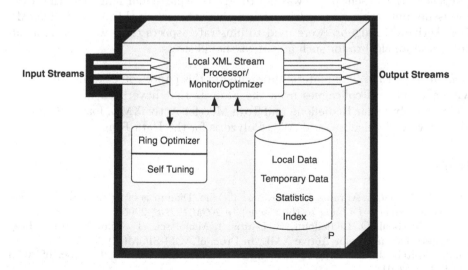

Fig. 5. Functional architecture

Another important element in the Figure 3 is the distinction between local query evaluation (inside each box) that is the responsibility of a local system, perhaps a relational system, and global query evaluation. The functional architecture of a peer query processor is shown in Figure 5. See the various components and in particular the local query optimizer and the local component performing global query optimization that collaborates with other peers to perform global query optimization. Essentially, this separation leads to physical plans that combine local query processing with distributed evaluation. Clearly, a collaboration between the two systems (local and global) is preferable but is unlikely to be widespread in the near future. This implies that we will have to view the local query optimizers as boxes with possibly different querying capabilities, in the same vein as mediation systems [14].

4   Conclusion

It is not necessary to insist on the importance of distributed data management. Recent years have seen the arrival of a number of software tools that participate in such activity: structured p2p network such as Chord or Pastry, XML repositories such as Xyleme or DBMonet, file sharing systems such as BitTorrent or Kazaa, distributed storage systems such as OceanStore or Google File System. content delivery network such as Coral or Akamai, multicast systems such as Bullet or Avalanche, Pub/Sub system such as Scribe or Hyper, application platform suites as proposed by Sun or Oracle for integrating software components, data integration as provided in warehouse or mediator systems.

A formal foundation for distributed data management is still to come. The purpose of the present paper was not to advertise particular languages that close the issue, but rather to encourage researchers to work in this area. ActiveXML and ActiveXML algebra were used to illustrate aspects that, we believe, a calculus and an algebra for such a context should stress.

Acknowledgments. The material presented in this paper comes from joint works with a number of colleagues from the projects that have been mentioned and most notably, Omar Benjelloun and Tova Milo for ActiveXML, Ioana Manolescu for ActiveXML Algebra, and Alkis Polyzotis for the Data Ring.

References

1. S. Abiteboul, Z. Abrams, S. Haar, and T. Milo. Diagnosis of asynchronous discrete event systems - Datalog to the rescue! In *ACM PODS*, 2005.
2. S. Abiteboul, O. Benjelloun, B. Cautis, I. Manolescu, T. Milo, N. Preda, Lazy Query Evaluation for Active XML, In Proc. of ACM SIGMOD 2004.
3. S. Abiteboul, O. Benjelloun, T. Milo, Positive Active XML, In Proc. of ACM PODS, 2004.
4. S. Abiteboul, P. Buneman, D. Suciu, Data on the Web, Morgan Kaufmann, 2000.
5. S. Abiteboul, A. Bonifati, G. Cobena, I. Manolescu, T. Milo, Active XML Documents with Distribution and Replication, In Proc. of ACM SIGMOD, 2003.

6. S. Abiteboul, R. Hull, and V. Vianu. *Foundations of Databases.* Addison-Wesley, Reading-Massachusetts, 1995.
7. Abiteboul, S., I. Manolescu, E. Taropa. A framework for distributed XML data management. In *Proc. EDBT.* 2006.
8. Serge Abiteboul, Neoklis Polyzotis, The Data Ring: Community Content Sharing In Proceedings of CIDR, 2007.
9. The ActiveXML project, INRIA, http://activexml.net.
10. The Object Database Standard: ODMG-93, editor R. G. G. Cattell, Morgan Kaufmann, San Mateo, California, 1994.
11. Sharma Chakravarthy, Jennifer Widom: Foreword: Special Issue on Active Database Systems. J. Intell. Inf. Syst. 7(2): 109-110. 1996.
12. H. Comon, M. Dauchet, R. Gilleron, F. Jacquemard, D. Lugiez, S. Tison, M. Tommasi, Tata, Tree Automata Techniques and Applications, www.grappa.univ-lille3.fr/tata/
13. The Edos Project, http://www.edos-project.org/
14. Laura M. Haas, Donald Kossmann, Edward L. Wimmers, and Jun Yang. Optimizing Queries Across Diverse Data Sources. In *vldb97*, pages 276–285, San Francisco, CA, USA, 1997. Morgan Kaufmann Publishers Inc.
15. M. Harren, J. Hellerstein, R. Huebsch, B. Thau Loo, S. Shenker, and I. Stoica. Complex queries in dht-based peer-to-peer networks. In *Peer-to-Peer Systems Int. Workshop*, 2002.
16. T. Milo, S. Abiteboul, B. Amann, O. Benjelloun, F. Dang Ngoc, Exchanging Intensional XML Data, In Proc. of ACM SIGMOD, 2003.
17. M.T. Ozsu, P. Valduriez, Principles of Distributed Database Systems, Prentice-Hall, 1999.
18. A. Muscholl, T. Schwentick, L. Segoufin, Active Context-Free Games, Symposium on Theoretical Aspects of Computer Science, 2004.
19. J.D. Ullman, Principles of Database and Knowledge Base Systems, Volume I, II, Computer Science Press, 1988.
20. The SOAP Specification, version 1.2, http://www.w3.org/TR/soap12/
21. Universal Description, Discovery and Integration of Web Services (UDDI), http://www.uddi.org/
22. The Extensible Markup Language (XML), http://www.w3.org/XML/
23. XML Typing Language (XML Schema), http://www.w3.org/XML/Schema
24. An XML Query Language, http://www.w3.org/TR/xquery/
25. The W3C Web Services Activity, http://www.w3.org/2002/ws/
26. The Web Services Description Language (WSDL), http://www.w3.org/TR/wsdl/

The Büchi Complementation Saga

Moshe Y. Vardi*

Rice University, Department of Computer Science, Rice University, Houston,
TX 77251-1892, U.S.A.
vardi@cs.rice.edu
http://www.cs.rice.edu/~vardi

Abstract. The complementation problem for nondeterministic word automata has numerous applications in formal verification. In particular, the language-containment problem, to which many verification problems are reduced, involves complementation. For automata on finite words, which correspond to safety properties, complementation involves determinization. The 2^n blow-up that is caused by the subset construction is justified by a tight lower bound. For Büchi automata on infinite words, which are required for the modeling of liveness properties, optimal complementation constructions are quite complicated, as the subset construction is not sufficient. We review here progress on this problem, which dates back to its introduction in Büchi's seminal 1962 paper.

1 Introduction

The complementation problem for nondeterministic word automata has numerous applications in formal verification. In order to check that the language of an automaton $\mathcal{A}_1$ is contained in the language of a second automaton $\mathcal{A}_2$, one checks that the intersection of $\mathcal{A}_1$ with an automaton that complements $\mathcal{A}_2$ is empty. Many problems in verification and design are reduced to language containment. In model checking, the automaton $\mathcal{A}_1$ corresponds to the system, and the automaton $\mathcal{A}_2$ corresponds to the property we wish to verify [21,37]. While it is easy to complement properties given in terms of formulas in temporal logic, complementation of properties given in terms of automata is not simple. Indeed, a word w is rejected by a nondeterministic automaton $\mathcal{A}$ if *all* runs of $\mathcal{A}$ on w rejects the word. Thus, the complementary automaton has to consider all possible runs, and complementation has the flavor of determinization.

For automata on finite words, determinization, and hence also complementation, is done via the subset construction [28]. Accordingly, if we start with a nondeterministic automaton with n states, the complementary automaton may have 2^n states. The exponential blow-up that is caused by the subset construction is justified by a tight lower bound: it is proved in [31] that for every $n > 1$, there exists a language L_n that is recognized by a nondeterministic automaton

* Supported in part by NSF grants CCR-9988322, CCR-0124077, CCR-0311326, and ANI-0216467, by BSF grant 9800096, and by a grant from the Intel Corporation. This paper is based on joint work with Orna Kupferman.

W. Thomas and P. Weil (Eds.): STACS 2007, LNCS 4393, pp. 12–22, 2007.

with n states, yet a nondeterministic automaton for the complement of L_n has at least 2^n states (see also [2]).

For Büchi automata on infinite words, which are required for the modeling of liveness properties, optimal complementation constructions are quite complicated, as the subset construction is not sufficient (but see erroneous claim in [25]). Due to the lack of a simple complementation construction, the user is typically required to specify the property by a deterministic Büchi automaton [21] (it is easy to complement a deterministic Büchi automaton), or to supply the automaton for the negation of the property [14]. Similarly, specification formalisms like ETL [38], which have automata within the logic, involve complementation of automata, and the difficulty of complementing Büchi automata is an obstacle to practical use [1]. In fact, even when the properties are specified in LTL, complementation is useful: the translators from LTL into automata have reached a remarkable level of sophistication (c.f., [5,33,10,11]). Even though complementation of the automata is not explicitly required, the translations are so involved that it is useful to checks their correctness, which involves complementation[1]. Complementation is interesting in practice also because it enables refinement and optimization techniques that are based on language containment rather than simulation [21][2]. Thus, an effective algorithm for the complementation of Büchi automata would be of significant practical value.

Efforts to develop complementation constructions for nondeterministic Büchi automata started early in the 60s, motivated by decision problems of second-order logics. Büchi introduced these automata in 1962 and described a complementation construction that involved a Ramsey-based combinatorial argument and a doubly-exponential blow-up in the state space [3]. Thus, complementing an automaton with n states resulted in an automaton with $2^{2^{O(n)}}$ states. In [32], an improved implementation of Büchi's construction is described, with only $2^{O(n^2)}$ states (see also [27]). Finally, in [29], Safra described a determinization construction, which also enables an $O(n^{O(n)})$ complementation construction, matching a lower bound of $n!$ described by Michel [23] (cf. [22]). Thus, from a theoretical point of view, some considered the problem solved since 1988, since we seem to have matching asymptotic upper and lower bounds.

Nevertheless, a careful analysis of the exact blow-up in Safra's and Michel's bounds reveals an exponential gap in the constants hiding in the $O()$ notations: while the upper bound on the number of states in the complementary automaton constructed by Safra is n^{2n}, Michel's lower bound involves only an $n!$ blow up, which is roughly $(n/e)^n$. This is in contrast with the case of automata on finite words, where, as mentioned above, the upper and lower bounds coincide. In the rest of this paper we describe more recent efforts to narrow this gap.

---

[1] For an LTL formula ψ, one typically checks that both the intersection of $\mathcal{A}_\psi$ with $\mathcal{A}_{\neg\psi}$ and the intersection of their complementary automata are empty.

[2] Since complementation of Büchi automata is complicated, current research is focused on ways in which fair simulation can approximate language containment [13], and ways in which the complementation construction can be circumvented by manually bridging the gap between fair simulation and language containment [15].

2 Background

Given an alphabet Σ, an *infinite word over* Σ is an infinite sequence $w = \sigma_0 \cdot \sigma_1 \cdot \sigma_2 \cdots$ of letters in Σ. An *automaton on infinite words* is $\mathcal{A} = \langle \Sigma, Q, Q_{in}, \rho, \alpha \rangle$, where Σ is the input alphabet, Q is a finite set of states, $\rho : Q \times \Sigma \to 2^Q$ is a transition function, $Q_{in} \subseteq Q$ is a set of initial states, and α is an acceptance condition (a condition that defines a subset of Q^ω). Intuitively, $\rho(q, \sigma)$ is the set of states that $\mathcal{A}$ can move into when it is in state q and it reads the letter σ. Since the transition function of $\mathcal{A}$ may specify many possible transitions for each state and letter, $\mathcal{A}$ is not *deterministic*.

A *run* of $\mathcal{A}$ on w is a function $r : \mathbb{N} \to Q$ where $r(0) \in Q_{in}$ (i.e., the run starts in an initial state) and for every $l \geq 0$, we have $r(l + 1) \in \rho(r(l), \sigma_l)$ (i.e., the run obeys the transition function). In automata over finite words, acceptance is defined according to the last state visited by the run. When the words are infinite, there is no such thing as a "last state", and acceptance is defined according to the set $Inf(r)$ of states that r visits *infinitely often*, i.e., $Inf(r) = \{q \in Q :$ for i.m. $l \in \mathbb{N}$, we have $r(l) = q\}$. As Q is finite, it is guaranteed that $Inf(r) \neq \emptyset$. The way we refer to $Inf(r)$ depends on the acceptance condition of $\mathcal{A}$. In *Büchi automata*, $\alpha \subseteq Q$, and r is accepting iff $Inf(r) \cap \alpha \neq \emptyset$. Dually, in *co-Büchi automata*, $\alpha \subseteq Q$, and r is accepting iff $Inf(r) \cap \alpha = \emptyset$.

Since $\mathcal{A}$ is not deterministic, it may have many runs on w. There are two, dual, ways in which we can refer to the many runs. When $\mathcal{A}$ is an *existential* automaton (or simply a *nondeterministic* automaton, as we shall call it in the sequel), it accepts an input word w iff there exists an accepting run of $\mathcal{A}$ on w. When $\mathcal{A}$ is a *universal* automaton, it accepts an input word w iff all the runs of $\mathcal{A}$ on w are accepting. The language of $\mathcal{A}$, denoted $\mathcal{L}(\mathcal{A})$ consists of all words accepted by $\mathcal{A}$.

We use three-letter acronyms to describe types of automata. The first letter describes the transition structure and is one of "N" (nondeterministic), and "U" (universal). The second letter describes the acceptance condition; in this paper we only consider "B" (Büchi) and "C" (co-Büchi). The third letter describes the objects on which the automata run; in this paper we are only concerned with "W" (infinite words). Thus, for example, NBW designates a nondeterministic Büchi word automaton and UCW designates a universal co-Büchi word automaton.

A lower bound for complementing NBW was established by Michel [23] (cf. [22]). Consider the alphabet $\Sigma_n = \{1, \ldots, n\}$. Let $w = a_0, a_1, \ldots$ be a word over Σ_n. An *infinite path in* w is a an infinite subsequence $a_{i_0}, a_{i_0+1}, a_{i_1}, a_{i_1+1}, \cdots$ such $a_{i_j+1} = a_{i_{j+1}}$ for $j \geq 0$; that is, an infinite path in w is an infinite subword of matching pairs of leters. Let L_n be the language of infinite words over Σ_n with infinite paths.

Theorem 1. [23]

- L_n can be defined using an n-state NBW.
- $\Sigma_n^\omega - L_n$ cannot be defined using an NBW with fewer than $n!$ states.

3   Complementation Via Ranks

In [18][3], the following approach for NBW complementation is described: in order to complement an NBW, first dualize the transition function and the acceptance condition, and then translate the resulting UCW automaton back to an NBW. By [26], the dual automaton accepts the complementary language, and so does the nondeterministic automaton we end up with. Thus, rather than determinization, complementation is based on a translation of universal automata to nondeterministic ones, which turns out to be simpler. (See also [35].)

Consider a UCW $\mathcal{A} = \langle \Sigma, Q, Q_{in}, \delta, \alpha \rangle$. The runs of $\mathcal{A}$ on a word $w = \sigma_0 \cdot \sigma_1 \cdots$ can be arranged in an infinite DAG (directed acyclic graph) $\mathcal{G}_w = \langle V, E \rangle$, where

 - $V \subseteq Q \times \mathbb{N}$ is such that $\langle q, l \rangle \in V$ iff some run of $\mathcal{A}$ on w has $r(l) = q$. For example, the first level of $\mathcal{G}_w$ contains the nodes $Q_{in} \times \{0\}$.
 - $E \subseteq \bigcup_{l \geq 0}(Q \times \{l\}) \times (Q \times \{l+1\})$ is such that $E(\langle q, l \rangle, \langle q', l+1 \rangle)$ iff $\langle q, l \rangle \in V$ and $q' \in \delta(q, \sigma_l)$.

Thus, $\mathcal{G}_w$ embodies exactly all the runs of $\mathcal{A}$ on w. We call $\mathcal{G}_w$ the *run DAG* of $\mathcal{A}$ on w, and we say that $\mathcal{G}_w$ is *accepting* if all its paths satisfy the acceptance condition α. Note that $\mathcal{A}$ accepts w iff $\mathcal{G}_w$ is accepting. We say that a node $\langle q', l' \rangle$ is a *successor* of a node $\langle q, l \rangle$ iff $E(\langle q, l \rangle, \langle q', l' \rangle)$. We say that $\langle q', l' \rangle$ is *reachable* from $\langle q, l \rangle$ iff there exists a sequence $\langle q_0, l_0 \rangle, \langle q_1, l_1 \rangle, \langle q_2, l_2 \rangle, \ldots$ of successive nodes such that $\langle q, l \rangle = \langle q_0, l_0 \rangle$, and there exists $i \geq 0$ such that $\langle q', l' \rangle = \langle q_i, l_i \rangle$. For a set $S \subseteq Q$, we say that a node $\langle q, l \rangle$ of $\mathcal{G}_w$ is an *S-node* if $q \in S$.

A short detour is now required. A *fair transition system* $M = (W, W_0, R, F)$ consists of a state set W (not necessarily finite), an initial state set $W_0 \subseteq W$, a transition relation $R \subseteq W^2$, and a *fair* state set $F \subseteq W$. An *infinite trace* of M is an infinite state sequence $w_0, w_1, \ldots$ such that $w_0 \in W_0$ and $(w_i, w_{i+1}) \in R$ for all $i \geq 0$. This trace is *fair* if $w_i \in F$ for infinitely many i's. We say that M *fairly terminates* if it has no fair infinite trace. Fair termination is a fundamental property of transition systems, as verification of linear temporal properties for transition systems can be reduced to fair-termination checking [36].

Emerson and Clarke characterized fair termination in terms of a nested fixpoint computation [6]. Let $X, Y \subseteq W$. Define $until(X, Y)$ as the set of states in X that can properly reach Y while staying in X. That is, $until(X, Y)$ consists of states x such that there is a sequence $x_0, \ldots, x_k$, $k > 0$, where $x_k \in Y$ and $x_i \in X$ for $0 \leq i < k$. Clearly, $until(X, Y)$ can be defined in terms of a least fixpoint. Consider now the following greatest fixpoint "algorithm", which we refer to by EC:

$Q \leftarrow W$
while change do
        $Q \leftarrow Q \cap until(Q, Q \cap F)$
endwhile
return $(W_0 \cap Q = \emptyset)$

---

[3] Preliminary version appeared in [17].

Emerson and Clarke showed that EC returns TRUE precisely when M fairly terminates. The intuition is that we can safely delete states that cannot be on a fair infinite trace because they cannot properly reach F even once. Note that the inner fixpoint, required to compute $until(Q, Q \cap F$ always converges in ω stages, since it concerns only finite traces, while the outer fixpoint may require transfinite stages to converge, when W is infinite. For finite transition systems, EC is a real algorithm for fair-termination detection [7], which is used widely in symbolic model checking [4].

A run DAG can be viewed as a fair transition system. Consider a UCW $\mathcal{A} = \langle \Sigma, Q, Q_{in}, \delta, \alpha \rangle$, with a run DAG $\mathcal{G}_w = \langle V, E \rangle$. The corresponding fair transition system is $M_w = (V, Q_{in} \times \{0\}, E, \alpha \times \mathbb{N})$. Clearly, $\mathcal{G}_w$ is accepting iff M_w fairly terminates. EC can therefore be applied to M_w. Using this characterization of acceptance, we can assign *ranks* to the nodes of V, as follows: a node is assigned rank i if it is deleted at the i-th iteration of the loop in EC. Since all nodes of $\mathcal{G}_w$ are reachable from $Q_{in} \times \{0\}$, all nodes will be assigned a rank if $\mathcal{G}_w$ is accepting. Intuitively, ranks measure the "progress" made by a node towards acceptance [16]. We can view these ranks as evidence that $\mathcal{G}_w$ is accepting. As we noted, however, transfinite ranks are required in general, while we desire finite ranks for the complementation construction.

To that end we refer to a heuristic improvement of EC, developed in [8], and referred to by OWCTY. Let $X \subseteq W$ be a set of states in a transition system $M = (W, W_0, R, F)$. By $next(X)$ we refer to states who has successors in X, that is, all states $x \in W$ such that there is a state $y \in W$ where $(x, y) \in R$ and $y \in X$. OWCTY is obtained from EC by adding an inner loop[4]:

```
Q ← W
while change do
    while change do
        Q ← Q ∩ next(Q)
    endwhile
    Q ← Q ∩ until(Q, Q ∩ F)
endwhile
return (W₀ ∩ Q = ∅)
```

Note that the additional inner loop deletes states that have no successor. Such states surely cannot lie on a fair infinite trace, which ensure that OWCTY is a correct characterization of fair termination. Surprisingly, while EC requires, in general, transfinitely many stages to converge, it is shown in [18] that when OWCTY is applied to fair transition systems of the form M_w for a UCW $\mathcal{A}$ with n states, the external loop always converges in at most n iterations. The crucial fact here is that each level of $\mathcal{G}_w$ has at most n nodes. This enables us to assign finite ranks to the nodes of $\mathcal{G}_w$ as follows (we count iterations from 0):

- Assign a node v rank $2i$ if it is deleted in the i-th iteration by the statement $Q \leftarrow Q \cap next(Q)$.

---

[4] The additional loop here precedes the inner statement of EC, while in [8] it succeeds it. This is not an essential change.

– Assign a node v rank $2i+$ if it is deleted in the i-th iteration by the statement $Q \leftarrow Q \cap until(Q, Q \cap F)$.

It is shown in [12,18] that precisely the ranks $0, \ldots, 2n - 2$ are needed (see also [16]).

We can now characterize accepting run DAGs in terms of ranks. Consider an n-state UCW $\mathcal{A} = \langle \Sigma, Q, Q_{in}, \delta, \alpha \rangle$, with a run DAG $\mathcal{G}_w = \langle V, E \rangle$. A C-ranking for $\mathcal{G}_w$ is a mapping $f : V \rightarrow \{0, \ldots, 2n - 2\}$ such that

1. For all nodes $\langle q, l \rangle \in V$, if $f(\langle q, l \rangle)$ is odd, then $q \notin \alpha$.
2. For all edges $\langle \langle q, l \rangle, \langle q', l + 1 \rangle \rangle \in E$, we have $f(\langle q', l + 1 \rangle) \leq f(\langle q, l \rangle)$.

Thus, a C-ranking associates with each node in $\mathcal{G}_w$ a rank so that the ranks along paths do not increase, and α-nodes get only even ranks. We say that a node $\langle q, l \rangle$ is an *odd node* if $f(\langle q, l \rangle)$ is odd. Note that each path in $\mathcal{G}_w$ eventually gets trapped in some rank. We say that the C-ranking f is an *odd C-ranking* if all the paths of $\mathcal{G}_w$ eventually get trapped in odd ranks. Formally, f is odd iff for all paths $\langle q_0, 0 \rangle, \langle q_1, 1 \rangle, \langle q_2, 2 \rangle, \ldots$ in $\mathcal{G}_w$, there is $l \geq 0$ such that $f(\langle q_l, l \rangle)$ is odd, and for all $l' \geq l$, we have $f(\langle q_{l'}, l' \rangle) = f(\langle q_l, l \rangle)$. Note that, equivalently, f is odd if every path of $\mathcal{G}_w$ has infinitely many odd nodes.

Lemma 1. [18] *The following are equivalent.*

1. *All paths of $\mathcal{G}_w$ have only finitely many α-nodes.*
2. *There is an odd C-ranking for $\mathcal{G}_w$.*

The fact that the nodes of a run DAG can be assigned finite ranks means that we can characterize acceptance using a variation of the subset construction, where each element of the subset also carries a rank. It is easy to check that the two conditions of C-ranking hold, since these involve only local conditions. Here is a first attempt to construct an NBW $\mathcal{A}'$ that is equivalent to the UCW $\mathcal{A}$. When $\mathcal{A}'$ reads a word w, it guesses a C-ranking for the run DAG $\mathcal{G}_w$ of $\mathcal{A}$ on w. At a given point of a run of $\mathcal{A}'$, it keeps in its memory a whole level of $\mathcal{G}_w$ and a guess for the ranks of the nodes at this level.

Before we define $\mathcal{A}'$, we need some notation. A *level ranking* for $\mathcal{A}$ is a function $g : Q \rightarrow \{0, \ldots, 2n - 2\}$, such that if $g(q)$ is odd, then $q \notin \alpha$. Let $\mathcal{R}$ be the set of all level rankings. For a subset S of Q and a letter σ, let $\delta(S, \sigma) = \bigcup_{s \in S} \delta(s, \sigma)$. Note that if level l in $\mathcal{G}_w$, for $l \geq 0$, contains the states in S, and the $(l + 1)$-th letter in w is σ, then level $l + 1$ of $\mathcal{G}_w$ contains the states in $\delta(S, \sigma)$. For two level rankings g and g' in $\mathcal{R}$, a set $S \subseteq Q$, and a letter σ, we say that g' *covers* $\langle g, S, \sigma \rangle$ if for all $q \in S$ and $q' \in \delta(q, \sigma)$, we have $g'(q') \leq g(q)$. Thus, if the nodes of level l contain exactly all the states in S, g describes the ranks of these nodes, and the $(l + 1)$-th letter in w is σ, then g' is a possible level ranking for level $l + 1$. Finally, for $g \in \mathcal{R}$, let $odd(g) = \{q : g(q) \text{ is odd}\}$. Thus, a state of Q is in $odd(g)$ if has an odd rank.

We can now try to define $\mathcal{A}'$ as follows. For the state set we take $Q' = 2^S \times \mathcal{R}$ and $Q'_{in} = Q_{in} \times \mathcal{R}$. Thus, a state of $\mathcal{A}'$ is simply a ranked subset of Q. Now we can define the transition function by $\delta'(\langle S, g \rangle, \sigma) = \{\langle \delta(S, \sigma), g' \rangle :$

g' covers $\langle g, S, \sigma \rangle \}$. This definition guarantees that $\mathcal{A}'$ is guessing a C-ranking of a run DAG $\mathcal{G}_w$. Unfortunately, this is not sufficient. To ensure that $\mathcal{G}_w$ is accepting we need to find an *odd* C-ranking. It is not clear how $\mathcal{A}'$ can check for oddness, which seems to be a global condition. To overcome this difficulty we use a technique due to [24], which uses a second subset construction to ensure that no path of $\mathcal{G}_w$ get stuck in an odd rank.

Let $\mathcal{A}' = \langle \Sigma, Q', Q'_{in}, \delta', \alpha' \rangle$, where

- $Q' = 2^Q \times 2^Q \times \mathcal{R}$, where a state $\langle S, O, g \rangle \in Q'$ indicates that the current level of the run DAG contains the states in S, the set $O \subseteq S$ contains states along paths that have not visited an odd node since the last time O has been empty, and g is the guessed level ranking for the current level.
- $Q'_{in} = \{Q_{in}\} \times \{\emptyset\} \times \mathcal{R}$.
- δ' is defined, for all $\langle S, O, g \rangle \in Q'$ and $\sigma \in \Sigma$, as follows.
  - If $O \neq \emptyset$, then

  $$\delta'(\langle S, O, g \rangle, \sigma) = \{\langle \delta(S, \sigma), \delta(O, \sigma) \setminus odd(g'), g' \rangle : g' \text{ covers } \langle g, S, \sigma \rangle \}.$$

  - If $O = \emptyset$, then

  $$\delta'(\langle S, O, g \rangle, \sigma) = \{\langle \delta(S, \sigma), \delta(S, \sigma) \setminus odd(g'), g' \rangle : g' \text{ covers } \langle g, S, \sigma \rangle \}.$$

- $\alpha' = 2^Q \times \{\emptyset\} \times \mathcal{R}$.

An easy analysis show that $\mathcal{A}'$ has at most $(6n)^n)$ states. This should be contrasted with the bound of n^{2n} that results from determinization [29].

Theorem 2. [18] *Let $\mathcal{A}$ be a UCW with n states. Then $\mathcal{A}'$ has at most $(6n)^n$ states and $\mathcal{L}(\mathcal{A}') = \mathcal{L}(\mathcal{A})$.*

A report on an implementation of this construction, which includes also many optimizations, can be found in [12].

4   Tight Rankings

While the upper bound bound of $(6n)^n$ described above is exponentially better than the bound of n^{2n} obtained via determinization, is is still exponentially far from the lower bound of $n!$. Recent results have improved both the upper and lower bounds.

For the upper bound, it was shown in [9] that the rank-based construction can be tightened. Consider a UCW $\mathcal{A}$ and a word $w \in \Sigma^\omega$ accepted by $\mathcal{A}$. For the run dag $\mathcal{G}_w$ of $\mathcal{A}$ on w, let $max\_rank(\mathcal{G}_w)$ be the maximal rank that a node in $\mathcal{G}_w$ gets. For a rank $j \in \{0, \ldots, 2n - 2\}$, let $[j]^{odd}$ be all odd ranks less than or equal to j.

Lemma 2. [9] *There is a limit level $l \geq 0$ such that for each level $l' > l$, and for all ranks $j \in [max\_rank(\mathcal{G}_w)]^{odd}$, there is a node $\langle q, l' \rangle$ such that $rank(q, l') = j$.*

Recall that a level ranking for $\mathcal{A}$ is a function $g : Q \to \{0, \ldots, 2n-2\}$, such that if $g(q)$ is odd, then $q \notin \alpha$. Let $max\_odd(g)$ be the maximal odd number in the range of g.

Definition 1. *We say that a level ranking g is* tight *if*

1. *the maximal rank in the range of g is odd, and*
2. *for all $j \in [max\_odd(g)]^{odd}$, there is a state $q \in Q$ with $g(q) = j$.*

Lemma 3. [9] *There is a level $l \geq 0$ such that for each level $l' > l$, the level ranking that corresponds to l' is tight.*

It follows that we can improve the earlier complementation construction and restrict the set $\mathcal{R}$ of possible level rankings to the set of tight level rankings. Since, however, the tightness of the level ranking is guaranteed only beyond the limit level l of $\mathcal{G}_w$, we also need to guess this level, and proceed with the usual subset construction until we reach it. Formally, we suggest the following modified construction.

Let $\mathcal{A} = \langle \Sigma, Q, Q_{in}, \delta, \alpha \rangle$ be a UCW, and let $\mathcal{R}_{tight}$ be the set of tight level rankings for $\mathcal{A}$. Let $\mathcal{A}' = \langle \Sigma, Q', Q'_{in}, \delta', \alpha' \rangle$, where

- $Q' = 2^Q \cup (2^Q \times 2^Q \times \mathcal{R}_{tight})$, where a state $S \in Q'$ indicates that the current level of the run DAG contains the states in S, and a state $\langle S, O, g \rangle \in Q'$ is similar to the states in the earlier construction; in particular, $O \subseteq S$.
- $Q'_{in} = \{Q_{in}\}$. Thus, the run starts in a "subset mode", corresponding to a guess that the limit level has not been reached yet.
- For all states in Q' of the form $S \in 2^Q$ and $\sigma \in \Sigma$, we have that

$$\delta'(S, \sigma) = \{\delta(S, \sigma)\} \cup \{\langle \delta(S, \sigma), \emptyset, g \rangle : \text{ and } g \in \mathcal{R}_{tight}\}.$$

Thus, at each point in the subset mode, $\mathcal{A}'$ may guess that the current level is the limit level, and move to a "subset+ranks" mode, where it proceeds as the NBW constructed earlier. Thus, for states of the form $\langle S, O, g \rangle$, the transition function is as described earlier, except that level rankings are restricted to tight ones.

Theorem 3. [9] *Let $\mathcal{A}$ be a UCW. Then $\mathcal{L}(\mathcal{A}') = \mathcal{L}(\mathcal{A})$.*

It remains to analyze carefully the complexity of this construction. Let $tight(n)$ be the number of tight level rankings for automata with n states. Is is easy to see that $\mathcal{A}'$ needs at most $3^n \cdot tight(n)$ states. A careful analysis, based on an asymptotic approximation of Stirling Numbers of The Second Kind [34], yields that $tight(n)$ is bounded by $(0.76n)^n$. We also have a factor of 3^n that results from the two subset constructions; recall that a state has the form $\langle S, O, g \rangle$, in which S and O are subsets of the state space of the original automaton, with $O \subseteq S$, and g is a tight level ranking. This analysis ignores possible relations between the pair $\langle S, O \rangle$ and the tight level ranking g associated with it.

Consider a state $\langle S, O, g \rangle$ of the NBW $\mathcal{A}'$ constructed. Since we are interested only in the ranks of states in S, we can assume without loss of generality that

g assigns the rank 0 to all states not in S. In addition, as O maintains the set of states that have not been visited an odd vertex, g maps all the states in O to an even rank. A careful combinatorial analysis now yields the following.

Theorem 4. [9] *Let $\mathcal{A}$ be a UCW with n states. Then there is an NBW $\mathcal{A}'$ with at most $(0.97n)^n$ states such that $\mathcal{L}(\mathcal{A}) = \mathcal{L}(\mathcal{A}')$.*

In particular, the upper bound is lower than n^n, which would have been a "clean" bound. Recent progress has also been made on the lower-bound front. It is shown in [39] that the complementary automaton needs to maintain all tight level rankings, resulting in a lower bound of $(0.76n)^n$, which is exponentially stronger than the previous bound of $n! \approx (n/e)^n$. An exponential bound remains between the upper bound of $(0.97n)^n$ and the lower bound of $(0.76n)^n$. Closing this gap is a tantalizing open question.

5 Concluding Remarks

Our focus in this paper was on the theoretical aspect of Büchi complementation. It is important to note that this is also an important practical problem. No verification tool so far supports the unrestricted use of Büchi automata as a specification formalism, due to the perceived difficulty of complementation. In spite of some recent progress in implementing Büchi complementation [12], more work needs to be done to make this practically viable.

It should also be noted that complementation is important for automata on infinite words with stronger acceptance conditions, such as generalized Büchi automata [20] and Streett automata [19]. In particular, Streett automata express strong fairness in a natural way. A Streett acceptance condition consists of a set of pairs (L, R) of sets of states. The requirement is that if a run visits L infinitely often, it also visits R infinitely often. The best known upper bound for complementing a Streett automaton with n states and k pairs is $(kn)^{O(kn)}$ [16,19,30]. The only known lower bound is of $(kn)^{O(n)}$ [39].

References

1. R. Armoni, L. Fix, A. Flaisher, R. Gerth, B. Ginsburg, T. Kanza, A. Landver, S. Mador-Haim, E. Singerman, A. Tiemeyer, M.Y. Vardi, and Y. Zbar. The For-Spec temporal logic: A new temporal property-specification logic. In *Proc. 8th International Conference on Tools and Algorithms for the Construction and Analysis of Systems*, volume 2280 of *Lecture Notes in Computer Science*, pages 296–211, Grenoble, France, April 2002. Springer-Verlag.
2. J.C. Birget. Partial orders on words, minimal elements of regular languages, and state complexity. *Theoretical Computer Science*, 119:267–291, 1993.
3. J.R. Büchi. On a decision method in restricted second order arithmetic. In *Proc. International Congress on Logic, Method, and Philosophy of Science. 1960*, pages 1–12, Stanford, 1962. Stanford University Press.

4. J.R. Burch, E.M. Clarke, K.L. McMillan, D.L. Dill, and L.J. Hwang. Symbolic model checking: 10^{20} states and beyond. *Information and Computation*, 98(2):142–170, June 1992.
5. N. Daniele, F. Guinchiglia, and M.Y. Vardi. Improved automata generation for linear temporal logic. In *Computer Aided Verification, Proc. 11th International Conference*, volume 1633 of *Lecture Notes in Computer Science*, pages 249–260. Springer-Verlag, 1999.
6. E.A. Emerson and E.M. Clarke. Characterizing correctness properties of parallel programs using fixpoints. In *Proc. 7th InternationalColloq. on Automata, Languages and Programming*, pages 169–181, 1980.
7. E.A. Emerson and C.-L. Lei. Temporal model checking under generalized fairness constraints. In *Proc. 18th Hawaii International Conference on System Sciences*, North Holywood, 1985. Western Periodicals Company.
8. K. Fisler, R. Fraer, G. Kamhi, M.Y. Vardi, and Z. Yang. Is there a best symbolic cycle-detection algorithm? In *7th International Conference on Tools and algorithms for the construction and analysis of systems*, number 2031 in Lecture Notes in Computer Science, pages 420–434. Springer-Verlag, 2001.
9. E. Friedgut, O. Kupferman, and M.Y. Vardi. Büchi complementation made tighter. *Int'l J. of Foundations of Computer Science*, 17(4):851–867, 2006.
10. P. Gastin and D. Oddoux. Fast LTL to büchi automata translation. In *Computer Aided Verification, Proc. 13th International Conference*, volume 2102 of *Lecture Notes in Computer Science*, pages 53–65. Springer-Verlag, 2001.
11. S. Gurumurthy, R. Bloem, and F. Somenzi. Fair simulation minimization. In *Computer Aided Verification, Proc. 14th International Conference*, volume 2404 of *Lecture Notes in Computer Science*, pages 610–623. Springer-Verlag, 2002.
12. S. Gurumurthy, O. Kupferman, F. Somenzi, and M.Y. Vardi. On complementing nondeterministic Büchi automata. In *12th Advanced Research Working Conference on Correct Hardware Design and Verification Methods*, volume 2860 of *Lecture Notes in Computer Science*, pages 96–110. Springer-Verlag, 2003.
13. T.A. Henzinger, O. Kupferman, and S. Rajamani. Fair simulation. *Information and Computation*, 173(1):64 81, 2002.
14. G.J. Holzmann. The model checker SPIN. *IEEE Trans. on Software Engineering*, 23(5):279–295, May 1997. Special issue on Formal Methods in Software Practice.
15. Y. Kesten, N. Piterman, and A. Pnueli. Bridging the gap between fair simulation and trace containment. In *Computer Aided Verification, Proc. 15th International Conference*, volume 2725 of *Lecture Notes in Computer Science*, pages 381–393. Springer-Verlag, 2003.
16. N. Klarlund. Progress measures for complementation of ω-automata with applications to temporal logic. In *Proc. 32nd IEEE Symp. on Foundations of Computer Science*, pages 358–367, San Juan, October 1991.
17. O. Kupferman and M.Y. Vardi. Weak alternating automata are not that weak. In *Proc. 5th Israeli Symp. on Theory of Computing and Systems*, pages 147–158. IEEE Computer Society Press, 1997.
18. O. Kupferman and M.Y. Vardi. Weak alternating automata are not that weak. *ACM Trans. on Computational Logic*, 2(2):408–429, July 2001.
19. O. Kupferman and M.Y. Vardi. Complementation constructions for nondeterministic automata on infinite words. In *Proc. 11th International Conf. on Tools and Algorithms for The Construction and Analysis of Systems*, volume 3440 of *Lecture Notes in Computer Science*, pages 206–221. Springer-Verlag, 2005.
20. O. Kupferman and M.Y. Vardi. From complementation to certification. *Theoretical Computer Science*, 305:591–606, 2005.

21. R.P. Kurshan. *Computer Aided Verification of Coordinating Processes*. Princeton Univ. Press, 1994.
22. C. Löding. Optimal bounds for the transformation of omega-automata. In *Proc. 19th Conference on the Foundations of Software Technology and Theoretical Computer Science*, volume 1738 of *Lecture Notes in Computer Science*, pages 97–109, December 1999.
23. M. Michel. Complementation is more difficult with automata on infinite words. CNET, Paris, 1988.
24. S. Miyano and T. Hayashi. Alternating finite automata on ω-words. *Theoretical Computer Science*, 32:321–330, 1984.
25. D.E. Muller. Infinite sequences and finite machines. In *Proc. 4th IEEE Symp. on Switching Circuit Theory and Logical design*, pages 3–16, 1963.
26. D.E. Muller and P.E. Schupp. Alternating automata on infinite trees. *Theoretical Computer Science*, 54:267–276, 1987.
27. J.P. Pécuchet. On the complementation of büchi automata. *Theor. Comput. Sci.*, 47(3):95–98, 1986.
28. M.O. Rabin and D. Scott. Finite automata and their decision problems. *IBM Journal of Research and Development*, 3:115–125, 1959.
29. S. Safra. On the complexity of ω-automata. In *Proc. 29th IEEE Symp. on Foundations of Computer Science*, pages 319–327, White Plains, October 1988.
30. S. Safra. Exponential determinization for ω-automata with strong-fairness acceptance condition. In *Proc. 24th ACM Symp. on Theory of Computing*, Victoria, May 1992.
31. W. Sakoda and M. Sipser. Non-determinism and the size of two-way automata. In *Proc. 10th ACM Symp. on Theory of Computing*, pages 275–286, 1978.
32. A.P. Sistla, M.Y. Vardi, and P. Wolper. The complementation problem for Büchi automata with applications to temporal logic. *Theoretical Computer Science*, 49:217–237, 1987.
33. F. Somenzi and R. Bloem. Efficient Büchi automata from LTL formulae. In *Computer Aided Verification, Proc. 12th International Conference*, volume 1855 of *Lecture Notes in Computer Science*, pages 248–263. Springer-Verlag, 2000.
34. N.M. Temme. Asimptotic estimates of Stirling numbers. *Stud. Appl. Math.*, 89:233–243, 1993.
35. W. Thomas. Complementation of Büchi automata revised. In J. Karhumäki, H. A. Maurer, G. Paun, and G. Rozenberg, editors, *Jewels are Forever*, pages 109–120. Springer, 1999.
36. M.Y. Vardi. Verification of concurrent programs - the automata-theoretic framework. *Annals of Pure and Applied Logic*, 51:79–98, 1991.
37. M.Y. Vardi and P. Wolper. Reasoning about infinite computations. *Information and Computation*, 115(1):1–37, November 1994.
38. P. Wolper. Temporal logic can be more expressive. *Information and Control*, 56(1–2):72–99, 1983.
39. Q. Yan. Lower bounds for complementation of ω-automata via the full automata technique. In *Proc. 33rd Intl. Colloq. on Automata, Languages and Pr ogramming*, volume 4052 of *Lecture Notes in Computer Science*, pages 589–600. Springer-Verlag, 2006.

Speed-Up Techniques for Shortest-Path Computations*

Dorothea Wagner and Thomas Willhalm

Universität Karlsruhe (TH)
Fakultät für Informatik
Institut für Theoretische Informatik
D-76128 Karlsruhe
{wagner,willhalm}@ira.uka.de
http://i11www.informatik.uni-karlsruhe.de/

Abstract. During the last years, several speed-up techniques for DIJK-STRA'S ALGORITHM have been published that maintain the correctness of the algorithm but reduce its running time for typical instances. They are usually based on a preprocessing that annotates the graph with additional information which can be used to prune or guide the search. Timetable information in public transport is a traditional application domain for such techniques. In this paper, we provide a condensed overview of new developments and extensions of classic results. Furthermore, we discuss how combinations of speed-up techniques can be realized to take advantage from different strategies.

1 Introduction

Computing shortest paths is a base operation for many problems in traffic applications. The most prominent are certainly route planning systems for cars, bikes and hikers, or timetable information systems for scheduled vehicles like trains and busses. If such a system is realized as a central server, it has to answer a huge number of customer queries asking for their best itineraries. Users of such a system continuously enter their requests for finding their "best" connections. Furthermore, similar queries appear as sub-problems in line planning, timetable generation, tour planning, logistics, and traffic simulations.

The algorithmic core problem that underlies the above scenario is a special case of the single-source shortest-path problem on a given directed graph with non-negative edge lengths. While this is obvious for route planning in street networks, different models and approaches have been presented to solve timetable information by finding shortest paths in an appropriately defined graph. The typical problem to be solved in timetable information is "given a departure and an arrival station as well as a departure time, which is the connection that arrives as early as possible at the arrival station?". There are two main approaches for

* Partially supported by the Future and Emerging Technologies Unit of EC (IST priority 6th FP) under contract no. FP6-021235-2 (project ARRIVAL).

W. Thomas and P. Weil (Eds.): STACS 2007, LNCS 4393, pp. 23–36, 2007.

modeling timetable information as shortest path problem, the time-expanded and the time-dependent approach. For an overview of models and algorithms for optimally solving timetable information we refer to [28].

In any case the particular graphs considered are huge, especially if the model used for timetable information expands time by modelling each event by a single vertex in the graph. Moreover, the number of queries to be processed within very short time is huge as well. This motivates the use of speed-up techniques for shortest-path computations. The main focus is to reduce the response time for on-line queries. In this sense, a speed-up technique is considered as a technique to reduce the search space of DIJKSTRA'S ALGORITHM e.g. by using precomputed information or inherent information contained in the data. Actually, often the underlying data contain geographic information, that is a layout of the graph is provided. Furthermore, in many applications the graph can be assumed to be static, which allows a preprocessing. Due to the size of the graphs considered in route planning or timetable information and the fact that those graphs are typically sparse, preprocessing space requirements are only acceptable to be linear in the number of nodes.

In this paper, we provide a systematic classification of common speed-up techniques and combinations of those. Our main intention is to give a concise overview of the current state of research. We restrict our attention to speed-up techniques where the correctness of the algorithms is guaranteed, i.e., that provably return a shortest path. However, most of them are heuristic with respect to the running time. More precisely, in the worst case, the algorithm *with* speed-up technique can be slower than the algorithm *without* speed-up technique. But experimental studies showed–sometimes impressive–improvements concerning the search front and consequently the running time. For most of these techniques, experimental results for different real-world graphs as well as generated graphs have been reported. However, as the effectiveness of certain speed-up techniques strongly depends on the graph data considered, we do not give a comparison of the speed-ups obtained. But we want to refer to the *9th DIMACS Implementation Challenge - Shortest Paths* where also experiments on common data sets were presented [7].

In the next section, we will provide some formal definitions and a description of DIJKSTRA'S ALGORITHM. Section 3 presents a classification of speed-up techniques for DIJKSTRA'S ALGORITHM and discusses how they can be combined.

2   Preliminaries

2.1   Definitions

A *(directed) graph* G is a pair (V, E), where V is a finite set of *nodes* and E is a set of *edges*, where an edge is an ordered pair (u, v) of nodes $u, v \in V$. Throughout this paper, the number of nodes $|V|$ is denoted by n and the number of edges $|E|$ is denoted by m. For a node $u \in V$, the number of outgoing edges $|\{(u, v) \in E\}|$ is called the *degree* of the node. A *path* in G is a sequence of nodes $(u_1, \ldots, u_k)$ such that $(u_i, u_{i+1}) \in E$ for all $1 \le i < k$. A path with $u_1 = u_k$ is called a *cycle*.

---

1 for all nodes $u \in V$ set $\text{dist}(u) := \infty$
2 initialize priority queue Q with source s and set $\text{dist}(s) := 0$
3 while priority queue Q is not empty
4   get node u with smallest tentative distance $\text{dist}(u)$ in Q
5   for all neighbor nodes v of u
7   set $\text{new-dist} := \text{dist}(u) + w(u,v)$
8   if $\text{new-dist} < \text{dist}(v)$
9   if $\text{dist}(v) = \infty$
10   insert neighbor node v in Q with priority new-dist
11   else
12   set priority of neighbor node v in Q to new-dist
13   set $\text{dist}(v) := \text{new-dist}$

Algorithm 1. DIJKSTRA'S ALGORITHM

Given edge weights $l : E \to \mathbb{R}$ ("lengths"), the *length of a path* $P = (u_1, \dots, u_k)$ is the sum of the lengths of its edges $l(P) := \sum_{1 \le i < k} l(u_i, u_{i+1})$. For two nodes $s, t \in V$, a *shortest s-t path* is a path of minimal length with $u_1 = s$ and $u_k = t$. The *(graph-theoretic) distance* $d(s,t)$ of s and t is the length of a shortest s-t path. A *layout* of a graph $G = (V, E)$ is a function $L : V \to \mathbb{R}^2$ that assigns each node a position in $\mathbb{R}^2$. The Euclidean distance between two nodes $u, v \in V$ is then denoted by $\|L(u) - L(v)\|$. A graph (without multiple edges) can have up to $O(n^2)$ edges. We call a graph *sparse*, if $m = O(n)$. In the following we assume that the graphs we are dealing with are large and one can only afford a memory consumption linear in the size of the graph. In particular, for large sparse graphs $O(n^2)$ space is not affordable.

2.2   Shortest Path Problem

Let $G = (V, E)$ be a directed graph whose edges are *weighted* by a function $l : E \to \mathbb{R}$. The *(single-source single-target) shortest-path problem* consists in finding shortest s-t path from a given source $s \in V$ to a given target $t \in V$. Note that the problem is only well defined for all pairs, if G does not contain negative cycles (cycles with negative length). In the presence of negative weights but not negative cycles, it is possible, using Johnson's algorithm [19], to convert in $O(nm + n^2 \log n)$ time the original edge weights $l : E \to \mathbb{R}$ to non-negative edge weights $l' : E \to \mathbb{R}_0^+$ that result in the same shortest paths. Hence, we can safely assume in the rest of this paper that edge weights are non-negative. We also assume throughout the paper that for all pairs $(s, t) \in V \times V$, the shortest path from s to t is unique. (This can be achieved by adding a small fraction to the edge weights, if necessary.)

The classical algorithm for computing shortest paths in a directed graph with non-negative edge weights is that of Dijkstra [6], independently discovered by Dantzig [2] (Algorithm 1). The algorithm maintains, for each node $v \in V$, a label $\text{dist}(v)$ with the current tentative distance. The algorithm uses a priority queue Q containing the nodes that build the current search horizon around s.

Nodes are either *unvisited* (i.e. $\text{dist}(u) = \infty$), in the priority queue, or *finished* (already removed from the priority queue). It is easy to verify that nodes are never reinserted in the priority queue if the extracted node u in line 4 is the node with the smallest tentative distance in the priority queue and all edge weights are non-negative. Thus, the labels are updated while the algorithm visits the nodes of the graph with non-decreasing distance from the source s.

In order to compute a shortest path tree, one has to remember that u is the predecessor of v if a shorter path to v has been found (i.e. between line 8 and 9). DIJKSTRA'S ALGORITHM computes the shortest paths to all nodes in the Graph. If only one shortest path is needed to a target node $t \in V$, the algorithm can stop if the target t is removed from the priority queue in line 4. If DIJKSTRA'S ALGORITHM is executed more than once, the initialization of dist in line 1 for each run can be omitted by introducing a global integer variable time and replacing the test $\text{dist}(v) = \infty$ by a comparison of the time with a time stamp for every node. See e.g., [33] for a detailed description.

The asymptotic time complexity of DIJKSTRA'S ALGORITHM depends on the choice of the priority queue. For general graphs, Fibonacci heaps [8] still provide the best theoretical worst-case time of $O(m + n \log n)$. For sparse graphs, binary heaps result in the same asymptotic time complexity. Even more, binary heaps are (1) easier to implement and (2) perform better for many instances in practice [25]. For special cases of edge weights, better algorithms are known. If edge weight are integral and bounded by a small constant, Dial's implementation [5] with an array of lists ("buckets") provides a priority queue where all operations take constant time. An extension with average linear complexity for uniformly distributed edge weights is presented in [9,26]. One might argue however, that the better a speed-up techniques works, the smaller the search front is, and the less important the priority queue is.

3   Speed-Up Techniques

In this section, we present *speed-up techniques* for DIJKSTRA'S ALGORITHM, i.e. modifications of the algorithm or graph that do not change the worst-case behavior but usually reduce considerably the number of visited nodes in practice. We shortly describe two classical speed-up techniques, *bidirectional search* and *goal-directed search*. Moreover, we give a classification of more recently presented techniques.

3.1   Bidirectional Search

Bidirectional search simultaneously performs two searches: a "normal", or forward, variant of the algorithm, starting at the source node, and a so-called reverse, or backward, variant of DIJKSTRA'S ALGORITHM, starting at the destination node. With the reverse variant, the algorithm is applied to the reverse graph, i.e., a graph with the same node set V as that of the original graph, and the reverse edge set $\overline{E} = \{(u, v) \mid (v, u) \in E\}$.

Let $d_f(u)$ be the distance labels of the forward search and $d_b(u)$ the labels of the backward search, respectively. The algorithm can be terminated when one node has been designated to be permanent by both the forward and the backward algorithm. Then, the shortest path is determined by the node u with minimum value $d_f(u) + d_b(u)$ and it can be composed of the shortest path from the start node s to u, (found by the forward search), and the shortest path from u to the destination t (found by the reverse search). Note that the node u itself is not necessarily marked as permanent by both searches.

One degree of freedom in bidirectional search is the choice whether a forward or backward step is executed. Common strategies are to choose the direction with the smaller priority queue, to select the direction with the smaller minimal distance in the priority queue, or simply alternate the directions. For a theoretical discussion of bidirectional search, see [24].

3.2   Goal-Directed Search or A^*

This technique, originating from AI [15], modifies the priority of active nodes to change the order in which the nodes are processed. More precisely, a goal-directed search adds to the priority $\texttt{dist}(u)$ a *potential* $p_t : V \rightarrow \mathbb{R}_0^+$ (often called *heuristic*) depending on the target t of the search. The modified priority of a node $v \in V$ is therefore $\texttt{dist}(v) + p_t(v)$. With a suited potential, the search can be pushed towards the target thereby reducing the running time while the algorithm still returns a shortest path. Intuitively speaking, one can compare a path in traffic network with a walk in a landscape. If you add a potential, the affected region is raised. If the added potential is small next to the target, you create a valley around the target. As walking downhill is easier than uphill, you are likely to hit the target sooner than without the potential added.

We will now use an alternative formulation of goal-directed search to discuss its correctness. Equivalently to modifying the priority, one can change the edge lengths such that the search is driven towards the target t. In this case, the weight of an edge $(u, v) \in E$ is replaced by $l'(u, v) := l(u, v) - p_t(u) + p_t(v)$. The length of a s-v path $P = (s = v_1, v_2, \ldots, v_{k+1} = v)$ is then

$$l'(P) = \sum_{i=1}^{k} l'(v_i, v_{i+1}) = \sum_{i=1}^{k} l(v_i, v_{i+1}) - p_t(v_i) + p_t(v_{i+1})$$

$$= -p_t(s) + p_t(v) + \sum_{i=1}^{k} l(v_i, v_{i+1})$$

$$= -p_t(s) + p_t(v) + l(P).$$

In particular, the length of an s-t path with modified edge lengths is the same up to the constant $-p_t(s) + p_t(t)$. Therefore, a path from s to t is a shortest s-t path according to l', if and only if it is a shortest s-t path according to l.

If all modified edge lengths $l'(u, v)$ are non-negative, we can apply DIJKSTRA'S ALGORITHMto the graph with modified edge lengths l' and get a shortest s-t path according to l. This leads to the following definition:

Definition 1. *Given a weighted graph* $G = (V, E), l : V \rightarrow \mathbb{R}_0^+$, *a potential* $p : V \rightarrow \mathbb{R}$ *is called* feasible, *if* $l(u, v) - p(u) + p(v) \geq 0$ *for all edges* $e \in E$.

Usually, potentials are used that estimate the distance to the target. In fact, it can be shown that a feasible potential p is a lower bound of the distance to the target t if $p(t) \leq 0$. Note that every feasible potential p can be transposed into an equivalent potential $p'(v) = p(v) - p(t)$ which is a lower bound of the distance to the target. We can therefore assume without loss of generality that the potential is indeed a lower bound. The tighter the bound is, the more the search is attracted to the target. In particular, a goal-directed search visits only nodes on the shortest path, if the potential is the distance to the target.

In an actual implementation of goal-directed search, you will most probably use the first formulation, namely to modify the priority with which nodes are inserted in the priority queue. This has the advantage that p is called (at most) once per edge instead of two calls. Furthermore, the distance labels of the nodes are unmodified. This improves the numerical stability and simplifies the handling of the labels (in particular in combinations with other speed-up techniques).

We will now present three scenarios and how to obtain feasible potentials in these cases:

Euclidean Distances. Assume a layout $L : V \rightarrow \mathbb{R}^2$ of the graph is available where the length of an edge is somehow correlated with the Euclidean distance of its end nodes. Then a feasible potential for a node v can be obtained using the Euclidean distance (the "flight distance") $\|L(v) - L(t)\|$ to the target t.

In case the edge lengths are in fact the Euclidean distances, the Euclidean distance $\|L(v) - L(t)\|$ itself is already a feasible potential, due to the triangular inequality. Using this potential, an edge that points directly towards the destination has a modified edge length of zero, while the modified length of an edge that points in the opposite direction is twice the distance. A theoretical analysis for various random graphs can be found in [35].

If the edge lengths are *not* the Euclidean distances of the end nodes, a feasible potential can be defined as follows: let v_{max} denote the maximum "edge-speed" $\|L(u) - L(v)\|/l(u, v)$, over all edges $(u, v) \in E$. The potential of a node u can now be defined as $p(u) = \|L(u), L(t)\|/v_{max}$. The maximum velocity can be computed in a preprocessing step by a linear scan over all edges. Numerical problems can be reduced if the maximum velocity is multiplied by $1 + \varepsilon$ for a small $\varepsilon > 0$. [37] presents how graph-drawing algorithms help in the case where a layout of the graph is not given beforehand.

This approach can be extended in a straight forward manner to other metric spaces than $(\mathbb{R}^2, \|\cdot\|)$. In particular, it is possible to use more than two dimensions or other metrics like the Manhattan metric. Finally, the expensive square root function to compute the Euclidean distance can be replaced by an approximation.

Landmarks. With preprocessing, it is possible to gather information about the graph that can be used to obtain improved lower bounds. In [10], a small fixed-sized subset $L \subset V$ of "landmarks" is chosen. Then, for all nodes $v \in V$, the distance $d(v, l)$ to all nodes $l \in L$ is precomputed and stored. These distances can be used to determine a feasible potential. For each landmark $l \in L$, we define the potential $p_t^{(l)}(v) := d(v, l) - d(t, l)$. Due to the triangle inequality $d(v, l) \le d(v, t) + d(t, v)$, the potential $p_t^{(l)}$ is feasible and indeed a lower bound for the distance to t. The potential is then defined as the maximum over all potentials: $p_t(v) := \max\{p_t^{(l)}(v); l \in L\}$. It is easy to show that the maximum of feasible potentials is again a feasible potential.

For landmarks that are situated next to or "behind" the target t, the lower bound $p_t^{(l)}(u)$ should be fairly tight, as shortest paths to t and l most probably share a common sub-path. Landmarks in other regions of the graph however, may attract the search to themselves. This insight justifies to consider, in a specific search from s to t, only those landmarks with the highest potential $p_t^{(l)}(u)$. The restriction of the landmarks in use has the advantage that the calculation of the potential is faster while its quality is improved.

An interesting observation is that using k landmarks is in fact very similar to using the maximum norm in a k-dimensional space. Each landmark corresponds to one dimension and, for a node, the distance to a landmark is the coordinate in the corresponding dimension. Such high-dimensional drawings have been used in [14], where they are projected to 2D using principal component analysis (PCA). This graph-drawing techniques has also been successfully used in [37] for goal-directed search and other geometric speed-up techniques.

Distances from Graph Condensation. For restricted shortest-path problems, performing a single run of an unrestricted DIJKSTRA'S ALGORITHM is a relatively cheap operation. Examples are travel planning systems for scheduled vehicles like busses or trains. The complexity of the problem is much higher if you take connections, vehicle types, transfer times, or traffic days into account. It is therefore feasible to perform a shortest-path computation to find tighter lower bounds [29]. More precisely, you run DIJKSTRA'S ALGORITHM on a condensed graph: The nodes of this graph are the stations (or stops) and an edge between two stations exists iff there is a non-stop connection. The edges are weighted by the minimal travel time. The distances of all v to the target t can be obtained by a single run of DIJKSTRA'S ALGORITHM from the target t with reversed edges. These distances provide a feasible potential for the time-expanded graph, since the distances are a feasible potential in the condensed graph and an edge between two stations in the time-expanded graph is at least as long as the corresponding edge in the condensed graph.

3.3 Hierarchical Methods

This speed-up technique requires a preprocessing step at which the input graph $G = (V, E)$ is enriched with additional edges representing shortest paths between certain nodes. The additional edges can be seen as "bridges" or "short-cuts" for DIJKSTRA'S ALGORITHM. These additional edges thereby realize new levels that step-by-step coarsen the graph. To find a shortest path between two nodes s

and t using a hierarchy, it suffices for DIJKSTRA'S ALGORITHM to consider a relatively small subgraph of the "hierarchical graph". The hierarchical structure entails that a shortest path from s to t can be represented by a certain set of upward and of downward edges and a set of level edges passing at a maximal level that has to be taken into account. Mainly two methods have been developed to create such a hierarchy, the *multi-level approach* [33,34,18,4] and *highway hierarchies* [31,32]. These hierarchical methods are already close to the idea of using precomputed shortest paths tables for a small number of very frequently used "transit nodes". Recently, this idea has been explored for the computation of shortest paths in road networks with respect to travel time [1].

Multi-Level Approach. The decomposition of the graph can be realized using separators $S_i \subset V$ for each level, called *selected nodes* at level i: $S_0 := V \supseteq S_1 \supseteq \ldots \supseteq S_l$. These node sets can be determined on diverse criteria. In a simple, but practical implementation, they consist of the desired numbers of nodes with highest degree in the graph. However, with domain-specific knowledge about the central nodes in the graph, better separators can be found. Alternatively, the planar separator theorem or betweenness centrality can be used to find small separators [18]. There are three different types of edges being added to the graph: *upward edges*, going from a node that is not selected at one level to a node selected at that level, *downward edges*, going from selected to non-selected nodes, and *level edges*, passing between selected nodes at one level. The weight of such an edge is assigned the length of a shortest path between the end-nodes.

In [4] a further enhancement of the multi-level approach is presented, which uses a precomputed auxiliary graph with additional information. Instead of a single multi-level graph, a large number of small partial graphs is precomputed, which are optimized individually. This approach results in even smaller query times than achieved by the original multi-level approach. On the other hand, however, a comparably heavy preprocessing is required.

Highway Hierarchies. A different approach presented by [31,32] is also based on the idea that only a "highway network" needs to be searched outside a the neighborhood of the source and the target node. Shortest path trees are used to determine a hierarchy. This has the advantage that no additional information like a separator is needed. Moreover, the use of highway hierarchies requires a less extensive preprocessing. The construction relies on a slight modification of DIJKSTRA'S ALGORITHM that ensures that a sub-path $u_i, \ldots, u_j$ of a shortest path $u_1, \ldots, u_i, \ldots, u_j, \ldots, u_k$ is always returned as the shortest path from u_i to u_j. These shortest paths are called *canonical*. Consider the sub-graph of G that consists of all edges in canonical shortest paths. The next level of the hierarchy is then induced by all nodes with degree at least two (i.e. the 2-core of the union of canonical shortest paths). Finally, nodes of degree 2 are then iteratively replaced by edges for a further contraction of the new level of the hierarchy.

3.4 Node and Edge Labels

Approaches based on node or edge labels use precomputed information as an indicator if a node or an edge has to be considered during an execution of DIJKSTRA'S ALGORITHM for a certain target node t.

Reach-Based Routing. Reach-based routing prunes the search space based on a centrality measure called "reach" [13]. Intuitively, a node in the graph is important for shortest paths, if it is situated in the middle of long shortest paths. Nodes that are only at the beginning or the end of long shortest paths are less central. This leads to the following formal definition:

Definition 2 (Reach). *Given a weighted graph $G = (V, E), l : E \rightarrow \mathbb{R}_0^+$ and a shortest s-t path P, the reach on the path P of a node $v \in P$ is defined as $r(v, P) := \min\{l(P_{sv}), l(P_{vt})\}$ where P_{sv} and P_{vt} denote the sub-paths of P from s to v and from v to t, respectively. The reach $r(v)$ of $v \in V$ is defined as the maximum reach for all shortest s-t paths in G containing v.*

In a search for a shortest s-t path P_{st}, a node $v \in V$ can be ignored, if (1) the distance $l(P_{sv})$ from s to v is larger than the reach of v and (2) the distance $l(P_{vt})$ from v to t is larger than the reach of v. While performing DIJKSTRA'S ALGORITHM, the first condition is easy to check, since $l(P_{sv})$ is already known. The second condition is fulfilled if the reach is smaller than a lower bound of the distance from v to t. (Suited lower bounds for the distance of a node to the target are already described for goal-directed search in Sect. 3.2.) Lines 7-13 of Algorithm 1 are therefore not performed if conditions (1) and (2) are surely fulfilled.

To compute the reach for all nodes, we perform a single-source all-target shortest-path computation for every node. With a modified depth first search on the shortest-path trees, it is easy to compute the reach of all nodes using the following insight: For two shortest paths P_{sx} and P_{sy} with a common node $v \in P_{sx}$ and $v \in P_{sy}$, we have

$$\max\{r(v, P_{sx}), r(v, P_{sy})\} = \min\{l(P_{sv}), \max\{l(P_{vx}), l(P_{vy})\}\}.$$

The preprocessing for sparse graphs needs therefore $O(n^2 \log n)$ time and $O(n)$ space. In case such a heavy preprocessing is not acceptable, [13] also describes how to compute upper bounds for the reach. As mentioned in [11], the reach criterion can be extended to edges, which even improves its effectiveness but also increases the preprocessing time.

Edge Labels. This approach attaches a label to each edge that represents all nodes to which a shortest path starts with this particular edge [22,23,27,33,36,38]. More precisely, we first determine, for each edge $(u, v) \in E$, the set $S(u, v)$ of all nodes $t \in V$ to which a shortest u-t path starts with the edge (u, v). The shortest path queries are then answered by DIJKSTRA'S ALGORITHM restricted to those edges (u, v) for which the target node is in $S(u, v)$. Similar to a traffic sign, the edge label shows the algorithm if the target node might be in the target region of the edge. It is easy to verify that such a pruned shortest-path computation returns a shortest path: If (u, v) is part of a shortest s-t path, then its sub-path from u to t is also a shortest path. Therefore, t must be in $S(u, v)$, because all nodes to which a shortest path starts with (u, v) are located in $S(u, v)$. The restriction of the graph can be realized on-line during the shortest-path computation by excluding those edges whose edge label does not contain the target node (line 5 of algorithm 1).

Geometric Containers. As storing all sets $S(u, v)$ would need $O(n^2)$ space, one can use a superset of $S(u, v)$ that can be represented with constant size. Using constant-sized edge labels, the size of the preprocessed data is linear in the size of the graph. Given a layout $L : V \to \mathbb{R}^2$ of the graph, an efficient and easy object type for an edge label associated to (u, v) is an *enclosing geometric object* of $\{L(t) \mid t \in S(u, v)\}$. Actually, the *bounding box*, i.e. the smallest rectangle parallel to the axes that contains $\{L(t) \mid t \in S(u, v)\}$ turns out to be very effective as geometric container [38]. The bounding boxes can be computed beforehand by running a single-source all-target shortest-path computation for every node. The preprocessing for sparse graphs needs therefore $O(n^2 \log n)$ time and $O(n)$ space.

Arc Flags. If you drop the condition that the edge labels must have constant size, you can get much better however. An approach that performs very well in practice [22,23,27], is to partition the node set in p regions with a function $r : V \longrightarrow \{1, \ldots, p\}$. Then an arc flag, i.e. a p-*bit-vector* where each bit represents one region is used as edge label. For an edge e, a region is marked in the p-bit-vector of e if it contains a node v with $v \in S(e)$.) Then the overall space requirement for the preprocessed data is $\Theta(p \cdot m)$. But an advantage of bit-vectors as edge labels is the insight that the preprocessing does not need to compute *all*-pairs shortest paths. Every shortest path from any node s outside a region R to a node inside a region R has to enter the region R at some point. As s is not a member of region R, there exists an edge $e = (u, v)$ such that $r(u) \neq r(v)$. It is therefore sufficient, if the preprocessing algorithm regards only the shortest paths to nodes v that are on the boundary of a region. These paths can be determined efficiently by a backward search starting at the boundary nodes. Usually, the number of boundary nodes is by orders of magnitude smaller than n. A crucial point for this type of edge labels is an appropriate partitioning of the node set. Using a layout of the graph, e.g. a *grid*, *quad-trees* or *kd-trees* can be used. In a general setup, a separator according to [21] is the best choice we are aware of [27].

3.5 Combining Speed-Up Techniques

It has been shown in various publications [3,11,12,16,17,30,31,32,33,37] that the full power of speed-up techniques is unleashed, if various speed-up techniques are combined. In [16,17] combinations of *bidirectional search*, *goal-directed search*, *multi-level approach* and *geometric container* are examined. For an experimental evaluation we refer to these papers. In this section, we concentrate on cases, where an effective combination of two speed-up techniques is not obvious. The extension to a combination of three or four techniques is straight forward, once the problem of combining two of them is solved. However, not every combination is useful, as the search space may not be decreased (much) by adding a third or fourth speed-up techniques.

Bidirectional Search and Goal-Directed Search. Combining goal-directed and bidirectional search is not as obvious as it may seem at first glance. [30] provides a counter-example to show that simple application of a goal-directed search forward and a "source-directed" search backward yields a wrong termination condition. However, the alternative condition proposed there has been shown in [20] to be quite inefficient, as the search in each direction almost reaches the source of the other direction. An alternative is to use the *same* potential in both directions. With a potential from Sect. 3.2, you already get a speed-up (compared to using either goal-directed or bidirectional search). But one can do better using a combination of potentials: if $p_s(v)$ is a feasible potential for the backward search, then $p_s(t) - p_s(v)$ is a feasible potential for the forward search (although not necessarily a good one). In order to balance the forward and the backward search, the average $\frac{1}{2}(p_t(v) + p_s(t) - p_s(v))$ is a good compromise [10].

Bidirectional Search and Hierarchical Methods. Basically, bidirectional search can be applied to the subgraph defined by the multi-level approach. In an actual implementation, that subgraph is computed on-the-fly during DIJKSTRA'S ALGORITHM: for each node considered, the set of necessary outgoing edges is determined. If a bidirectional search is applied to the multi-level subgraph, a symmetric, backward version of the subgraph computation has to be implemented: for each node considered in the backward search, the incoming edges that are part of the subgraph have to be determined. See [16,17] for an experimental evaluation. Actually, [31,32] takes this combination even further in that it fully integrates the two approaches. The conditions for the pruning of the search space are interweaved with the fact that the search is performed in two directions at the same time.

Bidirectional Search and Reach-Based Routing. The reach criterion $l(P_{sv}) \leq r(v) \vee l(P_{vt}) \leq r(v)$ can be used directly in the backward direction of the bidirectional search, too. In the backward search, $l(P_{vt})$ is already known whereas we have to use a lower bound instead of $l(P_{sv})$ to replace the first condition $l(P_{sv}) \leq r(v)$. However, even without using a geometric lower bound but only the known distances for pruning, [11] reports good results.

Bidirectional Search and Edge Labels. In order to take advantage of edge labels in both directions of a bidirectional search, a second set of edge labels is needed. For each edge $e \in E$, we compute the set $S(e)$ and the set $S_{rev}(e)$ of those nodes from which a shortest path ending with e exists. Then we store for each edge $e \in E$ appropriate edge labels for $S(e)$ and $S_{rev}(e)$. The forward search checks whether the target is contained $S(e)$, the backward search, whether the source is in $S_{rev}(e)$. See [16,17].

Goal-Directed Search and Highway Hierarchies. Already the original highway algorithm [31,32] accomplishes a bidirectional search. In [3] the highway hierarchies are further enhanced with goal-directed capabilities using potentials for forward and backward search based on landmarks. Unfortunately, the highway algorithm cannot abort the search as soon as an *s-t* path is found. However, another aspect of goal-directed search can be exploited, the pruning. As soon as an *s-t* path is found it yields an upper bound for the length of the shortest *s-t* path. Comparing upper and lower bound can then be used to prune the search. Altogether, the combination of highway hierarchies and landmarks brings less improvement than one might hope. On the other hand, using stopping the search as soon as an *s-t* path is found at the cost of losing correctness of the result (the *s-t* path found is not always the shortest *s-t* path) leads to an impressive speed-up. Moreover, almost all paths found are also shortest and, in the rare other cases the approximation error is extremely small.

Goal-Directed Search and Reach-Based Routing. Goal-directed search can also be applied to the subgraph that is defined by the reach criterion. However, some care is needed if the subgraph is determined on-line (which is the common way to implement it) with the restriction by the reach. In particular, one should choose an implementation of goal-directed search that doesn't change the distance labels of the nodes, as they are used to check the reach criterion. A detailed analysis of this combination can be found in [11]. Finally, in [12] the study of reach-based routing in combination with goal-directed search based on landmarks is continued.

4   Conclusion

We have summarized various techniques to speed-up DIJKSTRA'S ALGORITHM. All of them guarantee to return a shortest path but run considerably faster. After all, the "best" choice of a speed-up technique heavily depends on the availability of a layout, the size of the main memory, the amount of preprocessing time you are willing to spend, and last but not least on the graph data considered.

References

1. Bast, H., Funke, S., Matijevic, D., Sanders, P., Schultes, D.: In Transit to Constant Shortest-Path Queries in Road Networks. In Proc. Algorithm Engineering and Experiments (ALENEX'07), SIAM (2007) to appear.
2. Dantzig, G.: On the shortest route through a network. Mgnt. Sci. **6** (1960) 187–190
3. Delling, D., Sanders, P., Schultes, D., Wagner, D.: Highway Hierarchies Star. 9th DIMACS Implementation Challenge - Shortest Paths.
   http://www.dis.uniroma1.it/~challenge9/papers.shtml
4. Delling, D., Holzer, M., Müller, K., Schulz, F., Wagner, D.: High-Performance Multi-Level Graphs. 9th DIMACS Implementation Challenge - Shortest Paths.
   http://www.dis.uniroma1.it/~challenge9/papers.shtml
5. Dial, R.: Algorithm 360: Shortest path forest with topological ordering. Communications of ACM **12** (1969) 632–633

6. Dijkstra, E.W.: A note on two problems in connexion with graphs. Numerische Mathematik **1** (1959) 269–271
7. 9th DIMACS Implementation Challenge - Shortest Paths. http://www.dis.uniroma1.it/~challenge9/papers.shtml
8. Fredman, M.L., Tarjan, R.E.: Fibonacci heaps and their uses in improved network optimization algorithms. Journal of the ACM (JACM) **34** (1987) 596–615
9. Goldberg, A.V.: Shortest path algorithms: Engineering aspects. In Eades, P., Takaoka, T., eds.: Proc. International Symposium on Algorithms and Computation (ISAAC 2001). Volume 2223 of LNCS., Springer (2001) 502–513
10. Goldberg, A.V., Harrelson, C.: Computing the shortest path: A^* search meets graph theory. In: Proc. 16th Annual ACM-SIAM Symposium on Discrete Algorithms (SODA '05), 156–165
11. Goldberg, A.V., Kaplan, H., Werneck, R.: Reach for A^*: Efficient point-to-point shortest path algorithms. In Raman, R., Stallmann, M., eds.: Proc. Algorithm Engineering and Experiments (ALENEX'06), SIAM (2006) 129–143
12. Goldberg, A.V., Kaplan, H., Werneck, R.: Better Landmarks within Reach. In 9th DIMACS Implementation Challenge - Shortest Paths. http://www.dis.uniroma1.it/~challenge9/papers.shtml
13. Gutman, R.: Reach-based routing: A new approach to shortest path algortihms optimized for road networks. In Arge, L., Italiano, G.F., Sedgewick, R., eds.: Proc. Algorithm Engineering and Experiments (ALENEX'04), SIAM (2004) 100–111
14. Harel, D., Koren, Y.: A fast multi-scale method for drawing large graphs. Journal of graph algorithms and applications **6** (2002) 179–202
15. Hart, P.E., Nilsson, N.J., Raphael, B.: A formal basis for the heuristic determination of minimum cost paths. IEEE transactions on systems science and cybernetics **4** (1968) 100–107
16. Holzer, M., Schulz, F., Willhalm, T.: Combining speed up techniques for shortest-path computations. In Ribeiro, C.C., Martins, S.L., eds.: Experimental and Efficient Algorithms: Third International Workshop, (WEA 2004). Volume 3059 of LNCS., Springer (2004) 269–284
17. Holzer, M., Schulz, F., Wagner, D., Willhalm, T.: Combining speed-up techniques for shortest-path computations. ACM Journal of Experimental Algorithmics (JEA) **10**, (2005-2006) Article No. 2.05
18. Holzer, M., Schulz, F., Wagner, D.: Engineering multi-level overlay graphs for shortest-path queries. In Raman, R., Stallmann, M., eds.: Proc. Algorithm Engineering and Experiments (ALENEX'06), SIAM (2006) 156–170
19. Johnson, D.B.: Efficient algorithms for shortest paths in sparse networks. Journal of the ACM (JACM) **24** (1977) 1–13
20. Kaindl, H., Kainz, G.: Bidirectional heuristic search reconsidered. Journal of Artificial Intelligence Research **7** (1997) 283–317
21. Karypis, G.: METIS: Family of multilevel partitioning algorithms. http://www-users.cs.umn.edu/~karypis/metis/ (1995)
22. Köhler, E., Möhring, R.H., Schilling, H.: Acceleration of shortest path computation. In Nikoletseas, S.E., ed.: Experimental and Efficient Algorithms: 4th International Workshop, WEA 2005. Volume 3503 of LNCS., Springer (2005) 126–138
23. Lauther, U.: An extremely fast, exact algorithm for finding shortest paths in static networks with geographical background. In Raubal, M., Sliwinski, A., Kuhn, W., eds.: Geoinformation und Mobilität - von der Forschung zur praktischen Anwendung. Volume 22 of IfGI prints., Institut für Geoinformatik, Münster (2004) 219–230

24. Luby, M., Ragde, P.: A bidirectional shortest-path algorithm with good average-case behavior. Algorithmica **4** (1989) 551–567
25. Mehlhorn, K., Näher, S.: LEDA, A platform for Combinatorial and Geometric Computing. Cambridge University Press (1999)
26. Meyer, U.: Average-case complexity of single-source shortest-paths algorithms: lower and upper bounds. Journal of Algorithms **48** (2003) 91–134
27. Möhring, R.H., Schilling, H., Schütz, B., Wagner, D., Willhalm, T.: Partitioning graph to speed up dijkstra's algorithm. In Nikoletseas, S.E., ed.: Experimental and Efficient Algorithms: 4th International Workshop, WEA 2005. Volume 3503 of LNCS., Springer (2005) 189–202; Journal version to appear in ACM Journal on Experimental Algorithmics (JEA), **12** (2006).
28. Müller-Hannemann, M., Schulz, F., Wagner, D., Zaroliagis, C.: Timetable information: Models and algorithms. In: Geraets, F., Kroon, L., Schöbel, A., Wagner, D., Zaroliagis, C.: Algorithmic Methods for Railway Optimization, LNCS, to appear.
29. Müller-Hannemann, M., Weihe, K.: Pareto shortest paths is often feasible in practice. In Brodal, G., Frigioni, D., Marchetti-Spaccamela, A., eds.: Proc. 5th Workshop on Algorithm Engineering (WAE'01). Volume 2141 of LNCS., Springer (2001) 185–197
30. Pohl, I.: Bi-directional and heuristic search in path problems. Technical Report 104, Stanford Linear Accelerator Center, Stanford, California (1969)
31. Sanders, P., Schultes, D.: Highway hierarchies hasten exact shortest path queries. In Brodal, G.S., Leonardi, S., eds.: Proc. Algorithms ESA 2005: 13th Annual European Symposium. Volume 3669 of LNCS., Springer (2005) 568–579
32. Sanders, P., Schultes, D.: Engineering Highway hierarchies. In Assar, Y., Erlebach, T., eds.: Proc. Algorithms ESA 2006: 14th Annual European Symposium. Volume 4168 of LNCS., Springer (2006)
33. Schulz, F., Wagner, D., Weihe, K.: Dijkstra's algorithm on-line: An empirical case study from public railroad transport. ACM Journal of Experimental Algorithmics (JEA) **5**, (2000) Article No. 12.
34. Schulz, F., Wagner, D., Zaroliagis, C.: Using Multi-Level Graphs for Timetable Information. In: Mount, D. M., Stein, C. eds.: Proc. 4th Workshop Algorithm Engineering and Experiments (ALENEX'02). Volume 2409 of LNCS., Springer (2002) 43–59
35. Sedgewick, R., Vitter, J.S.: Shortest paths in Euclidean space. Algorithmica **1** (1986) 31–48
36. Wagner, D., Willhalm, T.: Geometric Speed-Up Techniques for Finding Shortest Paths in Large Sparse Graphs. In Di Battista, G., Zwick, U., eds.: Proc. Algorithms ESA 2003: 11th Annual European Symposium on Algorithms. Volume 2832 of LNCS., Springer (2003), 776–787
37. Wagner, D., Willhalm, T.: Drawing graphs to speed up shortest-path computations. In: Joint Proc. 7th Workshop Algorithm Engineering and Experiments (ALENEX 2005) and 2nd Workshop Analytic Algorithmics and Combinatorics (ANALCO 2005) 15–22
38. Wagner, D., Willhalm, T., Zaroliagis, C.: Geometric shortest path containers. ACM Journal on Experimental Algorithmics (JEA) **10**, (2005-2006) Article No. 1.03

Compact Forbidden-Set Routing

Bruno Courcelle and Andrew Twigg

[1] LaBRI, Bordeaux 1 University and CNRS
courcell@labri.fr
[2] Computer Laboratory, Cambridge University
andrew.twigg@cl.cam.ac.uk

Abstract. We study labelling schemes for X-constrained path problems. Given a graph (V, E) and $X \subseteq V$, a path is X-constrained if all intermediate vertices avoid X. We study the problem of assigning labels $J(x)$ to vertices so that given $\{J(x) : x \in X\}$ for any $X \subseteq V$, we can route on the shortest X-constrained path between $x, y \in X$. This problem is motivated by Internet routing, where the presence of routing policies means that shortest-path routing is not appropriate. For graphs of tree width k, we give a routing scheme using routing tables of size $O(k^2 \log^2 n)$. We introduce m-clique width, generalizing clique width, to show that graphs of m-clique width k also have a routing scheme using size $O(k^2 \log^2 n)$ tables.

Keywords: Algorithms, labelling schemes, compact routing.

1   Introduction

Given a graph $G = (V, E)$ where each vertex $u \in V$ has a set $S(u) \subseteq V$, a compact *forbidden-set routing scheme* is a compact routing scheme where all routes from u are (approximately) shortest paths in the (possibly disconnected) graph $G \setminus S(u)$. The problem is motivated by Internet routing, where nodes (routers) can independently set routing policies that assign costs to paths, thus making the shortest path not necessarily the most desirable. Shortest-path routing is well-understood, for example Thorup and Zwick [1] have given a compact routing scheme using $\tilde{O}(\sqrt{n})$ size tables, which is almost optimal for stretch-3 paths. On the other hand, very little is known about the complexity of forbidden-set routing. The only known algorithms for policy routing (such as BGP) use Bellman-Ford iteration to construct so-called stable routing trees – for each destination, a tree is rooted at that destination and packets are forwarded along it. Varadhan et al.[2] showed that the policies may conflict, forcing the algorithm to not converge. For general policies, Griffin et al.[3] showed that deciding if it will converge is NP-complete, and Feigenbaum and Karger et al.[4] showed that NP-completeness still holds for forbidden-set policies. This motivates the problem of designing efficient routing schemes that do not suffer from non-convergence, for simple classes of policy such as forbidden-set.

W. Thomas and P. Weil (Eds.): STACS 2007, LNCS 4393, pp. 37–48, 2007.

2 Preliminaries

Let $G = (V, E)$ be an undirected graph and $X \subseteq V$ a set of vertices (the extension to directed graphs is straightforward), and F be a set of edges. An (X, F)-*constrained path* is a path in G that does not use the edges of F and with no intermediate vertex in X (or simply X-constrained if F is empty). We denote by $G[Z]$ the subgraph of G induced by a set of vertices Z. We denote by $G_+[Z]$ the graph consisting of $G[Z]$ and weighted edges where an edge between x and y has weight d iff d is the length of a shortest path in G between x and y of length at least 2 with no intermediate vertex in Z. Between two vertices, one may have one edge without value and another one with value at least 2.

If we know the graph $G_+[Z]$, if $X \subseteq Z$ and every edge of F has its two ends in Z, we can get the length of a shortest (X, F)-constrained path in G between any $x, y \in Z$. The graph $G_+[Z]$ captures the separator structure of G since there is no edge between x, y in $G_+[X \cup \{x, y\}]$ iff X is a separator of x, y in G, thus the problem can be seen as constructing a distributed encoding of the separators of a graph. In all cases we say that we consider a *constrained path problem*.

Our objective is to label each vertex x of G by a label $J(x)$, as short as possible, in such a way that $G_+[Z]$ can be constructed from $\{J(x) : x \in Z\}$. If we can determine the lengths of shortest (X, F)-constrained paths from $\{J(x) : x \in Z\}$, where $X \subseteq Z$ and every edge of F has its two ends in Z, then we call $J(x)$ an (X, F)-*constrained distance labelling*.

The graph problem 'is there an X-constrained path from x to y?' is monadic second-order definable, so the result of Courcelle and Vanicat [5] implies that graphs of bounded clique width have a labelling with labels of $O(\log n)$ bits. However, the constant factor is a tower of exponentials in $cwd(G)$ and is impractical.

Our main result is a labelling scheme with labels of size $O(k^2 \log^2(n))$ where k is a bound on the *m-clique width* (*mcwd*) of the graph, a generalization of clique width that we will introduce. Since graphs with tree width (*twd*) k have *mcwd* at most $k + 3$, and graphs with clique width (*cwd*) k have *mcwd* at most k, the results follow for the case of tree width and clique width. Table 1 in [6] shows that the networks of some important major internet providers are of small tree width, between 10 and 20 and hence our constraint of dealing with graphs of small tree width or clique width is somehow realistic.

The labeling works as follows: given vertices between which we want to determine shortest paths and a set $Z \subseteq V$, we construct from $\{J(x) : x \in Z\}$ the weighted graph $G_+[Z]$. Then we can answer queries about 4-tuples (x, y, X, F) such that $X \cup \{x, y\} \subseteq Z$ and every edge of F has its two ends in Z by using only $G_+[Z]$: in particular the length of a shortest (X, F)-constrained path. The idea is not to repeat for each query the construction of $G_+[Y]$ for some set Y.

Our notation follows Courcelle and Vanicat [5]. For a finite set C of constants, a finite set F of binary function symbols, we let $T(F, C)$ be the set of finite well-formed terms over these two sets (terms will be discussed as labelled trees). The size $|t|$ of a term t is the number of occurrences of symbols from $C \cup F$. Its height $ht(t)$ is 1 for a constant and $1 + \max\{ht(t_1), ht(t_2)\}$ for $t = f(t_1, t_2)$.

Let a be a real number. A term t is said to be a-*balanced* if $ht(t) \leq a \log |t|$ (all logarithms are to base 2). Let t in $T(F_k, C_k)$ and $G = val(t)$, the graph obtained by evaluating t. For a node u in t, $val(t/u)$ is the subgraph represented by evaluating the subterm rooted at u.

3   The Case of Tree Width

Before presenting our main result on m-clique width graphs, we describe a labelling scheme for graphs of tree width k. A graph having tree width k can be expressed as the nondisjoint union of graphs of size $k + 1$, arranged as nodes in a tree such that the set of tree nodes containing some graph vertex forms a connected subtree of the tree (often called a *tree decomposition*). We shall work with a different, algebraic representation of graphs.

3.1   Balanced Tree Width Expressions

Every graph of tree width k can be represented by an algebraic expression (term). A j-*source graph* is a graph with at most j distinguished vertices called *sources*, each tagged with a unique label from $\{1, \ldots, j\}$. Courcelle [7][8] shows that a graph has tree width k iff it is isomorphic to $val(t)$ for some term t whose leaves are $(k + 1)$-source graphs and where every non-leaf node is labelled with one of the following operations, as illustrated in Figure 1.

- *Parallel composition*: The $(k + 1)$-source graph $(G \mathbin{//} H)$ is obtained from the disjoint union of $(k + 1)$-source graphs G and H where sources having the same label are fused together into a single vertex.
- *Erasure*: For $a \in \{1, \ldots, k + 1\}$, the unary operation $\mathrm{fg}_a(G)$ erases the label a and the corresponding source in G is no longer a source vertex.

As in Courcelle and Vanicat[5], we combine a parallel composition and a sequence of erasure operations to obtain a single binary operation, e.g. $\mathbin{//} \mathrm{fg}_{a,b}$. The term tree can be constructed given a tree decomposition of the graph – Corollary 2.1.1 of Courcelle [7] shows that given a tree decomposition of width k of a graph, it is possible to construct in linear time a term tree using at most $k+1$ source labels. The nodes of the term tree are the bags of the tree decomposition; hence the height and degree are unchanged.

The following result of Bodlaender shows how to obtain a balanced tree width expression with a small increase in tree width.

Lemma 1 (Bodlaender [9]). *Given a tree decomposition of width k and a graph G with n vertices, one can compute a binary tree decomposition of G of height at most $2 \log_{5/4}(2n)$ and width at most $3k + 2$ in time $O(n)$.*

3.2   Compact Forbidden-Set Routing for Small Tree Width

Assume we have an a-balanced term tree t for some constant a with $val(t) = G$, assume wlog assume that all sources are eventually erased in t. The vertices of

Parallel composition:

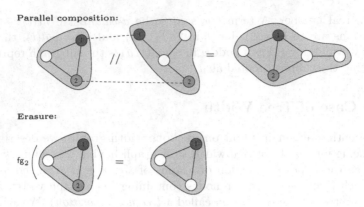

Erasure:

Fig. 1. The parallel composition and erasure operations for constructing graphs of tree width k

G are then in bijection with the erasure operations, so we shall use the same identifier u to refer to both a vertex in G and its unique corresponding erasure operation in t. We now describe a labelling $J(u)$ to compute the length of shortest X-constrained paths.

For a set $Y \subseteq \{1, \ldots, k+1\}$ of source labels and a $(k+1)$-source graph G, we denote by $G \setminus Y$ the induced subgraph of G obtained by removing the source vertices of G whose label is in Y. Every node u in t has a state $Q(u)$ associated with it, which for now assume to be the collection of graphs $\{val(t/u) \setminus Y : Y \subseteq \{1, \ldots, k+1\}\}$. As in Courcelle and Vanicat[5], the label $J(u)$ stores a string describing the *access path* from the root to the node in t representing u (rather than a leaf of t), and the state for every node adjacent to its access path (we assume that every vertex u is adjacent to its own access path). In addition, the label contains the source label of the node u in $val(t/u)$. If u has the source label s_u then the string is of the form

$$J(u) = (s_u, f_1, i_1, Q(s_{3-i_1}(u_1)), \ldots f_h, i_h, Q(s_{3-i_h}(u_h))$$

where h is the height of t, $f_1 \ldots f_h$ are the operations on the path, $i_1 \ldots i_h \in \{1, 2\}$ indicate whether to take the left or right branch and $s_1(u)$ (respectively $s_2(u)$) denote the left (respectively right) child of u in t. The states

$$Q(s_{3-i_1}(u_1))Q(s_{3-i_1}(u_2)) \ldots Q(s_{3-i_1}(u_h))$$

are the states of nodes adjacent to the access path for u. Since each set of at most $O(k)$ erasure operations can be identified with $O(k)$ bits and the term tree has height $O(\log n)$, the access path can be described using $O(k \log n)$ bits (excluding the space to store the states).

We now describe how to use the labelling to find the length of the shortest X-constrained path between u, v. Assume that $u, v \notin X$. For a vertex $x \in G$, we let $Path(x)$ be the path from the corresponding vertex x of t to the root. For a node u of t, let $X(u)$ be the subset of X whose corresponding erasure

CONSTRUCT-SOURCE-DISTANCE-GRAPH(G)

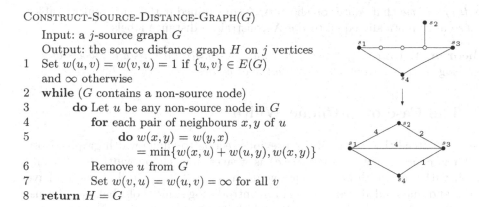

    Input: a j-source graph G
    Output: the source distance graph H on j vertices
1 Set $w(u,v) = w(v,u) = 1$ if $\{u,v\} \in E(G)$
    and ∞ otherwise
2 **while** (G contains a non-source node)
3   **do** Let u be any non-source node in G
4   **for** each pair of neighbours x,y of u
5   **do** $w(x,y) = w(y,x)$
                $= \min\{w(x,u) + w(u,y), w(x,y)\}$
6   Remove u from G
7   Set $w(v,u) = w(u,v) = \infty$ for all v
8 **return** $H = G$

Fig. 2. Constructing source distance graphs by contracting paths of non-source nodes

operations are all ancestors of u in t (i.e. the subset of X represented by sources in $val(t/u)$).

We construct the graph $Rep(t)[X]$ by adding the subgraphs $val(t/w) \setminus X(w)$ for each node $w \in t$ *adjacent* to an access path $Path(x)$ for $x \in X \cup \{u,v\}$ (the states *on* the access path will be reconstructed from these adjacent states). To each vertex $y \in Rep(t)[X]$, associate two pieces of information: a unique identifier $I(y)$ for the corresponding erasure node in t and the source label s_y of y in $val(t/y)$. Then add edges of length zero corresponding to parallel compositions between nodes $x,y \in Rep(t)[X]$ where $I(x) = I(y)$ and $s_x = s_y$. The length of the shortest X-constrained path between u,v in G equals the length of the shortest path in $Rep(t)[X]$ between two vertices x,y where x is a source corresponding to node u in G and y is a source corresponding to v in G.

Now we consider how to efficiently represent the state $Q(u)$. At first it might seem that one needs to store all $2^{O(k)}$ graphs, one for every set of deleted sources. From $val(t/u)$ we construct a compressed graph H called the *source distance graph* with the property that for any set Y of sources and sources x,y, the distance between x,y in $val(t/u) \setminus Y$ equals their distance in $H \setminus Y$. The graph is constructed by contracting paths of non-source vertices in $val(t/u)$, as in Figure 2. Since the edge weights in the source distance graph are in the range $[1,n]$, it can be represented using $O(k^2 \log n)$ bits. This gives labels $J(x)$ of size $O(k^2 \log^2 n)$ bits.

The correctness of the labelling scheme relies on the fact that the connectivity of sources in $G \mathbin{/\mkern-5mu/} H$ is completely determined by their connectivity in G and H: sources u,v are connected in $G \mathbin{/\mkern-5mu/} H$ iff there is a source labelled r in both G, H and paths $u - r$ in G and $r - v$ in H. For routing, we can augment the labelling to compute the next hop on the shortest X-constrained path by associating with each edge (x,y) in the source distance graph $Q(u)$ the next hop (possibly a non-source vertex) on the shortest non-source path represented by the contracted edges from x to y. We can then use this information to construct a *compact routing scheme* that routes on shortest X-constrained paths with routing tables of size asymptotically equal to the X-constrained distance labels.

Theorem 1. *Graphs of tree width k have X-constrained distance labels of size $O(k^2 \log^2 n)$ bits, where n is the number of vertices.*

4   The Case of m-Clique Width

We now extend the results of the previous section to clique width graphs. Note that the concept of tree width (*twd*) is weaker than clique width (*cwd*) : any graph with tree width k has clique width at most 3.2^{k-1} [10] but cliques have cwd 2 and unbounded twd. We begin by introducing some tools: balanced terms, the new notion of m-clique width and the main construction. Due to space restrictions, we outline our results and defer some details to a full version.

4.1   Balanced m-Clique Width Expressions

Let L be a finite set of vertex labels. A *multilabelled graph* is a triple $G = (V_G, E_G, \delta_G)$ consisting of a graph (V_G, E_G) and a mapping δ_G associating with each x in V_G the set of its labels, a subset of L. A vertex may have zero, one or several labels.

The following constants will be used: for $A \subseteq L$ we let **A** be a constant denoting the graph G with a single vertex u and $\delta_G(u) = A$. We write $\mathbf{A}(u)$ if we need to specify the vertex u. The following binary operations will be used: for $R \subseteq L \times L$, relabellings $g, h : L \longrightarrow \mathcal{P}(L)$ ($\mathcal{P}(L)$ is the powerset of L) and for multilabelled graphs G and H we define $K = G \otimes_{R,g,h} H$ iff G and H are disjoint (otherwise we replace H by a disjoint copy) where

$$V_K = V_G \cup V_H$$
$$E_K = E_G \cup E_H \cup \{\{v, w\} : v \in V_G, w \in V_H, R \cap (\delta_G(v) \times \delta_H(w)) \neq \varnothing\}$$
$$\delta_K(x) = (g \circ \delta_G)(x) = \{a : a \in g(b), b \in \delta_G(x)\} \text{ if } x \in V_G$$
$$\delta_K(x) = (h \circ \delta_H)(x) \text{ if } x \in V_H$$

As in the operations by Wanke [11] we add edges between two disjoint graphs, that are the 2 arguments of (many) binary operations. This is a difference with clique width [12] using a single binary operation.

Notation and definitions. We let F_L be the set of all binary operations $\otimes_{R,g,h}$ and C_L be the set of constants $\{\mathbf{A} : A \subseteq L\}$. Every term t in $T(F_L, C_L)$ denotes a multilabelled graph $val(t)$ with labels in L, and every multilabelled graph G is the value of such a term for large enough L. We let $mcwd(G)$ be the minimum cardinality of such a set L and call this number the *m-clique width* of G. We now compare $mcwd$ with cwd and twd [5,12].

Proposition 1. *For every unlabelled undirected graph G,*

$$mcwd(G) \leq twd(G) + 3$$
$$mcwd(G) \leq cwd(G) \ \leq \ 2^{mcwd(G)+1} - 1$$

It follows that the same sets of graphs have bounded clique width and bounded m-clique width. Our motivation for introducing m-clique width is that we can prove the following result:

Proposition 2. *There exists a constant a such that, every graph of m-clique width k is the value an a-balanced term in $T(F_L, C_L)$ for some set L of cardinality at most 2k.*

The proof is deferred to the full version. The above result is very useful since no such result is known for obtaining balanced clique width expressions.

4.2   Adjacency Labelling for m-Clique Width Graphs

For a vertex $x \in G$, let $Path(x)$ be the path $(u_m = x, u_{m-1}, ..., u_0)$ from the corresponding node x of t to the root $(=u_0)$. For a term t, let $m = ht(t)$ be its height. We now describe how to construct an adjacency labelling $I(x)$. Let $I(x) = (L_m, e_{m-1}, D_{m-1}, L_{m-1}, e_{m-2}, D_{m-2}, ..., e_0, D_0, L_0)$ where $L_m = A$ if $A \in C_{[k]}$ is the constant at leaf x in t; L_i is the set of labels of the vertex x in the graph $val(t/u_i)$ for $i = 0, ..., m$. For $i = 0, ..., m-1$, we define $e_i = 1$ if u_{i+1} is the left son of u_i and D_i is the set of labels $\{j'\}$ such that $(j, j') \in R$ for some j in L_{i+1} where $\otimes_{R,g,h}$ occurs at node u_i. Similarly, $e_i = 2$ if u_{i+1} is the right son of u_i and D_i is the set of labels $\{j'\}$ such that $(j', j) \in R$ for some j in L_{i+1} where $\otimes_{R,g,h}$ occurs at node u_i. Each label $I(x)$ has size $O(km)$ and is computable from t in time $O(k^2 ht(t))$, hence at most $O(nk^2 ht(t))$ to compute the entire labelling.

Fact 2. *From the sequences $I(x)$ and $I(y)$ for two distinct vertices x and y, one can determine whether they are linked in G by an edge.*

Proof. From the integers $e_{m-1}, ..., e_0, e'_{m'-1}, ..., e'_0$ in the sequences

$$I(x) = (L_m, e_{m-1}, D_{m-1}, L_{m-1}, e_{m-2}, D_{m-2}, ..., e_0, D_0, L_0)$$
$$I(y) = (L'_{m'}, e'_{m'-1}, D'_{m'-1}, L'_{m'-1}, ..., e'_0, D'_0, L'_0)$$

one can determine the position i in $Path(x)$ and $Path(y)$ of the least common ancestor u_i of x and y. Wlog we assume x below (or equal to) the left son of u_i. Then x and y are adjacent in G iff $D_i \cap L'_{i+1} \neq \emptyset$. This is equivalent to $D'_i \cap L_{i+1} \neq \emptyset$. Since the computations of Fact 2 take time $O(ht(t))$ for each pair x, y, we have the following.

Fact 3. *From $\{I(x) : x \in X\}$ for a set $X \subseteq V$, one can determine $G[X]$ in time $O(|X|^2 ht(t))$ (k is fixed).*

We have thus an *implicit representation* in the sense of Kannan et al.[13] for graphs of *mcwd* at most k, using labels of size $O(k \log n)$.   □

4.3   Enriching the Adjacency Labelling

We now show how to enrich $I(x)$ to achieve the following.

Proposition 3. *Fix k. For t in $T(F_k, C_k)$ with $G(V, E) = val(t)$ one can build a labelling J such that from $\{J(x) : x \in X\}$ for any $X \subseteq V$, one can determine $G_+[X]$ in polynomial time in $|X|$ and $ht(t)$.*

We shall now show how to do this with labels of size $O(k^2 \log^2(n))$ where k is the m-clique width of G. The basic idea is as follows. From $\{I(x) : x \in X\}$ for any $X \subseteq V$, one can reconstruct $G[X]$. For $G_+[X]$ we need paths going out of X, or at least their lengths. If u is a node of a path $Path(x)$ for some x in X, and w is a son of u not on any path $Path(y)$ for y in X, then we compute the lengths of at most k^2 shortest paths running through the subgraph of G induced on the leaves of t below w, and we insert this matrix of integers at the position corresponding to u in the label $J(x)$.

We shall work with a graph representation of terms in $T(F_k, C_k)$. With a term t in $T(F_k, C_k)$, we associate a graph $Rep(t)$ having directed and undirected edges. The vertices of $Rep(t)$ are the leaves of t and the pairs (u, i) for u a node of t and $i \in [k]$ that labels some vertex x in $val(t/u)$. The undirected edges are $(u_1, i) - (u_2, j)$ whenever u_1, u_2 are respectively the left and right sons of some u labelled by $\otimes_{R,g,h}$ and $(i, j) \in R$. The directed edges are of 3 types :

1. $u \longrightarrow (u, i)$ for u a leaf labelled by **A** and $i \in A$.
2. $(u_1, i) \longrightarrow (u, j)$ whenever u_1 is the left son of u, u is labelled by $\otimes_{R,g,h}$ and $j \in g(i)$.
3. $(u_2, i) \longrightarrow (u, j)$ whenever u_2 is the left son of u, u is labelled by $\otimes_{R,g,h}$ and $j \in h(i)$.

As an example, the left half of Figure 3 shows a term t (thick edges) and the graph $Rep(t)$ (fine edges). We use $\longrightarrow^*$ to denote a directed path; $\longleftarrow^*$ denotes the reversal of a directed path.

Fact 4. *For a vertex u of G below or equal to a node w of t, u has label i in $val(t/w)$ iff $u \longrightarrow^* (w, i)$ in $Rep(t)$.*

Fact 5. *For distinct vertices u, v of G : $u - v$ in G iff we have a mixed (directed/undirected) path $u \longrightarrow^* (w, i) - (w', j) \longleftarrow^* v$ in $Rep(t)$ for some w, w', i, j.*

We call such a path an *elementary path* of $Rep(t)$. A *walk* is a path where vertices may be visited several times. A *good walk* in $Rep(t)$ is a walk that is a concatenation of elementary paths. Its *length* is the number of undirected edges it contains (the number of elementary paths).

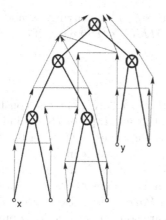 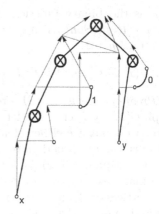

Fig. 3. A term t and the graph $Rep(t)$, and the graph $Rep(t)[\{x, y\}]$ with some valued edges from $Rep(t)_+[X]$

Fact 6. *There is a walk* $x - z_1 - \dots - z_p - y$ *in* G *iff there is in* $Rep(t)$ *a good walk*

$$W = x \longrightarrow^* - \longleftarrow^* z_1 \longrightarrow^* - \longleftarrow^* \dots \longrightarrow^* - \longleftarrow^* z_p \longrightarrow^* - \longleftarrow^* y$$

For a nonleaf vertex u, a *u-walk* in $Rep(t)$ is a walk that is formed of consecutive steps of a good walk W and is of the form

$$(u, i) \longleftarrow^* z \longrightarrow^* - \quad \longrightarrow^* \dots \longrightarrow^* (u, j)$$

where all vertices except the end vertices $(u, i), (u, j)$ are of the forms u, or w or (w, l) for w strictly below u in t. Its *length* is defined as the number of undirected edges.

We let $Min(u, i, j)$ be the smallest length of a u-walk from (u, i) to (u, j), or ∞ if no such u-walk exists. Clearly $Min(u, i, i) = 0$ ((u, i) is a vertex of $Rep(t)$, so Fact 4 applies). We let $MIN(u)$ be the $S \times S$ matrix of all such integers $Min(u, i, j)$, where S is the set of labels p such that (u, p) is a vertex of $Rep(t)$. It can be stored in space $O(k^2 \log n)$ since n bounds the lengths of shortest u-walks in $Rep(t)$.

Fact 7. *If in a good walk we replace a u-walk from* (u, i) *to* (u, j) *by another one also from* (u, i) *to* (u, j) *we still have a good walk.*

We are now ready to define $J(x)$ for x a vertex of G. We recall that $Path(x)$ is the path $(u_m = x, u_{m-1}, \dots, u_0)$ in t from a leaf x to the root u_0, and

$$I(x) = (L_m, e_{m-1}, D_{m-1}, L_{m-1}, e_{m-2}, D_{m-2}, \dots, e_0, D_0, L_0).$$

We let then

$$J(x) = (L_m, e_{m-1}, D_{m-1}, L_{m-1}, M_{m-1}, f_{m-1}, e_{m-2}, D_{m-2}, \dots, e_0, D_0, L_0, M_0, f_0)$$

where f_i is the binary function symbol (some $\otimes_{R,g,h}$) occurring at node u_i, $M_i = MIN(RightSon(u_i))$ if $e_i = 1$ and $M_i = MIN(LeftSon(u_i))$ if $e_i = 2$ for each $i = 0, ..., m - 1$.

Fact 8. *$J(x)$ has size $O(k^2 ht(t) \log(n))$.*

Proof (Proof of Proposition 3). From the set $\{J(x) : x \in X\}$, one can construct the graph $G[X]$ by Fact 3. We let $Rep(t)[X]$ be the subgraph of $Rep(t)$ induced by its vertices that are either elements of X (hence leaves of t), or of the form (w, i) if w is a son of a node u on a path $Path(x)$ for some x in X.

Because a sequence $J(x)$ contains the function symbols f_i and the index sets S of the matrices M_i, we can determine from it the edges of $Rep(t)$, not only between vertices of the form (u, i) for nodes u in $Path(x)$ but also between these vertices and those of the form (w, i) for w that are sons of such nodes u but are not necessarily in $Path(x)$.

It remains to determine the lengths of shortest good walks in $Rep(t)$ in order to get the valued edges of $G_+[X]$. We let $Rep(t)_+[X]$ be the graph $Rep(t)[X]$ augmented with the following integer valued undirected edges: $(u, i) - (u, j)$ valued by $Min(u, i, j)$ whenever this integer (possibly 0) is not ∞.

Example: For the term t in the left half of Figure 3 and $X = \{x, y\}$, the right half of the Figure shows the graph $Rep(t)[X]$ augmented with two valued edges $(u, i) - (u, j)$ for 2 of the 3 nodes u which are not on the paths $Path(x)$ and $Path(y)$ but are sons of nodes on these paths. These 3 nodes yield 5 vertices in the graph $Rep(t)[X]$. Each of these vertices has a loop with value 0 (these loops are not shown). We show the two non-loop edges labelled by 0 and 1.

The shortest good walks in $Rep(t)$ that define the valued edges of $G_+[X]$ are concatenations of edges of $Rep(t)[X]$ (which we have from the $J(x)$'s) and w-walks of minimal lengths for nodes w that are not on the paths $Path(x)$ but are sons of nodes on these paths. We need not actually know these w-walks exactly; we only need the minimal length of one of each type. This information is available from the matrices $MIN(w)$ which we have in the $J(x)$'s. We can thus build the valued graph $Rep(t)_+[X]$, and the desired values are lengths of shortest paths in the graph $Rep(t)_+[X]$ under the alternating edge constraints in Fact 5.

This proves Proposition 3.   □

Combining Propositions 2 and 3 gives the following.

Theorem 9. *For a graph G of m-clique width at most k on n vertices, one can assign to vertices labels $J(x)$ of size $O(k^2 \log^2 n)$ such that from $\{J(x) : x \in X\}$ for any set $X \subseteq V$, one can determine the graph $G_+[X]$ in time $O(|X|^3 \log n)$. The graph G must be given along with an mcwd expression of width at most k.*

The problem of determining for a given graph its m-clique width and the corresponding expression is likely to be NP-hard because the corresponding one for clique width is NP-complete [14]. A cubic algorithm that constructs non-optimal clique width expressions given by Oum [15] may be used.

4.4   Compact Forbidden-Set Routing for Small mcwd

We now describe how to use the labelling J to build a compact routing scheme. Recall that the construction of J is based on matrices that give for each node u of a term t the length of a shortest u-walk in $Rep(t)$ from (u, i) to (u, j). Storing the sequence of vertices of the corresponding path in G uses space at most space $n \log n$ instead of $\log n$ for each entry (assuming there are n vertices numbered from 1 to n, so that a path of length p uses space $p \log n$). The corresponding labelling $J'(x)$ uses for each x space $O(k^2 n \log^2 n)$.

We assume that $X \cup \{x, y\} \subseteq Z$ and every edge of F has its two endpoints in Z. For a compact routing scheme, it suffices to be able to construct the path in a distributed manner, by finding the next hop at each node. Here is such a construction, that for such a set $Z \subseteq V$ gives the length of a shortest (X, F)-constrained path from x to y together with z, the first one not in Z on the considered shortest path. For this, we need only store, in addition to the length of a shortest u-walk in $Rep(t)$ from (u, i) to (u, j) (in the matrix $MIN(u)$) its first and last vertices. This uses space $3 \log n$ instead of $\log n$ for each entry. The corresponding labelling $J''(x)$ uses for each x space $O(k^2 \log^2 n)$. This gives the following compact forbidden-set routing scheme.

Theorem 10. *Let each node have a forbidden set of size at most r. Then graphs of m-clique width at most k have a compact forbidden-set routing scheme using routing tables of size $O(rk^2 \log^2 n)$ bits and packet headers of size $O(rk^2 log^2 n)$ bits.*

Proof. Given an mcwd decomposition of $G = (V, E)$ of width at most k and a set $S(u) \subseteq V$ stored at each node u with $|S(u)| \leq r$, the routing table at u is the label J'' as above. To send a packet from u to v on an $S(u)$-constrained path, u writes into the packet header the label $J''(v)$ for the destination and the labels $\{J''(x) : x \in S(u)\}$. Then u forwards the packet to a neighbour w that minimizes the minimizes the distance from w to v, obtained as described above. Since the distances computed are exact distances, the packet always progresses towards the destination and will never loop. Note that if the paths are only approximately shortest, there may be loops – in this case, w adds its label $J''(w)$ to the packet header, setting $S'(u) = S(u) \cup \{w\}$ and we ask for the shortest $S'(u)$-constrained path from w to v. The price we pay here is that the packet headers grow with the length of the path.

In this case however, we may need to compute graphs $G_+[Z]$ for larger and larger sets Z. $\square$

5   Open Problems

A major problem is to get good bounds on planar graphs. Using the $O(\sqrt{n})$ recursive separator structure gives $\tilde{O}(n)$ bits per label, but we believe it is possible to do much better. We would also like to solve other constrained path problems using $G_+[X]$, using the separator structure that we encode.

References

1. Thorup, M., Zwick, U.: Compact routing schemes. In: SPAA '01: Proceedings of the thirteenth annual ACM symposium on Parallel algorithms and architectures, New York, NY, USA, ACM Press (2001) 1–10
2. Varadhan, K., Govindan, R., Estrin, D.: Persistent route oscillations in interdomain routing. Technical report, USC/ISI (1996)
3. Griffin, T.G., Shepherd, F.B., Wilfong, G.: The stable paths problem and interdomain routing. IEEE/ACM Trans. Netw. **10** (2002) 232–243
4. Feigenbaum, J., Karger, D., Mirrokni, V., Sami, R.: Subjective-cost policy routing. In: Lecture Notes in Computer Science. Volume 3828. (2005) 174–183
5. Courcelle, B., Vanicat, R.: Query efficient implementation of graphs of bounded clique-width. Discrete Applied Mathematics **131** (2003) 129–150
6. Gupta, A., Kumar, A., Thorup, M.: Tree based mpls routing. In: SPAA '03: Proceedings of the fifteenth annual ACM symposium on Parallel algorithms and architectures, New York, NY, USA, ACM Press (2003) 193–199
7. Courcelle, B. In: Graph decompositions. (2006) Chapter of a book in preparation. Available at www.labri.fr/perso/courcell/Textes/ChapitreDecArbos.pdf.
8. Arnborg, S., Courcelle, B., Proskurowski, A., Seese, D.: An algebraic theory of graph reduction. J. ACM **40** (1993) 1134–1164
9. Bodlaender, H.L.: NC-algorithms for graphs with small treewidth. In: Proc. 14th Workshop Graph-Theoretic Concepts in Computer Science WG'88, Springer-Verlag, Lecture Notes in Computer Science 344 (1989) 1–10
10. Corneil, D.G., Rotics, U.: On the relationship between clique-width and treewidth. SIAM J. Comput. **34** (2005) 825–847
11. Wanke, E.: k-nlc graphs and polynomial algorithms. Discrete Applied Mathematics **54** (1994) 251–266
12. Courcelle, B., Olariu, S.: Upper bounds to the clique width of graphs. Discrete Appl. Math. **101** (2000) 77–114
13. Kannan, S., Naor, M., Rudich, S.: Implicit representation of graphs. SIAM J. Discret. Math. **5** (1992) 596–603
14. Fellows, M.R., Rosamond, F.A., Rotics, U., Szeider, S.: Clique-width minimization is np-hard. In: STOC 2006: Proceedings of the thirty-eighth annual ACM symposium on Theory of computing, New York, NY, USA, ACM Press (2006)
15. il Oum, S.: Approximating rank-width and clique-width quickly. In Kratsch, D., ed.: WG. Volume 3787 of Lecture Notes in Computer Science., Springer (2005) 49–58

A New Bound for Pure Greedy Hot Potato Routing

Manfred Kunde

Technical University of Ilmenau, Institute for Theoretical Computer Science
kunde@tu-ilmenau.de

Abstract. We present a new bound for pure greedy hot potato routing on $n \times n$ mesh-connected arrays and $n \times n$ tori. For permutation problems the bound is $O(n\sqrt{n}\log n)$ steps which improves the for a long time known bound of $O(n^2)$. For the more general link-limited k-destination routing problem the bound is $O(n\sqrt{kn}\log n)$. The bound also holds for restricted pure greedy hot potato routing on $n \times n$ meshes with diagonals. The bound could be derived by a new technique where packets may have several identities.

1 Introduction

The problem of packet routing is basic in parallel and distributed computing. In this paper we study problems where each processor may be source of as many packets as it has links to direct neighbors and each processor is destination of at most k packets, $k \geq 1$. We call this type of problems link-limited k-destination routing. As a special case we get the well-known permutation routing where each node is source of at most one packet and destination of at most one packet.

A well-known routing strategy has become popular under the name hot potato routing where each processor does not store incoming packets besides they are destined for this processor [Bar64]. After arriving in a processor, due to a routing decision, the packets are sent immediately to neighboring processors (see Fig. 1). Hot potato routing algorithms have been observed to work well in practise and have been used in parallel machines such as the HEP multiprocessor [Smi81], the Connection machine [Hil85], and the Caltech Mosaic C [Sei92].

Several hot potato routing algorithms have been designed for mesh-connected arrays or meshes. In an $n \times n$ mesh (torus) each node is given as a pair (r, c), $1 \leq r, c \leq n$. A processor (r, c) lies in row r and in column c and has four direct neighbors in the interior of a mesh and on the border two or three direct neighbors. In a torus all the nodes are interior ones. On the 2-dimensional $n \times n$ torus Feige and Raghavan [FR92] gave an algorithm that solves any random destination problem in $2n + o(n)$ steps with high probability and presented a further algorithm that routes any permutation problem in $9n$ steps. Newman and Schuster [NS95] gave a deterministic algorithm based on sorting that solves permutation routing on an $n \times n$ mesh in $7n + o(n)$ steps. Kaufmann et al. [KLS] gave an improvement of this result to $3.5n + o(n)$ steps. Kaklamanis et al. [KKR]

W. Thomas and P. Weil (Eds.): STACS 2007, LNCS 4393, pp. 49–60, 2007.

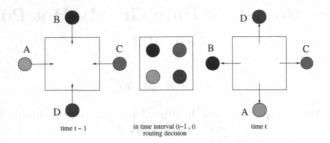

Fig. 1. Hot Potato Routing at step t

presented an algorithm that routes most of the permutations in $2n + o(n)$ steps. All these algorithms are pretty fast in theory. However, the control structures of these algorithms are too complicated and they are not used in practice, because they are not simple enough like the greedy algorithms. Borodin et al. [BRS97] gave a more practical and simple hot potato algorithm which runs an arbitrary permutation problem in $O(n^{3/2})$ steps in the worst-case. This algorithm routes each of the packets within the rows until a packet may enter its destination column. In this sense the algorithm is strictly dimension oriented. However, this algorithm is not greedy.

A hot potato routing algorithm is *greedy* [Bar64, BES95] if each node forwards each packet closer to its destination whenever this is possible, i.e. whenever the desired links are not already given to other packets. A packet that does not advance toward its destination is said to be *deflected*. The algorithm is called *pure greedy* if packets can be deflected only if their desired links are given to *advancing* packets. Greedy algorithms are attractive because they are quite simple and they are used and work quite well in practise. Only a little is known on upper bounds. Busch et al. [BHW00] presented a special algorithm that uses randomization to adjust packet priorities. It solves permutation problems in $O(n \log n)$ steps with high probability. In another paper the same authors [BHW00] studied the problem of many-to-one batch routing where each of the n^2 nodes is the source of at most one packet and a node may be the destination for many packets. Their algorithm needs $O(LB \log^3 n)$ steps with high probability where $LB \in \Omega(n)$ is a lower bound basing on the maximum path length and the maximum congestion of a given problem instance.

In general the so far best upper worst-case bound for greedy hot potato routing algorithms is $O(n^2)$ [BRS97, BHS98] and is known for more than a decade. The bound is far away from all experimental results. Indeed, there seems to be a huge gap between theoretical analysis and real behaviour. The situation is described by Ben-Dor et al. [BHS94] as follows: 'Although fairly simple greedy hot-potato algorithms perform very well in practice, they resist formal analysis attacks.' Ten years before Borodin and Hopcroft [BH85] already expressed themselves in a similiar way: 'Although experimentally the algorithm appears promising we have not been able to formally analyze its behaviour.'

In this paper we present for permutation problems a new upper bound of $O(n^{3/2} \log n)$ for quite natural pure greedy hot potato algorithms. The bound is derived by the help of a new proof technique which assigns different identities to each packet and analyzes the interactions between these identities. Moreover, for the more general link-limited k-destination routing problem we can give a bound of $O(n\sqrt{kn} \log n)$ steps for $n \times n$ meshes and tori. At the end of this paper it is shown that this bound is also valid for pure restricted greedy hot potato algorithms on meshes and tori with diagonals.

2   The Problem and Notations

For technical reasons we will concentrate in this section on $1-1$ routing problems on $n \times n$ meshes. That means, each processor is source of at most one packet and each node is destination of at most one packet. Each row (column) of processors is then destination of at most n packets. The direct neighbors of a processor (r,c), $1 \le r,c \le n$, have coordinates (i,j) with $|r - i| + |c - j| = 1$ and are each directly connected to node (r,c) with an incoming and an outgoing link. So, besides the border processors each node has four direct neighbors.

In time interval $(0,1)$, in the first step, each processor sends its own packet to a neighboring processor such that the distance to the packet's destination is shortened. From that on the following happens: in time interval $(t-1,t)$, $t \ge 2$, in step t, each processor inspects the at most 4 packets on the incoming links, makes a routing decision, and sends the packets on the outgoing links to directly neighboring processors (see Fig. 1). Packets which have reached their destinations are stored in the storage of the corresponding node and are no longer living in the system.

In the following we give the general scheme for the priorities of packets just for the moment when packets meet each other in a processor (see Fig. 1). For this purpose we classify packets with respect to their movements and directions they want to move. The wanted directions are those which shorten the distance to the corresponding destinations.

Forward packets (type (f)) are those which have moved towards their destination in the beginning of this step, *backward packets* (type (b)) are those which were deflected (that is they have moved away from their destination.) In a greedy algorithm all forward packets want to remain forward, that is they want further to shorten their distance to their target processor. All backward packets want to become forward packets.

A packet that is already either in its destination row or destination column is called *restricted* (type (r)). It is also called restricted if it is allowed to enter either its destination row or destination column. Restricted packets are not allowed to leave their destination row (or destination column), i.e. they remain restricted until they reach their target. Note that by this rule the algorithm is still greedy.

Packets which are not restricted are called *normal* (type (n)). Note that normal packets have two directions free to reduce the distance to their targets.

Restricted packets have priority over normal packets, and forward packets have higher priority against backward packets.

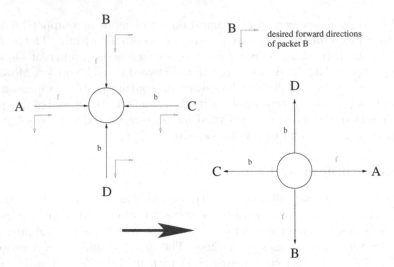

Fig. 2. Conflicts in the normal case

Since normal packets have two forward directions the worst scenario occurs when four normal packets have the same two forward directions. This can only happen when two backward packets meet two forward packets. In this case the two forward packets are preferred and travel towards their destinations while the backward packets are deflected and remain backward (see Fig. 2). Note that at latest in a corner processor a backward packet changes to a forward one. That means after at most $2n - 2$ steps a backward packet becomes a forward one.

From two restricted packets in a row (resp. column) which meet in a processor and want to travel along the same link one is a forward packet and the other a backward packet. The forward packet is prefered and reaches its destination within at most $n-1$ steps. The restricted backward packet will become a forward packet latest after $n-1$ steps in a border processor. All in all a restricted packet reaches its target after at most $2n - 2$ steps.

So clearly, normal packets want to become restricted and this can only happen when they arrive at a processor in their destination row or column. We only discuss the case for the column, the row case is analogous. If there is at most one restricted packet in that processor the packet can enter the column and is restricted from now on. However, in the case of two restricted packets the packet is deflected (as shown in Fig. 4 where packet C wants to enter column k). The former forward packet becomes a backward one. We say that the packet has suffered a *basic conflict*, since from this moment on the packet may be deflected several times until it becomes a forward packet again. In the case where one restricted packet meets two packets which want to enter the column, one of them enters and becomes restricted while the other one suffers a basic conflict and is deflected. In the following we handle this case as if two restricted packets have hindered a packet to enter the column.

In this sense normally two restricted packets at the same processor can generate basic conflicts for at most two other normal packets. A special case for

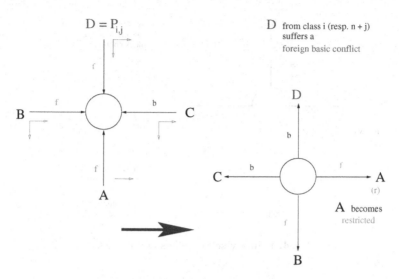

Fig. 3. Foreign basic conflicts

a basic conflict occurs when a restricted backward packet turns at the border and one or two packets from a border row try to enter the column. In this case each of them suffers a basic conflict generated by only one restricted packet. The situation is similiar to that when two packets from a border row want to enter the column: one becomes restricted and the other one suffers a basic conflict and is deflected.

Normally basic conflicts occur between packets which belong to the same destination column (or row). In the following rows and columns are also denoted as classes. Each packet belongs to its destination row and to its destination column. So each packet is member of 2 classes. To a deflected packet and a basic conflict belong a pair of restricted packets of the corresponding destination class (either a column or a row) or one restricted packet in the borderline case.

There is another type of basic conflict (see Fig. 3). When a packet A becomes restricted for a destination row (column) and two forward packets (B and D) not belonging to that row want to go in the same direction as packet A. When they have the same second free direction then only one (say B) can get that link and the other (D) is deflected. We then say that D suffers a *foreign basic conflict*. D is a witness for a packet of a foreign class, namely A, that becomes restricted. A is in a class which is different (foreign) from the classes of packet D. And we can say that the foreign packet A is responsible for this basic conflict. A is never again responsible for any conflict of this type.

By a basic conflict a packet turns from forward to backward. Note that after at most $2n - 2$ steps a backward packet becomes forward again. Within at most $2n - 2$ further steps a forward packet may either reach its target or becomes restricted or can become a backward packet only by a basic conflict. We will look at *phases* of $6n$ steps which consists of a *conflict phase* of the first $4n$ steps and a *leaving phase* of the last $2n$ steps. Note that all restricted packets of

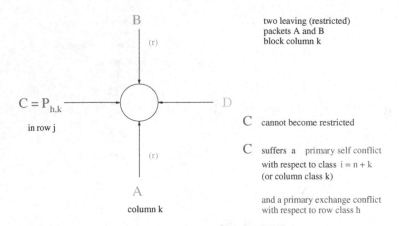

Fig. 4. Primary self conflicts and classes

the conflict phase will reach their targets latest in the leaving phase. A packet which survives a conflict phase of $4n$ steps is called a *surviving packet* and suffers at least one basic conflict. The first basic conflict of a surviving packet in the conflict part of a phase is called a *primary conflict*. (A surviving packet may leave the system in the next $2n$ steps, but this will play no role in the following analysis.) Packets which are restricted at the beginnig of the conflict phase or become restricted during the conflict phase are called *leaving packets* since they will have left the system latest during the leaving phase of $2n$ steps. Let phase t consists of steps $6nt, 6nt + 1, ..., 6nt + 4n, ..., 6n(t + 1) - 1$.

Let a packet with destination (i, j) be denoted by $P_{i,j}$. Then $P_{i,j}$ is member of row class i and column class j. In this sense packets have a kind of two identities which play a role in primary conflicts. In the following we will number the classes all together from 1 to $2n$, row class i becomes class i and column class j becomes class $n + j$.

Let $n_i(t)$ denote the number of packets in class i, $1 \leq i \leq 2n$, at the beginning of phase t, $t \geq 0$. So $n_i(0)$ is the number of packets in class i in the beginning at time 0. Let $l_i(t)$ denote the number of packets in class i, $1 \leq i \leq 2n$, which are already or become leaving packets during the conflict phase of phase t. Then

$$n_i(t + 1) \leq n_i(t) - l_i(t) \tag{1}$$

for all i and t. Note that each of the $n_i(t) - l_i(t)$ surviving packets suffers exactly one primary conflict.

A packet $P_{i,j}$ may have its primary conflict with either restricted packets of class i or of class $n + j$ or with a packet which becomes restricted in a foreign class. If packet $P_{i,j}$ suffers a primary conflict with restricted packets from its own class i (class $n + j$) then this conflict is called a *primary self conflict* with respect to class i (class $n + j$). The same conflict is called a *primary exchange conflict* with respect to the (orthogonal) class $n + j$ (class i). So self conflicts of a row are exchange conflicts for different columns, and self conflicts of a column are exchange conflicts for different rows (see Fig. 4). So each conflict of this type is regarded (and later counted) twice depending on the chosen identity of the corresponding packet $P_{i,j}$.

Let for phase t and class i $e_i(t)$ denote the number of surviving packets of class i that suffer a primary self conflict with restricted packets from class i and let $w_i(t)$ be the number of surviving packets of class i that suffer primary exchange conflicts with restricted packets from their own class $\neq i$. And let $f_i(t)$ be the number of surviving packets of class i that suffer a foreign primary conflict. Then $n_i(t) - l_i(t) = e_i(t) + w_i(t) + f_i(t)$, $1 \leq i \leq 2n$, or

$$n_i(t) = e_i(t) + w_i(t) + f_i(t) + l_i(t), \; 1 \leq i \leq 2n. \tag{2}$$

Here each packet and its primary conflict is counted twice. Since each primary self conflict is also a primary exchange conflict and vice versa we get

$$\sum_{i=1}^{2n} e_i(t) = \sum_{i=1}^{2n} w_i(t). \tag{3}$$

Let $N(t) = \sum_{i=1}^{2n} n_i(t)$ the (doubly counted) number of still existing packets at the beginning of phase t, and $L(t) = \sum_{i=1}^{2n} l_i(t)$ the (doubly counted) number of all leaving packets. Let $F(t) = \sum_{i=1}^{2n} f_i(t)$ be the (doubly counted) number of all foreign primary conflicts in phase t. As already said each packet that suffers a foreign primary conflict meets one leaving packet of a foreign class which is responsible for this conflict. Hence $F(t) \leq L(t)$. Note that again all conflicts and all packets are doubly counted which is due to membership of a packet in two classes. Then

$$N(t) = \sum_{i=1}^{2n} n_i(t) = \sum_{i=1}^{2n} e_i(t) + \sum_{i=1}^{2n} w_i(t) + \sum_{i=1}^{2n} f_i(t) + \sum_{i=1}^{2n} l_i(t)$$

$$= 2\sum_{i=1}^{2n} e_i(t) + F(t) + L(t) \leq 2\sum_{i=1}^{2n} e_i(t) + 2L(t). \tag{4}$$

The number of self conflicts of class i is bounded by the number of pairs of leaving packets, each pair may be responsible for up to two primary conflicts. Note that two restricted packets can meet in a class at most once. So the number of packets suffering a self conflict from these pairs is at most $2(l_i(t) - 1)l_i(t)/2 = l_i(t)^2 - l_i(t)$. At the boundary each turning restricted packet may also cause two self conflicts. Therefore the number of self conflicts is bounded by

$$e_i(t) \leq l_i(t)^2 + l_i(t). \tag{5}$$

3   The New Bound

Let for phase t $\alpha_i(t) = l_i(t)/n_i(t)^{1/2}$, i.e. $l_i(t) = \alpha_i(t)n_i(t)^{1/2}$ and $0 \leq \alpha_i(t) \leq n_i(t)^{1/2}$. If the factor $\alpha_i(t)$ is large then many packets of class i will leave the system and we will classify such a situation as good. In the following lemma the influence of these factors on the the number of still existing packets is given.

Lemma 1. $n_i(t+1)^{1/2} \leq n_i(0)^{1/2} - (1/2)\sum_{j=0}^{t} \alpha_i(j)$, $t \geq 0$.

Proof. By inequality (1) and the defintion of $\alpha_i(t)$ we get

$$n_i(t+1) \leq n_i(t) - l_i(t) = n_i(t) - \alpha_i(t)n_i(t)^{1/2} \leq n_i(t) - \alpha_i(t)n_i(t)^{1/2} + \alpha_i(t)^2/4$$

$$= (n_i(t)^{1/2} - \alpha_i(t)/2)^2 \quad \text{and therefore}$$

$$n_i(t+1)^{1/2} \leq n_i(t)^{1/2} - \alpha_i(t)/2 \leq n_i(t-1)^{1/2} - \alpha_i(t-1)/2 - \alpha_i(t)/2$$

$$\leq n_i(0)^{1/2} - (1/2)\sum_{j=0}^{t} \alpha_i(j) \ .$$

$\square$

Let $c > 0$ be a constant. A phase t is *c-good* for a class i if and only if $\alpha_i(t) \geq c$. In a certain sense in a c-good phase enough packets are leaving that class. If phase t is not c-good, then we say it is *c-bad* for class i.

Lemma 2. *Each class i has at most $g_i \leq (2/c)n_i(0)^{1/2}$ c-good phases.*

Proof. From the last lemma we know that

$$(1/2)\sum_{j=0}^{t} \alpha_i(j) \leq n_i(0)^{1/2} - n_i(t+1)^{1/2} \leq n_i(0)^{1/2} \ .$$

Let $g = g_i$ and $t_1,\ldots,t_g$ be all c-good phases for class i until phase t. That means, $\alpha_i(t_k) \geq c$ for all k, $1 \leq k \leq g$. Hence

$$(1/2)cg \leq (1/2)\sum_{k=1}^{g} \alpha_i(t_k) \leq (1/2)\sum_{j=0}^{t} \alpha_i(j) \leq n_i(0)^{1/2} \ .$$

$\square$

If for all classes all the phases are c-good then this lemma says that there are in total at most $O(\sqrt{n})$ phases and the routing is done in at most $O(\sqrt{n}n)$ steps. However, there might be also a lot of c-bad phases for the different classes. In the following let c be a constant with $c < 1/2$ and let $d = 2c^2 < 1/2$.

Lemma 3. *In a c-bad phase t for class i we have $e_i(t) < 2c^2n_i(t) = dn_i(t)$.*

Proof. If phase t is c-bad for class i we have $\alpha_i(t) < c$. Therefore

$$l_i(t)^2 + l_i(t) < c^2n_i(t) + cn_i(t)^{1/2} \ .$$

For $n_i(t)^{1/2} \leq 1/c$ we get $l_i(t) < cn_i(t)^{1/2} \leq 1$, i.e. $l_i(t) = 0$. In this case primary self conflicts do not occur. Therefore we may assume that $n_i(t)^{1/2} > 1/c$ or $cn_i(t)^{1/2} > 1$, from which we immediately get $cn_i(t)^{1/2} < c^2n_i(t)$. We already know by inequality (5) that $e_i(t) \leq l_i(t)^2 + l_i(t)$. Therefore

$$e_i(t) < c^2n_i(t) + cn_i(t)^{1/2} \leq 2c^2n_i(t) \ .$$

$\square$

In the following we show that the number of packets which have not reached their destinations is halved within at most $O(n\sqrt{n})$ steps. Let x be the last phase with $N(x) > (1/2)N(0)$, i.e. $N(x+1) \leq (1/2)N(0)$.

Lemma 4. *Let* $g = \max g_i$ *be the maximum number of c-good phases for all classes. Then*

$$x \in O(g) .$$

Proof. If $x \leq 2g$ we are done, so let $x > 2g$. Let $G_i = \{t | 0 \leq t \leq x, \alpha_i(t) \geq c\}$ be the set of c-good phases for class i among the first $x+1$ phases and $B_i = \{t | 0 \leq t \leq x, \alpha_i(t) \leq c\}$ be the set of c-bad phases for class i. Then $|G_i| + |B_i| = x+1$ and $|G_i| = g_i \leq g$. Then by the help of inequality (4)

$$\sum_{t=0}^{x} N(t) = \sum_{i=1}^{2n}\sum_{t=0}^{x} n_i(t) \leq 2\sum_{i=1}^{2n}\sum_{t=0}^{x} e_i(t) + 2\sum_{t=0}^{x} L(t)$$

$$\leq 2\sum_{i=1}^{2n}(\sum_{t \in G_i} e_i(t) + \sum_{t \in B_i} e_i(t)) + 2(N(0) - N(x+1)) .$$

Note that for a c-good phase t for class i we trivially have $e_i(t) \leq n_i(t)$ and for a c-bad phase t by Lemma 3 we get $e_i(t) < dn_i(t)$. Then for each class i

$$\sum_{t \in G_i} e_i(t) + \sum_{t \in B_i} e_i(t) \leq \sum_{t=0}^{g-1} n_i(t) + \sum_{t=g}^{x} dn_i(t) .$$

This follows from $n_i(t+1) \leq n_i(t)$ and $d < 1/2$ and by rearranging. Hence

$$\sum_{i=1}^{2n}\sum_{t=0}^{x} n_i(t) = \sum_{t=0}^{x} N(t) \leq 2\sum_{i=1}^{2n}(\sum_{t=0}^{g-1} n_i(t) + \sum_{t=g}^{x} dn_i(t)) + 2N(0)$$

and therefore

$$\sum_{t=g}^{x}\sum_{i=1}^{2n} n_i(t) \leq \sum_{t=0}^{g-1}\sum_{i=1}^{2n} n_i(t) + 2\sum_{t=g}^{x}\sum_{i=1}^{2n} dn_i(t) + 2N(0) \text{ or}$$

$$\sum_{t=g}^{x}(1 - 2d)N(t) \leq \sum_{t=0}^{g-1} N(t) + 2N(0) \leq (g+2)N(0)$$

Since $N(t) > N(0)/2$ for all $t \leq x$ we get

$$(x - g)(1 - 2d)N(0)/2 \leq (x - g + 1)(1 - 2d)N(0)/2 \leq (g+2)N(0)$$

und therefore

$$x \leq (g(3 - 2d) + 4)/(1 - 2d) \in O(g) .$$

$\square$

By Lemma 4 the number of good phases is bounded by $O(\sqrt{n})$. I. e. the number of surviving packets is halved within at most $O(\sqrt{n})$ phases. Since each phase consists of $O(n)$ steps we obtain the following theorem:

Theorem 1. *For permutation routing on an $n \times n$ grid the pure greedy hot potato routing algorithm needs at most $O(n\sqrt{n}\log n)$ steps.*

4   Extensions

Note that the above bound is also valid for $n \times n$ tori. In this case the duration of the phases can be halved because normal backward packets become forward ones after at most n steps and restricted backward packets turn into forward packets after at most $n/2$ steps. Furthermore, the bound also holds for $4 - 4$ routing problems on tori where in the beginning each processor contains at most 4 packets and is target of at most 4 packets. Note that in this case the maximal number of c-good phases is bounded by $(2/c)\sqrt{4n}$, which follows from Lemma 2 and $n_i(0) \leq 4n$. For meshes without wrap-around connections the problem has to be altered slightly. The number of packets in the beginning is limited by the number of direct neighbors and processors at the border have less than four direct neighbors. So let us view link-limited k-destination routing problems, as described in the introduction, where each node may be source of as many packets as it has links to direct neighbors and each processor is destination of at most k packets, $k \geq 1$. For such a problem a class (a row or a column) has at most kn members. In this case we get, again by Lemma 2, that the number of c-good phases is limited by $(2/c)\sqrt{kn}$ which is in $O(\sqrt{n})$ provided k is a constant.

Theorem 2. *For link-limited k-destination routing problems, $k \geq 1$, the pure greedy hot potato routing algorithm needs at most $O(n\sqrt{kn}\log n)$ steps on $n \times n$ meshes and tori.*

In the case of grids with diagonals in a greedy algorithm the packets would prefer to travel along the diagonal connections because this would shorten the distances to their targets mostly. If we agree that the hot potato algorithm is still pure greedy when each packet must try to get closer to its destination whenever this is possible then the concept of restricted packets must be changed. Consider the situation where two packets have arrived their destination column and want to enter their column in the same direction. In the case of grids without diagonals both packets become restricted, one becomes a forward packet while the other one becomes backward. In the case of diagonals the second packet may choose a free diagonal connection to get closer to its target. (See Fig. 5.) The status of being restricted with respect to its destination column or row or with respect to one of its destination diagonals is of some value for a packet because a restricted packet will reach its target within at most $2n$ steps. Let us call a hot potato algorithm pure restricted greedy when all packets that are already restricted remain restricted for their chosen either row, column or diagonal, even when it is backward. Also, if a packet has the chance to become restricted then it

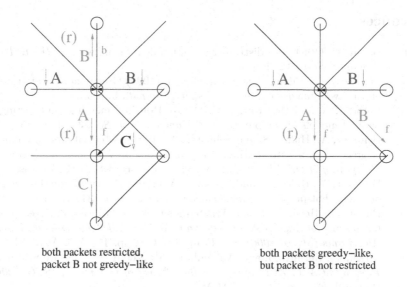

both packets restricted,
packet B not greedy-like

both packets greedy-like,
but packet B not restricted

Fig. 5. Diagonals: restricted vs. greedy-like

must enter its destination row, column or diagonal, even in the case it becomes backward. For this kind of algorithms we get the following result.

Theorem 3. *For link-limited k-destination routing problems, $k \geq 1$, the pure restricted greedy hot potato routing algorithm needs at most $O(n\sqrt{kn}\log n)$ steps on $n \times n$ meshes and tori with diagonals.*

In the case of grids with diagonals a packet belongs to four classes: to its destination row, to its destination column, and to its two destination diagonals. I.e. each packet has four identities. Since there are in total $4n - 2$ diagonals, $2n - 1$ for each slope, we have now classes with different numbers of processors. All in all we have now $6n - 2$ classes. As before let $n_i(t)$ denote the number of packets in class i in the beginning of phase t and let $N(t) = \sum_{i=1}^{6n-2} n_i(t)$. (In $N(t)$ each packet is counted four times.) Then we have $n_i(0) \leq kn$. Note that now each self conflict of a packet in a class i is an exchange conflict for 3 other classes $\neq i$ to which the packet also belongs. Therefore $3\sum_{i=1}^{6n-2} e_i(t) = \sum_{i=1}^{6n-2} w_i(t)$. Then

$$N(t) = \sum_{i=1}^{6n-2} n_i(t) = \sum_{i=1}^{6n-2} e_i(t) + \sum_{i=1}^{6n-2} w_i(t) + \sum_{i=1}^{6n-2} f_i(t) + \sum_{i=1}^{6n-2} l_i(t)$$

$$= 4\sum_{i=1}^{6n-2} e_i(t) + F(t) + L(t) \leq 4\sum_{i=1}^{6n-2} e_i(t) + 2L(t) .$$

The rest of the argumentation is then analogous to the case of grids without diagonals.

References

[Bar64]   Baran, P. (1964) On distributed communication networks. *IEEE Trans. Commun. Syst.*, **12**, 1–9.

[BES95]   Ben-Aroya, I., Eilam, T. and Schuster, A. (1995) Greedy hot-potato routing on the two-dimensional mesh. *Distrib. Comput.*, **9**, 3–19.

[BH85]   Borodin, A. and Hopcroft, J. E. (1985) Routing, merging, and sorting on parallel models of computation. *J. Comput. Syst. Sci.*, **30**, 130–145.

[BHS94]   Ben-Dor, A., Halevi, S. and Schuster, A. (1994) Potential function analysis of greedy hot-potato routing. In *Symposium on Principles of Distributed Computing (PODC '94)*, pp. 225–234, New York, USA, ACM Press.

[BHS98]   Ben-Dor, A., Halevi, S. and Schuster, A. (1998) Potential function analysis of greedy hot-potato routing. *Theory Comput. Syst.*, **31**, 41–61.

[BHW00]   Busch, C., Herlihy, M. and Wattenhofer, R. (2000) Randomized greedy hot-potato routing. In *Proc. 11th Ann. ACM-SIAM Symposium on Discrete Algorithms (SODA'2000)*, San Francisco, CA, pp. 458–466. ACM/SIAM.

[BHW00]   Busch, C., Herlihy, M. and Wattenhofer, R. (2000) Hard-potato routing. In *Proc. 32nd Ann. ACM Symp. on the Theory of Computing (STOC'2000)*, Portland, OR, pp. 278–285. ACM.

[BRS97]   Borodin, A., Rabani, Y. and Schieber, B. (1997) Deterministic many-to-many hot potato routing. *IEEE Trans. Parallel Distrib. Syst.*, **8**, 587–596.

[FR92]   Feige, U. and Raghavan, P. (1992) Exact analysis of hot-potato routing. In *Proc. 33rd Ann. Symp. Foundations of Computer Science (FOCS'92)*, Pittsburgh, PA, pp. 553–562. IEEE Computer Society Press.

[Hil85]   Hillis, W. D. (1985) *The Connection Machine*. MIT Press, Cambridge, MA.

[KKR]   Kaklamanis, C., Krizanc, D., and Rao, S. (1993) Hot-potato routing on processor arrays. *Proc. 5th Annual ACM Symp. on Parallel Algorithms and Architectures (SPAA'93)*, pp. 273–282.

[KLS]   Kaufmann, M., Lauer, H. and Schröder, H. (1994) Fast deterministic hot-potato routing on meshes. *Proc. 5th International Symp. on Algorithms and Computation (ISAAC)*, LNCS 834, pp. 333–541.

[NS95]   Newman, I. and Schuster, A. (1995) Hot-potato algorithms for permutation routing. *IEEE Trans. Parallel Distrib. Syst.*, **6**, 1168–1176.

[Sei92]   Seitz, C. L. (1992) Mosaic C: an experimental, fine-grain multicomputer. In *Proc. Int. Conf. Celebrating the 25th Anniversary of INRIA*, Paris, France, December. LNCS 653, pp. 69–85. Springer, New York.

[Smi81]   Smith, B. J. (1981) Architecture and applications of the HEP multiprocessor computer. *Soc. Photocopti. Instrum. Eng.*, **298**, 241–248.

Wavelength Management in WDM Rings
to Maximize the Number of Connections[*]

Ioannis Caragiannis

Research Academic Computer Technology Institute &
Department of Computer Engineering and Informatics
University of Patras, 26500 Rio, Greece

Abstract. We study computationally hard combinatorial problems arising from the important engineering question of how to maximize the
number of connections that can be simultaneously served in a WDM
optical network. In such networks, WDM technology can satisfy a set of
connections by computing a route and assigning a wavelength to each
connection so that no two connections routed through the same fiber are
assigned the same wavelength. Each fiber supports a limited number of w
wavelengths and in order to fully exploit the parallelism provided by the
technology, one should select a set connections of maximum cardinality
which can be satisfied using the available wavelengths. This is known as
the *maximum routing and path coloring* problem (maxRPC).

Our main contribution is a general analysis method for a class of iterative algorithms for a more general coloring problem. A lower bound
on the benefit of such an algorithm in terms of the optimal benefit and
the number of available wavelengths is given by a *benefit-revealing linear program*. We apply this method to maxRPC in both undirected and
bidirected rings to obtain bounds on the approximability of several algorithms. Our results also apply to the problem maxPC where paths instead
of connections are given as part of the input. We also study the profit
version of maxPC in rings where each path has a profit and the objective
is to satisfy a set of paths of maximum total profit.

1 Introduction

Combinatorial problems arising from high speed communication networks utilizing the Wavelength Division Multiplexing (WDM) technology have received
significant attention since the mid 90's. Such networks connect nodes through optical fibers. Each fiber can simultaneously carry different data streams provided
that each stream is carried on a different wavelength. In order to fully exploit
the capabilities of these networks, the same wavelength has to be used along a
path so that all necessary processing is performed on the optical domain and
slow opto-electronic conversions are avoided [20]. Given connection requests (i.e.,
transmitter-receiver pairs), the WDM technology establishes communication by

---

[*] This work was partially supported by the European Union under IST FET Integrated
Project 015964 AEOLUS.

W. Thomas and P. Weil (Eds.): STACS 2007, LNCS 4393, pp. 61–72, 2007.

finding a path from each transmitter to the corresponding receiver and assigning a wavelength to each path so that paths crossing the same fiber are using different wavelengths. The number of available wavelengths (i.e., the available optical bandwidth) is limited, so they have to be used efficiently.

The underlying WDM network can be modeled as an undirected graph assuming that each fiber can handle transmissions in both directions. WDM networks can also be modeled by bidirected graphs (i.e., directed graphs which contain a directed link (u, v) if and only if it contains (v, u)). Here, we assume that each fiber is dedicated to transmitting in one direction.

We use the term *connection* to denote a pair of a transmitter and a receiver that wish to communicate. Given a set of connections, a *routing* is a set of paths connecting each transmitter to the corresponding receiver. The *load* of a set of paths is the maximum number of paths crossing any link of the network. The load of a set of paths gives a lower bound on the number of wavelengths that are necessary to satisfy them. Combinatorial problems of interest are those which aim either to minimize the number of wavelengths (intuitively, we may think of the wavelengths as *colors*) for a set of connections or to maximize the number of connections that can be satisfied (also called *benefit*) given a limitation w on the number of available wavelengths. Formally, we define the following problems that abstract the most interesting engineering questions in WDM networks.

Routing and path coloring (RPC). Given a set of connections R on a network, find a routing P of R and a coloring of P with the minimum number of colors. When paths instead of connections are given on input, we have the *path coloring* (PC) problem.

Maximum routing and path coloring (maxRPC). Given a positive integer w and a set of connections R on a network, find a subset of R of maximum cardinality which has a routing that can be colored with at most w colors. When paths instead of connections are given on input, we have the *maximum path coloring* (maxPC) problem.

For general networks, the above problems have been proved to be hard to approximate. In particular, problems PC and maxPC are in general equivalent to minimum graph coloring and maximum independent set, two problems which are very unlikely to have efficient approximation algorithms. Although these results are disappointing from the practical point of view, the topologies deployed by the telecommunication industry are much simpler; trees, rings, and mesh-like planar networks are the most popular ones. In such networks, much better approximations are feasible. For example, in trees where unique paths correspond to connections, the above problems have algorithms which approximate the optimal solution within a constant factor (e.g., see [2,6,7,8]).

In this paper we focus on ring networks. Problem PC in rings is also known as *circular arc coloring* and has received significant attention in the literature (e.g., [3,10,13,14,22,23]). It has been proved to be NP-hard in [10]. The best general approximation algorithm has approximation ratio 3/2 [13] while better approximation algorithms exist in the case where the load of the set of paths is polylogarithmic on the ring size [14,15] or/and the minimum number of paths required to cover the whole ring is not very small [3,23]. Observe that the ring is the simplest topology where routing decisions can be part of the problems. Problem RPC is also known to be NP-hard [7]. The best known approximation algorithm has approximation ratio slightly smaller than 2 [5], while an algorithm with approximation ratio approaching $\frac{3}{2} + \frac{1}{2e} \approx 1.68394$ when the optimal number of colors is substantially large compared to the size of the ring has been presented in [15].

For general values of w, problems maxPC and maxRPC are NP-hard; their NP-hardness follow by the NP-hardness of problems PC and RPC, respectively. When $w = 1$, maxRPC is actually the problem of computing a maximum number of connections that can be routed through link-disjoint paths. Awerbuch et al. [1] (see also [24]) show that algorithms that iteratively call link-disjoint paths algorithms to compute solutions to maxRPC with arbitrary w have slightly worse approximation ratio than the ratio of the algorithm that is used to compute link-disjoint paths. In undirected and bidirected rings, link-disjoint paths of maximum size can be computed in polynomial-time yielding iterative algorithms with approximation ratio $\frac{e}{e-1} \approx 1.58198$ [24] (see also the discussion in [18]). The best known approximation algorithms for maxRPC (and maxPC) in undirected rings has approximation ratio $3/2$ [17,18] while an $11/7$-approximation algorithm for maxRPC in bidirected rings is presented in [18]. Interesting variants of the maxRPC and maxPC problems are their profit versions where connections (or paths) are associated with non-negative profits and the objective is to color with at most w colors a set of connections (or paths) with the maximum total profit. A simple iterative algorithm has approximation ratio 1.58198 in this case (the proof follows by extending the analysis of [1,24]). Li et al. [16] present a 2-approximation algorithm for a related problem which also has arbitrary load constraints on the links of the ring.

The aim of this paper is to improve the known approximability bounds for maxRPC and maxPC in rings. Before presenting our results, we give a brief overview of the ideas in [17,18]. The algorithm of [18] for the undirected case of maxRPC (similar ideas are used in [17] for maxPC) actually applies two different algorithms on the input instance and outputs the best among the two solutions. The first algorithm colors some of the connections on input with at most w colors by using the same color in at most two connections. This is done by a maximum matching computation on the graph which represents the compatibility of pairs of connections. Of course, this may lead to inefficient solutions if w is very small compared to the size of the optimal solution. In order to handle this case, another simple maxRPC algorithm is used whose performance increases as w decreases. This algorithm simply ignores one link of the ring and routes all connections so that no path uses this link. In this way an instance of maxPC on a chain network is obtained. maxPC in chains can be solved optimally in polynomial time by an algorithm of Carlisle and Lloyd [4]. By simple arguments, this second algorithm will color at most w connections less than those colored in an optimal solution of the original maxRPC instance. The same idea can be used in bidirected rings to color at most $2w$ connections less than those colored in an optimal solution.

In our algorithms, we also use this last algorithm to handle instances in which the optimal solution is much larger than w. We will refer to this algorithm as algorithm CL. In order to handle the most difficult case of large w, we will exploit iterative algorithms. Their main advantage compared to the maximum matching algorithm of [18] is that they can color more than two connections with the same color if this is feasible. We consider not only the *basic iterative algorithm* that iteratively computes link-disjoint paths but also more involved algorithms. We show that even the basic iterative algorithm combined with algorithm CL has approximation ratio $18/13 \approx 1.38462$ and $60/41 \approx 1.46341$ in undirected and bidirected rings, respectively, significantly improving the $\frac{e}{e-1}$ bound of [1,24] and the ratios of the algorithms in [17,18]. More involved iterative algorithms that use local search algorithms for computing *set packings* are proved to achieve approximation ratios $4/3$ and $719/509 + \epsilon \approx 1.41257$, respectively. We also study the profit version of maxPC and we present an algorithm based on linear programming and randomized rounding [19] with approximation ratio $1 + \frac{4}{3e} \approx 1.49015$, improving on the 1.58198 bound obtained by a simple iterative algorithm. Again, we use as a subroutine an algorithm of Carlisle and Lloyd [4] for solving the profit variant of maxPC in chains.

For the analysis of the algorithms for the non-profit version of the problems, we develop a new technique which is quite general and could be applied to many other contexts where we are given a set of elements together with subsets of elements that can be assigned the same color and the objective is to color the maximum number of elements using no more than w colors. In particular, we present the *benefit-revealing LP lemma* which provides lower bounds on the performance of iterative algorithms for such problems in terms of the size of the optimal solution, w, and the objective value of a linear program. This technique is motivated by studies of greedy-like algorithms for facility location problems [12] but, in contrast to [12], benefit-revealing LPs do not directly yield any bound on the approximation factor; this requires some additional case analysis.

The rest of the paper is structured as follows. In Section 2 we present the maxColoring problem which generalizes problems maxRPC and maxPC, define a class of iterative maxColoring algorithms, and present the benefit-revealing LP lemma for analyzing their performance. In Section 3, we present our maxRPC algorithms. The profit version of maxPC is studied in Section 4. Due to lack of space, most of the proofs have been omitted from this extended abstract.

2   Iterative Algorithms for the maxColoring Problem

The problems maxRPC and maxPC can be thought of as special cases of the maxColoring problem defined as follows. We are given an integer w, a set V and a set S of subsets of V called *compatible sets* (S is closed under subsets). The objective is to compute a subset of w disjoint sets of S whose union contains a maximum number of elements of V. In other words, we are seeking for an assignment of colors to as many elements of V as possible so that at most w different colors are used and, for each color, the set of elements colored with this color is a compatible set. The compatible sets can be given either explicitly or implicitly. For example, for $w = 1$ and by defining the compatible sets to be the independent sets of a graph, the problem is identical to the maximum independent set problem. In maxRPC instances, the compatible sets are all those sets of connections which have a routing so that the corresponding paths do not share the same fiber (i.e., sets of link-disjoint paths).

The maxColoring problem is strongly related to the problem of computing a compatible set of maximum size. A simple iterative algorithm repeatedly (i.e., w times) includes a compatible set of maximum size that does not contain elements that are contained in compatible sets selected before. Awerbuch et al. [1] (see also [24]) have shown that, using an algorithm that computes a compatible set of size at most ρ times smaller than the size of the maximum compatible set, the corresponding iterative algorithm has approximation ratio at most $\frac{1}{1-\exp(-1/\rho)}$. Even in the case where a compatible set of maximum size can be computed in polynomial time (this is trivial if all compatible sets are given explicitly), the approximation ratio of the iterative algorithm is $\frac{e}{e-1} \approx 1.58198$. In general, this bound is best possible. A maxColoring algorithm with strictly better approximation ratio could be executed repeatedly to approximate minimum set cover within a factor of $\alpha \ln n$ for some constant $\alpha < 1$, contradicting a famous inapproximability result due to Feige [9].

In this paper, we are interested in solutions of instances of the maxColoring problem when a compatible set of maximum size can be computed in polynomial time. We study the class of iterative maxColoring algorithms which try to accommodate elements of V by computing as many as possible disjoint compatible sets of the maximum size. This involves solving instances of the k-set packing problem. An instance of k-set packing consists of a set of elements V, a set S of subsets of V each containing exactly k elements, and the objective is to compute a maximum number of disjoint elements of S. A solution to this problem is called a k-set packing. A k-set packing is called *maximal* if it cannot be augmented by including another set of S without loosing feasibility. An iterative maxColoring algorithm works as follows:

INPUT: An integer w, a set V and a set of compatible sets $S \subseteq 2^V$.
OUTPUT: At most w disjoint sets $T_1, T_2, ...,$ of S.

1. Set $F := V$, $T := S$, $i := 1$ and denote by k the size of the largest compatible set in T.
2. While $i \leq w$ or $F \neq \emptyset$ do:
   (a) Compute a maximal k-set packing Π among the sets of T of cardinality k.
   (b) If $\Pi \neq \emptyset$ then
      i. Denote by $I_0, I_1, ..., I_{t-1}$ the compatible sets in Π and set $F' := \bigcup_{j=0}^{\min\{w-i,t-1\}} I_j$.
      ii. For $j := 0, ..., \min\{w - i, t - 1\}$, set $T_{i+j} := I_j$.
      iii. Set $F := F \setminus F'$, $T := T \setminus \bigcup_{S \in T : F' \cap S \neq \emptyset} S$ and $i := i + t$.
   (c) Set $k := k - 1$.

The algorithm that iteratively computes a compatible set of maximum size (henceforth called the *basic iterative algorithm*) can be thought of as an algorithm belonging to the above class of algorithms. In step 2a, it computes a maximal k-set packing by iteratively computing compatible sets of size k and removing from F the elements in the compatible sets computed. Since including a compatible set of size k may force at most k compatible sets of an optimal k-set packing to be excluded from the solution, this algorithm has approximation ratio k for solving the k-set packing problem. Using different methods for computing k-set packings, we obtain different algorithms. When the maximum compatible set has constant size κ, computing a maximal k-set packing can be done using a local search algorithm. Consider the set S of all compatible sets of V of size κ. A local search algorithm uses a constant parameter p (informally, this is an upper bound on the number of local improvements performed at each step) and, starting with an empty packing Π, repeatedly updates Π by replacing any set of $s < p$ sets of Π with $s + 1$ sets so that feasibility is maintained and until no replacement is possible. This algorithm is analyzed in [11].

Theorem 1 (Hurkens and Schrijver [11]). *The local search algorithm that computes k-set packings by performing at most p local improvements at each step has approximation ratio at most $\frac{k(k-1)^r-k}{2(k-1)^r-k}$ if $p = 2r - 1$ and $\frac{k(k-1)^r-2}{2(k-1)^r-2}$ if $p = 2r$.*

The next lemma relates the approximation ratio of iterative algorithms with the approximation ratio of the k-set packing algorithms used in step 2a.

Lemma 1 (Benefit-revealing LP). *Let Alg be an iterative maxColoring algorithm that uses ρ_k-approximation algorithms for computing maximal k-set packings in step 2a. Consider the execution of Alg on a maxColoring instance $(V, \mathcal{S}, w)$ and let $\mathcal{OPT} \subseteq V$ be an optimal solution for this instance. If Alg terminates by including elements of compatible sets of size $k = t$, then, for any $\lambda > t$, its benefit is at least*

$$\left(1 - \frac{t}{\lambda + 1}\right) |\mathcal{OPT}| + \left(t - \lambda + \frac{\lambda t}{\lambda + 1} + Z^*_{\lambda,t}\right) w$$

where $Z^*_{\lambda,t}$ is the maximum objective value of the following linear program

$$\text{maximize} \quad \left(1 - \frac{t}{\lambda + 1}\right) \sum_{i=t+1}^{\lambda-1} (\lambda - i)\gamma_i + \sum_{i=t+1}^{\lambda} \delta_i + \sum_{i=t+1}^{\lambda} \beta_i$$

$$\text{subject to:} \quad \left(1 - \frac{t}{\lambda + 1}\right) \sum_{i=t+1}^{j-1} \gamma_i + \delta_j \leq 1 - \frac{t}{j}, j = t + 2, ..., \lambda$$

$$\left(1 - \frac{t}{\lambda + 1}\right) \sum_{i=t+1}^{\lambda-1} \gamma_i + \delta_\lambda + \beta_\lambda \leq 1 - \frac{t}{\lambda + 1}$$

$$\left(1 - \frac{t}{\lambda + 1}\right) \gamma_j + \delta_{j+1} - \delta_j - \beta_j \geq 0, j = t + 1, ..., \lambda - 1$$

$$\frac{j}{\rho_j}\left(1-\frac{t}{\lambda+1}\right)\sum_{i=t+1}^{j-1}\gamma_i + \frac{j}{\rho_j}\delta_j + \beta_j \leq \frac{j-t}{\rho_j}, j = t+1,...,\lambda$$

$$\gamma_j \geq 0, j = t+1,...,\lambda-1$$

$$\delta_j, \beta_j \geq 0, j = t+1,...,\lambda$$

Lemma 1 can be extremely helpful for the analysis of the performance of iterative algorithms on instances of maxColoring where a maximum compatible set can be computed in polynomial time and, additionally, the ratio $|\mathcal{OPT}|/w$ is upper-bounded by a (small) constant. For these instances, the $\frac{e}{e-1}$ bound for the basic iterative algorithm following by the analysis in [1,24] can be improved. The new proofs are not particularly complicated and they require solving a few simple linear programs.

3   Applications to maxRPC

In the case of maxRPC, the ratio of the size of the optimal solution over the number of available wavelengths is not bounded in general. Hopefully, very simple algorithms are efficient when this ratio is large while iterative algorithms are proved to be efficient for small values of this ratio through the benefit-revealing LP analysis. So, all the maxRPC algorithms we describe in the section have the same structure. They execute algorithm CL and an iterative algorithm on the input instance and output the best among the two solutions.

We denote by CL-I the algorithm obtained by combining algorithm CL with the basic iterative algorithm that iteratively computes compatible sets of connections on undirected rings. The approximation ratio of algorithm CL-I is stated in the next theorem.

Theorem 2. *Algorithm* CL-I *has approximation ratio at most* 18/13 *for* maxRPC *in undirected rings.*

Note that this is already an improvement to the 3/2-approximation algorithm of [18]. Next we further improve the bound of Theorem 2 by using another simple iterative algorithm. For $k \geq 4$, algorithm I&3LS computes maximal k-set packings in the naive way (i.e., by mimicking the basic iterative algorithm). Maximum 2-set packings among compatible sets of 2 connections are computed using maximum matching computation while a 2-approximation algorithm is used to compute maximal 3-set packings among compatible sets of connections of size 3 (i.e., a local search algorithm performing 2 local improvements at each step). Algorithm CL-I&3LS simply calls both algorithms CL and I&3LS on the input instance and outputs the best among the two solutions.

Theorem 3. *Algorithm* CL-I&3LS *has approximation ratio at most* 4/3 *for* maxRPC *in undirected rings.*

Proof. Consider the application of algorithm CL-I&3LS on an instance of problem maxRPC consisting of a set of connections on an undirected ring supporting w

wavelengths. Denote by $\mathcal{OPT}$ an optimal solution. If $w \leq |\mathcal{OPT}|/4$, algorithm CL computes a solution of size at least $\frac{3}{4}|\mathcal{OPT}|$. We will also show that when $w \geq |\mathcal{OPT}|/4$, algorithm I&3LS computes a solution of size at least $\frac{3}{4}|\mathcal{OPT}|$.

We may assume that algorithm I&3LS has used all the w wavelengths when it terminates (if this is not the case, then algorithm I&3LS has optimal benefit). We distinguish between three cases depending whether the last wavelength is assigned to compatible sets of connections of size at least 3, 2, or 1. If all wavelengths are assigned to connections in compatible sets of size at least 3, then the benefit of algorithm I&3LS is at least $3w \geq \frac{3}{4}|\mathcal{OPT}|$.

For $\lambda = 3$ and $t = 2$, the benefit-revealing LP is simply to maximize $\delta_3 + \beta_3$ subject to $\frac{3}{2}\delta_3 + \beta_3 \leq \frac{1}{2}$ with $\delta_3, \beta_3 \geq 0$. This is trivially maximized to $1/2$ which yields that the benefit of algorithm I&3LS when it terminates by assigning the last wavelength to a compatible set of 2 connections is at least $\frac{1}{2}|\mathcal{OPT}| + w \geq \frac{3}{4}|\mathcal{OPT}|$.

For $\lambda = 3$ and $t = 1$, the benefit-revealing LP is

$$\text{maximize} \quad \frac{3}{4}\gamma_2 + \delta_2 + \delta_3 + \beta_2 + \beta_3$$
$$\text{subject to} \quad \frac{3}{4}\gamma_2 + \delta_3 - \delta_2 - \beta_2 \geq 0$$
$$\frac{3}{4}\gamma_2 + \delta_3 + \beta_3 \leq \frac{3}{4}$$
$$\frac{3}{4}\gamma_2 + \delta_3 \leq \frac{2}{3}$$
$$\delta_2 + \beta_2 \leq \frac{1}{2}$$
$$\frac{9}{8}\gamma_2 + \frac{3}{2}\delta_3 + \beta_3 \leq 1$$
$$\gamma_2, \delta_2, \delta_3, \beta_2, \beta_3 \geq 0$$

which is maximized to $5/4$ for $\gamma_2 = 2/3$, $\delta_2 = \delta_3 = 0$, $\beta_2 = 1/2$, and $\beta_3 = 1/4$. Hence, we obtain that the benefit of algorithm I&3LS when it terminates by assigning the last wavelength to a single connection is at least $\frac{3}{4}|\mathcal{OPT}|$.   □

Next we present algorithms that improve the $11/7$ approximation bound of [18] in bidirected rings. We denote by bCL-I the algorithm obtained by combining algorithm CL with the basic iterative algorithm that iteratively computes compatible sets of connections on bidirected rings. Its approximation ratio is stated in the next theorem.

Theorem 4. *Algorithm* bCL-I *has approximation ratio at most* $60/41$ *for* maxRPC *in bidirected rings.*

We can exploit local search algorithms for computing set packings among compatible sets of connections. Algorithm I&7LS uses the naive iterative algorithm to compute k-set packings for $k \geq 8$, while it uses the $k/2+\epsilon$-approximation local search algorithms to compute k-set packings for $k \in \{4, 5, 6, 7\}$. Optimal 3-set packings among compatible sets of connections of size 3 in bidirected rings are easy to compute using a maximum matching computation while 2-set packing is trivial since any set of 2 connections in a bidirected ring is a compatible set. Algorithm bCL-I&7LS simply calls both algorithms CL and I&7LS on the input instance and again outputs the best among the two solutions.

Theorem 5. *Algorithm* bCL-I&7LS *has approximation ratio at most* $719/509 + \epsilon$ *for* maxRPC *in bidirected rings.*

Note that we have made no particular attempt to design k-set packing algorithms among compatible sets of connections in rings with better approximation guarantees than those of the general set packing algorithms analyzed in [11]. Although, in general, improving the bounds in [11] is a long-standing open problem this may be easier by exploiting the particular structure of the ring. An algorithm for 4-set packing among compatible sets of 4 connections with approximation ratio strictly smaller than 2 would immediately yield an iterative algorithm with approximation ratio strictly better than $4/3$ for maxRPC in undirected rings. Similar improvements could be possible in bidirected rings as well.

4   Approximating the Profit Version of maxPC

By adapting the algorithms presented in Section 3 to work with paths instead of connections, we can obtain the same approximation bounds with those in Theorems 2 and 3 for the maxPC problem as well. Both results improve the 3/2-approximation algorithm of [17].

In the following we consider the profit version of the maxPC where together with each path we are given a non-negative profit and the objective is to select a w-colorable set of paths (or, equivalently, w disjoint compatible sets of paths) of maximum total profit. Again, we use two algorithms and pick the best solution. The first algorithm essentially mimics an algorithm of Carlisle and Lloyd [4] for the profit version of maxPC in chains applied to the paths not traversing a particular link e_0 of the ring. The second algorithm solves a linear programming relaxation of the problem maxPC and obtains a feasible integral solution by applying randomized rounding.

Given a set of paths P on a ring, denote by $\mathcal{I}$ the set of all compatible sets of paths in P. The problem can be expressed as the following integer linear program.

$$\text{maximize} \sum_{p \in P} c_p \sum_{I \in \mathcal{I}: p \in I} y_I$$

$$\text{subject to} \sum_{I \in \mathcal{I}: p \in I} y_I \leq 1, \forall p \in P$$

$$\sum_{I \in \mathcal{I}} y_I \leq w$$

$$y_I \in \{0, 1\}, \forall I \in \mathcal{I}$$

Although the above ILP has an exponential number of variables, we can solve its linear programming relaxation (obtained by relaxing the integrality constrained to $0 \leq y_I \leq 1$) by transforming it to a multicommodity flow problem. Denote by P_0 the subset of P containing the paths traversing link e_0. Consider the following network $N = (V(N), E(N))$ having two special nodes s and t, two nodes s_p and t_p for each path $p \in P_0$ and one node v_p for each path $p \in P \setminus P_0$. The nodes s and t have capacity w while all other nodes in $V(N)$ have unit capacity. For each pair of compatible paths p, q such that $p \in P_0$ and $q \in P \setminus P_0$, $E(N)$ contains the directed edges (s_p, v_q) and (v_q, t_p). For any two compatible paths $p, q \in P \setminus P_0$ such that path p is met prior to q when we walk clockwise on the ring starting from edge e_0, $E(N)$ contains the directed edge (v_p, v_q). For any path $p \in P \setminus P_0$, $E(N)$ contains the two directed edges (s, v_p) and (v_p, t). A directed path from s to t in N corresponds to a compatible set of paths in $P \setminus P_0$, while a directed path from node s_p to node t_p corresponds to a compatible set of paths containing the path $p \in P_0$. Denote by U_0 (resp. V_0) the set of nodes s (resp. t) and s_p (resp. t_p) for each $p \in P_0$.

Now, the maxPC problem with profits is equivalent to computing flows for each commodity (the flow for commodity corresponding to a node $u \in U_0$ has to be carried to the corresponding node in V_0) such that the capacity constraints are not violated (i.e., the flow entering/leaving any node in $V(N) \setminus \{s, t\}$ is at most 1 and the flow entering node t or leaving node s is at most w), the total flow of all commodities is at most w, and the quantity $\sum_{p \in P} c_p \sum_{u \in U_0} f_{v_p}^{(u)}$ is maximized. By $f_{v_p}^{(u)}$ we denote the flow for commodity corresponding to node $u \in U_0$ that is carried by the node v_p. In order to compute the values of the fractional variables in the solution of the LP relaxation, it suffices to decompose the flow of each commodity into flow paths and to set y_I equal to the flow carried by the flow path corresponding to compatible set I. The variables of compatible sets that correspond to flow paths carrying no flow are implicitly set to zero.

Denote by y^* the optimal solution to the LP relaxation of ILP. By ignoring the paths in P_0, we get an instance of the multicommodity flow problem with just one commodity. It can be easily seen that the constraint matrix of the corresponding LP is totally unimodular and, since the capacities are integral, this LP has an integral optimal extreme solution that can be computed in polynomial time [21]. In this way we obtain an integral feasible solution $\bar{y}$ for ILP which implicitly assigns zeros to all compatible sets that contain a path in P_0. Since this solution is optimal on the input instance consisting of the paths in $P \setminus P_0$, we obtain that the cost of $\bar{y}$ is

$$\sum_{p \in P \setminus P_0} c_p \sum_{I \in \mathcal{I}: p \in I} \bar{y}_I \geq \sum_{p \in P \setminus P_0} c_p \sum_{I \in \mathcal{I}: p \in I} y_I^* = \sum_{p \in P} c_p \sum_{I \in \mathcal{I}: p \in I} y_I^* - \sum_{p \in P_0} c_p \sum_{I \in \mathcal{I}: p \in I} y_I^*$$

In the following, we show how to obtain a good feasible solution for ILP by applying randomized rounding to its linear programming relaxation. The randomized rounding procedure works as follows. First, introduce dummy paths with zero profit that contain only e_0 into each compatible set I that does not contain any path in P_0 and whose variable has non-zero value in the fractional solution. Order the compatible sets $I \in \mathcal{I}$ whose fractional variable y_I^* is non-zero such that the compatible sets containing the same path of P_0 are consecutive. Let $I_1, I_2, ..., I_m$ be such an ordering. Let $W = \lceil \sum_{I \in \mathcal{I}} y_I^* \rceil$. Clearly, $W \leq w$. Pick W independent random variables $X_1, X_2, ..., X_W$ in range $(0, 1]$. Define

$$\mathcal{J} = \left\{ I_{j(t)} : \sum_{i=1}^{j(t)-1} y_{I_i}^* - t < X_t \leq \sum_{i=1}^{j(t)} y_{I_i}^* - t, \text{ for } t = 1, ..., W \right\}$$

So far, we have selected one compatible set for each of the w available colors. Since some of the paths may be contained in more than one compatible sets of $\mathcal{J}$, we apply the following procedure to guarantee that each path is contained in at most one compatible set. Consider each path that is contained in more than one compatible set of $\mathcal{J}$. Remove path p from all such compatible sets of $\mathcal{J}$ but one. Denote by $\mathcal{J}'$ the set of compatible sets obtained by the compatible sets of $\mathcal{J}$ in this way. Set $\hat{y}_I = 1$ for each $I \in \mathcal{J}'$ and $\hat{y}_I = 0$ for each $I \in \mathcal{I} \setminus \mathcal{J}'$.

Lemma 2. *The solution $\hat{y}$ obtained by applying the randomized rounding procedure on the optimal fractional solution y^* has expected cost*

$$E \left(\sum_{p \in P} c_p \sum_{I \in \mathcal{I}: p \in I} \hat{y}_I \right) \geq \left(1 - \frac{1}{e} \right) \sum_{p \in P} c_p \sum_{I \in \mathcal{I}: p \in I} y_I^* + \left(\frac{1}{e} - \frac{1}{4} \right) \sum_{p \in P_0} c_p \sum_{I \in \mathcal{I}: p \in I} y_I^*$$

Hence, we obtain that by selecting the best among the two solutions $\bar{y}$ and $\hat{y}$, we obtain a solution with expected total profit at least $\frac{3e}{8e+4}$ times the optimal profit. For any $\epsilon > 0$, we may repeat the method above $O(\frac{\log n}{\epsilon})$ times in order to obtain a solution with profit at least $\frac{3e}{3e+4+3e\epsilon}$ times the optimal profit, with probability at least $1 - 1/n$. The proof follows by a simple application of the Markov inequality. We obtain the following theorem.

Theorem 6. *For any $\epsilon > 0$, the algorithm described computes a $\left(1 + \frac{4}{3e} + \epsilon \right)$-approximate solution for the profit version of* maxPC *in rings in time polynomial on the input size and $1/\epsilon$.*

References

1. B. Awerbuch, Y. Azar, A. Fiat, S. Leonardi, and A. Rosen. Online competitive algorithms for call admission in optical networks. *Algorithmica*, 31(1), pp. 29-43, 2001.
2. I. Caragiannis, A. Ferreira, C. Kaklamanis, S. Perennes, and H. Rivano. Fractional path coloring with applications to WDM networks. In *Proceedings of the 29th International Colloquium on Automata, Languages, and Programming (ICALP '01)*, LNCS 2076, Springer, pp. 732-743, 2001.
3. I. Caragiannis and C. Kaklamanis. Approximate path coloring with applications to wavelength routing in WDM optical networks. In *Proceedings of the 21st Symposium on Theoretical Aspects of Computer Science (STACS '04)*, LNCS 2996, Springer, pp. 258-269, 2004.

4. M.C. Carlisle and E.L. Lloyd. On the k-coloring of intervals. *Discrete Applied Mathematics*, 59, pp. 225-235, 1995.
5. C. T. Cheng. Improved approximation algorithms for the demand routing and slotting problem with unit demands on rings. *SIAM Journal on Discrete Mathematics*, 17(3), pp. 384-402, 2004.
6. T. Erlebach and K. Jansen. The maximum edge-disjoint paths problem in bidirected trees. *SIAM Journal on Discrete Mathematics*, 14(3), pp. 326-366, 2001.
7. T. Erlebach and K. Jansen. The complexity of path coloring and call scheduling. *Theoretical Computer Science*, 255(1-2), pp. 33-50, 2001.
8. T. Erlebach, K. Jansen, C. Kaklamanis, M. Mihail, and P. Persiano. Optimal wavelength routing on directed fiber trees. *Theoretical Computer Science*, 221(1-2), pp. 119-137, 1999.
9. U. Feige. A threshold of $\ln n$ for approximating set cover. *Journal of the ACM*, 45(4), pp. 634-652, 1998.
10. M.R. Garey, D.S. Johnson, G.L. Miller, and C.H. Papadimitriou. The complexity of coloring circular arcs and chords. *SIAM Journal on Alg. Disc. Math.*, 1(2), pp. 216-227, 1980.
11. C. A. J. Hurkens and A. Schrijver. On the size of systems of sets every t of which have an SDR, with an application to the worst-case ratio of heuristics for packing problems. *SIAM Journal on Discrete Mathematics*, 2(1), pp. 68-72, 1989.
12. K. Jain, M. Mahdian, E. Markakis, A. Saberi, and V. V. Vazirani. Greedy facility location algorithms analyzed using dual fitting with factor-revealing LP. *Journal of the ACM*, 50(6), pp. 795-824, 2003.
13. I. Karapetian. On coloring of arc graphs. *Dokladi of the Academy of Sciences of the Armenian SSR*, 70(5), pp. 306-311, 1980. (in Russian)
14. V. Kumar. An approximation algorithm for circular arc coloring. *Algorithmica*, 30(3), pp. 406-417, 2001.
15. V. Kumar. Approximating circular arc colouring and bandwidth allocation in all–optical ring networks. In *Proceedings of the 1st International Workshop on Approximation Algorithms for Combinatorial Optimization Problems (APPROX '98)*, LNCS 1444, Springer, pp. 147–158, 1998.
16. J. Li, K. Li, L. Wang, and H. Zhao. Maximizing profits of routing in WDM networks. *Journal of Combinatorial Optimization*, 10, pp. 99-111, 2005.
17. C. Nomikos, A. Pagourtzis, S. Zachos. Satisfying a maximum number of pre-routed requests in all-optical rings. *Computer Networks*, 42, pp. 55-63, 2003.
18. C. Nomikos, A. Pagourtzis, S. Zachos. Minimizing request blocking in all-optical rings. In *Proceedings of the 22nd Annual Joint Conference of the IEEE Computer and Communications Societies (INFOCOM '03)*, 2003.
19. P. Raghavan and C.D. Thompson. Randomized rounding: a technique for provably good algorithms and algorithmic proofs. *Combinatorica*, 7, pp. 365–374, 1987.
20. R. Ramaswami and K. Sivarajan. Optical networks: A practical perspective. *Morgan Kauffman Publishers*, 1998.
21. A. Schrijver. Theory of Linear and Integer Programming. *Wiley and Sons*, 1998.
22. A. Tucker. Coloring a family of circular arcs. *SIAM Journal of Applied Mathematics*, 29(3), pp. 493–502, 1975.
23. M. Valencia-Pabon. Revisiting Tucker's algorithm to color circular arc graphs. *SIAM Journal on Computing*, 32(4), pp. 1067-1072, 2003.
24. P.J. Wan and L. Liu. Maximal throughput in wavelength-routed optical networks. *DIMACS Series in Discrete Mathematics and Theoretical Computer Science*, AMS, 46, pp. 15-26, 1998.

A First Investigation of Sturmian Trees

Jean Berstel[1], Luc Boasson[2], Olivier Carton[2], and Isabelle Fagnot[1]

[1] Institut Gaspard-Monge (IGM), Université de Marne-la-Vallée and CNRS,
Marne-la-Vallée
[2] Laboratoire d'informatique algorithmique: fondements et applications (LIAFA),
Université Denis-Diderot (Paris VII) and CNRS, Paris

Abstract. We consider Sturmian trees as a natural generalization of
Sturmian words. A Sturmian tree is a tree having $n+1$ distinct subtrees of
height n for each n. As for the case of words, Sturmian trees are irrational
trees of minimal complexity. We give various examples of Sturmian trees,
and we characterize one family of Sturmian trees by means of a structural
property of their automata.

1 Introduction

Sturmian words have been extensively studied for many years (see e.g. [4,5] for
recent surveys). We propose here an extension to trees.

A *Sturmian tree* is a complete labeled binary tree having exactly $n+1$ distinct
subtrees of height n for each n. Thus Sturmian trees are defined by extending
to trees one of the numerous equivalent definitions of Sturmian words. Sturmian
trees share the same property of minimal complexity than Sturmian words: indeed, if a tree has at most n distinct subtrees of height n for some n, then the
tree is rational, i.e. it has only finitely many distinct infinite subtrees.

This paper presents many examples and some results on Sturmian trees. The
simplest method to construct a Sturmian tree is to choose a Sturmian word and
to repeat it on all branches of the tree. We call this a uniform tree, see Fig. 1.
However, many other categories of Sturmian trees exist.

Contrary to the case of Sturmian words, and similarly to the case of epis-
turmian words, there seems not to exist equivalent definitions for the family of
Sturmian trees. This is due to the fact that, in our case, each node in a tree has
two children, which provides more degrees of freedom. In particular, only one of
the children of a node needs to be the root of a Sturmian tree to make the whole
tree Sturmian.

Each tree labeled with two symbols can be described by the set of words labeling paths from the root to nodes sharing a distinguished symbol. The (infinite)
minimal automaton of the language has quite interesting properties when the
tree is Sturmian. The most useful is that the Moore equivalence algorithm produces just one additional equivalence class at each step. We call these automata
slow.

We have observed that two parameters make sense in studying Sturmian trees:
the *degree* of a Sturmian tree is the number of disjoint infinite paths composed of

W. Thomas and P. Weil (Eds.): STACS 2007, LNCS 4393, pp. 73–84, 2007.
© Springer-Verlag Berlin Heidelberg 2007

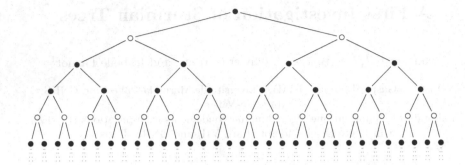

Fig. 1. The top of a uniform tree for the word $abaaba\cdots$. Node label a is represented by •, and label b is represented by ∘. This tree will be seen to have infinite degree and rank 0.

nodes which are all roots of Sturmian trees. The *rank* of a tree is the number of distinct rational subtrees it contains. Both parameters may be finite or infinite.

The main result of this paper is that the class of Sturmian trees of degree one and with finite rank can be described by infinite automata of a rather special form. The automata are obtained by repeating infinitely many often a distinguished path in some finite slow automaton, and intertwining consecutive copies of this path by letters taken from some Sturmian infinite word. Another property is that a Sturmian tree with finite degree at least 2 always has infinite rank.

The class of Sturmian trees seems to be quite rich. We found several rather different techniques to construct Sturmian trees. To the best of our knowledge, there is only one paper on Sturmian trees prior to the present one, by Carpi, De Luca and Varricchio [1].

2   Sturmian Trees

We are interested in complete labeled infinite binary trees, and we consider finite trees insofar as they appear inside infinite trees.

In the sequel, D denotes the alphabet $\{0,1\}$. A *tree domain* is a prefix-closed subset P of D^*. Any element of a tree domain is called a *node*. Let A be an alphabet. A *tree over* A is a map t from a tree domain P into A. The domain of the tree t is denoted $\mathrm{dom}(t)$. For each node w of t, the letter $t(w)$ is called the *label* of the node w. A *complete* tree is a tree whose domain is D^*. The *empty tree* is the tree whose domain is the empty set. A (finite or infinite) *branch* of a tree t is a (finite or infinite) word x over D such that each prefix of x is a node of t.

Example 1. (Dyck tree) Let A be the alphabet $\{a,b\}$. Let L be the set of Dyck words over $D = \{0,1\}$, that is the set of words generated by the context-free grammar with productions $S \to 0S1S + \varepsilon$. The *Dyck tree* is the complete tree defined by

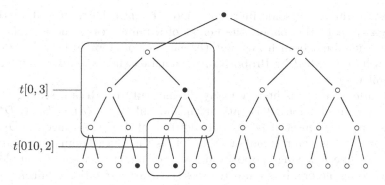

Fig. 2. The top of the Dyck tree of Example 1 and two of its factors, of height 3 and 2, respectively. Again, a is represented by • and b by ∘.

$$t(w) = \begin{cases} a & \text{if } w \in L, \\ b & \text{otherwise.} \end{cases} \tag{1}$$

The top of this tree is depicted in Fig. 2. The first four words ε, 01, 0101 and 0011 of L correspond to the four occurrences of the letter a as label on the top of the tree.

More generally, the *characteristic tree* of any language L over D is defined to be the tree t given by (1). Conversely, for any tree t over some alphabet A, and for any letter a in A, there is a language $L = t^{-1}(a)$ of words labeled with the letter a. The language $L = t^{-1}(a)$ is called the a *language of* t. In the sequel, we usually deal with the two-letter alphabet $A = \{a, b\}$, and we fix the letter a. We then say the *language of* t instead of the a-language.

We shall see that the a-languages of a tree t are regular if and only if the tree t is rational. For any word w and any language L, the expression $w^{-1}L$ denotes the set $w^{-1}L = \{x \mid wx \in L\}$. Let t be a tree over A and w be a word over D. We denote by $t[w]$ the tree with domain $w^{-1}\text{dom}(t)$ defined by $t[w](u) = t(wu)$ for each u in $w^{-1}\text{dom}(t)$. The tree $t[w]$ is sometimes written as $w^{-1}t$, for instance in [1]. If w is not a node of t, the tree $t[w]$ is empty. A tree of the form $t[w]$ is the *suffix* of t rooted at w. Suffixes are also called quotients or subtrees in the literature.

Let t be a tree over A and let w be a word over D. For a positive integer h, we denote by $D^{<h}$ the set $(\varepsilon + D)^{h-1}$ of words over D of length at most $h - 1$. We set $D^{<0} = \emptyset$.

Let h be a nonnegative integer. The *truncation* of a tree t at height h is the restriction of t to the domain $D^{<h}$. Any tree obtained by truncation is called a *prefix* of t. A *factor* of t is a prefix of a suffix of t. More precisely, for any word w and any nonnegative integer h, we denote by $t[w, h]$ the factor of height h rooted at w, that is the tree of domain $w^{-1}\text{dom}(t) \cap D^{<h}$ and defined by $t[w, h](u) = t(wu)$. A factor of height 0 is always the empty tree. A factor $t[w, 1]$ of height 1 can be identified with the letter $t(w)$ of A that labels its root. A prefix is a tree of the form $t[\varepsilon, h]$.

Factors of height h are sometimes considered to have height $h - 1$ in the literature (e.g. [1]). In this paper, the height of a finite tree is the number of nodes along a maximal branch and not the number of steps in-between. Our convention will be justified by Proposition 1 which extends a similar result for words in similar terms.

A tree is *rational* if it has finitely many distinct suffixes. Recall (see e.g. [2]) that a tree over an alphabet A is rational if and only if $t^{-1}(a) = \{w \in D^* \mid t(w) = a\}$ is a regular subset of D^* for each letter a of A. For instance the Dyck tree t of Example 1 is not rational since $t^{-1}(a)$ is the Dyck language which is not regular [6]. The following proposition gives a characterization of complete rational trees using factors. It extends to trees the characterization of ultimately periodic words by means of their subword complexity [3]. This statement appears in [1].

Proposition 1. *A complete tree t is rational if and only there is an integer h such that t has at most h distinct factors of height h.*

A complete tree is *Sturmian* if for any integer h, it has $h + 1$ factors of height h. Since the factors of height 1 are the letters $t(w)$ a Sturmian tree is defined over a two letter alphabet. In what follows, we always assume that this alphabet is $\{a, b\}$.

We will prove later that the Dyck tree given in Example 1 is indeed Sturmian. We start with some simpler examples of Sturmian trees.

In the first of these examples, the same infinite word is repeated along each branch of the tree.

Example 2. (Uniform trees) Let $x = x_0 x_1 x_2 \cdots$ be an infinite word over an alphabet A, where $x_0, x_1, x_2, \ldots$ are letters. The *uniform tree* of x is the complete tree t defined by $t(w) = x_{|w|}$. This means of course that all nodes of the same level n in the tree are labeled with the same symbol x_n. If x is a Sturmian word, then its uniform tree t is a Sturmian tree. Figure 1 shows the top of the uniform tree of the Fibonacci word $x = abaaba \cdots$.

Example 3. (Left branch tree) Let $x = x_0 x_1 x_2 \cdots$ be an infinite word over A, where $x_0, x_1, x_2, \ldots$ are letters. We define a complete tree t by $t(w) = x_{|w|_0}$. (Recall that $|w|_d$ is the number of occurrences of d in w.)

The label of each node w is the letter x_n of x, where n is the number of symbols 0 occurring on the path from the root to w. The label of the root node is x_0. If the label of w is x_n, the labels of $w0$ and $w1$ are respectively x_{n+1} and x_n.

In particular, the letters of the word x label the nodes of the leftmost branch of the tree, and all nodes on a rightmost branch share the same label. Figure 3 shows the top of the left branch tree of the Fibonacci word $x = abaaba \cdots$.

We write $x[n, h]$ for the factor $x_n x_{n+1} \cdots x_{n+h-1}$ of the word x. In Example 2, two factors $t[w, h]$ and $t[w', h]$ of height h are equal if and only if $x[|w|, h] = x[|w'|, h]$. In Example 3, $t[w, h]$ and $t[w', h]$ are equal if and only if

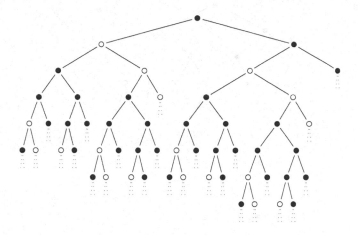

Fig. 3. The top of a left branch tree for the word $abaaba\cdots$

$x[|w|_0, h] = x[|w'|_0, h]$. It follows that in these examples, the tree t is Sturmian if and only if the word x is Sturmian.

Example 4. (Indicator tree) Let x be an infinite word over D. The *indicator tree* of x is the complete tree t defined by

$$t(w) = \begin{cases} a & \text{if } w \text{ is a prefix of } x, \\ b & \text{otherwise.} \end{cases}$$

In other terms, there is exactly one infinite path in t with all its nodes labeled by the letter a. The letters of this path are the letters of the word x. Equivalently, the indicator tree of the infinite word x is the characteristic tree of the language composed of its (finite) prefixes. Figure 4 shows the indicator tree of the Fibonacci word. It can be easily proved that x is a Sturmian word if and only if its indicator tree t is a Sturmian tree.

The following example is a variation on Example 4. For a finite word w and an infinite word x, we denote by $d(w, x)$ the integer $|w| - |u|$ where u is the longest common prefix of w and x.

Example 5. (Band indicator tree) Let x be an infinite word over D and let k be a non-negative integer. The *band indicator tree of width* k is the complete tree t defined by

$$t(w) = \begin{cases} a & \text{if } d(w, x) \leq k, \\ b & \text{otherwise.} \end{cases}$$

Again, x is a Sturmian word if and only if t is a Sturmian tree. The band indicator tree of width 0 is the indicator tree defined in Example 4, since $d(w, x) \leq 0$ if and only if w is a prefix of x.

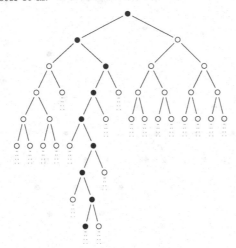

Fig. 4. The top of the indicator tree for the Fibonacci word 01001010 · · · . The only nodes labeled a are on the Fibonacci path.

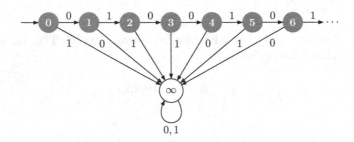

Fig. 5. Automaton accepting the prefixes of 01001010 · · · . All states excepted ∞ are final.

3   Rank and Degree

Recall that a *branch* of a tree is a (finite or infinite) word x over D such that each prefix of x is a node of the tree.

A node w of a tree t is called *rational* if the suffix $t[w]$ is a rational tree. It is called *irrational* otherwise. The *rank* of a tree t is the number of distinct rational suffixes of t. This number is either a nonnegative integer or infinite.

If w is an irrational node, then its prefixes also are irrational. Furthermore, at least one of the two words $w0$ and $w1$ also is irrational. The set of irrational nodes of a tree is a tree domain in which any finite branch is the prefix of an infinite branch.

The *degree* of a tree t is the number of infinite branches composed of irrational nodes. This number is either a nonnegative integer or infinite.

As a first example, consider the Dyck tree defined in Example 1. It has rank 1 and has infinite degree. A node w of this tree is rational if it is not a prefix of some Dyck word. The set of rational nodes is thus the set $L1D^*$ where L is the set of Dyck words. On the contrary, each branch in 00^*10^ω only contains irrational nodes. The degree of the Dyck tree is thus infinite.

Next, let t be the indicator tree of a Sturmian word x, as defined in Example 4. A node w of t is irrational if and only if it is a prefix of x. Thus, the word x itself is the only infinite branch composed of irrational nodes, and therefore the degree of this tree is 1. All rational subtrees are the same, so this tree has rank 1.

These examples show that there are Sturmian trees of degree 1 or of infinite degree. It turns out that there exist also Sturmian trees of finite degree greater than 1. In the final section, we construct a Sturmian tree of degree 2 but this construction is rather involved.

Here is a table summarizing the relations between degree and rank for Sturmian trees. A tree with rank 0 always has infinite degree since there is no rational node.

	rank	
degree	finite	infinite
1	*characterized in Theorem 1* Indicator tree (rank 1) Band width tree (rank $d+1$)	Example 8
≥ 2, finite	*empty by Proposition 4*	example not given here
infinite	Uniform tree (rank 0) Left branch tree (rank 0) Dyck tree (rank 1)	example not given here

The main result of the paper is the characterization of Sturmian trees of degree 1 and with finite rank by a structural property of the minimal automaton of its language.

4 Slow Automata

Let t be a complete tree over $\{a, b\}$. The *language* of t is the set $t^{-1}(a)$. We study properties of trees by considering automata recognizing their language. In particular, minimization of automata will play a central role.

We recall elementary properties of automata, just observing that they hold also when the set of states is infinite. We only use deterministic and complete automata. An *automaton* $\mathcal{A}$ over a finite alphabet D is composed of a state set Q, a set $F \subseteq Q$ of *final states*, and of a *next-state function* $Q \times D \to Q$ that maps (q, d) to a state denoted by $q \cdot d$. Given a distinguished state i, a word w over D is *accepted* by the automaton if the state $i \cdot w$ is final. When we emphasize the existence of state i, we call it the initial state as usual.

An automaton $\mathcal{B}$ is a *subautomaton* of an automaton $\mathcal{A}$ if its set of states is a subset of the set of states of $\mathcal{A}$ which is closed under the next-state function of $\mathcal{A}$.

Example 6. (*Dyck automaton*) The following automaton accepts the Dyck language. The set of states is $Q = \mathbb{N} \cup \{\infty\}$. The initial and unique final state is 0.

The next state function is given by $n \cdot 0 = n+1$ for $n \geq 0$, $n \cdot 1 = n-1$ for $n \geq 1$, $0 \cdot 1 = \infty$ and $\infty \cdot 0 = \infty \cdot 1 = \infty$. This automaton is depicted in Fig. 6. We call it the *Dyck automaton*. The singleton $\{\infty\}$ is the unique proper subautomaton of the Dyck automaton.

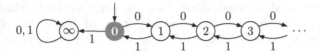

Fig. 6. Automaton of the Dyck language. State 0 is both the initial and the unique final state.

Given an arbitrary automaton $\mathcal{A}$, we define inductively a sequence $(\sim_h)_{h \geq 1}$ of equivalence relations on Q as follows.

$$q \sim_1 q' \iff (q \in F \iff q' \in F)$$
$$q \sim_{h+1} q' \iff (q \sim_h q' \text{ and } \forall d \in D \; q \cdot d \sim_h q' \cdot d)$$

These are well-known in the case of finite automata, and many properties extend to general automata. We call $\sim_h$ the *Moore equivalence* of order h. The *index* of $\sim_h$ is the number of equivalence classes of $\sim_h$. The Moore minimization algorithm consists in computing inductively the Moore equivalences.

The equivalence $\sim_{h+1}$ is a refinement of the equivalence $\sim_h$. Thus the index of $\sim_{h+1}$ is at least the index of $\sim_h$. An automaton is called *slow* if it is minimal and if the index of $\sim_h$ is at most $h+1$ for all $h \geq 1$. If $\sim_h$ and $\sim_{h+1}$ are different, that there is one class c of $\sim_h$ which gives raise to two classes in $\sim_{h+1}$. We say that $\sim_{h+1}$ *splits* class c, or that class c is *split* by $\sim_{h+1}$.

It is sometimes useful to distinguish, in a minimal automaton, two kinds of states. A state p is *rational* if it generates a finite subautomaton. States which are not rational are called *irrational*. In the minimal automaton associated to the language of a tree, a state is rational if and only if it corresponds to the root of a rational tree.

The following proposition shows that the classes of $\sim_h$ are in a one to one correspondence with the factors of t of height h.

Proposition 2. *Let t be a complete tree over $\{a, b\}$ and let $\mathcal{A}$ be an automaton over D accepting the language of t, with initial state i. For any words $w, w' \in D^*$ and any positive integer h, one has*

$$i \cdot w \sim_h i \cdot w' \iff t[w, h] = t[w', h].$$

Corollary 1. *Let t be a complete tree over $\{a, b\}$ and let $\mathcal{A}$ be an automaton over D accepting the language of t. The tree t is Sturmian iff the minimal automaton of its language is infinite and slow.*

5   Trees with Finite Rank

5.1   A Tree of Degree One

In this section, we give an example of a family of Sturmian trees with finite rank and of degree 1 by describing the family of automata accepting their languages. These (infinite) automata are based on a finite slow automaton. In this automaton, a path is distinguished (called a lazy path). The infinite automaton is obtained by repeating the lazy path and intertwining the copies with symbols taken from an infinite Sturmian word.

In the next section, we show that any Sturmian tree of degree 1 and with finite rank can be obtained in this way.

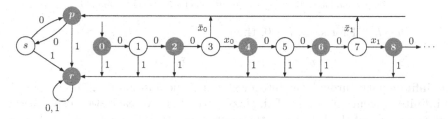

Fig. 7. A slow automaton $\hat{A}$ for the Fibonacci word $x_0 x_1 \cdots = 01001010 \cdots$. The final states are $p, r, 0, 2, 4, \cdots$.

Let $\mathcal{A} = (Q, \{i\}, F)$ be a finite deterministic automaton over the alphabet D with N states. We assume that $\mathcal{A}$ has the two following properties. First, $\mathcal{A}$ is *slow*. Recall that by definition, this means that the automaton is minimal and that the Moore minimization algorithm splits just one equivalence class into two new classes at each step.

Next, we suppose that there is a *lazy path* in $\mathcal{A}$. This is a path

$$\pi : q_0 \xrightarrow{a_0} q_1 \xrightarrow{a_1} q_2 \cdots q_{h-1} \xrightarrow{a_{h-1}} q_h$$

of length h, where q_0 and q_h are the two states which are separated in the last step in the Moore algorithm together with the condition that

$$q_{h-1} \cdot \bar{a}_{h-1} = q_0 \text{ or } q_h$$

where $\bar{a} = 1 - a$ for $a \in D$. If $N \geq 2$, the first of these conditions means that $q_0 \sim_{N-2} q_h$ and $q_0 \not\sim_{N-1} q_h$. As a consequence, the second property means that $q_{h-1} \cdot \bar{a}_{h-1}$ cannot be separated from $q_{h-1} \cdot \bar{a}_{h-1}$ before the very last step of the Moore algorithm.

Example 7. The automaton $\hat{A}$ given in Fig. 7 has a subautomaton $\mathcal{A}$ composed of the states $\{p, s, r\}$. This subautomaton is slow: the first partition is into $\{p, r\}$ and $\{s\}$, and the second partition is equality. The finite subautomaton $\mathcal{A}$ in Fig. 7 admits for example the lazy path $\pi : p \xrightarrow{0} s \xrightarrow{0} p \xrightarrow{0} s \xrightarrow{1} r$, and indeed $s \xrightarrow{0} p$. Here $h = 4$.

Given the finite slow automaton $\mathcal{A}$, the lazy path π and an infinite word $x = x_0 x_1 x_2 \cdots$ over D, we now define an infinite minimal automaton $\hat{\mathcal{A}}$ which accepts the set of nodes labeled a of a tree t. We will show that if x is a Sturmian word, then t is a Sturmian tree of degree 1. This automaton is the *extension* of $\mathcal{A}$ by π and x, and is denoted by $\hat{\mathcal{A}} = \mathcal{A}(\pi, x)$.

The set of states of $\hat{\mathcal{A}}$ is $Q \cup \mathbb{N}$. For convenience, we use a mapping $q : \mathbb{N} \to Q$ defined by $q(n) = q_{n \bmod h}$ for any $n \in \mathbb{N}$. Here and below $q_0, \ldots, q_h$ are the states of the lazy path of $\mathcal{A}$ and $a_0, \ldots, a_{h-1}$ are the letters labeling the path. The initial state of $\hat{\mathcal{A}}$ is 0 and its set of final states is $F \cup q^{-1}(F)$. The next-state function of $\mathcal{A}$ is extended to $\hat{\mathcal{A}}$ by setting, for $n \in \mathbb{N}$,

(α) if $n \not\equiv h - 1 \mod h$, then

$$n \cdot a_{n \bmod h} = n + 1, \qquad n \cdot \bar{a}_{n \bmod h} = q(n) \cdot \bar{a}_{n \bmod h}$$

(β) if $n = ih + h - 1$ for some $i \geq 0$, then

$$n \cdot x_i = n + 1, \qquad n \cdot \bar{x}_i = q_0$$

The infinite path through the integer states of the automaton $\hat{\mathcal{A}}$ is composed of an infinite sequence of copies of the lazy path of $\mathcal{A}$. For each state $q(n)$ inside each of the copies of the lazy path, the next-state for the "other" letter, that is the letter $\bar{a}_{n \bmod h}$, maps $q(n)$ back into $\mathcal{A}$. Two consecutive copies of the lazy path, say the ith and $i + 1$th, are linked together by the letter x_i of the infinite word x driving the automaton (see Fig. 7).

Proposition 3. *Let $\hat{\mathcal{A}} = \mathcal{A}(\pi, x)$ be the extension of the finite slow automaton $\mathcal{A}$ by a lazy path π and an infinite word x. If the word x is Sturmian, then $\hat{\mathcal{A}}$ defines a tree t which is Sturmian, of degree 1, and having finite rank.*

The tree defined by this automaton has degree 1 since the only irrational states are the integer states n and they all lie on a single branch. Its rank is the number of states of $\mathcal{A}$. We claim that this tree is also Sturmian.

5.2   Characterization

In this section, we give a characterization of Sturmian trees of degree 1 which have finite rank by describing the family of automata accepting their languages. These (infinite) automata are extensions of a finite automaton by a lazy path and a Sturmian word.

Theorem 1. *Let t be a Sturmian tree of degree one having finite rank, and let $\hat{\mathcal{A}}$ be the minimal automaton of the language of t. Then $\hat{\mathcal{A}}$ is the extension of a slow finite automaton $\mathcal{A}$ by a lazy path π and a Sturmian word x, i.e. $\hat{\mathcal{A}} = \mathcal{A}(\pi, x)$.*

Given a tree t and some Moore equivalence $\sim_h$ on its minimal automaton, it is convenient to call an equivalence class of $\sim_h$ an *irrational class* if it is entirely composed of irrational states. It is a *rational class* otherwise. A rational

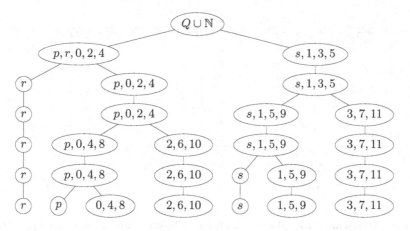

Fig. 8. The tree showing the evolution of the Moore equivalence relations on the automaton given in Fig. 7. Each level describes a partition. Each level has one class splitting into two classes at the next level.

class contains at least one rational state, and may contain even infinitely many irrational states.

Up to now, all our examples of Sturmian trees are of finite rank. It can be observed that for all of them the degree is either 1 or infinite. This is unavoidable.

Proposition 4. *The degree of a Sturmian tree with finite rank is either one or infinite.*

6   A Tree with Infinite Rank

There exist Sturmian trees with infinite rank. The following example gives a Sturmian tree with infinite rank and of degree 1.

Example 8. We define a tree by giving a (minimal) automaton accepting its language. The set of states of the automaton is $Q = \{n \in \mathbb{N} \mid n \geq 3\} \times \{0,1\}$. The set of final states is the set $\{(n,b) \in Q \mid n \equiv 0 \mod 2\}$. The set E of transitions is defined as follows. Let $n = 2^k m$ where $m \geq 1$ and $m \not\equiv 0 \mod 2$. The integer 2^k is then the greatest power of 2 which divides n.

$$(n,b) \cdot 0 = \begin{cases} (2^{k-1}+1,0) & \text{if } m=1 \text{ and } b=0 \\ (n+1,b) & \text{otherwise} \end{cases}$$

$$(n,b) \cdot 1 = \begin{cases} (3,0) & \text{if } k=0 \\ (4,0) & \text{if } k=1 \\ (4,0) & \text{if } k=2, m=1 \text{ and } b=0 \\ (2^{k-2}+1,0) & \text{if } k>2, m=1 \text{ and } b=0 \\ (2^{k-1}+1,0) & \text{otherwise} \end{cases}$$

In Fig. 9, we give a picture of this automaton; states of the form $(n,0)$ are drawn as circles $\textcircled{n}$ and states of the form $(n,1)$ as squares $\boxed{n}$.

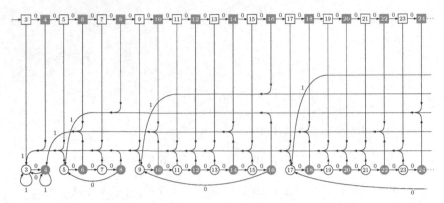

Fig. 9. Final states are dark. Observe the fractal-like structure, with a doubling of the size of each block.

7   Concluding Remarks

In this paper, we have introduced the notion of Sturmian trees. We have considered two parameters, the degree and the rank, and we have described Sturmian trees of finite rank and finite degree.

We have given several examples of Sturmian trees of finite rank and infinite degree. All these are in some sense easy. There exist more involved examples of trees in this family. Such examples may be constructed using more than one Sturmian word.

In this short note, we have presented only one Sturmian tree of infinite rank which is of degree one. Using some kind of fractal structure, we are able to build Sturmian trees of infinite rank and of degree two or more. Similarly, we know some Sturmian trees for which both degree and rank are infinite. None of these examples is given here due to the lack of space. They will be presented in a forthcoming full version.

References

1. A. Carpi, A. de Luca, and S. Varricchio. Special factors and uniqueness conditions in rational trees. *Theory of Computing Systems*, 34:375–395, 2001.
2. B. Courcelle. Fundamental properties of infinite trees. *Theoretical Computer Science*, 25:95–165, 1983.
3. E. M. Coven and G. A. Hedlund. Sequences with minimal block growth. *Mathematical Systems Theory*, 7:138–153, 1973.
4. M. Lothaire. *Algebraic Combinatorics on Words*, volume 90 of *Encyclopedia of Mathematics*. Cambridge University Press, 2002.
5. N. Pytheas-Fogg. *Substitutions in Dynamics, Arithmetics and Combinatorics*, volume 1794 of *Lecture Notes in Mathematics*. Springer-Verlag, 2002. Edited by V. Berthé, S. Ferenczi, C. Maudit and A. Siegel.
6. J. Sakarovitch. *Élements de théorie des automates*. Vuibert, 2003.

On the Size of the Universal Automaton of a Regular Language

Sylvain Lombardy

Université de Marne-la-Valle,
Institut Gaspard-Monge, UMR CNRS 8049,
77454 Marne-la-Valle Cedex 2
lombardy@univ-mlv.fr

Abstract. The universal automaton of a regular language is the maximal NFA without merging states that recognizes this language. This automaton is directly inspired by the factor matrix defined by Conway thirty years ago. We prove in this paper that a tight bound on its size with respect to the size of the smallest equivalent NFA is given by Dedekind's numbers. At the end of the paper, we deal with the unary case. Chrobak has proved that the size of the minimal deterministic automaton with respect to the smallest NFA is tightly bounded by the Landau's function; we show that the size of the universal automaton is in this case an exponential of the Landau's function.

Keywords: Regular languages, Universal Automaton, NFA Minimization.

1 Introduction

The computation of a minimal deterministic automaton (DFA) which recognizes a language given by any DFA is a well known procedure with small complexity ($O(n \log n)$ from [6]). For non deterministic automata (NFA) the problem is much harder (PSPACE complete from [8]). Several techniques have recently be developed to reduce the size of NFAs by merging states without changing the recognized language (*cf.* [7,2]).

In a recent paper, Câmpeanu, Sântean and Yu [1] state that for every regular language, every equivalent automaton larger than a constant depending on the language contains some states that can be merged without changing the accepted language. They give a huge bound for this constant, depending on the size of the minimal DFA. Grunsky, Kurganskyy and Potapov [5] have given a tight bound with respect to the size of the minimal DFA.

As this question is related to the NFA minimization, it is interesting to obtain a tight bound with respect to the minimal NFA.

We recall in Section 3 that the *universal automaton* of a language is the largest automaton that recognizes this language in which no states can be merged (*cf.* [11, Prop. 3]). In Section 4, we prove that the size of the universal automaton of a language recognized by a NFA with n states is bounded by $D(n)$, which is

W. Thomas and P. Weil (Eds.): STACS 2007, LNCS 4393, pp. 85–96, 2007.

the n-th number of Dedekind, *i.e.* the number of antichains in the power set of a set with n elements. We show that this bound is tight. In Section 5, we show a family $(\mathcal{Z}_n)$ of n states NFA that yield universal automata with $D(n)$ states, which implies that the bound is tight.

In Section 6, we address the one-letter case. The determinization of a one-letter NFA with n states can give a minimal DFA with $G(n)$ states [3], where $G(n)$ is the Landau's function, that is the maximal least common multiple of integers with sum n. We prove that the bound $2^{G(n)}$ on the size of the universal automaton with respect to the size of the smallest NFA is tight in the one-letter case.

2   Notations

We denote by A^* the free monoid generated by a set A. Elements of A^* are words, the identity of this monoid is the empty word 1_{A^*}. If X and Y are subsets of A^*, we define the product of X and Y by $X.Y = \{u.v \mid u \in X, v \in Y\}$.

If X is a set, we denote $\mathfrak{P}(X)$ the power set of X.

Definition 1. *We denote an automaton by a 5-tuple $\langle Q, A, E, I, T \rangle$, where Q is a finite set of states, A is a finite set of letters, E, the set of transitions, is a subset of $Q \times A \times Q$, and I (resp. T), the set of initial states (resp. terminal states), is a subset of Q.*

Definition 2. *Let $\mathcal{A} = \langle Q, A, E, I, T \rangle$ be an automaton. Let p be a state of $\mathcal{A}$ and a a letter. The set of successors (resp. predecessors) of p by a is $p \underset{\mathcal{A}}{\triangleright} a = \{q \in Q \mid (p, a, q) \in E\}$ (resp. $a \underset{\mathcal{A}}{\triangleleft} p = \{q \in Q \mid (q, a, p) \in E\}$), denoted $p \triangleright a$ (resp. $a \triangleleft p$) if there is no ambiguity. These notions are extended to subsets of states and words; for every letter a, and every word w,*

$$X \triangleright a = \bigcup_{p \in X} p \triangleright a, \qquad a \triangleleft X = \bigcup_{p \in X} a \triangleleft p,$$

$$X \triangleright 1_{A^*} = X, \qquad 1_{A^*} \triangleleft X = X, \tag{1}$$

$$X \triangleright aw = (X \triangleright a) \triangleright w, \qquad aw \triangleleft X = a \triangleleft (w \triangleleft X).$$

Obviously, q is in $p \triangleright w$ if and only if p is in $w \triangleleft q$.

Definition 3. *An automaton is deterministic if it has only one initial state and, for every letter, every state has at most one successor; an automaton is co-deterministic if it has only one final state and, for every letter, every state has at most one predecessor. An automaton is complete if, for every letter, every state has at least one successor.*

Definition 4. *Let $\mathcal{A} = \langle Q, A, E, I, T \rangle$ be an automaton and p a state of $\mathcal{A}$. The past of p in $\mathcal{A}$, $\mathsf{Past}(p)$ (or $\mathsf{Past}_{\mathcal{A}}(p)$), and the future of p in $\mathcal{A}$, $\mathsf{Fut}(p)$ (or $\mathsf{Fut}_{\mathcal{A}}(p)$), are defined as follows:*

$$\mathsf{Past}(p) = \{u \mid p \in I \triangleright u\}, \qquad \mathsf{Fut}(p) = \{v \mid p \triangleright v \cap T \neq \emptyset\}. \tag{2}$$

Remark 1. Let u and v be two words. The word $u.v$ is accepted by an automaton if and only if there exists a state p such that u is in $\mathsf{Past}(p)$ and v is in $\mathsf{Fut}(p)$.

Remark 2. If $\mathcal{A}$ is a deterministic automaton, and if p and q are two different states of $\mathcal{A}$, then $\mathsf{Past}(p) \cap \mathsf{Past}(q) = \emptyset$. In other words, if $\mathcal{A}$ is deterministic and complete, every word u of $\mathcal{A}$ belongs to the past of one and only one state.

Definition 5. *Let $\mathcal{A} = \langle Q, A, E, I, T \rangle$ be an automaton. The* determinized automaton of $\mathcal{A}$ *is the automaton $\mathcal{D} = \langle R, A, F, \{I\}, U \rangle$, where $R = \{I \triangleright w \mid w \in A^*\}$, $F = \{(X, a, X \underset{\mathcal{A}}{\triangleright} a) \mid X \in R, a \in A\}$ and $U = \{X \in R \mid X \cap T \neq \emptyset\}$. The* co-determinized *automaton of $\mathcal{A}$ is the automaton $\mathcal{C} = \langle S, A, G, J, \{T\} \rangle$, where $S = \{w \triangleleft T \mid w \in A^*\}$, $F = \{(a \underset{\mathcal{A}}{\triangleleft} X, a, X) \mid X \in S, a \in A\}$ and $J = \{X \in S \mid X \cap I \neq \emptyset\}$.*

Definition 6. *Let $\mathcal{A} = \langle Q, A, E, I, T \rangle$ and $\mathcal{B} = \langle R, A, F, J, U \rangle$ be two automata. A mapping μ from Q into R is a* morphism *of automata if and only if:*

$$\mu(I) \subseteq J, \quad \mu(T) \subseteq U, \quad and \ \mu(E) = \{(\mu(p), a, \mu(q)) \mid (p, a, q) \in E\} \subseteq F. \quad (3)$$

Proposition 1. *Let μ be a morphism from an automaton $\mathcal{A}$ into an automaton $\mathcal{B}$. Then, for every state p of $\mathcal{A}$,*

$$\mathsf{Past}_{\mathcal{A}}(p) \subseteq \mathsf{Past}_{\mathcal{B}}(\mu(p)), \quad \mathsf{Fut}_{\mathcal{A}}(p) \subseteq \mathsf{Fut}_{\mathcal{B}}(\mu(p)). \quad (4)$$

3   Universal Automaton

The universal automaton of a language has been defined by Conway [4] as a "factor matrix". A complete study of properties of this automaton can be found in [12]. We recall here its definition and some basic properties.

Definition 7. *Let L be a language of A^*. The set $\mathcal{F}(L)$ of* factorizations *of L in A^* is the set of a maximal pairs[1] of languages (X, Y) such that $X.Y$ is a subset of L.*

The universal automaton *of L is $\mathcal{U}_L = \langle \mathcal{F}(L), A, E, I, T \rangle$, with*

$$I = \{(X, Y) \in \mathcal{F}(L) \mid 1_{A^*} \in X\}, \quad T = \{(X, Y) \in \mathcal{F}(L) \mid X \subseteq L\},$$
$$E = \{((X, Y), a, (X', Y')) \in \mathcal{F}(L) \times a \times \mathcal{F}(L) \mid X.a \subseteq X'\}. \quad (5)$$

Remark 3. Due to the maximality of factorizations, the following equivalences hold for every factorization (X, Y) of L:

$$1_{A^*} \in X \Longleftrightarrow Y \subseteq L, \quad X \subseteq L \Longleftrightarrow 1_{A^*} \in Y,$$
$$\forall (X', Y') \in \mathcal{F}(L), \quad X.a \subseteq X' \Longleftrightarrow a.Y' \subseteq Y \Longleftrightarrow X.a.Y' \subseteq L \quad (6)$$

Remark 4. This automaton is not necessarily trim. It may have a non accessible state $(\emptyset, A^*)$ and a non co-accessible state $(A^*, \emptyset)$ if these pairs are factorizations.

---

[1] A pair (X, Y) of languages si larger or equal to a pair (X', Y') iff X' is a subset of X and Y' is a subset of Y.

Proposition 2. *The universal automaton of a regular language is a finite automaton.*

Factorizations of a rational language are recognized by the syntactic monoid of this language. Thus there is a finite number of factorizations. Besides, we shall give a construction of this automaton that induces the finiteness.

Proposition 3. *Let (X, Y) be a state of the universal automaton $\mathcal{U}_L$. Then*

$$\mathsf{Past}(X, Y) = X \quad and \quad \mathsf{Fut}(X, Y) = Y. \tag{7}$$

Corollary 1. *The universal automaton of a rational language L recognizes L.*

In this paper, we are particulary interested in the following property.

Proposition 4. *Let L be a rational language, and $\mathcal{A}$ be an automaton that recognizes L. Then there exists a morphism from $\mathcal{A}$ into the universal automaton of L.*

We explicitly define a mapping μ from states of $\mathcal{A}$ into $\mathcal{F}(L)$: $\mu(p) = (X_p, Y_p)$, with

$$X_p = \{u \in A^* \mid u.\mathsf{Fut}_{\mathcal{A}}(p) \subseteq L\}, \qquad Y_p = \{v \in A^* \mid X_p.v \subseteq L\}. \tag{8}$$

Notice that other mappings may be defined.

Definition 8. *An automaton $\mathcal{A}$ that recognizes a language L has some merging states if there exists a non injective morphism from $\mathcal{A}$ onto an automaton $\mathcal{B}$ that recognizes L.*

Remark 5. It is quite obvious that the automaton obtained by merging states with a morphism is equivalent to the automaton obtained by linking these states with ε-transitions. Our definition of merging states is therefore equivalent to Definition 2 in [1].

Proposition 5. *The universal automaton of a language L is the largest automaton that recognizes L with no merging states.*

The maximality of factorizations prevents from merging states of the universal automaton without changing the language. Conversely, there does not exist any larger automaton with no merging states that recognizes L, thanks to Proposition 4.

4   Maximal Size of the Universal Automaton

In order to compute an upper bound on the size of the universal automaton of a language L with respect to the number of states of a NFA that recognizes L, we give a construction of the universal automaton from an NFA. This construction is actually the same as the one which had been given in [10].

Definition 9. *Let Q be a set and R be a subset of $\mathfrak{P}(Q)$. The intersection closure $\mathcal{I}$ of R is the smallest subset of $\mathfrak{P}(Q)$ such that :*
i) Q is in $\mathcal{I}$ and R is a subset of $\mathcal{I}$,   *ii) if X and Y are in $\mathcal{I}$, so is $X \cap Y$.*

Proposition 6. *Let $\mathcal{D} = \langle Q, A, E, \{i\}, T \rangle$ be a deterministic automaton that recognizes a language L. Let $\mathcal{C} = \langle R, A, F, J, \{T\} \rangle$ be the co-determinized automaton of $\mathcal{D}$. The set of states R of $\mathcal{C}$ is a subset of $\mathfrak{P}(Q)$. Let $\mathcal{I}$ be the intersection closure of R. There is a one-to-one mapping:*

$$\varphi : \mathcal{I} \longrightarrow \mathcal{F}(L)$$
$$S \longmapsto (X_S, Y_S) = \left(\bigcup_{p \in S} \mathsf{Past}_{\mathcal{D}}(p), \bigcap_{p \in S} \mathsf{Fut}_{\mathcal{D}}(p) \right). \tag{9}$$

Proof. It is easy to prove by induction on the length of words that:

$$\mathsf{Past}_{\mathcal{C}}(P) = \bigcup_{p \in P} \mathsf{Past}_{\mathcal{D}}(p), \qquad \mathsf{Fut}_{\mathcal{C}}(P) = \bigcap_{p \in P} \mathsf{Fut}_{\mathcal{D}}(p). \tag{10}$$

a) $X_S . Y_S \subseteq L$. For every u in X_S, $p = i \underset{\mathcal{D}}{\rhd} u$ is in S. For every v in Y_S, v is in $\mathsf{Fut}_{\mathcal{D}}(p)$. Hence, $u.v$ is in L.

b) (X_S, Y_S) is a factorization. We show now that (X_S, Y_S) is maximal. Let u be a word which is not in X_S and such that $u.Y_S$ is included in L. Let $p_0 = i \underset{\mathcal{D}}{\rhd} u$. The state p_0 is not in S, otherwise u would be in X_S. As S is the intersection of some states of $\mathcal{C}$, there exists a state P de $\mathcal{C}$ such that $S \subseteq P$ and p_0 is not in P. Thus u is not in $\mathsf{Past}_{\mathcal{C}}(P)$. Let v be in $\mathsf{Fut}_{\mathcal{C}}(P)$; v is also in Y_S. The word $u.v$ is not in L, thus $u.Y_S \nsubseteq L$. Contradiction.

Let v be a word which is not in Y_S and such that $X_S.v$ is included in L. There exists a state p in S such that v is not in $\mathsf{Fut}_{\mathcal{D}}(p)$. Let u be in $\mathsf{Past}_{\mathcal{D}}(p)$. u is in X_S et $u.v$ is not in L; therefore, $X_S.v$ is not included in L. Contradiction.

c) The mapping φ is surjective.

Let (X, Y) be a factorization of L. Let $H = Y \underset{\mathcal{C}}{\lhd} T$ and let $S = \bigcap_{P \in H} P$: S is an element of $\mathcal{I}$. For every v in Y, S is a subset of $P = v \lhd T$, thus v is in Y_S. For every u in X, as $u.Y$ is included in L, u belongs to the past of every P in H. Thus, there is a state p in S such that u is in $\mathsf{Past}_{\mathcal{D}}(p)$; hence u is in X_S. We get $X \subseteq X_S$ and $Y \subseteq Y_S$, and, by maximality of (X, Y), these inclusions are equalities.

d) The mapping φ is injective.

Let S and S' be two different elements of $\mathcal{I}$. We can assume that S contains a state p which is not in S'. Let u be in $\mathsf{Past}_{\mathcal{D}}(p)$. The word u is in X_S, but not in $X_{S'}$. Hence $\varphi(S)$ is different from $\varphi(S')$. $\square$

This proposition shows that the size of the universal automaton with respect to the size of the minimal automaton of the language is at most 2^n. This bound is tight and an example of a language that illustrates this can be found in [5], or in Section 6 for unary languages. From Equations (7) and (9), if the empty set is an element of $\mathcal{I}$, the corresponding state in the universal automaton is not accessible. Hence the trim universal automaton contains at most $2^n - 1$ states. This gives a tight bound on the size of the maximal NFA without merging state with respect to the size of the minimal DFA. This result has previously be proved by Grunsky, Kurganskyy and Potapov [5].

Proposition 7 (Folklore). *Let A be an NFA with k states. Let D be the determinized automaton of A, with n states. Then $n \leqslant 2^k$ (including a non co-accessible state if the bound is reached).*

This proposition combined with Proposition 6 gives a straighforward upper bound for the size of the universal automaton with respect to any NFA that recognizes the language: $2^{2^n - 1}$. This bound is not tight; we give now a better one.

Definition 10. *Let X be an ordered set. An* upset V *of X is an upperly closed subset of X:*

$$\forall x \in V, \ \forall y \in X, \ x \leqslant y \Longrightarrow y \in V. \tag{11}$$

Notice that an upset may be empty and may also be equal to X itself. If Q is a set, $\mathfrak{P}(Q)$ or every subset of $\mathfrak{P}(Q)$ is naturally ordered by inclusion.

Proposition 8. *Let $A = \langle Q, A, E, I, T \rangle$ be an NFA. Let $D = \langle R, A, F, \{I\}, U \rangle$ be the determinized automaton of A. Let $C = \langle S, A, G, K, \{U\} \rangle$ be the co-determinized automaton of D. Every element of S is an upset of R.*

Proof. Let X and Y be two states of D such that $X \subseteq Y$. It holds $\mathsf{Fut}_D(X) = \bigcup_{p \in X} \mathsf{Fut}_A(p) \subseteq \bigcup_{p \in Y} \mathsf{Fut}_A(p) = \mathsf{Fut}_D(Y)$. Let P be a state of C which contains X. For every v in $\mathsf{Fut}_C(P)$, $P = v \underset{D}{\triangleleft} U$. As X is in P, v is in $\mathsf{Fut}_D(X)$, thus in $\mathsf{Fut}_D(Y)$. Hence, Y is in P. $\qquad\square$

From Proposition 6 and Proposition 8, we obtain the following result.

Proposition 9. *Let $A = \langle Q, A, E, I, T \rangle$ be an NFA that recognizes a language L. The universal automaton of L has at most $D(\mathsf{card}(Q))$ states, where $D(n)$ it the n-th Dedekind number.*

Proof. Let $n = \mathsf{card}(Q)$. $D(n)$ is equal to the number of upsets of $\mathfrak{P}(Q)$. If R is a subset of $\mathfrak{P}(Q)$, the number of its upsets is not larger than the number of upsets of $\mathfrak{P}(Q)$.

The intersection of two upsets is an upset. As, by Proposition 8, S is a set of upsets, the set $\mathcal{I}$ in Proposition 6, which is its intersection closure, is a set of upsets too. As $\mathcal{I}$ is in bijection with the set of states of the universal automaton, the number of states of the universal automaton of L has at most $D(n)$ states. $\qquad\square$

Remark 6. There is no closed form expression for $D(n)$, and its exact value is only known for n smaller than 9 (*cf.* [13]). However, Korshunov [9] has given an approximate expression of $D(n)$. For instance, if n is even,

$$D(n) \sim 2^{\binom{n}{n/2}} \exp\left(\binom{n}{n/2 - 1}(2^{-n/2} + n^2 2^{-n-5} - n 2^{-n-4})\right).$$

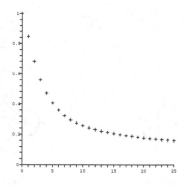

Fig. 1. The graph of $\dfrac{\log_2 D(n)}{2^n}$

Figure 1 is a visual comparison between $D(n)$ and the double exponential function $n \mapsto 2^{2^n}$.

Proposition 10. *Let $\mathcal{A} = \langle Q, A, E, I, T \rangle$ be an NFA that recognizes a language L. The number of states of the trim universal automaton of L is bounded by $D(\mathsf{card}(Q)) - 2$.*

Proof. Actually, if a state corresponds to the empty upset, it has an empty past and it is therefore not accessible. Likewise, if a state corresponds to the upset $\{\emptyset\}$, it has an empty future and it is therefore not co-accessible.   □

Example 1. We give here an example for the construction of the universal automaton. Let $\mathcal{Z}_2$ be the automaton of Figure 2 a). Let $\mathcal{D}_2$ be the determinized automaton of $\mathcal{Z}_2$, drawn on Figure 2 b). Each of its states is a subset of the set of states of $\mathcal{Z}_2$. We denote this set by a words whose letters are the element of the state: the word 01 stands for the set $\{0, 1\}$. The states of the universal automaton (Figure 2 c)) are upsets of the power set of states of $\mathcal{Z}_2$. The non accessible part of the universal automaton is drawn in gray. The automaton $\mathcal{Z}_2$ is an example of the worst case in the construction of the universal automaton. Actually, $D(2) = 6$.

Likewise, $D(3) = 20$ and we give a three-state automaton which recognizes a language whose universal automaton has twenty states: the automaton $\mathcal{Z}_3$ shown on Figure 3 a).

We denote an upset by the set of its minimal elements. For instance $0, 12$ means $\{\{0\}, \{0, 1\}, \{0, 2\}, \{1, 2\}, \{0, 1, 2\}\}$. More, as the number of transitions of the universal automaton is to high to allow to draw them all, a more compact description is drawn on Figure 3 c). Dotted arrows are epsilon transitions (which, strictly speaking, do not belong to the universal automaton); the transitions of the universal automaton are obtained as follows: there is a transition (p, a, q) in the universal automaton if and only if, on the figure, there are two states p' and

a)

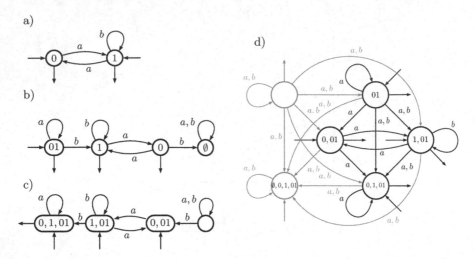

b)

c)

d)

Fig. 2. The construction of the universal automaton from $\mathcal{Z}_2$

q' such that there is a path of dotted arrows from p to p' and from q' to q and a transition labeled by a from p' to q'.

In the following section, we generalize this example to show that, for every n, there exists a n-state NFA that recognizes a language whose universal automaton has $D(n)$ states.

5   A Family of NFAs with Large Universal Automata

In this part, n is a positive integer and $\mathcal{Z}_n = \langle Q, A, E, I, T \rangle$ is the automaton defined by:

$$Q = \mathbb{Z}/n\mathbb{Z}; \qquad A = \{a, b\}; \qquad I = T = Q;$$
$$E = \{(p, a, p+1) \mid p \in Q\} \cup \{(p, b, p) \mid p \in Q \setminus \{0\}\}. \tag{12}$$

In the sequel, if X is a subset of Q, *i.e.* a subset of $\mathbb{Z}/n\mathbb{Z}$, for every integer k, we denote $X + k = \{x + k \mid x \in X\}$.

Lemma 1. *Let n be a positive integer. The determinized automaton of $\mathcal{Z}_n$ is $\mathcal{D}_n = \langle \mathfrak{P}(Q), A, F, \{Q\}, \mathfrak{P}(Q) \setminus \{\emptyset\} \rangle$, with:*

$$F = \{(X, a, X+1), (X, b, X \setminus \{0\}) \mid X \subseteq Q\}. \tag{13}$$

Proof. As every state of $\mathcal{A}$ is initial, the initial state of $\mathcal{D}$ is Q. As every state of $\mathcal{A}$ is terminal, every state of $\mathcal{D}$ different from $\emptyset$ is terminal.

If X is a subset of Q, $X \underset{\mathcal{A}}{\triangleright} a = \bigcup_{p \in X} p \underset{\mathcal{A}}{\triangleright} a = \bigcup_{p \in X} p + 1 = X + 1$; likewise, $X \underset{\mathcal{A}}{\triangleright} b = \bigcup_{p \in X, p \neq 0} p = X \setminus \{0\}$. This gives the set of transitions F of $\mathcal{D}$.

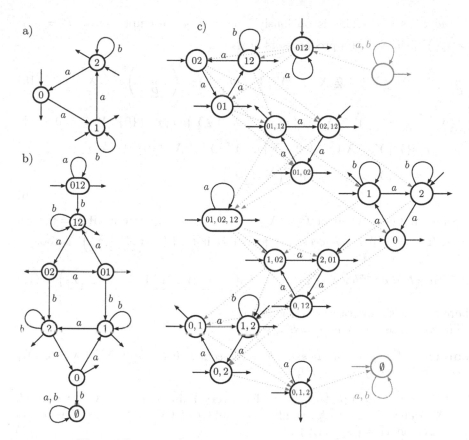

Fig. 3. The construction of the universal automaton from $\mathcal{Z}_3$

We show that every element of $\mathfrak{P}(Q)$ is an accessible state by induction on the number of elements. The set Q itself is the initial state of $\mathcal{D}$. Let assume that X is an accessible state. Let x be an element of X, we show that $X \smallsetminus \{x\}$ is accessible. Actually, $X \triangleright a^{n-x}ba^x = (X - x) \triangleright ba^x = ((X-x)\smallsetminus\{0\}) \triangleright a^x = ((X-x)\smallsetminus\{0\})+x = X\smallsetminus\{x\}$. Therefore, every element of $\mathfrak{P}(Q)$ is accessible.   □

For every subset X of Q, we denote $\underline{X} = \{Y \mid Y \subseteq X\}$, and $(\underline{X})^c = \mathfrak{P}(Q)\smallsetminus\underline{X}$; we can notice that $(\underline{X})^c$ is an upset of $\mathfrak{P}(Q)$.

Lemma 2. *Let* n *be a positive integer. The co-determinized automaton of* $\mathcal{D}_n$ *is* $\mathcal{C}_n = \langle S, A, G, K, V \rangle$*, with:*

$$S = \{(\underline{X})^c \mid X \in \mathfrak{P}(Q)\}; \qquad K = S\smallsetminus\{\emptyset\}; \qquad V = \{(\underline{\emptyset})^c\}$$
$$G = \{(\underline{X})^c, a, (\underline{Y})^c \mid (X, a, Y) \in F\}\cup\{(\underline{X \cup \{0\}})^c, b, (\underline{X})^c \mid X \subseteq Q\}. \tag{14}$$

Proof. As any state X of $\mathcal{D}_n$ different from $\emptyset$ is final, the state $t = (\underline{\emptyset})^c$ is the final state of $\mathcal{D}_n$. First, we show by induction on the word w that any state

$P = w \triangleleft t$ is in S. This is obviously true if w is the empty word: $P = t$. If $P = (\underline{X})^c$ is in S, so its predecessors are:

$$a \underset{c}{\triangleleft} (\underline{X})^c = \{a \underset{D}{\triangleleft} Y \mid Y \not\subseteq X\} = \{Y \mid Y \not\subseteq a \underset{D}{\triangleleft} X\} = \left(a \underset{D}{\triangleleft} X\right)^c = (\underline{X-1})^c; \quad (15)$$

$$b \underset{c}{\triangleleft} (\underline{X})^c = \{b \underset{D}{\triangleleft} Y \mid Y \not\subseteq X\} = \{Y \mid Y \not\subseteq X, 0 \notin Y\} \cup \{Y \cup \{0\} \mid Y \not\subseteq X, 0 \notin Y\}$$

$$= \{Y \mid Y \not\subseteq X \cup \{0\}, 0 \notin Y\} \cup \{Y' \mid Y' \not\subseteq X \cup \{0\}, 0 \in Y'\}$$

$$= \{Y \mid Y \not\subseteq X \cup \{0\}\} = \left(\underline{X \cup \{0\}}\right)^c.$$

$$(16)$$

We show that every element $P = (\underline{X})^c$ of S is co-accessible from t. If $X = \emptyset$, then $P = t$. If $P = (\underline{X})^c$ is co-accessible, for any x in Q, $P' = \left(\underline{X \cup \{x\}}\right)^c$ is too:

$$a^{n-x} b a^x \underset{c}{\triangleleft} P = a^{n-x} b \underset{c}{\triangleleft} (\underline{X-x})^c = a^{n-x} \underset{c}{\triangleleft} \left(\underline{(X-x) \cup \{0\}}\right)^c = \left(\underline{X \cup \{x\}}\right)^c. \quad (17)$$

Therefore the set of states of $\mathcal{C}_n$ is exactly S.

The initial set of $\mathcal{C}_n$ is $K = S \setminus \{\emptyset\}$. □

Lemma 3. *Let Q be a finite set. The intersection closure of $\{(\underline{X})^c \mid X \in \mathfrak{P}(Q)\}$ is exactly the set of upsets of $\mathfrak{P}(Q)$.*

Proof. Let $\mathcal{U}$ be an upset of $\mathfrak{P}(Q)$. For every Y in $\mathcal{U}$, for every X not in $\mathcal{U}$, $Y \not\subseteq X$. Hence, Y is in $(\underline{X})^c$ and $\mathcal{U}$ is a subset of $(\underline{X})^c$. Thus, as X is not in $(\underline{X})^c$, it comes $\mathcal{U} = \bigcap_{X \notin \mathcal{U}} (\underline{X})^c$. □

Therefore, for every integer n, the universal automaton of the language recognized by $\mathcal{Z}_n$ has exactly $D(n)$ states, and its trim part $D(n) - 2$ states. This, with Proposition 9, implies the following theorem.

Theorem 1. *Let $\mathcal{A} = \langle Q, A, E, I, T \rangle$ be an NFA that recognizes a language L. Let $D(n)$ be the n-th Dedekind number. The following tight bounds hold.*

i) The universal automaton of L has at most $D(\mathrm{card}(Q))$ states.
ii) The trim universal automaton of L has at most $D(\mathrm{card}(Q)) - 2$ states.

6   Unary Alphabets

We have seen that the composition of two algorithms (determinization and construction of the universal automaton) that may produce an exponential output yields an automaton with a number of states which is never a double exponential.

In the case of one-letter alphabet, the determinization algorithm has been shown not to be exponential. Actually, if $\mathcal{A}$ is a one-letter NFA with n states, the determinized automaton of $\mathcal{A}$ (and the minimal automaton of the accepted language) has at most $G(n)$ states (it cf. [3], where $G(n)$ is the Landau function

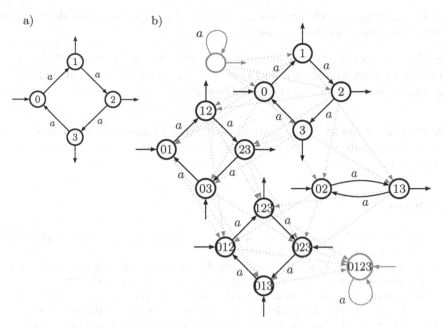

Fig. 4. The automaton $\mathcal{Y}_4$ and its universal automaton

of n, that is the maximal least common multiple of a set of integers with sum equal to n. We show that in this case, the universal automaton may have $2^{G(n)}$ states.

There exist an integer r and r numbers $k_1, .., k_r$ such that $k_1 + .. + k_r = n$ and $\mathsf{lcm}(k_1, k_2, ..., k_r) = G(n)$. Let Q be the disjoint union of $(Q_i = \mathbb{Z}/k_i\mathbb{Z})_{i \in [1;r]}$ and let $\mathcal{Y}_n = \langle Q, \{a\}, E, I, T \rangle$ be the automaton defined by:

$$I = \{0 \in Q_i \mid i \in [1;r]\}, \quad T = Q \smallsetminus I, \quad E = \{(p, a, p+1) \mid \exists i, p \in Q_i\}. \quad (18)$$

Lemma 4. *The determinized automaton of $\mathcal{Y}_n$ is isomorphic to the automaton $\mathcal{D}_n = \langle R, \{a\}, F, J, U \rangle$, with $R = \mathbb{Z}/G(n)\mathbb{Z}$, $J = \{0\}$, $U = R \smallsetminus J$ and $F = \{(p, a, p+1) \mid p \in R\}$.*

The states of the co-determinized automaton of $\mathcal{D}_n$ are all the subset of R with $\mathsf{card}(R) - 1$ elements. The intersection closure of this set of states is equal to $\mathfrak{P}(R)$. Hence, the universal automaton of the language recognized by $\mathcal{Y}_n$ has $2^{G(n)}$ states and the trim universal automaton has $2^{G(n)} - 2$ states.

Remark 7. Starting from a one-letter DFA with n states ($n > 1$), it is not possible to obtain a trim universal automaton with $2^n - 1$ states. The state corresponding to the empty set in the construction of Proposition 6 cannot be accessible. If the full set corresponds to a co-accessible state, it means that every state of the DFA is final, thus every word is accepted and the universal automaton has one state, or, if the DFA is not complete, the language is a finite prefix language and the universal automaton has n states. Therefore, the trim universal automaton has at most $2^n - 2$ states.

Example 2. Let $\mathcal{Y}_4$ be the automaton of Figure 4 a). It is equal to $\mathcal{D}_4$. The universal automaton, drawn on Figure 4 b), has $2^4 = 16$ states, including a non accessible state and a non co-accessible state.

Acknowledgement. I am grateful to Jacques Sakarovitch who introduced me the universal automaton a few years ago and who is always ready for any scientific discussion.

References

1. CÂMPEANU, C., SÂNTEAN, N., AND YU, S. Mergible states in large nfa. *Theoret. Comput. Sci. 330*, 1 (2005), 23–34.
2. CHAMPARNAUD, J.-M., AND COULON, F. NFA reduction algorithms by means of regular inequalities. *Theoret. Comput. Sci. 327*, 3 (2004), 241–253.
3. CHROBAK, M. Finite automata and unary languages. *Theoret. Comput. Sci. 47*, 2 (1986), 149–158. Errata in Theoret. Comput. Sci. 302 (2003) 497–498.
4. CONWAY, J. H. *Regular algebra and finite machines*. Mathematics series. Chapmann and Hall, London, 1971.
5. GRUNSKY, I., KURGANSKYY, O., AND POTAPOV, I. On a maximal nfa without mergible states. In *CSR* (2006), D. Grigoriev, J. Harrison, and E. A. Hirsch, Eds., vol. 3967, Springer, pp. 202–210.
6. HOPCROFT, J. E. An $n \log n$ algorithm for minimizing states in a finite automaton. In *Theory of machines and computations (Proc. Internat. Sympos., Technion, Haifa, 1971)*. Academic Press, New York, 1971, pp. 189–196.
7. ILIE, L., AND YU, S. Reducing NFAs by invariant equivalences. *Theoret. Comput. Sci. 306*, 1-3 (2003), 373–390.
8. JIANG, T., AND RAVIKUMAR, B. Minimal NFA problems are hard. *SIAM J. Comput. 22*, 6 (1993), 1117–1141.
9. KORSHUNOV, A. D. The number of monotone Boolean functions. *Problemy Kibernet.*, 38 (1981), 5–108, 272.
10. LOMBARDY, S. On the construction of reversible automata for reversible languages. In *ICALP 2002* (2002), P. Widmayer, F. Triguero Ruiz, R. Morales Bueno, M. Hennessy, S. Eidenbenz, and R. Conejo, Eds., vol. 2380 of *Lect. Notes Comp. Sci.*, Springer, pp. 170–182.
11. LOMBARDY, S., AND SAKAROVITCH, J. Star height of reversible languages and universal automata. In *LATIN 2002* (2002), S. Rajsbaum, Ed., vol. 2286 of *Lect. Notes Comp. Sci.*, Springer, pp. 76–90.
12. SAKAROVITCH, J. *Éléments de théorie des automates.* Les classiques de l'informatique. Vuibert, Paris, 2003. English translation to appear, Cambridge University Press.
13. WIEDEMANN, D. A computation of the eighth Dedekind number. *Order 8*, 1 (1991), 5–6.

Correlations of Partial Words*

Francine Blanchet-Sadri[1], Joshua D. Gafni[2], and Kevin H. Wilson[3]

[1] Department of Computer Science, University of North Carolina,
P.O. Box 26170, Greensboro, NC 27402–6170, USA
blanchet@uncg.edu
[2] Department of Mathematics, University of Pennsylvania,
Philadelphia, PA 19104–6395, USA
jgafni@sas.upenn.edu
[3] Department of Mathematics, University of Michigan,
Ann Arbor, MI 48109–1043, USA
khwilson@umich.edu

Abstract. *Partial words* are strings over a finite alphabet that may contain a number of "do not know" symbols. In this paper, we introduce the notions of binary and ternary correlations, which are binary and ternary vectors indicating the periods and weak periods of partial words. Extending a result of Guibas and Odlyzko, we characterize precisely which of these vectors represent the (weak) period sets of partial words and prove that all valid correlations may be taken over the binary alphabet. We show that the sets of all such vectors of a given length form distributive lattices under inclusion. We also show that there is a well defined minimal set of generators for any binary correlation of length n and demonstrate that these generating sets are the primitive subsets of $\{1, 2, ..., n-1\}$. Finally, we investigate the number of correlations of length n.

1 Introduction

Words, sequences or strings of symbols from a finite alphabet, arise naturally in several areas of mathematical sciences. Notions and techniques related to periodic structures in words find applications in virtually every area of theoretical and applied computer science, notably in text processing, data compression, coding, computational biology, string searching and pattern matching algorithms. Repeated patterns and related phenomena in words have played over the years a central role in the development of combinatorics on words, and have been highly valuable tools for the design and analysis of algorithms.

The first significant results on periodicity are the theorem of Fine and Wilf [9] and the critical factorization theorem [7]. These two fundamental results refer

---

* This material is based upon work supported by the National Science Foundation under Grant No. DMS–0452020. A World Wide Web server interface has been established at www.uncg.edu/mat/research/correlations for automated use of the program. We thank the referees of a preliminary version of this paper for their very valuable comments and suggestions.

W. Thomas and P. Weil (Eds.): STACS 2007, LNCS 4393, pp. 97–108, 2007.
© Springer-Verlag Berlin Heidelberg 2007

to two kinds of phenomena concerning periodicity: The theorem of Fine and Wilf considers the simultaneous occurrence of different periods in one string, whereas the critical factorization theorem relates local and global periodicity of strings. Starting from these basic classical results, the study of periodicity has grown along both directions. Reference [15] contains a systematic and self-contained exposition of this theory, including more recent significant results such as an unexpected theorem of Guibas and Odlyzko which gives the structure of the set of periods of a string [10].

In many practical applications, such as DNA sequence analysis, repetitions admit a certain variation between copies of the repeated pattern because of errors due to mutation, experiments, etc. Approximate repeated patterns, or repetitions where errors are allowed, are playing a central role in different variants of string searching and pattern matching problems. *Partial words*, or strings that may have a number of "do not know" symbols (also called "holes"), have acquired great importance in this context [11,12,13,14,17]. Another application area of current interest for the study of partial words is data communication where some information may be missing, lost, or unknown. In their seminal and fundamental work [1], Berstel and Boasson introduced this notion of partial word and proved a theorem analogous to the periodicity theorem of Fine and Wilf for the one-hole case. After them, Blanchet-Sadri and Hegstrom extended this result to partial words with two and three holes [5], and finally Blanchet-Sadri extended it to arbitrary partial words [2]. Blanchet-Sadri and co-authors have developed this line of research of periodicity on partial words and obtained the first algorithms in the context of partial words. In particular, they extended the critical factorization theorem to partial words with an arbitrary number of holes [4,6] and Guibas and Odlyzko's theorem to partial words with one hole [3].

In [10], Guibas and Odlyzko consider the period sets of strings of length n over a finite alphabet, and specific representations of them, *(auto)correlations*, which are binary vectors of length n indicating the periods. Among the possible 2^n bit vectors, only a small subset are valid correlations. There, they provide characterizations of correlations, asymptotic bounds on their number, and a recurrence for the *population size* of a correlation, that is, the number of strings sharing a given correlation. In [16], Rivals and Rahmann show that there is redundancy in period sets and introduce the notion of an *irreducible* period set. They prove that Γ_n, the set of all correlations of length n, is a lattice under set inclusion and does not satisfy the Jordan-Dedekind condition. They propose the first efficient enumeration algorithm for Γ_n and improve upon the previously known asymptotic lower bounds on the cardinality of Γ_n. Finally, they provide a new recurrence to compute the number of strings sharing a given period set, and exhibit an algorithm to sample uniformly period sets through irreducible period sets.

In the case of partial words, there are two notions of periodicity: one is that of *period*, the other is that of *weak period*. In this paper, we study the combinatorics of possible sets of periods and weak periods of partial words in a similar way as it was done for the structure of all global periods of words. In Section 3, we introduce the notions of binary and ternary correlations, which are binary and ternary vectors indicating the periods and weak periods of partial words. Extending the result of Guibas and Odlyzko, we characterize precisely which of these vectors represent the (weak) period sets of partial words and prove that all valid correlations may be taken over the binary alphabet. In Section 4, we show that the sets of all such vectors of a given length form distributive lattices under inclusion extending results of Rivals and Rahmann. We also show that there is a well defined minimal set of generators for any binary correlation of length n and demonstrate in Section 5 that these generating sets are the primitive subsets of $\{1, 2, ..., n - 1\}$. Finally, we investigate the number of correlations of length n.

2   Definitions, Notations, and Preliminary Results

Traditionally, a *(full) word* u is defined as a function $u : \{0, 1, \ldots, n-1\} \to A$ for some $n \geq 0$ and some nonempty, finite set A, called the *alphabet*. The *length* n is denoted $|u|$ and sometimes the word is written explicitly as $u = u(0)u(1) \cdots u(n-1)$. When $n = 0$ we say the word is *empty* and denote it by ε. We denote the set of all words of length n over the alphabet A by A^n and the set of all words over A by A^*.

A *partial word* is defined similarly except u is a *partial* function. We define $D(u)$ to be the *domain of* u, i.e., the set of $i \in \{0, 1, \ldots, n - 1\}$ such that $u(i)$ is defined. Moreover, we define the *companion of* u to be the full word $u_\diamond : \{0, 1, \ldots, n-1\} \to A \cup \{\diamond\}$ defined by $u_\diamond(i) = u(i)$ if $i \in D(u)$ and $u_\diamond(i) = \diamond$ otherwise. Finally we define $H(u) = [0, 1, \ldots, n-1] \setminus D(u)$ to be the set of *holes* of u. Throughout this paper u and $u_\diamond$ will be used interchangeably. For example, $u = abb\diamond bb\diamond a$ is a partial word where $D(u) = \{0, 1, 2, 4, 5, 7\}$ and $H(u) = \{3, 6\}$. We say that $A^n_\diamond$ is the set of partial words of length n over the alphabet A and that $A^*_\diamond$ is the set of *all* partial words (including ε) over the alphabet A.

Partial words allow for two weakenings of equality which we call containment and compatibility. We say that the partial word u is *contained in* the partial word v (denoted $u \subset v$) provided that $|u| = |v|$, $D(u) \subseteq D(v)$ and for all $i \in D(u)$ we have that $u(i) = v(i)$. As a weaker notion, we say that the partial words u and v are *compatible* (denoted $u \uparrow v$) provided that there exists another partial word w such that $u \subset w$ and $v \subset w$. An equivalent formulation of compatibility is that $|u| = |v|$ and for all $i \in D(u) \cap D(v)$ we have that $u(i) = v(i)$. As an example, $u = abb\diamond bb\diamond a$ and $v = \diamond bbab\diamond ba$ are compatible with $w = abbabbba$. For a partial word u, we denote by $C(u)$ the set of all partial words compatible with u. More specifically, $C(u) = \{v \mid u \uparrow v\}$.

We say that a partial word u is *(strongly) p-periodic* provided that $u(i) = u(j)$ for all $i, j \in D(u)$ with $i \equiv j \mod p$. Moreover, we say that all partial words have period 0. We denote the set of all periods of u which are less than $|u|$ by $\mathcal{P}(u)$. Similarly we say that a partial word u is *weakly p-periodic* provided that whenever $0 \leq i < n - p$ and $i, i+p \in D(u)$ we have $u(i) = u(i+p)$. We call the set of weak periods of u which are less than $|u|$ by $\mathcal{P}'(u)$. It is obvious that $\mathcal{P}(u) \subseteq \mathcal{P}'(u)$ and in the case of full words, $\mathcal{P}(u) = \mathcal{P}'(u)$ since $D(u) = \{0, 1, \ldots, |u|-1\}$. In general this equality does not hold. As an example, consider the partial word $ab\diamond bbb\diamond bbbb$, which is weakly 2-periodic but *not* 2-periodic. When $q \in \mathcal{P}'(u) \setminus \mathcal{P}(u)$ we say that u has a *strictly* weak period of q. Note that if for some n we have that $u, v \in A_\diamond^n$ and $u \subset v$, then $\mathcal{P}(v) \subseteq \mathcal{P}(u)$ and $\mathcal{P}'(v) \subseteq \mathcal{P}'(u)$.

We will say that the *greatest lower bound* of a pair of partial words u and v of length n is the partial word $u \wedge v$ with $D(u \wedge v) = \{0 \le i < n \mid i \in D(u) \cap D(v)$ and $u(i) = v(i)\}$ and $(u \wedge v)(i) = u(i) = v(i)$ for all $i \in D(u \wedge v)$. Consider for example the partial words $u = abbbbb\diamond a$ and $v = \diamond bbab\diamond ba$ where $u \wedge v = \diamond bb\diamond b\diamond\diamond a$. Note that $u \wedge v$ is constructed so that $(u \wedge v) \subset u$ and $(u \wedge v) \subset v$. Moreover, it is easily seen that $u \wedge v$ is *maximal* in the sense that for all partial words w which satisfy $w \subset u$ and $w \subset v$ we have that $w \subset (u \wedge v)$. One property we notice immediately about the greatest lower bound is that if $u, v \in A_\diamond^n$, then $\mathcal{P}(u) \cup \mathcal{P}(v) \subseteq \mathcal{P}(u \wedge v)$ and $\mathcal{P}'(u) \cup \mathcal{P}'(v) \subseteq \mathcal{P}'(u \wedge v)$.

For any $0 \le p < |u|$ and $0 \le i < p$, define $u_{i,p} = u(i)u(i+p)u(i+2p)\cdots$, the ith p-word of u. Clearly, $p \in \mathcal{P}(u)$ if and only if $u_{i,p}$ is 1-periodic for all $0 \le i < p$. Similarly, $p \in \mathcal{P}'(u)$ if and only if $u_{i,p}$ is weakly 1-periodic for all $0 \le i < p$.

3   Characterizations of Correlations

The major result of [10] was a complete characterization of the possible sets of periods for full words of arbitrary length. Guibas and Odlyzko stated their results not in terms of sets of periods but in terms of bit vectors which they called correlations. For a (full) word u, let v be the bit vector of length $|u|$ for which $v_i = 1$ whenever $i \in \mathcal{P}(u)$ and $v_i = 0$ otherwise. We call v the *correlation* of u. For example, the word $abbababbab$ has periods 5 and 8 and thus has correlation 1000010010. This representation gave them a useful method of representing sets of periods in concise ways and allowed them to prove the main result of their paper. We now recall their theorem, for which we will need a definition.

Definition 1. *A bit vector v of length n is said to satisfy the*

- *Forward propagation rule provided that for all $0 \le p < q < n$ such that $v_p = v_q = 1$ we have that $v_{p+i(q-p)} = 1$ for all integers i satisfying $2 \le i < (n-p)/(q-p)$,*
- *Backward propagation rule provided that for any nonnegative integers p and q less than n such that $0 \le p < q < 2p$ and $v_p = v_q = 1$ and $v_{2p-q} = 0$ we have that $v_{p-i(q-p)} = 0$ for all $i = 2, \ldots, \min\{p/(q-p), (n-p)/(q-p)\}$.*

Theorem 1. Guibas and Odlyzko [10] *For correlation v of length n the following are equivalent:*

1. *There exists a word over the binary alphabet with correlation v.*
2. *There exists a word over some alphabet with correlation v.*
3. *The correlation v satisfies the forward and backward propagation rules.*

Corollary 1. *For any alphabet A and any word $u \in A^*$, there exists a word $v \in \{a, b\}^*$ such that $\mathcal{P}(v) = \mathcal{P}(u)$.*

In this section, we follow the example of Guibas and Odlyzko and completely characterize the possible sets of periods and weak periods of partial words. To do so we first extend their definition of a "correlation" to incorporate the difference between strictly weak periods and strong periods, a difference which does not occur in the case of full words.

Definition 2. *Let P and Q be sets. We say that the pair (P, Q) is a ternary correlation of length n provided that there exists a partial word $u \in A_\diamond^n$ such that $P = \mathcal{P}(u)$ and $Q = \mathcal{P}'(u) \setminus \mathcal{P}(u)$. Such a pair we will denote by P/Q. For a given ternary correlation P/Q of length n, we define its correlation vector v to be the ternary vector for which $v_i = 1$ whenever $i \in P$, $v_i = 2$ whenever $i \in Q$, and $v_i = 0$ otherwise. We will say that $\mathcal{P}(v) = \{0 \le i < n \mid v_i = 1\}$ and $\mathcal{P}'(v) = \{0 \le i < n \mid v_i > 0\}$. When $Q = \varnothing$, we will call the correlation P/Q a binary correlation.*

We begin the process of characterizing the correlations of partial words by recording two facts. (1) The first formalizes a relatively obvious property of the periods of full words: For all integers $p \ge 0$ define $\langle p \rangle_n$ to be the set of nonnegative integers less than n which are multiples of p. Then for all $u \in A^n$,

$$\mathcal{P}(u) = \bigcup_{p \in P} \langle p \rangle_n$$

for some $P \subseteq \{0, 1, 2, \ldots, n-1\}$. (2) The second characterizes the relationship between partial words and the words which are compatible with them: If u is a partial word over an alphabet A, then

$$\mathcal{P}(u) = \bigcup_{w \in C(u) \cap A^*} \mathcal{P}(w)$$

For example, consider the partial word $u = abca\diamond cabca$ over the alphabet $A = \{a, b, c\}$. Then $\mathcal{P}(u) = \{3, 6, 9, 10\} = \mathcal{P}(w_1) \cup \mathcal{P}(w_2) \cup \mathcal{P}(w_3)$ where $w_1 = abcaacabca$, $w_2 = abcabcabca$ and $w_3 = abcaccabca$ are the words w satisfying $w \in C(u) \cap A^*$.

We are now ready to state the first part of our characterization theorem. This part of the theorem completely characterizes the set of binary correlations of all partial words. In the sequel, we only use the subscript n in $\langle p \rangle_n$ when its value is not clear from context.

Theorem 2. *For any finite collection $u_1, u_2, \ldots, u_k$ of full words of length n over an alphabet A, there exists a partial word w of length n over the alphabet $\{a, b\}$ with $\mathcal{P}(w) = \mathcal{P}'(w) = \mathcal{P}(u_1) \cup \mathcal{P}(u_2) \cup \cdots \cup \mathcal{P}(u_k)$.*

Proof. (Sketch) The case $k = 1$ follows from Corollary 1. Moreover, since ε is the only word of length 0, the case $n = 0$ forces $k = 1$ and so we assume that $k > 1$ and $n > 0$. Then from (1) we have that

$$\bigcup_{j=1}^{k} \mathcal{P}(u_j) = \bigcup_{p \in P} \langle p \rangle$$

for some $P \subseteq \{0, 1, \ldots, n-1\}$. Thus for all $1 \le j \le k$, we assume that $\mathcal{P}(u_j) = \langle p_j \rangle$ for some $0 \le p_j < n$.

With these assumptions, we move on to the case when $k = 2$. For notational clarity we set $u = u_1$, $v = u_2$, $\mathcal{P}(u) = \langle p \rangle$, and $\mathcal{P}(v) = \langle q \rangle$ for some $0 \le p < q < n$. Define

$$\omega_p = \begin{cases} ab^{n-1} & \text{if } p = 0 \\ (ab^{p-1})^k ab^{r-1} & \text{if } p > 0 \text{ and } r > 0 \\ (ab^{p-1})^k & \text{otherwise} \end{cases}$$

where $n = kp + r$ with $0 \le r < p$. Similarly define ω_q. Obviously $\mathcal{P}(\omega_p) = \langle p \rangle$ and $\mathcal{P}(\omega_q) = \langle q \rangle$. We claim that $\mathcal{P}(\omega_p \wedge \omega_q) = \mathcal{P}(\omega_p) \cup \mathcal{P}(\omega_q)$.

Moreover, we see that $\omega_p \wedge \omega_q$ has no strictly weak periods. Assume the contrary and let $\xi \in \mathcal{P}'(\omega_p \wedge \omega_q) \setminus \mathcal{P}(\omega_p \wedge \omega_q)$. Then there exist $i, j \in D(\omega_p \wedge \omega_q)$ such that $i \equiv j \bmod \xi$ and $(\omega_p \wedge \omega_q)(i) = a$ and $(\omega_p \wedge \omega_q)(j) = b$, and for all $0 \le k < n$ such that $k \equiv i \bmod \xi$ and k is strictly between i and j we have $k \in H(\omega_p \wedge \omega_q)$. Let k be such that $|i - k|$ is minimized (that is, if $i < j$ then k is minimal and if $i > j$ then k is maximal). This minimal distance is obviously ξ. Then p and q divide i and at least one of them divides k. But we see that only one of p and q divides k, for if both did then $(\omega_p \wedge \omega_q)(k) = a \ne \diamond$. Without loss of generality let $p | k$. But as $p | i$ and $p | k$, we have $p | |i - k| = \xi$. Then since ω_p is p-periodic, we have that $\omega_p(l) = \omega_p(i) = a$ for all $l \equiv i \bmod p$. But $j \equiv i \bmod \xi$ and $p | \xi$, so $j \equiv i \bmod p$. Therefore, $\omega_p(j) = a$ and thus $(\omega_p \wedge \omega_q)(j) \ne b$, a contradiction. Now let $k > 2$ and let $\{p_1, \ldots, p_k\} \subseteq \{0, 1, \ldots, n-1\}$ be the periods such that $\mathcal{P}(u_j) = \langle p_j \rangle$. We claim that $\mathcal{P}(\omega_{p_1} \wedge \cdots \wedge \omega_{p_k}) = \mathcal{P}(\omega_{p_1}) \cup \cdots \cup \mathcal{P}(\omega_{p_k})$ and that $\omega_{p_1} \wedge \cdots \wedge \omega_{p_k}$ has no strictly weak periods. □

Theorem 2 tells us that every union of possible correlations of full words over any alphabet is the correlation of a binary partial word. But (2) tells us that the period set of every partial word over any alphabet (including the binary alphabet) is the union of the period sets of all full words compatible with it. Thus, we have a bijection between these sets which we record as the following corollary.

Corollary 2. *The set of valid binary correlations $P/\varnothing$ of length n over the binary alphabet is precisely the set of unions of valid correlations of full words of length n over all nonempty alphabets.*

In light of (2), the following corollary is essentially a rephrasing of the previous corollary. But as a concept, this corollary is important enough to deserve special attention.

Corollary 3. *The set of valid binary correlations $P/\varnothing$ over an alphabet A with $|A| \ge 2$ is the set of valid binary correlations over the binary alphabet. Phrased differently, if u is a partial word over an alphabet A, then there exists a binary partial word v such that $\mathcal{P}(v) = \mathcal{P}(u)$.*

Theorem 2 and Corollaries 2 and 3 give us three equivalent characterizations of valid binary correlations of partial words over an arbitrary alphabet. They do not mention at all, though, the effect of strictly weak periods. The following theorem shows that the characterization is actually rather elegant.

Theorem 3. *A ternary correlation P/Q of length n is valid if and only if*

1. *P is the nonempty union of sets of the form $\langle p \rangle_n$,*
2. *For each $q \in Q$, there exists an integer $2 \leq m < \frac{n}{q}$ such that $mq \notin P \cup Q$.*

Proof. (*Sketch*) First, if $Q = \varnothing$ then we are in the case of Corollaries 2 and 3. Thus we consider only the case when $Q \neq \varnothing$. We begin by taking a triple (P, Q, n) satisfying the above conditions along with the assumption that n is at least 3 since the cases of zero-letter, one-letter, and two-letter partial words are trivial by simple enumeration considering all possible renamings of letters. So we may now define

$$\psi_Q = \bigwedge_{q \in Q} \psi_q \qquad \omega_P = \bigwedge_{p \in P} \omega_p$$

where $\psi_q = ab^{q-1} \diamond b^{n-q-1}$ with $1 \leq q < n$, $a, b \in A$ are distinct letters, and ω_p is as in the proof of Theorem 2. Notice that $0 \notin Q$ since $0 \in P$ and then $0m \in P$ for all integers m. Thus, ψ_Q is well-defined. Then we claim that $u = \omega_P \wedge \psi_Q$ is a partial word with correlation P/Q.

We claim that $P = \mathcal{P}(u)$ and since $P \cup Q \subseteq \mathcal{P}'(u)$ it suffices to show that if $q \in \mathcal{P}'(u) \setminus \mathcal{P}(u)$ then $q \subset Q$. Since $q \subset \mathcal{P}'(u) \setminus \mathcal{P}(u)$ we have that some $u_{i,q}$ contains both a and b. But the only possible location of a is 0, so we may write this as $u(0) = a$, $u(qj) = \diamond$, and $u(qk) = b$ for some $k \geq 2$ and $0 < j < k$. But notice then that u does not have period q so $q \notin P$. Thus, since $u(q) = \diamond$, we have that $q \in Q$ and have thus completed this direction of the theorem. Now consider the other direction, i.e., if we are given a partial word u with correlation P/Q, then P/Q satisfies our conditions. By Theorem 2 we have that the first condition must be met and we claim that the second condition must be met as well. $\qquad \square$

In analogy to Corollary 3, we record the following fact.

Corollary 4. *The set of valid ternary correlations P/Q over an alphabet A with $|A| \geq 2$ is the same as the set of valid ternary correlations over the binary alphabet. Phrased differently, if u is a partial word over an alphabet A, then there exists a binary partial word v with $\mathcal{P}(v) = \mathcal{P}(u)$ and $\mathcal{P}'(v) = \mathcal{P}'(u)$.*

We end this section with some consequences of Theorem 3. Having completely characterized the sets of binary and ternary correlations of partial words and having shown that all valid binary and ternary correlations may be taken as over the binary alphabet, we give these sets names. In the sequel we shall let Δ_n be the set of all valid binary correlations of partial words of length n and Δ'_n the set of valid ternary correlations of length n.

As a first consequence of Theorem 3 we notice that for a given ternary correlation $v \in \Delta'_n$, we have that $v_i \neq 2$ for all $i > \lfloor \frac{n-1}{2} \rfloor$. Another consequence of Theorem 3 is that for all $v \in \Delta_n$ we have that

$$\mathcal{P}(v) = \bigcup_{p \in P} \langle p \rangle_n$$

for some $P \subseteq \{0, 1, \ldots, n-1\}$, and we say that P *generates* the correlation v. One such P is $\mathcal{P}(v)$. But in general there are strictly smaller P which have this property. For example, if $v = 1001001101$ then $\mathcal{P}(v) = \{0, 3, 6, 7, 9\}$. While $P = \mathcal{P}(v)$ will generate this set, we see that $P = \{0, 3, 6, 7\}$, $\{3, 6, 7\}$, $\{0, 3, 7\}$, or $\{3, 7\}$ (among others) will as well. On the other hand, we see that there is a well defined *minimal* set of generators. That is, for every $v \in \Delta_n$ there is a set $R(v)$ such that for any set P which generates v we have that $R(v) \subseteq P$. Namely, this is the set of nonzero $p \in \mathcal{P}(v)$ such that for all $q \in \mathcal{P}(v)$ with $p \neq q$ we have that $q \nmid p$. For if there is q distinct from p such that $q|p$ then we have that all multiples of p are also multiples of q, i.e., $\langle p \rangle \subseteq \langle q \rangle$. Moreover, we see since there are no divisors of the elements of $R(v)$ in $\mathcal{P}(v)$ that the only $p \in \mathcal{P}(v)$ which can generate $r \in R(v)$ is r itself. Thus we have achieved minimality.

We will call $R(v)$ the *irreducible period set of* v. For partial words of length n, we define Φ_n to be the set of all irreducible period sets. Moreover, we see that there is an obvious bijective correspondence between Φ_n and Δ_n given by the function $R : \Delta_n \to \Phi_n$ in one direction and its inverse $E : \Phi_n \to \Delta_n$ defined as

$$E(P) = \bigcup_{p \in P} \langle p \rangle_n$$

4   Structural Properties of Δ_n, Δ_n' and Φ_n

In [16] Rivals and Rahmann defined the set of all valid correlations of full words of length n as Γ_n. They then defined a notion of irreducible period set based on forward propagation. Specifically, they noticed that (like partial words), some periods are implied by other periods because of the forward propagation rule. An example is that if a twelve-letter word has periods 7 and 9 then it must also have period 11 since $11 = 7 + 2(9 - 7)$. They then gave for any $v \in \Gamma_n$, conditions for a period set to be an irreducible period set associated with v and showed that this minimal set of periods exists and is unique. In the above example, $\{0, 7, 9, 11\}$ would correspond to $\{0, 7, 9\}$. The set of these irreducible period sets they called Λ_n.

Our notion of irreducible periods and Rivals and Rahmann's differ in a fundamental way. Specifically, their definition relied on forward propagation. This rule does not hold in the case of partial words. For example, the proof of Theorem 3 tells us that $abbbbbb \diamond b \diamond bb$ has periods 7 and 9 but does *not* have period 11. Thus, $\{7, 9, 11\}$ is irreducible in the sense of partial words, but not in the sense of full words.

The idea of reduction is still present though. And in [16] Rivals and Rahmann went on to show several structural properties of Γ_n and Λ_n. Specifically, they showed that Γ_n is a lattice under inclusion which does not satisfy the Jordan-Dedekind condition, a criterion which stipulates that all maximal chains between two elements of a poset are of equal length. Violating this condition implies that Γ_n is neither distributive, modular, nor a matroid. They also showed that while Λ_n is not a lattice that it *does* satisfy the Jordan-Dedekind condition as a poset.

Because of the analogies between Γ_n and Δ_n and Δ_n' as well as the analogies between Λ_n and Φ_n, we now investigate the structural properties of Δ_n, Δ_n'

and Φ_n. In order to highlight the differences between the cases of full words and partial words, the structure of this section closely follows the structure of the analogous section of [16]. In particular we show that both Δ_n and Δ'_n are distributive lattices under inclusion (suitably defined in the case of Δ'_n). On the other hand, we show that Φ_n is not a lattice but does satisfy the Jordan-Dedekind condition.

First, we blur the lines between the correlation *vector* $v \in \Delta_n$ and the associated set of periods $\mathcal{P}(v)$. Specifically, we say that for any $u, v \in \Delta_n$ we have that $u \subseteq v$ if and only if $\mathcal{P}(u) \subseteq \mathcal{P}(v)$ and $p \in u$ if and only if $p \in \mathcal{P}(u)$. Moreover, we define $u \cap v$ and $u \cup v$ to be the unique vectors with $\mathcal{P}(u \cap v) = \mathcal{P}(u) \cap \mathcal{P}(v)$ and $\mathcal{P}(u \cup v) = \mathcal{P}(u) \cup \mathcal{P}(v)$. It is easy to see that if $u, v \in \Delta_n$ then $u \cap v \in \Delta_n$ and $u \cup v \in \Delta_n$. Moreover, the pair $(\Delta_n, \subseteq)$ is a poset with a null element and a universal element. Namely the null element is 10^{n-1} and the universal element is 1^n. One of the theorems of [16] is that the set of correlations of full words form a lattice that does not satisfy the Jordan-Dedekind condition. Thus it is neither distributive nor modular. But since the meet and the join of binary correlations are the *set intersection* and *set union* of the correlations, we have the following theorem.

Theorem 4. *The poset $(\Delta_n, \subseteq)$ is a distributive lattice and thus satisfies the Jordan-Dedekind condition.*

Second, we expand our considerations to Δ'_n, the set of ternary correlations of partial words of length n, and show that Δ'_n is a lattice again with respect to inclusion, which we define suitably. Consider ternary correlations $u, v \in \Delta'_n$. We define the intersection of u and v as the ternary vector $u \cap v$ such that $\mathcal{P}(u \cap v) = \mathcal{P}(u) \cap \mathcal{P}(v)$ and $\mathcal{P}'(u \cap v) = \mathcal{P}'(u) \cap \mathcal{P}'(v)$. Equivalently we might say that $(u \cap v)_i = 0$ if either $u_i = 0$ or $v_i = 0$, 1 if $u_i = v_i = 1$, and 2 otherwise. Note that Δ'_n is closed under intersection.

We may define the union in the analogous way, specifically, for $u, v \in \Delta'_n$ we say that $\mathcal{P}(u \cup v) = \mathcal{P}(u) \cup \mathcal{P}(v)$ and that $\mathcal{P}'(u \cup v) = \mathcal{P}'(u) \cup \mathcal{P}'(v)$. Equivalently, $u \cup v$ is the ternary vector satisfying $(u \cup v)_i = 0$ if $u_i = v_i = 0$, 1 if either $u_i = 1$ or $v_i = 1$, and 2 otherwise. Unlike unions of binary correlations, the union of two ternary correlations is not necessarily again a ternary correlation. For example, consider the correlations $u = 102000101$ and $v = 100010001$. The union of these two correlations is $u \cup v = 102010101$, which violates the second condition of Theorem 3. Specifically, there is no $q \geq 2$ such that $(u \cup v)_{2q} = 0$. Finally, for $u, v \in \Delta'_n$ we say that $u \subseteq v$ provided that $\mathcal{P}(u) \subseteq \mathcal{P}(v)$ and $\mathcal{P}'(u) \subseteq \mathcal{P}'(v)$. Equivalently we may say that $u \subseteq v$ provided that whenever $u_i > 0$ we have that $u_i \geq v_i > 0$. Or more explicitly, $u \subseteq v$ provided that whenever $u_i = 1$ that $v_i = 1$ and whenever $u_i = 2$ that $v_i = 1$ or $v_i = 2$. Under these definitions, the pair $(\Delta'_n, \subseteq)$ is a poset with null element 10^{n-1} and universal element 1^n.

Theorem 5. *The poset $(\Delta'_n, \subseteq)$ is a lattice.*

Proof. (Sketch) First, Δ'_n is closed under intersection. Second, the pair $(\Delta'_n, \subseteq)$ is a poset. Now, we do not have the union of the two correlations to explicitly define the join. One method of proving that the join exists is to notice that the join of $u, v \in \Delta'_n$ is the intersection of all elements of Δ'_n which contain u and v. This intersection is guaranteed to be nonempty since Δ'_n contains a universal element. On the other hand, we can modify the union slightly such that we obtain the join constructively. Consider the example above in which $u = 102000101$ and $v = 100010001$ and $u \cup v = 102010101$. If we simply change $(u \cup v)_2$ from 2 to 1, then we will have created a valid ternary correlation. Calling this vector $u \vee v$ we see that $u \subseteq u \vee v$ and that $v \subseteq u \vee v$. Thus, we generalize this operator by defining $u \vee v$ to be the unique correlation satisfying $\mathcal{P}'(u \vee v) = \mathcal{P}'(u) \cup \mathcal{P}'(v)$ and $\mathcal{P}(u \vee v) = \mathcal{P}(u) \cup \mathcal{P}(v) \cup B(u \cup v)$ where $B(u \cup v)$ is the set of all $0 \leq q < n$ such that $(u \cup v)_q = 2$ and there exists no $k \geq 2$ such that $(u \cup v)_{kq} = 0$. That is, $B(u \cup v)$ is the set of positions in $u \cup v$ which do not satisfy the second condition of Theorem 3.

We claim that $u \vee v$ is the unique join of u and v (and thus justify our use of the traditional notation $\vee$ for our binary operation). Notice first that since $\mathcal{P}(u \cup v) = \mathcal{P}(u) \cup \mathcal{P}(v)$ and $\mathcal{P}'(u \cup v) = \mathcal{P}'(u) \cup \mathcal{P}'(v)$ that $u \cup v \subseteq u \vee v$. Thus we have that $u \subseteq u \cup v \subseteq u \vee v$ and that $v \subseteq u \cup v \subseteq u \vee v$. We also see that $u \vee v \in \Delta'_n$. This follows from the fact that if $p \in \mathcal{P}(u \vee v)$ then either $p \in \mathcal{P}(u) \cup \mathcal{P}(v)$ or for all $k \geq 1$ we have that $kp \in \mathcal{P}'(u) \cup \mathcal{P}'(v)$. In the first case, we then have that $\langle p \rangle \subseteq \mathcal{P}(u) \cup \mathcal{P}(v) \subseteq \mathcal{P}(u \vee v)$. In the second case, we see that all multiples of p are in $\mathcal{P}'(u) \cup \mathcal{P}'(v)$. Therefore, by the definition of $u \vee v$ and the fact that the multiples of all multiples of p are again multiples of p, we must have that $\langle p \rangle \subseteq \mathcal{P}(u \vee v)$. Thus, using the $\vee$ operator instead of the $\cup$ operator resolves all conflicts with Theorem 3 and so $u \vee v \in \Delta'_n$. From here it suffices to show that it is minimal.   □

Strangely, even though the join operation of Δ'_n is more complicated than the join operation of Δ_n, we still have that Δ'_n is distributive and thus satisfies the Jordan-Dedekind condition. This is stated in the following theorem.

Theorem 6. *The lattice $(\Delta'_n, \subseteq)$ is distributive and thus satisfies the Jordan-Dedekind condition.*

So unlike the lattice of correlations of full words which does not even satisfy the Jordan-Dedekind condition, the lattices of both binary and ternary correlations of partial words are distributive.

Finally we turn our attention to $\Phi_n = R(\Delta_n)$, the set of irreducible period sets of length n. For $n \geq 3$, we see immediately that the poset $(\Phi_n, \subseteq)$ is *not* a join-semilattice since the sets $\{1\}$ and $\{2\}$ will never have a join since $\{1\}$ is always maximal. On the other hand, we have that $(\Phi_n, \subseteq)$ *is* a meet-semilattice as it contains a null element $\varnothing$. The meet of two elements of Φ_n is simply their set theoretic intersection.

Proposition 1. *Φ_n satisfies the Jordan-Dedekind condition.*

Notice that while there is a natural bijection between the lattice Δ_n and the meet-semilattice Φ_n given above by the maps R and E, we see immediately that these maps are not morphisms. For example, consider the period sets $\{0, 1, 2, 3, 4\}$ and $\{0, 2, 4\}$. Then we see that $\{0, 1, 2, 3, 4\} \cap \{0, 2, 4\} = \{0, 2, 4\}$ for which the corresponding irreducible period set is $\{2\}$. But $R(\{0, 1, 2, 3, 4\}) = \{1\}$ and $R(\{0, 2, 4\}) = \{2\}$, a pair of irreducible period sets whose intersection is $\varnothing \neq \{2\}$.

5   Counting Correlations

In this section we look at the number of correlations of partial words of a given length. In the case of binary correlations, we give bounds and link the problem to one in number theory, and in the case of ternary correlations we give an exact count.

A *primitive set* of integers is a subset $S \subseteq \mathbb{N} = \{1, 2, \ldots\}$ such that for any two distinct elements $s, s' \in S$ we have that neither s divides s' nor s' divides s. We denote by $\mathbb{P}_n$ the set of finite primitive sets of integers at most n. As Φ_n and $\mathbb{P}_{n-1}$ coincide, we have the relation $\|\Delta_n\| = \|\Phi_n\| = \|\mathbb{P}_{n-1}\|$. So if we can count the number of finite primitive sets of integers less than n then we can count the number of binary correlations of partial words of length n. We present some results on approximating this number.

Theorem 7. Erdős [8] *Let S be a finite primitive set of size k with elements less than n. Then $k \leq \lfloor \frac{n}{2} \rfloor$. Moreover, this bound is sharp.*

This bound tells us that the number of primitive sets of integers with elements less than n is *at most* the number of subsets of $\{1, 2, \ldots, n-1\}$ of size at most $\lfloor \frac{n}{2} \rfloor$. Moreover, the sharpness of the bound gives us that $\|\Phi_n\| \geq 2^{\lfloor n/2 \rfloor}$. Thus we have that

$$\frac{\ln 2}{2} \leq \frac{\ln \|\Phi_n\|}{n} \leq \ln 2$$

In [10], Guibas and Odlyzko showed that as $n \to \infty$

$$\frac{1}{2 \ln 2} + o(1) \leq \frac{\ln \|\Gamma_n\|}{(\ln n)^2} \leq \frac{1}{2 \ln(3/2)} + o(1)$$

and in [16] Rivals and Rahmann improved the lower bound to

$$\frac{\ln \|\Gamma_n\|}{(\ln n)^2} \geq \frac{1}{2 \ln 2} \left(1 - \frac{\ln \ln n}{\ln n} \right)^2 + \frac{0.4139}{\ln n} - \frac{1.47123 \ln \ln n}{(\ln n)^2} + O\left(\frac{1}{(\ln n)^2} \right)$$

where Γ_n is the set of all valid correlations of full words. Thus the bounds we give, which show explicitly that $\ln \|\Delta_n\| = \Theta(n)$, demonstrate that the number of valid binary correlations of partial words is *much* greater than the number of valid correlations of full words.

We now show that the set of ternary correlations is actually much more tractable to count than the set of binary correlations. We first note two interesting consequences of Theorem 3: (1) Let u be a partial word of length n and let $p \in \mathcal{P}'(u)$. Then $p \in \mathcal{P}(u)$ if and only if $kp \in \mathcal{P}'(u)$ for all $0 \leq k < n/p$.

That is, a weak period is a strong period if and only if all of its multiples are also weak periods. (2) If $S \subseteq \{1, 2, \ldots, n-1\}$, then there is a unique ternary correlation $v \in \Delta'_n$ such that $\mathcal{P}'(v) = S \cup \{0\}$. We note that (2) agrees with the definition of the join forced upon us in Section 4. Considering all periods as *weak* periods and then determining which ones are actually strong periods is how we defined that operation. We note that (2) tells us as well that the cardinality of the set of ternary correlations is the same as the cardinality of the power set of $\{1, 2, \ldots, n-1\}$. And thus the equality $\|\Delta'_n\| = 2^{n-1}$ holds.

References

1. Berstel, J., Boasson, L.: Partial Words and a Theorem of Fine and Wilf. Theoret. Comput. Sci. **218** (1999) 135–141
2. Blanchet-Sadri, F.: Periodicity on Partial Words. Comput. Math. Appl. **47** (2004) 71–82
3. Blanchet-Sadri, F., Chriscoe, Ajay: Local Periods and Binary Partial Words: An Algorithm. Theoret. Comput. Sci. **314** (2004) 189–216 www.uncg.edu/mat/AlgBin
4. Blanchet-Sadri, F., Duncan, S.: Partial Words and the Critical Factorization Theorem. J. Combin. Theory Ser. A **109** (2005) 221–245 www.uncg.edu/mat/cft
5. Blanchet-Sadri, F., Hegstrom, Robert A.: Partial Words and a Theorem of Fine and Wilf Revisited. Theoret. Comput. Sci. **270** (2002) 401–419
6. Blanchet-Sadri, F., Wetzler, N.D.: Partial Words and the Critical Factorization Theorem Revisited. www.uncg.edu/mat/research/cft2
7. Césari, Y., Vincent, M.: Une Caractérisation des Mots Périodiques. C.R. Acad. Sci. Paris **268** (1978) 1175–1177
8. Erdös, P.: Note on Sequences of Integers No One of Which is Divisible by Another. J. London Math. Soc. **10** (1935) 126–128
9. Fine, N.J., Wilf, H.S.: Uniqueness Theorems for Periodic Functions. Proc. Amer. Math. Soc. **16** (1965) 109–114
10. Guibas, L.J., Odlyzko, A.M.: Periods in Strings. J. Combin. Theory Ser. A **30** (1981) 19–42
11. Kolpakov, R., Kucherov, G.: Finding Approximate Repetitions Under Hamming Distance. Lecture Notes in Comput. Sci. Vol. 2161. Springer-Verlag, Berlin (2001) 170–181
12. Kolpakov, R., Kucherov, G.: Finding Approximate Repetitions Under Hamming Distance. Theoret. Comput. Sci. **33** (2003) 135–156
13. Landau, G., Schmidt, J.: An Algorithm for Approximate Tandem Repeats. Lecture Notes in Comput. Sci. Vol. 684. Springer-Verlag, Berlin (1993) 120–133
14. Landau, G.M., Schmidt, J.P., Sokol, D.: An Algorithm for Approximate Tandem Repeats. J. Comput. Biology **8** (2001) 1–18
15. Lothaire, M.: Algebraic Combinatorics on Words. Cambridge University Press, Cambridge (2002)
16. Rivals, E., Rahmann, S.: Combinatorics of Periods in Strings. J. Combin. Theory Ser. A **104** (2003) 95–113
17. Schmidt, J.P.: All Highest Scoring Paths in Weighted Grid Graphs and Their Application to Finding All Approximate Repeats in Strings. SIAM J. Comput. **27** (1998) 972–992

Testing Convexity Properties of Tree Colorings

Eldar Fischer* and Orly Yahalom

Computer Science Department, Technion - IIT, Haifa 32000, Israel
{eldar, oyahalom}@cs.technion.ac.il

Abstract. A coloring of a graph is *convex* if it induces a partition of the vertices into connected subgraphs. Besides being an interesting property from a theoretical point of view, tests for convexity have applications in various areas involving large graphs. Our results concern the important subcase of testing for convexity in trees. This problem is linked, among other possible applications, with the study of phylogenetic trees, which are central in genetic research, and are used in linguistics and other areas. We give a 1-sided, non-adaptive, distribution-free ϵ-test for the convexity of tree colorings. The query complexity of our test is $O\left(\frac{k}{\epsilon}\right)$, where k is the number of colors, and the additional computational complexity is $O(n)$. On the other hand, we prove a lower bound of $\Omega(\sqrt{k/\epsilon})$ on the query complexity of tests for convexity in the standard model, which applies even for (unweighted) paths. We also consider whether the dependency on k can be reduced in some cases, and provide an alternative testing algorithm for the case of paths. Then we investigate a variant of convexity, namely *quasi-convexity*, in which all but one of the colors are required to induce connected components. For this problem we provide a 1-sided, non-adaptive ϵ-test with query complexity $O\left(\frac{k}{\epsilon^2}\right)$ and time complexity $O(n)$. For both our convexity and quasi-convexity tests, we show that, assuming that a query takes constant time, the time complexity can be reduced to a constant independent of n if we allow a preprocessing stage of time $O(n)$. Finally, we show how to test for a variation of convexity and quasi-convexity where the maximum number of connectivity classes of each color is allowed to be a constant value other than 1.

1 Introduction

Property testing deals with the following relaxation of decision problems: Given a fixed property P and an input f, one wants to decide whether f has the property or is 'far' from having the property. Formally, two input functions $f : \mathcal{D} \to \mathcal{F}$ and $f' : \mathcal{D} \to \mathcal{F}$ are said to be ϵ-*close* to each other if they differ in no more than $\epsilon|\mathcal{D}|$ places ($\mathcal{D}$ is assumed to be finite). f is called ϵ-*close to satisfying a property* P (or simply ϵ-*close to* P) if there exists an input f' that is ϵ-close to f and satisfies P. If f is not ϵ-close to P then we say that f is ϵ-*far from satisfying* P (or ϵ-*far from* P).

---

* Research supported in part by David and Miriam Mondry research fund and by an Israel Science Foundation grant number 55/03.

W. Thomas and P. Weil (Eds.): STACS 2007, LNCS 4393, pp. 109–120, 2007.

Property testing normally deals with functions with large domains and/or costly retrieval procedures. We assume here that the number of queries of the function values is the most limited resource, rather than the computation time (but we also address the computation time).

A property P is said to be (ϵ, q)-*testable* if there exists a (randomized) algorithm that, for every input function $f : \mathcal{D} \to \mathcal{F}$, queries the values of f on at most q points of $\mathcal{D}$, and with probability no smaller than $\frac{2}{3}$ distinguishes between the case where f has the property P and the case where f is ϵ-far from having the property P. If a property P is (ϵ, q)-testable with $q = q(\epsilon)$ (i.e. q is a function of ϵ only, and is independent of n) then we say that P is ϵ-*testable*. If P is ϵ-testable for every fixed $\epsilon > 0$ then we say that P is *testable*. We refer to the number of queries required by a given test as its *query complexity*.

Furthermore, a test is called *1-sided* if an input which has the property is accepted with probability 1. Otherwise, it is called *2-sided*. A test is said to be *adaptive* if some of the choices of the locations for which the input is queried may depend on the values (answers) of previous queries. Otherwise, if only the final decision to accept or reject depends on the query values, then the test is called *non-adaptive*.

The general notion of property testing was first formulated by Rubinfeld and Sudan [14], who were motivated mainly by its connection to the study of program checking. The study of this notion for combinatorial objects, and mainly for labelled graphs, was introduced by Goldreich, Goldwasser and Ron [3]. Property testing has since become quite an active research area, see e.g. the surveys [13] and [2].

1.1 Convex Colorings

Given a graph $G = (V, E)$ and a vertex coloring $c : V \to \{1, \ldots, k\}$ of G, define V_i as the set of vertices v in V such that $c(v) = i$. We say that c is *a convex coloring of G* if all the V_i's are connected sets (i.e., induce connected subgraphs).

Determining whether a graph coloring is convex is easy to solve in linear time with standard graph search techniques. However, when working with large data sets, a test which reads only a small part of the input would be desired, also at the cost of having some error probability and giving only an approximate answer. A possible application for testing convexity is considering the Internet graph, where the language in which a web page is written is regarded as its "color". We then may wish to determine whether the pages written in each language form a connected subgraph.

In this paper we consider testing for convexity as defined above, and several variants of this problem, on trees. A central motivation for this subcase is the study of phylogenetic (evolutionary) trees, which originated in genetics [11,15], but appears also in other areas, such as historical linguistics (see [12]). Whether our subjects of interest are biologic species, languages, or other objects, a phylogenetic tree specifies presumed hereditary relationships, representing different features with different colors. A convex coloring is a positive indication for the reliability of a phylogenetic tree, as it shows a reasonable evolutionary behavior.

Moran and Snir [9] studied *recoloring* problems, where the input is a colored tree and one has to find a close convex coloring of the tree. They gave several positive and negative results on exact and approximate algorithms. Our paper is the first, to the best of our knowledge, which approaches the property testing aspect of this topic.

Our input is always a fixed and known tree $T = (V, E)$. We test colorings c of T, where each query is a vertex $v \in V$ and the answer is its color $c(v)$. Note that the problems we deal with cannot be solved using connectivity testers such as those of Goldreich and Ron [4], as instead of looking at the structure of the graph we consider the values of the coloring function, while the graph structure is assumed to be known in advance and unchangeable.

1.2   Variants of Convexity

We provide tests for several variants of the convexity property defined above, the first of which is *quasi-convexity*. A coloring $c : V \to \{0, \ldots, k\}$ is called *quasi-convex* if the color components V_i are connected for colors $i \geq 1$, while V_0 is not necessarily connected. This property arises in various cases in which we are interested only in the connectivity of some of the color classes (and all the others may be considered as colored with 0). For example, regarding connectivity of Internet pages written in the same languages, we may not care about the connectivity of pages written in an unclear or esoteric language (e.g. Klingon).

In addition, we consider convexity and quasi convexity properties where we relax our requirement of having at most one color component from every color. A coloring $c : V \to \{1, \ldots, k\}$ is called *ℓ-convex* if the total number of color components that it induces is at most ℓ. Similarly, a coloring $c : V \to \{0, \ldots, k\}$ is called *ℓ-quasi-convex* if it induces at most ℓ color components for all colors $i > 0$. Similarly we discuss *list convexity* (and *list quasi-convexity*) where we have lists of upper bounds on the numbers of connected components of every color (or some of the colors).

1.3   Weighted and Distribution-Free Property Testing

Some distance functions, including the Hamming distance, have generalized weighted versions. For example, the cost of modifying the color of a vertex, which is constant under the Hamming distance, may be a function of the specific vertex. Such distance functions are discussed in [9] for convex colorings of phylogenetic trees. There, a high cost assigned to a vertex may imply a hypothesized high reliability of the color attributed to that vertex. Thus, if a "heavy" vertex must be recolored in order to acquire a convex coloring, then the presumed phylogenetic tree is more likely to be false. In other contexts, the cost function may represent the importance of certain vertices or the cost of modifying them.

A strict model for testing over the vertex-weighted distance is to consider a cost function which is unknown. This model, known as the *distribution-free model*, was introduced in [3] in the context of learning theory, and developed for property testing by Halevy and Kushilevitz [5,6]. A *distribution-free test* may attain a sample of the points of the domain of the input according to a fixed yet unknown distribution function (where each value obtained this way counts as a query). The cost of modifying a point in the input is equal to the probability of that point according to this distribution. Thus, the distance between two inputs is equal to the probability of obtaining a point on which they differ. Halevy and Kushilevitz provided efficient distribution-free tests for testing polynomiality and monotonicity of functions [5] and connectivity of graphs [6].

1.4   Our Results

We show that convexity of tree colorings is testable, providing a 1-sided, non-adaptive, distribution-free ϵ-test for every $\epsilon > 0$. The query complexity of our test is $O(k/\epsilon)$, where k is the number of colors, and the additional time complexity is $O(n)$. We further provide an alternative 1-sided, non-adaptive test for the standard (not weighted) model where the tree is a path, with query complexity $O(\sqrt{k}/\epsilon^3)$ and additional time complexity $\widetilde{O}(\sqrt{k}/\epsilon^3)$. On the negative side, we prove a lower bound of $\Omega(\sqrt{k}/\sqrt{\epsilon})$ on the query complexity of testing convexity of paths in the standard model.

For quasi-convexity of trees, we discuss the weighted, but not distribution-free case. For every $\epsilon > 0$, we provide a 1-sided, non-adaptive ϵ-test with query complexity $O(k/\epsilon^2)$, and additional time complexity $O(n)$.

In all the above algorithms, we show that the time complexity can be reduced to be polynomial in the query complexity (assuming that a query takes constant time) by allowing a preprocessing stage of time $O(n)$.

Finally, we provide (adaptive) 1-sided tests for the relaxed convexity problems for the weighted, though not distribution-free case. For ℓ-convexity we give a test with query complexity $\widetilde{O}(\ell/\epsilon)$ and time complexity $O(\ell n)$. For ℓ-quasi-convexity we provide a test with query complexity $\widetilde{O}(\ell/\epsilon^2)$ and time complexity $O(\ell n)$. Given a list of integers c_i, let ℓ denote their sum. Our test for list convexity has query complexity $\widetilde{O}(\ell/\epsilon)$ and computational complexity $O(\ell n)$. For list quasi-convexity, ℓ is the sum of c_i's only for the colors for which they are defined. For that property we give a test with query complexity $\widetilde{O}(\ell/\epsilon^2)$ and computational complexity $O(\ell n)$.

The rest of the paper is organized as follows: Section 2 is dedicated to the basic convexity problem. In Section 2.1 we give our distribution-free test for trees, with further implementation details given in Section 2.2. In Section 2.3 we present our lower bound for testing convexity, and section 2.4 we provide our specific convexity test for paths. Section 3 is dedicated to testing the quasi-convexity property. Finally, in Section 4 we consider relaxed convexity properties.

Due to space considerations, some of the proofs are omitted. Throughout the paper, we make no attempt to optimize the coefficients.

2 Testing Convexity on Trees

2.1 A Distribution-Free Convexity Test for Trees

In this section we assume that $\mu : V \rightarrow \mathbb{R}$ is a fixed yet unknown weight function satisfying $\mu(v) \geq 0$ for every $v \in V$ and $\sum_{v \in V} \mu(v) = 1$. For convenience, define $\mu(U) = \sum_{v \in U} \mu(v)$ for any $U \subseteq V$. The distance between two colorings c_1 and c_2 of T is defined as $\mu(\Delta_{c_1,c_2})$, where $\Delta_{c_1,c_2} = \{v \in V | c_1(v) \neq c_2(v)\}$.

Vertices u, w, v in T form a *forbidden subpath* if w is on the (simple) path between u and v and $c(u) = c(v) \neq c(w)$. Clearly, c is a convex coloring of T if and only if it does not contain any forbidden subpath.

Our test samples vertices according to the distribution function on V defined by μ and then queries their values. We note that the standard model of distribution-free testing allows queries of determined vertices, but our test will do better and use only sample vertices. To reject the input, the sample does not necessarily need to contain a forbidden subpath. Instead, the algorithm uses the information supplied by the queried vertices, together with the knowledge of the structure of the tree, to infer the existence of a forbidden subpath. The main idea behind the algorithm is that if a coloring is ϵ-far from being convex, then, with high probability, either a forbidden subpath is sampled or there exists a vertex that is a "crossroad" of two sampled subpaths with conflicting colors.

Algorithm 1

1. *Query* $\left\lceil \frac{8k \ln 12}{\epsilon} \right\rceil$ *vertices, where each vertex is independently chosen according to the distribution defined by μ. Let X denote the sample.*
2. *If X includes a forbidden subpath, reject.*
3. *Otherwise, if there exists $w \in V$ such that any value of $c(w)$ implies a forbidden subpath, reject. In other words, reject if there exist $w \in V$ and $u_1, u_2, v_1, v_2 \in X$ such that $c(u_1) = c(u_2) \neq c(v_1) = c(v_2)$, and w belongs to both the path between u_1 and u_2 and the path between v_1 and v_2.*
4. *Otherwise, accept.*

Theorem 2. *For every $\epsilon > 0$, Algorithm 1 is a 1-sided ϵ-test for convexity with query complexity $O(k/\epsilon)$ and time complexity $O(n)$. It can also be implemented in running time $\widetilde{O}(|X|) = \widetilde{O}(k/\epsilon)$ using a preprocessing stage of time $O(n)$.*

It is easy to see that the query complexity is as stated. We show how to implement the computational steps under the time complexity requirements stated in Section 2.2. Clearly, a convex coloring is always accepted by Algorithm 1, as it does not contain forbidden subpaths. It remains to show that every k-coloring which is ϵ-far from being convex is rejected with probability at least $\frac{2}{3}$.

For neighboring vertices u and v, we denote the connected component of $V \setminus \{u\}$ that contains v by $C_u^{(v)}$. Note that $C_u^{(v)}$ and $C_v^{(u)}$ form a partition of V. For any subset $U \subseteq V$ let the *i-weight* of U be the total weight of all *i*-vertices in U, and denote it by $\mu_i(U) \stackrel{\text{def}}{=} \mu(V_i \cap U)$. A color $i \in \{1, \ldots, k\}$ is called *abundant* if $\mu(V_i) \geq \epsilon/2k$. For an abundant color i, we say that a vertex $u \in V$

is *i-balanced* if the set $\{C_u^{(v)}|(u,v) \in E\}$ may be partitioned into two subsets, where the *i*-weight of the union of each subset is at least $\epsilon/8k$. We say that a vertex v is *heavy* if $\mu(v) \geq \epsilon/8k$. For every abundant color i, let B_i be the union of *i*-balanced vertices and heavy *i*-vertices.

Lemma 3. B_i *is a non-empty set for every abundant color i.*

Proof. Assume that there exists an abundant color i such that every $u \in V$ is not *i*-balanced and there are no heavy *i*-vertices. Note that in this case every $u \in V$ has a neighboring vertex v such that $C_u^{(v)}$ is of *i*-weight larger than $\epsilon/4k$ (as otherwise u is easily seen to be *i*-balanced). Consider u and v such that $C_u^{(v)}$ is of minimum *i*-weight among those whose *i*-weight is larger than $\epsilon/4k$ (and with a minimum number of vertices among the minimal weight $C_u^{(v)}$'s). There exists a neighbor w of v such that $C_v^{(w)}$ is of *i*-weight larger than $\epsilon/4k$. Due to the minimality of $C_u^{(v)}$, we must have $w = u$. Thus $C_v^{(u)}$ is of *i*-weight larger than $\epsilon/4k$, and, since there are no heavy *i*-vertices, the *i*-weight of $C_v^{(u)} \setminus \{u\}$ is at least $\epsilon/8k$. Therefore, both $C_u^{(v)}$ and $V \setminus \{C_u^{(v)} \cup \{u\}\}$ have *i*-weight of at least $\epsilon/8k$, and hence u is *i*-balanced. A contradiction.

Lemma 4. B_i *is a connected set for every abundant color i.*

Proof. Assume that there exist two vertices $u, v \in B_i$, and let w be on the path between u and v. Assuming that w is not a heavy *i*-vertex, we show that w is *i*-balanced. If u is a heavy *i*-vertex, then clearly $\mu_i(C_w^{(u)}) \geq \epsilon/8k$. Otherwise, u is *i*-balanced, and thus, $V \setminus \{u\}$ may be partitioned into two sets of connected components, the *i*-weight of each of which is at least $\epsilon/8k$. One of these sets does not contain $C_u^{(w)}$. Thus, $\mu_i(C_w^{(u)}) \geq \epsilon/8k$. Similarly, it follows that $\mu_i(C_w^{(v)}) \geq \epsilon/8k$, and hence w is *i*-balanced.

Proposition 5. *For every k-coloring c of T that is ϵ-far from being convex, there exist two abundant colors $i \neq j$ and a vertex u, such that $u \in B_i$ and $u \in B_j$.*

Proof. Notice first that there must be at least two abundant colors. Otherwise, as the total weight of vertices of non-abundant colors is smaller than ϵ, the convex coloring that assigns the only abundant color to all of the vertices is ϵ-close to c.

Suppose that the connected sets B_i are disjoint. We show a convex coloring c' of T that is ϵ-close to c, which leads to a contradiction. Define c' as follows. For every vertex v and abundant color i, let $d(v, B_i)$ denote the "walking" distance on T between v and B_i, i.e. the length of the path from v to (the connected) B_i. Color every vertex v with i such that $d(v, B_i)$ is minimal, choosing the minimal index i in case of a tie. In particular, we color all the vertices in B_i with i. One can show that c' is a convex coloring. We omit the proof in this version.

We now show that c' is ϵ-close to c. Consider a vertex w whose color has been changed from one abundant color i into another (abundant) color j. Surely $w \notin B_i$. Furthermore, either B_j is on the path between B_i and w or w is on the path between B_i and B_j. Consider the edge (u, v) on the path between B_i and B_j

where $u \in B_i$ and $v \notin B_i$. We call (u, v) the ij-bridge. Then $w \in C_u^{(v)}$. Now, let i and j be any distinct abundant colors and let (u, v) be the ij-bridge. Suppose that $\mu_i(C_u^{(v)}) \geq \epsilon/4k$. By the definition of B_i, v is not a heavy i-vertex, and thus $\mu_i(C_u^{(v)} \setminus \{v\}) > \epsilon/8k$. Since v is not i-balanced, we have $\mu_i(C_v^{(u)}) < \epsilon/8k$, but this is impossible, as u is i-balanced or heavy. We thus conclude that $\mu_i(C_u^{(v)}) < \epsilon/4k$ for every ij-bridge (u, v). To complete the proof of the proposition, we show that the number of ij-bridges in T is at most $2k$. The details are omitted here. It follows that the total weight of recolored vertices among those whose original color was abundant is less than $\epsilon/2$. Moreover, the total weight of vertices of non-abundant colors is smaller than $\epsilon/2$. Thus, c' is ϵ-close to c.

Proof of Theorem 2. We have shown that for every coloring that is ϵ-far from being convex, there exist $i \neq j$ and a vertex w such that $w \in B_i \cap B_j$. Clearly, w must be i-balanced or j-balanced or both. Suppose that w is not balanced with respect to one of the colors, say i. Then w must be a heavy i-vertex and j-balanced. In such a case $\mu(w) \geq \epsilon/8k$ and there exist two disjoint sets $W_1^j, W_2^j \subseteq V_j$, each of weight at least $\epsilon/8k$, such that every path between the vertices $v_1 \in W_1^j$ and $v_2 \in W_2^j$ passes through w. Hence, if the sample X contains w and at least one vertex from each of the sets W_1^j and W_2^j, then Algorithm 1 rejects the input in Step 2. The probability for any of the sets W_1^j and W_2^j or of w to not intersect the sample set X, is at most $(1 - \epsilon/8k)^{\frac{8k \ln 12}{\epsilon}}$. By the union bound, the algorithm will fail with probability at most $3(1 - \epsilon/8k)^{\frac{8k \ln 12}{\epsilon}} < 1/4$.

Otherwise, if w is both i-balanced and j-balanced, then there exist four disjoint sets $W_1^i, W_2^i \subseteq V_i$, $W_1^j, W_2^j \subseteq V_j$, each of weight at least $\epsilon/8k$, where w is in every path between vertices $u_1 \in W_1^i$ and $u_2 \in W_2^i$ as well as in every path between vertices $v_1 \in W_1^j$ and $v_2 \in W_2^j$. Algorithm 1 fails if at least one of the sets $W_1^i, W_2^i, W_1^j, W_2^j$ does not intersect the sample X, which occurs with probability at most $4(1 - \epsilon/8k)^{8k \ln 12/\epsilon} < 4 \exp(-\ln 12) = 1/3$.

2.2   Implementation of the Computation Step in Algorithm 1

We now specify a procedure implementing Steps 2 and 3 of Algorithm 1 in time $O(n)$. Later we explain briefly how the procedure can be completed in time $\widetilde{O}(|X|) = \widetilde{O}(k/\epsilon)$ if we allow a preprocessing stage of time $O(n)$. For $i = 1, \ldots, k$, let q_i be the number of i-vertices in the sample X. Clearly, the q_i's can be computed in time $O(|X|)$. Next, we arbitrarily select a root r for T and obtain a topological order of its nodes using Depth First Search from r, which can be done in time $O(n)$ (see e.g. [8]). We now consider the nodes in reverse topological order. This can be viewed as "trimming" leaves from the tree one by one.

Procedure 6. *For every v in reverse topological order of T, do:*

- *If $v \in X$ then set $a(v) = 1$; otherwise set $a(v) = 0$.*
- *If $v \in X$ then set $m(v) = c(v)$; otherwise set $m(v)$ to be null.*
- *For every child u of v such that $m(u)$ is not null:*

1. If $m(v)$ is not null and $m(v) \neq m(u)$ then reject the input and terminate.
2. Otherwise, set $m(v) = m(u)$ and $a(v) = a(v) + a(u)$.
- If $m(v)$ is not null and $a(v) = q_{m(v)}$ then set $m(v)$ to be null and $a(v) = 0$.

If the algorithm did not reject after going over all vertices, then accept.

As for every node v the running time is proportional to the number of its children, the total running time of Procedure 6 is $O(n)$. To prove its correctness, we show by induction that for every iteration on a node v, the procedure rejects if and only if v is a middle vertex of a forbidden subpath in X. Note that Procedure 6 performs significant processing only in nodes which are in X or are Least Common Ancestors (LCA's) of two or more members of X. This gives rise to the possibility of running it over a set that includes X and all of the LCA's of vertices in X. It can be shown that there exists such a set of size at most $2|X|$. Moreover, this set can be constructed in time $\widetilde{O}(|X|)$ after a preprocessing stage of time $O(n)$, using a constant time oracle that computes the LCA of two nodes in a tree (see [7], [16]). Running Procedure 6 over this set takes $O(|X|)$ time.

2.3   A Lower Bound for Testing Convexity

Theorem 7. *Every (adaptive) ϵ-test for convexity for every $\epsilon < 1/8$ must use more than $\sqrt{3\frac{(k-1)}{64\epsilon}}$ queries in the worst case. This is specifically true for trees which are (unweighted) paths.*

Proof. Our proof is based on Yao's method [17], see [2] for details. Let T be a path of length n. We present two distributions of k-colorings of a path T. D_P is a distribution of convex colorings and D_N is a distribution of colorings that are ϵ-far from being convex. For the proof, it suffices to show that any deterministic algorithm using $q \leq \sqrt{\frac{3(k-1)}{64\epsilon}}$ queries errs with probability larger than $\frac{1}{3}$ when trying to distinguish between D_P and D_N. Assume that k divides n. In the definitions below we divide T into k intervals of size n/k, such that all the vertices in each interval are colored with the same color. Without loss of generality, we assume that at most one vertex is queried from every interval.

Definition 8. *Let D_P be the distribution of inputs defined by uniformly choosing a permutation of all k colors and coloring the intervals accordingly.*

Definition 9. *Let $\widetilde{D_N}$ be the distribution where the inputs are selected by uniformly choosing $(1 - 8\epsilon)k$ colors to appear in one interval and $4\epsilon k$ colors to appear in two intervals. The placements of the colors are then chosen uniformly.*

Definition 10. *Let D_N be the conditional distribution of $\widetilde{D_N}$ on the event that the coloring chosen is ϵ-far from being convex.*

The main idea is based on the birthday problem. We show that a test which uses q queries is unlikely to query the same color more than once, and thus cannot distinguish between D_P and D_N. We use the auxiliary distribution $\widetilde{D_N}$ since its symmetric nature allows us to perform computations easily. The full proof will appear in a future journal version.

2.4   A Convexity Test for Paths

We present a convexity test for the special case where the tree T is a path, whose performance is better than that of Algorithm 1 when k is large with respect to $1/\epsilon^3$. We note that a colored path is essentially a string. The convexity property on strings is a special case of a regular language, and thus is known to be testable by Alon et. al [1]. However, the query complexity obtained there for convexity of a string over k colors would be super-exponential in k. We provide a more efficient test for this property. In fact, by Theorem 7, our algorithm is optimal up to a power of $\frac{1}{\epsilon}$. Theorem 12 below will be proved in a future journal version. The main idea of the proof is based on the birthday problem.

Algorithm 11

1. *Query* $q \geq \frac{256\sqrt{k}}{\epsilon^2}$ *vertices independently, uniformly at random.*
2. *Query* $x \geq \frac{5}{\epsilon} \ln 12$ *vertices uniformly and independently in every interval between two consecutive vertices queried in Step 1.*
3. *Reject if and only if the resulting sample contains a forbidden subpath.*

Theorem 12. *For every* $\epsilon > 0$, *Algorithm 11 is a 1-sided ϵ-test for convexity with query complexity* $O(\sqrt{k}/\epsilon^3)$. *The additional time complexity is* $\widetilde{O}(\sqrt{k}/\epsilon^3)$ *if the vertices in the path are sorted, and* $O(n)$ *otherwise.*

3   Quasi-convexity of Trees

We now formalize the notion of quasi-convexity. Let k be the number of colors whose vertices are required to induce connected components. Without loss of generality, we refer to all other vertices as having the color 0. Given a tree $T = (V, E)$ and a coloring $c : V \rightarrow \{0, 1, \ldots, k\}$, we define V_i, as before, as the set of vertices v in V with $c(v) = i$. If $c(v) > 0$ we say that v is *colored*. Otherwise, we say that v is *uncolored*. c is said to be *quasi-convex* if V_i is connected for $i = 1, \ldots, k$. Alternatively, vertices u, w, v in T form a *forbidden subpath* if w is on the (simple) path between u and v, $c(u) = c(v) > 0$ and $c(w) \neq c(v)$. c is a quasi-convex coloring of T if and only if it contains no forbidden subpaths as defined above. We assume that $\mu : V \rightarrow \mathbb{R}$ is a fixed and known weight function satisfying $\mu(v) \geq 0$ for every $v \in V$ and $\sum_{v \in V} \mu(v) = 1$. The distance between two colorings of T, and the components $C_u^{(v)}$, are defined as in Section 2.1.

Algorithm 13

1. *Query* $\lceil 48k/\epsilon \rceil$ *vertices, where each vertex is independently chosen according to the distribution defined by* μ. *Let* X *denote the sample.*
2. *If* X *includes a forbidden subpath, reject.*
3. *Otherwise, if there exists* $w \in V$ *such that any value of* $c(w)$ *implies a forbidden subpath, reject. In other words, reject if there exist* $w \in V$ *and* $u_1, u_2, v_1, v_2 \in X$ *such that* $c(u_1), c(u_2), c(v_1), c(v_2) > 0$ *and* $c(u_1) = c(u_2) \neq c(v_1) = c(v_2)$, *where* w *belongs both to the path between* u_1 *and* u_2 *and to the path between* v_1 *and* v_2.

4. *Otherwise, repeat the following $\lceil 146/\epsilon \rceil$ times independently:*
   - *Choose a vertex $w \in X$ uniformly at random. If w is colored, do nothing.*
   - *Otherwise, if w is uncolored, define a subtree T_w^i for every color i such that there are i-colored vertices in X, as follows. Let v_i be the neighbor of w that is on a path between w and an i-colored vertex in X (v_i is unique, as X does not contain a forbidden subpath). Now denote $T_w^i \stackrel{\text{def}}{=} C_{v_i}^{(w)}$ for every such v_i. Query $\log_{1/(1-\epsilon/8)} 8$ vertices in each T_w^i, where each vertex is independently chosen according to the distribution defined by μ conditioned on T_w^i.*
   - *Reject if the union of X and the recently queried vertices includes a forbidden subpath.*
5. *Otherwise, accept.*

Theorem 14. *For every $\epsilon > 0$, Algorithm 13 is a 1-sided ϵ-test for quasi-convexity with query complexity $O(k/\epsilon^2)$ and time complexity $O(n)$. This can be implemented in time $\widetilde{O}(k/\epsilon^2)$ with a preprocessing stage of time $O(n)$.*

It is easy to see that the query complexity is as stated. The computational steps are performed very similarly to those of Algorithm 1 (see Section 2.2). Clearly, a quasi-convex coloring is always accepted by the algorithm. It remains to show that every k-coloring that is ϵ-far from being quasi-convex is rejected with probability at least $\frac{2}{3}$. Note that Steps 1-3, which work similarly to Algorithm 1, may not suffice for detecting forbidden subpaths with an uncolored middle vertex. To discover these, we use the test in Step 4, which is in essence similar to the test for monotonicity on rooted trees presented in [10]. To complete the proof we also use ideas from the proof of Proposition 5 and other arguments.

4   Relaxed Convexity Properties

Given a tree $T = (V, E)$ and an integer $\ell > 0$, we say that a coloring $c : V \to \{1, \ldots, k\}$ is *ℓ-convex* if it induces at most ℓ color components. A coloring $c : V \to \{0, \ldots, k\}$ of T is called *ℓ-quasi-convex* if it induces at most ℓ components of colors $i > 0$. Given a list $c_1, \ldots, c_k$, of integers we say that a vertex coloring of T is *convex with respect to the list* $\langle c_1, \ldots, c_k \rangle$ if it induces at most c_i color components of every color $i = 1, \ldots, k$. If we allow some of the c_i's to be ∞, we say that the coloring is *quasi-convex with respect to the list* $\langle c_1, \ldots, c_k \rangle$.

We now sketch a test for ℓ-convexity on trees. Later we explain how to transform it into tests for ℓ-quasi-convexity, list convexity and list quasi-convexity.

Theorem 15. *There exists a 1-sided test for ℓ-convexity on trees with query complexity $\widetilde{O}(\ell/\epsilon)$ and time complexity $O(\ell n)$.*

Given a tree T and an integer $\ell > 0$, our algorithm maintains a set X of queried vertices and uses it to decompose T into subtrees that we call "interesting trees". We build the set X in such a way that the interesting trees intersect each other only on vertices of X. Each interesting tree has either one or two vertices in X.

Using the values of the vertices of X, we infer a lower bound CC on the number of color components in T. Our algorithm then tests individual interesting trees for the possible existence of more color components than implied by their vertices in X, which we call *defining* vertices.

Specifically, consider an interesting tree $T' = (V', E')$. If T' is defined by a single vertex $u \in X$ then we test it for homogeneity. Namely, we query a sample set of vertices in T' and accept if and only if they are all colored with $c(u)$. The same thing is done if T' is defined by two vertices $u, v \in X$ and $c(u) = c(v)$. If T' is defined by two vertices $u, v \in X$ and $c(u) \neq c(v)$, then we want to know if there is a convex coloring $c' : V' \to \{c(u), c(v)\}$ that is ϵ-close to c, such that $c'(u) = c(u)$ and $c'(v) = c(v)$. This is an instance of a variant of the convexity problem that we call *convexity under constraints*, in which we have a set of "constraint vertices". In this case the color of u and v is known and must not be changed. We prove that for this problem it is enough to run a test identical to Algorithm 1 except that the query set is augmented with the constraint vertices.

If the test of an interesting tree T' has rejected, it supplies us with witnesses for additional color components. We thus add them to X, remove T' from the set of interesting trees and replace it with the subtrees of T' defined by the newly found witnesses. We now accordingly increment our lower bound CC on the color components in T. On the other hand, if the test for T' has accepted, then we just remove T' from the set of interesting trees, as it is likely to be close to not containing additional color components. If at some point we have discovered more than ℓ color components, then the algorithm rejects the input. Otherwise, the algorithm terminates and accepts when there are no interesting trees left.

The full proof of **Theorem 15** will be given in a future version. In essence, we show that CC is a tight lower bound for the number of color components in T, and that for an ϵ-far coloring, more than ℓ color components are detected with high probability. The query and complexity bounds follow from the fact that CC is incremented whenever a new color component is found.

To test for ℓ-quasi-convexity, we use a test similar to the one described above, but here we use variants of the quasi-convexity algorithm for the interesting trees.

Theorem 16. *There exists a 1-sided test for ℓ-quasi-convexity on trees whose query complexity is $\widetilde{O}(\ell/\epsilon^2)$ and whose time complexity is $O(\ell n)$.*

Our tests for list convexity and list quasi-convexity are almost identical to those for ℓ-convexity and ℓ-quasi-convexity respectively. The main difference is that instead of the counter CC of the total number of color components discovered so far, we keep a counter CC_i for every color i with $c_i < \infty$.

Theorem 17. *Given a list $L = \langle l_1, \ldots, l_k \rangle$ of integers, there exists a 1-sided test for convexity with respect to L for trees, with query complexity $\widetilde{O}(\ell/\epsilon)$ and computational complexity $O(\ell n)$, where $\ell = \sum_{i=1,\ldots,k} l_i$.*

Theorem 18. *Given a list $L = \langle l_1, \ldots, l_k \rangle$ where every c_i is either an integer or ∞, there exists a 1-sided test for quasi-convexity with respect to L for trees, with query complexity $\widetilde{O}(\ell/\epsilon^2)$ and computational complexity $O(\ell n)$, where $\ell = \sum_{1 \leq i \leq k, \, l_i < \infty} l_i$.*

Acknowledgements

We thank Sagi Snir for introducing us to the topic of convex colorings. We also thank Ronitt Rubinfeld for helpful comments.

References

1. N. Alon, M. Krivelevich, Ilan Newman and M. Szegedy, Regular languages are testable with a constant number of queries, *Siam Journal on Computing* 30(6):1842–1862, 2001.
2. E. Fischer, The art of uninformed decisions: A primer to property testing, *Bulletin of the European Association for Theoretical Computer Science*, 75:97–126, Section 8, 2001. Also In *Current Trends in Theoretical Computer Science: The Challenge of the New Century*, G. Paun, G. Rozenberg and A. Salomaa (editors), World Scientific Publishing, Vol. I, 229–264, 2004.
3. O. Goldreich, S. Goldwasser and D. Ron, Propery testing and its connection to learning and approximation, *Journal of the ACM*, 45(4):653–750, 1998.
4. O. Goldreich and D. Ron, Property testing in bounded degree graphs, *Algorithmica*, 32, 302–343, 2002.
5. S. Halevy and E. Kushilevitz, Distribution-free property testing, In *Proceedings of the 7th RANDOM and the 6th APPROX*: 302–317, 2003.
6. S. Halevy and E. Kushilevitz, Distribution-free connectivity testing, In *Proceedings of the 8th RANDOM and the 7th APPROX*: 393–404, 2004.
7. D. Harel and R. E. Tarjan, Fast algorithms for finding nearest common ancestor, *SIAM Journal on Computing*, 13(2):338–355, 1984.
8. D. E. Knuth, *The Art of Computer Programming*, Vol. 1: Fundamental Algorithms, Addison-Wesley, 1968. Second edition, 1973.
9. S. Moran and S. Snir, Convex recolorings of phylogenetic trees: definitions, hardness results and algorithms, *Workshop on Algorithms and Data Structures (WADS)*:218–232, 2005. Also *Journal of Computer and System Sciences (JCSS)*, in press.
10. E. Fischer, E. Lehman, I. Newman, S. Raskhodnikova, R. Rubinfeld and A. Samorodnitsky, Monotonicity testing over general poset domains, *Proceedings of the 34th STOC*, pages 474–483, 2002.
11. B.M.E. Moret and T. Warnow, Reconstructing optimal phylogenetic trees: A challenge in experimental algorithmics, In: *Experimental Algorithmics, Lecture Notes in Computer Science 2547*, Springer Verlag, 2002, 163–180.
12. L. Nakhleh, T. Warnow, D. Ringe, and S.N. Evans, A comparison of phylogenetic reconstruction methods on an IE dataset, *Transactions of the Philological Society*, 3(2): 171–192, 2005.
13. D. Ron, Property testing (a tutorial), In: *Handbook of Randomized Computing* (S. Rajasekaran, P. M. Pardalos, J. H. Reif and J. D. P. Rolim eds), Vol II, 597–649, Kluwer Press, 2001.
14. R. Rubinfeld and M. Sudan, Robust characterization of polynomials with applications to program testing, *SIAM Journal on Computing*, 25(2):252–271, 1996.
15. C. Semple and M. Steel, *Phylogenetics*, Oxford University Press, 2003.
16. B. Schieber and U. Vishkin, On finding lowest common ancestors: Simplifications and parallelization, *SIAM Journal on Computing*, 17:1253–1262, 1988.
17. A. C. Yao, Probabilistic computation, towards a unified measure of complexity, In *Proceedings of the 18th IEEE FOCS*: 222–227, 1977.

Why Almost All k-Colorable Graphs Are Easy

Amin Coja-Oghlan[1], Michael Krivelevich[2], and Dan Vilenchik[3]

[1] Institute for Informatics, Humboldt-University, Berlin, Germany
`coja@informatik.hu-berlin.de`
[2] School Of Mathematical Sciences, Sackler Faculty of Exact Sciences,
Tel-Aviv University, Tel-Aviv, Israel
`krivelev@post.tau.ac.il`
[3] School of Computer Science, Sackler Faculty of Exact Sciences,
Tel-Aviv University, Tel-Aviv, Israel
`vilenchi@post.tau.ac.il`

Abstract. Coloring a k-colorable graph using k colors ($k \geq 3$) is a notoriously hard problem. Considering average case analysis allows for better results. In this work we consider the uniform distribution over k-colorable graphs with n vertices and exactly cn edges, c greater than some sufficiently large constant. We rigorously show that all proper k-colorings of most such graphs are clustered in one cluster, and agree on all but a small, though constant, number of vertices. We also describe a polynomial time algorithm that finds a proper k-coloring for $(1 - o(1))$-fraction of such random k-colorable graphs, thus asserting that most of them are "easy". This should be contrasted with the setting of very sparse random graphs (which are k-colorable *whp*), where experimental results show some regime of edge density to be difficult for many coloring heuristics. One explanation for this phenomena, backed up by partially non-rigorous analytical tools from statistical physics, is the complicated clustering of the solution space at that regime, unlike the more "regular" structure that denser graphs possess. Thus in some sense, our result rigorously supports this explanation.

1 Introduction

A *k-coloring* f of a graph $G = (V, E)$ is a mapping from its set of vertices V to $\{1, 2, ..., k\}$. f is a *proper coloring* of G if for every edge $(u, v) \in E$, $f(u) \neq f(v)$. The minimal k s.t. G admits a proper k-coloring is called the chromatic number, commonly denoted by $\chi(G)$. In this work we think of $k > 2$ as some fixed integer, say $k = 3$ or $k = 100$.

1.1 Phase Transitions, Clusters, and Graph Coloring Heuristics

The problem of properly k-coloring a k-colorable graph is one of the most famous NP-hard problems. The plethora of worst-case NP-hardness results for problems in graph theory motivates the study of heuristics that give "useful" answers for "typical" subset of the problem instances, where "useful" and "typical"

W. Thomas and P. Weil (Eds.): STACS 2007, LNCS 4393, pp. 121–132, 2007.

are usually not well defined. One way of evaluating and comparing heuristics is by running them on a collection of input graphs ("benchmarks"), and checking which heuristic usually gives better results. Though empirical results are sometimes informative, we seek more rigorous measures of evaluating heuristics. Although satisfactory approximation algorithms are known for several NP-hard problems, the coloring problem is not amongst them. In fact, Feige and Kilian [13] prove that no polynomial time algorithm approximates $\chi(G)$ within a factor of $n^{1-\varepsilon}$ for all input graphs G on n vertices, unless ZPP=NP.

When very little can be done in the "worst case", comparing heuristics' behavior on "typical", or "average", instances comes to mind. One possibility of rigourously modeling such "average" instances is to use random models. In the context of graph coloring, the $\mathcal{G}_{n,p}$ and $\mathcal{G}_{n,m}$ models, pioneered by Erdős and Rényi, might appear to be the most natural candidates. A random graph G in $\mathcal{G}_{n,p}$ consists of n vertices, and each of the $\binom{n}{2}$ possible edges is included w.p. $p = p(n)$ independently of the others. In $\mathcal{G}_{n,m}$, $m = m(n)$ edges are picked uniformly at random. Bollobás [7] and Łuczak [21] calculated the probable value of $\chi(\mathcal{G}_{n,p})$ to be whp [1] approximately $n \ln(1 - p)/(2 \ln(np))$ for $p \in [C_0/n, 0.99]$. Thus, the chromatic number of $\mathcal{G}_{n,p}$ is typically rather high (roughly comparable with the average degree np of the random graph) – higher than k, when thinking of k as some fixed integer, say $k = 3$, and allowing the average degree np to be arbitrarily large.

Remarkable phenomena occurring in the random graph $\mathcal{G}_{n,m}$ are **phase transitions**. With respect to the property of being k-colorable, such a phase transition takes place too. More precisely, there exists a threshold $d_k = d_k(n)$ such that graphs with average degree $2m/n > (1+\varepsilon)d_k$ do not admit any proper k-coloring whp, while graphs with a lower average degree $2m/n < (1 - \varepsilon)d_k$ will have one whp [1]. In fact, experimental results show that random graphs with average degree just below the k-colorability threshold (which are thus k-colorable whp) are "hard" for many coloring heuristics. One possible explanation for this empirical observation, backed up by partially non-rigorous analytical tools from statistical physics [22], is the surmise that k-colorable graphs with average degree just below the threshold show a **clustering phenomenon** of the solution space. That is, typically random graphs with density close to the threshold d_k have an exponential number of **clusters** of k-colorings. While any two k-colorings in distinct clusters disagree on at least εn vertices, any two k-colorings within one cluster coincide on $(1 - \varepsilon)n$ vertices. Furthermore, each cluster has a linear number of "frozen" vertices whose colors coincide in **all** colorings within that cluster.

Now, the algorithmic difficulty with such a clustered solution space seems to be that the algorithm does not "steer" into one cluster but tries to find a "compromise" between the colorings in distinct clusters, which actually is impossible. By contrast, the recent Survey Propagation algorithm can apparently cope with the existence of a huge number of clusters [9], though no rigorous analysis of the algorithm is known.

---

[1] Writing whp ("with high probability") we mean with probability tending to 1 as n goes to infinity.

In this work we consider the regime of denser graphs, i.e., the average degree will be by a constant factor higher than the k-colorability threshold. In this regime, almost all graphs are not k-colorable, and therefore we shall condition on the event that the random graph is k-colorable. Thus, we consider the most natural distribution on k-colorable graphs with given numbers n of vertices and m of edges, namely, the uniform distribution $\mathcal{G}_{n,m,k}^{\mathrm{uniform}}$. For $m/n \geq C_0$, C_0 a sufficiently large constant, we are able to **rigorously** prove that the space of all legal k-colorings of a typical graph in $\mathcal{G}_{n,m,k}^{\mathrm{uniform}}$ has the following structure.

- There is an exponential number of legal k-colorings, which are arranged in a **single cluster**.
- We describe a coloring algorithm, and using the same tools that provide the latter observation, we prove that it k-colors *whp* $\mathcal{G}_{n,m,k}^{\mathrm{uniform}}$ with $m \geq C_0 n$ edges using polynomial time.

Thus, our result shows that when a k-colorable graph has a single cluster of k-colorings, though its volume might be exponential, then typically, the problem is easy. This in some sense complements the results in [22] in a rigorous way (where it is conjectured that when the clustering is complicated, more sophisticated algorithms are needed). Besides, standard probabilistic calculations show that when $m \geq Cn \log n$, C a sufficiently large constant, a random k-colorable graph will have *whp* only one proper k-coloring; indeed, it is known that such graphs are even easier to color than in the case $m = O(n)$, which is the focus of this paper. A further appealing implication of our result is the fact that almost all k-colorable graphs, sparse or dense, can be efficiently colored. This extends a previous result from [24] concerning dense graphs (i.e., $m = \Theta(n^2)$).

1.2 Results and Techniques

A subset of vertices $U \subseteq V$ is said to be **frozen** in G if in every proper k-coloring of G, all vertices in U receive the same color. A vertex is said to be **frozen** if it belongs to a frozen subset of vertices. Here and throughout we consider two k-colorings to be the same if one is a permutation of the color classes of the other.

Theorem 1. *(clustering phenomena) Let G be random graph from $\mathcal{G}_{n,m,k}^{\mathrm{uniform}}$, $m \geq C_0(k)n$, $C_0(k)$ a sufficiently large constant that depends on k. Then whp G enjoys the following properties:*

1. *All but $e^{-\Theta(m/n)}n$ of the vertices are frozen.*
2. *The graph induced by the non-frozen vertices decomposes into connected components of at most logarithmic size.*
3. *Letting $\beta(G)$ be the number of proper k-colorings of G, we have $\frac{1}{n} \log \beta(G) = e^{-\Theta(m/n)}$.*

Theorem 2. *(algorithm) There exists a polynomial time algorithm that whp properly k-colors a random graph from $\mathcal{G}_{n,m,k}^{\mathrm{uniform}}$, $m \geq C_1(k)n$, $C_1(k)$ a sufficiently large constant that depends on k.*

It is not hard to see that Property 1 in Theorem 1 implies in particular that any two proper k-colorings of G differ on at most $e^{-\Theta(m/n)}n$ vertices.

In Theorem 1, our analysis gives for $C_0 = \Theta(k^4)$, and in Theorem 2, $C_1 = \Theta(k^6)$, but no serious attempt is made to optimize the power of k.

The Erdős-Rényi graph $\mathcal{G}_{n,m}$ and its well known variant $\mathcal{G}_{n,p}$ are both very well understood and have received much attention during the past years. However the distribution $\mathcal{G}_{n,m,k}^{\text{uniform}}$ differs from $\mathcal{G}_{n,m}$ significantly, as the event of a random graph in $\mathcal{G}_{n,m}$ being k colorable, when k is fixed, and $2m/n$ is some constant above the k-colorability threshold, is very unlikely. In effect, many techniques that have become standard in the study of $\mathcal{G}_{n,m}$ just do not carry over to $\mathcal{G}_{n,m,k}^{\text{uniform}}$ – at least not directly. In particular, the contriving event of being k-colorable causes the edges in $\mathcal{G}_{n,m,k}^{\text{uniform}}$ to be dependent. The inherent difficulty of $\mathcal{G}_{n,m,k}^{\text{uniform}}$ has led many researchers to consider the more approachable, but considerably less natural, **planted distribution** introduced by Kučera [20] and denoted throughout by $\mathcal{G}_{n,m,k}^{\text{plant}}$. In this context we can selectively mention [4,6,8,11,19]. In the planted distribution, one first fixes some k-coloring, and then picks uniformly at random m edges that respect this coloring. Due to the "constructive" definition of $\mathcal{G}_{n,m,k}^{\text{plant}}$, the techniques developed in the study of $\mathcal{G}_{n,m}$ can be applied to $\mathcal{G}_{n,m,k}^{\text{plant}}$ immediately, whence the model is rather well understood [4].

Of course the $\mathcal{G}_{n,m,k}^{\text{plant}}$ model is somewhat artificial and therefore provides a less natural model of random instances than $\mathcal{G}_{n,m,k}^{\text{uniform}}$. Nevertheless, devising new ideas for analyzing $\mathcal{G}_{n,m,k}^{\text{uniform}}$, in this paper we show that $\mathcal{G}_{n,m,k}^{\text{uniform}}$ and $\mathcal{G}_{n,m,k}^{\text{plant}}$ actually share many structural graph properties such as the existence of a single cluster of solutions. As a consequence, we can prove that a certain algorithm, designed with $\mathcal{G}_{n,m,k}^{\text{plant}}$ in mind, works for $\mathcal{G}_{n,m,k}^{\text{uniform}}$ as well. In other words, presenting new methods for analyzing heuristics on random graphs, we can show that algorithmic techniques invented for the somewhat artificial $\mathcal{G}_{n,m,k}^{\text{plant}}$ model extend to the canonical $\mathcal{G}_{n,m,k}^{\text{uniform}}$ model.

To obtain these results, we use two main techniques. As we mentioned, $\mathcal{G}_{n,m,k}^{\text{plant}}$ (and the analogous $\mathcal{G}_{n,p,k}^{\text{plant}}$ in which every edge respecting the planted k-coloring is included with probability p) is already very well understood, and the probability of some graph properties that we discuss can be easily estimated for $\mathcal{G}_{n,m,k}^{\text{plant}}$ using standard probabilistic calculations. It then remains to find a reasonable "exchange rate" between $\mathcal{G}_{n,m,k}^{\text{plant}}$ and $\mathcal{G}_{n,m,k}^{\text{uniform}}$. We use this approach to estimate the probability of "complicated" graph properties, which hold with extremely high probability in $\mathcal{G}_{n,m,k}^{\text{plant}}$. The other method is to directly analyze $\mathcal{G}_{n,p,k}^{\text{uniform}}$, crucially overcoming the edge-dependency issues. This method tends to be more complicated than the first one, and involves intricate counting arguments.

1.3   Related Work

As mentioned above, the k-colorability problem exhibits a sharp threshold phenomenon, in the sense that there exists a function $d_k(n)$ s.t. a random graph from $\mathcal{G}_{n,m}$ is *whp* k-colorable if $2m/n < (1 - \varepsilon)d_k(n)$ and is *whp* not k-colorable if $2m/n > (1+\varepsilon)d_k(n)$ (cf. [1]). For example, it is known that $d_3(n) \geq 4.03n$ [3] and $d_3(n) \leq 5.044n$ [2]. Therefore, a typical graph in $\mathcal{G}_{n,m}$ with $m = cn$ will not be k-colorable (when thinking of k as a fixed integer, say $k = 3$, and allowing the average degree c to be an arbitrary constant, say $c = 100$, or even a growing function of n). Therefore, when considering relatively dense random graphs, one should take care when defining the underlying distribution, e.g. consider $\mathcal{G}_{n,m,k}^{\text{plant}}$ or $\mathcal{G}_{n,m,k}^{\text{uniform}}$.

Almost all polynomial-time graph-coloring heuristics suggested so far for finding a proper k-coloring of the input graph (or return a failure), were analyzed when the input is sampled according to $\mathcal{G}_{n,p,k}^{\text{plant}}$, or various semi-random variants thereof (and similarly for other graph problems such as clique, independent set, and random satisfiability problems). Alon and Kahale [4] suggest a polynomial time algorithm, based on spectral techniques, that *whp* properly k-colors a random graph from $\mathcal{G}_{n,p,k}^{\text{plant}}$, $np \geq C_0 k^2$, C_0 a sufficiently large constant. Combining techniques from [4] and [11], Böttcher [8] suggests an expected polynomial time algorithm for $\mathcal{G}_{n,p,k}^{\text{plant}}$ based on SDP (semi-definite programming) for the same p values. Much work was done also on semi-random variants of $\mathcal{G}_{n,p,k}^{\text{plant}}$, e.g. [6,11,14,19].

On the other hand, very little work has been done on non-planted k-colorable graph distributions, such as $\mathcal{G}_{n,m,k}^{\text{uniform}}$. In this context one can mention the work of Prömel and Steger [23] who analyze $\mathcal{G}_{n,m,k}^{\text{uniform}}$ but with a parametrization which causes $\mathcal{G}_{n,m,k}^{\text{uniform}}$ to collapse to $\mathcal{G}_{n,m,k}^{\text{plant}}$, thus not shedding light on the setting of interest in this work. Similarly, Dyer and Frieze [12] deal with very dense graphs (of average degree $\Omega(n)$).

1.4 Paper's Structure

The rest of the paper is structured as follows. In Section 2 we present the algorithm Color that is used to prove Theorem 2. In Section 3 we discuss some properties that a typical graph in $\mathcal{G}_{n,m,k}^{\text{uniform}}$ possesses. Using these properties we then prove Theorem 1 in Section 4, and prove that the algorithm Color indeed meets the requirements of Theorem 2. Due to lack of space, most propositions are given without a proof, which can be found in complete in the journal version of this paper.

2   The Coloring Algorithm

In Section 3 we prove that a typical graph in $\mathcal{G}_{n,m,k}^{\text{uniform}}$ and in $\mathcal{G}_{n,m,k}^{\text{plant}}$ share many structural properties such as the existence of a single cluster of solutions. In effect, it will turn out that coloring heuristics that prove efficient for $\mathcal{G}_{n,m,k}^{\text{plant}}$ (e.g. [4,11]) are useful in the uniform setting as well. Therefore, our coloring algorithm builds on ideas from [4] and [11].

When describing the algorithm we have a sparse graph in mind, namely $m/n = c$, c a constant satisfying $c \geq C_0 k^6$ (in the denser setting where $m/n = \omega(1)$, matters actually get much simpler). For simplicity of exposition (to avoid the cumbersome floor and ceiling brackets) we assume that k divides n. The algorithm proceeds in several phases. First, using the Semi-Definite Programming ("SDP")-based subroutine SDPColor, a k-coloring of the vertices is obtained. This coloring may not be proper, but *whp* differs from a proper k-coloring on the colors of at most, say, $n/(200k)$ vertices. Next, this coloring is refined using an iterative recoloring procedure, after which the obtained coloring differs on the colors of at most $e^{-\Theta(m/n)}n$ vertices from some proper k-coloring. The next step is to obtain a partial but *correct* k-coloring of the graph (correct in the sense that the coloring can be completed to a proper k-coloring of the entire graph). This is done using a careful uncoloring procedure, in which the color of "suspicious" vertices is removed. Finally, the graph induced by the uncolored vertices is sparse enough so that *whp* the largest connected component in it is of at most logarithmic size. Therefore, one can simply use exhaustive search, separately in every connected component, to extract the k-coloring of the remaining vertices. Steps 2–5 are similar to the work in [4] on $\mathcal{G}_{n,p,k}^{\text{plant}}$, Step 1 is inspired by [8,11].

Color(G, k):
step 1: first approximation.
1. SDPColor(G, k).
step 2: recoloring procedure.
2. for $i = 1$ to $\log n$ do:
    2.a for all $v \in V$ simultaneously color v with the least popular
           color in $N_G(v)$.
step 3: uncoloring procedure.
3. while $\exists v \in V$ with <3 neighbors colored in some other color do:
    3.a uncolor v.
step 4: Exhaustive Search.
4. let $U \subseteq V$ be the set of uncolored vertices.
5. consider the graph $G[U]$.
    5.a if $\exists$ a connected component of size at least $\log n$ - fail.
    5.b otherwise, exhaustively color $G[U]$ according to $V \setminus U$.

We proceed by discussing the subroutine SDPColor in detail. The procedure is based on a SDP relaxation of the max k-cut problem ("partition the vertices in a given graph into k classes so as to maximize the number of edges that join vertices in different classes") suggested by Frieze and Jerrum [17]. For a graph $G = (V, E)$, $SDP_k(G)$ is defined as follows (here $\langle x, y \rangle$ stands for the scalar product of two vectors $x, y \in \mathbb{R}^{|V|}$):

$$SDP_k(G) = \max \sum_{(u,v)\in E} \frac{k-1}{k}(1 - \langle x_u, x_v \rangle) \quad \text{s.t.} \ \forall \, u, v \in V, \ \langle x_u, x_v \rangle \geq -\frac{1}{k-1},$$

where the max is taken over all families $(x_v)_{v \in V}$ of unit vectors in $\mathbb{R}^{|V|}$ (the vector x_v corresponds to the vertex v). Since SDP_k is a semi-definite program, its optimal value can be computed up to an arbitrary high precision $\varepsilon > 0$, in time polynomial in $|V|, k, \log \frac{1}{\varepsilon}$ (e.g. using the Ellipsoid algorithm [18]).

To get some intuition for the usefulness of SDP_k in the context of the coloring problem, consider the same objective function as $SDP_k(G)$ only restrict the x_v's to be one of $\{a_1, a_2, ..., a_k\}$, where a_i is the vector connecting the centroid of a simplex in $\mathbb{R}^{k-1}$ to its i'th vertex (scaled to be of length 1). It is not hard to see that for $i \neq j$, $\langle a_i, a_j \rangle = -\frac{1}{k-1}$, and that $\frac{k-1}{k}(1 - \langle a_i, a_j \rangle)$ is 1 if $i \neq j$ and 0 otherwise. Furthermore, if the graph is k-colorable, then $SDP_k = |E(G)|$, and therefore the assignment of the a_i's must imply the k color classes of some proper k-coloring (all vertices receiving the same a_i are placed in the same color class).

Thus, grouping vertices into color classes according to the distances between the vectors assigned to them by an optimal solution to $SDP_k(G)$, seems like a good heuristic to get a fair approximation of some proper k-coloring. This is done by the following procedure.

SDPColor(G, k):
```
1. solve SDP_k(G), and let (x_v)_{v∈V(G)} be the optimal solution.
2. for all choices of k distinct vectors x*_1, x*_2, ..., x*_k ∈ (x_v)_{v∈V(G)} do:
   2.a for every i ∈ [1..k] compute S_{x*_i} = {w ∈ V : ⟨x*_i, x_w⟩ ≥ 0.99}.
   2.b if for every i, |S_{x*_i}| ≥ n/k - n/(400k²) then:
      2.b.1 for every i, color S_{x*_i} in color i (break ties arbitrarily).
      2.b.2 color uncolored vertices in color 1.
      2.b.3 return the resulting coloring.
3. return failure
```

3 Properties of a Random Instance from $\mathcal{G}_{n,m,k}^{\text{uniform}}$

In this section we analyze the structure of a typical graph in $\mathcal{G}_{n,m,k}^{\text{uniform}}$.

3.1 Balancedly k-Colorable Graphs

We say that a graph G is ε-**balanced** if it admits a proper k-coloring in which every color class is of size $(1 \pm \varepsilon)\frac{n}{k}$. We say that a graph is **balancedly k-colorable** if it is 0-balanced.

In the common definition of $\mathcal{G}_{n,m,k}^{\text{plant}}$, all color classes of the planted k-coloring are of the same cardinality, namely n/k. Therefore, all graphs in $\mathcal{G}_{n,m,k}^{\text{plant}}$ have at least one balanced k-coloring (the planted one). Similarly, for the uniform case:

Proposition 1. *Let $m \geq (10k)^4$, then whp a random graph in $\mathcal{G}_{n,m,k}^{\text{uniform}}$ is 0.01-balanced.*

Therefore in order to prove Theorems 1 and 2 , we may just as well confine our discussion to 0.01-balanced k-colorable graphs. To simplify the presentation we will analyze the case $\varepsilon = 0$, namely $\mathcal{G}_{n,m,k}^{\text{uniform}}$ restricted to balancedly k-colorable graphs. Nevertheless, the result easily extends to any $\varepsilon \leq 0.01$ – details omitted. Somewhat abusing notation, from now on we use $\mathcal{G}_{n,m,k}^{\text{uniform}}$ to denote $\mathcal{G}_{n,m,k}^{\text{uniform}}$ restricted to *balancedly* k-colorable graphs. Propositions of similar flavor to Proposition 1 were proven in similar contexts, e.g. [23], and involve rather simple counting arguments.

3.2 Setting the Exchange Rate

Let $\mathcal{A}$ be some graph property (it would be convenient for the reader to think of $\mathcal{A}$ as a "bad" property). We start by determining the exchange rate for $Pr[\mathcal{A}]$ between the different distributions.

Notation. For a graph property $\mathcal{A}$ we use the following notation to denote the probability of $\mathcal{A}$ under the various distributions: $Pr^{\text{uniform},m}[\mathcal{A}]$ denotes the probability of property $\mathcal{A}$ occurring under $\mathcal{G}_{n,m,k}^{\text{uniform}}$, $Pr^{\text{planted},m}[\mathcal{A}]$ for $\mathcal{G}_{n,m,k}^{\text{plant}}$, and $Pr^{\text{planted},n,p}[\mathcal{A}]$ for $\mathcal{G}_{n,p,k}^{\text{plant}}$. We shall be mostly interested in the case $m = \binom{k}{2}\left(\frac{n}{k}\right)^2 p$, namely m is the expected number of edges in $\mathcal{G}_{n,p,k}^{\text{plant}}$. The following lemma, which is proved using rather standard probabilistic calculations, establishes the exchange rate for $\mathcal{G}_{n,p,k}^{\text{plant}} \to \mathcal{G}_{n,m,k}^{\text{plant}}$.

Lemma 1. *($\mathcal{G}_{n,p,k}^{\text{plant}} \to \mathcal{G}_{n,m,k}^{\text{plant}}$) Let $\mathcal{A}$ be some graph property, then if $m = \binom{k}{2}\left(\frac{n}{k}\right)^2 p$ it holds that*

$$Pr^{\text{planted},m}[\mathcal{A}] \leq O(\sqrt{m}) \cdot Pr^{\text{planted},n,p}[\mathcal{A}]$$

Next, we establish the exchange rate $\mathcal{G}_{n,m,k}^{\text{plant}} \to \mathcal{G}_{n,m,k}^{\text{uniform}}$, which is rather involved technically and whose proof embeds interesting results of their own – for example, bounding the expected number of proper k-colorings of a graph in $\mathcal{G}_{n,m,k}^{\text{uniform}}$.

Lemma 2. *($\mathcal{G}_{n,m,k}^{\text{plant}} \to \mathcal{G}_{n,m,k}^{\text{uniform}}$) Let $\mathcal{A}$ be some graph property, then*

$$Pr^{\text{uniform},m}[\mathcal{A}] \leq e^{ke^{-m/(6nk^3)}n} \cdot Pr^{\text{planted},m}[\mathcal{A}]$$

3.3 Coloring Using SDP

In this section we analyze the behavior of $SDP_k(G)$, where G is sampled according to $\mathcal{G}_{n,m,k}^{\text{uniform}}$. We start by analyzing SDP_k on $\mathcal{G}_{n,p,k}^{\text{plant}}$, then use the discussion in Section 3.2 to obtain basically the same behavior for $\mathcal{G}_{n,m,k}^{\text{uniform}}$. The following lemma appears in [8].

Lemma 3. *Let G be a random graph sampled according to $\mathcal{G}_{n,p,k}^{\text{plant}}$ with φ its planted k-coloring, $np \geq C_0 k^6$, C_0 a sufficiently large constant. Then with probability $(1 - e^{-n})$ SDPColor(G,k) obtains a k-coloring which differs from φ on the colors of at most $n/(200k)$ vertices.*

Proposition 2. *Let G be a random graph in $\mathcal{G}_{n,m,k}^{\text{uniform}}$, $m \geq C_0 k^6 n$, C_0 a sufficiently large constant. Then whp there exists a proper balanced k-coloring φ of G s.t. SDPColor(G,k) obtains a k-coloring which differs from φ on the colors of at most $n/(200k)$ vertices.*

Proof. Let $\mathcal{A}$ be "there exists no balanced k-coloring s.t. SDPColor(G,k) obtains a k-coloring which differs from it on the colors of at most $n/(200k)$ vertices", and set $m = \binom{k}{2}\left(\frac{n}{k}\right)^2 p$. Using the "exchange rate" technique:

$$Pr^{uniform,m}[\mathcal{A}] \underbrace{\leq}_{\text{Lemma 2}} e^{ke^{-m/(6nk^3)}n} \cdot Pr^{\text{planted},m}[\mathcal{A}] \underbrace{\leq}_{\text{Lemma 1}}$$

$$\sqrt{m} \cdot e^{ke^{-m/(6nk^3)}n} \cdot Pr^{\text{planted},n,p}[\mathcal{A}] \underbrace{\leq}_{\text{Lemma 3}} O(\sqrt{m}) \cdot e^{ke^{-m/(6nk^3)}n} \cdot e^{-n} = o(1).$$

The last inequality is due to $m \geq C_0 k^6 n/2$.

3.4 Dense Subgraphs

A random graph in $\mathcal{G}_{n,m,k}^{\text{plant}}$ (also in $\mathcal{G}_{n,m}$) *whp* will not contain a small yet unexpectedly dense subgraph. This property holds only with probability $1-1/poly(n)$, and therefore the "exchange rate" technique, implemented in Section 3.3 for example, is of no use in this case. Overcoming the edge-dependency issue, using an intricate counting argument, we directly analyze $\mathcal{G}_{n,p,k}^{\text{uniform}}$ to prove:

Proposition 3. *Let G be a random graph in $\mathcal{G}_{n,m,k}^{\text{uniform}}$, $m \geq C_0 k^2 n$, C_0 a sufficiently large constant. Then whp there exists no subgraph of G containing at most $n/(100k)$ vertices whose average degree is at least $m/(6nk)$.*

3.5 The Core Vertices

We describe a subset of the vertices, referred to as the *core vertices*, which plays a crucial role in the analysis of the algorithm and in the understanding of $\mathcal{G}_{n,m,k}^{\text{uniform}}$. Recall that a set of vertices is said to be frozen in G if in every proper k-coloring of G, all vertices of that set receive the same color. A vertex v is said to be frozen if it belongs to a frozen set. The notion of core captures this phenomenon. In addition, a core typically contains all but a small (though constant) fraction of the vertices. This implies that a large fraction of the vertices is frozen, a fact which must leave imprints on the structure of the graph. These imprints allow efficient heuristics to recover the k-coloring of the core. A second implication of this, is an upper bound on the number of possible k-colorings, and on the distance between every such two (namely, a catheterization of the cluster structure of the solution space).

There are several ways to define a core, we choose a constructive way. $\mathcal{H} = \mathcal{H}(\varphi, t)$ is defined using the following iterative procedure. Set $\mathcal{H} = V$, and remove all vertices v s.t. v has less than $(1 - 1/200)t$ neighbors in some color class other than $\varphi(v)$. Then, iteratively, while there exists a vertex v in $\mathcal{H}$, s.t. v has more than $t/200$ neighbors outside $\mathcal{H}$, remove v.

Proposition 4. *Let G be a random graph in $\mathcal{G}_{n,m,k}^{\text{uniform}}$, $m \geq C_0 k^4 n$, C_0 a sufficiently large constant, and set $t = (1-1/k)2m/n$. Then whp there exists a proper k-coloring φ s.t. $\mathcal{H} = \mathcal{H}(\varphi, t)$ enjoys the following properties (by $V_1, V_2 \ldots V_k$ we denote φ's k color classes):*

1. $|\mathcal{H}| \geq (1 - e^{-m/(20nk^3)})n$.
2. Every $v \in \mathcal{H} \cap V_i$ has the property that $e(v, \mathcal{H} \cap V_j) \geq 99t/100$ for all $j \in \{1, \ldots, k\} \setminus \{i\}$.
3. For all $v \in \mathcal{H}$ we have $e(v, V \setminus \mathcal{H}) \leq t/200$.
4. The graph induced by the vertices of $\mathcal{H}$ is uniquely k-colorable.

Observe that t is chosen to be the expected degree of a vertex $v \in V_i$ in color class V_j, $j \neq i$. Properties 2 and 3 follow immediately from the construction of $\mathcal{H}$. To obtain property 1 we first establish the following fact, which appears in [8] (with a complete proof).

Lemma 4. Let G be a graph sampled according to $\mathcal{G}_{n,p,k}^{\text{plant}}$, $np \geq C_0 k^4 n$, C_0 a sufficiently large constant, and let φ be its planted k-coloring. Then $Pr[|\mathcal{H}(\varphi, np/k)| \leq (1 - e^{-np/(40k^3)})n] \leq e^{-e^{-np/(40k^3)}n}$.

Using the "exchange rate" technique we obtain:

Proposition 5. Let G be a random graph in $\mathcal{G}_{n,m,k}^{\text{uniform}}$, $m \geq C_0 k^4 n$, C_0 a sufficiently large constant, and set $t = (1 - 1/k)2m/n$. Then whp there exists a proper k-coloring φ of G s.t. $|\mathcal{H}(\varphi, t)| \geq (1 - e^{-m/(20nk^3)})n$.

Lastly, we establish the frozenness property (property 4).

Proposition 6. Let G be a graph for which Proposition 3 holds. Then every core satisfying Properties 1 and 2 in Proposition 4 is uniquely k-colorable.

The next proposition ties between the core vertices and the approximation ratio of SDPColor, and is crucial to the analysis of the algorithm. The proposition follows by noticing that φ in Lemmas 3 and 4 is the same – the planted coloring, and then using the "exchange rate" technique on the combined property.

Proposition 7. Let G be a random graph in $\mathcal{G}_{n,m,k}^{\text{uniform}}$, $m \geq C_0 k^6 n$, C_0 a sufficiently large constant. Then whp there exists a proper k-coloring φ of G s.t. the coloring returned by SDPColor(G,k) differs from φ on the colors of at most $n/(200k)$ vertices, and there exists a core $\mathcal{H} = \mathcal{H}(\varphi, t)$ s.t. Proposition 4 holds for $\mathcal{H}$, where $t = (1 - 1/k)2m/n$ as in Proposition 4.

The next proposition characterizes the structure of the graph induced by the non-core vertices.

Proposition 8. Let G be a random graph in $\mathcal{G}_{n,m,k}^{\text{uniform}}$, $m \geq C_0 k^2 n$, C_0 a sufficiently large constant. Let $G[V \setminus \mathcal{H}]$ be the graph induced by the non-core vertices. Then whp the largest connected component in $G[V \setminus \mathcal{H}]$ is of size $O(\log n)$.

This fact is proven in [4] for $\mathcal{G}_{n,m,k}^{\text{plant}}$, however it holds w.p. $1 - 1/poly(n)$. Therefore the "exchange rate" technique is of no use. Thus, in the uniform case the analysis is much more involved due to dependency issues (an intricate counting argument). Full details are in the journal version.

4   Proofs of Theorems 1 and 2

Theorem 1 is an immediate corollary of Proposition 4, as it implies that all but $e^{-m/(20nk^3)}n$ of the vertices are uniquely colorable, and in particular are frozen. There are at most $k^{e^{-m/(20nk^3)}n} = \exp\{ne^{-\Theta(m/n)}\}$ possible ways to set the colors of the non-frozen vertices. Proposition 8 characterizes the graph induced by the non-core (which contain the non-frozen) vertices.

To prove Theorem 2, we prove that the algorithm Color meets the requirements of Theorem 2. In particular, we prove that if G is *typical* (in the sense that the properties discussed in Sections 3.3, 3.4, and 3.5 hold for it), then Color k-colors it properly in polynomial time. Since G is typical *whp* (the discussion in Section 3), Theorem 2 follows. The proofs of the following propositions can be found in [4], and are based on the discussion in Section 3 (while a similar discussion exists in [4] for the planted setting). In the following propositions we assume G is typical.

Proposition 9. *After the recoloring step ends, the core vertices $\mathcal{H}$ are colored according to the proper k-coloring promised in Proposition 7 – let φ denote this coloring.*

Proposition 10. *Assuming Proposition 9 holds, $\mathcal{H}$ survives the uncoloring step, and every vertex that survives the uncoloring step is colored according to φ.*

Proposition 11. *Assuming Proposition 10 holds, the exhaustive search completes in polynomial time with a legal k-coloring of the graph.*

5   Discussion

In this paper we explore the uniform distribution over k-colorable graphs with cn edges, c greater than some constant. We obtain a rather comprehensive understanding of the structure of the space of proper k-colorings of a typical graph in it, and describe a polynomial time algorithm that properly k-colors most such graphs.

The techniques of this paper apply to a number of further NP-hard problems, including random instances of k-SAT. More precisely, we can show that a uniformly distributed **satisfiable** k-SAT formula with sufficiently large, yet constant, clause-variable ratio (above the satisfiability threshold) typically exhibits a single cluster of exponentially many satisfying assignments. Our result implies that the algorithmic techniques developed for the planted k-SAT distribution [16,15] extend to the significantly more natural uniform distribution, thus improving Chen's [10] *exponential* time algorithm for the same problem. In addition, our result answers questions posed in [5]. Full details will appear in a separate paper.

Acknowledgements. we thank Uriel Feige for many useful discussions. Part of this work was done while the third author was visiting Humboldt University.

References

1. D. Achlioptas and E. Friedgut. A sharp threshold for k-colorability. *Random Struct. Algorithms*, 14(1):63–70, 1999.
2. D. Achlioptas and M. Molloy. Almost all graphs with 2.522n edges are not 3-colorable. *Elec. Jour. Of Comb.*, 6(1), R29, 1999.
3. D. Achlioptas and C. Moore. Almost all graphs with average degree 4 are 3-colorable. In *STOC '02*, pages 199–208, 2002.
4. N. Alon and N. Kahale. A spectral technique for coloring random 3-colorable graphs. *SIAM J. on Comput.*, 26(6):1733–1748, 1997.
5. E. Ben-Sasson, Y. Bilu, and D. Gutfreund. Finding a randomly planted assignment in a random $3CNF$. *manuscript*, 2002.
6. A. Blum and J. Spencer. Coloring random and semi-random k-colorable graphs. *J. of Algorithms*, 19(2):204–234, 1995.
7. B. Bollobás. The chromatic number of random graphs. *Combin.*, 8(1):49–55, 1988.
8. J. Böttcher. Coloring sparse random k-colorable graphs in polynomial expected time. In *Proc. 30th MFCS*, pages 156–167, 2005.
9. A. Braunstein, M. Mézard, M. Weigt, and R. Zecchina. Constraint satisfaction by survey propagation. *Computational Complexity and Statistical Physics*, 2005.
10. H. Chen. An algorithm for sat above the threshold. In *6th International Conference on Theory and Applications of Satisfiability Testing*, pages 14–24, 2003.
11. A. Coja-Oghlan. Coloring semirandom graphs optimally. In *Proc. 31st ICALP*, pages 383–395, 2004.
12. M. E. Dyer and A. M. Frieze. The solution of some random NP-hard problems in polynomial expected time. *J. Algorithms*, 10(4):451–489, 1989.
13. U. Feige and J. Kilian. Zero knowledge and the chromatic number. *J. Comput. and Syst. Sci.*, 57(2):187–199, 1998.
14. U. Feige and J. Kilian. Heuristics for semirandom graph problems. *J. Comput. and Syst. Sci.*, 63(4):639–671, 2001.
15. U. Feige, E. Mossel, and D. Vilenchik. Complete convergence of message passing algorithms for some satisfiability problems. In *RANDOM*, pages 339–350, 2006.
16. A. Flaxman. A spectral technique for random satisfiable 3CNF formulas. In *Proc. 14th ACM-SIAM Symp. on Discrete Algorithms*, pages 357–363, 2003.
17. A. Frieze and M. Jerrum. Improved approximation algorithms for MAX k-CUT and MAX BISECTION. *Algorithmica*, 18(1):67–81, 1997.
18. M. Grötschel, L. Lovász, and A. Schrijver. *Geometric algorithms and combinatorial optimization*, volume 2 of *Algorithms and Combinatorics*. Springer-Verlag, Berlin, second edition, 1993.
19. M. Krivelevich and D. Vilenchik. Semirandom models as benchmarks for coloring algorithms. In *ANALCO*, pages 211–221, 2006.
20. L. Kučera. Expected behavior of graph coloring algorithms. In *Proc. Fundamentals of Computation Theory*, volume 56 of *Lecture Notes in Comput. Sci.*, pages 447–451. Springer, Berlin, 1977.
21. T. Łuczak. The chromatic number of random graphs. *Combin.*, 11(1):45–54, 1991.
22. R. Mulet, A. Pagnani, M. Weigt, and R. Zecchina. Coloring random graphs. *Phys. Rev. Lett.*, 89(26):268701, 2002.
23. H. Prömel and A. Steger. Random l-colorable graphs. *Random Structures and Algorithms*, 6:21–37, 1995.
24. J. S. Turner. Almost all k-colorable graphs are easy to color. *J. Algorithms*, 9(1):63–82, 1988.

On Defining Integers in the Counting Hierarchy and Proving Arithmetic Circuit Lower Bounds

Peter Bürgisser[*]

Dept. of Mathematics, University of Paderborn, D-33095 Paderborn, Germany
pbuerg@upb.de

Abstract. Let $\tau(n)$ denote the minimum number of arithmetic operations sufficient to build the integer n from the constant 1. We prove that if there are arithmetic circuits for computing the permanent of n by n matrices having size polynomial in n, then $\tau(n!)$ is polynomially bounded in $\log n$. Under the same assumption on the permanent, we conclude that the Pochhammer-Wilkinson polynomials $\prod_{k=1}^{n}(X-k)$ and the Taylor approximations $\sum_{k=0}^{n}\frac{1}{k!}X^k$ and $\sum_{k=1}^{n}\frac{1}{k}X^k$ of exp and log, respectively, can be computed by arithmetic circuits of size polynomial in $\log n$ (allowing divisions). This connects several so far unrelated conjectures in algebraic complexity.

1 Introduction

The investigation of the complexity to evaluate polynomials by straight-line programs (or arithmetic circuits) is a main focus in algebraic complexity theory. Let the *complexity* $L_K(f)$ of a polynomial $f \in K[X_1, \ldots, X_m]$ over a field K be the minimum number of arithmetic operations $+, -, *, /$ sufficient to compute f from the variables X_i and constants in K. We call a sequence $(f_n)_{n\in\mathbb{N}}$ of univariate polynomials *easy to compute* if $L_K(f_n) = (\log n)^{\mathcal{O}(1)}$, otherwise *hard to compute* (usually n stands for the degree of f_n). For example, the sequence $(G_n^{(r)})_{n\in\mathbb{N}}$ of univariate polynomials over $K = \mathbb{C}$

$$G_n^{(r)} := \sum_{k=1}^{n} k^r X^k$$

is easy to compute, provided $r \in \mathbb{N}$. This is easily seen by computing the derivatives of the well-known formula $G_n^{(0)} = \frac{X^{n+1}-1}{X-1} - 1$ for the geometric series.

In a landmark paper [19], Strassen proved that various sequences (f_n) of specific polynomials like $f_n = \sum_{k=1}^{n} \exp(2\pi\sqrt{-1}/2^j)$ or $f_n = \sum_{k=1}^{n} 2^{2^k} X^k$ are hard to compute. Von zur Gathen and Strassen [11] showed that the sequence $(G_n^{(r)})$ is hard to compute if $r \in \mathbb{Q} \setminus \mathbb{Z}$. The complexity status of this sequence for negative integers r has ever since been an outstanding open problem, cf. Strassen [21, Problem 9.2]. More details and references on this can be found in [9, Chapter 9].

[*] Partially supported by DFG grant BU 1371 and Paderborn Institute for Scientific Computation (PaSCo).

W. Thomas and P. Weil (Eds.): STACS 2007, LNCS 4393, pp. 133–144, 2007.

In 1994 Shub and Smale [17] discovered the following connection between the complexity of univariate integer polynomials and the $P_{\mathbb{C}} \neq NP_{\mathbb{C}}$-hypothesis in the Blum-Shub-Smale model [6] over $\mathbb{C}$. For an integer polynomial $f \in \mathbb{Z}[X_1, \ldots, X_m]$, we define the *tau-complexity* $\tau(f)$ as $L_{\mathbb{Q}}(f)$, but allow only the constant 1 and disallow divisions. Clearly, $L_{\mathbb{Q}}(f) \leq \tau(f)$. The τ-*conjecture* claims the following connection between the number $z(f)$ of distinct integer roots of a univariate $f \in \mathbb{Z}[X]$ and the complexity $\tau(f)$:

$$z(f) \leq (1 + \tau(f))^c \tag{1}$$

for some universal constant $c > 0$ (compare also [21, Problem 9.2]). Shub and Smale [17] proved that the τ-conjecture implies $P_{\mathbb{C}} \neq NP_{\mathbb{C}}$. In fact, their proof shows that in order to draw this conclusion, it suffices to prove that for all nonzero integers m_n, the sequence $(m_n n!)_{n \in \mathbb{N}}$ of multiples of the factorials is hard to compute. Hereby we say that a sequence $(a(n))$ of integers is *hard to compute* iff $\tau(a(n))$ is not polynomially bounded in $\log n$.

It is plausible that $(n!)$ is hard to compute, otherwise factoring integers could be done in (nonuniform) polynomial time, cf. [20] or [5, p.126]. Lipton [14] strengthened this implication by showing that if factoring integers is "hard on average" (a common assumption in cryptography), then a somewhat weaker version of the τ-conjecture follows.

Resolving the τ-conjecture appears under the title "Integer zeros of a polynomial of one variable" as the fourth problem in Smale's list [18] of the most important problems for the mathematicians in the 21st century. Our main result confirms the belief that solving this problem is indeed very hard. In fact we prove that the truth of τ-conjecture (as well as a hardness proof for the other problems mentioned before) would imply the truth of another major conjecture in algebraic complexity.

A quarter of a century ago, Valiant [23,24] proposed an algebraic version of the P versus NP problem for explaining the hardness of computing the permanent. He defined the classes VP of polynomially computable and VNP of polynomially definable families of multivariate polynomials over a fixed field K and proved that the family (PER_n) of permanent polynomials is VNP-complete (if char$K \neq 2$). Recall that the *permanent* of the matrix $[X_{ij}]_{1 \leq i,j \leq n}$ is defined as

$$\text{PER}_n = \sum_{\pi \in S_n} X_{1\pi(1)} \cdots X_{n\pi(n)},$$

where the sum is over all permutations π of the symmetric group. Valiant's completeness result implies that VP $\neq$ VNP iff $(\text{PER}_n) \notin$ VP. The latter statement is equivalent to the the hypothesis that $L_K(\text{PER}_n)$ is not polynomially bounded in n, which is often called *Valiant's hypothesis* over K. (For a detailed account we refer to [7]).

Our main result stated below refers to a somewhat weaker hypothesis claiming that $\tau(\text{PER}_n)$ is not polynomially bounded in n (however, cf. Corollary 18).

Theorem 1. *Each of the statements listed below implies that the permanent of n by n matrices cannot be computed by constant-free and division-free arithmetic circuits of size polynomial in n: that is, $\tau(\text{PER}_n)$ is not polynomially bounded in n.*

1. *The sequence of factorials* $(n!)_{n \in \mathbb{N}}$ *is hard to compute.*
2. *The τ-conjecture of Shub and Smale [17,4] is true.*
3. *The sequence of Taylor approximations* $(\sum_{k=0}^{n} \frac{1}{k!} T^k)_{n \in \mathbb{N}}$ *of exp is hard to compute.*
4. *The sequence* $(G_n^{(r)}) = (\sum_{k=1}^{n} k^r T^k)_{n \in \mathbb{N}}$ *for a fixed negative integer r is hard to compute.*

This result gives some explanation why the attempts to prove the τ-conjecture or the hardness of the above specific sequences of integers or polynomials did not succeed. Astonishingly, the major open problems mentioned in Chapters 9 and 21 of [9] turn out to be closely related!

This theorem was essentially conjectured by the author in [7, §8.3]. Koiran [13] proved a weaker version of the statement regarding the factorials and proposed a couple of questions related to other sequences of integers. Our technique allows to answer these questions in the affirmative (Corollary 17).

The main new idea for the proof of Theorem 1 is the consideration of the counting hierarchy CH, which was introduced by Wagner [26]. This is a complexity class lying between PP and PSPACE that bears more or less the same relationship to #P as the polynomial hierarchy bears to NP. The counting hierarchy is closely tied to the theory of threshold circuits of bounded depth, cf. [2].

Beame et al. [3] presented parallel NC^1-algorithms for iterated multiplication and division of integers. Reif and Tate [16] observed that these algorithms can also be implemented by constant depth threshold circuits, placing these problems in the class TC^0. The question of the degree of uniformity required for these circuits was only recently solved in a satisfactory way by Hesse et al. [12], who showed that there are Dlogtime-uniform circuits performing these tasks. This result, scaled up to the counting hierarchy, is crucial for our study of sequences of integers definable in the counting hierarchy. In fact, for our purpose it is sufficient to have deterministic polylogarithmic time in the uniformity condition, which is somewhat easier to obtain. It is remarkable that, even though the statement of Theorem 1 involves only arithmetic circuits, its proof relies on uniformity arguments thus requiring the model of Turing machines.

A box at the end of a lemma etc. indicates that the proof had to be omitted for lack of space. A full version is available as ECCC Report TR06-113.

2 Preliminaries

2.1 The Counting Hierarchy

The (polynomial) counting hierarchy was introduced by Wagner [26] with the goal of classifying the complexity of certain combinatorial problems where counting is involved. It is best defined by means of a counting operator $\mathbf{C}\cdot$ that can be applied to complexity classes.

We denote by $\{0,1\}^* \times \{0,1\}^* \rightarrow \{0,1\}^*, (x,y) \mapsto \langle x,y \rangle$ a pairing function (e.g., by duplicating each bit of x and y and inserting 01 in between).

Definition 2. Let K be a complexity class. We define $\mathbf{C} \cdot K$ to be the set of all languages A such that there exist a language $B \in K$, a polynomial p, and a polynomial time computable function $f : \{0,1\}^* \to \mathbb{N}$ such that for all $x \in \{0,1\}^*$:

$$x \in L \iff |\{y \in \{0,1\}^{p(|x|)} \mid \langle x,y \rangle \in B\}| > f(x). \tag{2}$$

Remark 3. The operators $\exists \cdot$ and $\forall \cdot$ can be introduced in similar way by instead requiring $\exists y \in \{0,1\}^{p(|x|)} \langle x,y \rangle \in B$ and $\forall y \in \{0,1\}^{p(|x|)} \langle x,y \rangle \in B$, respectively. It is clear that $K \subseteq \exists \cdot K \subseteq \mathbf{C} \cdot K$ and $K \subseteq \forall \cdot K \subseteq \mathbf{C} \cdot K$.

By starting with the class $K = \mathsf{P}$ of languages decidable in polynomial time and iteratively applying the operator $\mathbf{C} \cdot$ we obtain the counting hierarchy.

Definition 4. The k-th level $\mathsf{C}_k\mathsf{P}$ of the counting hierarchy is recursively defined by $\mathsf{C}_0\mathsf{P} := \mathsf{P}$ and $\mathsf{C}_{k+1}\mathsf{P} := \mathbf{C} \cdot \mathsf{C}_k\mathsf{P}$ for $k \in \mathbb{N}$. One defines CH as the union of all classes $\mathsf{C}_k\mathsf{P}$.

We recall that the classes of the polynomial hierarchy PH are obtained from the class P by iteratively applying the operators $\exists \cdot$ and $\forall \cdot$. It follows from Remark 3 that the union PH of these classes is contained in CH. Also it is not hard to see that CH is contained in the class PSPACE of languages decidable in polynomial space.

Modifying Definition 2 we define $\mathbf{C}' \cdot K$ of a complexity class K by requiring the majority condition

$$x \in L \iff |\{y \in \{0,1\}^{p(|x|)} \mid \langle x,y \rangle \in B\}| > 2^{p(|x|)-1}.$$

instead of (2). It can be shown that this does not change the definition of the classes of the counting hierarchy $\mathsf{C}_k\mathsf{P}$, cf. Torán [22]. In particular, we obtain for $k = 1$ the definition of the familiar class PP (probabilistic polynomial time).

We recall also that the counting complexity class $\#\mathsf{P}$ consists of all functions $g : \{0,1\}^* \to \mathbb{N}$ for which there exist a language $B \in \mathsf{P}$ and a polynomial p such that for all $x \in \{0,1\}^*$: $g(x) = |\{y \in \{0,1\}^{p(|x|)} \mid \langle x,y \rangle \in B\}|$. Hence functions in $\#\mathsf{P}$ can be evaluated in polynomial time by oracle calls to PP.

Lemma 5. *The counting hierarchy collapses to* P *if* $\mathsf{PP} = \mathsf{P}$. *Moreover,* $\mathsf{PP} \subseteq \mathsf{P}/\mathsf{poly}$ *implies* $\mathsf{CH} \subseteq \mathsf{P}/\mathsf{poly}$. □

2.2 The Constant-Free Valiant Model

An *arithmetic circuit* over the field $\mathbb{Q}$ is an acyclic finite digraph, where all nodes except the input nodes have fan-in 2 and are labelled by $+, -, \times$ or $/$. The circuit is called *division-free* if there are no division nodes. The input nodes are labelled by variables from $\{X_1, X_2, \ldots\}$ or by constants in $\mathbb{Q}$. If all constants belong to $\{-1, 0, 1\}$, then the circuit is said to be *constant-free*. We assume that there is exactly one output node, so that the circuit computes a rational function in the obvious way. By the *size* of a circuit we understand the number of its nodes different from input nodes.

Definition 6. The *L-complexity* $L(f)$ of a rational polynomial f is defined as the minimum size of an arithmetic circuit computing f. The τ-*complexity* $\tau(f)$ of an integer polynomial f is defined as the minimum size of a divison-free and constant-free arithmetic circuit computing f.

Note that $L(f) \leq \tau(f)$. While $L(c) = 0$ for any $c \in \mathbb{Q}$, it makes sense to consider the τ-complexity of an integer k. For instance, one can show that $\log \log k \leq \tau(k) \leq 2 \log k$ for any $k \geq 2$, cf. [10].

In order to control the degree and the size of the coefficients of f we are going to put further restrictions on the circuits. The *(complete) formal degree* of a node is inductively defined as follows: input nodes have formal degree 1 (also those labelled by constants). The formal degree of an addition or subtraction node is the maximum of the formal degrees of the two incoming nodes, and the formal degree of a multiplication node is the sum of these formal degrees. The formal degree of a circuit is defined as the formal degree of its output node.

Valiant's algebraic model of NP-completeness [23,24] (see also [7]) explains the hardness of computing the permanent polynomial in terms of an algebraic completeness result. For our purposes, it will be necessary to work with a variation of this model. This constant-free model has been systematically studied by Malod [15]. We briefly present the salient features following Koiran [13].

Definition 7. A sequence (f_n) of polynomials belongs to the complexity class VP^0 iff there exists a sequence (C_n) of division-free and constant-free arithmetic circuits such that C_n computes f_n and the size and the formal degree of C_n are polynomially bounded in n.

Clearly, if $(f_n) \in \mathrm{VP}^0$ then $\tau(f_n) = n^{\mathcal{O}(1)}$. Moreover, it is easy to see that the bitsize of the coefficients of f_n is polynomially bounded in n. When removing in the above definition the adjective "constant-free", the original class VP over the field $\mathbb{Q}$ is obtained [15]. The counterpart to VP^0 is the following class.

Definition 8. A sequence $(f_n(X_1, \ldots, X_{u(n)}))$ of polynomials belongs to the complexity class VNP^0 iff there exists a sequence $(g_n(X_1, \ldots, X_{v(n)}))$ in VP^0 such that

$$f_n(X_1, \ldots, X_{u(n)})) = \sum_{e \in \{0,1\}^{v(n)-u(n)}} g_n(X_1, \ldots, X_{u(n)}, e_1, \ldots, e_{v(n)-u(n)}).$$

Replacing VP^0 by VP in this definition, we get the original class VNP over $\mathbb{Q}$. Valiant's algebraic completeness result implies that VP = VNP iff $(\mathrm{PER}_n) \in \mathrm{VP}$. The latter is equivalent to $L(\mathrm{PER}_n) = n^{\mathcal{O}(1)}$. In the constant-free setting, the situation seems more complicated. It is not clear that $\mathrm{VP}^0 = \mathrm{VNP}^0$ is equivalent to the hypothesis $\tau(\mathrm{PER}_n) = n^{\mathcal{O}(1)}$. Curiously, it is neither clear whether $(\mathrm{PER}_n) \in \mathrm{VP}^0$ and $\mathrm{VP}^0 = \mathrm{VNP}^0$ are equivalent. However, it is known that they become equivalent when considering arithmetic circuits using the additional constant $\frac{1}{2}$, cf. Koiran [13, Theorem 4.3] and the result below. Indeed, by inspection of Valiant's algebraic completeness proof one derives the following.

Theorem 9. *If $\tau(\mathrm{PER}_n) = n^{\mathcal{O}(1)}$, then for any family $(f_n) \in \mathrm{VNP}^0$ there exists a polyomially bounded sequence $(p(n))$ in $\mathbb{N}$ such that $\tau(2^{p(n)} f_n) = n^{\mathcal{O}(1)}$.* □

Valiant [23] developed a useful criterion for recognizing families in VNP^0, see also [7, Proposition 2.20]. This criterion has been "scaled down" by Koiran [13, Theorem 6.1] as follows.

Theorem 10. *Assume the map $a \colon \mathbb{N} \times \mathbb{N} \to \mathbb{N}, (n, j) \mapsto a(n, j)$ is in the complexity class #P/poly, where n, j are encoded in binary. Let $p \colon \mathbb{N} \to \mathbb{N}$ be polynomially bounded and satisfying $p(n) \geq n$ for all n. Consider the polynomial*

$$F_n(X_1, \ldots, X_{\ell(n)}) = \sum_{j=0}^{p(n)} a(n, j) X_1^{j_1} \cdots X_{\ell(n)}^{j_{\ell(n)}},$$

where $\ell(n) = 1 + \lfloor \log p(n) \rfloor$ and j_i denotes the bit of j of weight 2^{i-1}. Then there exists a sequence $(G_r(X_1, \ldots, X_r, N_1, \ldots, N_r, P_1, \ldots, P_r))$ in VNP^0 such that

$$F_n(X_1, \ldots, X_{\ell(n)}) = G_{\ell(n)}(X_1, \ldots, X_{\ell(n)}, n_1, \ldots, n_{\ell(n)}, p_1, \ldots, p_{\ell(n)}))$$

for all n, where n_i and p_i denote the bits of n and $p(n)$ of weight 2^{i-1}.

Lemma 11. *$\tau(\mathrm{PER}_n) = n^{\mathcal{O}(1)}$ implies that $\mathsf{PP} \subseteq \mathsf{P/poly}$.* □

3   Integers Definable in the Counting Hierarchy

We consider sequences of integers $a(n, k)$ defined for $n, k \in \mathbb{N}$ and $0 \leq k \leq q(n)$, where q is polynomially bounded, such that

$$\forall n > 1 \ \forall k \leq q(n) \quad |a(n, k)| \leq 2^{n^c} \tag{3}$$

for some constant c. We shall briefly refer to such sequences $a = (a(n, k))$ as being of *polynomial bitsize*. The falling factorials $a(n, k) = n(n-1) \cdots (n - k + 1)$ are an interesting example to keep in mind; note that $a(n, k) \leq 2^{n^2}$.

We shall write $|a| := (|a(n, k)|)$ for the sequence of absolute values of a. We assign to a sequence $a = (a(n, k))$ of polynomial bitsize the following languages with the integers n, k, j represented in binary (using $\mathcal{O}(\log n)$ bits):

$$\mathrm{Sgn}(a) := \{(n, k) \mid a(n, k) \geq 0\}$$
$$\mathrm{Bit}(|a|) := \{(n, k, j, b) \mid \text{the } j\text{-th bit of } |a(n, k)| \text{ equals } b \}.$$

The integer j can thus be interpreted as an address pointing to bits of $a(n, k)$. Because of (3), we have $j \leq n^c$ and thus $\log j = \mathcal{O}(\log n)$.

Definition 12. *A sequence a of integers of polynomial bitsize is called definable in the counting hierarchy CH iff $\mathrm{Sgn}(a) \in \mathsf{CH}$ and $\mathrm{Bit}(|a|) \in \mathsf{CH}$. If both $\mathrm{Sgn}(a)$ and $\mathrm{Bit}(|a|)$ lie in $\mathsf{CH/poly}$ then we say that a is definable in $\mathsf{CH/poly}$.*

This definition and all what follows extends to sequences $(a(n, k_1, \ldots, k_t))$ with a fixed number t of subordinate indices $k_1, \ldots k_t \leq n^{\mathcal{O}(1)}$ in a straightforward way. For the sake of simplifying notation we only state our results for the cases $t \in \{0, 1\}$.

Our next goal is to find a useful criterion for showing that specific sequences are definable in CH. Let $m \bmod p \in \{0, \ldots, p-1\}$ denote the remainder of m upon division by the prime p. We assign to $a = (a(n, k))$ and a corresponding constant $c > 0$ satisfying (3) the *Chinese remainder language*

$$\mathrm{CR}(a) := \{(n, k, p, j, b) \mid p \text{ prime}, p < n^{2c}, j\text{-th bit of } a(n, k) \bmod p \text{ equals } b \}.$$

Again, the integers n, k, p, j are to be represented in binary with $\mathcal{O}(\log n)$ bits. (We suppress the dependence of $\mathrm{CR}(a)$ on c to simplify notation.) Note that the absolute value $|a(n, k)| \leq 2^{n^c}$ is uniquely determined by the residues $a(n, k) \bmod p$ for the primes $p < n^{2c}$, since the product of these primes is larger than 2^{n^c} (for $n > 1$).

Theorem 13. *Let a be a sequence of integers of polynomial bitsize. Then a is definable in* CH *iff* $\mathrm{Sgn}(a) \in$ CH *and* $\mathrm{CR}(a) \in$ CH. *Moreover, a is definable in* CH/poly *iff* $\mathrm{Sgn}(a) \in$ CH/poly *and* $\mathrm{CR}(a) \in$ CH/poly.

PROOF. We first show that for nonnegative sequences a of polynomial bitsize

$$a \text{ is definable in CH} \Longleftrightarrow \mathrm{CR}(a) \in \mathsf{CH} \tag{4}$$

and similarly for the nonuniform situation.

By the Chinese Remainder Representation (CRR) of an integer $0 \leq X \leq 2^n$ we understand the sequence of bits indexed (p, j) giving the j-th bit of $X \bmod p$, for each prime $p < n^2$. (The length of this sequence is $\mathcal{O}(n^2)$.)

It was shown by Hesse et al. [12, Theorem 4.1] that there are Dlogtime-uniform threshold circuits of polynomial size and depth bounded by a constant D that on input the Chinese Remainder Representation of $0 \leq X \leq 2^n$ compute the binary representation of X. Let this circuit family be denoted by $\{\mathcal{C}_n\}$.

Suppose that a is a sequence of nonnegative integers satisfying (3). For $d \in \mathbb{N}$ consider the language L_d consisting of the binary encodings of (n, k, F, b), where F is the name of a gate on level at most d of the threshold circuit $\mathcal{C}_{n^c}$ and F evaluates to b on input the CRR of $a(n, k)$.

Claim. $L_{d+1} \in \mathsf{PP}^{L_d}$ for $0 \leq d < D$.

We argue as in [1]. Due to the Dlogtime-uniformity of the circuits we can check in linear time whether two gates F and G are connected (polynomial time would be sufficient for our purpose). Let F be a gate at level $d+1$. On input (n, k, F, b), we need to determine whether $(n, k, G, 1) \in L_d$ for a majority of the gates G connected to F. This is possible in PP^{L_d}, which proves the claim.

We can now show the direction from right to left of (4). Suppose that $\mathrm{CR}(a)$ is contained in the s-th level $\mathsf{C}_s\mathsf{P}$ of the counting hierarchy. This means that $L_0 \in \mathsf{C}_s\mathsf{P}$. Using the claim and the fact that $\mathsf{C}_{s+1}\mathsf{P} = \mathsf{PP}^{\mathsf{C}_s\mathsf{P}}$ (cf. Torán [22]) we conclude that $L_d \in \mathsf{C}_{s+d}\mathsf{P} \subseteq \mathsf{C}_{s+D}\mathsf{P}$. Applying this to the output gates of $\mathcal{C}_{n^c}$ we see that a is definable in CH. Similarly, if $\mathrm{CR}(a) \in \mathsf{C}_s\mathsf{P}/\mathrm{poly}$ we obtain $L_d \in \mathsf{C}_{s+d}\mathsf{P}/\mathrm{poly}$.

In order to show the direction from left to right of (4) we argue in the same way, using the fact that the reverse task of computing the CRR of $0 \le X \le 2^n$ from the binary representation of X can be accomplished by Dlogtime-uniform threshold circuits of polynomial size and constant depth, cf. [12, Lemma 4.1].

For completing the proof it now suffices to prove that

$$\mathrm{Sgn}(a) \in \mathsf{CH} \ \text{ and } \ \mathrm{CR}(a) \in \mathsf{CH} \Longleftrightarrow \mathrm{Sgn}(a) \in \mathsf{CH} \ \text{ and } \ \mathrm{CR}(|a|) \in \mathsf{CH}$$

and similarly for the nonuniform situation. However, this follows from the fact that $-X \bmod p$ can be computed from $X \bmod p$ in AC^0, cf. [25].   □

From the above criterion we can derive the following closure properties with respect to iterated addition, iterated multiplication, and integer division.

Theorem 14. *1. Suppose* $a = (a(n, k))_{n \in \mathbb{N}, k \le q(n)}$ *is definable in* CH, *where* q *is polynomially bounded. Consider*

$$b(n) := \sum_{k=0}^{q(n)} a(n, k), \quad d(n) := \prod_{k=0}^{q(n)} a(n, k).$$

Then $b = (b(n))$ *and* $d = (d(n))$ *are definable in* CH. *Moreover, if* a *is definable in* $\mathsf{CH}/\mathrm{poly}$, *then so are* b *and* d.

2. Suppose $(s(n))_{n \in \mathbb{N}}$ *and* $(t(n))_{n \in \mathbb{N}}$ *are definable in* CH *and* $t(n) > 0$ *for all* n. *Then the sequence of quotients* $(\lfloor s(n)/t(n) \rfloor)_{n \in \mathbb{N}}$ *is definable in* CH. *The analogous assertion holds for* $\mathsf{CH}/\mathrm{poly}$.

PROOF.   1. Iterated addition is the problem to compute the sum of n integers $0 \le X_1, \ldots, X_n < 2^n$ in binary. This problem is well known to be in Dlogtime-uniform TC^0, cf. [25]. By scaling up this result as in the proof of Theorem 13, we obtain the claim for b in the case where $a(n, k) \ge 0$.

For the general case we use that if a and b are two sequences of nonnegative integers definable in CH, then so is $a - b$, and similarly in the nonuniform situation. (This follows as in the proof of Theorem 13 by using [12, Lemma 4.3].)

The claim for the iterated multiplication will follow by scaling up the arguments in Hesse at al. [12] to the counting hierarchy. Suppose that a is definable in CH. First note that we can check for given n in CH whether all $a(n, k)$ are nonzero. We therefore assume w.l.o.g. that $a(n, k) \ne 0$ and write $a(n, k) = (-1)^{e(n,k)}|a(n, k)|$ with $e(n, k) \in \{0, 1\}$. By definition, the sequence $(e(n, k))$ is definable in CH. We have

$$d(n) = (-1)^{s(n)} \prod_k |a(n, k)| \quad \text{where } s(n) = \sum_{k=0}^{q(n)} e(n, k).$$

According to the first claim of the theorem, $(s(n))$ is definable in CH. Hence it suffices to prove the second claim for a nonnegative sequence a.

By Theorem 13 we know $CR(a) \in CH$ and it suffices to prove that $CR(d) \in CH$. Suppose d satisfies (3) with the constant $c > 0$. Let a prime $p \leq n^{2c}$ be given. We can find the smallest generator g of the cyclic group $\mathbb{F}_p^\times$ in P^{PH} by bisecting according to the following oracle in Σ_2 $(u < p)$:

$$\exists\, 1 \leq g < u \,\forall\, 1 \leq i < p \quad g^i \neq 1.$$

Note that g^i can be computed by repeated squaring in polynomial time.

Similarly, for a given $u \in \mathbb{F}_p^\times$, we can compute the discrete logarithm $0 \leq i < p$ defined by $u = g^i$ in P^{NP}. For given $k \leq q(n)$ let $\alpha(n,k)$ denote the discrete logarithm of $a(n,k) \bmod p$. By the previous reasonings we see that $(\alpha(n,k))$ is definable in CH. By part one of the theorem we conclude that $(\delta(n))$ defined by $\delta(n) = \sum_{k=0}^{q(n)} \alpha(n,k)$ is definable in CH. Hence $d(n) \bmod p = g^{\gamma(n)}$ is computable in CH. Similar arguments apply in the nonuniform case.

2. The claim for integer division follows as before by scaling up the arguments in Beame et al. [3] and Hesse et al. [12] to the counting hierarchy. $\qquad\square$

Corollary 15. *The sequence of factorials $(n!)$ and the sequence of falling factorials $(n(n-1)\cdots(n-k+1))_{k \leq n}$ are both definable in CH. Moreover, if $\sigma_k(z_1, \ldots, z_n)$ denotes the k-th elementary symmetric function in the variables $z_1, \ldots, z_n$, then the sequence $(\sigma_k(1, 2, \ldots, n))_{n \in \mathbb{N}, k \leq n}$ is definable in CH.* $\qquad\square$

4   Permanent Versus Integers and Univariate Polynomials

Theorem 16. *Consider a sequence $(a(n))_{n \in \mathbb{N}}$ of integers definable in $CH/poly$ and sequences*

$$f_n = \sum_{k=0}^{q(n)} b(n,k) X^k \in \mathbb{Z}[X], \quad g_n = \frac{1}{d(n)} f_n \in \mathbb{Q}[X]$$

of integer and rational polynomials, respectively, such that $(b(n,k))_{n \in \mathbb{N}, k \leq q(n)}$ and $(d(n))_{n \in \mathbb{N}}$ are definable in $CH/poly$ (in particular, q is polynomially bounded).

If $\tau(PER_n) = n^{\mathcal{O}(1)}$, then the following holds:

1. $\tau(a(n)) = (\log n)^{\mathcal{O}(1)}$.
2. $\tau(2^{e(n)} f_n) = (\log n)^{\mathcal{O}(1)}$ *for some polynomially bounded sequence $(e(n))$ in $\mathbb{N}$.*
3. $L(g_n) = (\log n)^{\mathcal{O}(1)}$.

PROOF. We assume that $\tau(PER_n) = n^{\mathcal{O}(1)}$. By Lemma 11 this yields $PP \subseteq P/poly$. According to Lemma 5, this implies that $CH \subseteq P/poly$.

1. Let $a(n) = \sum_{j=0}^{p(n)} a(n,j) 2^j$ be the binary representation of $a(n)$. Without loss of generality we may assume that the polynomially bounded function p satisfies $p(n) \geq n$. By assumption, we can decide $a(n,j) = b$ in $CH/poly$, where

n, j are given in binary. Because of the assumed collapse of the counting hierarchy we can decide $a(n, j) = b$ in P/poly. Consider the polynomial

$$A_n(Y_1, \ldots, Y_{\ell(n)}) = \sum_{j=0}^{p(n)} a(n, j) Y_1^{j_1} \cdots Y_{\ell(n)}^{j_{\ell(n)}},$$

where $\ell(n) = 1 + \lfloor \log p(n) \rfloor$ and j_i denotes the bit of j of weight 2^{i-1}. Note that

$$A_n(2^{2^0}, 2^{2^1}, \ldots, 2^{2^{\ell(n)-1}}) = a(n)$$

By Theorem 10 there is a family $(G_r(Y_1, \ldots, Y_r, N_1, \ldots, N_r, P_1, \ldots, P_r))$ in VNP^0 that satisfies for all n

$$A_n(Y_1, \ldots, Y_{\ell(n)}) = G_{\ell(n)}(Y_1, \ldots, Y_{\ell(n)}, n_1, \ldots, n_{\ell(n)}, p_1, \ldots, p_{\ell(n)}),$$

where n_i and p_i denote the bits of n and $p(n)$ of weight 2^{i-1}, respectively.

By Theorem 9 there exists a polynomially bounded sequence $(s(r))$ in $\mathbb{N}$ such that $\tau(2^{s(r)} G_r) = r^{\mathcal{O}(1)}$. This implies $\tau(2^{e(n)} G_{\ell(n)}) = (\log n)^{\mathcal{O}(1)}$, where $e(n) = s(\ell(n)) = (\log n)^{\mathcal{O}(1)}$. We conclude from the above that

$$2^{e(n)} a(n) = 2^{e(n)} G_{\ell(n)}(2^{2^0}, 2^{2^1}, \ldots, 2^{2^{\ell(n)-1}}, n_1, \ldots, n_{\ell(n)}, p_1, \ldots, p_{\ell(n)}),$$

hence $\tau(2^{e(n)} a(n)) \leq \tau(2^{e(n)} G_{\ell(n)}) + \ell(n) \leq (\log n)^{\mathcal{O}(1)}$. Lemma 4.4 in Koiran [13] implies $\tau(a(n)) \leq (2e(n) + 3)\tau(2^{e(n)} a(n))$. Altogether, $\tau(a(n)) = (\log n)^{\mathcal{O}(1)}$.

2. Let $b(n, k) = \sum_{j=0}^{p(n)} b(n, k, j) 2^j$ be the binary representation of $b(n, k)$. As before we assume $p(n) \geq n$ without loss of generality. Consider the polynomial

$$B_n(Y_1, \ldots, Y_{\ell(n)}, Z_1, \ldots, Z_{\lambda(n)}) = \sum_{j=0}^{p(n)} \sum_{k=0}^{q(n)} b(n, k, j) Y_1^{j_1} \cdots Y_{\ell(n)}^{j_{\ell(n)}} Z_1^{k_1} \cdots Z_{\lambda(n)}^{k_{\lambda(n)}},$$

where $\ell(n) = 1 + \lfloor \log p(n) \rfloor$, $\lambda(n) = 1 + \lfloor \log q(n) \rfloor$, and j_i, k_i denote the bit of j, k of weight 2^{i-1}, respectively. Note that

$$B_n(2^{2^0}, 2^{2^1}, \ldots, 2^{2^{\ell(n)-1}}, X^{2^0}, X^{2^1}, \ldots, X^{2^{2^{\lambda(n)-1}}}) = \sum_{k=0}^{q(n)} b(n, k) X^k = f_n.$$

By Theorem 10 there is a family $(G_r((X_1, \ldots, X_r), (N_1, \ldots, N_r), (P_1, \ldots, P_r)))$ in VNP^0 that satisfies for all n

$$B_n(Y, Z) = G_{\ell(n)+\lambda(n)}((Y, Z), (n_1, \ldots, n_{\ell(n)+\lambda(n)}), (p_1, \ldots, p_{\ell(n)}, q_1, \ldots, q_{\lambda(n)})),$$

where $(Y, Z) = (Y_1, \ldots, Y_{\ell(n)}, Z_1, \ldots, Z_{\lambda(n)})$ and n_i, p_i, and q_i denote the bits of n, $p(n)$, and $q(n)$ of weight 2^{i-1}, respectively. By Theorem 9 there exists a polynomially bounded sequence $(s(r))$ in $\mathbb{N}$ such that $\tau(2^{s(r)} G_r) = r^{\mathcal{O}(1)}$. This implies $\tau(2^{e(n)} G_{\ell(n)+\lambda(n)}) = (\log n)^{\mathcal{O}(1)}$, where $e(n) := s(\ell(n) + \lambda(n)) = (\log n)^{\mathcal{O}(1)}$. We conclude from the above that

$$\tau(2^{e(n)} f_n) \leq \tau(2^{e(n)} G_{\ell(n)+\lambda(n)}) + \ell(n) + \lambda(n) \leq (\log n)^{\mathcal{O}(1)}.$$

3. We know already that $\tau(2^{e(n)} f_n) = (\log n)^{\mathcal{O}(1)}$. By the first assertion, we have $\tau(d(n)) = (\log n)^{\mathcal{O}(1)}$. Using one division, we get $L(g_n) = (\log n)^{\mathcal{O}(1)}$. $\square$

PROOF OF THEOREM 1. Suppose that $\tau(\mathrm{PER}_n) = n^{\mathcal{O}(1)}$. The sequence of factorials $a(n) = n!$ is definable in CH according to Cor. 15. By Theorem 16(1) we get $\tau(n!) = (\log n)^{\mathcal{O}(1)}$. Consider the Pochhammer-Wilkinson polynomial

$$f_n = \prod_{k=1}^{n}(X - k) = \sum_{k=0}^{n}(-1)^k \sigma_k(1, 2, \ldots, n)\, X^{n-k},$$

which has exactly n integer roots. Cor. 15 implies that its coefficient sequence is definable in CH. By Theorem 16(2) we have $\tau(2^{e(n)} f_n) = (\log n)^{\mathcal{O}(1)}$ for some $(e(n))$. The polynomial $2^{e(n)} f_n$ violates the τ-conjecture. Consider now $g_n = \sum_{k=0}^{n} \frac{1}{k!} T^k = \frac{1}{n!} \sum_{k=0}^{n} n(n-1) \cdots (k+1)\, X^k$. According to Cor. 15, both the coefficient sequence and the sequence $(n!)$ of denominators are definable in CH. Theorem 16(3) implies $L(g_n) = (\log n)^{\mathcal{O}(1)}$. A similar argument works for $\sum_{k=1}^{n} k^r T^k$. □

The following application answers some questions posed by Koiran [13]. This result actually holds for a large class of integer sequences, so the choice of the sequences below is for illustration and just motivated by Koiran's question.

Corollary 17. *If one of the integer sequences* $(\lfloor 2^n e \rfloor)$, $(\lfloor 2^n \sqrt{2} \rfloor)$, *and* $(\lfloor (3/2)^n \rfloor)$ *is hard to compute, then* $\tau(\mathrm{PER}_n)$ *is not polynomially bounded in* n. □

Based on [8], we can prove a conditional implication refering to the original Valiant hypothesis (dealing with arithmetic circuits using divisions and arbitrary complex constants).

Corollary 18. *Assuming the generalized Riemann hypothesis,* $L_{\mathbb{C}}(\mathrm{PER}_n) = n^{\mathcal{O}(1)}$ *implies that* $L_{\mathbb{C}}(g_n) = (\log n)^{\mathcal{O}(1)}$, *where* g_n *is as in Theorem 16.* □

Acknowledgements. This work was triggered by discussions with Eric Allender, Johan Kjeldgaard-Pedersen, and Peter Bro Miltersen. I thank them, as well as Emmanuel Jeandel and Emanuele Viola, for useful comments.

References

1. E. Allender, P. Bürgisser, J. Kjeldgaard-Pedersen, and P. Miltersen. On the complexity of numerical analysis. In *Proc. 21st Ann. IEEE Conference on Computational Complexity*, pages 331–339, 2006.
2. E. Allender and K.W. Wagner. Counting hierarchies: polynomial time and constant depth circuits. In G. Rozenberg and A. Salomaa, editors, *Current trends in Theoretical Computer Science*, pages 469–483. World Scientific, 1993.
3. P.W. Beame, S.A. Cook, and H.J. Hoover. Log depth circuits for division and related problems. *SIAM J. Comput.*, 15(4):994–1003, 1986.
4. L. Blum, F. Cucker, M. Shub, and S. Smale. Algebraic Settings for the Problem "$P \neq NP$?". In *The mathematics of numerical analysis*, number 32 in Lectures in Applied Mathematics, pages 125–144. Amer. Math. Soc., 1996.
5. L. Blum, F. Cucker, M. Shub, and S. Smale. *Complexity and Real Computation*. Springer, 1998.

6. L. Blum, M. Shub, and S. Smale. On a theory of computation and complexity over the real numbers. *Bull. Amer. Math. Soc.*, 21:1–46, 1989.
7. P. Bürgisser. *Completeness and Reduction in Algebraic Complexity Theory*, volume 7 of *Algorithms and Computation in Mathematics*. Springer Verlag, 2000.
8. P. Bürgisser. Cook's versus Valiant's hypothesis. *Theoret. Comp. Sci.*, 235:71–88, 2000.
9. P. Bürgisser, M. Clausen, and M.A. Shokrollahi. *Algebraic Complexity Theory*, volume 315 of *Grundlehren der mathematischen Wissenschaften*. Springer Verlag, 1997.
10. W. de Melo and B. F. Svaiter. The cost of computing integers. *Proc. Amer. Math. Soc.*, 124(5):1377–1378, 1996.
11. J. von zur Gathen and V. Strassen. Some polynomials that are hard to compute. *Theoret. Comp. Sci.*, 11:331–336, 1980.
12. W. Hesse, E. Allender, and D.A. Barrrington. Uniform constant-depth threshold circuits for division and iterated multiplication. *J. Comput. System Sci.*, 65(4):695–716, 2002. Special issue on complexity, 2001 (Chicago, IL).
13. P. Koiran. Valiant's model and the cost of computing integers. *Comput. Complexity*, 13(3-4):131–146, 2004.
14. R.J. Lipton. Straight-line complexity and integer factorization. In *Algorithmic number theory*, number 877 in LNCS, pages 71–79. Springer Verlag, 1994.
15. G. Malod. *Polynômes et coefficients*. Phd thesis, Université Claude Bernard-Lyon 1, 2003. http://tel.ccsd.cnrs.fr/tel-00087399.
16. J.H. Reif and S.R. Tate. On threshold circuits and polynomial computation. *SIAM J. Comput.*, 21(5):896–908, 1992.
17. M. Shub and S. Smale. On the intractability of Hilbert's Nullstellensatz and an algebraic version of "NP ≠ P?". *Duke Math. J.*, 81:47–54, 1995.
18. S. Smale. Mathematical problems for the next century. In *Mathematics: frontiers and perspectives*, pages 271–294. Amer. Math. Soc., Providence, RI, 2000.
19. V. Strassen. Polynomials with rational coefficients which are hard to compute. *SIAM J. Comp.*, 3:128–149, 1974.
20. V. Strassen. Einige Resultate über Berechnungskomplexität. *Jahr. Deutsch. Math. Ver.*, 78:1–8, 1976.
21. V. Strassen. Algebraic complexity theory. In J. van Leeuwen, editor, *Handbook of Theoretical Computer Science*, volume A, chapter 11, pages 634–672. Elsevier Science Publishers B. V., Amsterdam, 1990.
22. J. Torán. Complexity classes defined by counting quantifiers. *J. Assoc. Comput. Mach.*, 38(3):753–774, 1991.
23. L.G. Valiant. Completeness classes in algebra. In *Proc. 11th ACM STOC*, pages 249–261, 1979.
24. L.G. Valiant. Reducibility by algebraic projections. In *Logic and Algorithmic: an International Symposium held in honor of Ernst Specker*, volume 30, pages 365–380. Monogr. No. 30 de l'Enseign. Math., 1982.
25. H. Vollmer. *Introduction to circuit complexity*. Texts in Theoretical Computer Science. An EATCS Series. Springer-Verlag, Berlin, 1999. A uniform approach.
26. K.W. Wagner. The complexity of combinatorial problems with succinct input representation. *Acta Inform.*, 23(3):325–356, 1986.

A New Rank Technique for Formula Size Lower Bounds

Troy Lee[*]

LRI, Université Paris-Sud
troyjlee@gmail.com

Abstract. We introduce a new technique for proving formula size lower bounds based on matrix rank. A simple form of this technique gives bounds at least as large as those given by the method of Khrapchenko, originally used to prove an n^2 lower bound on the parity function. Applying our method to the parity function, we are able to give an exact expression for the formula size of parity: if $n = 2^\ell + k$, where $0 \le k < 2^\ell$, then the formula size of parity on n bits is exactly $2^\ell(2^\ell + 3k) = n^2 + k2^\ell - k^2$. Such a bound cannot be proven by any of the lower bound techniques of Khrapchenko, Nečiporuk, Koutsoupias, or the quantum adversary method, which are limited by n^2.

1 Introduction

One of the most important open problems in complexity theory is to prove superlinear lower bounds on the circuit size of an explicit Boolean function. While this seems quite difficult, a modest amount of success has been achieved in the weaker model of formula size, a formula being a circuit where every gate has fan-out exactly one. The current best lower bound on the formula size of an explicit function is $n^{3-o(1)}$ [Hås98].

Besides proving larger lower bounds, many open questions remain about the formula size of basic Boolean functions—functions which are both very important in practice and are the constant companions of complexity theorists. One of the most startling such questions is the gap in our knowledge about the formula size of the majority function: the best lower bound is $\lceil n/2 \rceil^2$ while the best upper bound is $O(n^{4.57})$ [PPZ92]. Even in the monotone case, where a formula consists of only AND and OR gates, the best lower bound is $\lfloor n/2 \rfloor n$ [Rad97], while the best upper bound is $O(n^{5.3})$ by Valiant's beautiful construction [Val84].

One obstacle to proving larger formula size lower bounds seems to be what we call the n^2 barrier—most generic lower bound techniques seem to get stuck around n^2. The technique of Nečiporuk [Neč66] is limited to bounds of size $n^2/\log n$; the methods of Khrapchenko [Khr71], originally used to show a n^2 lower bound on the formula size of parity, Koutsoupias [Kou93], and the recent quantum adversary method [LLS06] all cannot prove lower bounds larger than

---

[*] Supported by a Rubicon grant from the Netherlands Organisation for Scientific Research (NWO). Part of this work conducted while at CWI, Amsterdam.

n^2; Karchmer, Kushilevitz, and Nisan [KKN95] introduce a promising technique based on linear programming but at the same stroke show that it cannot prove lower bounds larger than $4n^2$.

We introduce a new technique for proving formula size lower bounds based on matrix rank. Karchmer and Wigderson [KW88] show that formula size can be phrased as a communication complexity game, specifically as the communication complexity of a relation. Although matrix rank is one of the best tools available for proving lower bounds on the communication complexity of *functions* it has proved difficult to adapt to the relational case. Razborov [Raz90] uses matrix rank to show superpolynomial lower bounds on *monotone* formula size, but also shows [Raz92] that his method is limited to $O(n)$ bounds for general formulas.

While in its full generality our method seems difficult to apply, we give a simplified form which always gives bounds at least as large as the method of Khrapchenko, and even the quantum adversary method, and which *can* break the n^2 barrier: we apply it to the parity function and give an *exact expression* for the formula size of parity. Let $\oplus_n$ denote the parity function on n-bits, and let $L(f)$ denote the the number of leaves in a smallest formula which computes f.

Theorem 1. *If $n = 2^\ell + k$ where $0 \leq k < 2^\ell$, then*

$$L(\oplus_n) = 2^\ell(2^\ell + 3k) = n^2 + k2^\ell - k^2.$$

In Section 3 we present our method and show that it gives bounds at least as large as those of Khrapchenko. In Section 4 we apply the method to the parity function to prove Theorem 1. Finally, in Section 5 we look at the relative strength of different formula size techniques and show that the linear programming method of Karchmer, Kushilevitz, and Nisan [KKN95] is always at least as large as the quantum adversary method [LLS06].

2   Preliminaries

We will make use of Jensen's inequality. We will use the following form:

Lemma 1 (Jensen's Inequality). *Let $\phi : \mathbb{R} \to \mathbb{R}$ be a convex function and a_i a set of positive real numbers for $i = 1, \ldots, n$. Then*

$$\phi\left(\frac{\sum_{i=1}^n a_i x_i}{\sum_{i=1}^n a_i}\right) \leq \frac{\sum_{i=1}^n a_i \phi(x_i)}{\sum_{i=1}^n a_i}.$$

2.1   Linear Algebra

We will use some basic concepts from linear algebra. For a matrix A, let A^* be the transpose conjugate of A, that is $A^*[i,j] = \overline{A[j,i]}$. A matrix is Hermitian if $A = A^*$. We will use $\leq$ to refer to entrywise comparision of matrices: that is $A \leq B$ if $A[i,j] \leq B[i,j]$ for all (i,j). The shorthand $A \geq 0$ means that all entries of A are nonnegative. The rank of A, denoted by $\text{rk}(A)$, is the number of linearly independent columns of A. The trace of A, written $\mathrm{Tr}(A)$, is the sum of the diagonal entries of A. For a Hermitian n-by-n matrix A, let $\lambda_1(A) \geq \lambda_2(A) \geq \cdots \geq \lambda_n(A)$ be the eigenvalues of A. Let $\sigma_i(A) = \sqrt{\lambda_i(A^*A)}$ be the ith singular value of A.

We will make use of three matrix norms. The Frobenius norm is the ℓ_2 norm of a matrix thought of as a long vector—that is

$$\|A\|_F = \sqrt{\sum_{i,j} A[i,j]^2}.$$

Notice also that $\|A\|_F^2 = \mathrm{Tr}(A^*A) = \sum_i \sigma_i^2(A)$. We will also use the trace norm, $\|A\|_{tr} = \sum_i \sigma_i(A)$. Finally, the spectral norm $\|A\| = \sigma_1(A)$. A very useful relationship between Frobenius norm, trace norm, and rank is the following:

Lemma 2. *Let A be a n-by-m matrix with $n \leq m$.*

$$\left\lceil \frac{\|A\|_{tr}^2}{\|A\|_F^2} \right\rceil \leq \mathrm{rk}(A).$$

Proof. The rank of A equals the number of nonzero singular values of A. Thus by the Cauchy–Schwarz inequality,

$$\left(\sum_{i=1}^n \sigma_i\right)^2 \leq \mathrm{rk}(A) \cdot \sum_{i=1}^n \sigma_i^2.$$

As rank is an integer, we obtain

$$\left\lceil \frac{\|A\|_{tr}^2}{\|A\|_F^2} \right\rceil \leq \mathrm{rk}(A).$$

A useful tool to lower bound the trace norm is the following:

Lemma 3.
$$\|A\|_{tr} = \max_B \frac{|\mathrm{Tr}(A^*B)|}{\|B\|}.$$

For Theorem 1 we in fact need only the following simple bound on the trace norm: if there are k distinct rows $x_1, \ldots, x_k$ and k distinct columns $y_1, \ldots, y_k$ such that $A[x_i, y_i] = 1$ for all $1 \leq i \leq k$, then $\|A\|_{tr} \geq k$.

2.2   Formula Size and Communication Complexity

A formula is a binary tree with nodes labeled by AND and OR gates, and leaves labeled by literals, that is either a variable or its negation. The size of a formula is its number of leaves. The formula size of a Boolean function f, written $L(f)$, is the size of a smallest formula which computes f.

Karchmer and Wigderson [KW88] characterize formula size in terms of a communication game. Since this characterization, nearly all formula size lower bounds have been phrased in the language of communication complexity.

Let X, Y, Z be finite sets and $R \subseteq X \times Y \times Z$ a relation. In the communication problem for R, Alice is given some $x \in X$, Bob some $y \in Y$, and they wish to output some $z \in Z$ such that $(x, y, z) \in R$. A communication protocol is a binary tree with each internal node v labeled either by a function $a_v : X \to \{0, 1\}$ if Alice speaks at this node, or by a function $b_v : Y \to \{0, 1\}$ if Bob speaks. Each leaf is labeled by an element $z \in Z$. We say that a protocol P computes a relation R if for every $(x, y) \in X \times Y$, walking down the tree according to the functions a_v, b_v leads to a leaf labeled with z such that $(x, y, z) \in R$. We let $C^P(R)$ denote the number of leaves in a smallest protocol which computes R.

For a Boolean function $f : \{0, 1\}^n \to \{0, 1\}$, let $X = f^{-1}(0)$ and $Y = f^{-1}(1)$. We associate with f a relation $R_f \subseteq X \times Y \times [n]$, where $R_f = \{(x, y, i) : x \in X, y \in Y, x_i \neq y_i\}$.

Theorem 2 (Karchmer–Wigderson). $L(f) = C^P(R_f)$.

An important notion in communication complexity is that of a combinatorial rectangle. A combinatorial rectangle of $X \times Y$ is a set which can be expressed as $X' \times Y'$ for some $X' \subseteq X$ and $Y' \subseteq Y$. A set $S \subseteq X \times Y$ is called monochromatic for the relation R if there is some $z \in Z$ such that $(x, y, z) \in R$ for all $(x, y) \in S$. Let $C^D(R)$ be the number of rectangles in a smallest partition of $X \times Y$ into combinatorial rectangles monochromatic for R. We will often refer to this informally as the rectangle bound. A basic fact, which can be found in [KN97], is that $C^D(R) \leq C^P(R)$. The rectangle bound is also somewhat tight—Karchmer, Kushilevitz, and Nisan [KKN95] show that $C^P(R) \leq C^D(R)^{\log C^D(R)}$.

3   Rank Technique

One of the best techniques for showing lower bounds on the communication complexity of a function $f : X \times Y \to \{0, 1\}$ is matrix rank, originally used by [MS82]. If M_f is a matrix with rows labeled from X, columns labeled from Y and where $M_f[x, y] = f(x, y)$, then $\mathrm{rk}(M_f)$ lower bounds the number of leaves in a communication protocol for f.

Let X, Y, Z be finite sets and $R \subseteq X \times Y \times Z$ a relation. In order to apply the rank bound, we first restrict the relation to a (non-Boolean) function by means of what we call a selection function. A selection function $S : X \times Y \to Z$ for the relation R takes input (x, y) and outputs some z such that $(x, y, z) \in R$. That is, it simply selects one of the possible valid outputs of the relation on input (x, y). We let $R|_S = \{(x, y, z) : S(x, y) = z\}$.

Theorem 3. $C^P(R) = \min_S C^P(R|_S)$.

Proof. For any selection function S, we have $C^P(R) \leq C^P(R|_S)$, as a protocol for $R|_S$ is in particular a protocol for R.

To see $C^P(R) \geq \min_S C^P(R_S)$, let P be an optimal protocol for R. We define a selection function based on this protocol, that is, let $S(x, y) = z$ if and only if (x, y) lead to a leaf labeled z by P. Now the protocol P also solves $R|_S$ and the claim follows.

With the help of selection functions, we can now use rank as in the functional case.

Theorem 4. *Let $R \subseteq X \times Y \times Z$ be a relation. To a selection function S, we associate a set of matrices $\{S_z\}$ over $X \times Y$ where $S_z[x,y] = 1$ if $S(x,y) = z$ and $S_z[x,y] = 0$ otherwise. Then*

$$C^D(R) \geq \min_S \sum_{z \in Z} \mathrm{rk}(S_z).$$

Proof. Let $\mathcal{R}$ be an optimal rectangle partition of R satisfying $|\mathcal{R}| = C^D(\mathcal{R})$. We let $\mathcal{R}$ define a selection function in the natural way, setting $S(x,y) = z$ where z is the lexicographically least color of the rectangle in $\mathcal{R}$ which contains (x,y).

We now show for this particular choice

$$C^D(R) \geq \sum_{z \in Z} \mathrm{rk}(S_z),$$

which gives the theorem. Clearly $C^D(R)$ is equal to the sum over all z of the number of rectangles labeled z by the partition $\mathcal{R}$. Thus it suffices to show that $\mathrm{rk}(S_z)$ lower bounds the number of rectangles labeled by z. Consider some z and say that there are k monochromatic rectangles $B_1, \ldots, B_k$ labeled z. As each B_i is a combinatorial rectangle we can write it as $B_i = V_i \times W_i$ for $V_i \subseteq X$ and $W_i \subseteq Y$. Let v_i be the characteristic vector of V_i, that is $v_i[x] = 1$ if $x \in V_i$ and $v_i[x] = 0$ otherwise, and similarly for w_i with W_i. Then we can express S_z as $S_z = \sum_{i=1}^{k} v_i w_i^*$ and so $\mathrm{rk}(S_z) \leq k$.

In general, this bound seems quite difficult to apply because of the minimization over all selection functions. We will now look at a simplified form of this method where we get around this difficulty by using Lemma 2 to lower bound the rank.

Corollary 1. *Let $f : \{0,1\}^n \to \{0,1\}$ be a Boolean function, and let $X = f^{-1}(0), Y = f^{-1}(1)$. Let c_i be the number of pairs $(x,y) \in X \times Y$ which differ only in position i, and let $s_1, \ldots, s_n$ be n nonnegative integers which sum to $|X||Y|$. Then*

$$C^D(R_f) \geq \min_{\sum_i s_i = |X||Y|} \sum_i \left\lceil \frac{c_i^2}{s_i} \right\rceil.$$

Proof. By Theorem 4 and Lemma 2

$$C^D(R_f) \geq \min_S \sum_i \mathrm{rk}(S_i) \geq \min_S \sum_i \left\lceil \frac{\|S_i\|_{tr}^2}{\|S_i\|_F^2} \right\rceil. \tag{1}$$

For the c_i many (x,y) pairs which differ only in position i, any selection function S must choose i. As the string y differing from x only in position i is unique, this means that we can permute the rows and columns of S_i to obtain a matrix with trace at least c_i, and so $\|S_i\|_{tr} \geq c_i$. The Frobenius norm squared of a zero/one matrix is simply the number of ones, thus $\|S_i\|_F^2$ is simply the number of (x,y) pairs for which the selection function S chooses i. As the selection function is total, $\sum_i \|S_i\|_F^2 = |X||Y|$. The claim follows.

The simplified version of the rank method given in Corollary 1 is already strong enough to imply Khrapchenko's method, which works as follows. Let f be a Boolean function, and as before let $X = f^{-1}(0), Y = f^{-1}(1)$. Let C be the set of $(x, y) \in X \times Y$ which have Hamming distance one. Khrapchenko's bound is then $|C|^2/|X||Y|$.

Theorem 5. *The bound given in Corollary 1 is at least as large as that of Khrapchenko.*

Proof. Let c_i be the number of $(x, y) \in X \times Y$ which differ only in position i, and let $\{s_i\}$ be such that $\sum_i s_i = |X||Y|$ and which minimize the bound given in Corollary 1. We now apply Jensen's inequality, Lemma 1, with $\phi(x) = 1/x, x_i = s_i/c_i$, and $a_i = c_i$ to obtain

$$\sum_i \frac{c_i^2}{s_i} \geq \frac{(\sum_i c_i)^2}{\sum_i s_i} = \frac{|C|^2}{|X||Y|}.$$

4   Application to Parity

In this section, we look at an application of the rank technique to the parity function. For both the upper and lower bounds, we will use the communication complexity setting of Karchmer and Wigderson. In this setting, Alice is given some x with even parity, Bob some y with odd parity, and they wish to find some i such that $x_i \neq y_i$. We first show the upper bound.

Proposition 1. *Let $n = 2^\ell + k$, where $0 \leq k < 2^\ell$. Then $L(\oplus_n) \leq 2^\ell(2^\ell + 3k)$.*

Proof. The basic idea is binary search. First imagine that n is a power of two. Bob begins by saying the parity of the left half of y. Alice then says the parity of the left half of x. If these parities differ, then they continue playing on the left half, otherwise they continue playing on the right half. With each round they halve the size of the playing field, and use two bits of communication. Thus after $\log n$ rounds and $2 \log n$ bits of communication they determine an i on which x and y differ. This gives a formula of size n^2.

When n is not a power of two, then at some point Alice and Bob will not be able to split the playing field evenly between left and right halves. To govern how Alice and Bob decompose n, consider a binary tree with the following properties:

- The root is labeled by n.
- The label of a node equals the sum of its sons
- Each leaf is labeled by 1.

Any such tree gives a protocol of the above type in the following way:

- Alice and Bob begin at the root, Alice playing with x and Bob with y. If the left son of the root is n_1, then Alice and Bob exchange the parities of the first n_1 bits of x and y respectively. If these disagree, then they continue playing with the substrings consisting of the first n_1 bits of x and y respectively. If these agree then they continue playing on the last $n - n_1$ bits of x and y respectively.

– Say that Alice and Bob have arrived at node v playing with strings x' and y' respectively, and that the left son of v is labeled by n_1. Alice and Bob exchange the parities of the first n_1 bits of x' and y'. If these agree then they continue playing on the last $n - n_1$ bits of x' and y' respectively.

The following claim gives the number of leaves in such a protocol.

Claim. Let T be a binary decomposition of n as above. Then

$$L(\oplus_n) \leq \sum_{\ell \in T} 2^{\text{depth}(\ell)},$$

where the sum is taken over the leaves ℓ of T.

Proof. We count the number of transcripts. Consider a path from root to a leaf. At each step in this path, there are two messages that could lead to taking that step. Namely, if the step is a left step, then Alice and Bob disagree in parity at this step and thus the message exchange leading to this is either 01 or 10. Similarly, if the step is a right step then Alice and Bob agreed in parity at this step and the messages which could be exchanged are 00 or 11. Thus the total number of transcripts in the parity protocol from a given tree is $\sum_{\ell \in T} 2^{\text{depth}(\ell)}$.

We use this claim to prove Proposition 1. Consider a binary decomposition of n where the sons of any node labeled by an even number have the same value and the sons of any node labeled by an odd number differ by one. This decomposition will have $2k$ many leaves at depth $\ell + 1$ and $2^\ell - k$ many leaves at depth ℓ. The claim then gives

$$L(\oplus_n) \leq 2k(2^{\ell+1}) + (2^\ell - k)2^\ell = 2^\ell(2^\ell + 3k)$$

Proposition 2. *Let* $n = 2^\ell + k$*, where* $0 \leq k < 2^\ell$*. Then* $L(\oplus_n) \geq 2^\ell(2^\ell + 3k)$*.*

Proof. Let S be any selection function. For every i, there are 2^{n-1} entries of the matrix S_i which *must* be one, namely the entries x, y which differ only on position i. If S only assigns these entries to have the label i, then S_i is a permutation matrix and so has rank 2^{n-1}. Thus to reduce the rank of S_i, the selection function S must therefore assign more (x, y) pairs to also have the label i. The catch is that S must do this for all i simultaneously, and we will bound how well it can do this.

Notice that for parity on n-bits, $|X| = |Y| = 2^{n-1}$. For every i there are 2^{n-1} pairs (x, y) which differ only in position i. Thus applying Corollary 1 with $c_i = 2^{n-1}$ for all i, we obtain

$$C^D(R) \geq \min_{s_i : \sum_i s_i = 2^{2n-2}} \sum_{i=1}^n \left\lceil \frac{2^{2n-2}}{s_i} \right\rceil. \tag{2}$$

Notice that if we were to ignore the ceilings, then we are minimizing over a convex function $\phi(x) = 1/x$ and so Jensen's inequality gives that the minimum is obtained when all s_i are equal. In this case $s_i = 2^{2n-2}/n$ and so $\sum_i 2^{2n-2}/s_i = n^2$.

To get bound larger than n^2 we need to take the ceiling functions into account. If n is not a power of two, then $2^{2n-2}/n$ will not be an integer, whereas each s_i is an integer—this means that it is no longer possible to have all s_i values equal and $\sum_i s_i = 2^{2n-2}$. It is this imbalance that will lead to a larger lower bound.

We transform Equation (2) in a series of steps. First, notice that

$$\min_{s_i : \sum_i s_i = 2^{2n-2}} \sum_{i=1}^n \left\lceil \frac{2^{2n-2}}{s_i} \right\rceil = \min_{s_i' : \sum_i s_i' \leq 2^{2n-2}} \sum_{i=1}^n \left\lceil \frac{2^{2n-2}}{s_i'} \right\rceil. \tag{3}$$

The right hand side is clearly less than the left hand side as the minimization is taken over a larger set. The left hand side is less than the right hand side as given a solution $\{s_i'\}$ to the right hand side, we can obtain a solution to the left hand side which is not larger by setting $s_i = s_i'$ for $i = 1, \ldots, n-1$, and $s_n = 2^{2n-2} - \sum_{i=1}^{n-1} s_i' \geq s_n'$.

Now we observe that there is an optimal solution $\{s_i\}$ to Equation (refmin2) where each $2^{2n-2}/s_i$ is an integer, and so each s_i is a power of two. If $2^{2n-2}/s_i$ is not an integer, then we can set s_i' to the largest power of two less than s_i and $\lceil 2^{2n-2}/s_i \rceil = 2^{2n-2}/s_i'$, and the sum of s_i' does not increase.

Thus assume that each s_i is a power of two, say $s_i = 2^{a_i}$. We can now rewrite Equation (3) as

$$\min_{\substack{a_i \\ \sum_i 2^{a_i} \leq 2^{2n-2}}} \sum_i 2^{2n-2-a_i}$$

The values $\{a_i\}$ which achieve this minimum will maximize

$$\max_{\substack{a_i \\ \sum_i 2^{a_i} \leq 2^{2n-2}}} \sum_i a_i.$$

We now show that there is an optimal solution to this maximization problem where $|a_i - a_j| \leq 1$ for all i, j. If $a_i - a_j > 2$ then we can let $a_i' = a_i - 1$ and $a_j' = a_j + 2$, so that $a_i' + a_j' > a_i + a_j$ and $2^{a_j'} \leq 2^{a_j} + 2^{a_i - 1}$ so $2^{a_i'} + 2^{a_j'} \leq 2^{a_i} + 2^{a_j}$. If $a_i - a_j = 2$ then by setting $a_i' = a_i - 1$ and $a_j' = a_j + 1$ then we still have $a_i' + a_j' = a_i + a_j$, and have saved on weight, $2^{a_i'} + 2^{a_j'} < 2^{a_i} + 2^{a_j}$.

By performing these transformations, we can turn any solution into one where $|a_i - a_j| \leq 1$ and whose value is at least as good. Now if we have $|a_i - a_j| \leq 1$ and $\sum_i 2^{a_i} = 2^{2n-2}$, it follows that $a_i = 2n - \ell - 2$ for $2^\ell - k$ many values of i and $a_i = 2n - \ell - 3$ for $2k$ many values of i. This gives

$$\min_{a_i} \sum_{i=1}^n 2^{2n-2-a_i} = (2^\ell - k)2^\ell + 2k2^{\ell+1}$$

$$= 2^\ell (2^\ell + 3k).$$

5   Hierarchy of Techniques

In this section, we present two results clarifying the hierarchy of available techniques for proving lower bounds on formula size. Laplante, Lee, and Szegedy

[LLS06] show that the quantum adversary method gives bounds at least as large as the method of Koutsoupias [Kou93] which is in turn at least as large as the bound of Khrapchenko. Here we show that the linear programming bound of Karchmer, Kushilevitz, and Nisan [KKN95] and a slight variation of our bound, as presented in Equation (1), are both always at least as large as the quantum adversary method.

We first describe the methods in question. Karchmer, Kushilevitz, and Nisan notice that for a relation $R \subseteq X \times Y \times Z$ the rectangle bound $C^D(R)$ can be written as an integer program. Indeed, let $\mathcal{R}$ be the set of all rectangles which are monochromatic with respect to the relation R. To represent the relationship between inputs (x, y) and the rectangles of $\mathcal{R}$ we use a $|X| \cdot |Y|$-by-$|\mathcal{R}|$ incidence matrix A, where for $(x, y) \in X \times Y$ and $S \in \mathcal{R}$ we let $A[(x, y), S] = 1$ if $(x, y) \in S$. Now a set of rectangles can be described by a $|\mathcal{R}|$-length vector α, with each entry $\alpha[S] \in \{0, 1\}$. If α represents a partition, then $A\alpha = \mathbf{1}$, and the number of rectangles in such a partition is simply $\sum_S \alpha[S]$. Karchmer, Kushilevitz, and Nisan relax this integer program to a linear program by replacing the condition $\alpha[S] \in \{0, 1\}$ with $0 \leq \alpha[S] \leq 1$.

Definition 1 (Linear programming bound [KKN95]). *Let $f : \{0, 1\}^n \to \{0, 1\}$ be a Boolean function, R_f the relation corresponding to f, and α a vector indexed by rectangles monochromatic with respect to R_f. The linear programming bound, denoted $\mathrm{LP}(f)$, is then*

$$\mathrm{LP}(f) = \min_{\substack{\alpha : A\alpha = \mathbf{1} \\ 0 \leq \alpha[S] \leq 1}} \sum_S \alpha[S].$$

Ambainis [Amb02, Amb03] developed the quantum adversary method to prove lower bounds on bounded-error quantum query complexity. Laplante, Lee, and Szegedy show that the square of the adversary bound is lower bound on formula size. The adversary bound can be phrased as a maximization problem of the spectral norm of a matrix associated with f [BSS03].

Definition 2 (Adversary bound). *Let $f : \{0, 1\}^n \to \{0, 1\}$ be a Boolean function, and $X = f^{-1}(0)$ and $Y = f^{-1}(1)$. Let Γ be a $|X|$-by-$|Y|$ matrix, and let Γ_i be the matrix such that $\Gamma_i[x, y] = \Gamma[x, y]$ if $x_i \neq y_i$ and $\Gamma_i[x, y] = 0$ otherwise, for $1 \leq i \leq n$. Then*

$$\mathrm{ADV}(f) = \max_{\substack{\Gamma \geq 0 \\ \Gamma \neq 0}} \frac{\|\Gamma\|}{\max_i \|\Gamma_i\|}.$$

First we show that a slightly more sophisticated version of our bound Equation (1) is always at least as large as the quantum adversary method. A problem with Equation (1) is that it cannot take advantage of the fact that certain inputs to a function might be harder than others. To give a concrete example, the bound given by Equation (1) on the function $f : \{0, 1\}^{2n} \to \{0, 1\}$ on $2n$ bits which is just the parity of the first n bits is worse than the bound for parity on n bits. To remedy this, we let u be a unit vector of length $|X|$ and v be a unit vector of length $|Y|$ and consider the matrix $S_i \circ uv^*$ instead of the matrix S_i. As $\mathrm{rk}(S_i \circ uv^*) \leq \mathrm{rk}(S_i)$, we can again apply Theorem 4 and Lemma 2 to obtain

$$C^D(R_f) \geq \min_S \max_{\substack{u,v \\ \|u\|=\|v\|=1}} \sum_i \frac{\|S_i \circ uv^*\|_{tr}^2}{\|S_i \circ uv^*\|_F^2}. \tag{4}$$

Theorem 6. *The bound given by Equation (4) is at least as large as* $\mathrm{ADV}(f)^2$.

Proof. Starting from Equation (4) we first apply Jensen's inequality with $\phi(x) = 1/x$, $x_i = \|S_i \circ uv^*\|_F^2 / \|S_i \circ uv^*\|_{tr}$, and $a_i = \|S_i \circ uv^*\|_{tr}$ to obtain:

$$\min_S \max_{\substack{u,v \\ \|u\|=\|v\|=1}} \sum_i \frac{\|S_i \circ uv^*\|_{tr}^2}{\|S_i \circ uv^*\|_F^2} \geq \min_S \max_{\substack{u,v \\ \|u\|=\|v\|=1}} \frac{\left(\sum_i \|S_i \circ uv^*\|_{tr}\right)^2}{\sum_i \|S_i \circ uv^*\|_F^2}.$$

As the selection function is total we have $\sum_i \|S_i \circ uv^*\|_F^2 = \|uv^*\|_F^2 = 1$.

Now we use Lemma (3) to lower bound $\|S_i\|_{tr}$. One can think of the weight matrix Γ in the adversary bound as the matrix from Lemma (3) which witnesses that the trace norm of the S_i's is large:

$$\min_S \max_{\substack{u,v \\ \|u\|=\|v\|=1}} \left(\sum_i \|S_i \circ uv^*\|_{tr}\right)^2 \geq \min_S \max_{\substack{\Gamma \geq 0 \\ \Gamma \neq 0}} \max_{\substack{u,v \\ \|u\|=\|v\|=1}} \left(\sum_i \frac{|\mathrm{Tr}((\Gamma \circ S_i)vu^*|}{\|\Gamma \circ S_i\|}\right)^2$$

$$\geq \min_S \max_{\substack{\Gamma \geq 0 \\ \Gamma \neq 0}} \max_{\substack{u,v \\ \|u\|=\|v\|=1}} \left(\sum_i \frac{|\mathrm{Tr}((\Gamma \circ S_i)vu^*|}{\|\Gamma_i\|}\right)^2.$$

This step follows as $0 \leq \Gamma \circ S_i \leq \Gamma_i$ and for matrices A, B if $0 \leq A \leq B$ then $\|A\| \leq \|B\|$. We can now continue

$$\min_S \max_{\substack{\Gamma \geq 0 \\ \Gamma \neq 0}} \max_{\substack{u,v \\ \|u\|=\|v\|=1}} \left(\sum_i \frac{|\mathrm{Tr}((\Gamma \circ S_i)vu^*|}{\|\Gamma_i\|}\right)^2 \geq \min_S \max_{\substack{\Gamma \geq 0 \\ \Gamma \neq 0}} \max_{\substack{u,v \\ \|u\|=\|v\|=1}} \left(\frac{\sum_i \mathrm{Tr}((\Gamma \circ S_i)vu^*)}{\max_i \|\Gamma_i\|}\right)^2$$

$$= \max_{\substack{\Gamma \geq 0 \\ \Gamma \neq 0}} \max_{\substack{u,v \\ \|u\|=\|v\|=1}} \left(\frac{\mathrm{Tr}(\Gamma vu^*)}{\max_i \|\Gamma_i\|}\right)^2$$

$$= \max_{\substack{\Gamma \geq 0 \\ \Gamma \neq 0}} \left(\frac{\|\Gamma\|}{\max_i \|\Gamma_i\|}\right)^2.$$

Now we show that the bound given by the linear programming method is also always at least as large as that given by the adversary method.

Theorem 7. $\mathrm{LP}(f) \geq \mathrm{ADV}^2(f)$.

Proof. Let α be a solution to the linear program associated with f. By definition we have $\sum_{S:(x,y)\in S} \alpha[S] = 1$ for every (x,y). Let u,v be unit vectors such that $|u^*\Gamma v| = \|\Gamma\|$. We will need some notation to label submatrices of Γ and portions of u,v. For a combinatorial rectangle $S = U \times V$, let $\Gamma_S[x,y] = A[x,y]$ if $(x,y) \in S$

and $\Gamma[x, y] = 0$ otherwise. Similarly, let $u_S[x] = u[x]$ if $x \in U$ and $u_S[x] = 0$ otherwise, and similarly for v_S. Now

$$\|\Gamma\| = \sum_{x,y} \Gamma[x, y]u[x]v[y]$$

$$= \sum_{x,y} \sum_{S:(x,y)\in S} \alpha[S]\Gamma[x, y]u[x]v[y]$$

$$= \sum_{S} \alpha[S] \sum_{(x,y)\in S} \Gamma[x, y]u[x]v[y]$$

$$\leq \sum_{S} \alpha[S]\|\Gamma_S\|\|u_S\|\|v_S\|$$

$$\leq \left(\sum_{S} \alpha[S]\|\Gamma_S\|^2\right)^{1/2} \left(\sum_{S} \alpha[S]\|u_S\|\|v_S\|\right)^{1/2},$$

where the first inequality follows from the definition of spectral norm, and the second uses the Cauchy–Schwarz inequality. Notice that

$$\sum_{S} \alpha[S]\|\Gamma_S\|^2 = \sum_{x,y} \alpha[S]|u[x]|^2|v[y]|^2 = 1.$$

Thus

$$\|\Gamma\|^2 \leq \sum_{S} \alpha[S]\|\Gamma_S\|^2 \leq \max_{S} \|\Gamma_S\|^2 \sum_{S} \alpha[S],$$

and so

$$\sum_{S} \alpha[S] \geq \max_{\Gamma} \frac{\|\Gamma\|^2}{\max_S \|\Gamma_S\|^2} \geq \max_{\Gamma} \frac{\|\Gamma\|^2}{\max_i \|\Gamma_i\|^2}.$$

Acknowledgments

I would like to thank Anna Gál for helpful discussions on the topics of this paper, and the anonymous referees for many beneficial comments.

References

[Amb02] A. Ambainis. Quantum lower bounds by quantum arguments. *Journal of Computer and System Sciences*, 64:750–767, 2002.

[Amb03] A. Ambainis. Polynomial degree vs. quantum query complexity. In *Proceedings of the 44th IEEE Symposium on Foundations of Computer Science*, pages 230–239. IEEE, 2003.

[BSS03] H. Barnum, M. Saks, and M. Szegedy. Quantum decision trees and semidefinite programming. In *Proceedings of the 18th IEEE Conference on Computational Complexity*, pages 179–193, 2003.

[Hås98] J. Håstad. The shrinkage exponent is 2. *SIAM Journal on Computing*, 27:48–64, 1998.

[Khr71]   V.M. Khrapchenko. Complexity of the realization of a linear function in the case of Π-circuits. *Math. Notes Acad. Sciences*, 9:21–23, 1971.

[KKN95]   M. Karchmer, E. Kushilevitz, and N. Nisan. Fractional covers and communication complexity. *SIAM Journal on Discrete Mathematics*, 8(1):76–92, 1995.

[KN97]   E. Kushilevitz and N. Nisan. *Communication Complexity*. Cambridge University Press, 1997.

[Kou93]   E. Koutsoupias. Improvements on Khrapchenko's theorem. *Theoretical Computer Science*, 116(2):399–403, 1993.

[KW88]   M. Karchmer and A. Wigderson. Monotone connectivity circuits require super-logarithmic depth. In *Proceedings of the 20th ACM Symposium on the Theory of Computing*, pages 539–550, 1988.

[LLS06]   S. Laplante, T. Lee, and M. Szegedy. The quantum adversary method and classical formula size lower bounds. *Computational Complexity*, 15:163–196, 2006.

[MS82]   K. Melhorn and E. Schmidt. Las Vegas is better than determinism in VLSI and distributed computing. In *Proceedings of the 14th ACM Symposium on the Theory of Computing*, pages 330–337. ACM, 1982.

[Neč66]   E. I. Nečiporuk. A Boolean function. *Soviet Mathematics–Doklady*, 7:999–1000, 1966.

[PPZ92]   M. Paterson, N. Pippenger, and U. Zwick. Optimal carry save networks. In *Boolean function complexity*, pages 174–201. London Mathematical Society Lecture Note Series 169, Cambridge University Press, 1992.

[Rad97]   J. Radhakrishnan. Better lower bounds for monotone threshold formulas. *Journal of Computer and System Sciences*, 54(2):221–226, 1997.

[Raz90]   A. Razborov. Applications of matrix methods to the theory of lower bounds in computational complexity. *Combinatorica*, 10(1):81–93, 1990.

[Raz92]   A. Razborov. On submodular complexity measures. In M. Paterson, editor, *Boolean function complexity*, volume 169 of *London Math. Soc. Lecture Notes Series*, pages 76–83. Cambridge University Press, 1992.

[Val84]   L.G. Valiant. Short monotone formulae for the majority function. *Journal of Algorithms*, 5:363–366, 1984.

Hard Metrics from Cayley Graphs
of Abelian Groups

Ilan Newman and Yuri Rabinovich*

Computer Science Department, University of Haifa, Haifa 31905, Israel
ilan@cs.haifa.ac.il, yuri@cs.haifa.ac.il

Abstract. Hard metrics are the class of extremal metrics with respect to embedding into Euclidean Spaces: their distortion is as bad as it possibly gets, which is $\Omega(\log n)$. Besides being very interesting objects akin to expanders and good codes, with rich structure of independent interest, such metrics are important for obtaining lower bounds in Combinatorial Optimization, e.g., on the value of MinCut/MaxFlow ratio for multicommodity flows.

For more than a decade, a single family of hard metrics was known (see [10,3]). Recently, a different such family was found (see [8]), causing a certain excitement among the researchers in the area.

In this paper we present another construction of hard metrics, different from [10,3], and more general yet clearer and simpler than [8]. Our results naturally extend to NEG and to ℓ_1.

1   Introduction

A famous theorem of Bourgain [4] states that every metric space (X, d) of size n can be embedded into an Euclidean space with multiplicative distortion at most $\text{dist}(d \hookrightarrow \ell_2) = O(\log n)$. We call a metric space *hard* if $\text{dist}(d \hookrightarrow \ell_2) = \Omega(\log n)$.

When studying a special class of metric spaces, perhaps the most natural first question is whether this class contains hard metrics. Many fundamental results in the modern Theory of Finite Metric Spaces may be viewed as a negative answer to this question for some special important class of metrics. E.g., Arora et al. [1] (improving on Chawla et al. [5]) show this for Negative Type metrics, Klein et al. [9] for planar metrics, and Gupta et al. [6] for doubling metrics. For a long time (since Linial, London and Rabinovich [10] and Rabani and Aumann [3]), the only known family of hard metrics was, essentially, the shortest-path metrics of constant-degree expander graphs. It was even conjectured that in some vague sense this is always the case. Recently, however, Khot and Naor [8] constructed a different family of hard metrics by considering certain quotient spaces of $\mathbb{Z}_2^n$ equipped with the Hamming distance.

The starting point of the current research was a plausible conjecture that a *circular* metric cannot be hard, where by circular we mean a metric on the

---

* Supported in part by a grant ISF-247-020-10.5.

W. Thomas and P. Weil (Eds.): STACS 2007, LNCS 4393, pp. 157–162, 2007.

underlying space $\mathbb{Z}_n$, such that $d(a, b)$ depends solely on $((a-b) \mod n)$. Rather surprisingly, the conjecture turns out to be false, and, moreover, it fails not only for $\mathbb{Z}_n$, but for *any* Abelian group H. More precisely, it is always possible to choose a set A of generators for H, so that the shortest-path metric of the corresponding Cayley graph $G(H, A)$ is hard. In the special case of $\mathbb{Z}_2^n$, good sets of generators are closely related to error-correcting codes of constant rate and linear distance.

Our construction is both simple to describe and easy to analyze. It differs from that of [10,3], as the degree of such Cayley graphs is necessarily non-constant. It is more general than the construction of [8], since the latter, despite very different description and analysis, can be shown to produce the same mertic space as does our construction in the special case of $\mathbb{Z}_2^n$.

Note: Although in what follows we restrict the discussion to Euclidean Spaces, the same method shows the hardness of the metrics that we construct also with respect to much richer spaces of NEG, and consequently ℓ_1.

2   General Abelian Groups

Let G be a d-regular connected graph on n vertices, and let μ_G be its shortest-path metric. Our first step is to get a general lower bound on distortion of embedding μ_G into an Euclidean space. We use a standard (dual) method of comparing the so-called Poincare forms (see, e.g., [10,11], with further details therein). Consider the following projective quadratic form:

$$F(\Delta) = \frac{\sum_{(i,j)\in E(G)} \Delta^2(i, j)}{\sum_{i<j\in V(G)} \Delta^2(i, j)}$$

Then,

$$F(\mu_G) = \frac{|E|}{\binom{n}{2}\mathrm{Ave}(\mu_G^2)},$$

where $\mathrm{Ave}(\mu_G^2)$ is the average value of $\mu_G^2(i, j)$ over all pairs of vertices of G. On the other hand let δ be *any* Euclidean metric on $V(G)$, i.e., a metric of the form

$$\delta(i, j) = \|x^i - x^j\|_2, \quad \text{where } \{x^i\}_{i\in V(G)} \subset \mathbb{R}^m.$$

By a standard argument (see e.g., [11], Sect. 15.5), the minimum of $F(\delta)$ over all such δ's is precisely γ_G/n, where γ_G is the *spectral gap* of G, i.e., $(d - \lambda_G)$ where λ_G is the second largest eigenvalue of the adjacency matrix of G. If the minimum of $F(\delta)$ over all Euclidean metrics is larger than $F(\mu_G)$, we conclude that the square of distortion of any embedding of μ_G into an Euclidean space is at least the ratio between these two values:

Proposition 1.

$$\mathrm{dist}^2(\mu_G \hookrightarrow \ell_2) \geq \frac{n-1}{n} \cdot \frac{\gamma_G}{d} \cdot \mathrm{Ave}(\mu_G^2).$$

In particular,

Corollary 1. *If a graph G has a constant normalized spectral gap γ_G/d, and $\text{Ave}(\mu_G^2) = \Omega(\log^2 n)$, then the above method yields an $\Omega(\log n)$ lower bound on the distortion of embedding μ_G into an Euclidean space.*

In the following we shall deal solely with vertex-transitive graphs; let us remark that for such graphs $\text{Ave}(\mu_G^2) \approx \text{Diam}(G)^2$. Indeed, let r be the smallest radius such that the corresponding r-ball in μ_G contains at least $n/2$ vertices. Clearly, $\text{Ave}(\mu_G^2) \geq r^2/2$, while $\text{Diam}(G) \leq 2r + 1$. Thus, it suffices to ensure that the diameter of G is at least $\Omega(\log n)$.

Turning to Cayley graphs, it is well known that for (some) non-Abelian groups, there exist Cayley graphs with *constantly many* generators, and a constant spectral gap (see, e.g., [12], the section on Cayley expander graphs). Since the constant number of generators guarantees that the diameter is $\Omega(\log n)$, this yields a graph as required in Corollary 1. (This is precisely the construction used in [10,3]). For Abelian groups such construction is impossible, since in order to ensure a constant normalized gap γ_G/d, the number of generators must be at least $\Omega(\log n)$ (see, e.g., [12]). This might seem to be a problem, since, at least for general groups, that many generators may well cause the diameter be $O(\log n/\log\log n) = o(\log n)$. For Abelian groups, however, this does not happen! While the following simple fact is well known (see, e.g., [12], proof of Prop. 11.5), it has been apparently overlooked in the context of hard metrics. Let $h(p) = -p\log_2 p - (1 - p)\log_2(1 - p)$ be the entropy function.

Proposition 2. *Let H be an Abelian group of size n, and let $A \subset H$, $A = -A$, be a set of generators of size $d = c_0 \log_2 n$. Then, for any constant c_1 such that $(c_0 + c_1) \cdot h(c_1/(c_0 + c_1)) < 1$, the diameter of the corresponding Cayley graph $G(H, A)$ is $\geq c_1 \log_2 n$ for a large enough n.*

The proposition follows from the observation that the number of distinct endpoints of paths of of length l in G is at most $\binom{d+l}{l}$, since due to commutativity of G it is at most the number of partitions of a set of l (identical) elements to d (distinct) parts. Therefore, the number of points reachable by a path of length $\leq c_1 \log_2 n$ is at most

$$\sum_{l=0}^{c_1 \log_2 n} \binom{c_0 \log_2 n + l}{l} = 2^{h\left(\frac{c_1}{c_0+c_1}\right)\cdot(c_0+c_1)\cdot\log_2 n + o(\log n)} =$$

$$n^{(c_0+c_1)\cdot h\left(\frac{c_1}{c_0+c_1}\right)+o(1)} < n.$$

Thus, as long as the number of generators is $O(\log n)$, our only concern is getting a constant normalized spectral gap γ_G/d. This is summed up in the following theorem.

Theorem 1. *Let H be an Abelian group of size n, let $A \subset H$ be a symmetric set of generators of size $d = c_0 \log_2 n$ for a suitable universal constant c_0 (a 100 would certainly suffice) and let $G(H, A)$ be the corresponding Cayley graph. If the normalized spectral gap $\gamma_G/|A| = \Omega(1)$, then μ_G is a hard metric.*

It is well known that a random construction achieves this goal (see, e.g., [2], in particular the section on Abelian groups):

Proposition 3. *Let H be a an Abelian group of size n, and let $A \subset H$ be a random symmetric set of generators of size $d = c_0 \log_2 n$ for a suitable universal constant c_0 (a 100 would certainly suffice). Then, the corresponding Cayley graph $G(H, A)$ is almost surely connected, and has a normalized spectral gap ≥ 0.5.*

To prove the proposition, one needs first to realize that the eigenvectors of G are the *characters* of H, i.e., functions χ from H to the unit circle in $\mathbb{C}$, such that $\chi(a + b) = \chi(a) \cdot \chi(b)$. In particular, all such functions with the exception of the constant one (that corresponds to the eigenvalue d), sum up to 0. From here it is little more than an application of the Chernoff Bound. For an efficient deterministic construction of such A's see [13].

Combining Theorem 1 and Proposition 3, we arrive at the main result of this section:

Theorem 2. *Let $G = G(H, A)$ be a Cayley graph obtained by taking a random symmetric set of generators $A \subset H$ of size $d = c_0 \log_2 |H|$ for a suitable universal constant c_0. Then, the shortest-path metric of G is almost surely a hard metric.*

Remark: *It is natural to ask whether the Cayley graph whose shortest-path metric is hard, may have super-logarithmic degree. The answer is positive, and in fact for any Abelian H it is possible to get degree $O(n^{1-\epsilon})$ for any constant ϵ. We postpone the detailed discussion of this matter to the journal version of this paper.*

3   When the Group Is $\mathbb{Z}_2^n$

In this case the group is just an n-dimensional vector space over $\mathbb{Z}_2$. Any set of generators (vectors) A is automatically symmetric. Following the requirements of Corollary 1, we have to ensure three conditions: a constant normalized spectral gap, conectivity of $G(\mathbb{Z}_2^n, A)$, and $\Omega(n)$ diameter.

The construction is based on linear good codes. Let $\mathcal{C} \subset \mathbb{Z}_2^m$ be a linear code of *dimension* n, that is, $\mathcal{C}$ is generated by a set of n linearly independent m-dimensional vectors. The *distance* $D(\mathcal{C})$ of $\mathcal{C}$ is the minimum number of 1's in any $c \in \mathcal{C}$. $\mathcal{C}$ is said to be of linear distance if $D(\mathcal{C}) = \Omega(m)$. In addition, if $m = O(n)$ the code is said to have a *constant rate*.

Let M be an $n \times m$ matrix whose rows are a basis for $\mathcal{C}$ (such an M is called the generator matrix of $\mathcal{C}$) and let $A \subset \mathbb{Z}_2^n$, $|A| = m$, be the set of columns M. It is easy to see that for any such linear code, the graph $G(\mathbb{Z}_2^n, A)$ is connected due to the fact that the rank of M is n.

Proposition 4. *Let $\mathcal{C}$ be a linear code of linear distance and let M and A be the corresponding matrix and set of vectors as above. Then normalized spectral gap γ_G/n of $G(\mathbb{Z}_2^n, A)$ is constant. Conversely, any A with this property is necessarily the set of columns of a generator matrix of a linear code with linear distance.*

The proposition is a folklore (see e.g. [2], proof of Proposition 2). Here is a sketch of the proof.

Proof. The characters of $\mathbb{Z}_2^n$, indexed by the group elements, $\{\chi_u\}$, $u \in \mathbb{Z}_2^n$, are of the form

$$\chi_u(x) = (-1)^{\langle u,x \rangle},$$

where the inner product (with a slight abuse of notation) is (mod 2). Let $A \subset \mathbb{Z}_2^n$, $|A| = m$, be a set of generators (vectors), and let M_A be an $n \times m$ matrix over $\mathbb{Z}_2$ whose columns are the vectors of A. For a vector in $v \in \mathbb{Z}_2^m$ let $w(v)$ be the number of 1's in v. The second largest eigenvalue λ_G of $G(\mathbb{Z}_2^n, A)$ is

$$\lambda_G = \max_{u \neq 0} \sum_{a \in A} (-1)^{\langle u,a \rangle} = \max_{u \neq 0} \left\{ m - 2w(u^T M_A) \right\}.$$

Let $\mathcal{C} \subseteq \mathbb{Z}_2^n$ be a linear code generated by M_A, that is, all linear combinations of rows of M_A. Then $\mathcal{C} = \{u^T M_A\}_{u \in \mathbb{Z}_2^n} \subset \mathbb{Z}_2^m$ and hence $\lambda_G = m - 2D(\mathcal{C})$. Keeping in mind that $\gamma_G = m - \lambda_G$ we conclude that $\gamma_G = 2D(\mathcal{C})$. Therefore, $\gamma_G = \Omega(m)$ if and only $\mathcal{C}$ is a linear code of linear distace. $\qquad\square$

It remains to ensure that the diameter of $G(\mathbb{Z}_2^n, A)$ is $\Omega(n)$. By Proposition 2, this condition will necessarily hold provided $m = O(n)$, that is, if $\mathcal{C}$ is of constant rate. Thus,

Theorem 3. *Let $\mathcal{C}$ be a linear code of constant rate and linear distance, and $\dim(\mathcal{C}) = n$. Let M be an $n \times m$ matrix whose rows form a basis for $\mathcal{C}$, and let $A \subset \mathbb{Z}_?^n$, be the set of M's columns. Then the metric of $G(\mathbb{Z}_2^n, A)$ is hard.*

Such codes are at the core of the Coding Theory and they have received a considerable attention. Their existence has been established by numerous randomized and deterministic efficient constructions, with the first explicit construction due to Justesen [7].

We conclude the paper with a discussion of the construction of hard metrics due to Khot and Naor [8]. Let $\mathcal{C} \subset \mathbb{Z}_2^m$ be a linear code of constant rate and linear distance, of dimension n. Let $\mathcal{C}^\perp$ be the dual code, i.e., $\mathcal{C}^\perp = \{u | Mu = 0\}$ where M is the generator matrix of $\mathcal{C}$. Define an equivalence relation on $\mathbb{Z}_2^m$ by $x \equiv y$ iff $(x - y) \in \mathcal{C}^\perp$. Now, let X be a quotient metric space of $\mathbb{Z}_2^m$ equipped with the Hamming metric, with respect to $\equiv$. That is, the distance between two points a and b in X is the Hamming distance between the two corresponding cosets $A, B \subset \mathbb{Z}_2^m$. Khot and Naor show that X with the induced metric is hard.

Proposition 5. *The above construction is isometric to the construction described in Theorem 3.*

Proof. Let M be a matrix as in Theorem 3. Then X can be viewed as the image of $\mathbb{Z}_2^m$ under the linear mapping $\phi : \mathbb{Z}_2^m \to \mathbb{Z}_2^n$, $\phi(x) = Mx$. Define the *edges* of X as the images of Hamming edges of $\mathbb{Z}_2^m$ under ϕ. Clearly, the quotient metric of X is precisely the shortest-path metric of the resulting graph. The images of the Hamming edges are, however, precisely the column vectors of M, and the isometry follows. $\qquad\square$

Without diminishing the achievement of [8], which in addition to the result discussed here contains a number of other wonderful results, it appears that our construction, besides being more general, is simpler both in terms of description and analysis.

References

1. S.Arora, J.Lee, A.Naor. Euclidean distortion and the sparsest cut. in *Proceedings of the 37th Annual ACM Symposium on Theory of Computing, STOC'05*, pp.553–562, 2005.
2. N. Alon and Y. Roichman. Random Cayley graphs and expanders. *Random Structures Appl.*, 5:271–284, 1994.
3. Y. Aumann and Y. Rabani. An $O(\log k)$ Approximate min-cut max-flow theorem and approximation algorithm. *SIAM Journal on Computing*, 27(1):291–301, 1998.
4. Jean Bourgain. On Lipschitz embeddings of finite metric spaces in Hilbert space. *Israel Journal of Mathematics*, 52(1-2):46–52, 1985.
5. S.Chawla, A.Gupta, H.Rcke. Embeddings of negative-type metrics and an improved approximation to generalized sparsest cut. in Proceedings of the 16'th Annual ACM-SIAM Symposium on Discrete Algorithms, SODA'05., pp. 102-111, 2005.
6. A.Gupta, R.Krauthgamer, J.Lee. Bounded Geometries, Fractals, and Low-Distortion Embeddings. in *Proceedings of the 44th Annual Symposium on Foundations of CS, FOCS'03*, pp. 534-543, 2003.
7. J. Justesen, A class of constructive asymptotically good algebraic codes, *IEEE Transactions on Information*, 18:652-656, 1972.
8. S.Khot, A.Naor. Nonembeddability theorems via Fourier analysis. in *Proceedings of 46th Annual Symposium of FOCS 2005*:101-112, 2005.
9. P.Klein, S.Plotkin, and S.Rao. Excluded minors, network decomposition, and multicommodity flow. In *Proceedings of the 25th Annual ACM Symposium on Theory of Computing*, pages 682–690, 1993.
10. Nathan Linial, Eran London, and Yuri Rabinovich. The geometry of graphs and some of its algorithmic applications. *Combinatorica*, 15(2):215–245, 1995.
11. J.Matousek. Lectures on Discrete Geometry. Springer, 2002.
12. N.Linial, A.Wigderson Expander Graphs and their Applications. Bulletin of the American Math. Society, 43(4):439-561, 2006.
13. A.Wigderson, D.Xiao. Derandomizing the AW matrix-valued Chernoff bound using pessimistic estimators and applications. Electronic Colloquium on Computational Complexity, Report TR06-105, ISSN 1433-8092, 13th Year, 105th Report.

Broadcasting vs. Mixing and Information Dissemination on Cayley Graphs*

Robert Elsässer and Thomas Sauerwald

University of Paderborn
Institute for Computer Science
33102 Paderborn, Germany
{elsa,sauerwal}@upb.de

Abstract. One frequently studied problem in the context of information dissemination in communication networks is the broadcasting problem. In this paper, we study the following randomized broadcasting protocol: At some time t an information r is placed at one of the nodes of a graph G. In the succeeding steps, each informed node chooses one neighbor, independently and uniformly at random, and informs this neighbor by sending a copy of r to it.

First, we consider the relationship between randomized broadcasting and random walks on graphs. In particular, we prove that the runtime of the algorithm described above is upper bounded by the corresponding mixing time, up to a logarithmic factor. One key ingredient of our proofs is the analysis of a continuous-type version of the afore mentioned algorithm, which might be of independent interest. Then, we introduce a general class of Cayley graphs, including (among others) Star graphs, Transposition graphs, and Pancake graphs. We show that randomized broadcasting has optimal runtime on all graphs belonging to this class. Finally, we develop a new proof technique by combining martingale tail estimates with combinatorial methods. Using this approach, we show the optimality of our algorithm on another Cayley graph and obtain new knowledge about the runtime distribution on several Cayley graphs.

1 Introduction

Models and Motivation: The study of information spreading in large networks has various fields of application in distributed computing. Consider for example the maintenance of replicated databases on name servers in a large network [9]. There are updates injected at various nodes, and these updates must be propagated to all the nodes in the network. In each step, a processor and its neighbors check whether their copies of the database agree, and if not, they perform the necessary updates. In order to be able to let all copies of the database converge to the same content, efficient broadcasting algorithms have to be developed.

---

* This work was partially supported by German Science Foundation (DFG) Research Training Group GK-693 of the Paderborn Institute for Scientific Computation (PaSCo) and by the EU within the 6th Framework Programme under contract 001907 "Dynamically Evolving, Large Scale Information Systems" (DELIS).

W. Thomas and P. Weil (Eds.): STACS 2007, LNCS 4393, pp. 163–174, 2007.

There is an enormous amount of experimental and theoretical study of broadcasting algorithms in various models and on different networks. Several (deterministic and randomized) algorithms have been developed and analyzed. In this paper we only concentrate on the efficiency of randomized broadcasting and study the runtime of the *push model* [9] defined as follows. Place at some time t an information r on one of the nodes of a graph $G = (V, E)$. Then, in each succeeding time step, any *informed* vertex forwards a copy of r to a communication partner over an incident edge selected independently and uniformly at random. The advantage of randomized broadcasting is in its inherent robustness against several kinds of failures and dynamical changes compared to deterministic schemes that either need substantially more time [15] or can tolerate only a relatively small number of faults [19].

In this work we are particulary interested in the runtime of the push algorithm on *Cayley graphs*. A Cayley graph is given by a finite group $\mathfrak{G}$ and a set of generators $S \subseteq \mathfrak{G}$. The vertices are the group elements and there is an edge from an element a to an element b iff if $a = bs$ in $\mathfrak{G}$ for a generator $s \in S$.

This group theoretic model is often used for designing, analyzing, and improving symmetric interconnection networks. In designing interconnection networks, the objective is to construct large (vertex symmetric) graphs with small degree and diameter, high connectivity, and simple routing algorithms. Prominent examples that offer all these properties together are the Hypercube and the Star graph [1]. Other examples are explicit constructions of so called Ramanujan graphs, which are also obtained by using this group theoretic model [20].

An advantadge of analyzing Cayley graphs is that properties can be proved for the class as a whole, instead of proving some property for each network independently. Moreover, even for specific networks we can often derive properties algebraically and interpret them graph theoretically.

Related Work: Most papers dealing with randomized broadcasting analyze the runtime of the push algorithm in different graph classes. Pittel [21] proved that with a certain probability an information is spread to all nodes by the push algorithm within $\log_2 N + \ln N + O(1)$ steps in a complete graph K_N. Feige et al.[14] determined asymptotically optimal upper bounds for the runtime of this algorithm on random graphs, hypercubes and bounded degree graphs. In [12] we extended the results to Star graphs [2,1], i.e. after $O(\log N)$ steps any information is spread to all of the N nodes with high probability[1].

We should also note that several broadcasting models have been analyzed in some scenarios that allow nodes and/or edges to fail during the algorithm is executed (e.g. [18]). Most of these papers deal with the worst case asymptotic behavior of broadcasting algorithms when the failures are governed by an adversary, however, in some papers the random failure scenario is also considered. In [13] we established a robustness result w.r.t. the push algorithm against random failures in general graphs.

---

[1] When we write "with high probability" or "w.h.p." we mean with probability at least $1 - 1/N$. Accordingly, "with constant probability" or "w.c.p." means with probability at least $1 - O(1) > 0$.

Intuitively, rapid mixing implies fast broadcasting, but there is no (strong) bound on the runtime of the push algorithm, which uses mixing rates of Markov chains. In contrast to the push algorithm, mixing has been extensively studied in the past (e.g. [22,7,10,4]). Thus, one of our goals is to derive efficient bounds on the runtime of the push algorithm by using mixing rates of Markov chains.

There is also a long history of the analysis of Markov chains on Cayley graphs. Consider for example the so called *card shuffling process*. The main question is how many times must a deck of cards be shuffled until it is close to random. Using different shuffling rules, the problem reduces to random walks on certain Cayley graphs. We will give examples for card shuffling procedures in Section 5.

Our Results: The next section contains the basic notations and definitions needed in our further analysis. In Section 3 we show that the runtime of the broadcasting algorithm is upper bounded by the mixing time of the corresponding Markov chain, up to a logarithmic factor. Section 4 contains the introduction of a new class of graphs which contains prominent examples of Cayley graphs. It is shown that the push algorithm has an optimal runtime on all these graphs. Finally, in Section 5 we develop a powerful approach which enables us to extend the optimality results mentioned before. This technique combines Azuma-Hoefding type bounds with structural analysis of graphs. The last section contains our conclusions and points to some open problems. Due to space limitations, several proofs are omitted in this extended abstract.

2   Notation and Definitions

Let $G = (V(G), E(G))$ denote an unweighted, undirected, simple and connected graph, where $N := |V|$ denotes the size of the graph. In most cases, we will consider families of graphs $G(n) = (V_n, E_n)$, where $|V_n| \to \infty$ for $n \to \infty$. By $\mathrm{diam}(G)$ we denote the diameter of G and $N(v)$ is the neighbourhood of some vertex $v \in V(G)$. For an arbitrary vertex $u \in V(G)$, we denote by $N_r(u) := \{v \in V(G) \mid \mathrm{dist}(u, v) \le r\}$ the r-neighborhood around u. Furthermore, let δ be the minimum and Δ be the maximum degree.

Definition 1. *For any graph G and any integer $m \in \{1, \dots, \lfloor N/2 \rfloor\}$ define $E(m) = \min_{X \subseteq V(G), |X|=m} |E(X, X^c)|/|X|$. Here, $E(X, X^c)$ denotes the set of edges connecting X and its complement X^c.*

As mentioned in the introduction, in this paper we mainly consider the following randomized broadcasting algorithm (known as the push model [9]): Place at time $t = 0$ an information r on one of the nodes of the graph G. In the succeeding time steps (or rounds) each *informed* vertex forwards a copy of r to a communication partner over an incident edge selected independently and uniformly at random.

This algorithm will be shortly abbreviated by RBA$_d$, where d indicates that the time steps are discrete numbers (In Section 3 and 5 we will introduce some slightly modified versions of this algorithm). Throughout this paper, we denote by $I(t)$ the set of informed nodes at time t, and by $H(t)$ the set $V \setminus I(t)$.

Our main objective is to determine how many time steps are required to inform every node of G. Let $\mathsf{RT_d}(G,p) := \min\{t \in \mathbb{N} \mid \mathbf{Pr}\,[\,I(t) = V\,] \geq p\}$ denote the runtime of $\mathsf{RBA_d}$ in G, i.e. the number of time steps needed by the push algorithm to inform all vertices of G with probability p. Since every broadcasting algorithm requires $\max\{\log_2 N, \mathrm{diam}(G)\}$ rounds [14], we call $\mathsf{RBA_d}$ (asymptotically) optimal on G, if $\mathsf{RT_d}(G, 1 - 1/N) = O(\log N + \mathrm{diam}(G))$.

In the following, we will use basic notation of algebraic graph theory (cf. [5]).

Definition 2. *A (directed) Cayley graph $G = (\mathfrak{G}, S)$ is given by a finite group $\mathfrak{G}$ and a generating set $S = \{s_1, \ldots, s_n\}$. The set of vertices consists of elements of $\mathfrak{G}$ and there is an directed edge from u to v if and only if there exists a generator $s_i \in S$ such that $u = vs_i$.*

If the set of generators is closed under inverses, i.e. $S^{-1} = S$ (which will be always the case in this paper), the resulting Cayley graph $G = (\mathfrak{G}, S)$ can be also viewed as an undirected graph. In the following, $\mathfrak{G}_n$ will be always the symmetric group of n elements, denoted by $\mathfrak{S}_n$. For any distinct numbers $k_1, \ldots, k_i \in [1, n]$ let $\mathfrak{S}_n(k_1, \ldots, k_i) := \{\pi(n - i + j) = k_j, j \in \{1, \ldots, i\} \mid \pi \in \mathfrak{S}_n\}$.

3   Broadcasting vs. Mixing

In this section we are going to show that rapid mixing implies fast broadcasting. It will be important to consider a slightly different broadcasting algorithm, called $\mathsf{RBA_s}$ (s for subtimesteps) which is defined as follows.

In this model, the time axis is $\mathbb{T} = \mathbb{N} + \{i/N \mid i \in \{0, \ldots, N - 1\}\}$ At such a (sub)timestep $t \in \mathbb{T}$, one node of $V(G)$ is chosen uniformly at random and this node, provided that it is already informed, sends the information to some neighbor, again chosen uniformly at random. This model has the advantage that the waiting times between the transmission of some informed node are geometrically distributed with mean 1 and thus are oblivious. Denote by $\mathsf{RT_s}(G, 1 - 1/N)$ the runtime of this modified broadcasting algorithm. We say that a node $u \in V$ makes a transmission at time t, if node u is chosen by $\mathsf{RBA_s}$ at timestep t and sends the information to some neighbor.

The following theorem shows the equivalence of both introduced variants.

Theorem 1. *For any G we have $\mathsf{RT_s}(G, 1 - 1/N) = \Theta(\mathsf{RT_d}(G, 1 - 1/N))$.*

In order to derive a strong relationship between mixing and broadcasting, we first define the following Markov chain $\mathfrak{M}$ on a graph $G = (V, E)$. $\mathfrak{M}$ has state space $V(G)$, and its transition matrix is given by P where $p_{ii} = 1 - \alpha \deg(i)$, $p_{ij} = \alpha$ if $\{i, j\} \in E(G)$ and $p_{ij} = 0$ otherwise. Hereby, we set $\alpha = 1/(\Delta + 1)$ with Δ being the maximum degree in G. (P also corresponds to the diffusion matrix occurring in load balancing [11].) It is well-known that for our choice of α, the Markov chain $\mathfrak{M}$ is ergodic and reversible [11,22]. As usual, for any $k \in \mathbb{N}$, P^k denotes the k-step transition matrix.

For two given probability vectors $(\mu_i)_{i=1}^N$ and $(\nu_i)_{i=1}^N$ let

$$\|\mu - \nu\| = \frac{1}{2} \sum_{i=1}^N |\mu_i - \nu_i| = \max_{V' \subseteq V(G)} |\mu_{V'} - \nu_{V'}|$$

be the variation distance of these vectors [10]. Furthermore, we denote by

$$\text{MIX}_{\mathfrak{M}}(G, \epsilon) := \min\{t \in \mathbb{N} \mid \|P^t z - \pi\| \le \epsilon \text{ for any probability vector } z\},$$

the mixing time (or mixing rate) of $\mathfrak{M}$. Observe that due to the proper choices of the p_{ii}'s, the vector $(1/N, \dots, 1/N)$ is the stationary distribution corresponding to P. $\mathfrak{M}$ can be viewed as the Markov chain corresponding to a random walk on G, in which the transition probabilities are defined according to P.

Now we define the following random process on the graph G. Assume first that there are N indivisible unit size tokens $x_1, \dots, x_N$ distributed somehow on the nodes of the graph. At each time $t \in \{i + k/N \mid i \in \mathbb{N}, k \in \{0, \dots, N-1\}\}$ we choose one node of the graph, uniformly at random, and one of the tokens on this node is allowed to perform a transition according to the matrix P. Hereby, each token of any node has a priority value, and when a node is chosen, then only the token with highest priority on this node is allowed to perform the transition described above. At the beginning, the tokens on any node u are assigned priority values in the range $[1, l(0, u)]$ arbitrarily, where $l(0, u)$ denotes the *load* (i.e., the number of tokens) on node u at time 0. When a token x_j performs a transition according to P from some node u to node v, then x_j is assigned, after the transition, the lowest priority among all tokens being on v (please note that v and u might coincide).

According to the description above, let $h(t, x_j)$ denote the host of token x_j at time t. Furthermore, let $l(t, u)$ denote the load of any node $u \in V$ at time t.

We are now ready to define another Markov chain $\mathfrak{M}'$ based on the random process described above. $\mathfrak{M}'$ has state space $S(\mathfrak{M}') = \{(l(1), \dots, l(N)) \mid 0 \le l(i) \in \mathbb{N}, \sum_{i=1}^N l(i) = N\}$, and transition matrix P', where $p'_{i,j} = \alpha/N$ if there are two states s and s' such that $s = (l(1), \dots, l(i), \dots, l(j), \dots, l(N))$, $s' = (l(1), \dots, l(i) + 1, \dots, l(j) - 1, \dots, l(N))$, where $l(j) \ge 1$, and $\{i, j\} \in E$. Obviously, the Markov chain $\mathfrak{M}'$ simulates the random process described in the previous paragraphs. Since the transition matrix P' is symmetric, the stationary distribution equals the uniform distribution. Thus, the expected number of tokens equals 1 on each node in the stationary state.

Now we use the Markov chains introduced above to show the following.

Theorem 2. *For any graph $G = (V, E)$ it holds*

$$\text{RT}_s\left(G, 1 - \frac{1}{N}\right) \le O\left(\text{MIX}_{\mathfrak{M}}\left(G, \frac{1}{2N}\right) \cdot \log N\right).$$

Proof. For simplicity, let $m := \text{MIX}_{\mathfrak{M}}(G, 1/(2N))$. First, we show that if there are $\log N \le |I(t)| \le N/2$ informed nodes at timestep t, then there will exist $(1 + \Omega(1))|I(t)|$ informed nodes at timestep $t + m$, w.c.p. In this proof we derive a relationship between $\mathsf{RT_s}(G, 1 - 1/N)$ and the Markov chain $\mathfrak{M}'$, and show that by using $\mathfrak{M}'$ the information can be spread in time $O(m \cdot \log N)$ in G.

Now we consider the Markov chain $\mathfrak{M}$. We assume that there are N tokens distributed according to the stationary distribution of $\mathfrak{M}'$ at some time t. Let I be a fixed, connected set of nodes in G with $\log N \leq |I| \leq N/2$. Let $\mathcal{A}$ be set of tokens lying in I at timestep t, i.e., $\mathcal{A} := \{x_i \mid h(t, x_i) \in I\}$. Since $\mathbf{E}\left[\,|\mathcal{A}|\,\right] = |I|$, applying the Chernoff bounds [17], we get $\mathbf{Pr}\left[\,|\mathcal{A}| \geq |I|/2\,\right] \geq 1 - \exp(-\Omega(|I|))$.

We fix some token x_i on one of these nodes, and let this token perform a random walk according to P. Now we know that $\|P^m z - \pi\| \leq 1/(2N)$ for any probability vector z.

Let $D(i)$ denote the host of token x_i at time $t + m$ for some random instance $\mathcal{I}$ of $\mathfrak{M}$. Then, define

$$\mathcal{B} := \{x_i \in \mathcal{A} \mid D(i) \in H\}, \quad \mathcal{C} := \left\{x_i \in \mathcal{A} \mid |\{D(i) = D(j) \mid j \neq i\}| \leq 32\right\},$$

where $H = V \setminus I$. Due to (1) we have $\mathbf{Pr}\left[x_i \in \mathcal{B}\right] \geq \frac{N - |I|}{N} - \frac{1}{2N} \geq \frac{7}{16}$, whenever $|I| \leq N/2$ and $\mathbf{Pr}\left[x_i \in \mathcal{C}\right] \leq \binom{N}{32}\left(\frac{3}{2N}\right)^{32} \leq \frac{1}{1024}$. Again, by the Markov inequality we obtain that $\mathbf{Pr}\left[\,|\mathcal{B}| \geq 1/4|\mathcal{A}|\,\right] \geq 1/4$ and $\mathbf{Pr}\left[\,|\mathcal{C}| \geq 31/32|\mathcal{A}|\,\right] \geq 31/32$.

Now we consider the walks performed by all tokens according to $\mathfrak{M}'$, and take into account the delays induced by other tokens. We assume that at time t these tokens are distributed according to the stationary state of $\mathfrak{M}'$. Let $u_{i,t}, \ldots, u_{i,t+m}$ be the nodes visited by some fixed token x_i in steps $t, \ldots, t + m$, respectively, according to $\mathfrak{M}$ and instance $\mathcal{I}$. Let $f(u_{i,k})$ denote the number of time intervals $[j, j+1]$ in which node $u_{i,k}$ is not chosen by the random process described above while x_i resides on $u_{i,k}$. Since a node is not chosen in time interval $[j, j+1]$ with probability $(1 - 1/N)^N \approx 1/e$, the expected delay of token x_i is

$$\mathbf{E}\left[\Delta(i)\right] \leq \sum_{k=t}^{t+m} \mathbf{E}\left[l(u_{i,k}) + f(u_{i,k})\right] = \sum_{k=t}^{t+m} \mathbf{E}\left[\frac{e \cdot l(u_{i,k})}{e - 1}\right] \leq \frac{e(m+1)}{e - 1},$$

where $l(u_{i,k})$ is the load of node $u_{i,k}$ at the time when token x_i makes a transition to node $u_{i,k}$. Hence, token x_i reaches its destination after $32e(m+1)/(e-1) + m$ rounds, according to $\mathfrak{M}$ and instance $\mathcal{I}$, with probability at least $31/32$.

Now let $\mathcal{D} := \{x_i \mid \Delta(i) \leq 32e(m + 1)/(e - 1) \text{ and } x_i \in \mathcal{A}\}$, i.e., the set of tokens of A which reach their final destination after at most $32e \cdot (m + 1)/(e - 1) + m$ steps. Since $\mathbf{E}\left[\,|\mathcal{C}|\,\right] \geq |\mathcal{A}| \cdot 31/32$, the Markov inequality implies that $\mathbf{Pr}\left[\,|\mathcal{D}| \geq 13/16|\mathcal{A}|\,\right] \geq 5/6$. Putting all together, we get by the union bound

$$\mathbf{Pr}\left[|\mathcal{A}| \geq \frac{1}{2}|I| \;\wedge\; |\mathcal{B}| \geq \frac{3}{4}|\mathcal{A}| \;\wedge\; |\mathcal{C}| \geq \frac{31}{32}|\mathcal{A}| \;\wedge\; |\mathcal{D}| \geq \frac{13}{16}|\mathcal{A}|\right] \geq \frac{1}{32},$$

provided that N is large enough. Since $\mathcal{B}$, $\mathcal{C}$ and $\mathcal{D}$ are all subsets of $\mathcal{A}$ we have $|\mathcal{B} \cap \mathcal{C}| \geq |\mathcal{A}| - |\mathcal{A} \setminus \mathcal{B}| - |\mathcal{A} \setminus \mathcal{C}| - |\mathcal{A} \setminus \mathcal{D}| \geq |\mathcal{A}| - \frac{3}{4}|\mathcal{A}| - \frac{1}{32}|\mathcal{A}| - \frac{3}{16}|\mathcal{A}| = \frac{1}{32}|\mathcal{A}|$. Hence, at least $|\mathcal{A}|/32 \cdot 1/32 = |\mathcal{A}|/1024$ nodes of H will host a token of $\mathcal{A}$ within the time interval $[t, t + m + 32e(m + 1)/(e - 1)]$, with probability $1/32$.

Now we consider $\mathsf{RT_s}(G, 1 - 1/N)$. Since any node in the random process described by $\mathfrak{M}'$ forwards a token (according to P) in some substep iff there is a token on this node, $\mathsf{RT_s}$ is able to spread an information faster than the tokens, which perform movements according to $\mathfrak{M}'$. Hence, $|I(t + O(m))| = (1 + \Omega(1))|I(t)|$, whenever $\log N \leq |I(t)| \leq \frac{N}{2}$.

Similar techniques imply that $|H(t + O(m))| \leq (1 - \Omega(1))|H(t)|$, whenever $\log N \leq |H(t)| \leq \frac{N}{2}$. If $|I(t)| \leq O(\log N)$ or $|I(t)| \geq N - O(\log N)$, then w.c.p. at least one single node becomes informed in some step $t + O(m)$. Applying now the Chernoff bounds [6,17], we obtain the theorem. $\qquad\qquad\square$

However, for $G = K_{N/2} \times C_2$ we have $\mathsf{MIX}(G, 1/(2N)) = \Omega(N)$, but $\mathsf{RT_d}(G, 1 - 1/N) = \Theta(\log N)$ and thus a similar converse of Theorem 2 does not hold.

4   Broadcasting on Cayley Graphs

In this section we will prove that the $\mathsf{RBA_d}$ performs optimal on a certain class of Cayley Graphs which includes the Star Graph, Pancake Graph and Transposition Graph.

A vertex $v \in V$ in a graph $G = (V, E)$ is called α-approximated by the set $I(t)$, if $N_\alpha(v) \cap I(t) \neq \emptyset$. Furthermore, a vertex $v \in V$ is called contacted by a node $u \in V$ within some time interval $[a, b]$ (or conversely, u contacts v in time interval $[a, b]$) if there is a path $(u = u_1, u_2, \ldots, u_{m-1}, u_m = v)$ in V such that

$$\exists t_1 < t_2 < \cdots < t_{m-1} \in [a, b] \subseteq \mathbb{N} : \forall i \in [1, m-1] : u_i \text{ contacts } u_{i+1} \text{ in round } t_i.$$

Now we are ready to state the following theorem.

Theorem 3. *Assume that a family of Cayley graphs $G_n = (\mathfrak{S}_n, S_n)$ has the following properties:*

1. *for any $n \in \mathbb{N}$ it holds that $c_1 n^c \leq d(n) \leq c_2 n^c$, where $d(n)$ denotes the degree of G_n and $c_1, c_2, c \in \Theta(1)$,*
2. *$S_n \subseteq S_{n+1}$ for any $n \in \mathbb{N}$,*
3. *$\text{dist}(\tau, \mathfrak{S}_n(k)) := \min\{\text{dist}(\tau, \tau') \mid \tau' \in \mathfrak{S}_n(k)\} \leq c'$ for any $\tau \in \mathfrak{S}_n$, and $k \in [1, n]$, where c' is a constant,*
4. *$E(m) = \Omega(d(n))$ for any $m = O(n^{c \cdot c'})$.*

Then it holds that

$$\mathsf{RT_d}(G_n, 1 - \frac{1}{N}) \leq O(\log N).$$

Proof. Since any Cayley graph is vertex-transitive [5], we may assume w.l.o.g. that the identity id is informed at the beginning. The proof is divided into two parts. In the first part, we will show that after $t = O(\log N)$ steps it holds for any vertex $w \in V$ that $N_{\alpha n}(w) \cap I(t) \neq \emptyset$, w.h.p., where α is a properly chosen constant. This approximation will consist of $\beta := (1 - \alpha)n$ disjoint phases $\mathcal{P}_1, \ldots, \mathcal{P}_\beta$. To simplify notation let $\mathfrak{S}_n(i) := \mathfrak{S}_n(w_{n-i}, \ldots, w_n)$. Phase $\mathcal{P}_i$, $i \in \{1, \ldots, \beta\}$, begins when a node of $\mathfrak{S}_n(i - 1)$ becomes informed for the first time, and ends when the information jumps from the set $\mathfrak{S}_n(i - 1) \setminus \mathfrak{S}_n(i)$ to the set $\mathfrak{S}_n(i)$. Let X_i denote the random variable which represents the number of time steps needed by phase $\mathcal{P}_i$. Now, our goal is to derive an upper bound on X_i for an arbitrary fixed $i \in \{1, \ldots, \beta\}$.

First we count the number of steps needed to inform $\Omega(d(n)^{c'})$ vertices of $\mathfrak{S}_n(i-1)$. Since $i \leq (1-\alpha)n$, $S_{n-i} \subset S_n$, and $d(n-i) \geq c_1(n-i)^c$, each node of $\mathfrak{S}_n(i-1)$ has $\Omega(d(n))$ neighbors in $\mathfrak{S}_n(i-1)$. Due to assumption (4), a constant fraction of these inner edges, incident to nodes of $\mathfrak{S}_n(i-1) \cap I(t)$, are connected to nodes of $\mathfrak{S}_n(i-1) \cap H(t)$. Now, let p_v denote the probability that some node $v \in \mathfrak{S}_n(i-1) \cap H(t)$ becomes informed in step $t+1$. Since $p_v = d_{I(t)}(v)/d(n)$, where $d_{I(t)}(v)$ denotes the number of neighbors of v in $I(t)$, it holds that

$$\mathbf{E}\left[|(I(t+1) \setminus I(t)) \cap \mathfrak{S}_n(i-1)|\right] = \sum_{v \in \mathfrak{S}_n(i-1) \cap H(t)} \frac{d_{I(t)}(v)}{d(n)},$$

which equals $\Omega(|I(t) \cap \mathfrak{S}_n(i-1)|)$. This implies that

$$|I(t+1) \cap \mathfrak{S}_n(i-1)| \geq (1+\rho)|I(t) \cap \mathfrak{S}_n(i-1)|,$$

where $\rho = \Theta(1)$, w.c.p.

Now we assume that at some proper time t' it holds that $|I(t') \cap \mathfrak{S}_n(i-1)| \geq \delta d(n)^{c'}$, where δ is a constant. Due to assumption (3), we know that for all $v \in \mathfrak{S}_n(i-1)$ the distance to $\mathfrak{S}_n(i)$ is at most c'.

Let us now consider the propagation of the information in $\mathfrak{S}_n(i-1)$ towards $\mathfrak{S}_n(i)$. Recall, that from each node $v \in I(t') \cap \mathfrak{S}_n(i-1)$ exists a path to some node in $\mathfrak{S}_n(i)$ of length at most c'.

Now define $\mathcal{L}_1 := I(t') \cap \mathfrak{S}_n(i-1)$, $\mathcal{L}_2 := \{w \in \mathfrak{S}_n(i-1) \mid \text{dist}(w, \mathfrak{S}_n(i))) = c' - 1\}, \ldots, \mathcal{L}_{c'+1} := \mathfrak{S}_n(i)$. Assume w.l.o.g. that for each node $v \in I(t') \cap \mathfrak{S}_n(i-1)$ it holds $v \in \mathcal{L}_1$. Observe that $|\mathcal{L}_2| \geq |\mathcal{L}_1|/d(n)$, and generally $|\mathcal{L}_j| \geq \max\{1, |\mathcal{L}_1|/(d(n))^{j-1}\}$ for any j. Since any node of $\mathcal{L}_j$ has a neighbor in $\mathcal{L}_{j+1}$, and a node v of $\mathcal{L}_{j+1}$ becomes informed in some step $t''+1$ with probability $d_{I(t'')}(v)/d(n)$, it holds that

$$\mathbf{E}\left[|\mathcal{L}_{j+1} \cap I(t''+1)|\right] = \sum_{v \in \mathcal{L}_{j+1}} \frac{d_{I(t'')}(v)}{d(n)} \geq \frac{|\mathcal{L}_j \cap I(t'')|}{d(n)}$$

which implies $|\mathcal{L}_{j+1} \cap I(t' + O(1))| \geq \delta d(n)^{c'-j}$, w.c.p., provided that $|\mathcal{L}_j \cap I(t' + O(1))| \geq \delta d(n)^{c'-j+1}$. Summarizing, the time needed to complete $\mathcal{P}_i$ can be modelled by a sum of $O(\log d(n)^{c'} + c') = O(\log d(n))$ independent geometrically distributed random variables with constant mean. Recall, that we have $O(n)$ phases. Thus, applying the Chernoff-Bound [6,17] we conclude that some fixed vertex w is αn-approximated within $t_1 := O(n \log d(n)^{c'})$ steps with probability $1 - O(1/N^2)$. Using the Markov inequality we conclude that each vertex of G is αn-approximated at time t_1, w.h.p.

Using the techniques of [14] we obtain

$$|I(t_1)| \geq \frac{n!}{d(n)^{\alpha n+1}} \geq \frac{n!}{n^{(\alpha n+1)c}} \geq n^{n-2\alpha cn}.$$

Furthermore, to obtain a subset of informed nodes $\mathcal{A} \subseteq I(t_1)$ which only contains vertices being at distance at least αn from each other we get by the same arguments that $|\mathcal{A}| \geq |I(t_1)|/(d(n)^{\alpha n+1}) \geq n^{n-4\alpha nc}$.

Using similar arguments as above, it can be shown that for any pair of vertices $v, w \in V$ and any time t_2, there is a vertex $w' \in N_{\alpha n/2}(w)$ which contacts v within time interval $[t_2, t_2 + O(n \log d(n))]$, w.h.p.

In order to finish the proof we use similar techniques as in [12] which are omitted here due to space limitations. $\square$

It is now not too difficult to see that the class given in the previous theorem includes the following three well-known representatives of Cayley graphs.

Remark 1. The Star graph, Pancake graph and Transposition graph [2,1] satisfy the conditions of the Theorem 3.

5   A New Martingale-Based Technique

Definition 3. *[2] The Bubble sort graph is defined as* $B(n) = (\mathfrak{S}_n, S_n)$, *where* $S_n = \{(i\ (i+1)) \mid i \in \{1, \ldots, n-1\}\}$.

Since the diameter of a Bubble sort graph is obviously $\Omega(n^2)$, Theorem 3 is not applicable and new techniques have to be developed. First, we briefly summarize the research history of related random processes on these graphs.

In spite of very refined techniques designed for the analysis of shuffling cards procedures, the mixing time of the Bubble sort graph has been an open question for almost two decades. Finally in 2002, Wilson proved the mixing time $\Theta(n^3 \log n)$ which is asymptotically tight up to a small constant factor [23].

Additionally, Diaconis and Ram considered the following generalization. First, fix some parameter $p \in (0, 1)$. In each step, choose uniformly at random one pair of adjacent cards and flip a coin that is heads with probability p. If the coin comes up heads, then arrange the cards in the correct order. Otherwise, arrange them in the reverse order.

For $1/2 < p \leq 1$ this shuffling card procedure models a randomized version of Bubble sort. In particular, the stationary distribution of this Markov chain is no longer uniform. Rather surprisingly, Benjami et.al. [4] proved very recently that the mixing time decreases to $O(n^2)$ if $p \neq \frac{1}{2}$ and thereby affirmed a conjecture of Diaconis and Ram. To follow the notation of Benjami et.al., denote by $\mathcal{DA}(n, p)$ the aforementioned card shuffling procedure. Then their result can be formally stated as follows. For any $p > 1/2$ it holds $\mathsf{MIX}_{\mathcal{DA}(n,p)}(e^{-1}) \leq O(n^2)$. On the other hand, there is no cutoff [10] known yet. Thus, it is an open question of what magnitude is $\mathsf{MIX}_{\mathcal{DA}(n,p)}(1 - o(1))$. However, by transferring the result of Benjami et.al. to $\mathsf{RBA_s}$ and using refined martingale techniques, we will prove a tight concentration of the distribution of the runtime $\mathsf{RT_s}(G)$ around its mean.

Since $\mathsf{RBA_s}$ can simulate $\mathcal{DA}(n, p)$ we obtain the following result.

Lemma 1. $\mathsf{RBA_s}$ *informs some fixed node* v *within* $O(n^2)$ *rounds w.c.p.*

Our objective is to extend the Lemma above such that all nodes become informed after $O(n^2)$ rounds w.h.p.

To simplify the notation, we will analyze a slightly modified version of RBA_s, denoted by RBA_s'. Here, in each time step $t = 1, 2, \ldots \in \mathbb{N}$ one node is chosen uniformly at random and sends the information to some randomly chosen neighbor provided that it is already informed. Obviously, this is just a scaling of the time axis by a factor of N compared to RBA_s.

In the following, we fix some node $v \in V$. We make use of the following doob martingale [3] (sometimes also called exposure martingale). Let $Z_0 := \mathbf{E}\left[RT_s'(v)\right]$, where $RT_s'(v)$ is the random variable representing the runtime required to inform v. Furthermore define $Z_t := \mathbf{E}\left[RT_s'(v) \mid I(0), \ldots, I(t)\right] = \mathbf{E}\left[RT_s'(v) \mid I(t)\right]$. Thus, Z_t estimates the runtime conditioned on the set of informed nodes at time step t. Note that Z_t is a (random) function depending on $I(t)$. Moreover, if $Z_t \leq t$, then v has been informed and the sequence $Z_t, Z_{t+1}, \ldots$ becomes stationary. Additionally, for any two subsets $A \subseteq B \subseteq V$ we have

$$\mathbf{E}\left[RT_s'(v) \mid I(t) = A\right] \geq \mathbf{E}\left[RT_s'(v) \mid I(t) = B\right], \tag{1}$$

$$\mathbf{E}\left[RT_s'(v) \mid I(t-1) = A\right] + 1 = \mathbf{E}\left[RT_s'(v) \mid I(t) = A\right]. \tag{2}$$

Another building block will be the following concentration inequality.

Theorem 4. [8] Let $Z_0 \ldots, Z_t$ be a martingale w.r.t. the sequence $I(0), \ldots, I(t)$ such that for $1 \leq k \leq t$ it holds $|Z_k - Z_{k-1}| \leq M$, $\mathbf{Var}\left[Z_k \mid I(0), \ldots, I(k-1)\right] \leq \sigma_k^2$. Then for all $t \geq 0$ and $\lambda > 0$, $\mathbf{Pr}\left[|Z_t - Z_0| \geq \lambda\right] \leq 2e^{-\lambda^2/(\sum_{k=1}^t \sigma_k^2 + M\lambda/3)}$.

Let $RT_s'(u, v) := \min\{t \in \mathbb{N} \cup \{0\} \mid u \in I(t)\}$ conditioned on $I(0) = \{v\}$. and $\beta(G) := \max_{(u,v) \in E(G)} \mathbf{E}\left[RT_s'(u, v)\right]$. The following lemma improves the trivial bound $\beta(G) \leq \Delta(G) \cdot N$ for several graphs.

Lemma 2. Let G be any d-regular graph. If for any two adjacent nodes $u, v \in V$ there exist $\Theta(d)$ node-disjoint paths of length at most 3, then $\beta(G) \leq O(d^{2/3}N)$.

Note that the Transposition graph, Bubble sort graph and Hypercube satisfy the condition of this lemma. The following theorem relates the distribution of $Z_k - Z_{k-1}$ conditioned on Z_{k-1} to the combinatorial value $\beta(G)$.

Theorem 5. For any graph $G = (V, E)$ we have for all $k \in \mathbb{N} \backslash \{0\}$

$$-\beta(G) \leq Z_k - Z_{k-1} \leq 1 \quad and \quad \mathbf{Var}\left[Z_k \mid I(k-1)\right] \leq \beta(G).$$

Proof. Assume that $I(k-1) = I$ for a fixed I. We consider now two cases. In case of $I(k) = I$ we get $Z_k = Z_{k-1} + 1$ by (2). Secondly, if $I(k) = I \cup \{v\}$ for some $v \in N(u) \cap I^c, u \in I$, then

$$\mathbf{E}\left[RT_s'(v) \mid I(k-1) = I\right] \overset{(1)}{\leq} \mathbf{E}\left[\min_{j \in \mathbb{N} \cup \{0\}} \{v \in I(k-1+j)\} \,\Big|\, I(k-1) = \{u\}\right]$$

$$+ \mathbf{E}\left[RT_s'(v) \mid I(k) = I \cup \{v\}\right]$$

$$\overset{(2)}{=} \mathbf{E}\left[\min_{j \in \mathbb{N} \cup \{0\}} \{v \in I(j)\} \,\Big|\, I(0) = \{u\}\right]$$

$$+ \mathbf{E}\left[RT_s'(v) \mid I(k) = I \cup \{v\}\right]$$

and thus $\mathbf{E}\left[\mathsf{RT_s}'(v) \mid I(k) = I \cup \{v\}\right] - \mathbf{E}\left[\mathsf{RT_s}'(v) \mid I(k-1) = I\right] \geq -\beta(G)$. By the first inequality we know that Z_k is a random variable whose values are all in the interval $[Z_{k-1} - \beta(G), Z_{k-1} + 1]$. Moreover, by the martingale property we have $\mathbf{E}\left[Z_k \mid I(k-1)\right] = Z_{k-1}$. Thus, by some standard upper bound on the variance [16] we finally obtain $\mathbf{Var}\left[Z_k\right] \leq |-\beta(G) \cdot 1| = \beta(G)$.   □

Note that in all previous results $\mathsf{RT_s}'(v)$ can be replaced by $\mathsf{RT_s}'(G)$.

Theorem 6. *It holds that* $\mathsf{RT_d}(B(n), 1 - \frac{1}{N}) = \Theta(n^2)$. *Moreover, for any* $x < 2$ *we have that* $\mathbf{Pr}\left[\mathsf{RT_s}(B(n)) \leq \mathbf{E}\left[\mathsf{RT_s}(B(n))\right] + n^x\right] \leq O(\exp(-n^{2x-8/3}))$.

Proof. Fix some arbitrary node $w \in V(B(n))$. Due to Lemma 2 we have that $\beta(B(n)) = O(n^{2/3}N)$. Consequently by Theorem 5 it holds $\mathbf{Var}\left[Z_i - Z_{i-1/N}\right] = O(n^{2/3}N)$ and $|Z_i - Z_{i-1/N}| = O(n^{2/3}N)$. Then we apply Theorem 4 with $t = \mathbf{E}\left[\mathsf{RT_s}'(v)\right]$, $\sigma_i^2 \leq O(n^{2/3}N)$, $\lambda := \mathbf{E}\left[\mathsf{RT_s}'(v)\right] := \gamma n^2 N$, where $\gamma(n) = O(1)$ is some bounded function and obtain

$$\mathbf{Pr}\left[|Z_{2\mathbf{E}[\mathsf{RT_s}'(v)]} - \mathbf{E}\left[\mathsf{RT_s}'(v)\right]| \geq \lambda\right] \leq 2e^{-\lambda^2/(\sum_{k=1}^t \sigma_k^2 + M\lambda/3)},$$

$$\mathbf{Pr}\left[|Z_{2\lambda} - \lambda| \geq \lambda\right] \leq 2e^{\frac{-\gamma^2 N^2 n^4}{2N\gamma n^2(n^{2/3}N) + \gamma \cdot n^2 N \cdot n^{2/3} \cdot N}},$$

$$\mathbf{Pr}\left[Z_{2\lambda} \leq 2\lambda\right] \leq O(e^{\frac{-n^{12/3}}{n^{8/3}}}) \leq O(e^{-n^{4/3}}) \leq 1 - \frac{1}{N^2}.$$

Thus after 2λ time steps, each single node of $B(n)$ has received the information with probability $1 - (1/N)^2$. Hence by Markovs inequality $\mathsf{RT_s}'(B(n), 1 - \frac{1}{N}) = \Theta(Nn^2)$. The second claim is shown similarly.   □

It is worth mentioning that with the same techniques similar, but weaker tail estimates can be proven for Hypercubes, Star graphs and Pancake graphs.

6   Conclusions

In this paper we developed a new relationship between broadcasting and random walks, and proved that randomized broadcasting has optimal runtime on several classes of Cayley graphs. However, it would be still interesting whether the additional logarithmic factor in Theorem 2 can be reduced. It is also an open question on which graphs fast broadcasting implies fast mixing, though this has to be a more restricted class. Although the techniques introduced in Section 4 seem to be powerful, we could not apply it to all Cayley graphs considered in this paper. Our hope is that incorporating edge-expansion-based approaches would extend the applicability of this method.

Acknowledgments

We thank Peter Bürgisser for helpful suggestions concerning Section 5.

References

1. S. Akers, D. Harel, and B. Krishnamurthy. The star graph: An attractive alternative to the n-cube. In *Proc. of ICPP'87*, pages 393–400, 1987.
2. S. Akers and B. Krishnamurthy. A group-theoretic model for symmetric innterconnection networks. In *Proc. of ICPP'86*, pages 555–565, 1986.
3. N. Alon and J. H. Spencer. *The Probabilistic Method*. Wiley-Interscience Series in Discrete Mathematics and Optimization, 2000.
4. I. Benjamini, N. Berger, C. Hoffmann, and E. Mossel. Mixing times of the biased card shuffling and the asymmetric exclusion process. *Transactions of the American Mathematical Society*, 357:3013–3029, 2005.
5. N. Biggs. *Algebraic Graph Theory*. Cambridge University Press, 1993.
6. H. Chernoff. A measure of asymptotic efficiency for tests of a hypothesis based on the sum of observations. *Ann. Math. Stat.*, 23:493–507, 1952.
7. F. Chung. *Spectral Graph Theory*, volume 92 of *CBMS Regional conference series in mathematics*. American Mathematical Society, 1997.
8. F. Chung and L. Lu. Concentration inequalities and martingale inequalities — a survey. *Internet Mathematics (to appear)*.
9. A. Demers, D. Greene, C. Hauser, W. Irish, J. Larson, S. Shenker, H. Sturgis, D. Swinehart, and D. Terry. Epidemic algorithms for replicated database maintenance. In *Proc. of PODC'87*, pages 1–12, 1987.
10. P. Diaconis. *Group Representations in Probability and Statistics*, volume 11. Lecture notes-Monograph Series, 1988.
11. R. Diekmann, A. Frommer, and B. Monien. Efficient schemes for nearest neighbor load balancing. *Parallel Computing*, 25(7):789–812, 1999.
12. R. Elsässer and T. Sauerwald. On randomized broadcasting in star graphs. In *Proc. of WG'05*, pages 307–318, 2005.
13. R. Elsässer and T. Sauerwald. On the runtime and robustness of randomized broadcasting. In *Proc. of ISAAC'06*, pages 349–358, 2006.
14. U. Feige, D. Peleg, P. Raghavan, and E. Upfal. Randomized broadcast in networks. *Random Structures and Algorithm*, I(4):447–460, 1990.
15. L. Gasieniec and A. Pelc. Adaptive broadcasting with faulty nodes. *Parallel Computing*, 22:903–912, 1996.
16. M. Habib, C. McDiarmid, J. Ramirez-Alfonsin, and B. Reed. *Probabilistic Methods for Algorithmic Discrete Mathematics*. Algorithms and Combinatorics, 1991.
17. T. Hagerup and C. Rüb. A guided tour of chernoff bounds. *Information Processing Letters*, 36(6):305–308, 1990.
18. J. Hromkovič, R. Klasing, A. Pelc, P. Ruzicka, and W. Unger. *Dissemination of Information in Communication Networks*. Springer, 2005.
19. F. Leighton, B. Maggs, and R. Sitamaran. On the fault tolerance of some popular bounded-degree networks. In *Proc. of FOCS'92*, pages 542–552, 1992.
20. A. Lubotzky, R. Phillips, and P. Sarnak. Ramanujan graphs. *Combinatorica*, 8(3):261–277, 1988.
21. B. Pittel. On spreading rumor. *SIAM Journal on Applied Mathematics*, 47(1):213–223, 1987.
22. A. Sinclair and M. Jerrum. Approximate counting, uniform generation, and rapidly mixing markov chains. *Inform. and Comput.*, 82:93–113, 1989.
23. D. Wilson. Mixing times of lozenge tiling and card shuffling markov chains. *Annals of Applied Probability*, 14:274–325, 2004.

Light Orthogonal Networks
with Constant Geometric Dilation

Adrian Dumitrescu[1,*] and Csaba D. Tóth[2]

[1] Department of Computer Science, University of Wisconsin-Milwaukee, USA
ad@cs.uwm.edu
[2] Department of Mathematics, MIT, Cambridge, USA
toth@math.mit.edu

Abstract. An orthogonal network for a given set of n points in the plane is an axis-aligned planar straight line graph that connects all input points. We show that for any set of n points in the plane, there is an orthogonal network that (i) is *short* having a total edge length of $O(|T|)$, where $|T|$ denotes the length of a minimum Euclidean spanning tree for the point set; (ii) is *small* having $O(n)$ vertices and edges; and (iii) has *constant geometric dilation*, which means that for any two points u and v in the network, the shortest path in the network between u and v is at most constant times longer than the (Euclidean) distance between u and v.

1 Introduction

A typical problem in the theory of metric embeddings asks for a mapping from one metric space to another that distorts the distances between point pairs as little as possible. In this paper, we address the following problem about geometric dilation: Given a finite set S of points in the plane, find a small plane graph $G(S)$ containing S so that the distortion between the L_2 distance and the Euclidean shortest path distance between any two points (on edges or at vertices) of $G(S)$ is bounded by a constant.

A special case of this problem received frantic attention in the late 80s and early 90s in the context of geometric spanners [5,7,14,16] (see [13] for a survey). One of the latest results, due to Bose *et al.* [4], goes as follows: For any set S of n points in the plane, there is a plane graph H with four properties: (i) the vertex set of H is S, (ii) H has $O(1)$ maximum degree, (iii) the total length of the edges of H is $O(|T_S|)$, where $|T_S|$ is the length of the minimum Euclidean spanning tree for S, and (iv) for any two vertices $u, v \in S$ the (Euclidean) shortest path along H is at most $O(1)$ times longer than the distance between u and v. The last property is also referred to as constant *vertex-dilation*. Note that the graph H is sparse and the bound $O(|T_S|)$ is the best possible, since H has to be connected at least. Intuitively, this graph H corresponds to a road network that has constant *detour* (precise definition is below) between any two of n given cities.

---

* Research supported by NSF CAREER grant CCF-0444188.

W. Thomas and P. Weil (Eds.): STACS 2007, LNCS 4393, pp. 175–187, 2007.
© Springer-Verlag Berlin Heidelberg 2007

However, there may be pairs of points along the roads (halfway between cities) with arbitrarily large detour. In the current paper, we further extend the results in [4] and construct a graph G of constant geometric dilation, that is, constant detour between *any* two points of the graph (not just between vertices).

Let us first define the (geometric) dilation formally (see also [10,11]). Let G be an embedded planar graph whose edges are curves. Let $G \subseteq \mathbb{R}^2$ also denote the set of points covered by the edges and vertices of the embedded graph G. The *detour* between two points $u, v \in G$ (on edges or vertices of G) is the ratio between the length $d_G(p, q)$ of a Euclidean shortest path connecting u and v in G and their Euclidean distance $|uv|$. The supremum value of detours over all pairs of points, denoted $\delta(G)$, is called the *geometric dilation* of G:

$$\delta(G) := \sup_{u,v \in G} \frac{d_G(u, v)}{|uv|}.$$

In contrast, the *vertex-dilation* is $\max_{u,v \in V(G)} d_G(p, q)/|pq|$, where $V(G)$ is the vertex set of G. For instance, the dilation of a rectangle of aspect ratio $t \geq 1$ is $t + 1$, while its vertex-dilation is only $\frac{t+1}{\sqrt{t^2+1}}$.

For a set S of n points in the plane, we construct an *orthogonal network* $G = G(S)$, which is a planar straight line graph with $S \subseteq V(G)$ and with axis-parallel edges. $G(S)$ has constant geometric dilation and retains all the good properties listed above for H. We use only $O(n)$ Steiner points, thus $|V(G)| = O(n)$. The length of our network, that is the total length of the edges of G, is $|G| = O(|T_S|)$.

Theorem 1. *For every set S of n points in the plane, there is an orthogonal network G such that* (i) *its geometric dilation is at most c_1;* (ii) *it has at most $c_2 n$ vertices;* (iii) *its length is at most $c_3 |T_S|$. Here c_1, c_2, and c_3 are absolute constants.*

These constants are probably too large for designing a real-life orthogonal road network with small dilation for a given set of sites. Our priority was proving that such constants exist, rather than optimizing them.

Geometric spanners and vertex-dilation. Planar straight line graphs with constant vertex-dilation were thoroughly studied in the context of geometric spanners, motivated by VLSI design problems [13,17]. Chew [6] proved that the vertex-dilation of the rectilinear Delaunay triangulation of n points in the plane is at most $\sqrt{10}$; Dobkin *et al.* [9] gave a constant bound on vertex-dilation of the Euclidean Delaunay triangulation. Das and Joseph [7] found a large class of geometric graphs with this property, characterized by a certain *diamond property* similar to our concept of *lofty PLSGs* (see Def. 1). A lot of work has been done on finding "good" spanners: sparse and light graphs with constant vertex-dilation. Quite a few papers [1,3,5,16] present algorithms that compute, for a set S of n points in the plane, a graph G with vertex set S that has constant vertex-dilation, $O(n)$ edges, and $O(|T_S|)$ length. Das *et al.* [8] generalized the result to d-space. Some of these algorithms run in $O(n \log n)$ time, some compute graphs that are planar or have bounded maximal degree. Recently, Bose *et al.* [4] were able to combine all these properties. However, none of these papers provide any upper bound on the resulting *geometric* dilation. Aronov *et al.* [2] gave a tight worst-case bound on the vertex-dilation in terms of the number of edges of the graph used to connect n points.

Geometric dilation of planar point sets. The problem of embedding a given planar point set in a network of small geometric dilation, as well as the problem of computing or estimating the dilation of planar networks has only recently received attention. First attempts were made in designing efficient algorithms to compute the dilation of a polygonal curve [12,15]. Ebbers-Baumann *et al.* [11] proved that every finite point set can be embedded in a plane graph (with curved edges) of geometric dilation at most 1.678, and Dumitrescu *et al.* [10] showed that some point sets require geometric dilation strictly more than $\pi/2 \approx 1.5707$ (at least $(1 + 10^{-11})\pi/2$, to be precise).

2   Reduction to Axis-Aligned Polygons

Notation on planar straight line graphs and polygons. A *planar straight line graph* (PSLG) is a finite graph together with a planar embedding, where the vertices are distinct points and the edges are straight line segments, any pair of which being either disjoint or having a common endpoint. The complement $\mathbb{R}^2 \setminus G$ of a PSLG G may have several components, which are the *faces* of G. Since G is finite, exactly one face extends to infinity, while all other faces are *bounded*. The portion of G that lies on the boundary of a face f is the PSLG ∂f. If f is a simply connected region, then the PSLG ∂f is a *weakly simple polygon*, for convenience called *polygon* in this paper. A polygon P and its interior jointly form the polygonal domain $\text{dom}(P) \subset \mathbb{R}^2$. A subdivision of a polygon P is a PSLG G with $P \subset G \subset \text{dom}(P)$.

The *length* of a PSLG G, denoted $|G|$, is the total length of the edges of G. The *perimeter* of a (weakly simple) polygon P is the length of a shortest closed path that visits all vertices of P along the boundary. Since this closed path can traverse some edges twice, the perimeter of P is less than $2|P|$.

2.1   Our Algorithm in a Nutshell

We construct an orthogonal network for a given set S of n points in the plane (Fig. 1(a)). First, we reduce the problem to a polygon subdivision problem. We construct a constant factor approximation T_n of a minimum axis-aligned Steiner tree (MAST) of S. T_n retains a key property of a MAST, which we call *loftiness*. Intuitively, a PSLG G is lofty if nearby parallel edges do not form "narrow channels." Such narrow channels are undesirable because the detour between closest points on opposite sides of a channel is too large. We enclose T_n in an appropriate axis-aligned bounding square B, add a segment connecting T_n and B and thus obtain a *lofty* weakly simple polygon P (Fig. 1(b)). It suffices to subdivide P into polygonal faces of constant geometric dilation such that the total length and the number of vertices increase by at most constant factors.

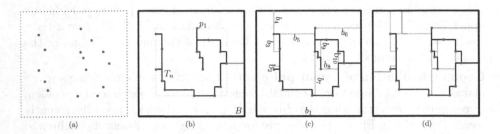

Fig. 1. The three main steps of our algorithm. (a) A point set; (b) a rectilinear Steiner tree T_n and a bounding square B; (c) a mountain subdivision; and (d) a refined subdivision into polygons of constant geometric dilation.

We augment P with new edges and vertices in two phases. The first phase decomposes a lofty axis-aligned polygon into lofty *pocketed mountain* polygons; see Def. 3 and Fig. 1(c). The advantage of mountains is that it is easy to approximate their dilation in terms of the detours of horizontal and vertical point pairs (see Lemma 2). In the second phase, we greedily decompose each pocketed mountain polygon into pocketed mountains of constant dilation in a top-down sweepline algorithm: Whenever the portion of a mountain above the sweepline has "critical" vertical or horizontal dilation, we insert new edges that separate this area and an adjacent buffer zone from the rest of the mountain (Fig. 1(d)). The buffer zones serve to make sure that the detour is bounded by a constant for points lying on the newly inserted edges.

2.2   Reduction to Axis-Aligned Subdivisions

Let P be a polygon. The *internal dilation* of P is $\delta_{\mathrm{int}}(P) = \sup d_G(u,v)/|uv|$ over all point pairs $u, v \in P$ such that the line segment uv lies in $\mathrm{dom}(P)$. To prove a constant bound on the geometric dilation in Theorem 1 part (i), it will suffice to bound the internal dilation of all polygonal faces of the final network. For this, recall a result of Ebbers-Baumann *et al.* [11] which says that the dilation of a plane graph G is attained for a pair u, v of *visible points* (where $u, v \in G$ but the relative interior of the segment uv is disjoint from G). In our final graph G, any pair of visible points lie on the boundary of a bounded (polygonal) face of G.

Theorem 2. *For every set S of n points in the plane, there is an axis-aligned subdivision G of a bounding square of S such that (i) the internal dilation of every bounded face of G is at most c_1; (ii) G has at most c_2n vertices; and (iii) $|G| \le c_3|T_S|$.*

2.3   Reduction to Lofty Axis-Aligned Polygons

Given a set S of n points in the plane, we first construct a Steiner spanning tree T_n with $S \subseteq V(T_n)$. Ideally, T_n should be the *minimum axis-aligned Steiner tree (MAST)* of S, which has at most $2n - 1$ vertices and whose length is at most $\sqrt{2}|T_S|$. Since the MAST problem is NP-complete [7], we construct T_n as an approximation of a MAST that retains three important properties: it has at most $2n - 1$ vertices, $\sqrt{2}|T_S|$ length, and is 2-lofty as defined below.

Definition 1. *Given an axis-aligned* PSLG *G and a parameter $\kappa \geq 1$, a κ-narrow channel is an axis-aligned rectangle r of aspect ratio at least κ such that (a) the two longer sides of r are contained in two parallel edges of G (but neither of these sides contains any vertex of G); (b) the interior of r is disjoint from G. (See Fig. 2(a).)*

An axis-aligned PSLG *G is κ-lofty, for $\kappa \geq 1$, if it does not admit any κ-narrow channel.*

By definition, if $\kappa_1 < \kappa_2$, and G is κ_1-lofty, then it is also κ_2-lofty. Note that a MAST T is κ-lofty for any $\kappa > 2$: If there were a κ-narrow channel r with $\kappa > 2$ for an MAST T, then one can construct a shorter axis-aligned Steiner tree by replacing a portion T along a longer side of r with the two shorter sides of r (see Fig. 2(a-b)).

It is not difficult to devise a constant-factor approximation to the MAST that is also 2-lofty. Start with an arbitrary input point $p_1 \in S$ and let $T_1 = \{p_1\}$ be a singleton graph. For every $i = 2, 3, \ldots, n$, construct an axis-aligned Steiner tree T_i on i points of S by extending T_{i-1}. If T_{i-1} is available, compute the minimum L_1 distance from T_{i-1} to remaining points and connect T_{i-1} to a closest point using at most two axis-parallel edges (forming an L-shape) and at most one Steiner point (the closest point in T_{i-1} or the joint of the L-shape). By Prim's result [18], the axis-parallel Steiner tree T_n is not longer than the minimum rectilinear spanning tree (which has no Steiner points but the edge length is measured in L_1 norm); which in turn is at most $\sqrt{2}$ times longer than the minimum spanning tree T_S.

The above approximation T_n is also 2-lofty: Assume that the two longer sides of a 2-narrow channel r lie along two parallel edges e_1 and e_2 of T_n. Refer to Fig. 2. We may assume that e_1 was created prior to e_2, and e_2 connects $q \in S$ to T_i. Since the aspect ratio of r is 2, the L_1 distance between q and e_1 is less then $|e_2|$. So e_2 is not part of a shortest axis-parallel path from q to T_i: a contradiction.

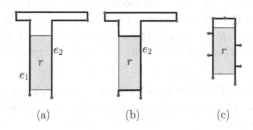

(a)   (b)   (c)

Fig. 2. (a-b) If an axis-aligned Steiner tree T is not 2-lofty, then it is not minimal. (c) This argument does not work if the two longer sides of r contains some vertices of T.

Let B' be the minimum axis-aligned bounding box of S, and let B be a bounding square of B' of side length $2|T_S|$ which extends B' by at least $|T_S|/2$ in each direction. Let now $P = P(B)$ be the PSLG formed by the union of B, T_n, and an axis-parallel segment connecting a vertex of T_n on B' to the closest point in B. Note that P is also 2-lofty, and we have $|P| \leq (4\cdot2+1+\sqrt{2})|T_S| = (9+\sqrt{2})|T_S|$. (The perimeter of P, however, is at most $(9+\sqrt{2})|T_S| + (1+\sqrt{2})|T_S| = (10 + 2\sqrt{2})|T_S|$.) P has at most $2n - 1 + 4 + 1 = 2n + 4$ vertices: T_n has at most $2n - 1$ vertices and there are 5 more vertices on the bounding box B. Note that P has exactly one bounded face which is is simply connected and which lies in the bounding square B. The following theorem immediately implies Theorem 2.

Theorem 3. *Every 2-lofty axis-aligned polygon P with n vertices has an axis-aligned subdivision G such that* (i) *the internal dilation of every face of G is at most c_1;* (ii) *G has at most a_2n vertices; and* (iii) *$|G| \leq a_3|P|$.*

3   Subdividing Axis-Aligned Lofty Polygons

In this section, we prove Theorem 3 and present an algorithm that constructs an axis-aligned subdivision G for an input 3-lofty axis-aligned polygon P with n vertices. This algorithm has two phases: First we decompose P into 3-lofty pocketed mountains in Subsection 3.1. In the second phase, we decompose 3-lofty pocketed mountains into axis-aligned polygons of bounded internal dilation (in Subsections 3.2 and 3.3).

In both phases, we add new edges and vertices to P. We charge every new vertex to old vertices (that is, vertices of P) such that each vertex of P is charged at most a_2 times. Similarly, we charge the length of every new edge to portions of edges of P of the same length such that each point of G is charged at most a_3 times.

3.1   Subdividing Lofty Polygons into Lofty Pocketed Mountains

We partition a 3-lofty axis-aligned polygon into 3-lofty *pocketed mountain* polygons defined below. We start with the definition of *mountain* polygons and attach *pockets* to them later.

Definition 2. *(see Fig. 4) A vertical mountain (alternatively, histogram) is an axis-aligned polygon P that has a special horizontal side b (base side) such that for every point $u \in P$ there is a vertical segment $uv \subset \text{dom}(P)$ that connects u to a point $v \in b$. Horizontal mountains (with a vertical base) are defined analogously.*

Our algorithm is a modified version of a standard algorithm that subdivides an axis-aligned polygon P into mountains. For completeness, we first present this standard algorithm. Its input is P and a *base* edge b.

   Rotate P to make b horizontal. Let $M(b)$ be the boundary polygon of the set of all points $x \in \mathbb{R}^2$ for which $\exists y \in b$ such that xy is vertical and $xy \subset \text{int}(P)$. Clearly, $M(b)$ is a mountain. If $P \neq M(b)$, then P decomposes into $M(b)$ and other faces, each of which has a unique edge that is adjacent to $M(b)$ but is not contained in edges of P. Recurse on each face, except for $M(b)$, independently, setting the base to be the edge adjacent to $M(b)$. (See Fig. 3.)

Fig. 3. The progress of the standard subdivision algorithm into mountains

Unfortunately this standard subdivision scheme may produce mountains $M(b)$ that are not 3-lofty. A narrow channel may be located either outside of $\text{dom}(M(b))$ along a vertical edge of $M(b)$, or in $\text{dom}(M(b))$ between two vertical edges of $M(b)$. To eliminate all narrow channels, we extend the faces of the graph G to fill adjacent narrow channels. Intuitively, we attach "pockets" to the mountains.

Definition 3. *(see Fig. 4) A vertical (horizontal) pocketed mountain is a polygon obtained from a vertical (horizontal) mountain M by replacing some segments s along M by a 3-path p_s such that $s \cup p_s$ forms a rectangle r_s (a pocket) lying outside $\text{dom}(M)$, where the side of r_s orthogonal to s has length at most $|s|/2$.*

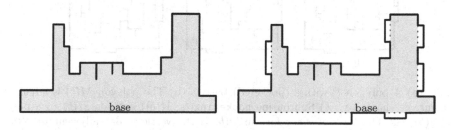

Fig. 4. A mountain polygon (left) and a pocketed mountain polygon (right)

Lemma 1. *Every axis-aligned 3-lofty polygon P with n vertices admits an orthogonal subdivision G, where: every face of G is a 3-lofty pocketed mountain; $|G| \leq 3|P|$; and G has at most $66n$ vertices.*

Proof. We describe a recursive algorithm, whose input is a polygon P and a base segment b contained in P, which computes a subdivision of P into 3-lofty pocketed mountains. Initially b is an arbitrary horizontal edge of P. Let $M(b)$ be the boundary polygon of the set of all points $x \in \mathbb{R}^2$ for which $\exists y \in b$ such that xy is vertical and $xy \subset \text{int}(P)$. See Fig. 5(a-b)). The graph $G = P \cup M(b)$ is a subdivision of P, in which $M(b)$ is a face. If $P = M(b)$, then the algorithm terminates, otherwise it modifies G in several steps to eliminate all κ-narrow channels, $\kappa \geq 3$. The main tool is the following *pocketing* subroutine, which extends a face f of G by attaching to it adjacent narrow channels.

pocketing(G, f) (see Fig. 5). Input: A PSLG G and a face f.
As long as G has a κ-narrow channel not contained in $\text{dom}(f)$ with $\kappa \geq 3$ and one of its long sides lying along ∂f, do:
Let r be such a narrow channel with maximal κ. Let r' be the rectangle obtained from r by removing two rectangles of aspect ratio 2 along its top and bottom sides. Delete the long side of r' that lies along ∂f and insert the two short sides of r' into G.

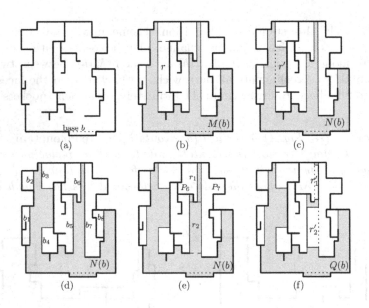

Fig. 5. (a) A polygon P with a (pocketed) base b. (b) The polygon $M(b)$ is adjacent to a narrow channel r. (c) Subroutine pocketing$(G, M(b))$ extends $M(b)$ to a polygon $N(b)$. (d) The base of every face in $\mathcal{P}(b)$ is the vertical edge adjacent to $N(b)$. (e) Narrow channels r_1 and r_2 in $\text{dom}(N(b))$. (f) Subroutines pocketing(G, P_6) and pocketing(G, P_7) splits $N(b)$ into several polygons $Q(b)$.

Apply pocketing$(G, M(b))$ (see Fig. 5(b-c)). Since P is 3-lofty, any narrow channel of G in the exterior of $\text{dom}(M(b))$ must lie between a vertical edge of $M(b)$ and a vertical edge of P. Note that the pockets are disjoint. Each step of the pocketing subroutine adds at most four new vertices (the four corners of r') and two new edges (the two horizontal sides of r'). The removal of two small rectangles from r along its horizontal sides guarantees that the new horizontal edges do not form 3-narrow channels with any other edge.

Let $N(b)$ denote the face of the resulting subdivision G that contains $M(b)$ (that is, $N(b)$ contains $M(b)$ and some adjacent pockets). Denote by $\mathcal{P}(b)$ the set of all faces of G except for $N(b)$. In each face $P' \in \mathcal{P}(b)$, choose a base b', which is the unique edge adjacent to $N(b)$ but not contained in P (Fig. 5(d)). Apply subroutine pocketing(G, P') for every $P' \in \mathcal{P}(b)$ successively (Fig. 5(e-f)). This destroys narrow channels lying in $\mathrm{dom}(N(b))$ by attaching pockets to the base sides of the faces in $\mathcal{P}(b)$. It may also split the face $N(b)$ into several faces: Let $Q(b)$ denote the polygon(s) obtained from $N(b)$ after this procedure. The graph G is a subdivision of polygon P into faces, where the faces of $Q(b)$ are pocketed mountains, and every base b' of other faces $P' \in \mathcal{P}(b)$ may have pockets attached. Apply this subdivision algorithm recursively with input (P', b') for every face $P' \in \mathcal{P}(b)$, independently. This completes the description of the algorithm.

Charging scheme for the length: We charge every edge created by our algorithm to a portion of the perimeter of P. Recall that each step of the pocketing subroutines removes a long side of a rectangle r' of aspect ratio at least 2 and inserts its two short sides. Clearly, this operation does not increase the length of the graph. Assume that the edge set of P is $E_0 = E(P)$. Let E_1 be the set of new edges constructed when building polygons $M(b)$ for all bases b in our algorithm. It is enough to charge the total length of edges in E_1 to the perimeter of P. Consider a step where the base b is horizontal, and the mountain $M(b)$ extends vertically above b. Charge the length of each edge $e \in E_1 \cap M(b)$ to the portion of the perimeter of P that is horizontally visible from e, and has the same length as e. (Note that the shorter edges of rectangles r' arising in pocketing subroutines are never charged.) Every point along the perimeter is charged at most once. Hence, $|G| \le |P| + 2|P| = 3|P|$.

Charging scheme for vertices: We count the number vertices created during the decomposition of polygon P with n vertices. Every edge in E_1 is incident to a reflex vertex of P; and every reflex vertex $v \in V(P)$ is incident to at most one edge of E_1 because if v is incident to a new edge of some mountain $M(b)$, then v becomes a convex vertex in the recursive steps. Hence, we have $|E_1| \le n$. Each edge of E_1 is incident to a vertex of P and a potentially new vertex, so the construction of polygons $M(b)$ increases the number of vertices by n. Each step of the pocketing subroutines increases the number of vertices by 4 (the corners of a rectangle r'). Next, we deduce an upper bound on the number of these steps. First consider the pockets created in subroutines pocketing$(G, M(b))$ for all bases b. Every such pocket lies between an edge of E_0 and a parallel edge of E_1, and every pair of parallel edges in $E_0 \times E_1$ corresponds to at most one pocket. If we draw a curve in each pocket that connects the two corresponding edges of E_0 and E_1, we obtain a planar bipartite graph on vertex set $E_0 \cup E_1$, which has less than $2|E_0 \cup E_1|$ edges by Euler's polyhedron theorem. Since $|E_0| + |E_1| \le n + n = 2n$, the number of pockets is less than $4n$. These pockets also split some edges of E_1 into several pieces; denote the set of these pieces by E_2. Each pocket partitions an edge of E_1 into two pieces, so we have $|E_2| \leq |E_1| + 4n \leq 5n$. Now consider the pockets created in subroutines $\mathtt{pocketing}(G, P')$ for all $P' \in \mathcal{P}(b)$. Each such pocket lies between an edge of E_2 and a parallel edge of $E_0 \cup E_2$. By a similar argument, the number of these pockets is at most $2(|E_0| + |E_2|) \leq 2(n + 5n) = 12n$. The subdivision G of the input polygon P has at most $n + n + 4(4n + 12n) = 66n$ vertices.   □

3.2   Subdividing Lofty Mountains

In this subsection, we present an algorithm to subdivide a 3-lofty mountain polygon into polygons of constant internal dilation. We extend this algorithm in the next subsection to 3-lofty *pocketed* mountains. The advantage of using mountains is that one can approximate their internal dilation in terms of special detours of axis-parallel segments. Consider a mountain M with a horizontal base side b. For every horizontal segment uv that lies in the polygonal domain $\mathrm{dom}(M)$ and $u, v \in M$, we denote by $d_M^*(u, v)$ the length of the (upper) arc between u and v along the perimeter of M that does not contain the base side.

Lemma 2. *The internal dilation of every vertical mountain M is upper bounded by $\max(\delta_H(M) + 1, \delta_V(M))$, where*

- $\delta_H(M) = \max_{uv} d_M^*(u, v)/|uv|$ *over all horizontal uv, with $u, v \in M$;*
- $\delta_V(M) = |M|/(2|\lambda(M)|)$, *where $\lambda(M)$ is the shortest vertical segment with endpoints on ∂M and whose interior lies in $\mathrm{int}(M)$.*

Proof. Consider two points $p, q \in M$ for which the internal dilation of M is attained. That is, $d_M(p, q)/|pq|$ is maximal over all segments pq that lie in the polygonal domain $\mathrm{dom}(M)$ and $p, q \in M$. We distinguish two cases: (1) either p or q lies in the base side, (2) neither p nor q lies in the base side.

If $p \in b$, then $q \notin b$ and so $|pq|$ is at least as long as $\lambda(M)$. Since $d_M(p, q)$ is less than $|M|/2$, we have $d_M(p, q)/|pq| \leq \delta_V(M)$. Assume that $p, q \notin b$. Denote

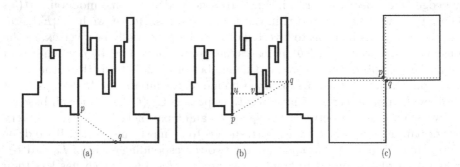

Fig. 6. (a-b) Approximating the internal dilation of a mountain in two cases. (c) For and x- and y-monotone axis-aligned polygon P, the internal dilation can be arbitrarily large even though $\delta_H(P)$ and $\delta_V(P)$ are bounded.

by $|pq|_H$ (resp., $|pq|_V$) the length of the horizontal (resp., vertical) component of segment pq. Let $\pi(p, q)$ be the staircase path between p and q whose vertical segments all lie in M (see Fig. 6). Clearly, we have $|\pi(p, q)| = |pq|_H + |pq|_V$. The graph distance $d_M(p, q)$ is at most the sum of the graph distances of the portions of $\pi(p, q)$, and for every portion above a horizontal segment uv, it is $d_M(u, v) \leq \delta_H(M)|uv|$. Hence, $d_M(p, q) \leq \delta_H(M)|pq|_H + |pq|_V < (\delta_H(M) + 1)|pq|$.   □

Note that the internal dilation of arbitrary axis-aligned polygons cannot be bounded in terms of detours of only horizontal and vertical point pairs. Fig. 6(c) shows that an x- and y-monotone polygon P can have arbitrarily large dilation even though the ratio $d_P(u, v)/|uv|$ is at most 3 for any horizontal or vertical segment uv.

In the remainder of this subsection, we present and analyze an algorithm for subdividing 3-lofty mountains into axis-aligned polygons with constant internal dilation. Our algorithm greedily chooses polygons for which the dilation bound of Lemma 2 is above a constant threshold. We prove the following.

Lemma 3. *Every 3-lofty mountain M with n vertices admits an orthogonal subdivision G, where: the internal dilation of every face of G is at most 45; $|G| \leq 2|P|$; and G has at most $52n$ vertices.*

Proof. We are given a vertical mountain M that lies above the x-axis, with the base side b on the x-axis. For every horizontal segment s, we define a *padding*, which is a rectangle of aspect ratio 3 whose top longer side is s. Let H denote the set of maximal horizontal segments uv where $u, v \in M$ and $uv \subset \mathrm{dom}(M)$. We subdivide M recursively into 3-lofty mountains as follows.

> Move a horizontal sweep line ℓ from the top of M down, and scan the segments of H lying along ℓ. We subdivide M if either of the following two events occurs.
> 1. If the padding of the segment uv intersects the base side b, then insert two vertical edges connecting u and v to the base side, and apply the `pocketing` subroutine to the face containing uv.
> 2. If $d_M^*(u, v) = 7|uv|$, then insert the lower, left, and right edges of the padding of uv, and apply the `pocketing` subroutine to the face containing uv.
>
> Recurse on each face of the resulting subdivision of M that lies in the closed halfplane below ℓ.

The analysis of our algorithm is available in the full version of this paper.   □

3.3 Subdividing Lofty Pocketed Mountains

In Subsection 3.1, we have subdivided a polygon into pocketed mountains, and in Subsection 3.2 we have subdivided mountains into polygons of constant dilation. It remains to show how to subdivide a *pocketed* mountain.

Lemma 4. *Every 3-lofty pocketed mountain P with n vertices admits an orthogonal subdivision G, where: the internal dilation of every face of G is at most 75; $|G| \leq 5|P|$; and G has at most 102n vertices.*

Proof. We are given a pocketed mountain P with n vertices corresponding to a mountain M and a set of disjoint pockets (see Def. 3). Recall that each pocket r has a common side $s(r)$ with M, and its sides orthogonal to $s(r)$ have length at most $|s(r)|/2$. Note also that M is shorter and has fewer vertices than P.

Subdivide M into polygons of bounded dilation as described in Subsection 3.2, and let G be the resulting network. Run the pocketing subroutine for the graph $G \cup P$ and each face of G (Subsection 3.1). This may attach all or some portions of each pocket to faces of G. Consider a maximal portion r' of a pocket r that has not been attached to any face of G. If the aspect ratio of r' is at most 3, then it is a rectangular face of dilation at most 4. If the aspect ratio of r' is $t \geq 3$, then G must have at least $\lfloor t/3 \rfloor$ vertices along $s(r')$. Subdivide r' by segments orthogonal to $s(r')$ into rectangles of aspect ratio at most 3. In this step, the number of vertices is at most doubled, and the length of $G \cup P$ increases by at most a factor of $\frac{7}{6}$. Pocketing can increase the perimeter of a face of G by a factor of at most $\frac{5}{3}$; and it can also increase the dilation by at most the same factor. □

Acknowledgments. We thank Ansgar Grüne and Minghui Jiang for interesting discussions on the topic. We are also grateful to an anonymous reviewer for several useful comments and observations.

References

1. I. Althöfer, G. Das, D. P. Dobkin, D. Joseph, and J. Soares, On sparse spanners of weighted graphs, *Discrete Comput. Geom.* **9** (1993), 81-100.
2. B. Aronov, M de Berg, O. Cheong, J. Gudmundsson, H. J. Haverkort, and A. Vigneron, Sparse geometric graphs with small dilation, in *Proc. 16th ISAAC*, vol. 3827 of LNCS, Springer, 2005, pp. 50–59.
3. S. Arya, G. Das, D. M. Mount, J. S. Salowe, and M. Smid, Euclidean spanners: short, thin, and lanky, in *Proc. 27th STOC*, 1995, ACM Press, pp. 489-498.
4. P. Bose, J. Gudmundsson, and M. Smid, Constructing plane spanners of bounded degree and low weight, *Algorithmica* **42** (2005), 249–264.
5. B. Chandra, G. Das, G. Narasimhan, J. Soares, New sparseness results on graph spanners, *Int. J. Comput. Geometry Appl.* **5** (1995), 125–144.
6. L. P. Chew, There are planar graphs almost as good as the complete graph, *J. Computer Sys. Sci.* **39** (1989), 205-219.
7. G. Das and D. Joseph, Which triangulations approximate the complete graph? in *Optimal Algorithms*, vol 401 of LNCS, Springer, 1989, pp. 168–192.
8. G. Das, G. Narasimhan, and J. S. Salowe, A new way to weigh malnourished Euclidean graphs, in *Proc. 6th SODA*, ACM Press, 1995, pp. 215–222.
9. D. P. Dobkin, S. J. Friedman, and K. J. Supowit, Delaunay graphs are almost as good as complete graphs, *Discrete Comput. Geom.* **5** (1990), 399-407.

10. A. Dumitrescu, A. Ebbers-Baumann, A. Grüne, R. Klein, and G. Rote, On the geometric dilation of closed curves, graphs, and point sets, *Comput. Geom.* **36** 2006, 16–38.
11. A. Ebbers-Baumann, A. Grüne, and R. Klein, On the geometric dilation of finite point sets, *Algorithmica* **44** (2006), 137–149.
12. A. Ebbers-Baumann, R. Klein, E. Langetepe, A. Lingas, A fast algorithm for approximating the detour of a polygonal chain, *Comput. Geom.* **27** (2004), 123–134.
13. D. Eppstein, Spanning trees and spanners, in *Handbook of Computational Geometry* (J. R. Sack and J. Urrutia, eds), North-Holland, Amsterdam, 2000, pp. 425–461.
14. M. Keil and C. A. Gutwin, Classes of graphs which approximate the complete Euclidean graph, *Discrete Comput. Geom.* **7** (1992), 13–28.
15. S. Langerman, P. Morin, and M. Soss, Computing the maximum detour and spanning ratio of planar chains, trees and cycles, in *Proc. 19th STACS*, vol. 2285 of LNCS, Springer, 2002, pp 250–261.
16. C. Levcopoulos and A. Lingas, There are planar graphs almost as good as the complete graphs and almost as cheap as minimum spanning trees, *Algorithmica* **8** (1992), 251–256.
17. J. MacGregor Smith & P. Winter, Computing in Euclidean geometry, in *Computational geometry and topological network design*, World Scientific, 1992, pp. 287-385.
18. R. C. Prim, Shortest connection networks and some generalizations, *Bell System Technical Journal* **36** (1957), 1389–1401.

Admissibility in Infinite Games

Dietmar Berwanger*

RWTH Aachen, Mathematical Foundations of Computer Science
52056 Aachen, Germany
berwanger@cs.rwth-aachen.de

Abstract. We analyse the notion of iterated admissibility, i.e., avoidance of weakly dominated strategies, as a solution concept for extensive games of infinite horizon. This concept is known to provide a valuable criterion for selecting among multiple equilibria and to yield sharp predictions in finite games. However, generalisations to the infinite are inherently problematic, due to unbounded dominance chains and the requirement of transfinite induction.

In a multi-player non-zero-sum setting, we show that for infinite extensive games of perfect information with only two possible payoffs (win or lose), the concept of iterated admissibility is sound and robust: all iteration stages are dominated by admissible strategies, the iteration is non-stagnating, and, under regular winning conditions, strategies that survive iterated elimination of dominated strategies form a regular set.

1 Introduction

Games are fundamental for the analysis of interaction between computational systems [19]. As a particularly effective model, sequential two-player zero-sum games of infinite duration are paradigmatic for capturing the nonterminating behaviour of reactive systems in interplay with their environment [22, 11]. For this class of games, a rich and powerful theory has been developed over the past fifty years: the semantics of most temporal and fixed-point logics translates into this framework, and the relevant algorithmic questions can be captured in terms of alternating ω-automata [20]. More recently, the research on multi-agent systems and on self-organising computational networks motivated the study of models with more than two players that are not necessarily in conflict. These investigations typically focus on the strategic choices of decision-makers rather than their sequential behaviour.

There are good reasons for investigating sequential games of infinite duration with more than two players. In supervisory control theory, the components of a distributed systems can be conceived as distinct players with the same payoff, rather than a coalition competing against the environment [2, 17]. In the context of autonomous agents, the framework captures models of infinite horizon. For the analysis of interaction in large networks, infinite multi-player games provide a basic model that takes into account the sequential, possibly nonterminating behaviour of the participating systems.

---

* This research was supported by the EU RTN 'GAMES' (www.games.rwth-aachen.de).

W. Thomas and P. Weil (Eds.): STACS 2007, LNCS 4393, pp. 188–199, 2007.

In this paper, we initiate a fundamental study addressing the question of rational behaviour in games of infinite duration that involve two or more players and are not strictly competitive. Concretely, we generalise the classical concept of iterated admissibility, that is well established in the theory of finite games [14, 7], to the framework of n-player non-zero-sum extensive games of perfect information over trees of countable depth. This concept is based on the notion of (weak) dominance. Considering two strategies r, s of a particular player, s dominates r if, against any choice of strategies of the other players, s performs at least as well as r, but there are cases in which s performs strictly better than r. As a basic principle of rationality it is assumed that, when a player takes all strategies of the other players in consideration, he will avoid playing dominated strategies. Accordingly, each player eliminates from his set of strategies those that are dominated. On the other hand, rationality is assumed to be common knowledge. Therefore each player understands which strategies his opponents eliminated, possibly discovering that some of his remaining strategies are again dominated when taking into account only admissible counter-strategies. This leads to the elimination of further strategies, and so on. For games with finite strategy spaces, the procedure stabilises after a finite number of stages; the solution concept postulating that outcomes of a game should involve only strategies that survive the iterated elimination is called iterated admissibility (a precise definition follows). Despite its simplicity, the analysis of this procedure required extensive efforts [9, 16, 1, 18]. An epistemic characterisation, justifying on the basis of the player's introspective abilities why outcomes should be iteratively admissible, was achieved recently [3], after having been open for a long time.

The generalisation of iterated admissibility to infinite strategy spaces is not obvious. Already at the elementary level, the avoidance of dominated strategies can lead to empty solutions, because maximally dominating strategies may not exist. For instance, in a game where two players simultaneously choose a natural number, with the greater number winning, any strategy choosing x is dominated by the strategy choosing $x + 1$. Unbounded dominance chains are problematic in general: it does not seem reasonable to eliminate a strategy unless some other strategy that dominates it survives. As a further difficulty, the elimination process may need infinitely many iterations to stabilise. In order to mitigate some of these apparent inconveniences, we will restrict our attention to games with qualitative payoffs, where a player may either win or lose. This setting covers a variety of situations significant in computer science.

We show that in the framework of infinite sequential games of perfect information with qualitative payoffs, the generalisation of iterated admissibility leads to a viable solution concept. For extensive games with winning conditions given by arbitrary sets of infinite paths, we prove that the procedure of simultaneous elimination of dominated strategies is sound, in the sense that every eliminated strategy is dominated by some surviving strategy. Further, we point out that the promoted solution is compatible with the sequential game structure: for any position reachable with admissible strategies, a strategy is admissible in the subgame rooted at that position if, and only if, it is the restriction of an admissible strategy in the original game. In particular, this means that admissibility does not feature non-credible threats. Although the iteration may not terminate in the general case, we still show that the procedure does not stagnate, in the sense that it generates a definitive solution for a maximal antichain in the game tree in a bounded number of stages.

Finally, we discuss iterated admissibility as a solution concept for ω-regular non-zero-sum graph games with n players. These are games played on the tree unravelling of a finite labelled graph with winning conditions given by ω-regular languages over the alphabet consisting of these labels. This framework is relevant for the specification, verification, and synthesis of finite-state controllers. Due to the non-stagnation property, the iteration on regular graph games always terminates after a finite number of steps. Strategies can be conceived as labelled ω-trees of finite branching. We show that, if we set out with ω-tree-regular sets of strategies, one for each player, the set of undominated strategies for any player is again regular. As a consequence, it follows that the set of iteratively admissible strategies in an ω-regular graph game is regular.

The area of infinite sequential games with non-zero-sum conditions or more than two players is largely unexplored. Related research focusses on Nash equilibrium and its refinements [5, 6, 21, 4, 8]. Nash equilibrium is the most prominent solution concept in the classical theory of non-cooperative games. It postulates that the collective decision of the players should be self-enforcing, in the sense that no one gains if he alone deviates. This concept has proved to be highly effective in explaining the outcome of games involving economic agents. However, in predicting and prescribing rational behaviour, Nash equilibria suffer from several shortcomings, some of which aggravate in the context of computational agents. One fundamental problem concerns games with multiple equilibria, where the interplay of strategies that are each consistent with some equilibrium may yield non-equilibrium outcomes (coordination failure). Justifications that players would coordinate on a particular equilibrium point often resort to evolutionary arguments that do not apply to computational agents [15]. Another problem is that Nash equilibria disregard the sequential structure of extensive games (non-credible threats). Besides constituting a solution concept on its own right, iterated admissibility provides basic criteria to exclude such implausible Nash equilibria and to mitigate the effect of coordination failures [13, 12].

The paper is organised as follows. In Section 2 we introduce basic notions and define the solution concept of iterated admissibility. Our principal technical tool is a value characterisation of admissibility developed in Section 3. Given a profile of strategy sets, the value for a particular player is a colouring of game positions that reflects the expectations of the player – to surely win, possibly win, or surely lose – when the play reaches that position, assuming that all players use strategies from the given sets. Using this characterisation, we show in Section 4 that the elimination procedure is sound and, in Section 5, that it produces a solution for an antichain of subgames whenever it is iterated over a bounded number of times. Finally, Section 6 is dedicated to ω-regular graph games. There, we show that iterated admissibility preserves regularity.

2   Basic Notions

We are concerned with games involving n players. We refer to a list of elements $x = (x^i)_{i<n}$, one for each player, as a *profile*. For any such profile, we write x^{-i} to denote the list $(x^j)_{j<n,i\neq j}$ of elements in x for all players except i. Given an element x^i and a list x^{-i}, we denote by (x^i, x^{-i}) the profile $(x^i)_{i<n}$. For clarity, we will always use superscripts to specify to which player an element belongs. If not quantified otherwise, we usually refer to player i meaning *any* player.

Definition 1. A game in *strategic form* is a structure $\Gamma = ((S^i)_{i<n}, (u^i)_{i<n})$ consisting of sets S^i of *strategies*, and *utility payoff* functions $u^i : \times_{i<n} S_i \to \mathbb{R}$, one for every player i.

When a game is played, each player i chooses a strategy $s^i \in S^i$, thus yielding a strategy profile $s = (s^i)_{i<n}$. The value $u^j(s)$ represents the payoff received by player j in this play. We denote by S the set of all strategy profiles $\times_{i<n} S^i$.

Every player is assumed to act rationally towards maximising his own payoff. A *solution concept* associates to any game a nonempty subset of strategy profiles that are consistent with this assumption. However, the notion of rationality is an informal one, allowing a variety of interpretations. We investigate a formalisation based on the notion of (weak) dominance.

Definition 2. Given two strategies $s^i, r^i \in S^i$ and a set $Q^{-i} \subseteq S^{-i}$, we say that s^i *dominates* r^i *on* Q^{-i}, if

$$u^i(s^i, t^{-i}) \geq u^i(r^i, t^{-i}) \text{ for all } t^{-i} \in Q^{-i}, \text{ and}$$

$$u^i(s^i, t^{-i}) > u^i(r^i, t^{-i}) \text{ for some } t^{-i} \in Q^{-i}.$$

For a set $Q \subseteq S$, we say that a strategy $s^i \in S^i$ is *admissible with respect to* Q, if no strategy in Q^i dominates s^i on Q^{-i}.

The idea is to postulate first that it is rational to avoid dominated strategies. Assuming common knowledge of rationality, all players need to be aware of this, and iteratively reevaluate their strategy sets. Different non-equivalent procedures have been proposed on the basis of this idea. Following [3], we opt for simultaneous maximal elimination.

Definition 3. For a game Γ, we define simultaneously for all players i:

- $Q_0^i := S^i$;
- $Q_{\alpha+1}^i := \{s^i \in Q_\alpha^i : s^i \text{ is admissible w.r.t } Q_\alpha\}$, for every ordinal α, and
- $Q_\lambda^i := \bigcap_{\alpha<\lambda} Q_\alpha^i$ for every limit ordinal λ.

A strategy $s^i \in Q_\alpha^i$ is called α-*admissible*. As the stages are decreasing, the induction reaches a fixed point $(Q_\infty^i)_{i<n}$. A strategy $s^i \in Q_\infty^i$ is called *iteratively admissible*.

Observe that, in contrast to most equilibrium concepts, iterative admissibility yields a *rectangular* set of strategy profiles, i.e., a Cartesian product of sets. Accordingly, whether the choice of a particular player is rational in our sense does not depend on the choices of the other players.

Extensive games of infinite horizon. As illustrated in the introduction, there is no hope that admissibility yields a meaningful solution for arbitrary infinite games. We will henceforth restrict our attention to a particular class of sequential games with perfect information.

Definition 4. A game in *extensive form* is a structure $\Gamma = (\mathcal{T}, (W^i)_{i<n})$, where $\mathcal{T}$ is a directed tree over a domain T of elements called *positions*, equipped with a partition $(T^i)_{i<n}$ of its non-terminal nodes, and each W^i is a set of maximal paths through $\mathcal{T}$, called the *winning set* of player i.

Game trees may be of arbitrary branching and of depth up to ω. We write $\preceq$ for the partial order associated to $\mathcal{T}$. When the game is played, the players form a maximal path through $\mathcal{T}$ starting from the root. Whenever a position p is reached, the player i to whose partition T^i it belongs, prolongs the path along some edge. Thus, *plays* are identified with maximal paths through $\mathcal{T}$. An *initial* play is a prefix of a play. The *length* of an initial play $\pi = p_0, p_1, \ldots, p_\ell$ is ℓ.

Definition 5. A *strategy* for player i is a function $s : T^i \to T$ that associates to every position in T^i a successor in $\mathcal{T}$.

Again, we denote the set of all strategies for player i by S^i. An (initial) play $p_0, p_1, \ldots$ *follows* a strategy $s^i \in S^i$, if for every $p_\ell \in T^i$, we have $p_{\ell+1} = s(p_\ell)$. A position $p \in T$ is *avoided* by s^i, if the unique initial play that ends at p does not follow s^i, otherwise p is *reachable* by s^i. Given a strategy set $Q^i \subseteq S^i$, we write $Q^i(p)$ for the subset of strategies in Q^i that do not avoid p. For $Q \subseteq S$, we define $Q(p)$ as the set of profiles $s \in Q$ with $s^i \in Q^i(p)$ for all $i < n$. We say that p is reachable in Q^i or in Q, if $Q^i(p)$ or $Q(p)$, respectively, is not empty. Two strategies $r^i, s^i \in S^i$ *agree* up to a position p, if for every $p' \preceq p$ with $p' \in T^i$, we have $r^i(p') = s^i(p')$; they *split* at p, if they agree up to p, but not on the immediate prolongation of the play, i.e., $r^i(p) \neq s^i(p)$.

Any strategy profile $s = (s^i)_{i<n}$ determines a unique play π which follows all of its components. This play is the *outcome* of the profile; in the 2-player case we denote it by $s^0{\hat{\ }}s^1$. A profile is winning for player i if its outcome is in W^i. In terms of utility, we have $u^i(\pi) = 1$ iff $\pi \in W^i$, otherwise $u^i(\pi) = -1$.

Given a game Γ and a position p, the *subgame* Γ_p is the game obtained by restricting all components of Γ to the positions comparable to p. We denote the restriction of a strategy $s^i \in S^i$ to this domain by $s^i|_p$. Given a strategy set $Q^i \subseteq S^i$, we define $Q^i|_p := \{s^i|_p : s^i \in Q^i(p)\}$. For a profile $Q \subseteq S$ of strategy sets, the restriction is defined component-wise $Q|_p = (Q^i|_p)_{i<n}$.

3   Value Characterisation

The main technical tool for our analysis is a characterisation of admissible strategies in terms of the value that a player can achieve in a given (restriction of the) strategy space. This characterisation also links rational behaviour in subgames with the original game. Whenever we refer to games in the sequel, we mean infinite extensive games.

Definition 6 (Value). Fix a game Γ and a rectangular set $Q \subseteq S$. The *value* of Q for player i is a function χ^i that maps every position p reachable in Q to an element of $\{-1, 0, 1\}$, as follows:

- $\chi^i(p) = 1$ (winning), if there exists a strategy $s^i \in Q^i(p)$ such that for any $t^{-i} \in Q^{-i}(p)$, the profile (s^i, t^{-i}) is winning for player i;

- $\chi^i(p) = -1$ (losing), if every profile in $Q(p)$ is losing for player i;

- $\chi^i(p) = 0$ (pending), otherwise.

First, we define a criterion that identifies well-formed restrictions of the strategy space in extensive games, which allows us to conceive a game position as a point where the player in turn may reassess his plan of action.

Definition 7 (Shifting). Given $s^i, r^i \in S^i$ and a position p up to which the two strategies agree, we denote by $s^i[p \leftarrow r^i]$ the strategy that agrees with r^i on every position comparable to p, and with s^i on any other position.

We say that a strategy set Q^i *allows shifting*, if for any $s^i, r^i \in Q^i$, and every position p up to which s^i and r^i agree, we have $s^i[p \leftarrow r^i] \in Q^i$. A rectangular set $Q \subseteq S$ of profiles allows shifting if all its components do.

The following lemma states that a strategy s dominates r if, and only if, from any position at which s and r disagree, either they both win or both lose, or s strictly improves over r.

Lemma 8. *Consider two strategies $s^i, r^i \in S^i$ and a rectangular set $Q \subseteq S$ that allows shifting. We denote the values of $\{s^i\} \times Q^{-i}$ and $\{r^i\} \times Q^{-i}$ for player i by χ^i_s and χ^i_r, respectively. Then, s^i dominates r^i on Q^{-i} if, and only if,*

(i) *for any position p at which r^i and s^i split, we have $\chi^i_s(p) \geq \chi^i_r(p)$, but at most one of $\chi^i_s(p)$ and $\chi^i_r(p)$ is 0, and*

(ii) *there exists a position p up to which s^i and r^i agree, where $\chi^i_s(p) > \chi^i_r(p)$.*

Proof. We only show here that the conditions are necessary, restricting to the case of two players with $i = 0$ and omitting the superscripts.

First, consider strategies $s, r \in S^0$ that violate condition (i), i.e., they split at some position p where the values are either $\chi_s(p) < \chi_r(p)$ or $\chi_s(p) = \chi_r(p) = 0$. In the former case, it follows that there exists a strategy $t \in Q^1$ that reaches p and further yields $s\hat{\ }t \notin W^0$ whereas $r\hat{\ }t \in W^0$. Hence s cannot dominate r on Q^1. In the latter case, since $\chi_s(p) < 1$, there exists a strategy $t \in Q^1(p)$ such that $s\hat{\ }t \notin W^0$. On the other hand, since $\chi_r(p) > -1$, there also exists a strategy $t' \in Q^1(p)$ such that $r\hat{\ }t' \in W^0$. Let $p' := r(p)$ be the position chosen by r, differing from $s(p)$. Since t, t' agree up to p, and Q^1 allows shifting, the strategy $\tau := t[p' \leftarrow t']$ is also in Q^1. But now $r\hat{\ }\tau = r\hat{\ }t' \in W^0$, whereas $s\hat{\ }\tau = s\hat{\ }t \notin W^0$, which shows that s does not dominate r on Q^1. Whenever two strategies s, r satisfy the first condition but not the second one, they shall have equal, but nonzero values at any splitting position p: either $\chi_s(p) = \chi_r(p) = 1$, or $\chi_s(p) = \chi_r(p) = -1$. It follows that for every $t \in Q^1$ we have $s\hat{\ }t \in W^0$ if, and only if, $r\hat{\ }t \in W^0$. Hence the strategies s and r are incomparable on Q^1. □

The characterisation of dominance extends to a characterisation of admissible strategies.

Lemma 9. *Let $Q \subseteq S$ be a rectangular set that allows shifting. Then, a strategy $s^i \in S^i$ is admissible with respect to Q if, and only if, the value of $\{s^i\} \times Q^{-i}$ for player i attains or exceeds that of Q at every reachable position.*

Proof. Again, we argue for the two-player case. Given a strategy $s \in S^0$, we denote the value of $\{s\} \times Q^1$ for player 0 by χ_s, and the value of $Q^0 \times Q^1$ by χ.

It is easy to verify that the stated condition is sufficient. To prove that it is necessary, let us consider a strategy $s \in Q^0$ and a position p of minimal depth where $\chi_s(p) < \chi(p)$. (Recall that χ_s is defined only for positions reachable in $\{s\} \times Q^1$.) By definition of the value function, there exists a strategy $r \in Q^0(p)$ that witnesses the value of $Q^0 \times Q^1$ at p, having $\chi_r(p) = \chi(p)$. In particular, r agrees with s up to p. Since Q^0 allows shifting, it also contains the strategy $\sigma := s[p \leftarrow r]$. We claim that σ dominates s on Q^1.

First, observe that for all positions p' incomparable to p, we have $\chi_\sigma(p') = \chi_s(p')$, whereas, for any p' comparable to p, we have $\chi_\sigma(p') = \chi_r(p')$. This already implies that the second condition of Lemma 8 is fulfilled: σ and s agree on p and $\chi_\sigma(p) = \chi_r(p) > \chi_s(p)$. The first condition of that lemma refers to the positions where σ and s split. We distinguish two cases. If $\chi_s(p) = 0$, there is only one split between s and σ that occurs immediately at p, where we know that $\chi_\sigma(p) > \chi_s(p)$. Otherwise, if $\chi_\sigma(p) = 1$, for any future position $p' \succeq p$ reached following σ, we have $\chi_\sigma(p') = 1$. Hence, whenever a split between σ and s occurs at such a position, we have $\chi_\sigma(p') \geq \chi_s(p')$. Accordingly, the first condition of Lemma 8 holds as well, allowing us to conclude that σ dominates s over Q^1.   □

This characterisation implies that if a rectangular set $Q \subseteq S$ allows shifting, the set of strategies $s^i \in Q^i$ admissible with respect to Q also allows shifting. By transfinite induction it follows that the value characterisation is valid throughout all iteration stages of admissibility.

Corollary 10. *For every ordinal α, the stage Q_α allows shifting.*

4   One-Step Soundness

Next, we show that in any nonempty stage there exist admissible strategies and every eliminated strategy is dominated by one of those.

Theorem 11. *For every $r^i \in Q_\alpha^i \setminus Q_{\alpha+1}^i$ there exists a strategy $s^i \in Q_{\alpha+1}^i$ that dominates r^i on Q_α^{-i}.*

Proof. In a two-player setting, assume $r \in Q_\alpha^0$ is a strategy dominated on Q_α^1. We construct an infinite chain $s_0, s_1, \cdots \in Q_\alpha^0$, starting with $s_0 := r$, where every strategy s_ℓ is either dominated by its successor $s_{\ell+1}$, or equal to it. Intuitively, $s_{\ell+1}$ follows s_ℓ for the first ℓ steps and then, if the value at the current position can be improved, it switches to a strategy that achieves this. In terms of the characterisation from Lemma 9, we thus ensure that $s_{\ell+1}$ attains the optimal value at any position p of depth at most ℓ that is reachable when the opponent plays in Q_α^1, i.e., $\chi_{s_{\ell+1}}(p) = \chi(p)$, with our usual notation for the value of $\{s_{\ell+1}\} \times Q_\alpha^1$ and $Q_\alpha^0 \times Q_\alpha^1$ for player 0. Concretely, we set out with $s := s_\ell$ and look at each position p of depth ℓ reachable in $\{s_\ell\} \times Q_\alpha^1$. In case $\chi_{s_\ell}(p) < \chi(p)$, by definition of the value function, there exists a strategy $s' \in Q_\alpha^0$ with $\chi_{s'}(p) = \chi(p)$, and we update $s := s[p \leftarrow s']$. By performing these shifts wherever appropriate, we finally obtain a strategy s that yields the optimal value $\chi(p)$ at every position of depth ℓ reachable in $\{s_\ell\} \times Q_\alpha^1$ while preserving the – already optimal – value of $\{s_\ell\} \times Q_\alpha^1$ at any shorter play, Since Q_α^0 allows shifting, $s \in Q_\alpha^0$, and we set $s_{\ell+1} := s$.

Observe that in the above construction every position p at which we shift is minimal with the property that $\chi(p) > \chi_{s_\ell}(p)$. By the same argument as in the proof of necessity in Lemma 9, it follows that $s[p \leftarrow s']$ dominates s on Q^1. Consequently, whenever shifts occurs between s_ℓ and $s_{\ell+1}$, the strategy $s_{\ell+1}$ dominates s_ℓ on Q_α^1 and, by transitivity, it dominates any previous strategy in the sequence. Also if, after some stage, the sequence stabilises, i.e., $s_\ell = s_k$ for every $k > \ell$, then s_ℓ is admissible with respect to $Q_\alpha^0 \times Q_\alpha^1$, according to Lemma 9. For the case in which the sequence does not stabilise, we consider its point-wise limit, i.e., the function σ assigning to position p of depth ℓ the value $\sigma(p) := s_{\ell+1}(p)$ (which further equals $s_k(p)$ for all $k > \ell$). Clearly, $\sigma \in S^0$. We can now verify that σ is admissible with respect to $Q_\alpha^0 \times Q_\alpha^1$, it belongs to Q_α^0, and dominates r on Q^1.   □

The above theorem implies that the elimination of dominated strategies will never evacuate all the strategies from a nonempty admissibility stage.

Corollary 12. *For every ordinal α, if $Q_\alpha \neq \emptyset$, then $Q_{\alpha+1} \neq \emptyset$.*

However, we remark that limit steps of the iteration may yield empty stages. As an example, consider a three-player game (an ω-centipede) with positions $p_0, p_1, \ldots$ all belonging to player 0 who can move from each p_k either to p_{k+1} or into a subgame Δ_k which stabilises after k stages with player 2 winning, player 1 pending, and player 0 losing. Further, let $p_0, p_1, \cdots \notin W^0$ so that the strategy $p_k \mapsto p_{k+1}$ is eliminated in the first stage. Since each stage Q_{n+1}^0 should avoid the subgames $\Delta_0, \ldots \Delta_k$, player 0 will eliminate strategies at every finite stage ending up with $Q_\omega^0 = \emptyset$.

5   Progress and Stabilisation

The example at the end of the previous section points out that the elimination of dominated strategies may require infinitely many iterations. In this section we provide an argument that mitigates this inconvenience, showing that the iteration actually never hangs: within a bounded number of stages, it always generates a definitive solution for some subgame. Towards this, we introduce a measure telling at which stage a subgame is solved from the viewpoint of player i, i.e., at which stage the iteration on that subgame closes.

Definition 13. Fix a game Γ. For a player i, the *closure* ordinal $\mathrm{cl}^i(p)$ of a position p is the smallest ordinal α such that, for every stage $\beta \geq \alpha$, if p is reachable in Q_β^i, then $Q_\beta^i|_p = Q_\alpha^i|_p$. We write $\mathrm{cl}(p)$ for the maximum $\mathrm{cl}^i(p)$ over all players $i < n$.

If a position p is reachable in Q_∞, then for $\alpha = \mathrm{cl}^i(p)$ we have $Q_\infty^i|_p = Q_\alpha^i|_p$, i.e., from p onwards, any strategy that is α-admissible is iteratively admissible. Conversely, if a position p becomes unreachable at some stage Q_α, then $\mathrm{cl}^i(p) \leq \alpha + 1$ for all players i. This can be interpreted as follows: when a play reaches p, it is apparent that the behaviour of some player is not $\alpha + 1$-admissible. Consequently the hypothesis of common knowledge of rationality (incorporating admissibility) must be dropped and the iteration halts.

The notion of a partial solution implicit in the consideration of closures is intimately related to subgames. When instead of the original game Γ, we refer to a subgame Γ_p, we write $(Q_p)_\alpha^i$ for the corresponding iteration stages and $\mathrm{cl}_p^i(\cdot)$ for the closure ordinals. The next lemma states that, for positions p reachable with admissible strategies, it does not matter whether we first iterate the elimination procedure on Γ and then restrict to the subgame Γ_p, or vice versa.

Lemma 14. *Let p be a position reachable in a stage Q_α. Then, with respect to the subgame Γ_p, we have $Q_\beta^i|_p = (Q_p)_\beta^i$ for every $\beta \leq \alpha$. If further $\mathrm{cl}^i(p) \leq \alpha$, then $\mathrm{cl}^i(p) = \mathrm{cl}_p^i(p)$.*

It follows that at most two iteration stages may pass without discovering a subgame that closes for at least one player.

Lemma 15. *If, for an ordinal α there is no position p with $\alpha \leq \mathrm{cl}^i(p) \leq \alpha + 1$, for some player i, then $Q_{\alpha+2} = Q_\infty$.*

Proof. We only sketch the argument. Notice that, if a subgame Γ_p does not close within two successive stages, the value χ of these stages does not change (if a position is found to be either winning or losing, it closes for the respective player within one more iteration step). Consequently, all subgames affected by the elimination of strategies in $Q_{\alpha+1} \setminus Q_{\alpha+0}$ are pending in Q_α and in $Q_{\alpha+1}$ and any eliminated strategy is losing in $Q_{\alpha+1}$. The strategies s, say of player 0, that are eliminated here are characterised as follows:

there exists a play $p_0, p_1, \cdots \notin W^0$ following s that reaches a position $p_k \in T^0$ with $\chi^0(p_k) = 0$ such that no $p_\ell \in T^{-0}$ for $\ell > k$ has a successor $p' \neq p_{\ell+1}$ with $\chi^0(p') \geq 0$.

If we now consider the next elimination step, it turns out that the above criterion does not apply to any further strategy, because the triggering conditions depend only on values that do not change. Therefore, $Q_{\alpha+2} \setminus Q_{\alpha+1} = \emptyset$. □

In the two-player case, whenever a game is closed for one player, it will also close for the other player within one step. With more players, the delay between closing stages can be arbitrary long. However, this delay can be bounded at least for some subgame.

Proposition 16. *Let p be a position reachable in a stage Q_α with $\mathrm{cl}(p) \geq \alpha$. Then, there exists a position p' reachable from p such that $\alpha \leq \mathrm{cl}(p') \leq \alpha + n$.*

Proof. By induction on n. First, apply Lemma 15 to the subgame Γ_{p_0} for $p_0 = p$, to find a reachable position p_1 which closes before $\alpha + 1$, for some player. Now, fix this player's strategy set and consider the subgame Γ_{p_1} as a game among $n - 1$ players to find a position $p_2 \succeq p_1$ that closes before $\alpha + 2$, and so on.   □

Applying Proposition 16 recursively for reachable subgames, we can conclude that the set of positions closed in any sequence of n iteration steps draws an antichain in the set of yet unresolved positions (with respect to the partial order of positions in the game tree).

Corollary 17. *Let $P(\alpha) := \{p \in T : \mathrm{cl}(p) > \alpha\}$ be the set of positions that are not yet closed at stage α. Then, for every α, the difference $P(\alpha) \setminus P(\alpha + n)$ contains a maximal antichain in $P(\alpha)$.*

6   Infinite Games on Finite Graphs

Finally, we discuss iterated admissibility on finite path-forming games with ω-regular objectives. Generalising the standard definition [10], we specify an n-player *graph game* as a finite directed graph $G = (V, E, (V^i)_{i<n})$ with a set of states V assigned to individual players according to the turn-partition $(V^i)_{i<n}$, and a set $E \in V \times V$ of edges. A play is an infinite path formed interactively on this graph starting from a fixed initial state and successively prolonged along edges chosen by the player to which the current state belongs. The objective of a player i is given by an ω-regular set of words $L_i \in V^\omega$ specifying the set of plays where he wins. We do not require the sets L_i to form a partition of V^ω. This model can be easily embedded into our extensive game setting by unravelling a graph G as a game tree $T(G)$ with positions corresponding to finite paths through G starting from the initial position. We say that a position $p \in T(G)$ *copies* a state $v \in G$, if p is an image of $v \in G$ under unravelling.

   Parity games provide a canonical model of ω-regular graph games. An n-player parity game is represented by a graph over an initial segment V of the natural numbers, equipped with subsets $\Omega^i \subseteq V$, one for each player i, that specify the winning condition for a play $v_0, v_1, \ldots$ as follows: player i wins the play, if the least priority appearing infinitely often in the sequence $v_0, v_1, \ldots$ belongs to Ω^i. In the classical framework of two-player zero-sum games, it is well known that every regular game can be equivalently translated into a parity game. This remains true in the n-player non-zero sum setting, in the following sense: for every regular game $\mathcal{G} = (G, (L^i)_{i<n})$, we can construct a parity game $\widehat{\mathcal{G}} = (\widehat{G}, (\Omega^i)_{i<n})$ together with an isomorphism h from $T(G)$ to $T(\widehat{G})$ that naturally extends to strategies such that $(s^0, \ldots, s^{n-1}) \in S$ is winning for a player i in $\mathcal{G}$ if, and only if, $\bigl(h(s^0), \ldots, h(s^{n-1})\bigr)$ is winning for i in $\widehat{\mathcal{G}}$; moreover, h preserves admissibility. Accordingly, the following results for parity games translate back to regular games.

The parity winning condition is prefix-independent: in a parity game $\mathcal{G}$, a play $v_0, v_1, \ldots$ is winning iff any suffix $v_k, v_{k+1}, \ldots$ is winning in the game $\mathcal{G}$ starting from v_k. Without loss of generality, a subgame Γ_p in the extensive form of a parity game can be identified with the game $\Gamma\!\restriction_p$ over the subtree of $\mathcal{T}(G)$ rooted at p. The value characterisation of admissible strategies then implies that the iterated elimination of dominated strategies in the extensive form of a parity game $\mathcal{G}$ evolves in the same way on any two subgames rooted at copies of the same state in $\mathcal{G}$, provided they are simultaneously reachable.

Lemma 18. *Consider the extensive-form game obtained by unravelling a parity game $\mathcal{G}$, and let $p, p' \in \mathcal{T}(G)$ be two copies of the same state in $\mathcal{G}$. Then, for any admissibility stage Q_α in which p and p' are both reachable, we have $Q_\alpha\!\restriction_p = Q_\alpha\!\restriction_{p'}$.*

In particular, if some position $p \in \mathcal{T}(G)$ closes with $\mathrm{cl}^i(p) = \alpha$, then every other copy $p' \preceq p$ of the same state also closes with $\mathrm{cl}^i(p') = \alpha$. By Proposition 16, in every sequence of n iterations, at least one position closes. Since the original parity game has finitely many states, the iteration for admissible strategies on its extensive form will terminate after finitely many stages.

Proposition 19. *The closure ordinal of an n-player parity game with m states is at most $n \cdot m$.*

Strategies in a parity game can be represented as colourings of the ω-tree obtained by unravelling the finite game graph. The initial set of strategy profiles is recognisable by an ω-tree automata. Given an automaton that recognises a regular set Q of strategy profiles we can construct, with some routine, an automaton that recognises the profiles consisting of strategies admissible with respect to Q.

Proposition 20. *In a regular game, let $Q \subseteq S$ be a Cartesian product of ω-tree regular sets. Then, the set of strategies $s \in Q^i$ that are admissible with respect to Q is ω-tree regular.*

Accordingly, in any regular game, the stage Q_α^i is regular, for any finite α. By Proposition 19, the iteration of admissible strategies on a regular game over a finite graph terminates after a bounded number of stages. We can hence conclude that iteratively admissible strategies on such games can be recognised by finite-state tree automata.

Theorem 21. *For every regular game over a finite graph, the set of iteratively admissible strategy profiles is ω-tree regular.*

References

[1] Krzysztof R. Apt. Order independence and rationalizability. In *TARK '05: Proc. Theoretical aspects of rationality and knowledge*, pages 22–38, 2005.

[2] André Arnold, Aymeric Vincent, and Igor Walukiewicz. Games for synthesis of controllers with partial observation. *Theoretical Comp. Science*, 303(1):7–34, 2003.

[3] Adam Brandenburger, Amanda Friedenberg, and H. Jerome Keisler. Admissibility in games. To appear.

[4] Krishnendu Chatterjee. Two-player nonzero-sum omega-regular games. In *CONCUR 2005 - Concurrency Theory*, volume 3653 of *LNCS*, pages 413–427. Springer, 2005.

[5] Krishnendu Chatterjee, Thomas A. Henzinger, and Marcin Jurdzinski. Games with secure equilibria. In *Proc. LICS 2004, Logic in Computer Science*, pages 160–169, 2004.

[6] Krishnendu Chatterjee, Rupak Majumdar, and Marcin Jurdzinski. On Nash equilibria in stochastic games. In *Proc. Computer Science Logic – CSL 2004*, volume 3210 of *LNCS*, pages 26–40. Springer, 2004.

[7] David Gale. A theory of n-person games with perfect information. *Proceedings of the National Academy of Sciences*, 39:495–501, 1953.

[8] Hugo Gimbert. *Jeux Positionels*. PhD thesis, Université Paris 7, 2006.

[9] Rodney J. Gretlein. Dominance elimination procedures on finite alternative games. *International Journal of Game Theory*, 12:107–113, 1983.

[10] Yuri Gurevich and Leo Harrington. Trees, automata and games. In *Proc. of the 14th Annual ACM Symposium on Theory of Computing, STOC '82*, pages 60–65. ACM, 1982.

[11] Thomas A. Henzinger. Games in system design and verification. In *Proc. Theoretical Aspects of Rationality and Knowledge (TARK-2005)*, 2005.

[12] John Hillas and Elon Kohlberg. Foundations of strategic equilibrium. In R.J. Aumann and S. Hart, editors, *Handbook of Game Theory with Economic Applications*, volume 3, chapter 42, pages 1597–1663. Elsevier, 2002.

[13] Elon Kohlberg and Jean-Francois Mertens. On the strategic stability of oquilibria. *Econometrica*, 54(5):1003–1037, September 1986.

[14] Duncan R. Luce and Howard Raiffa. *Games and Decisions*. Wiley, 1957.

[15] George J. Mailath. Do people play Nash equilibrium? Lessons from evolutionary game theory. *Journal of Economic Literature*, 36(3):1347–1374, 1998.

[16] Leslie M. Marx and Jeroen M. Swinkels. Order independence for iterated weak dominance. *Games and Economic Behavior*, 31(2):324–329, 2000.

[17] Swarup Mohalik and Igor Walukiewicz. Distributed games. In *FSTTCS'03*, volume 2914 of *LNCS*, pages 338–351, 2003.

[18] Lars Peter Østerdal. Iterated weak dominance and subgame dominance. *Journal of Mathematical Economics*, 41:637–645, 2005.

[19] Christos Papadimitriou. Algorithms, games, and the internet. In *STOC '01: Proc. ACM symposium on Theory of computing*, pages 749–753, 2001.

[20] Wolfgang Thomas. Infinite games and verification. In *Proc. CAV 2002 – Computer Aided Verification*, volume 2404 of *LNCS*, pages 58–64. Springer, 2002.

[21] Michael Ummels. Rational behaviour and strategy construction in infinite multiplayer games. Master's thesis, RWTH Aachen University, 2005.

[22] Igor Walukiewicz. A landscape with games in the background. In *Proc. Logic in Computer Science (LICS 2004)*, pages 356–366, 2004.

Pure Stationary Optimal Strategies
in Markov Decision Processes

Hugo Gimbert

LIX, Ecole Polytechnique, France[*]
hugo.gimbert@laposte.net

Abstract. Markov decision processes (MDPs) are controllable discrete event systems with stochastic transitions. Performances of an MDP are evaluated by a payoff function. The controller of the MDP seeks to optimize those performances, using optimal strategies.

There exists various ways of measuring performances, i.e. various classes of payoff functions. For example, average performances can be evaluated by a mean-payoff function, peak performances by a limsup payoff function, and the parity payoff function can be used to encode logical specifications.

Surprisingly, all the MDPs equipped with mean, limsup or parity payoff functions share a common non-trivial property: they admit *pure stationary* optimal strategies.

In this paper, we introduce the class of *prefix-independent* and *submixing* payoff functions, and we prove that any MDP equipped with such a payoff function admits pure stationary optimal strategies.

This result unifies and simplifies several existing proofs. Moreover, it is a key tool for generating new examples of MDPs with pure stationary optimal strategies.

1 Introduction

Controller synthesis. One of the central questions in system theory is the controller synthesis problem : given a controllable system and a logical specification, is it possible to control the system so that its behaviour meets the specification?

In the most classical framework, the transitions of the system are not stochastic and the specification is given in LTL or CTL*. In that case, the controller synthesis problem reduces to computing a *winning strategy* in a parity game on graphs [Tho95].

There are two natural directions to extend this framework.

First direction consists in considering systems with stochastic transitions [dA97]. In that case the controller wishes to maximize the *probability* that the specification holds. The corresponding problem is the computation of an *optimal strategy* in a Markov decision process with parity condition [CY90].

---

[*] This research was supported by Instytut Informatyki of Warsaw University and European Research Training Network: Games and Automata for Synthesis and Validation.

W. Thomas and P. Weil (Eds.): STACS 2007, LNCS 4393, pp. 200–211, 2007.

Second direction to extend the classical framework of controller synthesis consists in considering quantitative specifications [dA98, CMH06]. Whereas a logical specification specifies good and bad behaviours of the system, a quantitative specification evaluates performances of the system in a more subtle way. These performances are evaluated by a *payoff function*, which associates a real value with each run of the system. Synthesis of a controller which maximizes performances of the system corresponds to the computation of an *optimal strategy* in a *payoff game* on graphs.

For example, consider a logical specification that specifies that the system should not reach an error state. Then using a payoff function, we can refine this logical specification. For example, we can specify that the number of visits to the error states is as small as possible, or also that the average time between two occurrences of the error state is as long as possible. Observe that logical specifications are a special case of quantitative specifications, where the payoff function takes only two possible values, 1 or 0, depending whether or not the behaviour of the system meets the specification.

In the most general case, the transitions of the system are stochastic and the specification is quantitative. In that case, the controller wishes to maximize the *expected value* of the payoff function, and the controller synthesis problem consists in computing an optimal strategy in a Markov decision process.

Positional payoff functions. Various payoff functions have been introduced and studied, in the framework of Markov decision processes but also in the broader framework of two player stochastic games. For example, the discounted payoff [Sha53, CMH06] and the total payoff [TV87] are used to evaluate short-term performances. Long-term performances can be computed using the mean-payoff [Gil57, dA98] or the limsup payoff [MS96] that evaluate respectively average performances and peak performances. These functions are central tools in economic modelization. In computer science, the most popular payoff function is the parity payoff function, which is used to encode logical properties.

Very surprisingly, the discounted, total, mean, limsup and parity payoff functions share a common non-trivial property. Indeed, in any Markov decision process equipped with one of those functions there exists optimal strategies of a very simple kind : they are at the same time *pure* and *stationary*. A strategy is pure when the controller plays in a deterministic way and it is stationary when choices of the controller depend only on the current state, and not on the full history of the run. For the sake of concision, pure stationary strategies are called *positional* strategies, and we say that a payoff function itself is positional if in any Markov decision process equipped with this function, there exists an optimal strategy which is positional.

The existence of positional optimal strategies has algorithmic interest. In fact, this property is the key for designing several polynomial time algorithms that compute values and optimal strategies in MDPs [Put94, FV97].

Recently, there has been growing research activity about the existence of positional optimal strategies in non-stochastic two-player games with infinitely many states [Grä04, CN06, Kop06] or finitely many states [BSV04, GZ05]. The framework of this paper is different, since it deals with finite MDPs, i.e. one-player stochastic games with finitely many states and actions.

Our results. In this paper, we address the problem of finding a common property between the classical payoff functions introduced above, which explains why they are all positional. We give the following partial answer to that question.

First, we introduce the class of submixing payoff functions, and we prove that a payoff function which is submixing and prefix-independent is also positional (cf. Theorem 1).

This result partially solves our problem, since the parity, limsup and mean-payoff functions are prefix-independent and submixing (cf. Proposition 1).

Our result has several interesting consequences. First, it unifies and shortens disparate proofs of positionality for the parity [CY90], limsup [MS96] and mean [Bie87, NS03] payoff function (section 4). Second, it allows us to generate a bunch of new examples of positional payoff functions (section 5).

Plan. This paper is organized as follows. In section 2, we introduce notions of controllable Markov chain, payoff function, Markov decision process and optimal strategy. In section 3, we state our main result : prefix-independent and submixing payoff functions are positional (cf. Theorem 1). In the same section, we give elements of proof of Theorem 1. In section 4, we show that our main result unifies various disparate proofs of positionality. In section 5, we present new examples of positional payoff functions.

2   Markov Decision Processes

Let $\mathbf{S}$ be a finite set. The set of finite (resp. infinite) sequences on $\mathbf{S}$ is denoted $\mathbf{S}^*$ (resp. $\mathbf{S}^\omega$). A *probability distribution* on $\mathbf{S}$ is a function $\delta : \mathbf{S} \to \mathbb{R}$ such that $\forall s \in \mathbf{S}, \ 0 \leq \delta(s) \leq 1$ and $\sum_{s \in \mathbf{S}} \delta(s) = 1$. The set of probability distributions on $\mathbf{S}$ is denoted $\mathcal{D}(\mathbf{S})$.

2.1   Controllable Markov Chains and Strategies

Definition 1. *A controllable Markov chain* $\mathcal{A} = (\mathbf{S}, \mathbf{A}, (\mathbf{A}(s))_{s \in \mathbf{S}}, p)$ *is composed of:*

- *a finite set of states* $\mathbf{S}$ *and a finite set of actions* $\mathbf{A}$,
- *for each state* $s \in \mathbf{S}$, *a set* $\mathbf{A}(s) \subseteq \mathbf{A}$ *of actions available in* s,
- *transition probabilities* $p : \mathbf{S} \times \mathbf{A} \to \mathcal{D}(\mathbf{S})$.

When the current state of the chain is s, then the controller chooses an available action $a \in \mathbf{A}(s)$, and the new state is t with probability $p(t|s,a)$.

A triple $(s, a, t) \in \mathbf{S} \times \mathbf{A} \times \mathbf{S}$ such that $a \in \mathbf{A}(s)$ and $p(t|s,a) > 0$ is called a transition.

A *history* in $\mathcal{A}$ is an infinite sequence $h = s_0 a_1 s_1 \cdots \in \mathbf{S}(\mathbf{A}\mathbf{S})^\omega$ such that for each n, (s_n, a_{n+1}, s_{n+1}) is a transition. State s_0 is called the source of h. The set of histories with source s is denoted $\mathbf{P}_{\mathcal{A},s}^\omega$. A *finite history* in $\mathcal{A}$ is a finite sequence $h = s_0 a_1 \cdots a_{n-1} s_n \in \mathbf{S}(\mathbf{AS})^*$ such that for each n, (s_n, a_{n+1}, s_{n+1}) is a transition. s_0 is the source of h and s_n its target. The set of finite histories (resp. of finite histories with source s) is denoted $\mathbf{P}_{\mathcal{A}}^*$ (resp. $\mathbf{P}_{\mathcal{A},s}^*$).

A *strategy* in $\mathcal{A}$ is a function $\sigma : \mathbf{P}_{\mathcal{A}}^* \to \mathcal{D}(\mathbf{A})$ such that for any finite history $h \in \mathbf{P}_{\mathcal{A}}^*$ with target $t \in \mathbf{S}$, the distribution $\sigma(h)$ puts non-zero probabilities only on actions that are available in t, i.e. $(\sigma(h)(a) > 0) \implies (a \in \mathbf{A}(t))$. The set of strategies in $\mathcal{A}$ is denoted $\Sigma_{\mathcal{A}}$.

As explained in the introduction of this paper, certain types of strategies are of particular interest, such as *pure* and *stationary* strategies. A strategy is *pure* when the controller plays in a determnistic way, i.e. without using any dice, and it is *stationary* when the controller plays without using any memory, i.e. his choices only depend on the current state of the MDP, and not on the entire history of the play. Formally :

Definition 2. *A strategy $\sigma \in \Sigma_{\mathcal{A}}$ is said to be:*

- pure *if* $\forall h \in \mathbf{P}_{\mathcal{A}}^*$, $(\sigma(h)(a) > 0) \implies (\sigma(h)(a) = 1)$,
- stationary *if* $\forall h \in \mathbf{P}_{\mathcal{A}}^*$ *with target* t, $\sigma(h) = \sigma(t)$,
- positional *if it is pure and stationary.*

Since the definition of a stationary strategy may be confusing, let us remark that $t \in \mathbf{S}$ denotes at the same time the target state of the finite history $h \in \mathbf{P}_{\mathcal{A}}^*$ and also the finite history $t \in \mathbf{P}_{\mathcal{A},t}^*$ of length 1.

2.2 Probability Distribution Induced by a Strategy

Suppose that the controller uses some strategy σ and that transitions between states occur according to the transition probabilities specified by $p(\cdot|\cdot, \cdot)$. Then intuitively the finite history $s_0 a_1 \cdots a_n s_n$ occurs with probability

$$\sigma(s_0)(a_1) \cdot p(s_1|s_0, a_1) \cdots \sigma(s_0 \cdots s_{n-1})(a_n) \cdot p(s_n|s_{n-1}, a_n) \ .$$

In fact, it is also possible to measure probabilities of infinite histories. For this purpose, we equip $\mathbf{P}_{\mathcal{A},s}^{\omega}$ with a σ-field and a probability measure. For any finite history $h \in \mathbf{P}_{\mathcal{A},s}^*$, and action a, we define the sets of infinite plays with prefix h or ha:

$$\mathcal{O}_h = \{s_0 a_1 s_1 \cdots \in \mathbf{P}_{\mathcal{A},s}^{\omega} \mid \exists n \in \mathbb{N}, s_0 a_1 \cdots s_n = h\}$$

$$\mathcal{O}_{ha} = \{s_0 a_1 s_1 \cdots \in \mathbf{P}_{\mathcal{A},s}^{\omega} \mid \exists n \in \mathbb{N}, s_0 a_1 \cdots s_n a_{n+1} = ha\} \ .$$

$\mathbf{P}_{\mathcal{A},s}^{\omega}$ is equipped with the σ-field generated by the collection of sets $\mathcal{O}_h$ and $\mathcal{O}_{ha}$. In the sequel, a measurable set of infinite paths will be called an *event*. Moreover, when there is no risk of confusion, the events $\mathcal{O}_h$ and $\mathcal{O}_{ha}$ will be denoted simply h and ha.

A theorem of Ionescu Tulcea (cf. [BS78]) implies that there exists a unique probability measure $\mathbb{P}_s^{\sigma}$ on $\mathbf{P}_{\mathcal{A},s}^{\omega}$ such that for any finite history $h \in \mathbf{P}_{\mathcal{A},s}^*$ with target t, and for every $a \in \mathbf{A}(t)$,

$$\mathbb{P}_s^\sigma(ha \mid h) = \sigma(h)(a) \ , \tag{1}$$

$$\mathbb{P}_s^\sigma(har \mid ha) = p(r|t,a) \ . \tag{2}$$

We will use the following random variables. For $n \in \mathbb{N}$, and $t \in \mathbf{S}$,

$S_n(s_0a_1s_1\cdots) = s_n$	the $(n+1)$-th state,
$A_n(s_0a_1s_1\cdots) = a_n$	the n-th action,
$H_n = S_0A_1\cdots A_nS_n$	the finite history of the first n stages,
$N_t = |\{n > 0 : S_n = t\}| \in \mathbb{N} \cup \{+\infty\}$	the number of visits to state t. (3)

2.3   Payoff Functions

After an infinite history of the controllable Markov chain, the controller gets some payoff. There are various ways for computing this payoff.

Mean payoff. The mean-payoff function has been introduced by Gilette [Gil57] and is used to evaluate average performance. Each transition (s,a,t) of the controllable Markov chain is labeled with a daily payoff $r(s,a,t) \in \mathbb{R}$. An history $s_0a_1s_1\cdots$ gives rise to a sequence $r_0r_1\cdots$ of daily payoffs, where $r_n = r(s_n, a_{n+1}, s_{n+1})$. The controller receives the following payoff:

$$\phi_{\text{mean}}(r_0r_1\cdots) = \limsup_{n\in\mathbb{N}} \frac{1}{n+1}\sum_{i=0}^n r_i \ . \tag{4}$$

Discounted payoff. The discounted payoff has been introduced by Shapley [Sha53] and is used to evaluate short-term performance. Each transition (s,a,t) is labeled not only with a daily payoff $r(s,a,t) \in \mathbb{R}$ but also with a discount factor $0 \le \lambda(s,a,t) < 1$. The payoff associated with a sequence $(r_0, \lambda_0)(r_1, \lambda_1)\cdots \in (\mathbb{R} \times [0,1[)^\omega$ of daily payoffs and discount factors is:

$$\phi_{\text{disc}}^\lambda((r_0,\lambda_0)(r_1,\lambda_1)\cdots) = r_0 + \lambda_0 r_1 + \lambda_0\lambda_1 r_2 + \cdots \ . \tag{5}$$

Parity payoff. The parity payoff function is used to encode temporal logic properties [GTW02]. Each transition (s,a,t) is labeled with some priority $c(s,a,t) \in \{0,\ldots,d\}$. The controller receives payoff 1 if the highest priority seen infinitely often is odd, and 0 otherwise. For $c_0c_1\cdots \in \{0,\ldots,d\}^\omega$,

$$\phi_{\text{par}}(c_0c_1\cdots) = \begin{cases} 0 \text{ if } \limsup_n c_n \text{ is even,} \\ 1 \text{ otherwise.} \end{cases} \tag{6}$$

General payoffs. In the sequel, we will give other examples of payoff functions. Observe that in the examples we gave above, the transitions were labeled with various kinds of data: real numbers for the mean-payoff, couple of real numbers for the discounted payoff and integers for the parity payoff.

We wish to treat those examples in a unified framework. For this reason, we consider now that each controllable Markov chain $\mathcal{A}$ comes together with a finite set of colours $\mathbf{C}$ and a mapping $\text{col} : \mathbf{S} \times \mathbf{A} \times \mathbf{S} \to \mathbf{C}$, which colors transitions.

In the case of the mean payoff, transitions are coloured with real numbers hence $\mathbf{C} \subseteq \mathbb{R}$, whereas in the case of the discounted payoff colours are couples $\mathbf{C} \subseteq \mathbb{R} \times [0, 1[$ and for the parity game colours are integers $\mathbf{C} = \{0, \ldots, d\}$.

For an history (resp. a finite history) $h = s_0 a_1 s_1 \cdots$, the colour of the history h is the infinite (resp. finite) sequence of colours

$$\mathrm{col}(h) = \mathrm{col}(s_0, a_1, s_1) \, \mathrm{col}(s_1, a_2, s_2) \cdots .$$

Definition 3. *Let* $\mathbf{C}$ *be a finite set. A payoff function on* $\mathbf{C}$ *is a measurable[1] and bounded function* $\phi : \mathbf{C}^\omega \to \mathbb{R}$.

After an history h, the controller receives payoff $\phi(\mathrm{col}(h))$.

2.4   Values and Optimal Strategies in Markov Decision Processes

Definition 4. *A Markov decision process is a couple* $(\mathcal{A}, \phi)$, *where* $\mathcal{A}$ *is a controllable Markov chain coloured by a set* $\mathbf{C}$ *and* ϕ *is a payoff function on* $\mathbf{C}$.

Let us fix a Markov decision process $\mathcal{M} = (\mathcal{A}, \phi)$. After history h, the controller receives payoff $\phi(\mathrm{col}(h)) \in \mathbb{R}$. We extend the definition domain of ϕ to $\mathbf{P}^\omega_{\mathcal{A}, s}$:

$$\forall h \in \mathbf{P}^\omega_{\mathcal{A}, s}, \quad \phi(h) = \phi(\mathrm{col}(h)) .$$

The expected value of ϕ under the probability $\mathbb{P}^\sigma_s$ is called the *expected payoff* of the controller and is denoted $\mathbb{E}^\sigma_s[\phi]$. It is well-defined because ϕ is measurable and bounded. The *value of a state* s is the maximal expected payoff that the controller can get :

$$\mathrm{val}(\mathcal{M})(s) = \sup_{\sigma \in \Sigma_{\mathcal{A}}} \mathbb{E}^\sigma_s[\phi] .$$

A strategy σ is said to be *optimal* in $\mathcal{M}$ if for any state $s \in \mathbf{S}$,

$$\mathbb{E}^\sigma_s[\phi] = \mathrm{val}(\mathcal{M})(s) .$$

3   Optimal Positional Control

We are interested in those payoff functions that ensure the existence of positional optimal strategies. It motivates the following definition.

Definition 5. *Let* $\mathbf{C}$ *be a finite set of colors and* ϕ *a payoff function on* $\mathbf{C}^\omega$. *Then* ϕ *is said to be* positional *if for any controllable Markov chain* $\mathcal{A}$ *coloured by* $\mathbf{C}$, *there exists a positional optimal strategy in the MDP* $(\mathcal{A}, \phi)$.

Our main result concerns the class of payoff functions with the following properties.

---

[1] Relatively to the Borelian σ-field on $\mathbf{C}^\omega$.

Definition 6. *Let ϕ be a payoff function on $\mathbf{C}^\omega$. We say that ϕ is prefix-independent if for any finite word $u \in \mathbf{C}^*$ and infinite word $v \in \mathbf{C}^\omega$, $\phi(uv) = \phi(v)$. See [Cha06] for interesting results about concurrent stochastic games with prefix-independent payoff functions. We say that ϕ is submixing if for any sequence of finite non-empty words $u_0, v_0, u_1, v_1, \ldots \in \mathbf{C}^*$,*

$$\phi(u_0 v_0 u_1 v_1 \cdots) \leq \max\{\ \phi(u_0 u_1 \cdots)\ ,\ \phi(v_0 v_1 \cdots)\ \}\ .$$

The notion of prefix-independence is classical. The submixing property is close to the notions of *fairly-mixing* payoff functions introduced in [GZ04] and of *concave* winning conditions introduced in [Kop06]. We are now ready to state our main result.

Theorem 1. *Any prefix-independent and submixing payoff function is positional.*

The proof of this theorem is based on the 0-1 law and an induction on the number of actions. Due to space restrictions, we do not give details here, a full proof can be found in [Gim].

4   Unification of Classical Results

We now show how Theorem 1 unifies proofs of positionality of the parity [CY90], the limsup and liminf [MS96] and the mean-payoff [Bie87, NS03] functions.

The parity, mean, limsup and liminf payoff functions are denoted respectively $\phi_{\text{par}}, \phi_{\text{mean}}, \phi_{\text{lsup}}$ and ϕ_{linf}. Both ϕ_{par} and ϕ_{mean} have already been defined in subsection 2.3. ϕ_{lsup} and ϕ_{linf} are defined as follows. Let $\mathbf{C} \subseteq \mathbb{R}$ be a finite set of real numbers, and $c_0 c_1 \cdots \in \mathbf{C}^\omega$. Then

$$\phi_{\text{lsup}}(c_0 c_1 \cdots) = \limsup_n c_n$$

$$\phi_{\text{linf}}(c_0 c_1 \cdots) = \liminf_n c_n\ .$$

The four payoff functions $\phi_{\text{par}}, \phi_{\text{mean}}, \phi_{\text{lsup}}$ and ϕ_{linf} are very different. Indeed, ϕ_{lsup} measures the peak performances of the system, ϕ_{linf} the worst performances, and ϕ_{mean} the average performances. The function ϕ_{par} is used to encode logical specifications, expressed in MSO or LTL for example [GTW02].

Proposition 1. *The payoff functions ϕ_{lsup}, ϕ_{linf}, ϕ_{par} and ϕ_{mean} are submixing.*

Proof. Let $\mathbf{C} \subseteq \mathbb{R}$ be a finite set of real numbers and $u_0, v_0, u_1, v_1, \ldots \in \mathbf{C}^*$ be a sequence of finite non-empty words on $\mathbf{C}$. Define $u = u_0 u_1 \cdots \in \mathbf{C}^\omega$, $v = v_0 v_1 \cdots \in \mathbf{C}^\omega$ and $w = u_0 v_0 u_1 v_1 \cdots \in \mathbf{C}^\omega$. The following elementary fact immediately implies that ϕ_{lsup} is submixing.

$$\phi_{\text{lsup}}(w) = \max\{\phi_{\text{lsup}}(u), \phi_{\text{lsup}}(v)\}\ . \tag{7}$$

In a similar way, ϕ_{linf} is submixing since

$$\phi_{\text{linf}}(w) = \min\{\phi_{\text{linf}}(u), \phi_{\text{linf}}(v)\}\ . \tag{8}$$

Now suppose that $\mathbf{C} = \{0,\ldots,d\}$ is a finite set of integers and consider function ϕ_{par}. Remember that $\phi_{\mathrm{par}}(w)$ equals 1 if $\phi_{\mathrm{lsup}}(w)$ is odd and 0 if $\phi_{\mathrm{lsup}}(w)$ is even. Then using (7) we get that if $\phi_{\mathrm{par}}(w)$ has value 1 then it is the case of either $\phi_{\mathrm{par}}(u)$ or $\phi_{\mathrm{par}}(v)$. It proves that ϕ_{par} is also submixing.

Now let us consider function ϕ_{mean}. A proof that ϕ_{mean} is submixing already appeared in [GZ04], and we reproduce it here, updating the notations. Again $\mathbf{C} \subseteq \mathbb{R}$ is a finite set of real numbers. Let $c_0, c_1, \ldots \in \mathbf{C}$ be the sequence of letters of $\mathbf{C}$ such that $w = (c_i)_{i \in \mathbb{N}}$. Since word w is a shuffle of words u and v, there exists a partition (I_0, I_1) of $\mathbb{N}$ such that $u = (c_i)_{i \in I_0}$ and $v = (c_i)_{i \in I_1}$. For any $n \in \mathbb{N}$, let $I_0^n = I_0 \cap \{0,\ldots,n\}$ and $I_1^n = I_1 \cap \{0,\ldots,n\}$. Then for $n \in \mathbb{N}$,

$$
\frac{1}{n+1} \sum_{i=0}^{n} c_i = \frac{|I_0^n|}{n+1} \left(\frac{1}{|I_0^n|} \sum_{i \in I_0^n} c_i \right) + \frac{|I_1^n|}{n+1} \left(\frac{1}{|I_1^n|} \sum_{i \in I_1^n} c_i \right)
$$

$$
\leq \max \left\{ \frac{1}{|I_0^n|} \sum_{i \in I_0^n} c_i, \frac{1}{|I_1^n|} \sum_{i \in I_1^n} c_i \right\} .
$$

The inequality holds since $\frac{|I_0^n|}{n+1} + \frac{|I_1^n|}{n+1} = 1$. Taking the superior limit of this inequality, we obtain $\phi_{\mathrm{mean}}(w) \leq \max\{\phi_{\mathrm{mean}}(u), \phi_{\mathrm{mean}}(v)\}$. It proves that ϕ_{mean} is submixing. □

Since ϕ_{lsup}, ϕ_{linf}, ϕ_{par} and ϕ_{mean} are clearly prefix-independent, Proposition 1 and Theorem 1 imply that those four payoff functions are positional. Hence, we unify and simplify existing proofs of [CY90, MS96] and [Bie87, NS03]. In particular, we use only elementary tools for proving the positionality of the mean-payoff function, whereas [Bie87] uses martingale theory and relies on other papers, and [NS03] uses a reduction to discounted games, as well as analytical tools.

5 Generating New Examples of Positional Payoff Functions

We present three different techniques for generating new examples of positional payoff functions.

5.1 Mixing with the Liminf Payoff

In last section, we saw that peak performances of a system can be evaluated using the limsup payoff, whereas its worst performances are computed using the liminf payoff. The *compromise payoff* function is used when the controller wants to achieve a trade-off between good peak performances and not too bad worst performances. Following this idea, we introduced in [GZ04] the following payoff function. We fix a factor $\lambda \in [0,1]$, a finite set $\mathbf{C} \subseteq \mathbb{R}$ and for $u \in \mathbf{C}^\omega$, we define

$$
\phi_{\mathrm{comp}}^{\lambda}(u) = \lambda \cdot \phi_{\mathrm{lsup}}(u) + (1 - \lambda) \cdot \phi_{\mathrm{linf}}(u) .
$$

The fact that $\phi_{\mathrm{comp}}^{\lambda}$ is submixing is a corollary of the following proposition.

Proposition 2. *Let* $\mathbf{C} \subseteq \mathbb{R}$, $0 \leq \lambda \leq 1$ *and* ϕ *be a payoff function on* $\mathbf{C}$. *Suppose that* ϕ *is prefix-independent and submixing. Then the payoff function*

$$\lambda \cdot \phi + (1 - \lambda) \cdot \phi_{linf} \tag{9}$$

is also prefix-independent and submixing.

The proof is straightforward, using (8) above. According to Theorem 1 and Proposition 1, any payoff function defined by equation (9), where ϕ is either ϕ_{mean}, ϕ_{par} or ϕ_{lsup}, is positional. Hence, this technique enable us to generate new examples of positional payoffs.

5.2   The Approximation Operator

Consider an increasing function $f : \mathbb{R} \to \mathbb{R}$ and a payoff function $\phi : \mathbf{C}^\omega \to \mathbb{R}$. Then their composition $f \circ \phi$ is also a payoff function and moreover, if ϕ is positional then $f \circ \phi$ also is. Indeed, a strategy optimal for an MDP $(\mathcal{A}, \phi)$ is also optimal for the MDP $(\mathcal{A}, f \circ \phi)$.

An example is the threshold function $f = \mathbf{1}_{\geq 0}$ which associates 0 with strictly negative real numbers and 1 with positive number. Then $f \circ \phi$ indicates whether the performance evaluated by ϕ reaches the critical value of 0.

Hence any increasing function $f : \mathbb{R} \to \mathbb{R}$ defines a unary operator on the family of payoff functions, and this operator stabilizes the family of positional payoff functions. In fact, it is straightforward to check that it also stabilizes the sub-family of prefix-independent and submixing payoff functions.

5.3   The Hierarchical Product

Now we define a binary operator between payoff functions, which also stabilizes the family of prefix-independent and submixing payoff functions. We call this operator the *hierarchical product*.

Let ϕ_0, ϕ_1 be two payoff functions on sets of colours $\mathbf{C}_0$ and $\mathbf{C}_1$ respectively. We do not require $\mathbf{C}_0$ and $\mathbf{C}_1$ to be identical nor disjoints.

The hierarchical product $\phi_0 \rhd \phi_1$ of ϕ_0 and ϕ_1 is a payoff function on the set of colours $\mathbf{C}_0 \cup \mathbf{C}_1$ and is defined as follows. Let $u = c_0 c_1 \cdots \in (\mathbf{C}_0 \cup \mathbf{C}_1)^\omega$ and u_0 and u_1 the two projections of u on $\mathbf{C}_0$ and $\mathbf{C}_1$ respectively. Then

$$(\phi_0 \rhd \phi_1)(u) = \begin{cases} \phi_0(u_0) & \text{if } u_0 \text{ is infinite,} \\ \phi_1(u_1) & \text{otherwise.} \end{cases}$$

This definition makes sense : although each word u_0 and u_1 can be either finite or infinite, at least one of them must be infinite.

Let us give examples of use of hierarchical product.

For $e \in \mathbb{N}$, let 0_e and 1_e be the payoff functions defined on the one-letter alphabet $\{e\}$ and constant equal to 0 and 1 respectively. Let d be an odd number, and ϕ_{par} be the parity payoff function on $\{0, \ldots, d\}$. Then

$$\phi_{\mathrm{par}} = 1_d \rhd 0_{d-1} \rhd \cdots \rhd 1_1 \rhd 0_0 \ .$$

Another example of hierarchical product was given in [GZ05, GZ06], where we defined and establish properties about the *priority mean-payoff function*. This payoff function is in fact the hierarchical product of d mean-payoff functions. Remark that another way of fusionning the parity payoff and the mean-payoff functions has been presented in [CHJ05], and the resulting payoff function is not positional. In contrary, it turns out that the priority mean-payoff function is positional, as a corollary of Theorem 1, and the following proposition, whose proof is easy.

Proposition 3. *Let ϕ_0 and ϕ_1 be two payoff functions. If ϕ_0 and ϕ_1 are prefix-independent and submixing, then $\phi_0 \rhd \phi_1$ also is.*

5.4   Towards a Quantitative Specification Language?

In the previous section, we defined two unary operators and one binary operator over payoff functions. Moreover, we proved that the class of prefix-independent and submixing payoff functions is stable under these operators. As a consequence, if we start with the constant, the limsup, the liminf and the mean payoff functions, and we apply recursively our three operators, we get a huge family of sub-mixinf and prefix-independent payoff functions. According to Theorem 1, all those functions are positional.

We hope that this result is a first step towards a rich quantitative specification language. For example, using the hierarchical product, we can express properties such as: "Minimize the frequency of visits to error states. In the case where error states are visited only finitely often, maximize the peak performances." The positionality of those payoff functions gives hope that the corresponding controller synthesis problems are solvable in polynomial time.

6   Conclusion

In that paper, we have introduced the class of prefix-independent and submixing payoff functions, and we proved that they are positional. Moreover, we have defined three operators on payoff functions, that can be used to generate new examples of MDPs with positional optimal strategies.

There are different natural directions to continue this work.

First, most of the results of this paper can be extended to the broader framework of two-player zero-sum stochastic games with full information. This is ongoing work with Wiesław Zielonka, to be published soon.

Second, the results of the last section give rise to natural algorithmic questions. For MDPs equipped with mean, limsup, liminf, parity or discounted payoff functions, the existence of optimal positional strategies is the key for designing algorithms that compute values and optimal strategies in polynomial time [FV97]. For examples generated with the mixing operator and the hierarchical product, it seems that values and optimal strategies are computable in exponential time, but we do not know the exact complexity. Also it is not clear how to obtain efficient algorithms when payoff functions are defined using approximation operators.

To conclude, let us formulate the following conjecture about positional payoff functions. "Any payoff function which is positional for the class of non-stochastic one-player games is positional for the class of Markov decision processes".

Acknowledgments

I would like to thank Wiesław Zielonka for numerous discussions about payoff games on MDP's.

References

[Bie87]   K.-J. Bierth. An expected average reward criterion. *Stochastic Processes and Applications*, 26:133–140, 1987.

[BS78]   D. Bertsekas and S. Shreve. *Stochastic Optimal Control: The Discrete-Time Case*. Academic Press, 1978.

[BSV04]   H. Björklund, S. Sandberg, and S. Vorobyov. Memoryless determinacy of parity and mean payoff games: a simple proof, 2004.

[Cha06]   K. Chatterjee. Concurrent games with tail objectives. In *CSL'06*, 2006.

[CHJ05]   K. Chatterjee, T. A. Henzinger, and M. Jurdzinski. Mean-payoff parity games. In *LICS'05*, pages 178–187, 2005.

[CMH06]   K. Chatterjee, R. Majumdar, and T. A. Henzinger. Markov decision processes with multiple objectives. In *STACS'06*, pages 325–336, 2006.

[CN06]   T. Colcombet and D. Niwinski. On the positional determinacy of edge-labeled games. *Theor. Comput. Sci.*, 352(1-3):190–196, 2006.

[CY90]   C. Courcoubetis and M. Yannakakis. Markov decision processes and regular events. In *ICALP'90*, volume 443 of *LNCS*, pages 336–349. Springer, 1990.

[dA97]   L. de Alfaro. *Formal Verification of Probabilistic Systems*. PhD thesis, Stanford University, december 1997.

[dA98]   L. de Alfaro. How to specify and verify the long-run average behavior of probabilistic systems. In *LICS*, pages 454–465, 1998.

[FV97]   J. Filar and K. Vrieze. *Competitive Markov Decision Processes*. Springer, 1997.

[Gil57]   D. Gilette. Stochastic games with zero stop probabilities, 1957.

[Gim]   H. Gimbert. Pure stationary optimal strategies in Markov decision processes. http://www.lix.polytechnique.fr/~gimbert/recherche/ mdp_gimbert.ps.

[Grä04]   E. Grädel. Positional determinacy of infinite games. In *Proc. of STACS'04*, volume 2996 of *LNCS*, pages 4–18, 2004.

[GTW02]   E. Grdel, W. Thomas, and T. Wilke. *Automata, Logics and Infinite Games*, volume 2500 of *LNCS*. Springer, 2002.

[GZ04]   H. Gimbert and W. Zielonka. When can you play positionally? In *Proc. of MFCS'04*, volume 3153 of *LNCS*, pages 686–697. Springer, 2004.

[GZ05]   H. Gimbert and W. Zielonka. Games where you can play optimally without any memory. In *CONCUR 2005*, volume 3653 of *LNCS*, pages 428–442. Springer, 2005.

[GZ06]   H. Gimbert and W. Zielonka. Deterministic priority mean-payoff games as limits of discounted games. In *Proc. of ICALP 06*, LNCS. Springer, 2006.

[Kop06]   E. Kopczyński. Half-positional determinacy of infinite games. In *Proc. of ICALP'06*, LNCS. Springer, 2006.

[MS96]   A.P. Maitra and W.D. Sudderth. *Discrete gambling and stochastic games.* Springer-Verlag, 1996.

[NS03]   A. Neyman and S. Sorin. *Stochastic games and applications.* Kluwer Academic Publishers, 2003.

[Put94]   M. L. Puterman. *Markov Decision Processes: Discrete Stochastic Dynamic Programming.* John Wiley & Sons, Inc., New York, NY, USA, 1994.

[Sha53]   L. S. Shapley. Stochastic games. In *Proceedings of the National Academy of Science USA*, volume 39, pages 1095–1100, 1953.

[Tho95]   W. Thomas. On the synthesis of strategies in infinite games. In *Proc. of STACS'95,LNCS*, volume 900, pages 1–13, 1995.

[TV87]   F. Thuijsman and O. J. Vrieze. *The Bad Match, a total reward stochastic game*, volume 9. 1987.

Symmetries and the Complexity of Pure Nash Equilibrium*
Extended Abstract

Felix Brandt[1], Felix Fischer[1], and Markus Holzer[2]

[1] Institut für Informatik, Universität München, 80538 München, Germany
{brandtf,fischerf}@tcs.ifi.lmu.de
[2] Institut für Informatik, Technische Universität München, 85748 Garching, Germany
holzer@in.tum.de

Abstract. Strategic games may exhibit symmetries in a variety of ways. A common aspect, enabling the compact representation of games even when the number of players is unbounded, is that players cannot (or need not) distinguish between the other players. We define four classes of symmetric games by considering two additional properties: *identical payoff functions* for all players and the ability to *distinguish oneself* from the other players. Based on these varying notions of symmetry, we investigate the computational complexity of pure Nash equilibria. It turns out that in all four classes of games Nash equilibria can be computed in TC^0 when only a constant number of actions is available to each player, a problem that has been shown intractable for other succinct representations of multi-player games. We further show that identical payoff functions make the difference between TC^0-completeness and membership in AC^0, while a growing number of actions renders the equilibrium problem NP-complete for three of the classes and PLS-complete for the most restricted class for which the existence of a pure Nash equilibrium is guaranteed. Finally, our results extend to wider classes of *threshold symmetric* games where players are unable to determine the exact number of players playing a certain action.

1 Introduction

In recent years, the computational complexity of game-theoretic solution concepts, both in cooperative and non-cooperative game theory, has come under increasing scrutiny. A major obstacle when considering non-cooperative normal-form games with an unbounded number of players is the exponential size of the naive representation of payoffs. More precisely, a general game in normal-form with n players and k actions per player comprises $n \cdot k^n$ numbers. Computational statements over such large objects are somewhat dubious for two reasons, *cf.* [10]. First, the value of efficient, *i.e.*, polynomial-time, algorithms for problems

---

* This material is based upon work supported by the Deutsche Forschungsgemeinschaft under grant BR 2312/3-1.

W. Thomas and P. Weil (Eds.): STACS 2007, LNCS 4393, pp. 212–223, 2007.

whose input size is already exponential in a natural parameter (the number of players) is questionable. Secondly, most, if not all, "natural" multi-player games will hardly be given as multi-dimensional payoff matrices but rather in terms of some more intuitive (and compact) representation. A natural and straight-forward way to simplify the representation of multi-player games is to somehow formalize similarities between players. As a matter of fact, *symmetric games* have been studied since the early days of game theory, see, *e.g.*, [14, 4, 8]. The established definition states that a game is symmetric if the payoff functions of all players are *identical* and *symmetric* in the other players' actions, *i.e.*, it is impossible to distinguish between the other players [15, 7]. When explicitly look-ing at *multi-player* games, there are other conceivable notions of symmetry. For instance, dropping the requirement of identical payoff functions yields a more general class of multi-player games that still admits a compact representation.

In this paper, we define four classes of succinctly representable symmetric multi-player games and study the computational complexity of finding pure Nash equilibria in games belonging to these classes. It turns out that in all four classes equilibria can be found efficiently if only a constant number of actions is available to each player. Moreover, identical payoff functions for all players further reduce the computational complexity associated with pure Nash equilibria, an effect that is nullified as soon as there are two different payoff functions. Anonymity, *i.e.*, the fact that a player cannot (or does not) distinguish himself from the other players, does not seem to offer any computational advantage. Finally, computing equilibria becomes intractable in all four classes of symmetric games when the number of actions grows linearly in the number of players.

Unlike Nash equilibria in *mixed* strategies, *i.e.*, probabilistic combinations of actions, pure Nash equilibria are not guaranteed to exist. They nevertheless form an interesting subset of equilibria for three reasons. First, requiring randomiza-tion in order to reach a stable outcome has been criticized on various grounds. In multi-player games, where action probabilities in equilibrium can be irrational, randomization is particularly questionable. Secondly, the computation of pure equilibria, if they exist, may be tractable in cases where that of mixed ones is not. Finally, pure equilibria as computational objects are usually much smaller in size than mixed ones.

To date, most research on symmetries in games has concentrated on games that require identical payoff functions for all players, called *strongly* symmetric games in this paper. One of the reasons for this may have been the strong fo-cus of the early research in non-cooperative game theory on two-player games, where weak symmetry as defined in this paper does not impose any restric-tions. An early result by Nash implies the existence of a symmetric equilib-rium in (again, strongly) symmetric games [8].[1] Papadimitriou and Roughgarden capitalize on this existence result and show that a Nash equilibrium of a strongly symmetric game with n players and k actions can be computed in P if $k = O(\log n / \log \log n)$ [10]. While their related results about the tractability of

---

[1] More precisely, Nash shows that every game has an equilibrium that respects all symmetries of the game.

correlated equilibrium do not rely on identical payoff functions and hence apply to weakly symmetric games as well, this is not the case for their results about Nash equilibria. The aforementioned existence of *symmetric* Nash equilibria does neither extend to pure equilibria, nor does it hold for the classes of weakly symmetric and weakly anonymous games. For example, Figure 1 on page 217 shows a weakly symmetric game without a symmetric equilibrium.

We assume the reader to be familiar with the well-known chain of complexity classes $AC^0 \subset TC^0 \subseteq L \subseteq P \subseteq NP$, and the notions of constant-depth and polynomial-time reducibility, see, *e.g.*, [1, 5, 9]. AC^0 is the class of problems solvable by uniform constant-depth Boolean circuits with unbounded fan-in. TC^0 adds so-called threshold gates which output *true* if and only if the number of *true* inputs exceeds a certain threshold. L is the class of problems solvable by deterministic Turing machines using only logarithmic space. P and NP are the classes of problems that can be solved in polynomial time by deterministic and nondeterministic Turing machines, respectively. Furthermore, #P is the class of counting problems associated with polynomially balanced polynomial-time decidable relations. The class PLS of polynomial local search problems and an appropriate notion of reduction [6] will be introduced as needed.

The remainder of this paper is organized as follows: In the following section, we formally introduce four different notions of symmetry in strategic games and the solution concept of Nash equilibrium. The main results of this paper, including efficient algorithms as well as hardness results for all four symmetry classes, are given in Section 3. In Section 4, we provide additional results for a more general notion of symmetry. Section 5 concludes the paper and points to some open problems. The proofs to all theorems will be given in the full version of this paper.

2   Preliminaries

In this section, we formally define essential game-theoretic concepts, introduce four notions of symmetry in strategic multi-player games, and state several facts concerning these notions.

2.1   Strategic Games

An accepted way to model situations of strategic interaction is by means of a *normal-form game*, see, *e.g.*, [7].

Definition 1 (normal-form game). *A game in normal-form is a tuple $\Gamma = (N, (A_i)_{i \in N}, (p_i)_{i \in N})$ where N is a set of* players *and for each player $i \in N$, A_i is a nonempty set of* actions *available to player i, and $p_i : (\times_{i \in N} A_i) \to \mathbb{R}$ is a function mapping each action profile, i.e., combination of actions for all players, to a real-valued* payoff *for player i.*

A combination of actions $s \in \times_{i \in N} A_i$ is also called a profile of *pure strategies*. This concept can be generalized to *mixed strategy profiles* $s \in S = \times_{i \in N} S_i$, by letting players randomize over their actions. We have S_i denote the set of probability distributions over player i's actions, or *mixed strategies* available to player i. We further write $n = |N|$ for the number of players in a game, s_i for the ith strategy in profile s, and s_{-i} for the vector of all strategies in s but s_i.

2.2 Symmetries in Multi-player Games

A central aspect of our view on symmetry is the inability to distinguish between other players. We will therefore mainly talk about games where the set of actions is the same for all players and write $A = A_1 = \cdots = A_n$ and $k = |A|$, respectively, to denote this set and its cardinality. In the following definition, we formally introduce four classes of symmetric games by considering two additional characteristics: *identical payoff functions* for all players and the ability to *distinguish oneself* from the other players.

Definition 2 (symmetries). *Let $\Gamma = (N, (A_i)_{i \in N}, (p_i)_{i \in N})$ be a normal-form game, A a set of actions such that $A_i = A$ for all $i \in N$. For any permutation $\pi : N \to N$ of the set of players, let $\pi' : A^N \to A^N$ be the permutation of the set of action profiles given by $\pi'((a_1, \ldots, a_n)) = (a_{\pi(1)}, \ldots, a_{\pi(n)})$. Γ is called*

- *weakly symmetric if $p_i(s) = p_i(\pi'(s))$ for all $s \in A^N$, $i \in N$ and all π with $\pi(i) = i$,*
- *strongly symmetric if $p_i(s) = p_j(\pi'(s))$ for all $s \in A^N$, $i, j \in N$ and all π with $\pi(j) = i$,*
- *weakly anonymous if $p_i(s) = p_i(\pi'(s))$ for all $s \in A^N$, $i \in N$, and*
- *strongly anonymous if $p_i(s) = p_j(\pi'(s))$ for all $s \in A^N$, $i, j \in N$.*

It is easily verified that the class of strongly anonymous games are strictly contained in the intersection of strongly symmetric and weakly anonymous games, and that both of these are again strictly contained in the class of weakly symmetric games.

In the above definition, π' is an automorphism on the set of action profiles that preserves the number of players that play a particular action. Thus, an intuitive and convenient way to describe a symmetric game is in terms of the equivalence classes induced by π', or by the number of players playing the different actions in each of these classes. We use a notion introduced by Parikh in the context of context-free languages [11].

Definition 3 (commutative image). *Let $\Gamma = (N, (A_i)_{i \in N}, (p_i)_{i \in N})$ be a normal-form game, A a set of actions such that $A_i = A$ for all $i \in N$. Then, the commutative image of an action profile $s \in A^N$ is defined as $\#(s) = (\#(a, s))_{a \in A}$ where $\#(a, s) = |\{ i \in N \mid s_i = a \}|$.*

That is, $\#(a, s)$ denotes the number of players playing action a in action profile s, and $\#(s)$ is the vector of these numbers for all the different actions. This definition naturally extends to action profiles for subsets of the players.

The most basic way to specify a normal-form game is by means of a multidimensional table of payoffs for every single action profile. Certain games are succinctly representable simply because the payoff is the same for action profiles that are equivalent according to some equivalence relation, and needs only be specified once. For symmetric games, this equivalence relation is given by the number of players playing each action. The representation that lists the payoffs for every equivalence class will henceforth be referred to as the *naive representation* of a symmetric game. There are $\binom{n+k-1}{k-1}$ distributions of n players among k actions. Since these are exactly the equivalence classes of the set of action profiles for $n-1$ players under the commutative image, we have the following.

Fact 1. *A weakly symmetric game can be represented using at most* $n \cdot k \cdot \binom{n+k-2}{k-1}$ *numbers, and is representable using space polynomial in n if and only if k is bounded by a constant.*

On the other hand, the size of the game becomes super-polynomial in n even for the slightest growth of k. Nevertheless, space polynomial in n may still suffice to encode *certain classes* of symmetric games with a larger number of actions, using some kind of succinct representation.

2.3 Nash Equilibrium

One of the best-known solution concepts for strategic games is Nash equilibrium [8]. In a Nash equilibrium, no player is able to increase his payoff by *unilaterally* changing his strategy.

Definition 4 (Nash equilibrium). *A strategy profile $s \in S$ is called a* Nash equilibrium *if for each player $i \in N$ and each strategy $s_i' \in S_i$,*

$$p_i(s) \geq p_i((s_{-i}, s_i')).$$

A Nash equilibrium is called pure *if it is a pure strategy profile.*

For general games, simply checking the equilibrium condition for each action profile takes time polynomial in the size of their natural representation, *i.e.*, a table of payoffs for the different action profiles. Using a succinct representation for games where the size of the natural representation grows exponentially in the number of players, which is the case for $k \geq 2$ already, quickly renders the problem NP-complete, see, *e.g.*, [3, 13]. On the other hand, the polynomial size even of the naive representation for symmetric games with a constant number of actions might suggest that finding pure Nash equilibria is easy by a similar argument as above. This reasoning is flawed, however, since a single entry in the payoff table corresponds to an exponential number of action profiles, and it is very well possible that only a single one of them is a Nash equilibrium while all others are not. The weakly symmetric game given in Figure 1 illustrates this fact.

3 Solving Symmetric Games

In this section, we analyze the computational complexity associated with pure Nash equilibrium in symmetric games with a constant number of actions and a growing number of actions, respectively.

$(0,1,1)$	$(0,0,1)$
$(1,1,1)$	$(0,0,0)$

$(0,1,0)$	$(0,0,0)$
$(0,1,0)$	$(1,0,1)$

Fig. 1. A weakly symmetric game with a unique, non-symmetric Nash equilibrium at the action profile with payoff $(1,1,1)$. Players 1, 2, and 3 choose rows, columns, and tables, respectively. Outcomes are denoted as a vector of payoffs for the three players. Action profiles with the same commutative image as the equilibrium are shaded.

3.1 Games with a Constant Number of Actions

As we have noted earlier, the potential hardness of finding pure Nash equilibria in games with succinct representations stems from the fact that the number of action profiles that are candidates for being an equilibrium is exponential in the size of the representation of the game. While weakly symmetric games certainly satisfy this property, the following theorem states that the problem of deciding whether such a game possesses a pure Nash equilibrium is nevertheless tractable. The proof works by looking for a pure Nash equilibrium s with $\#(s) = x$. Fixing a particular x, we first compute numbers w_C of players for which each $C \subseteq A$ is the set of *potential* pure best responses in x (*i.e.*, every $a \in C$ is a best response for player i in some strategy profile s with $\#(s) = x$). We then check whether these numbers are consistent with x. The latter problem can be reduced to a directed integer flow problem with lower bounds in a network with fixed structure. Detailed proofs of this and all other theorems will be given in the full version of this paper.

Theorem 1. *Deciding whether a weakly symmetric or weakly anonymous game with a constant number of actions has a pure Nash equilibrium is TC^0-complete under constant-depth reducibility. Hardness holds even if there is only a constant number of payoffs and only two different payoff functions.*

In contrast to weakly symmetric games, if s is a Nash equilibrium of a *strongly* symmetric game, so are all t satisfying $\#(t) = \#(s)$. This is due to the fact that the payoff functions of all players, and thus the situation of all players playing the same action $a \in A$, is identical, as would be the situation of any other player exchanging actions with someone playing a. We exploit this property to show that deciding the existence of a Nash equilibrium in strongly symmetric games with a constant number of actions is strictly easier than for weakly symmetric or weakly anonymous games.

Theorem 2. *The problem of deciding whether a strongly symmetric game with a constant number of actions has a pure Nash equilibrium is in AC^0.*

As we have already said, strongly *anonymous* games always possess a pure Nash equilibrium, namely an action profile with maximum payoff for every player. We proceed to show that such an action profile, which has the additional property of maximizing social welfare, *i.e.*, the sum of payoffs for all players, can be found in AC^0.

Theorem 3. *The problem of finding a social-welfare-maximizing pure Nash equilibrium of a strongly anonymous game with a constant number of actions is in AC^0.*

3.2   Games with a Growing Number of Actions

To prove the theorems we have seen so far we could exploit the fact that for constant k the naive representation of a symmetric game, *i.e.*, in terms of payoff tables, is computationally equivalent to any kind of polynomially computable payoff function because the latter representation can be transformed into the former by means of a log-space reduction. This is no longer the case for unbounded k, because the size of the naive representation grows exponentially in n. However, a succinct representation of the payoff function, *e.g.*, a Boolean circuit, might exist for certain classes of games.

We will now show that deciding the existence of a pure Nash equilibrium in weakly and strongly symmetric and weakly anonymous games becomes NP-hard if the number of actions grows in n. For strongly anonymous games, which always have a Nash equilibrium, the associated search problem will be shown to be PLS-hard. In the following, we will only consider games where (i) the payoff *to all players* can be computed in polynomial time and (ii) a single player can check in polynomial time whether a particular action is a best response to a given action profile for the other players. Under this assumption, which is quite reasonable for "natural" games, we will be able to obtain membership in NP or PLS. All *hardness* results hold irrespective of this assumption. While there certainly are meaningful games with an exponential number of players or actions, the complexity in this case mainly stems from the sheer size of the game rather than the actual problem of finding a Nash equilibrium.

If the number of actions in a game is large enough, they can in principle be used to distinguish the players playing them. We will exploit this fact to prove the following theorem by a reduction from satisfiability of a Boolean circuit to the problem of deciding the existence of a pure Nash equilibrium in a special class of games. For a particular circuit C with inputs $M = \{1, \ldots, m\}$, we define a game Γ with players $N = M$ and actions $A = \{\, a_i^0, a_i^1 \mid i \in M \,\}$. An action profile s of Γ where $\#(a_i^0, s) + \#(a_i^1, s) = 1$ for all $i \in M$, *i.e.*, one where exactly one action of each pair a_i^0, a_i^1 is played, directly corresponds to an assignment c of C, the ith bit c_i of this assignment being $j \in \{0, 1\}$ if a_i^j is played. We can thus distinguish between the action profiles of Γ corresponding to a satisfying assignment of C, those corresponding to a non-satisfying assignment, and those not corresponding to an assignment at all.

Theorem 4. *Deciding whether a weakly anonymous or strongly symmetric game has a pure Nash equilibrium is NP-complete, even if the number of actions is linear in the number of players and there is only a constant number of different payoffs.*

By the previous theorem and by the inclusion relationships between the different classes of symmetric games, we also have the following.

Corollary 1. *Deciding whether a weakly symmetric game has a pure Nash equilibrium is NP-complete, even if the number of actions is linear in the number of players and there is only a constant number of different payoffs.*

The proof of Theorem 4 works by mapping satisfying assignments of a Boolean circuit to *a certain number* of pure Nash equilibria of a strategic game. Using this property, we can show that counting the number of Nash equilibria in the above classes of games is hard.

Corollary 2. *For weakly symmetric, weakly anonymous, and strongly symmetric games, counting the number of pure Nash equilibria is #P-complete, even if the number of actions is linear in the number of players and there is only a constant number of different payoffs.*

As we have already outlined above, every strongly anonymous game possesses a pure Nash equilibrium. Other games with this property, and the complexity of finding an equilibrium in this case, have recently been investigated by Fabrikant et al. [2]. Theorem 3 states that finding even a social-welfare-maximizing Nash equilibrium of a strongly anonymous game is very easy as long as the number of actions is bounded by a constant. If now the number of actions is growing but polynomial in the size of the input, an assumption we have made throughout the paper, we can start at an arbitrary action profile and check in polynomial time whether some player can change his action to increase the (common) payoff. If this is not the case, we have found an equilibrium. Otherwise, we can repeat the process for the new profile, resulting in a procedure called *best-response dynamics* in game theory. Since the payoff strictly increases in every step, we are guaranteed to find a Nash equilibrium in polynomial time if the number of different payoffs is polynomial. Conversely, we will show that, given a strongly anonymous game with a growing number of actions and an exponential number of different payoffs, finding a Nash equilibrium is at least as hard as finding a *locally optimal* solution to an NP-hard optimization problem. For this, we formally introduce the class of search problems for which a solution is guaranteed to exist by a local optimality argument.

Definition 5 (local search, PLS). *A local search problem is given by (i) a set $\mathcal{I}$ of instances, (ii) a set $\mathcal{F}(x)$ of feasible solutions for each $x \in \mathcal{I}$, (iii) an integer measure $\mu(S, x)$ for each $S \in \mathcal{F}(x)$, and (iv) a set $\mathcal{N}(S, x)$ of neighboring solutions for each $S \in \mathcal{F}(x)$. A solution is* locally optimal *if it does not have a strictly better neighbor, i.e., one with a higher or lower measure depending on the kind of optimization problem.*

A local search problem is in the class PLS of polynomial local search problems [6] if for every $x \in \mathcal{I}$ there exist polynomial time algorithms for (i) computing an initial feasible solution in $\mathcal{F}(x)$, (ii) computing the measure $\mu(S, x)$ of a solution $S \in \mathcal{F}$, and (iii) determining that S is locally optimal or finding a better solution in $\mathcal{N}(S, x)$.

A problem P in PLS is PLS-reducible *to another problem Q in PLS if there exist polynomial time computable functions Φ and Ψ mapping (i) instances x of P to instances $\Phi(x)$ of Q and (ii) solutions S of an instance $\Phi(x)$ of Q to* *solutions $\Psi(S, x)$ of the corresponding instance x of P such that locally optimal solutions are mapped to locally optimal solutions. A PLS reduction from P to Q is called* tight *[12] if for any instance x of P there exists a set $\mathcal{R} \subseteq \mathcal{F}(\Phi(x))$ with the following properties:*

1. $\mathcal{R}$ *contains all local optima of $\Phi(x)$.*
2. *For every $p \in \mathcal{F}(x)$, a solution $q \in \mathcal{R}$ satisfying $\Psi(q, x) = p$ can be computed in polynomial time.*
3. *Consider $q_0, q_1, \ldots, q_\ell \in \mathcal{F}(\Phi(x))$ such that $q_0, q_\ell \in \mathcal{R}$, $q_i \notin \mathcal{R}$ for all $0 < i < \ell$, $q_{i+1} \in \mathcal{N}(q_i, \Phi(x))$ for all $i < \ell$, and $\mu(q_i) > \mu(q_j)$ if $i > j$. Let $p = \Psi(q_0, x)$, $p' = \Psi(q_\ell, x)$. Then, either $p = p'$ or $p' \in \mathcal{N}(p, x)$.*

The proof of the following theorem works along similar lines as that of Theorem 4 to give a reduction from the PLS-complete problem FLIP.

Theorem 5. *The problem of finding a pure Nash equilibrium in a strongly anonymous game is PLS-complete, even if the number of actions is linear in the number of players.*

Implicit in the definition of PLS is a *standard algorithm* for finding a locally optimal solution for a given input $x \in \mathcal{I}$: start with an arbitrary feasible solution $S \in \mathcal{F}(x)$ and repeatedly find a strictly better neighbor until a locally optimal solution $T \in \mathcal{F}(x)$ has been found. The *standard algorithm problem* can be phrased as follows: given x, find the locally optimal solution T output by the standard algorithm on input x. By the proof of Theorem 5, we can draw some additional conclusions about the worst-case running time of the standard algorithm and about the hardness of the standard algorithm problem.

Corollary 3. *The standard algorithm for finding Nash equilibria in strongly anonymous games has an exponential worst-case running time. The standard algorithm problem is NP-hard.*

By a slight modification of the proof of Theorem 5, PLS-completeness, exponential worst-case running time of the standard algorithm, and NP-hardness of the standard algorithm problem can also be shown for general, *i.e.*, not necessarily symmetric, common payoff games with $k = 2$. This fact nicely illustrates the influence of symmetry on the hardness of finding (or deciding the existence of) a Nash equilibrium.

4   Threshold Symmetries

In order to extend the basic concept of symmetry as the indistinguishability of players, we will now consider games where the players cannot even observe the exact number of players playing a certain action, but only whether this number reaches certain *thresholds*. Let $\Gamma = (N, (A_i)_{i \in N}, (p_i)_{i \in N})$ be a normal-form game and A a set of actions such that $A_i = A$ for all $i \in N$. For $T \subseteq \{1, \ldots, n\}$, let $\sim_T \subseteq A^N \times A^N$ be defined as follows: $s \sim_T t$ if for all $a \in A$ and all $x \in T$, $\#(a, s) < x$ if and only if $\#(a, t) < x$. The relation $\sim_T$ naturally extends to action profiles for subsets of N. The following is easily verified.

Fact 2. *For any $T \subseteq \{1, \ldots, n\}$, $\sim_T$ is an equivalence relation on the set A^M of action profiles for players $M \subseteq N$.*

Based on $\sim_T$, we can give a more general version of Definition 2.

Definition 6 (threshold symmetry). *Let $\Gamma = (N, (A_i)_{i \in N}, (p_i)_{i \in N})$ be a normal-form game, A a set of actions such that $A_i = A$ for all $i \in N$. Let $T \subseteq \{1, \ldots, n\}$. Γ is called*

- *weakly T-symmetric if $p_i(s) = p_i(t)$ for all $i \in N$ and all $s, t \in A^N$ with $s_i = t_i$ and $s_{-i} \sim_T t_{-i}$,*
- *strongly T-symmetric if $p_i(s) = p_j(t)$ for all $i, j \in N$ and all $s, t \in A^N$ with $s_i = t_j$ and $s_{-i} \sim_T t_{-j}$,*
- *weakly T-anonymous if $p_i(s) = p_i(t)$ for all $i \in N$ and all $s, t \in A^N$ with $s \sim_T t$, and*
- *strongly T-anonymous if $p_i(s) = p_j(t)$ for all $i, j \in N$ and all $s, t \in A^N$ with $s \sim_T t$.*

For $T = \{1, \ldots, n\}$, these classes are equivalent to those of Definition 2. Moreover, we obtain *Boolean symmetry*, where payoffs only depend on the *support* of an action profile, *i.e.*, the actions that are played by at least one player, for $T = \{1\}$. In general, we call a game *threshold symmetric* for one of the above classes if it is T-symmetric for some T and the corresponding class.

Obviously, the number of payoffs that need to be written down for each player to specify a general weakly T-symmetric game is exactly the number of equivalence classes of $\sim_T$ for action profiles of the other players.

Fact 3. *A weakly T-symmetric game can be represented using at most $n \cdot k \cdot |A^{n-1}/ \sim_T|$ numbers, where $X/ \sim$ denotes the quotient set of set X by equivalence relation $\sim$. For Boolean weak symmetry, the number of equivalence classes equals the number of k-bit binary numbers where at least one bit is 1, i.e., $2^k - 1$. More generally, there cannot be more than $(|T| + 1)^k$ equivalence classes if $|T|$ is bounded by a constant (since for every action, the number of players playing this action must be between two thresholds), while for $T = \{n\}$ there are as few as $k + 1$. Hence, any T-symmetric game with constant $|T|$ is representable using space polynomial in n if $k = O(\log n)$.*

Using a similar construction as in the proof of Theorem 1, the existence of a pure Nash equilibrium in a threshold symmetric game can be decided in polynomial time if the number of actions grows at most logarithmically in the number of players.

Theorem 6. *For threshold symmetric games with $k = O(\log n)$ and a constant number of thresholds, deciding the existence of a pure Nash equilibrium is in P.*

On the other hand, all the games used in the proofs of Theorems 4 and 5 are Boolean. Action profiles corresponding to an assignment of a circuit trivially satisfy the conditions of Definition 6, since each action is played by either zero or one players. For all other action profiles, the conditions have to be checked individually. We thus have the following corollary.

Table 1. Complexity of pure Nash equilibrium in symmetric games

	$k = O(1)$	$k = O(n)$
weakly symmetric weakly anonymous	TC^0-complete	NP-complete
strongly symmetric strongly anonymous	in AC^0	PLS-complete

Corollary 4. *Deciding the existence of a pure Nash equilibrium is NP-complete for threshold weakly symmetric, threshold weakly anonymous, and threshold strongly symmetric games, even if thresholds are Boolean, the number of actions is linear in the number of players, and there is only a constant number of different payoffs. For the same classes, counting the number of pure Nash equilibria is #P-complete.*

For threshold strongly anonymous games, finding a pure Nash equilibrium is PLS-complete, even if thresholds are Boolean and the number of actions is linear in the number of players.

5   Conclusion and Future Work

In this paper, we have introduced four notions of symmetry in strategic multi-player games and investigated the computational complexity of finding pure Nash equilibria. This problem has been shown tractable for games with a constant number of actions, but intractable if the number of actions is linear in the number of players. It is worth noting that, for games with a constant number of actions, the Nash equilibrium problem happens to lie in NC^1 for all types of symmetry and is thus open to parallel computation. For games in which the number of actions grows slowly, e.g., logarithmically, in the number of players, the complexity remains open. The main results are summarized in Table 1.

In future work, it would further be interesting to investigate the notion of a *player type* to obtain efficient algorithms for more general classes of games. For example, games where indistinguishability holds only for players of the same type can be obtained by restricting Definition 2 to permutations that map players from a certain subset to players of the same set. We conjecture that using the algorithm of Theorem 1, pure Nash equilibria can still be found in polynomial time if the number of player types is constant. A different notion, such that players of the same type have identical payoff functions, does not seem to provide additional structure. As we have already shown, only two different payoff functions suffice to make the Nash equilibrium problem TC^0-hard for a constant number of actions and NP-hard for a growing number of actions. More generally, one might investigate games where payoffs are invariant under particular sets of permutations. For example, von Neumann and Morgenstern regard the number of permutations under which the payoffs of a game are invariant as a measure for the degree of symmetry [15]. The question is in how far the computational complexity of solving a game depends on the degree of symmetry.

Acknowledgements. We thank Jan Johannsen for enlightening discussions on circuit complexity and local search and Rob Powers for introducing the first author to the ambiguity of symmetry in games. We further thank the anonymous reviewers for useful comments.

References

1. A. K. Chandra, L. Stockmeyer, and U. Vishkin. Constant depth reducibility. *SIAM Journal on Computing*, 13(2):423–439, 1984.
2. A. Fabrikant, C. H. Papadimitriou, and K. Talwar. The complexity of pure Nash equilibria. In *Proceedings of the 36th Annual ACM Symposium on the Theory of Computing (STOC)*, pages 604–612. ACM Press, 2004.
3. F. Fischer, M. Holzer, and S. Katzenbeisser. The influence of neighbourhood and choice on the complexity of finding pure Nash equilibria. *Information Processing Letters*, 99(6):239–245, 2006.
4. D. Gale, H. W. Kuhn, and A. W. Tucker. On symmetric games. In H. W. Kuhn and A. W. Tucker, editors, *Contributions to the Theory of Games*, volume 1, pages 81–87. Princeton University Press, 1950.
5. D. S. Johnson. A catalog of complexity classes. In J. van Leeuwen, editor, *Handbook of Theoretical Computer Science*, volume A, chapter 2, pages 67–161. Elsevier, 1990.
6. D. S. Johnson, C. H. Papadimitriou, and M. Yannakakis. How easy is local search? *Journal of Computer and System Sciences*, 37:79–100, 1988.
7. R. D. Luce and H. Raiffa. *Games and Decisions: Introduction and Critical Survey*. Wiley, 1957.
8. J. F. Nash. Non-cooperative games. *Annals of Mathematics*, 54(2):286–295, 1951.
9. C. H. Papadimitriou. *Computational Complexity*. Addison-Wesley, 1994.
10. C. H. Papadimitriou and T. Roughgarden. Computing equilibria in multi-player games. In *Proceedings of the 16th Annual ACM-SIAM Symposium on Discrete Algorithms (SODA)*, pages 82–91. SIAM, 2005.
11. R. Parikh. On context-free languages. *Journal of the ACM*, 13(4):570–581, 1966.
12. A. A. Schäffer and M. Yannakakis. Simple local search problems that are hard to solve. *SIAM Journal on Computing*, 20(1):56–87, 1991.
13. G. Schoenebeck and S. Vadhan. The computational complexity of Nash equilibria in concisely represented games. In *Proceedings of the 7th ACM Conference on Electronic Commerce (ACM-EC)*. ACM Press, 2006.
14. J. von Neumann. Zur Theorie der Gesellschaftsspiele. *Mathematische Annalen*, 100: 295–320, 1928.
15. J. von Neumann and O. Morgenstern. *The Theory of Games and Economic Behavior*. Princeton University Press, 2nd edition, 1947.

Computing Representations of Matroids of Bounded Branch-Width

Daniel Král'*

Institute for Theoretical Computer Science (ITI),
Faculty of Mathematics and Physics, Charles University,
Malostranské náměstí 25,
118 00 Prague, Czech Republic
kral@kam.mff.cuni.cz

Abstract. For every $k \geq 1$ and two finite fields $\mathbb{F}$ and $\mathbb{F}'$, we design a polynomial-time algorithm that given a matroid $\mathcal{M}$ of branch-width at most k represented over $\mathbb{F}$ decides whether $\mathcal{M}$ is representable over $\mathbb{F}'$ and if so, it computes a representation of $\mathcal{M}$ over $\mathbb{F}'$. The algorithm also counts the number of non-isomorphic representations of $\mathcal{M}$ over $\mathbb{F}'$. Moreover, it can be modified to list all such non-isomorphic representations.

1 Introduction

Algorithmic matroid theory has recently attracted a lot of attention of researchers in particular in the area of algorithm for matroids with small width. Matroids are combinatorial structures that generalize the notions of graphs and linear independence of vectors. Similarly, as in the case of graphs, some hard problems (that cannot be solved in polynomial time for general matroids) can be efficiently solved for (representable) matroids of small width. Though the notion of tree-width generalizes to matroids [15], a more natural width parameter for matroids is the notion of *branch-width*. Let us postpone a formal definition of this width parameter to Section 2 and just mention at this point that the branch-width of matroids is linearly related with their tree-width, in particular, the branch-width of a graphic matroid is bounded by twice the tree-width of the corresponding graph.

The results obtained so far suggest that the algorithmic results generalize from graphs to matroids representable over finite fields but not to matroids that can be represented only over an infinite field or which are not representable at all. This is consistent with the structural results on matroids [6,7,8,9,10] that also suggest that matroids representable over finite fields are close to graphic matroids (and thus graphs) but general matroids can be quite different.

In the global perspective, one would like to be able for a matroid (with or without its representation) to decide whether it has bounded branch-width, whether

---

* Institute for Theoretical Computer Science (ITI) is supported as project 1M0545 by Czech Ministry of Education.

W. Thomas and P. Weil (Eds.): STACS 2007, LNCS 4393, pp. 224–235, 2007.

it is representable over a particular finite field and to compute one or several of its (possibly more) representations. In particular, the following problems naturally arise in this area:

1. Is it possible for $k \geq 1$ to decide in polynomial time whether the branch-width of a given matroid $\mathcal{M}$ is bounded by k and, if so, to find a branch-decomposition of $\mathcal{M}$ of small branch-width?
2. Is it possible for a field $\mathbb{F}$ and $k \geq 1$ to decide in polynomial time whether a matroid of branch-width at most k is representable over $\mathbb{F}$?
3. What problems (otherwise intractable) are polynomial-time solvable for matroids representable over finite fields that have bounded branch-width?

Another issue is how the matroid $\mathcal{M}$ is presented to an algorithm: it can be given as represented by an *oracle*, which is simply a function that for a given subset of elements of $\mathcal{M}$ determines whether it is independent, or by a representation over a field $\mathbb{F}$ which can be either finite or infinite (see Section 2 for more details on matroid representations). The complexity of algorithms for matroids is measured in terms of the number n of elements of an input matroid.

Let us now survey the status of the problems mentioned in the previous paragraph. The first problem is solved in a very satisfactory way: Oum and Seymour [16,17] constructed for fixed $k \geq 1$ an $O(n^4)$-algorithm which computes a branch decomposition of an oracle-given matroid with width at most $3k - 1$ or certifies that the branch-width of the input matroid is greater than k. Moreover, for fixed $k \geq 1$ and a fixed finite field $\mathbb{F}$, it can be tested in polynomial-time whether the branch-width of a matroid represented over $\mathbb{F}$ is at most k [12] and an optimal branch decomposition can be constructed [18]. Since it is possible to compute a good branch decomposition (if it exists) of any matroid in polynomial time, we can always assume that the matroid is presented with its decomposition.

Let us now focus on the status of the second problem. Seymour [22] showed that there is no sub-exponential algorithm to test whether an oracle-given matroid is binary, i.e., representable over GF(2). His result straightforwardly generalizes to any finite field and holds even if the input matroid has bounded branch-width. On the other hand, if the matroid is represented over rationals $\mathbb{Q}$, it can be tested in polynomial-time whether it is binary [21]. Since it is well known that if a matroid is binary, it has a unique representation over GF(2) and it is easy to find such a representation, we conclude that the answer to the second question is positive for $\mathbb{F} = GF(2)$ even if the branch-width of $\mathcal{M}$ is not restricted. On the other, for every finite field $\mathbb{F} \neq GF(2), GF(3)$ and every $k \geq 3$, the problem is NP-hard [14] for matroids with branch-width at most k.

A general answer to the third problem for matroids represented over finite fields was given in [11,13]: all MSOL-definable[1] properties can be tested in polynomial time for matroids represented over a fixed finite field with bounded branch-width. These result match analogous results [1,3,4,5] for graphs.

A property that a given matroid is representable over a fixed finite field can be defined in MSOL. Hence, the answer to the first half of the second question is positive if the matroid is given by its representation over a *finite* field

---

[1] MSOL stands for monadic second-order logic.

(note that the answer is negative if the matroid is given by an oracle or by its representation over $\mathbb{Q}$ as we explained earlier). Another way how to see that a representatibility over a fixed finite field $\mathbb{F}$ can be solved in polynomial time for matroids represented over another fixed finite field $\mathbb{F}'$ is to realize that the class of matroids representable over $\mathbb{F}$ is minor-closed and the matroids representable over $\mathbb{F}'$ with bounded branch-width are well-quasi-ordered [10]. This yields an $O(n^3)$-algorithm for testing whether a matroid of bounded branch-width which is represented over a finite field $\mathbb{F}'$ can be represented over another finite field $\mathbb{F}$. Also note that it is still open whether for every finite field $\mathbb{F}$, there exists a finite set of forbidden minors for $\mathbb{F}$-representatibility (a famous conjecture of Rota [20] asserts this to be the case) and thus the assertion of having bounded branch-width is essential.

The aim of this note is to provide a more complete answer for the other half of the second question in case that the input matroid is represented over a finite field $\mathbb{F}$. In particular, we show that there is a polynomial-time algorithm that for fixed finite fields $\mathbb{F}$ and $\mathbb{F}'$ and a fixed integer $k \geq 1$ decides whether a given matroid $\mathcal{M}$ represented over $\mathbb{F}$ with branch-width at most k can be represented over $\mathbb{F}'$ and if so, it finds its representation over $\mathbb{F}'$. Our algorithm can be modified to compute the number of non-isomorphic representations of $\mathcal{M}$ over $\mathbb{F}'$ and to list all such non-isomorphic representations.

The algorithm is divided into two steps—in the first step, we compute certain auxiliary matrices that fully determine the structure of a given matroid. This is the only place where a representation of $\mathcal{M}$ over $\mathbb{F}$ is used. In the second step, we use the matrices capturing the structure of $\mathcal{M}$ to verify the existence and in the positive case to construct a representation of $\mathcal{M}$ over $\mathbb{F}'$. Our algorithm similarly as algorithms of [11,12,13] implicitly involves rooted configurations as introduced in [10], and "structural finiteness" on cuts represented in the branch decomposition.

2 Definitions

In this section, we formally introduce all the notions used throughout the paper. We also refer the reader to the monographs [19,23] for further exposition on matroids. A *matroid* $\mathcal{M}$ is a pair $(X, \mathcal{I})$ where $\mathcal{I} \subseteq 2^X$. The elements of X are called *elements* of $\mathcal{M}$ and the sets contained in $\mathcal{I}$ are called *independent* sets. The set $\mathcal{I}$ is required to contain the empty set, to be hereditary, i.e., for every $X' \in \mathcal{I}$, $\mathcal{I}$ must contain all subsets of X', and to satisfy the exchange axiom: if X' and X'' are two sets of $\mathcal{I}$ such that $|X'| < |X''|$, then there exists $x \in X''$ such that $X' \cup \{x\} \in \mathcal{I}$. The *rank* of a set X', denoted by rank X', is the size of the largest independent subset of X' (it can be inferred from the exchange axiom that all inclusion-wise maximal independent subsets of $\mathcal{M}$ have the same size). In the rest, we often understand matroids as sets of elements equipped with a property of "being independent". Consistently with this view, $|\mathcal{M}|$ denotes the number of elements of $\mathcal{M}$ and rank $\mathcal{M}$ denotes the size of the largest independent set of $\mathcal{M}$.

Let us now introduce further notation related to matroids. If X' is a set of elements of $\mathcal{M}$, then $\mathcal{M} \setminus X'$ is the matroid obtained from $\mathcal{M}$ by *deleting* the elements of X', i.e., the elements of $\mathcal{M} \setminus X'$ are those not contained in X' and a subset X'' of such elements is independent in the matroid $\mathcal{M} \setminus X'$ if and only if X'' is independent in $\mathcal{M}$. The matroid $\mathcal{M}/X'$ which is obtained by *contraction* of X' is the following matroid: the elements of $\mathcal{M}/X'$ are those not contained in X' and a subset X'' of such elements is independent in $\mathcal{M}/X'$ if and only if rank $X' \cup X'' = $ rank $X' + $ rank X''. Finally, a *loop* of $\mathcal{M}$ is an element e of $\mathcal{M}$ such that rank $\{e\} = 0$ and a *bridge* is an element such that rank $\mathcal{M} \setminus \{e\} = $ rank $\mathcal{M} - 1$. A *separation* (A, B) is a partition of the elements of $\mathcal{M}$ into two disjoint sets and a separation is called a *k-separation* if rank $A + $ rank $B = $ rank $\mathcal{M} + k$ (note that in some literature such a separation is called a $(k+1)$-separation).

As mentioned in Introduction, matroids generalize the notion of linear independence of vectors. If $\mathbb{F}$ is a (finite or infinite) field, a mapping $\varphi : \mathcal{M} \rightarrow \mathbb{F}^d$ from the element set of $\mathcal{M}$ to a d-dimensional vector space over $\mathbb{F}$ is a *representation* of $\mathcal{M}$ if a set $\{e_1, \ldots, e_k\}$ of elements of $\mathcal{M}$ is independent in $\mathcal{M}$ if and only if $\varphi(e_1), \ldots, \varphi(e_k)$ are linearly independent vectors in $\mathbb{F}^d$. For a subset X of the elements of $\mathcal{M}$, $\varphi(X)$ denotes the linear subspace of $\mathbb{F}^d$ generated by the images of the elements of X. In particular, dim $\varphi(X) = $ rank X. Two representations φ_1 and φ_2 of $\mathcal{M}$ are isomorphic if there exists an isomorphism ψ of vector spaces $\varphi_1(\mathcal{M})$ and $\varphi_2(\mathcal{M})$ such that $\psi(\varphi_1(e))$ is a non-zero multiple of $\varphi_2(e)$ for every element e of $\mathcal{M}$. Next, we introduce additional notation for vector spaces over a field $\mathbb{F}$. If U_1 and U_2 are two linear subspaces of a vector space over $\mathbb{F}$, $U_1 \cap U_2$ is the linear space formed by all the vectors lying in both U_1 and U_2, and $\overline{U_1 \cup U_2}$ is the linear space formed by all the linear combinations of the vectors of U_1 and U_2, i.e., the linear hull of $U_1 \cup U_2$. Formally, $v \in \overline{U_1 \cup U_2}$ if and only if there exists α_1, α_2 and $v_1 \in U_1$ and $v_2 \in U_2$ such that $v = \alpha_1 v_1 + \alpha_2 v_2$.

A *branch decomposition* of a matroid $\mathcal{M}$ is a tree with all inner vertices of degree three and the leaves one-to-one corresponding to the elements of $\mathcal{M}$. Each edge e of the tree naturally splits the elements of $\mathcal{M}$ into two disjoint subsets X_1^e and X_2^e (the elements of each subset correspond to the leaves of the two subtrees obtained by removing e). The *width* of the branch decomposition is the maximum over all e of rank $X_1^e + $ rank $X_2^e - $ rank $\mathcal{M}$. If φ is a representation of $\mathcal{M}$ over a field $\mathbb{F}$, the width of the branch decomposition is also equal to the maximum of dim $\varphi(X_1^e) \cap \varphi(X_2^e)$ taken over all the edges e of the tree. The *branch-width* of a matroid $\mathcal{M}$ is the smallest width of a branch decomposition of $\mathcal{M}$.

In our considerations, it turns out to be useful to consider rooted branch decompositions of $\mathcal{M}$. A *rooted branch decomposition* of $\mathcal{M}$ is obtained from a branch decomposition of $\mathcal{M}$ by subdividing one of the edges of the tree and introducing a new vertex of degree one adjacent to the obtained vertex of degree two. We now root the tree at the new vertex of degree one and add a new element e_0 to $\mathcal{M}$. The element e_0 is a loop and is associated with the root of the tree. Throughout the paper, the vertices of the tree forming the rooted branch decomposition are referred as *nodes*, nodes of degree one different from the root are *leaves* and those of degree three are *inner nodes*. Note that each inner node has two children and a unique parent. Let us remark that adding a loop to $\mathcal{M}$ does not change any properties of $\mathcal{M}$ that we are interested in, in particular, the branch-width of $\mathcal{M}$ is preserved as well as its representatibility over any particular field $\mathbb{F}$.

3   Structural Observations

In this section, we establish some properties of matroids of bounded branch-width that can be represented over a finite field. We start with a lemma that has been implicitly used in most of algorithms for matroids of bounded branch-width, e.g., in those computing the Tutte polynomial. Since the proof of this lemma is a simple application of basic linear algebra facts, we decided to leave it to the reader.

Lemma 1. *Let (A, B) be a separation of a matroid $\mathcal{M}$ and let $\varphi : \mathcal{M} \to \mathbb{F}^d$, $d = \operatorname{rank} \mathcal{M}$, be a representation of $\mathcal{M}$ over a field $\mathbb{F}$. Let further C be the linear subspace $\varphi(A) \cap \varphi(B)$. For every subsets $A' \subseteq A$ and $B' \subseteq B$, the following holds:*

$$
\begin{aligned}
\operatorname{rank} A' \cup B' = {} & (\dim \varphi(A') - \dim \varphi(A') \cap C) + \\
& (\dim \varphi(B') - \dim \varphi(B') \cap C) + \\
& \dim \overline{(\varphi(A') \cap C) \cup (\varphi(B') \cap C)} \, .
\end{aligned}
$$

If (A, B) is a separation of a matroid $\mathcal{M}$, we say that subsets $A_1, A_2 \subseteq A$ are *B-indistinguishable* if for every $B' \subseteq B$,

$$
\operatorname{rank} B' \cup A_1 - \operatorname{rank} A_1 = \operatorname{rank} B' \cup A_2 - \operatorname{rank} A_2 \, .
$$

Note that subsets A_1 and A_2 are B-indistinguishable if and only if the identity on the elements of B is an isomorphism between the matroids $(\mathcal{M}/A_1) \backslash (A \backslash A_1)$ and $(\mathcal{M}/A_2) \backslash (A \backslash A_2)$. Also note that the relation of being B-indistinguishable is an equivalence relation and thus we can talk about *classes* of B-indistinguishable subsets of A.

If the matroid $\mathcal{M}$ has a representation $\varphi : \mathcal{M} \to \mathbb{F}^d$ over a field $\mathbb{F}$, Lemma 1 says that two subsets A_1 and A_2 are B-indistinguishable if for every subset $B' \subseteq B$,

$$
\dim \overline{(\varphi(B') \cap C) \cup (\varphi(A_1) \cap C)} = \dim \overline{(\varphi(B') \cap C) \cup (\varphi(A_2) \cap C)}
$$

where $C = \varphi(A) \cap \varphi(B)$. In particular, if $\varphi(A_1) \cap C = \varphi(A_2) \cap C$, the subsets A_1 and A_2 are B-indistinguishable, but the converse need not be true. If $|\mathbb{F}|$ is a finite field and C has dimension k, i.e., (A, B) is a k-separation, there are at most $|\mathbb{F}|^{k^2}$ possible linear subspaces $\varphi(A_i) \cap C$ and thus the following holds:

Lemma 2. *Let (A, B) be a k-separation of a matroid $\mathcal{M}$ that is representable over a finite field $\mathbb{F}$. There are at most $|\mathbb{F}|^{k^2}$ B-indistinguishable subsets of A.*

4 Algorithm

In this section, we describe our algorithm for computing representations matroids with bounded branch-width over finite fields. The input of the algorithm consists of a rooted branch decomposition with width k of a matroid $\mathcal{M}$ together with its representation $\varphi : \mathcal{M} \to \mathbb{F}^d$, $d = \text{rank } \mathcal{M}$, over a finite field $\mathbb{F}$. We assume throughout this section that $\mathcal{M}$ contains no loops except for the one corresponding to the root of the decomposition. This clearly does not decrease the generality of our results since the loops are always represented by the zero vectors.

As the first step, we compute for each inner node u_0 of the decomposition an auxiliary matrix M_{u_0} that determines the mutual relation between two parts of the matroid corresponding to the subtrees of the left and right child of u_0. We explain the structure of the matrices M_{u_0} in more detail in Subsection 4.1 where we also discuss how they are constructed. In Subsection 4.2, we show how to obtain a representation of $\mathcal{M}$ over any finite field $\mathbb{F}'$ (if it exists) with the aid of the constructed matrices. Throughout this section, we write A_{u_0} for the set of the elements of $\mathcal{M}$ corresponding to the leaves of the subtree of u_0 in the decomposition and B_{u_0} for the elements of $\mathcal{M}$ not contained in this subtree.

4.1 Computing Auxiliary Matrices

Fix an inner node u_0 of the decomposition and let u_1 and u_2 be its two children. The rows of the matrix M_{u_0} correspond to the classes of B_{u_1}-indistinguishable subsets of A_{u_1} and the columns correspond to the classes of B_{u_2}-indistinguishable subsets of A_{u_2}. If $A_1' \subseteq A_{u_1}$ and $A_2' \subseteq A_{u_2}$, the entry in the row corresponding to A_1' and the column corresponding to A_2' is labeled with

$$\text{rank } A_1' + \text{rank } A_2' - \text{rank } A_1' \cup A_2' \tag{1}$$

By the definitions of B_{u_1}-indistinguishability and B_{u_2}-indistinguishability, the value of (1) does not depend on the choice of subsets A_1' and A_2' in the two classes. The entry corresponding to A_1' and A_2' is further associated with the row/column of the matrix $M_{u'}$, where u' is the parent of u, that corresponds to the class of B_{u_0}-indistinguishable sets that contains $A_1' \cup A_2'$. Note that a single row/column of $M_{u'}$ can be (and usually is) associated with several different entries of M_{u_0}.

We now turn our attention to the actual computation of the matrices M_{u_0}. We first find for every node u_0 the list $\mathcal{L}_{u_0}^A$ of all linear subspaces of $\varphi(A_{u_0}) \cap \varphi(B_{u_0})$ that are equal to $\varphi(A') \cap \varphi(B_{u_0})$ for some $A' \subseteq A_{u_0}$. Let us describe this process in more detail. If u_0 is a leaf of the decomposition and the element e associated with it is a bridge of $\mathcal{M}$, the list $\mathcal{L}_{u_0}^A$ consists only of the zero subspace. If e is not a bridge, then the list $\mathcal{L}_{u_0}^A$ consists of the zero subspace and the linear subspace $\varphi(\{e\})$. If u_0 is an inner node with two children u_1 and u_2, then the list $\mathcal{L}_{u_0}^A$ is formed by all the linear subspaces equal to $\overline{U_1 \cup U_2} \cap \varphi(B_{u_0})$ for some $U_1 \in \mathcal{L}_{u_1}^A$ and $U_2 \in \mathcal{L}_{u_2}^A$. Since the lists $\mathcal{L}_{u_0}^A$ are formed by linear subspaces of a k-dimensional linear space over $\mathbb{F}$, $|\mathcal{L}_{u_0}^A| \leq |\mathbb{F}|^{k^2}$. Hence, the sizes of the lists $\mathcal{L}_{u_0}^A$ are bounded by a function of $\mathbb{F}$ and k only and we only perform a constant number of operations with linear subspaces over $\mathbb{F}$ for each node u_0 (if the field $\mathbb{F}$ and the branch-width k are fixed). Analogously, we can find the lists $\mathcal{L}_{u_0}^B$ of all linear subspaces equal to $\varphi(B') \cap \varphi(A_{u_0})$ for some $B' \subseteq B_{u_0}$.

Our next goal is to recognize B_{u_0}-indistinguishable sets. By the definition of B_{u_0}-indistinguishability, if two different subsets $A_1, A_2 \subseteq A_{u_0}$ correspond to the same set of $\mathcal{L}_{u_0}^A$, i.e.,

$$\varphi(A_1) \cap \varphi(B_{u_0}) = \varphi(A_2) \cap \varphi(B_{u_0}) = U \in \mathcal{L}_{u_0}^A,$$

then the sets A_1 and A_2 are B_{u_0}-indistinguishable. The converse need not be true. Still, we can now efficiently test whether two sets A_1 and A_2 are B_{u_0}-indistinguishable as follows: let $U_1 = \varphi(A_1) \cap \varphi(B_{u_0}) \in \mathcal{L}_{u_0}^A$ and $U_2 = \varphi(A_2) \cap \varphi(B_{u_0}) \in \mathcal{L}_{u_0}^A$. The sets A_1 and A_2 are B_{u_0}-indistinguishable if and only if

$$\dim \overline{U_1 \cup U} = \dim \overline{U_2 \cup U} \tag{2}$$

for every $U \in \mathcal{L}_{u_0}^B$. This condition can be efficiently tested since the size of $\mathcal{L}_{u_0}^B$ is bounded by a function of $\mathbb{F}$ and k. Hence, we can partition the list $\mathcal{L}_{u_0}^A$ into classes of linear subspaces that correspond to B_{u_0}-indistinguishable sets. Formally, two linear subspaces U_1 and U_2 of $\mathcal{L}_{u_0}^A$ are B_{u_0}-*equivalent* if (2) holds for every $U \in \mathcal{L}_{u_0}^B$. Note that two subsets A_1 and A_2 of A_{u_0} are B_{u_0}-indistinguishable if and only if the linear subspaces $\varphi(A_1) \cap \varphi(B_{u_0})$ and $\varphi(A_2) \cap \varphi(B_{u_0})$ are B_{u_0}-equivalent. Clearly, partitioning the lists $\mathcal{L}_{u_0}^A$ into classes of B_{u_0}-equivalent linear subspaces requires only a constant number of operations with linear subspaces over $\mathbb{F}$ at each node of the tree (under the assumption that $\mathbb{F}$ and k are fixed).

We are now ready to construct the matrix M_{u_0}. Let u_1 and u_2 be the two children of u_0 and u' the parent of u_0. The rows and columns of M_{u_0} correspond to the classes of B_{u_1}-equivalent linear subspaces of $\mathcal{L}_{u_1}^A$ and B_{u_2}-equivalent linear subspaces of $\mathcal{L}_{u_2}^A$. The entry of M_{u_0} corresponding to the class containing $U_1 \in \mathcal{L}_{u_1}^A$ and the class containing $U_2 \in \mathcal{L}_{u_2}^A$, is labelled with $\dim U_1 + \dim U_2 - \dim \overline{U_1 \cup U_2}$ and is associated with the row/column of $M_{u'}$ that corresponds to the class containing the linear subspaces of $\mathcal{L}_{u_0}^A$ that are B_{u_0}-equivalent $\overline{U_1 \cup U_2} \cap B_{u_0}$. Clearly, computing each of the matrices M_{u_0} requires a constant number of operations with linear subspaces over $\mathbb{F}$ at each node of the decomposition. Hence, we conclude that the entire process described in this subsection requires time at most $O(n^4)$ where n is the number of elements of $\mathcal{M}$ if we assume that we can decide the equality of m-dimensional linear spaces over $\mathbb{F}$ and compute their unions and intersections in time $O(m^3)$ (note that the rank of $\mathcal{M}$ cannot exceed n).

4.2 Computing Representations

Throughout this subsection, we assume that the matrices M_{u_0} as described in Subsection 4.1 have been constructed. We would like to point out that we do not use the original representation of $\mathcal{M}$ over $\mathbb{F}$ at all throughout this subsection and use only the auxiliary matrices to construct a representation of $\mathcal{M}$ over a given finite field $\mathbb{F}'$.

Let us consider a node u_0 of the branch decomposition and let ℓ_{u_0} be the number of the classes of B_{u_0}-indistinguishable subsets of A_{u_0}. Note that ℓ_{u_0} is also the number of rows/columns of $M_{u'}$ where u' is the parent of u_0 that correspond to A_{u_0}. Let further $k_{u_0} = \operatorname{rank} A_{u_0} + \operatorname{rank} B_{u_0} - \operatorname{rank} \mathcal{M}$.

If φ is a representation of $\mathcal{M} \setminus B_{u_0}$ in a vector space over $\mathbb{F}'$ and U is its k_{u_0}-dimensional linear subspace, the *type* of a representation φ with respect to U is an ℓ_{u_0}-tuple $[\mathcal{L}_1, \ldots, \mathcal{L}_{\ell_{u_0}}]$ where $\mathcal{L}_i$ is the set of all linear subspaces of U equal to $\varphi(A') \cap U$ for some $A' \subseteq A_{u_0}$ contained in the i-th class of B_{u_0}-indistinguishable subsets of A_{u_0}, $i = 1, \ldots, \ell_{u_0}$. The representation φ is *proper* with respect to U if the sets $\mathcal{L}_i$ are mutually disjoint and the dimensions of linear subspaces contained in the same $\mathcal{L}_i$ are equal. Observe that a restriction of any representation φ of $\mathcal{M}$ to A_{u_0} with $U = \varphi(A_{u_0}) \cap \varphi(B_{u_0})$ is proper with respect to U.

Finally, let us refine the notion of isomorphic representations. Two representations φ_1 and φ_2 of $\mathcal{M} \setminus B_{u_0}$ are *strongly isomorphic* with respect to U if they have the same type $[\mathcal{L}_1, \ldots, \mathcal{L}_{\ell_{u_0}}]$ and there exists an isomorphism ψ of the linear spaces $\varphi_1(A_{u_0})$ and $\varphi_2(A_{u_0})$ such that $\psi(\varphi_1(e))$ is a non-zero multiple of $\varphi_2(e)$ for each element e of A_{u_0}. Note that if φ_1 and φ_2 are strongly isomorphic, then they are also isomorphic representations of $\mathcal{M} \setminus B_{u_0}$, but the converse need not be true since the strong isomorphism requires that they agree on the linear subspaces of U corresponding to B_{u_0}-indistinguishable subsets of A_{u_0}.

Let us fix a linear space U_{u_0} over $\mathbb{F}'$ of dimension k_{u_0} for each inner node u_0. Our next step is to compute the number of strongly non-isomorphic representations of $\mathcal{M} \setminus B_0$ with respect to U_{u_0} for each type $[\mathcal{L}_1, \ldots, \mathcal{L}_{\ell_{u_0}}]$ of a possible proper representation. The linear subspaces U_{u_0} are fixed in order to allow us to be able to define the type of a representation and are not the actual subspaces $\varphi(A_{u_0}) \cap \varphi(B_{u_0})$ in the representation of $\mathcal{M}$ that we aim to construct. The numbers of representations of $\mathcal{M} \setminus B_{u_0}$ are computed in the bottom to top fashion in the branch decomposition as we explain further in more detail.

Handling leaves of the decomposition. We first handle the case that u_0 is a leaf of the branch decomposition. Let e be the element of $\mathcal{M}$ corresponding to u_0. If e is a bridge of $\mathcal{M}$, then the empty set and $\{e\}$ are B_{u_0}-indistinguishable, $k_{u_0} = 0$ and $\ell_{u_0} = 1$. Hence, there is a single possible type $[\mathcal{L}_1]$ of a proper representation of $\mathcal{M} \setminus B_{u_0}$ in which $\mathcal{L}_1$ is the set containing only the zero subspace of U_{u_0} and there is a single (up to a strong isomorphism) representation of $\mathcal{M} \setminus B_{u_0}$ of this type—any representation of e with a non-zero vector over $\mathbb{F}'$.

If e is not a bridge of $\mathcal{M}$, then $k_{u_0} = 1$ and the empty set and $\{e\}$ are B_{u_0}-indistinguishable. Hence, $\ell_{u_0} = 2$ and there is again a single possible type $[\mathcal{L}_1, \mathcal{L}_2]$ of a proper representation of $\mathcal{M} \setminus B_{u_0}$ in which $\mathcal{L}_1$ is the set containing only the zero subspace of U_{u_0} and $\mathcal{L}_2$ the set containing the linear space U_{u_0}. Clearly, there is a single (up to a strong isomorphism) representation of $\mathcal{M} \setminus B_{u_0}$ of this type.

Handling inner nodes of the decomposition. Assume now that u_0 is an inner node of the branch decomposition and let u_1 and u_2 be its two children. We now have to merge the representations of $\mathcal{M} \setminus B_{u_1}$ and $\mathcal{M} \setminus B_{u_2}$ (this is closely related to rooted configurations as described in [10]). Let U be a superspace of U_{u_0} of dimension $k_{u_1} + k_{u_2}$ (note that $k_{u_0} \leq k_{u_1} + k_{u_2}$ by submodularity of the rank function). For all possible identifications of U_{u_1} and U_{u_2} with k_{u_1}-dimensional and k_{u_2}-dimensional linear subspaces of U, we proceed as described in what follows.

We say that two types $[\mathcal{L}'_1, \ldots, \mathcal{L}'_{\ell_{u_1}}]$ and $[\mathcal{L}''_1, \ldots, \mathcal{L}''_{\ell_{u_2}}]$ are *weakly compatible* if for every $U' \in \mathcal{L}'_{i'}, 1 \leq i' \leq \ell_{u_1}$ and $U'' \in \mathcal{L}''_{i''}, 1 \leq i'' \leq \ell_{u_2}$,

$$\dim U' + \dim U'' - \dim \overline{U' \cup U''}$$

is equal to the entry in the i'-th row and i''-th column of M_{u_0}. Finally, let $\mathcal{L}_i$ for $i = 1, \ldots, \ell_{u_0}$ be the set of all linear subspaces equal to

$$\overline{U' \cup U''} \cap U_{u_0} \text{ for some } U' \in \mathcal{L}'_{i'}, 1 \leq i' \leq \ell_{u_1} \text{ and } U'' \in \mathcal{L}''_{i''}, 1 \leq i'' \leq \ell_{u_2}$$

such that the entry at the the i'-th row and i''-th column of M_{u_0} is associated with the i-th row/column of the matrix of the parent of u_0. If all the sets $\mathcal{L}_i$, $1 \leq i \leq \ell_{u_0}$, are disjoint and the subspaces contained in each $\mathcal{L}_i$ have the same dimension, we say that the types $[\mathcal{L}'_1, \ldots, \mathcal{L}'_{\ell_{u_1}}]$ and $[\mathcal{L}''_1, \ldots, \mathcal{L}''_{\ell_{u_2}}]$ are *strongly compatible*.

Observe now that representations of $\mathcal{M} \setminus B_{u_1}$ and $\mathcal{M} \setminus B_{u_2}$ form a representation of $\mathcal{M} \setminus B_{u_0}$ if and only if their types are weakly compatible. The condition of being strongly compatible is then equivalent to having a proper type with respect to B_{u_0}. The sum of the products of the numbers of strongly compatible representations of $\mathcal{M} \setminus B_{u_1}$ and $\mathcal{M} \setminus B_{u_2}$ with the same resulting (proper) type $[\mathcal{L}_1, \ldots, \mathcal{L}_{u_0}]$ yields after normalization (we have to divide by the number of isomorphic identifications of U_{u_1} and U_{u_2} with linear subspaces of U that fix U_{u_0}) the number of strongly non-isomorphic representations of $\mathcal{M} \setminus B_{u_0}$ with the type $[\mathcal{L}_1, \ldots, \mathcal{L}_{u_0}]$.

Handling the root of the decomposition. It remains to glue our observations together. Since the root u_r of the branch decomposition corresponds to a loop, U_{u_r} is the zero space and there is a single type of representations of $\mathcal{M} \setminus B_{u_r}$ associated with u_r. This type is $[\mathcal{L}_1]$ where $\mathcal{L}_1$ is a set consisting of the zero subspace only. The number of strongly non-isomorphic representations of $\mathcal{M} \setminus B_{u_r}$ of this type is the number of non-isomorphic representations of $\mathcal{M}$. Hence, we have just presented an algorithm for counting the number of non-isomorphic representations of $\mathcal{M}$ over $\mathbb{F}'$. Note that the number of mappings from $\mathcal{M}$ to an n-dimensional vector space over $\mathbb{F}'$, where n is the number of elements of $\mathcal{M}$, is at most $|\mathbb{F}'|^{n^2}$ and thus all the numbers involved in the computation are $O(n^2)$-bit numbers. In particular, our algorithm has running time polynomial in n.

If we just want to decide the existence of the representation over $\mathbb{F}'$, we can replace the numbers of strongly non-isomorphic representations in our computation with flags indicating their existence. In this way, we obtain an

$O(n)$-algorithm for computing the existence of a representation of $\mathcal{M}$ over $\mathbb{F}'$ (note that $\mathbb{F}'$ and the maximal branch-width of $\mathcal{M}$ are fixed) from the matrices M_{u_0}.

Finally, it is easy to modify the presented algorithm to either output one possible representation of $\mathcal{M}$ over $\mathbb{F}'$ (keeping the running time polynomial in $n = |\mathcal{M}|$) or to output all such non-isomorphic representations (in this case, each representation can be output in time polynomial in $|\mathcal{M}|$, but the running time of the algorithm need not be polynomial in $|\mathcal{M}|$ since the number of such representations could be exponential in $|\mathcal{M}|$).

4.3   Finale

The results of Subsections 4.1 and 4.2 can be combined to the following:

Theorem 1. *For every $k \geq 1$ and two finite fields $\mathbb{F}$ and $\mathbb{F}'$, there exists a polynomial-time algorithm that for a given matroid $\mathcal{M}$ of branch-width at most k that is represented over the field $\mathbb{F}$ decides whether $\mathcal{M}$ can be represented over $\mathbb{F}'$ and if so, it computes one of its representation over $\mathbb{F}'$. The algorithm also counts the number of non-isomorphic representations of $\mathcal{M}$ over $\mathbb{F}'$. Moreover, it can be modified to list all such non-isomorphic representations (in time linearly dependant on the number of such representations).*

Note that we have just presented an algorithm that shows that the problem of deciding and computing a representation over a finite field $\mathbb{F}'$ of matroid of branch-width at most k that is represented over $\mathbb{F}$ is fixed parameter tractable with respect to the parameters k, $|\mathbb{F}|$ and $|\mathbb{F}'|$. Let us also remark that our algorithm can be modified to match the results of Bagan [2], i.e., the algorithm first utilizes a preprocessing polynomial time and it then outputs each possible representation of $\mathcal{M}$ over $\mathbb{F}'$ with delay linear in the size of the representation.

5   Concluding Remarks

We would like to address a possibility of extending our algorithm to matroids that are not represented over a finite field. As discussed in Introduction, it is NP-hard to decide whether a matroid $\mathcal{M}$ represented over $\mathbb{Q}$ with branch-width three can be represented over a finite field $\mathbb{F}$, $\mathbb{F} \neq \mathrm{GF}(2), \mathrm{GF}(3)$. A possible extension would thus be to assume that $\mathcal{M}$ is guaranteed to be representable over $\mathbb{F}$:

Problem 1. For every $k \geq 1$ and every finite field $\mathbb{F}$, design a polynomial-time algorithm that for a matroid $\mathcal{M}$ represented over $\mathbb{Q}$ of branch-width at most k that is representable over $\mathbb{F}$ finds a representation of $\mathcal{M}$ over $\mathbb{F}$.

In Problem 1, one can also consider matroids that are given by an oracle, however, in this setting, we do not believe that such an algorithm could be designed.

Let us now have a closer look at Problem 1. The algorithm that we presented in Section 4 has two separate parts. In the first part, we compute auxiliary matrices M_{u_0} and in the second part, we just decide the existence and eventually compute the representations just using these matrices. Hence, we need the representation of $\mathcal{M}$ over a finite field only in the first part of our algorithm.

In order to compute the auxiliary matrices, we need to be able to recognize for a k-separation (A, B) of $\mathcal{M}$ which subsets $A_1, A_2 \subseteq A$ are B-indistinguishable. This test is equivalent to testing whether the matroids $(\mathcal{M}/A_1) \setminus (A \setminus A_1)$ and $(\mathcal{M}/A_2) \setminus (A \setminus A_2)$ are isomorphic and the identity on the elements of B is an isomorphism between them. We ask the reader to verify that the entire algorithm presented in Subsection 4.1 works even if each class of B_{u_0}-equivalent linear subspaces is represented by a single subset $A' \subseteq A$ which is B_{u_0}-indistinguishable from all subsets of A corresponding to B_{u_0}-equivalent linear subspaces.

Hence, the algorithm that we designed can be turned into a polynomial-time algorithm for computing representations of a matroid over a finite field from its representation over $\mathbb{Q}$ if the following algorithm exists:

Problem 2. For every $k \geq 1$ and every finite field $\mathbb{F}$, design a polynomial-time algorithm that decides whether a bijection between the elements of two matroids $\mathcal{M}_1$ and $\mathcal{M}_2$ represented over $\mathbb{Q}$, such that the branch-widths of $\mathcal{M}_1$ and $\mathcal{M}_2$ are at most k and both $\mathcal{M}_1$ and $\mathcal{M}_2$ are representable over $\mathbb{F}$, is an isomorphism between $\mathcal{M}_1$ and $\mathcal{M}_2$.

Note that if we dismiss the assumption that $\mathcal{M}_1$ and $\mathcal{M}_2$ are representable over $\mathbb{F}$, the algorithm described in Problem 2 does not exist. If it existed, this would imply that testing representatibility over a fixed finite field $\mathbb{F}$ can be solved in a polynomial time for matroids of bounded branch-width that are represented over $\mathbb{Q}$ which is an NP-hard problem.

Acknowledgement

The author would like to thank Jiří Fiala for fruitful discussions on algorithmic matroid theory, in particular on efficient computation of the Tutte polynomial, at various occasions in the spring of 2002, Ondřej Pangrác for sharing his insights into matroid theory, and Till Tantau for his computational complexity remarks. The author also thanks the anonymous referees for their helpful comments that helped to improve the clarity of presentation of the results in this note.

References

1. S. Arnborg, J. Lagergren, D. Seese: Easy problems for tree decomposable graphs, J. Algorithms 12 (1991), 308–340.
2. G. Bagan: MSO queries on tree decomposable structures are computable with linear delay, in: Proc. of CSL 2006, LNCS vol. 4207, Springer, Berlin, 2006, 167–181
3. H. Bodlaender: Dynamic programming algorithms on graphs with bounded tree-width, in: Proc. of ICALP 1988, LNCS. vol. 317, Springer, Berlin, 1988, 105–119.

4. B. Courcelle: The monadic second-order logic of graph I. Recognizable sets of finite graphs, Information and Computation 85 (1990), 12–75.
5. B. Courcelle: The expression of graph properties and graph transformations in monadic second-order logic, in: G. Rozenberg (ed.), Handbook of graph grammars and computing by graph transformations, Vol. 1: Foundations, World Scientific, 1997, 313–400.
6. J. Geelen, B. Gerards, G. Whittle: Tangles, tree decomposition and grids in matroids, preprint.
7. J. Geelen, B. Gerards, G. Whittle: On Rota's Conjecture and excluded minors containing large projective geometries, J. Combin. Theory Ser. B 96(3) (2006), 405–425.
8. J. Geelen, B. Gerards, G. Whittle: Excluding a planar graph from GF(q)-representable matroids, manuscript.
9. J. Geelen, B. Gerards, G. Whittle: Inequivalent representations of matroids I: An overview, in preparation.
10. J. Geelen, B. Gerards, G. Whittle: Branch-width and well-quasi-ordering in matroids and graphs, J. Combin. Theory Ser. B 84 (2002), 270–290.
11. P. Hliněný: On matroid properties definable in the MSO logic, in: Proc. of MFCS 2003, LNCS vol. 2747, Springer, Berlin, 2003, 470–479.
12. P. Hliněný: A parametrized algorithm for matroid branch-width, SIAM J. Computing 35(2) (2005), 259–277.
13. P. Hliněný: Branch-width, parse trees and monadic second-order logic for matroids, J. Combin. Theory Ser. B 96 (2006), 325–351.
14. P. Hliněný: On matroid representatibility and minor problems, in: Proc. of MFCS 2006, LNCS vol. 4192, Springer, Berlin, 2006, 505–516.
15. P. Hliněný, G. Whittle: Matroid tree-width, to appear in European Journal on Combinatorics.
16. S. Oum, P. Seymour: Certifying large branch-width, in: Proc. of SODA 2006, SIAM, 2006, 810–813.
17. S. Oum, P. Seymour: Approximating clique-width and branch-width, to appear in J. Combin. Theory, Ser. B.
18. S. Oum, P. Seymour: Testing branch-width, to appear in J. Combin. Theory, Ser. B.
19. J. G. Oxley: Matroid theory, Oxford University Press, 1992.
20. G.-C. Rota: Combinatorial theory, old and new, Actes du Congrès International de Mathématiciens, vol. 3, Gauthier-Villars, Paris, 1970, 229–233.
21. P. Seymour: Decomposition of regular matroids, J. Combin. Theory Ser. B 28 (1980), 305–359.
22. P. Seymour: Recognizing graphic matroids, Combinatorica 1 (1981), 75–78.
23. K. Truemper: Matroid decomposition, Academic Press, 1992.

Characterizing Minimal Interval Completions

Towards Better Understanding of Profile and Pathwidth (Extended Abstract)[*]

Pinar Heggernes[1], Karol Suchan[2,3], Ioan Todinca[2], and Yngve Villanger[1]

[1] Department of Informatics, University of Bergen, N-5020 Bergen, Norway
pinar@ii.uib.no, yngvev@ii.uib.no
[2] LIFO, Université d'Orleans, PB 6759, F-45067 Orleans Cedex 2, France
todinca@lifo.univ-orleans.fr, suchan@lifo.univ-orleans.fr
[3] Faculty of Applied Mathematics, AGH - University of Science and Technology,
Krakow, Poland

Abstract. Minimal interval completions of graphs are central in understanding two important and widely studied graph parameters: profile and pathwidth. Such understanding seems necessary to be able to attack the problem of computing these parameters. An interval completion of a given graph is an interval supergraph of it on the same vertex set, obtained by adding edges. If no subset of the added edges can be removed without destroying the interval property, we call it a minimal interval completion. In this paper, we give the first characterization of minimal interval completions. We present a polynomial time algorithm, for deciding whether a given interval completion of an arbitrary graph is minimal. If the interval completion is not minimal the algorithm can be used to extract a minimal interval completion that is a subgraph of the given interval completion.

1   Introduction

Interval graphs have a long list of applications in areas like biology, chemistry, and archeology, and many NP-complete graph problems are solvable in polynomial time on interval graphs [11]. Specifically, the problem of adding edges to a given input graph to obtain an interval graph, called an *interval completion* of the input graph, arises in Physical Mapping of DNA [10], Orthogonal Packing [6], and Sparse Matrix Computations [9]. For several applications, it is desirable to embed a given graph into an interval graph by adding as few edges as possible. Such an embedding is called a *minimum interval completion*, and the number of edges it contains is called the *profile* of the input graph. Another well known variant is to find an interval completion with the smallest possible maximum clique, which corresponds to the widely used graph parameter *pathwidth*. Many NP-complete graph problems are solvable on graphs whose pathwidth is bounded by a constant [1], thus it is an important task to compute the pathwidth of an input graph.

---

[*] This work is supported by the Research Council of Norway.

W. Thomas and P. Weil (Eds.): STACS 2007, LNCS 4393, pp. 236–247, 2007.

Both profile and pathwidth are well known and well studied graph parameters, and naturally both are NP-hard to compute [8,12]. There has been extensive work on computing these parameters for restricted graph classes [5], but our insight on how to handle arbitrary graphs is limited. One good news is that for both problems, the solutions can be found within the set of minimal interval completions. This is our main motivation to study minimal interval completions.

A minimal interval completion of an arbitrary graph can be computed in polynomial time [13], but still the knowledge about minimal interval completions is limited. Until now it was not known how to decide whether a given interval completion is minimal. In this paper, we solve exactly this problem. We characterize minimal interval completions, which enables us to answer whether or not a given interval completion is minimal, in polynomial time.[1]

Two other important and widely studied graph parameters are minimum fill and treewidth, and these are defined analogously to profile and pathwidth, by simply exchanging interval graphs with chordal graphs. As a comparison, minimal chordal completions were studied and a polynomial time algorithm for computing them was given already in 1976 [18], even before it was proved that minimum fill is NP-hard to compute [19]. Minimal chordal completions have several quite different characterizations, and some of these have proved useful in trying to compute minimum fill and treewidth [4,15], either by approximation algorithms [16] or by exact (fast) exponential time algorithms [7]. Following the history of chordal completions, our hope is that understanding and characterizing minimal interval completions will eventually lead to improved exact or approximation algorithms for computing profile and pathwidth.

In addition to characterizing minimal interval completions, we present the first polynomial time algorithm for making any given interval completion minimal by removing edges. Thus another impact of our results is that any output graph from a heuristic algorithm for computing profile or pathwidth can be enhanced by using our algorithm, which will produce a minimal interval completion that is a subgraph of the given initial interval completion. For practical purposes, such approaches have proved useful in connection with treewidth [2] and minimum fill [17], and can now be applied to pathwidth and profile by our results. Due to space limitations all proofs and some lemmas that only have applications in the proofs are excluded in this version; for a full version, see [14].

2   Definitions and Terminology

We work with simple and undirected graphs $G = (V, E)$, with vertex set $V(G) = V$ and edge set $E(G) = E$, and we let $n = |V|$, $m = |E|$. For a given vertex set $X \subset V$, $G[X]$ denotes the subgraph of G induced by the vertices in X. For simplicity, we will use $G - x$ instead of $G[V \setminus \{x\}]$, and $G - X$ instead of $G[V \setminus X]$. Similarly, when we remove a single edge xy or a set of edges D from G, we will use $G - xy$ and $G - D$ instead of the correct formal notation. A vertex set X is

---

[1] A polynomial time algorithm for computing minimal interval completions does not necessarily imply that this question can be answered in polynomial time.

a *clique* if $G[X]$ is a complete graph, and a *maximal clique* if no superset of X is a clique. The set of all maximal cliques of G is denoted by $\mathcal{K}(G)$.

The set of neighbors of a vertex x is denoted by $N_G(x) = \{y \mid xy \in E\}$, and the *closed neighborhood* is $N_G[x] = N_G(x) \cup \{x\}$. For a vertex set X, similarly, $N_G(X) = \{y \notin X \mid xy \in E \text{ and } x \in X\}$ and $N_G[X] = N_G(X) \cup X$. A vertex x is called simplicial if $N_G(x)$ is a clique in G.

Definition 1 ([1]). *A path-decomposition of an arbitrary graph* $G = (V, E)$ *is a sequence* $P = (X_1, X_2, \ldots, X_r)$ *of subsets of* V, *called* bags, *such that the following three conditions are satisfied.*

1. *Each vertex* x *appears in some bag.*
2. *For every edge* $xy \in E$ *there is a bag containing both* x *and* y.
3. *For every vertex* $x \in V$, *the bags containing* x *appear consecutively in* P.

Such a path decomposition can be constructed for any graph G, for example by taking a unique bag containing $V(G)$. The width of a decomposition is the maximum size of a bag, minus one, and the *pathwidth* of a graph is the minimum width over all possible path decomposition.

For interval graphs, special path decompositions exist such that each bag is a maximal clique, and the largest maximal clique gives the pathwidth. A graph is an *interval graph* if intervals can be associated to its vertices such that two vertices are adjacent if and only if their corresponding intervals overlap. Let us define more formally the special kind of path decompositions mentioned:

Definition 2. *A* clique-path *of a graph* G *is a permutation* $P = (K_1, \ldots, K_p)$ *of the maximal cliques of* G, *such that the maximal cliques containing* x *appear consecutively in* P, *for every vertex* x *of* G.

Theorem 1 ([11]). *A graph* G *is an interval graph if and only if if has a clique-path.*

In a given clique-path $P = (K_1, \ldots, K_p)$, the maximal cliques K_1 and K_p are called *leaf cliques* or *end cliques*. An interval graph has at most n maximal cliques.

Since the vertices of every maximal clique must appear together in some bag in every path decomposition, a clique-path is an optimal path decomposition for an interval graph, with respect to pathwidth. Interval graphs can be recognized, and their clique-paths can be computed, in linear time [3]. If a clique-path of an interval graph is given, then its interval representation can be easily obtained by assigning to each vertex x the interval consisting of the maximal cliques that contain x.

To any path-decomposition P of G, we can naturally associate an interval supergraph of G. Let `PathFill`(G, P) be the graph obtained by adding edges to G so that each bag of P becomes a clique. It is straight forward to verify that `PathFill`(G, P) is an interval supergraph of G for every path-decomposition P. In addition, we can obtain a clique-path of `PathFill`(G, P) by simply removing bags of P that are not maximal cliques of `PathFill`(G, P) or that are duplicates of other bags.

An interval supergraph $H = (V, E \cup F)$ of a given graph $G = (V, E)$, with $E \cap F = \emptyset$, is called an *interval completion*. The set F is called the set of *fill edges* of H. If there is no proper subset $F' \subset F$ such that $(V, E \cup F')$ is an interval graph, then H is called a *minimal interval completion* of G. With a weaker constraint, we say that H is a *quasi-minimal interval completion* of G if no single fill edge can be removed from H without destroying interval graph property. Simple examples exist to show that quasi-minimal interval completions are not necessarily minimal.

Finally, we would like to mention that clique-paths are useful also in connection with vertex separators. A vertex set $S \subset V$ is a *separator* if $G - S$ is disconnected. The set of connected components of $G - S$ is denoted by $C(G - S)$. Given two vertices u and v, S is a u, v-*separator* if u and v belong to different connected components of $G - S$. A u, v-separator S is *minimal* if no proper subset of S is a u, v-separator. In general, S is a *minimal separator* of G if there exist two vertices u and v in G such that S is a minimal u, v-separator. For a minimal separator S of G and C, a connected component of $G - S$ such that $N_G(C) = S$, we say that the set $B = S \cup C$ is a *block*.

Lemma 1 (see e.g. [11]). *Let H be an interval graph and let $P = (K_1, \ldots, K_p)$ be any clique path of H. A set of vertices S is a minimal separator of H if and only if S is the intersection of two maximal cliques of H that are consecutive in P.*

Assume that we are given an interval completion H of an arbitrary graph G. We want to find out whether H is a minimal interval completion. First we can start by trying to remove every single fill edge and test, in linear time, whether the remaining graph is an interval graph. After a number of steps (which is at most quadratic in the number of edges of H) we reach a quasi-minimal interval completion. Thus from now on, we assume that we are given a quasi-minimal interval completion H of G, and we want to decide whether it is minimal. If it is not minimal, we know that there is one that is minimal which is a strict subgraph of H, and before we finally find a minimal one, we might explore several strict interval subgraphs of H that are not minimal.

Let us give different names to these different interval completions of G. Let H_2 be the given quasi-minimal interval completion of G. If it is not minimal, let H_0 be a minimal interval completion of G that is a subgraph of H_2. Since we are only given G and H_2, and we do not know H_0, we will probably discover several intermediate graphs H_1, where H_1 is an interval completion of G that is a strict subgraph of H_2. Hence we have the following relations between these graphs: $E(G) \subset E(H_0) \subseteq E(H_1) \subset E(H_2)$. The first subset relation is proper because we can always check before start whether or not G is already an interval graph, in linear time. Even though we do not know H_0, we know that H_2 is a non-minimal and quasi-minimal interval completion of H_0. In the next section, we give useful properties about two interval graphs that have this relationship.

3   Folding Interval Graphs

Let H_0 be any interval graph (which is the unknown minimal interval completion of some given graph G in our case), and let H_2 be a non-minimal interval completion of H_0 (we think of it as being the given non-minimal but quasi-minimal interval completion of G). In this section we give an algorithm that computes any such completion H_2, given H_0. Of course, in our problem, we are given H_2 and not H_0. However, this algorithm provides the necessary understanding that will enable us to do the opposite operation; namely, computing H_0, given G and H_2.

Every permutation Q of the maximal cliques of H_0 defines an interval completion H_2 of H_0, as described by Algorithm FillFolding in Figure 1. Note that $Q(i)$ denotes the maximal clique in the ith position of Q.

Definition 3. *Let H be any interval graph, let Q be any permutation of the set of maximal cliques of H. We say that (H, Q) is a* folding *of H by Q.*

Algorithm FillFolding
Input: H_0 and Q;
Output: An interval completion H_2 of H_0;

$P_2 = Q$;
for each vertex x of H_0 **do**
    $s = \min\{i \mid x \in Q(i)\}$;
    $t = \max\{i \mid x \in Q(i)\}$;
    for $j = s + 1$ to $t - 1$ **do**
        $P_2(j) = P_2(j) \cup \{x\}$;
end-for
$H_2 = \text{PathFill}(H_0, P_2)$;

Fig. 1. The FillFolding algorithm

Lemma 2. *Given a folding (H_0, Q) of H_0, the graph $H_2 = FillFolding(H_0, Q)$ is an interval completion of H_0.*

The graph H_2 defined by a folding of H_0 is not necessarily a quasi-minimal interval completion of H_0. Nevertheless, by showing that any edge of $E(H_2) \setminus E(H_0)$ is contained in at least to maximal cliques of H_2, and carefull analysis of the relation ship between maximal cliques of H_0 and H_2 the following relationship between quasi-minimal interval completions and foldings are obtained.

Theorem 2. *Let H_2 be a quasi-minimal interval completion of an interval graph H_0. Then there exists a folding (H_0, Q) of H_0 such that $H_2 = FillFolding(H_0, Q)$.*

Given only the arbitrary graph G and a quasi-minimal interval completion H_2, we know by Theorem 2 that H_2 is defined by a folding of H_0, a minimal interval completion of G. In general it is difficult to find directly the graph H_0. Instead, we can analyze a sequence of interval completions that are between H_0 and H_2, where passing from one step to another needs a folding of a much more constrained nature than the general one – that we call *reduced folding*.

Definition 4. *Let (H_0, Q_0) be a folding. A clique $K \in Q$ is called a* pivot *in (H_0, Q_0) if there is a clique-path P_0 of H_0 where both cliques just next to K (one to the left, the other to the right) in P_0 are on the same side of K in Q_0.*

Definition 5. *A folding (H, Q) is said to be* reduced *if every pivot contains a simplicial vertex of H.*

Theorem 3. *Let H_2 be a quasi-minimal interval completion of H_0 defined by a folding (H_0, Q_0). Then there is an interval graph H_1 such that $H_0 \subseteq H_1 \subset H_2$, and $H_2 = \texttt{FillFolding}(H_1, Q_1)$ for some reduced folding (H_1, Q_1) of H_1.*

Lemma 3. *Let $H_2 = \texttt{FillFolding}(H_1, Q_1)$ for a reduced folding (H_1, Q_1). Then every pivot of (H_1, Q_1) contains a simplicial vertex in H_2, thus the pivot is contained in exactly one maximal clique of H_2.*

4   Unfolding

Let H_2 be a quasi-minimal interval completion with a clique-path P_2, obtained by the Algorithm `FillFolding` on (H_0, Q). For the analysis presented in this section, we need to fix a clique-path P_0 of H_0. The reason for this is that with the general definition of a pivot, a pivot K may have different neighbors in distinct clique-paths of H_0. So it may happen that the neighbors of K in P_0 appear at the same side of K in the permutation Q, whereas the neighbors of K in P_0', another clique-path of H_0, appear at different sides of K in Q. For the ease of argument, from now on we should think of a folding as a triple.

Definition 6. *Let H be an interval graph, P be a clique-path of H and Q be a permutation of its maximal cliques. The triple (H, Q, P) is a* folding.

The definition of a pivot becomes more constrained.

Definition 7. *Let (H_0, Q, P_0) be a folding. A clique $K \in Q$ is called a* pivot *in (H_0, Q, P_0) if both cliques just next to K in P_0 are on the same side of K in Q_0.*

Definition 8. *Let H_0 be an interval graph with a clique-path P_0. Let (H_0, Q, P_0) be a reduced folding. If Q contains just one pivot then it is called a* 1-folding. *If Q contains exactly 2 pivots, none of which is at an end of Q, then it is called a* 2-folding.

We show in this section that if the quasi-minimal completion H_2 of G is not minimal, there is an interval graph H_1 containing G and strictly contained in H_2 such that H_2 is obtained by a reduced 1-folding or a reduced 2-folding of H_1. In the next section we give a polynomial algorithm constructing H_1.

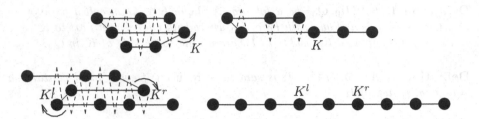

Fig. 2. Each circle represents a maximal clique in the input interval graph H_0, and each line provides the information that the two maximal cliques are consecutive in the clique path P_0 of H_0. The foldings are defined by the order of the maximal cliques from left to right. Arrows indicate in which direction a sub path is rotated around the pivot when we open a fold. The upper part demonstrates how to unfold when one of the extremal maximal cliques is a pivot, like K in this case. The lower part shows how to unfold when K^r is the rightmost pivot in Q and K^l is the leftmost pivot in Q that appears after K^r in P_0.

Let us sketch the main idea before getting into the technical details. The graph H_2 is equal to FillFolding(H_0, Q, P_0) for some smaller interval completion H_0 of G and some folding of H_0. Informally, we will slightly *unfold* (H_0, Q, P_0):

Definition 9. *A folding (H_0, Q', P_0) is an* unfolding *of (H_0, Q, P_0) if the set of pivots of (H_0, Q', P_0) is strictly contained into the set of pivots of (H_0, Q, P_0) and, moreover, the graph FillFolding(H_O, Q') is a (not necessarily strict) subgraph of FillFolding(H_0, Q).*

We will construct an unfolding (H_0, Q', P_0), having one or two pivots less than (H_0, Q, P_0). Then H_2 is obtained by a 1 or 2-folding of $H_1 =$ FillFolding(H_0, Q').

Theorem 4. *Let H_2 be a quasi-minimal, but not minimal interval completion of an arbitrary graph G. Then there exits a reduced folding (H_1, Q_1, P_1), with one (1-folding) or two (2-folding) pivots, with $E(G) \subseteq E(H_1) \subset E(H_2)$ and such that $H_2 =$ FillFolding(H_1, Q_1).*

Observation 1. *Let (H_0, Q_0, P_0) be a reduced 1-folding and let $H_2 =$ FillFolding(H_0, Q_0). Then its pivot is a maximal clique in H_2. Moreover, there is a clique path of H_2 such that this pivot corresponds to a leaf.*

The next results state that, if H_2 is a quasi-minimal interval completion of G and comes from a 1 or 2-folding of some H_1, there is an edge uv in $E(H_2) \setminus E(H_1)$ with special properties. In the next section, we shall ensure that the unfolding algorithm removes this edge.

Theorem 5. *Let $H_1 = (V, E_1)$, $H_2 = (V, E_2)$ be interval graphs and let (H_1, Q, P_1) be a 1 or 2-folding such that $H_2 =$ FillFolding(H_1, Q). If H_2 is a quasi-minimal but not minimal interval completion of H_1, then there is a fill edge uv, such that one of the pivots K is a u, v-separator in H_1. Moreover, in the clique path P_1, the vertices u and v appear on different sides of K.*

5   Extracting Minimal Interval Completions: The Algorithm

Let H_2 be a quasi-minimal interval completion of G and let H_0 be a minimal interval completion of G contained in H_2. Theorem 2 shows that there exists a folding (H_0, Q_0, P_0) that defines H_2, and by Theorem 4 there exists a reduced folding (H_1, Q_1, P_1) with one or two pivots that defines H_2. By Lemma 3 each pivot of (H_1, Q_1, P_1) is contained in exactly one maximal clique of H_2.

Let us now assume that (H_1, Q_1, P_1) is a folding such that every unfolding defines a graph with fewer edges than H_2. We will focus on finding an unfolding such that some fill edge uv is removed. The edge uv is chosen such that one of the pivots of (H_1, Q_1, P_1) is a u, v-separator in H_1 (see Theorem 5).

We will consider the cases of 1-folding and 2-folding separately. Let us first discuss the 1-folding case. Remember from Observation 1 that a maximal clique K of H_2 is a pivot in P_1 if (H_1, Q_1, P_1) is an 1-folding defining H_2.

Algorithm OneUnfolding
Input: A graph $G = (V, E)$, and an interval completion H_2 of G
Output: An interval completion H_1' of G such that
$E(H_1') \subset E(H_2)$ if H_2 is defined by a 1-folding of some H_1
$H_1' = H_2$ if no H_1 exists.

for each pair (Ω, u) where $\Omega \in \mathcal{K}(H_2)$ and $u \in V \setminus \Omega$
    Let C_u be connected comp of $G[V \setminus \Omega]$ containing u
    $H_1' \leftarrow (V, E(H_2[N_G[C_u]]) \cup E(H_2[V \setminus C_u]))$
    if H_1' is an interval graph and $E(H_1') \subset E(H_2)$ **then**
        return H_1'
return H_2

Fig. 3. Opening one pivot

Lemma 4. *Let $G = (V, E)$ be an arbitrary graph, and let H_1 and H_2 be two interval completions of G, such that $E(H_1) \subset E(H_2)$, H_2 is a quasi-minimal interval completion of H_1, and (H_1, Q_1, P_1) is a 1-folding that defines H_2. Then $H_1' = \text{OneUnfolding}(G, H_2)$ is an interval completion of G satisfying $E(H_1') \subset E(H_2)$.*

The two folding case is more complicated. First we define two vertex sets W^l and W^r by using G and H_2, and then these two vertex sets are used to obtain the unfolding of H_2. Several intermediate definitions are included in the definition of W^l and W^r. Figure 4 tries to give an indication of how these intermediate definitions relate to each other.

Let $H_2 = (V, E_2)$ be a quasi-minimal interval completion of a non-interval graph $G = (V, E)$. Suppose that H_2 is not minimal and choose the graph $H_1 = (V, E_1)$ such that $H_2 = \text{FillFolding}(H_1, Q)$, where (H_1, Q, P_1) is a reduced

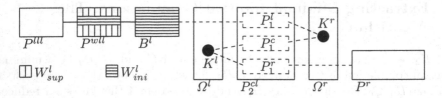

Fig. 4. The figure gives a sketch of how the defined maximal cliques, separators, and clique paths used to define W^l and W^r relate to each other. Two clique paths P^{lll} and P^{wll}, which are not needed for the definition of W^l and W^r, but provide a more detailed view of the situation in the figure are present: P^{wll} is the union of blocks of $H_2 \setminus S^l$ that have a non empty vertex intersection with W^l, while P^{lll} is given by the remaining blocks of P^{ll}.

2-folding and $E \subset E_1 \subset E_2$. Let P_2 be the clique path of H_2 obtained by the algorithm `FillFolding`(H_1, P_1). We can denote these clique paths as:

$$P_1 = P^l - -P_1^l - -K^r - -P_1^c - -K^l - -P_1^r - -P^r$$

$$P_2 = P^l - -\Omega^l - -P_2^c - -\Omega^r - -P^r$$

where K^l, K^r are the pivots and Ω^r, Ω^l are the maximal cliques of H_2 containing them. We have $K^l \subseteq \Omega^l, K^r \subseteq \Omega^r$.

Let S^l (S^r) be the separator between P^l and Ω^l $(\Omega^r$ and $P^r)$ in P_2. Notice that P^l, S^l, S^r, P^r appear also in P_1. Let B^l (B^r) be the interval of cliques that corresponds to the block of $H_2 - S^l$ $(H_2 - S^r)$ that is contained in P^l (P^r), the closest to Ω^l (Ω^r) in P_2. So we have:

$$P_2 = P^{ll} - -B^l - -\Omega^l - -P_2^c - -\Omega^r - -B^r - -P^{rr} \tag{1}$$

Notice that $C^l = V(B^l) \setminus \Omega^l$ $(C^r = V(B^r) \setminus \Omega^r)$ is a connected component of $H_2 - \Omega^l$ $(H_2 - \Omega^r)$. So, given H_2, Ω^l and Ω^r, we can efficiently compute the candidates for C^l and C^r. From now on we assume that $\Omega^l, \Omega^r, C^l, C^r, S^l, S^r$ are as described above. We want to find an unfolding of H_2, an interval graph $H_1' = (V, E(H_2[N_G[W^l] \cup S^l]) \cup E(H_2[N_G[W^r] \cup S^r]) \cup E(H_2 - (W^l \cup W^r)))$, with some well chosen W^l, W^r.

Let uv be an edge of $E(H_2) \setminus E(H_1)$. Like in Theorem 5, u and v are chosen such that one of the pivots of H_1, say K^r, separates u and v in H_1 and also in the clique path P_1. Suppose without loss of generality that u is in $V(P^l - -P_1^l) \setminus K^r$. In particular $u \notin \Omega^r$, and let C_u be the connected component of $G - \Omega^r$ containing the vertex u. Let $\mathcal{C}_v$ be the union of the connected components of $G - \Omega^r$ that contain or see the vertex v (we may have $v \in \Omega^r$, in which case there are several such components). Then we have:

Claim. C_u is contained in $V(P^l - -P_1^l) \setminus K^r$. $\mathcal{C}_v$ is contained in $V(P_1^c - -K^l - -P_1^r - -P^r)$. Moreover, u and v do not appear in K^r.

Definition 10.

$$W_{ini}^l = \bigcup \{C \mid C \in C(G - \Omega^r), C \cap B^l \neq \emptyset\} \cup C_u$$

$$W_{ini}^r = \bigcup \{C \mid C \in C(G - \Omega^l), C \cap B^r \neq \emptyset\}$$

When unfolding, we want the blocks corresponding to components of $H_2 - S^l$ that are in $P^{ll} - -B^l$ to stay blocks in $H_1' - S^l$. Let us investigate the connected components of $H_2 - S^l$. They induce a partition of $P^{ll} - -B^l$ into blocks of $H_2 - S^l$. Some of these blocks intersect connected components of $G - \Omega^r$ that are contained in W_{ini}^l. For example, all connected components of $G - \Omega^r$ that intersect B^l are also in W_{ini}^l. But there may be a block B^{lm} of $H_2 - S^l$ containing some components of $G - \Omega^r$ that are and some that are not in W_{ini}^l. In this case, B^{lm} is not a block of $H_1' - S^l$, where $H_1' = (V, E(H_2[N_G[W_{ini}^l]]) \cup E(H_2[N_G[W_{ini}^r]]) \cup E(H_2[V \setminus (W_{ini}^l \cup W_{ini}^r)]))$. In order to prevent this, we augment W_{ini}^l with W_{sup}^l, and W_{ini}^l with W_{sup}^l as defined below:

Definition 11.

$$W_{sup}^l =$$

$$\bigcup \{C \mid C \in C(G - \Omega^r), C \cap \Omega^l = \emptyset, N_{H_2}[C] \cap W_{ini}^l \neq \emptyset, N_{H_2}[C] \cap (W_{ini}^r \cup C_v) = \emptyset\}$$

$$W^l = W_{ini}^l \cup W_{sup}^l \tag{2}$$

$$W_{sup}^r = \bigcup \{C \mid C \in C(G - \Omega^l), C \cap \Omega^r = \emptyset, N_{H_2}[C] \cap W_{ini}^r \neq \emptyset, N_{H_2}[C] \cap W^l = \emptyset\}$$

$$W^r = W_{ini}^r \cup W_{sup}^r \tag{3}$$

We are now able to construct the unfolding.

Definition 12.

$$H_1' = (V, E(H_2[N_G[W^l] \cup S^l]) \cup E(H_2[N_G[W^r] \cup S^r]) \cup E(H_2 - (W^l \cup W^r))).$$

Lemma 5. *Let $G = (V, E)$ be an arbitrary graph, and let H_1 and H_2 be two interval completions of G, such that $E(H_1) \subset E(H_2)$, H_2 is a quasi-minimal interval completion of H_1, and (H_1, Q_1, P_1) is a 2-folding that defines H_2. Then $H_1' = \text{TwoUnfolding}(G, H_2)$ is an interval completion of G satisfying $E(H_1') \subset E(H_2)$.*

Lemmas 4 and 5 imply the main result of this paper. Algorithm Extract-MinimalIntervalCompletion is given in Figure 6.

Theorem 6. *There exists a polynomial time algorithm that, given an arbitrary graph G and an interval completion H_2 of G, computes a minimal interval completion H_1 of G, such that $E(H_1) \subseteq E(H_2)$.*

Algorithm TwoUnfolding
Input: A graph $G = (V, E)$, and an interval completion H_2 of G
Output: An interval completion H_1' of G such that
$\qquad E(H_1') \subset E(H_2)$ if H_2 is defined by a 2-folding of some $H_1 \subset H_2$
$\qquad H_1' = H_2$ if no H_1 exists.

for each tuple $(\Omega^l, \Omega^r, S^l, S^r, C^l, C^r, u, v)$
$\quad$ # Ω^l, Ω^r are maximal cliques of H_2
$\quad$ # S^l, S^r are minimal separators of H_2, contained in Ω^l and resp. Ω^r.
$\quad$ # C^l (C^r) is a component of $H_2 - S^l$ (resp. $H_2 - S^r$)
$\quad$ # u, v are vertices, $u \notin \Omega^r$
$\quad$ construct W^l using Equation 2
$\quad$ construct W^r using Equation 3
$\quad H_1' = (V, E(H_2[N_G[W^l] \cup S^l]) \cup E(H_2 - (W^l \cup W^r)) \cup E(H_2[N_G[W^r] \cup S^r]))$
$\quad$ **if** H_1' is an interval graph and $E(H_1') \subset E(H_2)$ **then**
$\qquad$ **return** H_1'
return H_2

Fig. 5. Opening two pivots

Algorithm ExtractMinimalIntervalCompletion
Input: A graph $G = (V, E)$, and an interval completion H_2 of G.
Output: A minimal interval completion H_1 of G, with $E(H_1) \subseteq E(H_2)$.

$H_1 = H_2$
$H_0 = G$
while $(H_0 \neq H_1)$
$\quad H_0 = H_1$
$\quad$ **for** each edge uv in $E(H_1) \setminus E(G)$
$\qquad$ **if** $H_1 - uv$ is an interval graph **then**
$\qquad\quad H_1 = H_1 - uv$
$\quad H_1 = \text{OneUnfolding}(G, H_1)$
$\quad H_1 = \text{TwoUnfolding}(G, H_1)$
return H_1

Fig. 6. Extracting a minimal interval completion

Let us point out that, by using as initial completion the complete graph, the algorithm ExtractingMinimalIntervalCompletion can obtain any of the minimal interval completions of G.

References

1. H. L. Bodlaender. A partial k-arboretum of graphs with bounded treewidth. *Theor. Comput. Sci.*, 209(1-2):1–45, 1998.
2. H. L. Bodlaender and A. M. C. A. Koster. Safe separators for treewidth. *Discrete Mathematics*, 306(3):337–350, 2006.

3. K. Booth and G. Leuker. Testing for the consecutive ones property, interval graphs, and graph planarity using PQ-tree algorithms. *J. Comput. Syst. Sci.*, 13:335–379, 1976.

4. V. Bouchitté and I. Todinca. Treewidth and minimum fill-in: Grouping the minimal separators. *SIAM J. Comput.*, 31:212–232, 2001.

5. J. Diaz, J. Petit, and M. Serna. A survey of graph layout problems. *ACM Comput. Surv.*, 34(3):313–356, 2002.

6. S. P. Fekete and J. Schepers. A combinatorial characterization of higher-dimensional orthogonal packing. *Math. Oper. Res.*, 29(2):353–368, 2004.

7. F. V. Fomin, D. Kratsch, and I. Todinca. Exact (exponential) algorithms for treewidth and minimum fill-in. In *ICALP*, volume 3142 of *LNCS*, pages 568–580. Springer, 2004.

8. M. R. Garey and D. S. Johnson. *Computer and Intractability: A Guide to the Theory of NP-Completeness*. W. H. Freeman, 1979.

9. A. George and J. W. Liu. *Computer Solution of Large Sparse Positive Definite.* Prentice Hall Professional Technical Reference, 1981.

10. P. W. Goldberg, M. C. Golumbic, H. Kaplan, and R. Shamir. Four strikes against physical mapping of dna. *Journal of Computational Biology*, 2(1):139–152, 1995.

11. M. C. Golumbic. *Algorithmic Graph Theory and Perfect Graphs*. Academic Press, San Diego, 1980.

12. J. Gustedt. On the pathwidth of chordal graphs. *Discrete Appl. Math.*, 45(3): 233–248, 1993.

13. P. Heggernes, K. Suchan, I. Todinca, and Y. Villanger. Minimal interval completions. In *ESA*, volume 3669 of *LNCS*, pages 403–414. Springer, 2005.

14. P. Heggernes, K. Suchan, I. Todinca, and Y. Villanger. Characterizing minimal interval completions. Towards better understanding of profile and pathwidth. Technical Report LIFO Research Report RR 2006-09, LIFO - University of Orleans, France., 2006.

15. H. Kaplan, R. Shamir, and R. E. Tarjan. Tractability of parameterized completion problems on chordal, strongly chordal, and proper interval graphs. *SIAM J. Comput.*, 28(5):1906–1922, 1999.

16. A. Natanzon, R. Shamir, and R. Sharan. A polynomial approximation algorithm for the minimum fill-in problem. *SIAM J. Comput.*, 30(4):1067–1079, 2000.

17. B.W. Peyton. Minimal orderings revisited. *SIAM J. Matrix Anal. Appl.*, 23(1):271–294, 2001.

18. D. Rose, R.E. Tarjan, and G. Lueker. Algorithmic aspects of vertex elimination on graphs. *SIAM J. Comput.*, 5:146–160, 1976.

19. M. Yannakakis. Computing the minimum fill-in is NP-complete. *SIAM J. Alg. Disc. Meth.*, 2:77–79, 1981.

The Complexity of Unions of Disjoint Sets

Christian Glaßer[1], Alan L. Selman[2,*],
Stephen Travers[1,**], and Klaus W. Wagner[1]

[1] Universität Würzburg, Germany
{glasser,travers,wagner}@informatik.uni-wuerzburg.de
[2] University at Buffalo, USA
selman@cse.buffalo.edu

Abstract. This paper is motivated by the open question whether the union of two disjoint NP-complete sets always is NP-complete. We discover that such unions retain much of the complexity of their single components. More precisely, they are complete with respect to more general reducibilities.

Moreover, we approach the main question in a more general way: We analyze the scope of the complexity of unions of m-equivalent disjoint sets. Under the hypothesis that $NE \neq coNE$, we construct degrees in NP where our main question has a positive answer, i.e., these degrees are closed under unions of disjoint sets.

1 Introduction

We report progress on the open question [Sel88] of whether the union of two disjoint NP-complete sets is NP-complete. Observe that this question has a negative answer if $P \subsetneq NP = coNP$, while it is not clear what to believe in the case that $NP \neq coNP$.

We prove that the union of two disjoint NP-complete sets belongs to the class $High_1$, the first level of Schöning's high hierarchy [Sch83]. Specifically, for every $k \geq 1$, if $A \in High_k$ and $B \in NP$ such that $A \cap B = \emptyset$, then $A \cup B \in High_k$. As a consequence [KS97], if A and B are disjoint NP-complete sets, then $A \cup B$ is a strongly-nondeterministic complete set for NP [Lon78].

In order to give further evidence that unions of disjoint NP-complete sets are not far from being NP-complete, we show that the union of an NP-complete set with a disjoint set in NP is nonuniformly NP-complete, under the following assumption: There exists a set $A \in NP$ such that A is not infinitely-often in coNP. Non-uniform reductions are of interest in cryptography, where they model an adversary who is capable of long preprocessing [BV97]. They also have applications in structural complexity theory. Agrawal [Agr02] and Hitchcock and Pavan

* This work was done while the author was visiting the Department of Computer Science at the University of Würzburg, Germany. Research supported in part by NSF grant CCR-0307077 and by the Alexander von Humboldt-Stiftung.
** Supported by the Konrad-Adenauer-Stiftung.

W. Thomas and P. Weil (Eds.): STACS 2007, LNCS 4393, pp. 248–259, 2007.
© Springer-Verlag Berlin Heidelberg 2007

[HP06] investigate non-uniform reductions and show under reasonable hypotheses that every many-one complete set for NP is also hard for length-increasing, non-uniform reductions.

Then we raise the more general question, given two many-one-equivalent, disjoint, sets A and B in NP, what can we say about the complexity of the union $A \cup B$. We call a set A m-idempotent if for all sets B and C,

$$(A \equiv_m^P B \equiv_m^P C) \wedge (B \cap C = \emptyset) \implies A \equiv_m^P B \cup C.$$

The set SAT is m-idempotent if and only if the union of two disjoint NP-complete sets always is NP-complete. We prove that every p-selective set that is not in P is m-idempotent. It follows readily that if NE $\neq$ coNE, then there exists $A \in$ NP $-$ coNP such that A is m-idempotent, and it follows that the class EXP contains m-idempotent sets.

Finally, we show that it is possible for the union of two disjoint sets to be harder than either of its components. We prove that if the polynomial hierarchy is infinite, then there exist sets A and B in NP(2) such that $A \equiv_m^P B$, $A \leq_m^P A \cup B$, and $A \cup B$ does not m-reduce to A. More precisely, we show this under the weaker assumption that the Boolean hierarchy over NP does not collapse to the second level.

To explore this possibility within NP, we show under an hypothesis that asserts strong immunity conditions that there exist disjoint sets $E, F \in$ NP $-$ coNP such that $E \equiv_m^P F$, but $E \cup F \not\leq_m^P E$.

Glasser et al. [GPSZ05] recently showed that all NP-complete sets are m-mitotic. This means that any NP-complete set A can be partitioned into disjoint NP-complete sets A_1, A_2. In a sense, the issue we are raising here, given two m-equivalent disjoint sets B_1 and B_2, how complex is the union $B_1 \cup B_2$, is to investigate the converse of that question.

2 Preliminaries

We recall basic notions. Σ denotes a finite alphabet with at least two letters, Σ^* denotes the set of all words, and $|w|$ denotes the length of a word w. A set $A \subseteq \Sigma^*$ is *nontrivial* if $A \neq \emptyset$ and $A \neq \Sigma^*$. A *tally set* is a subset of 0^*. The language accepted by a machine M is denoted by $L(M)$. The characteristic function of a set A is denoted by c_A. $\overline{L}$ denotes the complement of a language L and co$\mathcal{C}$ denotes the class of complements of languages in $\mathcal{C}$. 1NP [GW86] (also called US [BG82]) is the class of languages L for which there exists a nondeterministic polynomial-time-bounded machine M such that an input x belongs to L if and only if M on input x has exactly one accepting path. In contrast, UP is the class of languages L for which there exists a nondeterministic polynomial-time-bounded machine M such that $L = L(M)$ and on every input x, the machine M on input x has at most one accepting path [Val76].

FP denotes the class of functions computable in deterministic polynomial time. FP/poly is the superclass of FP that consists of all functions f for which there exists a total function $a : 0^* \to \Sigma^*$ such that

– there exists a polynomial p such that for all n, $|a(0^n)| \leq p(n)$, and
– there exists a $g \in \mathrm{FP}$ such that for all x, $f(x) = g(x, a(0^{|x|}))$.

The function a is called the *advice function*.

The *symmetric difference* of sets A and B is defined as $A \triangle B = (A - B) \cup (B - A)$. The complex version is defined as $\mathcal{C} \oplus \mathcal{D} = \{A \triangle B : A \in \mathcal{C}, B \in \mathcal{D}\}$. For a class of languages $\mathcal{C}$ which is closed under union and intersection, the *Boolean hierarchy over $\mathcal{C}$* [WW85] is the family of classes $\mathcal{C}(k)$ and $\mathrm{co}\mathcal{C}(k)$ where $k \geq 1$,

$$\mathcal{C}(k) =_{\mathrm{def}} \overbrace{\mathcal{C} \oplus \mathcal{C} \oplus \cdots \oplus \mathcal{C}}^{k \text{ times}}, \text{ and}$$
$$\mathrm{co}\mathcal{C}(k) =_{\mathrm{def}} \left\{ \overline{L} : L \in \mathcal{C}(k) \right\}.$$

The properties of Boolean hierarchies were studied by Köbler, Schöning, and Wagner [KSW87] and Cai et al. [CGH+88].

We recall standard polynomial-time reducibilities [LLS75]. A set B *many-one-reduces* to a set C (*m-reduces* for short; in notation $B \leq_m^P C$) if there exists a total, polynomial-time-computable function f such that for all strings x,

$$x \in B \iff f(x) \in C.$$

A set B *Turing-reduces* to a set C (*T-reduces* for short; in notation $B \leq_T^P C$) if there exists a deterministic polynomial-time-bounded oracle Turing machine M such that for all strings x,

$$x \in B \iff M \text{ with } C \text{ as oracle accepts the input } x.$$

A set B *2-disjunctively truth-table-reduces* to a set C (*2-dtt-reduces* for short; in notation $B \leq_{2-\mathrm{dtt}}^P C$) if there exists a total, polynomial-time-computable function $f : \Sigma^* \to \Sigma^* \times \Sigma^*$ such that for all strings x,

$$x \in B \iff \text{at least one word from the pair } f(x) \text{ belongs to } C.$$

A set B *non-uniformly many-one-reduces* to a set C (*non-uniformly m-reduces* for short; in notation $B \leq_m^{p/\mathrm{poly}} C$) if there exists a total function $f \in \mathrm{FP}/\mathrm{poly}$ such that for all strings x,

$$x \in B \iff f(x) \in C.$$

A set B *strongly nondeterministic Turing-reduces* to a set C [Lon78] (*snT-reduces* for short; in notation $B \leq_{\mathrm{snT}}^P C$) if there exists a nondeterministic polynomial-time-bounded oracle Turing machine M that on each computation path outputs exactly one symbol from $\{+, -, ?\}$ such that for all strings x,

$$x \in B \Rightarrow M^C \text{ on } x \text{ produces at least one } + \text{ and no } - \text{ and}$$
$$x \notin B \Rightarrow M^C \text{ on } x \text{ produces at least one } - \text{ and no } +.$$

If $B \leq_m^P C$ and $C \leq_m^P B$, then we say that B and C are *many-one-equivalent* (*m-equivalent* for short, in notation $B \equiv_m^P C$). Similarly, we define equivalence for other reducibilities. A set B is *many-one-hard* (*m-hard* for short) for a complexity class $\mathcal{C}$ if every $B \in \mathcal{C}$ m-reduces to B. If additionally $B \in \mathcal{C}$, then we say that B is *many-one-complete* (*m-complete* for short) for $\mathcal{C}$. Similarly, we define hardness and completeness for other reducibilities. We use the term $\mathcal{C}$-complete as an abbreviation for m-complete for $\mathcal{C}$.

Schöning [Sch83] defined a set $A \in$ NP to be *high* for Σ_k^P (the k-th level of the polynomial-time hierarchy) if $\Sigma_k^{P^A} = \Sigma_{k+1}^P$. High$_k$ is the class of languages that are high for Σ_k^P.

Disjoint sets A and B are called *p-separable* if there exists a set $S \in$ P (the separator) such that $A \subseteq S$ and $B \subseteq \overline{S}$. A set B is *m-mitotic* [AS84] if there exists an $S \in$ P such that $B \cap S$ and $B \cap \overline{S}$ are m-equivalent to B. B is *p-selective* [Sel79] if there exists a total function $f \in$ FP (the selector function) such that for all x and y, $f(x, y) \in \{x, y\}$ and if either of x and y belongs to B, then $f(x, y) \in B$.

Definition 1. *Let A be a set and $\mathcal{C}$ be a complexity class. The* reduction closure *and the* degree *of A (resp., $\mathcal{C}$) are defined as follows.*

$$\mathcal{R}_m^p(A) =_{\text{def}} \{B \mid B \leq_m^P A\},$$
$$\mathcal{R}_m^p(\mathcal{C}) =_{\text{def}} \bigcup_{A \in \mathcal{C}} \mathcal{R}_m^p(A),$$
$$\deg_m^P(A) =_{\text{def}} \{B \mid A \equiv_m^P B\},$$
$$\deg_m^P(\mathcal{C}) =_{\text{def}} \bigcup_{A \in \mathcal{C}} \deg_m^P(A).$$

It is easy to see that whenever a class $\mathcal{C}$ is closed under $\leq_m^P$, it then follows that $\deg_m^P(\mathcal{C}) = \mathcal{R}_m^p(\mathcal{C})$.

Definition 2. *Let $\mathcal{C}$ and $\mathcal{M}$ be complexity classes. We define*

$$\mathcal{C} \vee \mathcal{M} =_{\text{def}} \{A \cup B \mid A \in \mathcal{C}, B \in \mathcal{M}\},$$
$$\mathcal{C} \dot{\vee} \mathcal{M} =_{\text{def}} \{A \cup B \mid A \in \mathcal{C}, B \in \mathcal{M}, A \cap B = \emptyset\}.$$

Notice that the disjoint union used here is not the same concept as the marked union which is sometimes denoted by $\dot{\cup}$. The reason is that the latter leads to unions of disjoint p-separable sets, which does not have to be the case with $\dot{\vee}$. For instance, for all sets $A, B \in$ 1NP, it holds that $A \dot{\cup} B = 0A \cup 1B \in$ 1NP, implying that 1NP is closed under $\dot{\cup}$. Contrary to that, there exists an oracle relative to which 1NP $\dot{\vee}$ 1NP $\neq$ 1NP [GT06].

3   Unions of Disjoint NP-Complete Sets Are Not Easy

In this section we show that unions of disjoint NP-complete sets cannot be too easy. More precisely, we prove the following for disjoint NP-complete sets B and C.

1. $B \cup C$ is high for NP. Equivalently, $B \cup C$ is strongly nondeterministic-Turing-complete for NP [KS97].
2. Under a reasonable hypothesis, $B \cup C$ is non-uniformly many-one-complete for NP.

Our results show that unions of disjoint NP-complete sets remain complete with respect to more general reducibilities. This is evidence that unions of disjoint NP-complete sets retain much of the complexity of their single components.

As a byproduct, we obtain that the levels $1, 2, \ldots$ of the high-hierarchy are closed under disjoint unions with arbitrary NP-sets. Recently, Hitchcock and Pavan [HP06] showed that if NP does not have p-measure 0, then the levels 0 and 1 of the high-hierarchy are different.

3.1 Unions of Disjoint Sets from the High-Hierarchy

Lemma 1. *Let* $A, B \in \mathrm{NP}$ *such that* $A \cap B = \emptyset$. *Then* $\mathrm{NP}^A \subseteq \mathrm{NP}^{A \cup B}$.

Theorem 1. *Let* $k \geq 1$, $A \in \mathrm{High}_k$ *and* $B \in \mathrm{NP}$ *such that* $A \cap B = \emptyset$. *Then* $A \cup B \in \mathrm{High}_k$.

Corollary 1. *For all* $k \geq 1$, High_k *is closed under unions of disjoint sets.*

Corollary 2. *Let* $A, B \in \mathrm{NPC}$ *such that* $A \cap B = \emptyset$. *Then the set* $A \cup B$ *is* $\leq^{\mathrm{P}}_{\mathrm{snT}}$-*complete for* NP.

3.2 Uniformly Hard Languages in NP

Downey and Fortnow [DF03] studied languages that are uniformly hard for P. We here use a similar notion describing uniform-hardness for NP. In Section 3.1 we showed that the union of a disjoint NP-complete set and an arbitrary NP-set is high for NP. In this section we give further evidence that unions of disjoint NP-complete are not far from being NP-complete. To do so, we assume that NP contains uniformly hard languages, i.e., languages that are uniformly not contained in coNP. Under this hypothesis we show:

– For every NP-complete A and every $B \in \mathrm{NP}$ that is disjoint from A it holds that $A \cup B$ is nonuniformly NP-complete.

Definition 3. *Let* C *and* D *be complexity classes, and let* A *and* B *be subsets of* Σ^*.

1. $A \overset{\mathrm{i.o.}}{=} B \overset{df}{\Longleftrightarrow}$ *for infinitely many* n *it holds that* $A \cap \Sigma^n = B \cap \Sigma^n$.
2. $A \overset{\mathrm{i.o.}}{\in} C \overset{df}{\Longleftrightarrow}$ *there exists* $C \in C$ *such that* $A \overset{\mathrm{i.o.}}{=} C$.
3. $C \overset{\mathrm{i.o.}}{\subseteq} D \overset{df}{\Longleftrightarrow} C \overset{\mathrm{i.o.}}{\in} D$ *for all* $C \in C$.

The following result assumes the hypothesis that NP $\overset{\mathrm{i.o.}}{\not\subseteq}$ coNP. This is a believable assumption that says that (for sufficiently long formulas) not all tautologies of a given size have short proofs.

Theorem 2. *If* NP $\overset{i.o.}{\not\subseteq}$ coNP, *then for every* NP-*complete* A *and every* $B \in$ NP *that is disjoint to* A *it holds that* $A \cup B$ *is* $\leq_{\mathrm{m}}^{\mathrm{p/poly}}$-*complete for* NP.

4   The Complexity of Disjoint Unions

In this section, we abstract from the main question. We investigate how complex the union of two disjoint[1] equivalent NP sets can be, and we state interesting upper and lower bounds.

For any set A, we define the set $\mathcal{U}(A)$ which is the class of all sets which are m-equivalent to the union of two disjoint sets from the m-degree of A.

Definition 4. *For a set* A, *we define the class*

$$\mathcal{U}(A) =_{\mathrm{def}} \deg_{\mathrm{m}}^{\mathrm{P}}(\{C \cup D \mid C \cap D = \emptyset \wedge C \equiv_{\mathrm{m}}^{\mathrm{P}} D \equiv_{\mathrm{m}}^{\mathrm{P}} A\}).$$

The next theorem characterizes the scope of $\mathcal{U}(A)$. We state a technical lemma first.

Lemma 2. *Let* $\mathcal{K}$ *and* $\mathcal{M}$ *be complexity classes that are closed under* $\leq_{\mathrm{m}}^{\mathrm{P}}$. *Then the class* $\mathcal{K} \vee \mathcal{M}$ *is closed under* $\leq_{\mathrm{m}}^{\mathrm{P}}$ *as well.*

Theorem 3. *For all nonempty sets* A, *it holds that*

$$\deg_{\mathrm{m}}^{\mathrm{P}}(A) \subseteq \mathcal{U}(A) \subset \mathcal{R}_m^p(A) \vee \mathcal{R}_m^p(A).$$

Let A be a set and B and C be disjoint sets that are m-equivalent to A. In the next sections we will study the following phenomena:

- For some A, the union $B \cup C$ is always m-equivalent to A, no matter how B and C are chosen.
- For some A, the union $B \cup C$ can be less complex than A.
- For some A, the union $B \cup C$ can be more complex than A.

4.1   Disjoint Sets Whose Union Is at Most as Hard as the Single Components

In the following section, we consider m-equivalent, disjoint sets whose union is at most as complex as the single components. We prove that two extremes can occur:

- Unions of disjoint, m-equivalent NP sets can be equivalent to their single components (Theorem 5).
- Unions of disjoint, m-equivalent NP sets can be very easy, e.g. in P (Theorem 8).

---

[1] Note that the main question can easily be solved for non-disjoint unions of NP-complete sets: $0\mathrm{SAT} \cup 1\Sigma^*$ and $0\Sigma^* \cup 1\mathrm{SAT}$ are NPC sets whose union is in P.

Definition 5. *We say that a nontrivial set A is* m-idempotent *if the following holds for all sets B and C:*

$$(A \equiv_m^P B \equiv_m^P C) \wedge (B \cap C = \emptyset) \Longrightarrow A \equiv_m^P B \cup C.$$

Observe that a set A is m-idempotent if and only if $\deg_m^P(A) = \mathcal{U}(A)$; that is, the first inclusion in Theorem 3 is an equality. Furthermore, it is clear that whenever a set A is m-idempotent, the same holds for all sets $B \in \deg_m^P(A)$. It turns out that our main question can be formulated equivalently with the notion of m-idempotence.

Proposition 1. SAT *is m-idempotent if and only if the union of two disjoint* NP-*complete sets always is* NP-*complete.*

So it is open whether the sets in the highest degree of NP are m-idempotent. A more general question is to ask whether there exists a set $A \in$ NP such that the sets in the m-degree of A are m-idempotent. In other words, this is the question whether there is a set A in NP that has the least possible scope for $\mathcal{U}(A)$. Observe that such a set A must be in NP$-$P. Otherwise $0\Sigma^* \equiv_m^P (1\Sigma^* \cup \{\varepsilon\}) \equiv_m^P A$, which would imply that $\Sigma^* \equiv_m^P A$. This is a contradiction because A is nontrivial.

The next theorem states that the notion of p-selectivity can help us to find m-idempotent sets. More precisely, p-selectivity implies m-idempotence for any set outside the class P.

Theorem 4. *Let $A \notin$ P. If A is p-selective, then A is m-idempotent.*

The proof of Theorem 4 does also show that every degree having the property that all pairs of disjoint sets are p-separable is m-idempotent. It turns out that this holds in particular for degrees of p-selective sets. Moreover, if all pairs of disjoint sets in NP were p-separable, it would follow that P = UP [GS88] and that all sets in NP are m-idempotent. We refer to Fortnow and Rogers [FR02] for an analysis of this hypothesis. The next theorem gives a positive answer to the more general question whether NP contains m-idempotent sets under the assumption that NE $\neq$ coNE.

Theorem 5. *If* NE $\neq$ coNE, *there exists $A \in$ NP $-$ coNP such that A is m-idempotent.*

The class EXP contains m-idempotent sets unconditionally:

Theorem 6. *There exists an m-idempotent set $A \in$ EXP.*

We have shown that there are sets in EXP for which the first inclusion in Theorem 3 is an equality. Under a reasonable assumption, we have shown the same for NP. We now take a look at the second inclusion. The next proposition states that for nontrivial sets, at least one of the two inclusions has to be strict.

Proposition 2. *For any nontrivial set A, it holds that $\deg_m^P(A) \subsetneq \mathcal{R}_m^p(A)$.*

We will show that there exists a set $A \in \mathrm{NP}$ such that

$$\deg_m^P(A) \subsetneq \mathcal{U}(A) = (\mathcal{R}_m^p(A) \dot\vee \mathcal{R}_m^p(A)) - \{\emptyset\}$$

under the assumption that $\mathrm{P} \neq \mathrm{NP} \cap \mathrm{coNP}$.

We first prove that a set A cannot be m-idempotent if $\mathcal{R}_m^p(A)$ is closed under boolean operations.

Theorem 7. *If A is a nontrivial set and $\mathcal{R}_m^p(A)$ is closed under boolean operations then $\mathcal{U}(A) = \mathcal{R}_m^p(A) - \{\emptyset\}$.*

Proof. As $\mathcal{R}_m^p(A)$ is closed under boolean operations, it is easy to see that $\mathcal{R}_m^p(A) = \mathcal{R}_m^p(A) \dot\vee \mathcal{R}_m^p(A) = \mathcal{R}_m^p(A) \vee \mathcal{R}_m^p(A)$. Hence it follows from Theorem 3 that we only have to show $\mathcal{R}_m^p(A) - \{\emptyset\} \subseteq \mathcal{U}(A)$.

Let $E \in \mathcal{R}_m^p(A) - \{\emptyset\}$ and Σ be an alphabet such that $A \cup E \subseteq \Sigma^*$, let $a \notin \Sigma$ be a new letter, and let $\Delta =_{\mathrm{def}} \Sigma \cup \{a\}$. Say $E \leq_m^P A$ via function $h \in \mathrm{FP}$. Since $\mathcal{R}_m^p(A)$ is closed under complementation it follows that $\overline{A} \leq_m^P A$, say via function $h' \in \mathrm{FP}$, and hence $\overline{A} \equiv_m^p A$. So we can assume that $E \neq \Sigma^*$, since otherwise $E \in \mathcal{U}(A)$ holds trivially because $A \cup \overline{A} = \Sigma^*$.

Let $a_0, e_0 \in \Sigma^*$ such that $a_0 \notin A$ and $e_0 \notin E$.

We will define sets $A_0, A_1 \subseteq \Delta^*$ such that

- $A_0 \cap A_1 = \emptyset$,
- $A_0 \cup A_1 \equiv_m^P E$,
- $A_0 \equiv_m^P A_1 \equiv_m^P A$.

Notice that this implies $E \in \mathcal{U}(A)$.

We define $A_1 =_{\mathrm{def}} aA \cup E$ and $A_0 =_{\mathrm{def}} a(\Sigma^* - A)$. Clearly, $A_0 \cap A_1 = \emptyset$.

Claim 1. $A_0 \cup A_1 \equiv_m^P E$

Proof of the claim. It holds that $A_0 \cup A_1 = a\Sigma^* \cup E$. Let $f_1 : \Delta^* \to \Sigma^*$ be defined by

$$f_1(x) =_{\mathrm{def}} \begin{cases} x, & \text{if } x \in \Sigma^* \\ e_0, & \text{otherwise.} \end{cases}$$

Observe that $x \in a\Sigma^* \cup E \iff f_1(X) \in E$. As f_1 clearly is in FP, we have shown $A_0 \cup A_1 \leq_m^P E$. For the other direction, let $f_2 : \Sigma^* \to \Delta^*$ be defined by $f_2(x) = x$. Again, it is easy to see that $x \in E \iff f_2(x) \in a\Sigma^* \cup E$ and $f_2 \in \mathrm{FP}$. This proves the claim.

Claim 2. $A_0 \equiv_m^P A_1 \equiv_m^P A$

Proof of the claim. We will define functions $f_3, f_4, f_5 \in \mathrm{FP}$ such that $A_0 \leq_m^P A_1$ via f_3, $A_1 \leq_m^P A$ via f_4, and $A \leq_m^P A_0$ via f_5.

Define $f_3 : \Delta^* \to \Delta^*$ by

$$f_3(x) =_{\mathrm{def}} \begin{cases} ah'(z), & \text{if } x = az \text{ where } z \in \Sigma^* \\ e_0, & \text{otherwise.} \end{cases}$$

If $x \in A_0$, there exists $z \in \Sigma^* - A$ such that $x = az$. As h' reduces $\overline{A}$ to A, $ah'(z)$ is in A_1. If $x \notin A_0$, it either is of the form $x = az'$ where $z' \in A$ or $x \in \Delta^* - a\Sigma^*$. In the first case, $h'(z') \in \Sigma^* - A$, so $ah'(z) \notin A_1$. In the second case $f_3(x) = e_0 \notin A_1$. Obviously, $f_3 \in \mathrm{FP}$, hence $A_0 \leq_{\mathrm{m}}^{\mathrm{P}} A_1$.

We define $f_4 : \Delta^* \to \Sigma^*$ by

$$f_4(x) =_{\mathrm{def}} \begin{cases} z, & \text{if } x = az \text{ where } z \in \Sigma^* \\ h(x), & \text{if } x \in \Sigma^* \\ a_0, & \text{otherwise.} \end{cases}$$

If $x \in A_1$, either $x = az$ where $z \in A$ or $x \in E$. In the first case, $f_4(x) = z \in A$. In the second case, $f_4(x) = h(x) \in A$ since h reduces E to A. If $x \notin A_1$, we distinguish three cases:

1. Assume $x \in a(\Sigma^* - A)$, i.e. there exists $z' \in \Sigma^* - A$ such that $x = az'$. Then $f_4(x) = z' \notin A$.
2. Assume $x \in \Sigma^* - E$. Then $f_4(x) = h(x) \notin A$.
3. Assume $x \in (\Delta^* a \Delta^*) - (a\Sigma^*)$. Then $f_4(x) = a_0 \notin A$.

Together with $f_4 \in \mathrm{FP}$, we obtain $A_1 \leq_{\mathrm{m}}^{\mathrm{P}} A$.

Define $f_5 : \Sigma^* \to \Delta^*$ by $f_5(x) = ah'(x)$. If $x \in A$ then $h'(x) \in \Sigma^* - A$ hence $f_5(x) = ah'(x) \in a(\Sigma^* - A) \subseteq A_0$. If $x \notin A$ then $h'(x) \in A$ and hence $f_5(x) = ah'(x) \in A_0$. Obviously, $f_5 \in \mathrm{FP}$. This proves our claim.

As argued above, we have now shown that $E \in \mathcal{U}(A)$. This proves $\mathcal{R}_m^p(A) - \{\emptyset\} \subseteq \mathcal{U}(A)$. Altogether, we obtain $\mathcal{U}(A) = \mathcal{R}_m^p(A) - \{\emptyset\}$.   □

Corollary 3. *Let A be a nontrivial set. If $\mathcal{R}_m^p(A)$ is closed under boolean operations, then A is not m-idempotent.*

Consequently, no complete problem for a deterministic Turing-machine time or space complexity class can be m-idempotent. By Theorem 4, this also implies that no complete problem for a deterministic Turing-machine time or space complexity class except P can be p-selective.

The next theorem shows that unions of disjoints sets in NP can be much easier than the single components. In particular, there exists a degree $\deg_{\mathrm{m}}^{\mathrm{P}}(A)$ in NP − P such that all intermediate degrees can be reached by unions from disjoint sets from $\deg_{\mathrm{m}}^{\mathrm{P}}(A)$.

Theorem 8. *If $\mathrm{P} \neq \mathrm{NP} \cap \mathrm{coNP}$, then there exists a set $A \in (\mathrm{NP} \cap \mathrm{coNP}) - \mathrm{P}$ such that $\mathcal{U}(A) = \mathcal{R}_m^p(A) - \{\emptyset\} = \mathcal{R}_m^p(A) \dot\vee \mathcal{R}_m^p(A) - \{\emptyset\}$.*

By Proposition 2, the set A in Theorem 8 cannot be m-idempotent. Informally, the reason is that unions of sets in the degree of A can be too *easy* to be in the degree of A. As stated before, the question whether unions of NP-complete sets can be less than NP-complete is still open.

In the next section, we will show that the opposite can occur also, i.e. unions of equivalent sets can be harder than the original sets.

4.2   Disjoint Sets Whose Union Is Harder Than the Single Components

Buhrman, Hoene, and Torenvliet [BHT98] showed unconditionally that there exists an $A \in \text{EXP} - \text{P}$ such that A is not EXP-complete and not m-idempotent. Recall that due to Corollary 3, no EXP-complete problem can be m-idempotent.

Theorem 9. *[BHT98] Let C be m-complete for* EXP. *Then C can be split into A and B such that*

- $A, B \in \text{EXP}$,
- $A \equiv_m^p B$,
- $A \leq_m^p A \cup B = C$,
- $A \cup B$ *does not m-reduce to A, that means A, B are not m-complete for* EXP.

Corollary 4. *There exists $A \in \text{EXP}$ such that*

$$\deg_m^p(A) \subsetneq \mathcal{U}(A) \subseteq \mathcal{R}_m^p(A) \vee \mathcal{R}_m^p(A) = \text{EXP},$$

hence A is not m-idempotent.

In this case, the union of sets in $\deg_m^p(A)$ can be harder than A. We will identify degrees in Θ_2^p (more precisely, in the second level of the boolean hierarchy over NP) for which the same holds. After this, we will construct such sets within the class NP.

The *chromatic number* of a graph G (in notation $\text{cn}(G)$) is the smallest number k such that G is k-colorable.

Definition 6. *Let $\text{cn}(G)$ be the chromatic number of a graph G, and let $k \geq 1$. Then $\text{COLOR}_k =_{\text{def}} \{(G, a_1, \ldots, a_k) \mid G$ is a graph, $a_1 < \cdots < a_k$ and $\text{cn}(G) \in \{a_1, \ldots, a_k\}\}$.*

It is known that COLOR_k is $\leq_m^p$-complete for $\text{NP}(2k)$ [CGH+88]. Hence it follows that $\deg_m^p(\text{COLOR}_1) = \{A \mid A$ is m-complete for $\text{NP}(2)\}$ and that $\mathcal{R}_m^p(\text{COLOR}_1) \vee \mathcal{R}_m^p(\text{COLOR}_1) = \text{NP}(2) \vee \text{NP}(2)$.

Theorem 10. *There exist $\text{NP}(2)$-complete sets A and B such that*

- $A \leq_m^p A \cup B$,
- $A \cup B$ *does not m-reduce to A.*

unless the boolean hierarchy over NP *collapses to the second level.*[2]

Under the assumption that the boolean hierarchy over NP does not collapse, it follows that $\deg_m^p(\text{COLOR}_1) \subsetneq \mathcal{U}(\text{COLOR}_1)$. Hence, the NP(2)-complete sets are not m-idempotent. This indicates that the converse of Corollary 3 does not hold. COLOR_1 is an example for which $\mathcal{U}(\text{COLOR}_1)$ lies strictly between $\deg_m^p(\text{COLOR}_1)$ and $\mathcal{R}_m^p(\text{COLOR}_1) \vee \mathcal{R}_m^p(\text{COLOR}_1) - \{\emptyset\}$.

---

[2] This hypothesis is weaker than demanding that the polynomial hierarchy does not collapse.

Lemma 3. *For all sets A, the following are equivalent:*

1. $\mathcal{U}(A) \cap P \neq \emptyset$
2. $\mathcal{U}(A) \supseteq P - \{\emptyset\}$
3. $A \equiv_m^p \overline{A}$.

Theorem 11. *If the boolean hierarchy over NP does not collapse to NP(2), then it holds that*

$$\deg_m^p(\mathrm{COLOR}_1) \subsetneq \mathcal{U}(\mathrm{COLOR}_1) \subsetneq \mathcal{R}_m^p(\mathrm{COLOR}_1) \dot{\vee} \mathcal{R}_m^p(\mathrm{COLOR}_1) - \{\emptyset\}.$$

We now start our search inside NP. We prove under a stronger assumption that there exist m-equivalent disjoint sets E and F in NP such that $E \cup F$ is harder than E. In other words, we show under this assumption that there exists $E \in \mathrm{NP} - \mathrm{coNP}$ such that $\mathcal{U}(E) \not\subseteq \mathcal{R}_m^p(E)$. We then show that the existence of such a set E separates 2-dtt-reducibility from m-reducibility within NP. Consequently, it is not surprising that we need a stronger assumption to prove our result:

Definition 7. *A set L is* immune *to a complexity class C, or C-immune, if L is infinite and no infinite subset of L belongs to C. A set L is* bi-immune *to a complexity class C, or C-bi-immune, if both L and $\overline{L}$ are C-immune.*

Theorem 12. *If NP has NP ∩ coNP-bi-immune sets and NP ∩ coNP has P-bi-immune sets, then there exist disjoint sets $E, F \in \mathrm{NP} - \mathrm{coNP}$ such that $E \equiv_m^p F$, but $E \cup F \not\leq_m^p E$.*

The proof of Theorem 12 does also separate 2-dtt-reducibility from m-reducibility within NP:

Corollary 5. *If NP has NP ∩ coNP-bi-immune sets and NP ∩ coNP has P-bi-immune sets, then there exists $A, B \in \mathrm{NP} - \mathrm{coNP}$ such that such that $A \leq_{2-\mathrm{dtt}}^p B$, but $A \not\leq_m^p B$.*

References

[Agr02]   M. Agrawal. Pseudo-random generators and structure of complete degrees. In *IEEE Conference on Computational Complexity*, pages 139–147, 2002.

[AS84]   K. Ambos-Spies. P-mitotic sets. In E. Börger, G. Hasenjäger, and D. Roding, editors, *Logic and Machines*, volume 171 of *Lecture Notes in Computer Science*, pages 1–23. Springer-Verlag, 1984.

[BG82]   A. Blass and Y. Gurevich. On the unique satisfiability problem. *Information and Control*, 82:80–88, 1982.

[BH77]   L. Berman and J. Hartmanis. On isomorphism and density of NP and other complete sets. *SIAM Journal on Computing*, 6:305–322, 1977.

[BHT98]   H. Buhrman, A. Hoene, and L. Torenvliet. Splittings, robustness, and structure of complete sets. *SIAM Journal on Computing*, 27:637–653, 1998.

[BV97]   D. Boneh and R. Venkatesan. Rounding in lattices and its cryptographic applications. In *SODA*, pages 675–681, 1997.

[BWSD77]   R. V. Book, C. Wrathall, A. L. Selman, and D. P. Dobkin. Inclusion complete tally languages and the hartmanis-berman conjecture. *Mathematical Systems Theory*, 11:1–8, 1977.

[CGH+88]   J.-Y. Cai, T. Gundermann, J. Hartmanis, L. A. Hemachandra, V. Sewelson, K. W. Wagner, and G. Wechsung. The boolean hierarchy I: Structural properties. *SIAM Journal on Computing*, 17:1232–1252, 1988.

[DF03]   R. G. Downey and L. Fortnow. Uniformly hard languages. *Theoretical Computer Science*, 298(2):303–315, 2003.

[FR02]   L. Fortnow and J. Rogers. Separability and one-way functions. *Computational Complexity*, 11(3-4):137–157, 2002.

[GPSZ05]   C. Glaßer, A. Pavan, A. L. Selman, and L. Zhang. Redundancy in complete sets. In *Proceedings 23rd Symposium on Theoretical Aspects of Computer Science*, volume 3884 of *Lecture Notes in Computer Science*, pages 444–454. Springer-Verlag, 2006.

[GS88]   J. Grollmann and A. L. Selman. Complexity measures for public-key cryptosystems. *SIAM Journal on Computing*, 17(2):309–335, 1988.

[GT06]   C. Glaßer and S. Travers. Machines that can output empty words. In *Proceedings 31st Symposium on Mathematical Foundations of Computer Science*, volume 4162 of *Lecture Notes in Computer Science*, pages 436–446. Springer-Verlag, 2006.

[GW86]   T. Gundermann and G. Wechsung. Nondeterministic Turing machines with modified acceptance. In *Proceedings 12th Symposium on Mathematical Foundations of Computer Science*, volume 233 of *Lecture Notes in Computer Science*, pages 396–404. Springer-Verlag, 1986.

[HP06]   J. Hitchcock and A. Pavan. Comparing reductions to NP-complete sets. In *33rd International Colloquium on Automata, Languages and Programming*, volume 4051 of *Lecture Notes in Computer Science*, pages 465–476. Springer-Verlag, 2006.

[KS97]   J. Köbler and U. Schöning. High sets for NP. In *Advances in Algorithms, Languages, and Complexity*, pages 139–156, 1997.

[KSW87]   J. Köbler, U. Schöning, and K. W. Wagner. The difference and the truth-table hierarchies for NP. *RAIRO Inform. Théor.*, 21:419–435, 1987.

[LLS75]   R. E. Ladner, N. A. Lynch, and A. L. Selman. A comparison of polynomial time reducibilities. *Theoretical Computer Science*, 1:103–123, 1975.

[Lon78]   T. J. Long. *On some Polynomial Time Reducibilities*. PhD thesis, Purdue University, Lafayette, Ind., 1978.

[Sch83]   U. Schöning. A low and a high hierarchy within NP. *Journal of Computer and System Sciences*, 27(1):14–28, 1983.

[Sel79]   A. L. Selman. P-selective sets, tally languages, and the behavior of polynomial-time reducibilities on NP. *Mathematical Systems Theory*, 13:55–65, 1979.

[Sel88]   A. L. Selman. Natural self-reducible sets. *SIAM Journal on Computing*, 17(5):989–996, 1988.

[Val76]   L. G. Valiant. Relative complexity of checking and evaluation. *Information Processing Letters*, 5:20–23, 1976.

[WW85]   K. W. Wagner and G. Wechsung. On the boolean closure of NP. In *Proceedings International Conference on Fundamentals of Computation Theory*, volume 199 of *Lecture Notes in Computer Science*, pages 485–493. Springer-Verlag, 1985.

Kolmogorov-Loveland Stochasticity and Kolmogorov Complexity

Laurent Bienvenu

Laboratoire d'Informatique Fondamentale
39 rue Joliot-Curie, 13453 Marseille Cedex 13, France
Laurent.Bienvenu@lif.univ-mrs.fr

Abstract. Merkle et al. [11] that all Kolmogorov-Loveland stochastic infinite binary sequences have constructive Hausdorff dimension 1. In this paper, we go even further, showing that from an infinite sequence of dimension less than $\mathcal{H}(\frac{1}{2} + \delta)$ ($\mathcal{H}$ being the Shannon entropy function) one can extract by a selection rule a biased subsequence with bias at least δ. We also prove an analogous result for finite strings.

1 Introduction

In 1919 R. von Mises gave the first definition of algorithmic randomness, which was inspired by the law of large numbers. According to his definition, an infinite binary sequence α of zeroes and ones is said to be "random" (instead of "random sequence", von Mises used the term *collective*) if it is not biased, i.e. the frequency of zeroes goes to $\frac{1}{2}$, and if every sequence we can extract from α by an "admissible" selection rule is not biased. The second condition is important. Indeed, the infinite sequence 01010101010.... is not biased; however, and this is why no one would call it "random", the selection rule consisting in selecting the bits of even positions will select the subsequence 0000000...., which this time is biased. R. von Mises never made completely precise what he meant by admissible selection rule. When computability theory emerged two decades later, Church proposed a formal definition: he defined an admissible selection rule to be a (total) computable process which, having read the first n bits of an infinite binary sequence α, decides if it wants to select the next bit or not, and then reads it (of course, it is crucial that the decision to select the bit or not is made before reading the bit). The sequence of selected bits is the selected subsequence w.r.t. to the selection rule. Later, Kolmogorov and Loveland proposed a more permissive definition of an admissible selection rule: they argued that in Church's definition, the bits are read in order, which is too restrictive. Hence, they defined an admissible selection rule to be a (partial) computable process which, having read any n bits of an infinite binary sequence α, picks a bit that has not been read yet, decides whether it should be selected or not, and then reads it. Nowadays, the sequences α which are collectives w.r.t. to this last definition are called Kolmogorov-Loveland stochastic (KL-stochastic for short).

It turns out that even with this improvement, KL-stochasticity is too weak a notion of randomness. A method developed by van Lambalgen [16], which relies

W. Thomas and P. Weil (Eds.): STACS 2007, LNCS 4393, pp. 260–271, 2007.
© Springer-Verlag Berlin Heidelberg 2007

on randomness w.r.t. non-uniform probability measures, was used by A. Shen [14] to show that there exists a KL-stochastic sequence all of whose prefixes contain more zeroes than ones (this event has probability 0 for the uniform measure). In 1966, P. Martin-Löf introduced a notion of randomness which is now called Martin-Löf randomness and considered by many as the most satisfactory notion of algorithmic randomness. Its definition involved effective measure theory, but after the work of Levin, Chaitin and Schnorr, we know that Martin-Löf randomness can be characterized in terms of Kolmogorov complexity (we assume that the reader is familiar with this notion; if not, see [8]): an infinite binary sequence α is Martin-Löf random if $K(\alpha_0...\alpha_n) \geqslant n + O(1)$ (K being the prefix Kolmogorov complexity).

Now that we have this good notion of randomness, it is worth looking back at KL-stochasticity in the light of Kolmogorov complexity. For example:

Question 1. Do the initial segments of a KL-stochastic sequence have to be of high Kolmogorov complexity?

Question 2. Conversely, given a string α with some randomness deficiency (i.e. in the case where $K(\alpha_0...\alpha_n) \leqslant n - f(n)$ for some unbounded function f), can we quantify the maximal bias we can get by selecting a subsequence from α?

Concerning Question 1, the following two central theorems give a good picture of the situation:

Theorem 1 (Muchnik et al. [12]). *Let $f : \mathbb{N} \to \mathbb{N}$ be a computable function. If $f(n) = o(n)$, there exists a KL-stochastic sequence α such that*

$$K(\alpha_0...\alpha_n) \leqslant n - f(n) + O(1)$$

Theorem 2 (Merkle et al. [11]). *Let α be an infinite binary sequence. If*

$$\liminf_{n \to +\infty} \frac{K(\alpha_0...\alpha_n)}{n} < 1$$

then α is not KL-stochastic.

(as we will see later, the quantity $\liminf \frac{K(\alpha_0...\alpha_n)}{n}$ is called the constructive Hausdorff dimension of α).

Question 2 has been adressed in the case of finite binary sequences by Asarin [2], Durand and Vereshchagin in [5], who gave lower and upper bounds for the maximal bias one can extract from a sequence with a given randomness deficiency. However, not much is known in the case of infinite binary sequences. For example, Theorem 2 says nothing about the relation between the lim inf term and the maximal bias one can obtain by selecting a subsequence.

Both papers [11] and [5] use the same main three techniques, which are already present in [12] (where they were used to prove a weaker version of Theorem 2):

1. *Splitting technique.* Any sequence (finite or infinite) which has a linear randomness deficiency can be split into a finite number of subsequences such that

at least two of the subsequences have a linear randomness deficiency relatively to the other ones.

2. *Competing strategies.* Given two finite sequences u and v with known randomness deficiencies (say, respectively $K(u) = |u| - d_1$ and $K(v) = |v| - d_2$), one can construct (the construction depending only on d_1 and d_2, not on (u, v)) two strategies (the concept of strategy is formalized below) S_1 and S_2 such that: S_1 reads v and bets on u, S_2 reads u and bets on v, and either S_1 multiply its initial capital by a least 2^{d_1} or S_2 multiply its initial capital by at least 2^{d_2}. Hence, a good way to predict the bits of a string w with some random deficiency is to use the above technique 1 to split w into pieces such that two of them have some randomness deficiency and apply technique 2.

3. *Converting a strategy into a selection rule.* If a betting strategy wins on a sequence (finite or infinite) an amount of money which is expontential in the number of bets, one can construct from this strategy a selection rule which selects a biased subsequence.

Here we address Question 2 for both the finite and infinite cases. In section 2, we introduce some game-theoretic notions, and in particular the notion of (selective) betting strategy. We prove a refinement of the conversion of a strategy into a selection rule (Theorem 6), which will be of crucial use in the sequel.

In section 3, we start with an account of effective Hausdorff dimension. This is a well-known approach of algorithmic randomness, which was first introduced by Lutz [7], where he defines constructive Hausdorff dimension. We will also define Schnorr Hausdorff dimension, which was introduced by Downey et al. [4]. We then present our main result —Theorem 10— which is a quantitative version of the above Theorem 2, i.e. it relates explicitly the constructive Hausdorff dimension of a sequence to the maximal bias one can obtain by selecting a subsequence. More precisely, we provide a lower bound on this maximal bias, which we will prove to be optimal. We also give an interpretation of this result purely in terms of effective Hausdorff dimension.

Finally, in section 4, we will prove an analogous result in the framework of finite binary sequences, answering a question of Durand and Vereshchagin.

Before we move on to our discussion, we present the basic definitions and notation we will need in the sequel. We denote by 2^* the set of finite binary sequences, and by 2^ω the set of infinite ones. For every element $\alpha = \alpha_0\alpha_1\alpha_2...$ of 2^ω, and every $n, m \in \mathbb{N}$, we denote by $\alpha_{[n,m]}$ the string $\alpha_n\alpha_{n+1}...\alpha_m$. For all $u \in 2^*$, we denote by $u2^\omega$ the set of infinite sequences of which u is a prefix. We denote by $|u|$ the length of u.

We denote by $\sharp 0(\alpha, n)$ and $\sharp 1(\alpha, n)$ respectively the number of 0's and 1's among $\alpha_0..\alpha_{n-1}$. We set

$$Bias(\alpha) = \limsup_{n \to +\infty} \left| \frac{\sharp 0(\alpha, n)}{n} - \frac{1}{2} \right|$$

We denote by $\mathcal{H}(p)$ the entropy of the Bernoulli random variable with parameter p. Recall that for $p \in [0, 1]$, $\mathcal{H}(p) = -p \log p - (1 - p) \log(1 - p)$, and that $x \mapsto \mathcal{H}(\frac{1}{2} + x)$ is a decreasing bijection from $[0, \frac{1}{2}]$ to $[0, 1]$.

If Z is a subset of $\mathbb{N}$, and α, β are two elements of 2^ω, we call Z-join of α and β, and denote by $\alpha \oplus_Z \beta$, the element of 2^ω we get by merging α and β, placing the bits of β in positions i's such that $i \in Z$. Formally,

$$(\alpha \oplus_Z \beta)_i = \begin{cases} \alpha_{|\bar{Z} \cap \{0..i-1\}|} & \text{if } i \notin Z \\ \beta_{|Z \cap \{0..i-1\}|} & \text{if } i \in Z \end{cases}$$

If $Z = 2\mathbb{N} + 1$, we have $\alpha \oplus_Z \beta = \alpha_0 \beta_0 \alpha_1 \beta_1 ...$, and we abbreviate $\alpha \oplus_Z \beta$ by $\alpha \oplus \beta$.

If a set $A \subseteq \mathbb{N}$ is recursively enumerable, we denote by $A[\tau]$ the finite set containing the elements of A that appear during the first τ steps of a fixed enumeration of A.

2 Selection Rules vs Strategies

2.1 Selection Rules

We formalize the notion of selection rule we discussed above. A selection rule is a (partial) function $\sigma : 2^* \to \mathbb{N} \times \{\texttt{selects}, \texttt{scans}\}$.

We run a selection rule σ on a sequence α as follows. Let s_0 and h_0 be empty words, and p_0 be the empty set. We define s_n, h_n and p_n by induction. Informally, s_n represents the selected bits after n moves, h_n represents the history, i.e. the bits that have been read during the first n moves, and p_n the positions in α of these bits. At n-th move (by convention, there is a 0-th move):

- If $\sigma(h_n) = (k, \texttt{selects})$ and $k \notin p_n$, set $s_{n+1} = s_n \alpha_k$, $h_{n+1} = h_n \alpha_k$ and $p_{n+1} = p_n \cup \{k\}$.
- If $\sigma(h_n) = (k, \texttt{selects})$ and $k \in p_n$, or $\sigma(h_n) = (k, \texttt{scans})$, set $s_{n+1} = s_n$, $h_{n+1} = h_n \alpha_k$, and $p_{n+1} = p_n \cup \{k\}$.

(if for some n, $\sigma(h_n)$ is not defined, the selection process is immediately stopped). If infinitely many selections are performed, i.e. if the set $\{s_0, s_1, s_2, ...\}$ is infinite, the s_i's are prefixes of an infinite sequence β. In this case, we say that β is the subsequence of α selected by σ, which we write $\beta = \sigma[\alpha]$.

We say that α is Kolmogorov-Loveland stochastic if for every $\beta \in 2^\omega$ that can be selected from α by a computable selection rule, β satisfies the law of large numbers (i.e. $\lim \frac{\#0(\beta,n)}{n} = \frac{1}{2}$).

As we want to quantify the bias one can extract from a sequence by a computable selection rule, we will focus our attention on the quantity:

$$\delta_{max}^{sel}(\alpha) = \sup \left\{ Bias(\sigma[\alpha]) : \sigma \text{ computable selection rule} \right\}$$

Remark 3. *We made the choice to define selection rules by partial functions (and hence, by computable selection rule we mean partial computable selection rule). It turns out that, by an argument of W. Merkle [10], defining them to be total functions would not change the notion of KL-stochasticity nor would affect the quantity δ_{max}^{sel}.*

2.2 Strategies

In [12], Muchnik et al., trying to improve on the notion of KL-stochasticity, suggested to adopt a game-theoretic point of view. We follow their approach.

Let us consider the following game, where Player plays against a sequence $\alpha \in 2^\omega$. The goal for Player is to make money while trying to guess the bits of α. Initially, all the bits are hidden. At each move, Player selects a bit that is not yet revealed. He can either scan it, or bet on its value some (rational) fraction ρ of his current capital. If his guess is correct, his stake is doubled (i.e. his capital is multiplied by $(1 + \rho)$). If not, his stake is lost (i.e. his capital is multiplied by $(1 - \rho)$).

Formally, a selective strategy is a (partial) function $S : 2^* \to (\mathbb{N} \times \{\mathsf{scans}\}) \cup (\mathbb{N} \times \{0, 1\} \times (\mathbb{Q} \cap [0, 1]))$. If the range of S is contained in $\mathbb{N} \times \{0, 1\} \times (\mathbb{Q} \cap [0, 1])$ (i.e. S never scans), it is said to be a strategy.

We run a (selective) strategy S on a sequence α as follows: let h_0 be the empty word, and p_0 the empty set. Set $W_0 = 1$ (initial capital), and $N_0 = 0$ (number of bets). At n-th move:

- If $S(h_n) = (k, \mathsf{b}, \rho)$ and $k \notin p_n$, set $h_{n+1} = h_n \alpha_k$, $p_{n+1} = p_n \cup \{k\}$, $N_{n+1} = N_n + 1$. Also set $W_{n+1} = (1 + \rho)W_n$ if $\alpha_k = \mathsf{b}$ and $W_{n+1} = (1 - \rho)W_n$ otherwise.
- If $S(h_n) = (k, \mathsf{b}, \rho)$ and $k \in p_n$, or $S(h_n) = (k, \mathsf{scans})$, set $h_{n+1} = h_n \alpha_k$, $p_{n+1} = p_n \cup \{k\}$, $N_{n+1} = N_n$. Also set $W_{n+1} = W_n$.

We denote by V_m Player's capital after the m-th bet, that is: $V_m = W_n$ with $n = \min\{i : N_i = m\}$. We denote by $V_m(\alpha, S)$ Player's capital after the m-th bet, when playing against α according to the selective strategy S (note that this could be undefined). We finally call a triple (k, b, ρ) a bet.

Muchnik et al. defined an infinite sequence α to be unpredictable (we now say Kolmogorov-Loveland random) if there exists no computable strategy S such that $\limsup V_n(\alpha, S) = +\infty$ (here again, by Merkle's argument, it does not matter whether we take the strategies to be partial computable or total computable). While Kolmogorov-Loveland randomness is a priori weaker than Martin-Löf randomness, the two notions have been shown to be close ([12], [11]), and their equality remains a fundamental open question. We will not discuss Kolmogorov-Loveland randomness here, but we will use extensively the notion of selective strategy.

Remark 4. *One may think at first that the notions of selective strategy and strategy are equivalent, since scanning a bit is the same as betting 0 on it. This is true if we just want to define Kolmogorov-Loveland randomness (and indeed Muchnik et al. did not make our distinction between strategy and selective strategy). However, this would not be suitable for our purposes, as we want to distinguish the number of bets and the number of moves.*

It is a well-known fact that if a sequence α is biased, there exists a computable strategy S which makes money exponentially when betting on its bits. More precisely:

Proposition 5. *Let $\alpha \in 2^\omega$, and $\delta = Bias(\alpha)$. There exists a strategy S, computable with oracle δ, such that for all $t > \mathcal{H}(\frac{1}{2} + \delta)$:*

$$\limsup_{n \to +\infty} \frac{V_n(\alpha, S)}{2^{(1-t)n}} = +\infty$$

Proof: Without loss of generality, suppose that $\limsup \frac{\sharp 0(\alpha,n)}{n} = \frac{1}{2} + \delta$. Using the oracle δ, let us compute a sequence $\{\delta_n\}_{n \in \mathbb{N}}$ of rational numbers, converging to δ. Let S be the strategy which at the n-th move bets $(n, 0, 2\delta_n)$. We then have, for all n:

$$V_n(\alpha, S) = \prod_{\substack{0 \leqslant i \leqslant n-1 \\ \alpha_i = 0}} (1 + 2\delta_i) \prod_{\substack{0 \leqslant i \leqslant n-1 \\ \alpha_i = 1}} (1 - 2\delta_i)$$

Hence,

$$\frac{\log V_n(\alpha, S)}{n} = \frac{1}{n} \sum_{\substack{0 \leqslant i \leqslant n-1 \\ \alpha_i = 0}} \log(1 + 2\delta_i) + \frac{1}{n} \sum_{\substack{0 \leqslant i \leqslant n-1 \\ \alpha_i - 1}} \log(1 - 2\delta_i)$$

It follows that:

$$\limsup_{n \to +\infty} \frac{\log V_n(\alpha, S)}{n} = \left(\frac{1}{2} + \delta\right) \log(1 + 2\delta) + \left(\frac{1}{2} - \delta\right) \log(1 - 2\delta) = 1 - \mathcal{H}\left(\frac{1}{2} + \delta\right) \square$$

Schnorr [13] proved conversely that if there exists a selective strategy S which, playing against α, makes money exponentially in the number of bets, then there exists a computable selection rule which selects from α a biased subsequence (although he did not quite use the same terminology as ours). However, Schnorr proved this in a purely qualitative way. We strengthen Schnorr's theorem by proving the converse of Proposition 5.

Theorem 6. *Let $\alpha \in 2^\omega$. Suppose that there exists a real number s and a selective strategy S such that $\limsup \frac{V_n(\alpha, S)}{2^{(1-t)n}} = \infty$ for all $t > s$. Then, there exists a selection rule σ, computable with oracle s, such that the bias $\delta = Bias(\sigma[\alpha])$ is large enough to satisfy $\mathcal{H}(\frac{1}{2} + \delta) \leqslant s$.*

The basic idea of the proof is the following: by an argument of Ambos-Spies et al. [1], the above theorem would be easier to prove if S was only allowed to play moves of type $(k, \mathbf{scans})$ or $(k, 0, q)$, where q is a fixed constant. Indeed, in this case, let σ be the computable selection rule which simulates S, scanning a bit if S scans it, and selecting a bit if S bets on it. We then have for all n:

$$V_n(\alpha, S) = (1 + q)^{\sharp 0(\sigma[\alpha], n)} (1 - q)^{\sharp 1(\sigma[\alpha], n)}$$

i.e.

$$\frac{\log V_n(\alpha, S)}{n} = \frac{\sharp 0(\sigma[\alpha], n)}{n} \log(1 + q) + \frac{\sharp 1(\sigma[\alpha], n)}{n} \log(1 - q)$$

Setting $\delta = Bias(\sigma[\alpha])$, it follows that

$$\limsup_{n \to +\infty} \frac{\log V_n(\alpha, S)}{n} \leqslant \left(\frac{1}{2} + \delta\right) \log(1 + q) + \left(\frac{1}{2} - \delta\right) \log(1 - q)$$

By definition of S:

$$\limsup_{n \to +\infty} \frac{\log V_n(\alpha, S)}{n} \geqslant 1 - s$$

It follows that

$$1 - s \leqslant \left(\frac{1}{2} + \delta\right) \log(1 + q) + \left(\frac{1}{2} - \delta\right) \log(1 - q)$$

The function $x \mapsto \left(\frac{1}{2} + \delta\right) \log(1 + x) + \left(\frac{1}{2} - \delta\right) \log(1 - x)$ taking its maximum for $x = 2\delta$, we then have

$$1 - s \leqslant \left(\frac{1}{2} + \delta\right) \log(1 + 2\delta) + \left(\frac{1}{2} - \delta\right) \log(1 - 2\delta)$$

i.e.

$$s \geqslant \mathcal{H}(\frac{1}{2} + \delta)$$

Of course, our notion of strategy is not restricted as above. However, since the couples (value,stake) of the bets are contained in the compact set $\{0, 1\} \times [0, 1]$, we argue by a dichotomy technique that there must be some some condensation point $(\mathbf{b}, \bar{p})$ in the neighbourhood of which bets are often successfull. Applying the same kind of argument as above with $(\mathbf{b}, \bar{p})$ in place of $(0, q)$, we get the desired result.

3   Effective Hausdorff Dimension and Stochasticity

Let X be a subset of 2^ω, and $s \geqslant 0$. X is said to be an s-nullset if there exists a sequence $(C_n)_{n \in \mathbb{N}}$ of subsets of 2^* such that for all n:

$$X \subseteq \bigcup_{u \in C_n} u2^\omega \quad \text{and} \quad \sum_{u \in C_n} 2^{-s|u|} \leqslant 2^{-n} \tag{1}$$

The classical Hausdorff dimension of X is defined by:

$$\dim_H(X) = \inf\{s : X \text{ is a } s\text{-nullset}\}$$

(notice that for all $X \subseteq 2^\omega$, we have $\dim_H(X) \in [0, 1]$)

We now make things effective, following Lutz [7] and Downey et al. [4]:

A subset X of 2^ω is a constructive s-nullset if there exists a computable sequence $(C_n)_{n \in \mathbb{N}}$ of computably enumerable subsets of 2^* satisfying (1)

A subset X of 2^ω is a Schnorr s-nullset if there exists a computable sequence $(C_n)_{n\in\mathbb{N}}$ of computably enumerable subsets of 2^* satisfying (1) and such that the real numbers $\sum_{u\in C_n} 2^{-s|u|}$ are uniformly computable.

We can now define the constructive Hausdorff dimension $\dim_1(X)$ and the Schnorr Hausdorff dimension (also called computable Hausdorff dimension) $\dim_S(X)$:

$$\dim_1(X) = \inf\{s : X \text{ is a constructive } s\text{-nullset}\}$$

$$\dim_S(X) = \inf\{s : X \text{ is a Schnorr } s\text{-nullset}\}$$

Remark that by definition, for all $X \subseteq 2^\omega$, $\dim_H(X) \leqslant \dim_1(X) \leqslant \dim_S(X)$.

For a sequence $\alpha \in 2^\omega$, we abbreviate $\dim_1(\{\alpha\})$ by $\dim_1(\alpha)$ and $\dim_S(\{\alpha\})$ by $\dim_S(\alpha)$. The effective dimension of a singleton is not a trivial notion: although every singleton has classical Hausdorff dimension 0, the effectivity requirement can make a singleton have positive constructive (or Schnorr) dimension. In particular, Mayordomo proved an elegant characterization of constructive Hausdorff dimension in terms of Kolmogorov complexity (there had been some earlier results in this direction, see the discussion in [3]):

Theorem 7 (Mayordomo [9]). *For all $\alpha \in 2^\omega$:*

$$\dim_1(\alpha) = \liminf_{n\to+\infty} \frac{K(\alpha_{[0,n]})}{n}$$

Hausdorff dimension and its effective versions have a game-theoretic characterization. It involves the notion of martingale. A (normed) martingale is a total function $d : 2^* \to [0, +\infty)$ such that $d(\emptyset) = 1$ (here $\emptyset$ is the empty word) and for all $u \in 2^*$, $d(u) = \frac{d(u0)+d(u1)}{2}$.

A martingale is said to be s-successful on a sequence α if

$$\limsup_{n\to+\infty} \frac{d(\alpha_{[0,n]})}{2^{(1-s)n}} = +\infty$$

We have the following result, whose first part is due to Lutz [6] and second part to Downey et al. [4].

Theorem 8. *For all $X \subseteq 2^\omega$:*

$$\dim_H(X) = \inf\{s : \exists d \text{ martingale which } s\text{-succeeds on every } \alpha \in X\}$$

$$\dim_S(X) = \inf\{s : \exists d \text{ computable martingale which } s\text{-succeeds on every } \alpha \in X\}$$

Constructive dimension can also be characterized by game-theoretic concepts (see [7]), but we will not need such a characterization.

The first thing one should remark is that a martingale can be interpreted as the capital of a strategy which bets on every bit (in order). Indeed, if d is a martingale, define S_d by

$$S_d(u) = \begin{cases} (|u|, 0, \frac{d(u0)}{d(u)} - 1) & \text{if } d(u0) \geqslant d(u1) \\ (|u|, 1, \frac{d(u1)}{d(u)} - 1) & \text{if } d(u0) < d(u1) \end{cases}$$

We then have, for all $\alpha \in 2^\omega$ and all n:

$$V_n(\alpha, S_d) = d(\alpha_{[0,n-1]})$$

Obviously, d is computable if and only if S_d is. Hence, given a computable martingale and a computable selection rule, one can canonically construct a computable selective strategy corresponding to their composition. This remark, together with Proposition 5 and Theorem 6, yields a characterization of KL-stochasticity in terms of Schnorr dimension:

Proposition 9. *A sequence α is KL-stochastic iff for every sequence β selected from α by a computable selection rule, $\dim_S(\beta) = 1$*

We now turn our attention to the relation between constructive Hausdorff dimension and KL-stochasticity. We shall prove the main theorem of this section:

Theorem 10. *For all $\alpha \in 2^\omega$, $\mathcal{H}(\frac{1}{2} + \delta_{max}^{sel}(\alpha)) \leqslant \dim_1(\alpha)$*

The proof follows the three steps we mentioned in the introduction. First, we use a splitting argument. We prove:

Lemma 11. *Let $\alpha \in 2^\omega$ and s be such that $\dim_1(\alpha) \leqslant s$. There exists a recursive co-infinite $Z \subseteq \mathbb{N}$ such that, writing $\alpha = (\beta \oplus \beta') \oplus_Z \gamma$, we have:*

$$\dim_1^{(\gamma)}(\beta) \leqslant s \quad and \quad \dim_1^{(\gamma)}(\beta') \leqslant s$$

($\dim_1^{(\gamma)}$ is the dimension relative to the oracle γ).

Then, using the competing strategies technique, we get:

Lemma 12. *Let $\alpha, \beta, \gamma \in 2^\omega$ and s such that $\dim_1^{(\gamma)}(\alpha) \leqslant s$ and $\dim_1^{(\gamma)}(\beta) \leqslant s$. There exists a selective strategy S, computable with oracle (s, γ), such that for all $t > s$, $\limsup \frac{V_n(\alpha \oplus \beta, S)}{2^{(1-t)n}} = +\infty$.*

Lemma 11 and Lemma 12 yield:

Proposition 13. *Let $\alpha \in 2^\omega$ and s such that $\dim_1(\alpha) \leqslant s$. There exists a selective strategy S, computable with oracle s, such that for all $t > s$,*

$$\limsup_{n \to +\infty} \frac{V_n(\alpha, S)}{2^{(1-t)n}} = +\infty$$

Finally, converting the strategy S into a selection rule according to Theorem 6, the above proposition can be rephrased as follows:

Proposition 14. *Let $\alpha \in 2^\omega$ and s such that $\dim_1(\alpha) \leqslant s$. There exists a selection rule σ, computable with oracle s, such that, setting $\delta = Bias(\sigma[\alpha])$, we have $\mathcal{H}(\frac{1}{2} + \delta) \leqslant s$.*

To get Theorem 10 from Proposition 14, remark that in Proposition 14, if s is a rational number, σ is computable. Hence, let us take a decreasing sequence $\{s_m\}_m$ of rational numbers converging to s. For all m, by Proposition 14, there exists a computable strategy σ_m selecting a subsequence β with bias δ_m such that $\mathcal{H}(\frac{1}{2} + \delta_m) \leqslant s_m$. Setting $\delta = \sup_m \delta_m$, it follows that $\mathcal{H}(\frac{1}{2} + \delta) \leqslant s$, and hence $\mathcal{H}(\frac{1}{2} + \delta_{max}^{sel}(\alpha)) \leqslant s$.

The bound we give for $\delta_{max}^{sel}(\alpha)$ in Theorem 10 is optimal. Indeed, let us generate a sequence α by choosing its bits at random and independently, in such a way that for all i, the probability of α_i to be 1 is $\frac{1}{2} + \delta$. Then, with probability 1:

- Every sequence β selected from α by a computable selection rule has bias exactly δ (see van Lambalgen [16], Shen [14])

- $\lim \dfrac{K(\alpha_{[0,n]})}{n} = \mathcal{H}(\frac{1}{2} + \delta)$ (see Lutz [7])

Hence, for all α satisfying these two conditions, we have $\delta_{max}^{sel}(\alpha) = \delta$ and $\dim_1(\alpha) = \mathcal{H}(\frac{1}{2} + \delta)$.

Note that although the bound of Theorem 10 is optimal, there are some cases where $\mathcal{H}(\frac{1}{2} + \delta_{max}^{sel}(\alpha))$ is much smaller than $\dim_1(\alpha)$: take a Martin-Löf random sequence α and consider $\beta = \alpha \oplus_Z 0^\omega$ with $Z = \{n^2 : n \in \mathbb{N}\}$. In this case, $\delta_{max}^{sel}(\beta) = \frac{1}{2}$ (one just needs to select the bits whose position is in Z) which means $\mathcal{H}(\frac{1}{2} + \delta_{max}^{sel}(\beta)) = 0$, whereas $dim_1(\beta) = 1$.

The martingale characterization of Schnorr Hausdorff dimension, together with Proposition 14, provides the following relation between the two notions of effective dimension:

Proposition 15. *Let $\alpha \in 2^\omega$. There exists a selection rule σ, computable with oracle $\dim_1(\alpha)$, such that $\dim_S (\sigma[\alpha]) \leqslant \dim_1(\alpha)$.*

4   Kolmogorov-Loveland Stochasticity for Finite Binary Sequences

The study of Kolmogorov-Loveland stochasticity for finite sequences was initiated by E. Asarin [2]. The extension of Kolmogorov-Loveland stochasticity to finite sequences is more quantitative, i.e. contrary to infinite sequences, there is no clear separation between stochastic and non-stochastic. Rather, for each finte sequence u of length N, and each selection rule σ, there are three key-parameters:

- the Kolmogorov complexity of σ: $K(\sigma|N)$
- the size of the selected subsequence: $|\sigma[u]|$

- the bias of the selected subsequence: $Bias(\sigma[u]) = \left| \frac{\sharp 0(\sigma[u], N')}{N'} - \frac{1}{2} \right|$ (where $N' = |\sigma[u]|$)

The smaller the first, and the bigger the two others, the less stochastic u is. Asarin [2], Durand and Vereshchagin [5] proved respectively an upper bound and a lower bound of the bias one can obtain by selecting a subsequence of a sequence with some randomness deficiency, these bounds depending on the randomness deficiency, the Kolmogorov complexity of the selection rule and the size of the selected subsequence. Moreover, these bounds are very general as they require (almost) no restriction of their three parameters. We instead focus on a particular case, which we believe is very natural given the above discussion on infinite sequences: for a finite sequence u with randomness deficiency $(1 - s)|u|$, what bias can we obtain if we require the Kolmogorov complexity of the selection rule to be $O(1)$, and the size of the selected subsequence to be $\Omega(|u|)$? This question was raised by Durand and Vereshchagin (open question 1 of [5]). The following two theorems provide an answer to this question and show that in the case of finite sequences too, the constant δ such that $\mathcal{H}(\frac{1}{2} + \delta) = s$ is a threshold for the extraction of biased subsequences.

Theorem 16. *For all $s \in [0, 1]$ and all δ such that $\mathcal{H}(\frac{1}{2} + \delta) > s$, there exist real constants c_1, c_2 such that for all large enough N and every finite sequence u of length N satisfying $K(u) \leqslant sN$, there exists a selection rule σ such that*

$$K(\sigma|N) \leqslant c_1, \quad |\sigma[u]| \geqslant c_2 N \text{ and } Bias(\sigma[u]) \geqslant \delta$$

Theorem 17. *There is no tuple (s, δ, c_1, c_2), with $s \in [0, 1]$, $\mathcal{H}(\frac{1}{2} + \delta) < s$ and c_1, c_2 positive real constants such that for all large enough N and all finite sequence u of length N satisfying $K(u) \leqslant sN$, there exists a selection rule σ satisfying:*

$$K(\sigma|N) \leqslant c_1, \quad |\sigma[u]| \geqslant c_2 N \text{ and } Bias(\sigma[u]) \geqslant \delta$$

Acknowledgements. I would like to thank Bruno Durand, Serge Grigorieff and Alexander Shen for very helpful comments and discussions. I also thank Alexey Chernov and three anonymous referees for helping me improve the presentation of this paper.

References

1. K. Ambos-Spies, E. Mayordomo, Y. Wang, X. Zheng. *Resource-bounded dense genericity, stochasticity, and weak randomness.* Proceedings of the Thirteenth Symposium on Theoretical Aspects of Computer Science (STACS'96). Springer-Verlag Lecture Notes in Computer Science 1046:63-74 (1996).
2. E. Asarin. *Some properties of Kolmogorov Δ-random sequences.* Theory Probab. Appl. 32:507-508 (1987).
3. R. Downey, D. Hirschfeldt. *Algorithmic Randomness and complexity.* Book in preparation.
4. R. Downey, W. Merkle, J. Reimann. *Schnorr dimension.* Computability in Europe, Lecture Notes in Computer Science 3526: 6-105 (2005).
5. B. Durand, N. Vereshchagin. *Kolmogorov-Loveland stochasticity for finite strings.* Information Processing Letters. 91(6):263-269 (2004).

6. J. LUTZ. *Dimension in complexity classes.* Proc. 15th Conference on Computational Complexity, IEEE Computer Society 158-169 (2000).

7. J. LUTZ. *The dimensions of individual strings and sequences.* Information and Computation, 187(1):49-79 (2003).

8. M. LI, P. VITANYI. *An introduction to Kolmogorov complexity and its applications, second ed.* Graduate Texts in Computer Science, New York (1997).

9. E. MAYORDOMO. *A Kolmogorov complexity characterization of constructive Hausdorff dimension.* Information Processing Letters 84:1-3 (2002).

10. W. MERKLE. *The Kolmogorov-Loveland stochastic sequences are not closed under selecting subsequences.* Journal of Symbolic Logic 68: 1362-1376 (2003).

11. W. MERKLE, J.S. MILLER, A. NIES, J. REIMANN, F. STEPHAN. *Kolmogorov-Loveland Randomness and Stochasticity.* Ann. Pure Appl. Logic 138(1-3): 183-210 (2006).

12. AN.A. MUCHNIK, A.L. SEMENOV, V.A. USPENSKY. *Mathematical metaphysics of randomness.* Theor. Comput. Sci. 207, 2:263-317 (1998).

13. C.P. SCHNORR. *Zufälligkeit und Wahrscheinlichkeit.* Lecture Notes in Mathematics 218. Springer-Verlag Berlin-Heidelberg-New York (1971).

14. A. SHEN. *On relations between different algorithmic definitions of randomness.* Soviet Mathematics Doklady 38:316-319 (1989).

15. R. VON MISES. *Grundlagen der Wahrscheinlichkeitsrechnung.* Math. Z. 5:52-99 (1919).

16. M. VAN LAMBALGEN. *Random sequences.* Ph.D. thesis, Univ. of Amsterdam, Amsterdam (1987).

Bounded-Hop Energy-Efficient Broadcast in Low-Dimensional Metrics Via Coresets*

Stefan Funke and Sören Laue

Max-Planck-Institut für Informatik,
Stuhlsatzenhausweg 85, 66123 Saarbrücken, Germany

Abstract. We consider the problem of assigning powers to nodes of a wireless network in the plane such that a message from a source node s reaches all other nodes within a bounded number k of transmissions and the total amount of assigned energy is minimized. By showing the existence of a *coreset* of size $O((\frac{1}{\epsilon})^{4k})$ we are able to $(1+\epsilon)$-approximate the bounded-hop broadcast problem in time *linear* in n which is a drastic improvement upon the previously best known algorithm.

While actual network deployments often are in a planar setting, the experienced metric for several reasons is typically not exactly of the Euclidean type, but in some sense 'close'. Our algorithm (and others) also work for non-Euclidean metrics provided they exhibit a certain similarity to the Euclidean metric which is known in the literature as *bounded doubling dimension*. We give a novel characterization of such metrics also pointing out other applications such as space-efficient routing schemes.

1 Introduction

Radio networks connecting a number of stations without additional infrastructure have recently gained considerable interest. Since the sites often have limited power supply, the energy consumption of communication is an important optimization criterion.

In the first part of the paper we consider the following problem: Given a set P of points (stations) in $\mathbb{R}^2$ and a distinguished source point $s \in P$ (sender) we want to assign distances/ranges $r : P \rightarrow \mathbb{R}_{\geq 0}$ to the elements in P such that the resulting communication graph contains a branching rooted at s spanning all elements in P and with depth at most k (an edge (p, q) is present in the communication graph iff $r(p) \geq |pq|$). Goal is to minimize the total assigned energy $\sum_{p \in P} r(p)^\delta$, where δ is the *distance-power gradient* and typically a constant between 2 and 6 ($\delta = 2$ reflects the exact energy requirement for free space communication, larger values are used as popular heuristic model for absorption effects). Such a branching corresponds to a *broadcast* operation from station s to all other nodes in the network with bounded latency. This is one of the most basic communication tasks in a wireless radio network.

* This work was supported by the Max Planck Center for Visual Computing and Communication (MPC-VCC) funded by the German Federal Ministry of Education and Research (FKZ 01IMC01).

W. Thomas and P. Weil (Eds.): STACS 2007, LNCS 4393, pp. 272–283, 2007.

In Section 2 of this paper we construct a (k, ϵ)-*coreset* of size $O((\frac{1}{\epsilon})^{4k})$ for a given instance of a bounded-hop broadcast problem, that is, we identify a small subset of the original problem instance for which the solution translates to an almost as good solution of the original problem. Interestingly, the size of this 'problem sketch' only depends on k and the desired approximation quality $(1 + \epsilon)$ but is independent of n. Hence we can approximate the bounded-hop broadcast problem – even using a brute force algorithm – in time *linear* in n and only doubly exponential in k (in contrast to the result in [1] which is *triply* exponential in k where it is also an exponent of n).

For analytical purposes it is very convenient to assume that all network nodes are placed in the Euclidean plane; unfortunately, in real-world wireless network deployments, especially if not in the open field, the experienced energy requirement to transmit does not exactly correspond to some power of the Euclidean distance between the respective nodes. Buildings, uneven terrain or interference might affect the transmission characteristics. Nevertheless there is typically still a strong correlation between geographic distance and required transmission power. An interesting question is now how to model analytically this correlation. One possible way is to assume that the required transmission energies are powers of the distance values in some metric space containing all the network nodes, and that this metric space has some resemblance to a low-dimensional Euclidean space. Resemblance to low-dimensional Euclidean spaces can be described by the so-called *doubling dimension* [5]. The *doubling dimension* of a metric space (X, d) is the least value α such that any ball in the metric with arbitrary radius R can be covered by at most 2^α balls of radius $R/2$. Note that for any $\alpha \in \mathbb{N}$, the Euclidean space $\mathbb{R}^\alpha$ has doubling dimension $\Theta(\alpha)$. In Section 3 we consider the doubling dimension a bit more in-depth and give a novel characterization of such metrics based on *hierarchical fat decompositions* (HFDs). We then show how the algorithm for energy-efficient broadcast presented in Section 2 as well as other algorithms in the wireless networking context can be adapted to metric spaces of bounded doubling dimension. Interestingly, metrics of bounded doubling dimension are not a tight characterization of all the metrics that allow for well-behaved HFDs, that is, there are metrics which are *not* of bounded doubling dimension, still our and many other algorithms run efficiently. As a side result we show how such HFDs directly lead to well-separated pair decompositions of linear-size (such WSPDs were also constructed in a randomized fashion in [7]). Finally, in Section 4 we examine metrics of bounded doubling dimension that arise as shortest-path metrics in unweighted graphs (e.g. unit-disk communication graphs). We show that for such metrics, an HFD can be computed in near-linear time, and the latter can be instrumented to derive a simple deterministic routing scheme that allows for $(1 + \epsilon)$-stretch using routing tables of size $O((\frac{1}{\epsilon})^{O(\alpha)} \cdot \log^2 n)$ bits using a rather simple construction (compared to [3]).

Related Work

In [1] Ambühl et al. present an exact algorithm for solving the 2-hop broadcast problem with a running time of $O(n^7)$ as well as a polynomial-time approximation scheme for a fixed number of hops k and constant ϵ which has running time $O(n^\mu)$ where $\mu = O((k^2/\epsilon)^{2^k})$, that is, their algorithm is *triply* exponential in the number of hops (and this dependence shows up in the exponent of $n!$). Both their algorithms are for the low-dimensional *Euclidean* case. Metrics of bounded doubling dimension have been studied for quite some time, amongst others Talwar in [9] provides algorithms for such metrics that $(1 + \epsilon)$ approximate various optimization problems like TSP, k-median, and facility location. Furthermore he gives a construction of a well-separated pair decomposition for unweighted graphs of bounded doubling dimension α that has size $O(s^\alpha n \log n)$ (for doubling constant s). Based on that he provides compact representation schemes like approximate distance labels, a shortest path oracle, as well as a routing scheme which allows for $(1 + \epsilon)$-paths using routing tables of size $O((\frac{\log n}{\epsilon})^\alpha \log^2 n)$. An improved routing scheme using routing tables of size $O((1/\epsilon)^{O(\alpha)} \log^2 n)$ bits was presented in [3] by Chan et al., but the construction is rather involved and based on a derandomization of the Lovasz Local Lemma. Har-Peled and Mendel in [7] gave a randomized construction for a WSPD of *linear* size which matches the optimal size for the Euclidean case from Callahan and Kosaraju in [2].

2   Bounded-Hop Energy-Efficient Broadcast in $\mathbb{R}^2$

Given a set P of n nodes in the Euclidean plane, a *range assignment* for P is a function $r : P \rightarrow \mathbb{R}_{\geq 0}$. For a given range assignment r we define its overall power consumption as $\nu_r = \sum_{p \in P}(r(p))^\delta$. A range assignment r for a set P induces a *directed communication graph* $G_r = (P, E)$ such that for each pair $(p, q) \in P \times P$, the directed edge (p, q) belongs to E if and only if q is at distance at most $r(p)$ from p, i.e. $|pq| \leq r(p)$.

The *k-hop broadcast problem* is defined as follows. Given a particular source node s, G_r must contain a directed spanning tree rooted at source s to all other nodes $p \in P$ having depth at most k. W.l.o.g. we assume the largest Euclidean distance between the source node s and any other node $p \in P$ to be equal to 1. We say a range assignment r is *valid* if the induced communication graph G_r contains a directed spanning tree rooted at s with depth at most k; otherwise we call r *invalid*.

Definition 1. *Let P be a set of n points, $s \in P$ a designated source node. Consider another set S of points (not necessarily a subset of P). If for any valid range assignment $r : P \rightarrow \mathbb{R}_{\geq 0}$ there exist a valid range assignment $r' : S \rightarrow \mathbb{R}_{\geq 0}$ such that $\nu_{r'} \leq (1 + \epsilon) \cdot \nu_r$ and for any valid range assignment $r' : S \rightarrow \mathbb{R}_{\geq 0}$ there exists a valid range assignment $r : P \rightarrow \mathbb{R}_{\geq 0}$ such that $\nu_r \leq (1 + \epsilon) \cdot \nu_{r'}$ then S is called (k, ϵ)-**coreset** for (P, s).*

A (k, ϵ)-coreset for a problem instance (P, s) can hence be viewed as a problem sketch of the original problem. If we can show that a coreset of small size exists, solving the bounded-hop broadcast problem on this problem sketch immediately leads to an $(1 + \epsilon)^2$-solution to the original problem.

This definition of a coreset differs slightly from the definition of a coreset defined in previous papers. For example, the term coreset has been defined for k-median [6] or minimum enclosing disk [8]. However, in the case of the bounded-hop broadcast problem we have to consider two more issues. The first is feasibility. While any solution to the coreset for the k-median problem is feasible with respect to the original problem this is not the case for every coreset solution for the bounded-hop broadcast problem. The second issue is monotonicity. For the problem of the smallest enclosing disk the optimal solution does not increase if we remove points from the input. We do not have this property here. An optimal solution can increase or decrease if we remove points.

Our coreset construction is heavily based on the insight that for any valid range assignment r there exists an almost equivalent (in terms of total cost) range assignment r' where all assigned ranges are either zero or rather 'large'. We formalize this in the following structure lemma:

Lemma 1 (Structure Lemma). *Let r be a valid range assignment for (P, s) of cost ν_r. For any $0 < \epsilon < 1$ there exists a valid range assignment r' with either*
$$r'(p) = 0 \text{ or } r'(p) \geq (1 - \epsilon)\epsilon^{2k-2} \text{ and total cost } \nu_{r'} \leq \left(1 + \tfrac{\epsilon}{1-\epsilon}\right)^{\delta} \nu_r.$$

Proof: Let r be a valid range assignment. Consider a spanning tree rooted at s of depth at most k contained in the communication graph G_r. We call it the communication tree.

We will construct a valid range assignment r' from the given range assignment r. Initially, we set $r'(p) = r(p)$. After the first phase we will ensure $r'(s) \geq (1 - \epsilon)\epsilon^{k-1}$ and after the second phase we will ensure $r'(p) \geq (1 - \epsilon)\epsilon^{2k-2}$ for any node p.

The core idea to this construction is that if we have two nodes that are geometrically close to each other and one has a large power value $r(p)$ assigned to it and the other a rather small power value, we can safely increase the larger by a bit, remove the smaller one, and still have a valid power assignment. We apply this idea once in the opposite direction of the communication paths, i.e. towards the source node s (first phase) and once along the direction of the directed communication paths (second phase).

If $r(s) \geq (1 - \epsilon)\epsilon^{k-1}$ we are done with the first phase. Otherwise, there exists a directed path of length at least 1 from source node s to some node p having at most k hops. Let the nodes on this path be labeled $p = p_0, p_1, \ldots, p_l = s$, $l \leq k$ as in Figure 1. Note that $r(p_0)$ does not contribute to the length of this path as it is the last node on the directed path. On this path pick the node with largest index j such that $r(p_j) \geq (1 - \epsilon)\epsilon^{j-1}$. Such a node clearly exists as $\sum_{i=1}^{l} r(p_i) \geq 1$ and $\sum_{i=1}^{l}(1 - \epsilon)\epsilon^{i-1} < 1$. Setting $r'(s) = r(p_j)\left(1 + \tfrac{\epsilon}{1-\epsilon}\right)$ and $r'(p_i) = 0$ for $i = j \ldots l - 1$ as in figure 2 increases the cost $\nu_{r'}$ only slightly but still ensures a valid range assignment because

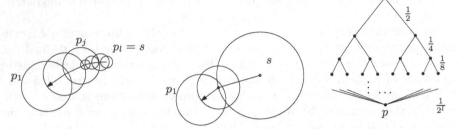

Fig. 1. Original range as-signment before the first phase
Fig. 2. Range assignment after the first phase
Fig. 3. A metric with un-bounded doubling dimen-sion but with bounded degree HFD

$$r'(s) = r(p_j)\left(1 + \frac{\epsilon}{1-\epsilon}\right) \geq r(p_j) + \epsilon^j > r(p_j) + \sum_{i=j+1}^{l}(1-\epsilon)\epsilon^{i-1} \qquad (1)$$

$$> r(p_j) + \sum_{i=j+1}^{l} r(p_i), \qquad (2)$$

i.e. we increased $r'(s)$ such that all nodes that could be reached by nodes $p_j, p_{j+1}, \ldots, p_{l-1}$ can now be reached directly by s.

In the second phase we can use an analogous argument starting from source node s. We assign each node p in the communication tree a level according to the number of hops to the source node s, where the source node s has level 0 and the leaves of the tree have level at most k. We distinguish two cases. In the first case $r'(s) = r(s)$, i.e. the value of the starting node s has not been increased. The other case occurs when it has been increased, i.e. $r'(s) > r(s)$.

Let us look at the first case. Consider all maximal paths $\{t_j\}$ in the commu-nication tree starting from node s where all nodes have $r(p) < (1-\epsilon)\epsilon^{k-1+i}$ if node p is on level i. We can set $r'(s) = r(s)(1 + \frac{\epsilon}{1-\epsilon})$ and $r'(p) = 0$ for all $p \in t_i$. Hence, we again maintain a valid range assignment and the next nodes p along the paths of the communication tree satisfy $r(p) \geq (1-\epsilon)\epsilon^{k-1+i}$ if node p is on level i. Applying the same reasoning iteratively to these nodes we finally have that for all nodes p either $r'(p) = 0$ or $r'(p) \geq (1-\epsilon)\epsilon^{k-1+i}$ for a node p on level i. Note that for nodes p on level k we can set $r'(p) = 0$. Hence, we have a valid range assignment r' with $r'(p) \geq (1-\epsilon)\epsilon^{2k-2}$.

Let us now consider the second case, when $r'(s) > r(s)$, i.e. the value of s has been increased in the first phase of the construction. Here we increased $r'(s)$ already in the first phase to at least $(1-\epsilon)\epsilon^{k-2}\left(1 + \frac{\epsilon}{1-\epsilon}\right) = \epsilon^{k-2}$. Hence, we can continue as in the first case without increasing $r'(s)$ anymore, because $\epsilon^{k-2} > \sum_{i=0}^{k}(1-\epsilon)\epsilon^{k-1+i}$ for $\epsilon < 1$.

The cost of the valid range assignment r' satisfies

$$\nu_{r'} = \sum_{p \in P} (r'(p))^{\delta} \leq \sum_{p \in P} \left(r(p) \left(1 + \frac{\epsilon}{1 - \epsilon} \right) \right)^{\delta} = \left(1 + \frac{\epsilon}{1 - \epsilon} \right)^{\delta} \nu_r \quad (3)$$

∎

Using the preceding Lemma it is now easy to come up with a small coreset by using a grid of width roughly an ϵ-fraction of the minimum non-zero range assigned in r'.

Lemma 2. *For any k-hop broadcast instance there exists a $(k, (\delta + 2)\epsilon)$-coreset of size $O((\frac{1}{\epsilon})^{4k})$.*

Proof: We will only sketch the main idea here. We place a grid of width $\Delta = \frac{1}{\sqrt{2}} \epsilon \cdot r_{min}$ on the plane, where $r_{min} = (1 - \epsilon) \epsilon^{2k-2}$. Notice, that the grid has to cover an area of radius 1 around the source only because the furthest distance from node s to any other node is 1. Hence its size is $O((\frac{1}{\epsilon})^{4k})$ for small ϵ. Now assign each point in P to its closest grid point. Let the coreset S be the set of grid points that had at least one point from P snapped to it. Applying the Structure Lemma 1 induces a relative error of $\left(1 + \frac{\epsilon}{1-\epsilon} \right)^{\delta}$. Since the grid induces an error of $(1 + \epsilon)$ the total relative error is bounded by $(1 + (\delta + 2)\epsilon)$. ∎

Unfortunately we are not aware of any efficient algorithm for computing even just a constant approximation to the bounded-hop broadcast problem. But since we were able to reduce the problem size to a constant independent of n, we can also employ a brute-force strategy to compute an optimal solution for the reduced problem (S, s), which in turn translates to an $(1+(\delta+2)\epsilon)^2$-approximate solution to the original problem since the reduced problem (S, s) is a $(k, (\delta+2)\epsilon)$-coreset.

When looking for a optimal, energy-minimal solution for S, it is obvious that each node needs to consider only $|S|$ different ranges. Hence, naively there are at most $|S|^{|S|}$ different range assignments to consider at all. We enumerate all these assignments and for each of them we check whether the induced communication graph contains a directed spanning tree of depth at most k rooted at the grid point corresponding to the original root node s, that is whether the respective range assignment is valid; this can be done in time $|S|^2$. Of all the valid range assignments we return the one of minimal cost.

Assuming the floor function a $(k, (\delta + 2)\epsilon)$-coreset S for an instance of the k-hop broadcast problem for a set of n radio nodes in the plane can be constructed in linear time. Hence we obtain the following corollary:

Corollary 1. *A $(1+(\delta+2)\epsilon)^2$-approximate solution to the k-hop energy-minimal broadcast problem on n points in the plane can be computed in time $O(n + |S|^{|S|}) = O\left(n + \left(\frac{1}{\epsilon} \right)^{4k(\frac{1}{\epsilon})^{4k}} \right)$.*

A simple observation allows us to improve the running time slightly. Since eventually we are only interested in an approximate solution to the problem, we are also happy with only approximating the optimum solution for the coreset S. Such an approximation for S can be found more efficiently by not considering all possible at most $|S|$ ranges for each grid point. Instead we consider as admissible ranges only 0 and $r_{\min} \cdot (1+\epsilon)^i$ for $i \geq 0$. That is, the number of different ranges a node can attain is at most $1 + \log_{1+\epsilon} r_{min}^{-1} \leq \frac{4k}{\epsilon} \cdot \log \frac{1}{\epsilon}$ for $\epsilon \leq 1$. This comes at a cost of a $(1+\epsilon)$ factor by which each individual assigned range might exceed the optimum. The running time of the algorithm improves, though, which leads to our main result in this section:

Corollary 2. *A $(1+(\delta+2)\epsilon)^3$-approximate solution to the k-hop energy-minimal broadcast problem on n points in the plane can be computed in time*

$$O\left(n + \left(\tfrac{4k}{\epsilon} \cdot \log \tfrac{1}{\epsilon}\right)^{|S|}\right) = O\left(n + \left(\tfrac{4k}{\epsilon}\right)^{\left(\tfrac{1}{\epsilon}\right)^{4k}}\right).$$

A $(1+\psi)$-approximate solution can be obtained by choosing $\epsilon = \theta(\psi/\delta)$.

3   Properties of Low-Dimensional Metrics

As mentioned in the introduction, the theoretical analysis of algorithms typically requires some simplifying assumptions on the problem setting. In case of wireless networking, a very common assumption is that all the network nodes are in the Euclidean plane, distances are the natural Euclidean distances, and the required transmission energy is some power of the Euclidean distance. This might be true for network deployments in the open field, but as soon as there are buildings, uneven terrain or interference, the effective required transmission power might be far higher. Still, it is true that there is a strong correlation between geographic/Euclidean distance and required transmission power. So how could we define the problem using less demanding assumptions but still be able to analytically prove properties of the algorithms and protocols of interest? One possible way is to assume that the required transmission energies are powers of distance values in some metric space on the network nodes, and that this metric space has some resemblance to a low-dimensional Euclidean space. "Resemblance to a low-dimensional Euclidean space" could be equivalent to the existence of a mapping into low-dimensional Euclidean space which more or less preserves distances (low distortion embeddings). Another means to capture similarity to low-dimensional Euclidean spaces is the so-called *doubling dimension*. The *doubling dimension* of a metric space (X, d) is the least value α such that any ball in the metric with arbitrary radius R can be covered by at most 2^α balls of radius $R/2$. Note that for any $\alpha \in \mathbb{N}$, the Euclidean space $\mathbb{R}^\alpha$ has doubling dimension $\Theta(\alpha)$. In the following we show that a metric of bounded doubling dimension exhibits not only this Euclidean-like covering property but also a respective *packing* property.

3.1   Metrics of Bounded Doubling Dimension

The fact that every ball can be covered by at most a constant number of balls of half the radius (covering property) induces the fact, that not too many balls of sufficiently large radius can be placed inside a larger ball (packing property). The following lemma states this fact precisely. (The same observation was made in Section 2 of [7] in the context of net-trees but was not explicitly stated in this general form.)

Lemma 3 (Packing Lemma). *Given a metric (X, d) with doubling constant k, i.e. every ball can be covered by at most k balls of half the radius, then, at most k pairwise disjoint balls of radius $r/2 + \epsilon$, for $\epsilon > 0$ can be placed inside a ball of radius r.*

Proof: Consider a ball B of radius r. Place a set $S = \{B_1, B_2, \ldots, B_l\}$ of pairwise disjoint balls each having radius $r/2 + \epsilon$ inside B. Let $C = \{b_1, b_2, \ldots, b_k\}$ be a set of balls of radius $r/2$ that cover the ball B. The distance between two centers of balls from S is at least $r + 2\epsilon > r$ as they are pairwise disjoint. Hence, every ball $b_i \in C$ can cover at most one center of a ball $B_j \in S$. Since every ball from the set S is covered and especially its center, we have $|S| \leq |C| = k$.   ∎

The same generalizes to arbitrary radii. If a ball B of radius R can be covered by at most k balls of radius r then there can be at most k pairwise disjoint balls of radius $r + \epsilon$ for $\epsilon > 0$ placed inside B. We will make use of this packing property at various places later.

3.2 Hierarchical Fat Decompositions (HFD)

Given an arbitrary metric (X, d), a *decomposition* is a partition of X into clusters $\{C_i\}$. A *hierarchical decomposition* is a sequence of decompositions $P_l, P_{l-1}, \ldots, P_0$, where each cluster in P_i is the union of clusters from P_{i-1}, $P_l = X$, and $P_0 = \{\{x\}|x \in X\}$, i.e. P_l is the single cluster containing X and every point forms one separate cluster in P_0.[1] We refer to clusters of P_i as clusters at level i. A hierarchical decomposition where each cluster of the same level i is contained in a ball of radius r_i, contains a ball of radius $\alpha \cdot r_i$, and $r_{i-1} \leq \beta \cdot r_i$ for constants α and $\beta < 1$ is called a *hierarchical fat decomposition* (HFD). Thus, in an HFD clusters are fat and the size of the clusters from different levels form a geometric sequence. We call a set *fat* if the ratio between an inscribed ball and a surrounding ball is bounded by a constant.

We will show how to construct an HFD for an arbitrary metric (X, d). Without loss of generality we assume $min_{p,q \in X} d(p, q) = 1$. We call $\Phi = max_{p,q \in X} d(p, q)$ the *spread* of X. We construct the HFD bottom-up. Let L_i be a set of points which we call landmarks of level i. With each landmark we associate a cluster $C_i(l) \subseteq X$.

On the lowest level we have $L_o = X$ and $C_0(l) = \{l\}$, i.e. each point forms a separate cluster. Obviously, each cluster is contained in a ball of radius 1 and contains a ball of radius $\frac{1}{2}$. Starting from the lowest level we construct the next level recursively as follows. For level i we compute a 4^i-independent maximal set (i.e. a maximal set with respect to insertion with the pairwise distance of at least 4^i) of landmarks L_i from the set L_{i-1} of landmarks from one level

---

[1] This is also known as a laminar set system as used frequently in the literature.

below. Hence, the distance between any two landmarks of level i is at least 4^i. We compute the Voronoi diagram VD of this set L_i and call the Voronoi cell of l $VC_i(l)$. The union of all clusters of landmarks from level $i - 1$ that fall in the region $VC_i(l)$ form the new cluster that we associate with landmark l, i.e. $C_i(l) = \bigcup_{p \in VC_i(l)} C_{i-1}(p)$. Obviously, each Voronoi cell contains a ball of radius $4^i/2$ and is contained in a ball of radius 4^i, since the set of landmarks L_i form a 4^i maximal independent set. Hence, each cluster on level i is contained in a ball of radius $\sum_{j=0}^{i} 4^j \le 4^{i+1}/3$ and each cluster contains a ball of radius $4^i/2 - \sum_{j=0}^{i-1} 4^i \ge 4^i/6$. Thus, we have constructed an HFD.

3.3   A Characterization of Metrics of Bounded Doubling Dimension

We say an HFD has degree d if the tree induced by the hierarchy has maximal degree d. The following theorem gives a characterization of metrics with bounded doubling dimension in terms of such HFDs.

Theorem 1. *A metric (X, d) has bounded doubling dimension if and only if all hierarchical fat decompositions of (X, d) have bounded degree.*

Proof: First, suppose metric (X, d) has bounded doubling dimension. Fix an arbitrary HFD for (X, d) and pick a cluster C. Since C is fat, it is contained in a ball of radius r_1 and it is the union of fat clusters $\{C_1, C_2, \ldots, C_l\}$. Each of them contains a ball of radius r_2. The ratio of the two radii r_1 and r_2 is bounded by a constant due to the definition of an HFD. Then, by the Packing Lemma 3 cluster C cannot contain more than a constant number of clusters from the level below. Hence, each HFD has bounded degree.

On the other hand, suppose (X, d) has no bounded degree. Then there exists a ball $B(x, r) = \{y | d(x, y) \le r\}$ that cannot be covered by a constant number of balls of half the radius r. We can construct an HFD, which has no bounded degree as follows. Consider an HFD constructed as in Section 3.2, where the set of landmarks always contains the point x. Consider the minimal cluster C that contains ball $B(x, r)$ and consider the set of children clusters $\{C_1, C_2, \ldots, C_l\}$ of C that are all contained in a ball of radius $r/2$. Due to the definition of an HFD the difference in the levels of these clusters is bounded by a constant. Since, the number of children clusters is not bounded, the HFD cannot have bounded degree. ∎

There are metrics however, that admit an HFD with bounded degree but do not have bounded doubling dimension. The following metric is such an example. Consider the complete binary tree of depth l and each edge from level $i - 1$ to level i having weight $\frac{1}{2^i}$ as in Figure 3. Let p be a node which is connected to all leaves with edge weights $\frac{1}{2^l}$. The shortest path metric induced by this graph does not have a bounded doubling dimension but admits an HFD with bounded degree. We can place 2^l disjoint balls of radius $\frac{1}{2^{l+1}}$, each having a leaf as its center, inside a ball of radius $\frac{1}{2^l}$ with center p. Hence, the metric cannot have bounded doubling dimension for arbitrary large l (Packing Lemma). On the other hand, it is easy to see that the metric has an HFD of degree 2.

An HFD with bounded degree immediately implies a well-separated pair decomposition (WSPD) of linear size in the number of input points. We just sketch the main idea here.

The construction follows closely the lines of [2]. If we replace in their construction the *fair split tree* by our hierarchical fat decomposition, we get the same bounds, apart from constant factors. All we need to show is that if a ball B of radius r is intersected by the surrounding balls of a set of clusters $S = \{C_1, C_2, \ldots, C_l\}$ with $C_j \cap C_j = \emptyset$ for $i \neq j$ and the parent of each cluster C_i has a surrounding ball of radius larger than r/c for a constant c, then the set S can only contain a constant number of clusters. But this is certainly true. The packing lemma 3 assures that there are just a constant number of clusters whose surrounding balls intersect a large ball B whose radius is larger by a constant. And as the HFD has bounded degree, these clusters have constant number of children clusters $S = \{C_1, C_2, \ldots, C_l\}$ all together. If we eliminate all clusters in the HFD that just have one children cluster we get that the number of well-separated pairs is linear in the number of input points and depends only on the constant c and the doubling dimension.

3.4   Optimizing Energy-Efficiency in Low-Dimensional Metrics

In the following we will briefly sketch how the algorithm presented in Section 2 can also be applied for metrics of bounded doubling dimension. Furthermore we show how an old result ([4]) can also be partly adapted from the Euclidean setting.

Energy-Efficient k-Hop Broadcast. The algorithm presented in Section 2 for broadcasting in the plane can be generalized to metrics with bounded doubling dimension. Obviously, the Structure Lemma 1 still holds since the triangle inequality holds. Now, instead of placing a planar grid, we construct an HFD for the nodes as in Section 3.2. The level of the decomposition where each cluster is contained in a ball of radius $r = \Delta/2$ replaces the grid in the approximation algorithm. As the metric has bounded doubling dimension, the HFD has bounded degree. Hence, there is just a constant number of clusters in the decomposition of this level. We can solve this instance in the same way as for the planar case.

Energy-Efficient k-Hop Paths. In [4] the authors considered the problem of computing an $(1 + \epsilon)$ energy-optimal path between a nodes s and t in a network in $\mathbb{R}^2$ which uses at most k hops. Again, as in Section 2, the assumption was that the required energy to transmit a message over Euclidean distance d is d^δ, for $\delta \geq 2$. Using a rather simple construction where the neighborhood of the query pair s and t was covered using a constant number of grid cells (depending only on k, δ, ϵ) such queries could be answered with a $(1 + \epsilon)$ guarantee in $O(\log n)$ time. Similarly to the bounded-hop broadcast, we can replace this grid by a respective level in a HFD. For bounded doubling dimension we then know that there are only a constant number of relevant grid cells and the algorithm can be implemented as in the Euclidean case. In [4] the construction was further refined by using a WSPD to actually precompute a linear number of k-hop paths which then could be accessed in $O(1)$ time for a query (independent of k, δ, ϵ). Generalizing this refinement is the focus of current research.

4   Computing HFDs in Shortest-Path Metrics

In wireless sensor networks, the employed network nodes are typically low-capability devices with simple computing and networking units. In particular, most of these devices do not have the ability to adjust the transmission power but always send within a fixed range. The graph representing the pairs of nodes that can communicate with each other is then a so-called *unit-disk graph* (UDG), where two nodes can exchange messages directly iff they are at distance of most 1. Typically UDGs are considered in the Euclidean setting, but they can be looked at in any metric space. Due to the fixed transmission power, saving energy by varying the latter is not possible. Still, indirectly, energy can be saved by for example better routing schemes which yield shorter (i.e. fewer hops) paths. In the following we briefly discuss how HFDs can be used to provide such efficient routing schemes. We first show how in case of unweighted graphs like UDGs, HFDs can be efficiently computed and then sketch how the structure of the HFDs can be exploited to allow for routing schemes with near-optimal path lengths using small routing tables at each node.

4.1   A Near-Linear Time Algorithm

Consider an unweighted graph $G = (V, E)$. All shortest paths define a shortest-path metric on the set of vertices. If the metric has bounded doubling dimension we can construct an HFD with bounded degree efficiently by employing the generic approach described in Section 3.2. At level i we need to construct an 4^i-independent maximal set of nodes L_i, the landmarks. This can be done greedily using a modified breadth-first search algorithm on the original graph G. At the same time we can compute the corresponding Voronoi diagram. We pick an arbitrary node n_1 and add it to the set L_i. In a breadth-first search we successively compute the set of nodes that have distance 1, 2, ... until we computed the set of nodes at distance 4^i. We mark each visited node as part of the Voronoi cell of node n_1 and store its distance to n_1. From the set of nodes at distance 4^i we pick a node n_2 and add it to L_i. Starting from node n_2 we again compute the set of nodes that have distance 1, 2, ... to the node n_2. Similarly, if a node is not assigned to a Voronoi cell, we assign it to n_2. If it has been assigned already to some other node but the distance to the other landmark is larger than to the current node n_2, we reassign it to the current node. We do this until no new landmark can be found and all nodes are assigned to its Voronoi cell.

We might visit a node or an edge several times, but as the metric has bounded doubling dimension, this happens only a constant number of times. Thus, the running time is $O(m + n)$ for one level and $O((m + n) \log n)$ for the whole construction of the HFD as there are $O(\log n)$ levels.

4.2   Hierarchical Routing in Doubling Metrics

The HFD constructed above implicitly induces a hierarchical naming scheme for all nodes of the network by building IP-type addresses which reflect in which child cluster of each level a node v is contained (remember that there are always only a constant number of children of each cluster). For example if v is contained in the top-most cluster 4, in the 2nd child of that top-most cluster and in the 5th child of that child, its name would be 4.2.5. Clusters can be named accordingly and will be prefixes of the node names. We now install routing tables at each node which allow for almost-shortest path routing in the network: For every cluster C with diameter D we store at all nodes in the network which have distance at most $O(D/\epsilon)$ from C a distance value (associated with the respective address of the cluster and a pointer to the predecessor on the shortest path to the cluster) to the boundary of C in the node's routing table. Now, when a message needs to be routed to a target node t and is currently at node p, p inspects its routing table and looks for an entry which is a as large as possible prefix of the target address. p then forwards the message to the adjacent neighbor which is associated with this routing table entry. A simple calculation shows that this yields paths which are at most a $(1 + \epsilon)$ factor longer than the optimal shortest path For the size of the routing table first consider an arbitrary node v and clusters of diameter at most D. Clearly there are at most $O((1/\epsilon)^{O(\alpha)})$ many such clusters which have distance less than $O(D/\epsilon)$ from v and have hence created a routing table entry at v. Overall there are only $\log n$ levels and each routing table entry has size $O(\log n)$ (since the maximum distance is n). Hence the overall size of the routing table of one node is $O((1/\epsilon)^{O(\alpha)} \log^2 n)$.

References

1. C. Ambühl, A. E. F. Clementi, M. Di Ianni, N. Lev-Tov, A. Monti, D. Peleg, G. Rossi, and R. Silvestri. Efficient algorithms for low-energy bounded-hop broadcast in ad-hoc wireless networks. In *STACS*, pages 418–427, 2004.
2. Paul B. Callahan and S. Rao Kosaraju. Algorithms for dynamic closest pair and n-body potential fields. In *SODA*, 1995.
3. Hubert T.-H. Chan, Anupam Gupta, Bruce M. Maggs, and Shuheng Zhou. On hierarchical routing in doubling metrics. In *SODA*, pages 762–771, 2005.
4. S. Funke, D. Matijevic, and P. Sanders. Approximating energy efficient paths in wireless multi-hop networks. In *ESA*, pages 230–241, 2003.
5. A. Gupta, R. Krauthgamer, and J. R. Lee. Bounded geometries, fractals, and low-distortion embeddings. In *FOCS*, 2003.
6. S. Har-Peled and S. Mazumdar. Coresets for k-means and k-median clustering and their applications. In *STOC*, pages 291–300, 2004.
7. S. Har-Peled and M. Mendel. Fast construction of nets in low dimensional metrics, and their applications. *SIAM Journal on Computing*, 35(5):1148–1184, 2006.
8. P. Kumar, J. S. B. Mitchell, and E. A. Yildirim. Approximate minimum enclosing balls in high dimensions using core-sets. *J. Exp. Algorithmics*, 8, 2003.
9. Kunal Talwar. Bypassing the embedding: algorithms for low dimensional metrics. In *STOC*, pages 281–290, 2004.

On the Complexity of Affine Image Matching[*]

Christian Hundt and Maciej Liśkiewicz[**]

Institut für Theoretische Informatik, Universität zu Lübeck, Germany
chundt/liskiewi@tcs.uni-luebeck.de

Abstract. The problem of image matching is to find for two given digital images A and B an admissible transformation that converts image A as close as possible to B. This problem becomes hard if the space of admissible transformations is too complex. Consequently, in many real applications, like the ones allowing nonlinear elastic transformations, the known algorithms solving the problem either work in exponential worst-case time or can only guarantee to find a local optimum. Recently Keysers and Unger have proved that the image matching problem for this class of transformations is NP-complete, thus giving evidence that the known exponential time algorithms are justified. On the other hand, allowing only such transformations as translations, rotations, or scalings the problem becomes tractable. In this paper we analyse the computational complexity of image matching for a larger space of admissible transformations, namely for all affine transformations. In signal processing there are no efficient algorithms known for this class. Similarly, the research in combinatorial pattern matching does not cover this set of transformations neither providing efficient algorithms nor proving intractability of the problem, although it is a basic one and of high practical importance. The main result of this paper is that the image matching problem can be solved in polynomial time even allowing all affine transformations.

1 Introduction

Image matching is a well studied problem in different research areas that arises in many application fields, for example, computer vision, medical imaging, pattern recognition, digital watermarking (for an overview we refer to [7,5,17,21]). Given two digital images A and B and some space $\mathcal{F}$ of admissible transformations, the IMAGE MATCHING PROBLEM is to find a transformation $f \in \mathcal{F}$ that changes A closest to B, i.e., that minimises the distortion between $f(A)$ and B. Thus, image matching determines how far image B is a distorted copy of image A according to a specific space of transformations.

We model a digital image A in a standard way as a two dimensional array over the finite set of integers $\Sigma = \{0, 1, \ldots, \sigma\}$ where each item A_{ij} represents a grey value of the pixel with coordinates (i, j). For simplicity's sake, assume $-N \leq i, j \leq N$, and let $A_{ij} = 0$, if either $|i| > N$ or $|j| > N$. We let $\mathcal{N} = \{-N, \ldots, 0, \ldots, N\}$

---

[*] Supported by DFG research grant RE 672/5-1.

[**] On leave from Instytut Informatyki, Uniwersytet Wrocławski, Poland.

W. Thomas and P. Weil (Eds.): STACS 2007, LNCS 4393, pp. 284–295, 2007.
© Springer-Verlag Berlin Heidelberg 2007

and call $\mathcal{N} \times \mathcal{N}$ the *support of the image* A. The pixel (i, j) is a unit square in the real plane $\mathbb{R}^2$ with the geometric center point (i, j). Thus the pixels for A cover a square area of size $(2N + 1) \times (2N + 1)$ with the geometric center point $(0, 0)$. A transformation f of an image A is an arbitrary injective mapping $f : \mathbb{R}^2 \to \mathbb{R}^2$. Transformations of particular importance from the image matching point of view fulfill some additional constraints like smoothness and elasticity and specifically such functions as rotations, scalings, translations, affine and some nonlinear elastic transformations play an important role in this area. Applying a transformation f to A we get the image $f(A)$, which is a two dimensional array over Σ with indices ranging the same interval as in A. The grey values of the pixels in $f(A)$ are determined by Nearest Neighbour Interpolation (NNI, for short) in which the grey value of the pixel (i, j) in $f(A)$ is equal to the value of the pixel (i', j') of the image A such that $f^{-1}(i, j)$ lies in the unit square with the geometric center point (i', j') (for an example see Fig. 1). For two images A and B of the same size the distortion between A and B is measured by $\sum \delta(A_{ij}, B_{ij})$ where $\delta(a, b)$ is a function charging mismatches, for example $\delta(a, b) = |a - b|$.

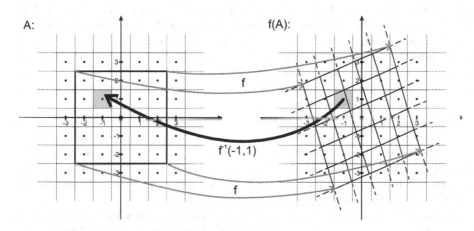

Fig. 1. Image A and the transformed image $f(A)$. The grey value of the pixel $(-1, 1)$ in $f(A)$ is equal to the value of the pixel $(-1, 1)$ of A since in $\mathbb{Z}^2$ the point $(-1, 1)$ is the closest one to the point $f^{-1}(-1, 1)$.

The crucial challenge in all image matching applications is that the IMAGE MATCHING PROBLEM is hard if the set of admissible transformations $\mathcal{F}$ is too complex. Subsequently, known algorithms for optimal or approximate solutions to the problem like the one used for nonlinear elastic transformations (see e.g. [24]) use exponential resources. Recently Keysers and Unger [18] have proved that the decision problem corresponding to the IMAGE MATCHING PROBLEM for this class of transformations is NP-complete, thus giving evidence that the known exponential time algorithms are justified. On the other hand, allowing only translations, rotations and scalings the problem becomes tractable [19,11,12,1,2,3].

For example, restricting the problem to rotations image matching can be solved in time $O(N^3)$. The main result of this paper is that the IMAGE MATCHING PROBLEM can be solved in polynomial time even allowing all invertible affine transformations. Recall, a transformation f over $\mathbb{R}^2$ is affine if $f(x) = \mathcal{A}x + t$ with $\mathcal{A}$ an $\mathbb{R}^{2\times 2}$-matrix and t an $\mathbb{R}^2$-vector.

1.1   Previous Work

In image processing, the classical approach to the IMAGE MATCHING PROBLEM for affine transformations is to transform the images A and B into a space where certain affine distortions correspond to simple translations. The advantage of that space is the IMAGE MATCHING PROBLEM becoming easy by exhaustive search in the set of translations. Take, for example, the polar map $p(A)$ of an image A. In $p(A)$ the pixel data is simply represented in a different coordinate system. Thereby the relation between image coordinates (i, j) and polar-map-coordinates (u, v) is given by $i = v\cos(u)$ and $j = v\sin(u)$. In the case of polar maps a rotation of the original image corresponds to a shifting of the related polar map with respect to coordinate u. Hence, if B is a rotated version of A, then their polar maps $p(A)$ and $p(B)$ are identical in the sense that they can be transformed into each other just by shifting. Additionally, the shifting distance between both maps gives the amount of rotation which would convert A into B. Hence, for solving the IMAGE MATCHING PROBLEM only for the set of rotations it suffices to compute the polar maps of A and B and then determine by brute force the shifting between both maps.

Another important example is the log-polar-map $lp(A)$ with transformation $i = e^v\cos(u), j = e^v\sin(u)$. In addition to rotation of the original image A, scaling is associated to translation in the corresponding log-polar-map $lp(A)$. The major drawback is that the map $lp(A)$ has to be exponentially large to preserve all image information of A. Thus, log-polar-maps are not an efficient tool for solving the IMAGE MATCHING PROBLEM.

The same disadvantages are shared by the log-log-map, which depending on the application is sometimes chosen instead of the log-polar-map. The log-log-map corresponds to the transformation $i = e^u$ and $j = e^v$ such that the image is represented in a way where aspect ratio is associated to translations. But here rotation of the original image is not associated to translation anymore.

Combinatorial pattern matching deals with image matching by using different means than image processing techniques. In this area discrete methods, rather than continuous analysis, are used. Restricting the space $\mathcal{F}$ of admissible transformations to rotations and scalings, the research in combinatorial pattern matching has been concentrated mainly on algorithms which for a given pattern image A and an image B, typically of a greater size, find all exact or close occurrences of $f(A)$ in B [19,11,12,1,2,3]. This problem is often called rotation (resp. scaling) invariant template matching in the signal processing literature. An obvious algorithm works in two phases. First, in the preprocessing step, it constructs a database $\mathcal{D}$ of all possible rotations of A. Then scanning the image B, for every pattern rotation in $\mathcal{D}$ find all its occurrences in B. The worst-case running time of the algorithm is $O(|\mathcal{D}|N^2 \log M)$ where M is the size of A and N is the size of B. In [1] it was proven that the number of different pattern rotations is $\Theta(M^3)$. Thus, the running time is $O(N^2 M^3 \log M)$. In a sequence of papers some improvements of this approach have been presented and currently the best known achievement due to Amir et al. [2] guarantees time complexity $O(N^2 M^2)$.

Some combinatorial pattern matching techniques have been used recently in computational geometry to solve matching problems in a geometric setting (see e.g. [15,23]). In geometric pattern matching, we are given two point sets A and B in Euclidian space and some space $\mathcal{F}$ of admissible transformations, and the problem is to find $f \in \mathcal{F}$ that transforms A closest to B under some distance measure (see [14] for a survey and [6,22] for some related problems).

Recently, Keysers and Unger [18] have considered the IMAGE MATCHING PROBLEM for elastic transformations and proved that for this class of transformations the problem is NP-complete. Elastic transformations are saddled with the constraint to preserve the neighbourhood relation of the pixels, hence, if two pixels are close in the source image, then the corresponding pixels in the transformed image have to be close as well. This is a natural condition which arise in many practical cases. Keysers and Unger show NP-completeness for the hardest constraint on elastic distortions where neighbouring pixels of the original image may not be more then one pixel apart in the transformed image. The IMAGE MATCHING PROBLEM becomes tractable without the elasticity constraint but nothing is known about the middle case where the constraint on the allowed elastic distortions is not as hard as assumed in [18], e.g., if we charge the difference of the distance between neighbouring pixels in the original image and the distance of the corresponding pixels in the transformed image by a smooth function.

In [20] we analysed various kinds of transformations under which the IMAGE MATCHING PROBLEM becomes intractable. However, we restricted the problem to the field of watermarking. In that setting not only the distortion between images has to be minimised during the matching process, but also a watermarking detector response has to be maximised. Development of algorithms which find matchings according to both criteria is one of the great challenges in the area of digital watermarking (see e.g. [7]).

1.2 Our Contribution

In this paper we analyse the IMAGE MATCHING PROBLEM where the set of admissible transformations is the set of all affine transformations.

The main result of this paper states that the IMAGE MATCHING PROBLEM can be solved in polynomial time if restricted to affine transformations. We present a polynomial time algorithm which on two input images A and B computes an affine transformation f such that the distortion between the transformed image $f(A)$ and image B is minimum. Since the polynomial for the time complexity has a far too high exponent to be practical, this is only the first step in developing an efficiently working algorithm but still an encouraging result.

Afterwards we generalise our result to higher dimensional image matching and to different methods of interpolations that we use to define the pixel values of the image $f(A)$ for a given image A and a transformation f. We summarise the result of this paper in the table below (here, N denotes the size of images):

	Complexity	
Allowed transformations	NN interpolation	Linear Interpolation
Scalings	N^3, e.g. [3]	P-time, this paper
Rotations	N^3, e.g. [12,2]	P-time, this paper
Affine transformations	P-time, this paper	
Elastic (threshold distance function)	NP-complete, [18]	
Elastic (smooth distance function)	open	

2 Preliminaries

The image A represents a function over the real plane $\mathbb{R}^2$ in a discrete way. Each element A_{ij} gives the function value for the argument (i,j). Normally the values for the intermediate arguments are defined by interpolation over A. Let $[\cdot]$ denote rounding all components of a vector, then we define the *Nearest Neighbour Interpolation* (NNI) as $\mathcal{I}(x) = [x]$.

Throughout the remainder of this paper let $\mathcal{F}$ denote the set of all invertible affine transformations. Despite the fact that A is transformed according to $f \in \mathcal{F}$, the actual definition of $f(A)$ is based on the inverse affine transformation f^{-1}. In the following we will for short simply use g as the inverse f^{-1} of affine transformation f.

We assume that there is a polynomial time computable function $\delta : \Sigma \times \Sigma \to \mathbb{N}$, measuring differences in grey values. Then for images A and B with support $\mathcal{N} \times \mathcal{N}$ we measure the *distortion* $\Delta(A, B)$ between A and B as the sum of pixel differences, i.e.,

$$\Delta(A, B) = \sum_{(i,j) \in \mathcal{N}^2} \delta(A_{ij}, B_{ij}).$$

We call the following optimisation problem the IMAGE MATCHING PROBLEM for affine distortions: For a given reference image A and a distorted image B, both of the same size $(2N + 1) \times (2N + 1)$, find an affine transformation $f \in \mathcal{F}$ minimising the distortion $\Delta(f(A), B)$.

Notice that the image matching problem considered by Keysers and Unger is different to our definition in that they regard the set of transformations f on B making $f(B)$ most similar to A. But this aspect is not important with affine transformation, since they can be inverted.

Additionally, Keysers and Unger use a distance d_d to charge the strength of distortion introduced by f. In our case, f is an affine transformation, and hence, these costs are approximately constant and do not have to be considered.

In [20] we also utilise a secondary distance D to additionally maximise the watermark detector response. But this does not apply to our case either, since we are not considering watermarking applications only.

3   Algorithm Development

We will develop a basic polynomial time strategy $\mathcal{S}$ for the IMAGE MATCHING PROBLEM of affine distorted images. The general idea of the strategy is simple. As we will show, the number of images $f(A)$ resulting from affine transformations of the image A is bounded polynomially with respect to the size of A, and the set of possible outcomes can be enumerated in polynomial time. The strategy $\mathcal{S}$ is as follows:

1. Create the database $\mathcal{D}$ for all possible affine transformations of A;
2. Set the error bound $D = \infty$;
3. For all affine transformations $f' \in \mathcal{D}$ do
    (a) Set $D' = \Delta(f'(A), B)$;
    (b) If $D' < D$ set $D = D'$ and $f = f'$;
4. Return f and exit.

In this section we show why Step 1 can be performed efficiently and that the loop can be repeated at most a polynomial number of times.

Let us first take a closer look at how the grey values of a distorted image $f(A)$ are determined by image A, affine transformation f and NNI. In the case of NNI the grey value at each coordinate in $f(A)$ is either zero or corresponds to the grey value of one grid coordinate in A. Denote by $\mathcal{G}$ the set of inverse transformations to $f \in \mathcal{F}$. Since $\mathcal{F}$ coincides with all invertible affine transformations, hence formally one has $\mathcal{G} = \mathcal{F}$. We use, however, the notation $\mathcal{G}$ to stress the fact that we look for an inverse transformation $g - f^{-1}$ rather than for transformation f itself. Obviously, $\mathcal{G}$ can not be enumerated, though the set $\{f(A) \mid f \in \mathcal{F}\}$ can be. Thus, our aim is to find a discretisation transferring $\mathcal{G}$ into discrete counterpart, which we will denote by Γ. Speaking formally, let $\Gamma = \{\gamma \mid \gamma : \mathcal{N} \times \mathcal{N} \to \mathcal{N} \times \mathcal{N} \cup \{\bot\}\}$. Then for every $g \in \mathcal{G}$ the discrete counterpart $\gamma_g \in \Gamma$ is defined as follows:

$$\gamma_g(i, j) = \begin{cases} [g(i,j)] & \text{if } [g(i,j)] \in \mathcal{N} \times \mathcal{N}, \\ \bot & \text{otherwise.} \end{cases}$$

If g is the inverse of some affine transformation f, then in γ_g all pixel coordinates $(i, j) \in \mathcal{N} \times \mathcal{N}$ of $f(A)$ are associated to the pixel of A nearest to $g(i, j)$. If such a pixel does not exist, then $\gamma_g(i, j) = \bot$. From γ_g and image A the transformed image $f(A)$ can be computed easily.

For affine transformations $\mathcal{A}x + t$ over $\mathbb{R}^2$, the matrix $\mathcal{A} = \left(\begin{smallmatrix} a_1 & a_2 \\ a_3 & a_4 \end{smallmatrix}\right)$ contains the four parameters a_1, a_2, a_3, a_4 and the vector $t = \left(\begin{smallmatrix} t_1 \\ t_2 \end{smallmatrix}\right)$ two additional parameters t_1 and t_2. Hence, each affine transformation can be characterised by a vector $(a_1, a_2, a_3, a_4, t_1, t_2)$ in $\mathbb{R}^6$ and each six-dimensional vector $(a_1, a_2, a_3, a_4, t_1, t_2)$ defines an affine transformation. However, not every vector in $\mathbb{R}^6$ describes a transformation $g \in \mathcal{G}$ (remember $\mathcal{G}$ coincides with all invertible affine transformations).

Now, for $p = (a_1, a_2, a_3, a_4, t_1, t_2) \in \mathbb{R}^6$ we define $\phi_p(x) = \left(\begin{smallmatrix} a_1 & a_2 \\ a_3 & a_4 \end{smallmatrix}\right) x + \left(\begin{smallmatrix} t_1 \\ t_2 \end{smallmatrix}\right)$ to be the corresponding affine transformation. We transfer the definition of γ over the space $\mathbb{R}^6$ as follows: $\gamma_p(i,j) = [\phi_p(i,j)]$ if $[\phi_p(i,j)] \in \mathcal{N} \times \mathcal{N}$, and otherwise we let $\gamma_p(i,j) = \bot$. Then we define $\mathcal{R}$ to be the equivalence relation on $\mathbb{R}^6$:

$$\mathcal{R} = \{(p,q) \mid p,q \in \mathbb{R}^6 \text{ and } \gamma_p = \gamma_q\}.$$

The relation $\mathcal{R}$ partitions $\mathbb{R}^6$ into subsets of points of equal discrete counterparts. The central concept of the data structure $\mathcal{D}$ is a partition of the space $\mathbb{R}^6$ according to the equivalence relation $\mathcal{R}$ and to find for each equivalence class C a point $p \in C$ such that $\phi_p \in \mathcal{G}$, if such a point exists. We will show that every equivalence class C is a convex polytope (hence, the structure of that partition is simple) and that there is only a polynomial number of classes to be considered.

3.1   Restricting the Problem to One Dimensions

Let $g \in \mathcal{G}$ and let $(a_1, a_2, a_3, a_4, t_1, t_2)$ be the corresponding parameter vector in $\mathbb{R}^6$. The discrete counterpart γ_g can be split into two independent mappings $\gamma_g^1 : \mathcal{N} \times \mathcal{N} \to \mathcal{N} \cup \{\bot\}$ and $\gamma_g^2 : \mathcal{N} \times \mathcal{N} \to \mathcal{N} \cup \{\bot\}$, each mapping one component of the pixel coordinates of $f(A)$ to the pixels of A. Reversely, the pair of one-dimensional mappings γ_g^1 and γ_g^2 can be combined to γ_g in the way that

$$\gamma_g(i,j) = \begin{cases} (\gamma_g^1(i,j), \gamma_g^2(i,j)) & \gamma_g^1(i,j) \neq \bot \text{ and } \gamma_g^2(i,j) \neq \bot, \\ \bot & \text{otherwise.} \end{cases}$$

Notice that γ_g^1 depends only on the parameters a_1, a_2 and t_1, while γ_g^2 depends solely on a_3, a_4 and t_2. We express this by writing $\gamma_{a_1 a_2 t_1}$ and $\gamma_{a_3 a_4 t_2}$ instead of γ_g^1 and γ_g^2. Furthermore the splitting of γ_g is symmetric in the way that if Γ^1 denotes all mappings γ_g^1 for the first component and Γ^2 denotes all mappings γ_g^2 for the second component, then $\Gamma^1 = \Gamma^2$.

Consequently, the partition of $\mathbb{R}^6$ can be described by a partition of $\mathbb{R}^3$ which is defined as follows. We consider the mapping $\gamma_{uvw} : \mathcal{N} \times \mathcal{N} \to \mathcal{N} \cup \{\bot\}$ where u, v, w correspond to either a_1, a_2, t_1 or a_3, a_4, t_2. From the definition of NNI we have:

$$\gamma_{uvw}(i,j) = \begin{cases} [ui + vj + w] & \text{if } [ui + vj + w] \in \mathcal{N}, \\ \bot & \text{otherwise.} \end{cases}$$

Define $\mathcal{X} = \{(p,q) \mid p,q \in \mathbb{R}^3 \text{ and } \gamma_p = \gamma_q\}$. Note that $\mathcal{R}$ and $\mathcal{X} \times \mathcal{X}$ correspond to each other in such a way that $(p,q) \in \mathcal{R}$ iff $((p_1, p_2, p_5), (q_1, q_2, q_5)) \in \mathcal{X}$ and $((p_3, p_4, p_6), (q_3, q_4, q_6)) \in \mathcal{X}$.

3.2   The One-Dimensional Problem

A key property of relation $\mathcal{X}$, we use for construction of the database $\mathcal{D}$, is that the equivalence classes of $\mathcal{X}$ are convex cells represented as the intersection of specific half-spaces in $\mathbb{R}^3$. The planes describing the half-spaces are defined as follows. For all pairs $(i,j) \in \mathcal{N} \times \mathcal{N}$ and all integers $i' \in [-N-1, N+1]$ let $H_{iji'} : ix + jy + z + (0.5 - i') = 0$ be the plane in $\mathbb{R}^3$, where x, y, and z are variables. Denote by $\mathcal{H}$ the set of all such planes $H_{iji'}$. Any Plane $H_{iji'} \in \mathcal{H}$ divides $\mathbb{R}^3$ into the two subspaces with $H_{iji'}(u, v, w) < 0$ and $H_{iji'}(u, v, w) \geq 0$. This corresponds directly to the rounding $[ui + vj + w]$ in γ_{uvw}.

Lemma 1. *Two points $s, s' \in \mathbb{R}^3$ belong to the same equivalence class of $\mathcal{X}$ iff for all $(i, j) \in \mathcal{N} \times \mathcal{N}$ and all $i' \in [-N - 1, N + 1]$ s and s' belong to the same half-subspace according to the partition of $\mathbb{R}^3$ by the plane $H_{iji'}$.*

Proof. Let $s = (u, v, w)$ and $s' = (u', v', w')$ be two parameter vectors from $\mathbb{R}^3$. By definition s and s' belong to the same equivalence class of $\mathcal{X}$, if and only if γ_{uvw} equals $\gamma_{u'v'w'}$.

$\Longrightarrow$: Let $\gamma_{uvw} = \gamma_{u'v'w'}$ hold but for a contradiction suppose that there is $(i, j) \in \mathcal{N} \times \mathcal{N}$ and $i' \in [-N - 1, N + 1]$ such that with respect to $H_{iji'}$, s and s' belong to different half-spaces of $\mathbb{R}^3$. Then, without loss of generality, it holds that $ui + vj + w - i' + 0.5 < 0$ and $u'i + v'j + w' - i' + 0.5 \geq 0$. But this means that $[ui + vj + w] < i'$ and $[u'i + v'j + w'] \geq i'$, which implies that γ_{uvw} and $\gamma_{u'v'w'}$ differ at least for the argument (i, j), a contradiction.

$\Longleftarrow$: Let for all $(i, j) \in \mathcal{N} \times \mathcal{N}$ and $i' \in [-N - 1, N + 1]$ s and s' belong to the same half-space of $\mathbb{R}^3$ with respect to $H_{iji'}$. Suppose for a contradiction that $\gamma_{uvw} \neq \gamma_{u'v'w'}$ for $(i, j) \in \mathcal{N} \times \mathcal{N}$. This means that there are numbers $i'_1, i'_2 \in \mathbb{Z}$ with (1) $ui + vj + w < i'_1 - 0.5$, (2) $u'i + v'j + w' \geq i'_2 - 0.5$, and (3) without loss of generality $i'_1 \leq i'_2$. This implies that $ui + vj + w < i'_2 - 0.5$. Either i'_1 or i'_2 must be in $\mathcal{N}$ since otherwise $\gamma_{uvw}(i, j) = \gamma_{u'v'w'}(i, j) = \bot$. Hence, if $i'_2 \leq N + 1$ then s and s' belong to different subspaces according to plane $H_{iji'_2}$ and else s and s' are still separated by $H_{ij(N+1)}$, a contradiction. $\qquad\square$

Thus, the subspaces of $\mathbb{R}^3$ corresponding to equivalence classes of $\mathcal{X}$ are convex cells bounded by planes. In that, the structure of $\mathcal{X}$ is not complex. By the limitations for i, j and i' the number of planes $H_{iji'}$ is $(2N + 1)^2(2N + 3)$ which is in $O(N^3)$. Any arrangement of planes from $\mathcal{H}$ partitions $\mathbb{R}^3$ into at most n convex cells where $n \leq \sum_{k=0}^{3} \binom{|\mathcal{H}|}{k} \in O(|\mathcal{H}|^3)$. Since there are $O(N^3)$ planes, the overall number of equivalence classes in $\mathcal{X}$ is bounded by $O(N^9)$. For detailed information on plane arrangements we refer the reader to Edelsbrunner [8] and de Berg et al. [9].

As all points of a cell C correspond to the same discretisation it suffices to choose just one representative of C for the database $\mathcal{D}$. The next lemma states that the coordinates for the representatives of each cell can be stored precisely and efficiently. However we shall omit the proof becasue of space limitations.

Lemma 2. *Consider a partition of $\mathbb{R}^3$ into convex cells by the planes from $\mathcal{H}$. Then every cell of the partition contains a representative with coordinates u, v, w which can be encoded by rational numbers with length $O(\log N)$.*

3.3 The Polynomial Time Algorithm

The central tool in strategy $\mathcal{S}$ is the data structure $\mathcal{D}$. Simply speaking $\mathcal{D}$ is a database that contains all discrete counterparts of affine transformations. We shall describe an algorithm *Init* which computes $\mathcal{D}$.

As described in Section 3.1 we can describe $\mathcal{R}$ by $\mathcal{X} \times \mathcal{X}$. Therefore we give an algorithm $Init'$ which computes a tree T' for the traversal of the equivalence classes of $\mathcal{X}$. Afterwards we describe how to efficiently compute a tree T from T' for the traversal of the equivalence classes of $\mathcal{R}$.

Consider $\mathbb{R}^3$ and its partition into convex cells by the planes from $\mathcal{H}$. For planes H and H' let $H' \parallel H$ denote that H' is parallel to H, and conversely let $H' \nparallel H$ denote that H' intersects H. Any plane in $H \in \mathcal{H}$ divides the space $\mathbb{R}^3$ into two half-spaces $H^- = \{(u,v,w) \mid H(u,v,w) < 0\}$ and $H^+ = \{(u,v,w) \mid H(u,v,w) \geq 0\}$. By Lemma 1 each cell corresponding to one equivalence class in $\mathcal{X}$ is either completely contained in H^- or in H^+.

If $H' \parallel H$, then $H' < H$ denotes that H' is contained in H^- and $H' > H$ that H' is contained in H^+. For each plane H in $\mathcal{H}$ let $\mathcal{H}_H^- = \{H' \in \mathcal{H} \mid H' \nparallel H$ or $(H' \parallel H$ and $H' < H)\}$ and $\mathcal{H}_H^+ = \{H' \in \mathcal{H} \mid H' \nparallel H$ or $(H' \parallel H$ and $H' > H)\}$.

We define the tree T' for traversing the cells of $\mathbb{R}^3$ by describing the algorithm $Init'$ which constructs T'. On input N, $Init'$ works as follows:

1. Create the plane arrangement $\mathcal{H}$ containing the planes $H_{iji'}$ for $(i,j) \in \mathcal{N} \times \mathcal{N}$ and $i' \in [-N - 1, N + 1]$.
2. Let r be the root of T'. Initialize a stack and push $(\mathcal{H}, r)$.
3. While the stack is not empty do:
   (a) Pop the top element $(\tilde{\mathcal{H}}, p)$ from the stack.
   (b) If $\tilde{\mathcal{H}} = \emptyset$ then the path from r to p in T' describes a convex cell C in $\mathbb{R}^3$. Compute the representative z of C and label p with z.
   (c) If $\tilde{\mathcal{H}} \neq \emptyset$ then
      i. create two nodes c_1 and c_2 and let p be their parent node,
      ii. choose an arbitrary $H \in \tilde{\mathcal{H}}$ and compute $\tilde{\mathcal{H}}_H^-$ and $\tilde{\mathcal{H}}_H^+$,
      iii. push $(\tilde{\mathcal{H}}_H^-, c_1)$ and $(\tilde{\mathcal{H}}_H^+, c_2)$ on the stack.
4. Return T', i.e., the labeled tree rooted at r.

The algorithm $Init'$ creates a tree, leaves of which represent the cells corresponding to the equivalence classes of $\mathcal{X}$. $Init'$ works in time $O(poly(N))$. To see this, notice that creating each node of T' takes time polynomial in N. In the case of interior nodes the most time consuming task is computing the sets $\mathcal{H}^-$ and $\mathcal{H}^+$. This is in the worst case quadratical according to the number of planes $O(N^3)$. In the case of leaves, vertex coordinates have to be computed, which can be done in polynomial time.

T' is a binary tree and has as many leaves as there are equivalence classes of $\mathcal{X}$. Subsequently, the number of nodes is limited by $O(N^9)$ and hence, $Init'$ runs in time polynomial with respect to N.

Remember that $\mathcal{X} \times \mathcal{X}$ gives the partition $\mathcal{R}$ of $\mathbb{R}^6$. To get T it suffices to augment every leaf of T' by the whole subtree T'. Any path in T from r to a leaf l defines two sets of parameters (u, v, w) and (u', v', w'). Setting $a_1 = u$, $a_2 = v$, $a_3 = u'$, $a_4 = v'$, $t_1 = w$ and $t_2 = w'$ gives a six-dimensional parameter $p = (a_1, a_2, a_3, a_4, t_1, t_2)$ in $\mathbb{R}^6$ representing one equivalence class of affine transformations.

The database $\mathcal{D}$ should be a list containing all possible affine transformations. Any path in $\mathcal{T}$ from root to leaf defines a set of parameters p and by that an affine transformation ϕ_p. To obtain $\mathcal{D}$ it suffices to traverse $\mathcal{T}$ in depth-first strategy. For every parameter vector p encountered, determine if ϕ_p is invertible. In the positive case compute the inverse and add it to the list $\mathcal{D}$. If ϕ_p is not invertible there are two cases to be distinguished. In the first case, p represents a class which contains only ϕ_p. Then no transformation has g as inverse with g and ϕ_p having the same discretisation. Thus, p can be discarded. In the second case, p is the center of a polyhedron in $\mathbb{R}^6$ and many other points belong to the same class. In that case one can easily find another representative q near p for the same class such that q can be stored efficiently and ϕ_q is invertible. The inversion of ϕ_p or ϕ_q can be done in polynomial time. Furthermore, the parameters for the resulting affine transformation can be stored in logarithmic space, too.

By the above results we may assume that there is a polynomial time algorithm $Init$ calling $Init'$ as a subroutine and computing the list $\mathcal{D}$ of all possible affine transformations.

Theorem 1. *The* IMAGE MATCHING PROBLEM *for affine distorted images and NNI can be solved in polynomial time.*

Proof. By Lemma 1 and Lemma 2 as well as the definition of the $Init$ algorithm for $\mathcal{D}$, the strategy $\mathcal{S}$ gives a polynomial time algorithm for the IMAGE MATCHING PROBLEM which works in time $\mathcal{O}(N^{18})$. □

4   Generalisations

In the previous section we studied a polynomial time algorithm for the IMAGE MATCHING PROBLEM for affine distorted two-dimensional images. We shall now follow two approaches for the generalisation of that result, namely considering higher dimensional images and different interpolation methods.

Even for k-dimensional images, the IMAGE MATCHING PROBLEM for affine distortion can be solved in polynomial time with respect to the input size. Nevertheless, the growth in complexity of a corresponding algorithm is exponential in k. We will consider images with support $\mathcal{N}^k$, affine transformation $f : \mathbb{R}^k \to \mathbb{R}^k$ with $f(x) = \mathcal{A}x + t$ where $\mathcal{A}$ is an invertible $\mathbb{R}^{k \times k}$-matrix and t is an $\mathbb{R}^k$-vector and the *Nearest Neighbour Interpolation* $\mathcal{I}(x) = [x]$ in k dimensions.

Theorem 2. *For any $k \in \mathbb{N}$, the* IMAGE MATCHING PROBLEM *for affine distorted k-dimensional images and NNI can be solved in polynomial time.*

The proof works like in the two-dimensional case taking into account that the problem is divided into k one-dimensional subproblems with enhanced parameter spaces each.

Another generalisation is the application of more complex interpolation. So far we used Nearest Neighbour Interpolation because of its simplicity. In NNI, the grey value of each pixel in $f(A)$ depends solely on one pixel in A. This made γ_g simply a mapping between pixel coordinates. However, if a more complex interpolation method is applied the pixel values of $f(A)$ may depend on more than one pixel of A. In general let $\mathcal{I} : \mathbb{R}^2 \times \mathbb{Z} \times \mathbb{Z} \to [0,1]$. Then for all pixels (i,j) the interpolated value $f(A)_{ij}$ with image A, affine transformation f and $\mathcal{I}$ is defined as $f(A)_{ij} = \left\lfloor \sum_{(i',j') \in \mathcal{N}^2} \mathcal{I}(f^{-1}(i,j),(i',j')) \, A_{i'j'} \right\rceil$.

In this generalised setting the IMAGE MATCHING PROBLEM can be solved by the following algorithm. On given images A and B do

1. Compute s, the least common multiple of the number set $\{0, \ldots, \sigma\}$;
2. Compute A_s by scaling the image A in each dimension by the factor s, therewith apply interpolation with $\mathcal{I}$;
3. Perform on A_s and B the polynomial time algorithm for the IMAGE MATCHING PROBLEM for NNI, yielding the optimal transformation $e(x) = \mathcal{A}x + t$;
4. Multiply e with the inverse scaling matrix corresponding to s yielding the affine transformation f, and return f.

Theorem 3. *The above algorithm for the IMAGE MATCHING PROBLEM for affine distortions with complex interpolation is correct and works in polynomial time.*

Because of space limitations we omit the proof. It is remarkable that the complexity remains in fact polynomial, but grows with σ by an enormously large factor. Even if σ is just 32, s is greater than 10^{14}. We restricted ourselves to two-dimensional images. However, the results can be easily carried out to images of higher dimension.

5   Conclusions and Further Work

In this paper we analysed the computational complexity of image matching for affine transformations and presented an exhaustive search polynomial time algorithm finding the optimal matching. We leave as open problem to give a nontrivial lower bound for the search space. Another interesting open question is the computational complexity of image matching for some other classes of admissible transformations like nonlinear elastic transformations with a smooth distance function.

Acknowledgement

The authors are grateful to Frank Balbach for stimulating discussions and for his careful reading of an early version of the paper. Also, the authors thank the anonymous referees for their remarks, which helped the authors in improving the presentation.

References

1. A. Amir, A. Butman, M. Crochemore, G. Landau, and M. Schaps, *Two-dimensional pattern matching with rotations*, Theor. Comput. Sci. 314(1-2), 2004, 173-187.
2. A. Amir, O. Kapah, and D. Tsur, *Faster Two dimensional pattern matching with rotations*, in Proc. CPM, LNCS 3109, 2004, 409-419.
3. A. Amir and E. Chencinski, *Faster two dimensional scaled matching*, in Proc. CPM, LNCS 4009, 2006, 200-210.
4. R. Baeza-Yates and G. Valiente, *An image similarity measure based on graph matching*, in Proc. SPIRE, IEEE CS Press, 2000, 28-38.
5. L.G. Brown, *A survey of image registration techniques*, ACM Computing Surveys 24(4), 1992, 325-376.
6. K. Claire, Y. Rabani, and A. Sinclair, *Low distortion maps between point sets*, in Proc. STOC, 2004, 272-280.
7. I. J. Cox, J.A. Bloom, and M.L. Miller, Digital Watermarking, Principles and Practice. *Morgan Kaufmann*, San Francisco, California, 2001.
8. H. Edelsbrunner, Algorithms in Combinatorial Geometry. *Springer Verlag*, 1987.
9. M. de Berg, M. van Kreveld, M. Overmars, and O. Schwarzkopf, Computational Geometry, Algorithms and Applications. *Springer Verlag*, 2000.
10. F. Deguillaume, S.V. Voloshynovskiy, and T. Pun, *Method for the estimation and recovering from general affine transforms in digital watermarking applications*, in Proc. SPIE Vol. 4675, 2002, 313-322.
11. K. Fredriksson and E. Ukkonen, *A rotation invariant filter for two-dimensional string matching*, In Proc. CPM, LNCS 1448, 1998, 118-125.
12. K. Fredriksson, G. Navarro, and E. Ukkonen, *Optimal exact and fast approximate two dimensional pattern matching allowing rotations*, in Proc. CPM, LNCS 2373, 2002, 235-248.
13. B.K.P. Horn, Robot Vision. *MIT Press*, Cambridge, Massachusetts, 1989.
14. P. Indyk, *Algorithmic aspects of geometric embeddings*, in Proc. FOCS, 2001, 10-33.
15. P. Indyk, R. Motwani, and S. Venkatasubramanian, *Geometric matching under noise: Combinatorial bounds and algorithms*, in Proc. SODA, 1999, 354-360.
16. J.R. Jensen, Introductory Digital Image Processing, A Remote Sensing Perspective. *Prentice-Hall*, Upper Saddle River, New Jersey, 1986.
17. R. Kasturi and R.C. Jain, Computer Vision: Principles. *IEEE Computer Society Press*, Los Alamitos, California, 1991.
18. D. Keysers and W. Unger, *Elastic image matching is NP-complete*, Pattern Recognition Letters 24(1-3), 2003, 445-453.
19. G. M. Landau and U. Vishkin, *Pattern matching in a digitized image*, Algorithmica, 12(3/4), 1994, 375-408.
20. M. Liśkiewicz and U. Wölfel, *On the intractability of inverting geometric distortions in watermarking schemes*, in Proc. IH, LNCS 3727, 2005, 176-188.
21. J.B.A. Maintz and M.A. Viergever, *A survey of medical image registration*, Medical Image Analysis 2(1), 1998, 1-36.
22. C. Papadimitriou and S. Safra, *The complexity of low-distortion embeddings between point sets*, in Proc. SODA, 2005, pp. 112-118.
23. L. Schulman and D. Cardoze, *Pattern matching for spatial point sets*, in Proc. FOCS, 1998, 156-165.
24. S. Uchida and H. Sakoe, *A monotonic and continuous two-dimensional warping based on dynamic programming*, Pattern Recognition, Vol. 1, 1998, 521-524.

On Fixed Point Equations over Commutative Semirings

Javier Esparza, Stefan Kiefer, and Michael Luttenberger

Universität Stuttgart
Institute for Formal Methods in Computer Science
Stuttgart, Germany
{esparza,kiefersn,luttenml}@informatik.uni-stuttgart.de

Abstract. Fixed point equations $\mathbf{x} = \mathbf{f}(\mathbf{x})$ over ω-continuous semirings can be seen as the mathematical foundation of interprocedural program analysis. The sequence $\mathbf{0}, \mathbf{f}(\mathbf{0}), \mathbf{f}^2(\mathbf{0}), \ldots$ converges to the least fixed point $\mu\mathbf{f}$. The convergence can be accelerated if the underlying semiring is commutative. We show that accelerations in the literature, namely Newton's method for the arithmetic semiring [4] and an acceleration for commutative Kleene algebras due to Hopkins and Kozen [5], are instances of a general algorithm for arbitrary commutative ω-continuous semirings. In a second contribution, we improve the $\mathcal{O}(3^n)$ bound of [5] and show that their acceleration reaches $\mu\mathbf{f}$ after n iterations, where n is the number of equations. Finally, we apply the Hopkins-Kozen acceleration to itself and study the resulting hierarchy of increasingly fast accelerations.

1 Introduction

Interprocedural program analysis is the art of extracting information about the executions of a procedural program without executing it, and fixed point equations over ω-continuous semirings can be seen as its mathematical foundation. A program can be mapped (in a syntax-driven way) to a system of fixed point equations over an abstract semiring containing one equation for each program point. Depending on the information on the program one wants to compute, the carrier and the abstract semiring operations can be instantiated so that the desired information is the least solution of the system. To illustrate this, consider a (very abstractly defined) program consisting of one single procedure X. This procedure can either do an action a and terminate, or do an action b and call itself twice. Schematically:

$$X \xrightarrow{a} \varepsilon \qquad X \xrightarrow{b} XX$$

The abstract equation corresponding to this program is

$$x = r_a + r_b \cdot x \cdot x \tag{1}$$

where $+$ and $\cdot$ are the abstract semiring operations. In order to compute the language $L(X)$ of terminating executions of the program, we instantiate the

W. Thomas and P. Weil (Eds.): STACS 2007, LNCS 4393, pp. 296–307, 2007.

semiring as follows: The carrier is $2^{\{a,b\}^*}$ (the set of languages over the alphabet $\{a,b\}$), $r_a = \{a\}$, $r_b = \{b\}$, $+$ is set union, and $\cdot$ is language concatenation. It is easy to prove that $L(X)$ is the least solution of (1) under this interpretation. But we can also be interested in other questions. We may wish to compute the *Parikh image* of $L(X)$, i.e., the set of vectors $(n_a, n_b) \in \mathbb{N}^2$ such that some terminating execution of the program does exactly n_a a's and n_b b's, respectively. For this, we take $2^{\mathbb{N}^2}$ as carrier, $r_a = \{(1,0)\}$, $r_b = \{(0,1)\}$, define $+$ as set union and $\cdot$ by $X \cdot Y = \{(x_a + y_a, x_b + y_b) \mid (x_a, x_b) \in X, (y_a, y_b) \in Y\}$. We may also be interested in quantitative questions. For instance, assume that the program X executes a with probability p and b with probability $(1-p)$. The probability that X eventually terminates is the least solution of (1) interpreted over $\mathbb{R}^+ \cup \{0, \infty\}$ with $r_a = p$, $r_b = (1-p)$, and the standard interpretation of $+$ and $\cdot$ (see for instance [3,4]). If instead of the probability of termination we are interested in the probability of the most likely execution, we just have to reinterpret $+$ as the max operator.

The semirings corresponding to all these interpretations share a property called ω-*continuity* [7]. This property allows to apply the Kleene fixed point theorem and to prove that the least solution of a system of equations $\mathbf{x} = \mathbf{f}(\mathbf{x})$ is the supremum of the sequence $\mathbf{0}, \mathbf{f}(\mathbf{0}), \mathbf{f}^2(\mathbf{0}), \ldots$, where $\mathbf{0}$ is the vector whose components are all equal to the neutral element of $+$. If the carrier of the semiring is finite, this yields a procedure to compute the solution. However, if the carrier is infinite, the procedure rarely terminates, and its convergence can be very slow. For instance, the approximations to $L(X)$ are all finite sets of words, while $L(X)$ is infinite. Another example is the probability case with $p = 1/2$; the least fixed point (the least solution of $x = 1/2x^2 + 1/2$) is 1, but $\mathbf{f}^k(0) \le 1 - \frac{1}{k+1}$ for every $k \ge 0$, which means that the Kleene scheme needs 2^i iterations to approximate the solution within i bits of precision[1].

Due to the slow convergence of $(\mathbf{f}^k(\mathbf{0}))_{k \ge 0}$, it is natural to look for "accelerations". Loosely speaking, an acceleration is a procedure of low complexity that on input $\mathbf{f}$ yields a function $\mathbf{g}$ having the same least fixed point $\mu\mathbf{f}$ as $\mathbf{f}$, but such that $(\mathbf{g}^k(\mathbf{0}))_{k \ge 0}$ converges faster to $\mu\mathbf{f}$ than $(\mathbf{f}^k(\mathbf{0}))_{k \ge 0}$. In [5], Hopkins and Kozen present a very elegant acceleration—although they do not use this term—that works for *every* commutative and idempotent ω-continuous semiring[2], i.e., for every ω-continuous semiring in which $\cdot$ is commutative and $+$ is idempotent (this is the case for both the Parikh image and the probability of the most likley computation). They prove that, remarkably, the acceleration is guaranteed to terminate. More precisely, they show that the fixed point is always reached after at most $\mathcal{O}(3^n)$ iterations, where n is the number of equations.

In this paper we further investigate the Hopkins-Kozen acceleration. In the first part of the paper we show that, in a certain formal sense, this acceleration was already discovered by Newton more than 300 years ago. In the arithmetic semiring, where the carrier is $\mathbb{R}^+ \cup \{0, \infty\}$ and $+$ and $\cdot$ have their usual mean-

---

[1] This example is adapted from [4].

[2] Actually, in [5] the result is proved for commutative Kleene algebras, an algebraic structure more general than our semirings (cf. Section 4.1).

ings, one can compute the least solution of $\mathbf{x} = \mathbf{f}(\mathbf{x})$ as a zero of $\mathbf{f}(\mathbf{x}) - \mathbf{x}$. Due to this connection, Newton's numerical method for approximating the zeros of a differentiable function (see [8]) can also be seen as an acceleration for the arithmetic case, which has been been studied by Etessami and Yannakakis [4] in a different context. Here we show that the Hopkins-Kozen acceleration and Newton's are two particular instances of an acceleration for equations over arbitrary commutative ω-continuous semirings [7] and, in this sense, "the same thing".

In a second contribution, we improve the $\mathcal{O}(3^n)$ bound of [5] and show that the acceleration is actually much faster: the fixed point is already reached after n iterations. Finally, in a third contribution we investigate the possibility of "accelerating the acceleration". We study a hierarchy $\{\mathcal{H}_i\}_{i \geq 1}$ of increasingly faster accelerations, with $\mathcal{H}_1$ as the Hopkins-Kozen acceleration, and show that k iterations of the i-th acceleration can already be matched by ki iterations of the basic acceleration.

In Section 2 we introduce commutative ω-continuous semirings following [7]. In Section 3 we introduce the Hopkins-Kozen acceleration and Newton's method. In Section 4 we present our generalisation and derive both the Hopkins-Kozen acceleration and Newton's method as particular cases. In Section 5 we prove that the Hopkins-Kozen acceleration terminates after n steps. The hierarchy of accelerations is studied in Section 6. Missing proofs can be found in a technical report [2].

2 ω-Continuous Semirings

A *semiring* is a quintuple $\langle A, +, \cdot, 0, 1 \rangle$ s.t.

  (i) $\langle A, +, 0 \rangle$ is a commutative monoid,
 (ii) $\langle A, \cdot, 1 \rangle$ is a monoid,
(iii) $a \cdot (b + c) = a \cdot b + a \cdot c$ and $(a + b) \cdot c = a \cdot c + b \cdot c$ for all $a, b, c \in A$,
 (iv) $0 \cdot a = a \cdot 0$ for all $a \in A$.

A semiring is

 — *commutative* if $a \cdot b = b \cdot a$ for all $a, b \in A$;
 — *idempotent* if $a + a = a$ for all $a \in A$;
 — *naturally ordered* if the relation $\leq$ given by $a \leq b \Leftrightarrow \exists c \in A : a + c = b$ is a partial order (this relation is always reflexive and transitive, but not necessarily antisymmetric);
 — *complete* if it is possible to define "infinite sums" as an extension of finite sums, that are associative, commutative and distributive with respect to $\cdot$ as are finite sums. The formal axioms are given in [7]. In complete semirings, the unary *-operator is defined by $a^* = \sum_{j \geq 0} a^j$. Notice that $a^* = 1 + aa^*$;
 — ω-*continuous* if it is naturally ordered, complete, and for all sequences $(a_i)_{i \in \mathbb{N}}$ with $a_i \in A$

$$\sup\left\{ \sum_{i=0}^{n} a_i \mid n \in \mathbb{N} \right\} = \sum_{i \in \mathbb{N}} a_i.$$

Notation 1. *We abbreviate commutative ω-continuous semiring to* cc-semiring.

Remark 1. For our proofs the existence and ω-continuity of *countable* sums is sufficient. While in the idempotent case there is the term of commutative *closed semirings* for such structures (see [6]), it seems that there is no such term in the non-idempotent case.

Examples of semirings include $\langle \mathbb{N} \cup \{0, \infty\}, +, \cdot, 0, 1 \rangle$, $\langle \mathbb{R}^+ \cup \{0, \infty\}, +, \cdot, 0, 1 \rangle$, $\langle \mathbb{N} \cup \{0, \infty\}, \min, +, \infty, 0 \rangle$ and $\langle 2^{\Sigma^*}, \cup, \cdot, \emptyset, \varepsilon \rangle$. They are all ω-continuous. The last two have an idempotent $+$-operation (min resp. $\cup$), and all but the last one are commutative.

2.1 Systems of Power Series

Let A be an ω-continuous semiring and let $\mathcal{X} = \{x_1, \ldots, x_n\}$ be a set of variables. We write $\mathbf{x}$ for the vector $(x_1, \ldots, x_n)^\top$. For every $i \in \{1, \ldots, n\}$, let $f_i(\mathbf{x})$ be a *(semiring) power series with coefficients in A*, i.e., a countable sum of products of elements of $A \cup \mathcal{X}$, and let $\mathbf{f}(\mathbf{x}) = (f_1(\mathbf{x}), \ldots, f_n(\mathbf{x}))^\top$. We call $\mathbf{x} = \mathbf{f}(\mathbf{x})$ a *system of power series over A*. A vector $\bar{\mathbf{x}} \in A^n$ with $\mathbf{f}(\bar{\mathbf{x}}) = \bar{\mathbf{x}}$ is called a *solution* or a *fixed point* of $\mathbf{f}$.

Given two vectors $\bar{\mathbf{x}}, \bar{\mathbf{y}} \in A^n$, we write $\bar{\mathbf{x}} \leq \bar{\mathbf{y}}$ if $\bar{x}_i \leq \bar{y}_i$ (w.r.t. the natural order of A) in every component. The *least fixed point of $\mathbf{f}$*, denoted by $\mu\mathbf{f}$, is the fixed point $\bar{\mathbf{x}}$ with $\bar{\mathbf{x}} \leq \bar{\mathbf{y}}$ for every fixed point $\bar{\mathbf{y}}$. It exists and can be computed by the following theorem.

Theorem 1 (Kleene fixed point theorem, cf. [7]). *Let $\mathbf{x} = \mathbf{f}(\mathbf{x})$ be a system of power series over an ω-continuous semiring. Then $\mu\mathbf{f}$ exists and $\mu\mathbf{f} = \sup_{k \in \mathbb{N}} \mathbf{f}^k(\mathbf{0})$.*

3   Two Acceleration Schemes

Loosely speaking, an acceleration is a procedure that on input $\mathbf{f}$ yields a function $\mathbf{g}$ having the same least fixed point $\mu\mathbf{f}$ as $\mathbf{f}$, but converging "faster" to it, meaning that $\mathbf{f}^k(\mathbf{0}) \leq \mathbf{g}^k(\mathbf{0})$ for every $k \geq 0$. In order to exclude trivial accelerations like $\mathbf{g}(\mathbf{x}) = \mu\mathbf{f}$, a formal definition should require the procedure to have low complexity with respect to some reasonable complexity measure. Since such a definition would take too much space and would not be relevant for our results, we only use the term "acceleration" informally.

We describe two accelerations for different classes of cc-semirings. Both of them are based on the notion of derivatives. Given a polynomial or a power series $f(\mathbf{x})$, its derivative $\frac{\partial f}{\partial x_i}$ with respect to the variable x_i is defined as follows, where $a \in A$ and g, g_j, h are polynomials or power series (see also [5]):

$$\frac{\partial a}{\partial x_i} = 0 \qquad \frac{\partial}{\partial x_i}(g + h) = \frac{\partial g}{\partial x_i} + \frac{\partial h}{\partial x_i} \qquad \frac{\partial}{\partial x_i}(g \cdot h) = \frac{\partial g}{\partial x_i} \cdot h + g \cdot \frac{\partial h}{\partial x_i}$$

$$\frac{\partial x_j}{\partial x_i} = \begin{cases} 0 & \text{if } i \neq j \\ 1 & \text{if } i = j \end{cases} \qquad \frac{\partial}{\partial x_i} \sum_{j \in \mathbb{N}} g_j = \sum_{j \in \mathbb{N}} \frac{\partial g_j}{\partial x_i}$$

The *Jacobian* of a vector $\mathbf{f}(\mathbf{x})$ is then the $n \times n$-matrix $\mathbf{f}'(\mathbf{x})$ given by $\mathbf{f}'(\mathbf{x})_{ij} = \dfrac{\partial f_i}{\partial x_j}$.

3.1 The Hopkins-Kozen Acceleration

In [5] Hopkins and Kozen introduce an acceleration of the Kleene procedure for *idempotent* cc-semirings and prove that it reaches the fixed point after finitely many steps. Given a system of power series $\mathbf{x} = \mathbf{f}(\mathbf{x})$, the *Hopkins-Kozen sequence* is defined by

$$\boldsymbol{\kappa}^{(0)} = \mathbf{f}(\mathbf{0}) \quad \text{and} \quad \boldsymbol{\kappa}^{(k+1)} = \mathbf{f}'(\boldsymbol{\kappa}^{(k)})^* \cdot \boldsymbol{\kappa}^{(k)}.$$

Theorem 2 (Hopkins and Kozen [5]). *Let $\mathbf{x} = \mathbf{f}(\mathbf{x})$ be a system of power series over an idempotent cc-semiring. There is a function $N : \mathbb{N} \to \mathbb{N}$ with $N(n) \in \mathcal{O}(3^n)$ s.t. $\boldsymbol{\kappa}^{(N(n))} = \mu\mathbf{f}$, where n is the number of variables of the system.*

Actually, [5] prove the theorem for commutative Kleene algebras, whose axioms are weaker than those of idempotent cc-semirings. There is no notion of infinite sums in the Kleene algebra axioms, especially the Kleene star operator $*$ and its derivative are defined axiomatically.

Example 1. Let $\langle 2^{\{a\}^*}, +, \cdot, 0, 1 \rangle$ denote the cc-semiring $\langle 2^{\{a\}^*}, \cup, \cdot, \emptyset, \{\varepsilon\} \rangle$. For simplicity, we write a^i instead of $\{a^i\}$. Consider the equation system

$$\mathbf{x} = \begin{pmatrix} x_1 \\ x_2 \end{pmatrix} = \begin{pmatrix} x_2^2 + a \\ x_1^2 \end{pmatrix} = \mathbf{f}(\mathbf{x}) \text{ with } \mathbf{f}'(\mathbf{x})^* = (x_1 x_2)^* \begin{pmatrix} 1 & x_2 \\ x_1 & 1 \end{pmatrix}.$$

The Hopkins-Kozen acceleration reaches the least fixed point $\mu\mathbf{f}$ after two steps:

$$\boldsymbol{\kappa}^{(0)} = (a, 0)^\top, \quad \boldsymbol{\kappa}^{(1)} = (a, a^2)^\top, \quad \boldsymbol{\kappa}^{(2)} = (a^3)^*(a, a^2)^\top.$$

It is easy to check that $\boldsymbol{\kappa}^{(2)}$ is a fixed point of $\mathbf{f}$. By Theorem 2 we have $\boldsymbol{\kappa}^{(2)} = \mu\mathbf{f}$.

3.2 Newton's Acceleration

Newton's method for approximating the zeros of a differentiable real function $\mathbf{g}(\mathbf{x})$ is one of the best known methods of numerical analysis. It computes the sequence

$$\mathbf{x}^{(0)} = \mathbf{s} \quad \text{and} \quad \mathbf{x}^{(k+1)} = \mathbf{x}^{(k)} - \mathbf{g}'(\mathbf{x}^{(k)})^{-1} \cdot \mathbf{g}(\mathbf{x}^{(k)}).$$

starting at the *seed* $\mathbf{s}$. Under certain conditions on $\mathbf{g}(\mathbf{x})$ and on the seed $\mathbf{s}$ (typically the seed must be "close enough" to the solution) the sequence converges to a solution of the equation $\mathbf{g}(\mathbf{x}) = \mathbf{0}$.

In order to approximate a solution of an equation system $\mathbf{x} = \mathbf{f}(\mathbf{x})$ over the reals, we can apply Newton's method to the function $\mathbf{g}(\mathbf{x}) = \mathbf{f}(\mathbf{x}) - \mathbf{x}$, which gives the sequence

$$\mathbf{x}^{(0)} = \mathbf{0} \quad \text{and} \quad \mathbf{x}^{(k+1)} = \mathbf{x}^{(k)} + (1 - \mathbf{f}'(\mathbf{x}^{(k)}))^{-1}(\mathbf{f}(\mathbf{x}^{(k)}) - \mathbf{x}^{(k)}).$$

4   An Acceleration for Arbitrary cc-Semirings

We show that the Hopkins-Kozen and Newton's accelerations are two instances of a general acceleration for arbitrary cc-semirings, which we call the cc-scheme. The proof relies on lemmata from [5] and [4], which we reformulate and generalise so that they hold for arbitrary cc-semirings.

The *cc-scheme* is given by:

$$\boldsymbol{\nu}^{(0)} = \mathbf{0} \quad \text{and} \quad \boldsymbol{\nu}^{(k+1)} = \boldsymbol{\nu}^{(k)} + \mathbf{f}'(\boldsymbol{\nu}^{(k)})^* \cdot \boldsymbol{\delta}(\boldsymbol{\nu}^{(k)}),$$

where $\boldsymbol{\delta}(\boldsymbol{\nu}^{(k)})$ is any vector s.t. $\boldsymbol{\nu}^{(k)} + \boldsymbol{\delta}(\boldsymbol{\nu}^{(k)}) = \mathbf{f}(\boldsymbol{\nu}^{(k)})$.
The scheme leaves the choice of $\boldsymbol{\delta}(\boldsymbol{\nu}^{(k)})$ free, but there is always at least one $\boldsymbol{\delta}(\boldsymbol{\nu}^{(k)})$ satisfying the condition (see Lemma 2 below).

The following theorem states that the cc-scheme accelerates the Kleene scheme $(\mathbf{f}^k(\mathbf{0}))_{k \in \mathbb{N}}$.

Theorem 3. *Let* $\mathbf{x} = \mathbf{f}(\mathbf{x})$ *be a system of power series over a cc-semiring. Then the iterates* $\boldsymbol{\nu}^{(k)}$ *of the cc-scheme exist and satisfy* $\mathbf{f}^k(\mathbf{0}) \leq \boldsymbol{\nu}^{(k)} \leq \mu\mathbf{f}$ *for all* $k \geq 0$.

The proof uses the following fundamental property of derivatives in cc-semirings:

Lemma 1 (Taylor's Theorem, cf. [5]). *Let* $\mathbf{f}(\mathbf{x})$ *and* $\mathbf{d}$ *be vectors of power series over a cc-semiring. Then*

$$\mathbf{f}(\mathbf{x}) + \mathbf{f}'(\mathbf{x}) \cdot \mathbf{d} \leq \mathbf{f}(\mathbf{x} + \mathbf{d}) \leq \mathbf{f}(\mathbf{x}) + \mathbf{f}'(\mathbf{x} + \mathbf{d}) \cdot \mathbf{d}.$$

The following lemma assures the existence of a suitable $\boldsymbol{\delta}(\boldsymbol{\nu}^{(k)})$ for each k.

Lemma 2. *Let* $\boldsymbol{\nu}^{(k)}$ *be the* k*-th iterate of the cc-scheme. For all* $k \geq 0$: $\mathbf{f}(\boldsymbol{\nu}^{(k)}) \geq \boldsymbol{\nu}^{(k)}$. *So, there is a* $\boldsymbol{\delta}(\boldsymbol{\nu}^{(k)})$ *such that* $\boldsymbol{\nu}^{(k)} + \boldsymbol{\delta}(\boldsymbol{\nu}^{(k)}) = \mathbf{f}(\boldsymbol{\nu}^{(k)})$.

What remains to show for Theorem 3 is $\mathbf{f}^k(\mathbf{0}) \leq \boldsymbol{\nu}^{(k)} \leq \mu\mathbf{f}$ (cf. [2]).

In the rest of the section we show that the Hopkins-Kozen acceleration and Newton's acceleration are special cases of the cc-scheme.

4.1   Idempotent cc-Semirings

If addition is idempotent, we have $x \leq y$ iff $x + y = y$, as $x \leq y$ implies that there is a d with $x + d = y$ so that $x + y = x + (x + d) = x + d = y$. By Lemma 2 we have $\boldsymbol{\nu}^{(k)} \leq \mathbf{f}(\boldsymbol{\nu}^{(k)})$. In the cc-scheme (see above) we therefore may choose $\boldsymbol{\delta}(\boldsymbol{\nu}^{(k)}) = \mathbf{f}(\boldsymbol{\nu}^{(k)})$. Moreover, since $\mathbf{f}'(\boldsymbol{\nu}^{(k)})^* \geq \mathbf{1}$ by the definition of the Kleene star and since $\boldsymbol{\nu}^{(k)} \leq \mathbf{f}(\boldsymbol{\nu}^{(k)})$ by Lemma 2 we get

$$\boldsymbol{\nu}^{(k)} \leq \mathbf{f}(\boldsymbol{\nu}^{(k)}) \leq \mathbf{f}'(\boldsymbol{\nu}^{(k)})^* \cdot \mathbf{f}(\boldsymbol{\nu}^{(k)})$$

and by idempotence

$$\boldsymbol{\nu}^{(k)} + \mathbf{f}'(\boldsymbol{\nu}^{(k)})^* \cdot \mathbf{f}(\boldsymbol{\nu}^{(k)}) = \mathbf{f}'(\boldsymbol{\nu}^{(k)})^* \cdot \mathbf{f}(\boldsymbol{\nu}^{(k)}) .$$

So the cc-scheme collapses in the idempotent case to

$$\boldsymbol{\nu}^{(0)} = \mathbf{0} \quad \text{and} \quad \boldsymbol{\nu}^{(k+1)} = \mathbf{f}'(\boldsymbol{\nu}^{(k)})^* \cdot \mathbf{f}(\boldsymbol{\nu}^{(k)}).$$

In other words, $\boldsymbol{\nu}^{(k+1)}$ results from $\boldsymbol{\nu}^{(k)}$ by applying the operator $\mathcal{N}_\mathbf{f}(\mathbf{x}) := \mathbf{f}'(\mathbf{x})^* \cdot \mathbf{f}(\mathbf{x})$. Recall that the Hopkins-Kozen sequence is given by

$$\boldsymbol{\kappa}^{(0)} = \mathbf{f}(\mathbf{0}) \quad \text{and} \quad \boldsymbol{\kappa}^{(k+1)} = \mathbf{f}'(\boldsymbol{\kappa}^{(k)})^* \cdot \boldsymbol{\kappa}^{(k)}.$$

So it is obtained by repeatedly applying the Hopkins-Kozen operator $\mathcal{H}_\mathbf{f}(\mathbf{x}) := \mathbf{f}'(\mathbf{x})^* \cdot \mathbf{x}$, starting from $\mathbf{f}(\mathbf{0})$. While the two sequences are not identical, the following theorem shows that they are essentially the same.

Theorem 4.

1. *For all* $k > 0 : \boldsymbol{\kappa}^{(k-1)} \le \boldsymbol{\nu}^{(k)} \le \boldsymbol{\kappa}^{(k)}$.
2. *For all* $k \ge 0 : \boldsymbol{\kappa}^{(k)} = \mathcal{H}_\mathbf{f}^k(\mathbf{f}(\mathbf{0})) = \mathcal{N}_\mathbf{f}^k(\mathbf{f}(\mathbf{0}))$.

4.2   The Semiring over the Nonnegative Reals

We now consider the cc-semiring $\langle \mathbb{R}^+ \cup \{0, \infty\}, +, \cdot, 0, 1\rangle$. In order to instantiate the cc-scheme, we have to choose $\boldsymbol{\delta}(\boldsymbol{\nu}^{(k)})$ so that $\boldsymbol{\nu}^{(k)} + \boldsymbol{\delta}(\boldsymbol{\nu}^{(k)}) = \mathbf{f}(\boldsymbol{\nu}^{(k)})$ holds. By Lemma 2 we have $\boldsymbol{\nu}^{(k)} \le \mathbf{f}(\boldsymbol{\nu}^{(k)})$, and so we can take $\boldsymbol{\delta}(\boldsymbol{\nu}^{(k)}) = \mathbf{f}(\boldsymbol{\nu}^{(k)}) - \boldsymbol{\nu}^{(k)}$. The cc-acceleration becomes

$$\boldsymbol{\nu}^{(0)} = \mathbf{0} \quad \text{and} \quad \boldsymbol{\nu}^{(k+1)} = \boldsymbol{\nu}^{(k)} + \mathbf{f}'(\boldsymbol{\nu}^{(k)})^* \cdot (\mathbf{f}(\boldsymbol{\nu}^{(k)}) - \boldsymbol{\nu}^{(k)}).$$

It is easy to see that for any nonnegative real-valued square matrix $\mathbf{A}$, if $\sum_{k \in \mathbb{N}} \mathbf{A}^k = \mathbf{A}^*$ has only finite entries, then $(1 - \mathbf{A})^{-1}$ exists and equals $\mathbf{A}^*$. If this is the case for $\mathbf{A} = \mathbf{f}'(\boldsymbol{\nu}^{(k)})^*$, then Newton's method coincides with the cc-acceleration for the reals and thus converges to $\mu\mathbf{f}$. In [4] Etessami and Yannakakis give sufficient conditions for $\mathbf{f}'(\boldsymbol{\nu}^{(k)})^* = (1 - \mathbf{f}'(\boldsymbol{\nu}^{(k)}))^{-1}$ when $\mathbf{f}$ is derived from a recursive Markov chain.

5   Convergence Speed in Idempotent Semirings

In the first subsection we want to analyse how many steps the Newton iteration or, equivalently, the Hopkins-Kozen iteration needs to reach $\mu\mathbf{f}$ when we consider an idempotent cc-semiring $\langle A, +, \cdot, 0, 1\rangle$, i.e. we have the additional equation $1 + 1 = 1$. In the subsequent subsection we then generalise the obtained results to the setting of commutative Kleene algebras.

5.1   Idempotent cc-Semirings

In this subsection $\mathbf{f}$ again denotes a system of n power series in the variables $\mathcal{X} = \{x_1, \ldots, x_n\}$, i.e. we have $f_i(\mathbf{x}) = \sum_{\iota \in \mathbb{N}^n} c_\iota^{(i)} \mathbf{x}^\iota$, where $\mathbf{x}^\iota$ denotes the product $x_1^{\iota_1} \cdot \ldots \cdot x_n^{\iota_n}$ and $c_\iota^{(i)} \in A$ for all $\iota \in \mathbb{N}^n$ and $1 \le i \le n$. We define the concept of *derivation trees* of our system $\mathbf{f}$ as in formal language theory.

Notation 2. *In the following, if u is a node of a tree t, we identify u with the subtree of t rooted at u. In particular, t is also used to denote t's root. The height $h(t)$ of t is defined as usual, e.g. a tree consisting only of a single node has height 0.*

Definition 1. *A partial derivation tree t of x_i is a labelled tree satisfying:*

- *every node of t is labelled by either an element of A or an element of $\mathcal{X}$,*
- *its root is labelled by x_i, and*
- *for each node u of t labeled by some variable x_k the following holds: Let $p_u(\mathbf{x})$ be the product of the labels of u's children. Then p_u is a summand of f_k, i.e. there exists a $\iota \in \mathbb{N}^n$ with $c_\iota^{(k)} \neq 0$ and $c_\iota^{(k)} \mathbf{x}^\iota = p_u(\mathbf{x})$.*

We call a partial derivation tree t a derivation tree if no leaf of t is labelled by a variable. The yield $Y(t)$ of a derivation tree t is the product of the labels of its leaves.

As in the case of formal languages we have the following

Theorem 5.

1. *The sum of yields of all derivation trees of x_i with height $\leq h$ equals $(\mathbf{f}^h(\mathbf{0}))_i$.*
2. *The sum of yields of all derivation trees of x_i equals $(\mu\mathbf{f})_i$.*

In the following we show that because of commutativity and idempotence already a special class of derivation trees is sufficient to reach $\mu\mathbf{f}$.

Definition 2 (cf. Fig. 5.1). *The dimension $\dim(t)$ of a tree t is defined by:*

1. *A tree of height 0 or 1 has dimension 0.*
2. *Let t be a tree of height $h(t) > 1$ with children $c_1, c_2, \ldots, c_s$ where $\dim(c_1) \geq \dim(c_2) \geq \ldots \dim(c_s)$. Let $d_1 = \dim(c_1)$. If $s > 1$, let $d_2 = \dim(c_2)$, otherwise let $d_2 = 0$. Then we define*

$$\dim(t) := \begin{cases} d_1 + 1 & \text{if } d_1 = d_2 \\ d_1 & \text{if } d_1 > d_2. \end{cases}$$

Note that for a derivation tree t we have $h(t) > \dim(t)$.

Definition 3. *Let t be a derivation tree. We denote with $V(t)$ the number of distinct variables appearing as labels in t. We call t compact if $\dim(t) \leq V(t)$.*

In the following, we state two central lemmata that lead to the main result of this section. Lemma 3 tells us that it is sufficient to consider only compact derivation trees. Lemma 4 shows the connection between the dimension of a derivation tree and the Hopkins-Kozen sequence.

Lemma 3. *For each derivation tree t of x_i there is a compact derivation tree t' of x_i with equal yield.*

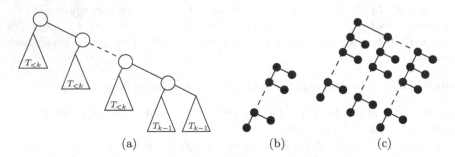

Fig. 1. (a) shows the general structure of a tree of dimension k, where $T_{<k}$ (T_{k-1}) represents any tree of dimension $< k$ $(= k - 1)$. (b) and (c) give some idea of the topology of one-, resp. two-dimensional trees in general.

Lemma 4. *Let t be a derivation tree of x_i s.t. $\dim(t) \leq k$. Then $Y(t) \leq (\boldsymbol{\kappa}^{(k)})_i$.*[3]

The proof of Lemma 3 bears some similarity to the proof of the pumping lemma for context free languages. Let us call a partial derivation tree a *pumping* tree (p-tree) if it has exactly one leaf which bears the same label as its root and all other leaves are labelled by elements of A. Because of commutativity, reallocating such a p-tree from one subtree of t to another one does not change t's yield. We use a reallocation procedure to inductively reduce the dimension of t's subtrees, which eventually results in decreasing the dimension of t itself.

Theorem 6. *Let $\mathbf{f} : A^n \to A^n$ be a system of power series over an idempotent cc-semiring $\langle A, +, \cdot, 0, 1 \rangle$. Then $\mu\mathbf{f} = \boldsymbol{\kappa}^{(n)}$.*

Proof. First recall that by Theorem 3 ($\boldsymbol{\nu}^{(k)} \leq \mu\mathbf{f}$) and Theorem 4 ($\boldsymbol{\kappa}^{(k-1)} \leq \boldsymbol{\nu}^{(k)} \leq \boldsymbol{\kappa}^{(k)}$) we have $\boldsymbol{\kappa}^{(n)} \leq \mu\mathbf{f}$. Obviously, $V(t) \leq n$ for every derivation tree t of x_i. Lemma 3 allows to assume that t is compact, i.e. $\dim(t) \leq V(t) \leq n$. Lemma 4 thus implies $Y(t) \leq (\boldsymbol{\kappa}^{(n)})_i$. Therefore the sum of yields of derivation trees of x_i is less than or equal to $(\boldsymbol{\kappa}^{(n)})_i$. But Theorem 5 tells us that this sum is already $(\mu\mathbf{f})_i$. Hence $\mu\mathbf{f} \leq \boldsymbol{\kappa}^{(n)} \leq \mu\mathbf{f}$. $\square$

Remark 2. The bound of this theorem is tight as can be shown by a generalisation of Example 1: If $\mathbf{f}(\mathbf{x}) = (x_2^2 + a, x_3^2, \ldots, x_n^2, x_1^2)^\top$, then $(\boldsymbol{\kappa}^{(k)})_1 = a$ for $k < n$, but $a^{2^n} \leq (\boldsymbol{\kappa}^{(n)})_1 = (\mu\mathbf{f})_1$.

5.2   Generalisation to Commutative Kleene Algebras

Notation 3. Let M be any set. Then RExp_M denotes the set of regular expressions *generated by* the elements of M. We write $R_M : \mathsf{RExp}_M \to 2^{M^*}$ for their canonical interpretation *as languages.*

---

[3] In fact one can similarly show that $(\boldsymbol{\kappa}^{(k)})_i$ equals exactly the sum of yields of all derivation trees of x_i of dimension less than or equal to k.

For this subsection, let $\mathbf{f}$ denote a system of n *regular expressions* $f_i \in \mathsf{RExp}_{K \cup \mathcal{X}}$. We are again interested in the least solution $\mu \mathbf{f}$ of $\mathbf{x} = \mathbf{f}(\mathbf{x})$, but this time over the *commutative Kleene algebra* $\langle K, +, \cdot,^*, 0, 1 \rangle$. A *commutative Kleene algebra* is an idempotent commutative semiring $\langle K, +, \cdot, 0, 1 \rangle$ where the *-operator is only required to satisfy these two equations for all $a, b, c \in K$:

$$1 + aa^* \leq a^* \quad \text{and} \quad a + bc \leq c \rightarrow b^* a \leq c.$$

In [5] it is proved that $\mu \mathbf{f}$ can be computed by applying the Hopkins-Kozen operator $\mathcal{H}_{\mathbf{f}}$ to $\mathbf{f}(\mathbf{0})$ for a finite number of times. In addition, $\mathcal{H}_{\mathbf{f}}^i(\mathbf{f}(\mathbf{0})) \leq \mu \mathbf{f}$ for all $i \in \mathbb{N}$.

As in the setting of cc-semirings the Hopkins-Kozen operator is defined by $\mathcal{H}_{\mathbf{f}}(\mathbf{x}) = \mathbf{f}'(\mathbf{x})^* \mathbf{x}$. For $\mathcal{H}$ to be well defined over Kleene algebras, one has to define the partial derivatives $\frac{\partial}{\partial x_j}$ over $\mathsf{Reg}_{K \cup \mathcal{X}}$. This is done in [5] just as in the case of cc-semirings (see the beginning of Section 3), however the equation for the $\sum$-operator is replaced by the axiom $\frac{\partial \alpha^*}{\partial x_j} = \alpha^* \frac{\partial \alpha}{\partial x_j}$ for $\alpha \in \mathsf{RExp}_{K \cup \mathcal{X}}$.

We lift the result of the previous subsection to commutative Kleene algebras, improving the $\mathcal{O}(3^n)$ bound in [5]. More precisely we show that

$$\mathbf{f}(\mathcal{H}_{\mathbf{f}}^n(\mathbf{f}(\mathbf{0}))) = \mathcal{H}_{\mathbf{f}}^n(\mathbf{f}(\mathbf{0})). \tag{2}$$

In order to prove (2) we appeal to Redko's theorem [1] that essentially states that an equation of terms over any commutative Kleene algebra holds if it holds under the *canonical commutative interpretation*. See [2] for a technical justification of this fact. Let Σ be the finite set of elements of K appearing in $\mathbf{f}$. The canonical commutative interpretation $\mathsf{c}_\Sigma : \mathsf{RExp}_\Sigma \rightarrow 2^{\mathbb{N}^\Sigma}$ is then defined by $\mathsf{c}_\Sigma(\alpha) = \{\#w \mid w \in R_\Sigma(\alpha)\}$, where $\#w$ is the Parikh-vector of $w \in \Sigma^*$, i.e. $a \in \Sigma$ appears exactly $(\#w)_a$-times in w. We omit the subscript of c_Σ in the following. The idempotent cc-semiring of sets of Parikh-vectors $\mathcal{C}_\Sigma$ is defined by $\mathcal{C}_\Sigma = \langle 2^{\mathbb{N}^\Sigma}, \cup, +, \emptyset, \{\mathbf{0}\} \rangle$ with $A + B = \{a + b \mid a \in A, b \in B\}$ for all $A, B \subseteq \mathbb{N}^\Sigma$ and $\sum S = \bigcup S$ for all $S \subseteq 2^{\mathbb{N}^\Sigma}$. By Redko's theorem, we can prove (2) by showing $\mathsf{c}(\mathbf{f}(\mathcal{H}_{\mathbf{f}}^n(\mathbf{f}(\mathbf{0})))) = \mathsf{c}(\mathcal{H}_{\mathbf{f}}^n(\mathbf{f}(\mathbf{0})))$ over $\mathcal{C}_\Sigma$.

For any function $g : \mathsf{RExp}_\Sigma \rightarrow \mathsf{RExp}_\Sigma$, let g^c denote the commutative interpretation of g as a map over $\mathcal{C}_\Sigma$, i.e. $\mathsf{c}(g(\alpha)) = g^\mathsf{c}(\mathsf{c}(\alpha))$ for all $\alpha \in \mathsf{RExp}_\Sigma$. In particular $\mathsf{c}(\alpha^*) = \bigcup_{i \in \mathbb{N}} \mathsf{c}(\alpha^i)$. Notice that this definition is consistent with the axiomatic definition of derivatives of *-expressions, since

$$\mathsf{c}(\frac{\partial}{\partial x_i}(\alpha^*)) = \mathsf{c}(\alpha^* \frac{\partial}{\partial x_i}(\alpha)) = \bigcup_{j \in \mathbb{N}} \mathsf{c}(\alpha^j) \frac{\partial}{\partial x_i}(\mathsf{c}(\alpha)) = \frac{\partial}{\partial x_i} \bigcup_{j \in \mathbb{N}} \mathsf{c}(\alpha^j) = \frac{\partial}{\partial x_i}(\mathsf{c}(\alpha^*)).$$

We then have $(\mathcal{H}_{\mathbf{f}})^\mathsf{c} = \mathcal{H}_{\mathbf{f}^\mathsf{c}}$. Furthermore, by Theorem 6, $\mathcal{H}_{\mathbf{f}^\mathsf{c}}^n(\mathbf{f}^\mathsf{c}(\emptyset))$ solves the equation system $\mathbf{x} = \mathbf{f}^\mathsf{c}(\mathbf{x})$ over $\mathcal{C}_\Sigma$. Combined, we have

$$\mathsf{c}(\mathbf{f}(\mathcal{H}_{\mathbf{f}}^n(\mathbf{f}(\mathbf{0})))) = \mathbf{f}^\mathsf{c}((\mathcal{H}_{\mathbf{f}}^n)^\mathsf{c}(\mathbf{f}^\mathsf{c}(\emptyset))) = \mathbf{f}^\mathsf{c}(\mathcal{H}_{\mathbf{f}^\mathsf{c}}^n(\mathbf{f}^\mathsf{c}(\emptyset))) = \mathcal{H}_{\mathbf{f}^\mathsf{c}}^n(\mathbf{f}^\mathsf{c}(\emptyset)) = \mathsf{c}(\mathcal{H}_{\mathbf{f}}^n(\mathbf{f}(\mathbf{0}))).$$

This proves the following theorem.

Theorem 7. *Let* $\mathbf{f} \in \mathsf{RExp}_{K \cup \mathcal{X}}^n$ *define a system* $\mathbf{x} = \mathbf{f}(\mathbf{x})$ *over a commutative Kleene algebra* $\langle K, +, \cdot,^*, 0, 1 \rangle$. *Then* $\mu \mathbf{f} = \kappa^{(n)}$.

6   A Hierarchy of Accelerations

In this section we apply the Hopkins-Kozen acceleration to itself. Let $\mathbf{x} = \mathbf{f}(\mathbf{x})$ be an equation system of degree-2-polynomials over a commutative Kleene algebra. Any polynomial equation system (even with *-expressions) can be reduced to this "Chomsky normal" form by introducing auxiliary variables.

Recall the Hopkins-Kozen operator $\mathcal{H}_{\mathbf{f}}(\mathbf{x}) = \mathbf{f}'(\mathbf{x})^*\mathbf{x}$. As shown in [5] and in the previous section, the sequence $\mathcal{H}_{\mathbf{f}}^i(\mathbf{f}(\mathbf{0}))$ is "faster" than $\mathbf{f}^i(\mathbf{f}(\mathbf{0}))$ to the extent that the fixed point iteration of $\mathcal{H}_{\mathbf{f}}$ reaches $\mu\mathbf{f}$ in a finite number of steps, whereas the fixed point iteration of $\mathbf{f}$ may not reach $\mu\mathbf{f}$. We study in this section how fast accelerations $\mathcal{H}_{\mathcal{H}_{\mathbf{f}}}, \mathcal{H}_{\mathcal{H}_{\mathcal{H}_{\mathbf{f}}}}, \ldots$ are compared to $\mathcal{H}_{\mathbf{f}}$. We write $\mathcal{H}_1$ for $\mathcal{H}_{\mathbf{f}}$ and $\mathcal{H}_{i+1}$ for $\mathcal{H}_{\mathcal{H}_i} = (\frac{\partial}{\partial\mathbf{x}}(\mathcal{H}_i(\mathbf{x})))^*\mathbf{x}$. In the following we mean $\mathcal{H}_{\mathbf{f}}$ when the subscript of $\mathcal{H}$ is omitted. Our hierarchy theorem states that using $\mathcal{H}_i$ once amounts to using $\mathcal{H}$ i-times:

Theorem 8. *For all* $i \geq 1$: $\mathcal{H}_i(\mathbf{x}) = \mathcal{H}^i(\mathbf{x})$.

Combined with Theorem 6 we conclude that the least fixed point $\mu\mathbf{f}$ can be computed by (a) iteratively applying $\mathcal{H}$ to $\mathbf{f}(\mathbf{0})$ (n times) or (b) computing the operator $\mathcal{H}^n$ and applying it to $\mathbf{f}(\mathbf{0})$ once or (c) computing the operator $\mathcal{H}_n$ and applying it to $\mathbf{f}(\mathbf{0})$ once. A discussion which method is most appropriate depends on the the particular applications and is beyond the scope of this paper.

Example 2. We continue Example 1 where we have shown that $\mathcal{H}^2(\mathbf{f}(\mathbf{0})) = \mu\mathbf{f}$. Now we illustrate Theorem 8 by showing that $\mathcal{H}_2(\mathbf{f}(\mathbf{0})) = \mu\mathbf{f}$. We have

$$\mathcal{H}(\mathbf{x}) = \mathbf{f}'(\mathbf{x})^*\mathbf{x} = (x_1 x_2)^* \begin{pmatrix} x_1 + x_2^2 \\ x_1^2 + x_2 \end{pmatrix} ,$$

$$\mathcal{H}'(\mathbf{x}) = (x_1 x_2)^* \begin{pmatrix} 1 + x_2^3 & x_1^2 + x_2 \\ x_2^2 + x_1 & 1 + x_1^3 \end{pmatrix} ,$$

$$\mathcal{H}'(\mathbf{f}(\mathbf{0})) = \begin{pmatrix} 1 & a^2 \\ a & 1 + a^3 \end{pmatrix} \quad \text{and} \quad \mathcal{H}'(\mathbf{f}(\mathbf{0}))^* = (a^3)^* \begin{pmatrix} 1 & a^2 \\ a & 1 \end{pmatrix} .$$

So $\mathcal{H}_2(\mathbf{f}(\mathbf{0})) = \mathcal{H}'(\mathbf{f}(\mathbf{0}))^*\mathbf{f}(\mathbf{0}) = (a^3)^* \begin{pmatrix} a \\ a^2 \end{pmatrix} = \mu\mathbf{f}$.

7   Conclusions

We have studied the Hopkins-Kozen acceleration scheme for solving fixed point equations $\mathbf{x} = \mathbf{f}(\mathbf{x})$ over commutative Kleene algebras [5]. We have shown that, maybe surprisingly, the scheme is tightly related to Newton's method for approximating a zero of a differentiable real function. Loosely speaking, the scheme is the result of generalising Newton's method to commutative ω-continuous semi-rings in a very straightforward way, and then instantiating this generalisation to the case in which addition is idempotent. In the proof we very much profit from a result by Etessami and Yannakakis on using Newton's method to solve fixed point equations derived from recursive Markov chains [4]. At the same time, our result extends Etessami and Yannakakis' result to arbitrary commutative ω-continuous semirings, a much more general algebraic setting.

We have also proved that the Hopkins-Kozen scheme terminates after n iterations for a system of n equations, improving on the $O(3^n)$ bound of [5]. As in [5], our bound holds for arbitrary commutative Kleene algebras.

Finally, we have studied the result of applying the scheme to itself, leading to a sequence of faster and faster accelerations. The Hopkins-Kozen scheme can be "arbitrarily faster" than the basis scheme derived from Kleene's theorem (the scheme computing $(\mathbf{f}^k(\mathbf{0}))_{k\geq 0}$) because it is guaranteed to terminate, while Kleene's scheme is not. We have shown that, on the contrary, the reduction in the number of iterations achieved by subsequent accelerations is very moderate: one iteration of the scheme obtained by applying k times the acceleration to itself is already matched by k iterations of the Hopkins-Kozen scheme.

Our work can be extended in several directions. Our proof of the new bound relies on formal languages concepts, and is therefore very non-algebraic. We intend to search for an algebraic proof. We also plan to investigate accelerations for the non-commutative case.

Acknowledgements

We thank Volker Diekert for helpful discussions and the anonymous referees for useful comments.

References

1. J.H. Conway. *Regular Algebra and Finite Machines*. Chapman and Hall, 1971.
2. J. Esparza, S. Kiefer, and M. Luttenberger. On fixed point equations over commutative semirings. Technical report, 2006.
3. J. Esparza, A. Kučera, and R. Mayr. Model checking probabilistic pushdown automata. In *LICS 2004*. IEEE Computer Society, 2004.
4. K. Etessami and M. Yannakakis. Recursive Markov chains, stochastic grammars, and monotone systems of nonlinear equations. In *STACS*, pages 340–352, 2005.
5. M. W. Hopkins and D. Kozen. Parikh's theorem in commutative Kleene algebra. In *Logic in Computer Science*, pages 394–401, 1999.
6. D. Kozen. On Kleene algebras and closed semirings. In B. Rovan, editor, *Proc. Math. Found. Comput. Sci.*, volume 452 of *Lecture Notes in Computer Science*, pages 26–47, Banska-Bystrica, Slovakia, 1990. Springer-Verlag.
7. W. Kuich. *Handbook of Formal Languages*, volume 1, chapter 9: Semirings and Formal Power Series: Their Relevance to Formal Languages and Automata, pages 609 – 677. Springer, 1997.
8. J.M. Ortega. *Numerical Analysis: A Second Course*. Academic Press, New York, 1972.

An Exponential Lower Bound for
Prefix Gröbner Bases in Free Monoid Rings

Andrea Sattler-Klein

Technische Universität Kaiserslautern, Fachbereich Informatik
Postfach 3049, 67653 Kaiserslautern, Germany
sattler@informatik.uni-kl.de

Abstract. We show by an example that the number of reduction steps
needed to compute a prefix Gröbner basis in a free monoid ring by interreduction can in fact be exponential in the size of the input. This
answers an open question posed by Zeckzer in [Ze00].

Keywords: algorithms, computational complexity, rewriting, Gröbner
bases.

1   Introduction

The importance of the theory of Gröbner bases for ideals in commutative polynomial rings over fields as introduced by Buchberger in 1965 has led to various
generalizations. An important one is the theory of prefix Gröbner bases introduced by Madlener and Reinert in [MaRe93] (see also [Re95]) for handling right-
ideals in monoid and groups rings. Their work generalizes the theory introduced
by Mora for Gröbner bases in non-commutative polynomial rings [Mo86] (see
also [Mo94]) and has recently been further generalized to modules over monoid
rings in [AcKr06].

Based on the ideas of Madlener and Reinert, Zeckzer has developed the system
MRC, a system for computing prefix Gröbner bases in monoid and group rings
(see [ReZe98],[ReZe99],[Ze00]). In [Ze00] Zeckzer also analyzed the complexity
of some related problems and algorithms. The general procedure for computing
prefix Gröbner bases does not terminate in general, since it may happen that for
the given input no finite prefix Gröbner basis exists. Therefore, Zeckzer restricted
his attention to the case of prefix Gröbner bases in free monoid rings, since in
this case termination of the procedure is guaranteed. For special cases he derived
some exponential upper bounds as well as some exponential lower bounds for
the time complexity of the algorithm, where the later ones depend essentially on
the underlying field.

The algorithm for computing prefix Gröbner bases in free monoid rings is
based on rewriting techniques. If we do not take into account the field operations performed then the time needed by the algorithm corresponds to the
number of reduction steps that are performed. Therefore, it is interesting to establish bounds for the number of reduction steps that have to be performed by

W. Thomas and P. Weil (Eds.): STACS 2007, LNCS 4393, pp. 308–319, 2007.

the algorithm. In [Ze00] Zeckzer also studied this aspect. For all of his examples the computation of prefix Gröbner bases can be done with only polynomial many reduction steps provided an appropriate strategy is used. Based on this observation he asked the following question which is the first one in his list of open problems formulated on page 242:

"Is there a strategy such that prefix Gröbner basis computation can be done with only polynomial many prefix reduction steps?"

In the following we will answer this question in the negative by showing an example where the corresponding algorithm always needs exponentially many reduction steps independently of the strategies used within. For doing this, we will first investigate reduction strategies and characterize a strategy that is optimal for left-normalized prefix Gröbner bases. On the one hand, this result is interesting on its own. On the other hand, it is very useful for the proof of our main example.

Due to lack of space we will omit all proofs in the following. We refer to the full version of the paper for the proofs (see [Sa07]).

2 Preliminaries

In the following we introduce the basic definitions and foundations that are needed when considering prefix Gröbner bases in free monoid rings from a rewriter's point of view. For further reading concerning prefix Gröbner bases we refer to [MaRe93], [Re95] and [Ze00].

Let Σ be a finite alphabet and let K be a computable field. Then Σ^* denotes the set of all *strings (words)* over Σ including the empty string ε, i.e., Σ^* is the free monoid generated by Σ. For $u, v \in \Sigma^*$ and $\Gamma \subseteq \Sigma^*$, $u\Gamma v$ denotes the set $\{ uwv \mid w \in \Gamma \}$. Moreover, for a set $\Gamma \subseteq \Sigma^*$ and a number $n \in \mathbb{N}_0$, Γ^n denotes the set $\{ u_1 u_2 ... u_n \mid u_1, u_2, ..., u_n \in \Gamma \}$. An ordering $>$ on Σ^* is called *admissible* if $u > v$ implies $xuy > xvy$ for all $u, v, x, y \in \Sigma^*$, and it is called *wellfounded* if there is no infinite descending chain $u_1 > u_2 > u_3 > ...$. For a finite set $\Gamma \subseteq \Sigma^*$ and a total ordering on Σ^*, $max_> \Gamma$ denotes the largest string of Γ w.r.t. $>$.

The *free monoid ring* $K[\Sigma^*]$ is the ring of all formal sums (called *polynomials*) $\sum_{i=1}^{n} \alpha_i * w_i$ ($n \in \mathbb{N}_0$) with *coefficients* $\alpha_i \in K - \{0\}$ and *terms* $w_i \in \Sigma^*$ such that for all $i, j \in \{1, ..., n\}$ with $i \neq j$, $w_i \neq w_j$ holds. The products $\alpha_i * w_i$ ($\alpha_i \in K - \{0\}$, $w_i \in \Sigma^*$) are called *monomials* and the set of all terms occurring in a polynomial p is denoted by $T(p)$. Instead of $1 * w_i$ we will also sometimes simply write w_i. For a polynomial $p = \sum_{i=1}^{n} \alpha_i * w_i$, a string $x \in \Sigma^*$ and $\beta \in K$, $\beta \cdot p \circ x$ denotes the polynomial $\sum_{i=1}^{n} (\beta \cdot \alpha_i) * w_i x$. Moreover, for a finite set $\Gamma \subseteq \Sigma^*$, $\sum \Gamma$ denotes the polynomial $\sum_{w \in \Gamma} 1 * w$.

A pair $(\alpha * t, r)$ with $\alpha \in K - \{0\}$, $t \in \Sigma^*$ and $r \in K[\Sigma^*]$ is called a *rule*. Given a total wellfounded admissible ordering $>$ on Σ^* we associate with each non-zero polynomial $p \in K[\Sigma^*]$ a rule $(l, r) \in K\Sigma^* \times K[\Sigma^*]$ with $l = \alpha * t$ ($\alpha \in K - \{0\}$, $t \in \Sigma^*$), namely the one that satisfies the following two properties: 1. $l - r = p$, 2.

(l, r) is *compatible* with $>$, i.e., $t > s$ for all $s \in T(r)$. Accordingly, we associate with a set $F \subseteq K[\Sigma^*]$ of polynomials the set of corresponding rules that are compatible with $>$. For a rule $(l, r) \in K\Sigma^* \times K[\Sigma^*]$ we also write $l \to r$. If the coefficient of the left-hand side of a rule (l, r) associated with a polynomial p is 1 then (l, r) as well as p are called *monic*. A set of rules $\mathcal{R} \subseteq K\Sigma^* \times K[\Sigma^*]$ is called *monic* if each rule of $\mathcal{R}$ is monic.

A set of rules $\mathcal{R} \subseteq K\Sigma^* \times K[\Sigma^*]$ induces a reduction relation $\to_\mathcal{R}$ on $K[\Sigma^*]$ which is defined in the following way: For $p, q \in K[\Sigma^*]$, $p \to_\mathcal{R} q$ if and only if there exists a rule $(\alpha * t, r) \in \mathcal{R}$ (with $\alpha \in K$ and $t \in \Sigma^*$), a monomial $\beta * s$ in p (with $\beta \in K, s \in \Sigma^*$) and a string $x \in \Sigma^*$ such that 1. $tx = s$ and 2. $q = p - \beta * s + (\beta \cdot \alpha^{-1}) \cdot r \circ x$. We also write $p \xrightarrow{\beta * s}_\mathcal{R} q$ in this case to indicate the monomial that is substituted by the reduction step and say that the rule $\alpha * t \to r$ *(prefix) reduces p to q* in one step. If $\alpha * t \to r$ (with $\alpha \in K, t \in \Sigma^*$ and $r \in K[\Sigma^*]$) is a rule, $\beta \in K$ and $x \in \Sigma^*$ then $(\beta \cdot \alpha) * tx \to_\mathcal{R} \beta \cdot r \circ x$ is called an *instance* of the rule $\alpha * t \to r$. A polynomial $p \in K[\Sigma^*]$ is called *(prefix) reducible* w.r.t. a set of rules $\mathcal{R} \subseteq K\Sigma^* \times K[\Sigma^*]$ if there exists a polynomial $q \in K[\Sigma^*]$ with $p \to_\mathcal{R} q$. Otherwise, p is called $\mathcal{R}$-irreducible.

As usually, $\to_\mathcal{R}^*$ denotes the reflexive and transitive closure of $\to_\mathcal{R}$, i.e., $p \to_\mathcal{R}^* q$ means that p can be reduced to q in n reduction steps for some $n \in \mathbb{N}_0$. We also write $p \to_\mathcal{R}^n q$ if p reduces to q in n steps and we denote by $D_{\to_\mathcal{R}}(p, q)$ the minimum of the set $\{n \in \mathbb{N}_0 \mid p \to_\mathcal{R}^n q\}$ in this case. If $p \to_\mathcal{R}^* q$ holds, then q is called a *descendant* of p. An irreducible descendant of p is called a *normal form* of p. If p has a unique normal form w.r.t. $\mathcal{R}$ then this normal form is denoted by $NF_\mathcal{R}(p)$. Moreover, $\leftrightarrow_\mathcal{R}^*$ denotes the reflexive, symmetric and transitive closure of $\to_\mathcal{R}$. Two sets of rules $\mathcal{R}, \mathcal{S} \subseteq K\Sigma^* \times K[\Sigma^*]$ are called *equivalent* if $\leftrightarrow_\mathcal{R}^* = \leftrightarrow_\mathcal{S}^*$.

If $(\alpha * t, r_1)$ and $(\beta * s, r_2)$ $(\alpha, \beta \in K$ and $t, s \in \Sigma^*)$ are two rules of $\mathcal{R} \subseteq K\Sigma^* \times K[\Sigma^*]$ such that $t = sx$ for some $x \in \Sigma^*$ then $(r_1, (\alpha \cdot \beta^{-1}) \cdot r_2 \circ x)$ is a *critical pair* (of $\mathcal{R}$) and the corresponding polynomial $r_1 - (\alpha \cdot \beta^{-1}) \cdot r_2 \circ x$ is called a *(prefix) S-polynomial* (of $\mathcal{R}$). A set of rules $\mathcal{R} \subseteq K\Sigma^* \times K[\Sigma^*]$ is called *confluent* if for all $p, q, r \in K[\Sigma^*]$ the following holds: If q and r are descendants of p then they are *joinable* in $\mathcal{R}$, i.e., they have a common descendant w.r.t. $\mathcal{R}$. Moreover, $\mathcal{R}$ is called *noetherian* (or *terminating*) if no infinite chain of the form $p_0 \to_\mathcal{R} p_1 \to_\mathcal{R} p_2 \to_\mathcal{R} \ldots$ exists. If $\mathcal{R}$ is compatible with a total wellfounded admissible ordering then it is noetherian. If in addition, each critical pair of $\mathcal{R}$ is joinable in $\mathcal{R}$, or in other words, each S-polynomial of $\mathcal{R}$ is $\mathcal{R}$-reducible to 0, then $\mathcal{R}$ is confluent. $\mathcal{R} \subseteq K\Sigma^* \times K[\Sigma^*]$ is called *left-normalized* if for all $(l, r) \in \mathcal{R}$, l is irreducible w.r.t. $\mathcal{R} - \{(l, r)\}$. Moreover, $\mathcal{R}$ is called *right-normalized* if for all $(l, r) \in \mathcal{R}$, r is irreducible w.r.t. $\mathcal{R}$ and it is called *interreduced* if it is left- and right-normalized.

Let $F \subseteq K[\Sigma^*]$ be a set of non-zero polynomials, let $>$ be a total wellfounded admissible ordering on Σ^* and let $\mathcal{R} \subseteq K\Sigma^* \times K[\Sigma^*]$ be the associated set of rules. Then a set of rules $\mathcal{S} \subseteq K\Sigma^* \times K[\Sigma^*]$ is called a *prefix Gröbner basis* for F (or for $\mathcal{R}$) w.r.t. $>$ if the following holds: 1. $\leftrightarrow_\mathcal{S}^* = \leftrightarrow_\mathcal{R}^*$, 2. $\mathcal{S}$ is compatible with $>$, 3. $\mathcal{S}$ is confluent. If $\mathcal{S}$ is a prefix Gröbner basis for a set

$F \subseteq K[\Sigma^*]$, then a polynomial p is an element of the right-ideal generated by F if and only if its uniquely determined $\mathcal{S}$-normal form is equal to 0. For a set $F \subseteq K[\Sigma^*]$ ($\mathcal{R} \subseteq K\Sigma^* \times K[\Sigma^*]$) of non-zero polynomials (of rules) and a given total wellfounded admissible ordering $>$ on Σ^* there exists a uniquely determined finite, monic set $\mathcal{R}^* \subseteq K\Sigma^* \times K[\Sigma^*]$ that is an interreduced prefix Gröbner basis for F ($\mathcal{R}$) w.r.t. $>$. Since in a left-normalized set $\mathcal{R} \subseteq K\Sigma^* \times K[\Sigma^*]$ there are no critical pairs, any left-normalized set $\mathcal{R} \subseteq K\Sigma^* \times K[\Sigma^*]$ compatible with some total wellfounded admissible ordering $>$ is a prefix Gröbner basis. On the other hand, the set $\mathcal{R}$ associated with $F \subseteq K[\Sigma^*]$ and $>$ can be effectively transformed in a finite prefix Gröbner basis for F by normalizing the left-hand sides.

Obviously, if in a set $\mathcal{R} \subseteq K\Sigma^* \times K[\Sigma^*]$ of rules, each rule $(\alpha * t, r)$ (with $\alpha \in K, t \in \Sigma^*$) is replaced by $(1 * t, \alpha^{-1} * r)$ then the resulting system is a monic system that is equivalent to $\mathcal{R}$. Therefore, we will assume in the following that the rules of a set $\mathcal{R} \subseteq K\Sigma^* \times K[\Sigma^*]$ are always monic ones.

Since for our complexity analysis we will not take into account the field operations that have to be performed we define the size of a set of rules independently of the coefficients occurring: The *size* of the empty word is defined by $size(\epsilon) := 1$, while the *size* of a nonempty word w is its length. Moreover, for a non-zero polynomial $p \in K[\Sigma^*]$, the size is defined by $size(p) := \sum_{t \in T(p)} size(t)$ and for $p = 0$, $size(p) := 1$. Further, for a set $\mathcal{R} \subseteq K\Sigma^* \times K[\Sigma^*]$ of rules, $size(\mathcal{R})$ is defined as $\sum_{(l,r) \in \mathcal{R}}(size(l) + size(r))$.

3   Reduction Strategies

It is a well known fact that for a given prefix Gröbner basis $\mathcal{R} \subseteq K\Sigma^* \times K[\Sigma^*]$ and a given polynomial $p \in K[\Sigma^*]$, the number of reduction steps needed to compute a normal form of p w.r.t. $\mathcal{R}$ can be exponential in the size of the input.

Examples of this kind can be found for instance in [Ze00]. Note that the corresponding prefix Gröbner bases $\mathcal{R}_n$ considered in the literature are compatible with some length-lexicographical ordering, but not with the length ordering. However, it is not difficult to see that even for a length ordering a similar example can be constructed as our first example shows.

Example 1.
Let K be an arbitrary computable field, let $\Sigma = \{\, g, f, x, y \,\}$ and let $> \subseteq \Sigma^* \times \Sigma^*$ be the length ordering on Σ^*. Moreover, for $n \in \mathbb{N}_0$, let $\mathcal{R}_n \subseteq K\Sigma^* \times K[\Sigma^*]$ be defined as follows:

$$\mathcal{R}_n = \{\, g^2 f \rightarrow x + y \,\} \cup \{\, g^{2i+2} f \rightarrow g^{2i} fx + g^{2i} fy \mid 1 \leq i \leq n \}.$$

Then for all $n \in \mathbb{N}_0$, $\mathcal{R}_n$ is compatible with $>$ and left-normalized. Hence, it is a prefix Gröbner basis. Moreover, for all $n \in \mathbb{N}_0$ the following holds:

1. $size(\mathcal{R}_n) = 3n^2 + 10n + 5$

2. $NF_{\mathcal{R}_n}(g^{2n+2}f) = \sum\{x, y\}^{n+1}$

3. $D_{\rightarrow \mathcal{R}_n}(g^{2n+2}f, \sum\{x, y\}^{n+1}) = 2^{n+1} - 1$

This example as well as those given in the literature lead to the following question: Can similar phenomena occur when a fixed prefix Gröbner basis $\mathcal{R}$ is considered? Or is the length of a reduction sequence with respect to a fixed prefix Gröbner basis $\mathcal{R}$ bounded by a polynomial?

The next example illustrates that such a polynomial bound does not exist in general even if the given prefix Gröbner basis is interreduced and moreover, even if it is compatible with a length-ordering, in addition. Moreover, the example shows that the number of reduction steps needed for normalizing a polynomial with respect to a given interreduced prefix Gröbner basis $\mathcal{R}$ can essentially depend on the reduction strategy used.

Example 2.
Let K be an arbitrary computable field, let $\Sigma = \{a, b, c, d, g\}$ and let $> \subseteq \Sigma^* \times \Sigma^*$ be the length ordering on Σ^*. Moreover, let $\mathcal{R} \subseteq K\Sigma^* \times K[\Sigma^*]$ be defined as follows:

$$\mathcal{R} = \{\, ab \to a+d,\ ac \to a+d,\ db \to a+d,\ dc \to a+d,\ ag \to 0,\ dg \to 0\,\}.$$

Then $\mathcal{R}$ is an interreduced prefix Gröbner basis that is compatible with $>$ and we have for all $n \in \mathbb{N}_0$:

1. $a(bc)^n g \to_{\mathcal{R}}^{2^{2n+1}-1} 0$

2. $a(bc)^n g \to_{\mathcal{R}}^{\leq 4n+1} 0$

As the proof of the example shows (see [Sa07]), exponentially many reduction steps are needed to reduce the term $a(bc)^n g$ $(n \in \mathbb{N}_0)$ to its normal form if always a minimal (w.r.t. $>$) reducible monomial is reduced first. Since for all $n \in \mathbb{N}_0$, the number of terms occurring in a reduction sequence starting with $a(bc)^n g$ is linear in n and since the corresponding coefficients are always 1, there must exist at least one monomial that is reduced exponentially many times. One such monomial is $1 * dg$ for instance.

On the other hand, the lengths of the reduction sequences starting with $a(bc)^n g$ $(n \in \mathbb{N}_0)$ can be bounded by a linear function if always a maximal (w.r.t. $>$) reducible term is reduced first. Analysis of the corresponding reduction sequences shows that in this case any monomial is reduced at most once in a sequence.

Does there exist a reduction strategy that is optimal for prefix Gröbner basis in that it always leads to normalizing reduction sequences that are of minimal length?

The above observations suggest to investigate the reduction strategy preferring large terms (w.r.t. $>$) in this context. To this end we introduce the following definition.

Definition 1.
Let K be an arbitrary computable field, let Σ be an alphabet, let $>$ be a total admissible wellfounded ordering on Σ^* and let $\mathcal{R} \subseteq K\Sigma^* \times K[\Sigma^*]$ be a set of rules compatible with $>$. Then the relation $\hookrightarrow_{\mathcal{R}} \subseteq K[\Sigma^*] \times K[\Sigma^*]$ is defined

as follows: If $p, q \in K[\Sigma^*]$, then $p \hookrightarrow_\mathcal{R} q$ iff $p \xrightarrow[\alpha*t]{}_\mathcal{R} q$ where $t = max_>\{s \in T(p) \mid s$ is $\rightarrow_\mathcal{R}$-reducible$\}$ and $\alpha \in K$.

Moreover, based on this definition $\xrightarrow{\hookrightarrow}_\mathcal{R}$, $\hookrightarrow_\mathcal{R}^*$, $\hookrightarrow_\mathcal{R}^n$ and $D_{\hookrightarrow_\mathcal{R}}$ are defined analogously to $\xrightarrow[\alpha*t]{}_\mathcal{R}$, $\rightarrow_\mathcal{R}^*$, $\rightarrow_\mathcal{R}^n$ and $D_{\rightarrow_\mathcal{R}}$.

And in fact, it turns out that the observation made in Example 2 can be generalized: In a $\hookrightarrow_\mathcal{R}$-reduction sequence, for each term t a monomial of the form $\alpha * t$ will be reduced at most once. More precisely, the following holds:

Lemma 2.
Let K be an arbitrary computable field, let Σ be an alphabet, let $>$ be a total admissible wellfounded ordering on Σ^* and let $\mathcal{R} \subseteq K\Sigma^* \times K[\Sigma^*]$ be a set of rules compatible with $>$. Moreover, let $p_0, p_1, p_2 \in K[\Sigma^*]$ be polynomials and let $\alpha_0 * t_0, \alpha_1 * t_1$ be monomials.

If $p_0 \xrightarrow[\alpha_0*t_0]{\hookrightarrow}_\mathcal{R} p_1 \xrightarrow[\alpha_1*t_1]{\hookrightarrow}_\mathcal{R} p_2$ *then* $t_0 > t_1$.

Corollary 3.
Let K be an arbitrary computable field, let Σ be an alphabet, let $>$ be a total admissible wellfounded ordering on Σ^* and let $\mathcal{R} \subseteq K\Sigma^* \times K[\Sigma^*]$ be a set of rules compatible with $>$. Moreover, let $p_0, p_1, p_1, p_2 \in K[\Sigma^*]$ be polynomials and let $\alpha_0 * t_0, \alpha_1 * t_1$ be monomials.

If $p_0 \xrightarrow[\alpha_0*t_0]{\hookrightarrow}_\mathcal{R} p_1 \hookrightarrow_\mathcal{R}^* \bar{p}_1 \xrightarrow[\alpha_1*t_1]{\hookrightarrow}_\mathcal{R} p_2$ *then* $t_0 > t_1$.

This fact might suggest that the $\hookrightarrow_\mathcal{R}$-reduction strategy is always very efficient. However, this is not true in general: As our next example illustrates it is possible to construct a sequence of prefix Gröbner bases S_n ($n \in \mathbb{N}_0$) and a sequence of polynomials p_n ($n \in \mathbb{N}_0$) such that the length of each normalizing $\hookrightarrow_{S_n}$-sequence starting with p_n grows exponentially in n while a shortest normalizing $\rightarrow_{S_n}$-reduction sequence for p_n is of constant length.

Example 3.
Let K be an arbitrary computable field, let $\Sigma = \{g, f, x, y, a, b, c, d\}$ and let $> \subseteq \Sigma^* \times \Sigma^*$ be any length-lexicographical ordering on Σ^*. Moreover, for $n \in \mathbb{N}_0$, let $\mathcal{R}_n \subseteq K\Sigma^* \times K[\Sigma^*]$ and $S_n \subseteq K\Sigma^* \times K[\Sigma^*]$ be defined as follows:

$$\mathcal{R}_n = \{g^2 f \rightarrow x + y\} \cup \{g^{2i+2} f \rightarrow g^{2i} fx + g^{2i} fy \mid 1 \leq i \leq n\}$$

$$\cup \{g^{2(n+1)+2} f \rightarrow g^{2(n+1)} fx + g^{2(n+1)} fy + d\}$$

$$\cup \{xx \rightarrow 0, xy \rightarrow 0, yx \rightarrow 0, yy \rightarrow 0\}$$

$$S_n = \mathcal{R}_n \cup \{a^{2n+8} \rightarrow b^{2n+7}, b^{2n+7} \rightarrow c^{2n+6}, b^{2n+7} \rightarrow d, c^{2n+6} \rightarrow g^{2n+4} f\}$$

Then for all $n \in \mathbb{N}_0$, S_n is a prefix Gröbner basis that is compatible with $>$ and for $p_n = a^{2n+8} + b^{2n+7} + (-1) * c^{2n+6} + (-1) * d$ we have:

1. $size(S_n) = 3n^2 + 30n + 78$

2. $NF_{S_n}(p_n) = 0$

3. $D_{\rightarrow_{S_n}}(p_n, 0) = 3$

4. $D_{\hookrightarrow_{S_n}}(p_n, 0) \geq 2^{n+3} + 1$

As mentioned above if a reduction sequence is not a $\hookrightarrow$-sequence, then it may happen that a fixed term t will be reduced many times in the same reduction sequence. This fact can lead to very inefficient reduction processes as shown in Example 2. Nevertheless, as the Example 3 illustrates this fact can also be very advantageous: If the term t can be reduced using different rules, then doing this can lead to an essential abbreviation in the corresponding $\hookrightarrow$-sequence.

However, if this situation does not arise, i.e., if it is either not possible or not allowed to reduce different occurrences of a term t using different rules during a reduction sequence then the $\hookrightarrow$-relation is a reduction strategy that is optimal with regard to the length of the normalizing reduction sequences. To prove this we will make use of the following technical lemma.

Lemma 4.
Let K be an arbitrary computable field, let Σ be an alphabet, let $>$ be a total admissible wellfounded ordering on Σ^* and let $\mathcal{R} \subseteq K\Sigma^* \times K[\Sigma^*]$ be a set of rules that is compatible with $>$. Moreover, let $k \geq 0$, let $p, p_1, \hat{p} \in K[\Sigma^*]$ be polynomials where $\hat{p}$ is $\mathcal{R}$ -irreducible, let $\alpha \in K$, $s \in \Sigma^*$ and $l \to r$ a rule of $\mathcal{R}$ such that the following conditions hold:

1. $p \xrightarrow[\alpha * s]{} \{l \to r\} \; p_1$

2. $p_1 \hookrightarrow_{\mathcal{R}}^k \hat{p}$ where for any $\beta \in K$ the monomial $\beta * s$ is either not reduced in the $\hookrightarrow_{\mathcal{R}}$-sequence or only with the rule $l \to r$

Then the following holds:

$$p \hookrightarrow_{\mathcal{R}}^{\leq k+1} \hat{p}$$

where for any term $t \in \Sigma^*$, if there exists a coefficient $\beta \in K$ such that $\beta * t$ is reduced with the rule $l' \to r'$ in this sequence, then there is a coefficient $\zeta \in K$ such that the monomial $\zeta * t$ is also reduced in the sequence $p \xrightarrow[\alpha * s]{} \{l \to r\} \; p_1 \hookrightarrow_{\mathcal{R}}^k \hat{p}$ with the rule $l' \to r'$.

The idea of the proof of Lemma 4 is to rearrange the reduction steps appropriately such that the resulting sequence is a $\hookrightarrow$-sequence. To this end the step $\xrightarrow[\alpha * s]{} \{l \to r\}$ has to be put on the right place in the list of $\hookrightarrow$-steps. Doing this can result in shortening the original sequence due to the fact that at the moment when the $\xrightarrow[\alpha * s]{} \{l \to r\}$ -step should be applied, the term s may no longer occur in the current polynomial.

By an iterated application of the construction used in the proof of Lemma 4, on the last non-$\hookrightarrow_{\mathcal{R}}$-reduction step we can transform any $\to_{\mathcal{R}}$-sequence into a corresponding $\hookrightarrow_{\mathcal{R}}$-sequence that is either as long as the original sequence or even shorter.

Theorem 5.
Let K be an arbitrary computable field, let Σ be an alphabet, let $>$ be a total admissible wellfounded ordering on Σ^* and let $\mathcal{R} \subseteq K\Sigma^* \times K[\Sigma^*]$ be a set of rules that is compatible with $>$. Moreover, let $k \geq 0$, let $p, \hat{p} \in K[\Sigma^*]$ be polynomials where $\hat{p}$ is $\mathcal{R}$ -irreducible such that

$p \to_{\mathcal{R}}^{k} \hat{p}$ *where for each term t, a monomial of the form $\beta * t$ is either not reduced in the $\to_{\mathcal{R}}$-sequence or always with the same rule.*

Then the following holds:

$$p \hookrightarrow_{\mathcal{R}}^{\leq k} \hat{p} \, .$$

At a first sight, the restriction on the reduction sequence $p \to_{\mathcal{R}}^{k} \hat{p}$ in Theorem 5 might seem to be rather artificial. But, in practice these conditions are usually fulfilled: In existing implementations of reduction methods for prefix Gröbner bases, such as in the system MRC (see e.g. [Ze00]) for instance, a rule for reducing a reducible monomial $\alpha * t$ is usually chosen independently from the coefficient α.

However, if $\mathcal{R}$ is left-normalized then the condition on the reduction sequence $p \to_{\mathcal{R}}^{k} \hat{p}$ in Theorem 5 is obviously fulfilled, since then for each $\mathcal{R}$-reducible term t there exists exactly one rule in $\mathcal{R}$ that is applicable. Thus, Theorem 5 shows that when analyzing the derivational complexity $D_{\to_{\mathcal{R}}}$ of a left-normalized prefix Gröbner basis $\mathcal{R}$ with regard to the normalizing sequences, it suffices to consider the normalizing $\hookrightarrow_{\mathcal{R}}$-reduction sequences since these sequences are of minimal length. Moreover, for a left-normalized prefix Gröbner basis $\mathcal{R}$ any reduction sequence of the form $p \hookrightarrow_{\mathcal{R}}^{*} NF_{\mathcal{R}}(p)$ is uniquely determined.

Theorem 6.
Let K be an arbitrary computable field, let Σ be an alphabet, let $>$ be a total admissible wellfounded ordering on Σ^{*} and let $\mathcal{R} \subseteq K\Sigma^{*} \times K[\Sigma^{*}]$ be a left-normalized prefix Gröbner basis compatible with $>$. Then for all $p \in K[\Sigma^{*}]$ the following holds:

$D_{\to_{\mathcal{R}}}(p, NF_{\mathcal{R}}(p))$ *is equal to the length of the uniquely determined reduction sequence $p \hookrightarrow_{\mathcal{R}}^{*} NF_{\mathcal{R}}(p)$.*

We will make use of this result in the next section when analyzing the complexity of the computation of prefix Gröbner bases by interreduction.

3.1 Computation of Interreduced Prefix Gröbner Bases

A terminating set $\mathcal{R} \subseteq K\Sigma^{*} \times K[\Sigma^{*}]$ of rules is a prefix Gröbner basis if and only if all S-polynomials of $\mathcal{R}$ can be reduced with the rules of $\mathcal{R}$ to zero. Hence, in particular, any left-normalized, terminating set $\mathcal{R} \subseteq K\Sigma^{*} \times K[\Sigma^{*}]$ is a prefix Gröbner basis. On the other hand, a set $\mathcal{R} \subseteq K\Sigma^{*} \times K[\Sigma^{*}]$ that is compatible with some total admissible wellfounded ordering $>$, but not a prefix Gröbner basis can be transformed into an equivalent prefix Gröbner basis by left-normalizing $\mathcal{R}$ w.r.t. $>$ (see [Mo86],[Re95]).

In practice, interreduced, i.e., left- and right-normalized, prefix Gröbner bases are usually considered since in general, the additional simplification of the right-hand sides of the rules leads to "smaller" systems which often allow shorter reduction sequences. To compute an interreduced prefix Gröbner basis for a set $\mathcal{R} \subseteq K\Sigma^{*} \times K[\Sigma^{*}]$ compatible with some total admissible wellfounded ordering $>$ the following interreduction algorithm is usually used (see e.g. [Ze00]).

ALGORITHM 1: PGB

INPUT: A total admissible wellfounded ordering $>$ on Σ^* and a non-empty
          set $\mathcal{R} \subseteq K\Sigma^* \times K[\Sigma^*]$ compatible with $>$.
OUTPUT: An interreduced prefix Gröbner basis $\mathcal{B}$ of $\mathcal{R}$ compatible with $>$.

begin
while there is a $(l,r) \in \mathcal{R}$ such that $l - r$ is reducible w.r.t. $\mathcal{R} - \{(l,r)\}$ **do**
    begin
       $\mathcal{R} := \mathcal{R} - \{(l,r)\}$;
       $\bar{p} := \text{NORMALIZE } (l - r, \mathcal{R})$;
       if $\bar{p} \neq 0$ **then** $\mathcal{R} := \mathcal{R} \cup \{ \text{MAKE\_RULE}(\bar{p}, >) \}$;
    end;
$\mathcal{B} := \mathcal{R}$;
end

where for a polynomial p and for a set of rules $\mathcal{R}$, the subprocedure NORMALIZE computes a normal form of p w.r.t. $\mathcal{R}$ and where for a polynomial p and a total admissible wellfounded ordering $>$, the subprocedure MAKE_RULE transforms p in the corresponding rule w.r.t. $>$.

What is the time complexity of this algorithm?

Of course, the number of reduction steps needed to interreduce a set $\mathcal{R}$ w.r.t. an appropriate ordering $>$ by the algorithm PGB can essentially depend on the strategies used within, more precisely, on the strategy used for normalizing polynomials and on the strategy used to select the rule that will be reduced next. In [Ze00] Zeckzer has studied the time complexity of the algorithm PGB. He analyzed many examples and observed that there is no obvious strategy for the algorithm PGB that always leads to only polynomial many reduction steps, although for all of his examples the number of reduction steps needed by the algorithm PGB is bounded by a polynomial function.

We will prove that such a strategy does not exist by giving an example where the algorithm PGB always needs exponentially many reduction steps independently of the strategies used within.

Before explaining our main example we want to emphasize the following interesting phenomenon: In general, left-normalizing a set $\mathcal{R}$ may need many more reduction steps than interreducing the set. For instance, if we extend in Example 1 the systems $\mathcal{R}_n$ $(n \in \mathbb{N}_0)$ by the rule $g^{2n+2}ff \to 0$ then left-normalization of the extended system $\mathcal{R}'_n$ corresponds to normalizing the polynomial $g^{2n+2}ff$ and hence, requires an exponential number of reduction steps (cf. Example 1, p. 311).

Nevertheless, it is possible to interreduce the system $\mathcal{R}'_n$ in such a way that only polynomially many reduction steps are needed: To this end we first right-normalize the set $\mathcal{R}_n$. This can be done in a polynomial number of reduction steps if the rules are considered in increasing order with respect to the size of their left-hand sides. Using this right-normalized system it is then possible to compute the $\mathcal{R}_n$-normal form of $g^{2n+2}ff$ using one reduction step only.

However, as our next example shows even interreduction of a set $\mathcal{R}$ according to the algorithm PGB can require exponentially many reduction steps.

Theorem 7.
Let K be an arbitrary computable field, let $\Sigma = \{g, f, G, F, x, y, h, b\}$ and let $> \subseteq \Sigma^* \times \Sigma^*$ be any length-lexicographical ordering on Σ^*. Moreover, for $n \geq 1$, let

$$\mathcal{S}_n = \mathcal{R}_n \cup \mathcal{R}'_n$$
$$\cup \{b^{2n+4} \to g^{2n+2}f, \, b^{2n+4}h \to G^{2n+2}Fh + x, \, xh \to y\}$$

where

$$\mathcal{R}_n = \{g^2f \to x + y\} \cup \{g^{2i+2}f \to g^{2i}fx + g^{2i}fy \mid 1 \leq i \leq n\},$$
$$\mathcal{R}'_n = \{G^2F \to x + y\} \cup \{G^{2i+2}F \to G^{2i}Fx + G^{2i}Fy \mid 1 \leq i \leq n\}.$$

Then for all $n \geq 1$ the following holds:

1. *$\mathcal{S}_n$ is compatible with $>$.*

2. *$size(\mathcal{S}_n) = 6n^2 + 28n + 30$*

3. *Given $(\mathcal{S}_n, >)$ as input the algorithm PGB performs*

$$\geq 2^{n/2}$$

reduction steps, independently of the strategies used within.

4. *Given $(\mathcal{S}_n, >)$ as input the algorithm PGB generates the interreduced prefix Gröbner basis*

$$\mathcal{S}_n^* = \{g^{2i+2}f \to 0 \mid 0 \leq i \leq n\} \cup \{G^{2i+2}F \to 0 \mid 0 \leq i \leq n\}$$
$$\cup \{b^{2n+4} \to 0, \, x \to 0, \, y \to 0\}.$$

We want to emphasize one interesting aspect of the last example: All rules of $\mathcal{S}_n$ except the rule $b^{2n+4}h \to G^{2n+2}Fh + x$ are left-normalized w.r.t. the other rules. Moreover, interreduction of the system $\mathcal{S}_n - \{b^{2n+4}h \to G^{2n+2}Fh + x\}$, that is right-normalization of the set $\mathcal{S}_n - \{b^{2n+4}h \to G^{2n+2}Fh + x\}$, can be performed by using only polynomially many reduction steps. Nevertheless, the resulting interreduced system contains exponentially many monomials and in order to generate the system $\mathcal{S}_n^*$ all the monomials of the right-hand sides have to be reduced to 0. Thus, exponentially many reduction steps will be needed to generate the set $\mathcal{S}_n^*$ even if we proceed as described.

4   Concluding Remarks

We have studied the time complexity of the algorithm PGB which generates prefix Gröbner bases in free monoid rings by interreduction and derived by an example an exponential lower bound for the number of reduction steps that are needed in general. This gives an answer to the first of the open problems formulated in [Ze00].

Obviously, the complexity of an algorithm based on the kind of prefix reduction considered here can essentially depend on the following two parameters: 1. The underlying field K. 2. The underlying wellfounded ordering $>$.

We want to emphasize that these two parameters do not play an important role in the example that we have used to prove the exponential lower bound. First of all, the example works for an arbitrary computable field. Secondly, it is based on an arbitrary length-lexicographical ordering on the given alphabet. In fact, all rules that will be generated by the algorithm PGB are even compatible with the length-ordering. In practice, the orderings used for computing prefix Gröbner bases belong either to the class of length-lexicographical orderings, to the class of Knuth-Bendix orderings (which is a superclass of the previous one) or to the class of syllable orderings, which means these are those that are also usually used for completing string rewriting systems (see [Ze00]). It is not difficult to see that our example also works for any syllable ordering satisfying $b > g > G > h > x > y$ for instance. Thus the derived lower bound holds for almost all settings that are of practical interest.

Since in Theorem 7 the computable field K can be chosen arbitrarily, the example also gives a partial answer to the second open problem formulated by Zeckzer in [Ze00] asking for the time complexity of prefix Gröbner bases computation in $\mathbb{Z}_2[\Sigma^*]$. For $K = \mathbb{Z}_p$ where $p > 2$ and for $K = \mathbb{Q}$, Zeckzer proved an exponential lower bound for the time needed to compute interreduced prefix Gröbner bases by showing that the size of an interreduced system can grow exponentially in the size of the input system in such a way that exponentially many coefficients have to be computed separately. Nevertheless, the number of reduction steps that will be performed by the algorithm PGB is bounded by a polynomial function in Zeckzer's examples.

However, Theorem 7 shows that even in the case $K = \mathbb{Z}_2$ in general it is not possible to compute interreduced prefix Gröbner bases in polynomial time by using the algorithm PGB. Thus, one question that arises is whether or not there exists a more efficient algorithm for the computation of prefix Gröbner bases in $\mathbb{Z}_2[\Sigma^*]$.

Another question that arises is how good the lower bound derived for the algorithm PGB in this paper is in fact. In [Ze00] Zeckzer has derived an exponential upper bound for the algorithm PGB for the class of length-lexicographical orderings and for the class of Knuth-Bendix orderings, respectively. His results show that the lower bound derived here is rather sharp. However, for the class of syllable orderings it is still an open problem to derive a (non-trivial) upper bound for the number of reduction steps performed by the algorithm PGB.

Acknowledgement. I would like to thank the referees for their valuable comments.

References

[AcKr06]   Peter Ackermann and Martin Kreuzer. Gröbner Basis Cryptosystems. *AAECC (17)* (2006), pp. 173–194.

[MaRe93]   Klaus Madlener and Birgit Reinert. On Gröbner Bases in Monoid and Group Rings. *Proc. ISSAC'93*, pp. 54–263. ACM Press, 1993.

[Mo86]   Theo Mora. Gröbner Bases for Non-Commutative Polynomial Rings. *Proc. AAECC-3 (1986)*, LNCS 229, pp. 353–362. Springer, 1986.

[Mo94]   Theo Mora. An Introduction to Commutative and Noncommutative Gröbner Bases. *Theoretical Computer Science 134* (1994), pp. 131–173.

[Re95]   Birgit Reinert. *On Gröbner Bases in Monoid and Group Rings*. PhD thesis, Universität Kaiserslautern, 1995.

[ReZe98]   Birgit Reinert and Dirk Zeckzer. MRC - A System for Computing Gröbner Bases in Monoid and Group Rings. Presented at the *6th Rhine Workshop on Computer Algebra*. Sankt Augustin, 1998.

[ReZe99]   Birgit Reinert and Dirk Zeckzer. MRC - Data Structures and Algorithms for Computing in Monoid and Group Rings. *Applicable Algebra and Engineering, Communications and Computing 10(1)*, pp. 41–78, 1999.

[Sa07]   Andrea Sattler-Klein. An Exponential Lower Bound for Prefix Gröbner Bases in Free Monoid Rings. *Internal Report*, Universität Kaiserslautern, to appear in 2007.

[Ze00]   Dirk Zeckzer. *Implementation, Applications, and Complexity of Prefix Gröbner Bases in Monoid and Group Rings*. PhD thesis, Universität Kaiserslautern, 2000.

A Cubic Kernel for Feedback Vertex Set

Hans L. Bodlaender

Department of Information and Computing Sciences, Utrecht University, P.O. Box
80.089, 3508 TB Utrecht, the Netherlands
hansb@cs.uu.nl

Abstract. In this paper, it is shown that the FEEDBACK VERTEX SET
problem on unweighted, undirected graphs has a kernel of cubic size. I.e.,
a polynomial time algorithm is described, that, when given a graph G
and an integer k, finds a graph H and integer $k' \leq k$, such that H has
a feedback vertex set with at most k' vertices, if and only if G has a
feedback vertex set with at most k vertices, and H has at most $O(k^3)$
vertices and edges. This improves upon a result by Burrage et al. [8] who
gave a kernel for FEEDBACK VERTEX SET of size $O(k^{11})$.

One can easily make the algorithm constructive, and transform a minimum size feedback vertex set of H with at most k' vertices into a minimum size feedback vertex set of G. The kernelization algorithm can be
used as a first step of an FPT algorithm for FEEDBACK VERTEX SET,
but also as a preprocessing heuristic for the problem.

1 Introduction

The FEEDBACK VERTEX SET problem is a classic and fundamental graph problem, with several applications. See e.g., [13] for an overview paper on this and
related problems. In this paper, we consider the undirected and unweighted case
of the problem. I.e., we are given an undirected graph $G = (V, E)$, and an inte-
ger k, and ask if there is a set of vertices S with $|S| \leq k$, such that each cycle
of G contains at least one vertex from S. To facilitate the description of the
algorithms, we allow G to have parallel edges.

As in [12,18], we consider the *fixed parameter* case of this problem; i.e., k is
seen as the *parameter*, and is considered to be small. For more information on
fixed parameter tractability, see [12,18]. A parameterized problem with input I
and parameter k is said to be *fixed parameter tractable* (i.e., in FPT), if there
is an algorithm that solves the problem in $p(|I|, k) \cdot f(k)$ time, where p is a
polynomial and f an arbitrary function. FEEDBACK VERTEX SET is one of the
problems, known to be fixed parameter tractable. The problem was first shown
to be in FPT by Downey and Fellows [11]. In a series of papers, faster FPT algorithms were obtained [4,12,2,20,16,21,15,10]. The currently best known bounds
(concentrating on the function of k), are a probabilistic algorithm that finds with
high probability the feedback vertex set of size at most k, if existing, and uses
$O(4^k kn)$ time [2], and a deterministic algorithm that uses $O(10.567^k p(n))$ time
(p a polynomial) [10] (see also [15].) An exact algorithm for FEEDBACK VERTEX
SET with a running time of $O(1.8899^n)$ was recently found by Razgon [22].

W. Thomas and P. Weil (Eds.): STACS 2007, LNCS 4393, pp. 320–331, 2007.
© Springer-Verlag Berlin Heidelberg 2007

Kernelization is a technique that yields a proof that a problem belongs to FPT (assuming it is known that the problem is decidable), and that gives mathematical insight to the commonly used technique of *preprocessing*. A kernelization algorithm takes an input-parameter pair, and transforms it to an equivalent input-parameter pair (called the *kernel*), such that for the latter, the size of the input is a function of the (possibly new) parameter, and the new parameter is at most the old parameter. The kernelization algorithm is supposed to run in time that is both polynomial in the size of the input and the value of the parameter. If we have a kernel, then we can run any existing algorithm on the kernel, and obtain an algorithm that uses $O(p(n, k) + f(k))$ time, p a polynomial and f some function.

In a certain sense, kernelization is the very often used technique of preprocessing with in addition a mathematical guarantee on the quality of the preprocessing (the size of the input that remains after the preprocessing.) So, kernelization is for preprocessing what approximation algorithms are for heuristics (i.e., an approximation algorithm can be seen as a heuristic with a guarantee for the quality.)

The long open problem whether there existed a kernel of size polynomial in k for FEEDBACK VERTEX SET was recently resolved by Burrage et al. [8], who obtained a kernel for FEEDBACK VERTEX SET with $O(k^{11})$ vertices. In this paper, we improve on the size of this kernel, and show that FEEDBACK VERTEX SET has a kernel with $O(k^3)$ vertices. The kernelization algorithm uses the 2-approximation algorithm for FEEDBACK VERTEX SET of [1] or [3] as a first step, and then uses a set of relatively simple reduction rules. A combinatorial proof shows that if no rule can be applied, then the graph has $O(k^3)$ vertices, k the parameter in the reduced instance.

Some of the techniques in this paper were taken from, or inspired by techniques from [8]. Missing proofs can be found in [7].

2 Preliminaries

We allow graphs to have parallel edges; we let $\{w, v\}$ denote the same edge as $\{v, w\}$. A pair of vertices $\{v, w\}$ is called a *double edge* in a graph $G = (V, E)$, if E contains at least two edges of the form $\{v, w\}$. $\{v, w\}$ is a *non-edge*, if there is no edge of the form $\{v, w\}$ in E, and is a *non-double edge*, if there is at most one edge of the form $\{v, w\}$ in E. A set of vertices $W \subseteq V$ is a *feedback vertex set* in $G = (V, E)$, if $G[V - W]$ is a forest, i.e., for each cycle in G, there is at least one vertex on the cycle that belongs to W.

If there is a double edge $\{v, w\}$, then these form a cycle of length two. Thus, each feedback vertex set W must contain v or w. We will use this fact frequently in the paper, i.e., when we want to ensure for a pair v, w that v or w belongs to each feedback vertex set, we take a double edge $\{v, w\}$.

Two paths are said to be *vertex disjoint*, if all their internal vertices are different. (I.e., we allow that vertex disjoint paths share endpoints.)

3   A Kernelization Algorithm for Feedback Vertex Set

We assume that we have as input a graph $G = (V, E)$, and an integer k. The algorithm either returns *no*, in which case we are sure that G has no feedback vertex set of size at most k, or a pair (G', k'), such that G has a feedback vertex set of size at most k, if and only if G' has a feedback vertex set of size k'. (Instead of returning *no*, we could instead output a clique with $k + 3$ vertices.) The algorithm runs in time, polynomial in $|V| + |E|$ and in k. The number of vertices and edges in G' is bounded by $O(k^3)$. It is also possible to give a constructive version, i.e., one where we can turn a minimum size feedback vertex set of G' of size at most k' into a minimum size feedback vertex set of G in polynomial time. This will be discussed in Section 3.3.

The algorithm has two phases: an initialization phase, and an improvement and reduction phase. During the algorithm, we maintain a graph G, initially the input graph, and an integer k. During both phases, we possibly could determine that the graph has no feedback vertex set of value k, and return *no*. In the improvement and reduction phase, we possibly may decrease the value of k. When this happens, we restart the initialization phase, but now with the smaller number k and the modified graph.

During the algorithm, we have two special sets of vertices, called A and B. These play the following roles: A will be invariantly a feedback vertex set of G, and B will be the vertices in $V - A$ that have a double edge to a vertex in A.

3.1   Initialization Phase

We assume that we are given a graph $G = (V, E)$, and an integer k. If $k = 0$, then we return *yes*, if G is a forest, and *no* otherwise. So, suppose $k \geq 1$.

The first step of the kernelization algorithm is to run the approximation algorithm of Bafna et al. [1] or the algorithm of Becker and Geiger [3]. These algorithms have a performance ratio of 2. Suppose this approximation algorithm returns a feedback vertex set A of G. If $|A| > 2k$, then from the performance ratio it follows that there is no feedback vertex set of size at most k, and we return *no*.

Otherwise, we continue with the next step, and also initialize the set B as $B = \{w \in V - A \mid \exists v \in A : \text{there are at least two edges } \{v, w\} \in E\}$. I.e., if there is a double edge between a vertex $v \in A$ and a vertex $w \notin A$, then w is added to B. This can be done in $O(|V| + |E|)$ time using bucket sort.

3.2   Improvement and Reduction Rules

In this section, we give a number of improvement and reduction rules. Improvement rules add double edges to G; reduction rules remove edges and or vertices from G.

Each of the rules transforms the pair (G, k). We say that a rule is *safe*, if, whenever it transforms (G, k) to (G', k'), we have that G has a feedback vertex set of size k, if and only if G' has a feedback vertex set of size k'. In addition, we require that A is invariantly a feedback vertex set in the graph. We will show that each of the given rules is safe. For several rules, their safeness uses the following simple principle, earlier also used in [8].

Proposition 1. *Let $G = (V, E)$, and $v \in V$, such that there is at least one feedback vertex set W in G of minimum size with $v \in W$. Then a rule that removes v and its incident edges from G, and decreases k by one is safe.*

In our description below, we assume always that we restart the initialization phase, whenever k is decreased by one. This just simplifies some counting arguments (in particular, it ensures that $|A| \leq 2k$); it is also possible to give a variant without such restarts. We first give some simple rules, whose safeness is easy to see. Many are taken from [8].

Rule 1 Islet Rule
If v has degree zero, then remove v from G.

Rule 2 Twig Rule
If v has degree one, then remove v and its incident edge from G.

Rule 3 Triple Edge Rule
If there are three or more parallel edges of the form $\{v, w\}$, then remove all but two of these edges.

As a result of the **Triple Edge** rule, we have between each pair of vertices either 0, 1, or 2 edges when this rule cannot be applied.

Rule 4 Degree Two Rule
Suppose v has degree two. Let the edges, incident to v be $\{v, w\}$ and $\{v, x\}$. If $w = x$, then remove v and w, and their incident edges; decrease k by one, and restart the initialization phase. Otherwise, remove v, its incident edges, and add an edge $\{w, x\}$ to G. If $\{w, x\}$ becomes a double edge, and $w \in A$, $x \notin A \cup B$, then add x to B. If $\{v, w\}$ becomes a double edge, and $x \in A$, $w \notin A \cup B$, then add w to B.

Note that the **Degree Two** rule can create a parallel edge. An important rule is the **Improvement** rule. It is inspired by the improvement rule, used in [5,6,9] in the context of algorithms to compute treewidth.

Rule 5 Improvement Rule
Suppose $v \in A$, $w \in V$, $v \neq w$. Suppose there is no double edge between v and w, and that there are at least $k + 2$ vertex disjoint paths from v to w in G. Then add two edges $\{v, w\}$ to G. If $v \notin A \cup B$, then put w in B.

For a given pair of vertices, $v, w \in V$, one can compute in polynomial time the maximum number of vertex disjoint paths from v to w, using standard flow techniques. Nagamochi and Ibaraki [17] gave an algorithm that uses $O(k^2 n)$ time for checking if there are k vertex disjoint paths between a given pair of vertices. See also [23, Chapter 9]. Lemma 1 shows that the **Improvement** rule is safe.

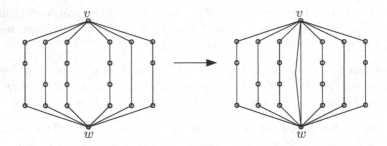

Fig. 1. The Improvement Rule

Lemma 1. *Suppose there are at least $k + 2$ vertex disjoint paths from v to w in G. For each feedback vertex set S of size at most k, $v \in S$ or $w \in S$.*

Proof. If S is a feedback vertex set of size at most k and $v, w \notin S$, then at least two paths from v to w do not contain a vertex in S. These paths and v and w form a cycle; contradiction.   □

Rule 6 Flower Rule
Let $v \in A$. Suppose there is a collection of at least $k + 1$ cycles in G, such that each pair of cycles intersects only in v.
Then remove v and all its incident edges from G, and decrease k by one. Restart the initialization phase with the new graph and new value of k.

I.e., we look for a set of cycles, that are vertex disjoint, except that they intersect in the vertex v. Lemma 2 formulates the **Flower** rule as a special case of *generalized matching*, hence it can be checked in polynomial time, see e.g., [14].

Lemma 2. *Let $G' = (V', E')$ be the graph obtained from G by adding to each vertex $w \neq v$ two new vertices w_1 and w_2, with edges $\{w_1, w_2\}$, $\{w_1, w\}$, and $\{w_2, w\}$. There is a collection of $k + 1$ cycles in G such that each pair of cycles intersects only in v, if and only if there is a set of edges $F' \subseteq E'$, such that v is incident to exactly $2k + 2$ edges in F', each new vertex is incident to one edge in F', and each vertex $w \in V - \{v\}$ is incident to exactly two edges in F'.*

Safeness of the **Flower** rule follows from the next lemma.

Lemma 3. *Let $v \in A$. Suppose there is a collection of at least $k + 1$ cycles in G such that no two different cycles in the collection share another vertex except v. Then v belongs to each feedback vertex set S in G of size at most k.*

Proof. Consider a feedback vertex set S in G with $v \notin S$. Then, each cycle in the collection contains a vertex in S, and these are all different vertices, so $|S| \geq k + 1$.   □

A simple special case of the **Flower** rule is the following.

Rule 7 Large Double Degree Rule

Suppose $v \in V$, such that there are at least $k+1$ vertices w with $\{v, w\}$ a double edge. Then remove v and its incident edges, and decrease k by one. Restart the initialization phase with the new graph and new value of k.

To describe the two abdication rules, we introduce some additional terminology. This terminology will also be used in the counting arguments.

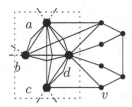

Fig. 2. Example of the Abdication Rules: a and d govern the drawn piece. The first abdication rule will remove the edge $\{a, u\}$; the second abdication rule will remove d and all edges incident to c. After these step, more reduction rules can be applied.

A *piece* is a connected component of $G[V - A - B]$. Let X be the set of vertices of a piece. The *border* of this piece is the set of vertices in $A \cup B$ that is adjacent to a vertex in X. A vertex v in the border of a piece *governs* the piece, if it has a double edge to each other vertex $w \neq v$ in the border of the piece.

Rule 8 First Abdication Rule

Suppose $v \in A \cup B$ governs a piece with vertex set X. If there is exactly one edge with one endpoint v and one endpoint in X, (i.e., one edge of the form $\{v, w\}$ with $w \in X$), then remove this edge $\{v, w\}$ with $w \in X$ from G.

As a result of the **First Abdication** rule, v will no longer belong to the border of the piece.

Lemma 4. *The* **First Abdication** *rule is safe.*

Proof. Let v, w, X be as in the **First Abdication** rule. Let G' be the graph, obtained by removing the edge $\{v, w\}$.

We claim that for each set $S \subseteq V$, S is a feedback vertex set in G, if and only if S is a feedback vertex set in G'. If S is a feedback vertex set in G, then, S is also a feedback vertex set in the subgraph G'. Suppose S is a feedback vertex set in G'. Each cycle in G that is not a cycle in G' uses the edge $\{v, w\}$. Hence, if $v \in S$, S is also a feedback vertex set in G. Suppose $v \notin S$. As v governs the piece X, all vertices in the border of the piece except v must belong to S. Each cycle that uses the edge $\{v, w\}$ uses besides v one other border vertex of the piece (as v has only one edge to the piece, and the vertex set of a piece induces a tree), and thus contains a vertex in S. So, again S is a feedback vertex set. As removing the edge $\{v, w\}$ does not change the collection of feedback vertex sets, the rule is safe. $\square$

Rule 9 Second Abdication Rule

Suppose $v \in A \cup B$ governs a piece with vertex set X. If there are at least two edges with one endpoint v and one endpoint in X, then remove v and all its incident vertices from G, and decrease k by one. Restart the initialization phase with the new graph and new value of k.

It is straightforward to see that we can check in polynomial time whether an abdication rule is possible for given G, A, B. Safeness of the **Second Abdication** rule follows from Lemma 5.

Lemma 5. *Suppose $v \in A \cup B$ governs a piece with vertex set X. Suppose there are at least two edges with one endpoint v and one endpoint in X. Then there is a minimum size feedback vertex set in G that contains v.*

Consider a piece with vertex set X with border set Y, such that for each pair of disjoint vertices in Y, there is a double edge. Consider what happens when we apply the abdication rules to this piece. Each vertex in Y governs the piece. If $v \in Y$ has one edge to the piece, this edge will be removed, and v no longer is in the border of X. If $v \in Y$ has two or more edges to the piece, then v itself is removed. Thus, after all the vertices in Y have been handled, the border of X will be empty. A piece with an empty border is a connected component of G that is a tree: it is a subgraph of $G[V - A]$ and hence does not have a cycle. Now, repeated application of the **Twig** rule, and then an application of the **Islet** rule will remove all vertices in the piece.

Above, we have seen that the given rules remove each piece for which there is a double edge between each pair of disjoint vertices in its border. A direct consequence of this is the following lemma.

Lemma 6. *Suppose none of the Rules 1 – 9 can be applied to G. Suppose $Y \subseteq V$ is the border of a piece in G. Then there are two disjoint vertices $v, w \in Y$ such that $\{v, w\}$ is not a double edge.*

A graph $G = (V, E)$, with sets A, B, and integer k is called *a reduced instance*, if none of the rules 1 – 9 is applicable anymore. We show that reduced instances have $O(k^3)$ vertices and edges.

Lemma 7. *In a reduced instance, there are at most $2k$ vertices in A and at most $2k^2$ vertices in B.*

Proof. We start with a set A of size at most $2k$. During the algorithm, we recompute A whenever k is changed.

Each vertex in B has at least one neighbor in A to which it has a double edge, but no vertex in A has more than k neighbors to which it has a double edge, otherwise the **Large Double Degree** rule can be applied. So the result follows.   □

We construct an auxiliary graph, which we call the B-piece graph. In the B-piece graph, there are two types of vertices: each vertex in B is a vertex in the B-piece graph, and for each piece, there is a vertex representing the piece in the B-piece graph. The B-piece graph is bipartite, with an edge between a vertex $v \in B$ and a vertex x representing a piece, if B is in the border of the piece.

Lemma 8. *(i) The B-piece graph is a forest.*
(ii) Let $v \in B$ be in the border of a piece with vertex set X. Then there is at exactly one edge from v to a vertex in X.

Lemma 9. *Suppose we have a reduced instance. There are at most $8k^3 + 9k^2 + k$ pieces.*

Proof. (Sketch.) We associate each piece to a non-double edge in its border (cf. Lemma 6. To a pair $v, w \in A$, we can associate at most $k + 1$ pieces, otherwise there are $k + 2$ disjoint paths from v to w, and the **Improvement** rule would have created a double edge $\{v, w\}$. To a pair $v, w \in B$, we can associate at most one piece, otherwise the B-piece graph is a forest. We omit from this abstract the more detailed counting of the number of pieces associated with pairs $\{v, w\}$, $v \in A$, $w \in B$. □

We now count the number of vertices and edges in the pieces. To do so, we consider subsets of the vertices in pieces. $C \subseteq V \setminus (A \cup B)$ is the set of vertices in a piece that are adjacent to a a vertex in $A \cup B$. Vertices in $D = V \setminus (A \cup B \cup C)$ are only adjacent to vertices in $C \cup D$. As $C \cup D$ induces a forest, and vertices in D have degree at least three in G and hence in $G[C \cup D]$, and as a forest has less vertices of degree three than it has leaves, $|D| < |C|$.

To estimate C, we define for each $v \in A \cup B$, $C_v = \{w \in C \mid \{v, w\} \in E\}$ as the set of vertices in pieces, adjacent to v. The sets C_v are partitioned into two sets, $C_{v,1}$, and $C_{v,\geq 2}$. $C_{v,1}$ is the set of the vertices $w \in C_v$, such that w is the only vertex in its piece that is adjacent to v. $C_{v,\geq 2} = C_v - C_{v,1}$ is the set of vertices $w \in C_v$, such that the piece of w has at least one other vertex, also adjacent to v.

We give a number of different lemmas that give bounds on the size of these sets. In each case, we assume we have a reduced instance. For omitted proofs, see [7].

Lemma 10. *Let $v \in A$. $|C_{v,1}| \leq 3k^2 + 3k - 1$.*

Proof. Consider a vertex $w \in C_{v,1}$, and the piece containing w. As v does not govern this piece (otherwise the **First Abdication** rule would be applicable), there is a vertex $x \in (A \cup B) - \{v\}$, in the border of the piece for which the pair $\{v, x\}$ is not a double edge. For each $w \in C_{v,1}$, we associate w with such a vertex x in the border of the piece of w with $x \neq v$ and $\{v, x\}$ is not a double edge.

No vertex $x \in A \cup B$ has more than $k + 1$ vertices associated to it. Suppose x has $k + 2$ or more vertices in $C_{v,1}$ associated to it. For each vertex w in $C_{v,1}$, associated to x, we take the path, starting at v, and moving through the piece containing w to x. As each of these paths uses a different piece, we have $k + 2$ vertex disjoint paths from v to x, and hence the **Improvement** rule will add the double edge $\{v, x\}$. However, if $\{v, x\}$ is a double edge, no vertices in $C_{v,1}$ will be associated to x, contradiction.

There are at most k vertices in $A \cup B$ that have two or more vertices associated to it. Suppose we have at least $k + 1$ vertices in $A \cup B$ that have two or more vertices associated with it. For each vertex x in $A \cup B$ that has two or more vertices associated with it, we build a cycle as follows. Suppose X_1, X_2 are pieces containing vertices associated to x. Start at v, more through X_1 to x, move from x through X_2 to v. As all pieces used by these cycles are different, these cycles only intersect at v, and thus the **Flower** rule applies. This contradicts the assumption that we have a reduced instance.

Now we can count the number of vertices in $C_{v,1}$, or, equivalently, the total over all $x \in A \cup B - \{v\}$ of the number of vertices associated to x. There are at most $|A| + |B| - 1$ vertices to which one vertex is associated. There are at most k vertices in $A \cup B - \{v\}$ to which two or more vertices are associated, and to each, at most $k + 1$ vertices are associated. This gives a total of at most $2k + 2k^2 - 1 + k(k + 1) = 3k^2 + 3k - 1$. □

Lemma 11. *Let $v \in A$. $|C_{v, \geq 2}| \leq k^2 + 3k + 3$.*

Proof. (Sketch.) If for some $v \in A$, $|C_{v, \geq 2}| > k^2 + 3k + 3$, then a detailed construction shows that we can build a collection of $k + 1$ cycles that only share v. Hence, the **Flower** rule can be applied, and the instance is not reduced. □

Lemma 12. $\sum_{v \in B} |C_v| \leq 8k^3 + 11k^2 + k - 1$.

Proof. By Lemma 8, if $v \in B$, then $C_{v, \geq 2} = \emptyset$. So, for all $v \in B$, $C_v = C_{v,1}$.

Suppose $w \in C_{v,1}$, $v \in B$. The B-piece graph has an edge from v to the piece that contains w. As w is the only vertex in this piece incident to v, we can associate this edge to w. Now each vertex in $\bigcup_{v \in B} C_v$ has at least one edge from the B-piece graph associated to it, and hence $|\bigcup_{v \in B} C_v|$ is at most the number of edges of the B-piece graph. As the B-piece graph is a forest (Lemma 8), the number of edges in this graph is smaller than the number of vertices, which equals $|B|$ plus the number of pieces. By Lemmas 7 and 9, the result follows. □

Theorem 1. *In a reduced instance, there are $O(k^3)$ vertices and $O(k^3)$ edges.*

Proof. We have $|A| = O(k)$, $|B| = O(k^2)$. For each $v \in A$, $|C_v| \leq |C_{v,1}| + |C_{v, \geq 2}| = O(k^2)$. Thus $|C| = O(k^3)$, and hence $|D| = O(k^3)$.

As $G[V - A]$ is a forest, there are $O(|V - A|) = O(k^3)$ edges with no endpoint in A. Thus, we only need to count the edges with at least one endpoint in A. There are $O(|A|^2) = O(k^2)$ edges with both endpoints in A and $O(|A| \cdot |B|) = O(k^3)$ edges with one endpoint in A and one endpoint in B. By definition, there are no edges between vertices in A and vertices in D. If there is an edge $\{v, w\}$, $v \in A$, $w \in C$, then $w \in C_v$, and there is no parallel edge to this one (otherwise $w \in B$, so the number of edges in $A \times C$ equals $\sum_{v \in A} |C_v| = O(k^3)$. □

Theorem 2. *There is a polynomial time algorithm, that, given a graph G and an integer k, finds a graph H with $O(k^3)$ vertices and edges, such that G has a* *feedback vertex set with at most k vertices, if and only if H has a feedback vertex set with at most k vertices.*

Obtaining a fast implementation, e.g., with a proper choice of data structures, is an interesting issue. In this paper, we concentrated on the combinatorial aspects, and refrained from discussion such implementation issues and the precise asymptotic running time of the kernelization algorithm.

3.3 A Constructive Version

It is not hard to transform the algorithm to a constructive one. Place each vertex, removed by the **Self-loop** rule, **Flower** rule, **Second Abdication** rule, or **Large Double Degree** rule is placed in a set S. Suppose the kernelization algorithm transforms the pair (G, k) to a pair (G', k'). Then, if W is a minimum size feedback vertex set in G' of size at most k', then $W \cup S$ is a minimum size feedback vertex set in G.

4 Discussion

In this paper, we showed that the FEEDBACK VERTEX SET problem on undirected graphs has a kernel of size $O(k^3)$.

Several variants of the algorithm are also possible. E.g., we can refrain from doing a restart after k has been decreased. Also, some rules can be replaced by other rules, e.g., the **Flower** rule can be replaced by a rule, that applies the 2-approximation algorithm of [1] or [3] to a weighted variant, with v weight $2k + 1$, and all other vertices weight one. If this approximation algorithm gives a solution of weight at least $2k + 1$, then v must be part of any optimal solution, and thus we remove v, decrease k by one, and restart the initialization phase. See the full paper [7] for a further discussion. It would be interesting to perform an experimental evaluation of this, and similar algorithms for FEEDBACK VERTEX SET kernelization. What techniques will give fast algorithms and/or small kernel sizes. How well do these algorithms perform on data obtained from real-life applications? We can also use the kernelization algorithm as a preprocessing heuristic, using for k the best upper bound known for the minimum size feedback we have from one or more heuristics.

It is to be expected that with small (or larger) changes, improvements to the constant in the $O(k^3)$ bound on the kernel size are possible. It is also to be expected that in a similar way, we can obtain a kernel for the case where vertices have integer weights with the parameter k an upper bound on the sum of the weights of the vertices in the vertex set.

We end the paper with mentioning two open problems.

- Is there a kernel for FEEDBACK VERTEX SET of size $o(k^3)$? See e.g., the discussion in [8].
- Is it possible to carry over the techniques to the related LOOP CUT SET problem? In this problem, we are given a directed (acyclic) graph $G = (V, A)$,

and ask for a minimum size set of vertices S, such that the undirected graph, obtained by first removing all arcs whose tail is in S, and then dropping direction of edges, is a forest. This problem is motivated by the algorithm of Pearl [19] for computing inference in probabilistic networks. See e.g., [3,2].

- The DIRECTED FEEDBACK VERTEX SET problem and FEEDBACK ARC SET problems, where we look for a minimum size set of vertices or arcs in a directed graph G, such that each cycle in G contains a vertex or arc in the set, are still not known to be in FPT. Membership in FPT of these problems is a long outstanding open problem. As having a kernel for these problems would imply membership in FPT, it is probably very hard to find a kernelization algorithm for these problems.

Acknowledgments

I thank Mike Fellows, Eelko Penninkx and Richard Tan for discussions and suggestions.

References

1. V. Bafna, P. Berman, and T. Fujito. A 2-approximation algorithm for the undirected feedback vertex set problem. *SIAM J. Disc. Math.*, 12:289–297, 1999.
2. A. Becker, R. Bar-Yehuda, and D. Geiger. Randomized algorithms for the loop cutset problem. *J. Artificial Intelligence Research*, 12:219–234, 2000.
3. A. Becker and D. Geiger. Optimization of Pearl's method of conditioning and greedy-liker approximation algorithms for the vertex feedback set problem. *Acta Informatica*, 83:167–188, 1996.
4. H. L. Bodlaender. On disjoint cycles. *Int. J. Found. Computer Science*, 5(1):59–68, 1994.
5. H. L. Bodlaender. A linear time algorithm for finding tree-decompositions of small treewidth. *SIAM J. Comput.*, 25:1305–1317, 1996.
6. H. L. Bodlaender. Necessary edges in k-chordalizations of graphs. *Journal of Combinatorial Optimization*, 7:283–290, 2003.
7. H. L. Bodlaender. A cubic kernel for feedback vertex set. Technical Report UU-CS-2006-042, Department of Information and Computing Sciences, Utrecht University, Utrecht, The Netherlands, 2006.
8. K. Burrage, V. Estivill-Castro, M. R. Fellows, M. A. Langston, S. Mac, and F. A. Rosamond. The undirected feedback vertex set problem has a poly(k) kernel. In H. L. Bodlaender and M. A. Langston, editors, *Proceedings 2nd International Workshop on Parameterized and Exact Computation, IWPEC 2006*, pages 192–202. Springer Verlag, Lecture Notes in Computer Science, vol. 4169, 2006.
9. F. Clautiaux, J. Carlier, A. Moukrim, and S. Négre. New lower and upper bounds for graph treewidth. In J. D. P. Rolim, editor, *Proceedings International Workshop on Experimental and Efficient Algorithms, WEA 2003*, pages 70–80. Springer Verlag, Lecture Notes in Computer Science, vol. 2647, 2003.

10. F. K. H. A. Dehne, M. R. Fellows, M. A. Langston, F. A. Rosamond, and K. Stevens. An $o(2^{O(k)}n^3)$ fpt algorithm for the undirected feedback vertex set problem. In L. Wang, editor, *Proceedings 11th International Computing and Combinatorics Conference COCOON 2005*, pages 859–869. Springer Verlag, Lecture Notes in Computer Science, vol. 3595, 2005.

11. R. G. Downey and M. R. Fellows. Fixed-parameter tractability and completeness. *Congressus Numerantium*, 87:161–178, 1992.

12. R. G. Downey and M. R. Fellows. *Parameterized Complexity*. Springer, 1998.

13. P. Festa, P. M. Pardalos, and M. G. C. Resende. Feedback set problems. In *Handbook of Combinatorial Optimization, Vol. A.*, pages 209–258, Amsterdam, the Netherlands, 1999. Kluwer.

14. A. M. H. Gerards. Matching. In M. O. Ball et al., editor, *Handbooks in Operations Research and Management Sciences, Volume 7, Network Models*, chapter 3, pages 135–224. Elsevier Science, Amsterdam, 1995.

15. J. Guo, J. Gramm, F. Hüffner, R. Niedermeier, and S. Wernicke. Improved fixed-parameter algorithms for two feeback set problems. In *Proc. 9th Int. Workshop on Algorithms and Data Structures WADS 2004*, pages 158–168. Springer Verlag, Lecture Notes in Computer Science, vol. 3608, 2004.

16. I. A. Kanj, M. J. Pelmajer, and M. Schaefer. Parameterized algorithms for feedback vertex set. In R. G. Downey and M. R. Fellows, editors, *Proccedings 1st International Workshop on Parameterized and Exact Computation, IWPEC 2004*, pages 235–248. Springer Verlag, Lecture Notes in Computer Science, vol. 3162, 2004.

17. H. Nagamochi and T. Ibaraki. A linear-time algorithm for finding a sparse k-connected spanning subgraph of a k-connected graph. *Algorithmica*, 7:583–596, 1992.

18. R. Niedermeier. *Invitation to fixed-parameter algorithms*. Oxford Lecture Series in Mathematics and Its Applications. Oxford University Press, 2006.

19. J. Pearl. *Probablistic Reasoning in Intelligent Systems: Networks of Plausible Inference*. Morgan Kaufmann, Palo Alto, 1988.

20. V. Raman, S. Saurabh, and C. R. Subramanian. Faster fixed parameter tractable algorithms for undirected feedback vertex set. In *Proceedings 13th International Symposium on Algorithms and Computation, ISAAC 2002*, pages 241 – 248. Springer Verlag, Lecture Notes in Computer Science, vol. 2518, 2002.

21. V. Raman, S. Saurabh, and C. R. Subramanian. Faster algorithms for feedback vertex set. *Proceedings 2nd Brazilian Symposium on Graphs, Algorithms, and Combinatorics, GRACO 2005, Electronic Notes in Discrete Mathematics*, 19:273–279, 2005.

22. I. Razgon. Exact computation of maximum induced forest. In L. Arge and R. Freivalds, editors, *10th ScandinavianWorkshop on Algorithm Theory, SWAT 2006*, pages 160–171. Springer Verlag, Lecture Notes in Computer Science, vol. 4059, 2006.

23. A. Schrijver. *Combinatorial Optimization. Polyhedra and Efficiency*. Springer, Berlin, 2003.

The Union of Minimal Hitting Sets: Parameterized Combinatorial Bounds and Counting

Peter Damaschke

School of Computer Science and Engineering
Chalmers University, 41296 Göteborg, Sweden
ptr@cs.chalmers.se

Abstract. We study how many vertices in a rank-r hypergraph can belong to the union of all inclusion-minimal hitting sets of at most k vertices. This union is interesting in certain combinatorial inference problems with hitting sets as hypotheses, as it provides a problem kernel for likelihood computations (which are essentially counting problems) and contains the most likely elements of hypotheses. We give worst-case bounds on the size of the union, depending on parameters r, k and the size k^* of a minimum hitting set. (Note that $k \geq k^*$ is allowed.) Our result for $r = 2$ is tight. The exact worst-case size for any $r \geq 3$ remains widely open. By several hypergraph decompositions we achieve nontrivial bounds with potential for further improvements.

Keywords: algorithms, parameterization, combinatorial inference, counting, hypergraph transversals.

1 Introduction

A quite general and fundamental type of inference problem is to conclude a set of causes from a set of observed effects. We are given a set V of n *causes*, a set E of *effects*, a relation $R \subset V \times E$, and a set $O \subset E$ of *observed* effects. (A cause or effect is either present or absent.) We consider two models which we denote $(\forall)$ and $(\exists)$. Under $(\forall)$, each present cause v generates *all* effects e with $(v, e) \in R$. Under $(\exists)$, each present cause v generates *some* effects e with $(v, e) \in R$. We suppose no interference, i.e., causes generate effects independently. We want to infer the set C of present causes. Since each $e \in O$ must be explained by some cause, this is just a *hitting set* problem in a certain *hypergraph*: Under $(\exists)$, any $C \subseteq V$ containing some v from each $V(e) := \{v : (v, e) \in R\}$, $e \in O$, is a valid hypothesis, i.e., candidate for set C. In other words, constraint $|C \cap V(e)| \geq 1$ must be satisfied for all $e \in O$. Hitting sets are also called *transversals*, of the hypergraph with vertex set V and hyperedges $V(e)$, $e \in O$. Under $(\forall)$ we can first discard all $v \in V$ for which not all $e \in E$, $(v, e) \in R$ are in O. Then we are back to the hitting set problem, with the remaining causes. Besides constraints $|C \cap V(e)| \geq 1$, $e \in O$, we may know some *a priori* bound k on the number of

W. Thomas and P. Weil (Eds.): STACS 2007, LNCS 4393, pp. 332–343, 2007.

present causes, giving the constraint $|C| \leq k$. We may know further constraints $|C \cap Y| \leq k$ or $|C \cap Y| \geq k$ for several $Y \subset V$ and integers k, however, we will focus on hitting sets with one total size limit k, because this setting appears naturally, e.g., in diagnostics (cf. references in [11]).

An example is the reconstruction of unknown mixtures of proteins by peptide mass fingerprinting and a database of mass spectra [7]. (The following exposition is simplified, to stress the connection to hitting sets. We ignore possible experimental and database errors which just require slight extensions of the model. For background information on peptide mass fingerprinting see [1].) In order to avoid costly isolation of proteins prior to identification, one may digest the entire mixture by certain enzymes. Proteins are split in peptides whose masses are identified by mass spectrometry. Checking the mass spectrum of the given mixture against a database of mass spectra of candidate proteins, one can in principle compute the mixtures that are consistent with the observed masses. A mixture is known to contain at most a certain number of proteins (think of 30-50), being a small fraction of proteins listed in the database (think of thousands). Assuming that all masses of peptides of present proteins occur in the measured spectrum, model ($\forall$) applies. We first discard all candidate proteins having non-observed peptide masses. For many $e \in O$ there remains only one candidate protein with a peptide of mass e, that is: $V(e) - \{v\}$. We put aside these v (they must be present in any possible mixture), along with all e where $(v, e) \in R$. This trivial preprocessing leaves us with a small hitting set problem instance. The number k of further (unsure) proteins can be considerably smaller than the mixture size.

Combinatorics alone cannot infer which of the many hypotheses (hitting sets of size at most k) explains the data correctly, thus we want a summary of all consistent solutions, rather than one particular solution (cf. the general discussions in [4,8]), as a basis for further investigations, i.e., conducting additional informative experiments that finally point to a unique or most likely solution. But what is a useful summary? Plain enumerations are in general big and hardly comprehensible. Some compressed representation is preferable. Following [12], the *version space* of an inference problem is the family of all hypotheses consistent with the data. A set C in the version space is called *most specific (most general)* if no proper subset (superset) of C is in the version space. These extremal hypotheses determine the version space. In our case, it consists of all hitting sets of size *at most* k, or *k-hitting sets* for short, hence the most specific hypotheses are the *minimal k-hitting sets*. (Distinguish carefully between inclusion-*minimal*, and *minimum* cardinality.) The most general hypotheses are those sets of size k that extend some minimal hitting set. Still, there can be too many different minimal k-hitting sets, but they heavily overlap. On the other hand, in inference tasks as above we are in the first place interested in evidence for presence or absence of every single $v \in V$. A natural approach, especially if no solution is preferred *a priori*, is to *count* for each v the hypotheses in the version space with and without v. This yields posterior probabilities for the presence of causes.

(The approach can be adapted to more complicated priors by weighting, to joint presence of several causes, etc.)

In the following we study the abstract problem. We are given a hypergraph with n vertices, and a number $k \ll n$. Throughout the paper, $U(k)$ *denotes the union of all minimal k-hitting sets, and k^* the minimum size of a hitting set.* In Section 2 we show that, once $U(k)$ is known, one can easily count all k-hitting sets containing any specific $v \in V$, and that all vertices not in $U(k)$ appear in the same (least!) number of k-hitting sets. Which means that $U(k)$ is a kernel for the counting problem, and vertices in $U(k)$ are the most likely candidates for present causes. These preliminaries motivate the study of: $|U(k)|$, the complexity of computing $U(k)$, and of counting all hitting sets of a given size. Obviously, these problems include as a special case the problem of computing k^*, which is NP-complete, and even unlikely to be fixed-parameter tractable (FPT), with k^* itself as the parameter [3]. However, for hypergraphs of fixed *rank r* (maximum size of a hyperedge), enumerating the minimal k-hitting sets is FPT [8]. Enumeratiing and counting small vertex covers is also addressed in [9,4].

Small ranks are common in our inference problem. Often, many effects e are characteristic for only a few possible causes each, that is, hyperedges $V(e)$ are small. If, in a practical problem instance, the rank is not small enough for efficient hitting set computations, we may fix a small threshold r and, in the first place, restrict our instance to those $e \in O$ with $|V(e)| \leq r$. By ignoring constraints the version space can grow by extra hypotheses that could be ruled out when the whole data set O was taken into account. But, on the positive side, the restricted instance becomes computationally feasible, and the skipped constraints may be considered afterwards in an *ad hoc* way for the concrete instance. Intuitively, constraints $|C \cap Y| \geq 1$ with large Y are less powerful and will not affect the version space too much. Due to this discussion we study the aforementioned problems for hypergraphs of fixed (usually very small) rank r.

Note that our problems are void if $r = 1$, and in case $r = 2$ we are faced with k-vertex covers in graphs. In [8] we proved that $U(k)$ has less than $\min(rk^r, kr^k)$ vertices and can be computed in linear time in the size of the hypergraph (but exponential time in the parameters). The more interesting part is when $k > r$. To be precise, we proved $|U(k)| \leq (r-1)k^r + k$ and gave simple examples where $|U(k)| = \Theta(k^r)$, with a tiny factor depending on r. An open question is: *How large can $U(k)$ actually be, in the worst case?* In view of the role of $U(k)$, better upper bounds are desirable, including the constant for any fixed r. In the rest of the paper we make new contributions to this question.

For the vertex cover case ($r = 2$) we found in [8] that $|U(k)| \leq \frac{1}{4}k^2 + O(k)$, which is a tight bound as a function of k. In Section 3 below we "stratify" this result, taking also the relation between k and k^* into account: We prove the tight bound $(k - k^* + 2)k^*$. To our best knowledge, previous related work has considered only the case $k = k^*$: An upper bound for the union of minimum vertex covers, in relation to the size of a minimum vertex cover and maximum matching, is given in [2]. (Results in [2] are formulated in terms of stable sets, i.e., complements of vertex covers.) In the same paper, NP-hardness of computing

$U(k^*)$ is proved. This hardness result already for $r = 2$ adds further motivation to using the parameterized framework. The bound on $|U(k^*)|$ has been further improved in [6] (among many other results).

In Section 4 we turn to general r. Using some hypergraph decomposition we improve the factor in $|U(k)| = O(k^r)$ from $r - 1$ to essentially $\log_2 r$. Actually, our result is stronger. We relate $|U(k)|$ to the number h of hyperedges in an equivalent reduced hypergraph and show $|U(k)| \leq \log_2 r \cdot h$ if $h = \Theta(k^r)$, and due to an earlier result we have $h \leq k^r$. (If $h = o(k^r)$ then $|U(k)|$ is smaller anyhow.) Hence, improved bounds on h would further reduce $|U(k)|$, too, but this part must be left for further research. By a somewhat different decomposition we get even sharper results for $r \leq 6$. Section 5 points out open questions.

2 A Kernel for Counting Small Hitting Sets

In this section we show how to use $U(k)$ to count the k-hitting sets containing any given vertex. For any h with $k^* \leq h \leq k$, let $s(h)$ be the number of different hitting sets $D \subseteq U(k)$ such that $|D| = h$. For any vertex v let $s_v(h)$ be the number of different hitting sets $D \subseteq U(k)$ such that $|D| = h$ and $v \in D$.

Lemma 1. *The number of different k-hitting sets containing a fixed vertex v equals*
$$\sum_{h=k^*}^{k} s_v(h) \sum_{i=0}^{k-h} \binom{n-|U(k)|}{i} \ \text{if } v \in U(k), \text{ and}$$
$$\sum_{h=k^*}^{k} s(h) \sum_{i=0}^{k-1-h} \binom{n-1-|U(k)|}{i} \ \text{if } v \notin U(k).$$

Proof. Every k-hitting set extends some minimal k-hitting set $C \subseteq U(k)$ possibly by further vertices. Since $|C| \geq k^*$, any k-hitting set shares at least k^* vertices with $U(k)$. In order to count all k-hitting sets containing some v we just have to consider the different hitting sets in $U(k)$ of each cardinality h, and add all possible combinations of at most $k - h$ vertices outside $U(k)$. $\square$

Corollary 1. *All vertices $v \notin U(k)$ belong to exactly the same number of different k-hitting sets, and this number is smaller than that for any $v \in U(k)$.*

This follows from Lemma 1 by direct comparison of terms. For the problem of counting how many solutions contain a certain vertex v we give the following reduction. Note that the counts are different only for $v \in U(k)$, thus $|U(k)|$ determines how many different values have to be computed.

Proposition 1. *Consider a hypergraph with n vertices, and hyperedges of total size M (sum of cardinalities, regardless of intersections). Say, some algorithm counts the hitting sets with exactly h vertices in a hypergraph of n vertices in $T(n, h)$ time, where T is some monotone function. Then we can compute, for all vertices v, the number of k-hitting sets that contain v, within time $O(|U(k)| \cdot (M + (k - k^* + 1) \cdot T(|U(k)|, k)))$, plus the time for computing $U(k)$ itself.*

Proof. Do the following separately (from scratch) for each $v \in U(k)$ and for one (arbitrary) $v \notin U(k)$.

(1) Take the given hypergraph and delete the hyperedges containing v, but keep the other vertices therein.

(2) Delete all vertices outside $U(k)$ from all hyperedges.

(3) Count the hitting sets of size $h - 1$, for all $k^* \leq h \leq k$.

(4) Use the formulae in Lemma 1 with the so obtained $s_v(h)$ and $s(h)$.

Correctness is easy to establish, from the definition of D, Lemma 1 and Corollary 1. The time bound follows from the monotonicity of T. Time $O(M)$ suffices for the auxiliary operations in (1) and (2), and the binomial coefficients for step (4) can be precomputed. □

How complicated are the subroutines of this algorithm? As mentioned earlier, computing $U(k)$ and counting *all* hitting sets of a given size are FPT in parameters k, r. The basic idea for counting is to branch on carefully selected vertices and thus obtain a repetition-free enumeration of the hitting sets. Branching can be stopped when the "residual" hypergraphs are simple enough for counting the hitting sets directly in polynomial time. A complexity result for the *enumeration* of k-vertex covers is in [4]: A structure computable in $O^*(1.47^k)$ time is used to output the smallest vertex covers successively with linear delay. The same construction can be used to count all vertex covers with h vertices in $O^*(1.47^h)$ time. Similar nontrivial bounds for any fixed rank $r > 2$ would be interesting. The state-of-the-art techniques for k-hitting sets (as in [10,11]) do not directly yield counting results, as several reduction rules do not apply here.

3   The Union of Minimal Vertex Covers of Bounded Size

For a subset X of vertices in a graph, $N(X)$ denotes the set of all vertices with a neighbor in X. If X is independent then $N(X) \cap X = \emptyset$. The following simple lemma holds for minimal (not necessarily minimum!) vertex covers.

Lemma 2. *Let C be a fixed minimal vertex cover. Let D be any other minimal vertex cover, and $I := C \setminus D$. Then we have $D = (C \setminus I) \cup N(I)$. Consequently, D is uniquely determined by I.*

Proof. Straightforward. Omitted due to space limitations. □

It follows $|U(k)| \leq (k + 1)k^*$: Take some C with k^* vertices, and observe that $|N(v)| \leq k$ for each $v \in C$ that appears in some $I = C \setminus D, |D| \leq k$. Below we will improve this bound, but already now we can limit the complexity of computing $U(k)$ to $O(k^* k)$ instances of the vertex cover (optimization) problem. Finding a minimum vertex cover is FPT, the currently best time bound is in [5].

Theorem 1. *Computing $U(k)$ in a graph G has at most the complexity of computing the following items: (1) one minimum vertex cover in G, (2) one minimum vertex cover in $O(k^* k)$ subgraphs, each being of size $O(k^* k)$ and computable in polynomial time.*

Proof. Compute a minimum vertex cover C, using your favorite FPT algorithm. If some vertex in C has degree larger than k, it must be in every k-vertex cover, thus, remove that vertex and all incident edges, reducing the problem to an instance with $k := k - 1$. Repeat this elimination step recursively until all degrees in C are bounded by the current k. This eventually gives a minimum vertex cover C' in the remaining graph G' and a number $k' \leq k^*$ such that all vertices in C' have degree at most k' in G'. By Lemma 2, the union of all minimal vertex covers in G' is entirely in $C' \cup N(C')$. This finally restricts the problem to a kernel of no more than $(k + 1)k^*$ vertices v. For each v in this kernel do the following (from scratch). Decide that v be in the vertex cover, delete all incident edges, and find out whether the remainder of the kernel has a $(k' - 1)$-vertex cover, again using your favorite FPT algorithm. The result says whether $v \in U(k)$ or not. □

The following result improves the simple bound on $|U(k)|$ especially when k is close to k^*. It also absorbs Theorem 3 from [8] as a special case.

Theorem 2. *We have* $|U(k)| \leq (k - k^* + 2)k^*$, *and this bound is tight.*

Proof. To establish the lower bound, consider the disjoint union of k^* stars, each with a central vertex connected to $x + 1$ leaves, where $x = k - k^*$. The centers build a minimum vertex cover and, obviously, minimal vertex covers of size $k = k^* + x$ involve all the $(x + 2)k^* = (k - k^* + 2)k^*$ vertices.

We are going to prove the upper bound. Let C be some fixed vertex cover of size k^*. By Lemma 2, any other minimal vertex cover D (of any size) has the form $D = (C \setminus I) \cup N(I)$. Since $I = C \setminus D$ is in the complement of a vertex cover, I is an independent set, hence $I \cap N(I) = \emptyset$. Conversely, each independent set $I \subseteq C$ yields a vertex cover $D = (C \setminus I) \cup N(I)$. Since C has minimum size, $|N(I) \setminus C| \geq |I|$ holds for every independent set $I \subseteq C$. For making $|D| \leq k = k^* + x$ true, it must be $|N(I) \setminus C| \leq |I| + x$.

Due to these necessary conditions, we call an independent set $I \subseteq C$ a *replacement set* if $|N(I) \setminus C| \leq |I| + x$ and $(C \setminus I) \cup N(I)$ is actually a minimal vertex cover, in particular, no vertex from $C \setminus I$ can be removed without uncovering some edge. Now it suffices to prove the following

Claim: The union of the $N(I) \setminus C$ of all replacement sets I has at most $(x+1)k^*$ vertices.

Let $I_1, I_2, I_3, \ldots$ be a non-extendible sequence of replacement sets such that $I_{t+1} \not\subseteq \bigcup_{j=1}^{t} I_j$ for each $t \geq 1$. It suffices to prove the Claim for replacement sets in this sequence, as the $N(I) \setminus C$ for further replacement sets I cannot contribute more vertices to the union. Define $\Delta_t := \bigcup_{j=1}^{t} N(I_j) \setminus C$. We shall prove that $|\Delta_t| \leq |\bigcup_{j=1}^{t} I_j| + xt$. Since our sequence can consist of at most k^* replacement sets, this would imply the Claim and finish the proof.

We apply induction on t. Induction base $t = 1$ is true by the definition of replacement sets. Suppose that our induction hypothesis holds for some t. The induction step has to show $|\Delta_t \cup (N(I_{t+1}) \setminus C)| \leq |(\bigcup_{j=1}^{t} I_j) \cup I_{t+1}| + x(t + 1)$.

Since $I' := (\bigcup_{j=1}^{t} I_j) \cap I_{t+1}$ is contained in a replacement set, I' is an independent set, thus $|N(I') \setminus C| \geq |I'|$. Furthermore, note that for any vertex sets

$A, B \subseteq C$ in a graph the trivial relation $N(A \cap B) \setminus C \subseteq N(A) \cap N(B) \setminus C$ holds. In particular, $N(I') \setminus C \subseteq \Delta_t \cap N(I_{t+1}) \setminus C$. For the cardinalities we get

$$\left| (\bigcup_{j=1}^{t} I_j) \cap I_{t+1} \right| = |I'| \leq |N(I') \setminus C| \leq |\Delta_t \cap N(I_{t+1}) \setminus C|.$$

Since $|\Delta_t| \leq |\bigcup_{j=1}^{t} I_j| + xt$ by the induction hypothesis for t, and $|N(I_{t+1}) \setminus C| \leq |I_{t+1}| + x$ (replacement set), the induction hypothesis for $t+1$ follows:

$$|\Delta_t \cup (N(I_{t+1}) \setminus C)| = |\Delta_t| + |N(I_{t+1}) \setminus C| - |\Delta_t \cap (N(I_{t+1}) \setminus C)|$$

$$\leq |\bigcup_{j=1}^{t} I_j| + xt + |I_{t+1}| + x - \left| (\bigcup_{j=1}^{t} I_j) \cap I_{t+1} \right| = \left| (\bigcup_{j=1}^{t} I_j) \cup I_{t+1} \right| + x(t+1).$$

$\square$

Lemma 2 has another nice consequence. In [8] we computed a repetition-free concise description (suitably defined) of all minimal k-vertex covers in $O^*(1.74^k)$ time. (A more "dirty" description that tolerates redundant vertex covers is obtained much easier in $O(1.62^k)$ time.) By Lemma 2, we get an explicit enumeration faster if $2^{k^*} < 1.74^k$, that is, if $k > 1.25k^*$: Compute some minimum vertex cover C, and test for all independent sets $I \subseteq C$ whether $(C \setminus I) \cup N(I)$ is a minimal k-vertex cover. (For every I, the time is polynomial in k as it suffices to consider vertices of degree at most k.) However, for $k < 1.25k^*$ the concise description is still more efficient.

4   The Union of Minimal Hitting Sets of Bounded Size in Hypergraphs of Bounded Rank

The *degree* of a vertex in a hypergraph is the number of hyperedges it belongs to. Theorem 7 in [8] can be rephrased as follows:

Theorem 3. *For any hypergraph G of rank r, and integer k, there exists a hypergraph G' of rank r on the same vertex set such that: G' has exactly the same minimal k-hitting sets as G, and all vertex degrees in G' are at most k^{r-1}.*

The proof is done by a reduction process that computes G' from G in polynomial time. If there is a k-hitting set at all, it also follows immediately:

Corollary 2. *G' contains at most k^r hyperedges which cover at most $(r-1)k^r + k$ vertices. Hence the last expression also bounds $|U(k)|$ in G' (and thus in G).*

In this section we will much improve the constant factor $r - 1$, for any r. The number k^r of hyperedges in Corollary 2 is a tight bound: Take r disjoint sets of k vertices and choose one vertex from each set, in all possible ways. However, this example has only kr vertices, each with degree k^{r-1}. The basic observation leading to better upper bounds on $|U(k)|$ is that hypergraphs with large $|U(k)|$ must also have many vertices of small degrees, and then, existence of k-hitting sets imposes further restrictions. The largest $|U(k)|$ we could find is $\frac{(r-1)^{r-1}}{r!r^{r-1}}k^r \approx \frac{1}{er!}k^r$: Take a set C of roughly $\frac{r-1}{r}k$ vertices and create $\frac{1}{r}k$ hyperedges for every $D \subset C$ with $|D| = r - 1$, by adding $\frac{1}{r}k$ different single vertices to D. In fact, each vertex of such a hypergraph is in some minimal k-hitting set. Note that almost all vertices in these examples have degree 1, so that we get (approximately) $|U(k)|$ hyperedges. We will prove that, on the other hand, $|U(k)|$ is at most $\log_2 r$ times the number of hyperedges in the reduced hypergraph G'.

We need some technical preparations. In a *t-uniform* hypergraph, all hyperedges have the same size t. A subset X of vertices *cuts* a hyperedge e if neither $X \cap e = \emptyset$ nor $X \supseteq e$.

Lemma 3. *Any t-uniform hypergraph possesses a subset X of vertices that cuts all hyperedges, subject to a fraction of at most $1/2^{t-1}$.*

Proof. Put vertices in X independently with probability $1/2$. Then a hyperedge is either disjoint to X or contained in X, respectively, with probability $1/2^t$. Hence some of these cases appears with probability $1/2^{t-1}$. By linearity of expectation, an expected fraction of $1/2^{t-1}$ of all hyperedges is not cut by X. Finally, since our random X has not cut this expected number of hyperedges, there *exists* an X that has not cut at most this number of hyperedges.   □

Lemma 4. *Let H be a minimal hitting set in a hypergraph G. Partition the family of hyperedges of G into s subfamilies. (Every hyperedge is put in one subfamily.) Then there exist H_i such that $H = H_1 \cup \ldots \cup H_s$, and H_i is a minimal hitting set of the ith subfamily.*

Proof. Straightforward. Omitted due to space limitations.   □

Now we are ready for an improved asymptotic upper bound, relating $|U(k)|$ to the number of hyperedges therein. Notice that our construction only serves to prove the bound, hence it does not need to be efficient.

Theorem 4. *(1) In hypergraphs of rank r with $h = \Theta(k^r)$ hyperedges, we have that $|U(k)| \leq (1 + o(1))\log_2 r \cdot h$. Consequently, (2) in any hypergraph with rank r we have that $|U(k)| \leq (1 + o(1))\log_2 r \cdot k^r$.*

Proof. First note that (2) follows in fact from (1). By Theorem 3 it suffices to consider the reduced hypergraph with all vertex degrees bounded by k^{r-1}, and $h \leq k^r$. If $h > \frac{1}{r}k^r = \Theta(k^r)$, we can apply (1). If h is smaller, then the trivial relation $|U(k)| \leq rh$ gives (2) as well. Next we are going to prove (1).

Our construction involves some free parameters we will fix afterwards. For some integer d, a vertex in G is *d-thin* (*d-fat*) if its degree is smaller than d (at least d). Suppose that our hypergraph G with at most h hyperedges contains $(1-a)rh$ d-thin vertices (i.e., factor a is defined by that.) Clearly, the sum of vertex degrees in G is at most rh. Hence at most $\frac{a}{d}rh$ vertices are d-fat.

We *diminish* the hyperedges of G as follows: From every hyperedge with at least t d-thin vertices, we select t such vertices arbitrarily. In the resulting t-uniform hypergraph we take a set X as in Lemma 3 and delete the vertices of X from G. If a hyperedge has more than t d-thin vertices, we also delete one of these surplus vertices. Let G_0 be the so obtained hypergraph. G_0 has still at most h hyperedges and $\frac{a}{d}rh$ d-fat vertices. All hyperedges from G with more than t d-thin vertices are *diminished* by construction, i.e., they have lost some vertices. From the hyperedges with exactly t d-thin vertices, a fraction of $u/2^{t-1}$, $u \leq 1$ is *undiminished*, by Lemma 3. Let $b_<, b_=, b_>$ be the number of hyperedges of G with $< t, = t, > t$ d-thin vertices, respectively, divided by h. Note that $b_< + b_= + b_> = 1$. Summation of all worst-case bounds yields that the undiminished hyperedges together have less than $(\frac{a}{d}r + b_<(t-1) + \frac{b_= ut}{2^{t-1}})h$ vertices. By definition, every diminished hyperedge has size at most $r-1$ in G_0. At most $(b_= + b_>)(1-u)h/2^{t-1}$ diminished hyperedges in G_0 do not have d-thin vertices anymore, also by Lemma 3.

Now, consider any minimal k-hitting set H in G. We decompose the family of hyperedges of G into three subfamilies: undiminished hyperedges, diminished hyperedges retaining some d-thin vertices in G_0, and diminished hyperedges without d-thin vertices in G_0. By Lemma 4 there exist $A, B, C \subseteq H$ which are minimal hitting sets of these three subfamilies in the mentioned order, with $H = A \cup B \cup C$. Trivially, A is contained in the union of undiminished hyperedges, which has at most $(\frac{a}{d}r + b_<(t-1) + \frac{b_= ut}{2^{t-1}})h$ vertices as stated above. Similarly, C is contained in the union of diminished hyperedges that lose all d-thin vertices. This union is of size at most $(b_= + b_>)(1-u)\frac{r}{2^{t-1}}h$ (namely, r times the number of these hyperedges).

Encasing also B in a small enough vertex set (independent of the set H it comes from!) is more complicated. We shall construct from B some minimal hitting set B_0 of the diminished hyperedges in G_0, and then use B_0, its relationship to B, and the smaller rank $r-1$, to bound the number of hyperedges that may intersect B. Start with $B_0 := B$. Next, every vertex v in B_0 that does no longer exist in G_0 is deleted from B_0. Since B was minimal, some hyperedge in the subfamily (diminished, with some d-thin vertex left) that contained v does no longer intersect B_0. Since v was d-thin, this affects at most $d-1$ hyperedges, for each v. From each temporarily uncovered hyperedge we insert instead in B_0 some d-thin vertex of G_0. These newly added vertices in B_0 can make other vertices in B_0 redundant, i.e., unnecessary for hitting any hyperedge in the subfamily. In this case we remove some redundant vertices one-by-one from B_0, until B_0 is again a *minimal* hitting set. This is our final B_0.

In the worst case we have $|B| = k$, each vertex in B had to be replaced by $d-1$ others, and no vertex got redundant. Thus, $|B_0| \leq (d-1)k$. Since B_0 is in the union of minimal hitting sets of that size, in a hypergraph of diminished hyperedges, we conclude from the loose bound in Corollary 2 that B_0 is contained in a fixed set of $O((k(d-1))^{r-1}) = O(\frac{(d-1)^{r-1}}{k}k^r)$ vertices, with a factor depending on r only. Since $h = \Theta(k^r)$, we can write this as $O(\frac{(d-1)^{r-1}}{k}h)$. It remains to count the vertices v in all possible B that do not occur in the sets

B_0. These are deleted vertices and redundant vertices in some B. For any such v, some other vertex in any hyperedge containing v must remain in the hitting set B_0. More specifically: A deleted v is in the same hyperedge with some d-thin $w \in B_0$, and a redundant v became redundant because of a new d-thin vertex $w \in B_0$ in the same hyperedge, as v was not redundant before in B. In summary, each $v \in B \setminus B_0$ is assigned to some d-thin $w \in B_0$ in the same hyperedge of G. Since all these w are d-thin, belong to a fixed set as specified above, and G has rank r, the union of all B is bounded in size by $O(\frac{r(d-1)^r}{k}h)$.

Summing up all bounds, the union of all minimal k-hitting sets has at most

$$\left(\frac{a}{d}r + b_<(t-1) + \frac{b_= ut}{2^{t-1}} + (b_= + b_>)(1-u)\frac{r}{2^{t-1}} + O\left(\frac{r(d-1)^r}{k} \right) \right) h \qquad (1)$$

vertices. Recall that $a \le 1$, $u \le 1$ and $b_< + b_= + b_> = 1$. These parameters depend on the hypergraph and cannot be chosen, but it is safe to take the worst case. In contrast, we can freely choose d and t. The first and last summand in (1) play no role for the asymptotics: As k grows, we can have $d \to \infty$ and make the last term go to 0 at the same time, and by $d \to \infty$ the first term goes to 0, too. For fixed t we have to maximize $b_<(t-1) + \frac{b_= ut}{2^{t-1}} + (b_= + b_>)(1-u)\frac{r}{2^{t-1}}$. Since $b_=$ appears in two terms and $b_>$ in one of them, we can set $b_> = 0$, and with $b := b_<$ the expression simplifies to

$$b(t-1) + \frac{(1-b)ut}{2^{t-1}} + (1-b)(1-u)\frac{r}{2^{t-1}}. \qquad (2)$$

Note that our variables b, u form three coefficients $b, (1-b)u, (1-b)(1-u)$, being arbitrary nonnegative numbers that sum up to 1. Hence the maximum of (2) is $\max\{t-1, \frac{t}{2^{t-1}}, \frac{r}{2^{t-1}}\}$. Finally we choose t so as to minimize this maximum. This gives the result. $\square$

Due to $|U(k)| = \Theta(k^r)$, we define $f(r)$ to be the smallest factor where $|U(k)| \le f(r)k^r + o(k^r)$. Trivially, $f(1) = 1$, and in [8] we got $f(2) = \frac{1}{4}$. Theorem 4 implies $f(r) \le \log_2 r$ for large enough r, and the proof also yields specific bounds for fixed r: $f(3) \le \frac{3}{2}$, $f(r) \le 2$ for $4 \le r \le 8$, $f(r) \le \frac{r}{4}$ for $9 \le r \le 12$, $f(r) \le 3$ for $13 \le r \le 24$, etc. In the remainder of this section we prove better upper bounds for r up to 6 through a different hypergraph decomposition.

Let H be a fixed minimum hitting set in a hypergraph G of rank r. Unlike case $r = 2$, we call $I \subseteq H$ a replacement set if there exists a minimal hitting set H' such that $I = H \setminus H'$, and $|H'| \le k$. Let I be any fixed replacement set. We define a hypergraph $G(I)$ whose hyperedges are the sets $e \setminus I$, for all hyperedges e in G with $\emptyset \ne e \cap H \subseteq I$. Vertices in a gypergraph are w.l.o.g. the vertices contained in its hyperedges. (Since we are interested in hitting sets, we may ignore isolated vertices.)

We decompose $G(I)$ into several hypergraphs G_J, each equipped with a sub-family of the hyperedges of $G(I)$, as follows. G_J is defined as the hypergraph of rank $r - j$ $(j = |J|)$, consisting of those hyperedges $e \setminus J$ of $G(I)$ with $e \cap H = J$. (Note that G_J is the same for each $I \supseteq J$, hence we do not need subscript I.)

Lemma 5. *For any fixed I, any minimal hitting set H' with $H \setminus H' = I$ contains vertices only from H and from minimal hitting sets of the G_J, $J \subseteq I$, $0 < |J| < r$.*

Proof. Straightforward from Lemma 4. Omitted due to space limitations.   □

Theorem 5. *The union of all minimal k-hitting sets in a hypergraph of rank 3 has at most $\frac{1}{4} k^* (k^2 + (k^*)^2) + k^* k$ vertices.*

Proof. Consider a minimum hitting set H, thus $k^* = |H|$. For each $v \in H$ let I_v be some maximum replacement set with $x_v \in I_v$, and $x_v = |I_v|$. (We can assume that I_v exists, since a vertex of H in no replacement set belongs to every minimal hitting set, and putting these vertices aside we get a reduced instance with smaller k and k^*.) We define $x = \max_v x_v$. For each v we distinguish $x_v - 1$ two-vertex sets J with $v \in J \subseteq I_v$. Due to Lemma 5, all vertices of $U(k)$ are in H or in minimal hitting sets of the G_J, $1 \le |J| \le 2$.

The G_J with $|J| = 1$ contribute together at most $\frac{1}{4} \sum_{v \in H} (k - k^* + x_v)^2$ vertices to $U(k)$. This because the G_J have rank 2, at most $k - k^* + x_v$ vertices outside H are allowed in every minimal hitting set of G_J, $J = \{v\}$, and $f(2) = \frac{1}{4}$.

The G_J with $|J| = 2$ have rank 1. Thus, every vertex in G_J, $|J| = 2$, $J \subseteq I$ (any replacement set) must be in every hitting set that extends $H \setminus I$, limiting the *total* number of vertices in all these G_J, $J \subseteq I$, to $k - k^* + |I|$.

We apply this observation in two ways: All G_J of distinguished sets J, $|J| = 2$, contribute together at most $k^*(k - k^* + x) \le k^* k$ vertices to $U(k)$. Each of the remaining G_J with $|J| = 2$, these are fewer than $\frac{1}{2}((k^*)^2 - \sum_{v \in H} x_v)$ pairs, contributes at most $k - k^* + x$ vertices to $U(k)$. Altogether we obtain

$$|U(k)| \le \frac{1}{4} \sum_{v \in H} (k - k^* + x_v)^2 + \frac{1}{2} \left((k^*)^2 - \sum_{v \in H} x_v\right)(k - k^* + x) + k^* k.$$

After rewriting $(k^*)^2 = \sum_{v \in H} k^*$, algebraic manipulation easily yields

$$|U(k)| \le \frac{1}{4} k^* (k^2 - (k^*)^2 + 2k^* x) + \frac{1}{4} \sum_{v \in H} x_v (x_v - 2x) + k^* k.$$

Since the middle term is negative, and $x \le k^*$, we get the claimed result.   □

We believe that this is not yet optimal. Note especially that the optimal bound for $r = 2$ (Theorem 2) is linear in $k - k^*$ for any fixed k^*. An intriguing question is whether a similar bound with factor $k - k^*$ in the main term holds also for $r = 3$ (whereas the result in Theorem 5 is always cubic). This would be interesting when limits k close to k^* are used.

Corollary 3. *We have $f(3) \le \frac{1}{2}$, $f(4) \le \frac{19}{24}$, $f(5) \le \frac{9}{8}$, $f(6) \le \frac{779}{480}$.*

Proof. Consider $r = 3$. For any fixed k, our bound from Theorem 5 is maximized when $k^* = k$, and then it becomes $\frac{1}{2} k^3$, hence $f(3) \le \frac{1}{2}$. Next, Lemma 5 implies

$$|U(k)| \le k + \sum_{j=1}^{r-1} \binom{k}{j} f(r - j) k^{r-j} \le k + \sum_{j=1}^{r-1} \frac{f(r - j)}{j!} k^r.$$

Neglect of the lower-order term k gives the recursion $f(r) \leq \sum_{j=1}^{r-1} \frac{f(r-j)}{j!}$ that we apply to $r = 4, 5, 6$.   □

Unfortunately, this recursive formula grows exponentially in r. But the bounds for $r \leq 6$ are considerably better than those from the general Theorem 4.

5   Conclusions

The union $U(k)$ of minimal k-hitting sets is useful in combinatorial inference. We have $|U(k)| = O(k^r)$ in hypergraphs of rank r, but the factor depending on r is open. We have significantly improved a previous upper bound, using some intricate hypergraph decompositions, but still there seems to be a fundamental lack of understanding of these kernels. We believe that the techniques introduced here are more powerful than what the current results exhibit. Bounds on the number of hyperedges in the kernel would further reduce the bounds on $|U(k)|$, too. Finally, the parameterized complexity of counting k-hitting sets in hypergraphs of rank r deserves investigation.

Acknowledgment. This work has been initiated and partially supported by the *Combinatorial Search Algorithms in Bioinformatics* group at the University of Bielefeld, led by Ferdinando Cicalese, through his Sofja Kovalevskaja Award 2004 from the Alexander von Humboldt Foundation.

References

1. V. Bafna, K. Reinert. Mass spectrometry and computational proteomics, in: *Encyclopedia of Genetics, Genomics, Proteomics and Bioinformatics*, Wiley 2005
2. E. Boros, M.C. Golumbic, V.E. Levit. On the number of vertices belonging to all maximum stable sets of a graph, *Discrete Appl. Math.* 124 (2002), 17-25
3. J. Chen, X. Huang, I.A. Kanj, G. Xia. Strong computational lower bounds via paramterized complexity, *J. Comp. and System Sci.* 72 (2006), 1346-1367
4. J. Chen, I.A. Kanj, J. Meng, G. Xia, F. Zhang. On the effective enumerability of NP problems, 2nd IWPEC 2006, *LNCS* 4169, 215-226
5. J. Chen, I.A. Kanj, G. Xia. Improved parameterized upper bounds for vertex cover, *31st MFCS 2006, LNCS 4162*, 238-249
6. M. Chlebik, J. Chlebikova. Crown reductions for the minimum weighted vertex cover problem, ECCC Report 101 (2004), to appear in *Discrete Appl. Math.*
7. F. Cicalese, Center for Biotechnology, Univ. Bielefeld (personal communication)
8. P. Damaschke. Parameterized enumeration, transversals, and imperfect phylogeny reconstruction, *Theoretical Computer Science* 351 (2006), 337-350, special issue of selected papers from *IWPEC 2004*
9. H. Fernau. On parameterized enumeration, *COCOON 2002, LNCS* 2387, 564-573
10. H. Fernau. A top-down approach to search-trees: Improved algorithmics for 3-hitting set. *ECCC* Report 073 (2004)
11. H. Fernau. Parameterized algorithms for hitting set: The weighted case, *6th CIAC 2006, LNCS* 3998, 332-343
12. T. Mitchell. *Machine Learning*, McGraw-Hill 1997

An Optimal, Edges-Only Fully Dynamic Algorithm for Distance-Hereditary Graphs⋆

Marc Tedder and Derek Corneil

Department of Computer Science, University of Toronto,
10 King's College Road, Room 3302, Toronto, Ontario, Canada, M5S 3G4
{mtedder,dgc}@cs.toronto.edu

Abstract. The problem of dynamically recognizing a class of graphs has received much attention recently. Given an input graph and a sequence of operations (vertex and edge additions and deletions) to be performed on that graph, the algorithm must determine after each operation if the resulting graph is still a member of the class in question. This paper presents the first dynamic recognition algorithm for distance-hereditary graphs. The algorithm handles edge additions and deletions, and is optimal in that each operation can be performed in constant time. In doing so, the paper completely characterizes when an edge can be added to and removed from a distance-hereditary graph with the result remaining distance-hereditary, and develops a new representation for these graphs in terms of cographs.

Keywords: dynamic algorithm, graph recognition, distance-hereditary, cograph.

1   Introduction

Many networks are dynamic in nature: networks expand and contract; hubs and transition lines fail and are repaired or replaced. The underlying graph sees these changes as additions and deletions of vertices and edges. Throughout these changes the network must continue to function properly, which often means the underlying graph must maintain some property – connectivity, for instance. The dynamic recognition problem for a family of graphs is related. The input is a triple $\langle G, \sigma, \Pi \rangle$; G is the initial graph, σ is a sequence of operations (vertex and edge additions and deletions) to apply to G, and Π is a family of graphs for which membership is to be verified after each operation; the algorithm halts after the first operation where membership in Π no longer holds. Such an algorithm usually operates by maintaining a representation of the graph as it changes, which it uses to verify membership in Π. The running time of these algorithms is the worst-case time required for a single operation. Dynamic graph algorithms

---

⋆ This research was partially funded by the Natural Science and Engineering Research Council (NSERC) of Canada and the Ontario Graduate Scholarship (OGS) program.

W. Thomas and P. Weil (Eds.): STACS 2007, LNCS 4393, pp. 344–355, 2007.

that accommodate addition and deletion of both vertices and edges are called *fully dynamic*; those only allowing edge addition and deletion are said to be *edges-only fully dynamic*.

The problem of dynamically recognizing a family of graphs has received considerable attention recently. All of [1,2,3,4,5,6,7,8,9,10,11] dynamically recognize a class of graphs in one way or another. This is useful in a network setting since membership in a class of graphs confers certain desirable properties. The distance-hereditary graphs, for example, ensure that all induced paths between a pair of vertices have the same length. This paper presents the first dynamic graph algorithm for (connected) distance-hereditary graphs. We give an optimal, edges-only fully dynamic graph algorithm where Π is membership in the class of (connected) distance-hereditary graphs; the algorithm is optimal in that each operation can be performed in constant time.

2 Preliminaries

All graphs in this paper are simple and undirected. The distance-hereditary graphs in this paper are all connected. The edge $\{x, y\}$ is specified as xy; $G - xy$ is the graph G with xy removed, and $G + xy$ is the graph G with xy added. References to a component could be to the set of vertices defined by the component or to the graph induced by the component; the meaning will be clear from the context.

A collection of sets S is arboreal if for any two sets $s, s' \in S$, either $s \subseteq s'$, $s' \subset s$, or $s \cap s' = \emptyset$. Let $E(S) = \{e | \exists s \in S \text{ such that } e \in s\}$. An arboreal collection of sets can be organized in a forest: the vertices of each tree are the elements of $S \cup E(S)$; the parent of a vertex is the smallest set in S that properly contains that vertex.

A vertex is universal to a set of vertices S if it is adjacent to all vertices in S; a vertex is isolated from S if it is not adjacent to any vertex in S. When $x \in S$, x is universal to S when x is adjacent to every vertex in $S - \{x\}$; similarly for x isolated from S. A module is a set of vertices M such that every vertex not in M is either universal to M or isolated from M.

Non-leaf vertices of a tree are referred to as the *internal vertices* of the tree.

A two-way connection between a pair of objects refers to a pointer from one object to the other, along with a second pointer in the opposite direction.

The algorithm assumes it is supplied with pointers to the endpoints of the edge to be added or deleted.

All other definitions and notation used in this paper can be found in the book of West [12].

2.1 Cographs

Cographs are those graphs not containing an induced P_4. The modular decomposition tree (see [13,14]) of a cograph is called its *cotree*. Each internal vertex of a cotree is labeled by 1 or 0, with the labels alternating on any path from the root to a leaf, starting with 1 at the root when the graph is connected, and 0 when disconnected. The following follows from the definition of modular decomposition and will be used in the paper:

Remark 1. Two vertices in a cograph are adjacent if and only if their least common ancestor in the graph's cotree is labeled by 1.

2.2 Distance-Hereditary Graphs

A graph G is distance-hereditary when the distance between any two vertices in any connected induced subgraph is the same as in G.

Hangings are an important algorithmic tool for distance-hereditary graphs. A hanging of a graph G with respect to one of its vertices, v, is a division of G into horizontal and vertical subgraphs. The horizontal subgraph is the disjoint union of the graphs $G[L^i]$, where L^i is the set of vertices distance i from v. The vertical subgraph consists of the vertices of G and the edges between different L^i's. In this paper the terms level and layer are used interchangeably for each L^i; a reference to L^i could mean the set of vertices itself or the graph induced by the set, the meaning being clear from the context.

Notation. For any hanging of a graph, the following is used:

- $N^i(x) = N(x) \cap L^i$. The notion of a *closed-neighbourhood* is extended: $N^i[x] = N^i(x) \cup \{x\}$.
- If $x \in L^i$, then $N^-(x) = N^{i-1}(x)$; this is called the *up-neighbourhood* of x. An up-neighbourhood is *non-trivial* when $|N^-(x)| > 1$, and *trivial* otherwise. Notation is abused somewhat when the up-neighbourhood has cardinality one: $N^-(x) = y$ is used instead of $N^-(x) = \{y\}$.
- Subscripts are sometimes added to make clear the graph to which these objects belong. For example, $N_G^-(x)$ is the up-neighbourhood of x in G, while $N_H^-(x)$ is the up-neighbourhood of x in H.

Definition 1. *Fix a hanging of a graph G. Two vertices x and y are tied with respect to this hanging if there exists a vertex z such that $x, y \in N^-(z)$; in this case x and y are said to be tied via z.*[1]

Bandelt and Mulder [15], Hammer and Maffray [16], and D'atri and Moscarini [17] independently characterized distance-hereditary graphs in terms of their hangings. The Bandelt and Mulder characterization is used in this paper:

Theorem 1. *[15] Fix a hanging of a graph G. Then G is distance-hereditary if and only if the following all hold:*

1. *For any two vertices x and y in the same component of L^i, $N^-(x) = N^-(y)$.*
2. *Each level is a cograph.*
3. *For $v \in L^i$, if $x, y \in N^-(v)$ belong to different components C and C' of L^{i-1}, then $C \cup C' \subseteq N^-(v)$ and $N^-(x) = N^-(y)$.*

---

[1] This definition differs from what is traditionally seen in the literature.

4. If x and y belong to different components of L^i then either $N^-(x) \subseteq N^-(y)$, $N^-(y) \subset N^-(x)$, or $N^-(x) \cap N^-(y) = \emptyset$.
5. For $v \in L^i$, if $x, y \in N^-(v)$ belong to the same component of L^{i-1}, then any vertex of L^{i-1} not in $N^-(v)$ is either adjacent to both x and y or to neither.

The next fact follows from conditions 3 and 5 of Theorem 1:

Remark 2. If $z \in L^{i+1}$, then $N^-(z)$ is a module of $G[L^i]$.

Hammer and Maffray [16] defined a relation $\approx$ on the vertices of a distance-hereditary graph:

Definition 2. [16] Fix a hanging of a distance-hereditary graph G. Then $x \approx y$ with respect to this hanging if and only if $x, y \in L^i$ and either x and y are in the same component of $G[L^i]$ or are tied with respect to the hanging.

Remark 3. [16] The relation $\approx$ is an equivalence relation.

Notation. The equivalence class of x with respect to $\approx$ is denoted $[x]$.

The next fact follows from conditions 1 and 3 of Theorem 1:

Remark 4. If $x, y \in [x]$, then $N^-(x) = N^-(y)$.

3 The Representation

In this section we outline the representation employed by our algorithm. Let G be a distance-hereditary graph; fix a hanging of G; consider an arbitrary level L^i and the set,

$$S = \{N^-(x) | x \in L^{i+1}, |N^-(x)| > 1\} \cup$$
$$\{\{u\} | u \in L^i, \nexists x \in L^{i+1}, u \in N^-(x), |N^-(x)| > 1\}.$$

Conditions 1 and 4 of Theorem 1 imply that S is an arboreal collection of sets; hence, its elements can be organized in a forest. If x and y are leaves of the same tree in this forest, then there is at least one $z \in L^{i+1}$ such that $x, y \in N^-(z)$. So by conditions 1 and 3 of Theorem 1, $N^-(x) = N^-(y)$; in this sense, we can speak of each of these trees as having an up-neighbourhood; note that distinct trees can have the same up-neighbourhood. Unifying the trees with the same up-neighbourhood under a common root still leaves a forest; call each of these unified trees a *common parent tree* (*CPT*), and use $CPT_G(x)$ to denote the *CPT* of x in G; Fig. 1 provides an example.

Let T be some *CPT* of level L^i, and consider one of its internal vertices, call it s. Recall that s corresponds to $N^-(z)$ for some $z \in L^{i+1}$. Also note that s can have two types of children: those that are themselves up-neighbourhoods, and those that are vertices of L^i – internal vertices of T and leaves of T, respectively; let $c_1, \ldots, c_k$ be s's children of the first type, and $c_{k+1}, \ldots, c_\ell$ its children of the second type. Form the graph G_s as follows: the vertices are $s, c_1 \ldots, c_\ell$;

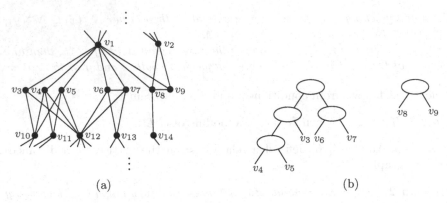

Fig. 1. (a) Three levels in a distance-hereditary graph; (b) the CPT's of the second level

adjacencies are defined according to G: c_j is adjacent to $c_{j'}$ if and only if $\exists x \in c_j$ and $\exists y \in c_{j'}$ such that x and y are adjacent in G.[2] Using the fact that $G[L^i]$ is a cograph (condition 2 of Theorem 1), we can easily show that G_s is a cograph. Hence, for each internal node s of a CPT, we can associate a cograph G_s; note that some vertices in a CPT participate in two such cographs (non-root internal CPT vertices) while others only participate in one (the root and leaves of a CPT). The cotrees of these cographs compose our representation.

The cotrees can be stored in the natural way: each child with a pointer to its parent, with siblings in a doubly-linked list, and a link from the parent to the head of this sibling list. Our algorithm requires additional pointers. As mentioned above, each CPT has a unique up-neighbourhood, and this up-neighbourhood corresponds to an internal vertex of some other CPT. Let T be a CPT and r its root; in addition to the pointers r requires for its cograph G_r, we will also have it maintain a two-way connection with the CPT vertex corresponding to its up-neighbourhood. These additional pointers link the cotrees and serve to differentiate roots, leaves, and internal vertices of CPT's.

If there are n vertices in G, there can be at most n distinct up-neighbourhoods. The number of CPT vertices is therefore linear in n, and since the size of a cotree is linear in the size of the graph it encodes, the representation used by the algorithm is linear in the size of G.

4   Edge Deletion

4.1   Safely Deleting Edges from Distance-Hereditary Graphs

Given a distance-hereditary graph G, our algorithm must determine when $G - xy$ is distance-hereditary, and must do so using our representation. Consider the case where $N_G^-(x) = y$ and x is not tied. Say $y \in L^i$, $x \in L^{i+1}$, and let C be the

---

[2] We are abusing notation somewhat. One of c_j and $c_{j'}$ might not be a set, in which case they correspond to a vertex of G and should be thought of as singleton sets.

component of x in $G[L^{i+1}]$; let $G_{C,y}$ be $G[C \cup \{y\}]$. By condition 1 of Theorem 1, y is universal in $G_{C,y}$; combining this with condition 2 allows us to conclude that $G_{C,y}$ is a cograph.

Consider $G_{C,y} - xy$; what happens when this is not a cograph? Then it contains a P_4 on which x and y must reside (non-consecutively). Let p be such a P_4, and suppose z and w are the other vertices on p. Now, w and z are non-adjacent but connected, and $G_{C,y}$ is a cograph, so there must be a $u \in C$ adjacent to both w and z. We know u and x are adjacent as otherwise $\{x, z, u, w\}$ would induce a P_4, contradicting $G_{C,y}$ being a cograph. But then in $G - xy$ either condition 3 or 5 of Theorem 1 is violated by $\{x, u, z, w\}$, meaning $G - xy$ is not distance-hereditary. Hence, $G_{C,y} - xy$ being a cograph is necessary for $G - xy$ being distance-hereditary. It turns out that this is also sufficient (the proof can be found in [18]):

Theorem 2. *Assume $N_G^-(x) = y$ and that x is not tied. Say $y \in L^i$ and $x \in L^{i+1}$, and let C be the component of x in L^{i+1} in G, and $G_{C,y}$ the subgraph of G induced by the vertices of $C \cup \{y\}$. Then $G - xy$ is distance-hereditary if and only if $G_{C,y} - xy$ is a cograph.*

So in this case our algorithm need only use its representation to verify that $G_{C,y} - xy$ is a cograph. This is made simpler by the following lemma, which reduces things to a question of adjacencies in G:

Lemma 1. *$G_{C,y} - xy$ is a cograph if and only if for all $q \in [x]_G - N_G^{i+1}(x)$, q is universal to $N_G^{i+1}(x)$.*

Proof. (Necessity:) Assume $G_{C,y} - xy$ is a cograph. Suppose there is a $q \in [x]_G - N_G^{i+1}(x)$, and for contradiction let $w \in N_G^{i+1}(x)$ be a vertex not adjacent to q. Since x is not tied, $C = [x]_G$; thus, $q \in C$. But then $\{x, y, w, q\}$ induces a P_4 in $G_{C,y} - xy$, a contradiction.

(Sufficiency:) Assume for all $q \in [x]_G - N_G^{i+1}(x)$, that q is universal to $N_G^{i+1}(x)$. For contradiction, suppose $G_{C,y} - xy$ is not a cograph. Then $G_{C,y} - xy$ has a P_4, say p. With G distance-hereditary, $G_{C,y}$ must be a cograph by conditions 1 and 2 of Theorem 1. So x and y must both reside on p. Let z and w be the other vertices on p. Note that y is adjacent to both z and w, by condition 1 of Theorem 1. So without loss of generality, $p = x, z, y, w$. But then $w \in C - N_G^{i+1}(x) = [x]_G - N_G^{i+1}(x)$, and w is not adjacent to $z \in N_G^{i+1}(x)$, a contradiction. $\square$

The preceding lemma says that when $|[x]_G| = 1$, $G - xy$ is distance-hereditary. However, $G - xy$ is disconnected when $|[x]_G| = 1$, so our algorithm should halt in this case. The vertex x is not tied – not a member of a non-trivial up-neighbourhood – and therefore a child of the root of its CPT, meaning x is a vertex of G_r, where r is the root of its CPT. With $|[x]_G| = 1$, we also know x is only adjacent to r in G_r. Such a graph can only be described by the cotree in Fig. 2(a); moreover, it is clear that this configuration implies $|[x]_G| = 1$.

Since the configuration in Fig. 2(a) can be verified in constant time, we will concentrate on the case where $|[x]_G| > 1$. As before, x must be a vertex in

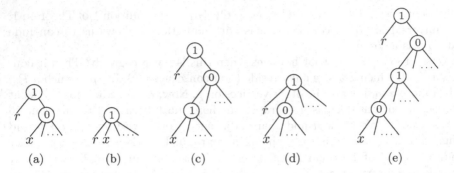

Fig. 2. The five possibilities for G_r when $N^-(x) = y$, x is not tied, and $G - xy$ is distance-hereditary

G_r since it is not tied. It not being tied also means $[x]_G = C$, where C is the component of x in its level. Fig.'s 2(b)-(d) give four possibilities for the cotree of G_r. In the first two, x must be universal to $[x]_G$; clearly, these are the only two possibilities for this occurring, the first when the leaves of $CPT_G(x)$ are all in $[x]_G$, the second when they are not. In the third configuration, $[x]_G - N_G^{i+1}(x)$ is non-empty and forms a join with $N_G^{i+1}(x)$; furthermore, when the all the leaves of $CPT_G(x)$ are in $[x]_G$, this is the only configuration that can describe this scenario. In the fourth configuration, if c is a child of r in $CPT_G(x)$, then $c \notin [x]_G$ precisely when it descends from x's great-grandparent (but not grandparent) in the cotree. This leaves for consideration the graph described by the cotree rooted at x's grandparent, which is the same as the third configuration but with r removed. Hence,

Lemma 2. *When $N_G^-(x) = y$ and x is not tied, $G - xy$ is distance-hereditary if and only if G_r is described by one of the four configurations in Fig.'s 2(b)-(d).*

With a pointer to x, each of these configurations can be checked in constant time, which gives us the following:

Corollary 1. *It can be determined in constant time if $G - xy$ is distance-hereditary when $N_G^-(x) = y$ and x is not tied.*

So far we have looked at deleting xy where $N_G^-(x) = y$ and x is not tied. We must also consider the cases where $N_G^-(x) = y$ and x is tied; where $y \in N_G^-(x)$ and $|N_G^-(x)| > 1$; and where x and y reside in the same level. Luckily, the obvious necessary conditions for $G - xy$ being distance-hereditary also end up being sufficient for these, just as they were in the first case, with the proofs closely following the one provided there (the statement of the conditions can be found in [18]). Still more, each set of conditions can be reduced to the existence of (constant time verifiable) local configurations in our representation, just as with the first case.

These configurations also help us distinguish the cases. In Fig. 2, for example, x is a vertex of G_r and thus not tied, while access to r is easily obtained via

x. Through the two-way connection r maintains with $N_G^-(x)$, we can check in constant time if $N_G^-(x) = y$. Similar steps identify the other cases. Complete details of this and the other cases can be found in [18].

Lemma 3. *The algorithm can distinguish the different cases for deletion in constant time, and in each, determine if $G - xy$ is distance-hereditary in constant time.*

4.2 Updating the Representation

Having determined that $G - xy$ is distance-hereditary, our algorithm must then update its representation to account for the removal of xy. Fig. 3(a) displays three levels of a distance-hereditary graph G. In it, $|C| > 1$, where C is the component of x in its level; $N_G^-(x) = y$; x is tied and universal to $[x]_G$; and $N_G^-(z_j) = [x]_G$ and $N_G^-(u_j) = [x]_G - \{x\}$, for all j. It can be shown that $G - xy$ is distance-hereditary in this case (see [18]).

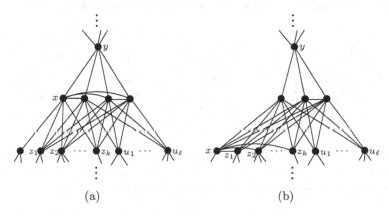

(a)   (b)

Fig. 3. (a): Three levels of a distance-hereditary graph; (b): the levels with xy removed

Figure 3(b) shows what happens when xy is removed. Since x's up-neighbourhood changes, so too must its CPT. Let p be the parent of x in $CPT_G(x)$, and p' its grandparent. In this example, x has exactly one sibling in $CPT_G(x)$, call it s. Note that $N_G^-(z_j) = p$ and $N_G^-(u_j) = s$, for all j; hence, p ceases to exist in $G - xy$, while s persists. So three changes are required of the representation: the deletion of G_p (without deleting x), the removal of p from $G_{p'}$, and the addition of s to $G_{p'}$. The first is easy. Regarding the last two, note that because $s \subset p$, the modularity of p in $G[L^{i+1}]$ (see fact 2) means p can simply be replaced by s in $G_{p'}$. These changes are constant time operations with the supplied pointer to x.

With x removed from $CPT_G(x)$, we now must add it to its new CPT. Since they share an up-neighbourhood in $G - xy$, the z_j's, u_j's, and x must be made to share a CPT. Let T_z be $CPT_G(z_j)$ and r_z its root; let T_u be $CPT_G(u_j)$ and r_u its root. The algorithm adds x to T_z, then merges the result with T_u.

Observe that x is not tied in $G - xy$, so it is a child of r_z in T_z – it must be made a vertex of G_{r_z}. Also observe that x is universal to the $z'_j s$ – universal to the leaves of T_z – and so universal in G_{r_z}. In other words, we must make x a sibling of r_z in the cotree of G_{r_z}. This can be done in constant time since access to r_z can be obtained in constant time through its two-way connection with p.

Let $T_{x,z}$ be the result of adding x to T_z; note that r_z is the root of $T_{x,z}$. Merging $T_{x,z}$ and T_u means creating a new root r and making the children of r_z and r_u its only children. In terms of our representation, this means creating a new vertex r, creating the graph G_r (which consists of the vertices of G_{r_z} and G_{r_u} minus z and u), and deleting G_{r_z} and G_{r_u}. The first of these tasks is easy, and the second task will be performed in such a way that both it and the third task will be constant time operations: G_r will be built from G_{r_z} and G_{r_u}.

The adjacencies between the vertices in G_{r_z} remain the same there as in G_r, as do those in G_{r_u}. Since T_z and T_u were distinct CPT's in G, none of the leaves of T_z are adjacent to those of T_u; this means no vertex of G_{r_z} is adjacent to a vertex of G_{r_u} in G_r (recall that x is not adjacent to any u_j in G or $G - xy$). This gives us enough information to form G_r from G_{r_z} and G_{r_u}.

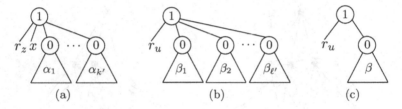

(a)   (b)   (c)

Fig. 4. (a): G_{r_z} after x has been added. (b)-(c): the two possibilities for G_{r_u}: when r_u has more than one sibling (b) and when r_u has exactly one sibling (c). Note that some of the α's and β's could be empty, that is, could be leaves.

Figure 4(a) shows G_{r_z} after adding x, while (b) and (c) show the two possibilities for G_{r_u}. From these configurations, and the adjacencies just described, the possibilities for G_r are those described in Fig. 5. Access to r_u can be obtained in constant time through its two-way connection with s; so, if the bold objects represent new data items, and all other items are reused, a constant time merge can clearly be obtained. Deleting G_{r_z} and G_{r_u} is now easy since only r_z and r_u remain of those graphs, respectively.

The preceding discussion was intended to illustrate the deletion of xy when $N_G^-(x) = y$ with x tied and $|C| > 1$, where C is the component of x in $G[L^{i+1}]$. What is true in this example – x not being tied in $G - xy$, the leaves of $CPT_G(z_j)$ being the vertices by which x is tied in G, and x being universal to these vertices in $G - xy$ – is easily seen to hold in general. However, it may be that $\ell = 0$; that is, there could be no vertex u with $N_G^-(u) = [x]_G - \{x\}$. In this case, removing x from $CPT_G(x)$ is slightly different since x has siblings other than s', but the steps are similar. Also, the algorithm need not merge $T_{x,z}$ with T_u: it can stop with the formation of $T_{x,z}$.

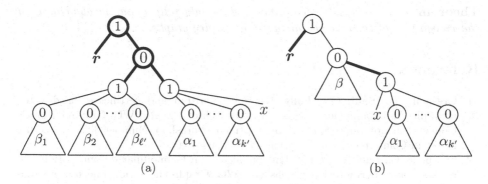

Fig. 5. (a): G_{r_u} when G_{r_u} is described by Fig. 4(b); (c): G_{r_u} when G_{r_u} is described by Fig. 4(c)

When $N_G^-(x) = y$ and x is tied with $|C| = 1$, x moves to L^{i+3} in $G - xy$. Following the approach employed above – using the definitions of the structures involved, the configurations that must be present (because $G - xy$ is distance-hereditary), and making careful reuse of existing data objects – allows for constant time updating in this case too. In fact, the same technique yields constant time updating procedures for the other three major cases – when $N_G^-(x) = y$ and x is not tied, when $y \in N_G^-(x)$ and $|N_G^-(x)| > 1$, and when x and y reside in the same level; complete details can be found in [18]. The following is a consequence of this and Lemma 3:

Lemma 4. *There exists a constant time dynamic graph algorithm recognizing (connected) distance-hereditary graphs under a sequence of edge deletions.*

5 Edge Addition

Edge addition can be handled in much the same way as edge deletion: first characterize when it is "safe" to add an edge to a distance-hereditary graph; reduce these conditions to configurations in the representation, all of which can be verified in constant time; then use the presence of these configurations, the definitions of the constructs involved, and carefully reuse existing structures to accomplish the updating of the representation in constant time.

The process is divided into four cases: adding an edge within a layer, between adjacent layers, between layers distance-two apart, and between layers distance-three apart. Adding an edge between layers more than distance-three apart necessarily creates a hole – induced cycle of length at least five – which is forbidden for distance-hereditary graphs (see [15,16]). The conditions for each case appear in the appendix; details of their verification and the updating required afterwards can be found in [19]. Combining this with Lemma 4 provides the main result of the paper:

Theorem 3. *There exists an optimal, edges-only fully dynamic algorithm for the recognition of (connected) distance-hereditary graphs.*

References

1. Crespelle, C., Paul, C.: Fully dynamic algorithm and certificate for directed cographs. In Hromkovic, J., Nagl, M., Westfechtel, B., eds.: WG: Graph-Theoretic Concepts in Computer Science, International Workshop. Number 3353 in Lecture Notes in Computer Science, Springer (2004) 93–104
2. Crespelle, C., Paul, C.: Fully dynamic algorithm for modular decomposition and recognition of permutation graphs. In: WG: Graph-Theoretic Concepts in Computer Science, International Workshop. (2005)
3. Corneil, D., Perl, Y., Stewart, L.: A linear recognition algorithm for cographs. Siam J. Comput. **14** (1985) 926–934
4. Deng, X., Hell, P., Huang, J.: Linear-time representation algorithms for proper circular-arc graphs and proper interval graphs. SIAM J. Comput. **25** (1996) 390–403
5. Hsu, W.L.: On-line recognition of interval graphs in $O(m + n\log n)$ time. In: Selected papers from the 8th Franco-Japanese and 4th Franco-Chinese Conference on Combinatorics and Computer Science, London, UK, Springer-Verlag (1996) 27–38
6. Hell, P., Shamir, R., Sharan, R.: A fully dynamic algorithm for recognizing and representing proper interval graphs. SIAM J. Comput. **31** (2001) 289–305
7. Ibarra, L.: A fully dynamic algorithm for recognizing interval graphs using the clique-separator graph. Technical report, University of Victoria (2001)
8. Ibarra, L.: Fully dynamic algorithms for chordal graphs. In: SODA '99: Proceedings of the tenth annual ACM-SIAM symposium on Discrete algorithms, Philadelphia, PA, USA, Society for Industrial and Applied Mathematics (1999) 923–924
9. Jamison, B., Olariu, S.: Recognizing P_4-sparse graphs in linear time. Siam J. Comput **21** (1992) 381–406
10. Nikolopoulos, S.D., Palios, L., Papadopoulos, C.: A fully dynamic algorithm for the recognition of P_4-sparse graphs. In: WG: Graph-Theoretic Concepts in Computer Science, International Workshop. (2006)
11. Shamir, R., Sharan, R.: A fully dynamic algorithm for modular decomposition and recognition of cographs. Discrete Applied Mathematics **136** (2004) 329–340
12. West, D.B.: Introduction to Graph Theory. 2nd. edn. Prentice Hall Inc., Upper Saddle River, NJ (2001)
13. Brandstadt, A., Le, V.B., Spinrad, J.P.: Graph classes: a survey. Society for Industrial and Applied Mathematics, Philadelphia, PA, USA (1999)
14. Dahlhaus, E., Gustedt, J., McConnell, R.M.: Efficient and practical modular decomposition. In: SODA '97: Proceedings of the eighth annual ACM-SIAM symposium on Discrete algorithms, Philadelphia, PA, USA, Society for Industrial and Applied Mathematics (1997) 26–35
15. Bandelt, H., Mulder, H.: Distance-hereditary graphs. J. Comb. Theory Ser. B **41** (1986) 182–208
16. Hammer, P.L., Maffray, F.: Completely separable graphs. Discrete Appl. Math. **27** (1990) 85–99

17. D'Atri, A., Moscarini, M.: Distance-hereditary graphs, steiner trees, and connected domination. SIAM J. Comput. **17** (1988) 521–538
18. Tedder, M.: An optimal algorithm recognizing distance-hereditary graphs under a sequence of edge deletions. Master's thesis, University of Toronto (2006)
19. Tedder, M.: An optimal, edges-only fully-dynamic algorithm recognizing distance-hereditary graphs. In preparation (2006)

A Search Algorithm for the Maximal Attractor of a Cellular Automaton

Enrico Formenti[1] and Petr Kůrka[1,2]

[1] Laboratoire I3S, Université de Nice Sophia Antipolis,
2000, route des Lucioles, Les Algorithmes - bât Euclide B, BP 121,
06903 Sophia Antipolis - Cedex, France
[2] Center for Theoretical Study, Charles University in Prague,
Jilská 1, CZ-11000 Praha 1, Czechia

Abstract. We present an algorithm that finds the maximal attractor (limit set) of those cellular automata whose maximal attractor is a sofic subshift.

Keywords: cellular automata, limit sets, sofic subshifts.

1   Introduction

The maximal attractor (limit set) is one of its most intensively studied structures in cellular automata theory [1,2,3]. It is the intersection of all forward images of the state space. A cellular automaton is called stable, if the maximal attractor is attained in a finite number of forward images. In this case, the maximal attractor is a sofic subshift, and its structure can be obtained by an algorithm. However, the problem whether a cellular automaton is stable is undecidable (Culik, Pachl and Yu [4]), the set of stable cellular automata being only recursively enumerable.

The maximal attractor of an unstable cellular automaton may but need not be sofic. In fact, its language complexity may be arbitrarily high. The only constraint is that the complement of its language is recursively enumerable (Culik, Hurd and Yu [1]). There are other constraints of dynamical nature: The maximal attractor contains a homogenous configuration $i.e.$ of the form $a^{\mathbb{Z}}$ (see Hurley [5]) and it is chain-mixing for the shift (see Formenti and Kůrka [6]).

To determine the maximal attractor of a given cellular automaton is not always a simple task. One can estimate the maximal attractor from above by the forward images of the state space, but it is undecidable whether this procedure ever ends. In the present paper we propose a method for the construction of the maximal attractor from bellow. The key role in this procedure is played by signal subshifts (see Kůrka [7]) which are infinite subshifts consisting of weakly periodic configurations of a given period (p,q), $i.e.$, satisfying $F^q \sigma^p(x) = x$. Signal subshifts are of finite type and can be easily computed. All signal subshifts are contained in the maximal attractor.

Our algorithm works for some cellular automata with a finite number of signal subshifts. From them, we build their join - a larger subshift which is still

W. Thomas and P. Weil (Eds.): STACS 2007, LNCS 4393, pp. 356–366, 2007.

included in the maximal attractor. Then, we construct the forward images of the join, obtaining an increasing sequence of subshifts included in the maximal attractor. If this procedure stops in finite time, we test a special condition of decreasing preimages. A subshift has decreasing preimages, if the preimage of any word not in the language contains a shorter word which is not in the language. This condition is decidable, and a subshift which satifies it already includes whole maximal attractor. While our algorithm is not (and cannot be) universal, it works for a large class of cellular automata.

2   Subshifts and Cellular Automata

For a finite alphabet A, denote by $A^* := \bigcup_{n \geq 0} A^n$ the set of words over A. The length of a word $u = u_0 \ldots u_{n-1} \in A^n$ is denoted by $|u| := n$. The word of zero length is λ. We say that $u \in A^*$ is a subword of $v \in A^*$ ($u \sqsubseteq v$) if there exists k such that $v_{k+i} = u_i$ for all $i < |u|$. We denote by $u_{[i,j)} = u_i \ldots u_{j-1}$ and $u_{[i,j]} = u_i \ldots u_j$ subwords of u associated to intervals. We denote by $A^{\mathbb{Z}}$ the space of A-**configurations**, or doubly-infinite sequences of letters of A equipped with the metric $d(x,y) := 2^{-n}$, where $n = \min\{i > 0 : x_i \neq y_i \text{ or } x_{-i} \neq y_{-i}\}$.

The **shift map** $\sigma : A^{\mathbb{Z}} \to A^{\mathbb{Z}}$ is defined by $\sigma(x)_i := x_{i+1}$. For any nonzero $u \in A^*$ we have a σ-periodic configuration $u^{\mathbb{Z}} \in A^{\mathbb{Z}}$ defined by $(u^{\mathbb{Z}})_i = u_{|i| \bmod |u|}$ for $i \in \mathbb{Z}$. A **subshift** is a nonempty subset $\Sigma \subseteq A^{\mathbb{Z}}$, which is closed and strongly σ-invariant, i.e., $\sigma(\Sigma) = \Sigma$.

For a subshift Σ there exists a set $D \subseteq A^*$ of forbidden words such that $\Sigma = \Sigma_D := \{x \in A^{\mathbb{Z}} : \forall u \sqsubseteq x, u \notin D\}$. A subshift is uniquely determined by its **language**

$$\mathcal{L}(\Sigma) := \bigcup_{n \geq 0} \mathcal{L}^n(\Sigma), \quad \text{where} \quad \mathcal{L}^n(\Sigma) := \{u \in A^n : \exists x \in \Sigma, u \sqsubseteq x\}.$$

A subshift $\Sigma \subseteq A^{\mathbb{Z}}$ is **transitive**, if for any words $u, v \in \mathcal{L}(\Sigma)$ there exists $w \in A^*$ such that $uwv \in \mathcal{L}(\Sigma)$.

If $x \in A^{\mathbb{Z}}$ is a configuration and $I \subseteq \mathbb{Z}$ is an interval, denote by $x_{|I} : I \to A$ the restriction of x to I. The extended language of Σ is

$$\tilde{\mathcal{L}}(\Sigma) = \{x_{|I} : x \in \Sigma, \quad I \subseteq \mathbb{Z} \text{ is an interval}\}.$$

A cellular automaton is a continuous map $F : A^{\mathbb{Z}} \to A^{\mathbb{Z}}$ which commutes with the shift map, i.e., $F\sigma = \sigma F$. For a cellular automaton F there exists a **local rule** $f : A^{d+1} \to A$ such that $F(x)_i = f(x_{[i-m,i-m+d]})$ for some **memory** $m \in \mathbb{Z}$ and **diameter** $d \geq 0$. The local rule can be extended to a map $f : A^* \to A^*$ by $f(u)_i := f(u_{[i,i+d]})$ for $0 \leq i < |u| - d$. The maximal attractor (limit set) of a cellular automaton F is $\Omega_F = \bigcap_{n \geq 0} F^n(A^{\mathbb{Z}})$.

3   Sofic Subshifts

A subshift $\Sigma \subseteq A^{\mathbb{Z}}$ is **sofic** if its language $\mathcal{L}(\Sigma)$ is regular. Sofic subshifts are usually described by labelled graphs. A **labelled graph** over an alphabet A is a structure $G = (V, E, s, t, l)$, where V is a finite set of vertices, E is a finite set of edges, $s, t : E \to V$ are the **source** and **target maps**, and $l : E \to A$ is a **labelling function**. A finite or infinite word $w \in E^* \cup E^{\mathbb{Z}}$ is a **path** in G if $t(w_i) = s(w_{i+1})$ for all i. The source and target of a finite path $w \in E^n$ are $s(w) := s(w_0)$, $t(w) := t(w_{n-1})$. The **label** of a path is defined by $l(w)_i := l(w_i)$. A subshift Σ is sofic if there exists a labelled graph G such that $\Sigma = \Sigma_G$ is the set of labels of all doubly infinite paths in G. In this case we say that G is a **presentation** of Σ (see e.g. Lind and Marcus [8], or Kitchens [9]). Among all presentations of a sofic subshift there exists a minimal one which corresponds to the minimal deterministic finite automaton which recognizes its language.

A labelled graph $G = (V, E, s, t, l)$ is **connected** if for any two vertices $q, r \in V$ there exists a path $w \in E^*$ from q to r. A **subgraph** of a graph G is a graph $G' = (V', E', s', t', l')$, such that $V' \subseteq V$, $E' = \{e \in E : s(e) \in V' \,\&\, t(e) \in V'\}$, and s', t', l' coincide respectively with s, t, l on E'. A **connected component** of G is a subgraph of G which is connected and maximal with this property. The subshift of a connected graph is transitive. Conversely, every transitive sofic subshift $\Sigma \subseteq A^{\mathbb{Z}}$ has a connected presentation.

A subshift Σ is of **finite type** (SFT), if $\Sigma = \Sigma_D$ for some finite set $D \subseteq A^*$ of forbidden words. A forbidden word is minimal if it does not contain another forbidden words as factor. The order $\mathfrak{o}(\Sigma)$ of a SFT is the length of its longest minimal forbidden word. A configuration $x \in A^{\mathbb{Z}}$ belongs to Σ iff $x_{[i, i+\mathfrak{o}(\Sigma))} \in \mathcal{L}(\Sigma)$ for all $i \in \mathbb{Z}$. Any SFT is sofic: if $p = \mathfrak{o}(\Sigma) - 1$, the **canonical graph** $G = (V, E, s, t, l)$ of Σ is given by $V = \mathcal{L}^p(\Sigma)$, $E = \mathcal{L}^{p+1}(\Sigma)$, $s(u) = u_{[0,p)}$, $t(u) = u_{[1,p]}$ and $l(u) = u_p$.

We say that a labelled graph G is p**-distinguishing**, if for any two paths $v, w \in E^p$ with $t(v) = t(w)$ we have $l(v) = l(w)$. In this case there exist labelling functions $\nu : V \to A^p$ and $\pi : E \to A^{p+1}$. For $q \in V$ we have $\nu(q) = u$ iff there exists a path $v \in E^p$ such that $t(v) = q$ and $l(v) = u$. For $e \in E$ we have $\pi(e) = u$ iff there exists a path $w \in E^{p+1}$ such that $w_p = e$ and $l(w) = u$. Any sofic subshift has a p-distinguishing presentation for any $p > 0$. If $G = (V, E, s, t, l)$ is a presentation of Σ, we define a graph $G' = (V', E', s', t', l')$, where $V' \subseteq E^p$ is the set of paths of G of length p, $E' \subseteq E^{p+1}$ is the set of paths of G of length $p + 1$, s' and t' are the prefix and suffix maps and $l'(u) = l(u_p)$. Then G' is a p-distinguishing presentation of Σ.

Given two sofic subshifts $\Sigma_0, \Sigma_1 \subseteq A^{\mathbb{Z}}$, their union and intersection (provided non-empty) are sofic subshifts. Moreover there exists an algorithm which constructs a presentation of $\Sigma_0 \cup \Sigma_1$ and $\Sigma_0 \cap \Sigma_1$ from those of Σ_0 and Σ_1. It is also decidable whether $\Sigma_0 \subseteq \Sigma_1$. Given a labelled graph G it is decidable whether Σ_G is a SFT (see Lind and Marcus [8], page 94).

Proposition 1. *Let $\Sigma \subseteq A^{\mathbb{Z}}$ be a sofic subshift and $F : A^{\mathbb{Z}} \to A^{\mathbb{Z}}$ a cellular automaton with local rule $f : A^{d+1} \to A$. Then $F(\Sigma)$ and $F^{-1}(\Sigma)$ are sofic subshifts, and there exists an algorithm which constructs their graphs from the local rule f and a graph of Σ.*

Proof. Let $G = (V, E, s, t, l)$ be a presentation of Σ. Let V_0 be the set of paths of G of length d, and let E_0 be the set of paths of G of length $d+1$. define the source

and target maps by $s_0(u) = u_{[0,d)}$, $t_0(u) = u_{[1,d]}$. Then $G_0 = (V_0, E_0, s_0, t_0, f)$ is
a presentation of $F(\Sigma)$.
Set $E_1 = \{(e, u) \in E \times A^{d+1} : l(e) = f(u)\}$, and define s_1, t_1 by $s_1(e, u) =$
$(s(e), u_{[0,d)})$, $t_1(e, u) = (t(e), u_{[1,d]})$. Finally set $V_1 = s_1(E_1) \cup t_1(E_1) \subseteq V \times A^d$
and define the labelling function by $l_1(e, u) = u_d$. Then $G_1 = (V_1, E_1, s_1, t_1, l_1)$
is a presentation of $F^{-1}(\Sigma)$.

4   Join of Subshifts

Definition 1. *Given an integer $c \geq 0$, the c-join $\Sigma_0 \overset{c}{\vee} \Sigma_1$ of subshifts $\Sigma_0, \Sigma_1 \subseteq$
$A^{\mathbb{Z}}$ consists of all configurations $x \in A^{\mathbb{Z}}$ such that either $x \in \Sigma_0 \cup \Sigma_1$, or there
exist integers b, a such that $b - a \geq c$, $x_{(-\infty,b)} \in \tilde{\mathcal{L}}(\Sigma_0)$, and $x_{[a,\infty)} \in \tilde{\mathcal{L}}(\Sigma_1)$.*

Examples of joins of subshifts are given in Figure 4 and 5.

Proposition 2. *The c-join of two subshifts is a subshift and the operation of
c-join is associative. A configuration $x \in A^{\mathbb{Z}}$ belongs to $\Sigma_1 \overset{c}{\vee} \cdots \overset{c}{\vee} \Sigma_n$ iff there
exist integers $k > 0$, $1 \leq i_1 < i_2 < \cdots < i_k \leq n$, and intervals $I_1 = (a_1, b_1)$, $I_2 =$
$[a_2, b_2), \ldots, I_k = [a_k, b_k)$ such that $a_1 = -\infty$, $b_k = \infty$, $a_j < a_{j+1}$, $b_j < b_{j+1}$,
$b_j - a_{j+1} \geq c$, and $x_{|I_j} \in \tilde{\mathcal{L}}(\Sigma_{i_j})$.*

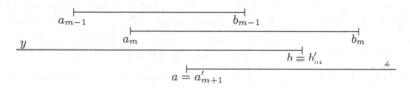

Fig. 1. Associativity of the join

Proof. It is clear that the c-join of two subshifts is a subshift. We prove by
induction the formula for $\Sigma_1 \overset{c}{\vee} \cdots \overset{c}{\vee} \Sigma_n$. Let $x \in (\Sigma_1 \overset{c}{\vee} \cdots \overset{c}{\vee} \Sigma_{n-1}) \overset{c}{\vee} \Sigma_n$, so
there exists $y \in \Sigma_1 \overset{c}{\vee} \cdots \overset{c}{\vee} \Sigma_{n-1}$, $z \in \Sigma_n$ and integers a, b such that $x_{(-\infty,b)} =$
$y_{(-\infty,b)}$, $x_{[a,\infty)} = z_{[a,\infty)}$ and $b - a \geq c$. By the induction hypothesis there exist
integers k and intervals $I_1, \ldots I_k$ such that $y_{|I_j} \in \tilde{\mathcal{L}}(\Sigma_{i_j})$. Let m be the unique
index such that $b_{m-1} < b \leq b_m$ (see Figure 1). Set $i'_j := i_j$ for $j \leq m$ and
$i'_{m+1} = n$. For $k \leq m + 1$ define intervals $I'_j := [a'_j, b'_j)$ by

$$a'_j := \begin{cases} a_j & \text{for } j \leq m \\ \max\{a, a_m + 1\} & \text{for } j = m + 1 \end{cases}, \quad b'_j := \begin{cases} b_j & \text{for } j < m \\ b & \text{for } j = m \\ \infty & \text{for } j = m + 1 \end{cases}$$

Then clearly $x_{|I'_j} \in \tilde{\mathcal{L}}(\Sigma_{i'_j})$ and $b'_j - a'_{j+1} = b_j - a_{j+1} \geq c$ for $j < m$. If $a'_{m+1} =$
$a_m + 1$, then $b'_m - a'_{m+1} = b - a_m - 1 \geq b_{m-1} - a_m \geq c$. If $a'_{m+1} = a$, then
$b'_m - a'_{m+1} = b - a \geq c$. Similarly it can be shown that the formula holds for
$x \in \Sigma_1 \overset{c}{\vee} (\Sigma_2 \overset{c}{\vee} \cdots \overset{c}{\vee} \Sigma_n)$ provided it holds for $z \in \Sigma_2 \overset{c}{\vee} \cdots \overset{c}{\vee} \Sigma_n$. This proves
associativity.   □

Proposition 3. *Let $\Sigma_0, \Sigma_1 \subseteq A^{\mathbb{Z}}$ be sofic subshifts and $c \geq 0$. Then $\Sigma_0 \overset{c}{\vee} \Sigma_1$ is a sofic subshift and there exists an algorithm which constructs its presentation from those of Σ_i.*

Proof. Let $G_i = (V_i, E_i, s_i, t_i, l_i)$ be c-distinguishing presentations of Σ_i, and assume that $V_0 \cap V_1 = \emptyset$ and $E_0 \cap E_1 = \emptyset$. We have labelling functions $\pi_i : E_i \to A^{c+1}$. Set $V = V_0 \cup V_1$,

$$E = E_0 \cup E_1 \cup \{(e_0, e_1) \in E_0 \times E_1 : \pi_0(e_0) = \pi_1(e_1)\}.$$

The source, target and label maps extend s_i, t_i, l_i. For the new edges we have $s(e_0, e_1) = s_0(e_0)$, $t(e_0, e_1) = t_1(e_1)$, $l(e_0, e_1) = l_0(e_0) = l_1(e_1)$. Then $\Sigma_G = \Sigma_0 \overset{c}{\vee} \Sigma_1$. $\qquad\square$

5   Signal Subshifts

Definition 2. *Let $F : A^{\mathbb{Z}} \to A^{\mathbb{Z}}$ be a cellular automaton. A configuration $x \in A^{\mathbb{Z}}$ is **weakly periodic**, if $F^q \sigma^p(x) = x$ for some $q > 0$ and $p \in \mathbb{Z}$. We call (p, q) the **period** of x and p/q its speed. Let $\Sigma_{(p,q)} := \{x \in A^{\mathbb{Z}} : F^q \sigma^p(x) = x\}$ be the set of all weakly periodic configurations with period (p, q). A **signal subshift** is any infinite $\Sigma_{(p,q)}$.*

Remark that $\Sigma_{(p,q)}$ is closed and σ-invariant, so it is a subshift provided it is nonempty. Moreover, $\Sigma_{(p,q)}$ is F-invariant and $F : \Sigma_{(p,q)} \to \Sigma_{(p,q)}$ is bijective, so $\Sigma_{(p,q)} \subseteq \Omega_F$. If $\Sigma_{(p,q)}$ is finite, it consists only of σ-periodic configurations. Figures 4 and 5 show some examples of signal subshifts.

Proposition 4. *Let $F : A^{\mathbb{Z}} \to A^{\mathbb{Z}}$ be a cellular automaton with diameter d and memory m, so $F(x)_i = f(x_{[i-m, i-m+d]})$.*

(1) If $\Sigma_{(p,q)}$ is nonempty, then it is a subshift of finite type.
(2) If $\Sigma_{(p,q)}$ is infinite, then $m - d \leq p/q \leq m$.
(3) If $p_0/q_0 < p_1/q_1$, then $\Sigma_{(p_0,q_0)} \cap \Sigma_{(p_1,q_1)} \subseteq \{x \in A^{\mathbb{Z}} : \sigma^p(x) = x\}$, where $p = q(\frac{p_1}{q_1} - \frac{p_0}{q_0})$ and $q = \mathrm{lcm}(q_0, q_1)$ (the least common multiple).

Proof. (1) Set $D := \{u \in A^{dq+1} : f^q(u) \neq u_{mq-p}\}$. Then $\Sigma_{(p,q)} = \Sigma_D$.

(2) If $x \in \Sigma_{(p,q)}$, then $x_i = f^q(x_{[i+p-mq, i+p-mq+dq]})$. If $p - mq + dq < 0$, then there exists a function $g : A^{mq-p} \to A^{mq-p}$ such that $x_{[i+p-mq+1, i]} = g(x_{[i+p-mq, i-1]})$ for every $i \in \mathbb{Z}$. This is possible only if x is σ-periodic. Moreover, the period of x is bounded, so $\Sigma_{(p,q)}$ is finite. The proof is similar for $p > mq$.

(3) Set $p_2 = qp_0/q_0$, $p_3 = qp_1/q_1$. If $x \in \Sigma_{(p_0,q_0)} \cap \Sigma_{(p_1,q_1)}$, then $\sigma^{-p_2}(x) = F^q(x) = \sigma^{-p_3}(x)$, so $\sigma^{p_2-p_3}(x) = x$. $\qquad\square$

A positively expansive CA[1] has no signal subshifts (see [7] for a proof). The shift cellular automaton $\sigma : A^{\mathbb{Z}} \to A^{\mathbb{Z}}$ has the unique signal subshift $\Sigma_{(-1,1)} = A^{\mathbb{Z}}$. A cellular automaton with infinitely many signal subshifts with infinitely many speeds has been constructed in [7].

---

[1] A CA f is positively expansive iff there exists $\varepsilon > 0$ such that for all $x, y \in A^{\mathbb{Z}}$, $x \neq y$ implies that there exists an integer n such that $d(f^n(x), f^n(y)) > \varepsilon$.

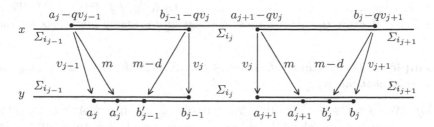

Fig. 2. Preimage of a configuration in the join

Theorem 5. *Consider a cellular automaton $F : A^{\mathbb{Z}} \to A^{\mathbb{Z}}$ and the signal sub-shifts $\Sigma_{(p_1,q_1)}, \ldots, \Sigma_{(p_n,q_n)}$ with decreasing speeds, i.e., $p_i/q_i > p_j/q_j$ for $i < j$. Set $q := \mathrm{lcm}\{q_1, \ldots q_n\}$ (the least common multiple). There exists $c \geq 0$ such that for $\Sigma := \Sigma_{(p_1,q_1)} \overset{c}{\vee} \cdots \overset{c}{\vee} \Sigma_{(p_n,q_n)}$ we have $\Sigma \subseteq F^q(\Sigma)$ and therefore $\Sigma \subseteq \Omega_F$.*

Proof. Let m be the memory of F and d its diameter. If $i < j$ then $m - d \leq \frac{p_j}{q_j} < \frac{p_i}{q_i} \leq m$, so $0 < \frac{p_i}{q_i} - \frac{p_j}{q_j} \leq d$. Set

$$c := \max\left\{ q\left(\frac{p_j}{q_j} - \frac{p_i}{q_i} + d\right) : i < j \ \& \ \Sigma_i \cap \Sigma_j \neq \emptyset \right\} \geq 0$$

Let $y \in \Sigma$, $1 \leq i_1 < i_2 \cdots < i_k \leq n$ and let $I_1 = (a_1, b_1], \ldots, I_k = [a_k, b_k)$ be intervals such that the restrictions $y_{|I_j}$ belong to $\tilde{\mathcal{L}}(\Sigma_{(p_{i_j}, q_{i_j})})$. Let $v_j := p_{i_j}/q_{i_j}$ be the speed of the i_j-th signal. The configurations in $\Sigma_{i_j} \cap \Sigma_{i_{j+1}}$ are σ-periodic with period $n_j := q(v_j - v_{j+1})$. Let u be the prefix of $y_{|I_j}$ of length n_{j-1} and let v be the suffix of $y_{|I_j}$ of length n_j. Since $c \geq n_{j-1}$ and $c \geq n_j$, we get $y^{(j)} = u^{\mathbb{N}}(y_{|I_j})v^{\mathbb{N}} \in \Sigma_{(p_{i_j}, q_{i_j})}$ and $F^q \sigma^{qv_j}(y^{(j)}) = y^{(j)}$. Set $J_j = [a_j - qv_{j-1}, b_j - qv_{j+1})$. For the endpoints of these intervals we get $(b_j - qv_{j+1}) - (a_{j+1} - qv_j) = b_j - a_{j+1} + qn_j \geq c$. There exists a unique configuration x such that $x_{|J_j} = \sigma^{qv_j}(y^{(j)})_{|J_j}$. We show $F^q(x) = y$. Set $a'_j := a_j + q(m - v_{j-1})$, $b'_j := b_j + q(m - d - v_{j+1})$ (see Figure 2). For $a'_j \leq k \leq b'_j$ we have

$$F^q(x)_k = f^q(x_{[k-qm, k-qm+qd]}) = f^q(\sigma^{qv_j}(y^{(j)})_{[k-qm, k-qm+qd]})$$
$$= F^q \sigma^{qv_j}(y^{(j)})_k = (y^{(j)})_k = y_k$$

We have $b'_j - a'_{j+1} = b_{j-1} - a_j - q(v_{j+1} - v_j + d) \geq c - c = 0$, so the intervals $[a'_j, b'_j)$ cover whole $\mathbb{Z}$, and $F^q(x) = y$. Thus $\Sigma \subseteq F^q(\Sigma)$. It follows that for any $k > 0$ we have $\Sigma \subseteq F^{kq}(\Sigma) \subseteq F^{kq}(A^{\mathbb{Z}})$, so $\Sigma \subseteq \Omega_F$. $\qquad\square$

6 Decreasing Preimages

Definition 3. *Let $f : A^{d+1} \to A$ be a local function of a cellular automaton. We say that a subshift $\Sigma \subseteq A^{\mathbb{Z}}$ has m-**decreasing preimages**, if for each $u \in A^* \setminus \mathcal{L}(\Sigma)$, each $v \in f^{-m}(u)$ contains as a subword a word $w \in A^* \setminus \mathcal{L}(\Sigma)$*

such that $|w| < |u|$ *(the condition is satisfied trivially if* $f^{-m}(u) = \emptyset$*). We say that* Σ *has* **decreasing preimages**, *if it has m-decreasing preimages for some* $m > 0$.

Example 1. *The maximal attractor of the ECA128* $F(x)_i = x_{i-1}x_ix_{i+1}$ *has decreasing preimages.*

Proof. We have $\Omega_F = \{x \in A^{\mathbb{Z}} : \forall n > 0, 10^n1 \not\sqsubseteq x\}$. If $u \in A^* \setminus \mathcal{L}(\Omega_F)$, then it contains 10^n1 as a subword, and each preimage v of u contains $10^{n-2}1$ as a subword. $\qquad\square$

Example 2. *There exists a cellular automaton such that* $\Omega_F(A^{\mathbb{Z}})$ *does not have decreasing preimages.*

```
3 0 3 0 0 3 0 0 0 3 1 1 2 3 0 0 0 0 3 0 1 1 2 3 1 1 1 1 3 2 1 1 0 3
3 1 3 0 1 3 0 0 1 3 1 2 0 3 0 0 0 1 3 0 1 2 0 3 1 1 1 2 3 2 1 1 1 3
3 2 3 0 2 3 0 0 2 3 2 0 1 3 0 0 0 2 3 0 2 0 1 3 1 1 2 0 3 2 1 1 2 3
3 2 3 1 0 3 0 1 0 3 2 0 2 3 0 0 1 0 3 1 0 0 2 3 1 2 0 1 3 2 1 2 0 3
3 2 3 1 1 3 0 1 1 3 2 1 0 3 0 0 1 1 3 1 0 1 0 3 2 0 0 2 3 2 2 0 1 3
3 2 3 1 2 3 0 1 2 3 2 1 1 3 0 0 1 2 3 1 0 1 1 3 2 0 1 0 3 2 2 0 2 3
3 2 3 2 0 3 0 2 0 3 2 1 2 3 0 0 2 0 3 1 0 1 2 3 2 0 1 1 3 2 2 1 0 3
3 2 3 2 1 3 1 0 1 3 2 2 0 3 0 1 0 1 3 1 0 2 0 3 2 0 1 2 3 2 2 1 1 3
3 2 3 2 2 3 1 0 2 3 2 2 1 3 0 1 0 2 3 1 1 0 1 3 2 0 2 0 3 2 2 1 2 3
3 2 3 2 2 3 1 1 0 3 2 2 2 3 0 1 1 0 3 1 1 0 2 3 2 1 0 1 3 2 2 2 0 3
3 2 3 2 2 3 1 1 1 3 2 2 2 3 0 1 1 1 3 1 1 1 0 3 2 1 0 2 3 2 2 2 1 3
3 2 3 2 2 3 1 1 2 3 2 2 2 3 0 1 1 2 3 1 1 1 1 3 2 1 1 0 3 2 2 2 2 3
```

Fig. 3. Nondecreasing preimages

Proof. The alphabet is $A = \{0, 1, 2, 3\}$, $d = 2$, $m = -1$, and the transition table $f : A^3 \to A$ is given by

$$x02 : 1, \quad x03 : 1, \quad x12 : 2, \quad x13 : 2, \quad 02x : 0, \quad 12x : 0,$$

where $x \in A$ and the first applicable rule is used, otherwise the letter is unchanged. The letter 3 is stationary, and the binary value of a word $u \in \{0, 1, 2\}^*$ between two threes increases by one every two time steps out of three. Let x be a configuration such that $x_{(-\infty,0]} = 0^{\mathbb{N}}3$. Then for each n, the sequence $f^i(x)_{[-n,0]}$ is eventually periodic with preperiod $n - 1$ and period $p_n = 3 \cdot 2^{n-1}$, so $F^{n-1+p_n}(x)_{[-n,0]} = F^{n-1}(x)_{[-n,0]}$ (see Figure 3). It follows that $F^i(x)_{[-n,0]} \in \mathcal{L}(\Omega_F)$ for $i \geq n-1$. On the other hand, if $u \in \{0, 1, 2\}^n \setminus \{2^n\}$, then $3u3 \notin \mathcal{L}(\Omega_F)$. In particular, if $n > 1$ then no word $3F^i(x)_{[-n,0]}$ belongs to $\mathcal{L}(\Omega_F)$. Thus $u = 3F^{n-1}(x)_{[-n,0]} \notin \mathcal{L}(\Omega_F)$, but for $m < p_n$ we have

$$v = 3^{m+1}F^{n-1+p_n-m}(x)_{[-n,0]}3^m \in f^{-m}(u)$$

and each subword of v of length $|u| = n + 2$ belongs to $\mathcal{L}(\Omega_F)$. $\qquad\square$

Proposition 6. *If a subshift $\Sigma \subseteq A^{\mathbb{Z}}$ has decreasing preimages, then $\Omega_F \subseteq \Sigma$.*

Proof. By the assumption, if $u \in A^* \backslash \mathcal{L}(\Sigma)$ and $u \in \mathcal{L}(\Omega_F)$, then each $v \in f^{-m|u|}$ contains as a subword $w \in A^* \backslash \mathcal{L}(\Sigma)$ with $|w| = 0$. This is a contradiction, since $w = \lambda \in \mathcal{L}(\Sigma)$. Thus $f^{-m|u|}(u)$ is empty and $u \notin \mathcal{L}(\Omega_F)$. Thus $\mathcal{L}(\Omega_F) \subseteq \mathcal{L}(\Sigma)$ and $\Omega_F \subseteq \Sigma$. □

Proposition 7. *There exists an algorithm, which decides whether for a given cellular automaton and given $m > 0$, a given sofic subshift has m-decreasing preimages.*

Proof. By the assumption both $\mathcal{L}(\Sigma)$ and $\mathcal{L}(F^{-m}(\Sigma))$ are regular languages. It follows that the language

$$L = \{v \in A^* : f^m(v) \notin \mathcal{L}(\Sigma), \forall k \le md + 1, v_{[k,k+|v|-md-1)} \in \mathcal{L}(\Sigma)\}$$

is regular too and we can construct its recognizing finite automaton from that of $\mathcal{L}(\Sigma)$. Since L is empty iff Σ has m-decreasing f-preimages, we get the deciding procedure. □

Corollary 8. *Let F be a cellular automaton, let $\Sigma_1, \ldots, \Sigma_n$ be signal subshifts with decreasing speeds, and set $q := \operatorname{lcm}(q_1, \ldots, q_n)$. If $F^{kq}(\Sigma_1 \overset{c}{\vee} \cdots \overset{c}{\vee} \Sigma_n)$ has decreasing preimages for some k, c, then $\Omega_F = F^{kq}(\Sigma_1 \overset{c}{\vee} \cdots \overset{c}{\vee} \Sigma_n)$.*

Proposition 9. *The set of cellular automata whose maximal attractor is a sofic subshift with decreasing preimages is recursively enumerable.*

Proof. Generate successively all sofic subshifts, verify whether they are strongly invariant and whether they have decreasing preimages. □

While the algorithm based on Proposition 9 is rather time-consuming, and would not give practical results, there is a faster algorithm based on signal subshifts and their join. Given a local rule f with diameter d and memory m, consider the procedure Omega(f,m,n) which performs the following steps:

procedure Omega(f,m,n)

1. Construct all signal subshifts with periods (p_i, q_i) such that $q_i \le n$, and $(m - d)q_i \le p_i \le mq_i$. Denote by q the least common multiple of q_i.
2. Order the signal subshifts obtained in step 1 by decreasing speeds and construct their c-join Σ, where c is given in the proof of Theorem 5.
3. Construct $F^q(\Sigma), F^{2q}(\Sigma), \ldots$ and test whether $F^{kq}(\Sigma) = F^{(k+1)q}(\Sigma)$.
4. If step 3 ends with $F^{kq}(\Sigma) = F^{(k+1)q}(\Sigma)$, verify whether $F^{kq}(\Sigma)$ has decreasing preimages. If so, $\Omega_F = F^{kq}(\Sigma)$ has been found.

The procedure Omega(f,m,n) may fail to give a result if it repeats indefinitely step 3, or if step 4 gives the negative result. To get a procedure not depending on n, one can perform concurrently procedures Omega(f,m,1), Omega(f,m,2)..., so that by time $n(n+1)/2$, n steps of Omega(f,m,1) have been performed, $n - 1$ steps of Omega(f,m,2), etc. The algorithm ends whenever one of the procedures

`Omega(f,m,n)` stops, otherwise it runs indefinitely. The implementation of this algorithm is currently under progress.

7 Examples

Example 3 (ECA 128). *The product rule* $F(x)_i = x_{i-1}x_ix_{i+1}$.

We have two (nontransitive) signal subshifts (see Figure 4)

$$\Sigma_{(1,1)} = \{x \in A^{\mathbb{Z}} : 10 \not\sqsubseteq x\}, \quad \Sigma_{(-1,1)} = \{x \in A^{\mathbb{Z}} : 01 \not\sqsubseteq x\}.$$

Their intersection is the finite subshift $\{0^{\mathbb{Z}}, 1^{\mathbb{Z}}\}$. The maximal attractor is constructed in Figure 4. In the first row, 1-distinguishing presentations for $\Sigma_{(1,1)}$ and $\Sigma_{(-1,1)}$ are constructed. Their join is constructed in the second row. In the third row, the minimal presentation of $\Sigma_{(1,1)} \overset{1}{\vee} \Sigma_{(-1,1)}$ is given. As it has decreasing preimages, it equals Ω_F.

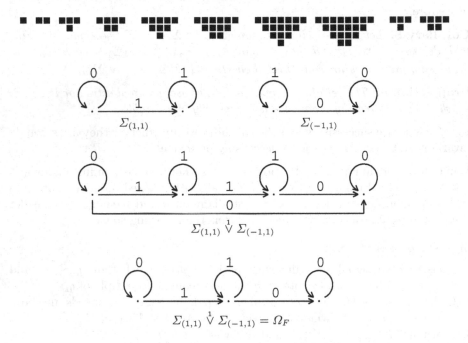

Fig. 4. ECA 128 and its signal subshifts

Example 4 (ECA 184). *The traffic rule* $F(x)_i = 1$ *iff* $x_{[i-1,i]} = 10$ *or* $x_{[i,i+1]} = 11$.

We have two signal subshifts (see Figure 5) representing holes and jams

$$\Sigma_{(1,1)} = \{x \in A^{\mathbb{Z}} : 11 \not\sqsubseteq x\} \cup \{1^{\mathbb{Z}}\}$$
$$\Sigma_{(-1,1)} = \{x \in A^{\mathbb{Z}} : 00 \not\sqsubseteq x\} \cup \{0^{\mathbb{Z}}\}.$$

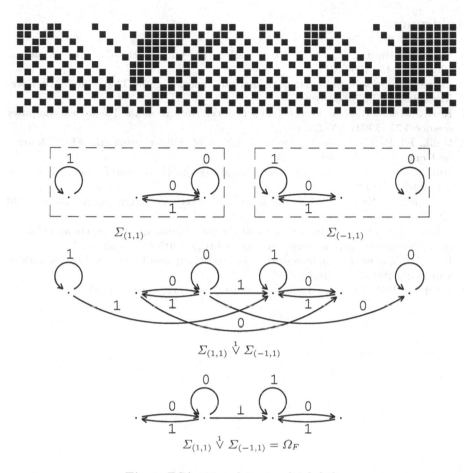

Fig. 5. ECA 184 and its signal subshifts

Their intersection is the finite subshift $\{0^{\mathbb{Z}}, 1^{\mathbb{Z}}, (01)^{\mathbb{Z}}, (10)^{\mathbb{Z}}\}$. There is one more (nontransitive) signal subshift $\Sigma_{(0,1)} = \{x \in A^{\mathbb{Z}} : \forall i < j, x_i \leq x_j\}$. The maximal attractor is constructed in Figure 5. In the first row, 1-distinguishing presentations for $\Sigma_{(1,1)}$ and $\Sigma_{(-1,1)}$ are constructed. Their join is constructed in the second row. In the third row, the minimal presentation of $\Sigma_{(1,1)} \overset{1}{\vee} \Sigma_{(-1,1)}$ is given. As it has decreasing preimages, it equals Ω_F.

Acknowledgments

The research was partially supported by the Research Program CTS MSM 0021620845.

References

1. Culik, K., Hurd, L.P., Yu, S.: Computation theoretic aspects of cellular automata. Physica D **45** (1990) 357–378
2. Maass, A.: On sofic limit sets of cellular automata. Ergodic Theory and Dynamical Systems **15** (1995) 663–684
3. Kari, J.: Rice's theorem for the limit sets of cellular automata. Theoretical computer science **127** (1994) 229–254
4. Culik, K., Pachl, J., Yu, S.: On the limit set of cellular automata. SIAM Journal on Computing **18** (1989) 831–842
5. Hurley, M.: Attractors in cellular automata. Ergodic Theory and Dynamical Systems **10** (1990) 131–140
6. Formenti, E., Kůrka, P.: Subshift attractors of cellular automata. Nonlinearity **20** (2007) 1–13
7. Kůrka, P.: On the measure attractor of a cellular automaton. Discrete and Continuous Dynamical Systems **Supplement volume 2005** (2005) 524–535
8. Lind, D., Marcus, B.: An introduction to symbolic dynamics and coding. Cambridge University Press, Cambridge (1995)
9. Kitchens, B.P.: Symbolic Dynamics. Springer-Verlag, Berlin (1998)

Universal Tilings

Grégory Lafitte[1] and Michael Weiss[2],[*]

[1] Laboratoire d'Informatique Fondamentale de Marseille (LIF), CNRS – Université de Provence, 39, rue Joliot-Curie, F-13453 Marseille Cedex 13, France
[2] Centre Universitaire d'Informatique, Université de Genève, 24, rue Général Dufour, 1211 Genève 4, Switzerland

Abstract. Wang tiles are unit size squares with colored edges. To know if a given finite set of Wang tiles can tile the plane while respecting colors on edges is undecidable. Berger's proof of this result shows the equivalence between tilings and Turing machines and thus tilings can be seen as a computing model. We thus have tilings that are Turing-universal, but there lacks a proper notion of universality for tilings. In this paper, we introduce natural notions of universality and completeness for tilings. We construct some universal tilings and try to make a first hierarchy of tile sets with a universality criteria.

1 Introduction

Tilings were first introduced by Wang [Wan01]. A tile is a unit size square with colored edges. Two tiles can be assembled if their common edge has the same color. A finite set of tiles is called a tile set. To tile consists of assembling tiles from a tile set on the grid $\mathbb{Z}^2$.

Wang was the first to conjecture that if a tile set tiles the plane, then it tiles it in a periodic way. Another famous problem is to know whether a tile set tiles the entire plane or not. It is called the *domino problem*. Berger proved the undecidability of the domino problem by constructing an aperiodic set of tiles, *i.e.*, a tile set that can generate only non-periodic tilings [Ber66]. Simplified proofs can be found in [Rob71] and later [AD96]. As a corollary, Berger's result shows that Wang's conjecture is false. The main argument of this proof was to simulate the behaviour of a given Turing machine with a tile set, in the sense that the Turing machine M stops on an instance ω if and only if the tile set $\tau_{\langle M, \omega \rangle}$ does not tile the plane. Hanf and later Myers [Mye74, Han74] have strengthened this and constructed a tile set that has only non-recursive tilings.

From this, we have that there exists tile sets that can generate only non-periodic tilings of the plane, and others, that can generate only non-recursive tilings of the plane. But in all those cases, Durand [Dur99] proved that if a tile set tiles the plane, then it can tile the plane in a quasiperiodic way, *i.e.*, a tiling where each pattern appears regularly along the tiling.

---

[*] This author has been supported by the FNS grant 200020-105515.

The core main result from Berger's theorem is that tilings are Turing equivalent and so, there is a notion of computability for tilings. The tilings' computability can be studied from different points of view. One of them is universality. A universal Turing machine is a machine that can simulate all other Turing machines. We have to move away from Turing universality and see more specifically how can universality be defined for tilings. Asking the question of universality for tilings is equivalent to asking the question of how a tiling computes because we expect from a universal tiling to be able to give back the process of computation of each tiling. So, how can a tiling simulate another tiling?

In order to answer our question, we introduce different notions to tackle the search for natural universality. The main thing about tilings' computability consists in the way the tiles are assembled to tile the plane. So, we can see a given tiling T from different scales. The lowest scale is the tiling. By partitioning a given tiling into rectangles of same size, we obtain another tiling, where the tiles are the rectangular patterns. It is the tiling T seen from a higher scale. By this principle, we define strong reductions and weak reductions. By those reductions, we reach our goal : we have a notion of simulation.

We are now able to define universality and completeness for tilings. Since we have two kinds of reductions (*weak and strong*) and that a tiling can be universal for all the tilings (*dense*), or just for one tiling for each tile set (*sparse*), then we have four kinds of universality.

The main goal of this paper is to show the existence or the non-existence of the different universality notions. We will construct a complete tile set, *i.e.*, a tile set such that for each tiling P, our complete tile set can generate a tiling Q with $P \trianglelefteq Q$. We prove that a tile set is complete if and only if it generates a universal weak tiling.

The main result is to construct a strong universal tiling that can simulate, for each tile set τ, a countable infinity of tilings from τ. That is the strongest result we can obtain, because having a strongly dense universal tiling, *i.e.*, a tiling that simulates all tilings, is impossible, because there is a countable set of reductions but an uncountable set of tilings. Those results yield a classification on tile sets that is actually a hierarchy.

In the first part, we introduce the different notions used along the paper (pattern sets, reductions, completeness, universalities) and prove some obvious results from those definitions. The second part concentrates on completeness, by relating it to universality, and by constructing our first complete tile set. The last part explains universality, by constructing weak and strong universal tilings, and by giving some results following from those. Lastly we construct a non-periodic tile set that generates a universal tiling and propose a classification of the different universality and completeness notions seen along the paper.

2   Notions of Tilings' Universality and Completeness

First, we give the definitions of the basic notions of tilings. A tile is an oriented unit size square with colored edges from C, where C is a finite set of colors. A tile set is a finite set of tiles. To tile consists of placing the tiles of a given tile set on the grid $\mathbb{Z}^2$ such that two adjacent tiles share the same color on their common edge. Since a tile set can be described with a finite set of integers, then we can enumerate the tile sets, and τ_i will designate the ith tile set.

Let τ be a tile set. A tiling P generated by τ is called a τ-tiling. It is associated to a tiling function f_P where $f_P(x, y)$ gives the tile at position (x, y) in P. In this paper, when we will say: "Let P be a tiling", we mean that there exists a tile set τ such that P is a τ-tiling of the plane. The set of all tilings is $\mathfrak{T}$. A pattern m is a finite tiling. If it is generated by τ, we call it a τ-pattern. A pattern m is associated to a tiling partial function f_m, defined on a finite subset of $\mathbb{N}^2$ such that $f_m(x, y)$ gives the tile at the position (x, y) in m. A finite set of rectangular τ-patterns is a τ-pattern set. We explain how to tile the plane with a pattern set.

Definition 1. *A pattern set M of $\{a \times b\}$ τ-patterns tiles the plane if there exists $0 \le c < a$, $0 \le d < b$ and a function $f_{P_M} : \{c + k_1 a \mid k_1 \in \mathbb{Z}\} \times \{d + k_2 b \mid k_2 \in \mathbb{Z}\} \longrightarrow M$ such that the function $f^{\tau}_{P_M} : \mathbb{Z}^2 \longrightarrow \tau$ defined by: $f^{\tau}_{P_M}(c + k_1 a + x, d + k_2 b + y) = f_{(f_{P_M}(c + k_1 a, d + k_2 b))}(x, y)$ for all $0 \le x < a$ and $0 \le y < b$, is a τ-tiling function of the plane. Here, $f_{(f_{P_M}(c + k_1 a, d + k_2 b))}$ is the tiling partial function of the pattern $f_{P_M}(c + k_1 a, d + k_2 b)$. With the same notation as above, we define the function $s_{P_M} : \mathbb{Z}^2 \to M$ by $s_{P_M}(k_1, k_2) = f_{P_M}(c + k_1 a, d + k_2 b)$.*

This definition explains in a formal way what we expect intuitively. To tile the plane with a pattern set consists in putting the patterns side by side in a subgrid of $\mathbb{Z}^2$ in such a way that color matching is respected. By analogy with tilings, we say that P_M is a M-tiling and it is associated to the pattern tiling function f_{P_M}.

The second function in the definition, s_{P_M}, is another way to define P_M: if $s_{P_M}(x, y)$ gives the pattern m_i, then $s_{P_M}(x + 1, y)$ gives the pattern that touches m_i on its east side in P_M. The same is true for the south, north and west side of a pattern in P_M.

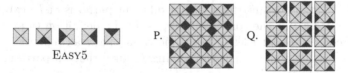

EASY5   P.   Q.

Fig. 1. An EASY5-tiling P and a pattern tiling Q extracted from it

In the previous definition, we used a tiling function $f^{\tau}_{P_M}$. It can be associated to a τ-tiling P because $f^{\tau}_{P_M}$ is defined from $\mathbb{Z}^2$ to τ and respects the color matching. So, we have a strong connection between P and P_M because both of them give rise to the same geometric tiling Q (by geometric tiling, we mean the grid $\mathbb{Z}^2$ filled with the appropriate tiles). That is one of the main notions of this paper. A given tiling can be seen from different heights. Here, P is the smallest height, the unit size level. P_M is a higher level, the $\{a \times b\}$ level. Obviously, a tiling of the plane can be seen with an infinity of different scales. From this infinity of different ways to see a tiling, we expect to obtain a notion of universality for tilings.

More formally, let M be a τ-pattern set, Q be a M-tiling and P be a τ-tiling. We say that Q is extracted[1] from P if $f_Q^\tau = f_P$ (figure 1). P describes the geometric tiling with unit size squares while Q describes it with $\{a \times b\}$-patterns.

From the above notions, we are able to define intuitively what we mean by tilings' reductions. From a given tiling P, we can extract an infinity of pattern tilings. Let P' be one of them. By definition, there exists a pattern set M such that P' is a M-tiling. M is a finite set of $\{a \times b\}$ patterns. We can associate to M a tile set τ with a function $R : M \to \tau$ such that two patterns m_1 and m_2 match if and only if the tiles $R(m_1)$ and $R(m_2)$ match in the same way. It can be easily shown that any pattern set can be associated to a tile set with this property. With R we can build a τ-tiling Q defined by: $f_Q(x, y) = R \circ s_{P'}(x, y)$. Since P' is extracted from P, and since Q works as P' works, so Q can be thought to be "easier" than P. That is our idea of reduction, and now we define it more formally:

Definition 2. *Let P be a τ-tiling and Q be a τ'-tiling.*

Q reduces strongly to P, denoted by $Q \trianglelefteq P$ if there exists a set of τ-patterns M, a M-tiling P' extracted from P and a function $R : M \longrightarrow \tau'$ such that $\forall (x, y) \in \mathbb{Z}^2$, $R \circ s_{P'}(x, y) = f_Q(x, y)$. R is called the reduction core function and its size is the size of the patterns of M, i.e., $size(R) \in \mathbb{N}^2$.

Q reduces weakly to P, denoted by $Q \preccurlyeq P$, if there exists a set of τ_i-patterns M, a M-tiling P' extracted from P and a function $R : M \longrightarrow \tau'$ such that for any $\{p \times q\}$-pattern m of Q there exists $a, b \in \mathbb{Z}^2$ such that $m(x, y) = R \circ s_{P'}(a + x, b + y)$ for all $0 \leq x < p$, $0 \leq y < q$.

When we want to specify R we denote the reduction by $\trianglelefteq^R$ or $\preccurlyeq^R$.

As we have seen above, if $Q \trianglelefteq P$ then we can extract from P a pattern tiling P' that simulates Q in the sense that the patterns of P' represent the tiles of Q. We will say that Q is the tiling *associated* to the pattern tiling P' or that P' *simulates* Q. The important thing is that different patterns of P' can represent the same tile of Q. But the converse is impossible by definition (a pattern of P' cannot represent different tiles of Q). Concerning the weak reduction, if $Q \preccurlyeq P$ then we can extract from P a pattern tiling P' such that all patterns of Q are simulated somewhere in P'.

We can extend naturally our strong reduction definition to patterns. Let A be a τ-pattern and B be a τ'-pattern. We say that $A \trianglelefteq B$ if we can extract from B a M-tiling B' that simulates A, where M is a set of τ'-patterns. For patterns,

---

[1] We note that in most papers on tilings the word *extract* is already used in the following sense: if a tile set can tile square patterns of ever-increasing sizes, then it can tile the plane; one can *extract* from this set of patterns a tiling of the plane. In this paper, extract will, most of the time, refer to the pattern tiling taken from a given tiling. It is specified when we use *extract* to mean "extraction of a tiling from a set of patterns of ever-increasing sizes".

the weak reduction is equivalent to the strong reduction since weak reduction is locally equivalent to strong reduction.

Those reductions have the following property:

Lemma 1. $\trianglelefteq$ *and* $\preccurlyeq$ *are preorders on* $\mathfrak{T}$, *where* $\mathfrak{T}$ *is the set of all possible tilings.*

We do not have an order on $\mathfrak{T}$, because the antisymmetric property is not respected: we can find two tilings P and Q such that $P \trianglelefteq Q$ and $Q \trianglelefteq P$ but $P \not\equiv Q$ (By $P \not\equiv Q$ we mean that P and Q are not the representation of the same tiling up to a color permutation, or, in an equivalent way, that there is no trivial reduction of size $(1,1)$ between P and Q).

With the definition of reduction, we can now define the notions of completeness and universality.

Definition 3. *Let* $\mathcal{A}$ *be a set of tilings. A tile set* τ *is* $\mathcal{A}$-*complete if for any tiling* $P \in \mathcal{A}$, *there exists a* τ-*tiling* Q *such that* $P \trianglelefteq Q$. *If* $\mathcal{A} = \mathfrak{T}$ *then* τ *is called complete.*

This completeness notion is natural in the sense that it corresponds to what one would expect: any tiling can be reduced to some instance tiling of our complete tile set in such a way that to answer any question about our tiling it suffices to study the instance tiling of our complete tile set.

We expect from a universal tiling to have in its construction much of the information of all the other tilings. For tilings, we have different ways to define the information contained in a given tiling and can distinguish mainly two kinds of information for a tiling. The first, and the most natural, is the tiling itself (how it is built). The second consists in studying the different patterns that appear in the tiling. Those two ways to consider a tiling's information give rise to two ways to consider universality. Does a tiling contain enough information to explain the behaviour of all other tilings (we call it *strong dense universality*), or only the behaviour of a tiling for each tile set (*strong sparse universality*)? Does a tiling contain enough information to simulate all the patterns of any tiling (*weak dense universality*) or only the patterns of a tiling for each tile set (*weak dense universality*)?

With this motivation, we have the following definitions:

Definition 4. *Let* P_u *be a* τ-*tiling.* P_u *is:*

- strongly dense universal *if for any tiling* Q, $Q \trianglelefteq P_u$,
- strongly sparse universal *if for all* τ', *there exists a* τ'-*tiling* Q, *such that* $Q \trianglelefteq P_u$,
- weakly dense universal *if for any tiling* Q, $Q \preccurlyeq P_u$,
- weakly sparse universal *if for all* τ', *there exists a* τ'-*tiling* Q, *such that* $Q \preccurlyeq P_u$.

We have the following properties:

Lemma 2. *1.* P_u *strongly (resp. weakly) dense universal* $\Rightarrow$ P_u *strongly (resp. weakly) sparse universal.*

2. P_u *strongly dense (resp. sparse) universal* $\Rightarrow$ P_u *weakly dense (resp. sparse)*
   universal.
3. $\lhd$ *preserves universalities.*
4. $\preccurlyeq$ *preserves weak universality.*

We will show the existence or the non-existence of these universality notions after the following section.

3   Completeness

The following theorem shows how complete tile sets and universal tilings relate.

Theorem 1. *Assuming the existence of at least one complete tile set and one weakly dense universal tiling, we have:*
  Let τ be a tile set. τ is complete if and only if there exists a weakly dense universal τ-tiling.

Proof. [$\Rightarrow$]: Let τ be a complete tile set and P_u be a weakly dense universal tiling. Since τ is complete, there exists a τ-tiling P such that $P_u \lhd P$. $\lhd$ preserves weak universality, therefore P is a weakly universal τ-tiling.
  [$\Leftarrow$]: Let P_u be a weakly universal τ-tiling. By definition, for any tiling P there exists R such that $P \preccurlyeq^R P_u$. We consider the set of patterns $\{A_i\}_{i>0}$ where A_i is the $\{i \times i\}$-pattern of P centered around $(0,0)$. By definition, there exists a set of patterns $\{B_i\}_{i>0}$ of P_u such that $A_i \lhd B_i$ for all i. We can extract from the set of patterns $\{B_i\}_{i>0}$ of ever-increasing sizes, a τ-tiling P' such that $P \lhd P'$; and so, τ is complete.

We now exhibit our first complete tile set. We can easily prove that the tile set EASY5 (figure 1) is complete. In order to do this, we just have to see that we can encode any tile set with square EASY5-patterns such that the EASY5-patterns have a code on their borders that represent the tiles of the tile set. Then, we just have to assemble the patterns in the same way that the tiles, that they represent, are assembled in the tiling.

Theorem 2. EASY5 *is complete.*

We have a stronger result for complete tile sets: if τ is a complete tile set, then for each tiling P, there exists an uncountable set of τ-tilings to which P reduces.
  It would be interesting to find a non-trivial complete tile set, *e.g.*, a complete tile set that has only non-periodic tilings. We will construct such a tile set in theorem 6. For now, we construct a more complex complete tile set that we will use later on.
  Since Berger's proof of the undecidability of the domino problem, it is known that we can simulate a Turing machine with a tiling. We briefly recall how to do this.
  Some tiles are used to transmit a symbol of the alphabet of the Turing machine, some are used to show that the state q_i will act on the symbol a_j at the

next step and finally, some are used to represent the transitions of the Turing machine. More details of this construction can be found in [AD96].

We will now build a Turing machine M such that the space×time diagram of the computation of $M(\omega)$ gives a rectangular pattern that simulates a tile from the tile set $\tau_{|\omega|}$ (the $|\omega|^{th}$ tile set).

Our Turing machine works with a semi-infinite tape. A typical input is $\omega = x\$^n$ where $x \in \{0,1\}^*$ and n depends on $|x|$. The length of ω represents the code of the tile set we are working with, and the first part of ω, x, is the code of a color of the set of color of $\tau_{|\omega|}$. We know that we can encode a tile set, $i.e.$, by giving it an unique number or code in a same way that we do for Turing machines. So the first step consists in decoding $|\omega|$ to find the different tiles that compose $\tau_{|\omega|}$. Then we check if x is the code of a color of $\tau_{|\omega|}$. If yes, we choose in a non-deterministic way a tile t of $\tau_{|\omega|}$ such that the color of its south side is x. We can build our Turing machine such that after m steps of computation, the k next steps of the computation are used to write the code of the west/east[2] color of t (n and k depending only on $|\omega|$), $i.e.$, in the space×time diagram of the Turing machine, the first column from time $m + 1$ to $m + k$ represents the code of the color of the west side of t. The tiles that are not between the $(m+1)^{th}$ and the $(m+k)^{th}$ lines are all the blank tile $\sqcup$. We do the same for the east/west side (depending on the first choice we made), $i.e.$, in the space×time diagram of the Turing machine, the last column from time $m' + 1$ to $m' + k$ represents the code of the color of the east side of t (m' depending only on $|\omega|$). The p last steps of computation are used to write the code of the color of the north side of t completed with \$'s and $\square$'s. For later usage, we precise that our Turing machine M does nothing when the entrance is the empty word. This means that its corresponding space×time diagram will be a rectangular space filled by blank tiles.

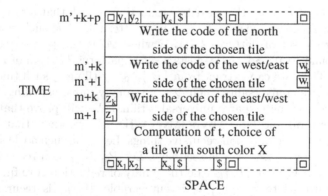

SPACE

Fig. 2. The space×time diagram of M

The figure 2 represents the space×time diagram of our Turing machine. In addition, we construct the Turing machine such that for two inputs of size p the

---

[2] Our algorithm chooses in a non-determistic way either the west or the east side. This non-determinism is essential for east/west matching of two diagrams.

machine uses exactly $s(p)$ of space and $t(p)$ of time. With this construction, we are certain that two space×time diagrams have the same size if and only if the inputs have the same lengths. That guarantees that the simulations of two tiles from the same tile set give two diagrams of the same size. So, two diagrams will match on their north/south side if and only if the two tiles that they simulate match on their north/south side. For the east/west border the match rules are different. During the computation, we can choose to write first the east color or the west color. Then, two diagrams will match on their east/west border if and only if the tiles they represent match on their east/west border, and if during the computation, the two Turing machines they represent have done different non-deterministic choices.

The idea is now to associate this Turing machine to its corresponding tiling, called τ_u. By construction, τ_u generates patterns that correspond to the space× time diagram of the simulation of a tile. We have a tiling that gives $\{s \times t\}$-patterns such that two patterns match if and only if they represent two tiles, from the same tile set, that match. Hence, we can simulate with this tile set any behaviour of any tile set. Therefore, τ_u is complete.

4   Universality

We now study the different universality notions defined above. We give some results about universality before constructing our first universal tiling.

Theorem 3.   *1. If $P_u \preccurlyeq P$, where P_u is a strongly universal tiling and P is a*
   τ-tiling, then there exists a strongly universal τ-tiling.
   2. Let P_u be a tiling. If P_u is strongly universal, then P_u is non-recursive.

Proof. **1.** If $P_u \preccurlyeq P$, then there exists a reduction R such that for any $\{n_1 \times n_2\}$-pattern A of P_u there exists a $\{m_1 \times m_2\}$-pattern B of P such that $A \trianglelefteq^R B$. We consider the set of patterns $\{A_i\}_{i>0}$ where A_i is the $\{i \times i\}$-pattern of P_u centered around $(0,0)$. So, there exists a set of patterns $\{B_i\}_{i>0}$ of P_u such that $A_i \trianglelefteq B_i \,\forall i$. Thus, we can extract from $\{B_i\}_{i>0}$ a τ-tiling Q such that $P_u \trianglelefteq^R Q$. Since $\trianglelefteq$ preserves universality, then Q is a strongly universal tiling.
2. Let P_u be a strongly sparse universal τ-tiling. We will prove that P_u is non-recursive. By Hanf and later Myers [Mye74, Han74], we know that there exists tile sets that produce only non-recursive tilings. Let τ' be such a tile set. Suppose that P_u is recursive, *i.e.*, f_{P_u} is recursive. Let P_{nr} be a non-recursive τ'-tiling such that $P_{nr} \trianglelefteq P_u$. Let $\{R_i\}_{i \geq 1}$ be the family of reduction core functions from a set of τ-patterns to τ'. $\{R_i\}_{i \geq 1}$ is enumerable. If f_{P_u} is recursive, we can compose it with the reductions $\bar{R}_i$ and obtain the recursive tiling functions of all τ'-tilings that reduce to P_u. By definition P_{nr} reduces strongly to P_u, thus one of those recursive tiling functions defines P_{nr}. This is a contradiction, hence P_u is non-recursive.

The first result we obtain, concerning the different universality notions, is the non-existence of strongly dense universal tilings. This is due to a countability argument. We only have a countable set of possible reductions for a given tiling, but an uncountable set of tilings.

Theorem 4. *Strongly dense universal tilings do not exist.*

We now study the weak version of universality for tilings. The idea of the construction is to build our tiling in the same way that we can construct a Turing machine simulating every step of all the Turing machines by simulating at step i the first i computing steps of the first i Turing machines. Similarly, we construct a weakly dense universal tiling that enumerates all possible patterns of all tilings. They are countable so we can simulate all of them in the same tiling. Thus, we obtain the following result:

Theorem 5. *There exists a weakly dense universal tiling.*

Of course, weak dense universality implies weak sparse universality.

We still have a last universality notion to study: strong sparse universality, *i.e.*, a tiling that can simulate at least one tiling for each tile set. We can still use the EASY5 tile set to show the non-emptiness of this class. In the following theorem, we propose a non-periodic tile set that will generate a strongly sparse universal tiling, that is universal in a more "natural" way than EASY5.

Theorem 6. *There exists a non-periodic tile set that generates a strongly sparse universal tiling.*

Proof. The idea is to simulate a Turing machine in an aperiodic tiling. For this, we use Robinson's tiling. We give some explanations on how to force the computation of a Turing Machine in Robinson's tiling. We again refer the reader to [Rob71] and [AD96] for a detailed construction.

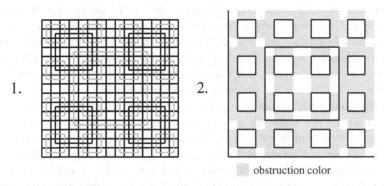

obstruction color

Fig. 3. The hierarchical structure and the obstruction zone in Robinson's tiling

The main idea is to use the hierarchical pattern construction that is generated by Robinson's tiling. It gives rise to $2^n - 1$ square patterns (figure 3.1). We note that two squares of sizes $2^{2n} - 1$ and $2^{2m} - 1$ cannot intersect if $n \neq m$. The idea is to compute a given Turing machine in the squares of size $2^{2n} - 1$.

In order to do this, the squares of size $2^{2n} - 1$ send an obstruction color outside their borders. That is an intuitive fact that we can do this with a tiling but it is a quite technical result to prove. Figure 3.2 shows the hierarchical construction with the obstruction tiles.

In this figure there appears white spaces, *i.e.*, areas without obstruction color spaces. Those spaces are called free. Those white spaces are the computation spaces, where the Turing machine M will be simulated. On each free tile, we superimpose the tiles representing our Turing machine as we explained in section 3. The tiles that are obstructed in one direction (horizontally or vertically) will transmit the information of the computation of our Turing machine in the other direction. By construction, the tiles that are obstructed in both direction have no information to transmit. Thus, we can impose to the lowest free spaces of a square to start the simulation of our Turing machine on an empty tape with a given state. Then, by transmission of the information horizontally and vertically, we will simulate in each square of size $2^{2n} - 1$, the first steps of our Turing machine.

We now take the Turing machine M described in figure 2. We built it to force that on any input of length n, if M stops, then it stops using exactly $s(n)$ spaces and $t(n)$ steps. We modify it to permit that $t(n) = k \times s(n) = k \times n^2, \forall n$. Since we work in linear space and time, we can modify M to satisfy those conditions.

We also modify Robinson's tiling by simulating any tile of Robinson's tiling with patterns of size $\{1 \times k\}$. The k is the same constant that relates the time function and the space function of M. The tiling that we obtain is Robinson's tiling stretched horizontally with a factor k. Thus, in each square of size $2^{2n} - 1$, we will have the equivalent of a square of size $n^2 \times (k\, n^2)$ of free tiles.

Now, we just have to simulate our Turing machine M in these spaces. We can force the south-west free tile of any square pattern to be the tile that simulates M on state q_0. We force that the tiles that touch the south border of the square represent any of the four symbols $\{0, 1, \$, \square\}$. Then, the computation of M on this input will say if it was a correct input, and will halt in exactly $t(n)$ steps and $s(n)$ spaces if it was correct. We can force that the computation tiles match the north board of the square if and only if they are in a final state. Thus, we fill the free tiles of a square if and only if the input was $x\$^n\square^m$, such that x is the code of a color of $\tau_{|x|+n}$ and the computation uses $|x| + n + m$ spaces and halts after $k \times (|x| + n + m)$ steps to give a simulation of a tile of $\tau_{|x|+n}$.

With this construction, we fill any pattern of a given size with the simulations of some tiles from the same tile set. To guarantee that this simulation works, we modify the obstruction color sent by the squares outside their borders. We add four kinds of obstruction colors: $c_0, c_1, c_\$$ and $c_\square$, representing the four symbols $\{0, 1, \$, \square\}$. For example, the obstruction color $c_\$$ will be sent if the first tile inside the square is a computation tile, and is a tile representing the symbol \$. Thus, all the squares of a given size will represent a tiling P of a certain tile set because we have guaranteed that the matching rules were respected. Then, P reduces to our construction.

The last point consists in checking that at least one tiling for each tile set will reduce to our construction. It is the case because in our construction of M, we guarantee that each number represents a tile set, and thus, for each tile set, there exists a unique size of rectangular free spaces where the tile set will be simulated and so, any tile set that tiles the plane has a tiling that reduces to our construction. We have specified that our Turing machine does nothing when the entrance is the empty word. Its special space×time diagram corresponds to the blank tile. Thus, all the free spaces of a given square size will be filled with blank tiles. It is used when a tile set does not tile the plane to guarantee that our final universal tiling will tile the plane.

In this theorem, we constructed a tiling P_1 that simulates a tiling for each tile set. For a given tile set τ_i, we can choose the τ_i-tiling that we will simulate in P_1. At a certain step of our computation, our tiling P_1 will simulate its own tile set. We can imagine that we will simulate a τ_i tiling P_2 which is a strongly sparse universal tiling such that P_2 simulates for any tile set τ_i another τ_i-tiling than the τ_i-tiling simulated in P_1. Thus, by transitivity, with this construction, P_1 simulates at least 2 tilings for each tile set. At a certain point P_2 will also simulate its own tile set, *etc.* By iterating this process, we can build a tiling that simulates for each tile set τ a countable infinity of τ-tilings.

The following theorem gives the conditions needed by a tile set to generate a universal tiling that simulates a countable infinity of tilings for each tile set.

Theorem 7. *Let τ be a tile set. If for any countable set $A = \{P_1, P_2, P_3, \ldots \mid P_j$ is a τ_j-tiling $\forall j\}$ there exists a τ-tiling P_A such that $P_j \trianglelefteq P_A$ for all $P_j \in A$, then there exists a strongly sparse universal τ-tiling P_u such that for all τ_j there exists a countable infinite set $A_j = \{P_{j_1}, P_{j_2} P_{j_3}, \ldots\}$ of τ_j-tilings such that $P_{j_k} \trianglelefteq \Gamma_u$ for all j, k. We say that a tiling has the universal infinity property ('UIP') if it satisfies the conditions of this theorem.*

Proof. Let τ be a tile set that satisfies the hypothesis of the theorem. Since τ is a tile set, there exists i such that $\tau = \tau_i$. We consider the set A_1 composed of P_1^1, P_2^1, $\ldots$ such that, for all j, P_j^1 is a τ_j-tiling and P_i^1 is a τ_i-tiling that simulates all tilings of the set A_2. By induction, we define A_n to be composed of P_1^n, P_2^n, $\ldots$ such that, for all j, P_j^n is a τ_j-tiling and P_i^n is a τ_i-tiling that simulates all tilings of the set A_{n+1}.

If we choose the sets A_n in such a way that $A_n \cap A_m = \emptyset$ for all n, m, then by simulating all tilings of the set A_1, P_u will simulate a countable infinity of tilings for each tile set.

Since in theorem 6 we can choose the tiling that we want to simulate for a given tile set, EASY5 and the tile set of theorem 6 have the universal infinity property. We can see that a tile set with *UIP* has the highest class of universality. The following theorem shows that this property is equivalent to other notions mentionned above.

Theorem 8. *The following statements are equivalent:*
1. τ has the universal infinity property;
2. τ is complete;
3. τ generates a weakly dense universal tiling.

Proof. $1 \Rightarrow 2$: Let τ be a tile set with the universal infinity property. Then, for any subset $A = \{P_1, P_2, \ldots\}$, where P_j is a τ_j-tiling, there exists a τ-tiling P such that $P_i \trianglelefteq P$ for all $P_i \in A$. Thus, for any tiling Q, there exists a τ-tiling P such that $Q \trianglelefteq P$. So, τ is complete.

$1 \Leftarrow 2$: Let τ be a complete tile set and τ' a tile set with the universal infinity property. Since τ is complete, for any τ'-tiling P_k there exists a τ-tiling Q_k such that $P_k \trianglelefteq Q_k$. Since the theorem 6 shows the existence of at least one tile set with the universal infinity property, then we can reduce all of its tilings to our complete tile set τ and thus, τ has the universal infinity property.

$2 \Leftrightarrow 3$: By theorem 1.

We have shown that completeness, generating weak dense universality and universal infinity property are equivalent. In fact, it is the finest universality class we can get, based on our reduction notion. We call this class $[UIP]$.

The class $[UIP]$ is really interesting in the sense that two tile sets τ and τ' of $[UIP]$ have the following property: for any τ-tiling P, there exists an infinity of τ'-tilings $\{Q_i\}_{i>0}$ such that $P \trianglelefteq Q_i$. In a certain way, the tile sets of $[UIP]$ generate tilings with the same behaviour.

In figure 4, we illustrate the obtained classification of the different universality and completeness notions seen along the paper.

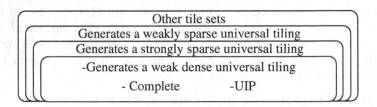

Fig. 4. The universality classification for tile sets

To clarify this classification, we aim to show that some non-periodic tile sets do not belong to $[UIP]$. To prove this, we recall the quasiperiodic function associated to a tiling. For a given tiling P, the quasiperiodic function G_P gives for each n, the smallest m such that any pattern of size n in P appears at least once in any $m \times m$-square pattern of P. Of course, G_P is not a total function for all P. We can have a tiling Q where a given pattern of size s appears only once in Q and thus, $G_Q(s)$ will not be defined. Nevertheless, Durand [Dur99] showed that if a tile set tiles the plane, then it can tile it in a quasiperiodic way, *i.e.*, the quasiperiodic function associated to this tiling is total.

We have the following results:

Theorem 9. *Let P and Q be two tilings of the plane. If there does not exist $c \in \mathbb{N}$ such that $G_Q(cn) > G_P(n) \; \forall n$, then $P \ntrianglelefteq Q$.*

Proof. Suppose that $P \trianglelefteq Q$ with a reduction of size (a, b). That means that any $\{c \times d\}$-pattern of P is simulated by a $\{ca \times bd\}$-pattern of Q. By the theorem's condition, there exists at least one n such that $G_Q(a \times b \times n) < G_P(n)$. Thus there exists a pattern m of P of size n that appears less frequently in P than any pattern of Q of size $a \times b \times n$ appears in Q. Hence, no pattern of Q of size $a \times b \times n$ can represent the pattern m and thus, $P \not\trianglelefteq Q$.

Since [CD04], we know that there exists tile sets that generate only tilings with a non-recursive quasiperiodic function. Thus, if P is a universal strong tiling, then G_P cannot be recursive. Since Robinson's tile set gives rise only to tilings with recursive quasiperiodic functions, Robinson's tilings are not universal.

5   Concluding Remarks

We have shown that there exists a strongly sparse universal tiling that can simulate a countable infinity of tilings for each tile set. That is the strongest universality notion we can get. In fact, having a tile set with this property is equivalent to completeness and to generating a weakly sparse universal tiling. But we have also shown that there is no strongly universal tiling that simulates all tilings, because of an argument of countability.

The constructions were generated by the trivial tile set EASY5. But we also show that even non-periodic tile sets can generate universality and be complete. There remains the question: are all non-periodic tile sets, that generate only tilings with a non-recursive quasiperiodic function, complete?

Acknowledgements

We warmly thank Jacques Mazoyer for his startling remarks and all his advices, and Bruno Durand for the stimulating discussions.

References

[AD96]   ALLAUZEN (C.) et DURAND (B.), *The Classical Decision Problem*, appendix A: "Tiling problems", p. 407–420. Springer, 1996.

[Ber66]   BERGER (R.), « The undecidability of the domino problem », *Memoirs of the American Mathematical Society*, vol. 66, 1966, p. 1–72.

[CD04]   CERVELLE (J.) et DURAND (B.), « Tilings: recursivity and regularity », *Theoretical Computer Science*, vol. 310, n° 1-3, 2004, p. 469–477.

[CK97]   CULIK II (K.) et KARI (J.), « On aperiodic sets of Wang tiles », in *Foundations of Computer Science: Potential - Theory - Cognition*, p. 153–162, 1997.

[DLS01]   DURAND (B.), LEVIN (L. A.) et SHEN (A.), « Complex tilings », in *Proceedings of the Symposium on Theory of Computing*, p. 732–739, 2001.

[Dur99]   DURAND (B.), « Tilings and quasiperiodicity », *Theoretical Computer Science*, vol. 221, n° 1-2, 1999, p. 61–75.

[Dur02]   DURAND (B.), « De la logique aux pavages », *Theoretical Computer Science*, vol. 281, n° 1-2, 2002, p. 311–324.

[Han74]   HANF (W. P.), « Non-recursive tilings of the plane. I », *Journal of Symbolic Logic*, vol. 39, n° 2, 1974, p. 283–285.

[Mye74]   MYERS (D.), « Non-recursive tilings of the plane. II », *Journal of Symbolic Logic*, vol. 39, n° 2, 1974, p. 286–294.

[Rob71]   ROBINSON (R.), « Undecidability and nonperiodicity for tilings of the plane », *Inventiones Mathematicae*, vol. 12, 1971, p. 177–209.

[Wan61]   WANG (H.), « Proving theorems by pattern recognition II », *Bell System Technical Journal*, vol. 40, 1961, p. 1–41.

[Wan62]   WANG (H.), « Dominoes and the $\forall\exists\forall$-case of the decision problem », in *Proceedings of the Symposium on Mathematical Theory of Automata*, p. 23–55, 1962.

On the Complexity of Unary
Tiling-Recognizable Picture Languages*

Alberto Bertoni[1], Massimiliano Goldwurm[1], and Violetta Lonati[1]

Dipartimento di Scienze dell'Informazione, Università degli Studi di Milano
Via Comelico 39/41, 20135 Milano – Italy
{bertoni,goldwurm,lonati}@dsi.unimi.it

Abstract. We give a characterization, in terms of computational complexity, of the family REC_1 of the unary picture languages that are tiling recognizable. We introduce quasi-unary strings to represent unary pictures and we prove that any unary picture language L is in REC_1 if and only if the set of all quasi-unary strings encoding the elements of L is recognizable by a one-tape nondeterministic Turing machine that is space and head-reversal linearly bounded. In particular, the result implies that the family of binary string languages corresponding to tiling-recognizable square languages lies between $NTIME(2^n)$ and $NTIME(4^n)$. This also implies the existence of a nontiling-recognizable unary square language that corresponds to a binary string language recognizable in nondeterministic time $O(4^n \log n)$.

Classification: automata and formal languages, computational complexity.

Keywords: unary picture languages, tiling systems, Turing machine head reversal.

1 Introduction

Picture languages have been introduced in the literature as two-dimensional extension of traditional string languages, a picture being a two-dimensional array of elements from a finite alphabet. They have been originally considered as formal models for image processing in connection with problems of pattern recognition. Several classical tools and concepts have been used to classify picture languages and study their properties: regular expressions [8], grammars [12], automata [6], logic formulas [5].

One of the main effort in this area is to capture the notion of recognizability. In particular, various notions of two-dimensional finite automaton have been proposed and studied in the literature [6,7]. An interesting formal model for the recognition of picture languages is given by the so-called tiling systems introduced in [3], which are based on projection of local properties. A tiling system τ is defined by a finite set Θ of square pictures of size 2 together with a projection

---

* This work has been supported by the Project M.I.U.R. COFIN "Automata and formal languages: mathematical and application driven studies".

W. Thomas and P. Weil (Eds.): STACS 2007, LNCS 4393, pp. 381–392, 2007.

between alphabets. Roughly speaking, a language is recognized by τ if each of its elements can be obtained as a projection of a picture whose subpictures of size 2 belong to Θ. The class of picture languages recognized by such systems satisfy relevant properties, which resemble classical properties of regular string languages [4].

A special case is represented by pictures over a one-letter alphabet: in this case only the shape of the picture is relevant, and hence a unary picture is simply identified by a pair of positive integers. In this context, a general goal is to define techniques to describe families of recognizable languages, or to construct examples of non-recognizable languages [4,7]. For instance, families of tiling-recognizable unary picture languages are introduced in [4] by means of integer functions or in [2] by means of special regular expressions, whereas in [7] two-dimensional automata are used to recognize unary languages and several strategies to explore pictures are presented.

In this work we give a complexity result concerning the unary picture languages recognized by tiling systems. We characterize such a family by means of non-deterministic Turing machines that are space and head-reversal bounded. More precisely, we introduce a notion of quasi-unary strings to represent pairs of positive numbers and we prove that a unary picture language L is tiling recognizable if and only if the set of all quasi-unary strings encoding the sizes of the elements of L is recognizable by a one-tape non-deterministic Turing machine M that works within $\max(n, m)$ space and executes at most $\min(n, m)$ head reversals, on the input representing the pair (n, m).

In particular for the case of squares, this result allows us to relate the recognizability of unary square pictures to nondeterministic time complexity bounds. Informally, it shows that the complexity of the binary encodings of tiling-recognizable unary square picture languages is located between $\mathrm{NTIME}(2^n)$ and $\mathrm{NTIME}(4^n)$. This yields a large variety of examples of picture languages that are tiling recognizable. For instance, all sets of binary encodings of NP problems correspond to tiling-recognizable (unary square) picture languages.

Also, our characterization allows us to use separating results on time complexity classes as a tool for defining recognizable and non-recognizable unary picture languages. In particular, using a property proved in [11], we show the existence of a unary square language that is not tiling recognizable, but corresponds to a binary string language recognizable in nondeterministic time $O(4^n \log n)$.

2   Preliminaries on Picture Languages

Given a finite alphabet Σ, a *picture* (or *two-dimensional string*) over Σ is either a two-dimensional array (i.e., a matrix) of elements of Σ or the *empty picture* λ. The set of all pictures over Σ is denoted by Σ^{**}; a *picture language* (or *two-dimensional language*) over Σ is a subset of Σ^{**}.

Given a picture $p \in \Sigma^{**}$, we use r_p and c_p to denote the number of rows and columns of p, respectively. The pair $(\mathrm{r}_p, \mathrm{c}_p)$ is called the *size* of p. By definition we have $\mathrm{r}_p > 0$ and $\mathrm{c}_p > 0$, except for the empty picture λ that has size $(0, 0)$. The symbol in p with coordinates (i, j) is denoted by $p(i, j)$, for every $1 \leq i \leq r_p$ and $1 \leq j \leq c_p$. If $r_p = c_p$, then p is called a *square picture* and the *size* of p is simply r_p. A *square language* is a picture language containing only square pictures. If the alphabet Σ is a singleton, then the pictures over Σ^{**} are called *unary pictures*. A *unary picture language* is a subset of Σ^{**}, where Σ is a singleton.

For any picture $p \in \Sigma^{**}$ of size (m, n), we use $\hat{p}$ to denote a new picture of size $(m + 2, n + 2)$ obtained by surrounding p with a special boundary symbol $\sharp \notin \Sigma$. Such boundary will be useful when describing scanning strategies for pictures.

Many operations can be defined between pictures and picture languages. In particular, we recall the operations of row and column concatenation. Let p and q be pictures over Σ^{**} of size (r_p, c_p) and (r_q, c_q), respectively. If $r_p = r_q$, we define the column concatenation $p \oplus q$ between p and q as the picture of size $(r_p, c_p + c_q)$ whose i-th row equals the concatenation of the i-th rows of p and q, for every $1 \leq i \leq r_p$. If $c_p = c_q$, we define the row concatenation $p \ominus q$ analogously. Clearly, $\oplus$ and $\ominus$ are partial operations over the set Σ^{**}. These definitions can be extended to picture languages and iterated: for every language $L \subseteq \Sigma^{**}$, we set $L^{0\oplus} = L^{0\ominus} = \{\lambda\}$, $L^{i\oplus} = L \oplus L^{(i-1)\oplus}$ and $L^{i\ominus} = L \ominus L^{(i-1)\ominus}$, for every $i \geq 1$. Thus, one can define the *row* and *column closures* as the transitive closures of $\oplus$ and $\ominus$:

$$L^{*\oplus} = \bigcup_{i \geq 0} L^{i\oplus} \qquad L^{*\ominus} = \bigcup_{i \geq 0} L^{i\ominus},$$

which can be seen as a sort of *two-dimensional Kleene star*. Another useful operation is the so-called *rotation*: given $p \in \Sigma^{**}$, its rotation p^R is the picture of size (c_p, r_p) defined by $(p^R)_{ij} = p_{r_p+1-j,i}$.

From the recognizability view point, various approaches have been proposed. In particular, here we consider the class REC and its definition in terms of tiling systems [3,4]. First, we recall the definition of *local picture language*.

Definition 1. *A tile is a square picture of size 2; for every picture p, $T(p)$ denotes the set of all tiles that are subpictures of p. A picture language $L \subseteq \Gamma^{**}$ is called* local *if there exists a finite set Θ of tiles over the alphabet $\Gamma \cup \{\sharp\}$ such that $L = \{p \in \Gamma^{**} \mid T(\hat{p}) \subseteq \Theta\}$. In this case we write $L = \mathcal{L}(\Theta)$.*

We also need the notion of projection of pictures and picture languages. Let $\pi : \Gamma \to \Sigma$ be a mapping between two alphabets. Given a picture $p \in \Gamma^{**}$, the *projection* of p by π is the picture $\pi(p) \in \Sigma^{**}$ such that $\pi(p)\,(i, j) = \pi(p(i, j))$ for every pair of coordinates i, j. Analogously, the projection of a language $L \subseteq \Gamma^{**}$ by π is the set $\pi(L) = \{\pi(p) \mid p \in \Gamma^{**}\} \subseteq \Sigma^{**}$.

Definition 2. *A tiling system is a 4-tuple $\tau = \langle \Sigma, \Gamma, \Theta, \pi \rangle$ where Σ and Γ are two finite alphabets, Θ is a finite set of tiles over the alphabet $\Gamma \cup \{\sharp\}$ and $\pi : \Gamma \to \Sigma$ is a projection. A picture language is* tiling recognizable *if there exists a tiling system $\langle \Sigma, \Gamma, \Theta, \pi \rangle$ such that $L = \pi(\mathcal{L}(\Theta))$. REC is the class of picture languages that are tiling recognizable.*

Notice in particular that any local language is tiling recognizable.

The class REC satisfies some remarkable properties. For instance it can be defined as the class of languages recognized by online tessellation automata, that are special acceptors related to cellular automata [6]; they can be expressed by formulas of existential monadic second order [5]; they can be defined by means of regular-like expressions based on certain composition rules between pictures [4]. In particular we will use the fact that REC is closed with respect to the operations $\cup, \ominus, \oplus, {}^{*\ominus}, {}^{*\oplus}, {}^{R}$.

Finally, since we are interested in unary pictures, we also introduce the following

Definition 3. REC_1 *is the subclass of* REC *containing the unary picture languages that are tiling recognizable.*

3   Characterization of Rec_1

In this section, we state our main result, that is a characterization of the class of unary picture languages that are tiling recognizable.

To this aim, consider the alphabet $\Sigma = \{\circ\}$ and notice that any unary picture $p \in \{\circ\}^{**}$ is identified by its size, that is by the pair (r_p, c_p). Thus, unary pictures (i.e. pairs of positive integers) can be encoded by quasi-unary strings as follows. We consider the set of unary strings over Σ

$$U = \{\circ^n \mid n > 0\}$$

and the following sets of strings that are unary except for one special letter h or v (not occurring in first position):

$$Q_h = \{\circ^n h \, \circ^k \mid n > 0, k \geq 0\},$$
$$Q_v = \{\circ^n v \, \circ^k \mid n > 0, k \geq 0\}.$$

We call *quasi-unary string* over the alphabet $\{\circ, h, v\}$ any string in $Q = U \cup Q_h \cup Q_v$. The length of any quasi-unary string x is denoted as usual by $|x|$, whereas we use ${}_\circ|x|$ to denote the length of the longest prefix of x in $\circ^+$. The use of symbols h and v allows us to distinguish among squares, horizontal (with more columns than rows), and vertical rectangles. Thus, a quasi-unary string $x \in Q_h$ represents the unary horizontal rectangle of size $({}_\circ|x|, |x|)$; $x \in Q_v$ represents the unary vertical rectangle of size $(|x|, {}_\circ|x|)$; whereas $x \in U$ represents the unary square of size $|x|$.

Summarizing the previous definitions, the encoding ϕ from unary pictures to quasi-unary strings can be stated as follows: for every picture $p \in \{\circ\}^{**}$, we have

$$\phi(p) = \begin{cases} \circ^{r_p} \, h \, \circ^{c_p - r_p - 1} & \text{if } r_p < c_p \\ \circ^{r_p} & \text{if } r_p = c_p \\ \circ^{c_p} \, v \, \circ^{r_p - c_p - 1} & \text{if } r_p > c_p \end{cases}$$

Notice that $|\phi(p)| = \max(r_p, c_p)$, while ${}_\circ|\phi(p)| = \min(r_p, c_p)$.

Now, let us introduce the complexity classes of quasi-unary languages that we shall use to characterize the class of tiling-recognizable unary languages.

Definition 4. NSPACEREV$_Q$ *is the class of quasi-unary string languages that can be recognized by 1-tape nondeterministic Turing machines working within $|x|$ space and executing at most $_o|x|$ head reversals, for any input x in Q.*

Our main theorem can then be stated as follows:

Theorem 1. *A unary picture language L is in REC$_1$ if and only if $\phi(L)$ belongs to NSPACEREV$_Q$.*

The proof of Theorem 1 is split into two parts. In section 4 we prove that if L is in REC$_1$, then $\phi(L)$ belongs to NSPACEREV$_Q$, whereas in Section 5 we prove the inverse.

4   Recognizability Implies the Complexity Bound

In this section we prove that, if L is a tiling-recognizable unary picture language, then $\phi(L)$ is in NSPACEREV$_Q$. In order to prove such a result, let Θ be a finite set of tiles over some alphabet Γ, and consider the following problem.

SIZE REPRESENTABILITY (Θ)
Instance: a quasi-unary string $x \in Q$.
Question: does there exist $p \in \mathcal{L}(\Theta)$ whose size is represented by x?

Lemma 1. *The problem* SIZE REPRESENTABILITY (Θ) *is in* NSPACEREV$_Q$ *for every finite set of tiles Θ.*

Proof. We define a Turing machine M for the SIZE REPRESENTABILITY problem, that nondeterministically tries to generate some $p \in \mathcal{L}(\Theta)$ of the required size. First of all, M establishes if $x \in Q_h$, $x \in Q_v$, or $x \in U$. This can be done nondeterministically without head reversals. If $x \in Q_h$ or $x \in U$, then the generation is performed row by row, otherwise the generation has to be done column by column. The input is accepted if and only if such a generating process can be accomplished. We describe in details only the steps executed in the case $x \in Q_h$; the other cases are similar and are left to the reader.

The working alphabet Γ' of M contains the symbols $\circ, h, v, \sharp$ $\flat$, all the pairs $(a, b) \in (\Gamma \cup \{\sharp\}) \times (\Gamma \cup \{\sharp\})$, and their marked versions $\overline{(a, b)}$ and $\widetilde{(a, b)}$. The symbols (a, b) shall be used in correspondence with a pair of adjacent symbols in some column of the picture p generated during the computation; the overlined symbols shall be used as bookmarks at the $_o|x|$-th cell, tildes shall be used to implement a counter.

The machine M works only on the portion of the tape containing the input x, which we call the *working portion* of the tape. The computation behaves as follows:

1. First of all, M reads the tape rightwards until the first blank, nondeterministically replacing each input symbol according to Θ, whenever such a replacement is possible. More precisely:

- the leftmost symbol is replaced by some pair $(\sharp, a)$ such that the tile t_1 in the figure below belongs to Θ;
- any next symbol is replaced by some pair $(\sharp, b)$ in such a way that, for each pair of consecutive pairs $(\sharp, b)$ and $(\sharp, b')$, the tile t_2 in the figure belongs to Θ (the position of the symbol h is preserved by using overlined pairs);
- the rightmost symbol $\circ$ is replaced by some pair $(\sharp, c)$ such that the tile t_3 in the figure belongs to Θ. At any position, if no replacement is allowed, then M halts and rejects.

$$t_1 = \begin{array}{|c|c|} \hline \sharp & \sharp \\ \hline \sharp & a \\ \hline \end{array} \qquad\qquad t_2 = \begin{array}{|c|c|} \hline \sharp & \sharp \\ \hline b & b' \\ \hline \end{array} \qquad\qquad t_3 = \begin{array}{|c|c|} \hline \sharp & \sharp \\ \hline c & \sharp \\ \hline \end{array}$$

2. M changes direction and reads all the working portion of the tape without head reversals, replacing each symbol (a, b) by (b, c) in such a way that the ending symbols and each pair of consecutive symbols do respect Θ (as in point 1). Such a procedure is repeated $(_\circ|x| - 1)$-many times. Observe that this task can be performed by using the first $(_\circ|x|)$ cells of the tape (those that precede some overlined symbol of Γ') and marking one cell with a tilde at each repetition. Also during this phase, if no replacement is allowed, then M halts and rejects.
3. After the $(_\circ|x| - 1)$-th repetition of step 2, M changes direction and reads all the working portion of the tape again, without head reversals. Now each symbol (a, b) is replaced by $(b, \sharp)$ according to Θ, and whenever no replacement is allowed, then M halts and rejects.

The input x is accepted if and only if the procedure can be concluded, that is, if and only if there exists a picture $p \in \mathcal{L}(\Theta)$ of size $(_\circ|x|, |x|)$. Since the machine M works exactly in space $|x|$ and executes exactly $_\circ|x|$ head reversals, the proof is complete.

Theorem 2. *If L is a unary picture language in* REC$_1$, *then* $\phi(L)$ *belongs to* NSPACEREV$_Q$.

Proof. Let $\langle \{\circ\}, \Gamma, \Theta, \pi \rangle$ be a tiling system for L, and consider the Turing machine M that solves the problem SIZE REPRESENTABILITY(Θ). Now notice that π maps all symbols of Γ to $\circ$, that is π forgets the content of p and preserves only its size. Thus $x \in \phi(L) = \phi(\pi(\mathcal{L}(\Theta)))$ means that there is a picture in $\mathcal{L}(\Theta)$ whose size is represented by x. Therefore M exactly recognizes the set $\phi(L)$ and this concludes the proof.

5 The Complexity Bound Implies Recognizability

To prove the inverse of Theorem 2, we first introduce an auxiliary picture language, associated with the accepting computations of a 1-tape nondeterministic

Turing Machine. A similar approach is used in [3] to prove that the emptiness problem for the family REC is undecidable.

5.1   The Accepting-Computation Language of a Turing Machine

Let M be a 1-tape nondeterministic Turing machine M, and let Σ and Λ be the input and the working alphabet (Λ contains the blank symbol $\flat$). We denote by Q the set of states, which includes the initial state q_0 and a unique accepting state q_{yes}. Also let $\delta : Q \times \Lambda \to 2^{Q \times \Lambda \times \{+,-\}}$ be the transition function of M. Without loss of generality, we assume M can never print the blank symbol $\flat$, and hence $(q, c, x) \in \delta(p, a)$ implies $c \neq \flat$. Then, set $\Lambda_Q = \{\sigma_q \mid \sigma \in \Lambda, q \in Q\}$, a configuration of M is a string $C = x\sigma_q y \in \Lambda^* \Lambda_Q \Lambda^*$ which represents the instantaneous description of the machine where $x\sigma y$ is the work portion of the tape, q is the current state and the head scans the cell containing σ on the right of x. If $q = q_0$ and x is the empty string, then C is the initial configuration of M on input σy. If $q = q_{yes}$ then C is an accepting configuration. We assume the machine halts in every accepting configuration.

Given two configurations C and D of M, we write $C \rhd D$ whenever M can go from C to D without head reversals, possibly by several distinct moves. We call *run* such a sequence of moves.

We define an accepting computation[1] of M on input $x \in \Sigma^*$ as a string of the form

$$W = W_1 \rhd W_2 \rhd \cdots \rhd W_n$$

such that all W_j's are configurations of M, W_1 is the initial configuration on input x, W_n is an accepting configuration, $W_i \rhd W_{i+1}$ holds for each $i = 1, \ldots, n-1$, and there is a head reversal at W_i for every $1 < i < n$, that is, in the runs from W_{i-1} to W_i and from W_i to W_{i+1}, the head moves to opposite directions.

Given an accepting computation W, let $m = \max_i |W_i|$ and consider the picture of size $n \times m$ containing the string W_i (possibly followed by $\flat$'s) on the i-th row, for $1 \le i \le n$. Notice that, from such a picture, one can recover the input and the sequence of runs but not the complete step-by-step computation on the same input.

The *accepting-computation language* of M is defined as the set $A(M)$ of all pictures corresponding to any accepting computation of M. Note that every accepting computation W of M corresponds to a picture $w \in A(M)$ such that $r_w - 2$ equals the number of head reversals executed in W (corresponding to $W_2, \cdots, W_{n-1}$) and c_w is the space used in W.

Example 1. Let M be a Turing machine such that $\{a, b, c\}$ is the input and working alphabet, $Q = \{1, 2, 3, 4, 5, y\}$ is the set of states, y is the accepting state. Then, consider the sequence of moves represented in the following table, where $(\sigma', q', *) \in \delta(\sigma, q)$:

---

[1] We remark that usually the term computation refers to a description of the sequence of all single moves the machine executes. Rather, here we refer to this concept using the expression *step-by-step computation*.

q	0	1	4	2	1	4	5	1	4	0	2	3	2	4	2	0
σ	a	b	a	c	b	c	a	b	c	b	c	a	b	a	a	c
q'	1	4	2	1	4	5	1	4	0	2	3	2	4	2	0	y
σ'	c	a	c	b	a	b	c	a	b	a	b	b	a	c	b	b
$*$	+	+	+	+	+	−	−	+	+	+	+	−	−	+	−	−

The picture w associated to such a computation $W = W_1 \triangleright W_2 \triangleright \cdots \triangleright W_7$ is given by

a_0	b	a	c	b	c	c	a	$\rightarrow W_1$
c	a	c	b	a	c_4	c	a	$\rightarrow W_2$
c	a	c	b_1	c	b	c	a	$\rightarrow W_3$
c	a	c	a	b	a	b	a_3	$\rightarrow W_4$
c	a	c	a	b	a_4	a	b	$\rightarrow W_5$
c	a	c	a	b	c	a_2	b	$\rightarrow W_6$
c	a	c	a	b_y	b	b	b	$\rightarrow W_7$

with $w =$ shown at the left of the above grid.

Proposition 1. *The accepting-computation language of a 1-tape nondeterministic Turing machine is in* REC.

Sketch of the proof. One can prove that, for every given 1-tape nondeterministic Turing machine M, the accepting-computation language L of M is the projection of a suitable language L' in REC. The complete proof of this fact is omitted because of space constraints. Here we just say that, given M, for every picture $w \in L$ it is possible to define a new picture $w' \in L'$ by marking some symbols of w, so that w' encodes all information about the step-by-step computation of M on input w. Then, since such a computation can be described *locally* (the head touches only two cells at each step), L' can be recognized by a tiling system. Hence, L is in REC, too.   □

5.2   Overlap of Picture Languages

We now introduce a partial operation in the set of all picture languages (over all alphabets). Given two picture languages L_1 and L_2, we consider every pair of pictures $p \in L_1$ and $q \in L_2$ with the same size and having the first row in common, and we glue them along the first row. The collection of all these pairs is called the *overlap* $L_1 \diamond L_2$.

More formally, given two pictures p and q of the same size (n, m), let $p \times q$ be the picture such that $(p \times q)(i, j) = (p(i, j), q(i, j))$ for every $1 \leq i \leq n$ and $1 \leq j \leq m$. Then, the overlap of L_1 and L_2 is defined as

$$L_1 \diamond L_2 = \{ p \times q \mid p \in L_1, q \in L_2, \mathsf{r}_p = \mathsf{r}_q, \mathsf{c}_p = \mathsf{c}_q,$$
$$p(1, j) = q(1, j) \text{ for every } 1 \leq j \leq \mathsf{c}_p \}$$

Proposition 2. *Given two picture languages in* REC, *their overlap is still in* REC.

Proof. Let L_1 and L_2 be two picture languages over the alphabets Σ_1 and Σ_2, respectively, and assume that they are in REC. Then, for each $i \in \{1, 2\}$, there exists a tiling system $\langle \Sigma_i, \Gamma_i, \Theta_i, \pi_i \rangle$ recognizing L_i. Set

$$\text{Top}(\Theta_i) = \{t \in \Theta_i \mid t = \begin{array}{|c|c|} \hline \sharp & \sharp \\ \hline a & b \\ \hline \end{array} \text{ where } a, b \in \Gamma_i \cup \{\sharp\}\}$$

and let $\text{Left}(\Theta_i)$, $\text{Right}(\Theta_i)$, and $\text{Bottom}(\Theta_i)$ be defined analogously. Also, define $\text{Inner}(\Theta_i)$ as the set of tiles of Θ_i that do not belong to any of the previous set. Now, let $\Gamma = \Gamma_1 \times \Gamma_2$ and define Θ as the union of the sets $\text{Inner}(\Theta)$, $\text{Left}(\Theta)$, $\text{Right}(\Theta)$, $\text{Bottom}(\Theta)$, $\text{Top}(\Theta)$, where:

$$\text{Inner}(\Theta) = \{ \begin{array}{|c|c|} \hline (a_1, a_2) & (b_1, b_2) \\ \hline (c_1, c_2) & (d_1, d_2) \\ \hline \end{array} \mid \begin{array}{|c|c|} \hline a_i & b_i \\ \hline c_i & d_i \\ \hline \end{array} \in \text{Inner}(\Theta_i), \ i \in \{1, 2\}\},$$

$$\text{Left}(\Theta) = \{ \begin{array}{|c|c|} \hline \sharp & (a_1, a_2) \\ \hline \sharp & (b_1, b_2) \\ \hline \end{array} \mid \begin{array}{|c|c|} \hline \sharp & a_i \\ \hline \sharp & b_i \\ \hline \end{array} \in \text{Left}(\Theta_i), \ i \in \{1, 2\} \},$$

$\text{Bottom}(\Theta)$ and $\text{Right}(\Theta)$ are defined similarly, whereas $\text{Top}(\Theta)$ is given by

$$\text{Top}(\Theta) = \{ \begin{array}{|c|c|} \hline \sharp & \sharp \\ \hline (a_1, a_2) & (b_1, b_2) \\ \hline \end{array} \mid \begin{array}{|c|c|} \hline \sharp & \sharp \\ \hline a_i & b_i \\ \hline \end{array} \in \text{Top}(\Theta_i), \ i \in \{1, 2\} \text{ and }$$

$$\pi_1(a_1) = \pi_2(a_2), \pi_1(b_1) = \pi_2(b_2)\}.$$

Finally, set $\pi = \pi_1 \times \pi_2$, that is, for each pair $(a_1, a_2) \in \Gamma$, set $\pi(a_1, a_2) = (\pi_1(a_1), \pi_2(a_2))$. Clearly, $\langle \Sigma_1 \times \Sigma_2, \Gamma, \Theta, \pi \rangle$ is a tiling system recognizing the overlap of L_1 and L_2.

We are now able to prove the second part of Theorem 1.

Theorem 3. *Given any unary picture language L, if the quasi-unary string language $\phi(L)$ is in NSPACEREV_Q, then L is tiling recognizable.*

Proof. Since $\phi(L)$ is in NSPACEREV_Q, it is recognized by a 1-tape nondeterministic Turing machine M that works in $|x|$ space for any input $x \in Q$, and executes at most $o|x|$ head reversals during each computation. Thus, the accepting-computation language $A(M)$ of such a Turing machine is in REC, by Proposition 1, and so is the language $\bar{A}$ obtained from $A(M)$ by replacing the symbol $\circ_{q_0}$ by $\circ$ in the upper-leftmost cell of each picture in $A(M)$. As a consequence, the following language is in REC, too:

$$A' = \bar{A} \ominus \left(\not{b}^{*\Theta} \right)^{*\text{①}}$$

(observe that any picture in A' can be seen as a picture in $\bar{A}$ possibly extended downwards with rows of blanks).

Now, let us introduce some special picture languages that shall be used to bind the size of a picture, (i.e., they play the role of *mask languages*). Let E_s be the set of all unary squares and set

$$E_h = E_s \oplus h^{*\ominus} \oplus \circ^{**} \quad \text{and} \quad E_v = E_s \oplus v^{*\ominus} \oplus \circ^{**}.$$

In other words, any $p \in E_s \cup E_h$ contains, on each row, the quasi-unary string representing its own size, while if $p \in E_v$, then p contains, on each row, the quasi-unary string representing the size of p^R. Moreover consider the picture languages

$$L_s = A' \diamond E_s, \qquad L_h = A' \diamond E_h \quad \text{and} \quad L_v = (A' \diamond E_v)^R.$$

and set $L' = L_s \cup L_h \cup L_v$.

By Proposition 2, also L' is tiling recognizable, and it turns out that $L = \pi(L')$. Indeed, by the previous definition, we have that any quasi-unary string x representing a picture of $\pi(L')$ is an accepted input of M, and hence it also represents a picture in L. Thus, L and $\pi(L')$ being unary, we get $\pi(L') \subseteq L$.

On the other hand, assume $p \in L$. First of all, notice that $\phi(p)$ is accepted by M, hence there exists $a \in \bar{A}$ having $\phi(p)$ on the first row and such that $c_a = \max(r_p, c_p)$ and $r_a \leq \min(r_p, c_p)$. Let $a' \in A'$ be the extension of a that has exactly $\min(r_p, c_p)$ rows, and notice that a' is a horizontal rectangle or a square, independently of the shape of p. Moreover, consider the picture $u_p = \phi(p)^{\circ|x|\ominus}$. Notice that, if p is a horizontal rectangle, then $u_p \in E_h$; if p is a vertical rectangle, then $u_p \in E_v$, otherwise, if p is a square, $u_p \in E_s$. In any case, u_p has the same size as a'. Hence, if p is a square or a horizontal rectangle, then we have $p = \pi(a' \diamond u_p)$; otherwise we have $p = \pi((a' \diamond u_p)^R)$. In all cases, $p \in \pi(L')$ and hence $L \subseteq \pi(L')$. Thus, $L = \pi(L')$ is in REC$_1$ and this concludes the proof.

6   Square Languages

In this last section we focus on unary square languages, that is on unary picture languages whose elements are all squares. As should be clear at this moment of the exposition, square languages are nothing but sets of positive integers, and so far we represented them by unary strings over the alphabet $\{\circ\}$. In the following definition, we introduce a subclass of NSPACEREV$_Q$ that concerns only square languages and their representation.

Definition 5. NSPACEREV$_U$ *is the class of unary string languages that can be recognized by 1-tape nondeterministic Turing machines working within n space and executing at most n head reversals, for any input of length n.*

Integers can also be represented with the classical binary encoding and this suggest to define the binary complexity class corresponding to the previous definition.

Definition 6. NSPACEREV$_B$ *is the class of binary string languages that can be recognized by 1-tape nondeterministic Turing machines working within 2^n space and executing at most 2^n head reversals, for any input of length n.*

Notice that the families NSPACEREV_U and NSPACEREV_B are related to the well-known time complexity classification. In particular, denoting by $\text{NTIME}_U(f(n))$ (resp. $\text{NTIME}_B(f(n))$) the class of unary (resp. binary) string languages that can be recognized by 1-tape nondeterministic Turing machines working within $f(n)$ time for any input of length n, we have the following relations:

$$\text{NTIME}_U(n) \subseteq \text{NSPACEREV}_U \subseteq \text{NTIME}_U(n^2),$$

$$\text{NTIME}_B(2^n) \subseteq \text{NSPACEREV}_B \subseteq \text{NTIME}_B(4^n). \tag{1}$$

Theorem 1 can then be re-stated using these new classes, obtaining the following corollary.

Corollary 1. *Given a unary square language L, the following statements are equivalent:*

- *L is in REC_1,*
- *$\{\circ^{r_p} \mid p \in L\} \in \text{NSPACEREV}_U$,*
- *$\{Bin(r_p) \mid p \in L\} \in \text{NSPACEREV}_B$,*

where $Bin(n)$ is the binary encoding of the positive integer n.

The previous corollary provides a useful tool to verify whether a unary square language is tiling recognizable. For instance, it proves that the set of unary square pictures whose size is a prime number is in REC_1, since it is well-known that the set of prime numbers is recognizable in polynomial time[1]. More generally, if π is a NP problem, let L_π be the language of all binary encodings of positive instances of π. Then, the picture language $\{p \in \circ^{**} \mid \exists x \in L_\pi \text{ such that } Bin(r_p) = 1x\}$ belongs to REC_1.

A further, more complex, tiling-recognizable picture language can be built by considering INEQ(RE,2), i.e. the inequality problem of regular expressions with squaring, studied by Meyer and Stockmeyer in [9,10]. It is known that this problem is complete in the class $\text{NEXPTIME} = \bigcup_{c \geq 1} \text{NTIME}(2^{cn})$ and hence it is not even included in NP by well-known separation results [11]. It is not difficult to prove that a rather natural binary encoding of INEQ(RE,2) belongs to $\text{NTIME}_B(2^n)$ and hence, by the previous corollary and Equation 1, the corresponding family of unary square pictures is tiling recognizable.

Another consequence of Corollary 1 concerns the construction of unary square languages that are not tiling recognizable. For instance one can prove the existence of a unary square language that is not tiling recognizable, but such that the set of binary encoding of its sizes is not too far (from a complexity view point) from the class NSPACEREV_B. In order to present such an example, for any function $f : \mathbb{N} \to \mathbb{R}^+$, let us define $2t\text{-NTIME}_B(f)$ as the class of binary string languages that are recognizable by 2-tape nondeterministic Turing machines working within time $f(n)$ on every input of length n.

Proposition 3. *There exists a unary square picture language $L \notin \text{REC}_1$ such that the string language $S = \{x \in \{0,1\}^* \mid 1x = Bin(r_p) \text{ for a picture } p \in L\}$ belongs to $2t\text{-NTIME}_B(4^n \log n)$.*

Proof. The existence of such language is guaranteed by a property proved in [11]. If $T_1, T_2 : \mathbb{N} \to \mathbb{R}^+$ are two running-time functions such that $T_1(n+1)/T_2(n)$ tends to 0 as n goes to infinity, then there exists a language $S \subseteq \{0,1\}^*$ that belongs to 2t-$\text{NTIME}_B(T_2(n))$ but does not belong to 2t-$\text{NTIME}_B(T_1(n))$. Setting $T_1(n) = 4^n$, $T_2(n) = 4^n \log n$, and observing that 2t-$\text{NTIME}_B(4^n) \supseteq \text{NSPACEREV}_B$, by Theorem 1 we have that S is in 2t-$\text{NTIME}_B(4^n \log n)$ whereas L cannot be tiling recognizable.

Concluding, we observe that a natural problem arising from our characterization result is whether a separation property, similar to the one proved in [11], also holds for complexity classes defined by bounding the number of head reversals. This would lead to simpler unary picture languages that are not tiling recognizable.

References

1. M. Agrawal, N. Kayal, N. Saxena. PRIMES is in P. *Annals of Mathematics*, 160(2): 781-793, 2004.
2. M. Anselmo, D. Giammarresi, M. Madonia. Regular expressions for two-dimensional languages over one-letter alphabet. In *Proc. 8th DLT*, C.S. Calude, E. Calude and M.J. Dinneen (Eds.), LNCS 3340, 63–75, Springer-Verlag, 2004.
3. D. Giammarresi, A. Restivo. Recognizable picture languages. *Int. J. Pattern Recognition and Artificial Intelligence*, Special Issue on Parallel Image Processing, 31–42, 1992.
4. D. Giammarresi, A. Restivo. Two-dimensional languages. In *Handbook of Formal Languages*, G. Rosenberg and A. Salomaa (Eds.), Vol. III, 215 – 268, Springer-Verlag, 1997.
5. D. Giammarresi, A. Restivo, S. Seibert, W. Thomas. Monadic second order logic over rectangular pictures and recognizability by tiling system. *Information and Computation*, 125(1):32–45, 1996.
6. K. Inoue, I. Takanami. A survey of two-dimensional automata theory. In *Proc. 5th Int. Meeting of Young Computer Scientists*, J. Dasson, J. Kelemen (Eds.), LNCS 381, 72–91, Springer-Verlag, 1990.
7. J. Kari, C. Moore. New results on alternating and non-deterministic two-dimensional finite state automata. In *Proc. 18th STACS*, A. Ferreira, H. Reichel (Eds.), LNCS 2010, 396–406, Springer-Verlag, 2001.
8. O. Matz. Regular expressions and context-free grammars for picture languages. In *Proc. 14th STACS*, LNCS 1200, 283–294, Springer-Verlag, 1997.
9. A.R. Meyer and L.J. Stockmeyer. The equivalence problem for regular expressions with squaring requires exponential space. Proc. 13th Annual IEEE Symp. on Switching and Automata Theory 125-129, 1972.
10. A.R. Meyer and L.J. Stockmeyer. Words problems requiring exponential time. Proc. 5th ACM Symp. on Theory of Computing 1-9, 1973.
11. J. I. Seiferas, M. J. Fischer, A. R. Meyer. Separating nondeterministic time complexity classes. *Journal of ACM*, 25(1): 146–167, 1978.
12. R. Siromoney. Advances in array languages. In *Graph-grammars and their applications to Computer Science*, Ehrig et al. Eds., LNCS 291, 549–563, Springer-Verlag, 1987.

A Characterization of Strong Learnability in the Statistical Query Model*

Hans Ulrich Simon

Fakultät für Mathematik, Ruhr-Universität Bochum, 44780 Bochum, Germany
simon@lmi.rub.de

Abstract. In this paper, we consider Kearns' [4] Statistical Query Model of learning. It is well known [3] that the number of statistical queries, needed for "weakly learning" an unknown target concept (i.e. for gaining significant advantage over random guessing) is polynomially related to the so-called Statistical Query dimension of the concept class. In this paper, we provide a similar characterization for "strong learning" where the learners final hypothesis is required to approximate the unknown target concept up to a small rate of misclassification. The quantity that characterizes strong learnability in the Statistical Query model is a surprisingly close relative of (though not identical to) the Statistical Query dimension. For the purpose of proving the main result, we provide other characterizations of strong learnability which are given in terms of covering numbers and related notions. These results might find some interest in their own right. All characterizations are purely information-theoretical and ignore computational issues.

1 Introduction

Kearns' Statistical Query (SQ) model [4] is an elegant abstraction from Valiant's PAC learning model [7]. In this model, instead of having direct access to random examples (as in the PAC learning model) the learner obtains information about random examples via an oracle that provides estimates of various statistics about the unknown concept. Kearns showed that any learning algorithm that is successful in the SQ model can be converted, without much loss of efficiency, into a learning algorithm that is successful in the PAC learning model despite noise uniformly applied to the class labels of the examples. In the same paper where Kearns showed that SQ learnability implies noise-tolerant PAC learnability, he developed SQ algorithms for almost all concept classes known to be efficiently learnable in the PAC learning model. This is why the SQ model attracted a lot of attention in the Computational Learning community.

---

* This work was supported in part by the IST Programme of the European Community, under the PASCAL Network of Excellence, IST-2002-506778. This publication only reflects the authors' views. Part of this work was done during a visit of the Helsinki Institute of Information Technology.

W. Thomas and P. Weil (Eds.): STACS 2007, LNCS 4393, pp. 393–404, 2007.
© Springer-Verlag Berlin Heidelberg 2007

Blum et al. [3] have shown that the number of statistical queries, needed for weakly learning a concept class, is polynomially related to the largest number of pairwise "almost orthogonal" concepts from this class (the so-called SQ dimension). Ke Yang [8] presented an alternative (stronger but polynomially related) lower bound on the number of statistical queries. It is stated in terms of the eigenvalues of the correlation matrix associated with the concept class. The problem of characterizing strong learnability in the SQ model was left open in these papers.

Köbler and Lindner [5] characterized strong learnability in the SQ model in terms of the so-called "general dimension" (a variant of the abstract combinatorial dimension from [1]). The general dimension can be viewed as the number of queries needed when the SQ oracle behaves like a uniform non-adaptive adversary that returns answers according to a fixed scheme (the *same* scheme for all learners). Köbler and Lindner show that this number is polynomially related to the number of queries needed in the worst-case where the SQ oracle behaves like an adaptive and non-uniform adversary (the strongest adversary of the particular learner). Loosely speaking, the result by Köbler and Lindner tells that the handicap of being non-adaptive and uniform does not make the adversary substantially weaker. The general dimension has no algebraic flavor. In contrast, the results in this paper make extensive use of algebraic properties of the correlation matrix associated with the concept class. We conjecture that our results can also serve as a tool for the computation of the general dimension.

Models related to the SQ model: We would like to mention briefly that the SQ model has a predecessor: the model of "Learning by Distances" [2]. The former model is a special case of the latter (but the inventors of the latter model did not reveal the relation to noise-tolerant learning).

The SQ model is furthermore equivalent to a conceptually simpler model where statistical queries (as they were originally defined by Kearns) are replaced by "correlation queries". For the purpose of our theoretical analysis, the simpler model is more convenient. For this reason, we do not bother the reader with the definition of the original model. Instead we define the SQ model in section 2 directly within the Correlation Query framework. The reader interested in the formal proof of equivalence between the two models is referred to [6].

In the original model by Kearns, "concepts" and "query functions" are ± 1-valued. In this paper, it will be more convenient to deal with real-valued functions instead. The traditional setting of concept learning (with binary functions) will however be subsumed as a special case.

Structure of the paper: In section 2, we provide the reader with rigorous definitions and notations (including the notions of weak and strong learning in the SQ model). Section 3 briefly reviews the known bounds on the number of statistical queries and the known characterization of weak learnability in terms of the (Weak) Statistical Query dimension (SQdim). In section 4, we define the Strong Statistical Query dimension (SQDim*) and present a characterization of strong learnability in terms of this dimension. It should be stressed that, although SQDim* is a close relative of SQdim, the mathematical analysis of strong learnability in the SQ model is much more involved than the preceding analysis of weak learnability.

2   Definitions and Notations

Concept Learning: A *concept* is a function f of the form $f : X \rightarrow \{\pm1\}$. A concept class, denoted as $\mathcal{F}$, is a set of concepts. Throughout this paper, X is a finite set called the *domain*. An element $x \in X$ is called an *instance*. A labeled instance $(x, b) \in X \times \{\pm1\}$ is called an *example for f* if $b = f(x)$. $D : X \rightarrow [0, 1]$ denotes a mapping that assigns probabilities to instances such that $D(x) \geq 0$ for all $x \in X$ and $\sum_{x \in X} D(x) = 1$. Notations $\Pr_D[\cdot]$ and $\mathbb{E}_D[\cdot]$ refer to the probability of an event and to the expectation of a random variable, respectively. A function $h : X \rightarrow \{\pm1\}$ (not necessarily from $\mathcal{F}$) is called a *(binary) hypothesis*. Informally, the goal of a learner for concept class $\mathcal{F}$ is to infer from "partial information" about an unknown *target concept* $f_* \in \mathcal{F}$ a hypothesis h_* whose probability of misclassification, $\Pr_D[h(x) \neq f(x)]$, is small. A notion that helps to keep track of the progress made by the learner is the so-called "version space". Formally, the *version space* is a subclass $\mathcal{F}' \subseteq \mathcal{F}$ of the concept class (initially $\mathcal{F}' = \mathcal{F}$) that consists of all concepts being consistent with the partial information that is currently available to the learner. The formal notion of "partial information" depends on the learning model in consideration. The reader might perhaps be familiar with the PAC learning model [7] where the information given to the learner consists of random examples for the unknown target concept. In this paper, we will be mainly concerned with the SQ model that is outlined in the remainder of this section.

Correlation Matrix: The real-valued functions on domain X form an $|X|$-dimensional vector space that can be equipped with the following inner product:

$$\langle h_1, h_2 \rangle_D := \sum_{x \in X} D(x) h_1(x) h_2(x) = \mathbb{E}_D[h_1(x) h_2(x)]$$

This inner product induces the so-called *D-norm*: $\|h\|_D := \langle h, h \rangle_D$. Note that $\|h\|_D = 1$ if h is a ±1-valued function, and $\|h\|_D \leq 1$ if h is a function with values in $[-1, 1]$. In the sequel, $\mathcal{F}$ denotes a class of real-valued functions, and $C_{\mathcal{F}} \in [-1, 1]^{\mathcal{F} \times \mathcal{F}}$ such that $C_{\mathcal{F}}[f_1, f_2] := \langle f_1, f_2 \rangle_D$ denotes the *correlation matrix* induced by $\mathcal{F}$. Note that $C_{\mathcal{F}}$ is positive semidefinite.

Ingredients of the SQ Model: Notions $\mathcal{F}, X, D, f_*$ are understood as in the general concept learning framework except that $\mathcal{F}$ is a function class (with concept classes as a special case). The learner has access to random examples only indirectly through queries that are answered by an oracle. To this end, let $\mathcal{Q}$ denote a function class from which the learner picks its so-called query functions and its final hypothesis. Throughout the paper, we assume that $\mathcal{F} \subseteq \mathcal{Q}$ and that $1 \leq B < \infty$ is an upper bound on the D-norm of functions from $\mathcal{Q}$. A *query* is of the form (h, τ) where $h \in \mathcal{Q}$ and $\tau > 0$. τ is called the *tolerance parameter*. Upon such a query, the oracle returns a τ-*approximation* for $\langle h, f_* \rangle_D$, i.e. it returns a number c that satisfies

$$\langle h, f_* \rangle_D - \tau \le c \le \langle h, f_* \rangle_D + \tau \ . \tag{1}$$

Like in the general framework of concept learning, the learner will stop at some point and return a final hypothesis $h_* \in Q$. We will measure the "efficiency" of the learner by the number of queries that it passes to the oracle (in the worst-case) and by the smallest tolerance parameter τ that is ever used during learning. We will measure the "success" of the learner by the correlation between the target function f_* and the final hypothesis h_*.

Statistical Learning Complexity: We say that $q = q(\tau, \gamma)$ queries are sufficient to learn $\mathcal{F}$ with query functions and final hypothesis chosen from Q if there exists a learning procedure L (with unbounded computational resources) that achieves the following. For every possible target function $f_* \in \mathcal{F}$ and for every possible policy for the oracle (subject to (1)), L asks at most $q-1$ queries (with tolerance parameter set to τ or a larger value) until it comes up with a final hypothesis $h_* \in Q$ (a kind of q-th query function) whose correlation with f_* is at least γ. $\mathrm{SLC}_{\mathcal{F},Q}(\tau, \gamma)$ denotes the smallest number of queries that is sufficient for that purpose. If Q consists of all functions of the form $h : X \to \mathbb{R}$ such that $\|h\|_D \le 1$, we simply write $\mathrm{SLC}_{\mathcal{F}}(\tau, \gamma)$.[1]

Parameterized Classes, Weak and Strong Learnability: A parameterized function class is of the form $\mathcal{F} = \cup_{n \ge 1} \mathcal{F}_n$. Similarly, $Q = \cup_{n \ge 1} Q_n$. We say that $\mathcal{F}$ is *weakly learnable* in the SQ model with query functions and final hypothesis chosen from Q if there exist functions $\gamma(n) > 0$ and $\tau(n) > 0$ such that $1/\gamma(n)$, $1/\tau(n)$, and $\mathrm{SLC}_{\mathcal{F}_n, Q_n}(\tau(n), \gamma(n))$ are polynomially bounded in n. We say that $\mathcal{F}$ is *strongly learnable* in the SQ model with query functions and final hypothesis chosen from Q if there exists a function $\tau(n, \varepsilon) > 0$ such that $1/\tau(n, \varepsilon)$ and $\mathrm{SLC}_{\mathcal{F}_n, Q_n}(\tau(n), 1 - \varepsilon)$ are polynomially bounded in n and $1/\varepsilon$.

Notations and Facts from Matrix Theory: Although we assume some familiarity with basic concepts from matrix theory, we provide the reader with a refreshment of his or her memory and fix some notation. The Euclidean norm of a vector $u \in \mathbb{R}^d$ is denoted as $\|u\|$. The real eigenvalues of a symmetric matrix A are denoted as $\lambda_1(A) \ge \lambda_2(A) \ge \lambda_3(A) \ge \cdots$. We finally would like to mention the following fact (known as Geršgorin's Disc Theorem): for any $(d \times d)$-matrix M with complex entries, the union of discs,

$$\bigcup_{i=1}^{d} \left\{ z \ \middle| \ |z - M_{i,i}| \le \sum_{j:1 \le j \le d, j \ne i} |M_{i,j}| \right\} ,$$

covers all (complex) eigenvalues of M. Here, $|\cdot|$ denotes the absolute value of a complex number. The theorem holds in particular for symmetric real-valued matrices where all eigenvalues are reals.

---

[1] An analogous convention is made in the sequel for other notions depending on Q.

3   Known Bounds on the Number of Statistical Queries

The following beautiful result by Ke Yang presents a lower bound on statistical learning complexity in terms of the eigenvalues of the correlation matrix $C_{\mathcal{F}}$.

Theorem 1 ([8]). *Assume that all query and target functions have D-norm at most 1. Then,* $\sum_{i=1}^{\text{SLC}_{\mathcal{F}}(\tau,\gamma)} \lambda_i(C_{\mathcal{F}}) \geq |\mathcal{F}| \cdot \min\{\gamma^2, \tau^2\}$.

Definition 1 (Covering Number). *A set of functions* $h_1, \ldots, h_k \in \mathcal{Q}$ *is called a* τ-cover *of* $\mathcal{F}$ *if, for every function* $f \in \mathcal{F}$, *there exists an index* $i \in \{1, \ldots, k\}$ *such that* $\langle f, h_i \rangle_D \geq \tau$. *We denote the size of the smallest* τ-cover *by* $\text{CNum}_{\mathcal{F}, \mathcal{Q}}(\tau)$.

The following result is easy to infer from Ke Yang's proof of Theorem 1:

Corollary 1. *Assume that* $\tau \leq \gamma$. *Then,* $\text{SLC}_{\mathcal{F}}(\tau, \gamma) \geq \text{CNum}_{\mathcal{F}}(\tau)$ *and*

$$\sum_{i=1}^{\text{CNum}_{\mathcal{F}}(\tau)} \lambda_i(C_{\mathcal{F}}) \geq |\mathcal{F}| \cdot \tau^2 \ . \tag{2}$$

Definition 2 (Weak SQ Dimension). *Let* $\text{SQDim}_{\mathcal{F}}$ *denote the largest number* d *such that* $\mathcal{F}$ *contains functions* $f_1, \ldots, f_d$ *with the following property:[2]*

$$\forall 1 \leq i < j \leq d : \ |\langle f_i, f_j \rangle_D| < \frac{1}{d-1} \tag{3}$$

Let $d := \text{SQDim}_{\mathcal{F}}$. Consider a maximal sequence $f_1, \ldots, f_s \in \mathcal{F}$ with the property that $|\langle f_i, f_j \rangle_D| < 1/d$ for all $1 \leq i < j \leq s$. These functions form a $1/d$-cover (because, otherwise, the sequence could be extended). Thus, $s \geq \text{CNum}_{\mathcal{F}, \mathcal{F}}(1/d)$. On the other hand, $s \leq d$ (because, otherwise, the sequence witnesses that $\text{SQDim}_{\mathcal{F}} \geq d+1$). We conclude that the following holds (provided that $\mathcal{F} \subseteq \mathcal{Q}$):

$$\text{SQDim}_{\mathcal{F}} \geq \text{CNum}_{\mathcal{F}, \mathcal{F}}\left(\frac{1}{\text{SQDim}_{\mathcal{F}}}\right) \geq \text{CNum}_{\mathcal{F}, \mathcal{Q}}\left(\frac{1}{\text{SQDim}_{\mathcal{F}}}\right) \ . \tag{4}$$

Ke Yang [8] inferred from Theorem 1 that for $d = \text{SQDim}_{\mathcal{F}}$ the following (slight improvement on an older result from [3]) holds:

$$\text{SLC}_{\mathcal{F}}(d^{-1/3}, d^{-1/3}) \geq \frac{1}{2} \cdot d^{1/3}$$

From Corollary 1, one can infer a slightly more general result:

Corollary 2. *Assume* $\tau \leq \gamma$. *Then,*

$$\text{SLC}_{\mathcal{F}}(\tau, \gamma) \geq \text{CNum}_{\mathcal{F}}(\tau) \geq \frac{1}{2} \cdot \tau^2 \cdot \text{SQDim}_{\mathcal{F}} \ .$$

---

[2] If we replace $1/(d-1)$ on the right hand side of (3) by $1/d^3$, we obtain the original definition (from [3]) of the SQ dimension of $\mathcal{F}$.

Weak learnability in the SQ model can be perfectly characterized in terms of the weak SQ dimension:

Corollary 3 ([3]). *A parameterized function class $\mathcal{F} = \cup_{n \geq 1} \mathcal{F}_n$ is weakly learnable in the SQ-model if and only if the growth rate of $\mathrm{SQDim}_{\mathcal{F}_n}$ is polynomially bounded in n.*

Proof. Direction "only if" is obvious from Corollary 2. Direction "if" easily follows from (4). □

4 Strong Learnability in the SQ Model

It is well-known that there exist concept classes that are weakly, but not strongly, learnable. These classes will have a reasonably small SQ dimension. This rules out the possibility of characterizing strong learnability in the SQ model by the weak SQ dimension. As for strong learnability, we need, on one hand, stronger lower bounds and, on the other hand, (reasonably well) matching upper bounds. It turns out that satisfactory (lower and upper) bounds are obtained in terms of the SQ dimension of classes of the form

$$\mathcal{F} - g := \{f - g : f \in \mathcal{F}\}$$

provided that the set of "admissible shift functions" g is carefully chosen. A serious technical obstacle is the fact that possibly $\mathrm{SLC}_{\mathcal{F}-g,\mathcal{Q}}(\tau, \gamma) > \mathrm{SLC}_{\mathcal{F},\mathcal{Q}}(\tau, \gamma)$ such that lower bounds on $\mathrm{SLC}_{\mathcal{F}-g,\mathcal{Q}}(\tau, \gamma)$ are not necessarily lower bounds on $\mathrm{SLC}_{\mathcal{F},\mathcal{Q}}(\tau, \gamma)$. We shall proceed as follows:

- As for the upper bound, we will pursue a "halving strategy" where the learner proceeds in stages and, at any fixed stage, tries to "halve" the current version space. This will lead to the notion of "statistical halving complexity" $\mathrm{SHC}_{\mathcal{F},\mathcal{Q}}(\tau)$.
- As for the lower bound, we will exploit the fact that the statistical halving complexity is invariant under shifts such that lower bounds on $\mathrm{SHC}_{\mathcal{F}-g,\mathcal{Q}}(\tau)$ *are* lower bounds on $\mathrm{SHC}_{\mathcal{F},\mathcal{Q}}(\tau)$.
- Shift functions g that lead to "unbiased" classes $\mathcal{F} - g$ will play a crucial role.

The remainder of this section is devoted to the statement and proof of the main result.

4.1 Central Definitions and Main Result

The following definition is tailored such that a learner with a γ-nontrivial version space is actually *forced* to "halve" it in order to achieve a correlation of at least γ with the target function. This prepares the ground for relating statistical learning and statistical halving complexity to each other.

Definition 3 (Trivial Subclasses). *We say that $\mathcal{F}' \subseteq \mathcal{F}$ is a $(\gamma, \mathcal{Q})$-trivial subclass of $\mathcal{F}$ if there exists a function $h \in \mathcal{Q}$ that has a correlation of at least γ with at least half of the functions in $\mathcal{F}'$. The remaining subclasses of $\mathcal{F}$ are said to be $(\gamma, \mathcal{Q})$-nontrivial.*

Definition 4 (Unbiased Function Classes and Admissible Functions). *The average of the functions in $\mathcal{F}$ is given by*

$$B_{\mathcal{F}} := \frac{1}{|\mathcal{F}|} \sum_{f \in \mathcal{F}} f \ .$$

$\mathcal{F}$ is called unbiased *if $B_{\mathcal{F}}(x) = 0$ for every $x \in X$. A function $g : X \to \mathbb{R}$ is called $(\gamma, \mathcal{Q})$-admissible for $\mathcal{F}$ if it has the form $g = B_{\mathcal{F}'}$ for a $(\gamma, \mathcal{Q})$-nontrivial subclass $\mathcal{F}'$ of $\mathcal{F}$.*

The following (obvious) result sheds some light on the significance of the preceding definitions:

Lemma 1. *1. $\mathcal{F} - B_{\mathcal{F}}$ is unbiased.*
2. For every function $h : X \to \mathbb{R}$, the correlation between h and the functions from an unbiased class (like, for example, $\mathcal{F} - B_{\mathcal{F}}$) is zero on the average.

Here comes the central new notion that allows for a characterization of strong learnability in the SQ model.

Definition 5 (Strong SQ Dimension). *The strong SQ dimension associated with $\mathcal{F}$ and $\mathcal{Q}$ is the function*

$$\text{SQDim}_{\mathcal{F},\mathcal{Q}}^{*}(\gamma) := \sup_{\mathcal{F}'} \text{SQDim}_{\mathcal{F}'-B_{\mathcal{F}'}} \ ,$$

where $\mathcal{F}'$ ranges over all $(\gamma, \mathcal{Q})$-nontrivial subclasses of $\mathcal{F}$. In addition, we define

$$\text{SQDim}_{\mathcal{F},\mathcal{Q}}^{**}(\gamma) := \sup_{g} \text{SQDim}_{\mathcal{F}-g} \geq \text{SQDim}_{\mathcal{F},\mathcal{Q}}^{*}(\gamma) \ ,$$

where g ranges over all functions that are $(\gamma, \mathcal{Q})$-admissible for $\mathcal{F}$.[3]

With these definitions, our main result reads as follows:

Theorem 2. *Assume that all query and target functions have D-norm at most 1. A parameterized function class $\mathcal{F} = \cup_{n \geq 1}\mathcal{F}_n$ is strongly learnable in the SQ-model with query functions and final hypothesis chosen from $\mathcal{Q} = \cup_{n \geq 1}\mathcal{Q}_n$ if and only if the growth rate of $\text{SQDim}_{\mathcal{F}_n,\mathcal{Q}_n}^{*}(1 - \varepsilon)$ is polynomially bounded in n and $1/\varepsilon$.*

---

[3] Throughout the paper, the default value for a supremum ranging over the empty set is 1.

4.2   A Detour on Halving Complexity and Half-Covering Numbers

As explained in the beginning of section 4, statistical halving complexity will be the right notion for our purpose because of its invariance to shifts. Here comes the formal definition:

Definition 6 (Statistical Halving Complexity). $\mathrm{SHC}_{\mathcal{F},\mathcal{Q}}(\tau)$ *denotes the smallest number of queries that is sufficient to "halve" function class $\mathcal{F}$ in the sense that at most half of the functions from $\mathcal{F}$ are consistent with the answers that are received from the oracle. We furthermore define*

$$\mathrm{SHC}^*_{\mathcal{F},\mathcal{Q}}(\tau,\gamma) := \sup_{\mathcal{F}'} \mathrm{SHC}_{\mathcal{F}',\mathcal{Q}}(\tau)$$

where $\mathcal{F}'$ ranges over all $(\gamma,\mathcal{Q})$-nontrivial subclasses of $\mathcal{F}$.

Note that a subclass might be harder to halve than the class itself. It is however obvious that, for every function $g : X \to \mathbb{R}$,

$$\mathrm{SHC}_{\mathcal{F},\mathcal{Q}}(\tau) = \mathrm{SHC}_{\mathcal{F}-g,\mathcal{Q}}(\tau) \ . \tag{5}$$

The following notion relates to statistical halving complexity pretty much as the covering number relates to statistical learning complexity:

Definition 7 (Half-Covering Number). *A set of functions $h_1,\ldots,h_k \in \mathcal{Q}$ is called a τ-half-cover of $\mathcal{F}$ if, for at least half of the functions $f \in \mathcal{F}$, there exists an index $i \in \{1,\ldots,k\}$ such that $\langle f,h_i\rangle_D \geq \tau$. We denote the size of the smallest τ-half-cover by $\mathrm{HCNum}_{\mathcal{F},\mathcal{Q}}(\tau)$.*

Recall that B denotes an upper bound on the D-norm of query functions. The following result is the analogue to Corollary 1:

Theorem 3. $\mathrm{SHC}_{\mathcal{F},\mathcal{Q}}(\tau) \geq \mathrm{HCNum}_{\mathcal{F},\mathcal{Q}}(\tau)$ *and*

$$\sum_{i=1}^{\mathrm{HCNum}_{\mathcal{F},\mathcal{Q}}(\tau)} \lambda_i(C_{\mathcal{F}}) \geq \frac{|\mathcal{F}|}{2} \cdot \frac{\tau^2}{B^2} \ .$$

The proof is a slight modification of Ke Yang's proof of Theorem 1. We briefly note that

$$\mathrm{SHC}_{\mathcal{F},\mathcal{Q}}(\tau) \overset{(5)}{=} \mathrm{SHC}_{\mathcal{F}-g,\mathcal{Q}}(\tau) \overset{Th.3}{\geq} \mathrm{HCNum}_{\mathcal{F}-g,\mathcal{Q}}(\tau) \ . \tag{6}$$

We will see in Lemmas 2 and 4 that SLC is closely related to SHC*. Furthermore, SHC* can be shown to be closely related to the following variants of half-covering numbers:

$$\mathrm{HCNum}^*_{\mathcal{F},\mathcal{Q}}(\tau,\gamma) := \sup_{\mathcal{F}'} \mathrm{HCNum}_{\mathcal{F}'-B_{\mathcal{F}'},\mathcal{Q}}(\tau)$$

$$\mathrm{HCNum}^{**}_{\mathcal{F},\mathcal{Q}}(\tau,\gamma) := \sup_{\mathcal{F}'} \sup_{g:X\to\mathbb{R}} \mathrm{HCNum}_{\mathcal{F}'-g,\mathcal{Q}}(\tau)$$

In both definitions, $\mathcal{F}'$ ranges over all $(\gamma,\mathcal{Q})$-nontrivial subclasses of $\mathcal{F}$.

Lemma 2. $\text{SLC}_{\mathcal{F},\mathcal{Q}}(\tau,\gamma) \geq \text{SHC}^*_{\mathcal{F},\mathcal{Q}}(\tau,\gamma) \geq \text{HCNum}^{**}_{\mathcal{F},\mathcal{Q}}(\tau,\gamma)$.

Proof. The second inequality is obtained by applying (6) to every $(\gamma,\mathcal{Q})$-nontrivial subclass $\mathcal{F}' \subseteq \mathcal{F}$.
The first inequality can be seen as follows. If there exists no $(\gamma,\mathcal{Q})$-nontrivial subclass of $\mathcal{F}$, it holds because $\text{SLC}_{\mathcal{F},\mathcal{Q}}(\tau,\gamma) \geq 1$. Otherwise, consider a $(\gamma,\mathcal{Q})$-nontrivial subclass $\mathcal{F}' \subseteq \mathcal{F}$ such that $\text{SHC}_{\mathcal{F}',\mathcal{Q}}(\tau) = \text{SHC}^*_{\mathcal{F},\mathcal{Q}}(\tau,\gamma)$. It is easily seen that

$$\text{SLC}_{\mathcal{F},\mathcal{Q}}(\tau,\gamma) \geq \text{SLC}_{\mathcal{F}',\mathcal{Q}}(\tau,\gamma) \geq \text{SHC}_{\mathcal{F}',\mathcal{Q}}(\tau) ,$$

where the second inequality holds thanks to the $(\gamma,\mathcal{Q})$-non-triviality of $\mathcal{F}'$.   □

In order to establish an upper bound on SHC^* in terms of HCNum^*, we have to work harder. Imagine a learner who received the information that the target function, f_*, has a correlation of at least τ with query function h. If the vast majority of concepts shared this property with f_*, the learner would make only little progress. If, however, the correlation between h and the functions of the current version space is zero on the average, then, as compensation for the functions with correlation at least τ, there will be a certain fraction of concepts that correlate negatively with h and that fall out of the version space. This explains why the fact that $\mathcal{F}\ B_{\mathcal{F}}$ is unbiased will play a central role in the proof of the following result:

Lemma 3. $\text{SHC}^*_{\mathcal{F},\mathcal{Q}}(\tau/4,\gamma) < 2/\tau + \text{HCNum}^*_{\mathcal{F},\mathcal{Q}}(2\tau,\gamma)$.

Proof. Consider a $(\gamma,\mathcal{Q})$-nontrivial subclass $\mathcal{F}' \subseteq \mathcal{F}$ such that $\text{SHC}^*_{\mathcal{F},\mathcal{Q}}(\tau/4,\gamma) = \text{SHC}_{\mathcal{F}',\mathcal{Q}}(\tau/4)$. (The case that no such subclass exists is trivial.) Recall that $\text{SHC}_{\mathcal{F}',\mathcal{Q}}(\tau/4) = \text{SHC}_{\mathcal{F}'-B_{\mathcal{F}'},\mathcal{Q}}(\tau/4)$ such that we can focus on the halving problem for $\mathcal{F}' - B_{\mathcal{F}'}$. We proceed by case analysis.

Case 1: $\exists h \in \mathcal{Q} : |\{f \in \mathcal{F}' : \langle h, f - B_{\mathcal{F}'}\rangle_D \geq 3\tau/2\}| \geq |\mathcal{F}'|/2$.
Pass $(h,\tau/4)$ to the oracle. If it returns a value smaller than than $5\tau/4$ such that the true correlation with the target function is smaller than $3\tau/2$, then, by our case assumption, we have halved $\mathcal{F}'$ at the expense of one query only. So let us assume that the oracle returns a value of at least $5\tau/4$ such that the true correlation with the target function from $\mathcal{F}' - B_{\mathcal{F}'}$ must be at least τ. Let α denote the fraction of functions from $\mathcal{F}' - B_{\mathcal{F}'}$ whose correlation with h is at least τ such that the version space shrinks by factor α. According to Lemma 1, the average correlation between h and functions from $\mathcal{F}' - B_{\mathcal{F}'}$ is zero. It follows that $\alpha\tau + (1-\alpha)(-1) \leq 0$, or equivalently, $\alpha \leq 1/(1+\tau)$.

Case 2: $\forall h \in \mathcal{Q} : |\{f \in \mathcal{F}' : \langle h, f - B_{\mathcal{F}'}\rangle_D \geq 3\tau/2\}| < |\mathcal{F}'|/2$.
Consider the smallest (2τ)-half-cover, say $h_1,\ldots,h_k \in \mathcal{Q}$, for $\mathcal{F}' - B_{\mathcal{F}'}$. Clearly, $k \leq \text{HCNum}^*_{\mathcal{F},\mathcal{Q}}(2\tau,\gamma)$. Pass $(h_1,\tau/4),\ldots,(h_k,\tau/4)$ to the oracle. If it ever returns a value of at least $7\tau/4$, then the true correlation with the target function is at least $3\tau/2$ and, according to our case assumption, the version space shrinks immediately by factor $1/2$. If the oracle returns only values smaller than $7\tau/4$, then the true correlation is smaller than 2τ and, by the definition of a (2τ)-half-cover, $\mathcal{F}' - B_{\mathcal{F}'}$ is halved after the k-th query.

The punch-line of this discussion is that, either we can shrink $\mathcal{F}' - B_{\mathcal{F}'}$ by factor $1/(1+\tau)$ at the expense of a single query, or we can halve $\mathcal{F}' - B_{\mathcal{F}'}$ at the expense of at most $\mathrm{HCNum}^*_{\mathcal{F},\mathcal{Q}}(2\tau, \gamma)$ queries. In the former case, we are not quite done with halving $\mathcal{F}' - B_{\mathcal{F}'}$ but we can iterate the procedure. Since $1/(\tau+1)^{2/\tau} < 1/2$, the theorem follows. □

Putting Lemmas 2 and 3 together, it follows that SHC* can be "sandwiched" by HCN*:

$$\mathrm{HCNum}^*_{\mathcal{F},\mathcal{Q}}(\tau, \gamma) \leq \mathrm{HCNum}^{**}_{\mathcal{F},\mathcal{Q}}(\tau, \gamma) \leq \mathrm{SHC}^*_{\mathcal{F},\mathcal{Q}}(\tau, \gamma) < \frac{1}{2\tau} + \mathrm{HCNum}^*_{\mathcal{F},\mathcal{Q}}(8\tau, \gamma)$$
(7)

For the purpose of sandwiching SLC by SHC*, we state the following result:

Lemma 4. $\mathrm{SLC}_{\mathcal{F},\mathcal{Q}}(\tau, \gamma - 2\tau) \leq \mathrm{SHC}^*_{\mathcal{F},\mathcal{Q}}(\tau, \gamma) \cdot \lfloor \log |\mathcal{F}| \rfloor$.

Proof. As long as the current version space $\mathcal{F}'$ is not $(\gamma, \mathcal{Q})$-trivial, we can use $\mathrm{SHC}_{\mathcal{F}',\mathcal{Q}}(\tau, \gamma) \leq \mathrm{SHC}^*_{\mathcal{F},\mathcal{Q}}(\tau, \gamma)$ queries to halve it. If the current version space $\mathcal{F}'$ is $(\gamma, \mathcal{Q})$-trivial, we can use the function $h \in \mathcal{Q}$ with correlation at least γ to at least half of the functions in $\mathcal{F}'$ as query function. The value returned by the oracle will either prove that h has correlation at least $\gamma - 2\tau$ with the target function or it will halve the version space. In the former case, we can output h as the final hypothesis. In the latter case, we enter the next stage. We conclude that either we identify the target function exactly after $\lfloor \log |\mathcal{F}| \rfloor$ halving-stages or we have found a function with correlation at least $\gamma - 2\tau$ on the way. □

Combining Lemma 2 and Lemma 4, we obtain

$$\mathrm{SHC}^*_{\mathcal{F},\mathcal{Q}}(\tau, \gamma) \leq \mathrm{SLC}_{\mathcal{F},\mathcal{Q}}(\tau, \gamma) \leq \mathrm{SHC}^*_{\mathcal{F},\mathcal{Q}}(\tau, \gamma + 2\tau) \cdot \lfloor \log |\mathcal{F}| \rfloor .$$
(8)

4.3   Proof of the Main Result

Theorem 2 is a direct consequence of the three lemmas below and of the previous "sandwich-results" (inequalities (7) and (8)). Lemma 5 implies that parameterized classes with a super-polynomial strong SQ dimension are not strongly learnable. Lemmas 6 and 7 imply that parameterized classes with a polynomially bounded strong SQ dimension are strongly learnable.

Lemma 5. *Let* $d := \mathrm{SQDim}^{**}_{\mathcal{F},\mathcal{Q}}(1 - \varepsilon)$. *If* $\varepsilon^2 \cdot d \geq 640$, *then the following holds:*

$$\mathrm{HCNum}^{**}_{\mathcal{F},\mathcal{Q}}\left(\tau, 1 - \frac{\varepsilon}{4}\right) \geq \frac{1}{40} \cdot \tau^2 \cdot d$$

Proof. Choose a $(1 - \varepsilon, \mathcal{Q})$-nontrivial subclass $\mathcal{F}' \subseteq \mathcal{F}$ and set $g := B_{\mathcal{F}'}$ such that $\mathrm{SQDim}^{**}_{\mathcal{F},\mathcal{Q}}(1 - \varepsilon) = \mathrm{SQDim}_{\mathcal{F}-g}$. Furthermore choose $f_1, \ldots, f_d \in \mathcal{F}$ such that the the absolute values of the pairwise correlations of $f_1 - g, \ldots, f_d - g$ are smaller than $1/(d - 1)$. The following three claims are proven in the full paper:

Claim 1: The correlation between g and any function from $\mathcal{Q}$ is bounded by $1 - \varepsilon/2$.

Claim 2: Let $\mathcal{F}'' := \{f_1, \ldots, f_d\}$. Then, $\lambda_1(C_{\mathcal{F}''-g}) < 5$.
Claim 3: $\mathcal{F}''$ is $(1 - \varepsilon/4, \mathcal{Q})$-nontrivial.

We are now in the position to complete the proof of the lemma. We can conclude from the $(1 - \varepsilon/4, \mathcal{Q})$-non-triviality of $\mathcal{F}''$ that $\text{HCNum}^{**}_{\mathcal{F},\mathcal{Q}}(\tau, 1 - \varepsilon/4) \geq \text{HCNum}_{\mathcal{F}''-g,\mathcal{Q}}(\tau)$. We can furthermore conclude from Theorem 3 (with $\mathcal{F}'' - g$ in the role of $\mathcal{F}$, and $B = 2$) and Claim 2 that

$$5 \cdot \text{HCNum}_{\mathcal{F}''-g,\mathcal{Q}}(\tau) > \lambda_1(C_{\mathcal{F}''-g}) \cdot \text{HCNum}_{\mathcal{F}''-g,\mathcal{Q}}(\tau) \geq \frac{d}{8} \cdot \tau^2 .$$

Division by 5 yields the lemma. □

Lemma 6. Let $d := \text{SQDim}^*_{\mathcal{F},\mathcal{Q}}(1 - \varepsilon)$ and assume that[4]

$$\tilde{\mathcal{Q}} := \{f - B_{\mathcal{F}'} : f \in \mathcal{F}, \mathcal{F}' \subseteq \mathcal{F}\} \subseteq \mathcal{Q} . \tag{9}$$

Then, the following holds:

$$\text{HCNum}^*_{\mathcal{F},\mathcal{Q}}\left(\frac{1}{d}, 1 - \varepsilon\right) \leq d$$

Proof. Choose a $(1 - \varepsilon, \mathcal{Q})$-nontrivial subclass $\mathcal{F}' \subseteq \mathcal{F}$ and set $g := B_{\mathcal{F}'}$ such that

$$\text{HCNum}^*_{\mathcal{F},\mathcal{Q}}\left(\frac{1}{d}, 1 - \varepsilon\right) = \text{HCNum}_{\mathcal{F}'-g,\mathcal{Q}}\left(\frac{1}{d}\right) .$$

Let $d' := \text{SQDim}_{\mathcal{F}'-g}$. Since $\mathcal{F}'$ is $(1 - \varepsilon, \mathcal{Q})$-nontrivial, we can conclude that $d' \leq d$. Furthermore, by assumption (9), $\mathcal{F}' - g \subseteq \tilde{\mathcal{Q}} \subseteq \mathcal{Q}$. The proof is now completed as follows:

$$\text{HCNum}_{\mathcal{F}'-g,\mathcal{Q}}\left(\frac{1}{d}\right) \leq \text{CNum}_{\mathcal{F}'-g,\mathcal{Q}}\left(\frac{1}{d}\right) \leq \text{CNum}_{\mathcal{F}'-g,\mathcal{Q}}\left(\frac{1}{d'}\right) \overset{(4)}{\leq} d' \leq d$$

□

Assumption (9) is not essential for the following reason: if $\mathcal{F}$ is strongly learnable in the SQ model with query functions and final hypothesis chosen from $\mathcal{Q} \cup \tilde{\mathcal{Q}}$, then $\mathcal{F}$ is already strongly learnable in the SQ model with query functions and final hypothesis chosen from $\mathcal{Q}$. This is an immediate consequence of the following

Lemma 7. *A query of the form $(\tilde{h}, \tau)$ such that $\tilde{h} \in \tilde{\mathcal{Q}}$ can be simulated by means of $O(1/\tau^2)$ queries of the form $(h, \tau/3)$ such that $h \in \mathcal{F}$.*

Proof. According to the definition of $\tilde{\mathcal{Q}}$, $\tilde{h} = f - B_{\mathcal{F}'}$ for some function $f \in \mathcal{F}$ and a subclass $\mathcal{F}' \subseteq \mathcal{F}$. Let f_* denote the unknown target function. Query $(f, \tau/3)$ provides us with a $\tau/3$-approximation $\hat{c}_1$ of $\langle f, f_* \rangle_D$. $\langle B_{\mathcal{F}'}, f_* \rangle_D$ is the average correlation between the target function and a function from $\mathcal{F}'$. Hoeffding

---

[4] Assumption (9) looks strange. See however Lemma 7 below for a justification.

bounds imply that there exist $O(1/\tau^2)$ functions in $\mathcal{F}'$ such that their average correlation with f_* equals $\langle B_{\mathcal{F}'}, f_* \rangle_D$ up to an additive term $\tau/3$. If we get to know these $O(1/\tau^2)$ correlations only up to another additive term $\tau/3$ (the tolerance parameter), the resulting estimation, say $\hat{c}_2$, for $\langle B_{\mathcal{F}'}, f_* \rangle_D$ will be only a $2\tau/3$-approximation. Clearly, $\hat{c}_1 - \hat{c}_2$ is a τ-approximation of $\langle \tilde{h}, f_* \rangle_D$. This shows that $O(1/\tau^2)$ queries with tolerance $\tau/3$ and query functions from $\mathcal{F}$ are sufficient to simulate the query $(\tilde{h}, \tau)$. □

Our results imply the following lower and upper bound on the statistical halving complexity in terms of the strong SQ dimension $d := \mathrm{SQDim}^*_{\mathcal{F}, \mathcal{Q}}(1 - \varepsilon)$:

$$\mathrm{SHC}^*_{\mathcal{F}, \mathcal{Q}}\left(\tau, 1 - \tfrac{\varepsilon}{4}\right) \overset{L.2}{\geq} \mathrm{HCNum}^{**}_{\mathcal{F}, \mathcal{Q}}\left(\tau, 1 - \tfrac{\varepsilon}{4}\right) \overset{L.5}{\geq} \tfrac{1}{40} \cdot \tau^2 \cdot d$$

$$\mathrm{SHC}^*_{\mathcal{F}, \mathcal{Q}}\left(\tfrac{1}{8d}, 1 - \varepsilon\right) \overset{L.3}{<} 4d + \mathrm{HCNum}^*_{\mathcal{F}, \mathcal{Q}}\left(\tfrac{1}{d}, 1 - \varepsilon\right) \overset{L.6}{\leq} 5 \cdot d$$

The inequality marked "L.6" is only valid under assumption (9). Without this assumption, we have to replace $5 \cdot d$ by $O(d/\tau^2)$. The gap between the lower and the upper bound is not tremendous but it would be interesting to know whether it can be narrowed.

Acknowledgments. Thanks to Heikki Mannila, Esko Ukkonen, and Aristides Gionis for helpful discussions. Thanks to the anonymous referees for their comments and suggestions, for pointing my attention to the paper by Köbler and Lindner about the general dimension (and for fixing a flaw in the first version of the paper).

References

1. José L. Balcázar, Jorge Castro, and David Guijarro. A new abstract combinatorial dimension for exact learning via queries. *Journal of Computer and System Sciences*, 64(1):2–21, 2002.
2. Shai Ben-David, Alon Itai, and Eyal Kushilevitz. Learning by distances. *Information and Computation*, 117(2):240–250, 1995.
3. Avrim Blum, Merrick Furst, Jeffrey Jackson, Michael Kearns, Yishai Mansour, and Steven Rudich. Weakly learning DNF and characterizing statistical query learning using Fourier analysis. In *Proceedings of the 26th Annual Symposium on Theory of Computing*, pages 253–263, 1994.
4. Michael Kearns. Efficient noise-tolerant learning from statistical queries. *Journal of the Association on Computing Machinery*, 45(6):983–1006, 1998.
5. Johannes Köbler and Wolfgang Lindner. A general dimension for approxmately learning boolean functions. In *Proceedings of the 13th International Conference on Algorithmic Learning Theory*, pages 139–148, 2002.
6. Hans Ulrich Simon. Spectral norm in learning theory: some selected topics. In *Proceedings of the 17th International Conference on Algorithmic Learning Theory*, pages 13–27, 2006. Invited Talk.
7. Leslie G. Valiant. A theory of the learnable. *Communications of the ACM*, 27(11):1134–1142, 1984.
8. Ke Yang. New lower bounds for statistical query learning. *Journal of Computer and System Sciences*, 70(4):485–509, 2005.

On the Consistency of Discrete Bayesian Learning

Jan Poland

Graduate School of Information Science and Technology
Hokkaido University, Japan
jan@ist.hokudai.ac.jp
http://www-alg.ist.hokudai.ac.jp/~jan

Abstract. This paper accomplishes the last step in a series of consistency theorems for Bayesian learners based on discree hypothesis class, being initiated by Solomonoff's 1978 work. Precisely, we show the generalization of a performance guarantee for Bayesian stochastic model selection, which has been proven very recently by the author for finite observation space, to countable and continuous observation space as well as mixtures. This strong result is (to the author's knowledge) the first of this kind for stochastic model selection. It states almost sure consistency of the learner in the realizable case, that is, where one of the hypotheses/models considered coincides with the truth. Moreover, it implies error bounds on the difference of the predictive distribution to the true one, and even loss bounds w.r.t. arbitrary loss functions. The set of consistency theorems for the three natural variants of discrete Bayesian prediction, namely marginalization, MAP, and stochastic model selection, is thus being completed for general observation space. Hence, this is the right time to recapitulate all these results, to present them in a unified context, and to discuss the different situations of Bayesian learning and its different methods.

1 Introduction

"When you have eliminated the impossible, whatever remains must be the truth." This famous quote describes the induction principle of Sherlock Holmes, whose observations and conclusions are always correct. Real world observations usually lack this desirable property, instead they are *noisy*. Thus, Bayes' rule, *eliminating the improbable*, has emerged as a successful induction principle in practice. This paper aims at collecting and generalizing statements of the form: "When you have eliminated the improbable, whatever remains is almost sure to behave like the truth." We will give different but tightly connected forms of this assertion: Asymptotic almost sure consistency results and bounds on the error of a predictor based on Bayes' rule.

The main technical result of this paper is the generalization of the consistency theorem for Bayesian stochastic model selection, obtained recently for finite observation space [1], to continuous observation space. It will be proven

W. Thomas and P. Weil (Eds.): STACS 2007, LNCS 4393, pp. 405–416, 2007.

in Section 3. This completes a series of recent performance guarantees obtained for all three fundamental ways of Bayesian learning. It therefore motivates a comparative presentation of all these results, discussing the basics of Bayesian learning, the fundamental variants of Bayesian induction, and the state of the art of Bayesian learning theorems. This is subject of the next section.

2   Bayesian Learning

Bayes' famous rule,

$$P(H|D) = \frac{P(D|H) \cdot P(H)}{P(D)}, \tag{1}$$

says how the probability of a hypothesis H is updated after observing some data D. Still, different specific induction setups can use Bayes' rule. First, there are different possibilities to define the input space, the observation space, and the hypothesis space. Second, a hypothesis class endowed with a probability distribution can be used for induction in principally three different ways.

The reader should keep in mind that Bayes' rule is no theorem in general. Under the assumption that hypotheses and data are *both* sampled from a joint probability distribution that coincides with the prior $P(H)$, (1) would be a theorem. However, Bayes' rule is commonly not applied under such an assumption, in particular the distribution $P(H)$ on the hypotheses is usually merely a *belief distribution*, there is no probabilistic sampling mechanism generating hypotheses assumed. Hence, Bayes' rule is motivated intuitively in the first place. Still, many optimality results and performance guarantees have been shown for Bayesian induction (e.g. in [2,3,4]), including the results of the present work.

2.1   Hypotheses, History, Inputs, Observation Spaces

Let $\mathcal{X}$ be the observation space. We work in an *online prediction setup in discrete time*, that is, in each time step $t = 1, 2, \ldots$, an observation $x_t \in \mathcal{X}$ is revealed to the learner. The task of the learner will be to predict x_t *before* he observes it. One question of fundamental technical impact concerns the structure of the observation space $\mathcal{X}$. We restrict our attention to the two most important cases of (a) $\mathcal{X}$ being discrete (finite or countable) and (b) continuous $\mathcal{X} \subset \mathbb{R}^d$ for suitable dimension $d \in \mathbb{N}$.

A *hypothesis* ν specifies a probability distribution on the observation space $\mathcal{X}$. In the simplest case, it does not depend on any input, these hypotheses represent the assumption that the observed data is independently identically distributed (i.i.d.). In all other cases, there is some *input space* $\mathcal{Z}$, and a hypothesis maps inputs to distributions on $\mathcal{X}$. In fact, technically, the inputs play no role at all, as we will see in the following. We therefore may assume the existence of an arbitrary input space $\mathcal{Z}$ without any structure (which may consist of just one point, meaning that there are no inputs at all), and inputs are generated by an arbitrary process. This covers (even more than) two of the most important learning setups: *Classification*, where the data is conditionally i.i.d. given the inputs, and *prediction of non-i.i.d. sequences*, where in each time step t, we may define the input $z_t = (x_1, \ldots, x_{t-1})$ to be the observation history seen so far. Generally, we will denote the history of inputs *and* observations by

$$h_{1:t-1} = h_{<t} = (z_1, x_1, z_2, x_2, \ldots, z_{t-1}, x_{t-1})$$

(observe that two pieces of notation have been introduced here).

Now, a hypothesis is formally defined as a function

$$\nu : \mathcal{Z} \to \mathcal{M}^1_{D+C}(\mathcal{X}).$$

Here, $\mathcal{M}^1_{D+C}(\mathcal{X})$ denotes the probability distributions on $\mathcal{X} \subset \mathbb{R}^d$, that are mixtures of discrete distributions (with nonzero mass concentrated on single points) and distributions with continuous density functions. We make this restriction mainly because we wish to be able to define all subsequent quantities, in particular Bayesian posteriors, effortlessly and uniquely (except perhaps on a set of measure zero).[1] In particular, we have

$$\int d\nu(\cdot|z) = 1 \text{ for all } z \in \mathcal{Z}.$$

Note that we consistently use this integral notation, also for discrete observation space (in which case the integral is in reality a sum).

A Bayesian learner is always based on a *hypothesis class* $\mathcal{C} = \{\nu_1, \nu_2, \ldots\}$. In this work with the title "discrete Bayesian learning", we restrict to discrete, i.e. finite or countable, hypothesis classes (and in the notation we assume a countable hypothesis class from now on, without loss of generality). Before the learning process starts, each hypothesis $\nu \in \mathcal{C}$ is endowed with a prior weight $w_\nu \in (0, 1)$, such that $\sum_{\nu \in \mathcal{C}} w_\nu = 1$.

Hypothesis classes considered in statistics are usually *continuously parameterized*. One motivation to study discrete classes is that they are technically simpler, so they can serve as a basis for the more advanced continuous case. In the continuous case, some Bayesian predictors such as MAP (see below) are not consistent at all, while others such as MML (minimum message length) [5,6] and MDL (minimum description length) [7] require appropriate discretization. Also, countable hypothesis classes always admit stronger performance guarantees than possible for their continuously parameterized counterparts. In particular, we will be able to show almost sure consistency, whereas only convergence in probability holds in the continuous case (e.g. in [3,4,8]). Another important motivation to consider discrete hypothesis classes, studied in depth in Algorithmic Information Theory, lies in the fact that computers can – even in the limit – handle at most discrete (or discretized) classes, also if the original model was continuously parameterized. We do not discuss this point in detail here, see e.g. [9,10].

We rewrite Bayes' rule (1) using new notation: For a hypothesis $\nu \in \mathcal{C}$, current prior weights $w_{\nu'}(h_{<t})$ of all hypotheses $\nu' \in \mathcal{C}$ depending on the history $h_{<t}$, input z_t, and observation x_t, we set the posterior weight of ν to

---

[1] It easy to see that the continuity assumption can be immediately slightly lifted.

$$w_\nu(h_{1:t}) = \frac{\nu(x_t|z_t) \cdot w_\nu(h_{<t})}{\sum_{\nu' \in \mathcal{C}} \nu'(x_t|z_t) \cdot w_{\nu'}(h_{<t})}, \qquad (2)$$

Note that we actually need to distinguish three variants of Bayes' rule (not to be confused with the three variants of Bayesian prediction discussed below): In the case of discrete observation space, the quantities $\nu'(x|z)$ (and therefore also the sum in the denominator) are probabilities, while for continuous observation space, they are densities. Finally, if at least one hypothesis $\nu \in \mathcal{C}$ is a mixture of a discrete and a continuous distribution, then *all* $\nu'(x|z)$ must be treated as mixtures in the following way: If for an observation $x \in \mathcal{X}$, there is a hypothesis assigning non-zero mass to x, then the $\nu'(x|z)$ are treated as probabilities (and all hypotheses assigning merely a non-zero density to that particular x will get posterior weight 0). Otherwise, the $\nu'(x|z)$ are treated as densities.

2.2 Three Fundamental Variants of Bayesian Prediction

Given a set of hypotheses $\mathcal{C}$ and some observed data $h_{1:t} = (z_1, x_1, \ldots, z_t, x_t)$, a legitimate question is asking which of the hypotheses in $\mathcal{C}$ has actually generated the data. It is clear that this question might not be well-defined if the process generating the data, which we will call μ in the sequel, is *not* member of $\mathcal{C}$. Actually, one can immediately construct examples where any Bayesian learner produces very undesirable results in this non-realizable learning setup (see [11] for sophisticated examples). In this work, we will restrict to the *realizable* case, where the true distribution generating the observations is contained in the class, $\mu \in \mathcal{C}$. (But recall that this only refers to the distribution of the observation *given* the inputs, we do not need any assumption on the generation of the inputs z_t). Of course, the learner does not know in advance which element of $\mathcal{C}$ is the true distribution μ.

However, hypothesis identification has technical difficulties. For instance, consider the case where two hypothesis are in $\mathcal{C}$ that make (almost) identical predictions, one of them being the true one. Then it is (almost) impossible to identify the right one, but if we just want to make predictions, we need not care: Choosing any of the two will yield (almost) perfect predictions.

So from now on, we restrict our focus to prediction. That is, for given history $h_{<t}$ and current input $z_t \in \mathcal{Z}$, we are interested in a *predictive distribution*[2] on the observation space $\mathcal{X}$ that comes as closely to the truth as possible. Our hypothesis class endowed with the Bayesian posterior $(w_{\nu'}(h_{<t})_{\nu' \in \mathcal{C}})$ offers us *three fundamental* ways to obtain such a prediction:

1. **Marginalization.** If we apply Bayes' rule (1) to the modified setting where the next observation x_t takes the place of the hypothesis H, then, as an easy computation shows, we get a predictive distribution $\xi(x_t|z_t, h_{<t})$ by integrating the predictions of *all* hypotheses w.r.t. the current posterior:

---

[2] In many prediction tasks, a single value is required as prediction, rather than a distribution. Such a single prediction can be derived from a predictive distribution, e.g. by minimizing a risk function, as briefly discussed at the end of Section 2.4.

$$\xi(x|z_t, h_{<t}) = \sum_{\nu' \in \mathcal{C}} w_{\nu'}(h_{<t})\nu'(x|z_t). \tag{3}$$

2. **Maximum a posteriori (MAP).** If we are interested in a *single hypothesis'* prediction, then we may choose the *hypothesis with maximal a-posteriori belief value*, abbreviated as MAP hypothesis:

$$\nu^*_{h_{<t}} = \arg\max_{\nu \in \mathcal{C}}\{w_\nu(h_{<t})\} \quad \text{and} \quad m(x_t|z_t, h_{<t}) = \nu^*_{h_{<t}}(x_t|z_t), \tag{4}$$

where the latter $m(x_t|z_t, h_{<t})$ is the MAP prediction.

3. **Stochastic model selection.** The third possibility is to randomize and sample a hypothesis according to the probability distribution defined by the current posterior. This *stochastic model selection* can be formally written as

$$\Xi(x_t|z_t, h_{<t}) = \tilde{N}(x_t|z_t) \text{ where } \tilde{N} \in \mathcal{C} \tag{5}$$

$$\text{and } \mathbf{P}(\tilde{N} = \nu') = w_{\nu'}(h_{<t}) \text{ for all } \nu' \in \mathcal{C}.$$

Note that for given history $h_{<t}$, the first two methods are deterministic, while stochastic model selection uses additional randomness.

All three prediction methods are practically important. In particular, stochastic model selection is related to some learning algorithms for statistical models, in particular Monte Carlo methods. There are other possibilities than the stated three to use a Bayesian hypothesis class for prediction. MAP is tightly related to MML and MDL, but the terms MML and MDL are (also) used for (slightly, in the case of discrete hypothesis class) different concepts [12,7]. Also, there is a "dynamic" variant of MAP defined in [10], where a MAP hypothesis is chosen for each possible outcome x_t. Anyway: many, if not most, Bayesian prediction methods can be roughly grouped into the three principles "integrate over all hypothesis", "take the hypothesis with the best current score", and "select one hypothesis at random according to the current belief distribution". And we hold (but that is a matter of taste) that the above representants are the simplest and most natural of the prediction methods to consider.

2.3   Performance Guarantees for Bayesian Learners

We are now ready to state the performance guarantees for the three Bayesian learners defined in (3), (4), and (5). We start with the technically easiest case of marginalization (3). Actually, this result has been originally discovered by Solomonoff [13] within the context of Algorithmic Information Theory.

Recall that $\mu \in \mathcal{C}$ is the true distribution generating the data, and ξ is the marginalization predictor. The *Hellinger distance* between the ξ-predictions and μ-predictions at time t is given by

$$h_t^2(\mu, \xi) := \int d\big(\sqrt{\mu(\cdot|z_t)} - \sqrt{\xi(\cdot|z_t, h_{<t})}\big)^2. \tag{6}$$

It clearly depends on the history $h_{<t}$ and the current input z_t. Our main technical results are all stated as cumulative (i.e., over $t = 1, \ldots, \infty$) bounds on the Hellinger distance (that is, *errors*) of the predictive probabilities to the truth.

Theorem 1. *If $\mu \in C$, then for any sequence of inputs $z_1, z_2, \ldots,$*

$$\sum_{t=1}^{\infty} \mathbf{E}_\mu h_t^2(\mu, \xi) \leq \log w_\mu^{-1} \tag{7}$$

holds, where $\log$ denotes the natural logarithm and w_μ is the prior weight of the true distribution. $\mathbf{E}_\mu$ refers to the fact that the expectation is taken w.r.t. the true distribution μ, i.e., all observations are generated w.r.t. μ conditional to the inputs, and this expectation is computed.

It should not be surprising that the quantity w_μ appears on the r.h.s. and therefore has an impact on how large the error on the l.h.s. can grow. After all, if the Bayesian learner assigns a high prior weight to the true distribution, the error should be small. The remarkable fact is the *logarithmic* dependence in w_μ. As by Kraft's inequality, the logarithm of a weight can be interpreted as its description length, (7) is a very strong result asserting that the cumulative error never exceeds the description length of the true distribution. In a sense: When finding the truth single-handedly, our error is at most the number of bits a teacher needs to tell us the truth.

Although the proof of the theorem is very simple using (12) below, we omit it due to space constraints and because it has been given several times. Actually, one can use different techniques to show the result: The standard procedure exploits the the dominance property of the Bayes mixture, a possible alternative uses a potential function. The latter is the way we will choose to prove the assertions for stochastic model selection below.

Results for MAP (4) similar to Theorem 1 have been shown in [10].

Theorem 2. *Assume $\mu \in C$. Suppose that, for any history with nonzero probability density, the hypotheses always admit the specification of a (not necessarily unique) MAP hypothesis ν^*. This is satisfied for instance if all hypotheses correspond to continuous probability densities that are uniformly bounded. Then*

$$\sum_{t=1}^{\infty} \mathbf{E}_\mu h_t^2(\mu, m) \leq 21 w_\mu^{-1}. \tag{8}$$

The proof uses telescoping and dominance. The most remarkable (and worrying) fact here is the bound $O(w_\mu^{-1})$ on the r.h.s. While the logarithm in (7) is sufficiently small to be of practical significance, the exponentially larger quantity $O(w_\mu^{-1})$ is generally huge. One can construct examples where this bound is sharp [14]. Fortunately, this does not necessarily imply that the MAP predictions are bad, the actual error is smaller in many important cases. Still, there are situations where MAP predictions tend to be "unbalanced" and therefore unfavorable compared to marginalization. Stochastic model selection often gives better results in such cases.

Before concentrating on stochastic model selection for the remainder of this paper, we briefly discuss implications of the bounds stated so far.

2.4   Almost Sure Consistency and Other Implications

One important consequence of any finite bound on the expected cumulative Hellinger error is *almost sure consistency* of the predictor in the Hellinger sense. That is, the Hellinger distance of the predictive to the true distribution tends to zero almost surely (see e.g. [10]). In case of a finite or countable observation space $\mathcal{X}$, this implies in particular convergence of all predictive probabilities $\xi(x_t|z_t, h_{<t})$ to the true probabilities $\mu(x_t|z_t)$. In case of a continuous observation space, the predicted probability masses of any measurable subset of $\mathcal{X}$ converges to the true mass. However, we cannot conclude the convergence of moments, e.g. the expectation, without making further assumptions.

Other implications of Theorems 1 and 2 are *loss bounds* of a Bayes-optimal decision maker based on the predictive distribution, w.r.t. arbitrary loss functions. Assertions like [10, Theorem 27] are easily obtainable. Due to space constraints, we do not discuss this issue further here.

3   Stochastic Model Selection

The corresponding theorem for stochastic model selection (5), which is the main technical result of this paper, reads as follows.

Theorem 3. *Assume $\mu \in \mathcal{C}$. Then, for any sequence of inputs $z_1, z_2, \ldots$,*

$$\sum_{t=1}^{\infty} \mathbf{E}_{\mu}\mathbf{E}_{\Xi} h_t^2(\xi, \Xi) < (1 + \Pi)\left[\log(1 + \mathcal{H}) - \log(w_\mu)\right] \tag{9}$$

holds. The quantities $\mathcal{H}$ and Π, the Shannon entropy and the μ-entropy potential of the hypothesis class, are defined below. $\mathbf{E}_\Xi$ serves as a reminder that the Ξ-predictor is randomized.

The quantity $\mathcal{H}$ in the theorem is the Shannon entropy of the hypothesis class w.r.t. the current posterior distribution,

$$\mathcal{H}(h_{<t}) = \mathcal{H}\big([w_\nu(h_{<t})]_{\nu \in \mathcal{C}}\big) = -\sum_{\nu \in \mathcal{C}} w_\nu(h_{<t})\log w_\nu(h_{<t}).$$

If we write just $\mathcal{H}$ as in the theorem, this corresponds to the prior (or, below in the proofs, to the current posterior). Moreover, we define the current *entropy potential of the hypothesis class relative to the true distribution* μ as

$$\Pi\big((w_\nu)_{\nu \in \mathcal{C}}\big) = \sup\Big\{\mathcal{H}\big((\tfrac{\tilde{w}_\nu}{\sum_{\nu'}\tilde{w}_{\nu'}})_{\nu \in \mathcal{C}}\big) : \tilde{w}_\mu = w_\mu \wedge \tilde{w}_\nu \leq w_\nu \; \forall \nu \in \mathcal{C} \setminus \{\mu\}\Big\} \tag{10}$$

and $\Pi(h_{<t}) = \Pi\big([w_\nu(h_{<t})]_{\nu \in \mathcal{C}}\big)$ This can be paraphrased as "worst-case entropy of the class under all possible Bayesian updates where the true distribution

always has evidence value 1". We use the same convention as before: writing just Π corresponds to the prior, or, in the proofs below, to the current posterior.

It was shown in [1] that $\Pi \leq \mathcal{H}w_\mu^{-1}$ always holds. This implies in particular that Π is finite if and only if $\mathcal{H}$ is finite. Moreover, the bound in (9) is, in the worst case, not much worse than the corresponding bound for MAP (8). However, the desirable relation $\Pi = O(-\log w_\mu)$ holds if the tails of the prior are *sufficiently light* [1]. So in these cases, stochastic model selection performs almost as well as marginalization (7).

As the triangle inequality is valid for the Hellinger distance, Theorem 3 shows in particular almost sure consistency of prediction by stochastic model selection, provided that the Shannon entropy $\mathcal{H}$ of the hypothesis class is finite. Lower bounds that essentially match (9) have been given in [1].

Proof of Theorem 3. This follows immediately from the three subsequent Lemmata, which are generalizations of their counterparts in [1]: (11) and (13) are chained, and their expected sum is taken from $t = 1, \ldots, T$. Then the assertion follows immediately, because $\mathcal{P}(h_{1:T}) \geq 0$ always holds. Lemma 6 finally makes sure that Lemma 5 and therefore (13) are applicable.   □

Lemma 4. *If the current entropy of the hypothesis class is finite, $\mathcal{H}(h_{<t}) < \infty$, then, for any input z_t,*

$$\mathcal{H}(h_{<t}) - \mathbf{E}_{x_t \sim \xi(\cdot|z_t, h_{<t})}\mathcal{H}(h_{1:t}) \geq \mathbf{E}h_t^2(\xi, \Xi). \tag{11}$$

Proof. It is a well-known fact, shown e.g. in [15, p. 178], that the Hellinger distance of two probability distributions μ and ν on $\mathcal{X}$ never exceeds their Kullback-Leibler divergence:

$$h^2(\mu, \nu) = \int d(\sqrt{\mu(\cdot)} - \sqrt{\nu(\cdot)})^2 \leq \int d\mu(\cdot) \log \frac{\mu(\cdot)}{\nu(\cdot)}. \tag{12}$$

Therefore, we have

$$\mathcal{H}(h_{<t}) - \mathbf{E}_{x_t \sim \xi(\cdot|z_t, h_{<t})}\mathcal{H}(h_{1:t}) = \sum_{\nu \in \mathcal{C}} w_\nu(h_{<t}) \int d\nu(x|z_t) \log \frac{\nu(x|z_t)}{\xi(x|z_t, h_{<t})}$$

$$\geq \sum_{\nu \in \mathcal{C}} w_\nu(h_{<t})h^2(\xi, \nu) = \mathbf{E}h_t^2(\xi, \Xi).   □$$

Lemma 5. *Assume $\mu \in \mathcal{C}$. Suppose that we have some continuous function $B((w_\nu)_{\nu \in \mathcal{C}}) = B(h_{<t})$, depending in a continuous way on the current posterior and therefore depending on the history, with the following properties:*

(i) $B(h_{<t}) \geq \mathcal{H}(h_{<t})$ *(dominates the entropy)*,

(ii) $\mathbf{E}_{x_t \sim \mu(\cdot|z_t)}B(h_{1:t}) \leq B(h_{<t})$ *(expectation decreases)*,

(iii) *the value of $B(h_{<t})$ can be approximated arbitrarily closely by restricting to a finite model class.*

Then, for any history and current input, consider the potential function

$$\mathcal{P}(h_{<t}) = [\mathcal{K}(h_{<t}) + \log(1 + \mathcal{H}(h_{<t}))](1 + B(h_{<t})),$$

with $\mathcal{K}(h_{<t}) = -\log w_\mu(h_{<t})$ being the complexity potential. *Then we have*

$$\mathcal{P}(h_{<t}) - \mathbf{E}_{x_t \sim \mu(\cdot|z_t)}\mathcal{P}(h_{1:t}) \geq \mathcal{H}(h_{<t}) - \mathbf{E}_{x_t \sim \xi}\mathcal{H}(h_{1:t}). \tag{13}$$

Proof. The assertion has been already proven for finite $\mathcal{X}$ [1, Lemma 11]. In order to show the generalization, we may decompose $\mathcal{X}$ into two subsets $\mathcal{X} = \mathcal{X}^{\text{discrete}} \cup \mathcal{X}^{\text{continuous}}$, where $\mathcal{X}^{\text{discrete}}$ is the at most countable set of points where any of the distributions in $\mathcal{C}$ has a non-zero mass concentration. We can prove the assertion for the discrete and the continuous parts separately. The discrete part follows simply by approximating, so we focus on the continuous part and assume without loss of generality that all distributions are (piecewise) continuous probability densities.

We show the assertion by assuming the contrary

$$\mathbf{E}_{x_t \sim \mu(\cdot|z_t)}\mathcal{P}(h_{1:t}) - \mathcal{P}(h_{<t}) > \mathbf{E}_{x_t \sim \xi}\mathcal{H}(h_{1:t}) - \mathcal{H}(h_{<t}) \tag{14}$$

and obtaining a contradiction. Dropping the history $h_{<t}$ from the notation, (14) is equivalent to

$$\mathbf{E}_{x \sim \mu}\mathcal{P}(x) - \mathcal{P} > \mathbf{E}_{x \sim \xi}\mathcal{H}(x) - \mathcal{H} + 11\varepsilon \text{ for some } \varepsilon > 0. \tag{15}$$

We may assume without loss of generality that $\mathcal{X}$ is *compact*, and that there is a number $R > 0$ such that

$$\max_{x \in \mathcal{X}}\mathcal{H}(x)\xi(x) \leq R \text{ and } \max_{x \in \mathcal{X}}\xi(x) \leq R. \tag{16}$$

To see this, just choose $\tilde{\mathcal{X}} \subset \mathcal{X}$ compact and sufficiently large, such that both (16) and $\mathbf{E}_{x \sim \xi|\tilde{\mathcal{X}}}\mathcal{H}(x) \geq \mathbf{E}_{x \sim \xi}\mathcal{H}(x) - \varepsilon$ hold, this is possible because $\xi(x)\mathcal{H}(x)$ is integrable w.r.t. the Lebesgue measure λ. Then, replace $\mathcal{X}$ by $\tilde{\mathcal{X}}$ and (15) by

$$\mathbf{E}_{x \sim \mu}\mathcal{P}(x) - \mathcal{P} > \mathbf{E}_{x \sim \xi}\mathcal{H}(x) - \mathcal{H} + 10\varepsilon. \tag{17}$$

Next, we argue that we may even assume without loss of generality that $\mathcal{C}$ is *finite*. To this aim, first start with approximating $\mathcal{P}(x)$ by a step function $\tilde{\mathcal{P}}(x)$ that is piecewise constant on relatively compact subsets $A_1, A_2, \ldots, A_n \subset \mathcal{X}$ and takes only finitely many (namely n) values $\tilde{y}_1, \ldots, \tilde{y}_n > 0$. We choose $\tilde{\mathcal{P}}(x)$ such that it is dominated by $\mathcal{P}(x)$, with the property

$$\mathbf{E}_{x \sim \mu}\tilde{\mathcal{P}}(x) \geq \mathbf{E}_{x \sim \mu}\mathcal{P}(x) - \varepsilon.$$

This is possible since $\mathcal{P}(x)$ is measurable and non-negative.

We choose an even smaller step function $\underline{\mathcal{P}}(x)$ that is likewise constant on $A_1, \ldots, A_n$ and is strictly dominated by $\tilde{\mathcal{P}}(x)$, such that

$$\mathbf{E}_{x \sim \mu}\underline{\mathcal{P}}(x) \geq \mathbf{E}_{x \sim \mu}\mathcal{P}(x) - 2\varepsilon \tag{18}$$

and $\underline{P}(x) = \tilde{P}(x) - \varepsilon_i = \tilde{y}_i - \varepsilon_i := y_i$ for $x \in A_i$, where $\varepsilon_i > 0$ for all $1 \leq i \leq n$. Then, for each $x \in A_1$, $B(x)$ and therefore $\mathcal{P}(x)$ can be approximated with finitely many hypotheses. Since $\mathcal{P}(x) \geq \tilde{y}_i$, we can find a finite set of hypotheses $\mathcal{F}(x)$ such that $\mathcal{P}^{\tilde{\mathcal{F}}}(x) > y_i$ for any $\tilde{\mathcal{F}} \supset \mathcal{F}(x)$, where $\mathcal{P}^{\tilde{\mathcal{F}}}(x)$ denotes the potential computed with only the hypotheses in $\tilde{\mathcal{F}}$. Since $\mathcal{P}^{\tilde{\mathcal{F}}}(\cdot)$ is continuous (while $\tilde{\mathcal{F}}$ is fixed), we have that $\mathcal{P}^{\tilde{\mathcal{F}}}(\tilde{x}) > y_i$ holds even within an open superset $\tilde{x} \in \mathcal{U}(x)$ of x. For each $x \in A_1$, there is such an open $\mathcal{U}(x)$, and they form an open cover of $\bar{A}_1$. Since $\bar{A}_1$ is compact, there is a finite subcover $\mathcal{U}(x_1) \cup \ldots \cup \mathcal{U}(x_m) \supset A_1$. We may choose $\mathcal{F}_1 = \mathcal{F}(x_1) \cup \ldots \cup \mathcal{F}(x_m)$ in order to obtain a finite set of hypotheses approximating $\mathcal{P}(x)$ sufficiently closely on all of A_1.

Analogous approximations $\mathcal{F}_2, \ldots, \mathcal{F}_n$ are obtained for all other $A_2, \ldots, A_n$. Also, we choose a finite set of hypotheses $\mathcal{F}_0 \subset \mathcal{C}$ such that all supersets $\tilde{\mathcal{F}} \supset \mathcal{F}_0$ approximate the prior $\mathcal{P}$ up to ε. Take the union $\mathcal{F} = \mathcal{F}_0 \cup \mathcal{F}_1 \cup \ldots \cup \mathcal{F}_n$. Then, from (18), we conclude that

$$\mathbf{E}_{x \sim \mu} \underline{P}(x) - \mathcal{P}^{\tilde{\mathcal{F}}} > \mathbf{E}_{x \sim \mu} P(x) - \mathcal{P} - 3\varepsilon.$$

and $\mathcal{P}^{\tilde{\mathcal{F}}}(x) \geq \underline{P}(x)$ for all $x \in \mathcal{X}$ and any $\tilde{\mathcal{F}} \supset \mathcal{F}$. We make sure that $\mu \in \mathcal{F}$.

We perform the same construction an approximation of $\mathcal{H}(x)$ from above. Since $\mathcal{X}$ was already assumed to be compact, the constant function R, which dominates $\xi(x)\mathcal{H}(x)$ according to (16) is integrable w.r.t. the Lebesgue measure λ. Therefore, we may refine the partitioning $(A_i)_{i=1}^k$ of $\tilde{X}$, obtaining a new partitioning $(\tilde{A}_i)_{i=1}^m$ of $\tilde{X}$, such that $\mathcal{H}(x)\xi(x)$ is approximated from above within ε by functions constant on each $\tilde{A}_i$. We may choose the approximators $\overline{\mathcal{H}}(x)$ and $\overline{\xi}(x)$ slightly larger, such that they need only finitely many hypotheses. We incorporate these hypotheses into $\mathcal{F}$.

Altogether, this shows that we may indeed assume that $\mathcal{C}$ is finite, if we replace (17) with

$$\mathbf{E}_{x \sim \mu} \underline{P}(x) - \mathcal{P} > \mathbf{E}_{x \sim \overline{\xi}} \overline{\mathcal{H}}(x) - \mathcal{H} + 4\varepsilon, \tag{19}$$

knowing that $\underline{P}(x) \leq P(x)$ and $\overline{\mathcal{H}}(x) \geq \mathcal{H}(x)$ for all $x \in \mathcal{X}$.

In the next step, we further decrease $\mathcal{X}$ a tiny little bit and define $\underline{\mathcal{X}} \subset \mathcal{X}$ such that

$$\nu(\underline{\mathcal{X}}) < 1 \text{ for all (finitely many!) } \nu \in \mathcal{C}. \tag{20}$$

Set $\underline{A}_i = A_i \cap \underline{\mathcal{X}}$ for all $1 \leq i \leq n$. While choosing $\underline{\mathcal{X}}$, we make sure that it is not too small. Namely, we assert

$$\mu(A_i)\left(1 - \frac{\varepsilon}{2y_i}\right) < \mu(\underline{A}_i) \text{ for all } 1 \leq i \leq n, \tag{21}$$

$$\mathbf{E}_{x \sim \mu|_{\underline{\mathcal{X}}}} \underline{P}(x) \geq \mathbf{E}_{x \sim \mu} \underline{P}(x) - \varepsilon, \text{ and} \tag{22}$$

$$1 - \xi(\underline{\mathcal{X}}) < \frac{\varepsilon}{2 \log |\mathcal{C}|}, \tag{23}$$

where $|\mathcal{C}|$ is the number of hypotheses in $\mathcal{C}$.

In the last step, construct a refining partition $(A_i')_{i=1}^k$ of $(\tilde{A}_i \cap \underline{\mathcal{X}})_{i=1}^m$ and lower and upper approximations $\underline{\nu}, \overline{\nu}$ for each $\nu \in \mathcal{C}$, with the following properties:

$$\int_{\underline{\mathcal{X}}} \overline{\nu} < 1 \text{ for all } \nu \in \mathcal{C}, \text{ possible due to (20)}, \tag{24}$$

$$\int_{\underline{A}_i} \underline{\mu} \geq \mu(\underline{A}_i)\left(1 - \frac{\varepsilon}{y_i}\right) \text{ for all } 1 \leq i \leq n, \text{ possible due to (21)}, \tag{25}$$

$$1 - \int_{\underline{\mathcal{X}}} \underline{\xi} < \frac{\varepsilon}{\log |\mathcal{C}|}, \text{ possible due to (23)}. \tag{26}$$

Now choose (with λ being the Lebesgue measure)

$$\mathcal{X}' = \{0, 1, \ldots, k\}, \qquad\qquad x_i' = \arg\min_{x \in A_i'} \mathcal{P}(x) \text{ for all } 1 \leq i \leq k,$$

$$\nu_i' = \nu(x_i')\lambda(A_i') \quad (1 \leq i \leq k, \nu \in \mathcal{C}), \qquad \nu_0' = 1 - \sum_{i=1}^k \nu_i' \text{ for all } \nu \in \mathcal{C},$$

$$\mathcal{H}_i' = \mathcal{H}\left(\left(\frac{w_\nu \nu_i'}{\sum_{j=0}^k w_\nu \nu_j'}\right)_{\nu \in \mathcal{C}}\right) = \mathcal{H}(x_i'), \quad \mathcal{P}_i' = \mathcal{P}\left(\left(\frac{w_\nu \nu_i'}{\sum_{j=0}^k w_\nu \nu_j'}\right)_{\nu \in \mathcal{C}}\right) = \mathcal{P}(x_i').$$

By (24), each ν' is in fact a measure on $\mathcal{X}'$. Justifying the following estimations with the respective equations before, we have

$$\sum_{i=0}^{l_0} \mu_i' \mathcal{P}_i' - \mathcal{P} \geq \sum_{i=1}^{l_0} \mu_i' \mathcal{P}_i' - \mathcal{P} \qquad \geq \mathbf{E}_{\mu|\underline{x}} \mathcal{P} - \mathcal{P} \qquad \overset{(25)}{\geq} \mathbf{E}_{\mu|\underline{x}} \mathcal{P} - \mathcal{P} - \varepsilon$$

$$\overset{(22)}{\geq} \mathbf{E}_\mu \mathcal{P} - \mathcal{P} - 2\varepsilon \overset{(19)}{\geq} \mathbf{E}_{\overline{\xi}} \overline{\mathcal{H}} - \mathcal{H} + 2\varepsilon \quad \geq \mathbf{E}_{\underline{\xi}|\underline{x}} \overline{\mathcal{H}} - \mathcal{H} + 2\varepsilon$$

$$\geq \sum_{i=1}^k \xi_i' \mathcal{H}_i' - \mathcal{H} + 2\varepsilon \overset{(26)}{\geq} \sum_{i=0}^k \xi_i' \mathcal{H}_i' - \mathcal{H} + \varepsilon.$$

The last estimate is true since $\mathcal{H}_0' \leq \log |\mathcal{C}|$ holds. This is the desired contradiction to the finite case. □

The next Lemma states that the entropy potential in fact satisfies the requirement on the function B from the previous Lemma. From the conditions $(i) - (iii)$, we only need to verify (ii), as (i) and (iii) are obviously true.

Lemma 6. *For any history $h_{<t}$ and current input z_t,*

$$\mathbf{E}_{x_t \sim \mu(\cdot|z_t)} \Pi(h_{1:t}) \leq \Pi(h_{<t}).$$

Proof. This follows from a reduction to the finite case [1, Theorem 16] that is similar and simpler than the proof of the previous Lemma. □

References

1. Poland, J.: The missing consistency theorem for Bayesian learning: Stochastic model selection. In: Algorithmic Learning Theory, 16h International Conference, ALT (LNAI 4264). (2006) 259–273
2. Blackwell, D., Dubins, L.: Merging of opinions with increasing information. Annals of Mathematical Statistics **33** (1962) 882–887
3. Clarke, B.S., Barron, A.R.: Information-theoretic asymptotics of Bayes methods. IEEE Trans. Inform. Theory **36** (1990) 453–471
4. Barron, A.R., Rissanen, J.J., Yu, B.: The minimum description length principle in coding and modeling. IEEE Trans. Inform. Theory **44** (1998) 2743–2760
5. Wallace, C.S., Boulton, D.M.: An information measure for classification. Computer Jrnl. **11** (1968) 185–194
6. Wallace, C.S., Dowe, D.L.: Minimum Message Length and Kolmogorov Complexity. Computer Journal **42** (1999) 270–283
7. Rissanen, J.J.: Fisher Information and Stochastic Complexity. IEEE Trans. Inform. Theory **42** (1996) 40–47
8. Barron, A.R., Cover, T.M.: Minimum complexity density estimation. IEEE Trans. Inform. Theory **37** (1991) 1034–1054
9. Hutter, M.: Universal Artificial Intelligence: Sequential Decisions based on Algorithmic Probability. Springer, Berlin (2004)
10. Poland, J., Hutter, M.: Asymptotics of discrete MDL for online prediction. IEEE Transactions on Information Theory **51** (2005) 3780–3795
11. Grünwald, P., Langford, J.: Suboptimal behaviour of Bayes and MDL in classification under misspecification. In: 17th Annual Conference on Learning Theory (COLT). (2004) 331–347
12. Comley, J.W., Dowe, D.L.: Minimum message length and generalized Bayesian nets with asymmetric languages. In Grünwald, P., Myung, I.J., Pitt, M.A., eds.: Advances in Minimum Description Length: Theory and Applications. (2005) 265–294
13. Solomonoff, R.J.: Complexity-based induction systems: comparisons and convergence theorems. IEEE Trans. Inform. Theory **24** (1978) 422–432
14. Poland, J., Hutter, M.: MDL convergence speed for Bernoulli sequences. Statistics and Computing **16** (2006) 161–175
15. Borovkov, A.A., Moullagaliev, A.: Mathematical Statistics. Gordon & Breach (1998)

VPSPACE and a Transfer Theorem over the Reals

Pascal Koiran and Sylvain Perifel

LIP*, École Normale Supérieure de Lyon
{Pascal.Koiran,Sylvain.Perifel}@ens-lyon.fr

Abstract. We introduce a new class VPSPACE of families of polynomials. Roughly speaking, a family of polynomials is in VPSPACE if its coefficients can be computed in polynomial space. Our main theorem is that if (uniform, constant-free) VPSPACE families can be evaluated efficiently then the class $PAR_\mathbb{R}$ of decision problems that can be solved in parallel polynomial time over the real numbers collapses to $P_\mathbb{R}$. As a result, one must first be able to show that there are VPSPACE families which are hard to evaluate in order to separate $P_\mathbb{R}$ from $NP_\mathbb{R}$, or even from $PAR_\mathbb{R}$.

Keywords: computational complexity, algebraic complexity, Blum-Shub-Smale model, Valiant's model.

1 Introduction

Two main categories of problems are studied in algebraic complexity theory: evaluation problems and decision problems. A typical example of an evaluation problem is the evaluation of the permanent of a matrix, and it is well known that the permanent family is complete for the class VNP of "easily definable" polynomial families [18]. Deciding whether a multivariate polynomial has a real root is a typical example of a decision problem. This problem is NP-complete in the Blum-Shub-Smale model of computation over the real numbers [1,2].

The main purpose of this paper is to provide a transfer theorem connecting the complexity of evaluation and decision problems. This paper is therefore in the same spirit as [11]. In that paper, we showed that if certain polynomials can be evaluated efficiently then certain decision problems become easy. The polynomials considered in [11] are those that can be written as exponential-size products of polynomials that are easy to compute (see [11] for a precise definition) over some field K. The decision problems under consideration are those that are in NP in the structure $(K, +, -, =)$, in which multiplication is not allowed.

In the present paper we work with a larger class of polynomial families, which we call VPSPACE. Roughly speaking, a family of polynomials (of possibly exponential degree) is in VPSPACE if its coefficients can be evaluated in polynomial

---

* UMR 5668 ENS Lyon, CNRS, UCBL, INRIA.

W. Thomas and P. Weil (Eds.): STACS 2007, LNCS 4393, pp. 417–428, 2007.
© Springer-Verlag Berlin Heidelberg 2007

space. For instance, we show that resultants of systems of multivariate polynomial equations form a VPSPACE family. Our main result is that if (uniform, constant-free) VPSPACE families can be evaluated efficiently then the class PAR$_\mathbb{R}$ of decision problems that can be solved in parallel polynomial time over the real numbers collapses to P$_\mathbb{R}$. This result relies crucially on a combinatorial lemma due to Grigoriev [9] and especially on its effective version, recently established in [5]. The class PAR$_\mathbb{R}$ plays roughly the same role in the theory of computation over the reals as PSPACE in discrete complexity theory. In particular, it contains NP$_\mathbb{R}$ [1] (but the proof of this inclusion is much more involved than in the discrete case). It follows from our main result that in order to separate P$_\mathbb{R}$ from NP$_\mathbb{R}$, or even from PAR$_\mathbb{R}$, one must first be able to show that there are VPSPACE families which are hard to evaluate. This seems to be a very challenging lower bound problem, but it is still presumably easier than showing that the permanent is hard to evaluate.

Organization of the paper. Section 2 recalls some notions and notations from algebraic complexity (Valiant's model, the Blum-Shub-Smale model). A uniform version of the class VPSPACE is defined in Section 3. The next two sections of the paper are devoted to the transfer theorem. Section 4 deals with sign conditions, an important tool from computational real algebraic geometry. The transfer theorem is stated at the beginning of Section 5, and proved thereafter.

Some of the proofs can be found in the full version of this paper [12]. In addition, the full version contains several other results. In particular, it is shown that resultants of multivariate polynomial systems form a VPSPACE family. The definition of the nonuniform class VPSPACE is given and the hypothesis that VPSPACE families are easy to evaluate is discussed. It is shown that (assuming the generalized Riemann hypothesis) this hypothesis is equivalent to: VP = VNP and P/poly = PSPACE/poly. The conjunction of these two equalities is an extremely strong assumption: by results from [3] (see [10]), it implies, assuming again GRH, that NC/poly = PSPACE/poly. This conjunction of equalities is still apparently consistent with our current understanding of complexity theory. We also discuss the uniform, constant-free version of the hypothesis that VPSPACE families are easy to evaluate. It turns out that this stronger hypothesis implies that PSPACE collapses to the polynomial-time uniform version of NC. Such a dramatic collapse of complexity classes looks extremely unlikely, but as far as we know it cannot be refuted with the current methods of complexity theory.

2   Preliminaries

The notions of boolean complexity theory that we use are quite standard. In the present section, we focus on algebraic complexity.

2.1   The Blum-Shub-Smale Model

In contrast with boolean complexity, algebraic complexity deals with other structures than $\{0, 1\}$. In this paper we will focus on the ordered field $(\mathbb{R}, +, -, \times, \leq)$ of the real numbers. Although the original definitions of Blum, Shub and Smale [2,1] are in terms of uniform machines, we will follow [16] by using families of algebraic circuits to recognize languages over $\mathbb{R}$, that is, subsets of $\mathbb{R}^\infty = \bigcup_{n \geq 0} \mathbb{R}^n$.

An algebraic circuit is a directed acyclic graph whose vertices, called gates, have indegree 0, 1 or 2. An input gate is a vertex of indegree 0. An output gate is a gate of outdegree 0. We assume that there is only one such gate in the circuit. Gates of indegree 2 are labelled by a symbol from the set $\{+, -, \times\}$. Gates of indegree 1, called test gates, are labelled "≤ 0?". The size of a circuit C, in symbols $|C|$, is the number of vertices of the graph.

A circuit with n input gates computes a function from $\mathbb{R}^n$ to $\mathbb{R}$. On input $\bar{u} \in \mathbb{R}^n$ the value returned by the circuit is by definition equal to the value of its output gate. The value of a gate is defined in the usual way. Namely, the value of input gate number i is equal to the i-th input u_i. The value of other gates is then defined recursively: it is the sum of the values of its entries for a $+$-gate, their difference for a $-$-gate, their product for a $\times$-gate. The value taken by a test gate is 0 if the value of its entry is > 0 and 1 otherwise. We assume without loss of generality that the output is a test gate. The value returned by the circuit is therefore 0 or 1.

The class $\mathsf{P}_\mathbb{R}$ is the set of languages $L \subseteq \mathbb{R}^\infty$ such that there exists a tuple $\bar{a} \in \mathbb{R}^p$ (independent of n) and a P-uniform family of polynomial-size circuits (C_n) satisfying the following condition: C_n has exactly $n + p$ inputs, and for any $\bar{x} \in \mathbb{R}^n$, $\bar{x} \in L \Leftrightarrow C_n(\bar{x}, \bar{a}) = 1$. The P-uniformity condition means that C_n can be built in time polynomial in n by an ordinary (discrete) Turing machine. Note that $\bar{a}$ plays the role of the machine constants of [1,2].

As in [4], we define the class $\mathsf{PAR}_\mathbb{R}$ as the set of languages over $\mathbb{R}$ recognized by a PSPACE-uniform family of algebraic circuits of polynomial depth (and possibly exponential size), with constants $\bar{a}$ as for $\mathsf{P}_\mathbb{R}$. Note at last that we could also define similar classes without constants $\bar{a}$. We will use the superscript 0 to denote these constant-free classes, for instance $\mathsf{P}_\mathbb{R}^0$ and $\mathsf{PAR}_\mathbb{R}^0$.

2.2   Valiant's Model

In Valiant's model, one computes polynomials instead of recognizing languages. We thus use arithmetic circuits instead of algebraic circuits. A book-length treatment of this topic can be found in [3].

An arithmetic circuit is the same as an algebraic circuit but test gates are not allowed. That is to say we have indeterminates $x_1, \ldots, x_{u(n)}$ as input together with arbitrary constants of $\mathbb{R}$; there are $+$, $-$ and $\times$-gates, and we therefore compute multivariate polynomials.

The polynomial computed by an arithmetic circuit is defined in the usual way by the polynomial computed by its output gate. Thus a family (C_n) of arithmetic circuits computes a family (f_n) of polynomials, $f_n \in \mathbb{R}[x_1, \ldots, x_{u(n)}]$. The class $\mathsf{VP}_{\mathsf{nb}}$ defined in [13] is the set of families (f_n) of polynomials computed by a family (C_n) of polynomial-size arithmetic circuits, i.e., C_n computes f_n and there exists a polynomial $p(n)$ such that $|C_n| \leq p(n)$ for all n. We will assume without loss of generality that the number $u(n)$ of variables is bounded by a polynomial function of n. The subscript "nb" indicates that there is no bound on the degree of the polynomial, in contrast with the original class VP of Valiant where a polynomial bound on the degree of the polynomial computed by the circuit is required. Note that these definitions are nonuniform. The class Uniform $\mathsf{VP_{nb}}$ is obtained by adding a condition of polynomial-time uniformity on the circuit family, as in Section 2.1.

The class VNP is the set of families of polynomials defined by an exponential sum of VP families. More precisely, $(f_n(\bar{x})) \in \mathsf{VNP}$ if there exists $(g_n(\bar{x}, \bar{y})) \in \mathsf{VP}$ and a polynomial p such that $|\bar{y}| = p(n)$ and $f_n(\bar{x}) = \sum_{\bar{\epsilon} \in \{0,1\}^{p(n)}} g_n(\bar{x}, \bar{\epsilon})$.

We can also forbid constants from our arithmetic circuits in unbounded-degree classes, and define constant-free classes. The only constant allowed is 1 (in order to allow the computation of constant polynomials). As for classes of decision problems, we will use the superscript 0 to indicate the absence of constant: for instance, we will write $\mathsf{VP_{nb}^0}$ (for bounded-degree classes, we are to be more careful; see [13]).

Note at last that arithmetic circuits are at least as powerful as boolean circuits in the sense that one can simulate the latter by the former. Indeed, we can for instance replace $\neg u$ by $1 - u$, $u \wedge v$ by uv, and $u \vee v$ by $u + v - uv$. This proves the following classical lemma.

Lemma 1. *Any boolean circuit C can be simulated by an arithmetic one of size at most $3|C|$, in the sense that on boolean inputs, both circuits output the same value.*

3   The Class VPSPACE

3.1   Definition

We fix an arbitrary field K. The definition of VPSPACE will be stated in terms of *coefficient function*. A monomial $x_1^{\alpha_1} \cdots x_{u(n)}^{\alpha_{u(n)}}$ is encoded in binary by $\alpha = (\alpha_1, \ldots, \alpha_{u(n)})$ and will be written $\bar{x}^\alpha$.

Definition 1. *Let (f_n) be a family of multivariate polynomials with integer co-efficients. The coefficient function of (f_n) is the function a whose value on input (n, α, i) is the i-th bit $a(n, \alpha, i)$ of the coefficient of the monomial $\bar{x}^\alpha$ in f_n. Furthermore, $a(n, \alpha, 0)$ is the sign of the coefficient of the monomial $\bar{x}^\alpha$. Thus f_n can be written as*

$$f_n(\bar{x}) = \sum_\alpha \left((-1)^{a(n,\alpha,0)} \sum_{i \geq 1} a(n, \alpha, i) 2^{i-1} \bar{x}^\alpha \right).$$

The coefficient function is a function $a : \{0,1\}^* \to \{0,1\}$ and can therefore be viewed as a language. This allows us to speak of the complexity of the coefficient function.

Definition 2. *The class* Uniform $\mathsf{VPSPACE^0}$ *is the set of all families (f_n) of multivariate polynomials $f_n \in K[x_1, \ldots, x_{u(n)}]$ satisfying the following requirements:*

1. *the number $u(n)$ of variables is polynomially bounded;*
2. *the polynomials f_n have integer coefficients;*
3. *the size of the coefficients of f_n is bounded by $2^{p(n)}$ for some polynomial p;*
4. *the degree of f_n is bounded by $2^{p(n)}$ for some polynomial p;*
5. *the coefficient function of (f_n) is in* PSPACE.

We have chosen to define first Uniform VPSPACE^0, a uniform class without constants, because this is the main object of study in this paper. In keeping with the tradition set by Valiant, however, the class VPSPACE, defined in the full version of this paper [12], is nonuniform and allows for arbitrary constants.

3.2   An Alternative Characterization

Let Uniform VPAR^0 be the class of families of polynomials computed by a PSPACE-uniform family of constant-free arithmetic circuits of polynomial depth (and possibly exponential size). This in fact characterizes Uniform VPSPACE^0.

Proposition 1. *The two classes* Uniform VPSPACE^0 *and* Uniform VPAR^0 *are equal.*

Proof. Let (f_n) be a Uniform VPSPACE^0 family. In order to compute f_n by an arithmetic circuit of polynomial depth, we compute all its monomials in parallel and sum them in a divide-and-conquer-fashion. The resulting family of arithmetic circuits is uniform due to the uniformity condition on (f_n).

For the converse, take an arithmetic circuit of polynomial depth. We show that we can build a boolean circuit of polynomial depth which takes as input the encoding α of a monomial and computes the coefficient of $\bar{x}^\alpha$. We proceed by induction, computing the coefficient of $\bar{x}^\alpha$ for each gate of the original arithmetic circuit. For the input gates, this is easy. For a +-gate, it is enough to add both coefficients. For a gate $a \times b$, we compute in parallel the sum of the cd over all the monomials $\bar{x}^\beta$ and $\bar{x}^\gamma$ such that $\beta + \gamma = \alpha$, where c is the coefficient of $\bar{x}^\gamma$ in the gate a, and d the coefficient of $\bar{x}^\beta$ in the gate b. The whole boolean circuit remains uniform and of polynomial depth. Therefore, the coefficient function is in PSPACE by the "parallel computation thesis".   □

We see here the similarity with PAR$_\mathbb{R}$, which by definition are those languages recognized by uniform algebraic circuits of polynomial depth. But of course there is no test gate in the arithmetic circuits of Uniform VPSPACE^0.

4   Sign Conditions

4.1   Definition

Given are s polynomials $f_1, \ldots, f_s \in \mathbb{Z}[x_1, \ldots, x_n]$. A sign condition is merely an s-tuple $S \in \{-1, 0, 1\}^s$. Intuitively, the i-th coordinate of S represents the sign of f_i: -1 for < 0, 0 for 0, and 1 for > 0. Accordingly, the sign condition of a point $\bar{x} \in \mathbb{R}^n$ is the tuple $S \in \{-1,0,1\}^s$ such that $S_i = -1$ if $f_i(\bar{x}) < 0$, $S_i = 0$ if $f_i(\bar{x}) = 0$ and $S_i = 1$ if $f_i(\bar{x}) > 0$.

Of course some sign conditions are not realizable, in the sense that the polynomials can nowhere take the corresponding signs (think for instance of $x^2 + 1$ which can only take positive values over $\mathbb{R}$). We say that a sign condition is *satisfiable* if it is the sign condition of some $\bar{x} \in \mathbb{R}^n$ and we call N the number of satisfiable sign conditions. The key result detailed in the next section is that among all possible sign conditions, there are few satisfiable ones (i.e. N is small), and there exists a polynomial space algorithm to enumerate them all.

4.2 A PSPACE Algorithm for Sign Conditions

The following theorem will prove to be a central tool in our proofs. The bound on the number of satisfiable sign conditions follows from the Thom-Milnor bounds [14] (see Grigoriev [8, Lemma 1]); the enumeration algorithm is from Renegar [17, Prop. 4.1].

Theorem 1. *Let $f_1, \ldots, f_s \in \mathbb{Z}[x_1, \ldots, x_n]$ be s polynomials of maximal degree d, and whose coefficients have bit size $\leq L$. Then:*

1. *there are $N = (sd)^{O(n)}$ satisfiable sign conditions;*
2. *there is an algorithm using work space $(\log L)[n \log(sd)]^{O(1)}$ which, on input $(f_1, \ldots, f_s)$ in dense representation, and (i,j) in binary, outputs the j-th component of the i-th satisfiable sign condition.*

If S is the i-th satisfiable sign condition produced by this enumeration algorithm, we say that the *rank* of S is i (the rank is therefore merely the index of the sign condition in the enumeration). Note that if $d = 2^{n^{O(1)}}$, $s = 2^{n^{O(1)}}$ and $L = 2^{n^{O(1)}}$ as will be the case, then the work space of the algorithm is polynomial in n.

4.3 Enumerating All Possibly Tested Polynomials

In the execution of an algebraic circuit, the values of some polynomials at the input $\bar{x}$ are tested to zero. If two points $\bar{x}$ and $\bar{y}$ have the same sign condition with respect to all polynomials possibly tested to zero, then they will either both belong to the language, or both be outside of it: indeed the results of all the tests will be the same during the execution of the circuit. Therefore we can handle sign conditions (i.e. boolean words) instead of algebraic inputs.

Note that in order to find the sign condition of the input $\bar{x}$, we have to be able to enumerate in polynomial space all the polynomials that can ever be tested to zero in some computation of an algebraic circuit. This is done as in [7, Th. 3].

Proposition 2. *Let C be a constant-free algebraic circuit with n variables and of depth d.*

1. *The number of different polynomials possibly tested to zero in some computation of C is $2^{d^2 O(n)}$.*

2. *There exists an algorithm using work space* $(nd)^{O(1)}$ *which, on input C and integers (i, j) in binary, outputs the j-th bit of the i-th of these polynomials.*

The proof can be found in the full version of this paper [12]. Note that this proposition can also be useful when our algebraic circuit is not constant-free: it is enough to replace the constants by fresh variables. The only risk is indeed to take more polynomials into account since we have replaced specific constants by generic variables.

5   A Transfer Theorem

In this section we prove our main result.

Theorem 2. Uniform $\mathsf{VPSPACE}^0$ = Uniform $\mathsf{VP}_{\mathsf{nb}}^0 \implies \mathsf{PAR}_{\mathbb{R}}^0 = \mathsf{P}_{\mathbb{R}}^0$.

Note that the collapse of the constant-free class $\mathsf{PAR}_{\mathbb{R}}^0$ to $\mathsf{P}_{\mathbb{R}}^0$ implies the collapse of $\mathsf{PAR}_{\mathbb{R}}$ to $\mathsf{P}_{\mathbb{R}}$: just replace constants by new variables in order to transform a $\mathsf{PAR}_{\mathbb{R}}$ problem into a $\mathsf{PAR}_{\mathbb{R}}^0$ problem, and then replace these variables by their orignal values in order to transform a $\mathsf{P}_{\mathbb{R}}^0$ problem into a $\mathsf{P}_{\mathbb{R}}$ problem.

Let $A \in \mathsf{PAR}_{\mathbb{R}}^0$: it is decided by a uniform family (C_n) of constant-free algebraic circuits of polynomial depth. For convenience, we fix n and work with C_n. For the proof of Theorem 2 we will need to find the sign condition of the input $\bar{x}$ with respect to the polynomials $f_1, \ldots, f_s$ of Proposition 2, that is to say, with respect to all the polynomials that can be tested to zero in an execution of C_n. We denote by N the number of satisfiable sign conditions with respect to $f_1, \ldots, f_s$.

Note that most of the forthcoming results depend on the polynomials $f_1, \ldots, f_s$, therefore on the choice of C_n. For instance, once C_n and $f_1, \ldots, f_s$ are chosen, the satisfiable sign conditions are fixed and we will speak of the i-th satisfiable sign condition without referring explicitly to the polynomials $f_1, \ldots, f_s$.

In order to find the sign condition of the input, we will give a polynomial-time algorithm which tests some $\mathsf{VPSPACE}$ family for zero. Here is the formalized notion of a polynomial-time algorithm with $\mathsf{VPSPACE}$ tests.

Definition 3. *A polynomial-time algorithm with* Uniform $\mathsf{VPSPACE}^0$ *tests is a* Uniform $\mathsf{VPSPACE}^0$ *family* $(f_n(x_1, \ldots, x_{u(n)}))$ *together with a uniform constant-free family* (C_n) *of polynomial-size algebraic circuits endowed with special test gates of indegree $u(n)$, whose value is 1 on input $(a_1, \ldots, a_{u(n)})$ if $f_n(a_1, \ldots, a_{u(n)}) \leq 0$ and 0 otherwise.*

Observe that a constant number of Uniform $\mathsf{VPSPACE}^0$ families can be used in the preceding definition instead of only one: it is enough to combine them all in one by using "selection variables". The following Theorem 3 is the main result en route to showing the transfer theorem. It is proved via successive lemmas in Sections 5.1 to 5.3: we proceed as in [9] but constructively.

Theorem 3. *There is a polynomial-time algorithm with* Uniform $\mathsf{VPSPACE}^0$ *tests that, on input $\bar{x}$, computes the rank of the sign condition of $\bar{x}$ with respect to $f_1, \ldots, f_s$.*

5.1   Truncated Sign Conditions

A truncated sign condition is merely an element T of $\{0,1\}^s$. Contrary to full sign conditions, only the two cases $= 0$ and $\neq 0$ are distinguished. We define in a natural way the truncated sign condition T of a point $\bar{x}$: $T_i = 0$ if and only if $f_i(\bar{x}) = 0$.

Of course, there are fewer satisfiable truncated sign conditions than full ones, and of course there exists a polynomial space algorithm to enumerate them. Furthermore, truncated sign conditions can be viewed as subsets of $\{1, \ldots, s\}$ (via the convention $k \in T \iff T_k = 1$), therefore enabling us to speak of inclusion of truncated sign conditions.

We fix an order $\leq_T$ compatible with inclusion and easily computable in parallel, e.g. the lexicographic order. Let us call $T^{(i)}$ the i-th satisfiable truncated sign condition with respect to this order.

Lemma 2. *There is an algorithm using work space polynomial in n which, on input $(f_1, \ldots, f_s)$ in dense representation, and (i,j) in binary, outputs the j-th component of $T^{(i)}$ (the i-th satisfiable truncated sign condition with respect to $\leq_T$).*

Proof. It is enough to use the algorithm of Theorem 1, followed by a fast parallel-sorting procedure, for instance Cole's parallel merge-sort algorithm [6].   □

Note that the truncated sign condition of the input $\bar{x}$ is the maximal truncated satisfiable sign condition T satisfying $\forall i, T_i = 1 \Rightarrow f_i(\bar{x}) \neq 0$. Hence we have to find a maximum. This will be done by binary search.

Lemma 3. *There is a* Uniform VPSPACE^0 *family (g_n) of polynomials satisfying, for real $\bar{x}$ and boolean i,*

$$g_n(\bar{x}, i) = \prod_{j \leq i} \Big(\sum_{k \notin T^{(j)}} f_k(\bar{x})^2 \Big).$$

Proof. Lemma 2 asserts that deciding whether $k \notin T^{(j)}$ is in PSPACE.

Then we use twice the closure of Uniform VPSPACE^0 under exponential sum and product (see the full version of this paper [12]).   □

Proposition 3. *There is a polynomial-time algorithm with* Uniform VPSPACE^0 *tests which on input $\bar{x}$ outputs the rank m of its truncated sign condition $T^{(m)}$.*

Proof. The algorithm merely consists in performing a binary search thanks to the polynomials of Lemma 3: if the truncated sign condition of the input $\bar{x}$ is $T^{(m)}$, then $\prod_{j \leq i}(\sum_{k \notin T^{(j)}} f_k(\bar{x})^2) = 0$ if and only if $m \leq i$. By making i vary, we find m in a number of steps logarithmic in the number of satisfiable truncated sign conditions, i.e. in polynomial time.   □

5.2 Binary Search for the Full Sign Condition

We say that a (full) sign condition S is compatible with the truncated sign condition T if $\forall i, T_i = 0 \Leftrightarrow S_i = 0$ (i.e. they agree for "$= 0$" and for "$\neq 0$"). Let N' denote the number of (full) satisfiable sign conditions compatible with the truncated sign condition of the input $\bar{x}$. Obviously, $N' \leq N$. The following lemma is straightforward after Lemma 2 and Theorem 1.

Lemma 4. *There is an algorithm using work space polynomial in n which, on input (i, j, k), ouputs the j-th bit of the i-th satisfiable sign condition compatible with $T^{(k)}$.*

Since we know the truncated sign condition of $\bar{x}$ after running the algorithm of Proposition 3, we know which polynomials vanish at $\bar{x}$. We can therefore discard the zeros in the (full) compatible satisfiable sign conditions. Hence we are now concerned with two-valued sign conditions, that is, elements of $\{-1, 1\}^{s'}$ with $s' \leq s$. In what follows arithmetic over the field of two elements will be used, hence it will be simpler to consider that our sign conditions have values among $\{0, 1\}$ instead of $\{-1, 1\}$: 0 for > 0 and 1 for < 0. Thus sign conditions are viewed as vectors over $\{0, 1\}$, or alternately as subsets of $\{1, \dots, s'\}$. The set $\{0, 1\}^{s'}$ is endowed with the inner product $u.v = \sum_i u_i v_i \pmod 2$, and we say that u and v are orthogonal whenever $u.v = 0$ (see [5]).

The following proposition from [5] will be useful. It consists in an improvement of the result of [9]: first (and most importantly), it is constructive, and second, the range $[N'/2 - \sqrt{N'}/2, N'/2 + \sqrt{N'}/2]$ here is much better than the original one $[N'/3, 2N'/3]$.

Proposition 4. *Let V be a set of N' vectors of $\{0, 1\}^{s'}$.*

1. *There exists a vector u orthogonal to at least $N'/2 - \sqrt{N'}/2$ and at most $N'/2 + \sqrt{N'}/2$ vectors of V.*
2. *Such a vector u can be found on input V by a logarithmic space algorithm.*

Our aim is to find the sign condition of $\bar{x}$. We will use Proposition 4 in order to divide the cardinality of the search space by two at each step. This is based on the following observation: if $u \in \{0, 1\}^{s'}$, the value of the product $\prod_{j \in u} f_j(\bar{x})$ is negative if the inner product of u and the sign condition of $\bar{x}$ is 1, and is positive otherwise. The idea is then to choose u judiciously so that the number of satisfiable sign conditions having the same inner product with u as the sign condition of $\bar{x}$ is halved at each step. Therefore, in a logarithmic number of steps, the sign condition of $\bar{x}$ will be uniquely determined. This gives the following algorithm for finding the sign condition of $\bar{x}$.

- Let E be the set of all the satisfiable sign conditions.
- While E contains more than one element, do
  - Find by Proposition 4 a vector u orthogonal to at least $|E|/2 - \sqrt{|E|}/2$ and at most $|E|/2 + \sqrt{|E|}/2$ vectors of E.
  - Let b be the result of the test "$\prod_{j \in u} f_j(\bar{x}) < 0$?".

- Let the new E be the set of all sign conditions in E which have inner product b with u.
- Enumerate all the satisfiable sign conditions and find the one that produces exactly the same results as in the loop: this is the sign condition of $\bar{x}$.

Note that the number of steps is $O(\log N')$, which is polynomial in n. The last step of this algorithm (namely, recovering the rank of the sign condition of $\bar{x}$ from the list of results of the loop) is detailed in Section 5.3.

We now show how to perform this algorithm in polynomial time with Uniform $\mathsf{VPSPACE}^0$ tests. The main technical difficulty is that according to Definition 3 we can use only one $\mathsf{VPSPACE}$ family, whereas we want to make adaptive tests. We therefore have to store the intermediate results of the preceding tests in some variables $\bar{c}$ (a "list of choices") of the $\mathsf{VPSPACE}$ polynomial. Proposition 4 shows that, by reusing space, there exists a logspace algorithm that, given any set V of N' vectors together with a "list of choices" $c \in \{0,1\}^l$ (with $l = O(\log N')$), enumerates $l + 1$ vectors $u^{(1)}, \ldots, u^{(l+1)}$ satisfying the following condition $(\star)$:

- $u^{(1)}$ is orthogonal to at least $N'/2 - \sqrt{N'}/2$ and at most $N'/2 + \sqrt{N'}/2$ vectors of V.
- Let $V_i \subseteq V$ be the subset of all the vectors $v \in V$ satisfying $\forall j \leq i, v.u^{(j)} = c_j$. Then the vector $u^{(i+1)}$ is orthogonal to at least $|V_i|/2 - \sqrt{|V_i|}/2$ and at most $|V_i|/2 + \sqrt{|V_i|}/2$ vectors of V_i.

Note that $|V_i|$ is roughly divided by 2 at each step, so the number of steps is $O(\log N')$. In particular, since s' and N' are simply exponential, the following lemma is easily derived by combining what precedes with Lemma 4.

Lemma 5. *There is an algorithm using work space polynomial in n which, on input (i, j, k, c) in binary, outputs the j-th bit of $u^{(i)} \in \{0,1\}^{N'}$, where the vectors $u^{(1)}, \ldots, u^{(l+1)}$ satisfy condition $(\star)$ for the input consisting of:*

- *the set V of the N' (full) satisfiable sign conditions compatible with $T^{(k)}$,*
- *together with the list of choices $c \in \{0,1\}^l$.*

Lemma 6. *There exists a Uniform $\mathsf{VPSPACE}^0$ family (h_n) satifsying, for real $\bar{x}$ and boolean (i, k, c):*

$$h_n(\bar{x}, i, k, c) = \prod_{j \in u^{(i)}} f_j(\bar{x}),$$

where $u^{(1)}, \ldots, u^{(l+1)}$ are defined as in Lemma 5 (in particular they depend on $T^{(k)}$).

Proof. Lemma 5 asserts that deciding whether $j \in u^{(i)}$ is done in polynomial space. The closure of Uniform $\mathsf{VPSPACE}^0$ under exponential products (see [12]) then concludes the proof.   □

Therefore, by a Uniform $\mathsf{VPSPACE}^0$ test, one is able to know the sign of the polynomial $h_n(\bar{x}, i, k, c) = \prod_{j \in u^{(i)}} f_j(\bar{x})$. As mentioned before, this gives us the inner product of $u^{(i)}$ and the (full) sign condition of $\bar{x}$: this sign is < 0 if and only if the inner product is 1. By beginning with $c = 0 \cdots 0$ (step 1), and at step $i \geq 2$ letting $c_{i-1} = 1$ if and only if the preceding test was < 0, the number of sign conditions that have the same inner products as that of $\bar{x}$ is divided by (roughly) two at each step. At the end, we therefore have a list of choices c that only the sign condition of $\bar{x}$ fulfills. This proves the following lemma.

Lemma 7. *There is a polynomial-time algorithm with* Uniform VPSPACE^0 *tests which on input $\bar{x}$ outputs the list of choices c (defined as above) which uniquely characterizes the sign condition of $\bar{x}$, provided we know the rank k of the truncated sign condition $T^{(k)}$ of $\bar{x}$.*

We are now able to recover the rank of the sign condition of $\bar{x}$ from this information, as explained in the next section.

5.3   Recovering the Rank of the Sign Condition

Lemma 8. *There is an algorithm using work space polynomial in n which, on input $c \in \{0, 1\}^l$ (a list of choices) and k, outputs the rank of a satisfiable sign condition compatible with $T^{(k)}$ that fulfills the list of choices c.*

Proof. In polynomial space we recompute all the vectors $u^{(i)}$ as in Lemma 5, then we enumerate all the sign conditions thanks to Theorem 1 until we find one that fulfills the list of choices c.   □

The proof of Theorem 3 follows easily from Proposition 3 and Lemmas 7–8.

5.4   A Polynomial-Time Algorithm for PAR$_\mathbb{R}$ Problems

Remember that $A \in$ PAR$_\mathbb{R}^0$ and (C_n) is a uniform family of polynomial-depth algebraic circuits deciding A.

Lemma 9. *There is a (boolean) algorithm using work space polynomial in n which, on input i (the rank of a satisfiable sign condition), decides whether the elements of the i-th satisfiable sign condition S are accepted by the circuit C_n.*

Proof. We follow the circuit C_n level by level. For test gates, we compute the polynomial f to be tested. Then we enumerate the polynomials $f_1, \ldots, f_s$ as in Proposition 2 for the circuit C_n and we find the index j of f in this list. By consulting the j-th bit of the i-th satisfiable sign condition with respect to $f_1, \ldots, f_s$ (which is done by the polynomial-space algorithm of Theorem 1), we therefore know the result of the test and can go on like this until the output gate.   □

Theorem 4. *Let $A \in$ PAR$_\mathbb{R}^0$. There exists a polynomial-time algorithm with* Uniform VPSPACE^0 *tests that decides A.*

Proof. A is decided by a uniform family (C_n) of polynomial depth algebraic circuits. On input $\bar{x}$, thanks to Theorem 3 we first find the rank of the sign condition of $\bar{x}$ with respect to the polynomials $f_1, \ldots, f_s$ of Proposition 2. Then we conclude by Lemma 9.   □

Theorem 2 follows immediately from this result. One could obtain other versions of these two results by changing the uniformity conditions or the role of constants.

References

1. L. Blum, F. Cucker, M. Shub, and S. Smale. *Complexity and Real Computation.* Springer-Verlag, 1998.
2. L. Blum, M. Shub, and S. Smale. On a theory of computation and complexity over the real numbers: NP-completeness, recursive functions and universal machines. *Bulletin of the American Mathematical Society*, 21(1):1–46, 1989.
3. P. Bürgisser. *Completeness and Reduction in Algebraic Complexity Theory.* Number 7 in Algorithms and Computation in Mathematics. Springer, 2000.
4. O. Chapuis and P. Koiran. Saturation and stability in the theory of computation over the reals. *Annals of Pure and Applied Logic*, 99:1–49, 1999.
5. P. Charbit, E. Jeandel, P. Koiran, S. Perifel, and S. Thomassé. Finding a vector orthogonal to roughly half a collection of vectors. Available from http://perso.ens-lyon.fr/pascal.koiran/publications.html. Accepted for publication in *Journal of Complexity*, 2006.
6. R. Cole. Parallel merge sort. *SIAM J. Comput.*, 17(4):770–785, 1988.
7. F. Cucker and D. Grigoriev. On the power of real Turing machines over binary inputs. *SIAM Journal on Computing*, 26(1):243–254, 1997.
8. D. Grigoriev. Complexity of deciding Tarski algebra. *Journal of Symbolic Computation*, 5:65–108, 1988.
9. D. Grigoriev. Topological complexity of the range searching. *Journal of Complexity*, 16:50–53, 2000.
10. P. Koiran. Valiant's model and the cost of computing integers. *Computational Complexity*, 13:131–146, 2004.
11. P. Koiran and S. Perifel. Valiant's model: from exponential sums to exponential products. In *Mathematical Foundations of Computer Science*, volume 4162 of *Lecture Notes in Computer Science*, pages 596–607. Springer-Verlag, 2006.
12. P. Koiran and S. Perifel. VPSPACE and a Transfer Theorem over the Reals. 2006. Available from http://prunel.ccsd.cnrs.fr/ensl-00103018.
13. G. Malod. *Polynômes et coefficients.* PhD thesis, Université Claude Bernard Lyon 1, July 2003.
14. J. Milnor. On Betti numbers of real varieties. *Proceedings of the American Mathematical Society*, 15(2):275–280, 1964.
15. C. H. Papadimitriou. *Computational Complexity.* Addison-Wesley, 1994.
16. B. Poizat. *Les petits cailloux.* Aléas, 1995.
17. J. Renegar. On the computational complexity and geometry of the first-order theory of the reals, part 1. *Journal of Symbolic Computation*, 13:255–299, 1992.
18. L. G. Valiant. Completeness classes in algebra. In *Proc. 11th ACM Symposium on Theory of Computing*, pages 249–261, 1979.
19. L. G. Valiant, S. Skyum, S. Berkowitz, and C. Rackoff. Fast parallel computation of polynomials using few processors. *SIAM Journal on Computing*, 12(4):641–644, 1983.

On Symmetric Signatures in Holographic Algorithms

Jin-Yi Cai[1],[*] and Pinyan Lu[2],[**]

[1] Computer Sciences Department, University of Wisconsin
Madison, WI 53706, USA
jyc@cs.wisc.edu
[2] Department of Computer Science and Technology, Tsinghua University
Beijing, 100084, P.R. China
lpy@mails.tsinghua.edu.cn

Abstract. In holographic algorithms, *symmetric signatures* have been particularly useful. We give a complete characterization of these symmetric signatures over all bases of size 1. These improve previous results [4] where only symmetric signatures over the Hadamard basis (special basis of size 1) were obtained. In particular, we give a complete list of Boolean symmetric signatures over bases of size 1.

It is an open problem whether signatures over bases of higher dimensions are strictly more powerful. The recent result by Valiant [18] seems to suggest that bases of size 2 might be indeed more powerful than bases of size 1. This result is with regard to a restrictive counting version of #SAT called #Pl-Rtw-Mon-3CNF. It is known that the problem is #P-hard, and its mod 2 version is ⊕P-hard. Yet its mod 7 version is solvable in polynomial time by holographic algorithms. This was accomplished by a suitable symmetric signature over a basis of size 2 [18]. We show that the same unexpected holographic algorithm can be realized over a basis of size 1. Furthermore we prove that 7 is the only modulus for which such an "accidental algorithm" exists.

1 Introduction

Valiant has recently developed the theory of matchgate computations and holographic algorithms [13,15]. This is a novel methodology to design polynomial time algorithms. With this methodology, for some seemingly exponential time computations, one can design a custom made process to carry out exponentially many cancellations so that the computation can actually be done in polynomial time. Frequently the technical content of this design process amounts to finding a suitable *signature*.

These algorithms can appear quite unintuitive and exotic. So far, the main impact of this new theory is not so much as solving every day algorithmic

[*] Supported by NSF CCR-0208013 and CCR-0511679.
[**] Supported by the National Natural Science Foundation of China Grant 60553001 and the National Basic Research Program of China Grant 2007CB807900,2007CB807901.

W. Thomas and P. Weil (Eds.): STACS 2007, LNCS 4393, pp. 429–440, 2007.
© Springer-Verlag Berlin Heidelberg 2007

problems, but rather pointing out the existence of some unexpected ways of doing computation. Thus, to us, the most intriguing aspect of the new theory is its broader implication in complexity theory. A case in point is the following restrictive version of #SAT (the problem of counting satisfying assignments), called #Pl-Rtw-Mon-3CNF. Here we consider only planar Boolean formulae in Conjunctive Normal Form with 3 variables in each clause. Furthermore we assume each variable appears positively (Monotone) and in exactly two clauses (Read twice). (This problem can also be stated naturally as a Vertex Cover problem on 2-3-regular planar bipartite graphs.) #Pl-Rtw-Mon-3CNF has been studied before, including its approximate versions [7,6,1]. It is known to be #P-hard. Moreover counting the satisfying assignments modulo 2 for such formulae is ⊕P-hard. However, Valiant [18] showed that a surprising polynomial time (he called it an "accidental") algorithm exists for this counting problem mod 7, denoted #$_7$Pl-Rtw-Mon-3CNF, using holographic algorithms. What makes this work is a particular *symmetric signature* exists over the field $\mathbf{Z}_7$. This is what Valiant called an "accidental or freak object" [18].[1]

Suppose we all believe P $\neq$ NP. Unless and until a proof of P $\neq$ NP is found, one should regard this as an open problem. Then it is reasonable to ask where do we derive our confidence in this assertion. Certainly this is not due to any strong unconditional lower bound. We believe this confidence is based on the fact that all existing algorithmic approaches do not seem to tackle a myriad of NP-hard problems. Valiant's new theory of holographic algorithms challenges us to re-examine this belief critically. To put it bluntly, if you haven't seen these "exotic" or "accidental" algorithms, and haven't looked closely at how such algorithms behave, then how do you know such algorithms do not exist for one NP-hard problem? As Valiant pointed out [15], "any proof of P $\neq$ NP may need to explain, and not only to imply, the unsolvability" of NP-hard problems in this framework.

Valiant actually introduced two related theories, first, matchgate / matchcircuit [13], and second, holographic algorithms [15]. In the first theory, the basic notion is a matchgate and its *character*, defined by Pfaffians. He used this theory to simulate a fragment of quantum computations. In the second, a new ingredient was added, that of a linear vector basis through which computation is expressed. In this second theory, the matchgates are assumed to be planar, and each matchgate is associated with a *signature* defined by the Perfect Matching polynomial PerfMatch. Then the computation is ultimately done in terms of the Fisher-Kasteleyn-Temperley (FKT) method [8,9,12] via the *Holant Theorem* [15]. After the development from [3,4], a certain unification of the two theories was achieved. Basically, using the algebraic properties of Pfaffians, we were able to achieve a complete characterization of *realizable* characters in [3]. In [4] an equivalence theorem was proved for matchgates/characters on the one hand and

---

[1] From Valiant [18]: "... the situation with the P = NP question is not dissimilar to that of other unresolved enumerative conjectures in mathematics. The possibility that accidental or freak objects in the enumeration exist cannot be discounted, if the objects in the enumeration have not been systematically studied previously."

planar-matchgates/signatures on the other, thereby the characterization theorem also applies to planar matchgates and their *standard signatures*. In this paper, we will use these results.

Due to space limitations, we will omit most definitions, and refer the readers to [13,15,3,4,2]. A *planar matchgate* $\Gamma = (G, X, Y)$ is a weighted graph $G = (V, E, W)$ with a planar embedding, having external nodes, the input nodes X and the output nodes Y, placed on the outer face. Define PerfMatch$(G) = \sum_M \prod_{(i,j) \in M} w_{ij}$, where the sum is over all perfect matchings M. The *standard signature*, $u = u(\Gamma)$, is defined to be a $2^{|Y|} \times 2^{|X|}$ matrix whose entries are indexed by subsets $X' \subseteq X$ and $Y' \subseteq Y$, and the entry at (row Y', column X') is $u_Z = $ PerfMatch$(G - Z)$, where $Z = X' \cup Y'$. Here $G - Z$ denotes the subgraph of G obtained by removing the subset of nodes in Z (and all their incident edges). Matchgates with only output nodes are called *generators*. Matchgates with only input nodes are called *recognizers*.

In the design of holographic algorithms so far, the most useful signatures have been the so-called *symmetric signatures*. A symmetric signature is one where u_Z only depends on the cardinality of Z; we denote this by $\sigma_{|Z|}$. Thus, a symmetric signature of a generator or a recognizer with k external nodes can be identified with a vector of $k + 1$ entries $\sigma = [\sigma_0, \sigma_1, \ldots, \sigma_k]$. The ingenious idea of holographic algorithms is that one can transform the standard signatures under a linear transformation of the basis vectors. Under this transformation, the symmetric signature will remain a symmetric signature, but will have a clear combinatorial meaning. E.g., $\sigma = [0, 1, 1, 1]$ will mean a Boolean OR. These combinatorial interpretations, when applied with the Holant Theorem [15], lead to polynomial time algorithms. The symmetric signatures are responsible for a majority of the interesting polynomial time algorithms in the new theory.

To understand the limit of holographic algorithms, and to develop a substantial theory for this new methodolgy, we must come to grips with what can or cannot be done by signatures of matchgates, under *all possible* basis transformations. This is still a rather remote goal. For now we can only say something intelligent on symmetric signatures, and over bases of size 1.

In this paper, we give a complete characterization of symmetric signatures over bases of size 1. Our characterization is valid for all fields with characteristic $p \neq 2$. These improve previous results [4] where only symmetric signatures over the Hadamard basis, which is a special basis of size 1, were obtained. In [4], those results were proved using properties of Krawtchouk polynomials. Here we are able to prove a much stronger results without the use of these special polynomials. We also give a complete list of Boolean symmetric signatures over bases of size 1.

It is an open problem whether signatures over bases of higher dimensions are strictly more powerful. The recent result by Valiant [18] seems to suggest that this might be the case. He considered a restrictive version of #SAT, called #Pl-Rtw-Mon-3CNF: To count the number of satisfying assignments for a planar monotone read-twice 3CNF formula. The problem is #P-hard for counting [6,1] and ⊕P-hard for counting mod 2. But Valiant showed that it is solvable by an exotic holographic algorithm for counting mod 7. In order to do that, he used a suitable signature, with a basis of size 2. We show that the same holographic algorithm for $\#_7$Pl-Rtw-Mon-3CNF can be realized over a basis of size 1. Furthermore we prove that 7 is the only modulus for which such an "accidental algorithm" exists.

2   Holographic Algorithms for $\#_7$Pl-Rtw-Mon-3CNF

We briefly review some background information on holographic algorithms.

We use the tensor theoretic treatment for matchgates (see [2]). Let $\mathbf{b}$ denote the standard basis for two dimensional space (or size 1), $\mathbf{b} = [e_0, e_1] = \left[\begin{pmatrix} 1 \\ 0 \end{pmatrix}, \begin{pmatrix} 0 \\ 1 \end{pmatrix} \right]$. Consider another basis $\beta = [n, p] = \left[\begin{pmatrix} n_0 \\ n_1 \end{pmatrix}, \begin{pmatrix} p_0 \\ p_1 \end{pmatrix} \right]$. Let T be the transformation matrix from $\mathbf{b}$ to β, where $T = \begin{bmatrix} n_0 & p_0 \\ n_1 & p_1 \end{bmatrix}$, and $\beta = \mathbf{b}T$. For convenience, denote $T = (t_j^i)$ and $T^{-1} = (\tilde{t}_j^i)$. (Upper index is for row and lower index is for column.)

Each generator (with n output nodes) is associated with a contravariant tensor $\mathbf{G}$. Each recognizer (with n input nodes) is associated with a covariant tensor $\mathbf{R}$. The standard signature of a matchgate is the expression of its matchgate tensor under the standard basis for the tensor product space. Under a basis transformation $\beta = \mathbf{b}T$, these tensors take different forms, and transform either *contravariantly* or *covariantly*.

More concretely, the contravariant tensor $\mathbf{G}$ of a generator transforms under the basis transformation $\beta = \mathbf{b}T$ as

$$(G')^{i'_1 i'_2 \dots i'_n} = \sum G^{i_1 i_2 \dots i_n} \tilde{t}_{i_1}^{i'_1} \tilde{t}_{i_2}^{i'_2} \cdots \tilde{t}_{i_n}^{i'_n} \tag{1}$$

Here the entry of the standard signature $G^{i_1 i_2 \dots i_n} = \mathrm{PerfMatch}(G - Z)$, and the bit string $i_1 i_2 \dots i_n$ denotes subset Z. Correspondingly, the covariant tensor $\mathbf{R}$ of a recognizer transforms as

$$(R')_{i'_1 i'_2 \dots i'_n} = \sum R_{i_1 i_2 \dots i_n} t_{i'_1}^{i_1} t_{i'_2}^{i_2} \cdots t_{i'_n}^{i_n} \tag{2}$$

(where the sum is with all matching upper and lower indices.)

Let's consider $\#$Pl-Rtw-Mon-3CNF. We are given a planar formula in 3CNF form, where each variable appears positively, and appearing in exactly 2 clauses. By being a planar formula [10] our formula can be drawn as a planar bipartite graph (L, R, E), where each variable x is represented by a node in L, and each clause C is represented by a node in R, such that they are connected iff x appears in C. Because it is a Read-twice 3CNF, each node in L has degree 2, and each node in R has degree 3.

Now we replace each node in L by a generator with 2 outputs, and replace each node in R by a recognizer with 3 inputs, and connect each generator output and recognizer input in the natural way. This means that, suppose x appears in

C, and $G[x]$ and $R[C]$ are the generator and recognizer for x and C respectively, then there is an edge (with assigned weight 1) connecting one output of $G[x]$ and one input of $R[C]$.

This is called a matchgrid Ω. If Ω has g generators $G[i]$ and r recognizers $R[j]$, and $w(= 2g = 3r)$ connecting wires, the beautiful *Holant Theorem* of Valiant [15] states that under *any basis* β,

$$\text{Holant}(\Omega) = \text{PerfMatch}(G), \tag{3}$$

where

$$\text{Holant}(\Omega) = \sum_{x \in \beta^{\otimes f}} \{ [\Pi_{1 \le i \le g} G[i]^x] \cdot [\Pi_{1 \le j \le r} R[j]_x] \}. \tag{4}$$

(In tensor language, this is called a contraction.)

Now imagine we were able to find a generator matchgate G, a recognizer matchgate R, and a basis β over the field of complex numbers $\mathbf{C}$, such that G has a signature $[1, 0, 1]$ and R has a signature $[0, 1, 1, 1]$. Note that the signature $[1, 0, 1] = 1n \otimes n + 0(n \otimes p + p \otimes n) + 1p \otimes p$ has the clear combinatorial meaning of two equal signals nn or pp, and $[0, 1, 1, 1]$ has the Boolean meaning of OR. Thus the exponential sum represented by $\text{Holant}(\Omega)$ in (4) counts exactly the number of satisfying assignments of the original Boolean formula, since each such assignment contributes exactly one to the sum defining $\text{Holant}(\Omega)$.

However, $\text{Holant}(\Omega)$ is not computed by its defining expression (4), but rather as $\text{PerfMatch}(G)$ in (3) by the Holant Theorem. Notice how fragments of actual Boolean assignments to the 3CNF formula, represented by the signature entries, got all "mixed up holographically" by the transformation in (1) and (2), so that each fragment is split into exponentially many "shares" which then get summed up in (3). The latter can be computed in polynomial time by the FKT method. Now if we were able to find such matchgates and a basis over $\mathbf{C}$ such that the (symmetric) signatures have the desired form, it would have collapsed #P to P.

However, Valiant showed that one *can* find such matchgates and a basis over $\mathbf{Z}_7$, but a larger basis of size 2 is used (we will not formally define this notion for space limitations). The resulting Holant counts the number of satisfying assignments modulo 7. This is surprising, especially because it is known that the problem modulo 2 is $\oplus$P-hard.

In the rest of this section we prove that the problem can be solved using a basis of size 1. Moreover, modulo 7 is the only modulus for which this is possible.

Theorem 1. *For $\mathbf{Z}_7$ and for basis $\beta = [n, p] = \left[\binom{n_0}{n_1}, \binom{p_0}{p_1} \right] = \left[\binom{1}{6}, \binom{3}{5} \right]$, there is a generator for $[1, 0, 1]$ and a recognizer for $[0, 1, 1, 1]$.*

Remark: We recall that the notation is for symmetric signatures. Thus for a generator, $[1, 0, 1]$ denotes $(1, 0, 0, 1)^{\mathrm{T}}$ in dimension 4, and for a recognizer, $[0, 1, 1, 1]$ denotes $(0, 1, 1, 1, 1, 1, 1, 1)$ in dimension 8.

Proof: It is a simple fact that the standard signature $(3, 0, 0, 5)^{\mathrm{T}}$ is realizable by a generator matchgate with 2 outputs. This can be shown directly by a direct construction [15] or it follows from the general theory of standard signature realizability theorem in terms of matchgate identities [15,3,4]. Similarly the standard signatures $[0,3,0,5]$ is realizable by a recognizer, with 3 inputs.

A simple calculation shows that $n \otimes n + p \otimes p = (3,0,0,5)^T$ for the chosen basis β over $\mathbf{Z}_7$. Thus the generator has signature $[1,0,1]$ under the basis β.

As a recognizer, its signature u_β w.r.t. the basis β and its standard signature u are related by the equation

$$u_\beta = uT^{\otimes 3}, \qquad \text{where} \qquad T = \begin{bmatrix} n_0 & p_0 \\ n_1 & p_1 \end{bmatrix}.$$

We can calculate its signature w.r.t. β, and we find the symmetric signature $[r_0, r_1, r_2, r_3]$, where
$r_0 = 3 \times 3n_0^2 n_1 + 5n_1^3 = 0$,
$r_1 = 3(n_0^2 p_1 + 2n_0 n_1 p_0) + 5n_1^2 p_1 = 1$,
$r_2 = 3(p_0^2 n_1 + 2p_0 p_1 n_0) + 5p_1^2 n_1 = 1$,
$r_3 = 3 \times 3p_0^2 p_1 + 5p_1^3 = 1$.
Therefore this matchgate recognizes $[0,1,1,1]$. □

Corollary 1. *There is a polynomial time algorithm for $\#_7$Pl-Rtw-Mon-CNF.*

For bases of size 1, we can further prove that a similar technique can not be applied to any other $\#_k$Pl-Rtw-Mon-3CNF problem unless $k = 7$. This result may highlight the true "accidental" nature of the polynomial time algorithm for $\#_7$Pl-Rtw-Mon-3CNF. (The proof is omitted here, and is given in the full paper[5].)

Theorem 2. *Characteristic 7 is the unique characteristic of a field for which there is a common basis of size 1 for generating $[1,0,1]$ and recognizing $[0,1,1,1]$.*

3   Symmetric Signatures

In this section we give a closed form solution to characterize all symmtric signatures of generators and recognizers, under any basis of size 1. Our closed form applies to complex numbers $\mathbf{C}$ and to all fields with characteristic p greater than the arity n of the matchgate. Since we can calculate (t_j^i) and $(\tilde{t}_j^i)$ from $[n,p]$, we need only consider recognizers. The situation for generators is similar.

In tensor analysis we have the following proposition, which is straightfarward from (1)(2).

Proposition 1. *If a tensor $\mathbf{T}$ is symmetric in one basis, it is still symmetric after transforming to other basis.*

Since we focus on the case of two dimensional space $\mathbf{V}$ spanned by $\{e_0, e_1\}$, all the symmetric tensors in $\mathbf{V}^{\otimes n}$ form a $n + 1$ dimensional space, which can be denoted by $\sigma = [\sigma_0, \sigma_1, \ldots, \sigma_n]$. The symmetric signature transforms as follows under a basis transformation:

$$\sigma'_{k'} = \sum_k \sigma_k a_{k'}^k, \tag{5}$$

where

$$a^k_{k'} = \sum_{s=0}^{k} \binom{k'}{s}\binom{n-k'}{k-s}(t^1_1)^s(t^0_1)^{k'-s}(t^1_0)^{k-s}(t^0_0)^{n-k-k'+s}. \tag{6}$$

We can rewrite (6) as

$$a^k_{k'} = (t^0_1)^{k'}(t^0_0)^{n-k'}\sum_{s=0}^{k}\binom{k'}{s}\binom{n-k'}{k-s}\left(\frac{t^1_1 t^0_0}{t^0_1 t^1_0}\right)^s\left(\frac{t^1_0}{t^0_0}\right)^k. \tag{7}$$

A matchgate is called an even or an odd matchgate, precisely when it has an even or an odd number of nodes. The parity consideration is crucial in signatures of matchgates, as they are defined in terms of perfect matchings. More subtle, but just as important, are the *matchgate identities* [15,3]. From the work of [3,4] we know the following precise information regarding symmetric standard signatures.

Lemma 1. *Suppose Γ is an even matchgate, with symmetric standard signature $\sigma = [\sigma_0, \sigma_1, \ldots, \sigma_n]$. Then for all odd i, $\sigma_i = 0$, and there exist constants r_1, r_2 and λ, such that $\sigma_{2i} = \lambda \cdot (r_1)^{[n/2]-i} \cdot (r_2)^i$.*

Lemma 2. *Suppose Γ is an odd matchgate, with symmetric standard signature $\sigma = [\sigma_0, \sigma_1, \ldots, \sigma_n]$. Then for all even i, $\sigma_i = 0$, and there exist constants r_1, r_2 and λ, such that $\sigma_{2i+1} = \lambda \cdot (r_1)^{[(n-1)/2]-i} \cdot (r_2)^i$.*

Let's substitute $r_1 = b^2$ and $r_2 = c^2$ (if necessary in an extension field). Since $b = 0$ and $c = 0$ is trivial, we assume at least one of them is non-zero.

Case 1: even n and even matchgate
In this case, we have $\sigma_k = \lambda b^{n-k}c^k$, $\forall k$ even, and $\sigma_k = 0$, $\forall k$ odd. From (5) and (7) we get:

$$\sigma'_{k'} = \sum_{k=0}^{n}\sigma_k a^k_{k'}$$

$$= \lambda \sum_{k \ even} b^{n-k}c^k a^k_{k'}$$

$$= \lambda(t^0_1)^{k'}(t^0_0)^{n-k'}\sum_{k \ even} b^{n-k}c^k\left[\sum_{s=0}^{k}\binom{k'}{s}\binom{n-k'}{k-s}\left(\frac{t^1_1 t^0_0}{t^0_1 t^1_0}\right)^s\left(\frac{t^1_0}{t^0_0}\right)^k\right]$$

$$= \lambda(t^0_1)^{k'}(t^0_0)^{n-k'}\sum_{s=0}^{n}\binom{k'}{s}\left(\frac{ct^1_1}{t^1_1}\right)^s b^{k'-s}\left[\sum_{k \ even,\ k\geq s}\binom{n-k'}{k-s}b^{n-k'-k+s}\left(\frac{ct^1_0}{t^0_0}\right)^{k-s}\right].$$

Now the second sum within the brackets is

$$\sum_{k \ even,\ k\geq s}\binom{n-k'}{k-s}b^{n-k'-k+s}\left(\frac{ct^1_0}{t^0_0}\right)^{k-s} = \frac{1}{2}\left[\left(b+\frac{ct^1_0}{t^0_0}\right)^{n-k'}\pm\left(b-\frac{ct^1_0}{t^0_0}\right)^{n-k'}\right],$$

Choose $+$ if s is even and $-$ if s is odd.

Therefore, we have

$$\sigma'_{k'} = \frac{1}{2}\lambda(t_1^0)^{k'}(t_0^0)^{n-k'}\left[\left(b+\frac{ct_0^1}{t_0^0}\right)^{n-k'}+\left(b-\frac{ct_0^1}{t_0^0}\right)^{n-k'}\right]\left[\sum_{s\ even}^{n}\binom{k'}{s}\left(\frac{ct_1^1}{t_1^0}\right)^{s}b^{k'-s}\right]$$

$$+\frac{1}{2}\lambda(t_1^0)^{k'}(t_0^0)^{n-k'}\left[\left(b+\frac{ct_0^1}{t_0^0}\right)^{n-k'}-\left(b-\frac{ct_0^1}{t_0^0}\right)^{n-k'}\right]\left[\sum_{s\ odd}^{n}\binom{k'}{s}\left(\frac{ct_1^1}{t_1^0}\right)^{s}b^{k'-s}\right]$$

$$=\frac{1}{2}\lambda(t_1^0)^{k'}[(bt_0^0+ct_0^1)^{n-k'}+(bt_0^0-ct_0^1)^{n-k'}]\cdot\frac{1}{2}\left[\left(b+\frac{ct_1^1}{t_1^0}\right)^{k'}+\left(b-\frac{ct_1^1}{t_1^0}\right)^{k'}\right]$$

$$+\frac{1}{2}\lambda(t_1^0)^{k'}[(bt_0^0+ct_0^1)^{n-k'}-(bt_0^0-ct_0^1)^{n-k'}]\cdot\frac{1}{2}\left[\left(b+\frac{ct_1^1}{t_1^0}\right)^{k'}-\left(b-\frac{ct_1^1}{t_1^0}\right)^{k'}\right]$$

$$=\frac{1}{2}\lambda[(bt_0^0+ct_0^1)^{n-k'}(bt_1^0+ct_1^1)^{k'}+(bt_0^0-ct_0^1)^{n-k'}(bt_1^0-ct_1^1)^{k'}].$$

Case 2: odd n and even matchgate

In this case, we have $\sigma_k = \lambda b^{n-1-k}c^k$, $\forall k$ even, and $\sigma_k = 0$,$\forall k$ odd. From (5) and (7) we get:

$$\sigma'_{k'} = \sum_{k=0}^{n}\sigma_k a_{k'}^k = \lambda\sum_{k\ even}b^{n-1-k}c^k a_{k'}^k. \tag{8}$$

If $b \neq 0$, let $\lambda' = \lambda/b$, we can have the similar calculation as Case 1 and get the following form:

$$\sigma'_{k'} = \frac{1}{2}\lambda'[(bt_0^0+ct_0^1)^{n-k'}(bt_1^0+ct_1^1)^{k'}+(bt_0^0-ct_0^1)^{n-k'}(bt_1^0-ct_1^1)^{k'}]. \tag{9}$$

Otherwise $b = 0$, then $\sigma_{n-1} = \lambda c^{n-1}$, and $\sigma_k = 0$, $\forall k \neq n-1$. In this subcase, let $\lambda' = \lambda c^{n-1} = \sigma_{n-1}$. The only non-zero term in (5) is when $k = n-1$ and further more the only non-zero terms in (6) are when $s = k'$ and $s = k'-1$:

$$\sigma'_{k'} = \sum_{k=0}^{n}\sigma_k a_{k'}^k$$

$$= \sigma_{n-1}a_{k'}^{n-1}$$

$$= \lambda'((n-k')(t_1^1)^{k'}(t_0^1)^{n-1-k'}t_0^0 + k'(t_1^1)^{k'-1}t_1^0(t_0^1)^{n-k'}).$$

The situations of case 3 "odd n and odd matchgate" and case 4 "even n and odd matchgate" are similar with case 1 and case 2. Detail is omitted here and is given in the full paper [5].

To sum up, we get the following theorem: (We assume the characteristic of the field is not 2)

Theorem 3. *A symmetric signature* $[x_0, x_1, \ldots, x_n]$ *for a recognizer is realizable under the basis* $\beta = [n, p] = \left[\binom{n_0}{n_1}, \binom{p_0}{p_1}\right]$ *iff it takes one of the following forms:*

- Form 1: there exist (arbitrary) constants λ, s, t and ϵ where $\epsilon = \pm 1$, such that for all $i, 0 \leq i \leq n$,

$$x_i = \lambda[(sn_0 + tn_1)^{n-i}(sp_0 + tp_1)^i + \epsilon(sn_0 - tn_1)^{n-i}(sp_0 - tp_1)^i]. \quad (10)$$

- Form 2: there exist (arbitrary) constants λ, such that for all $i, 0 \leq i \leq n$,

$$x_i = \lambda[(n - i)n_0(p_1)^i(n_1)^{n-1-i} + ip_0(p_1)^{i-1}(n_1)^{n-i}]. \quad (11)$$

- Form 3: there exist (arbitrary) constants λ, such that for all $i, 0 \leq i \leq n$,

$$x_i = \lambda[(n - i)n_1(p_0)^i(n_0)^{n-1-i} + ip_1(p_0)^{i-1}(n_0)^{n-i}]. \quad (12)$$

Similarly we can prove

Theorem 4. *A symmetric signature* $[x_0, x_1, \ldots, x_n]$ *for a generator is realizable under the basis* $\beta = [n, p] = \left[\begin{pmatrix} n_0 \\ n_1 \end{pmatrix}, \begin{pmatrix} p_0 \\ p_1 \end{pmatrix} \right]$ *iff it takes one of the following forms:*

- Form 1: there exist (arbitrary) constance λ, s, t and ϵ where $\epsilon = \pm 1$, such that for all $i, 0 \leq i \leq n$,

$$x_i = \lambda[(sp_1 - tp_0)^{n-i}(-sn_1 + tn_0)^i + \epsilon(sp_1 + tp_0)^{n-i}(-sn_1 - tn_0)^i]. \quad (13)$$

- Form 2: there exist (arbitrary) constants λ, such that for all $i, 0 \leq i \leq n$,

$$x_i = \lambda[(n - i)p_1(n_0)^i(-p_0)^{n-1-i} - in_1(n_0)^{i-1}(-p_0)^{n-i}]. \quad (14)$$

- Form 3: there exist (arbitrary) constants λ, such that for all $i, 0 \leq i \leq n$,

$$x_i = \lambda[-(n - i)p_0(-n_1)^i(p_1)^{n-1-i} + in_0(-n_1)^{i-1}(p_1)^{n-i}]. \quad (15)$$

We wish to obtain another characterization of realizable symmetric signatures. First, we deal with some degenerate cases. The following three cases are called degenerate:

- In Form 1, $sn_0 + tn_1 = 0$ or $sn_0 - tn_1 = 0$.
- In Form 2, $n_1 = 0$.
- In Form 3, $n_0 = 0$.

In Form 1, if $sn_0 + tn_1 = 0$ and $sn_0 - tn_1 = 0$, then all the realizable signatures take the following form (λ is arbitrary):

$$[0, 0, \cdots, 0, \lambda]. \quad (16)$$

In Form 1, if $sn_0 + tn_1 = 0$ and $sn_0 - tn_1 \neq 0$, or $sn_0 + tn_1 \neq 0$ and $sn_0 - tn_1 = 0$, then all the realizable signatures take the following form (a, q, λ are arbitrary):

$$[a, aq, aq^2, \cdots, aq^{n-1}, \lambda]. \quad (17)$$

Notice that (16) is a special case of (17), we will not consider (16) later.

In Form 2, if $n_1 = 0$, then all the realizable signatures take the following form (λ_1, λ_2 is arbitrary):

$$[0, 0, \cdots, 0, \lambda_1, \lambda_2]. \tag{18}$$

In form 3, if $n_0 = 0$, then all the realizable signatures take the following form (λ_1, λ_2 is arbitrary):

$$[0, 0, \cdots, 0, \lambda_1, \lambda_2]. $$

This is the same as (18).

Besides these degenerate cases, we can rewrite the sequence defined in Form 1 as $x_i = A\alpha^i + B\beta^i$, and the sequence defined Form 2 or Form 3 as $x_i = \alpha^i(Ai + B)$. Both are solutions to **second-order homogeneous linear recurrences** ($x_i = ax_{i-1} + bx_{i-2}$). To sum up in a more symmetric way, we have the following theorem: (We assume the the characteristic of the field $p \neq 2$ and $p \nmid n$.)

Theorem 5. *A symmetric signature* $[x_0, x_1, \cdots, x_n]$ *is realizable on some basis of size 1 iff there exists three constants* a, b, c *(not all zero), such that* $\forall k, 0 \leq k \leq n - 2$,

$$ax_k + bx_{k+1} + cx_{k+2} = 0. \tag{19}$$

Proof

"$\Rightarrow$":

Since $[x_0, x_1, \cdots, x_n]$ is realizable, from Theorem 3 (4), x_i takes one of the forms in Theorem 3 (4). If it is degenerate as (17), we can let $a = -q, b = 1, c = 0$. If it is degenerate as (18), we can let $a = 1, b = 0, c = 0$. Otherwise it is a second-order homogeneous linear recurring sequence $x_i = a_0 x_{i-1} + b_0 x_{i-2}$, we can let $a = b_0, b = a_0, c = -1$. Therefore if $[x_0, x_1, \cdots, x_n]$ is realizable on some basis of size 1 , there exists three constants a, b, c (not all zero), such that $\forall k, 0 \leq k \leq n - 2, ax_k + bx_{k+1} + cx_{k+2} = 0$.

"$\Leftarrow$":

If $c = 0$ and $b = 0$, then $a \neq 0$. From (19), we know $x_k = 0$, $\forall k, 0 \leq k \leq n - 2$. So $\{x_i\}$ takes the form (18), which is realizable.

If $c = 0$ and $b \neq 0$, form (19) we have $ax_k + bx_{k+1} = 0$, $\forall k, 0 \leq k \leq n - 2$. Let $q = -a/b$, we have $x_{k+1} = x_k q$, $\forall k, 0 \leq k \leq n - 2$. Therefore $\{x_i\}$ takes the form (17), which is realizable.

Otherwise $c \neq 0$, substituting $a_0 = -b/c, b_0 = -a/c$, we have $x_{k+2} = a_0 x_{k+1} + b_0 x_k$, $\forall k, 0 \leq k \leq n - 2$. The characteristic equation is $x^2 - a_0 x - b_0 = 0$. Let α, β be the two roots of the characteristic equation. If $\alpha \neq \beta$, we can calculate A, B such that $x_i = A\alpha^i + B\beta^i$, $\forall i, 0 \leq i \leq n$. If $A = B = 0$, then $x_i = 0$, $\forall i, 0 \leq i \leq n$, which trivially realizable. If $A = 0$ and $B \neq 0$ (the case $B = 0$ and $A \neq 0$ is similar), then $x_i = B\beta^i$. Let $\epsilon = s = 1, t = 0, \lambda = B/2, n_0 = 1, p_0 = \beta, n_1 = 0, p_1 = 1$ in (10), we know it is realizable. Otherwise $AB \neq 0$, let $\lambda = \epsilon = s = t = 1$ in (10), we have the following equations:

$$n_0 + n_1 = \sqrt[n]{A} \tag{20}$$

$$n_0 - n_1 = \sqrt[n]{B} \tag{21}$$

$$p_0 + p_1 = \alpha \sqrt[n]{A} \tag{22}$$

$$p_0 - p_1 = \beta \sqrt[n]{B} \tag{23}$$

From the above equations, we can get the value of n_0, n_1, p_0, p_1 and we conclude that $x_i = A\alpha^i + B\beta^i$ is realizable.

If $\alpha = \beta$ we can calculate A, B such that $x_i = \alpha^i(Ai + B)$, $\forall i, 0 \le i \le n$. If $\alpha = 0$ or $A = 0$, the above argument shows it is realizable. Otherwise let $\lambda = n_1 = 1, p_1 = \alpha, n_0 = \frac{B}{n}, p_0 = A\alpha + \frac{B\alpha}{n}$ in form (11), we conclude that $x_i = \alpha^i(Ai + B)$ is realizable. $\qquad\square$

Corollary 2. *Over the complex numbers* **C** *as well as all fields* **F** *of characteristic $p > 3$, every signature $[x_0, x_1, x_2, x_3]$ is realizable on some basis of size 1.*

Proof: View $r_1 = (x_0, x_1, x_2), r_2 = (x_1, x_2, x_3)$ as two vectors in 3-dimension Euclid space. Geometrically, there exists a non-zero vector $r_0 = (a, b, c)$ such that $r_0 \perp r_1$ and $r_0 \perp r_2$. That is $ax_0 + bx_1 + cx_2 = 0$ and $ax_1 + bx_2 + cx_3 = 0$. From Theorem 5, we know that $[x_0, x_1, x_2, x_3]$ is realizable. $\qquad\square$

4 Boolean Symmetric Signatures

In this section, we consider the realizability of a special family of symmetric signatures, which we call boolean symmetric signatures (BSS).

Definition 1. *A signature of a generator or a recognizer is called a Boolean Symmetric Signature (BSS) iff it is symmetric $[x_0, x_1, \ldots, x_n]$ and $\forall i \in [n], x_i \in \{0, 1\}$.*

From Corollary 2 and Theorem 5 , we can conclude that:

Theorem 6. *When $n \le 3$, all BSS are realizable.*

When $n \ge 4$, the set of realizable BSS is rather sparse. More precisely we have the following theorem:

Theorem 7. *When $n \ge 4$, a BSS $[x_0, x_1, \ldots, x_n]$ is realizable on some basis of size 1 iff it has one of the following forms ($\lambda, \lambda_1, \lambda_2 \in \{0, 1\}$ is arbitrary):* $[\lambda_1, 0, 0, \cdots, 0, \lambda_2]$, $[1, 1, \cdots, 1, \lambda]$, $[\lambda, 1, 1, \cdots, 1]$, $[0, 0, \cdots, 0, \lambda_1, \lambda_2]$, $[\lambda_1, \lambda_2, 0, 0, \cdots, 0]$, $[1, 0, 1, 0, \cdots, 0(1)]$, $[0, 1, 0, 1, \cdots, 0(1)]$

Proof: From Theorem 5, we can check that all the forms are all realizable.

Using theorem 5 and checking all the possible values of x_0, x_1, x_2, x_3, we can prove that these forms are the only possible cases. Detail is omitted here and is given in the full paper [5] $\qquad\square$

Acknowledgments

We would like to thank Leslie Valiant for many comments and questions, particularly for pointing out a mistake in an earlier draft. We also thank

Andrew Yao, and his group of students in Tsinghua University, while the first author visited Tsinghua and gave lectures.

References

1. R. Bubley, and M. Dyer, Graph orientations with no sink and an approximation for a hard case of #SAT, ACM SODA , (1997) 248-257.
2. J-Y. Cai and V. Choudhary. Valiant's Holant Theorem and Matchgate Tensors. In Proceedings of TAMC 2006. Lecture Notes in Computer Science vol. 3959. pp 248-261. Also available as ECCC TR05-118.
3. J-Y. Cai and V. Choudhary. On the Theory of Matchgate Computations. *Submitted*. Also available as ECCC TR06-018.
4. J-Y. Cai and V. Choudhary. Some Results on Matchgates and Holographic Algorithms. In Proceedings of ICALP 2006, Part I. Lecture Notes in Computer Science vol. 4051. pp 703-714. Springer.
5. J-Y. Cai and Pinyan Lu. On Symmetric Signatures in Holographic Algorithms. Available at Electronic Colloquium on Computational Complexity Report TR06-135.
6. H.B. Hunt and M.V. Marathe, V. Radhakrishnan and R.E. Stearns. The complexity of planar counting problems. SIAM J. Comput. 27:4 (1998) 1142-1167.
7. H. B. Hunt III and R. E. Stearns. The complexity of very simple Boolean formulas with applications. SIAM J. Comput., 19:1 (1990) 44-70.
8. P. W. Kasteleyn. The statistics of dimers on a lattice. *Physica*, 27: 1209-1225 (1961).
9. P. W. Kasteleyn. Graph Theory and Crystal Physics. In *Graph Theory and Theoretical Physics*, (F. Harary, ed.), Academic Press, London, 43-110 (1967).
10. D. Lichtenstein, Planar formulae and their uses. SIAM J. on Computing 11 (1982) 329-343.
11. K. Murota. Matrices and Matroids for Systems Analysis, Springer, Berlin, 2000.
12. H. N. V. Temperley and M. E. Fisher. Dimer problem in statistical mechanics – an exact result. *Philosophical Magazine* 6: 1061– 1063 (1961).
13. L. G. Valiant. Quantum circuits that can be simulated classically in polynomial time. *SIAM Journal on Computing*, 31(4): 1229-1254 (2002).
14. L. G. Valiant. Expressiveness of Matchgates. *Theoretical Computer Science*, 281(1): 457-471 (2002). See also 299: 795 (2003).
15. L. G. Valiant. Holographic Algorithms (Extended Abstract). In *Proc. 45th IEEE Symposium on Foundations of Computer Science*, 2004, 306–315. A more detailed version appeared in Electronic Colloquium on Computational Complexity Report TR05-099.
16. L. G. Valiant. Holographic circuits. In *Proc. 32nd International Colloquium on Automata, Languages and Programming*, 1–15, 2005.
17. L. G. Valiant. Completeness for parity problems. In *Proc. 11th International Computing and Combinatorics Conference*, 2005.
18. L. G. Valiant. Accidental Algorithms. In *Proc. 47th Annual IEEE Symposium on Foundations of Computer Science* 2006, 509–517.

Randomly Rounding Rationals with Cardinality Constraints and Derandomizations

Benjamin Doerr

Max–Planck–Institut für Informatik, Saarbrücken, Germany

Abstract. We show how to generate randomized roundings of rational vectors that satisfy hard cardinality constraints and allow large deviations bounds. This improves and extends earlier results by Srinivasan (FOCS 2001), Gandhi et al. (FOCS 2002) and the author (STACS 2006). Roughly speaking, we show that also for rounding arbitrary rational vectors randomly or deterministically, it suffices to understand the problem for $\{0, \frac{1}{2}\}$ vectors (which typically is much easier). So far, this was only known for vectors with entries in $2^{-\ell}\mathbb{Z}$, $\ell \in \mathbb{N}$.

To prove the general case, we exhibit a number of results of independent interest, in particular, a quite useful lemma on negatively correlated random variables, an extension of de Werra's (RAIRO 1971) coloring result for unimodular hypergraphs and a sufficient condition for a unimodular hypergraph to have a perfectly balanced non-trivial partial coloring.

We also show a new solution for the general derandomization problem for rational matrices.

1 Introduction and Results

Randomized rounding is one of the core primitives in randomized algorithmics. In the last few years it was observed that dependent randomized rounding has some important advantages over the classical, independent variant. Of particular interest are randomized roundings that satisfy cardinality constraints. In this paper, we continue earlier work on how to generate such randomized roundings. We improve the results of Srinivasan [Sri01a] and Gandhi et al. [GKPS02] in terms of run-time and generality, and own work [Doe06] in that we allow arbitrary rational numbers instead of only those having a finite binary expansion. This work is a continuation of [Doe06]. Though we try to give as much details as possible, some more general information on randomized rounding and cardinality constraints has to be found there.

1.1 Randomized Rounding

A central problem in different areas is to round a vector x to an integer one y in such a way that the rounding errors $|(Ax)_i - (Ay)_i|$, $i \in [m] := \{1, \ldots, m\}$, are small for some given $m \times n$ matrix A. This problem has to be solved if the solution of the relaxation of an integer linear program has to be retransformed into in integer one, but also in other algorithmic applications where the linear

W. Thomas and P. Weil (Eds.): STACS 2007, LNCS 4393, pp. 441–452, 2007.
© Springer-Verlag Berlin Heidelberg 2007

program is less visible (e.g., Gnewuch, Srivastav and the author [DGS05] used it to construct evenly distributed point sets for numerical integration purposes).

A highly successful approach to such rounding problems is the one of *randomized rounding* introduced by Raghavan and Thompson [RT87, Rag88]. Here the integer vector y is obtained from x by rounding each component j independently with probabilities derived from the fractional part of x_j. In particular, if $x \in [0,1]^n$, we have $\Pr(y_j = 1) = x_j$ and $\Pr(y_j = 0) = 1 - x_j$ independently for all $j \in [n]$.

Since the components are rounded independently, the rounding error $|(Ax)_i - (Ay)_i|$ in constraint i is a sum of independent random variables. Thus it is highly concentrated around its mean, which by choice of the probabilities is zero. Large deviation bounds like the Chernoff inequality allow to quantify such violations and thus yield performance guarantees.

The corresponding derandomization problem is to transform this randomized approach into deterministic rounding algorithms that keep the rounding errors $|(Ax)_i - (Ay)_i|$ below some threshold.

1.2   Hard Constraints

Whereas the independence in rounding the variables ensures that the rounding errors $|(Ax)_i - (Ay)_i|$ are small, it is very weak in guaranteeing that a constraint is satisfied without error. We call a constraint *hard constraint* if we require our solution to satisfy it without violation. In this paper, we are mainly concerned with *cardinality constraints*. These are constraints on unweighted sums of variables. Naturally, we assume that these constraints form a totally unimodular system (cf. Section 2).

Hard cardinality constraints of this type occur frequently in diverse areas of optimization. Some examples of rounding problems with hard constraints include routing applications ([RT91, Sri01a]), many flow problems ([RT87, RT91]), partial and capacitated covering problems ([GKPS02, GHK+06]), and different approaches to the digital halftoning problem ([STT01, Doe04b, Doe04a]).

At FOCS 2001, Srinivasan [Sri01a] presented a way to compute randomized roundings that respect the constraint that the sum of all variables remains unchanged (one *global cardinality constraint*) and fulfill some negative correlation properties. This approach was then extended by Gandhi, Khuller, Parthasarathy and Srinivasan [GKPS02] to obtain degree preserving randomized roundings of edge weights in bipartite graphs. By this we mean that the sum of weights of all edges incident with some vertex is not changed by the rounding. The roundings of Gandhi et al. also fulfill negative correlation properties, but only on sets of edges incident with a common vertex.

Both Srinivasan [Sri01a] and Gandhi et al. [GKPS02] do not consider the derandomization problem. For the bipartite edge weight rounding problem, Ageev and Sviridenko [AS04] state that any randomized rounding algorithm "will be too sophisticated to admit derandomization".

This problem was overcome in the author's last years STACS paper [Doe06]. Among other results, we gave a simpler way to generate the randomized roundings used in [Sri01a] and [GKPS02]. One consequence was that this approach could be derandomized easily. However, this new approach only worked for numbers that have a finite binary expansion.

1.3 Our Contribution

In this paper, we extend the work of [Doe06] in that we can now treat arbitrary rational numbers. More precisely, we show that if we can generate randomized roundings with cardinality constraints and large deviation bounds for all $\{0, \frac{1}{2}\}$ vectors, then we can do so for arbitrary rational vectors. The same is true for the derandomization problem.

This result is interesting from the theoretical point of view in that it shows that rounding arbitrary rationals is not too much different from rounding numbers having finite binary expansion, but also from the practical point of view. Since the $\{0, \frac{1}{2}\}$ case, both randomized and derandomized, for many problems is quite easy (cf. again [Doe06]), our result immediately yields a simpler and often faster way to generate the randomized roundings used in Srinivasan [Sri01a], Gandhi et al. [GKPS02], Sadakane, Takki-Chebihi and Tokuyama [STT01] and [Doe04b].

Also, there are some problems where rational number with small denominator naturally occur and have to be rounded. Klein and the author [DK06] have some related results on the controlled rounding problem from statistics. However, these results are different from ours in that no large deviation bounds were obtained (one of the key difficulties we had to overcome). Also, there a rounding problem with a particular structure was regarded, whereas we allow any totally unimodular hard constraint matrix for which $\{0, \frac{1}{2}\}$ rounding can be computed.

To establish the randomized construction, we prove several result of independent interest, namely a quite useful lemma on negatively correlated random variables (Lemma 1), an extension of de Werra's result on the multi-color discrepancy of unimodular hypergraphs (Lemma 2) and a necessary condition for a unimodular hypergraph to have a zero-discrepancy non-trivial partial coloring (Lemma 4).

In the last section of this paper, we extend the derandomization result of [Doe06] to arbitrary non-negative rational matrices. This derandomization problem used to be a long-standing open problem until its solution by Srivastav and Stangier [SS96]. Note that Raghavan's derandomization [Rag88] needs to compute the exponential function and in consequence in the RAM model only works for binary matrices (as pointed out in Section 2.2 of his paper).

The solution in [SS96] is complicated, resulting in an $O(mn^2 \log(mn))$ runtime for $m \times n$ matrices (and a 30 pages paper). This was partially overcome in [Doe06], where a simple $O(mn\ell)$ time derandomization was given for matrices all whose entries are multiples of $2^{-\ell}$. For general matrices, it was argued that before-hand one can round the matrix to the one that only has such entries and pay for this through an extra additional error of $2^{-\ell}n$ in the large deviation bound. Hence, to get this extra error small, one typically has to accept an extra logarithmic factor in the run time.

In this paper, give a simple derandomization for arbitrary non-negative matrices. If $p \in \mathbb{N}$ is a common denominator of the matrix entries, it has run time $O(mn \log p)$. For small p, this is clearly superior.

2   Randomized Rounding, Constraints and Correlation

For a number r write $[r] = \{n \in \mathbb{N} \mid n \leq r\}$, $\lfloor r \rfloor = \max\{z \in \mathbb{Z} \mid z \leq r\}$, $\lceil r \rceil = \min\{z \in \mathbb{Z} \mid z \geq r\}$ and $\{r\} = r - \lfloor r \rfloor$. We write $z \approx r$ if $z \in \{\lfloor r \rfloor, \lceil r \rceil\}$. We use these notations for vectors as well (component-wise).

Let $x \in \mathbb{R}$. A real-valued random variable y is called *randomized rounding of* x if $\Pr(y = \lfloor x \rfloor + 1) = \{x\}$ and $\Pr(y = \lfloor x \rfloor) = 1 - \{x\}$. Since only the fractional parts of x and y are relevant, we usually have $x \in [0, 1]$. In this case, we have

$$\Pr(y = 1) = x,$$
$$\Pr(y = 0) = 1 - x.$$

For $x \in \mathbb{R}^n$, we call $y = (y_1, \ldots, y_n)$ *randomized rounding of* x if y_j is a randomized rounding of x_j for all $j \in [n]$.

The algorithmic concept of randomized rounding can be formulated as follows: Fix a number $n \in \mathbb{N}$, the number of variables to be rounded. Let $X \subseteq [0, 1]^n$. This is the set of vectors for which we allow randomized rounding. Typically, this will be $[0, 1]^n$ or a suitably rich subset thereof. A family $(\Pr_x)_{x \in X}$ of probability distributions on $\{0, 1\}^n$ is called *randomized rounding*, if for all $x \in X$, a sample y from $\Pr_x$ is a randomized rounding of x.

As described in the introduction, we are interested in roundings that satisfy some hard constraints. Though usually we will only regard cardinality constraints (requiring the sum of some variable to be unchanged), it will be convenient to encode hard constraints in a matrix B. Our aim then is that a rounding y of x satisfies $By = Bx$. Of course, if Bx is not integral, this can never be satisfied. We therefore relax the condition to $By \approx Bx$. If y is a randomized rounding of x, this is equivalent to saying that By is a randomized rounding of Bx.

Besides satisfying hard constraints we still want to keep other rounding errors small (as does independent randomized rounding). A useful concept here is the one of negative correlation.

Let $X_j, j \in S$, be a family of random variables taking values in some finite set Ω. We call the $X_j, j \in S$, *negatively correlated* if

$$\forall S_0 \subseteq S \, \forall \omega \in \Omega : \Pr(\forall j \in S_0 : X_j = \omega) \leq \prod_{j \in S_0} \Pr(X_j = \omega).$$

As shown in [PS97], negative correlation of binary variables implies the usual Chernoff-Hoeffding bounds on large deviations.

It turns out that hard constraints and negative correlation cannot always be achieved simultaneously. We therefore restrict ourselves to negative correlation on certain sets of variables. Let $\mathcal{S} \subseteq 2^{[n]}$ be closed under taking subsets, that is, $S_0 \subseteq S \in \mathcal{S}$ implies $S_0 \in \mathcal{S}$.

Definition 1. *We call* $(\Pr_x)$ *randomized rounding with respect to* B *and* $\mathcal{S}$, *if for all* x *a sample* y *from* $\Pr_x$ *satisfies the following.*

(A1) *y is a randomized rounding of x.*
(A2) *By is a randomized rounding of Bx.*
(A3) *For all $S \in \mathcal{S}$, $\forall b \in \{0,1\} : \Pr(\forall j \in S : y_j = b) \leq \prod_{j \in S} \Pr(y_j = b)$.*

In this language, we know the following. Clearly, independent randomized rounding is a randomized rounding with respect to the empty matrix B and $\mathcal{S} = 2^{[n]}$. Srinivasan [Sri01a] showed that for the $1 \times n$ matrix $B = (1 \ldots 1)$, randomized roundings with respect to B and $\mathcal{S} = 2^{[n]}$ exist and can be generated in time $O(n)$. Let $G = (V, E)$ be a bipartite graph and $B = (b_{ij})_{\substack{i \in V \\ j \in E}}$ its vertex-edge-incidence matrix. For $v \in V$ let $E_v = \{e \in E \,|\, v \in e\}$. Gandhi et al. [GKPS02] showed that there are randomized roundings with respect to B and $\mathcal{S} = \{E_0 \,|\, \exists v \in V : E_0 \subseteq E_v\}$. They can be generated in time $O(mn)$. From [Doe03, Doe04b], we have that if B is totally unimodular, then randomized roundings with respect to B and $\mathcal{S} = \emptyset$ exist. Recall that a matrix is totally unimodular if each square submatrix has determinant -1, 0 or 1. If B is not totally unimodular, then not even for $X = \{0, \frac{1}{2}\}^n$ a randomized rounding $(\Pr_x)_{x \in X}$ with respect to B and $\mathcal{S} = \emptyset$ exists.

Throughout the paper let $A \in [0,1]^{m_A \times n}$ and $x \in [0,1]^n$. Let B be a totally unimodular $m_B \times n$ matrix.

3   Rounding Rationals

In this section, we show that arbitrary rational vectors have randomized roundings with respect to B and $\mathcal{S}$ if all half-integral vectors do.

For convenience, let us abbreviate $Z_p := \{0, \frac{1}{p}, \frac{2}{p}, \ldots, \frac{p-1}{p}\}$ and $\overline{Z}_p = Z_p \cup \{1\}$. Also, we write $\mathrm{nint}(x)$ to denote the number of non-integral entries of the vector x. We will need to solve integer systems of linear equations over a totally unimodular matrix. Clearly, this can be done in polynomial time. Since in many cases, a particular structure of the matrix is known, we prefer not to use a general bound, but rather explicitly denote by $c(B, n)$ the time complexity to solve an integer linear system over a submatrix of B having n columns.

Theorem 1. *Assume that for each $x \in \{0, \frac{1}{2}\}^n$ there is a randomized rounding y of x with respect to B and $\mathcal{S}$.*

(a) *For each $x \in Z_p^n$ there is a randomized rounding y of x with respect to B and $\mathcal{S}$.*
(b) *If each of the half-integral roundings in the assumption can be generated in time at most T, then the rounding in the conclusion can be generated in expected time $O((T + pc(B, n))p^2 \log n)$.*
(c) *If each of the half-integral roundings in the assumption can be generated in time at most $O(T\,\mathrm{nint}(x)/n)$, that is, linear in the number of non-integers, and also $c(B, k) = O(c(B, n)k/n)$ is at least linear in k, then the rounding in the conclusion can be generated in expected time $O((T + pc(B, n))p^2)$.*

To prove the theorem, besides some elementary facts on random walks, we need a number of non-trivial lemmas (Lemma 1, 2 and 4), which are of independent interest for various reasons. For reasons of space, all proofs had to be omitted. The following lemma, roughly speaking, shows that the expected product of negatively correlated random variables is at most the product of the expectations of the variables. This lemma (again) shows the power of the concept of negative correlation.

Lemma 1. *Let* $\varepsilon_1, \ldots, \varepsilon_n$ *be negatively correlated and uniformly distributed* $-1, 1$ *random variables. Let* $x_1, \ldots, x_n \in [0, 1]$ *and* $d_1, \ldots, d_n \in \mathbb{R}$ *such that* $0 \le d_j \le x_j$ *for all* $j \in [n]$*. Then*

$$E\left(\prod_{j \in [n]} (x_j + \varepsilon_j d_j) \right) = \sum_{z \in \{-1,1\}^n} \Pr(\varepsilon = z) \prod_{j \in [n]} (x_j + z_j d_j) \le \prod_{j \in [n]} x_j.$$

The lemma above would have been easier if we assumed negative association instead of correlation. However, as pointed out in [Doe06], some of the distributions we use are not negativly associated.

The following result extends an old result of de Werra [dW71], namely that unimodular hypergraphs have p–color discrepancy less than one.

Lemma 2. *Let* B *be a totally unimodular* $m_B \times n$ *matrix and* $x \in \overline{Z}_p^n$ *such that* $Bx \in \mathbb{Z}^{m_B}$*. Then there are* $x^{(1)}, \ldots, x^{(p)} \in \{0, \frac{1}{p}\}^n$ *such that*

(i) $x = \sum_{k=1}^p x^{(k)}$*;*
(ii) $\forall k \in [p] : Bx^{(k)} = \frac{1}{p}Bx$*;*
(iii) $\forall i \in [n], k \in [p] : x_i = 0 \Rightarrow x_i^{(k)} = 0$*.*

They can be computed in time $O(pc(B, \mathrm{nint}(x))$*.*

Without proof, we state the following elementary fact.

Lemma 3. *Let* I *be an even cardinality subset of* $[p]$ *drawn uniformly at random. Let* $\emptyset \neq J \subset [p]$*. Then* $\Pr(|I \cap J| \text{ odd}) = \frac{1}{2}$*.*

The final ingredient of the proof of Theorem 1 is the following.

Lemma 4. *Let* B *be a totally unimodular* $m_B \times n$ *matrix and* $x \in \overline{Z}_p^n$*. Then there is a random* $x' \in Z_2^n$ *such that*

(i) *for all* $i \in [n]$*,* $x_i' = \frac{1}{2} \Rightarrow x_i \notin \{0, 1\}$*;*
(ii) *for all* $i \in [m_B]$*,* $(Bx)_i \in \mathbb{Z} \Rightarrow (Bx')_i \in \mathbb{Z}$*;*
(iii) *for all* $i \in [n]$ *such that* $x_i \notin \{0, 1\}$*,* $\Pr(x_i' = \frac{1}{2}) = \frac{1}{2}$*.*

Such an x' *can be generated in time* $O(pc(B, \mathrm{nint}(x)))$*.*

The result above also answers a very natural question concerning colorings of hypergraphs. It is known that the vertices of unimodular hypergraphs (those, which have a totally unimodular incidence matrix) can be two-colored with discrepancy at most one, that is, in such a way that in each hyperedge, the number of red vertices deviates from that of blue vertices by at most one (which occurs exactly for odd cardinality hyperedges).

A non-trivial question is whether one can two-color only some vertices, but with discrepancy zero, that is, in a way that each hyperedge has exactly the same number of vertices in both colors. This is known as partial coloring and frequently used in iterative coloring procedures. The lemma above shows that partial coloring is possible if one can assign weights to the vertices in such a way that all weights are multiples of $1/p$ and the total weight of each hyperedge is an integer. We end this deviation by adding, but not proving, that this condition is also necessary.

We are now ready to prove Theorem 1.

Proof. Let $x \in Z_p^n$. We claim that the following algorithm does the job:

1. $y^{(0)} := x$, $t := 0$
2. while $y^{(t)} \notin \{0,1\}^n$ do
3.   compute $x' \in \{0, \frac{1}{2}\}^n$ from $y^{(t)}$ as in Lemma 4
4.   generate y' as randomized rounding of x' with respect to B and $\mathcal{S}$
5. $y^{(t+1)} := y^{(t)} + \frac{2}{p}(y' - x')$
6. $t := t + 1$
7. output $y := y^{(t)}$

Let us first argue that the resulting y is a randomized rounding of x. Let $i \in [n]$. Is it easy to check from the algorithm that the following invariant is maintained: $y_i^{(t)} \in \overline{Z}_p$, $E(y_i^{(t)}) = x_i$ and $\Pr(|y_i^{(t)} - x_i| < 1) = 1$. Since also $\Pr(y_i \in \mathbb{Z}) - 1$, we see that y_i is a randomized rounding of x_i.

Since B is a $-1, 0, 1$ matrix, basically the same line of argument shows that By is a randomized rounding of Bx. Note that here condition (ii) of Lemma 4 is crucial. It ensures that once $(By^{(t)})_i$ becomes integral, it never changes. Before that, just by construction, $(By^{(t)})_i$ changes in steps of $\frac{1}{p}$ only.

Let $S \in \mathcal{S}$. By induction on t, we prove $E(\prod_{i \in S} y_i^{(t)}) \leq \prod_{i \in S} x_i$. There is nothing to show for $t = 0$. For $t \geq 1$, we compute

$$E(\prod_{i \in S} y_i^{(t)}) = \sum_{z \in \overline{Z}_p^n} \Pr(y^{(t-1)} = z) E(\prod_{i \in S} y_i^{(t)} \mid y^{(t-1)} = z)$$

$$\leq \sum_{z \in \overline{Z}_p^n} \Pr(y^{(t-1)} = z) \prod_{i \in S} y_i^{(t-1)} = E(\prod_{i \in S} y_i^{(t-1)}) \leq \prod_{i \in S} x_i,$$

where the first inequality follows from Lemma 1 and the negative correlation of the ± 1 random variables $2(y_i' - x_i')$, and the second one from induction hypothesis.

We omit the run time analysis for reasons of space. The key observations is that a single component of $y^{(t)}$ does a random walk on $\{0, \frac{1}{p}, \ldots, 1\}$ with absorbing barriers 0 and 1.   □

If the denominator p in the theorem above can be written as product of smaller integers $p = p_1 \ldots p_\ell$, we may apply the above reasoning on the factors separately and gain a substantial run-time improvement. In particular, the p^2 term becomes $\sum_{k=1}^{\ell} p_k^2$. For reasons of space, we omit the details.

4 Derandomizations

We now show how the rounding approach described in the previous section can be derandomized using a classical derandomization in each iteration. Since the errors in each iteration may add, the total error bound is of larger order than in the randomized setting. It depends on the circumstances whether this can be tolerated or whether it is preferable to round x to a vector having finite binary expansion (typically of length $\log n$) and use the approach of [Doe06].

A *derandomization of a randomized rounding* (with constant c) is an algorithm that computes for given $A \in [0,1]^{m_A \times n}$ and $x \in [0,1]^n$ a $y \in \{0,1\}^n$ such that for all $i \in [m_A]$,

$$|(Ax)_i - (Ay)_i| \leq c\sqrt{\max\{(Ax)_i, \ln(2m_A)\} \ln(2m_A)}.$$

It thus achieves (with minor loss) the existential bounds given by randomized rounding.

A number of derandomizations are known. We sketch some results relevant in the following and refer to the successor [Doe06] of this paper for more details. The classical derandomization by Raghavan [Rag88] via so-called pessimistic estimators runs in time $O(m_A n)$ and achieves a constant of $c = e - 1$. In the RAM model, it works for all $A \in \{0,1\}^{m_A \times n}$ and $x \in ([0,1] \cap \mathbb{Q})^n$. If one allows precise computations with real numbers in constant time (in particular exponential functions), then this extends to arbitrary $A \in [0,1]^{m_A \times n}$. As discussed in the introduction, Srivastav and Stangier [SS96] give a derandomization for all $A \in ([0,1] \cap \mathbb{Q})^{m_A \times n}$ in the RAM model, though at the price of an increased run-time of $O(m_A n^2 \log(m_A n))$. The constant here is $c = \sqrt{3}$. In [Doe06], this result was improved to a run time of $O(m_A n \log n)$. The constant in this case is $4(e-1)(1+o(1))$.

Theorem 2. *Let $A \in [0,1]^{m_A \times n}$ and B be totally unimodular. Let $\mathcal{A}$ be an algorithm which for any $x \in \{0, \frac{1}{2}, 1\}^n$ computes a rounding y of x such that $By \approx Bx$ and*

$$\forall i \in [m_A] : |(Ax)_i - (Ay)_i| \leq c\sqrt{\max\{(Ax)_i, \ln(2m_A)\} \ln(2m_A)}.$$

Then for each $x \in \mathbb{Z}_p^n$, a rounding y such that $By \approx Bx$ and

$$\forall i \in [m_A] : |(Ax)_i - (Ay)_i| \leq \tfrac{1}{2}cp(\ln(n)+1)\sqrt{\max\{\tfrac{p}{2}(Ax)_i, \ln(2m_A)\} \ln(2m_A)}$$

can be computed by $\frac{1}{2}p^2(\ln(n)+1)$ times invoking $\mathcal{A}$ and solving a system of linear equations over B. If the complexity $c(\mathcal{A}, n)$ of the first and $c(B, n)$ of the latter in fact is proportional to the number of non-integers of x, then a run time of $O(p^2 \log(p)(c(\mathcal{A}, n) + pc(B, n)))$ can be achieved.

Derandomizing Lemma 3 yields the following deterministic version of Lemma 4.

Lemma 5. *Let B be a totally unimodular $m_B \times n$ matrix and $x \in \overline{Z}_p^n$. Then a $x' \in Z_2^n$ such that*

(i) for all $i \in [n]$, $x_i' = \frac{1}{2} \Rightarrow x_i \neq 0$;
(ii) for all $i \in [m_B]$, $(Bx)_i \in \mathbb{Z} \Rightarrow (Bx')_i \in \mathbb{Z}$;
(iii) $|\{i \in [n] \mid x_i' = \frac{1}{2}\}| \geq \frac{1}{2}|\{i \in [n] \mid x_i \neq 0, 1\}|$;

can be computed in time $O(pc(B, \text{nint}(x)))$.

Derandomizing the algorithm given in the proof of Theorem 1 is now the heart of the following proof of Theorem 2.

Proof. For all $x \in \overline{Z}_p^n$, let $w(x) = \sum_{i=1}^n p^2 x_i(1 - x_i)$. We analyse the following algorithm.

1. $y^{(0)} := x$, $t := 0$
2. while $y^{(t)} \notin \{0,1\}^n$ do
3.   compute $x' \in \{0, \frac{1}{2}\}^n$ from $y^{(t)}$ as in Lemma 5
4.   compute y' as rounding of x' as in the assumptions of the theorem
5.   if $w(y^{(t)} + \frac{2}{p}(y' - x')) \leq w(y^{(t)} + \frac{2}{p}(-y' + x'))$
        then $y^{(t+1)} := y^{(t)} + \frac{2}{p}(y' - x')$
        else $y^{(t+1)} := y^{(t)} + \frac{2}{p}(-y' + x')$
6. $t := t + 1$
7. output $y := y^{(t)}$

Since the output y of this algorithm could also have been generated by the algorithm in the proof of Theorem 1 (assuming suitable random choices and noting that $2x' - y'$ is an as good rounding of x' as is y'), we immediately see that $y \approx x$ and $By \approx Bx$. Hence it remains to show the large deviations bound and the run-time.

The large deviation bounds will depend heavily on the final value of t, so let us estimate this first. To this end, we first analyze the behaviour of the weight function w in step 5 of the algorithm. For all $r \in Z_p$, we have

$$p^2(r + \tfrac{1}{p})(1 - r - \tfrac{1}{p}) + p^2(r - \tfrac{1}{p})(1 - r + \tfrac{1}{p}) = 2p^2 r(1 - r) - 2.$$

Since we chose the alternative leading to a smaller weight in line 5, we have $w(y^{(t+1)}) \leq w(y^{(t)}) - \text{nint}(x')$. By construction, we have $\text{nint}(x') \geq \frac{1}{2}\text{nint}(y^{(t)}) \geq \frac{2}{p^2}w(y^{(t)})$. We conclude that $w(y^{(t+1)}) \leq w(y^{(t)})(1 - 2/p^2)$. Hence $w(y^{(p^2 \ln(n)/2)}) \leq w(y^{(0)})/n \leq p^2/4$. Now since $\text{nint}(x')$ is always at least one, we see that another at most $p^2/4$ iterations suffice to reduce the weight to zero, which means that $y^{(t)}$ is integral. Hence our algorithm terminates after at most $t = \frac{1}{2}p^2(\ln(n) + 1)$ iterations.

By construction,

$$\left|(Ay^{(t+1)})_i - (Ay^{(t)})_i\right| \leq \tfrac{2}{p}c\sqrt{\max\{(Ax')_i, \ln(2m_A)\}\ln(2m_A)}$$

$$\leq \tfrac{2}{p}c\sqrt{\max\{\tfrac{p}{2}(Ax)_i, \ln(2m_A)\}\ln(2m_A)}.$$

The large deviation bound now follows from the triangle inequality. The proof
of the run-time bound is omitted.   □

5 Application of the General Scheme

In this section, we analyse what the above methods yield for some of the randomized roundings with hard constraints regarded so far. We start with the simplest
example of disjoint cardinality constraints.

5.1 Disjoint Constraints

Throughout this subsection let $B \in \{0,1\}^{m_B \times n}$ and $\|B\|_1 := \max_j \sum_i |b_{ij}| = 1$.
For the generation of the roundings, this is a microscopic extension of Srini-
vasan's [Sri01a] setting, who regarded a single cardinality constraint involving
all variables.

Let us assume that B is stored in some $O(n)$ space datastructure allowing
amortized linear time enumerations of the sets $\{j \in [n] \mid b_{ij} = 1\}$ for all $i \in [m_B]$.
Then it is easy to see that $c(B, k) = O(k)$. From [Doe06], we already know that
the $\{0, \frac{1}{2}\}$ case can be solved highly efficiently. For any $x \in \{0, \frac{1}{2}\}^n$, a randomized
rounding with respect to B and $2^{[n]}$ can be generated in time $O(\text{nint}(x))$. Hence
Theorem 1 yields the following.

Theorem 3. *For any* $x \in Z_p^n$, *a randomized rounding with respect to* B *and*
$2^{[n]}$ *can be generated in time* $O(p^2 n)$.

We now derandomize the construction above. Again, the $\{0, \frac{1}{2}\}$ case was settled
in [Doe06]. For convenience, let us restrict ourselves to $0, 1$ matrices, so that
we can apply Raghavan's derandomization (cf. Section 4). Then for all $A \in
\{0,1\}^{m_A \times n}$ and $x \in \{0, \frac{1}{2}\}^n$ a rounding y of x such that $By \approx Bx$ and

$$\forall i \in [m_A] : |(Ax)_i - (Ay)_i| \leq 2(e-1)\sqrt{\max\{(Ax)_i, \ln(4m_A)\} \ln(4m_A)}$$

can be computed in time $O(\text{nint}(x))$. Combining this with Theorem 2, we obtain
the following derandomized version of Srinivasan's results.

Theorem 4. *Let* $A \in \{0,1\}^{m_A \times n}$. *Let* $x \in Z_p^n$. *Then in time* $O(p^3 \log(p)n)$ *a
binary vector* y *can be computed such that* $By \approx Bx$ *and*

$$\forall i \in [m_A] : |(Ax)_i - (Ay)_i| \leq (e-1)p(\ln(n)+1)\sqrt{\max\{\tfrac{p}{2}(Ax)_i, \ln(4m_A)\} \ln(4m_A)}.$$

Note that the run time above is linear in n. This cannot be achieved with the
approach in [Doe06]. If we approximate x by an element of $Z_{2^\ell}^n$ and then use
the result from [Doe06], we have to choose ℓ at least logarithmic in n to keep
the errors inflicted by the approximation small. Thus we would end up with a
run-time of $\Theta(n \log n)$.

5.2   Bipartite Edge Weight Rounding

In this subsection, we consider sets of cardinality constraints where each variable may be contained in up to two constraints. We use the graph theoretic language of Gandhi et al. [GKPS02]. Let $G = (V, E)$ be a bipartite graph with edge weights $w : E \to Z_p$. Let $B \in \{0, 1\}^{V \times E}$ such that $(Bw)_v = \sum_{e \ni v} w(e)$ for all $v \in V$. Let $\mathcal{S} = \{E_0 \subseteq E \mid \exists v \in V \; \forall e \in E_0 : v \in e\}$. In [Doe06], we showed that for any $w \in \{0, \frac{1}{2}\}^E$, a randomized rounding with respect to B and $\mathcal{S}$ can be generated in time $O(\text{nint}(w))$.

The more interesting part is efficiently computing the half-integral vector as in Lemma 4. However, since we know the structure of the hard constraints, this also can be done directly in linear time.

Lemma 6. Let $w \in Z_p^E$. Then we can compute in time $O(\text{nint}(w))$ an $x' : E \to \{0, \frac{1}{2}\}$ such that

(i) $x'_e \neq 0 \Rightarrow w_e \neq 0$;
(ii) $(Bw)_v \in \mathbb{N}_0 \Rightarrow (Bx')_v \in \mathbb{N}_0$;
(iii) $w_e \neq 0 \Rightarrow \Pr(x'_e = \frac{1}{2}) \geq \frac{1}{2}$.

Hence again Theorem 1 yields the following.

Theorem 5. For any $w \in Z_p^E$, a randomized rounding with respect to B and $\mathcal{S}$ can be generated in time $O(p^2 n)$.

Note that the time complexity here is superior to the $O(|E||V|)$ bound of Gandhi et al. [GKPS02], unless p is large.

Let us derandomize this result. For Lemma 6, this is again easy using the known structure of the constraints. Derandomizing the $\{0, \frac{1}{2}\}$ case was settled in [Doe06]. Together with Theorem 2, we obtain the following derandomization of the result of Gandhi et al. [GKPS02]

Theorem 6. Let $A \in \{0, 1\}^{m_A \times E}$ such that for each $i \in [m_A]$ there is a $v \in V$ such that for all $e \in E$, $e \ni v$ whenever $a_{iv} \neq 0$. Let $x \in Z_p^E$. Then in time $O(p^3 \log(p)n)$ a binary vector y can be computed such that $By \approx Bx$ and

$$\forall i \in [m_A] : |(Ax)_i - (Ay)_i| \leq (e-1)p(\ln(|E|)+1)\sqrt{\max\{\tfrac{p}{2}(Ax)_i, \ln(4m_A)\}\ln(4m_A)}.$$

6   General Derandomization

In this section, we give a simple derandomization for the case that the constraint matrix A is rational and we do not have hard constraints. Note that such would in many cases not lead to additional problems. As demonstrated in [Doe06], in the $\{0, \frac{1}{2}\}$ case the problem with hard constraints can be reduced to one without.

Theorem 7. Let $A \in \overline{Z}_p^{m \times n}$ and $x \in ([0, 1] \cap \mathbb{Q})^n$. Let $\ell = \lfloor \log_2 p \rfloor$. Then in time $O(mn\ell)$ in the RAM model, a $y \in \{0, 1\}^n$ can be computed such that for all $i \in [m]$,

$$|(Ax)_i - (Ay)_i| \leq 4(e-1)\sqrt{\max\{(Ax)_i, \ln(2(\ell+1)m)\}\ln(2(\ell+1)m)}.$$

Proof. Write $A = \sum_{k=0}^{\ell} \frac{2^k}{p} A^{(k)}$ with $A^{(k)} \in \{0,1\}^{m \times n}$ for all $k \in [\ell] \cup \{0\}$. Apply Raghavan's derandomization (cf. Section 4) to the $(\ell + 1)m \times n$ matrix obtained from stacking the $A^{(k)}$. With some care in the calculations, the result follows. $\square$

References

[AS04]   A. A. Ageev and M. I. Sviridenko. Pipage rounding: a new method of constructing algorithms with proven performance guarantee. *J. Comb. Optim.*, 8:307–328, 2004.

[DGS05]   B. Doerr, M. Gnewuch, and A. Srivastav. Bounds and constructions for the star-discrepancy via δ-covers. *Journal of Complexity*, 21:691–709, 2005.

[DK06]   B. Doerr and C. Klein. Unbiased rounding of rational matrices. In *FSTTCS 2006*, volume 4337 of *LNCS*, pages 200–211, 2006. Springer-Verlag.

[Doe03]   B. Doerr. Non-independent randomized rounding. In *SODA 2003*, pages 506–507, 2003.

[Doe04a]   B. Doerr. Global roundings of sequences. *Information Processing Letters*, 92:113–116, 2004.

[Doe04b]   B. Doerr. Nonindependent randomized rounding and an application to digital halftoning. *SIAM Journal on Computing*, 34:299–317, 2004.

[Doe06]   B. Doerr. Generating randomized roundings with cardinality constraints and derandomizations. In *STACS 2006*, volume 3884 of *LNCS*, pages 571–583, 2006. Springer-Verlag.

[dW71]   D. de Werra. Equitable colorations of graphs. *Rev. Française Informat. Recherche Opérationnelle*, 5(Ser. R-3):3–8, 1971.

[GHK+06]   R. Gandhi, E. Halperin, S. Khuller, G. Kortsarz, and A. Srinivasan. An improved approximation algorithm for vertex cover with hard capacities. *J. Comput. Syst. Sci.*, 72:16–33, 2006.

[GKPS02]   R. Gandhi, S. Khuller, S. Parthasarathy, and A. Srinivasan. Dependent rounding in bipartite graphs. In *FOCS 2002*, pages 323–332, 2002.

[PS97]   A. Panconesi and A. Srinivasan. Randomized distributed edge coloring via an extension of the Chernoff-Hoeffding bounds. *SIAM J. Comput.*, 26:350–368, 1997.

[Rag88]   P. Raghavan. Probabilistic construction of deterministic algorithms: Approximating packing integer programs. *J. Comput. Syst. Sci.*, 37:130–143, 1988.

[RT87]   P. Raghavan and C. D. Thompson. Randomized rounding: A technique for provably good algorithms and algorithmic proofs. *Combinatorica*, 7:365–374, 1987.

[RT91]   P. Raghavan and C. D. Thompson. Multiterminal global routing: a deterministic approximation scheme. *Algorithmica*, 6:73–82, 1991.

[Sri01a]   A. Srinivasan. Distributions on level-sets with applications to approximations algorithms. In *FOCS 2001*, pages 588–597, 2001.

[SS96]   A. Srivastav and P. Stangier. Algorithmic Chernoff-Hoeffding inequalities in integer programming. *Random Structures & Algorithms*, 8:27–58, 1996.

[STT01]   K. Sadakane, N. Takki-Chebihi, and T. Tokuyama. Combinatorics and algorithms on low-discrepancy roundings of a real sequence. In *ICALP 2001*, volume 2076 of *LNCS*, pages 166–177, 2001. Springer-Verlag.

Cheating to Get Better Roommates in a Random Stable Matching

Chien-Chung Huang

Dartmouth College
villars@cs.dartmouth.edu

Abstract. This paper addresses strategies for the stable roommates problem, assuming that a stable matching is chosen at random. We investigate how a cheating man should permute his preference list so that he has a higher-ranking roommate probabilistically.

In the first part of the paper, we identify a necessary condition for creating a new stable roommate for the cheating man. This condition precludes any possibility of his getting a new roommate ranking higher than all his stable roommates when everyone is truthful. Generalizing to the case that multiple men collude, we derive another impossibility result: given any stable matching in which a subset of men get their best possible roommates, they cannot cheat to create a new stable matching in which they all get strictly better roommates than in the given matching.

Our impossibility result, considered in the context of the stable marriage problem, easily re-establishes the celebrated Dubins-Freedman Theorem. The more generalized Demange-Gale-Sotomayor Theorem states that a coalition of men and women cannot cheat to create a stable matching in which everyone of them gets a strictly better partner than in the Gale-Shapley algorithm (with men proposing). We give a sharper result: a coalition of men and women cannot cheat together so that, in a newly-created stable matching, every man in the coalition gets a strictly better partner than in the Gale-Shapley algorithm while none of the women in the coalition is worse off.

In the second part of the paper, we present two cheating strategies that guarantee that the cheating man's new probability distribution over stable roommates majorizes the original one. These two strategies do not require the knowledge of the probability distribution of the cheating man. This is important because the problem of counting stable matchings is #P-complete. Our strategies only require knowing the set of stable roommates that the cheating man has and can be formulated in polynomial time. Our second cheating strategy has an interesting corollary in the context of stable marriage with the Gale-Shapley algorithm. Any woman-optimal strategy will ensure that every woman, cheating or otherwise, ends up with a partner at least as good as when everyone is truthful.

1 Introduction

In the stable roommates problem [4], $2n$ people are to be assigned to n rooms, each of which accommodates two of them. Each man $m \in \mathcal{R}$ (following convention, we assume that all participants in $\mathcal{R}$ are male) has a strictly-ordered

W. Thomas and P. Weil (Eds.): STACS 2007, LNCS 4393, pp. 453–464, 2007.
© Springer-Verlag Berlin Heidelberg 2007

preference list in which he ranks all other men in $\mathcal{R} - \{m\}$. Given any matching, two men preferring each other to their assigned roommates comprise a *blocking pair*. A matching without blocking pairs is *stable*. For a man $m \in \mathcal{R}$, man m' is called his stable roommate if there exists any stable matching containing the couple $\{m, m'\}$; otherwise, m' is an unstable roommate for him.

The stable roommates problem is more general than the stable marriage problem [4]. However, unlike stable marriage, whose strategic aspects have been investigated extensively [2,5,6,9,10,14,16], the cheating strategies for the stable roommates problem have not received much attention.

In contrast to stable marriage, the stable roommates problem does not always allow stable matchings. In this work, we assume that in the given problem instance, stable matchings do exist and that one is chosen at random. Supposing that a participant has complete knowledge of all others' preferences, we study what can be done to his preference list so that he gets a better roommate probabilistically.

Major Results of This Work. The first part of our paper identifies a necessary condition for the cheating man m to make an unstable roommate m' who ranks higher than his lowest-ranking stable roommate become a stable one. This condition demands that, in the falsified list, m' has to rank higher than at least one of m's stable roommates, say m'', and m'' originally ranks higher than m' in the truthful list of m. Hence, this condition rules out any chance of the cheating man obtaining a roommate ranking higher than all his stable roommates.

We then generalize to the case of multiple men forming a coalition. Given any stable matching in which a subset of men all get their best possible roommates, we prove that they cannot cheat together to create a stable matching in which they all get strictly better roommates than in the given matching. In the context of the stable marriage problem with the Gale-Shapley algorithm, our impossibility result easily re-establishes the celebrated Dubins-Freedman Theorem [2]: A coalition of men cannot cheat together and all get better partners. The more general Demange-Gale-Sotomayor Theorem [1] states that a coalition of men and women cannot cheat together and all get better partners than in the Gale-Shapley algorithm. In fact, we have a sharper result: a coalition of men and women cannot cheat together so that in a newly-created stable matching, every man in the coalition gets a strictly better partner than in the Gale-Shapley stable matching, while no woman involved in the coalition is worse off.

In the second part of the paper, assuming that a stable matching is chosen *uniformly* at random, we exhibit two strategies that ensure the cheating man to have a new probability distribution over stable roommates which majorizes the original one. Here we define the term "probability majorization" as follows. Let $P_i(m)$ and $P'_i(m)$ be the probabilities of m's getting his i-th ranking roommate in a uniformly random stable matching, when he is truthful and otherwise. P' majorizes P if for $1 \leq t \leq n$, $\sum_{i=1}^{t} P'_i(m) \geq \sum_{i=1}^{t} P_i(m)$. The first strategy guarantees that in all the newly-created stable matchings, he gets the best possible stable roommate; moreover, it can be formulated in constant time. The second strategy is an optimal strategy for the cheating man to destroy low-ranking stable roommates. We use the term "optimal" in the sense that if our second strategy cannot eliminate someone, say m_k, as a stable roommate of m, then there does not exist any other strategy to achieve this without causing someone else ranking lower than m_k to become a new (and unwanted) roommate. In the context of stable marriage with the Gale-Shapley algorithm, our second strategy has the auxiliary consequence that any optimal cheating strategy for a sole cheating woman (Teo, Sethuraman and Tan suggested how to formulate such a strategy in [16]) will ensure her to get one of her original stable partners and every other woman to get a partner ranking at least as high as when everyone is truthful. This fact was also independently discovered by Sethuraman and Teo [15]. Our second strategy costs $O(n^4)$ time.

Our two strategies do not need to know the probability distribution over stable roommates of the cheating man. The only knowledge required is the set of roommates he has; this can be obtained in $O(n^2)$ time [3]. We think strategies not involving the knowledge of the exact probability distribution are important, because to obtain the exact probability distribution can be computationally expensive. For one thing, if we want to enumerate the set of stable matchings, Knuth [13] pointed out the number of stable matchings can be exponential; for the other, supposing we know the set of possible stable roommates of the cheating man, it is very unlikely we can count the number of stable matchings for each of his stable roommate in polynomial time, otherwise, in polynomial time, we can count the total number of stable matchings, which has been proved by Irving and Leather [12] to be a #P-complete problem.

Related Work. The stable roommates problem, along with the stable marriage problem, was formulated by Gale and Shapley [4]. They proved that stable matchings always exist for the latter, but not necessarily for the former. Knuth [13] posed the open problem of finding an algorithm for the stable roommates problem; this problem was solved by Irving [11]. The book of Gusfield and Irving [7] is probably the best reference for algorithmic issues on the stable roommates problem. Some group cheating strategies for the random stable matching in the marriage case are explored in [9]. For strategic behavior in the stable matching problem, Roth and Sotomayor have a rather detailed treatment in [14].

Structure of the Paper. Section 2 presents a necessary condition for a cheating man to get a new stable roommate. In Section 3, we discuss the more general case of multiple men colluding, and we exhibit a number of impossibility results. In Sections 4 and 5, we present the two cheating strategies for a cheating man that make his new probability distribution majorize the original one. Finally, in Section 6, we draw the conclusion and discuss some open questions.

Notation and Terminology. Throughout this paper, we refer to the cheating man as m. His preference list is decomposed as $(U_0(m), m_1, U_1(m), m_2, \cdots, U_{k-1}(m), m_k, U_k(m))$, where m_i, $1 \leq i \leq k$ is his set of stable roommates and $U_j(m), 0 \leq j \leq k$ constitute his (ordered) subset of unstable roommates. When referring to the roommate of a particular person $m^\dagger$ in the matching M, we write $M(m^\dagger)$. As a shorthand for the preference list of m, we often write $(P_{L,M}(m),$

$M(m), P_{R,M}(m))$, where M is any matching, stable or otherwise. $P_{L,M}(m)$ is the sub-list containing all the men ranking higher than $M(m)$; and similarly for $P_{R,M}(m)$. Colloquially, we often say the elements of $P_{L,M}(m)$ $(P_{R,M}(m))$ are the men on the left (respectively, right) of $M(m)$. Given an ordered list A, $\pi_r(A)$ is any permutation of A; suppose A and B are ordered lists, $\prod_r(A,B)$ is an arbitrary combination of A and B such that the elements of A and of B retain their original order in the combined list.

In m's preference list, if m' ranks strictly higher than m'', we write $m' \succ_m m''$. If $m' \succeq_m m''$, then either $m' \succ_m m''$, or $m' = m''$. If m falsifies his list such that m' ranks higher than m'', we write $m' \succ_m^f m''$. When everyone is truthful, we refer to the collection of their preference lists as "true" lists. When any one of them lies, the resulting lists are referred to as "falsified." Given two matchings M and M', if a subset of men $G \subseteq \mathcal{R}$ all prefer M to M' or are indifferent, we write $M \succeq_G M'$; if all of them strictly prefer M to M', we write $M \succ_G M'$.

As we will switch back and forth between stable roommate and stable marriage, we also introduce notation for the latter problem. The collection of men and women are $\mathcal{M}$ and $\mathcal{W}$. The men-optimal/women-pessimal matching (found by the Gale-Shapley men-proposing algorithm) is $M_{\mathcal{M}}$; analogously, the women-optimal/men-pessimal matching is $M_{\mathcal{W}}$. Throughout this work, when we refer to the Gale-Shapley algorithm, we implicitly assume the men-proposing version.

2   In Search of a New Roommate

In this section, we study how to create a new stable roommate for the cheating man.

Targeting a Roommate Ranking Higher than All Stable Roommates. To motivate our cheating strategy, assume that the cheating man m hopes to get a new roommate $m_0 \in U_0(m)$ who ranks higher than all of his stable roommates. However, the feeling is not reciprocal and m ranks lower than all of m_0's stable roommates (otherwise, $\{m, m_0\}$ would block some stable matching). Is there a strategy for m to make m_0 his new stable roommate? Unfortunately for him, we will answer in the negative in the following discussion.

Proposition 1. *Let M be any stable matching. If m submits a preference list of the form $(\pi_r(P_{L,M}(m) - X), M(m), \pi_r(P_{R,M}(m) \cup X))$, where $X \subseteq P_{L,M}(m)$, the matching M remains stable with regard to the falsified lists.*

This proposition states that man m can shift some men from the left to the right of $M(m)$ without worrying about losing $M(m)$ as a stable roommate. The next proposition identifies a strategy which is *not* effective for creating a new stable roommate.

Proposition 2. *Suppose M^ϕ is an unstable matching with regard to the true lists. Moreover, m falsifies his list so that M^ϕ becomes stable. Then it is impossible that the falsified list of m is of the form:*
$$(\pi_r(P_{L,M^\phi}(m) \cup X), M^\phi(m), \pi_r(P_{R,M^\phi}(m) - X)), \text{ where } X \subseteq P_{R,M^\phi}(m).$$

Proposition 2 eliminates all but one possible strategy: the cheating man m shifts some subset of men ranking higher than m_0 to the right of m_0 in his falsified list. This might create the chance of making an unstable matching $M^\phi \supset \{m, m_0\}$ become stable. This is possible if in M^ϕ, with regard to the true lists, all blocking pairs involve m. We now present our first primary result. Its full proof can be found in [8].

Lemma 1. *Let M be a stable matching and $M^\phi(m)$ be an unstable roommate of m with regard to the true lists. Suppose $M^\phi(m) \succ_m M(m)$ and all blocking pairs for M^ϕ involve m. Then at least one of the blocking pairs $\{m, m_x\}$ is a stable pair and $m_x \succ_m M^\phi(m)$.*

Proof. (Sketch) We remark that if m wishes to make $M^\phi(m)$ a stable roommate, by Proposition 2, he has to submit a falsified list of the form $(P_{L,M^\phi}(m) - X, M^\phi(m), \prod_r(P_{R,M^\phi}(m), X))$, where $X \subseteq P_{L,M^\phi}(m)$. Moreover, by Proposition 1, M remains stable with regard to the falsified lists.

Our proof plan is as follows: with regard to the falsified lists, we introduce an algorithm that transforms the stable matching M into another stable matching $M^\flat$ such that $M^\flat(m) \succ_m M(m)$ and $M^\flat(m) \in X$. Finally, we prove that $M^\flat$ is also stable with regard to the true lists, thereby arriving at the conclusion. $\square$

Specializing Lemma 1 to the case that the cheating man m is getting his highest-ranking stable roommate in M, we get the conclusion that a new stable matching M^ϕ, in which $M^\phi(m) = m_0 \succ_m M(m) = m_1$ cannot be realized by shifting some men ranking higher than m_0 to the right of m_0 in the falsified list.

Theorem 1. *Given any stable roommates instance in which stable matchings exist, a sole cheating man cannot create a new stable roommate ranking higher than all his stable roommates by any strategy.*

An interesting corollary follows from Lemma 1 and Proposition 1.

Corollary 1. *Suppose the cheating man m submits a preference list of the form $(\pi_r(U_0(m)), m_1, \pi_r(U_1(m)), m_2, \cdots, m_{k-1}, \pi_r(U_{k-1}(m)), m_k, U_k(m))$. Then the set of stable matchings remain identical to the case when everyone is truthful.*

We remark that this corollary does not consider permuting $U_k(m)$. In fact, it is possible that by permuting $U_k(m)$ alone a new stable roommate is formed. But obviously, m has no interest in creating a new roommate of such low rank.

A Necessary Condition for Creating a New Stable Roommate. Our attempt at making $m_0 \in U_0(m)$ a new stable roommate has been thwarted. Suppose m now realizes the difficulty of getting m_0; he compromises his ideal and considers creating another stable roommate ranking between m_1 and m_k. How can he achieve this? As mentioned in the proof of Lemma 1, after we apply the algorithm to get another stable matching $M^\flat$ from the given stable matching M, the cheating man m ends up with $M^\flat(m) \in X$, where X is the set of men ranking higher than $M^\phi(m)$ being shifted to the right of $M^\phi(m)$. This suggests a necessary condition of making M^ϕ stable.

Theorem 2. *Let $m_{i+\epsilon} \in U_i(m)$, where $1 \leq i \leq k-1$, be an unstable roommate of the cheating man m. A necessary (but not sufficient) condition of making $m_{i+\epsilon}$ a new stable roommate is that at least one original stable roommate ranking higher than $m_{i+\epsilon}$ has to become lower-ranked than $m_{i+\epsilon}$ in the falsified list of m.*

3   Multiple Men Cheat Together

In this section, we generalize to the case of multiple cheaters. Propositions 1 and 2 can be adapted straightforwardly and will be used in the proofs.

Theorem 3. *Let M be a stable matching. Suppose M^ϕ is an unstable matching such that $M^\phi \succeq_G M$ where $G \subseteq \mathcal{R}$, moreover, there exists a non-empty subset $G' \subseteq G$ such that men in G' get their highest-ranking roommates in M and $M^\phi \succ_{G'} M$. If there do not exist strategies for men in $G - G'$ to make M^ϕ a stable matching, then there does not exist any strategy for men in G collectively to make M^ϕ become stable.*

Proof. By the generalized version of Proposition 2, the only possible strategy for man $m_\gamma \in G - G'$ to make M^ϕ stable is to falsify his list in the form $(\pi_r(P_{L,M^\phi}(m_\gamma) - X), M^\phi(m_\gamma), \pi_r(P_{R,M^\phi}(m_\gamma), X))$, where $X \subseteq P_{L,M^\phi}(m_\gamma)$. If after all men in $G - G'$ have falsified their lists in this way, M^ϕ becomes stable, the theorem is trivially true. Therefore, we assume M^ϕ remains unstable after all men in $G - G'$ falsify their lists. Now choose any man $m'_\gamma \in G'$. By Theorem 1, there does not exist any strategy for man m'_γ to make $M^\phi(m'_\gamma)$ a new stable roommate. So however m'_γ permutes his list, M^ϕ remains unstable. The same argument applies to the rest of the men in G' and so we have the theorem.   □

Theorem 3 leads to several interesting corollaries.

Corollary 2. *Let M be any stable matching in which a non-empty subset $G \subseteq \mathcal{R}$ of men are matched to their highest-ranking stable roommates. There does not exist any strategy for the men in G to create a new stable matching M^ϕ in which every man in G gets a better roommate than in M.*

In the context of the stable marriage problem, the celebrated Dubins-Freedman Theorem [2] can be easily re-established by Corollary 2.

Corollary 3. (Dubins-Freedman Theorem): *In the stable marriage problem, a coalition of men cannot falsify their preference lists so that everyone of them gets a strictly better partner than in the men-optimal matching.*

Proof. Choose any subset of men $G \subseteq \mathcal{M}$. Apply Corollary 2 to G and the men-optimal matching $M_\mathcal{M}$.   □

A stronger theorem by Demange, Gale and Sotomayor [1] states that a coalition of men and women cannot cheat together so that *everyone of them* gets a strictly better partner than in the men-optimal matching $M_\mathcal{M}$. We give a sharper result.

Corollary 4. *In the stable marriage problem, a coalition of men and women cannot falsify their preference lists to create a stable matching in which every man in the coalition gets a strictly better partner than in the original men-optimal matching, while none of the women involved in the coalition is worse off.*

Proof. Let $G \subset \mathcal{M} \cup \mathcal{W}$ be a coalition of men and women. Since in the men-optimal matching $M_{\mathcal{M}}$, men already have their best possible partners, by Theorem 3, a new stable matching M' that $M' \succeq_G M_{\mathcal{M}}$ and $M' \succ_{G \cap \mathcal{M}} M_{\mathcal{M}}$ can only be created by the falsified lists of women in $G \cap \mathcal{W}$. So we suppose all women in $G \cap \mathcal{W}$ falsify their lists and M' becomes a new stable matching.

To make M' stable, by the generalized version of Proposition 2, the only effective strategy for each woman $w \in G \cap \mathcal{W}$ is that she submits a falsified list of the form $(\pi_r(P_{L,M'}(w) - X), M'(w), \pi_r(P_{R,M'}(w) \cup X))$, where $X \subseteq P_{L,M'}(w)$. Let the falsified list of w be P_w. We create another falsified list P'_w, which only differs from P_w in that all members in $P_{R,M'}(w)$ are restored to their original order in the truthful list of w. By the generalized version of Proposition 1, if we replace P_w with P'_w, the matching M' remains stable. The reason for this pre-processing will be clear shortly.

We make the following two observations. (1) In the Gale-Shapley algorithm, women only receive proposals from men ranking *lower* than their $M_{\mathcal{M}}$-partners. Given $w \in G \cap \mathcal{W}$, since $M'(w) \succeq_w M_{\mathcal{M}}(w)$, in her falsified list, how she moves about men ranking higher than $M'(w)$ does not affect the execution of the Gale-Shapley algorithm. (2) Given $w \in G \cap \mathcal{W}$, in P'_w, men in $P_{R,M'}(w)$ have the same relative order as in woman w's truthful list. Therefore, women, whether in G or not, will make entirely the same decision about rejecting and accepting men as when everyone is truthful. Combining the two observations, we conclude that applying the Gale-Shapley algorithm to the falsified lists will lead to the original matching $M_{\mathcal{M}}$.

Finally, if M' can become stable by the falsified lists of women in $G \cap \mathcal{W}$, then the men in $G \cap \mathcal{M}$ get better partners in M' than in $M_{\mathcal{M}}$. The men-optimality of the latter (since it is produced by the Gale-Shapley algorithm) is then violated. This finishes the proof. □

This result again manifests the difficulty of men cheating. If a coalition of men try to lobby some women to falsify their lists also (on the premise that none of the women involved will be worse off), there still does not exist any chance of forming a successful strategy for them. The only way for a coalition of men to get better partners in a new stable matching is that they ask for the collaboration of other fellow men, as has been shown in [9].

4   Strategy A

We return to the theme of the strategies for a sole cheating man m. Supposing a stable matching is chosen uniformly at random, in this section and the next, we present two strategies for him so that his probability distribution over stable roommates majorizes the original one.

By Theorem 1, there is nothing more the cheating man m can do to get any member in $U_0(m)$. Nonetheless, these unapproachable men still serve a purpose. If we move all of them en masse to the immediate right of m_1, there is a chance that more stable matchings containing $\{m, m_1\}$ are thus created (since men in $U_0(m)$ constitute potential blocking pairs to unstable matchings containing $\{m, m_1\}$). However, if these men are moved to the right of m_i, $i > 1$, other new stable matchings containing $\{m, m_2\}, \{m, m_3\}, \cdots \{m, m_i\}$ may crop up, which is not as a good outcome as we simply "squeeze" $U_0(m)$ between m_1 and $U_1(m)$. From the above discussion, the following strategy is immediate:

Theorem 4. (Strategy A): *Suppose the cheating man m submits a falsified list of the form $(m_1, \pi_r(U_0(m)), U_1(m), m_2, P_{M,R}(m))$ where $M \supset \{m, m_2\}$. For m, the new probability distribution over roommates majorizes the original one when everyone is truthful. More generally, such a list will majorize the probability distribution induced by any list of m in the following form $(U_0(m) - X, m_1, \prod_r(X, P_{R,M'}(m)))$, where $X \subseteq U_0(m)$ and $M' \supset \{m, m_1\}$.*

5   Strategy B

We introduce another strategy which destroys low-ranking stable roommates of the cheating man m. In this section, when we say we *destroy* a stable roommate m_i, we mean the cheating man m manipulates his preference list so that all stable matchings containing $\{m, m_i\}$ become unstable. We call m_i *destructible* if m can destroy m_i without other stable roommates ranking lower than m_i being formed.

To build up some intuition, assume that our preliminary goal is to destroy all stable matchings containing $\{m, m_k\}$. By Proposition 1, this can only be achieved by shifting some men from $U_k(m)$ to the left of m_k. But this move involves some risk: some of these shifted men in $U_k(m)$ may become new stable roommates of m, which is a worse outcome for him.

We define three categories for the members in $U_k(m)$:

Definition 1. *$U_k(m)$ is decomposed into (interleaving) ordered subsets $A \cup B \cup C$. For a man $m^\dagger \in U_k(m)$, let man m submit a falsified list of the form $(U_0(m), m_1, U_1(m), m_2, \cdots, U_{k-1}(m), m^\dagger, m_k, U_k(m) - m^\dagger)$, then:*

- *$m^\dagger \in A$, if m_k is no longer a stable roommate and $m^\dagger$ does not become a new stable roommate of m.*
- *$m^\dagger \in B$, if m_k remains a stable roommate but $m^\dagger$ does not become a new stable roommate of m.*
- *$m^\dagger \in C$, if $m^\dagger$ becomes a new stable roommate of m, while m_k remains/is no longer a stable roommate of m.*

The following algorithm suggests a procedure to systematically make all stable matchings containing $\{m, m_k\}$ become unstable without creating any new unwanted stable roommate in $U_k(m)$.

We outline the general idea of the algorithm **Destroy-Bad** before proving its mathematical properties. The first part of the algorithm is concerned with

0:	Algorithm **Destroy-Bad**: Input $(U_0(m), m_1, \cdots, U_{k-1}(m), m_k, U_k(m))$
1:	**For All** $m^\dagger \in U_k(m)$
2:	Shift $m^\dagger$ to the immediate left of m_k. Observe whether $m^\dagger$ is in A, B, or in C.
3:	**If** $A \neq \emptyset$ **Then** /* In this case, m_k is destructible.
4:	Output the list $(U_0(m), m_1, \cdots, U_{k-1}(m), m_a, m_k, U_k(m) - m_a)$, where $m_a \in A$.
5:	**If** $B \neq \emptyset$ **Then**
6:	**If** $P' = (U_0(m), m_1, \cdots, U_{k-1}(m), \pi_r(B), m_k, U_k(m) - B)$ destroys m_k **Then** Output P'
7:	**Else**
8:	**For All** $m^\dagger \in U_k(m) - B$
9:	**If** $P'' = (U_0(m), m_1, \cdots, U_{k-1}(m), \pi_r(B), m^\dagger, m_k, U_k(m) - B - m^\dagger)$ destroys m_k
10:	**Then** Output P''
11:	Output P'
12:	**If** $C = U_k(m)$ **Then** Output the input preference list $(U_0(m), m_1, \cdots, U_{k-1}(m), m_k, U_k(m))$

Fig. 1. Algorithm **Destroy-Bad**: Given a preference list, this algorithm returns a new preference list which: (1) if m_k is destructible, destroys m_k without causing any man ranking lower than m_{k-1} to become a new stable roommate; (2) if m_k is indestructible, ensures m has a new probability distribution over his roommates which majorizes the original one

identifying which group, as defined in Definition 1, the members in $U_k(m)$ fall into. Note the fact that we shift $m^\dagger$ to the "immediate" left of m_k. This artifice preserves the maximum likelihood of preventing $m^\dagger$ from becoming a new stable roommate of m.

If group A is not empty, we achieve our goal trivially. If B is not empty, we shift all of its members to the immediate left of m_k. The idea is that, even though separately, each of them is unable to destroy m_k, their combined presence on the left of m_k might succeed. There might be a concern that, when being moved en masse, some of the men in B may become new stable roommates of m. We will prove shortly that this is not the case.

Supposing the combined efforts of B on the left of m_k cannot destroy m_k, we still need to check one more time the status of the remaining members in $U_k(m)$. Some of them, say m_c, can be transformed from a member of C to a member of A (but not B, as we will prove later on). The reason is that more members of B being on the left of m_c might serve as more potential blocking pairs to matchings containing $\{m, m_c\}$. Given that, there is still one more caveat here. One might imagine that after we shift "more than one" members in $U_k(m) - B$ to the left of m_k, we might have more chance of destroying m_k while still avoiding any member in $U_k(m) - B$ being shifted from becoming new (and unwanted) stable roommates. We shall also discuss why this is not the case below.

Finally, suppose the algorithm finds that $A = \emptyset$ and $B \neq \emptyset$, and unfortunately, shifting B to the left of m_k still cannot destroy m_k. The cheating man m still should adopt the new preference list suggested by Algorithm **Destroy-Bad**. The reason is that the more members that we shift to the left of m_k, the more likely we are able to destroy stable matchings containing $\{m, m_k\}$ (but not all of them). Destroying stable matchings containing $\{m, m_k\}$ helps for our probability majorization purpose.

Optimality of Strategy B. We prove the correctness of Algorithm **Destroy-Bad** and a number of mathematical properties of the members of $U_k(m)$. We first show that men in B being moved together will not cause any of them to become a new stable roommate of m.

Lemma 2. *Let $U_k(m)$ be decomposed into interleaving ordered subsets $A \cup B \cup C$ as defined in Definition 1. Suppose $|B| \geq 1$ and let m submit a list of the form $(U_0(m), m_1, \cdots, U_{k-1}(m), \pi_r(B), m_k, U_k(m) - B)$. Then there are no new stable matchings containing $\{m, m_b\}$ where $m_b \in B$. Moreover, suppose $A = \emptyset$ and in the new preference list, all members of B are shifted to the immediate left of m_k but m_k remains a stable roommate of m. All members in $U_k(m) - B$ can only belong to group A or group C.*

Proof. For the first part, the case of $|B| = 1$ is trivial. As to the case of $|B| > 1$, we prove by contradiction. Sort men in B in arbitrary order $(m_{b1}, m_{b2}, \cdots, m_{bx})$. We shift m_{b1} to the immediate left of m_k, and then shift m_{b2} to the immediate left of m_{b1} and so forth. By Proposition 2, if after m_{bi} is moved, he does not become a new stable roommate, the subsequent shifts involving $m_{b(i+1)}, m_{b(i+2)}, \cdots$ will not change the status of m_{bi}. Thus, we only need to worry about the man in B who is being shifted at this point.

Let m_{bi} be the first man becoming a new stable roommate of m in the process. We refer to the preference list at this point as P_i. We then create another list P_i' which differs from P_i in that $m_{b1}, m_{b2}, \cdots m_{b(i-1)}$ are shifted back to their original positions in $U_k(m)$. By the definition of group B, $\{m, m_{bi}\}$ is not part of a stable matching given P_i'. However, based on P_i, $\{m, m_{bi}\}$ is part of a stable matching. Combining the two facts, we violate Proposition 1.

For the second part, if there is any member $m^\dagger \in U_k(m) - B$ belonging to group B, i.e., in the preference list $P_m' = (U_0(m), m_1, \cdots, U_{k-1}(m), \pi_r(B), m^\dagger, m_k, U_k(m) - B - m^\dagger)$, $m^\dagger$ is not a stable roommate but m_k still is. We create another preference list by shifting all members of B back to their original places. Then, $m^\dagger$ becomes a stable roommate of m but originally in P_m', all members of B are unstable roommates. Thus we violate Theorem 2. □

As alluded to previously, there might be a concern that the members in C, being shifted in a group, instead of individually, between B and m_k, might succeed in destroying m_k without causing any of themselves to become a stable roommate of m. The following lemma dissipates this concern.

Lemma 3. *Let $U_k(m)$ be decomposed into interleaving ordered subsets $A \cup B \cup C$ as defined in Definition 1. Suppose $C = U_k(m)$. Given any subset $C' \subseteq C$, let the cheating man m submit a preference list of the form $(U_0(m), m_1, \cdots, U_{k-1}(m), \pi_r(C'), m_k, C - C')$, then there exists at least one man in C' who becomes a new stable roommate of m.*

Proof. We prove by contradiction. We choose the *minimal* set $C' \subseteq C$ such that a falsified list of the stated form violates this lemma (no new stable roommates in C' are formed). Sorting the members in C' in arbitrary order $(m_{c1}, m_{c2}, \cdots, m_{cx})$, we shift m_{c1} to the immediate left of m_k, and then m_{c2} to the immediately left of m_{c1} and so forth. We claim that after each round i of this operation, $1 \leq i < x$, at least one man in $\{m_{c1}, m_{c2}, \cdots, m_{ci}\}$ is a stable roommate of m (otherwise, the minimality of C' is violated). Only in the last round x, shifting m_{cx} to the immediate left of $m_{c(x-1)}$, all men in C' are not stable roommates of m. Let the preference list at this point be P_x. We create another preference list P'_x in which all men in C', except m_{cx}, are shifted back to their original positions in $U_k(m)$. By the definition of group C, given P'_x, m_{cx} is a stable roommate of m. But in P_x, he is not. Combining these two facts, we violate Proposition 2. □

We now show that Algorithm **Destroy-Bad** is an optimal strategy in the sense that if the combined members of B cannot destroy m_k, m_k must be indestructible. The full proof of the following theorem can be found in [8].

Theorem 5. *(Strategy B): Algorithm **Destroy-Bad** is an optimal strategy for the cheater m to destroy m_k. Moreover, the preference list output by Algorithm **Destroy-Bad** will not cause any stable matching containing $\{m, m_i\}$, where $1 \le i \le k - 1$, to become unstable.*

Some Implications of Strategy B. It is obvious that Algorithm **Destroy-Bad** can be repeatedly applied; moreover, every time a stable roommate m_i is destroyed, m_{i-1} becomes a new lowest-ranking stable roommate of m. We can use this idea to prove the following corollary. The full proof can be found in [8].

Corollary 5. *In the stable marriage problem with the Gale-Shapley algorithm, a woman-optimal strategy will cause every woman, cheating or otherwise, to get a partner ranking at least as high as when everyone is truthful.*

By Corollary 5, women have common interest in cheating. When a woman cheats to get herself a better partner, she is also doing all other women a favor (and all men a disfavor).

Algorithm **Destroy-Bad** can be applied repeatedly to destroy as many low-ranking stable roommates as possible. The first part of Algorithm **Destroy-Bad** (identifying which group the members in $U_k(m)$ fall into) has to linearly check at most $O(n)$ people. For each member, this checking can be done in time $O(n^2)$ by Feder's algorithm [3]. Since there are at most $O(n)$ stable roommates, Algorithm **Destroy-Bad** needs to be applied at most the same amount of rounds. Summing up, Strategy B takes $O(n^4)$ time.

6   Conclusion

In this paper, we identified a necessary condition for a sole cheating man to get a new stable roommate. We also presented a number of impossibility results for a coalition of cheating men in the context of both stable roommates and stable marriage. When a stable matching is chosen uniformly at random, we exhibited two strategies that induce a new probability distribution majorizing the original one.

There is an interesting algorithmic issue closely related to our basic assumption. To our knowledge, so far there does not exist an efficient algorithm for finding a nearly-uniformly random stable matching. Indeed, even for the simpler stable marriage, no such algorithm appears to be known. It is well known that the stable matchings for an instance of stable marriage constitute a distributive lattice (possibly of exponential size) [7]. Since every distributive lattice is the lattice of ideals of some partially ordered set, we can ask the following more general question: given a poset P, is there a randomized polynomial-time algorithm for sampling an ideal of P from a nearly uniform probability distribution?

Acknowledgment

I thank my adviser Peter Winkler for many helpful discussions. I am also indebted to two anonymous reviewers who gave detailed comments on my submitted version. One of them especially directed my attention to the algorithmic issue of the random stable matching and pointed out an incorrect remark I made about counting stable matchings.

References

1. G. Demange, D. Gale, and M. Sotomayor. A further note on the stable matching problem. *Discrete Applied Mathematics*, 16:217–222, 1987.
2. L. Dubins and D. Freedman. Machiavelli and the Gale-Shapley algorithm. *American Mathematical Monthly*, 88:485–494, 1981.
3. T. Feder. A new fixed point approach for stable networks and stable marriages. *Journal of Computer and System Sciences*, 1:233–294, 1992.
4. D. Gale and L. Shapley. College admissions and the stability of marriage. *American Mathematical Monthly*, 69(1):9–15, 1962.
5. D. Gale and M. Sotomayor. Ms. Machiavelli and the stable matching problem. *American Mathematical Monthly*, 92:261–268, 1985.
6. D. Gale and M. Sotomayor. Some remarks on the stable matching problem. *Discrete Applied Mathematics*, 11:223–232, 1985.
7. D. Gusfield and R. Irving. *The Stable Marriage Problem*. The MIT Press, 1989.
8. C.-C. Huang. Cheating to get better roomates in a random stable matching. Technical Report TR2006-582, Computer Science Department, Dartmouth College, 2006.
9. C.-C. Huang. Men cheating in the Gale-Shapley stable matching algorithm. In *14th Annual European Symposium on Algorithms (ESA)*, 2006.
10. N. Immorlica and M. Mahdian. Marriage, honesty, and stability. In *Proceedings of the Sixteenth Annual ACM-SIAM Symposium on Discrete Algorithms (SODA)*, pages 53–62, 2005.
11. R. Irving. An efficient algorithm for the stable room-mates problem. *Journal of Algorithms*, 6:577–595, 1985.
12. R. Irving and P. Leather. The complexity of counting stable marriages. *SIAM Journal on Computing*, 15:655–667, 1986.
13. D. Knuth. *Mariages stables et leurs relations avec d'autre problèmes combinatoires*. Les Presses de l'université de Montréal, 1976.
14. A. Roth and M. Sotomayor. *Two-sided matching: A study in game-theorectic modeling and analysis*. Cambridge University Press, 1990.
15. J. Sethuraman. Private communication, 2006.
16. C.-P. Teo, J. Sethuraman, and W.-P. Tan. Gale-Shapley stable marriage problem revisited: Strategic issues and applications. *Management Science*, 47:1252–1267, 2001.

A Deterministic Algorithm for Summarizing Asynchronous Streams over a Sliding Window

Costas Busch[1] and Srikanta Tirthapura[2]

[1] Department of Computer Science
Rensselaer Polytechnic Institute, Troy, NY 12180, USA
buschc@cs.rpi.edu
[2] Department of Electrical and Computer Engineering
Iowa State University, Ames, IA 50010, USA
snt@iastate.edu

Abstract. We consider the problem of maintaining aggregates over recent elements of a massive data stream. Motivated by applications involving network data, we consider *asynchronous* data streams, where the observed order of data may be different from the order in which the data was generated. The set of recent elements is modeled as a *sliding timestamp window* of the stream, whose elements are changing continuously with time. We present the first *deterministic* algorithms for maintaining a small space summary of elements in a sliding timestamp window of an asynchronous data stream. The summary can return approximate answers for the following fundamental aggregates: *basic count*, the number of elements within the sliding window, and *sum*, the sum of all element values within the sliding window. For basic counting, the space taken by our summary is $O(\log W \cdot \log B \cdot (\log W + \log B)/\epsilon)$ bits, where B is an upper bound on the value of the basic count, W is an upper bound on the width of the timestamp window, and ϵ is the desired relative error. Our algorithms are based on a novel data structure called *splittable histogram*. Prior to this work, randomized algorithms were known for this problem, which provide weaker guarantees than those provided by our deterministic algorithms.

1 Introduction

Many massive data sets naturally occur as *streams*; elements of a stream are visible to the processor in a sequence, one after another, and random access is impossible. Often, streams are too large to be stored in memory, and have to be processed in a single pass using extremely limited workspace, typically much smaller than the size of the data. Examples include IP packet streams observed by internet routers, a stream of stock quotes observed by an electronic stock exchange, and a sequence of sensor observations observed by an aggregator. In spite of the volume of the data and a highly constrained model of computation, in all the above applications it is important to maintain reasonably accurate estimates of aggregates and statistics on the data.

W. Thomas and P. Weil (Eds.): STACS 2007, LNCS 4393, pp. 465–476, 2007.
© Springer-Verlag Berlin Heidelberg 2007

In many applications, only the most recent elements of a stream are important. For example, in a stream of temperature readings obtained from a sensor network, it may be necessary to maintain the moving average of the temperature over the last 1 hour. In network monitoring, it is useful to track aggregates such as the volume of traffic originating from a particular subnetwork over a recent window of time. Motivated by such applications, there has been extensive work [1,6,7,2,5,9] on designing algorithms to compute aggregates over a *sliding window* of the most recent elements of a data stream.

Most previous work on computing aggregates over a stream has focused on a *synchronous* data stream where it is assumed that the order of arrival of elements in the data aggregator is the same as the time order of their generation. However, in many applications, especially those involving network data, this may not be the case. Data streams may be *asynchronous*, and the order of arrival of elements may not be the same as their order of generation. For example, nodes in a sensor network generate observations that are aggregated at the *sink* node. When data is being transmitted to the sink, different observations may experience different delays in reaching the sink due to the inherent asynchrony in the network. Thus, the received order of observations at the sink may be different from the time order in which data was generated. If each data item had a timestamp that was tagged at the time of generation, the sink may observe a data stream whose elements are not arriving in increasing order of timestamps. Asynchronous data streams are inevitable anytime two streams of observations, say A and B, fuse with each other and data processing has to be done on the stream formed by the interleaving of A and B. Even if individual streams A or B are not inherently asynchronous, i.e. elements within A or within B arrive in increasing order of timestamps, when the streams are fused, the stream could become asynchronous. For example, if the network delay in receiving stream B is greater than the delay in receiving elements in stream A, then the aggregator may consistently observe elements with earlier timestamps from B after elements with more recent timestamps from A.

We consider the problem of maintaining aggregates over recent elements of an asynchronous data stream. An asynchronous stream is modeled as a sequence of elements $R = d_1, d_2, \ldots, d_n$ observed by an aggregator node, where d_1 is the element that was received the earliest and d_n is the element that was received most recently. Each element is a tuple $d_i = (v_i, t_i)$ where v_i is the value of the observation, and t_i is a timestamp, tagged at the time the value was generated. Let c denote the current time at the aggregator. We are interested in all elements that have a timestamp within w of the current time, i.e. all elements in the set $R_w = \{d = (v, t) \in R \mid t \in [c - w, c]\}$. Since this window of allowed timestamps $[c - w, c]$ is constantly changing with the current time c, we call it a *sliding timestamp window*. When the context is clear, we sometimes use the term sliding timestamp window to refer to the set R_w.

Definition 1. *For $0 < \epsilon < 1$, an ϵ-approximation to a number X is a number Y such that $|X - Y| \leq \epsilon X$.*

Contributions. We present the first deterministic algorithms for summarizing asynchronous data streams over a sliding window. We first consider a fundamental aggregate called the *basic count*, which is simply the number of elements within the sliding window. We present a data structure that can summarize an asynchronous stream in a small space and is able to provide a provably accurate estimate of the basic count. More precisely, let W denote an upper bound on the window size and B denote an upper bound on the basic count. For any $\epsilon \in (0, 1)$, we present a summary of the stream that uses space $O(\log W \cdot \log B \cdot (\log W + \log B)/\epsilon)$ bits. For any window size $w \leq W$ presented at the time of query, the summary can return an ϵ-approximation to the number of elements whose timestamps are in the range $[c - w, c]$ and arrive in the aggregator no later than c, where c denotes the current time. The time taken to process a new stream element is $O(\log W \cdot \log B)$ and the time taken to answer a query for basic count is $O(\log B + \frac{\log W}{\epsilon})$.

We next consider a generalization of basic counting, the *sum* problem. In a stream whose observations $\{v_i\}$ are positive integer values, the sum problem is to maintain the sum of all observations within the sliding window, $\sum_{\{(v,t) \in R \mid t \in [c-w,c]\}} v$. Our summary for the sum provides similar guarantees as for basic counting. For any $\epsilon \in (0, 1)$ the summary for the sum uses space $O(\log W \cdot \log B \cdot (\log W + \log B)/\epsilon)$ bits, where W is an upper bound on the window size, and B is an upper bound on the value of the sum. For any window size $w \leq W$, the summary can return an ϵ-approximation to the sum of all element values within the sliding window $[c - w, c]$. The time taken to process a new stream element is $O(\log W \cdot \log B)$ and the time taken to answer a query for the sum is $O(\log B + \frac{\log W}{\epsilon})$.

It is easy to verify that even on a synchronous data stream, a stream summary that can return the exact value of the basic count within the sliding window must use $\Omega(W)$ space in the worst case. The reason is that using such a summary one can reconstruct the number of elements arriving at each instant within the sliding window. Hence, to achieve space efficiency it is necessary to introduce approximations. Datar *et. al.* [5] show lower bounds for the space complexity of approximate basic counting on a synchronous stream. They show that if a summary has to return an ϵ-approximation for the basic count on distinct timestamp elements, then it should use space at least $\Omega(\log^2 W/\epsilon)$. Since the synchronous stream is a special case of an asynchronous stream, the above lower bound of $\Omega(\log^2 W/\epsilon)$ applies to approximate basic counting over asynchronous streams too. To compare our results for basic counting with this lower bound, let us consider the case when the timestamps of the elements are unique. In such a case, $\log B = O(\log W)$, since the value of the basic count cannot exceed W, and thus the space required by our summary is $O(\log^3 W/\epsilon)$.

Techniques. Our algorithm for basic counting is based on a novel data structure that we call a *splittable histogram*. The data structure consists of a small number of histograms that summarize the elements within the sliding window at various granularities. Within each histogram, the elements in the sliding window are grouped into buckets, that are each responsible for a certain range of timestamps.

Arriving elements are placed in appropriate buckets within this histogram. When a bucket becomes "heavy", i.e. gets too many elements, it is *split* in half to produce two buckets of smaller sizes, each responsible for a smaller range of timestamps. Buckets may be recursively split if the again become too heavy due to future insertions. A key technical ingredient is the analysis of the error resulting from this recursive splitting of buckets. In contrast, earlier uses of histograms in processing data streams over a sliding window, for example, Datar *et al.* [5] and Arasu and Manku [1] have all been based on *merging* smaller histogram buckets into larger ones, rather than splitting them as we do here.

Comparison to Prior Work. Prior to our work, deterministic algorithms were known for summarizing synchronous streams over a sliding window [5,7], but only randomized algorithms were known for summarizing asynchronous streams. In a previous work, Tirthapura, Xu and Busch [12] presented randomized algorithms for summarizing asynchronous streams over a sliding window. Their summary yields an (ϵ, δ)-approximation for the *sum* problem and for basic counting, i.e. the answer returned is within a relative error ϵ of the actual answer with probability at least $1 - \delta$; this is a weaker guarantee that is provided by the deterministic algorithm. The space used by their algorithm for the sum is $O((\frac{1}{\epsilon^2})(\log \frac{1}{\delta})(\log W \log B))$, where W is a bound on the maximum window size, B is an upper bound on the value of the sum, ϵ is the relative error, and δ is the failure probability. When compared with our deterministic algorithm, which uses space $O(\log W \cdot \log B \cdot (\log W + \log B)/\epsilon)$, the randomized algorithm arguably takes more space, since $(\log W + \log B)$ is typically smaller than $(\frac{1}{\epsilon})(\log \frac{1}{\delta})$. Thus, the deterministic algorithm that we present here not only gives a stronger guarantee than the randomized one but also (arguably) uses lesser space. Nevertheless, the randomized algorithm in [12] has the advantage of being more flexible and it can be used for other aggregates, including the median and quantiles.

Related Work. With the exception of [12], earlier work on summarizing data streams over a sliding window have all considered the case of *synchronous* streams, where the stream elements appear in increasing order of timestamps. Datar *et al.* [5] were the first to consider basic counting over a sliding window under synchronous arrivals. They present a deterministic algorithm for summarizing synchronous streams which is based on a data structure called the *exponential histogram*. This summary can give an ϵ-approximate answer for basic counting, sum and other aggregates. For a sliding window size of maximum size W, and an ϵ relative error, the space taken by the exponential histogram for basic counting is $O(\frac{1}{\epsilon} \log^2 W)$, and the time taken to process each element is $O(\log W)$ worst case, and $O(1)$ amortized. Their summary for the sum of elements within the sliding window has space complexity $O(\frac{1}{\epsilon} \log W (\log W + \log m))$, and worst case time complexity of $O(\log W + \log m)$ where m is an upper bound on the value of an item. Gibbons and Tirthapura [7] gave an improved algorithm for basic counting that uses the same space as in [5], but whose time per element is $O(1)$ worst case. Since then, there has been much work on summarizing synchronous data streams to approximate various aggregates over a sliding window, including

Arasu and Manku [1] on frequency counts and quantiles, Babcock *et al.* [2] on variance and k-medians, Feigenbaum *et al.* [6] on the diameter of a set of points. Much other recent work on data stream algorithms has been surveyed in [10].

2   Basic Counting

For basic counting, the values of the stream elements do not matter, so the stream is essentially a sequence of timestamps $R = t_1, t_2, \ldots, t_n$. The timestamps may not be distinct and do not necessarily arrive in an increasing order. Let c denote the current time. The goal is to maintain a sketch of R which will provide an answer for the following query: for a user-provided $w \leq W$, which is given at the time of the query, return the number of elements in the current timestamp window $[c - w, c]$.

2.1   Algorithm

We assume that timestamps are non-negative integers. The universe of possible timestamps is divided into intervals $I_0, I_1, \ldots$ of length W each; $I_0 = [0, W - 1], I_1 = [W, 2W - 1], \ldots, I_k = [kW, (k + 1)W - 1], \ldots$. A separate data structure D_i is maintained for each interval I_i, and all timestamps belonging in I_i are inserted into D_i. If c is the current time, then any timestamp that is less than $c - W$ will never be useful for a query, whether current or future. Thus we only need to maintain data structures D_i for those I_i that intersect $[c - W, c]$. It is easy to verify that there exists $j \geq 0$ such that $[c - W, c] \subset I_j \cup I_{j+1}$. Thus, the only data structures that are needed at time c are D_j and D_{j+1}, and the algorithm only needs to maintain two such data structures at any time. When a query is asked for the basic count over a timestamp window of width $w \leq W$, there are two possibilities:

(1) The window $[c - w, c]$ is completely contained within I_j, i.e. $[c - w, c] \subseteq I_j$. In this case D_j is queried for the number of elements in the range $[c - w, c]$, and this estimate is returned by the algorithm.

(2) The window $[c - w, c]$ falls partially in I_j and in I_{j+1}. In such a case, the algorithm consults D_j for the number of elements in the range $[c - w, (j+1)W - 1]$ and consults D_{j+1} for the number of timestamps in the range $[(j + 1)W, c]$, and returns the sum of the two estimates. If each estimate is within an ϵ relative error of the correct value, their sum is also within an ϵ relative error of the total number of elements in the sliding timestamp window.

In the remainder of this section, we discuss the algorithms for maintaining and querying data structure D_0. Other D_is can be maintained similarly. For D_0 we assume that all timestamps are in the range $[0, W - 1]$. Without loss of generality, we assume W is a power of 2 (since W only needs to be an upper bound on the window size, it is always acceptable to increase it without affecting the correctness). Let B be an upper bound on the number of elements with timestamps in $I_0 = [0, W - 1]$. Let $M = \lceil \log B \rceil$, and $\alpha = \left\lceil (1 + \log W) \cdot \frac{2 + \epsilon}{\epsilon} \right\rceil$ where ϵ is the desired relative error.

Intuition: Our algorithm is based on a novel data structure *splittable histogram*, which we introduce here. Data structure D_0 consists of $M + 1$ histograms $S_0, S_1, \ldots, S_M$. Each histogram S_i consists of no more than α *buckets*. Each bucket in S_i is a tuple $b = \langle w(b), l(b), r(b) \rangle$ where: which is $(1)[l(b), r(b)] \subseteq [0, W-1]$ is the range of all timestamps the bucket is responsible for and $(2)w(b)$ is the *weight* of the bucket which is an estimate of the number of elements with timestamps in the range $[l(b), r(b)]$.

The timestamp ranges of different buckets within S_i are disjoint. For each $i = 0, \ldots, M$, we maintain the following invariant for S_i: *If S_i has two or more buckets, then the weight of every bucket in S_i is in the range $[2^i, 2^{i+1} - 1]$, except for those buckets which are responsible for a single timestamp.* Intuitively, if $i_1 > i_2$, then histogram S_{i_1} contains "coarser' information about the distribution of elements than does S_{i_2}, since it uses buckets of a larger size. Modulo some significant details, this setup is similar to the one used in Datar *et. al.* [5] and Gibbons and Tirthapura [7] to process synchronous streams.

An arriving element with timestamp t is inserted into every S_i, $i = 0, \ldots, M$. Within S_i, the element is inserted into a bucket b which is responsible for the timestamp of the element $(t \in [l(b), r(b)])$, and the weight $w(b)$ of the bucket is incremented. Since stream elements are arriving asynchronously, the bucket into which the arriving element is inserted may not be the bucket responsible for the most recent timestamps. This is a fundamental departure from the way histograms were employed to process synchronous streams in previous work [5,7]. The algorithms in [5,7] rest on the fact that an arriving element is always inserted into the most recent bucket. Thus, when the size of the most recent bucket exceeds 2^i, the most recent bucket is "closed" and a new bucket is created to hold future elements.

In our case, since elements arriving in the future may fall into a bucket which is not the most recent bucket, we are unable to "close" a bucket. Thus, due to arrival of elements in an arbitrary order, the weight of a bucket may increase and may reach 2^{i+1}, causing it to become too heavy. A heavy bucket of the form $\langle 2^{i+1}, l, r \rangle$ is "split" into two lighter buckets $\langle 2^i, l, (l + r + 1)/2 - 1 \rangle$ and $\langle 2^{i+1}, (l + r + 1)/2, r \rangle$, each of which has half the weight of the original bucket, and is responsible for half the timestamp range of the original bucket.

Clearly, this splitting is inaccurate, since in the earlier grouping of all 2^{i+1} elements into a single bucket, the information about the timestamps of the individual elements has already been lost, and assigning half the elements of the bucket into half the timestamp range may be incorrect. The key intuition here is that *the error due to this split is controlled, and is no more than 2^i at each bucket resulting from the split.* Any future insertions of elements in the timestamp range $[l, r]$ are considered more carefully, since they are being inserted into buckets whose timestamp ranges are smaller. The buckets resulting from the split may further increase in weight due to future insertions, and may split recursively. The error due to splitting may accumulate, but only to a limited extent, as we prove. A bucket resulting from $\log W$ recursive splits is responsible for only a single timestamp, since the range of timestamps for a bucket decreases by a factor of 2 during every split, and the initial bucket is responsible for a timestamp range of length W. A bucket that is responsible for a single timestamp is treated as a special case, and is not split further, even if its weight increases beyond 2^{i+1}.

Due to the splits, the number of buckets within S_i may increase beyond α, in which case we only maintain the α buckets that are responsible for the most recent timestamps. Given a query for the basic count in window $[c - w, c]$, the different S_is are examined in increasing order of i. For smaller values of i, S_i may have already discarded some buckets that are responsible for timestamps in $[c - w, c]$. But, there will always be a level $\ell \leq M$ that will have all buckets intersecting the range $[c - w, c]$ (this is formally proved in Lemma 2). The algorithm selects the earliest such level to answer the basic counting query, and we show that the resulting relative error is within ϵ.

The algorithm for basic counting is given below. Algorithm 1 describes the initialization of the data structure, Algorithm 2 describes the steps taken to process a new element with a timestamp t, and Algorithm 3 describes the procedure for answering a query for basic count.

Algorithm 1. Basic Counting: Initialization

$\quad \alpha \leftarrow \lceil (1 + \log W) \cdot \frac{2 + \epsilon}{\epsilon} \rceil$, where ϵ is the desired relative error;
$\quad S_0 \leftarrow \phi;\ T_0 \leftarrow -1;$

$\quad$ **for** $i = 1, \ldots, M$ **do**
$\quad\quad$ S_i is a set with a single element $\langle 0, 0, W - 1 \rangle$;
$\quad\quad$ $T_i \leftarrow -1;$
$\quad$ **end**

2.2   Proof of Correctness

Let c denote the current time. We consider the contents of sets S_i and the values of T_i at time c. For any time t, $0 \leq t \leq c$, let s_t denote the number of elements with timestamps in the range $[t, W - 1]$ which arrive until time c. For level i, $0 \leq i \leq M$, e_t^i is defined as follows.

Definition 2.
$$e_t^i = \sum_{\{b \in S_i \mid l(b) \geq t\}} w(b)$$

Lemma 1. *For any level $i \in [0, M]$, for any t such that $T_i < t \leq c$, $|s_t - e_t^i| \leq 2^i \cdot (1 + \log W)$*

Proof. For level $i = 0$ we have $s_t = e_t^0$, since each element x with timestamp t', where $t \leq t' \leq W - 1$, is counted in the bucket $b = \langle w(b), t', t' \rangle$ which is a member of S_0 at time c. Thus, $|s_t - e_t^0| = 0$.

Algorithm 2. Basic Counting: When an element with timestamp t arrives

```
// level 0
if there is bucket ⟨w(b), t, t⟩ ∈ S₀ then
    Increment w(b);
else
    Insert bucket ⟨1, t, t⟩ into S₀;
end
```

// level 0
if there is bucket $\langle w(b), t, t \rangle \in S_0$ then
    Increment $w(b)$;
else
    Insert bucket $\langle 1, t, t \rangle$ into S_0;
end

// level i, $i > 0$
for $i = 1, \ldots, M$ do
    if there is bucket $b = \langle w(b), l(b), r(b) \rangle \in S_i$ with $t \in [l(b), r(b)]$ then
        Increment $w(b)$;
        if $w(b) = 2^{i+1}$ and $l(b) \neq r(b)$ then
            // bucket too heavy, split
            // note that a bucket is not split
            // if it is responsible for only a single time stamp
            New bucket $b_1 = \langle 2^i, l(b), \frac{l(b)+r(b)+1}{2} - 1 \rangle$;
            New bucket $b_2 = \langle 2^i, \frac{l(b)+r(b)+1}{2}, r(b) \rangle$;
            Delete b from S_i;
            Insert b_1 and b_2 into S_i;
        end
    end
end

// handle overflow
for $i = 0, \ldots, M$ do
    if $|S_i| > \alpha$ then
        // overflow
        Discard bucket $b^* \in S_i$ such that $r(b^*) = \min_{b \in S_i} r(b)$;
        $T_i \leftarrow r(b^*)$;
    end
end

Algorithm 3. Basic Counting: Query(w)

Input: w, the width of the query window, where $w \leq W$
Output: An estimate of the number of elements with timestamps in $[c - w, c]$
        where c is the current time
Let $\ell \in [0, \ldots, M]$ be the smallest integer such that $T_\ell < c - w$;
return $\sum_{\{b \in S_\ell | l(b) \geq c - w\}} w(b)$;

Consider now some level $i > 0$. We can construct a binary tree A whose nodes are all the buckets that appeared in S_i up to current time c. Let $b_0 = \langle 0, 0, W-1 \rangle$ be the initial bucket which is inserted into S_i during initialization (Algorithm 1). The root of A is b_0. For any bucket $b \in A$, if b is split into two buckets b_l and b_r, then b_l and b_r will appear as the respective left and right children of b in A. Note that in A a node is either a leaf or has exactly two children. Tree A

has depth at most $\log W$ (the root is at depth 0), since every time that a bucket splits the time period divides in half, and the smallest time period is a discrete time step. For any node $b \in A$ let $A(b)$ denote the subtree with root b; we will also refer to this as the subtree of b.

Consider now the tree A at time c. The buckets in S_i appear as the $|S_i|$ rightmost leaves of A. Let S_i' denote the set of buckets in S_i with $l(b) \geq t$. clearly, $e_t^i = \sum_{b \in S_i'} w(b)$. The buckets in S_i' are the $|S_i'|$ rightmost leaves of A. Suppose that $S_i' \neq \emptyset$ (the case $S_i' = \emptyset$ is discussed below). Let b' be the leftmost leaf in A among the buckets in S_i'. Let p denote the path in A from the root to b'. For the number of nodes $|p|$ of p it holds $|p| \leq 1 + \log W$. Let H_1 (H_2) be the set that consists of the right (left) children of the nodes in p, such that these children are not members of the path p. Note that $b' \notin H_1 \cup H_2$. The union of b' and the leaves in the subtrees of H_2 ($\cup_{b \in H_2} A(b)$) constitute the nodes in S_i'. Further, each bucket $b \notin S_i'$ is in a leaf in a subtree of H_2.

Consider some element x with timestamp t'. Initially, when x arrives it is *initially assigned* to the bucket b which t' belongs to. If b splits to two (children) buckets b_1 and b_2, then we can assume that x is *assigned* arbitrarily to one of the two new buckets arbitrarily. Even through x's timestamp may belong to b_1, x may be assigned to b_2, and vice-versa. If again the new bucket splits, x is assigned to one of its children, and so on. Note that x is always assigned to a leaf of A.

At time c, we can write

$$e_t^i = s_t + |X_1| - |X_2 \cup X_3|, \tag{1}$$

such that: X_1 is the set of elements with timestamps in $[0, t-1]$ which are assigned to buckets in S_i'; X_2 is the set of elements with timestamps in $[l(b'), W-1]$ which are assigned to buckets outside of S_i'; and, for $t < l(b')$, X_3 is the set of elements with timestamps in $[t, l(b')-1]$ which are assigned to buckets outside of S_i', while for $t = l(b')$, $X_3 = \emptyset$. Note that the sets X_1, X_2, X_3 are disjoint.

First, we bound $|X_1|$. Consider some element $x \in X_1$ with timestamp in $[0, t-1]$ which at time c appears assigned to a leaf bucket $b_l \in S_i'$. Since $b_l \in S_i'$, t cannot be a member of the time range of b_l, that is, $t \notin [l(b_l), r(b_l)]$. Thus, x could not have been initially assigned to b_l. Suppose that $b_l \neq b'$. Then, there is a node $\widehat{b} \in H_1$ such that b_l is the leaf of the subtree $A(\widehat{b})$. None of the nodes in $A(\widehat{b})$ contain t in their time range, since all the leaves of $A(\widehat{b})$ are members of S_i'. Therefore, x could not have been initially assigned to $A(\widehat{b})$. Thus, x is initially assigned to a node $b_p \in p' = p - \{b'\}$, since x could not have been assigned to any node in the subtrees of H_2 which would certainly bring x outside of S_i'. Similarly, if $b_l \neq b'$, x is initially assigned to a node $b_p \in p'$. Since at most 2^{i+1} elements are initially assigned to the root, and at most 2^i elements are initially assigned to each of the subsequent nodes of p', we get:

$$|X_1| \leq 2^i \cdot (|p'| - 1) + 2^{i+1} = 2^i \cdot |p| \leq 2^i \cdot (1 + \log W). \tag{2}$$

With a similar analysis (the details are omitted due to space constraints) in can be shown that:

$$|X_2 \cup X_3| \le 2^i \cdot (1 + \log W). \tag{3}$$

Combining Equations 1, 2, and 3 we can bound $s_t - e_t^i$:

$$-2^i \cdot (1 + \log W) \le -|X_1| \le s_t - e_t^i \le |X_2 \cup X_3| \le 2^i \cdot (1 + \log W).$$

Therefore, $|s_t - e_t^i| \le 2^i \cdot (1 + \log W)$. In case $S_i' = \emptyset$, $e_t^i = s_t - |X_3| = 0$, and the same bound follows immediately. □

Lemma 2. *When asked for an estimate of the number of timestamps in $[c-w, c]$
(1)There exists a level $i \in [0, M]$ such that $T_i < c - w$, and
(2)Algorithm 3 returns e_{c-w}^ℓ where $\ell \in [0, M]$ is the smallest level such that $T_\ell < c - w$.*

The proof of Lemma 2 is omitted due to space constraints, and can be found in the full version [3]. Let ℓ denote the level used by Algorithm 3 to answer a query for the number of timestamps in $[c - w, c]$. From Lemma 2 we know ℓ always exists.

Lemma 3. *If $\ell > 0$, then $s_{c-w} \ge \frac{(1+\log W) \cdot 2^\ell}{\epsilon}$.*

Proof. If $\ell > 0$, it must be true that $T_{\ell-1} \ge c - w$, since otherwise level $\ell - 1$ would have been chosen. Let $t = T_{\ell-1} + 1$. Then, $t > c - w$, and thus $s_{c-w} \ge s_t$. From Lemma 1, we know $s_t \ge e_t^{\ell-1} - (1 + \log W) \cdot 2^{\ell-1}$. Thus we have:

$$s_{c-w} \ge e_t^{\ell-1} - (1 + \log W) \cdot 2^{\ell-1} \tag{4}$$

We know that for each bucket $b \in S_{\ell-1}$, $l(b) \ge t$. Further we know that each bucket in $S_{\ell-1}$ has a weight of at least $2^{\ell-1}$ (only the initial bucket in $S_{\ell-1}$ may have a smaller weight, but this bucket must have split, since otherwise $T_{\ell-1}$ would still be -1). Since there are α buckets in $S_{\ell-1}$, we have:

$$e_t^{\ell-1} \ge \alpha 2^{\ell-1} \ge (1 + \log W) \cdot \frac{2 + \epsilon}{\epsilon} \cdot 2^{\ell-1} \tag{5}$$

The lemma follows from Equations 4 and 5. □

Theorem 1. *The answer returned by Algorithm 3 is within an ϵ relative error of s_{c-w}.*

Proof. Let X denote the value returned by Algorithm 3. If $\ell = 0$, it can be verified that Algorithm 3 returns exactly s_{c-w} (proof omitted due to space constraints). If $\ell > 0$, from Lemmas 1 and 2, we have $|X - s_{c-w}| \le (1 + \log W) \cdot 2^\ell$. Using Lemma 3, we get $|X - s_{c-w}| \le \epsilon \cdot s_{c-w}$ as needed. □

Theorem 2. *The worst case space required by the data structure for basic counting is $O((\log W \cdot \log B) \cdot (\log W + \log B)/\epsilon)$ where B is an upper bound on the value of the basic count, W is an upper bound on the window size w, and ϵ is the desired upper bound on the relative error. The worst case time taken by Algorithm 2 to process a new element is $O(\log W \cdot \log B)$, and the worst case time taken by Algorithm 3 to answer a query for basic counting is $O(\log B + \frac{\log W}{\epsilon})$.*

The proof is omitted due to space constraints, and can be found in the full version [3].

3   Sum of Positive Integers

We now consider the maintenance of a sketch for the *sum*, which is a generalization of basic counting. The stream is a sequence of tuples $R = d_1 = (v_1, t_1), d_2 = (v_2, t_2), \ldots, d_n = (v_n, t_n)$ where the v_is are positive integers, corresponding to the observations, and t_is are the timestamps of the observations. Let c denote the current time. The goal is to maintain a sketch of R which will provide an answer for the following query. For a user provided $w \le W$ that is given at the time of the query, return the sum of the values of stream elements that are within the current timestamp window $[c - w, c]$. Clearly, basic counting is a special case where all v_is are equal to 1.

An arriving element (v, t), is treated as v different elements each of value 1 and timestamp t, and these v elements are inserted into the data structure for basic counting. Finally, when asked for an estimate for the sum, the algorithm for handling a query in basic counting (Algorithm 3) is used. The correctness of this algorithm for the sum follows from the correctness of the basic counting algorithm (Theorem 1). The space complexity of this algorithm is the same as the space complexity of basic counting, the only difference being that the number of levels in the algorithm for the sum is $M = \lceil \log B \rceil$, where B is an upper bound on the value of the sum within the sliding window (in the case of basic counting, B was an upper bound on the number of elements within the window).

If naively executed, the time complexity of the above procedure for processing an element (v, t) could be large, since v could be large. The time complexity of processing an element can be reduced by directly computing the final state of the basic counting data structure after inserting all the v elements. The intuition behind the faster processing is as follows. The element (v, t) is inserted into each of the $M + 1$ levels. In each level $i, i = 0, \ldots, M$, the v elements are inserted into S_i in *batches* of unit elements $(1, t)$ taken from (v, t). A batch contains enough elements to cause the current bucket containing timestamp t to split. The next batch contains enough elements from v to cause the new bucket containing timestamp t to split, too, and so on. The process repeats until a bucket containing timestamp t cannot split further. This occurs when at most $O(\max(v/2^i, \log W))$ batches are processed (and a similar number of respective new buckets is created), since at most $O(2^i)$ elements from v are processed at each iteration in a batch, and a bucket can be recursively split at most $\log W$ times until it is responsible for only one timestamp, at which point no further splitting can occur (and any remaining elements are directly inserted into this bucket). The complete algorithm for processing (v, t) and its analysis can be found in the full version of the paper [3], where it is proved that upon receiving element (v, t), the algorithm for the sum simulates the behavior of Algorithm 2 upon receiving v elements each with a timestamp of t.

Theorem 3. *The worst case space required by the data structure for the sum is* $O((\log W \cdot \log B)(\log W + \log B)/\epsilon)$ *bits where* B *is an upper bound on the value of the sum,* W *is an upper bound on the window size* w, *and* ϵ *is the desired upper bound on the relative error. The worst case time taken by the algorithm for the sum to process a new element is* $O(\log W \cdot \log B)$, *and the time taken to answer a query for the sum is* $O(\log B + (\log W)/\epsilon)$.

References

1. A. Arasu and G. Manku. Approximate counts and quantiles over sliding windows. In *Proc. ACM Symposium on Principles of Database Systems (PODS)*, pages 286–296, 2004.
2. B. Babcock, M. Datar, R. Motwani, and L. O'Callaghan. Maintaining variance and k-medians over data stream windows. In *Proc. 22nd ACM Symp. on Principles of Database Systems (PODS)*, pages 234–243, June 2003.
3. C. Busch and S. Tirthapura. A deterministic algorithm for summarizing asynchronous streams over a sliding window. Technical report, Iowa State University, 2006. Available at http://archives.ece.iastate.edu/view/year/2006.html.
4. G. Cormode, F. Korn, S. Muthukrishnan, and D. Srivastava. Space- and time-efficient deterministic algorithms for biased quantiles over data streams. In *Proc. ACM Symposium on Principles of Database Systems*, pages 263–272, 2006.
5. M. Datar, A. Gionis, P. Indyk, and R. Motwani. Maintaining stream statistics over sliding windows. *SIAM Journal on Computing*, 31(6):1794–1813, 2002.
6. J. Feigenbaum, S. Kannan, and J. Zhang. Computing diameter in the streaming and sliding-window models. *Algorithmica*, 41:25–41, 2005.
7. P. Gibbons and S. Tirthapura. Distributed streams algorithms for sliding windows. *Theory of Computing Systems*, 37:457–478, 2004.
8. S. Guha, D. Gunopulos, and N. Koudas. Correlating synchronous and asynchronous data streams. In *Proc.9th ACM International Conference on Knowledge Discovery and Data Mining (KDD)*, pages 529–534, 2003.
9. A. Manjhi, V. Shkapenyuk, K. Dhamdhere, and C. Olston. Finding (recently) frequent items in distributed data streams. In *Proc. IEEE International Conference on Data Engineering (ICDE)*, pages 767–778, 2005.
10. S. Muthukrishnan. *Data Streams: Algorithms and Applications*. Foundations and Trends in Theoretical Computer Science. Now Publishers, August 2005.
11. U. Srivastava and J. Widom. Flexible time management in data stream systems. In *Proc. 23rd ACM Symposium on Principles of Database Systems (PODS)*, pages 263–274, 2004.
12. S. Tirthapura, B. Xu, and C. Busch. Sketching asynchronous streams over a sliding window. In *Proc. 25th annual ACM symposium on Principles of distributed computing (PODC)*, pages 82–91, 2006.

Arithmetizing Classes Around NC^1 and L

Nutan Limaye, Meena Mahajan, and B.V. Raghavendra Rao

The Institute of Mathematical Sciences, Chennai 600 113, India
{nutan,meena,bvrr}@imsc.res.in

Abstract. The parallel complexity class NC^1 has many equivalent models such as bounded width branching programs. Caussinus et.al[10] considered arithmetizations of two of these classes, $\#NC^1$ and $\#BWBP$. We further this study to include arithmetization of other classes. In particular, we show that counting paths in branching programs over visibly pushdown automata has the same power as $\#BWBP$, while counting proof-trees in logarithmic width formulae has the same power as $\#NC^1$. We also consider polynomial-degree restrictions of SC^i, denoted sSC^i, and show that the Boolean class sSC^1 lies between NC^1 and L, whereas sSC^0 equals NC^1. On the other hand, $\#sSC^0$ contains $\#BWBP$ and is contained in FL, and $\#sSC^1$ contains $\#NC^1$ and is in SC^2. We also investigate some closure properties of the newly defined arithmetic classes.

1 Introduction

The parallel complexity class NC^1, comprising of languages accepted by logarithmic depth, polynomial size, bounded fan in Boolean circuits, is of fundamental interest in circuit complexity. NC^1 is known to be contained within logarithmic space L. The classes NC^1 and L have many equivalent characterizations. Bounded width branching programs BWBP, as well as bounded width circuits SC^0, (both of polynomial size), were shown by Barrington [6] to be equivalent to NC^1, while it it is folklore that poly size $O(\log n)$ width circuits SC^1 equals L.

However, arithmetizations of these classes are not necessarily equivalent. In [10], Caussinus et al proposed three arithmetizations of NC^1: (1) counting proof-trees in an NC^1 circuit, (2) computation by a poly size log depth circuit over $+$ and $\times$, and (3) counting paths in a nondeterministic bounded width branching program. It is straightforward to see that the first two definitions of function classes, over $\mathbb{N}$, coincide (see for instance [25,27]); and this class is denoted $\#NC^1$. It is shown in [10] that the third class, $\#BWBP$, is contained in $\#NC^1$, though the converse inclusion is still open. (However, the arithmetizations over $\mathbb{Z}$ are shown to coincide.) Also, using the programs over monoids framework, [10] observe that $\#BWBP$ equals $\#BP\text{-}NFA$, the class of functions that count the number of accepting paths in a nondeterministic finite-state automaton NFA when run on the output of a deterministic branching program. It is known (see e.g. [3,27]) that $\#NC^1$ has Boolean poly size circuits of depth $O(\log n \log^* n)$ and is thus very close to NC^1. It follows from more recent results [11] that $\#NC^1$ is contained in FL; see e.g. [3].

W. Thomas and P. Weil (Eds.): STACS 2007, LNCS 4393, pp. 477–488, 2007.

We continue this study here (and also extend it to L) by arithmetizing other Boolean classes also known to be equivalent to NC^1. The first extension we consider is from NFA to VPA. Visibly pushdown automata (VPA) are ϵ-moves-free pushdown automata whose stack behaviour (push/pop/no change) is dictated solely by the input letter under consideration. They are also referred to as input-driven pda, and have been studied in [18,8,14,5] etc. In [14], languages accepted by such pda are shown to be in NC^1, while in [5] it is shown that such pda can be determinized. Thus they lie properly between regular languages and deterministic context-free languages, and membership is complete for NC^1. The arithmetic version we consider is #BP-VPA, counting the number of accepting paths in a VPA, when run on the output of a deterministic branching program. Clearly, this contains #BP-NFA; we show that in fact the two are equal. Thus adding a stack to an NFA but restricting its usage to a visible nature adds no power to the closure of the class under projections.

Next we consider arithmetic formulae. It is known that formulae F (circuits with fanout 1 for each gate) and even log width formulae LWF have the same power as NC^1 [16]. Applying either of definition (1) or (2) above to formulae give the function classes #F and #LWF. It is known [9] that #LWF $\subseteq$ #F = #NC^1. We show that this is in fact an equality. Thus even in the arithmetic setting, LWF have the full power of NC^1.

Next we consider bounded width circuits. SC is the class of polynomial size poly log width (width $O(\log^i n)$ for SC^i) circuits, and corresponds in the uniform setting to a simultaneous time-space bound. (SC stands for Steve's Classes, named after Stephen Cook who proved the first non-trivial result about polynomial time log-squared space PLoSS, i.e. SC^2, in [12]. See for instance [17]). It is known that SC^0 equals NC^1 [6]. However, this equality provably does not carry over to the arithmetic setting, since it is easy to see that even SC^0 over $\mathbb{N}$ can compute values that have exponentially long representation. So we consider the restriction to polynomial degree, denoted by sSC^0, before arithmetizing to get #sSC^0. We note that in the Boolean setting, this is not a restriction at all; sSC^0 equals NC^1 as well. However, the arithmetization does not appear to collapse to either of the existing classes. We show that #sSC^0 lies between #BWBP and FL.

The polynomial-degree restriction of SC^0 immediately suggests a similar restriction on all the SC^i classes. We thus explore the power of sSC^i and sSC, the polynomial-degree restrictions of SC^i and SC respectively, and their corresponding arithmetic versions #sSC^i and #sSC. This restriction automatically places the corresponding classes in LogCFL and #LogCFL, since LogCFL is known to equal languages accepted by polynomial size polynomial degree circuits [23,21], and since the arithmetic analogue also holds [25,19]. Thus we have a hierarchy of circuit classes between NC^1 and LogCFL. Other hierarchies sitting in this region are poly size branching programs of poly log width, limited by NL in LogCFL, and poly size log depth circuits with AND fan in 2 and OR fan in poly log, limited by SAC^1 which equals LogCFL [24]; see [26]. In both of these hierarchies, [26] establishes closure under complementation. For sSC^i, we have a weaker result: co-sSC^i is contained in sSC^{2i}.

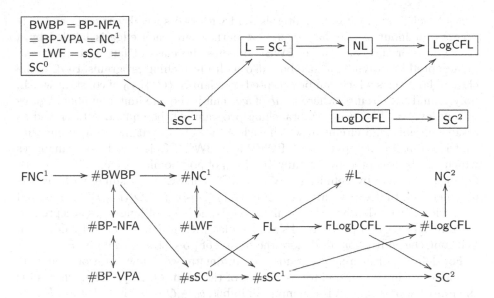

Fig. 1. Boolean classes and their arithmetizations

It is not clear what power the Boolean class sSC^1 possesses: is it strong enough to equal SC^1, or is the polynomial degree restriction crippling enough to bring it down to SC^0=NC^1? We show that all of #NC^1 is captured by #sSC^1, which is contained in Boolean SC^2. The maximal fragments of NC hitherto known to be in SC were LogDCFL [22,13,15] and randomized log space RL [20]; we do not know how this fragment compares with them. In fact, turning the question around, studying sSC is an attempt to understand fragments of NC that lie within SC.

Our main results can be summarized in Figure 1. It shows that corresponding to Boolean NC^1, there are three naturally defined arithmetizations, while the correct arithmetization of L is still not clear. We also show that the three arithmetizations of NC^1 coincide under modulo tests, for any fixed modulus.

A key to understanding function classes better is to investigate their closure properties. We present some such results concerning #sSC^i.

This paper is organized as follows. Definitions and notation are presented in Section 2. Sections 3 and 4 present the bounds on #BP-VPA and #LWF, respectively. Section 5 introduces and presents bounds involving sSC^i and #sSC^i. Some closure properties of these classes are presented in Section 6, where also the collapse of the modulus test classes NC^1= ⊕NC^1 = ⊕BWBP = ⊕sSC^0 follows.

2   Preliminaries

By NC^1 we denote the class of languages which can be accepted by a family $\{C_n\}_{n\geq0}$ of polynomial size $O(\log n)$ depth bounded circuits, with each gate having a constant fan-in. A branching program is a layered acyclic graph G with edges labeled by constants or literals, and with two special vertices s and t. It accepts an input x if it has an $s \leadsto t$ path where each edge is labeled by a true literal or the constant 1. BWBP denotes the class of languages that can be accepted by polynomial size bounded width branching programs. BWC is the class of languages which can be accepted by a family $\{C_n\}_{n \geq 0}$ of constant width, polynomial size circuits, where *width* of a circuit is the maximum number of gates at any level of the circuit. A branching program can be equivalently viewed as a skew circuit i.e, a circuit in which each AND gate has at most one input wire that is not a circuit input; hence BWBP is in BWC. SC^i is the class of languages which can be accepted by a family $\{C_n\}_{n \geq 0}$ of polynomial size circuits of width $O((\log n)^i)$. Thus by definition, BWC = SC^0. For SC^i we assume, without loss of generality, that every gate has fan-in $O(1)$ (fan-in $f = O((\log n)^i)$ is replaced by a width $O(1)$, depth $O(f)$ circuit). LWF is the class of languages accepted by a family $\{F_n\}_{n \geq 0}$ of polynomial size formulae with width bounded by $O(\log n)$. Without the width bound, denote the family of poly size formula by F.

For defining branching programs over automata, we follow notation from [10]. A nondeterministic automaton is a tuple of the form $(Q, \Delta, q_0, \delta, F)$, where Q is the finite set of states, Δ is the input alphabet, $q_0 \in Q$ is the initial state, $F \subseteq Q$ is the set of accepting states and $\delta : Q \times \Sigma \rightarrow \mathcal{P}(Q)$.

A projection $P = (\Sigma, \Delta, S, B, E)$ over Δ is a family $P = (P_n)_{n \in N}$ of n-projections over Δ, where an n-projection over Δ is a finite sequence of pairs (i, f) with $1 \leq i \leq n$ and $f : \Sigma \rightarrow \Delta$. The length of the sequence is denoted by S_n, its j-th instruction by $(B_n(j), E_n(j))$ where $S : \mathbb{N} \rightarrow \mathbb{N}$, $B : \mathbb{N} \times \mathbb{N} \rightarrow \mathbb{N}$, $E : \mathbb{N} \times \mathbb{N} \rightarrow \Delta^\Sigma$. B pulls out a letter $x_{B_{|x|}(j)} \in \Sigma$ from the input x and E projects it to a letter in the alphabet Δ. Thus the string $x \in \Sigma^*$ is projected to a string $P(x) \in \Delta^*$. FDLOGTIME uniformity for the projections is assumed.

A branching program over an automaton N is a projection $P = (\Sigma, \Delta, S, B, E)$. It accepts $x \in \Sigma^*$ if N accepts $P(x)$. BP-NFA is the class of languages recognized by uniform poly length branching programs over a nondeterministic automaton[1].

A visibly pushdown automaton (VPA) is a pda $M = (Q, Q_{in}, \Delta, \Gamma, \delta, Q_F)$ working over an input alphabet Δ that is partitioned as $(\Delta_c, \Delta_r, \Delta_{int})$. Q is a finite set of states, $Q_{in}, Q_F \subseteq Q$ are the sets of initial and final states respectively, Γ is the stack alphabet containing a special bottom-of-stack marker $\perp$, and acceptance is by final state. The transition function δ is constrained so that: If $a \in \Delta_c$, then $\delta(p, a) = (q, \gamma)$ (push move, independent of top-of-stack). If $a \in \Delta_r$, then $\delta(p, a, \gamma) = q$ (pop move), and $\delta(p, a, \perp) = q$ (pop on empty stack). If $a \in \Delta_{int}$, then $\delta(p, a) = q$ (internal move, independent of top-of-stack). The input letter completely dictates the stack movement. Also the pda is assumed to be ϵ-move-free, while δ is allowed to be non-deterministic.

BP-VPA is the class of all languages recognized by uniform polynomial length branching programs over a VPA.

In [6], Barrington showed that NC^1= BWBP= BWC. As observed in [10], BWBP coincides with BP-NFA; thus NC^1= BP-NFA. Istrail and Zivkovic showed

---

[1] In [10], this class is called BP. We introduce this new notation to better motivate the next definition, of BP-VPA.

in [16] that NC^1= LWF. In [14], Dymond showed that acceptance by VPAs can be checked in NC^1, and hence BP-VPA= NC^1. Thus

Lemma 1 ([6,10,16,14]). NC^1= BWBP= SC^0= LWF= BP-NFA= BP-VPA

The corresponding arithmetic classes are defined as follows:

$$\#\mathsf{BWBP} = \{f : \{0,1\}^n \to \mathbb{N} \mid f = \#s \rightsquigarrow t \text{ paths in a BWBP}\}$$

$$\#\mathsf{NC}^1 = \left\{ f : \{0,1\}^n \to \mathbb{N} \mid \begin{array}{l} f \text{ can be computed by a poly size} \\ O(\log n) \text{ depth bounded fan in circuit} \\ \text{over } \{+, \times, 1, 0, x_i, \overline{x_i}\}. \end{array} \right\}$$

$$\#\mathsf{BP\text{-}NFA} = \left\{ f : \{0,1\}^n \to \mathbb{N} \mid \begin{array}{l} f(x) = \#\mathrm{accept}(P_n, x) \text{ for some uni-} \\ \text{form poly length BP } P \text{ over an NFA} \\ N \end{array} \right\}$$

Here, $\#\mathrm{accept}(P, x)$ denotes the number of distinct accepting paths of N on the projection of x, $P(x)$.

For each of these counting classes, the corresponding Gap classes are defined by allowing the constant -1 in the circuit.

Though the above classes are all equal in the Boolean setting, in the arithmetic setting the equivalences are not established, and strict containments are also not known. The best known relationships among these classes are as below.

Lemma 2 ([10]).
FNC^1 $\subseteq$ #BWBP = #BP-NFA $\subseteq$ #NC^1 $\subseteq$ GapBWBP = GapNC^1 $\subseteq$ L.

3 Counting Accepting Runs in Visibly Pushdown Automata

We introduce a natural arithmetization of BP-VPA, by counting the number of accepting paths in a VPA rather than in an NFA. Given a uniform poly length branching program P over a VPA M, $\#\mathrm{accept}(P, x)$ denotes the number of distinct accepting paths of M on the projection of x.

Definition 1. $\#\mathsf{BP\text{-}VPA} = \left\{ f : \{0,1\}^n \to \mathbb{N} \mid \begin{array}{l} f(x) = \#accept(P_n, x) \text{ for} \\ \text{some uniform poly length BP} \\ P \text{ over a VPA } M \end{array} \right\}$

The main result of this section is that adding a visible pushdown to an NFA adds no power to the corresponding counting class. That is,

Theorem 1. #BP-NFA= #BP-VPA

Proof. #BP-NFA$\subseteq$ #BP-VPA is obvious from the definition. To show #BP-VPA$\subseteq$ #BP-NFA, we place #BP-VPA in #BWBP below, and then use Lemma 1.

Let $f \in$ #BP-VPA. There exists a uniform polynomial length branching program P over a VPA $M = (Q, \Delta, Q_{in}, \Gamma, \delta, Q_F)$. Let input w be projected to $P(w) = x \in \Delta^n$, where $\Delta = (\Delta_c, \Delta_r, \Delta_{int})$, $|x| = n$. So $f(w) = \#acc_M(x)$.

The strategy is as follows. We first construct an equivalent VPA M' that never needs to perform a pop on an empty stack. A TC^0 circuit transforms x to a string y over a larger alphabet, such that $\#acc_M(x) = \#acc_{M'}(y)$. This latter quantity, $\#acc_{M'}(y)$, is counted by paths in a BWBP G whose edges are labeled by NC^1 predicates involving M' and y. Thus each edge can be replaced by an equivalent BWBP, and the whole graph is still a BWBP.

The VPA $M' = (Q', \Delta'', Q'_{in}, \Gamma', \delta', Q'_F)$ is essentially the same as M. It has two new input symbols A, B, and a new stack symbol X. A is a push symbol on which X is pushed, and B is a pop symbol on which X is expected and popped. M' has a new state q' that is the only initial state. M' expects an input from $A^* \Delta^* B^*$. On the prefix of A's it pushes X's. When it sees the first letter from Δ, it starts behaving like M. The only exception is when M performs a pop move on $\perp$, M' can perform the same move on $\perp$ or on X. On the trailing suffix of B's it pops X's. It is straightforward to design δ' from δ.

The TC^0 circuit does the following. It counts the difference d between the number of push and pop symbols in $A^n x$. It then outputs $y = A^n x B^d$. By the way M' is constructed, it should be clear that $\#acc_M(x) = \#acc_{M'}(y)$ and that M', on y, never pops on an empty stack. In fact y is *well-matched*, i.e. for every push there exists a corresponding pop and vice versa.

We now describe the layered directed acyclic graph G, with nodes s, t such that $\#_G s \rightsquigarrow t = \#acc_{M'}(y)$. It will be clear that G can be constructed in NC^1.

Let $V = \{(q, X, i) \mid q \in Q' \cup \{g\}, X \in \Gamma' \cup \{\perp\}, (g \notin Q'), 0 \le i \le (n+1)\}$. At layer 0 we need only the vertex labeled $s = (q', \perp, 0)$. Layer i, for $1 \le i \le n$, contains vertices of the form $(q, X, i) \ \forall q \in Q'$ and $\forall X \in \Gamma'$. At layer $n + 1$, we keep only $t = (g, \perp, n + 1)$. This describes the vertex set of G. Note that every layer has a constant number of vertices. The vertex labels are intended to denote *surface configurations* of M', i.e. state, top-of-stack, tape head position. For VPAs, the tape head position is also the time-stamp.

Now we describe the edge set of G. The edges should trace out computations of M'. Thus if $(q, Z') \in \delta'(p, y_i)$ for $y_i \in \Delta'_c$, then we put an edge from $(p, Z, i-1)$ to (q, Z', i) for each Z. Also, if $(q, Z) \in \delta'(p, y_i)$ for $y_i \in \Delta'_{int}$, then we put an edge from $(p, Z, i-1)$ to (q, Z, i) for each Z. The problematic case is when $y_i \in \Delta'_r$. If $q \in \delta'(p, y_i, Z)$, then we want to put an edge from $(p, Z, i-1)$ to (q, Z', i). But we don't know Z'; it is the stack symbol that is uncovered when Z is popped.

In TC^0, first find the matching symbol j, $j < i$, such that $y_j \in \Delta_c$ and the symbol Z pushed by M' while reading y_j is popped while reading y_i. Since y is well-matched, this matching symbol is uniquely defined. Note that the stack never dips below Z between $y_{j+1}...y_{i-1}$. M' can go from $(p, Z, i-1)$ to (q, Z', i) and hence we should put this edge in G if and only if for some $p', p'' \in Q'$,

(a) $(p'', Z) \in \delta'(p', y_j)$ (so there is an edge from $(p', Z', j-1)$ to (p'', Z, j)),
(b) M' can move from (p'', Z) to (p, Z) on reading the string $y_{j+1}...y_{i-1}$ (and without dipping below Z on the stack),
(c) $q \in \delta'(p, y_i, Z)$, and
(d) M' can reach the configuration $(p', Z', j-1)$ starting from $s = (q', \perp, 0)$ and reading the string $y_1...y_{j-1}$.

(a) and (c) are determined by a simple lookup of δ'. (b) and (d) are in NC^1, and hence in deterministic BWBP, since the following is established in [14].

Proposition 1 ([14]). *Determining whether a pair of height-matched surface configurations of a* VPA *is realizable (one is reachable from the other without dipping below the given stack top) is in* NC^1.

(b) is already in the required form to use this result. To check (d), we need to pad the string $y_1...y_{j-1}$ with appropriate number of extra copies of B to get a well-matched string, and then check realizability. As argued above, this can be done in TC^0. Thus, the AND of the four conditions is recognised by a deterministic BWBP. We insert this BWBP in G, identifying its start and sink vertices with $(p, Z, i-1)$ and (q, Z', i).

Also put all the edges of the form $\langle (p, \bot, n), (g, \bot, n+1) \rangle$ provided $p \in F'$

This completely describes the graph G. Simple induction proves that the number of accepting paths in the VPA M equals $\#_G s \rightsquigarrow t$.   □

4 Counting Proof Trees in (Log Width) Formula

We show that the result of [16], log width formula capture NC^1, holds in the arithmetized setting too. This result is crucially used in showing Theorem 4.

Definition 2. $\#\mathsf{F} = \left\{ f : \{0,1\}^n \to \mathbb{N} \;\middle|\; \begin{array}{l} f \text{ can be computed by a poly size} \\ \text{formula over } \{+, \times, 1, 0, x_i, \overline{x_i}\}. \end{array} \right\}$

$\#\mathsf{LWF} = \left\{ f : \{0,1\}^n \to \mathbb{N} \;\middle|\; \begin{array}{l} f \text{ can be computed by a poly size } O(\log n) \\ \text{width formula over } \{+, \times, 1, 0, x_i, \overline{x_i}\}. \end{array} \right\}$

Theorem 2. $\#\mathsf{LWF} = \#\mathsf{F} = \#\mathsf{NC}^1$

Proof. Clearly, $\#\mathsf{LWF} \subseteq \#\mathsf{F}$. It follows from [9] (see also [3]) that $\#\mathsf{F}$ is in $\#\mathsf{NC}^1$. To show that $\#\mathsf{NC}^1$ is in $\#\mathsf{LWF}$, we observe that the construction of Lemma 2 in [16], establishing that NC$^1 \subseteq$ LWF, preserves proof-trees.   □

5 Polynomial Degree Small-Width Circuits and Their Arithmetization

We now consider arithmetization of SC. A straightforward arithmetization of any Boolean circuit class over $(\wedge, \vee, x_i, \overline{x_i}, 0, 1)$ is to replace each $\vee$ gate by a $+$ gate and each $\wedge$ gate by a $\times$ gate. In the case of SC^0 (SC^i in general), this enables the circuit to compute infeasible values (i.e exponential sized values), which makes the class uninteresting. Hence we propose bounded degree versions of these classes and then arithmetize them. The degree of a circuit is the maximum degree of any gate in it, where the degree of a leaf is 1, the degree of an $\vee$ or $+$ gate is the maximum of the degrees of its children, and the degree of a $\wedge$ or $\times$ gate is the sum of the degrees of its children.

Definition 3. sSC^i *is the class of languages accepted by Boolean circuits of polynomial size, $O(\log^i n)$ width and polynomial degree.*

$\#sSC^i$ is the class of functions computed by arithmetic circuits of polynomial size, $O(\log^i n)$ width and polynomial degree. Equivalently, it is the class of functions counting the number of proof trees in an sSC^i circuit.

$$sSC = \bigcup_{i \geq 0} sSC^i \qquad\qquad \#sSC = \bigcup_{i \geq 0} \#sSC^i$$

Note that SC circuits can have internal NOT gates as well; moving the negations to the leaves only doubles the width. However, when we restrict degree as in sSC, we explicitly disallow internal negations. The circuits have only AND and OR gates, and constants and literals appear at leaves.

It is known that polynomial-size circuits of polynomial degree, irrespective of width or depth, characterize LogCFL, which is equivalent to semi-unbounded log depth circuits SAC^1, and hence is contained in NC^2 [23,21,24]. This equivalence also holds in the arithmetic settings for $\#$ and for Gap, see [25,19,4]. Thus

Proposition 2. *For all $i \geq 0$,*
(1) $sSC^i \subseteq$ LogCFL.   (2) $\#sSC^i \subseteq \#$LogCFL.   (3) $GapsSC^i \subseteq$ GapLogCFL

A BP can be viewed as a skew circuit, and a skew circuit's degree is bounded by its size; so BWBP is contained in sSC^0. But $SC^0 =$ BWBP $= NC^1$. Thus

Proposition 3. $sSC^0 = SC^0 = NC^1$.

If such an equality ($sSC^i = SC^i$) holds for any other level $i \geq 2$, it would bring a larger chunk of SC into the NC hierarchy.

We now show that the individual bits of each $\#sSC^i$ function can be computed in polynomial time using $O(\log^{i+1})$ space. However, the Boolean circuits constructed may not have polynomial degree.

Theorem 3. *For all $i \geq 0$, $\#sSC^i \subseteq GapsSC^i \subseteq SC^{i+1}$*

Proof. We show how to compute $\#sSC^i$ in SC^{i+1}. The result for Gap follows since subtraction can be performed in SC^0.

Let $f \in \#sSC^i$. Let d be the degree bound for f. Then the value of f can be represented using $d \in n^{O(1)}$ bits. By the Chinese Remainder Theorem, f can be computed exactly from its residues modulo the first $O(d^{O(1)})$ primes, each of which has $O(\log d) = O(\log n)$ bits. These primes are small enough that they can be found in log space. Further, due to [11], the computation of f from its residues can also be performed in L= SC^1; see also [2]. If the residues can be computed in SC^k, then the overall computation will also be in SC^k because we can think of composing the computations in a sequential machine with a simultaneous time-space bound.

It thus remains to compute $f \bmod p$ where p is a small prime. Consider a bottom-up evaluation of the $\#sSC^i$ circuit, where we keep track of the values of all intermediate nodes modulo p. The space needed is $\log p$ times the width of the circuit, that is, $O(\log^{i+1} n)$ space, while the time is clearly polynomial.   □

In particular, bits of an #sSC^0 function can be computed in SC^1, which equals L. On the other hand, similar to the discussion preceding Proposition 3, we know that #BWBP is contained in #sSC^0. Thus

Corollary 1. FNC^1 ⊆ #BWBP ⊆ #sSC^0 ⊆ FL.
GapNC^1 = GapBWBP ⊆ GapsSC^0 ⊆ FL.

We cannot establish any direct connection between #sSC^0 and #NC^1. Thus this is potentially a third arithmetization of the Boolean class NC^1, the other two being #BWBP and #NC^1.

We also do not know whether sSC^1 properly restricts SC^1=L. Even if it does, it cannot fall below NC^1, since NC^1 = sSC^0(Proposition 3). We note that this holds in the arithmetic setting as well:

Theorem 4. #NC^1 ⊆ #sSC^1.

Proof. From Theorem 2, we know that #NC^1 equals #LWF. But an LWF has log width and has poly degree since it is a formula; hence #LWF is in #sSC^1. □

Since sSC is sandwiched between NC^1 and LogCFL, both of which are closed under complementation, it is natural to ask whether the levels of sSC are closed under complement. While we are unable to show this, we show that for each i, co-sSC^i is contained in sSC^{2i}; thus sSC as a whole is closed under complement.

Theorem 5. *For each $i \geq 1$, co-sSC^i is contained in sSC^{2i}.*

Proof. Our approach for complementing sSC^i is similar to that of [7] for complementing LogCFL. ([7] uses inductive counting on the circuit equivalent of LogCFL, semi-unbounded log depth circuits.) However, one problem is that the construction of [7] uses NC^1 circuits for threshold internally, and if we use these directly, the degree will blow up. So for the thresholds, we use the construction from [26]. A careful analysis of the parameters then yields the result.

Let C_n be a boolean circuit of length l, width $w = O(\log^i n)$ and degree p. Without loss of generality, assume that C_n has only ∨ gates at odd levels and ∧ gates at even levels. Also assume that all gates have fan in 2 or less. If an input literal is read by a gate at level k, the literal is counted as a gate at level $k - 1$. We construct a boolean circuit C_n', which computes C_n. C_n' contains a copy of C_n. Besides, for each level k of C_n, C_n' contains the gates $cc(g|c)$ where g is a gate at level k of C_n and $0 \leq c \leq w$, and gates $count(c, k)$ for $0 \leq c \leq w$. These represent the conditional complement of g assuming the count at the previous level is c, and verifying that the count at level k is c, and are defined as follows:

$$cc(g|c) = \begin{cases} cc(a_1|c) \vee cc(a_2|c), & \text{if } g = a_1 \wedge a_2 \\ Th^c(b_1, \cdots, b_j), & \text{if } g = a_1 \vee a_2 \end{cases}$$

where $b_1, \cdots, b_j$ range over all gates at the previous level except a_1 and a_2.

$$count(c, k) = \begin{cases} Th1(c, k) \wedge \bigvee_{d=0}^{w}[count(d, k - 1) \wedge Th0(c, k, d)] & \text{if } k > 0 \\ 1 \text{ if } k = 0, c = \# \text{ of inputs with value 1 at level 0} \\ 0 \text{ otherwise} \end{cases}$$

Th^c is the c-threshold value of its inputs , $Th1(c, k) = Th^c$ of all original gates at current level, $Th0(c, k, d)$ is Th^{k-c} of all $cc(g|d)$ at the current level. Finally, the output gate of C'_n is $comp(g) = \bigvee_{c=0}^{w} Count(c, l-1) \wedge cc(g|c)$, where g is the output gate of C_n, at level l. Correctness follows from the analysis in [7].

A crucial observation, used also in [7], is that any root-to-leaf path goes through at most two threshold blocks.

To achieve small width and small degree, we have to be careful about how we implement the thresholds. Since the inputs to the threshold blocks are computed in the circuit, we need monotone constructions. We do not know whether monotone NC^1 is in monotone sSC^0. But for our purpose, the following is sufficient: Lemma 4.3 of [26] says that any threshold on K bits can be computed by a monotone branching program of width $O(K)$ and size $O(K^2)$ (hence degree $O(K^2)$). The thresholds we use have $K = O(w^2)$. The threshold blocks can be staggered so that the $O(w^2)$ extra width appears as an additive rather than multiplicative factor. Hence the width of C'_n is $O(w^2)$.

Let q be the degree of a threshold block; $q \in O(K^2) \in O(w^4)$. If the inputs to a threshold block come from computations of degree p, then the overall degree is pq. A $cc(g|c)$ gate is a threshold block applied to gates of C_n at the previous level, and these gates all have degree at most p. So the $cc(g|c)$ gate has degree at most pq. Also, the degree of a $count(c, k)$ gate is bounded by the sum of (1) the degree of a $count(c, k-1)$ gate, (2) the degree of a threshold block applied to gates of C_n, and (3) the degree of a threshold block applied to $cc(g|c)$ gates. Hence it is bounded by $p^{O(1)}w^{O(1)}l$, where l is the depth of C_n. Thus, the entire circuit has polynomial degree.   □

6   Extensions and Closure Properties

In this section, we show that some closure properties that hold for $\#NC^1$ and $\#BWBP$ also hold for $\#sSC^0$. (Construction details are omitted due to space restrictions.) The simplest closures are under addition and multiplication, and it is straightforward to see that $\#sSC^0$ is closed under these. The next are weak sum and weak product: add (or multiply) the value of a two-argument function over a polynomially large range of values for the second argument. (See [10,27] for formal definitions.) A simple staggering of computations yields:

Lemma 3. For each $i \geq 0$, $\#sSC^i$ is closed under weak sum and weak product.

$\#NC^1$ and $\#BWBP$ are known to be closed under decrement $f \ominus 1 = \max\{f - 1, 0\}$ and under division by a constant $\lfloor \frac{f}{m} \rfloor$. ([1] credits Barrington with this observation for $\#NC^1$.) We show that these closures hold for $\#sSC^0$ as well. The following property will be useful.

Proposition 4. For any f in $\#sSC^0$ or $\#NC^1$, and for any constant m, the value $f \mod m$ is computable in FNC^1.

Lemma 4. $\#sSC^0$ is closed under decrement and under division by a constant.

Another consequence of Proposition 4 can be seen as follows. We have three competing arithmetizations of the Boolean class NC^1. The most natural one is #NC^1, defined by arithmetic circuits. It contains #BWBP, which is contained in #sSC^0, though we do not know the relationship between #NC^1 and #sSC^0. Applying a "> 0?" test to any yields the same class, NC^1. We show that applying a "$\equiv 0 \bmod p$?" test to any also yields the same language class, namely NC^1.

Definition 4. *For a function class #C, Mod$_p$C denotes the class of languages L such that for some $f \in$ #C, $\forall x \in \Sigma^*$: $x \in L \Longleftrightarrow f(x) \equiv 0 \bmod p$.*

Theorem 6. *For any fixed p, Mod$_p$BWBP = Mod$_p$sSC^0 = Mod$_p$NC^1 = NC^1.*

Proof. From Proposition 4, for $f \in \{$#sSC^0, #BWBP, #NC$^1\}$, and a constant m, the value $[f(x) \bmod m]$ can be computed in FNC^1. Hence the predicate $[f(x) \equiv 0 \bmod m]$ can be computed in NC^1.   □

Another natural way to produce boolean circuits from arithmetic circuits is by allowing the circuit to perform test-for-zero operations. Such circuits, known as *Arithmetic-Boolean* circuits, were introduced by von zur Gathen, and have been studied in the literature; see e.g. [28,9,3]. We extend this by looking at bounded width restrictions.

Definition 5. *Let C be any of the arithmetic circuit classes studied above. Then Arith-Bool C is defined to be the set of languages accepted by circuits from C with the following additional gates, and with Boolean output. (Here y is either a constant or a literal.)*

$$test(f) = \begin{cases} 0 & if\ f = 0 \\ 1 & otherwise \end{cases} \qquad select(f_0, f_1, y) = \begin{cases} f_0 & if\ y = 0 \\ f_1 & if\ y = 1 \end{cases}$$

Assigning $deg(select(f_0, f_1, y)) = 1 + \max\{deg(f_0), deg(f_1)\}$ and $deg(test(f)) = deg(f)$, we have the following,

Lemma 5. *(1) Arith-Bool#NC^1 = #NC^1.[3] (2) Arith-Bool#BWBP = #BWBP. (3) Arith-Bool#sSC^0 = #sSC^0*

However, for the Gap classes, we do not have such a collapse. Analogous to the definitions of SPP and SPL, define a class SNC^1: it consists of those languages L for which the characteristic function χ_L is in GapNC^1. Then we have:

Lemma 6. *Arith-BoolGapNC^1 = GapNC^1 if and only if SNC^1 = C$_=$NC^1.*

References

1. M. Agrawal, E. Allender, and S. Datta. On TC^0, AC^0, and arithmetic circuits. *Journal of Computer and System Sciences*, 60(2):395–421, 2000.
2. E. Allender. The division breakthroughs. *BEATCS: Bulletin of the European Association for Theoretical Computer Science*, 74, 2001.
3. E. Allender. Arithmetic circuits and counting complexity classes. In *Complexity of Computations and Proofs*, Quaderni di Matematica Vol. 13, pages 33–72, 2004.

4. E. Allender, J. Jiao, M. Mahajan, and V. Vinay. Non-commutative arithmetic circuits: depth reduction and size lower bounds. *Theoretical Computer Science*, 209:47–86, 1998.
5. R. Alur and P. Madhusudan. Visibly pushdown languages. In *STOC*, pages 202–211, 2004.
6. D. Barrington. Bounded-width polynomial-size branching programs recognize exactly those languages in NC^1. *JCSS*, 38(1):150–164, 1989.
7. A. Borodin, S. Cook, P. Dymond, W. Ruzzo, and M. Tompa. Two applications of inductive counting for complementation problems. *SIAM Journal of Computation*, 18(3):559–578, 1989.
8. B. V. Braunmuhl and R. Verbeek. Input-driven languages are recognized in log n space. In *Proc. FCT, LNCS*, pages 40–51, 1983.
9. S. Buss, S. Cook, A. Gupta, and V. Ramachandran. An optimal parallel algorithm for formula evaluation. *SIAM J. Comput.*, 21(4):755–780, 1992.
10. H. Caussinus, P. McKenzie, D. Thérien, and H. Vollmer. Nondeterministic NC^1 computation. *JCSS*, 57:200–212, 1998.
11. A. Chiu, G. Davida, and B. Litow. Division in logspace-uniform NC^1. *RAIRO Theoretical Informatics and Applications*, 35:259–276, 2001.
12. S. A. Cook. Deterministic CFL's are accepted simultaneously in polynomial time and log squared space. In *STOC*, pages 338–345, 1979.
13. P. Dymond and S. Cook. Complexity theory of parallel time and hardware. *Information and Computation*, 80:205–226, 1989.
14. P. W. Dymond. Input-driven languages are in $\log n$ depth. In *Information Processing Letters*, pages 26, 247–250, 1988.
15. H. Fernau, K.-J. Lange, and K. Reinhardt. Advocating ownership. In V. Chandru and V. Vinay, editors, *Proc. 16th FST&TCS, LNCS 1180*, pages 286–297, 1996.
16. S. Istrail and D. Zivkovic. Bounded width polynomial size Boolean formulas compute exactly those functions in AC^0. *Infor. Proc. Letters*, 50:211–216, 1994.
17. D. S. Johnson. A catalog of complexity classes. In J. van Leeuwen, ed., *Handbook of Theoretical Computer Science, Volume A*, pages 67–161. 1990.
18. K. Mehlhorn. Pebbling mountain ranges and its application to DCFL-recognition. In *Proc. 7th ICALP*, pages 422–432, 1980.
19. R. Niedermeier and P. Rossmanith. Unambiguous auxiliary pushdown automata and semi-unbounded fan-in circuits. *Inform. and Comp.*, 118(2):227–245, 1995.
20. N. Nisan. RL $\subseteq$ SC. *Computational Complexity*, 4(11):1–11, 1994.
21. W. Ruzzo. Tree-size bounded alternation. *Journal of Computer and System Sciences*, 21:218–235, 1980.
22. S.Cook. Characterizations of pushdown machines in terms of time-bounded computers. *Journal of Assoc. Comput. Mach.*, 18:4–18, 1971.
23. I. Sudborough. On the tape complexity of deterministic context-free language. *Journal of Association of Computing Machinery*, 25(3):405–414, 1978.
24. H. Venkateswaran. Properties that characterize LogCFL. *Journal of Computer and System Sciences*, 42:380–404, 1991.
25. V. Vinay. Counting auxiliary pushdown automata and semi-unbounded arithmetic circuits. In *Proc. Structure in Complexity Theory Conference*, pages 270–284, 1991.
26. V. Vinay. Hierarchies of circuit classes that are closed under complement. In *Proc. 11th Annual IEEE Conference on Computational Complexity*, pages 108–117, 1996.
27. H. Vollmer. *Introduction to Circuit Complexity: A Uniform Approach*. Springer-Verlag New York Inc., 1999.
28. J. von zur Gathen and G. Seroussi. Boolean circuits versus arithmetic circuits. *Information and Computation*, 91(1):142–154, 1991.

The Polynomially Bounded
Perfect Matching Problem Is in NC²*

Manindra Agrawal[1], Thanh Minh Hoang[2], and Thomas Thierauf[3]

[1] IIT Kanpur, India
[2] Ulm University, Germany
[3] Aalen University, Germany

Abstract. The *perfect matching problem* is known to be in **P**, in randomized **NC**, and it is hard for **NL**. Whether the perfect matching problem is in **NC** is one of the most prominent open questions in complexity theory regarding parallel computations.

Grigoriev and Karpinski [GK87] studied the perfect matching problem for bipartite graphs with polynomially bounded permanent. They showed that for such bipartite graphs the problem of deciding the existence of a perfect matchings is in **NC²**, and counting and enumerating all perfect matchings is in **NC³**. For general graphs with a polynomially bounded number of perfect matchings, they show both problems to be in **NC³**.

In this paper we extend and improve these results. We show that for any graph that has a polynomially bounded number of perfect matchings, we can construct all perfect matchings in **NC²**. We extend the result to weighted graphs.

1 Introduction

Whether there is an **NC**-algorithm for testing if a given graph contains a perfect matching is an outstanding open question in complexity theory. The problem of deciding the existence of a perfect matching in a graph is known to be in **P** [Edm65], in randomized **NC²** [MVV87], and in nonuniform **SPL** [ARZ99]. This problem is very fundamental for other computational problems (see e.g. [KR98]). Another reason why a derandomization of the perfect matching problem would be very interesting is, that it is a special case of the polynomial identity testing problem.

Since no **NC**-algorithm is known for testing the existence of perfect matchings in a common graph, some special cases of the perfect matching problem have been investigated intensively. For example, **NC**-algorithms have been found the perfect matching problem for regular bipartite graphs [LPV81], dense graphs [DHK93], strongly chordal graphs [DK86] and planar graphs [Kas67, Vaz89]. The unique perfect matching problem is considered in [HMT06].

Grigoriev and Karpinski [GK87] considered the perfect matching problem for bipartite graphs with polynomially bounded number of perfect matchings, i.e. a

---

* Supported by DFG grant Scho 302/7-1.

W. Thomas and P. Weil (Eds.): STACS 2007, LNCS 4393, pp. 489–499, 2007.

promise problem. They showed that the decision version of the perfect matching problem for such graphs is solvable in $\mathbf{NC}^2$. and that all perfect matchings for such graphs can be constructed in $\mathbf{NC}^3$. For general graphs, their techniques bring both problems into $\mathbf{NC}^3$.

We extend the result of Grigoriev and Karpinski [GK87] to arbitrary weighted graphs and improve the upper bound to $\mathbf{NC}^2$. That is, we show that on input of some graph G one can construct all perfect matchings of G in $\mathbf{NC}^2$, if G has a polynomially bounded number of perfect matchings. We show the result for bipartite graphs in Section 3 and then extend it to general graphs in Section 4. In Section 5 we generalize our techniques to graphs with polynomially bounded weights.

When we restrict ourselves to the decision version or the counting version of the problem, we get logspace counting classes inside $\mathbf{NC}^2$ as upper bounds for these problems.

2   Preliminaries

Let $G = (V, E)$ be an undirected graph. A *matching in* G is a set $M \subseteq E$, such that no two edges in M have a vertex in common. A matching M is called *perfect* if every vertex occurs as an endpoint of some edge in M. Define

$$PM(G) = \{\, M \mid M \text{ is a perfect matching in } G \,\}.$$

Bipartite Graphs. Let G be bipartite, that is we can partition the nodes into $V = L \cup R$ such that there are no edges in L and in R. We assume w.l.o.g. that $|L| = |R| = n$, otherwise G has no perfect matching. The *bipartite adjacency matrix of* G is the $n \times n$ matrix $A = (a_{i,j})$, where

$$a_{i,j} = \begin{cases} 1 & \text{if } (i,j) \in E, \text{ for } i \in L \text{ and } j \in R, \\ 0 & \text{otherwise.} \end{cases}$$

The *bipartite Tutte matrix of* G is the $n \times n$ matrix $T = (t_{i,j})$, where

$$t_{i,j} = a_{i,j} \, x_{i,j},$$

for indeterminates $x_{i,j}$. The determinant of T is

$$\det(T) = \sum_{\pi \in S_n} \text{sign}(\pi) \prod_{i=1}^{n} a_{i,\pi(i)} \, x_{i,\pi(i)}.$$

$\det(T)$ is a multi-linear polynomial. Each non-vanishing term $\text{sign}(\pi) \prod_{i=1}^{n} x_{i,\pi(i)}$ corresponds to one perfect matching $M_\pi = \{\, (i,\pi(i)) \mid 1 \le i \le n \,\} \in PM(G)$. In particular we have

Theorem 1 (Tutte 1952). *Let G be a bipartite graph. G has a perfect matching iff* $\det(T) \neq \mathbf{0}$.

General Graphs. Let G be a graph with n nodes. W.l.o.g. assume that n is even, otherwise G has no perfect matchings. Let $A = (a_{i,j})$ be the $n \times n$ adjacency matrix of G. Note that A is symmetric. The skew-symmetric *Tutte matrix* of G is the $n \times n$ matrix $T = (t_{i,j})$, where

$$t_{i,j} = \begin{cases} a_{i,j}\, x_{i,j}, & \text{if } i \leq j, \\ -a_{j,i}\, x_{j,i}, & \text{otherwise}, \end{cases}$$

for indeterminates $x_{i,j}$. The Pfaffian of T is

$$\mathrm{pf}(T) = \sum_{M \in PM(G)} \mathrm{sign}(M) \cdot \prod_{\substack{(i,j)\,\in\,M \\ i < j}} a_{i,j}\, x_{i,j}.$$

The sign is defined as follows. Consider perfect matching

$$M = \{(i_1, j_1), (i_2, j_2), \ldots, (i_k, j_k)\} \in PM(G)$$

for $k = n/2$. By convention, we have $i_l < j_l$ for all l. The *sign of* M is defined as the sign of the permutation

$$\begin{pmatrix} 1 & 2 & 3 & 4 & \cdots & n-1 & n \\ i_1 & j_1 & i_2 & j_2 & \cdots & i_k & j_k \end{pmatrix} \in S_n$$

It is known that the sign of M does not depend on the order in which the edges are given, i.e. the sign is well defined.

$\mathrm{pf}(T)$ is a multi-linear polynomial. Each non-vanishing term $\mathrm{sign}(M)$. $\prod_{\substack{(i,j)\,\in\,M \\ i<j}} x_{i,j}$ corresponds to one perfect matching $M \in PM(G)$. The Pfaffian and the determinant of a matrix are known to be closely related.

Theorem 2. $\det(T) = \mathrm{pf}^2(T)$.

In particular we have

Theorem 3 (Tutte 1952). *Graph G has a perfect matching iff* $\det(T) \neq 0$.

Linear Algebra. The following matrix is called a *Vandermonde matrix*

$$V = \begin{pmatrix} 1 & 1 & \cdots & 1 \\ a_1 & a_2 & \cdots & a_n \\ a_1^2 & a_2^2 & \cdots & a_n^2 \\ \vdots & \vdots & & \vdots \\ a_1^{n-1} & a_2^{n-1} & \cdots & a_n^{n-1} \end{pmatrix}.$$

It is known that

$$\det(V) = \prod_{i \neq j}(a_i - a_j).$$

Hence, in the case when $a_1, a_2, \ldots, a_n$ are pairwise distinct the matrix V is nonsingular. The inverse can be written as

$$V^{-1} = \frac{1}{\det(V)} \mathrm{adj}(V),$$

where $\mathrm{adj}(V)$ is the adjoint of V.

Complexity Classes. The classes $\mathbf{NC}^k$, for fixed k, consists of families of Boolean circuit with $\wedge$-, $\vee$-gates of fan-in 2, and $\neg$-gates, of depth $O(\log^k n)$ and of polynomial size. $\mathbf{NC} = \cup_{k \geq 0} \mathbf{NC}^k$.

Standard arithmetic operations like addition, subtraction, multiplication and integer division are known to be in $\mathbf{NC}^1$. Many problems from linear algebra like computing powers of a matrix are in $\mathbf{NC}^2$. A break-through result was that the determinant of a matrix is computable in $\mathbf{NC}^2$ [Ber84].

For a nondeterministic Turing machine M, we denote the number of accepting and rejecting computation paths on input x by $acc_M(x)$ and by $rej_M(x)$, respectively. The difference of these two quantities is gap_M, i.e., for all x: $gap_M(x) = acc_M(x) - rej_M(x)$. The complexity class $\mathbf{GapL}$ is defined as the set of all functions $gap_M(x)$, where M is a nondeterministic logspace bounded Turing machine. Most notably, we have

Theorem 4. [Dam91, Tod91, Vin91, Val92] *The determinant of an integer matrix is complete for* $\mathbf{GapL}$.

And similarly for the Pfaffian we have

Theorem 5. [MSV99] *The Pfaffian of an integer matrix is complete for* $\mathbf{GapL}$

$\mathbf{GapL}$ is closed under addition, subtraction, and multiplication. It is not known to be closed under integer division. In particular, consider the inverse of matrix like in the above example, $V^{-1} = \frac{1}{\det(V)} \mathrm{adj}(V)$. The entries of the adjoint matrix are determinants and can therefore be computed in $\mathbf{GapL}$. But we don't know whether the entries of V^{-1} can be computed in $\mathbf{GapL}$ too because of the division by $\det(V)$. However, with the adjoint matrix we have the entries of $\det(V)V^{-1}$ in $\mathbf{GapL}$.

The class $\mathbf{C}_{=}\mathbf{L}$ (*Exact Counting in Logspace*) is the class of sets A for which there exists a function $f \in \mathbf{GapL}$ such that $\forall x : x \in A \Longleftrightarrow f(x) = 0$. A problem complete for $\mathbf{C}_{=}\mathbf{L}$ is the singularity problem, where one has to decide whether the determinant of an integer matrix is zero. $\mathbf{C}_{=}\mathbf{L}$ is closed under union and intersection, but is not known to be closed under complement.

Problems that can be expressed as a (unbounded) boolean combination of sets from $\mathbf{C}_{=}\mathbf{L}$ are captured by the class $\mathbf{AC}^0(\mathbf{C}_{=}\mathbf{L})$ of sets being $\mathbf{AC}^0$-reducible to $\mathbf{C}_{=}\mathbf{L}$. Allender, Beals, and Ogihara [ABO99] defined and studied this class. They show for example that the problem to decide whether a system of linear equations has a solution is complete for $\mathbf{AC}^0(\mathbf{C}_{=}\mathbf{L})$. We have the following inclusions.

$$\mathbf{NL} \subseteq \mathbf{C}_{=}\mathbf{L} \subseteq \mathbf{AC}^0(\mathbf{C}_{=}\mathbf{L}) \subseteq \mathbf{NC}^2.$$

Cook [Coo85] defined the class DET as the class of sets that are $\mathbf{NC}^1$-reducible to the determinant. Since the determinant is complete for $\mathbf{GapL}$, we denote DET by $\mathbf{NC}^1(\mathbf{GapL})$. We have $\mathbf{NC}^1(\mathbf{GapL}) \subseteq \mathbf{NC}^2$.

3   Bipartite Graphs

In this section we prove the following theorem.

Theorem 6. *All perfect matchings of a bipartite graph with a polynomially bounded number of perfect matchings can be constructed in $\mathbf{NC}^2$.*

Let $G = (V, E)$ be a bipartite graph with $|V| = 2n$ nodes and let $A = (a_{i,j})$ be the bipartite adjacency matrix of G. Let p be a polynomial and assume that G has at most $p(n)$ perfect matchings. Define

$$b_{i,j}^{(m)}(x) = a_{i,j} \; p_{i,j} \; x^{m^{ni+j} \bmod r},$$

where $p_{i,j}$ are pairwise different primes, x is an indeterminate, r is a prime such that $r > n^2 p^2(n)$, and $0 \leq m < r$. We can choose $\max\{\, p_{i,j} \mid 1 \leq i, j \leq n \,\} = O(n^3)$ by the Prime Number Theorem. For $1 \leq m < r$ define matrices

$$B_m(x) = \left(b_{i,j}^{(m)}(x) \right).$$

The determinant of $B_m(x)$ is a polynomial $d_m(x)$, where

$$d_m(x) = \det(B_m(x)) = \sum_{\pi \in S_n} \mathrm{sign}(\pi) \prod_{i=1}^{n} a_{i,\pi(i)} \; p_{i,\pi(i)} \; x^{m^{ni+\pi(i)} \bmod r}$$

$$= \sum_{\pi \in S_n} \mathrm{sign}(\pi) (\prod_{i=1}^{n} a_{i,\pi(i)} \; p_{i,\pi(i)}) \; x^{e_m(\pi)},$$

where $e_m(\pi) = \sum_{i=1}^{n}(m^{ni+\pi(i)} \bmod r)$ are the exponents of x in $d_m(x)$.

The crucial point here is, that the summands of $e_m(\pi)$ are taken modulo r. Therefore the degree of polynomial $d_m(x)$ is bounded by $D = n(r - 1)$, which is a polynomial in n. Without the mod r we would have exponential degree. On the other hand, without the mod r, for any $\pi \in S_n$ the exponent of x is unique. We show in the following that this also holds modulo r, at least for some m.

Lemma 1. *Let $\pi_1, \ldots, \pi_t \in S_n$ for some $t \leq p(n)$. Then there exists an $m < r$ such that $e_m(\pi_i) \neq e_m(\pi_j)$, for all $i \neq j$.*

Proof. The values $e_m(\pi_i)$ can be seen as evaluations of polynomials over the field $\mathbb{Z}_r$ in the following way. Define

$$q_\pi(z) = \sum_{i=1}^{n} z^{ni+\pi(i)}.$$

Then we have $e_m(\pi_i) \equiv q_\pi(m) \pmod r$, for any m. To prove the lemma, we have to show that $q_{\pi_i}(m) \not\equiv q_{\pi_j}(m) \pmod r$, for some $m < r$ and for all $i \neq j$.

Notice first that $q_{\pi_i} \neq q_{\pi_j}$, for any $i \neq j$. Now the degree of the q-polynomials is bounded by $n^2 + n \leq 2n^2$. Hence any two of them can agree on at most $2n^2$ points. Thus in any field of size larger than $\binom{t}{2} 2n^2$ we have a point where all polynomials q_{π_i} pairwise differ. Note that

$$\binom{t}{2} 2n^2 \leq t^2 n^2 \leq p^2(n) n^2 < r.$$

Hence there is an appropriate m in $\mathbb{Z}_r$. $\square$

It follows that if G has t perfect matchings for some $t \leq p(n)$, then there exists an $m < r$ such that polynomial $d_m(x)$ has precisely t terms. That is,

$$d_m(x) = \sum_{k=0}^{D} c_k^{(m)} x^k,$$

where precisely t of the coefficients $c_k^{(m)}$ are non-zero. Moreover, the non-zero coefficients are of the form

$$c_k^{(m)} = \text{sign}(\pi) \prod_{i=1}^{n} p_{i,\pi(i)}$$

for some $\pi \in S_n$ such that $k = e_m(\pi)$. We want to compute these coefficients.

Define the Vandermonde matrix $V = (v_{i,j})$ by $v_{i,j} = i^j$, for $0 \leq i, j \leq D$. Define vectors

$$d_m = (d_m(0) \ \ d_m(1) \ \cdots \ d_m(D))^T$$
$$c_m = (c_0^{(m)} \ \ c_1^{(m)} \ \cdots \ c_D^{(m)})^T$$

The evaluation of polynomial $d_m(x)$ at points $0, \ldots, D$ can now be written as

$$d_m = V c_m.$$

Therefore we obtain the coefficient vector by the equation

$$c_m = V^{-1} d_m.$$

By the latter equation, c_m can be computed in $\mathbf{NC}^2$.

Lemma 2. $c_m \in \mathbf{NC}^2$.

Proof. The matrices V and $B_m(x)$ can be computed in $\mathbf{NC}^1$ for any $x \leq D$. Vector d_m can be computed by computing the determinant of matrix $B_m(x)$ for different values of x, which is in $\mathbf{NC}^2$ by Theorem 4. Also, V^{-1} can be computed in $\mathbf{NC}^2$. $\square$

The final step is to determine the prime factors $p_{i,j}$ of the non-zero coefficients in $\boldsymbol{c}_m$, because these factors define perfect matchings as explained above. Given a non-zero $c_k^{(m)}$, we can test in $\mathbf{NC}^1$ whether $c_k^{(m)} \equiv 0 \pmod{p_{i,j}}$ since all $p_{i,j}$ are $O(n^3)$. In summary, we can construct all perfect matchings of G in $\mathbf{NC}^2$ if we have the right value of m.

To find the right value for m, we compute $\boldsymbol{c}_m$ for all $m \in \{1, \ldots, r-1\}$ in parallel. We can take any m such that $\boldsymbol{c}_m$ has a maximum number of non-zero entries. The procedure remains in $\mathbf{NC}^2$.

In fact, we get a slightly better upper bound. Note first that the entries of all vectors $\det(V)\boldsymbol{c}_m = \mathrm{adj}(V)\boldsymbol{d}_m$ can be computed in $\mathbf{GapL}$. Having all these values, the remaining computation can be done in $\mathbf{NC}^1$. Recall in particular that integer division is in $\mathbf{NC}^1$ [CDL01].

Suppose we want to know only whether there exists some perfect matching (*decision problem*) or count the number of perfect matchings (*counting problem*). For the decision problem it suffices to determine whether $\boldsymbol{c}_m$ is non-zero for some m. Note that this is equivalent to $\det(V)\boldsymbol{c}_m$ being non-zero. For the counting problem we have to count the number of non-zero entries of $\boldsymbol{c}_m$, for an m such that $\boldsymbol{c}_m$ has a maximum number of non-zero entries.

Corollary 1. *For bipartite graphs with a polynomially bounded number of perfect matchings*

1. *the decision problem is in* $\mathbf{coC_=L}$,
2. *the counting problem is in* $\mathbf{AC}^0(\mathbf{C_=L})$,
3. *the construction problem is in* $\mathbf{NC}^1(\mathbf{GapL})$.

4   General Graphs

In this section we extend Theorem 6 to non-bipartite graphs.

Theorem 7. *All perfect matchings of a graph with a polynomially bounded number of perfect matchings can be constructed in* $\mathbf{NC}^2$.

Let $G = (V, E)$ be an undirected graph with $|V| = n$ nodes. We assume that n is even, otherwise G has no perfect matchings. Let $A = (a_{i,j})$ be the adjacency matrix of G. Let p be a polynomial and assume that G has at most $p(n)$ perfect matchings. We define matrices $B_m(x) = \left(b_{i,j}^{(m)}(x)\right)$ in a similar fashion as before. The definition is now according to the Tutte matrix of G:

$$b_{i,j}^{(m)}(x) = \begin{cases} a_{i,j}\, p_{i,j}\, x^{m^{ni+j} \bmod r}, & \text{if } i \leq j, \\ -a_{j,i}\, p_{j,i}\, x^{m^{nj+i} \bmod r}, & \text{otherwise,} \end{cases}$$

for pairwise different primes $p_{i,j}$ of size $O(n^3)$, an indeterminate x, a prime r such that $r > n^2 p^2(n)$, and $1 \leq m < r$.

The Pfaffian of $B_m(x)$ is a polynomial $p_m(x)$, where

$$p_m(x) = \text{pf}(B_m(x)) = \sum_{M \in PM(G)} \text{sign}(M) \cdot \prod_{\substack{(i,j) \in M \\ i < j}} a_{i,j} \, p_{i,j} \, x^{m^{ni+j} \bmod r}$$

$$= \sum_{M \in PM(G)} \text{sign}(M) \cdot \left(\prod_{\substack{(i,j) \in M \\ i < j}} a_{i,j} \, p_{i,j} \right) x^{e_m(M)},$$

where

$$e_m(M) = \sum_{\substack{(i,j) \in M \\ i < j}} (m^{ni+j} \bmod r)$$

are the exponents of x in $p_m(x)$. Similar as in Lemma 1 we have that there is some $m < r$ where the exponents $e_m(M)$ pairwise differ.

Note that $e_m(M) \leq (r-1)n/2$. Let $D = (r-1)n/2$. Then we can write

$$p_m(x) = \sum_{k=0}^{D} c_k^{(m)} x^k.$$

Define the Vandermonde matrix $V = (v_{i,j})$ by $v_{i,j} = i^j$, for $0 \leq i, j \leq D$. Define vectors

$$\boldsymbol{p}_m = (p_m(0) \;\; p_m(1) \;\; \cdots \;\; p_m(D))^T$$
$$\boldsymbol{c}_m = (c_0^{(m)} \;\; c_1^{(m)} \;\; \cdots \;\; c_D^{(m)})^T$$

As in the bipartite case we have $\boldsymbol{p}_m = V\boldsymbol{c}_m$, from which we get $\boldsymbol{c}_m = V^{-1}\boldsymbol{p}_m$. By Theorem 5, $\boldsymbol{c}_m$ can be computed in $\mathbf{NC}^2$.

Corollary 2. *For graphs with a polynomially bounded number of perfect matchings,*

1. *the decision problem is in* $\mathbf{coC_=L}$,
2. *the counting problem is in* $\mathbf{AC}^0(\mathbf{C_=L})$,
3. *the construction problem are in* $\mathbf{NC}^1(\mathbf{GapL})$.

5   Weighted Graphs

In this section we extend Theorem 7 to graphs with small weights. Let $G = (V, E)$ be an undirected graph with $|V| = n$ nodes. Let $A = (a_{i,j})$ be the adjacency matrix of G and $W = (w_{i,j})$ be the symmetric matrix that gives weight $w_{i,j}$ to edge (i, j), where all weights are polynomially bounded in n.

There are several variants of problems we might consider: the *minimal perfect matching problem* asks for a perfect matching of minimum weight. In its promise version, we assume that there are at most polynomially many perfect matching of minimum weight. Analogously, there is the *maximum perfect matching problem*.

But actually, we can solve a more general problem. It suffices that for some weight w there are at most $p(n)$ many perfect matching of weight w, for some polynomial p.

Theorem 8. *Let G be a weighted graph with polynomially bounded weights such that G has a polynomially bounded number of perfect matchings of some weight w. Then all perfect matchings of G of weight w can be constructed in $\mathbf{NC}^2$.*

Define matrices $B_m(x,y) = \left(b_{i,j}^{(m)}(x,y) \right)$ in two variables x and y that incorporate the weights of G:

$$b_{i,j}^{(m)}(x,y) = \begin{cases} a_{i,j}\ p_{i,j}\ y^{w_{i,j}}\ x^{m^{ni+j}}\bmod r, & \text{if } i \leq j, \\ -a_{j,i}\ p_{j,i}\ y^{w_{j,i}}\ x^{m^{nj+i}}\bmod r, & \text{otherwise,} \end{cases}$$

for pairwise different primes $p_{i,j}$ of size $O(n^3)$, indeterminates x and y, a prime r such that $r > n^2 p^2(n)$, and $1 \leq m < r$.

The Pfaffian of $B_m(x,y)$ is a polynomial $p_m(x,y)$, where

$$p_m(x,y) = \mathrm{pf}(B_m(x,y)) = \sum_{M \in PM(G)} \mathrm{sign}(M) \cdot \prod_{\substack{(i,j)\,\in\,M \\ i<j}} a_{i,j}\ p_{i,j}\ y^{w_{i,j}}\ x^{m^{ni+j}}\bmod r$$

$$= \sum_{M \in PM(G)} \mathrm{sign}(M) \cdot \Big(\prod_{\substack{(i,j)\,\in\,M \\ i<j}} a_{i,j}\ p_{i,j} \Big)\ y^{w(M)}\ x^{e_m(M)}$$

where $e_m(M) = \sum_{\substack{(i,j)\,\in\,M \\ i<j}} (m^{ni+j} \bmod r)$. By a similar argument as in Lemma 1 we have that there is some $m < r$ where the exponents $e_m(M)$ pairwise differ, and this suffices for our purpose.

The degree of x in $p_m(x,y)$ is bounded by $(r-1)n/2$. Let $d = (r-1)n/2 + 1$, so that the degree of x in $p_m(x,y)$ is strictly less than d. We transform $p_m(x,y)$ into polynomial $P_m(x)$ with just one variable by setting

$$P_m(x) = p_m(x, x^d).$$

Then we have

$$P_m(x) = \sum_{M \in PM(G)} \mathrm{sign}(M) \cdot \Big(\prod_{\substack{(i,j)\,\in\,M \\ i<j}} a_{i,j}\ p_{i,j} \Big)\ x^{dw(M)+e_m(M)}$$

By our choice of d we have $d > e_m(M)$. Let w be any fixed weight and consider a perfect matching M of weight w. Then we have

$$dw < dw + e_m(M) < d(w+1).$$

That is, the degrees of x in $P_m(x)$ for perfect matchings of different weights w are in disjoint intervals of the form $(dw, d(w+1))$. Let D be the degree of $P_m(x)$.

We have $D \le d w_{\max}$, where $w_{\max}$ is the maximum weight of any matching. Note that $w_{\max} \le \max\{\, w_{i,j} \mid 1 \le i, j \le n \,\} n/2$. Let

$$P_m(x) = \sum_{k=0}^{D} c_k^{(m)} x^k.$$

We have seen in Section 4 how to determine the coefficients $c_k^{(m)}$ and how to get the perfect matchings from these coefficients in $\mathbf{NC}^2$. Note that the perfect matchings of weight w are represented by the coefficients $c_k^{(m)}$ for $dw < k < d(w+1)$.

Now, if there are at most $p(n)$ perfect matchings of weight w, then all of these will be listed by our $\mathbf{NC}^2$-circuit. Note however that we might list perfect matchings of other weights as well. In case that the promise is for the minimum (or maximum) weight perfect matching, we may discard non-optimal perfect matchings.

6   Open Problems

We have the polynomial bound on the number of perfect matchings given as a promise. Clearly the ultimate goal is to get rid of the promise and to put the perfect matching problem in $\mathbf{NC}^2$. We conjecture that, modulo some small modifications, our approach works for the general case. It remains to prove this.

Acknowledgments

We thank Eric Allender for clarifying various subtleties concerning logspace computations.

References

[ABO99]   E. Allender, R. Beals, and M. Ogihara. The complexity of matrix rank and feasible systems of linear equations. *Computational Complexity*, 8:99 –126, 1999.

[ARZ99]   E. Allender, K. Reinhardt, and S. Zhou. Isolating, matching, and counting: uniform and nonuniform upper bounds. *Journal of Computer and System Sciences*, 59:164–181, 1999.

[Ber84]   S. Berkowitz. On computing the determinant in small parallel time using a small number of processors. *Information Processing Letters*, 18:147–150, 1984.

[CDL01]   A. Chiu, G. Davida, and B. Litow. Division in logspace-uniform $\mathbf{NC}^1$. *RAIRO Theoretical Informatics and Applications*, 35:259–276, 2001.

[Coo85]   S. Cook. A taxonomy of problems with fast parallel algorithms. *Information and Control*, 64:2–22, 1985.

[Dam91]   C. Damm. DET $= \mathrm{L}^{(\#L)}$. Technical Report Informatik-Preprint 8, Fachbereich Informatik der Humboldt-Universität zu Berlin, 1991.

[DHK93] E. Dahlhaus, P. Hajnal, and M. Karpinski. On the parallel complexity of hamiltonian cycles and matching problem in dense graphs. *Journal of Algorithms*, 15:367–384, 1993.

[DK86] E. Dahlhaus and M. Karpinski. The matching problem for strongly chordal graphs is in **NC**. Technical Report 855-CS, University of Bonn, 1986.

[Edm65] J. Edmonds. Maximum matching and a polyhedron with 0-1 vertices. *Journal of Research National Bureau of Standards*, 69:125–130, 1965.

[GK87] D. Grigoriev and M. Karpinski. The matching problem for bipartite graphs with polynomially bounded permanent is in **NC**. In *28th Annual IEEE Symposium on Foundations of Computer Science (FOCS)*, pages 166–172. IEEE Computer Society Press, 1987.

[HMT06] T. M. Hoang, M. Mahajan, and T. Thierauf. On the Bipartite Unique Perfect Matching Problem. In *Automata, Languages and Programming, 33rd International Colloquium, (ICALP)*, Lecture Notes in Computer Science 4051, pages 453–464. Springer-Verlag, 2006.

[Kas67] P. W. Kastelyn. Graph theory and crystal physics. In F. Harary, editor, *Graph Theory and Theoretical Physics*, pages 43–110. Academic Press, 1967.

[KR98] M. Karpinski and W. Rytter. *Fast Parallel Algorithms for Graph Matching Problems*. Oxford University Press, 1998.

[LPV81] G. Lev, M. Pippenger, and L. Valiant. A fast parallel algorithm for routing in permutation networks. *IEEE Transactions on Computers*, C-30:93–100, 1981.

[MSV99] M. Mahajan, P. Subramanya, and V Vinay. A combinatorial algorithm for pfaffians. In *5th Annual International Conference on Computing and Combinatorics (COCOON)*, Lecture Notes in Computer Science 1627, pages 134–143. Springer-Verlag, 1999.

[MVV07] K. Mulmuley, U. Vazirani, and V. Vazirani. Matching is as easy as matrix inversion. In *19th ACM Symposium on Theory of Computing*, pages 345–354. ACM Press, 1987.

[Tod91] S. Toda. Counting problems computationally equivalent to the determinant. Technical Report CSIM 91-07, Dept. of Computer Science and Information Mathematics, University of Electro-Communications, Chofu-shi, Tokyo 182, Japan, 1991.

[Val92] L. Valiant. Why is boolean complexity theory difficult. In M.S. Paterson, editor, *Boolean Function Complexity*, London Mathematical Society Lecture Notes Series 169. Cambridge University Press, 1992.

[Vaz89] V. Vazirani. NC algorithms for computing the number of perfect matchings in $K_{3,3}$-free graphs and related problems. *Information and computation*, 80(2):152–164, 1989.

[Vin91] V Vinay. Counting auxiliary pushdown automata and semi-unbounded arithmetic circuits. In *6th IEEE Conference on Structure in Complexity Theory*, pages 270–284, 1991.

Languages with Bounded Multiparty Communication Complexity*

Arkadev Chattopadhyay[1], Andreas Krebs[2], Michal Koucký[3], Mario Szegedy[4], Pascal Tesson[5], and Denis Thérien[1]

[1] School of Computer Science, McGill University, Montreal
{achatt3, denis}@cs.mcgill.ca
[2] Universität Tübingen, Germany
mail@krebs-net.de
[3] Mathematical Institute, Academy of Sciences, Czech Republic
koucky@math.cas.cz
[4] Rutgers University, New Jersey
szegedy@cs.rutgers.edu
[5] Laval University, Québec
pascal.tesson@ift.ulaval.ca

Abstract. We study languages with bounded communication complexity in the multiparty "input on the forehead model" with worst-case partition. In the two-party case, languages with bounded complexity are exactly those recognized by programs over commutative monoids [19]. This can be used to show that these languages all lie in shallow ACC⁰.

In contrast, we use coding techniques to show that there are languages of arbitrarily large circuit complexity which can be recognized in constant communication by k players for $k \geq 3$. However, we show that if a language has a neutral letter and bounded communication complexity in the k-party game for some fixed k then the language is in fact regular. We give an algebraic characterization of regular languages with this property. We also prove that a symmetric language has bounded k-party complexity for some fixed k iff it has bounded two party complexity.

1 Introduction

The "input on the forehead" multiparty model of communication, introduced by Chandra, Furst and Lipton [7], is a powerful tool in the study of branching programs [2,6,7] and shallow-depth Boolean circuits (among many others [11,13,14]). However, it is still, in many regards, not well-understood as both upper bounds [1,12] and lower bounds [2,7,18] for the model appear very challenging. In particular, good lower bounds on the k-party non-interactive communication complexity of an explicit function f when $k > \log n$ have long been sought since they would

* Supported in part by the NSF (M. Szegedy), NSERC (A. Chattopadhyay, P. Tesson, D. Thérien), FQRNT (D. Thérien), grant GA-CR 201/05/0124, ITI-1M0545 (M. Koucký) and the A.V. Humboldt Foundation (P. Tesson and D. Thérien). We thank Pavel Pudlák for suggesting the use of the Hales-Jewett Theorem.

W. Thomas and P. Weil (Eds.): STACS 2007, LNCS 4393, pp. 500–511, 2007.
© Springer-Verlag Berlin Heidelberg 2007

yield size-lower bounds for ACC^0 circuits computing f [9], and even more modest lower bounds $\Omega(\log^3 n)$ for particular functions like Disjointness in the three-party setting would imply separation of different proof systems [5].

We obtain significant insight into the multiparty model by focusing on functions that have bounded k-party complexity, where $k \geq 3$ is an arbitrary constant. For the two-party model, languages with bounded communication complexity have many nice characterizations [19] implying, in particular, that any language with bounded two-party complexity can be computed by very shallow ACC^0 circuits. In contrast, we show in Section 3 that there are languages with arbitrarily large uniform circuit complexity whose three-party communication complexity is bounded by a constant even for the worst-case partition of the input instances among the players. An analogous result for non-uniform circuit complexity can also be derived. These languages are constructed using specially crafted *error-correcting codes*. Because of these results, we cannot expect to obtain characterizations of languages of bounded multiparty complexity which are as nice as those for the two-player case.

There are several key features that make the multiparty communication model so powerful: first, every input bit is seen by several players, second, every $(k-1)$-tuple of input positions is seen by at least one of the k players, and third, all players know the partitioning of the input, i.e., they know which positions they actually see. Multiparty communication complexity upper bounds typically rely heavily on all these properties. If we remove the first two properties then we obtain essentially the multiparty "input in the hand" model which is computationally even weaker than the two-party communication model. To understand how crucial the last property is, we consider two restricted classes of languages/functions in which this advantage is in some sense taken away.

First, we consider in Section 4 languages with a *neutral letter* [4,3], i.e. a letter which can be inserted or deleted at will in an input word without affecting its membership in the language. We show that every such language having bounded k-party communication complexity for some fixed k is regular. Furthermore, we characterize this class of regular languages in terms of algebraic properties of their minimal automaton. Our results indicate that the presence of a neutral letter is thus a severe handicap in the multiparty game and suggests that it might be easier to prove communication complexity lower bounds under this assumption.

Finally, in Section 5 we use the Ramsey-like theorem of Gallai [10] to prove that for any fixed $k \geq 3$ the *symmetric* functions that can be computed in bounded k-party communication complexity by k-players are exactly the symmetric functions that have bounded 2-party complexity.

In Section 2 we show, using a Ramsey-theoretical argument reminiscent of [7], that k parties need to exchange $\omega(1)$ bits of communication to verify that their k inputs in $\{0,1\}^n$ represent a partition of $[n]$. This result is of independent interest and also gets used in two of our proofs later.

Due to lack of space, we omit proofs of Lemmas 11, 17 and 23. These proofs are contained in the more complete version [8].

2   Multiparty Communication Complexity

The multiparty model of communication complexity was first introduced by Chandra, Furst and Lipton [7]. In this game, k players $P_1, \ldots, P_k$ wish to collaborate to compute a function $f : \Sigma^n \to \{0,1\}$. The n input letters are partitioned into k sets $X_1, \ldots, X_k \subseteq [n]$ and each participant P_i knows the values of all the inputs *except* the ones of X_i. This game is often referred to as the "input on the forehead" model since it is convenient to picture that player i has the letters of X_i written on his forehead, available to everyone but himself. Players exchange bits, according to an agreed upon protocol, by writing them on a public blackboard. The protocol specifies whose turn it is to speak, and what the player broadcasts is a function of the communication history and the input he has access to. The protocol's output is a function of what is on the blackboard after the protocol's termination. We denote by $D_k(f)$ the k-party communication complexity of f, i.e. the number of bits exchanged in the *best* protocol for f on the worst case input and for the worst-case partition of inputs. More generally, we consider functions $f : \Sigma^* \to \{0,1\}$ and thus view $D_k(f)$ as a function of input length.

The information available to individual players overlaps a lot since any input letter is known to $k-1$ of the k players. Thus, the power of the multiparty model increases with the number of players involved as the fraction of inputs available to each player increases.

A subset S of $\Sigma^{X_1 \times \cdots \times X_k}$ is a *cylinder in the ith dimension* if membership in S is independent of the ith coordinate, i.e. if for all $x_1, x_2, \ldots, x_k$ and any x_i' we have $(x_1, \ldots, x_i, \ldots, x_k) \in S$ if and only if $(x_1, \ldots, x_i', \ldots, x_k) \in S$. We say that S is a *cylinder intersection* if $S = \bigcap_{1 \le i \le k} S_i$ where S_i is a cylinder in the ith dimension. A cylinder intersection is called f-*monochromatic* if the function f evaluates to the same value on every input instance in the intersection. The following lemma underlies all lower bound arguments for the multiparty model:

Lemma 1 (see [13]). *Let $f : \Sigma^{X_1 \times \cdots \times X_k} \to \{0,1\}$ be a function of k-inputs. Any k-party communication protocol of cost c computing f partitions the input space into at most 2^c f-monochromatic cylinder intersections, each intersection corresponding to a possible communication exchange by players.*

We say that a set of k elements of $\Sigma^{X_1 \times \cdots \times X_k}$ forms a *star* if it is of the form:

$$(x_1', x_2, \ldots, x_k), (x_1, x_2', \ldots, x_k), \ldots, (x_1, x_2, \ldots, x_k')$$

where the x_i are values for the input bits letters in X_i for each i with $x_i \neq x_i'$. In that case, we call $(x_1, x_2, \ldots, x_k)$ the *center* of this star. These notions lead to a useful characterization of cylinder intersections.

Lemma 2 (see [13,7]). *A set $S \subseteq \Sigma^{X_1 \times \cdots \times X_k}$ is a cylinder intersection if and only if the center of any star contained in S is itself an element of S.*

A k-rectangular reduction r from $L \subseteq \{0,1\}^{n \times k}$ to $K \subseteq \{0,1\}^{l(n) \times k}$ is a k-tuple of functions $(r_1, \ldots, r_k)$ with each $r_i : \{0,1\}^n \to \{0,1\}^{l(n)}$ such that $(x_1, \ldots, x_k) \in L$ iff $(r_1(x_1), \ldots, r_k(x_k)) \in K$. The *length* of the reduction is ℓ.

Observation 3. *Let $L \subseteq \{0,1\}^{n \times k}$ and $K \subseteq \{0,1\}^{l(n) \times k}$ be languages such that there exists a rectangular reduction r from L to K of length l. Then, the communication complexity of L for the partition for which r exists is at most $D_k(K)(l(n))$.*

Lower bounds for the k-party communication complexity of the functions $Part_k$ and $GIP_{k,p}$ will be particularly useful. Both functions take as input an $n \times k$ Boolean matrix A and we think of the ith column of A as representing a subset x_i of $[n] = \{1, \dots n\}$. We define $Part_k(A) = 1$ iff each row contains exactly one 1 (i.e. the x_i form a partition of $[n]$) and $GIP_{k,p} = 1$ iff the number of all-1 rows of A (i.e. the size of the intersection of the x_i) is divisible by p. It is clear that for the k-party game the worst input partition for $GIP_{k,p}$ and $Part_k$ is the one where player P_i holds the bits of column i on his forehead.

Lemma 4 ([2,11]). $D_k(GIP_{k,p}) = \Omega(n)$ *for all constants* $k, p \geq 2$.

More precisely, the best known lower bound for $GIP_{k,p}$ is $\Omega(n/4^k)$ and holds even for k growing as a function of n but we only consider the case where k is constant.

We establish a lower bound on the k-party communication complexity of $Part_k$ by applying a Ramsey-theoretical result known as the Hales-Jewett Theorem. The n-tuples $v^1, \dots, v^t \in [t]^n$ are said to form a *combinatorial line* if the v^j are distinct and for each $1 \leq i \leq n$ either all the v^j agree on co-ordinate i (i.e. $v_i^j = v_i^{j'}$ for all $1 \leq j \leq j' \leq t$) or we have $v_i^j = j$ for all $1 \leq j \leq t$.

Theorem 5 (Hales-Jewett [10]) *For any integers c, t there exists an integer $n = HJ(c,t)$ such that if all vectors in $[t]^n$ are colored with c colors then there is a monochromatic combinatorial line $v^1, \dots, v^t$ (i.e. a line whose elements all were assigned the same color).*

We now prove:

Lemma 6. *For all* k, $D_k(Part_k) = \omega(1)$.

Proof. Consider the input as a collection of k subsets of $[n]$. Consider any input $(S_1, \dots, S_k)$ that is *accepted* by a protocol for $Part_k$. For every $1 \leq j \leq n$, the element j lies in exactly one of the S_i. Using this observation, these inputs can be put in one-to-one correspondence with n-tuples in $[k]^n$. As an example for $k = 3$ and $n = 4$, we have $Part_3(\{4\}, \{1,3\}, \{2\}) = 1$ and this input corresponds to the n-tuple $(2, 3, 2, 1)$.

Suppose that the k-party communication complexity of $Part_k$ is bounded, for some k, by a constant c. To every input accepted by a protocol for $Part_k$, (i.e. to every element in $[k]^n$), we assign one of 2^c colors corresponding to the communication history resulting from that particular input. If n is large enough then by the Hales-Jewett Theorem this set contains a monochromatic combinatorial line $v^1, \dots, v^k$. Let $T \subseteq [n]$ be the (non-empty) set of positions on which the v^j differ and for each $i \leq k$ denote as S_i the set of positions on which all the v^j are i. By definition of the above one-to-one correspondence, we have that $T, S_1, \ldots, S_k$ form a partition of $[n]$ and all the inputs $(S_1 \cup T, S_2, \ldots S_k)$, $(S_1, S_2 \cup T, \ldots S_k)$, $\ldots, (S_1, S_2, \ldots S_k \cup T)$ induce the same communication history. By Lemma 2, and since these inputs form a star, their center $(S_1, S_2, \ldots S_k)$ *also* induces that same communication and must thus belong to $Part_k$. However $S_1 \cup \ldots \cup S_k = [n] - T \neq [n]$ so we get a contradiction.

The proof of Lemma 6 only considers those instances of $Part_k$ in which any two subsets held by the k players are disjoint. Further, it is easily verified that the input instance (the center of the star) on which the players are forced to make an error, also has this disjointness property. These observations yield the following slightly stronger result: define the promised problem $RPart_k^n$ to be $Part_k^n$ with the promise that the k sets given to players are pairwise disjoint and are subsets of $[n]$.

Corollary 7. *For each k, $RPart_k^n$ cannot be solved using c bits of communication whenever $n \geq HJ(k, 2^c)$.*

Note that an $n \times k$ matrix A belongs to $Part_k$ iff none of its rows contains two 1 and the total number of 1 entries in A is n. If $k \geq 3$ then k players can check the first condition using k bits of communication since any pair of input bits is accessible to at least one player. They are then left with verifying that the sum of the input bits is n which can, surprisingly, be achieved with a communication cost much less than the trivial $O(\log n)$ [7].

3   Functions with Bounded Multiparty Complexity but High Time/Space Complexity

In this section we exhibit languages of arbitrarily large computational complexity but with bounded multiparty communication complexity. For a language L and an *encoding* $C : \{0,1\}^* \to \{0,1\}^*$, we denote by $C(L)$ the set $\{C(x); \ x \in L\}$. We prove that for a suitably chosen error-correcting code C, any language L is such that its encoding $C(L)$ has bounded multiparty communication complexity. We will choose C such that the corresponding encoding and decoding function are efficiently computable and hence the complexities of L and $C(L)$ will be closely related.

As a warm-up, we start with the *unary encoding* C_U defined as follows: for $x \in \{0,1\}^*$, $C_U(x) = 0^x 10^{2^n - x - 1}$, where n is the length of x and x is interpreted as an integer between 0 and $2^n - 1$. Hence, C_U encodes bit strings of length n into strings of length 2^n having a single 1 in a one-to-one way.

Lemma 8. *For any language L and integer $k \geq 3$, $D_k(C_U(L)) \leq 3$.*

Proof. Without loss of generality $k = 3$. On an input w that is split among the three parties, the players need to verify two things: 1) whether w is a valid encoding of some string x, and 2) whether the corresponding string x is in L. To verify the first property the players only need to check whether at least one of them sees a 1 and whether none of them sees two or more 1s. They can communicate their observations regarding this using six bits in total. Next, one of the players who sees the one, determines the unique string x with $C_U(x) = w$. He can do this solely based on the position of the one since he knows how w is partitioned. This player can also determine whether $x \in L$ and hence $w \in C_U(L)$. He communicates his conclusion to the other parties by sending one more bit. Hence in total players exchange at most seven bits. The protocol can be optimized so that each player simultaneously sends one bit of information for the total of three bits.

The disadvantage of the unary encoding is its inefficiency: because codewords are exponentially longer than the words they encode, we cannot provide efficient reductions between L and $C(L)$. A better encoding can be obtained by concatenating Reed-Solomon codes with the unary encoding. In the 3-party scenario at least one of the parties has on its forehead at least a $1/3$-fraction of the input. Hence, if the chosen encoding has the property that from an arbitrary $1/3$-fraction of the input the whole word can be reconstructed (assuming the input is an encoding of some word, i.e., assuming that the input is a codeword) the other two parties can reconstruct the whole input and verify whether the parts on remaining foreheads are consistent with such an input. With the proper choice of parameters Reed-Solomon codes have this property.

Let n be a large enough integer, $m = \lceil \log_2 3n \rceil$ and $d = n/m$. Any string $x \in \{0,1\}^n$ can be interpreted as a sequence of d elements from $GF[2^m]$. Define p_x to be the degree $d-1$ polynomial over $GF[2^m]$ whose coefficients are given by x. Define the Reed-Solomon encoding by $C_{RS}(x) = p_x(g_0)p_x(g_1)\cdots p_x(g_{3d-1})$, where $GF[2^m] = \{g_0, g_1, \ldots, g_{2^m-1}\}$, and we will encode each g_i as a binary string in $\{0,1\}^m$. Furthermore, define the concatenation of the Reed-Solomon encoding with the unary encoding by $C_{RS \circ U}(x) = C_U(p_x(g_0)) \cdots C_U(p_x(g_{3d-1}))$. Codewords thus consist of $3d$ blocks of 2^m bits (corresponding to the $3d$ symbols of the Reed-Solomon encoding) with each block containing exactly one 1. Thus, $C_{RS \circ U}$ encodes strings of length n into strings of length $O(n^2)$. Furthermore, $C_{RS \circ U}$ can be encoded and decoded in polynomial time and so the languages L and $C_{RS \circ U}(L)$ are polynomial-time equivalent. Note that the decoding task at hand does not require us to perform error correction in the usual sense: we simply want to identify if an input is a codeword (since we reject all words that are not codewords) and we only care about decoding true codewords.

Lemma 9. *For any language L and any $k \geq 3$, $D_k(C_{RS \circ U}(L)) \leq 6$*

Proof. Without loss of generality $k = 3$ as all but the first two players can pretend they are the same party. Let $m = \lceil \log_2 3n \rceil$ and $d = n/m$. To check if an input is a codeword, the players can easily check that there are never two 1s in a single block of input bits. They cannot, however, verify at constant cost that each of the $3d$ blocks contains *at least* one 1 since this task is essentially the partition problem whose complexity we lower bounded in Lemma 6. We proceed differently: an input w of length $3d \cdot 2^m$ can only be a codeword if at least one player (say player 1) has on its forehead at least d ones and this player can be identified with three bits of communication. These d ones determine d elements of $GF[2^m]$ hence players 2 and 3 can each privately reconstruct from them the unique degree $d - 1$ polynomial p that coincides with these elements. Players 2 and 3 now know that if the input is a codeword then it must be the one corresponding to p and player 2 can check that the bits on player 3's forehead are consistent with that hypothesis while player 3 can similarly cross-check the input bits on player 2's forehead. If this cross-checking procedure is successful, player 2 can determine the unique x such that $p_x = p$, verify $x \in L$ and send the result to all parties. Overall, only six bits of communication suffice to decide if the input is from $C_{RS \circ U}(L)$.

As an immediate corollary to this lemma and the fact that the complexity of $C_{RS \circ U}(L)$ is polynomially related to the complexity of L we obtain:

Corollary 10. *The class of languages with bounded multi-party communication complexity contains languages with arbitrarily large time and space complexity.*

In order to obtain also languages with essentially the largest possible circuit complexity we need codes that map n bits into $O(n)$ bits. We can obtain such codes by concatenating Reed-Solomon codes with codes provided by the following lemma and the unary code C_U.

Lemma 11 (see [8]). *For any integer $n \geq 1$, there exists a linear map C_8 : $\{0,1\}^n \rightarrow GF[8]^{39n}$ such that every $w \in C_8(\{0,1\}^n)$ is uniquely determined by any one-third of its coordinates.*

By concatenating C_{RS} with C_8 and C_U we obtain the code $C_{RS \circ 8 \circ U}$ with polynomial time encoding and decoding that maps n bit strings into $O(n)$ bit strings.

Corollary 12. *For any $k \geq 3$, the class of languages with bounded k-party communication complexity contains languages with $2^{\Omega(n)}$ circuit complexity.*

4   Languages with a Neutral Letter

A language $L \in \Sigma^*$ is said to have a *neutral letter* e if for all $u, v \in \Sigma^*$ we have $uv \in L$ iff $uev \in L$. Thus, adding or deleting e anywhere in a word w does not affect membership in L. If a language has a neutral letter then membership in L cannot depend, as in Lemma 8, on having specific value on a specific input position and, at least intuitively, this seems to take away a lot of the power inherent to the multiparty communication model. The neutral letter hypothesis was helpful in obtaining length lower bounds on bounded-width branching programs [4] and was central to the Crane-Beach Conjecture [3]. In this section, we give a precise characterization of languages with a neutral letter that have bounded k-party complexity for some fixed k. We first show that all such languages must be regular and then characterize them in terms of algebraic properties of their minimal automaton.

4.1 Proving Regularity

Let $C \geq 0$ be an integer and let $\mathcal{G}$ be a family of functions over Σ^* with finite range R. We say that inputs with length at most C *determine* the functions of $\mathcal{G}$ if every function $g : \Sigma^{\leq C} \to R$ has at most one extension to Σ^* in $\mathcal{G}$. Now, let $\mathcal{C}_{k,c}$ be the family of functions with a neutral letter and k-party communication complexity at most c. We show:

Lemma 13. *Functions of $\mathcal{C}_{k,c}$ are determined by inputs of length at most $C = HJ(k, 2^{2c})$, a constant.*

We obtain this lemma as a corollary to

Lemma 14. *For any $C > 0$ if the functions of $\mathcal{C}_{k,c}$ are not determined by inputs of size C then $RPart_k^n$ can be solved by k parties with $2c$ communication, where $n \geq C$ is some number.*

Lemma 14 and Corollary 7 together imply Lemma 13 immediately.

Proof. (Lemma 14) For any word $w \in \Sigma^*$, we shall denote by w_e the word obtained from w by deleting all occurrences of e in w. The ith letter of w will be denoted by w^i. Also, for k words $w_1, \ldots, w_k$, each of length ℓ, let $w = w_1 \Diamond \ldots \Diamond w_k$ denote the word obtained by interleaving the k words in the following way : $|w| = \ell k$ and for all $1 \leq i \leq \ell k$, $w^i = w_{j+1}^m$ if $i = (m-1)k + j$ with $0 \leq j < k$. Let us assume that f and g are in $\mathcal{C}_{k,c}$, such that they are not identical, but the minimal string $v \in \{\Sigma - e\}^*$ such that $f(v) \neq g(v)$ has length at least C. We show below a k party protocol that solves $RPart_k^{|v|}$ by communicating at most $2c$ bits.

Our protocol will work using a k-rectangular reduction r to language $H \subset \Sigma^{|v| \times k}$, where $(y_1, \ldots, y_k) \in H$ iff $v = (y_1 \Diamond \cdots \Diamond y_k)_e$. Consider an instance of $RPart_k^{|v|}$ in which player i's forehead holds a $|v|$ bit vector representing set I_i. Then, $I_i \cap I_j = \emptyset$ if $i \neq j$. We define r_i as follows : let $y_i = r_i(I_i)$. Then, $y_i^j = v^j$ if $j \in I_i$, otherwise $y_i^j = e$. The simple observation that is key to our argument, is that $(y_1 \Diamond \cdots \Diamond y_k)_e$ is v if $\cup_{i=1}^k I_i = [|v|]$ and otherwise it is a word u, where $|u| < |v|$. This shows that r is indeed a reduction from $RPart_k^{|v|}$ to H.

The observation above and the property of v (i.e. $f(u) = g(u)$, whenever $|u| < |v|$) imply the following : $y = y_1 \Diamond \ldots \Diamond y_k$ is in H iff $f(y) \neq g(y)$. The condition $f(y) \neq g(y)$ can be checked with $2c$ bits of communication by running the c-bit protocol on f and g separately. Thus, $2c$ bits of communication are enough to solve H and hence $RPart_k^{|v|}$.

Let $f : \Sigma^* \to \{0, 1\}$ be a function in $\mathcal{C}_{k,c}$: For a word $w \in \Sigma^*$, we define the function $f_w : \Sigma^* \to \{0, 1\}$ by $f_w(z) = f(wz)$. Note that each f_w is also in $\mathcal{C}_{k,c}$. Applying Lemma 13, the functions $\{f_w\}$ are determined by inputs of length at most $C = HJ(k, 2^{2c})$. It follows that the equivalence relation on Σ^* defined by $u \sim v$ iff $f(uz) = f(vz)$ for all $z \in \Sigma^*$ has at most $2^{(|\Sigma|-1)^C}$ equivalence classes. It is well-known that if $\sim$ has finite index then f is regular and we obtain

Theorem 15. *If f is a function with a neutral letter such that $D_k(f) = O(1)$ for some fixed k, then f is regular.*

4.2   Regular Languages with Bounded Complexity

A monoid M is a set with a binary associative operation and a distinguished identity element 1_M. A language $L \subseteq \Sigma^*$ is *recognized* by a finite monoid M if there is a morphism ϕ from the free monoid Σ^* to M and a set $F \subseteq M$ such that $L = \phi^{-1}(F)$. A restatement of Kleene's Theorem states that L is regular iff it is recognized by some finite monoid. If L is regular, the *syntactic monoid* $M(L)$ of L is the transformation monoid of L's minimal automaton [15] and is the smallest monoid recognizing L.

The *word problem* for M is the function *eval* which maps a string $w = w_1 \ldots w_n \in M^*$ to the product $eval(w_1 \ldots w_n) = w_1 \cdot w_2 \cdots \cdots w_n$. We define the k-party *communication complexity of M*, denoted $D_k(M)$ as the communication complexity of its word problem. Two of the authors gave a complete classification result for the two-party communication complexity of finite monoids [20] and this led to a similar classification for the two-party complexity of regular languages. The communication complexity of monoids was first studied in [17] from which we use the following:

Lemma 16. *Let L be a regular language with a neutral letter and let $M = M(L)$ be its syntactic monoid. Then for any $k \geq 2$ we have $D_k(L) = \Theta(D_k(M))$.*

A finite group is *nilpotent* if it is the direct product of p-groups and a monoid lies in the class $\overline{\mathbf{G_{nil}}}$ if all its subgroups are nilpotent. The class $\mathbf{DO}$ consists of monoids satisfying the identity $(xy)^\omega (yx)^\omega (xy)^\omega = (xy)^\omega$.

Lemma 17. *If M is a finite monoid outside of $\mathbf{DO}$ then $D_k(M) = \omega(1)$ for all k.*

The lemma is proved in the full version of our paper (see [8]): we show that if M lies outside $\mathbf{DO}$ then for any k there exists a rectangular reduction of linear length from either $GIP_{k,p}$ or $Part_k$ to the word problem of M.

Theorem 18 ([17]). *Let G be a group. If G is in $\mathbf{G_{nil}}$ then there exists a constant $k \geq 2$ such that $D_k(G) = O(1)$. Otherwise $D_k(G) = \Omega(n)$ for all k.*

In this case also, the lower bound is obtained through a rectangular reduction from $GIP_{k,p}$ to the word problem of any non-nilpotent finite group. The upper bound, on the other hand, stems from a combinatorial description of languages recognized by nilpotent groups. We say that a word $u = a_1 \ldots a_t$ with $a_i \in \Sigma$ is a *subword* of the word w if w can be factorized as $w_0 a_1 w_1 \ldots w_{t-1} a_t w_t$ and we denote by $\binom{w}{u}$ the number of such factorizations. We say that a language L *counts subwords of length k modulo m* if membership of w in L depends on the values modulo m of $\binom{w}{u_1}, \ldots, \binom{w}{u_t}$ for some u_i with $|u_i| \leq k$. One can show that the syntactic monoid of a regular language L is a nilpotent group iff there exist $k, m \geq 2$ such that L counts subwords of length k modulo m [22].

For $a \in \Sigma$ and $L, K \subseteq \Sigma^*$, the concatenation LaK is said to be *perfectly unambiguous* if $L \subseteq (\Sigma - \{a\})^*$ or $K \subseteq (\Sigma - \{a\})^*$. If LaK is perfectly unambiguous then any $w \in LaK$ can be uniquely factorized as $w_L a w_K$ with $w_L \in L$ and $w_K \in K$ since the a can only be the first or last occurrence of a in w. Let

$\mathcal{V}_\Sigma$ be the smallest class of regular languages over Σ that contains both the subword-counting languages and the languages Σ_0^* for each $\Sigma_0 \subseteq \Sigma$ and which is closed under Boolean operations and perfectly unambiguous concatenations. The next lemma can be inferred from [20].

Lemma 19. *A language $L \subseteq \Sigma^*$ is recognized by a monoid in $\mathbf{DO} \cap \overline{\mathbf{G_{nil}}}$ iff it is in $\mathcal{V}_\Sigma$.*

We can now give a characterization of monoids that have bounded multiparty communication complexity for some suitably large constant k.

Theorem 20. *Let $L \subseteq \Sigma^*$ be a regular language with a neutral letter and syntactic monoid M. If M lies in $\mathbf{DO} \cap \overline{\mathbf{G_{nil}}}$ then there exists a constant k such that $D_k(L) = O(1)$. Otherwise, we have $D_k(L) = \omega(1)$ for all k.*

Proof. To obtain the upper bound, it suffices to show, by Lemma 19, that every language in $\mathcal{V}_\Sigma$ has bounded k-party complexity for some k and we argue from the definition of $\mathcal{V}_\Sigma$.

First, any language Σ_0^* has bounded two-party communication complexity since players only need to check that the input letters they have access to indeed belong to Σ_0. Furthermore, if K counts subwords of length k modulo m, then $D_{k+1}(K) = O(1)$ because any k-tuple of input letters is available to at least one player in the $(k+1)$-party game and the value of $\binom{w}{u}$ modulo m can thus be computed with communication $k \cdot \lceil \log m \rceil$ if $|u| \leq k$. Clearly, Boolean combinations of languages with bounded k-party complexity also have bounded k-party complexity and it remains to show that if L and K have bounded k-party complexity and $L \subseteq (\Sigma - \{a\})^*$ then LaK has bounded $(k+1)$-party complexity. Players proceed as follows: each party broadcasts the identity of the player which, in their opinion, holds on the forehead the first occurrence of a in the input. This requires $k \cdot \lceil \log k \rceil$ bits of communication and the player holding that first occurrence will be the only dissenting voice since that letter is seen by all other parties. Since $k+1 \geq 3$, the k remaining players now know the position of the first a and they simulate the k-party protocols for L and K on the prefix and suffix at constant cost.

For the lower bound, if M is not in $\mathbf{DO}$ then $D_k(M) = \omega(1)$ for all k by Lemma 17. If M contains a non-nilpotent group G then $D_k(G) = \Omega(n)$ for all k by Theorem 18 and we clearly have $D_k(M) \geq D_k(G)$. So for all k, we have $D_k(M) = \omega(1)$ and, by Lemma 16, $D_k(L) = \omega(1)$.

Combining this result with Theorem 15 we get

Theorem 21. *If L is a language with a neutral letter and bounded k-party communication complexity for some fixed k then L is regular and $M(L) \in \mathbf{DO} \cap \overline{\mathbf{G_{nil}}}$.*

Note that the class $\mathbf{DO} \cap \overline{\mathbf{G_{nil}}}$ is decidable. Also, the corresponding regular languages have a nice logical characterization [21] and one can see from the definition of $\mathcal{V}_\Sigma$ that they all lie in ACC^0.

5   Symmetric Functions

For $w \in \Sigma^*$, we denote as $|w|_a$ the number of occurrences of a in w. A function $f : \Sigma^* \to \{0,1\}$ is *symmetric* if its value depends only on the values $|w|_a$ for $a \in \Sigma$. Intuitively $k \geq 3$ parties computing a symmetric function only get limited benefits from the features of the multiparty model since their protocol cannot significantly rely on the precise set of input positions accessible to each player or on the fact that any $(k-1)$-tuple of bits is seen by one party. We formalize this idea by showing that any symmetric f with bounded k-party complexity for a fixed k in fact has bounded two-party complexity.

Let us first deal with functions with boolean inputs. To any symmetric function $f : \{0,1\}^n \to \{0,1\}$, we will naturally associate the function $\widehat{f} : \{0, \ldots, n\} \to \{0,1\}$ such that $f(x) = \widehat{f}(|x|_1)$ for every $x \in \{0,1\}^n$ and say that f is (ℓ, r, p)–*periodic* if $\widehat{f}(a) = \widehat{f}(a + p)$ for $\ell \leq a \leq n - r$.

Theorem 22. *If $f : \{0,1\}^n \to \{0,1\}$ is symmetric and has bounded k-party communication complexity then in fact f has bounded two-party complexity.*

In the full version (see [8]), we extend this theorem to symmetric functions with non-Boolean domains. The result in the Boolean case is established through the next lemma. Recall that a *simultaneous protocol* is one in which each player sends a single message to an extra party (the *referee*) who then computes the answer solely based on the messages he received. In particular, the message sent by a party does not depend on messages sent by other parties. Since a k-party protocol of communication cost c can be easily turned into a k-party simultaneous protocol with cost $ck2^c$, functions of bounded complexity in the simultaneous model are exactly those with bounded complexity in the standard model.

Lemma 23. *For any constants k, c with $k \geq 1$ there exists an integer $N_{k+1} = N(k+1, c)$ such that every symmetric boolean function $f : \{0,1\}^n \to \{0,1\}$ that has a $k+1$-party simultaneous protocol of complexity c for the input partition in which players $X_1, \ldots, X_k$ each get N_{k+1} bits and player X_{k+1} gets the remaining $n - kN_{k+1}$ bits is (ℓ, r, p)-periodic for some $\ell, r \leq kN_{k+1}$ and some $p \leq N_{k+1}$.*

Theorem 22 then follows by observing that an (ℓ, r, p)-periodic function has 2-party simultaneous communication complexity roughly $2 \cdot \lceil \log(\ell + r + p) \rceil$. The proof of Lemma 23, given in the full version ([8]), proceeds by induction on k. The base case is due to [19] and our induction step uses a non-trivial "player elimination" technique (as in [16]). More precisely, we use the Ramsey-like theorem of Gallai [10] to show that if f has a $(k + 1)$-party protocol of bounded cost then there exists a large set of inputs $\mathcal{P}$ for the foreheads of the first k players on which player P_{k+1} always sends the same communication. This renders the $(k + 1)$st player irrelevant if the input lies in $\mathcal{P}$ and allows the use of the induction hypothesis.

References

1. A. Ambainis. Upper bounds on multiparty communication complexity of shifts. In *Proc. 13th STACS*, pages 631–642, 1996.
2. L. Babai, N. Nisan, and M. Szegedy. Multiparty protocols, pseudorandom generators for logspace, and time-space trade-offs. *JCSS*, 45(2):204–232, 1992.
3. D. A. M. Barrington, N. Immerman, C. Lautemann, N. Schweikardt, and D. Thérien. First order expressibility of languages with neutral letters or: The Crane Beach conjecture. *JCSS*, 70(2):101–127, 2005.
4. D. A. M. Barrington and H. Straubing. Superlinear lower bounds for bounded-width branching programs. *JCSS*, 50(3):374–381, 1995.
5. P. Beame, T. Pitassi, and N. Segerlind. Lower bounds for Lovász-Schrijver systems and beyond follow from multiparty communication complexity. In *ICALP*, pages 1176–1188, 2005.
6. P. Beame and E. Vee. Time-space tradeoffs multiparty communication complexity and nearest neighbor problems. In *34th STOC*, pages 688–697, 2002.
7. A. K. Chandra, M. L. Furst, and R. J. Lipton. Multi-party protocols. In *STOC'83*, pages 94–99, 1983.
8. A. Chattopadhyay, A. Krebs, M. Koucký, M. Szegedy, P. Tesson and D. Thérien. Languages with bounded multiparty communication complexity. In *ECCC* TR06-118, 2006.
9. M. Goldmann and J. Håstad. Monotone circuits for connectivity have depth $(\log n)^{2-o(1)}$. *SIAM J. Comput.*, 27(5):1283–1294, 1998.
10. R. L. Graham, B. L. Rotschild, and J. H. Spencer. *Ramsey Theorey*. Series in Discrete Mathematics. Wiley Interscience, 1980.
11. V. Grolmusz. Separating the communication complexities of MOD m and MOD p circuits. In *Proc. 33rd FOCS*, pages 278–287, 1992.
12. V. Grolmusz. The BNS lower bound for multi-party protocols in nearly optimal. *Information and Computation*, 112(1):51–54, 1994.
13. E. Kushilevitz and N. Nisan. *Communication Complexity*. Cambridge University Press, 1997.
14. N. Nisan. The communication complexity of treshold gates. In *Combinatorics, Paul Erdös is Eighty, Vol. 1*, pages 301–315, 1993.
15. J.-E. Pin. Syntactic semigroups. In *Handbook of language theory*, volume 1, chapter 10, pages 679–746. Springer Verlag, 1997.
16. P. Pudlák. An application of Hindman's theorem to a problem on communication complexity. *Combinatorics, Probability and Computing*, 12(5–6):661–670, 2003.
17. J.-F. Raymond, P. Tesson, and D. Thérien. An algebraic approach to communication complexity. *ICALP*, 1443:29–40, 1998.
18. R. Raz. The BNS-Chung criterion for multi-party communication complexity. *Computational Complexity*, 9(2):113–122, 2000.
19. M. Szegedy. Functions with bounded symmetric communication complexity, programs over commutative monoids, and ACC. *JCSS*, 47(3):405–423, 1993.
20. P. Tesson and D. Thérien. Complete classifications for the communication complexity of regular languages. *Theory of Computing Systems*, 38(2):135–159, 2005.
21. P. Tesson and D. Thérien. Restricted two-variable sentences, circuits and communication complexity. In *ICALP* pages 526–538, 2005.
22. D. Thérien. Subword counting and nilpotent groups. In *Combinatorics on Words: Progress and Perspectives*, pages 195–208. Academic Press, 1983.

New Approximation Algorithms for Minimum Cycle Bases of Graphs

Telikepalli Kavitha[1], Kurt Mehlhorn[2], and Dimitrios Michail[2]

[1] Indian Institute of Science, Bangalore, India
kavitha@csa.iisc.ernet.in
[2] Max-Planck-Institut für Informatik, Saarbrücken, Germany
{mehlhorn,michail}@mpi-inf.mpg.de

Abstract. We consider the problem of computing an approximate minimum cycle basis of an undirected edge-weighted graph G with m edges and n vertices; the extension to directed graphs is also discussed. In this problem, a $\{0,1\}$ incidence vector is associated with each cycle and the vector space over $\mathbb{F}_2$ generated by these vectors is the cycle space of G. A set of cycles is called a cycle basis of G if it forms a basis for its cycle space. A cycle basis where the sum of the weights of the cycles is minimum is called a minimum cycle basis of G. Cycle bases of low weight are useful in a number of contexts, e.g. the analysis of electrical networks, structural engineering, chemistry, and surface reconstruction.

We present two new algorithms to compute an approximate minimum cycle basis. For any integer $k \geq 1$, we give $(2k-1)$-approximation algorithms with expected running time $O(kmn^{1+2/k} + mn^{(1+1/k)(\omega-1)})$ and deterministic running time $O(n^{3+2/k})$, respectively. Here ω is the best exponent of matrix multiplication. It is presently known that $\omega < 2.376$. Both algorithms are $o(m^\omega)$ for dense graphs. This is the first time that any algorithm which computes sparse cycle bases with a guarantee drops below the $\Theta(m^\omega)$ bound.

We also present a 2-approximation algorithm with $O(m^\omega \sqrt{n \log n})$ expected running time, a linear time 2-approximation algorithm for planar graphs and an $O(n^3)$ time 2.42-approximation algorithm for the complete Euclidean graph in the plane.

1   Introduction

Let $G = (V, E)$ be an undirected connected graph with m edges and n vertices. A *cycle* of G is any subgraph of G where each vertex has even degree. Associated with each cycle C is an *incidence vector* x, indexed on E, where for any $e \in E$, x_e is 1 if e is an edge of C and 0 otherwise. The vector space over $\mathbb{F}_2$ generated by the incidence vectors of cycles is called the *cycle space* of G. It is well known that this vector space has dimension $N = m - n + 1$, where m is the number of edges of G and n is the number of vertices. A maximal set of linearly independent cycles is called a *cycle basis*. The edges of G have non-negative weights assigned to them. A cycle basis where the sum of the weights of the cycles is minimum is called a *minimum cycle basis* of G. We use the abbreviation MCB to refer

W. Thomas and P. Weil (Eds.): STACS 2007, LNCS 4393, pp. 512–523, 2007.

to a minimum cycle basis. Minimum cycle bases are of considerable practical importance and therefore the problem of computing an MCB has received considerable attention. An early paper is by Stepanec [1]. Horton [2] presented the first polynomial time algorithm. Faster and/or alternative algorithms were later presented by de Pina [3], Golynski and Horton [4], Berger et al. [5], and Kavitha et al. [6]. The current fastest algorithm [6] has running time $O(m^2n+mn^2\log n)$. Implementations are discussed in [7,8,9].

An important application of the MCB problem is the construction of sparse systems when solving problems in electrical networks [10,3,5]. Other applications are in structural engineering [11], chemistry and biochemistry [12], and surface reconstruction from point clouds [13]. In most applications, the computation of an MCB is a preprocessing step. The use of an MCB ensures sparseness and translates into faster running times of the main algorithm. Unfortunately, even the fastest exact minimum cycle basis algorithm has a running time of $\Theta(m^2n + mn^2\log n)$. This may dominate the running time of the application.

However, most applications can work with any cycle basis and any constant factor approximate minimum cycle basis may be substituted for a minimum cycle basis without much affect on the application. In [6] an α-approximation algorithm for any $\alpha > 1$ is presented for the MCB problem; its running time is $o(m^2n + mn^2\log n) + \Theta(m^\omega)$, where ω is the exponent of matrix multiplication. It is known [14] that $\omega < 2.376$. The time bound of $\Theta(m^\omega)$ is still prohibitive for some of the applications. It results from Gaussian elimination on $m \times m$ linear systems.

We present a new approximation approach which leads to vastly improved time bounds. In particular, for any integer $k \geq 1$, we give two $(2k - 1)$ approximation algorithms with expected running time $O(kmn^{1+2/k} + mn^{(1+1/k)(\omega-1)})$ and deterministic running time $O(n^{3+2/k})$, respectively. Both algorithms are $o(m^\omega)$ for sufficiently dense graphs, the first algorithm for number of edges $m > \max(n^{1+1/k}, \sqrt[\omega-1]{kn^{1+2/k}})$ and the second algorithm for $m > n^{\frac{3}{\omega}+\frac{2}{k\omega}} = n^{1.26+\frac{0.84}{k}}$. The first algorithm is faster for sparser graphs and the second algorithm for denser graphs. More precisely, the second algorithm is faster for $m > n^{4-\omega+\frac{3-\omega}{k}}$ which with the current upper bound on ω is $m > n^{1.624+\frac{0.624}{k}}$.

Our algorithms work in two phases. The first phase is a very fast computation of a large number of cycles (all but $O(n^{1+1/k})$ cycles) in an approximate MCB. The second part is a more expensive computation of the remaining cycles. We present two different ways for computing these remaining cycles, leading to the above two algorithms, each faster for different graph densities. Only the second phase needs a null space computation; it is a null space computation of a square system of size $O(n^{1+1/k})$. Our new algorithms are fast even when implemented without fast matrix multiplication. Furthermore, by combining the techniques of both the algorithms, we get an even faster algorithm at the expense of a larger approximation factor.

We also present a 2-approximation algorithm with $O(m^\omega\sqrt{n\log n})$ expected running time. For sparse graphs, this is subcubic. Moreover, we develop very fast approximation algorithms for some special graph classes. For planar graphs we give a linear time 2-approximation algorithm and for the complete Euclidean graph in the plane we give a 2.42-approximation algorithm with running time $O(n^3)$. In higher dimensions we give a k-approximation algorithm for any $k > 1$ with running time $O(s^d n^3 \log n)$ where $s = 4(k+1)/(k-1)$ and d is the fixed dimension.

The minimum cycle basis problem for directed graphs is less studied. Polynomial time algorithms are given in [15,16,17,18]. The fastest deterministic algorithm [17] has running time $O(m^3 n + m^2 n^2 \log n)$ and there is a Monte Carlo algorithm [18,17] with running time $O(m^2 n + mn^2 \log n)$. Some of our algorithms generalize to directed graphs. We give a deterministic $(2k-1)$-approximation algorithm with running time $O(n^{4+3/k})$, a Monte Carlo $(2k-1)$-approximation algorithm with running time $O(n^{3+2/k})$, and a 2-approximation algorithm with expected running time $O(m^\omega \sqrt{n} \log n)$.

Preliminaries. Let T be any spanning tree in $G(V, E)$, let $e_1, \ldots, e_N$ be the edges of $E \setminus T$ in some arbitrary but fixed order, and let $e_{N+1}, \ldots, e_m$ be the edges in T in some arbitrary but fixed order. We frequently view cycles in terms of restricted incidence vectors[1], that is, each cycle is a vector in $\{0, 1\}^N$.

We use S and R to denote subsets of $E \setminus T$. Each such subset gives rise to an incidence vector in $\{0, 1\}^N$. We use $\langle C, S \rangle$ to denote the standard inner product of vectors C and S. We say that a vector S is *orthogonal* to C if $\langle C, S \rangle = 0$. In the field $\mathbb{F}_2$, $\langle C, S \rangle = 1$ if and only if C contains an odd number of edges of S.

For a cycle C, we use $w(C) = \sum_{e \in C} w(e)$ to denote its weight. We use $w_G(\text{MCB})$ to denote the weight of a minimum cycle basis of graph G. When it is clear by the context we omit G and write $w(\text{MCB})$. The following lemma gives us a lower bound on $w(\text{MCB})$. See [6] for a proof.

Lemma 1 (de Pina [3]). *Let $R_1, \ldots, R_N$ be linearly independent vectors in $\{0, 1\}^N$ and let A_i be a shortest cycle in G such that $\langle A_i, R_i \rangle = 1$. Then $\sum_{i=1}^{N} w(A_i) \leq w(\text{MCB})$.*

The sets $R_i = \{e_i\}$, $1 \leq i \leq N$, are clearly independent. The shortest cycle C with $\langle C, R_i \rangle = 1$ consists of the edge e_i plus the shortest path in $G \setminus \{e_i\}$ connecting its endpoints. We use SC_i to denote this cycle. The cycle exists, since there is always the spanning tree path in $E \setminus \{e_i\}$ connecting the endpoints of e_i. Let $\text{SC} = \{SC_i \mid 1 \leq i \leq N\}$ be the shortest cycle multiset and let $w(\text{SC}) = \sum_{C \in \text{SC}} w(C)$ be its weight. By applying Lemma 1 to the cycles in SC, we obtain Lemma 2.

Lemma 2. $w(\text{SC}) \leq w(\text{MCB})$.

---

[1] For a cycle C, use C to denote its incidence vector in $\{0, 1\}^N$ (restricted to $e_1, \ldots, e_N$) and C^* to denote its incidence vector in $\{0, 1\}^m$. Consider a set of cycles $C_1, \ldots, C_k$. Clearly, if the vectors C_1^* to C_k^* are dependent, then so are the vectors C_1 to C_k. Conversely, assume that $\sum_i \lambda_i C_i = 0$. Then $C = \sum_i \lambda_i C_i^*$ contains only edges in T. Moreover, since C is a sum of cycles, each vertex has even degree with respect to C. Thus, $C = 0$ and hence linear dependence of the restricted incidence vectors implies linear dependence of the full incidence vectors. Thus we may restrict attention to the restricted incidence vectors when discussing questions of linear independence.

2   The New Approach

Our approximation algorithms are motivated by the shortest cycle multiset lower bound (Lemma 2). We fix a parameter $\lambda \leq N$ and construct a set of linearly independent cycles $C_1, \ldots, C_\lambda$ such that $w(C_i) \leq (2k-1) \cdot w(SC_i)$ for $1 \leq i \leq \lambda$. In the second phase, we extend the partial basis to a full basis. We offer two alternatives for the second phase. Let $t = 2k - 1$.

Now we give the details of the first phase. We construct the cycles $C_1, \ldots, C_\lambda$ using a sparse t-spanner of G. A *multiplicative* t-spanner of a graph G is a subgraph $G'(V, E')$, $E' \subseteq E$ such that for any $u, v \in V$ we have $w(\mathrm{SP}_{G'}(u, v)) \leq t \cdot w(\mathrm{SP}_G(u, v))$ where $\mathrm{SP}_G(u, v)$ denotes a shortest path in G from u to v. When it is clear from the context we omit the subscript G and write $\mathrm{SP}(u, v)$. Let $G'(V, E')$ be such a t-spanner of G. Since we can always add the edges in the spanning tree T to E', we may assume $T \subseteq E'$. We also assume that the edges are indexed such that $E \setminus E' = \{e_1, \ldots, e_\lambda\}$.

For each edge $e_i = (u, v) \in E \setminus E'$, let C_i be formed by e_i and $\mathrm{SP}_{G'}(u, v)$. The cycles C_i, $1 \leq i \leq \lambda$ are clearly independent since e_i is contained in precisely C_i. We have $w(C_i) = w(e_i) + w(\mathrm{SP}_{G'}(u, v)) \leq w(e_i) + t \cdot w(\mathrm{SP}_G(u, v)) \leq t \cdot w(SC_i)$.

The running time of phase 1 is easily estimated. As pointed out by Althöfer et al. [19] every weighted undirected graph on n vertices has a $(2k-1)$-spanner with $O(n^{1+1/k})$ edges where $k \geq 1$ is an integer. Such a spanner can be constructed using an algorithm similar to Kruskal's algorithm for constructing minimum spanning trees. In order to build the spanner, consider all edges of the graph in non-decreasing order of weight, adding each edge to the spanner if its endpoints are not already connected, in the spanner, by a path using at most $2k - 1$ edges. At any stage, the spanner is a $(2k - 1)$-spanner of the edges already considered, and its unweighted girth is at least $2k + 1$, so it has only $O(n^{1+1/k})$ edges. The above procedure can be implemented in $O(mn^{1+1/k})$ time.

In the above spanner we are going to perform λ shortest path computations, one for each edge of G that is not in the spanner. Using Dijkstra's algorithm we need $O(\lambda \cdot (n^{1+1/k} + n \log n))$ time and since $\lambda \leq m$ we can compute both the spanner and the λ linearly independent cycles in time $O(mn^{1+1/k})$. We should mention that there are faster algorithms to construct similar spanners, see for example [20]. However, the construction by Althöfer et al. suffices for our purposes.

3   The Remaining Cycles

In the preceding section we computed most of the cycles of an approximate minimum cycle basis. We are left with computing the remaining cycles. The number of additional cycles is $N - \lambda$. Note that this is exactly the dimension of the cycle space of the spanner G'. We present two different algorithms. The first approach uses all the edges in G to construct the remaining cycles while the second approach uses only the edges $e_{\lambda+1}, \ldots, e_m$ of the spanner.

3.1   The First Approach

We first need to briefly review the algorithm in [6] in order to compute a minimum cycle basis; it refines a previous algorithm by de Pina [3]. The algorithm is recursive. We immediately describe the modification of the algorithm needed for our purposes.

The general step adds some number k of cycles to a partial basis PB of size α. This step takes as input an integer $k \geq 1$, and k linearly independent vectors $S_{\alpha+1}, \ldots, S_{\alpha+k}$ orthogonal to the cycles in PB. These vectors, viewed as sets, have the additional property that $S_{\alpha+i} \cap \{e_{\alpha+1}, \ldots, e_N\} = \{e_{\alpha+i}\}$ for $1 \leq i \leq k$. The step updates $S_{\alpha+1}, \ldots, S_{\alpha+k}$ and returns k cycles $Z_{\alpha+1}, \ldots, Z_{\alpha+k}$ such that $\langle Z_i, S_j \rangle = \delta_{ij}$ for $\alpha + 1 \leq i \leq j \leq \alpha + k$ (here δ_{ij} is 1 if $i = j$ and 0 otherwise). The update has the additional property that it does not affect the orthogonality w.r.t the partial basis PB. Observe, that the cycles PB $\cup \{Z_{\alpha+1}, \ldots, Z_{\alpha+k}\}$ are linearly independent. To see this note that for any $1 \leq i \leq k$, $\langle Z_{\alpha+i}, S_{\alpha+i} \rangle = 1$ while any cycle C in the span of PB $\cup \{Z_{\alpha+1}, \ldots, Z_{\alpha+i-1}\}$ has $\langle C, S_{\alpha+i} \rangle = 0$.

The top level call: We call the recursive procedure with the partial basis of phase 1, namely PB $= \{C_1, \ldots, C_\lambda\}$ and ask it to compute $\mu = N - \lambda$ additional cycles. Let us write the $C_1, \ldots, C_\lambda$ in the form of a $\lambda \times N$ matrix with one row per cycle. Then

$$\begin{pmatrix} C_1 \\ \vdots \\ C_\lambda \end{pmatrix} = \begin{pmatrix} I_\lambda & B \end{pmatrix} \tag{1}$$

where I_λ is the $\lambda \times \lambda$ identity matrix and B is a $\lambda \times \mu$ matrix. The matrix has this form since each of the edges e_i for $1 \leq i \leq \lambda$ belongs only to the cycle C_i. Set

$$\begin{pmatrix} S_{\lambda+1} \cdots S_{\lambda+\mu} \end{pmatrix} = \begin{pmatrix} B \\ I_\mu \end{pmatrix}. \tag{2}$$

Then the product of the matrix of C's on the left side of Equation (1) and the matrix of S's on the left side of Equation (2) is $B + B = 0$, i.e., the S's are orthogonal to the C's. Moreover, $S_{\lambda+i} \cap \{e_{\lambda+1}, \ldots, e_N\} = e_{\lambda+i}$ for $1 \leq i \leq \mu$. The running time required to compute this null space basis is the time required to output the already known matrix B. By using some sparse representation of the vectors we need at most $O(\lambda \cdot \mu)$ time. In the general case $\lambda \leq m$ and $\mu = N - \lambda \in O(n^{1+1/k})$. Thus, initialization of phase 2 needs $O(mn^{1+1/k})$ time.

The recursive case, $k \geq 2$: Let $\ell = \lceil k/2 \rceil$. We first call the algorithm recursively with ℓ and $S_{\alpha+1}$ to $S_{\alpha+\ell}$. The call will return cycles $Z_{\alpha+1}$ to $Z_{\alpha+\ell}$ and updated sets $S_{\alpha+1}$ to $S_{\alpha+\ell}$. We next update the sets $S_{\alpha+\ell+1}$ to $S_{\alpha+k}$. The set $S_{\alpha+j}$, $\ell + 1 \leq j \leq k$, is replaced by a sum $S_{\alpha+j} + \sum_{1 \leq i \leq \ell} \beta_{ji} S_{\alpha+i}$ where the β_{ji} are chosen such that the updated $S_{\alpha+j}$ becomes orthogonal to the cycles $Z_{\alpha+1}$ to $Z_{\alpha+\ell}$. Observe that orthogonality to the cycles in PB is not affected. The update step is implemented using fast matrix multiplication and takes time $O(mk^{\omega-1})$. The final step is to call the algorithm recursively for the remaining cycles. We therefore have the following recursion for the running time: $T(k) = T(\lceil k/2 \rceil) + T(\lfloor k/2 \rfloor) + O(mk^{\omega-1})$ for $k \geq 2$. This solves to $T(k) = k \cdot T(1) + O(mk^{\omega-1})$. We call the algorithm with $k = \mu$ and hence have total running time $\mu \cdot T(1) + O(m\mu^{\omega-1})$.

The base case, $k = 1$: The algorithm computes a t-approximate shortest[2] cycle C with $\langle C, S_{\alpha+1} \rangle = 1$. The shortest cycle C with $\langle C, S_{\alpha+1} \rangle = 1$ can be computed as follows. We set up an auxiliary graph $G^\dagger$ with two copies, say v' and v'', for each vertex v, and two copies e' and e'' for each edge $e = (u, v) \in E$. If $e \in S_{\alpha+1}$, the copies are (u', v'') and (u'', v') and if $e \notin S_{\alpha+1}$, the copies are (u', v') and (u'', v''). Then a shortest cycle C with $\langle C, S_{\alpha+1} \rangle = 1$ corresponds to a shortest path connecting the two copies of some vertex v minimized over all v. Such a path can be found by n shortest path computations in the auxiliary graph. In order to compute a t-approximate shortest cycle C with $\langle C, S_{\alpha+1} \rangle = 1$ we compute t-approximate single source shortest paths between n pairs of vertices.

We need to perform a total of μn approximate shortest path computations. Therefore, we require a faster algorithm than constructing a spanner. We use an *approximate distance oracle*. Thorup and Zwick [20] constructed a structure which answers $(2k-1)$-approximate shortest path queries in time $O(k)$. The structure requires space $O(kn^{1+1/k})$ and can be constructed in expected time $O(kmn^{1/k})$.

Using such a construction, we bound $T(1)$ by the cost of computing the approximate distance oracle ($O(kmn^{1/k})$ expected time) and the cost of performing n queries to the oracle. Each query costs $O(k)$ and thus a total cost of $O(nk)$. Forming the actual cycle can be done in time linear to its length which is $O(n)$. Thus, $T(1) = O(kmn^{1/k})$ and therefore $T(\mu) = O(\mu kmn^{1/k} + m\mu^{\omega-1})$. Since $\mu \in O(n^{1+1/k})$ we get a bound of $O(kmn^{1+2/k} + mn^{(1+1/k)(\omega-1)})$.

Approximation guarantee. We prove that the computed set of cycles is a t-approximation of the MCB. Consider the vectors $S_{\lambda+1}, \ldots, S_N$ at the end of the algorithm and define $S_i = \{e_i\}$ for $1 \leq i \leq \lambda$. Then each C_i, $1 \leq i \leq N$, is a t-approximation of the shortest cycle in G having odd intersection with S_i. All we need to show is Lemma 3. Then the approximation guarantee follows from Lemma 1.

Lemma 3. *The vectors $S_1, \ldots, S_N$ are linearly independent.*

Proof. Consider any i. We have $\langle C_i, S_i \rangle = 1$ and $\langle C_i, S_j \rangle = 0$ for all $j \geq i+1$. The latter holds for $j > \lambda$ by the invariants of the recursive procedure and it holds for $i < j \leq \lambda$ since C_i consists of edge e_i and edges in the spanner (which have index greater than λ) and $S_j = \{e_j\}$. Thus, S_i is independent of the $S_{i+1}, \ldots, S_N$ and the lemma follows.

Theorem 1. *For any integer $k \geq 1$, a $(2k-1)$-approximate MCB can be computed in expected time $O(kmn^{1+2/k} + mn^{(1+1/k)(\omega-1)})$ in undirected weighted graphs. An $O(\log n)$-approximate MCB in expected time $O(mn^{\omega-1} + mn \log n)$.*

---

[2] The original algorithm in [6] constructs a shortest cycle.

3.2   The Second Approach

Our second algorithm to compute the remaining cycles of our cycle basis, just computes a minimum cycle basis of the t-spanner G'. The dimension of the cycle space of G' is $\mu = N - \lambda$ and thus we have the right number of cycles. Let $C_{\lambda+1}, \dots, C_N$ be an MCB of G'. Cycles $\{C_1, \dots, C_\lambda\} \cup \{C_{\lambda+1}, \dots, C_N\}$ are by definition linearly independent and we are also going to prove that they form a t-approximation of an MCB of G.

For $1 \le i \le \lambda$, we have $C_i = e_i + p_i$, where p_i is a shortest path in G' between the endpoints of e_i. In order to show that cycles $C_1, \dots, C_N$ are a t-approximation of the MCB, we again define appropriate linearly independent vectors $S_1, \dots, S_N \in \{0,1\}^N$ and use Lemma 1. Consider the exact algorithm in [6] executing with the t-spanner G' as its input. Other than the cycles $C_{\lambda+1}, \dots, C_N$, the algorithm also returns vectors $R_{\lambda+1}, \dots, R_N \in \{0,1\}^{N-\lambda}$ such that $\langle C_i, R_j \rangle = 0$ for $\lambda + 1 \le i < j \le N$ and C_i is a shortest cycle in G' such that $\langle C_i, R_i \rangle = 1$ for $\lambda + 1 \le i \le N$. Moreover, the $(N - \lambda) \times (N - \lambda)$ matrix whose j-th row is R_j is lower triangular with 1 in its diagonal. This implies that the R_j's are linearly independent. Given any vector $S \in \{0,1\}^N$ let $\tilde{S}$ be the projection of S onto its last $N - \lambda$ coordinates. In other words, if S is an edge set of G, then let $\tilde{S}$ be the edge set restricted only to the edges of G'. We define S_j for $1 \le j \le N$ as follows. Let $S_1, \dots, S_\lambda$ be the first λ unit vectors of $\{0,1\}^N$. For $\lambda + 1 \le j \le N$ define S_j as:

$$S_j = (-\langle \tilde{C}_1, R_j \rangle, \dots, -\langle \tilde{C}_\lambda, R_j \rangle, R_{j,1}, R_{j,2}, \dots, R_{j,(N-\lambda)}),$$

where $R_{j,1}, \dots, R_{j,(N-\lambda)}$ are the coordinates of the vector $R_j \in \{0,1\}^{N-\lambda}$. Note that the vectors S_j for $1 \le j \le N$, defined above, are linearly independent. This is because the $N \times N$ matrix whose j-th row is S_j is lower triangular with 1's in its diagonal. The above definition of S_j's is motivated by the property that for each $1 \le i \le \lambda$, we have $\langle C_i, S_j \rangle = -\langle \tilde{C}_i, R_j \rangle + \langle \tilde{C}_i, R_j \rangle = 0$, since the cycle C_i has 0 in all first λ coordinates, except the i-th coordinate, which is 1. Lemma 4, shown below, together with Lemma 1, implies the correctness of our approach.

Lemma 4. *Consider the above defined S_j for $1 \le j \le N$ and let D_j be the shortest cycle in G such that $\langle D_j, S_j \rangle = 1$. Cycle C_j has weight at most t times the weight of D_j.*

Proof. This is obvious for $1 \le j \le \lambda$ since D_j is a shortest cycle in G which uses edge e_j and $C_j = e_j + p_j$, where p_j is a t-approximate shortest path between the endpoints of e_j. Consider now D_j for $\lambda + 1 \le j \le N$. If D_j uses any edge e_i for $1 \le i \le \lambda$ we replace it with the corresponding shortest path in the spanner. This is the same as saying consider the cycle $D_j + C_i$ instead of D_j. Let $D'_j = D_j + \sum_{1 \le i \le \lambda}(e_i \in D_j)C_i$ where $(e_i \in D_j)$ is 1 if $e_i \in D_j$ and 0 if $e_i \notin D_j$. Then

$$\langle D'_j, S_j \rangle = \langle D_j, S_j \rangle + \sum_{1 \le i \le \lambda} (e_i \in D_j)\langle C_i, S_j \rangle.$$

But recall that our definition of S_j ensures that $\langle C_i, S_j \rangle = 0$ for $1 \leq i \leq \lambda$. This implies that $\langle D'_j, S_j \rangle = \langle D_j, S_j \rangle = 1$. But D'_j by definition has 0 in the first λ coordinates and $\tilde{S}_j = R_j$, which in turn implies that $\langle \tilde{D}'_j, R_j \rangle = 1$.

C_j is a shortest cycle in G' such that $\langle C_j, R_j \rangle = 1$. Thus, C_j has weight at most the weight of $\tilde{D}'_j$, and by construction, D'_j has weight at most t times the weight of D_j.

Thus, we have shown that the cost of our approximate basis is at most t times the cost of an optimal basis. As a t-spanner we will again use a $(2k-1)$-spanner. The best time bound in order to compute an MCB is $O(m^2 n + mn^2 \log n)$ and since a $(2k - 1)$-spanner has at most $O(n^{1+1/k})$ edges the total running time becomes $O(n^{3+2/k})$.

Theorem 2. *A $(2k-1)$-approximate MCB, for any integer $k \geq 1$, in a weighted undirected graph can be computed in time $O(n^{3+2/k})$. An $O(\log n)$-approximate MCB can be computed in time $O(n^3 \log n)$.*

Further results. By combining the two approaches we can get even faster algorithms in the expense of an increased approximation ratio. Due to space restrictions, details of this and several following results can be found in the full version of this paper.

Our techniques for $2k-1$ approximate minimum cycle basis can also be applied to the minimum cycle basis problem in directed graphs. The problem definition is described in Section 4.1. We simply state our results here.

Theorem 3. *For any integer $k \geq 1$, a $(2k - 1)$ approximate MCB of a directed graph with non-negative edge weights can be computed in time $O(n^{4+3/k})$. If we allow randomization it can be computed, with high probability, in time $O(n^{3+2/k})$.*

For some classes of graphs which admit better spanners, our approaches lead to very fast approximation algorithms. For the complete Euclidean graph in two dimensions we get a 2.42 approximation in time $O(n^3)$. Similar results can be obtained in higher (but fixed) dimensions. For planar graphs we get a linear time 2 approximation by just returning the list of bounded faces.

Practical considerations. Both approaches (Section 3.1 and 3.2) use fast matrix multiplication. However, they are also efficient even when used without fast matrix multiplication. This fact has high practical value since high performance fast matrix multiplication libraries are difficult to implement. Instead of the $O(m^2 n + mn^2 \log n)$ algorithm to compute an MCB in G', use the $O(m^3 + mn^2 \log n)$ algorithm from [3], which is the fastest algorithm to compute an MCB without fast matrix multiplication.

Theorem 4. *A $(2k - 1)$-approximate MCB, for any integer $k \geq 1$, can be computed in an undirected weighted graph without fast matrix multiplication in expected $O(kmn^{1+2/k} + mn^{2+2/k})$ and deterministic $O(n^{3+3/k})$ time respectively.*

Both our algorithms are $o(m^\omega)$ for sufficiently dense graphs and appropriate values of k. Moreover, they are easy to implement efficiently. Preliminary experiments suggest a significant speedup in practice.

4   A 2-Approximation Algorithm

For any undirected (connected) graph $G = (V, E)$ with n vertices and m edges, Horton [2] defined a set of $O(mn)$ cycles and proved that it contains an MCB. An MCB can be found by determining the least weight $N = m - n + 1$ linearly independent cycles from this set, using Gaussian elimination. We define a set of $O(m\sqrt{n}\log n)$ cycles and show that it contains a 2-approximate minimum cycle basis; our set is a subset of Horton's set. Again, the basis is extracted from the set by determining the least weight N linearly independent cycles in it.

For a vertex $x \in V$ and an edge $e = (u, v) \in E$, let $C[x, e] = SP(x, u) + e + SP(v, x)$ be the cycle consisting of the edge e and the shortest paths from x to its endpoints. Horton's collection consists of the cycles $C[x, e]$ for all $x \in V$ and $e \in E$. We use a subset of Horton's collection.

Definition 1. *For $v, x \in V$ and $S \subset V$, bunch(v, S) consists of all vertices closer to v than to any vertex in S and cluster(x, S) consists of all vertices v with $x \in$ bunch(v, S).*

Lemma 5 (Thorup and Zwick [21]). *Given a weighted graph $G = (V, E)$ and $0 < q < 1$, one can compute a set $S \subset V$ of size $O(nq\log n)$ in expected time $O(m/q \log n)$ such that $|cluster(x, S)| = 1/q$ for all $x \in V$.*

We take a value $q = 1/\sqrt{n\log n}$ here and first compute in expected time $O(m\sqrt{n}\log^{3/2} n)$ a set $S \subset V$ of $O(\sqrt{n\log n})$ vertices as given in Lemma 5. This ensures that $cluster(v, S)$ has size $\sqrt{n\log n}$ for all $v \in V$. Also, $bunch(v, S)$ for all v can be computed in expected time $O(m/q)$ [20], which is $O(m\sqrt{n\log n})$. We use two types of cycles:

- the $O(m\sqrt{n\log n})$ cycles $C[s, e]$ for all $s \in S$ and $e \in E$,
- the cycles $C[u, e]$ for each $u \in V$ and $e = (v, w) \in E$ and either v or w in $bunch(u, S)$. The number of such cycles is $\sum_{u \in V} \sum_{v \in bunch(u,S)} \deg(v)$. This is the same as $\sum_{v \in V} \deg(v) \cdot |cluster(v, S)|$, which is $\sqrt{n\log n} \sum_{v \in V} \deg(v) = m\sqrt{n\log n}$.

Thus, our collection has $O(m\sqrt{n\log n})$ cycles. We need to show that it contains a 2-approximate cycle basis. Let $B_1, \ldots, B_N$ be the minimum cycle basis of G determined by Horton's algorithm in order of increasing weight, i.e., $w(B_1) \leq w(B_2) \leq \cdots \leq w(B_N)$. We show that each $B_i = \sum_{C \in \mathcal{C}_i} C$ where $\mathcal{C}_i$ is a subset of our collection and each cycle in $\mathcal{C}_i$ has cost at most $2w(B_i)$. This implies that our collection contains N linearly independent cycles $A_1, \ldots, A_N$ with $w(A_i) \leq 2 \cdot w(B_i)$ for $i = 1, \ldots, N$. Assume otherwise and let j be minimal such that $\cup_{i \leq j} \mathcal{C}_i$ contains less than j linearly independent vectors with $w(A_i) \leq 2 \cdot w(B_i)$ for $i = 1, \ldots, j$. Then $j \geq 1$ and $\cup_{i \leq j-1} \mathcal{C}_i$ contains at least $j-1$ linearly independent vectors with $w(A_i) \leq 2 \cdot w(B_i)$ for $i = 1, \ldots, j - 1$. Also, $\cup_{i \leq j} \mathcal{C}_i$ spans $\{B_1, \ldots, B_i\}$ and hence contains at least i linearly independent vectors. Thus, it contains a vector A_j linearly independent from $\{A_1, \ldots, A_{j-1}\}$. Furthermore, $A_j \in \mathcal{C}_i$ for some $i \leq j$ and hence $w(A_j) \leq 2w(B_i) \leq 2w(B_j)$, a contradiction.

Consider any B_i. If B_i belongs to our collection, we set $\mathcal{C}_i = \{B_i\}$. Otherwise, $B_i = C[u, e]$ where $e = (v, w)$ and neither v nor w is in $bunch(u, S)$. Let $s \in S$ be the nearest vertex in S to u. Then, $w(\mathrm{SP}(s, u)) \leq w(\mathrm{SP}(u, v))$ and $w(\mathrm{SP}(s, u)) \leq w(\mathrm{SP}(u, w))$.

For any edge $f \in B_i$, the cycle $C(s, f)$ is in our collection and furthermore $B_i = \sum_{f \in B_i} C(s, f)$ since the paths from s to the endpoints of the edges in B_i appear twice in this sum and cancel out. We set $\mathcal{C}_i = \{C(s, f) \mid f \in B_i\}$. It remains to show $w(C(s, f)) \leq 2w(B_i)$ for all $f \in B_i$. We distinguish cases.

Assume first that $f \neq e$. Then $f \in \mathrm{SP}(u, v)$ or $f \in \mathrm{SP}(u, w)$. We may assume w.l.o.g. that the former is the case. Then $w(C(s, f)) \leq w(\mathrm{SP}(s, u)) + w(\mathrm{SP}(u, v)) + w(\mathrm{SP}(v, s))$ since $C(s, f)$ consists of f and the shortest paths from s to the endpoints of f and $w(\mathrm{SP}(v, s)) \leq w(\mathrm{SP}(s, u)) + w(\mathrm{SP}(u, v))$ by the triangle inequality. Thus $w(C(s, f)) \leq 2(w(\mathrm{SP}(s, u)) + w(\mathrm{SP}(u, v))) \leq 2w(B_i)$ since $w(\mathrm{SP}(s, u)) \leq w(\mathrm{SP}(u, w))$.

Assume next that $f = e$. Then $w(C(s, f)) = w(\mathrm{SP}(s, v)) + c(e) + w(\mathrm{SP}(w, s)) \leq w(\mathrm{SP}(s, u)) + w(\mathrm{SP}(u, v)) + c(e) + w(\mathrm{SP}(s, u)) + w(\mathrm{SP}(u, w)) \leq 2w(\mathrm{SP}(u, v)) + c(e) + 2w(\mathrm{SP}(u, w)) \leq 2w(B_i)$.

We sort our collection in non-decreasing order of weight and do Gaussian elimination on their incidence vectors, restricted to the N edges $e_1, \ldots, e_N$. This determines the least weight N linearly independent cycles in our collection. The time taken for the Gaussian elimination step, which is the most expensive step in our algorithm, is $O(m^\omega \sqrt{n \log n})$ using fast matrix multiplication.

Theorem 5. *A 2-approximate MCB in an undirected graph G with non-negative edge weights can be computed in expected time $O(m^\omega \sqrt{n \log n})$.*

4.1 Extension to Directed Graphs

The above algorithm also holds for directed graphs. A cycle in a directed graph is a cycle in the underlying undirected graph with edges traversable in both directions. A $\{-1, 0, 1\}$ edge incidence vector is associated with each cycle: edges traversed by the cycle in the right direction get 1 and edges traversed in the opposite direction get -1. The cycle space is the space generated by these cycle vectors over $\mathbb{Q}$. Note that the weight of a cycle is simply the sum of the weight of its edges, independent of the orientation of these edges. Let $C = (e_1, \ldots, e_k)$ be a cycle in a directed graph and let $e_i = (u_i, u_{i+1})$. Then we can write $C = \sum_{i=1}^{k} \mathrm{SP}(s, u_i) + e_i + \mathrm{SP}(u_{i+1}, s)$ where $u_{k+1} = u_1$, since $\mathrm{SP}(s, u_i)$ cancels $\mathrm{SP}(u_i, s)$. Note that $\mathrm{SP}(a, b)$ for us here need not be a directed path - it is a shortest path in the underlying undirected graph between a and b. However, the incidence vector of this path in the directed graph would contain -1's corresponding to edges which are traversed in the reverse direction. All the steps in the above construction go through for directed minimum cycle bases too and we have a collection of $O(m\sqrt{n \log n})$ cycles which is a superset of a 2-approximate directed minimum cycle basis.

However, when we do Gaussian elimination, we are no longer over $\mathbb{F}_2$ and so the numbers could grow large. So we can no longer claim that the time taken for

Gaussian elimination is $O(m^\omega \sqrt{n} \log n)$. But if we choose a prime p uniformly at random from a collection of small primes and do the arithmetic in Gaussian elimination modulo p, then our cost remains $O(m^\omega \sqrt{n} \log n)$ and we will show that with high probability we determine the cycles of a 2-approximate MCB.

Arithmetic modulo p. The problem with doing arithmetic modulo any number p is that the least weight N linearly independent cycles in our collection could turn out to be *linearly dependent* modulo p. That is, the determinant of the $N \times N$ matrix M, defined by incidence vectors of these N cycles, is a multiple of p. In that case, our algorithm is not guaranteed to return a 2-approximate minimum cycle basis.

Now we will use the property that all the entries in the matrix M are $-1, 0, 1$, to show a bounded error when p is a prime chosen uniformly at random from a collection $P = \{p_1, \ldots, p_{N^2}\}$ of N^2 distinct primes, where each $p_i \geq \sqrt{N}$. It follows from Hadamard's inequality that the absolute value of the determinant of M is at most $N^{N/2}$, since each of the N rows is a vector in $\{-1, 0, 1\}^N$. Thus, at most N elements of P can be divisors of $\det(M)$. So the probability that a random element of P divides $\det(M)$ is $\leq N/N^2 = 1/N$. So with probability $1 - 1/N$, arithmetic modulo p yields the least weight N linearly independent cycles from the collection of $O(m\sqrt{n} \log n)$ cycles.

The value of $\pi(r)$, the number of primes less than r, is given by $r/6 \log r \leq \pi(r) \leq 8r/\log r$ [22]. So all the primes $p_1, \ldots, p_{N^2}$ are $\tilde{O}(N^2)$, and computing them takes $\tilde{O}(N^2)$ time using a sieving algorithm. Arithmetic modulo p ensures that all numbers are $\tilde{O}(N^2)$ and we can assume that arithmetic on $O(\log N)$ bit numbers takes $O(1)$ time. It follows that addition, subtraction and multiplication in $\mathbb{Z}_p$ can be implemented in unit time since p is $\tilde{O}(N^2)$. However, we also need to implement division efficiently. Once p is chosen, we compute the multiplicative inverses of all elements in $\mathbb{Z}_p^*$ by the extended Euclid's gcd algorithm by solving $ax = 1 \pmod{p}$ for each $a \in \mathbb{Z}_p^*$. This takes time $O(\log p)$ for each element and hence $O(p \log p) = \tilde{O}(N^2)$ for all the elements. Thus, we have shown the following theorem.

Theorem 6. *A 2-approximate minimum cycle basis can be computed with high probability in expected time $O(m^\omega \sqrt{n} \log n)$ in an directed graph G with n vertices, m edges and non-negative edge weights.*

5   Conclusions

In this paper we design faster algorithms for computing approximate minimum cycle basis of undirected graphs. To the best of our knowledge it is the first time that sparse cycle bases with a guarantee are computed in $o(m^\omega)$ time. Our techniques extend also to the directed version of the minimum cycle basis problem in which the base field is $\mathbb{Q}$ instead of $\mathbb{F}_2$. We present very fast approximate algorithms for this version as well.

References

1. Stepanec, G.F.: Basis systems of vector cycles with extremal properties in graphs. Uspekhi Mat. Nauk **19** (1964) 171–175
2. Horton, J.D.: A polynomial-time algorithm to find a shortest cycle basis of a graph. SIAM Journal of Computing **16** (1987) 359–366
3. de Pina, J.: Applications of Shortest Path Methods. PhD thesis, University of Amsterdam, Netherlands (1995)
4. Golynski, A., Horton, J.D.: A polynomial time algorithm to find the minimum cycle basis of a regular matroid. In: SWAT. (2002)
5. Berger, F., Gritzmann, P., de Vries, S.: Minimum cycle basis for network graphs. Algorithmica **40**(1) (2004) 51–62
6. Kavitha, T., Mehlhorn, K., Michail, D., Paluch, K.E.: A faster algorithm for minimum cycle basis of graphs. In: 31st International Colloquium on Automata, Languages and Programming, Finland. (2004) 846–857
7. Huber, M.: Implementation of algorithms for sparse cycle bases of graphs. Technical report, Technische Universität München (2002) http://www-m9.ma.tum.de/dm/cycles/mhuber.
8. Kreisbasenbibliothek CyBaL. http://www-m9.ma.tum.de/dm/cycles/cybal (2004)
9. Mehlhorn, K., Michail, D.: Implementing minimum cycle basis algorithms. In: WEA. Volume 3503 of LNCS. (2005) 32–43
10. Swamy, M.N.S., Thulasiraman, K.: Graphs, Networks, and Algorithms. John Wiley & Sons, New York (1981)
11. Cassell, A.C., Henderson, J.C., Ramachandran, K.: Cycle bases of minimal measure for the structural analysis of skeletal structures by the flexibility method. In: Proc. Royal Society of London Series A. Volume 350. (1976) 61–70
12. Gleiss, P.M.: Short Cycles, Minimum Cycle Bases of Graphs from Chemistry and Biochemistry. PhD thesis, Fakultät Für Naturwissenschaften und Mathematik der Universität Wien (2001)
13. Tewari, G., Gotsman, C., Gortler, S.J.: Meshing genus-1 point clouds using discrete one-forms. Computers and Graphics (2006) to appear.
14. Coppersmith, D., Winograd, S.: Matrix multiplications via arithmetic progressions. Journal of Symb. Comput. **9** (1990) 251–280
15. Kavitha, T., Mehlhorn, K.: A polynomial time algorithm for minimum cycle basis in directed graphs. In: STACS 2005. Volume 3404 of LNCS. (2005) 654–665
16. Liebchen, C., Rizzi, R.: A greedy approach to compute a minimum cycle basis of a directed graph. Inf. Process. Lett. **94**(3) (2005) 107–112
17. Hariharan, R., Kavitha, T., Mehlhorn, K.: A faster deterministic algorithm for minimum cycle basis in directed graphs. In: Proceedings of ICALP. Volume 4051 of LNCS. (2006) 250–261
18. Kavitha, T.: An $\tilde{O}(m^2 n)$ randomized algorithm to compute a minimum cycle basis of a directed graph. In: Proceedings of ICALP, LNCS 3580. (2005) 273–284
19. Althöfer, I., Das, G., Dobkin, D., Joseph, D., Soares, J.: On sparse spanners of weighted graphs. Discrete Comput. Geom. **9**(1) (1993) 81–100
20. Thorup, M., Zwick, U.: Approximate distance oracles. In: ACM Symposium on Theory of Computing. (2001) 183–192
21. Thorup, M., Zwick, U.: Compact routing schemes. In: Proceedings of 13th ACM Symposium on Parallel Algorithms and Architecture. (2001) 1–10
22. Apostol, T.M.: Introduction to Analytic Number Theory. Springer-Verlag (1997)

On Completing Latin Squares

Iman Hajirasouliha[1], Hossein Jowhari[1], Ravi Kumar[2], and Ravi Sundaram[3]

[1] Simon Fraser University, Burnaby, BC, Canada V5A 1S6
{ihajiras,hjowhari}@cs.sfu.ca
[2] Yahoo! Research, Sunnyvale, CA 94089, USA
ravikumar@yahoo-inc.com
[3] Northeastern University, Boston, MA 02115, USA
koods@ccs.neu.edu

Abstract. We present a $(\frac{2}{3} - \epsilon)$-approximation algorithm for the partial latin square extension (PLSE) problem. This improves the current best bound of $1 - \frac{1}{e}$ due to Gomes, Regis, and Shmoys [5]. We also show that PLSE is APX-hard.

We then consider two new and natural variants of PLSE. In the first, there is an added restriction that at most k colors are to be used in the extension; for this problem, we prove a tight approximation threshold of $1 - \frac{1}{e}$. In the second, the goal is to find the largest partial Latin square embedded in the given partial Latin square that can be extended to completion; we obtain a $\frac{1}{4}$-approximation algorithm in this case.

1 Introduction

Latin squares are elementary combinatorial objects that have been studied for a long time [14]. Informally, a Latin square is an $n \times n$ grid, where each cell is filled with a number in $\{1, \ldots, n\}$ and each number occurs exactly once in every row and every column. A partially filled latin square (PLS) is an $n \times n$ grid, where each cell is either empty or filled with a number in $\{1, \ldots, n\}$ and each number occurs at most once in every row and every column. Besides being interesting objects from a mathematical point of view, PLSs have found applications in statistical design, error-correcting codes, and more recently, optical routing. Sudoku puzzles, one of the current fads, are PLSs with additional properties.

To motivate an algorithmic study of PLSs, consider their applications in optical routers [1]. Routers in an optical network are connected by fiber optic links that support a certain number of wavelengths. Each router has some input and output links and is capable of switching wavelengths to avoid conflicts in fiber links. Suppose the router has n input and n output ports and each link can carry n different wavelengths. The snapshot of an active router can be modeled by a PLS as follows. Associate each input port with a row and each output port with a column in the PLS and consider a light signal that comes from the input port i and is routed to the output port j with the new wavelength of k. This can be reflected by assigning k to the cell (i, j) in the PLS.

The question of how much can we increase the utilization of the router is precisely the problem of assigning numbers to the empty cells in a PLS; this is the

W. Thomas and P. Weil (Eds.): STACS 2007, LNCS 4393, pp. 524–535, 2007.

PLS extension problem (PLSE). Colbourn [2] showed that the decision version of PLSE is NP-complete. Kumar, Russell, and Sundaram [10] presented two approximation algorithms for PLSE that achieves factors $\frac{1}{3}$ and $\frac{1}{2}$ (see Section 2 for definition of approximation). Gomes, Regis, and Shmoys [5] obtained an LP-based approximation algorithm that achieves a factor $1 - \frac{1}{e}$, which is currently the best known.

Consider the following two natural variants of the PLSE problem. In the k-PLSE problem, the goal is to use at most k different numbers to fill the empty cells in a PLS. This problem arises in optical routers when we wish to invest in at most k new wavelengths, say because of resource considerations. In the c-PLSE problem, the goal is to find the largest PLS embedded in the given PLS that can be extended to completion. This problem arises naturally when we wish to build out an existing network to completion while retaining as much of the existing infrastructure as possible. To the best of our knowledge, neither k-PLSE nor c-PLSE has been studied before.

1.1 Main Results

We obtain a $(\frac{2}{3} - \epsilon)$-approximation algorithm for the PLSE problem. This improves the current best bound of $1 - \frac{1}{e}$ due to Gomes, Regis, and Shmoys [5]. Our algorithm is based on local search and we analyze its performance by appealing to a packing bound of Hurkens and Schrijver [8]. We also show that PLSE is APX-hard, thereby strengthening the NP-hardness result of Colbourn [2].

We then study the k-PLSE problem. For this problem, we first show a natural greedy algorithm that achieves an approximation factor $\frac{1}{2}$. We also show that a randomized rounding procedure applied on the LP formulation of the problem achieves a factor $1 - \frac{1}{e} - \epsilon$. Moreover we show that this is almost the best possible, i.e. no polynomial-time algorithm for k-PLSE can achieve factor better than $1 - \frac{1}{e} + \epsilon$ unless P = NP.

Finally, for the c-PLSE problem, based on a theorem of Ryser [14], we present a $\frac{1}{4}$-approximation algorithm.

2   Preliminaries

Let $[n] = \{1, \ldots, n\}$. A *partial Latin square* (PLS) of order n is an $n \times n$ array whose cells are empty or contain a color from $[n]$, with the restriction that no color is repeated in a row or column. When the PLS has no empty cells it is simply called a *latin square* (LS). We denote the content of the (i, j)-th cell in the PLS L by $L(i, j)$. The number of non-empty cells of L is denoted $|L|$.

A PLS L' is an *extension* of a PLS L if $L'(i, j) = L(i, j)$ holds for all non-empty cells $L(i, j)$; we denote this by $L \preceq L'$. Naturally, L' can be obtained by coloring some of the empty cells in L, while maintaining the coloring restriction.

The *partial Latin square extension* problem (PLSE) is, given a PLS L, color the maximum number of empty cells in L using colors in $[n]$, i.e., find PLS L' such that $L' \succeq L$ and $|L'|$ is maximized. The *k-partial latin square extension* problem (k-PLSE) is, given a PLS L of order n, color the maximum number of empty cells in L by colors in $[n]$ such that at most k colors are used in the coloring. Note that, the colors originally present in L are counted when and only when they are used again in L'. It is clear that PLSE is the same as n-PLSE. The *c-partial latin square extension* problem (c-PLSE) is, given a PLS L of order n, find the largest $c, 0 \leq c \leq 1$, such that L contains a PLS L' with $|L'| = c|L|$ and L' can be extended to completion. It is clear that when an instance of c-PLSE has $c = 1$ it means that it can be extended to completion.

A ρ-approximation to these problems is to find a PLS L' such that $|L'|$ is within ρ of the optimum solution to the problem, where $0 < \rho \leq 1$.

2.1 The 3EDM Problem

To facilitate the presentation of our results, we define the following new problem called *3EDM*: given a tripartite graph, this problem corresponds to finding the largest number of edge disjoint triangles in the graph. Similarly, in the *k-3EDM* problem, the goal is to find the largest number of edge disjoint triangles in a tripartite graph, with the constraint that at most k vertices from the third partition are touched by the triangles. We argue that 3EDM and PLSE problems are equivalent, i.e., there are value-preserving reductions from PLSE to 3EDM and vice versa.

Theorem 1. *The PLSE and 3EDM problems are equivalent.*

Proof. The reduction from PLSE to 3EDM is straightforward. Given an $n \times n$ instance L of PLSE, create a tripartite graph G with $3 \times n$ vertices as follows. The first partition in G represents the n rows, the second represents the n columns, and the third represents the n colors. For each empty cell (i, j) in L and each candidate color k that can be assigned to this cell, place a triangle between the vertices i, j, k in G. It is easy to see that L can be extended to t additional cells if and only if G has t edge-disjoint triangles.

Conversely, we show that there is a value-preserving reduction from 3EDM to PLSE. Let $G = (U \cup V \cup W, E)$ be a tripartite graph and let $n = \max\{|U|, |V|, |W|\}$. We construct a PLS L of order $3n$ such that maximum number of edge disjoint triangles in G equals the maximum number of entries that can be filled in L and vice versa.

First we assume that every edge in G is contained in at least one triangle, since edges that are not present in at least one triangle can always be removed without affecting the solution. Next we assume that $|V| = |U| = |W| = n$, since isolated vertices can be added to G without changing the solution. Let $U = \{u_1, \ldots, u_n\}, V = \{v_1, \ldots, v_n\}$, and $W = \{w_1, \ldots, w_n\}$. Let L be an empty PLS of order $3n$; think of L as being composed of square blocks $A_1, \ldots, A_9$, each of dimension $n \times n$; here the blocks are numbered in the row-major order. Now we turn L into a PLS such that the entry (i, j) in L is empty and can be filled with color $k \leq n$ if the triangle (u_i, v_j, w_k) exists in G.

Let R_i be the index set of vertices in W such that u_i is not connected to them. For each $r \in R_i$, we fill an empty entry in the i-th row of A_2 with color r. Note that we can do this for all $i = 1, \ldots, n$ without creating a conflict. Similarly let C_j be the index set of vertices in W such that v_j is not connected to them. For each $c \in C_j$, we fill one of the empty entries in the j-th column of A_4 with c. Now it is easy to see that we can fill the entry (i, j) in L with color $k \leq n$ if the triangle (u_i, v_j, w_k) appears in G. However it is possible to fill these entries with colors greater than n. To circumvent this problem, we use the additional blocks in the following way.

Let A'_1 be the subset of entries in A_1 such that $(i, j) \in A'_1$ if the edge (u_i, v_j) does not appear in G. We fill in the entries in A'_1 with colors from the set $\{n + 1, \ldots, 2n\}$; this will ensure that the non-edge (u_i, v_j) does not contribute to the PLSE solution. After this step, let A_{1j} be the set of colors appearing in j-th column of A_1. For every $r \in \{n + 1, \ldots, 2n\}$, if $r \notin A_{1j}$, then we place r in an empty entry in the j-th column of A_7. This way, we ensure that none of the colors in $\{n + 1, \ldots, 2n\}$ can be used to fill the empty entries of A_1. Analogously, the block A_3 is used to ensure that none of the colors in $\{2n + 1, \ldots, 3n\}$ can be used to fill the empty entries of A_1; this can be easily achieved by setting A_3 to be a complete Latin square with entries from $\{2n + 1, \ldots, 3n\}$. Now it suffices to fill in the remaining entries greedily except that we have to avoid filling the entries of A_2, A_4, and A_7 with colors from $\{1, \ldots, n\}$. We can block A_2 and A_4 w.r.t $\{1, \ldots, n\}$ by placing appropriate colors in A_6 and A_8. We fill the empty entries in A_7 with colors from the set $\{2n + 1, \ldots, 3n\}$). Now all entries except the empty ones in A_1 are either filled or blocked and we can place k in (i, j) if and only if the triangle (u_i, v_j, w_k) exists in G. This completes the proof. $\square$

In a similar manner, we can show that

Corollary 1. *The k-PLSE and k-3EDM problems are equivalent.*

3   Improved Bounds for the PLSE Problem

In this section we obtain a $(\frac{2}{3} - \epsilon)$-approximation algorithm for the PLSE problem; this improves the $(1 - \frac{1}{e})$-approximation algorithm of Gomes, Regis, and Shmoys [5]. We then show that the PLSE problem is APX-hard.

3.1   A Local Search Algorithm

First, we state a well-known result of Hurkens and Schrijver [8].

Theorem 2 (Hurkens–Schrijver [8]). *Let m, n, k, t be positive integers with $k \geq 3$. Let $E_1, \ldots, E_m$ be subsets of a set V of size n such that*

1. *each element of V is contained in at most k of the sets $E_1, \ldots E_m$ and*
2. *any collection of at most t sets among $E_1, \ldots E_m$ has a system of distinct representatives in V.*

Then we have

$$\frac{m}{n} \leq \begin{cases} \frac{k(k-1)^r - k}{2(k-1)^r - k} & \text{if } t = 2r - 1 \\ \frac{k(k-1)^r - 2}{2(k-1)^r - 2} & \text{if } t = 2r. \end{cases}$$

We present a simple local search-based approximation algorithm for PLSE by obtaining an algorithm for 3EDM.

Theorem 3. *For any $\epsilon > 0$, there is a $(\frac{2}{3} - \epsilon)$-approximation algorithm for the 3EDM problem.*

Proof. Let G be the given graph with n vertices. Fix a $t \geq 1$. Start with any collection of edge-disjoint triangles from G. Iteratively perform local search by replacing any sub-collection of $s \leq t$ triangles in the current solution with $s + 1$ triangles from the graph such that the collection continues to be edge disjoint.

It is obvious that the above heuristic run in polynomial time since the collection grows by at least one in each step and its size is upper bounded by n^2. Let OPT denote the largest collection of edge disjoint triangles in G.

Now, we apply Theorem 2 to our situation by taking the sets $E_1, \ldots, E_m$ to be the edge disjoint triangles of OPT and Z to be the collection of edge disjoint triangles found by our heuristic with edge intersection representing containment, i.e., we say E_i contains z_j, an element of Z, when the intersection of the triangle in OPT corresponding to E_i with the triangle corresponding to z_j contains at least an edge of the original graph.

Observe that both the conditions of Theorem 2 are met.

1. Since each of the two collections of triangles, the set corresponding to $E_1, \ldots, E_m$ as well as the set corresponding to Z are edge disjoint therefore it follows that each E_i can intersect at most 3 z_j and vice versa.

2. By the termination condition of the heuristic, every collection of t elements from $E_1, \ldots, E_m$ must have a system of distinct representatives in Z, i.e., intersect at least t triangles from Z for otherwise we could replace $s \leq t$ triangles from Z with at least $s + 1$ triangles from $E_1, \ldots, E_m$.

Hence, when the heuristic terminates, the size of the collection as a fraction of $|\text{OPT}|$ is at least $(2 - \frac{3}{2^r})/(3 - \frac{3}{2^r})$ if $t = 2r - 1$ and $(2 - \frac{2}{2^r})/(3 - \frac{2}{2^r})$ if $t = 2r$. The proof is complete.   □

Note that the running time of the heuristic increases the closer we wish to get to $\frac{2}{3}$. In particular to beat the existing bound of $1 - \frac{1}{e}$ [5], we can run the heuristic with any $t \geq 7$. Naively implemented, the running time of the heuristic in this case is $O(n^{26})$ since we are picking upto 8 triangles at a time from a maximum possible collection of $O(n^3)$ triangles upto $O(n^2)$ times. From Theorem 1, we get

Corollary 2. *For any fixed $\epsilon > 0$ there exists a polynomial time algorithm that approximates PLSE to within $\frac{2}{3} - \epsilon$.*

3.2 APX-Hardness

In this section we show that 3EDM is APX-hard. We prove that in the reduction of Holyer [7], if we restrict the input 3SAT instances to the instances of 5-OCC-MAX-3SAT—each variable occurs exactly five times in the formula—then the reduction becomes gap preserving. Feige [4] proved that there is a constant ϵ such that it is not possible to distinguish between satisfiable instances of

5-OCC-MAX-3SAT and ones where at most ϵ fraction of clauses are satisfiable, unless P = NP. (The Holyer's reduction was also used in [9] to prove the APX-hardness of a variant of cycle covering. For sake of completeness here we repeat the definitions. To avoid the confusion we use the notation used in [7,9].)

Theorem 4. *3EDM is APX-hard.*

Proof. Let the graph $H_{3,p}$ be a graph with p^2 vertices where $V = \{(x_1 + x_2 + x_3) \in Z_n^3 \mid x_1 + x_2 + x_3 \equiv 0(\text{mod } p)\}$ and two vertices $(x_1, x_2, x_3), (y_1, y_2, y_3)$ are connected if there are distinct i, j, and k such that $x_i \equiv y_i(\text{mod } p), x_j \equiv y_j + 1(\text{mod } p)$ and $x_k \equiv y_k - 1(\text{mod } p)$. As has been pointed out in [2], if we choose p so that $p \equiv 0(\text{mod } 3)$, then the graph becomes tripartite. The crucial point is that there are just two ways to partition $H_{3,p}$ into triangles; this will serve as a switch for modeling a truth assignment. We call the first a T-partition and the second an F-partition. We define a *patch* to be an induced subgraph in $H_{3,p}$ that consists of the triangle in center with three other triangles surrounding it. When the central triangle belongs to a T-partition, we call it a T-patch and otherwise an F-patch.

Let $\aleph$ be an instance of 5-OCC-MAX-3SAT that consists of $m = (5/3)n$ clauses $C = (C_1, \ldots, C_m)$ defined over n variables $x_1, \ldots, x_n$ where each C_j consists of three literals $\ell_{j,1}, \ell_{j,2}$, and $\ell_{j,3}$. For each variable x_i in $\aleph$ we create a graph X_i that is a copy of $H_{3,6}$. Also corresponding to each literal $\ell_{j,k}$ we create a graph $C_{j,k}$ that is a copy of $H_{3,6}$. Now we glue the graphs in the following way. If $\ell_{j,k} = x_i$, then we glue an F-patch of X_i with an F-patch of $C_{j,k}$ and otherwise (when $\ell_{j,k} = \bar{x}_i$) we glue an F-patch of X_i with a T-patch of $C_{j,k}$. We also glue $C_{j,1}, C_{j,2}$, and $C_{j,3}$ together at an F-patch from them and then remove the edge of the central triangle in the F-patch. Note that we have chosen $p = 6$ so that we have enough disjoint number of patches, also to ensure that the resulted graph is tripartite, we arbitrarily color each copies of $H_{3,6}$ with three colors and then we glue the vertices with the same color. Let G_j be the graph after gluing together the graphs $C_{j,1}, C_{j,2}$, and $C_{j,3}$. The following facts have been shown in [7].

1. In order to partition all of the edges in G_j, exactly one of the graphs $C_{j,1}, C_{j,2}$, and $C_{j,3}$ should be F-partitioned.
2. If $\ell_{j,1} = x_i$, then it is not possible that $C_{j,k}$ and X_i are both F-partitioned. If $\ell_{j,k} = \bar{x}_i$ then it is not possible that $C_{j,k}$ is F-partitioned and X_i is T-partitioned.

These facts imply

Lemma 1. *The edges of the graph G_j can be partitioned into triangles if and only if one of the literals in C_j is true.*

Let t_1 be the number of edge-disjoint triangles in $H_{3,6}$ and let t_2 be the number of edge-disjoint triangles in G_j. Lemma 1 indicates that if $\aleph$ is satisfiable, then there are $nt_1 + 5/3nt_2 = c_1n$ edge-disjoint triangles in the final graph, where c_1 is a constant. On the other hand if $\aleph$ is not satisfiable, then for each unsatisfiable clause C_j we have two possibilities: there is one edge that has been left or the there is one edge left in one of graphs corresponding to the variables involving in C_j. Since each variable is in at most two unsatisfied clause (otherwise we can switch it), we can conclude that if there are $(1-\epsilon)5/3n$ unsatisfiable clauses in $\aleph$, then we can have at most $t_1 n + 5/3 t_2 n - 5/6(1-\epsilon)n = c_2 n$ edge-disjoint triangles, where $c_2 < c_1$. This shows that there is a constant $\alpha < c_2/c_1$ such that if we can α-approximate the number of edge-disjoint triangles in tripartite graphs, then we can distinguish between satisfiable instances of 5-OCC-MAX-3SAT and instances that at most ϵ fraction of them are satisfiable. This completes the proof.   □

Corollary 3. *PLSE is APX-hard.*

4   The k-PLSE Problem

In this section we study the k-PLSE problem. First we present a simple greedy algorithm that approximates to within a factor $\frac{1}{2}$. Next we show a randomized approximation algorithm that achieves a factor $1 - \frac{1}{e} - \epsilon$. Finally, we prove that k-PLSE is hard to approximate to within a factor $1 - \frac{1}{e} + \epsilon$.

4.1   A Greedy Algorithm

Let M_i be the largest matching that extends the existing matching associated with color i. Pick color j such that $|M_j| = \max\{|M_1|, \ldots, |M_n|\}$, breaking ties arbitrarily. Fill the cells in M_j with color j and repeat until k colors are used.

Theorem 5. *The greedy algorithm approximates k-PLSE to within a factor $\frac{1}{2}$.*

Proof. Let OPT $= \{(i, j, k)\}$ where the cell (i, j) has color k in the optimal solution. Similarly we define S as the set of triples that represents the solution returned by the greedy algorithm. For each triple $(i, j, k) \in$ OPT we determine a triple $(i', j', k') \in S$ as accountable. We make the assignment in the order of following three cases.

1. $x = (i, j, k) \in$ OPT and $y = (i, j, k') \in S$. In this case, y is accountable for x.
2. $x = (i, j, k) \in$ OPT but the cell (i, j) is left uncolored in the greedy solution while there exists a triple $(i', j', k) \in S$. Let T_k and T'_k be the set of triples representing the cells colored with k in OPT and S respectively. Some of the triples in T_k have already been considered and hence have their own accountable. Consider the iteration that greedy algorithm uses color k. Since the greedy algorithm picks the largest matching, for each unassigned triple in T_k, we can pick a distinct triple in T'_k as accountable.
3. $x = (i, j, k) \in$ OPT and the cell (i, j) is left uncolored in the greedy solution. Moreover, the greedy algorithm has not used color k. To analysis this case, let $\overline{T}_k$ be the set of cells with this condition. Also let $C = c_1, \ldots, c_t$ be the set of colors that appear in OPT but not in S. Assume that we have ordered the colors with respect to size of $\overline{T}_{c_i}$ (decreasing order). We similarly define

C' for the greedy solution where the ordering is based on the number of cells colored, i.e. the size of $T'_{c'_i}$ (decreasing order). Note that $|C| = |C'|$ thus we can assign c_i to c'_i for each $1 \geq i \geq t$. It is easy to see that $|T'_{c'_t}| > |\overline{T}_{c_1}|$ and hence for each $1 \geq i \geq t$ we have $|T'_{c'_i}| > |\overline{T}_{c_i}|$. This implies that for each cell in $\overline{T}_{c_i}$ we can assign a distinct cell in $T'_{c'_i}$ as accountable. Note that before making these assignments, the triples in S representing the cells with color in C' are accountable to at most one triple in OPT and hence at the end they are accountable to at most two triples.

The above arguments show that at the end of the assignments, we do not have a triple in S that is accountable for more than two triples in OPT. This completes the proof of the theorem.   □

We now show an examples where the above analysis is tight. Let $k = 3$ and consider the PLS

	2	3	
2			1
3			2
	1	2	

. The greedy algorithm first chooses color 4 and if it decides to color the main diagonal. By this choice, at most 4 cells can be filled while the optimum solution can be shown to color 8 cells.

4.2   A $(1 - \frac{1}{e} - \epsilon)$-Approximation Algorithm

In this section we modify the LP formulation for PLSE problem defined in [5] to get a $(1 - \frac{1}{e} - \epsilon)$-approximation for the k-PLSE problem. Let $\mathcal{M}_c$ be the set of all matchings that extend the matching associated with color c and y_{cM} be the indicator variable associated with matching $M \in \mathcal{M}_c$. The modified formulation is:

$$\text{maximize} \quad \sum_{c=1}^{n} \sum_{M \in \mathcal{M}_c} |M| y_{cM} \tag{1}$$

$$\text{subject to} \quad \forall c = 1, \ldots, n : \quad \sum_{M \in \mathcal{M}_c} y_{cM} = 1$$

$$\forall i, j = 1, \ldots, n : \quad \sum_{c=1}^{n} \sum_{M \in \mathcal{M}_c : (i,j) \in M} y_{cM} \leq 1$$

$$\sum_{c=1}^{n} \sum_{M \in \mathcal{M}_c : |M| > 0} y_{cM} \leq k$$

$$y_{cM} \geq 0$$

Note that the above LP has an exponential number of variables but only a polynomial number of constraints. In [5] they solve this by showing its equivalence to the related assignment LP; however, they also state that it can be solved by using the ellipsoid method. We follow this latter approach and provide a sketch of this technique; details can be found in [6]. We transform the above LP into its equivalent dual, which has a polynomial number of variables and an exponential number of constraints, and solve it using the ellipsoid with a separation oracle. The separation oracle solves the matching problem in an appropriately defined bipartite graph to find violated constraints. This gives us a non-degenerate basic feasible solution to the dual as well as the corresponding set of tight constraints. Using complementary slackness we obtain the set of non-zero variables in the primal (of which there will only be a polynomial number) and solve the primal constraints to get a non-degenerate basic feasible primal solution.

Now we round the primal solution as in [5] to get one matching for each color, except that before rounding, we multiply each variable in the LP solution by $1 - \epsilon$. Note that we can do this rounding even though there are an exponential number of primal variables because in the primal solution only a polynomial number of them will be non-zero. Furthermore, we can use the Chernoff bound to guarantee that at most k matchings with different colors have been picked with some constant probability.

Theorem 6. *Let $k \geq \frac{2}{\epsilon^2}(1 - \epsilon)(\ln \frac{1}{\delta})$, $0 < \epsilon \leq \frac{1}{2}$, and $0 \leq \delta \leq 1$. There is a randomized $(1 - \frac{1}{e} - \epsilon)$-approximation algorithm for k-PLSE that succeeds with probability at least $1 - \delta$.*

Proof. Let y^* be the optimal solution for the above LP and $\bar{y}$ be the solution obtained from y^* after multiplying each variable by $1 - \epsilon$. Now for each color c, we pick a matching from the set $\mathcal{M}_c$ such that matching y_{cM} is picked with probability $\bar{y}_{cM}$. If two or more matchings share cell (i, j) we color (i, j) arbitrary with the color of one those matchings. Let OPT and OPT' be the cost of $y*$ and $\bar{y}$ respectively. According to the argument in [5], the cost of solution produced by the above rounding procedure is at least $(1 - \frac{1}{e})$OPT'. Since OPT' $= (1 - \epsilon)$OPT, we conclude that the cost of final solution is at least $(1 - \epsilon)(1 - \frac{1}{e})$OPT $\geq (1 - \frac{1}{e} - \epsilon)$OPT. It remains to prove that the solution is feasible, i.e., at most k different colors have been picked. Let $s = \sum_{c=1}^{n} \sum_{M \in \mathcal{M}_c : |M| > 0} \bar{y}_{cM}$. We have $E(s) \leq (1 - \epsilon)k$ and since s is the sum of a set of independent random variables, we can apply the version of Chernoff bound used in [11] to bound the tail of s. Given $0 \leq \epsilon' \leq 1$ such that $\epsilon' = \frac{\epsilon}{1-\epsilon}$, we have,

$$\Pr[s > k] = \Pr[s > (1 + \epsilon')(1 - \epsilon)k] \leq \exp\left(-\frac{(1 + \epsilon)(1 + \epsilon')^2 k}{2}\right) \leq \delta.$$

After simplification, we have $\Pr[s > k] < \delta$ when $k \geq \frac{2}{\epsilon^2}(1 - \epsilon)(\ln \frac{1}{\delta})$. This completes the proof. □

Note that if we settle for some constant probability of success, we can use brute force search for values of k less than $\frac{2}{\epsilon^2}(1 - \epsilon)(\ln \frac{1}{\delta})$.

4.3   Hardness

We show that the k-PLSE problem is hard to approximate to within $1 - \frac{1}{e} + \epsilon$, unless P = NP.

Theorem 7. *For any $\epsilon > 0$, k-3EDM is not approximable to within $1 - 1/e + \epsilon$, unless P = NP.*

Proof. We use the Max-k-Cover problem for the reduction. In the *Max-k-Cover* problem, we are given several subsets of a ground set and we are asked to pick k subsets that cover most of the ground set elements. Feige [4] proved that no polynomial time algorithm for Max-k-Cover can have approximation ratio better than $1 - \frac{1}{e}$, unless P = NP.

Given an instance of Max-k-Cover with the ground set $\{e_1, \ldots, e_n\}$ and subsets $S_1, \ldots, S_m$, we construct the tripartite graph $G = (U \cup V \cup W, E)$ in the following way. Let $|U| = |V| = n$ and $|W| = m$. We place a perfect matching between U and V where the edge (u_i, v_i) correspond to the element e_i. Now if $e_i \in S_k$ we connect u_i and v_i to w_k, thereby creating the triangle (u_i, v_i, w_k). It is easy to see that every solution to the given instance of Max-k-Cover problem corresponds to a solution to the k-3EDM problem and vice versa.   □

Corollary 4. *For any $\epsilon > 0$, k-PLSE is not approximable to within $1 - 1/e + \epsilon$, unless P = NP.*

5   The c-PLSE Problem

In this section we present a $\frac{1}{4}$-approximation algorithm for the c-PLSE problem.

Theorem 8. *There exists a polynomial-time algorithm that approximates the c-PLSE problem to within a factor $\frac{1}{4}$.*

Proof. We show a stronger result, namely, every partial Latin square with T filled cells has a subset with size of at least $T/4$ filled cells that can be extended to completion.

Let P be a partial Latin square of order n with t filled cells. We distinguish two cases. $n = 2m$: we divide the square into four blocks of size $m \times m$ and then pick the block that has more filled cells ($\geq T/4$). By permuting rows and columns, we exchange the picked block with the left upper hand block and then clear the other cells. It is easy to see that we can complete the upper-left block in any order. And for completing the square we invoke a famous theorem of Ryser ([12], also [14, Theorem 17.4]) that we state for the sake of completeness.

Theorem 9 (Ryser [12]). *Let A be a partial Latin square of order n in which cell (i, j) is filled if and only if $i \leq r$ and $j \leq s$ Then A can be completed if and only if $N(i) \geq r + s - n$ for $i = 1, \ldots, n$, where $N(i)$ denotes the number of elements of A that are equal to i.*

By Ryser's theorem (letting $r = s = m$), the square is guaranteed to be extendible to completion.

The proof for the situation when $n = 2m + 1$ is similar except that here we divide the square into four blocks of size $m \times (m - 1)$ with one cell left in the center of square. If the cell which is left in the center is not empty, we permute the rows and columns so that it becomes an empty cell. Again we pick the block with more filled cells and using Ryser's Theorem (let $r = m, s = m + 1$), we are done.   □

We make the following remarks on the above theorem. Using the above approach it is not possible to get better than a $\frac{1}{2}$ approximation. Consider a square of order $2n$. Place a LS from the colors $\{1, \ldots, n\}$ in the upper left section of the square and similarly, place a LS from colors $\{n+1, \ldots, 2n\}$ in the bottom-right section. It is easy to see that this is a blocked PLS and moreover in order to obtain a completable subset of the filled cells, we have to cancel at least $\frac{n^2}{4}$ of the filled cells (In order to place a number in the empty cells at least one filled cell should be canceled). In fact the combinatorial version of the c-PLSE problem is in of itself a very interesting problem — what is the largest fraction f, $0 < f < 1$ such that every PLS with T filled cells contains a PLS with at least fT filled cells that can be extended to completion? We conjecture that the right answer is $f = \frac{1}{2}$.

6   Conclusions

We defined two new and natural problems - k-PLSE and c-PLSE. We obtained simple approximation algorithms for the PLSE, k-PLSE and c-PLSE problems. We also showed APX-hardness for PLSE and a $(1 - \frac{1}{e})$-hardness of approximation for k-PLSE. Our result for PLSE is an improvement over the best known and our result for k-PLSE is the best possible.

The main open problem is to improve the approximation ratio for PLSE. Obtaining an *explicit* constant hardness of approximation is also an interesting problem. Although there is a $(1 - \frac{1}{e})$ hardness result for k-PLSE, the further improvement for approximation of PLSE is not unlikely as the hardness of k-PLSE seems to be of a different origin—for example, the worst-case instance for k-PLSE is an easy instance for PLSE.

Embedding PLSs in LSs with the same order and with minimum loss of elements poses many new directions and open problems. We conjecture that the tight constant in Theorem 8 is $\frac{1}{2}$.

References

1. R. A. Barry and P. A. Humblet. Latin routers, design and implementation. *IEEE/OSA Journal of Lightwave Technology*, pages 891–899, 1993.
2. C. J. Colbourn. The complexity of completing partial latin squares. *Discrete Applied Mathematics*, 8:25–30, 1984.

3. T. Evans. Embedding incomplete latin squares. *American Mathematical Monthly*, 67:958–961, 1960.
4. U. Feige. A threshold of ln n for approximating set cover. *Journal of the ACM*, 45(4):634–652, 1998.
5. C. P. Gomes, R. G. Regis, and D. B. Shmoys. An improved approximation algorithm for the partial latin square extension problem. *Operations Research Letters*, 32(5):479–484, 2004.
6. M. Grötschel, L. Lovász, and A. Schrijver. *Geometric Algorithms and Combinatorial Optimization*. Springer-Verlag, 1988.
7. I. Holyer. The NP-completeness of some edge-partition problems. *SIAM Journal on Computing*, 10(4):713–717, 1981.
8. C. A. J. Hurkens and A. Schrijver. On the size of systems of sets every t of which have an SDR, with an application to the worst-case ratio of heuristics for packing problems. *SIAM Journal on Discrete Mathematics*, 2(1):68–72, 1989.
9. N. Immorlica, M. Mahdian, and V. S. Mirrokni. Cycle cover with short cycles. In *Proceedings of the 22nd Annual Symposium on Theoretical Aspects of Computer Science*, pages 641–653, 2005.
10. R. Kumar, A. Russell, and R. Sundaram. Approximating latin square extensions. *Algorithmica*, 24(2):128–138, 1999.
11. P. Raghavan and C.D. Thompson. Randomized rounding: A technique for provably good algorithms and algorithmic proofs. *Combinatorica* 7(4): 365-374, 1987.
12. H. J. Ryser. A combinatorial theorem with an application to latin rectangles. *Proceedings of the American Mathematical Society*, 2:550–552, 1951.
13. B. Smetaniuk. A new construction on Latin squares I. A proof of the Evans conjecture. *Ars Combinatoria*, XI:155–172, 1981.
14. J. H. van Lint and R. M. Wilson. *A Course in Combinatorics*. Cambridge University Press, 1992.

Small Space Representations for Metric Min-Sum k-Clustering and Their Applications[*]

Artur Czumaj[1] and Christian Sohler[2]

[1] Department of Computer Science, University of Warwick, Coventry CV7 4AL, U.K.
czumaj@dcs.warwick.ac.uk
[2] Heinz Nixdorf Institute and Department of Computer Science, University of
Paderborn, 33102 Paderborn, Germany
csohler@upb.de

Abstract. The *min-sum k-clustering* problem is to partition a metric space (P, d) into k clusters $C_1, \ldots, C_k \subseteq P$ such that $\sum_{i=1}^{k} \sum_{p,q \in C_i} d(p, q)$ is minimized. We show the first efficient construction of a *coreset* for this problem. Our coreset construction is based on a new adaptive sampling algorithm. Using our coresets we obtain three main algorithmic results.

The first result is a sublinear time $(4+\epsilon)$-approximation algorithm for the min-sum k-clustering problem in metric spaces. The running time of this algorithm is $\widetilde{O}(n)$ for any constant k and ϵ, and it is $o(n^2)$ for all $k = o(\log n / \log \log n)$. Since the description size of the input is $\Theta(n^2)$, this is *sublinear* in the input size.

Our second result is the first *pass-efficient data streaming algorithm* for min-sum k-clustering in the distance oracle model, i.e., an algorithm that uses $poly(\log n, k)$ space and makes 2 passes over the input point set arriving as a data stream.

Our third result is a *sublinear-time* polylogarithmic-factor-approximation algorithm for the min-sum k-clustering problem for arbitrary values of k.

To develop the coresets, we introduce the concept of α-*preserving metric embeddings*. Such an embedding satisfies properties that (a) the distance between any pair of points does not decrease, and (b) the cost of an optimal solution for the considered problem on input (P, d') is within a constant factor of the optimal solution on input (P, d). In other words, the idea is find a metric embedding into a (structurally simpler) metric space that approximates the original metric up to a factor of α *with respect to a certain problem*. We believe that this concept is an interesting generalization of coresets.

1 Introduction

Clustering problems deal with the task of partitioning an input set of objects into subsets called *clusters*. In typical applications as they occur in bioinformatics,

[*] Research supported in part by NSF ITR grant CCR-0313219, by EPSRC grant EP/D063191/1, and by DFG grant Me 872/8-3.

W. Thomas and P. Weil (Eds.): STACS 2007, LNCS 4393, pp. 536–548, 2007.

pattern recognition, data compression, data mining, etc., clustering algorithms are either used to find certain patterns in large data sets or to find a lossy representation of the data that still maintains important features of the original data set. Ideally, objects in the same cluster are "similar" while objects in different clusters are not. To measure similarity between objects one typically defines a metric on the set of objects. The closer the objects are in this metric, the more similar they are, i.e., the metric is a measure of dissimilarity of objects. One of the most natural definitions of clustering is to minimize the intra cluster dissimilarity of objects. This problem is known as the *min-sum k-clustering* problem and has received considerably attention in the past [3,7,8,11,16,22,23]. Min-sum k-clustering is the *dual problem* to another well-known problem, the *Max-k-cut problem* (see, e.g., [9,16]), where the goal is to maximize the inter cluster dissimilarity.

Unlike many other classical clustering problems, like k-median and k-means clustering, in min-sum k-clustering it is possible that clusters of different densities "overlap". This makes the problem significantly different from k-median and k-means, and combinatorially challenging. In many scenarios the property that the clusters may "overlap" can give a better clustering, for example, it can be used to detect *outliers*.

In typical applications of clustering, the data sets to be clustered tend to be very large. Therefore, the *scalability* to massive data sets is one of the most important requirements a good clustering algorithm should satisfy. In this context, even if polynomial-time algorithms may be efficient for small and medium-sized inputs, they may become impractical for input sizes of several gigabytes. For example, when we consider approximation algorithms for clustering problems in metric spaces then they typically run in time $\Omega(n^2)$, where n is the number of input points. Clearly, such a running time is not feasible for massive data sets. Similarly, we do not have several gigabytes of main memory available and our algorithm cannot maintain the entire input in main memory, what calls for the use of data streaming algorithm that passes only few times over the data. Our goal is to develop clustering algorithms that require *near linear (in n) running time* and/or *polylogarithmic space* and not more than a few passes over the input.

1.1 Related Work

The *min-sum k-clustering problem* was first formulated by Sahni and Gonzales [22]. It is known to be $\mathcal{NP}$-hard and there is a 2-approximation algorithm by Guttman-Beck and Hassin [11] with runtime $n^{O(k)}$. Bartal et al. [3] presented an $O(\epsilon^{-1} \log^{1+\epsilon} n)$-approximation algorithm running in time $n^{2+O(1/\epsilon)}$ and Fernandez de la Vega et al. [8] gave an $(1 + \epsilon)$-approximation algorithm with the runtime $O(n^{3k}2^{O(\epsilon^{-k^2})})$. For points in $\mathbb{R}^d$, Schulman [23] introduced an algorithm for distance functions ℓ_2^2, ℓ_1 and ℓ_2 that computes a solution that is either within $(1 + \epsilon)$ of the optimum or that disagrees with the optimum in at most an ϵ fraction of points. For the basic case of $k = 2$ (complement to the Max-Cut), Indyk [16] gave an $(1 + \epsilon)$-approximation algorithm that runs in time $O(2^{1/\epsilon^{O(1)}} n (\log n)^{O(1)})$, e.g., sublinear in the input description size. In [7], the authors analyze the quality of uniform random sampling for the min-sum k-clustering problem.

Sublinear time algorithms for clustering problems. A number of sublinear time algorithms have been developed for other clustering problems. For the k-median problem (in general metrics), the quality of random sampling has been investigated in [7]. Other sublinear time algorithms have been developed in [14,21] and $\widetilde{O}(nk)$ algorithms for the k-median problem in metric spaces have been presented in [20,24]. In [1], a sublinear time algorithm to estimate the cost of the facility location problem has been developed.

Data streaming algorithms for clustering problems. Several data streaming algorithms have been designed for clustering problems in Euclidean and general metric spaces.

For a data stream of points from the *Euclidean* space $\mathbb{R}^d$ one can compute a $(1+\epsilon)$-approximation for k-median and k-means clustering in space polynomial in $\log n, k$, and ϵ and exponential in d [12]. This result was improved to polynomial dependence in d in [6]. In [17] the study of dynamic geometric data streams was initiated. In this model the input points come from the discrete space $\{1, \ldots, \Delta\}^d$ and the stream consists of insert and delete operations. It was shown in [17] that a $(1+\epsilon)$-approximation for the k-median problem can, in principle, be computed in small space. However, the running time to compute the approximation from the summary was prohibitively large. Using a different approach, it was shown in [9] how to quickly get a $(1+\epsilon)$-approximation for k-median, k-means and Max-Cut in the dynamic model. For facility location a $O(d \log^2 \Delta)$-approximation has been given in [17]. For *general metric spaces*, there are constant factor approximation algorithms for k-center [4] and k-median [5,10,24].

Coresets for other clustering problems. The concept of *coresets* has been playing a critical role in the recent developments of efficient clustering algorithms. Informally, a coreset is a small weighted point set that approximates a larger unweighted point set with respect to a certain (clustering) problem. For some *geometric* problems, like k-center or k-median clustering, coresets with size independent of the number of points and the dimension of the underlying Euclidean space exist [2]. Other coreset constructions for low-dimensional Euclidean spaces have been developed and used to improve existing approximation algorithms and develop data streaming clustering algorithms [9,12,13]. It is even possible to compute a coreset for the k-median clustering problem, whose number of points is independent of the dimension [6].

To the best of our knowledge, previous approximation techniques for k-means and k-median like [2,18,19] as well as the combination of the coreset construction from [6] with the bicriteria approximation from [3] and the analysis of [7] cannot be used to obtain coresets for min-sum k-clustering and the related balanced k-median problem.

1.2   New Contributions

In this paper we construct small space representations for approximately good solutions for the min-sum k-clustering problem and the related *balanced k-median* problem, which is known to be within a factor 2 of the solution for the min-sum k-clustering problem. We apply our constructions to design new efficient algorithms for these problems. In particular, we develop a new adaptive sampling scheme for balanced k-median. Based on this sampling scheme we obtain an α-preserving embedding and a coreset for the balanced k-median and min-sum k-clustering problem. Our constructions run in near linear time and can be implemented to use small space. Using the developed tools, we obtain three main algorithmic results.

First, we present a *sublinear time* constant factor approximation algorithm for the case that k is small, i.e., $k = o(\log n / \log \log n)$. For this choice of k, our algorithm runs in $O(n \cdot k \cdot (k \log n / \epsilon)^{O(k)})$ time and computes a $(4+\epsilon)$-approximation for the min-sum k-clustering problem. For $\omega(1) \leq k \leq O(\frac{\log n}{\log \log n})$, this is the first constant-factor polynomial-time approximation algorithm for this problem. Note that the running time of this algorithm is *sublinear* in the full description size of the metric space, which is $\Theta(n^2)$. Furthermore, we can speed-up the algorithm to run in time $\widetilde{O}(n\,k) + (k \log n)^{O(k)}$ and still achieve a constant (but slightly worse one) factor approximation (this has been deferred to the full version of the paper).

Our second result is a 2-*pass data streaming* algorithm that is a constant-factor approximation for the min-sum k-clustering problem, that is, an algorithm that uses $poly(\log n, k)$ space and requires two passes over the point set P, which arrives in an arbitrary order. The output of the algorithm is a succinct representation of the clustering. One more pass is needed to assign each point to the corresponding cluster. This is the first data streaming algorithm for this problem.

Our third result is a $(\log n)^{O(1)}$-approximation algorithm for min-sum k-clustering that runs in $\widetilde{O}(n \cdot k^{O(1)})$ time; hence, its running time is sublinear even for large values of k. This result almost matches the approximation guarantee of the best polynomial-time algorithm for this problem for large k due to Bartal et al. [3], and at the same time, it significantly improves the runtime.

New concepts and techniques. To obtain our first result we develop a new adaptive random sampling algorithm PARTITIONINGSCHEME. This algorithm computes a set S of $poly(k, \log n, 1/\epsilon)$ points that contains k centers, which (together with the right partition of points) are a $(2 + \epsilon)$-approximation to the balanced k-median problem. Then we use a variation of exhaustive search together with a modified algorithm for the minimum cost assignment problem to find the best centers in S. The idea to compute a small set of points that contain good centers has been previously used in the context of k-median clustering [24]. However, both, our algorithm and its analysis for the *balanced k-median* are substantially different from previous work.

To obtain our second and the third algorithmic result, we introduce the concept of α-preserving embedding, which we believe is interesting beyond the applications in this paper. To define the concept of an α-*preserving embedding*, let Π be a minimization problem defined on finite metric spaces such that the cost of any solution does not decrease when the distances in the metric space are increased. Given two metric spaces (P, d) and (P, d'), we say that (P, d) has an α-preserving embedding into (P, d'), if *(i)* for every two points $p, q \in P$ it holds $d(p, q) \leq d'(p, q)$, and *(ii)* the cost of an optimal solution for instance (P, d) is within factor α of the cost of an optimal solution for instance (P, d'). We use α-preserving embeddings to develop a *coreset* construction for the balanced k-median and min-sum k-clustering problem. Such a coreset can be seen as a small-space representation of the input metric space (P, d) that changes the cost of an optimal solution by at most a constant factor and does not improve the cost of other (bad) solutions significantly.

2   Preliminaries

Let (P, d) be a finite metric space and let $n = |P|$. For $S \subseteq P$ and $p \in P$ we will define $d(p, S) = \min_{q \in S} d(p, q)$. The *min-sum k-clustering* problem is to partition P into k sets (*clusters*) $C_1, \ldots, C_k$ such that $\sum_{i=1}^{k} \sum_{p,q \in C_i} d(p, q)$ is minimized. It is known that this problem is within a factor two approximation (cf. [3, Claim 1]) of the *balanced k-median* problem, which is to find a set $\mathcal{C} = \{c_1, \ldots, c_k\} \subseteq P$ of k points (*centers*) and a partition of P into sets $C_1, \ldots, C_k$ that minimizes $\sum_{i=1}^{k} |C_i| \cdot \sum_{p \in C_i} d(p, c_i)$.

Since min-sum k-clustering and balanced k-median approximate each other to within a factor of 2, in our analysis, we will focus mostly on the latter problem.

For any set $\mathcal{C} = \{c_1, \ldots, c_k\}$ of k points (centers) in P, we define

$$cost_k(P, \mathcal{C}) = \min_{\substack{\text{partition of } P \text{ into} \\ C_1 \cup C_2 \cup \cdots \cup C_k}} \sum_{i=1}^{k} |C_i| \cdot \sum_{p \in C_i} d(p, c_i) \ .$$

We abbreviate the cost of cluster C_i with associated center c_i as $cost(C_i) = cost_1(C_i, \{c_i\})$.

A *balanced k-median* of P is a set $\mathcal{C}^* = \{c_1^*, \ldots, c_k^*\}$ of k points (centers) in P that minimizes the value of $cost_k(P, \mathcal{C}^*)$. We will use Opt_k to denote the cost of a *balanced k-median* for P. Next, we introduce the notions of kernels and points close to kernels.

Definition 1. *Let $\mathcal{C}^* = \{c_1^*, \ldots, c_k^*\}$ be a balanced k-median and let $C_1^*, \ldots, C_k^*$ be the corresponding optimal partition of P. We define the* kernel $Kern(C_i^*)$ *of cluster C_i^* as*

$$Kern(C_i^*) = \left\{ p \in C_i^* \ : \ d(p, c_i^*) \leq (1 + \epsilon) \cdot \frac{cost(C_i^*)}{|C_i^*|^2} \right\} \ .$$

We say that a point p is close *to $Kern(C_i^*)$, if $d\left(p, Kern(C_i^*)\right) \leq \frac{\epsilon}{k} \cdot \frac{Opt_k}{|C_i^*|^2}$.*

The next lemma follows easily from the triangle inequality.

Lemma 1. *Let $C^* = \{c_1^*, \ldots, c_k^*\}$ be a balanced k-median and let $C_1^*, \ldots, C_k^*$ be the corresponding optimal partition of P. Let $C = \{c_1, \ldots, c_k\}$ be any set of points such that each c_i is close to $Kern(C_i^*)$. Then $cost_k(P, C) \leq (2 + 2\epsilon) \cdot Opt_k$.*

Furthermore, simple counting arguments give the following.

Lemma 2. *For every i, $|Kern(C_i^*)| \geq \frac{\epsilon}{1+\epsilon} \cdot |C_i^*|$.*

The balanced k-median problem is defined similarly to another standard problem of k-median. The difference is that in the k-median problem, our goal is to find a set $C^* = \{c_1^*, \ldots, c_k^*\}$ of k centers in P and a partition of P into $C_1, \ldots, C_k$ that minimize $\sum_{i=1}^{k} \sum_{p \in C_i} d(p, c_i)$. We will use the well-known and easy fact that if c_{med} is the cost of an optimal solution of k-median for P, then $c_{med} \leq Opt_k \leq |P| \cdot c_{med}$.

3   New Sampling-Based Partitioning Scheme

In this section we develop a partitioning scheme that with high probability finds a set S of size $\tilde{O}(k \log n / \epsilon^3)$ that contains a point close to $Kern(C_i^*)$ for every cluster C_i^* of an optimal solution. By Lemma 1, it follows that these points contain k centers that provide a good approximation to a balanced k-median. In the next section we will see how to compute a $(2 + \epsilon)$-approximation for the balanced k-median from this set.

Algorithm RANDOMPARTITION. Our partitioning scheme uses algorithm RANDOMPARTITION. This algorithm gets a "guess" $\widetilde{Opt_k}$ for the cost Opt_k of an optimal solution and a parameter ℓ, which can be viewed as a "guess" for the cluster size. Given these parameters, the algorithm selects a set $S \subseteq P$ using simple adaptive sampling. As we prove later in Lemma 4, if our "guess" $\widetilde{Opt_k}$ for Opt_k is good then for every cluster C_i^* of size $(1 - \epsilon) \cdot \ell \leq |C_i^*| \leq \ell$, set S contains, with high probability, a point p that is close to $Kern(C_i^*)$. RANDOMPARTITION is parameterized by s, which is closely related to the sample size and will be specified later. (We assume that $d(p, \emptyset) = +\infty$.)

RANDOMPARTITION $(P, s, \widetilde{Opt_k}, \ell)$
    for each $p \in P$ **do**
        if $d(p, S) > \frac{\epsilon}{k} \cdot \frac{\widetilde{Opt_k}}{\ell^2}$ **then** with probability $\min\left\{\frac{s}{\epsilon \cdot \ell}, 1\right\}$ put p into S
    return S

The running time of algorithm RANDOMPARTITION is $O(n \cdot |S|)$. Therefore now, we want to find an upper bound on the size of the sample set S.

Lemma 3. *Let $0 < \varrho < 1$ be arbitrary. Let $\widetilde{Opt_k} \geq Opt_k / 2$. Then, for $s \geq \frac{15 \cdot \epsilon^2 \cdot \ln(1/\varrho)}{k}$ we have $|S| \leq \frac{6 \cdot s \cdot k}{\epsilon^2} + k$ with probability at least $1 - \varrho$.*

Proof. Let $C_1^*, \ldots, C_k^*$ be an optimal partition of P and let $c_1^*, \ldots, c_k^*$ be the corresponding optimal centers. We denote by $t = \frac{\epsilon}{k} \cdot \frac{\widetilde{Opt_k}}{\ell^2}$ the threshold for the distance to the set S used in the **if**-statement of algorithm RANDOMPARTITION. We use the following simple fact that follows directly from the triangle inequality.

Claim 1. *For each center c_i^*, S contains at most one point p with $d(p, c_i^*) \leq t/2$.*

It follows immediately that there can be at most k points in S with distance at most $t/2$ to one of the cluster centers. We say that a point $p \in P$ is an *outlier*, if it has distance more than $t/2$ to every cluster center. We next analyze the number of outliers.

Claim 2. *The number of outliers is at most $4 \cdot \ell \cdot k/\epsilon + k \cdot \ell$.*

Proof. Let us call a cluster *small*, if it has at most ℓ points. Otherwise, we call a cluster *large*. The overall number of points in small clusters is at most $k \cdot \ell$ and so the number of outliers in small clusters is at most $k \cdot \ell$. Any outlier in a large cluster contributes with at least $\ell \cdot t/2$ to the cost of an optimal solution. Therefore, there can be at most $Opt_k/(t \cdot \ell/2) \leq 2 \cdot \widetilde{Opt_k}/(t \cdot \ell/2) = 4 \cdot \ell \cdot k/\epsilon$ outliers in large clusters. The claim follows by summing up the number of outliers in small and large clusters. $\square$

Algorithm RANDOMPARTITION picks every outlier with probability at most $\min\left\{\frac{s}{\epsilon \cdot \ell}, 1\right\}$. If $\frac{s}{\epsilon \cdot \ell} > 1$, then $s > \epsilon \cdot \ell$. Since by Claim 1, the cardinality of S is bounded by the number of outliers plus k, we get

$$|S| \leq 4 \cdot \ell \cdot k/\epsilon + k \cdot \ell + k \leq 6 \cdot \ell \cdot k/\epsilon + k = \frac{6 \cdot \epsilon \cdot \ell \cdot k}{\epsilon^2} + k \leq \frac{6 \cdot s \cdot k}{\epsilon^2} + k .$$

Hence, we only have to consider the case when $\frac{s}{\epsilon \cdot \ell} \leq 1$. Let Out denote the set of outliers. For $1 \leq Y_i \leq |Out|$, let Y_i denote an independent 0-1-random variable with $\mathbf{Pr}[Y_i = 1] = \frac{s}{\epsilon \cdot \ell}$. We get $\mathbf{Pr}\left[|S \cap Out| > 6 \cdot \frac{s \cdot k}{\epsilon^2}\right] \leq \mathbf{Pr}\left[\sum_{i=1}^{|Out|} Y_i > 6 \cdot \frac{s \cdot k}{\epsilon^2}\right]$.

Clearly, the latter probability is maximized by maximizing $|Out|$. Let $M = 5 \cdot \ell \cdot k/\epsilon$. Since by Claim 2, $|Out| \leq 4 \cdot \ell \cdot k/\epsilon + k \cdot \ell \leq M$, we have $\mathbf{Pr}[\sum_{i=1}^{|Out|} Y_i > 6 \cdot \frac{s \cdot k}{\epsilon^2}] \leq \mathbf{Pr}[\sum_{i=1}^{M} Y_i > 6 \cdot \frac{s \cdot k}{\epsilon^2}]$. Let us study the latter probability. We have, $\mathbf{E}[\sum_{i=1}^{M} Y_i] = \frac{s}{\epsilon \cdot \ell} \cdot M = \frac{5 \cdot s \cdot k}{\epsilon^2}$. Now we can apply Chernoff bounds. We get

$$\mathbf{Pr}\left[\sum_{i=1}^{M} Y_i > 6\frac{sk}{\epsilon^2}\right] = \mathbf{Pr}\left[\sum_{i=1}^{M} Y_i > (1 + 1/5)\mathbf{E}[\sum_{i=1}^{M} Y_i]\right] \leq e^{-(1/5)^2 \mathbf{E}[\sum_{i=1}^{M} Y_i]/3} \leq \varrho$$

for $s \geq \frac{15 \, \epsilon^2 \, \ln(1/\varrho)}{k}$. Thus, $\mathbf{Pr}\left[|S| \leq 6\frac{sk}{\epsilon^2} + k\right] \geq \mathbf{Pr}\left[|S \cap Out| \leq 6\frac{sk}{\epsilon^2}\right] \geq 1 - \varrho$. $\square$

Our next lemma shows that in our sampling algorithm, with a high probability, every optimal cluster has at least one point that is close to its kernel and that is in S.

Lemma 4. *Let $\widetilde{Opt_k} \leq Opt_k$, $\epsilon \leq 1/2$ and $(1 - \epsilon) \cdot \ell \leq |C_i^*| \leq \ell$. Then, $\mathbf{Pr}[\exists p \in S : p \text{ is close to } Kern(C_i^*)] \geq 1 - \varrho \text{ for } s \geq 4 \cdot \ln(1/\varrho).$*

Proof. Let p be an arbitrary point in P that is not close to $Kern(C_i^*)$. By definition, we have then $d(p, Kern(C_i^*)) > \frac{\epsilon}{k} \cdot \frac{Opt_k}{|C_i^*|^2} \geq \frac{\epsilon}{k} \cdot \frac{\widetilde{Opt_k}}{\ell^2}$. Now, if no point in S is close to $Kern(C_i^*)$, then for every point p in $Kern(C_i^*)$ we have $d(p, S) > \frac{\epsilon}{k} \cdot \frac{\widetilde{Opt_k}}{\ell^2}$ and hence, every point from $Kern(C_i^*)$ was considered for being taken into S. Thus, the probability that S has no point that is close to $Kern(C_i^*)$ is at most $\mathbf{Pr}[\sum_{j=1}^{|Kern(C_i^*)|} Y_i = 0]$, where the Y_i are 0–1-random variables with $\mathbf{Pr}[Y_i = 1] = \frac{s}{\epsilon \cdot \ell}$. This yields:

$$\mathbf{Pr}\Big[\sum_{j=1}^{|Kern(C_i^*)|} Y_i = 0 \Big] = \Big(1 - \frac{s}{\epsilon \cdot \ell}\Big)^{|Kern(C_i^*)|} \leq \Big(1 - \frac{s}{\epsilon \cdot \ell}\Big)^{\epsilon \cdot \ell / 4} \leq e^{-s/4} .$$

Hence, the lemma follows with $s = 4 \cdot \ln(1/\varrho)$. $\qquad\square$

Partitioning scheme. Now we present our partitioning scheme. First, we use the fact that the cost c_{med} of an α-approximation for k-median provides us with a lower bound of c_{med}/α and an upper bound of $c_{med} \cdot n$ for balanced k-median. We apply an $\widetilde{O}(n\,k)$-time constant-factor approximation algorithm for k-median to compute an approximate solution to this problem (see, e.g., [10,14,24]). Next, we are trying to guess the right value $\widetilde{Opt_k}$ for Opt_k. We use $\widetilde{Opt_k} \approx c_{med} \cdot n$ as a first guess for the cost of an optimal solution. Then, we run RANDOMPARTITION for $\ell = 1, \lceil (1 + \epsilon) \rceil, \lceil (1 + \epsilon)^2 \rceil, \ldots, n$ and build the union of the returned sets. Next, we halve our guess $\widetilde{Opt_k}$ for the cost of the optimal solution and proceed in a similar way until, eventually, RANDOMPARTITION returns a set which is larger than the bound from Lemma 3. If s is sufficiently large then we know at this point that with high probability our current guess $\widetilde{Opt_k}$ is smaller than $Opt_k/2$. Therefore, in the previous iteration (for the previous guess $\widetilde{Opt_k}$ of Opt_k), we had $\widetilde{Opt_k} \leq Opt_k$, in which case we use properties of the set S proven in Lemma 4.

```
PARTITIONINGSCHEME(P, s)
    Compute cost c_med of an α-approximation for k-median in O(n · k) time
    for i = ⌈log(α · n)⌉ downto 0 do
        S_i ← ∅
        for j = 0 to ⌈log_{1+ε} n⌉ do
            X = RANDOMPARTITION(P, s, 2^i · c_med/α, ⌈(1 + ε)^j⌉)
            if |X| > 6 · (s·k)/ε² + k then return S_{i+1}
            S_i ← S_i ∪ X
    return S_0
```

Theorem 1. *Let $N = (2 + \log(\alpha \cdot n)) \cdot (2 + \log_{1+\epsilon} n)$. Run Algorithm* PARTITIONINGSCHEME *with parameter $s \geq 4 \ln(2Nk/\delta) = O(\log(k \cdot \log n/(\delta \cdot \epsilon)))$. Then the algorithm runs in time $O(\frac{n \cdot \log^2 n \cdot k \cdot s}{\epsilon^3})$ and finds a set S of $O(\frac{s \cdot k \cdot \log n}{\epsilon^3})$ points in P such that with probability at least $1 - \delta$, there is a set $\mathcal{C}$ of k points in S for which $cost(P, \mathcal{C}) \leq (2 + \epsilon) \cdot Opt_k$.*

4   Poly-time Constant Factor Approximation for Small k

In this section we will show how the result from Theorem 1 can be used to obtain a polynomial-time constant factor approximation for balanced k-median for all values of $k = O(\log n/\log\log n)$. The underlying idea of our algorithm is that if we have a good guess for a possible set of candidates for centers, then we can find an almost optimal partition for this set, which will yield a good approximation for balanced k-median.

We consider the problem of finding a constant factor approximation for balanced k-median for a given *fixed* set of k centers. Let $\mathcal{C} = (c_1,\ldots,c_k)$ be a sequence of k cluster centers and consider an integer k-tuple $\langle N_1,\ldots,N_k\rangle$ with $\sum_{i=1}^{k} N_i = n$. Tokuyama and Nakano [25] showed that in time $O(n\,k) + \widetilde{O}(\sqrt{n}\,k^{2.5})$ one can find a partition of a set P into subsets $C_1^*,\ldots,C_k^*$ with $|C_i^*| = N_i$ for every i, that minimizes $cost_k(P,\mathcal{C}) = \sum_{i=1}^{k}|C_i^*|\sum_{p\in C_i^*} d(p,c_i)$. This algorithm can be used to solve balanced k-median for a fixed set of k-centers by considering all possible values of N_i. However, its running time would be $\Omega(n^k)$, which is prohibitively expensive. We describe now a $\mathcal{O}(1)$-approximation algorithm which has a significantly better runtime.

Let us fix $\mathcal{C} = (c_1,\ldots,c_k)$. Our goal is to partition P into k subsets $C_1,\ldots,C_k$ for which the cost of the clustering $\sum_{i=1}^{k}|C_i|\sum_{p\in C_i} d(p,c_i)$ is close to $cost_k(P,\mathcal{C})$, i.e., to the optimal cost, and which can be found by applying the algorithm from [25] with the sizes of all clusters to be powers of $(1+\epsilon)$.

Our idea is simple. Instead of calling the algorithm of Tokuyama and Nakano [25] with the sizes of all clusters $N_1,\ldots,N_k$ we do it with the sizes of clusters $\lambda_1,\ldots,\lambda_k$, where each λ_i is of the form $\lfloor(1+\epsilon)^m\rfloor$ for an integer m, and $N_i \leq \lambda_i < (1+\epsilon)\cdot N_i$. The "fake" points of each set are to be chosen from a set of additional points, from the set $\mathbb{O}_\ell$ for an appropriate value of ℓ. Here, for every integer ℓ we define set $\mathbb{O}_\ell$ to be the set of ℓ points such that for every $u \in \mathbb{O}_\ell$ and for every c_i, we have $d(u,c_i) = 0$. Observe that with such a definition of set $\mathbb{O}_\ell$ (and in particular, the requirement that $d(u,c_i) = 0$ for every $u \in \mathbb{O}_\ell$ and for every c_i) we will not obtain a metric instance of the problem, but the algorithm of Tokuyama and Nakano [25] will still work.

Theorem 2. *For every $\varepsilon \leq 1/8$, there is a randomized algorithm for balanced k-median that finds a $(2+\varepsilon)$-approximate solution in time $(O(n\,k) + \widetilde{O}(\sqrt{n}\,k^{2.5}))\cdot (O(k\log^2 n\,\log(n/\varepsilon)/\varepsilon^4))^k$. The algorithm fails with probability at most $1/poly(n)$. It returns also a $(4+\varepsilon)$-approximation for min-sum k-clustering.*

5 α-Preserving Embeddings and Coresets

Let Π be any minimization problem on metric spaces that is *monotone with respect to distances*, i.e., if the distances in the metric space increase then the cost of an optimal solution for Π does not decrease. An embedding from a metric space (P,d) into (P,d') is α-*preserving for* Π if *(a)* the distance between any pair of points does not decrease, and *(b)* the cost of an optimal solution of Π for (P, d') is at most α times that for (P, d).

The concept of α-preserving embeddings can be viewed as a generalization of coresets. In a coreset one tries to reduce the complexity of a problem by reducing the size of the input set in such a way that the considered problem is only slightly affected. The goal of α-preserving embeddings is to carry this idea over to metric embeddings. In this context, the complexity of a problem can be reduced by mapping a metric to a simpler metric in such a way that the considered problem is still approximated.

5.1 $(6 + \epsilon)$-Preserving Embedding for Balanced k-Median

We begin with a $(6+\epsilon)$-preserving embedding into a *shortest path metric* (P, d_G) on a graph $G = (P, E)$ consisting of $poly(k, \log n, 1/\epsilon)$ stars whose centers (which we call *anchor points*) are connected in a clique.

Let G be the graph whose edges are defined by the following procedure:

- Choose the set of anchor points to be the set S computed by PARTITION-INGSCHEME.
- Every pair of anchor points $p, q \in S$ is connected by an edge with distance the same as in the metric space (P, d), i.e., $d_G(p, q) = d(p, q)$.
- Every point $p \in P \setminus S$ is connected by an edge to the nearest anchor point; the cost of this edge is the same as in the metric space (P, d).

Lemma 5. *The embedding of (P, d) into (P, d_G) as described above is a $(6 + \epsilon)$-preserving embedding for the balanced k-median problem.*

5.2 Coresets for Balanced k-Median

In this section, we will design a coreset for balanced k-median for a given input metric. We use the following notation of a coreset for balanced k-medians.

Definition 2 (α-coresets). *Let (P, d) be a metric space with $|P| = n$. Let $Q = \{q_1, \ldots, q_s\} \subseteq P$ be a set of $poly(\log n)$ points with integer weights $w_1, \ldots, w_s$ that sum up to n. Let $\alpha_1 \cdot \alpha_2 \leq \alpha$ be positive parameters. A metric space (Q, d') is an α-coreset for (P, d) for balanced k-median, if there is a mapping $\tau : P \to Q$ with $|\tau^{-1}(q_i)| = w_i$ such that*

- *for every partition of P into sets $C_1, \ldots C_k$ and centers $c_1, \ldots, c_k \in Q$:*

$$\frac{1}{\alpha_1} \cdot \sum_{i=1}^{k} |C_i| \sum_{p \in C_i} d(p, c_i) \leq \sum_{i=1}^{k} |C_i| \sum_{p \in C_i} d'(\tau(p), \tau(c_i)) \ ,$$

- *there exists a partition $C_1, \ldots, C_k$ of P and centers $c_1, \ldots, c_k$ such that*

$$\sum_{i=1}^{k} |C_i| \sum_{p \in C_i} d'(\tau(p), \tau(c_i)) \leq \alpha_2 \cdot Opt_k \ .$$

Construction. To construct the coreset, we consider the graph G defined in Section 5.1, and modify some of its distances and group some of its vertices together. We begin with computing a constant approximation to the cost c_{med} of the k-median problem and use $\widetilde{Opt}_k = n \cdot c_{med}$ as a rough approximation of the cost of the balanced k-median. Then, we increase all edge distances smaller than $\epsilon \cdot \widetilde{Opt}_k/(c_{med} \cdot n^3)$ to the value of $\epsilon \cdot \widetilde{Opt}_k/(c_{med} \cdot n^3)$; it is easy to see that this transformation increases the cost of the optimal solution by not more than a factor of $(1 + \epsilon)$. Next, let F be the set of edges connecting anchor points to non-anchor points, $F = \{(u, v) \in G : u \in S \text{ and } v \in P \setminus S\}$. We round the distances corresponding to these edges up to the next power of $(1 + \epsilon)$. Clearly, this changes the cost of any solution by at most $(1 + \epsilon)$ and only increases edge weights. Since there can be no edges in F with cost more than Opt_k, there are at most $O(\log(n/\epsilon)/\epsilon)$ different edge weights.

Let H denote the graph with these modified distances and let d_H denote the shortest path metric on H. We group the points from $P \setminus S$ incident to the same anchor point $p \in S$ by their edge weights in H. This way, we obtain $O(\log(n/\epsilon)/\epsilon)$ groups V_j^p such that each q in V_j^p is incident to $p \in S$ via an edge with cost w_j. Since all points in V_j^p have equal distance to p, we would like to replace them by a single weighted vertex with weight $|V_j^p|$. The only difficulty stems from the fact that the points in V_j^p have pairwise distance $2 \cdot w_j$ in H and this distance is reduced to 0 when we join them. To reduce this effect, we subdivide V_j^p into groups $V_{j,1}^p, \ldots, V_{j,t}^p$ of size $|V_j^p|/t$ for $t = 32 \cdot (k/\epsilon)^{3/2}$ (for simplicity, we assume that $|V_j^p|/t$ is integral). Each group $V_{j,\ell}^p$, $1 \le \ell \le t$, is replaced by a single vertex of weight $|V_j^p|/t$. Let us define the mapping τ according to this replacement, i.e., every anchor point is mapped to the corresponding anchor point, every non-anchor point is mapped by τ to its replacement. Let us call the resulting new graph H' and let $d_{H'}$ be the shortest path metric induced by H'. H' has $|S| = O(k \log n \log(n/\epsilon)/\epsilon^3)$ anchor points, $O(|S| t \log(n/\epsilon)/\epsilon)$ other points, and $O(|S|)^2 + O(t k \log n \log^2(n/\epsilon)/\epsilon^4)$ edges. In particular, if we set $t = 32 \cdot (k/\epsilon)^{3/2}$, then H' has $O(k^{2.5} \log n \log^2(n/\epsilon)/\epsilon^{5.5})$ points and $O((k^2 \log n \log^2(n/\epsilon)/\epsilon^5) \cdot (\log n + \sqrt{k/\epsilon}))$ edges.

Theorem 3. *The shortest path metric on the weighted graph H' defined above is a $(6 + \epsilon)$-coreset (Q, d') for the balanced k-median problem. It can be computed in $\widetilde{O}(n \cdot k \cdot \ln(1/\delta)/\epsilon^3)$ time with probability $1 - \delta$. It is also a $(12 + \epsilon)$-coreset (Q, d') for the min-sum k-clustering problem.*

6   2-Pass Streaming Algorithm

We present here an application of our coresets to design the first efficient *streaming* algorithm for min-sum k-clustering and balanced k-median. A streaming algorithm for a problem in a metric space (P, d) takes as its input set P as a read-only sequence of points $p_1, \ldots, p_n$ given one-by-one in an arbitrary order. It can evaluate $d(p, q)$ in constant time for any two points p, q stored in local memory. The capacity of the local memory is polylogarithmic. A c-pass streaming algorithm is an algorithm that makes c passes over the input sequence. Using our results from previous sections, we design a 2-pass streaming algorithm for balanced k-median and min-sum k-clustering. Our algorithm begins with computing the coreset from Theorem 3. To do this, we first observe that RANDOMPARTITION is a data streaming algorithm. We can implement PARTITIONINGSCHEME by executing all calls to RANDOMPARTITION in parallel. This yields a one pass algorithm to compute the set S. During the first pass we can also compute a constant factor approximation for the cost of k-median using the algorithm from [5]. In a second pass we compute for every point in P its distance to the nearest neighbor in S and round it up to the next power of $(1 + \epsilon)$. From this representation we compute our coreset and from the coreset we find (an implicit representation of) a constant approximation to min-sum k-clustering using a variation of the algorithm from Theorem 2.

Theorem 4. *There is a 2-pass, $O(1)$-approximation algorithm for min-sum k-clustering and balanced k-median. The algorithm uses $poly(\log n, k)$ space. The time to compute the clustering is $O(k \log n))^{O(k)}$.*

7 Sublinear-Time Polylog-Approximation Factor Algorithm

In Section 4, we presented a very fast algorithm that finds a $(2+\epsilon)$-approximation for balanced k-median and $(4+\epsilon)$-approximation for min-sum k-clustering. The runtime of this algorithm is $o(n^2)$ (and hence, sublinear) for all values $k \leq (\frac{1}{4} - o(1)) \cdot \frac{\log n}{\log(\log n/\epsilon)}$. A natural question is if we can apply similar techniques to obtain good polynomial-time approximation algorithms for larger values of k, in particular, for $k = \omega(\frac{\log n}{\log \log n})$. Prior to our work, for values $k = \omega(1)$, the best polynomial-time algorithm achieved the approximation ratio of $O(c \log^{1+1/c} n)$ [3], for an arbitrary constant $c > 0$; the runtime is $\Omega(n^{2+O(1/c)})$. We can combine the arguments from [3] with the techniques developed in previous sections to obtain an algorithm that has a similar approximation guarantee as that in [3], but which at the same time has superior running time.

Let us define an extension of balanced k-median: *splittable weighted balanced k-median*. Let Q be a set of N points in a metric space. Let $w : Q \to \mathbb{N}$ be a function associating a multiplicity of every point in Q and let Q^* be the multiset defined by taking every point $q \in Q$ with multiplicity $w(q)$. The *splittable weighted balanced k-median* problem for Q is to solve the balanced k-median problem for Q^*, i.e., to find a set of k points $c_1, \ldots, c_k$ in Q^* and a partition of Q^* into $Q_1^*, \ldots, Q_k^*$ that minimizes $\sum_{i=1}^{k} |Q_i^*| \cdot \sum_{q \in Q_i^*} d(q, c_i)$. By combining our coreset construction with an extension of the analysis of an approximation algorithm for balanced k-median of Bartal et al. [3] to the splittable weighted balanced k-median problem, we can prove the following.

Theorem 5. *There is a randomized $(\log n)^{O(1)}$-approximation algorithm for balanced k-median and min-sum clustering that runs in $O(n\, k^{O(1)} (\log n)^{O(1)})$ time. The algorithm fails with probability at most $\frac{1}{poly(n)}$.*

References

1. M. Bădoiu, A. Czumaj, P. Indyk, and C. Sohler. Facility location in sublinear time. *ICALP*, pp. 866–877, 2005.
2. M. Bădoiu, S. Har-Peled, and P. Indyk. Approximate clustering via core-sets. *STOC*, pp. 250–257, 2002.
3. Y. Bartal, M. Charikar, and D. Raz. Approximating min-sum k-clustering in metric spaces. *STOC*, pp. 11–20, 2001.
4. M. Charikar, C. Chekuri, T. Feder, and R. Motwani. Incremental clustering and dynamic information retrieval. *STOC*, pp. 626–635, 1997.
5. M. Charikar, L. O'Callaghan, and R. Panigrahy. Better streaming algorithms for clustering problems. *STOC*, pp. 30–39, 2003.
6. K. Chen. On k-median clustering in high dimensions. *SODA*, pp. 1177–1185, 2006.
7. A. Czumaj and C. Sohler. Sublinear-time approximation for clustering via random sampling. *ICALP*, pp. 396–407, 2004.
8. W. Fernandez de la Vega, M. Karpinski, C. Kenyon, and Y. Rabani. Approximation schemes for clustering problems. *STOC*, pp. 50–58, 2003.
9. G. Frahling and C. Sohler. Coresets in dynamic geometric data streams. *STOC*, pp. 209–217, 2005.
10. S. Guha, N. Mishra, R. Motwani, and L. O'Callaghan. Clustering data streams. *FOCS*, pp. 359–366, 2000.
11. N. Gutmann-Beck and R. Hassin. Approximation algorithms for min-sum p-clustering. *Discrete Applied Mathematics*, 89:125–142, 1998.
12. S. Har-Peled and S. Mazumdar. Coresets for k-means and k-medians and their applications. *STOC*, pp. 291–300, 2004.
13. S. Har-Peled and A. Kushal. Smaller coresets for k-median and k-means clustering. *SoCG*, pp. 126–134, 2005.
14. P. Indyk. Sublinear time algorithms for metric space problems. *STOC*, pp. 428–434, 1999.
15. P. Indyk. A sublinear time approximation scheme for clustering in metric spaces. *FOCS*, pp. 154–159, 1999.
16. P. Indyk. *High-Dimensional Computational Geometry*. PhD thesis, Stanford, 2000.
17. P. Indyk. Algorithms for dynamic geometric problems over data streams. *STOC*, pp. 373–380, 2004.
18. A. Kumar, Y. Sabharwal, and S. Sen. A simple linear time $(1 + \varepsilon)$-approximation algorithm for k-means clustering in any dimensions. *FOCS*, pp. 454–462, 2004.
19. A. Kumar, Y. Sabharwal, and S. Sen. Linear time algorithms for clustering problems in any dimensions. *ICALP*, pp. 1374–1385, 2005.
20. R. Mettu and G. Plaxton. Optimal time bounds for approximate clustering. *Machine Learning*, 56(1-3):35–60, 2004.
21. A. Meyerson, L. O'Callaghan, and S. Plotkin. A k-median algorithm with running time independent of data size. *Machine Learning*, 56(1–3): 61–87, July 2004.
22. S. Sahni and T. Gonzalez. P-complete approximation problems. *JACM*, 23:555–566, 1976.
23. L. J. Schulman. Clustering for edge-cost minimization. *STOC*, pp. 547–555, 2000.
24. M. Thorup. Quick k-median, k-center, and facility location for sparse graphs. *SIAM Journal on Computing*, 34(2):405–432, 2005.
25. T. Tokuyama and J. Nakano. Geometric algorithms for the minimum cost assignment problem. *Random Structures and Algorithms*, 6(4):393–406, 1995.

An Optimal Tableau-Based Decision Algorithm for Propositional Neighborhood Logic

Davide Bresolin, Angelo Montanari, and Pietro Sala

Department of Mathematics and Computer Science, University of Udine, Italy
{bresolin,montana,sala}@dimi.uniud.it

Abstract. In this paper we focus our attention on the decision problem for Propositional Neighborhood Logic (PNL for short). PNL is the proper subset of Halpern and Shoham's modal logic of intervals whose modalities correspond to Allen's relations *meets* and *met by*. We show that the satisfiability problem for PNL over the integers is NEXPTIME-complete. Then, we develop a sound and complete tableau-based decision procedure and we prove its optimality.

1 Introduction

Temporal logics play an important role in several areas of computer science, including artificial intelligence, specification and automatic verification of programs, and temporal databases. Even though interval-based temporal logics provide a natural framework for representing and reasoning about time, most work has been devoted to point-based ones, which generally show a better computational behavior. In this paper, we focus our attention on the propositional fragment of the interval logic of temporal neighborhood (PNL for short) [4,5]. We devise a NEXPTIME tableau-based decision procedure for PNL over the integers (or a subset of them) and we prove its optimality.

Various propositional and first-order interval temporal logics have been proposed in the literature (a comprehensive survey can be found in [6]). The most significant propositional ones are Halpern and Shoham's Modal Logic of Time Intervals (HS) [8], Venema's CDT logic [7,13], and Moszkowski's Propositional Interval Temporal Logic (PITL) [12]. Unfortunately, all of them turn out to be undecidable. Halpern and Shoham's logic has been shown to be undecidable for several classes of linear and branching orders [8]. Venema's CDT is powerful enough to embed HS, and thus it is undecidable (at least) over the same classes of orders. Finally, PITL has been shown to be undecidable over discrete linear orders by Moszkowski [12]; its undecidability over dense linear orders easily follows from the undecidability of the *Begin/End* (BE) fragment of HS [6,9].

To get decidability, severe syntactic and/or semantic restrictions have been imposed to interval-based temporal logics to make it possible to reduce them to point-based ones [10]. One can get decidability by making a suitable choice of the interval modalities. This is the case with the $B\overline{B}$ (*Begin/Begun by*) and $E\overline{E}$ (*End/Ended by*) fragments of HS [6]. As an alternative, decidability can

W. Thomas and P. Weil (Eds.): STACS 2007, LNCS 4393, pp. 549–560, 2007.
© Springer-Verlag Berlin Heidelberg 2007

be achieved by constraining the classes of temporal structures over which the interval logic is interpreted. This is the case with the so-called Split Logics (SLs) [11]. Finally, another possibility is to constrain the relation between the truth value of a formula over an interval and its truth value over subintervals of it. As an example, one can constrain a propositional variable to be true over an interval if and only if it is true at its starting point (*locality*) or if and only if it is true over all its subintervals (*homogeneity*) [12]. All these approaches differ in the nature of the restrictions they impose, but they have a common feature: they replace every interval with a point and, accordingly, interval-based temporal operators with point-based ones. Hence, as pointed out in [10], the problem of proving the decidability of interval logics without taking advantage of such a replacement remains largely unexplored.

A first result in this direction has been obtained by Bresolin et al. in [1,3], where the decidability of the future fragment of PNL (RPNL for short) over the natural numbers is established. They basically prove that an RPNL formula is satisfiable if and only if there exist a finite model, or an ultimately periodic (infinite) one, with a finite representation of *bounded size*. In both cases, such a model can be built starting from any model satisfying the formula by progressively removing exceeding points from it until the desired bound is reached. The removal of a point d from a model causes the removal of all intervals either beginning or ending at it. Since RPNL features only future time modalities, the removal of intervals beginning at d is not critical. On the contrary, the removal of intervals ending at d may introduce "defects", that is, there may be existential future temporal formulae that are not satisfied anymore. However, by properly choosing the point d to remove, we can guarantee that there exist sufficiently many points in the future of d which allows us to fix such defects (by possibly changing the truth value of formulas over intervals ending at them) without introducing new defects.

In this paper, we generalize the proof for RPNL to full PNL by showing that a PNL formula is satisfiable if and only if there exist a finite model or an infinite one with a finite representation of *bounded size*. As in the case of RPNL, such a model can be obtained by removing exceeding points from a given model satisfying the formula, but the removal process turns out to be much more involved. In contrast with the case of RPNL, the removal of a point d from a PNL model may affect the satisfiability of formulae over intervals in the past as well as in the future of d. Hence, to fix the defects possibly caused by the removal of d, we must guarantee that there exist sufficiently many points with the same characteristics as d both in the future and in the past of d. Moreover, we must be sure that changing the valuation of intervals that either end or start at these points does not generate new defects. In the following, we show that this can actually be done.

The paper is organized as follows. In Section 2 we introduce syntax and semantics of PNL. Then, in Section 3 we prove the decidability of PNL over the integers (or a subset of them). In Section 4 we describe an optimal NEXPTIME tableau-based decision procedure, and we prove its soundness and completeness.

Conclusions provide an assessment of the work and outline future research directions. The details of missing proofs can be found in [2].

2   Propositional Neighborhood Logic

In this section, we give syntax and semantics of PNL interpreted over the set $\mathbb{Z}$ of the integers or over a subset of it. To this end, we introduce some preliminary notions. Let $\mathbb{D} = \langle D, < \rangle$ be a strict linear order isomorphic to $\mathbb{Z}$ (or to a subset of it). A *strict interval* on $\mathbb{D}$ is an ordered pair $[d_i, d_j]$ such that $d_i, d_j \in D$ and $d_i < d_j$. The set of all strict intervals over $\mathbb{D}$ will be denoted by $\mathbb{I}(\mathbb{D})^-$ (here we conform to the notation proposed in [5], where $^-$ is used to denote the lack of point intervals, that is, intervals of the form $[d_i, d_i]$). The pair $\langle \mathbb{D}, \mathbb{I}(\mathbb{D})^- \rangle$ is called a *strict interval structure*. For every pair of intervals $[d_i, d_j], [d_i', d_j'] \in \mathbb{I}(\mathbb{D})^-$, we say that $[d_i', d_j']$ is a *right* (resp., *left*) *neighbor* of $[d_i, d_j]$ if and only if $d_j = d_i'$ (resp., $d_j' = d_i$).

The language of (Strict) *Propositional Neighborhood Logic* (PNL for short) consists of a set AP of propositional letters, the connectives $\neg$ and $\vee$, and the modal operators $\langle A \rangle$ and $\langle \overline{A} \rangle$. The other connectives, as well as the logical constants $\top$ (true) and $\bot$ (false), can be defined as usual. The *formulae* of PNL, denoted by $\varphi, \psi, \ldots$, are recursively defined by the following grammar:

$$\varphi ::= p \mid \neg\varphi \mid \varphi \vee \varphi \mid \langle A \rangle \varphi \mid \langle \overline{A} \rangle \varphi.$$

We denote by $|\varphi|$ the length of φ, that is, the number of symbols in φ (in the following, we shall use $|\ |$ to denote the cardinality of a set as well). Whenever there are no ambiguities, we call a PNL formula just a formula. A formula of the forms $\langle A \rangle \psi$, $\neg \langle A \rangle \psi$, $\langle \overline{A} \rangle \psi$, or $\neg \langle \overline{A} \rangle \psi$ is called a *temporal formula* (from now on, we identify $\neg \langle A \rangle \neg \psi$ with $[A]\psi$ and $\neg \langle \overline{A} \rangle \neg \psi$ with $[\overline{A}]\psi$).

A *model* for a PNL formula is a pair $\mathbf{M} = \langle \langle \mathbb{D}, \mathbb{I}(\mathbb{D})^- \rangle, \mathcal{V} \rangle$, where $\langle \mathbb{D}, \mathbb{I}(\mathbb{D})^- \rangle$ is a strict interval structure and $\mathcal{V} : \mathbb{I}(\mathbb{D})^- \longrightarrow 2^{AP}$ is a *valuation function* assigning to every interval the set of propositional letters true over it. Given a model $\mathbf{M} = \langle \langle \mathbb{D}, \mathbb{I}(\mathbb{D})^- \rangle, \mathcal{V} \rangle$ and an interval $[d_i, d_j] \in \mathbb{I}(\mathbb{D})^-$, the semantics of PNL is defined recursively by the *satisfiability relation* $\Vdash$ as follows:

- for every propositional letter $p \in AP$, $\mathbf{M}, [d_i, d_j] \Vdash p$ iff $p \in \mathcal{V}([d_i, d_j])$;
- $\mathbf{M}, [d_i, d_j] \Vdash \neg\psi$ iff $\mathbf{M}, [d_i, d_j] \not\Vdash \psi$;
- $\mathbf{M}, [d_i, d_j] \Vdash \psi_1 \vee \psi_2$ iff $\mathbf{M}, [d_i, d_j] \Vdash \psi_1$ or $\mathbf{M}, [d_i, d_j] \Vdash \psi_2$;
- $\mathbf{M}, [d_i, d_j] \Vdash \langle A \rangle \psi$ iff $\exists d_k \in D$ such that $d_k > d_j$ and $\mathbf{M}, [d_j, d_k] \Vdash \psi$;
- $\mathbf{M}, [d_i, d_j] \Vdash \langle \overline{A} \rangle \psi$ iff $\exists d_k \in D$ such that $d_k < d_i$ and $\mathbf{M}, [d_k, d_i] \Vdash \psi$.

We place ourselves in the most general (and difficult) setting where there are not constraints on the valuation function. As an example, given an interval $[d_i, d_j]$, it may happen that $p \in \mathcal{V}([d_i, d_j])$ and $p \notin \mathcal{V}([d_i', d_j'])$ for all intervals $[d_i', d_j']$ (strictly) contained in $[d_i, d_j]$.

3   Labeled Interval Structures and Satisfiability

In this section we introduce some preliminary notions and we establish some basic results on which our tableau method for PNL relies (an intuitive account of them can be found in [3]).

Let φ be a PNL formula to be checked for satisfiability and let AP be the set of its propositional letters.

Definition 1. *The* closure $\mathrm{CL}(\varphi)$ *of* φ *is the set of all subformulae of* $\langle A \rangle \varphi$ *and of their negations (we identify* $\neg\neg\psi$ *with* ψ*).*

As it will become clear later, we put the formula $\langle A \rangle \varphi$ and its negation in $\mathrm{CL}(\varphi)$ to avoid that the removal process could delete all intervals over which φ holds.

Definition 2. *The* set of *temporal formulae of* φ *is the set* $\mathrm{TF}(\varphi) = \{\zeta \in \mathrm{CL}(\varphi) : \zeta = \langle A \rangle \psi$ *or* $\zeta = [A]\psi$ *or* $\zeta = \langle \overline{A} \rangle \psi$ *or* $\zeta = [\overline{A}]\psi\}$.

By induction on the structure of φ, we can easily prove that, for every formula φ, $|\mathrm{CL}(\varphi)|$ is less than or equal to $2 \cdot (|\varphi| + 1)$, while $|\mathrm{TF}(\varphi)|$ is less than or equal to $2 \cdot |\varphi|$. We are now ready to introduce the notion of φ-atom.

Definition 3. *A* φ-atom *is a set* $A \subseteq \mathrm{CL}(\varphi)$ *such that:*

- *for every* $\psi \in \mathrm{CL}(\varphi)$, $\psi \in A$ *iff* $\neg\psi \notin A$;
- *for every* $\psi_1 \vee \psi_2 \in \mathrm{CL}(\varphi)$, $\psi_1 \vee \psi_2 \in A$ *iff* $\psi_1 \in A$ *or* $\psi_2 \in A$.

We denote the set of all φ-atoms by $\mathcal{A}_\varphi$. We have that $|\mathcal{A}_\varphi| \leq 2^{|\varphi|+1}$. Atoms are connected by the following binary relation.

Definition 4. *Let* LR_φ *be a relation such that for every pair of atoms* $A_1, A_2 \in \mathcal{A}_\varphi$, $A_1 \ LR_\varphi \ A_2$ *if and only if (i) for every* $[A]\psi \in \mathrm{CL}(\varphi)$, *if* $[A]\psi \in A_1$ *then* $\psi \in A_2$ *and (ii) for every* $[\overline{A}]\psi \in \mathrm{CL}(\varphi)$, *if* $[\overline{A}]\psi \in A_2$ *then* $\psi \in A_1$.

We now introduce a suitable labeling of interval structures based on φ-atoms.

Definition 5. *A* φ-labeled interval structure *(LIS for short) is a pair* $\mathbf{L} = \langle \langle \mathbb{D}, \mathbb{I}(\mathbb{D})^- \rangle, \mathcal{L} \rangle$, *where* $\langle \mathbb{D}, \mathbb{I}(\mathbb{D})^- \rangle$ *is an interval structure and* $\mathcal{L} : \mathbb{I}(\mathbb{D})^- \to \mathcal{A}_\varphi$ *is a labeling function such that, for every pair of neighboring intervals* $[d_i, d_j], [d_j, d_k] \in \mathbb{I}(\mathbb{D})^-$, $\mathcal{L}([d_i, d_j]) \ LR_\varphi \ \mathcal{L}([d_j, d_k])$.

If we interpret the labeling function as a valuation function, LISs represent *candidate models* for φ. The truth of formulae devoid of temporal operators and that of $[A]/[\overline{A}]$ formulae indeed follow from the definition of φ-atom and LR_φ, respectively. However, to obtain a model for φ, we must also guarantee the truth of $\langle A \rangle / \langle \overline{A} \rangle$ formulae. To this end, we introduce the notion of fulfilling LIS.

Definition 6. *A* φ-labeled interval structure $\mathbf{L} = \langle \langle \mathbb{D}, \mathbb{I}(\mathbb{D})^- \rangle, \mathcal{L} \rangle$ *is fulfilling if and only if (i) for every temporal formula* $\langle A \rangle \psi \in \mathrm{TF}(\varphi)$ *and every interval* $[d_i, d_j] \in \mathbb{I}(\mathbb{D})^-$, *if* $\langle A \rangle \psi \in \mathcal{L}([d_i, d_j])$, *then there exists* $d_k > d_j$ *such that* $\psi \in \mathcal{L}([d_j, d_k])$ *and (ii) for every temporal formula* $\langle \overline{A} \rangle \psi \in \mathrm{TF}(\varphi)$ *and every interval* $[d_i, d_j] \in \mathbb{I}(\mathbb{D})^-$, *if* $\langle \overline{A} \rangle \psi \in \mathcal{L}([d_i, d_j])$, *then there exists* $d_k < d_i$ *such that* $\psi \in \mathcal{L}([d_k, d_i])$.

The next theorem proves that for any given formula φ, the satisfiability of φ is equivalent to the existence of a fulfilling LIS with an interval labeled by φ.

Theorem 1. *A formula φ is satisfiable if and only if there exists a fulfilling LIS* $\mathbf{L} = \langle \langle \mathbb{D}, \mathbb{I}(\mathbb{D})^- \rangle, \mathcal{L} \rangle$ *with $\varphi \in \mathcal{L}([d_i, d_j])$ for some $[d_i, d_j] \in \mathbb{I}(\mathbb{D})^-$.*

The implication from left to right is straightforward; the opposite implication is proved by induction on the structure of the formula.

From now on, we say that a fulfilling LIS $\mathbf{L} = \langle \langle \mathbb{D}, \mathbb{I}(\mathbb{D})^- \rangle, \mathcal{L} \rangle$ *satisfies* φ if and only if there exists an interval $[d_i, d_j] \in \mathbb{I}(\mathbb{D})^-$ such that $\varphi \in \mathcal{L}([d_i, d_j])$. Since (the domain of) fulfilling LISs satisfying φ may be arbitrarily large or even infinite, we must find a way to finitely establish their existence. In the following, we first give a bound on the size of finite fulfilling LISs that must be checked for satisfiability, when searching for finite φ-models; then, we show that we can restrict ourselves to infinite fulfilling LISs with a finite bounded representation, when searching for infinite φ-models.

Definition 7. *Given a LIS $\mathbf{L} = \langle \langle \mathbb{D}, \mathbb{I}(\mathbb{D})^- \rangle, \mathcal{L} \rangle$ and a point $d \in D$, we define the set of* future temporal requests *of d as the set* $\mathrm{REQ}_f^{\mathbf{L}}(d) = \{ \langle A \rangle \xi, [A]\xi \in \mathrm{TF}(\varphi) : \exists d' \in D(\langle A \rangle \xi, [A]\xi \in \mathcal{L}([d', d]))\}$ *and the set of* past temporal requests *of d as the set* $\mathrm{REQ}_p^{\mathbf{L}}(d) = \{ \langle \overline{A} \rangle \xi, [\overline{A}]\xi \in \mathrm{TF}(\varphi) : \exists d' \in D(\langle \overline{A} \rangle \xi, [\overline{A}]\xi \in \mathcal{L}([d, d']))\}$. *The set of* temporal requests *of d is defined as* $\mathrm{REQ}^{\mathbf{L}}(d) = \mathrm{REQ}_p^{\mathbf{L}}(d) \cup \mathrm{REQ}_f^{\mathbf{L}}(d)$.

We denote by REQ_φ the set of all possible sets of requests. It is not difficult to show that $|\mathrm{REQ}_\varphi|$ is equal to $2^{\frac{|\mathrm{TF}(\varphi)|}{2}}$.

Definition 8. *Given a LIS $\mathbf{L} = \langle \langle \mathbb{D}, \mathbb{I}(\mathbb{D})^- \rangle, \mathcal{L} \rangle$, $D' \subseteq D$, and $\mathcal{R} \in \mathrm{REQ}_\varphi$, we say that $\mathcal{R}$ occurs n times in D' if and only if there exist exactly n distinct points $d_{i_1}, \ldots, d_{i_n} \in D'$ such that $\mathrm{REQ}^{\mathbf{L}}(d_{i_j}) = \mathcal{R}$, for all $1 \leq j \leq n$.*

We describe now the process of removing a point from a LIS. Given $\mathbf{L} = \langle \langle \mathbb{D}, \mathbb{I}(\mathbb{D})^- \rangle, \mathcal{L} \rangle$ and $d \in D$, let $\mathbf{L}_{-d}$ be the set of all LIS $\mathbf{L}' = \langle \langle \mathbb{D}', \mathbb{I}(\mathbb{D}')^- \rangle, \mathcal{L}' \rangle$ such that $D' = D \setminus \{d\}$ and $\mathrm{REQ}^{\mathbf{L}'}(\overline{d}) = \mathrm{REQ}^{\mathbf{L}}(\overline{d})$, for all $\overline{d} \in D \setminus \{d\}$. $\mathbf{L}$ and $\mathbf{L}'$ do not necessarily agree on the labeling of intervals, but they agree on the sets of requests of points.

Given a fulfilling LIS $\mathbf{L}$ and a point d, it is not guaranteed that $\mathbf{L}_{-d}$ contains a fulfilling LIS. The removal of d indeed causes the removal of all intervals either beginning or ending at it and thus there can be a point $\overline{d} < d$ (resp., $\overline{d} > d$) such that there exists a formula $\langle A \rangle \psi \in \mathrm{REQ}_f^{\mathbf{L}}(\overline{d})$ (resp., $\langle \overline{A} \rangle \psi \in \mathrm{REQ}_p^{\mathbf{L}}(\overline{d})$) which is fulfilled in $\mathbf{L}$, but not in any $\mathbf{L}' \in \mathbf{L}_{-d}$. The following lemma provides a sufficient condition for preserving the fulfilling property when removing a point from $\mathbf{L}$.

Lemma 1. *Let $\mathbf{L} = \langle \langle \mathbb{D}, \mathbb{I}(\mathbb{D})^- \rangle, \mathcal{L} \rangle$ be a fulfilling LIS, f be the number of $\langle A \rangle$-formulae in $\mathrm{TF}(\varphi)$, and p be the number of $\langle \overline{A} \rangle$-formulae in $\mathrm{TF}(\varphi)$. If there exists a point $d_e \in D$ such that (i) there exist at least $f \cdot p + p$ distinct points $d < d_e$ such that $\mathrm{REQ}^{\mathbf{L}}(d) = \mathrm{REQ}^{\mathbf{L}}(d_e)$ and (ii) there exist at least $f \cdot p + f$ distinct points $d > d_e$ such that $\mathrm{REQ}^{\mathbf{L}}(d) = \mathrm{REQ}^{\mathbf{L}}(d_e)$, then there is one fulfilling LIS $\widehat{\mathbf{L}} \in \mathbf{L}_{-d_e}$.*

Proof. Let $\mathbf{L} = \langle \langle \mathbb{D}, \mathbb{I}(\mathbb{D})^- \rangle, \mathcal{L} \rangle$ be a fulfilling LIS and let $d_e \in D$ be a point such that there exist at least $f \cdot p + p$ distinct points $d < d_e$ such that $\mathrm{REQ}^{\mathbf{L}}(d) = \mathrm{REQ}^{\mathbf{L}}(d_e)$ and at least $f \cdot p + f$ distinct points $d > d_e$ such that $\mathrm{REQ}^{\mathbf{L}}(d) = \mathrm{REQ}^{\mathbf{L}}(d_e)$. We define $\mathbb{D}' = \langle D \setminus \{d_e\}, < \rangle$ and $\mathcal{L}' = \mathcal{L}|_{\mathbb{I}(\mathbb{D}')^-}$ (the restriction of $\mathcal{L}$ to the intervals on $\mathbb{D}'$). The pair $\mathbf{L}' = \langle \langle \mathbb{D}', \mathbb{I}(\mathbb{D}')^- \rangle, \mathcal{L}' \rangle$ is obviously a LIS in $\mathbf{L}_{-d_e}$, but, as already pointed out, it is not necessarily a fulfilling one. We show how the defects possibly caused by the removal of d_e can be fixed one-by-one by properly redefining $\mathcal{L}'$.

Consider the case of a point $d < d_e$ and a formula $\langle A \rangle \psi \in \mathrm{REQ}^{\mathbf{L}}_f(d)$ such that $\psi \in \mathcal{L}([d, d_e])$ and there are no $\overline{d} \in D \setminus \{d_e\}$ such that $\psi \in \mathcal{L}'([d, \overline{d}])$ (the symmetric case of $d > d_e$ and $\langle \overline{A} \rangle \psi \in \mathrm{REQ}^{\mathbf{L}}_p(d)$ can be dealt with in the same way). Let $R = \{d_r \in D : d_r > d_e \wedge \mathrm{REQ}^{\mathbf{L}}(d_r) = \mathrm{REQ}^{\mathbf{L}}(d_e)\}$. To satisfy the request $\langle A \rangle \psi \in \mathrm{REQ}^{\mathbf{L}}(d)$ we change the labeling of an interval $[d, d_r]$, for a suitable $d_r \in R$. However, to avoid that such a change makes one or more requests in $\mathrm{REQ}^{\mathbf{L}}_p(d_r)$ no more satisfied, we preliminarily redefine the labeling $\mathcal{L}'$. First, we take a minimal set of points $P^{d_e} \subseteq D \setminus \{d_e\}$ such that, for every $\langle \overline{A} \rangle \psi \in \mathrm{REQ}^{\mathbf{L}}_p(d_e)$ there exists a point $d_i \in P^{d_e}$ such that $\psi \in \mathcal{L}([d_i, d_e])$. We call P^{d_e} the set of *preserved past points for* d_e. Then, for every point $d_i \in P^{d_e}$, let $F^{d_i} \subseteq D \setminus \{d_e\}$ be a minimal set of points such that, for every $\langle A \rangle \psi \in \mathrm{REQ}^{\mathbf{L}}_f(d_i)$ there is a point $d_f \in F^{d_i}$ such that $\psi \in \mathcal{L}([d_i, d_f])$. We call F^{d_i} the set of *preserved future points for* d_i.

Let G be the set of points $R \setminus \bigcup_{d_i \in P^{d_e}} F^{d_i}$. By the minimality requirements, $|P^{d_e}|$ is bounded by p and $|F^{d_i}|$, for each $d_i \in P^{d_e}$, is bounded by f. Hence, $|\bigcup_{d_i \in P^{d_e}} F^{d_i}| \leq f \cdot p$ and, by Condition (ii), $|G|$ is greater than or equal to f. Now, we can use points in G to fulfill $\langle A \rangle \psi \in \mathrm{REQ}^{\mathbf{L}}_f(d)$, without generating new defects, as follows. Since $\mathrm{REQ}^{\mathbf{L}}_f(d)$ contains at most f $\langle A \rangle$-formulae, there exists at least one point $d_g \in G$ such that the atom $\mathcal{L}'([d, d_g])$ either fulfills no $\langle A \rangle$-formulae or it fulfills only $\langle A \rangle$-formulae which are also fulfilled by an φ-atom $\mathcal{L}'([d, d_k])$ for some d_k. Let d_g one of such "useless" points. We can redefine $\mathcal{L}'([d, d_g])$ by putting $\mathcal{L}'([d, d_g]) = \mathcal{L}([d, d_e])$, thus fixing the problem for $\langle A \rangle \psi \in \mathrm{REQ}^{\mathbf{L}}_f(d)$. Since $\mathrm{REQ}^{\mathbf{L}}(d_g) = \mathrm{REQ}^{\mathbf{L}}(d_e)$, such a change has no impact on the right neighboring intervals of $[d, d_g]$. On the contrary, there may exist one or more $\langle \overline{A} \rangle$-formulae in $\mathrm{REQ}^{\mathbf{L}}_p(d_g)$ which, due to the change in the labeling of $[d, d_g]$, are not satisfied anymore. In such a case, however, we can recover satisfiability, without introducing any new defect, by putting $\mathcal{L}'([d_i, d_g]) = \mathcal{L}([d_i, d_e])$ for all $d_i \in P^{d_e}$.

In the same way, we can fix all possible other defects caused by the removal of d_e. Let $\widehat{\mathbf{L}} = \langle \langle \mathbb{D}', \mathbb{I}(\mathbb{D}') \rangle, \widehat{\mathcal{L}} \rangle$ be the resulting LIS. It is immediate to show that $\widehat{\mathbf{L}}$ is fulfilling and it belongs to $\mathbf{L}_{-d_e}$. $\square$

By taking advantage of Lemma 1, we can prove the following theorem.

Theorem 2. *Let* $\mathbf{L} = \langle \langle \mathbb{D}, \mathbb{I}(\mathbb{D})^- \rangle, \mathcal{L} \rangle$ *be a* finite fulfilling *LIS that satisfies* φ, f *be the number of* $\langle A \rangle$-*formulae in* $\mathrm{TF}(\varphi)$, *and* p *be the number of* $\langle \overline{A} \rangle$-*formulae in* $\mathrm{TF}(\varphi)$. *Then, there exists a* finite fulfilling *LIS* $\widehat{\mathbf{L}} = \langle \langle \widehat{\mathbb{D}}, \mathbb{I}(\widehat{\mathbb{D}})^- \rangle, \widehat{\mathcal{L}} \rangle$ *that satisfies*

φ such that, for every $\widehat{d}_i \in \widehat{D}$, $\text{REQ}^{\widehat{L}}(\widehat{d}_i)$ occurs at most $m = 2fp + f + p$ times in $\widehat{D}$.

Let us consider now the case of infinite (fulfilling) LISs. We start with a classification of points belonging the domain of the structure.

Definition 9. *Given an infinite LIS* $\mathbf{L} = \langle \langle \mathbb{D}, \mathbb{I}(\mathbb{D})^- \rangle, \mathcal{L} \rangle$, *we partition the points in D into the following sets:*

- $Fin(\mathbf{L})$ *is the set of all points $d \in D$ such that $\text{REQ}^{\mathbf{L}}(d)$ occurs finitely many times in D;*
- $Inf_l(\mathbf{L})$ *is the set of all points $d \in D$ such that $\text{REQ}^{\mathbf{L}}(d)$ occurs infinitely many times in D, but there exists a point d_{max} such that, for all $d' > d_{max}$, $\text{REQ}^{\mathbf{L}}(d') \neq \text{REQ}^{\mathbf{L}}(d)$;*
- $Inf_r(\mathbf{L})$ *is the set of all points $d \in D$ such that $\text{REQ}^{\mathbf{L}}(d)$ occurs infinitely many times in D, but there exists a point d_{min} such that, for all $d' < d_{min}$, $\text{REQ}^{\mathbf{L}}(d') \neq \text{REQ}^{\mathbf{L}}(d)$;*
- $Inf(\mathbf{L})$ *is the set of all points $d \in D$ such that $\text{REQ}^{\mathbf{L}}(d)$ occurs infinitely many times in D and, for every point d', there exists $d'' < d'$ such that $\text{REQ}^{\mathbf{L}}(d'') = \text{REQ}^{\mathbf{L}}(d)$ and there exists $d''' > d'$ such that $\text{REQ}^{\mathbf{L}}(d''') = \text{REQ}^{\mathbf{L}}(d)$.*

The following definition captures a particular subclass of infinite LISs that enjoy a finite representation.

Definition 10. *An infinite LIS* $\mathbf{L} = \langle \langle \mathbb{D}, \mathbb{I}(\mathbb{D})^- \rangle, \mathcal{L} \rangle$ *is ultimately periodic, with left period l, infix i and right period r, if and only if there exists $d_0 \in D$ such that for all $k < 0$, $\text{REQ}^{\mathbf{L}}(d_k) = \text{REQ}^{\mathbf{L}}(d_{k-l})$ and for all $k \geq 0$, $\text{REQ}^{\mathbf{L}}(d_{i+k}) = \text{REQ}^{\mathbf{L}}(d_{i+k+r})$.*

The following theorem proves that if there exists an infinite fulfilling LIS that satisfies φ, then there exists also an ultimately periodic fulfilling LIS that satisfies it. Furthermore, it provides a bound to the left period, infix, and right period of such a fulfilling LIS which closely resembles the one that we established for finite ones.

Theorem 3. *Let* $\mathbf{L} = \langle \langle \mathbb{D}, \mathbb{I}(\mathbb{D})^- \rangle, \mathcal{L} \rangle$ *be an infinite fulfilling LIS that satisfies φ, f be the number of $\langle A \rangle$-formulae in $\text{TF}(\varphi)$, and p be the number of $\langle \overline{A} \rangle$-formulae in $\text{TF}(\varphi)$. Then, there exists an ultimately periodic fulfilling LIS $\widehat{\mathbf{L}} = \langle \langle \widehat{\mathbb{D}}, \mathbb{I}(\widehat{\mathbb{D}})^- \rangle, \widehat{\mathcal{L}} \rangle$, with left period l, infix i and right period r, such that*

1. *for every $d_j \in Fin(\widehat{\mathbf{L}})$, $\text{REQ}^{\widehat{\mathbf{L}}}(d_j)$ occurs at most $m = 2fp + f + p$ times in D;*

2. *for every $d_j \in Inf_r(\widehat{\mathbf{L}})$, $\text{REQ}^{\widehat{\mathbf{L}}}(d_j)$ occurs exactly $fp + p$ times in I, where I is the set of points in the infix part of $\widehat{\mathbf{L}}$;*

3. *for every $d_j \in Inf_l(\widehat{\mathbf{L}})$, $\text{REQ}^{\widehat{\mathbf{L}}}(d_j)$ occurs exactly $fp + f$ times in I;*

4. *for all points $d_j \in Inf(\hat{\mathbf{L}})$, $d_j \notin I$;*

5. *$r \leq |\mathrm{REQ}_\varphi|$ and $l \leq |\mathrm{REQ}_\varphi|$;*

6. *for every $d_j \in Fin(\mathbf{L})$ and every formula $\langle A \rangle \psi \in \mathrm{REQ}_f^{\hat{\mathbf{L}}}(d_j)$, there exists a point $d_h \leq d_{i+(f \cdot p+f) \cdot r}$ such that $\psi \in \hat{\mathcal{L}}([d_j, d_h])$;*

7. *for every $d_j \in Fin(\mathbf{L})$ and every formula $\langle \overline{A} \rangle \psi \in \mathrm{REQ}^{\hat{\mathbf{L}}}(d_j)$, there exists a point $d_h \geq d_{-(f \cdot p+p) \cdot l}$ such that $\psi \in \hat{\mathcal{L}}([d_h, d_j])$*

that satisfies φ.

4   A Tableau-Based Decision Procedure for PNL

In this section we define a tableau method for PNL over the integers (or a subset of them). We begin with some basic definitions.

Given a formula φ, let $m = 2fp + f + p$, where f (resp. p) is the number of $\langle A \rangle$-formulae (resp. $\langle \overline{A} \rangle$-formulae) in $CL(\varphi)$. A tableau for PNL is a special *decorated tree* $\mathcal{T}$. For each node n in a branch B, the *decoration* $\nu(n)$ is a tuple $\langle [d_i, d_j], A_n, \mathrm{REQ}_n, \mathbb{D}_n, x \rangle$, where:

- $[d_i, d_j] \in \mathbb{I}(\mathbb{D}_n)^-$;
- $\mathrm{REQ}_n : \mathbb{D}_n \mapsto \mathrm{REQ}_\varphi$ is a *request function*;
- $\mathbb{D}_n = \langle D_n, < \rangle$ is a finite linear order;
- $A_n \in \mathcal{A}_\varphi$ is such that: *(i)* for all $[A]\psi \in \mathrm{REQ}_n(d_i)$, $\psi \in A_n$, *(ii)* for all $[\overline{A}]\psi \in \mathrm{REQ}_n(d_j)$, $\psi \in A_n$, *(iii)* for all $\psi \in A_n$, if $\psi = \langle \overline{A} \rangle \xi$ or $\psi = [\overline{A}]\xi$, then $\psi \in \mathrm{REQ}_n(d_i)$, and *(iv)* for all $\psi \in A_n$, if $\psi = \langle A \rangle \xi$ or $\psi = [A]\xi$, then $\psi \in \mathrm{REQ}_n(d_j)$;
- $x \in \{R, L, F\}$, where R, L, and F respectively stand for right blocked, left blocked, and free.

The root r of the tree is decorated by the *empty decoration* $\langle \emptyset, \emptyset, \emptyset, \emptyset, F \rangle$.

Given a node $n \in B$, decorated with $\langle [d_i, d_j], A_n, \mathrm{REQ}_n, \mathbb{D}_n, x \rangle$, and a future existential formula $\langle A \rangle \psi \in A_n$, we say that $\langle A \rangle \psi \in A_n$ is *fulfilled on B* if and only if there exists a node $n' \in B$ such that $\nu(n') = \langle [d_j, d_k], A_{n'}, \mathrm{REQ}_{n'}, \mathbb{D}_{n'}, x \rangle$ and $\psi \in A_{n'}$. Conversely, we say that a past existential formula $\langle \overline{A} \rangle \psi \in A_n$ is *fulfilled on B* if and only if there exists a node $n' \in B$ such that $\nu(n') = \langle [d_k, d_i], A_{n'}, \mathrm{REQ}_{n'}, \mathbb{D}_{n'}, x \rangle$ and $\psi \in A_{n'}$. A node n is said to be *active on B* if and only if A_n contains at least one (future or past) existential formula which is not fulfilled on B.

Expansion rules. Let B a branch of a decorated tree $\mathcal{T}$. We denote by $\mathbb{D}_B$ and REQ_B the linear order and the request function of the decoration of the last node in B, respectively. Moreover, let d_l and d_r be the minimum and maximum element of $\mathbb{D}_B$, respectively. The *expansion rules* for B are:

1. *Right step rule*: if there exists an active node $n \in B$, with $\nu(n) = \langle [d_i, d_j], A_n, \mathrm{REQ}_n, \mathbb{D}_n, x \rangle$ and a non-fulfilled future existential formula in A_n, then extend $\mathbb{D}_B$ to $D' = \mathbb{D}_B \cup \{d_{r+1}\}$, with $d_{r+1} > d_r$. Then, take an atom A' such

that A_n LR_φ A' and extend REQ_B to $\mathrm{REQ}' : D' \mapsto \mathrm{REQ}_\varphi$ in such a way that for all $[\overline{A}]\psi \in \mathrm{REQ}'(d_{r+1})$, $\psi \in A'$ and for all $\psi \in A'$, if $\psi = \langle A \rangle \xi$ or $\psi = [A]\xi$, then $\psi \in \mathrm{REQ}'(d_{r+1})$. Finally, add an immediate successor n' to the last node in B decorated as follows:

- if the number p of points $d \in D'$ with $\mathrm{REQ}'(d) = \mathrm{REQ}'(d_{r+1})$ is less than or equal to m, then $\nu(n') = \langle [d_j, d_{r+1}], A', \mathrm{REQ}', \mathbb{D}', F \rangle$;
- otherwise ($p = m + 1$), $\nu(n') = \langle [d_j, d_{r+1}], A', \mathrm{REQ}', \mathbb{D}', R \rangle$.

2. *Left step rule*: if there exists an active node $n \in B$, with $\nu(n) = \langle [d_i, d_j], A_n,$ $\mathrm{REQ}_n, \mathbb{D}_n, x \rangle$ and a non-fulfilled past existential formula in A_n, then extend D_B to $D' = D_B \cup \{d_{l-1}\}$, with $d_{l-1} < d_l$. Then, take an atom A' such that A' LR_φ A_n and extend REQ_B to $\mathrm{REQ}' : D' \mapsto \mathrm{REQ}_\varphi$ in such a way that for all $[A]\psi \in \mathrm{REQ}'(d_{l-1})$, $\psi \in A'$ and for all $\psi \in A'$, if $\psi = \langle \overline{A} \rangle \xi$ or $\psi = [\overline{A}]\xi$, then $\psi \in \mathrm{REQ}'(d_{l-1})$. Finally, add an immediate successor n' to the last node in B decorated as follows:

- if the number p of points $d \in D'$ with $\mathrm{REQ}'(d) = \mathrm{REQ}'(d_{l-1})$ is less than or equal to m, then $\nu(n') = \langle [d_{l-1}, d_i], A', \mathrm{REQ}', \mathbb{D}', F \rangle$;
- otherwise ($p = m + 1$), $\nu(n') = \langle [d_{l-1}, d_i], A', \mathrm{REQ}', \mathbb{D}', L \rangle$.

3. *Fill-in rule*: if there exist two points $d_i < d_j$ such that there are no nodes in B decorated with the interval $[d_i, d_j]$ and there exists a decoration $\langle [d_i, d_j], A',$ $\mathrm{REQ}_B, \mathbb{D}_B, F \rangle$, then expand B by adding an immediate successor n', with such a decoration, to the last node in B.

All rules expand the branch B with a new node. However, while the left and right step rules add a new point d to D_B and decorate the new node with a new interval beginning or ending at d, the fill-in rule decorates it with a new interval whose endpoints already belong to D_B.

Expansion strategy. Given a decorated tree $\mathcal{T}$ and a branch B, we say that B is *right-blocked* if there exists a node n decorated with $\langle [d_i, d_j], A_n, \mathrm{REQ}_n, \mathbb{D}_n, R \rangle$, while it is *left-blocked* if there exists a node n decorated with $\langle [d_i, d_j], A_n, \mathrm{REQ}_n,$ $\mathbb{D}_n, L \rangle$. A branch is *blocked* if it is both left and right blocked.

An expansion rule is *applicable on B* if B is non-blocked and the application of the rule generates a new node. The *branch expansion strategy* for a branch B is the following one:

1. if the fill-in rule is applicable, apply the fill-in rule to B and, for every possible choice for the decoration, add an immediate successor to the last node in B;
2. if the fill-in rule is not applicable and there exist two points $d_i < d_j \in D_B$ such that there are no nodes in B decorated with $[d_i, d_j]$, *close* the branch;
3. if B is not right-blocked and the right-step rule is applicable, then apply it to B and, for every possible choice for the decoration, add an immediate successor to the last node in B;
4. if B is not left-blocked and the left-step rule is applicable, then apply it to B and, for every possible choice for the decoration, add an immediate successor to the last node in B.

Tableau. Let φ be the formula to be checked for satisfiability and let $\langle[d_0,d_1], A_1, \text{REQ}_1, \{d_0,d_1\}, F\rangle, \ldots, \langle[d_0,d_1], A_k, \text{REQ}_k, \{d_0,d_1\}, F\rangle$ be the set of decorations with $\langle A\rangle\varphi \in \text{REQ}_i(d_0)$. The *initial tableau* for φ consists of the root, with the empty decoration, and k immediate successors $n_1, \ldots n_k$. For each $1 \leq i \leq k$, n_i is decorated by $\langle[d_0,d_1], A_i, \text{REQ}_i, \{d_0,d_1\}, F\rangle$. A *tableau* for φ is any decorated tree $\mathcal{T}$ obtained by expanding the initial tableau for φ through successive applications of the branch-expansion strategy to existing branches, until the branch-expansion strategy cannot be applied anymore.

Fulfilling branches. Given a branch B of a tableau $\mathcal{T}$ for φ, we say that B is a *fulfilling branch* if and only if B is not closed and one of the following conditions holds:

1. B does not contain active nodes (finite model case);

2. B is right blocked and there exists at least one formula $\langle A\rangle\psi$ not fulfilled in B (right unbounded model case). Moreover, let d_r be the greatest point in D_B. By the blocking condition, $\text{REQ}_B(d_r)$ is repeated $m + 1$ times in D_B. Let d_k be the greatest point in D_B, with $d_k < d_r$, such that $\text{REQ}_B(d_k) = \text{REQ}_B(d_r)$. The set $\{d_{k+1}, \ldots, d_r\}$, called *fulfilling right period*, satisfies the following conditions:

   (a) for all $d_i, d_j \in \{d_{k+1}, \ldots, d_r\}$, there exists an atom A_{ij} such that *(i)* for all $[A]\psi \in \text{REQ}_B(d_i)$, $\psi \in A_{ij}$, and *(ii)* for all $[\overline{A}]\psi \in \text{REQ}_B(d_j)$, $\psi \in A_{ij}$;

   (b) for all $d_i \in \{d_{k+1}, \ldots, d_r\}$ and $\langle A\rangle\psi \in \text{REQ}_B(d_i)$, there exist a point $d_j \in \{d_{k+1}, \ldots, d_r\}$ and an atom A_{ij} such that *(i)* $\psi \in A_{ij}$, *(ii)* for all $[A]\xi \in \text{REQ}_B(d_i)$, $\xi \in A_{ij}$, and *(iii)* for all $[\overline{A}]\xi \in \text{REQ}_B(d_j)$, $\xi \in A_{ij}$;

   (c) for all $d_i \leq d_k$ such that $\text{REQ}_B(d_i)$ does not occur in the right period, all $\langle A\rangle$-formulae in $\text{REQ}_B(d_i)$ are fulfilled in B.

3. B is left blocked and there exists at least one formula $\langle\overline{A}\rangle\psi$ not fulfilled in B (left unbounded model case). Moreover, let d_l be the smallest point in D_B. By the blocking condition, $\text{REQ}_B(d_l)$ is repeated $m + 1$ times in D_B. Let d_k be the smallest point in D_B, with $d_k > d_l$, such that $\text{REQ}_B(d_k) = \text{REQ}_B(d_l)$. The set $\{d_l, \ldots, d_{k-1}\}$, called *fulfilling left period*, satisfies the following conditions:

   (a) for all $d_i, d_j \in \{d_l, \ldots, d_{k-1}\}$, there exists an atom A_{ij} such that *(i)* for all $[A]\psi \in \text{REQ}_B(d_i)$, $\psi \in A_{ij}$, and *(ii)* for all $[\overline{A}]\psi \in \text{REQ}_B(d_j)$, $\psi \in A_{ij}$;

   (b) for all $d_i \in \{d_l, \ldots, d_{k-1}\}$ and $\langle\overline{A}\rangle\psi \in \text{REQ}_B(d_i)$, there exists a point $d_j \in \{d_l, \ldots, d_{k-1}\}$ and an atom A_{ji} such that *(i)* $\psi \in A_{ji}$, *(ii)* for all $[A]\xi \in \text{REQ}_B(d_j)$, $\xi \in A_{ji}$, and *(iii)* for all $[\overline{A}]\xi \in \text{REQ}_B(d_i)$, $\xi \in A_{ji}$;

   (c) for all $d_i \geq d_k$ such that $\text{REQ}_B(d_i)$ does not occur in the left period, all $\langle\overline{A}\rangle$-formulae in $\text{REQ}_B(d_i)$ are fulfilled in B.

4. if B is both right and left blocked, Conditions 2. and 3. must hold.

The decision procedure works as follows: given a formula φ, it constructs a tableau T for φ and it returns "satisfiable" if and only if there exists at least one fulfilling branch in T.

4.1 Soundness and Completeness

Soundness and completeness of the proposed method can be proved as follows. Soundness is proved by showing how to construct a fulfilling LIS satisfying φ from a fulfilling branch B in a tableau T for φ (by Theorem 1, it follows that φ has a model). The proof must encompass both the case of non-blocked branches (finite case) and of blocked ones (infinite case). Proving completeness consists in showing that for any satisfiable formula φ, there exists a fulfilling branch B in any tableau T for φ. Given a model for φ and the corresponding fulfilling LIS **L**, we prove the existence of a fulfilling branch in T by exploiting Theorems 2 and 3.

Theorem 4. *Given a formula φ and a tableau T for φ, if there exists a fulfilling branch in T, then φ is satisfiable.*

Theorem 5. *Given a satisfiable formula φ, there exists a fulfilling branch in every tableau T for φ.*

The proofs of the theorems can be found in [2].

4.2 Optimality of the Proposed Method

In this section we provide a precise characterization of the computational complexity of the satisfiability problem for PNL.

As for the computational complexity of the proposed decision procedure, observe that, by the blocking condition, after at most $|\operatorname{REQ}_\varphi| \cdot m + 1$ applications of the step rules, the expansion strategy cannot be applied anymore to a branch. Moreover, given a branch B, between two successive applications of the step rules, the fill-in rule can be applied at most k times, being k the number of points in D_B (as a matter of fact, k is exactly the number of applications of the step rules up to that point). Since $m = 2fp + p \leq 2 \cdot |\operatorname{TF}(\varphi)|^2 + |\operatorname{TF}(\varphi)|$, we have that m is polynomial in the length of φ, while $|\operatorname{REQ}_\varphi|$ is exponential in it. If $|\varphi| = n$, the length of any branch B of a tableau T for φ is bounded by $\left(|\operatorname{REQ}_\varphi| \cdot (2 \cdot |\operatorname{TF}(\varphi)|^2 + |\operatorname{TF}(\varphi)|)\right)^2 = 2^{O(n)}$, that is, the length of a branch is exponential in $|\varphi|$. This implies that the satisfiability problem for PNL can be solved by a (nondeterministic) algorithm that guesses a fulfilling branch B for the formula φ in nondeterministic exponential time.

To give a NEXPTIME lower bound to the complexity of the satisfiability problem for PNL we can exploit the computational complexity results for the future-only fragment of PNL [3]. NEXPTIME-hardness of RPNL is proved by reducing the exponential tiling problem to the satisfiability problem for RPNL. Since RPNL is a fragment of PNL, the reduction presented in [3] proves NEXPTIME-hardness of PNL as well.

Theorem 6. *The satisfiability problem for RPNL is NEXPTIME-complete.*

5   Conclusions

In this paper, we focussed our attention on interval logics of temporal neighborhood. We addressed the satisfiability problem for Propositional Neighborhood Logic (PNL), interpreted over the integers (or a subset of them), and we showed that it is NEXPTIME-complete. Moreover, we developed a sound and complete tableau-based decision procedure for PNL and we proved its optimality. As for possible extensions of the method, we are working on its generalization to the whole class of linear orders as well as to other specific classes of temporal structures, such as dense ones.

References

1. D. Bresolin and A. Montanari. A tableau-based decision procedure for Right Propositional Neighborhood Logic. In *Proc. of TABLEAUX 2005: 14th Conference on Automated Reasoning with Analytic Tableaux and Related Methods*, volume 3702 of *LNAI*, pages 63–77, Koblenz, Germany, September 2005. Springer.
2. D. Bresolin, A. Montanari, and P. Sala. An optimal tableau-based decision algorithm for Propositional Neighborhood Logic. Technical report, Dipartimento di Matematica e Informatica, Università di Udine, Italy, 2006.
3. D. Bresolin, A. Montanari, and G. Sciavicco. An optimal decision procedure for Right Propositional Neighborhood Logic. *Journal of Automated Reasoning*, 2006. DOI10.1007/s10817-006-9051-0.
4. Z. Chaochen and M. R. Hansen. An adequate first order interval logic. In W.P. de Roever, H. Langmaak, and A. Pnueli, editors, *Compositionality: the Significant Difference*, number 1536 in LNCS, pages 584–608. Springer, 1998.
5. V. Goranko, A. Montanari, and G. Sciavicco. Propositional interval neighborhood temporal logics. *Journal of Universal Computer Science*, 9(9):1137–1167, 2003.
6. V. Goranko, A. Montanari, and G. Sciavicco. A road map of interval temporal logics and duration calculi. *Journal of Applied Non-Classical Logics*, 14(1–2):9–54, 2004.
7. V. Goranko, A. Montanari, G. Sciavicco, and P. Sala. A general tableau method for propositional interval temporal logics: theory and implementation. *Journal of Applied Logic*, 4(3):305–330, 2006.
8. J. Halpern and Y. Shoham. A propositional modal logic of time intervals. *Journal of the ACM*, 38(4):935–962, 1991.
9. K. Lodaya. Sharpening the undecidability of interval temporal logic. In *Proc. of 6th Asian Computing Science Conference*, volume 1961 of *LNCS*, pages 290–298. Springer, 2000.
10. A. Montanari. Propositional interval temporal logics: some promising paths. In *Proc. of the 12th International Symposium on Temporal Representation and Reasoning (TIME)*, pages 201–203. IEEE Computer Society Press, 2005.
11. A. Montanari, G. Sciavicco, and N. Vitacolonna. Decidability of interval temporal logics over split-frames via granularity. In *Proc. of the 8th European Conf. on Logic in Artificial Intelligence*, volume 2424 of *LNAI*, pages 259–270. Springer, 2002.
12. B. Moszkowski. *Reasoning about digital circuits*. Tech. rep. stan-cs-83-970, Dept. of Computer Science, Stanford University, Stanford, CA, 1983.
13. Y. Venema. A modal logic for chopping intervals. *Journal of Logic and Computation*, 1(4):453–476, 1991.

Bounded-Variable Fragments of Hybrid Logics

Thomas Schwentick and Volker Weber

Fachbereich Informatik, Universität Dortmund, Germany
{thomas.schwentick,volker.weber}@udo.edu

Abstract. Hybrid logics extend modal logics by first-order concepts, in particular they allow a limited use of variables. Unfortunately, in general, satisfiability for hybrid formulas is undecidable and model checking is **PSPACE**-hard. It is shown here that on the linear frame $(\omega, <)$, the restriction to one name, although expressively complete, has **EXPSPACE**-complete satisfiability and polynomial time model-checking.

For the upper bound, a result of independent interest is found: Nonemptiness for alternating two-way Büchi automata with one pebble is **EXPSPACE**-complete.

1 Introduction

Hybrid logics extend modal and temporal logics by first-order concepts. They aim at bringing together good properties of both sides, e.g., do be reasonably expressive and yet decidable. There has been a lot of fundamental research on hybrid logics over the last years and their applications range from verification tasks to reasoning about semistructured data [5].

One of the most well known hybrid languages is $\mathcal{HL}(\downarrow, @)$, which extends modal logics by three concepts. Nominals are names for states of a model, i.e., they correspond to constants in first-order logic. The @-operator allows to express that a formula holds at a named state. Finally, the $\downarrow$-operator binds variables to the current state, creating on the fly names that can be referenced by the @-operator. These concepts clearly increase the expressive power, although they preserve the modal perspective. Unfortunately, satisfiability of $\mathcal{HL}(\downarrow, @)$ is undecidable [1] and model checking is **PSPACE**-complete [5].

These results are with respect to arbitrary structures. However, as in most applications models are either linear or have a branching structure, there has been some research in hybrid logics over such structures [2,6,15].

In this work, we focus on linear, initial, and discrete structures, as they occur in linear time model checking. Previous work showed that $\mathcal{HL}(\downarrow, @)$ is decidable over these structures, referred to as the *frame of the natural numbers*, but with non-elementary complexity [6]. In the light of this high complexity there have been successful attempts to identify more tractable cases, like restricting formulas to existential fragments [6], disallowing certain patterns in formulas, or allowing only models of bounded width [18].

We take a different approach here, reminiscent of a successful line of research in classical logic, namely restricting the number of variables. Our main result is

W. Thomas and P. Weil (Eds.): STACS 2007, LNCS 4393, pp. 561–572, 2007.
© Springer-Verlag Berlin Heidelberg 2007

that the one-variable fragment of $\mathcal{HL}(\downarrow, @)$ has a satisfiability problem with elementary complexity, tractable model checking problem, and is still expressively complete over the frame of the natural numbers. In contrast, the two-variable fragment shares the non-elementary complexity with the full logic.

The proof of the upper bound for the one-variable fragment is by the automata theoretic approach. Starting from [24], there has been quite some work by Vardi and others using alternating (one-way) Büchi automata for linear time model checking (see also [21]).

We use alternating *two-way* Büchi automata which, in order to simulate the one variable, are further equipped with a pebble. Alternating two-way automata have been already used for similar purposes in previous work [22,16,13]. In particular, it was shown in [13] that their non-emptiness problem is in **PSPACE**. We show here that with one pebble the complexity is in **EXPSPACE**. We think that this result is of general interest, especially for the automata theoretic approach to temporal logics.

We start with basic definitions in Section 2. Section 3 contains the automata theoretic results, while Section 4 is devoted to the bounded variable fragments of hybrid logic. We conclude in Section 5.

We thank Henrik Björklund, Thomas Schneider, and the referees for many insightful comments and suggestions.

2   Preliminaries

In this section, we give the basic definitions for hybrid logics and Büchi automata.

2.1   Hybrid Logics

The syntax of the hybrid logics we consider is defined as follows.

Definition 2.1. Let $\mathsf{PROP} = \{p, q, \ldots\}$, $\mathsf{NOM} = \{i, j, \ldots\}$, $\mathsf{SVAR} = \{x, y, \ldots\}$ be disjoint, countable sets of *proposition symbols*, *nominals*, and *state variables*, respectively, and let ATOM denote $\mathsf{PROP} \cup \mathsf{NOM} \cup \mathsf{SVAR}$.

The formulas of the *hybrid language* $\mathcal{HL}(\downarrow, @)$ are as follows.

$$\varphi := \top \mid a \mid \neg\varphi \mid \varphi \wedge \psi \mid \mathbf{F}\varphi \mid @_t\varphi \mid \downarrow x.\varphi$$

where $a \in \mathsf{ATOM}$, $t \in \mathsf{NOM} \cup \mathsf{SVAR}$, and $x \in \mathsf{SVAR}$.

The *hybrid temporal language* $\mathcal{HTL}(\downarrow, @)$ has also formulas of the form $\mathbf{P}\varphi$. We use the common notations for the duals of the modalities, namely $\mathbf{G}\varphi$ for $\neg\mathbf{F}\neg\varphi$ and $\mathbf{H}\varphi$ for $\neg\mathbf{P}\neg\varphi$. By omitting $\downarrow$ or $@$ from $\mathcal{HL}(\downarrow, @)$, we indicate the fragments without the respective operators.

As an example, $\theta = \downarrow x.(\mathbf{F} \downarrow y.(b \wedge @_x\mathbf{G}(\mathbf{F}y \rightarrow a)))$ is an $\mathcal{HL}(\downarrow, @)$ formula.

As for modal and temporal logics, semantics is defined by *Kripke structures*.

Definition 2.2. A *hybrid model* $\mathcal{M}$ is a tuple (M, R, V) consisting of a non-empty set M of *states*, a binary *accessibility relation* R on M, and a *valuation* $V : \mathsf{PROP} \cup \mathsf{NOM} \rightarrow 2^M$, such that $V(i)$ is a singleton for every $i \in \mathsf{NOM}$.

For a given model $\mathcal{M}$, an *assignment* is a mapping $g : \mathsf{SVAR} \to M$. By g_m^x we denote the assignment that is identical to g, except that x is mapped to m. By $[V, g]$ we denote the disjoint union of the functions V and g.

The semantics of $\mathcal{HTL}(\downarrow, @)$ is defined as follows:

$$\mathcal{M}, g, m \models a \quad\quad \text{iff} \quad m \in [V, g](a),\ a \in \mathsf{ATOM}$$
$$\mathcal{M}, g, m \models \neg\varphi \quad\quad \text{iff} \quad \mathcal{M}, g, m \not\models \varphi$$
$$\mathcal{M}, g, m \models \varphi \wedge \psi \quad \text{iff} \quad \mathcal{M}, g, m \models \varphi \text{ and } \mathcal{M}, g, m \models \psi$$
$$\mathcal{M}, g, m \models \mathbf{F}\varphi \quad\quad \text{iff} \quad \text{for some } n \in M : mRn \text{ and } \mathcal{M}, g, n \models \varphi$$
$$\mathcal{M}, g, m \models \mathbf{P}\varphi \quad\quad \text{iff} \quad \text{for some } n \in M : nRm \text{ and } \mathcal{M}, g, n \models \varphi$$
$$\mathcal{M}, g, m \models @_t\varphi \quad\quad \text{iff} \quad \mathcal{M}, g, [V, g](t) \models \varphi$$
$$\mathcal{M}, g, m \models\, \downarrow x.\varphi \quad\quad \text{iff} \quad \mathcal{M}, g_m^x, m \models \varphi$$

A formula φ is called *satisfiable* if there is a model $\mathcal{M}$, an assignment g for $\mathcal{M}$, and a state $m \in M$ such that $\mathcal{M}, g, m \models \varphi$.

The semantics is defined with respect to arbitrary Kripke structures, but most applications require models with a linear or branching structure. In this paper, we only consider the case of linear, initial, and discrete models, i.e., models based on the frame[1] $(\mathbb{N}, <)$ of the natural numbers with $<$ as accessibility relation.

On these frames, the example formula θ above is equivalent to the strict version of the $\mathcal{LTL}$ formula $a\mathbf{U}b$.

By $\mathcal{HTL}(\downarrow^k, @)$ we denote the set of $\mathcal{HTL}(\downarrow, @)$ formulas which use at most k variables. We note that, over the natural numbers, $\mathcal{HTL}(\downarrow, @)$ and $\mathcal{HTL}(\downarrow)$ are equivalent as one can simply substitute $@_x\varphi$ by $\mathbf{FP}(x \wedge \varphi)$. Thus we obtain the following.

Lemma 2.3. *Over the natural numbers: For every $\mathcal{HTL}(\downarrow^1, @)$-formula φ of length n, there is an equivalent $\mathcal{HTL}(\downarrow^1)$-formula ψ of length $O(n)$.*

2.2 Automata

For a given nonempty alphabet Σ, an *infinite word* is an infinite sequence $\sigma_1, \sigma_2, \ldots$ of symbols from Σ.

A *nondeterministic (one-way) Büchi automaton* A is a tuple $(Q, \Sigma, Q^0, \delta, F)$, where Q is a finite set of states, Σ is a finite alphabet, $Q^0 \subseteq Q$ is a set of initial states, $\delta : Q \times \Sigma \to 2^Q$ is a transition function, and $F \subseteq Q$ is the set of accepting states.

A *run* r of A on an infinite word $w = \sigma_1, \sigma_2, \ldots$ is a sequence of states $q_1, q_2, \ldots$, such that $q_1 \in Q^0$ and $q_{i+1} \in \delta(q_i, \sigma_i)$. A run r is *accepting* if some accepting state occurs infinitely often in r, i.e., if $\inf(r) \cap F \neq \emptyset$. An infinite word w is accepted by A if there is an accepting run of A on w. The language accepted by A is the set of all infinite words accepted by A and denoted $L(A)$.

---

[1] The tuple (M, R) is traditionally called a *frame*.

Proposition 2.4 ([23]). *Non-emptiness of non-deterministic Büchi automata is complete for* **NL**.

An *alternating one-pebble Büchi automaton* is an automaton which has a head that can move along the input string in both directions. It can drop its pebble at a position and it can lift the pebble again if its head is at the pebble position. Furthermore, without affecting head or pebble, it can universally or existentially branch into two independent sub-computations. More formally, it is a tuple $(Q, \Sigma, q^0, \delta, F)$, such that Q is a finite set of states, Σ is a finite alphabet, $q^0 \in Q$ is the initial state, $F \subseteq Q$ is the set of accepting states, and
$$\delta : Q \times \Sigma \to (Q \times Q \times \{\wedge, \vee, \text{lift}\}) \cup (Q \times \{\text{left}, \text{right}, \text{drop}\})$$
is a transition function.

A *configuration* $(q, i, j) \in Q \times \mathbb{N} \times (\mathbb{N} \cup \{\bot\})$ of A consists of a state, the position of the head, and the position of the pebble, where '$\bot$' means that the pebble is not placed. A *run* ρ of A on an infinite word $w = \sigma_1, \sigma_2, \ldots$ is a possibly infinite tree whose nodes are labeled with configurations.

This tree must be compatible with the transition function. For example, for every node v labeled by a state (q, i, j),

- if $\delta(q, \sigma) = (q', \text{left})$, v has a child with configuration $(q, i - 1, j)$;
- if $\delta(q, \sigma) = (q_1, q_2, \wedge)$, v has two children labelled (q_1, i, j) and (q_2, i, j);
- if $\delta(q, \sigma) = (q_1, q_2, \vee)$, v has a child, labelled by (q_1, i, j) or (q_2, i, j).

Nodes v of the second kind are called *universal*, nodes of the third kind *existential*. A run is *accepting* if every infinite branch[2] contains infinitely many configurations with labels from F. Acceptance of A is defined as usual.

It is easy to see that this definition is essentially equivalent to a more liberal one, in which transitions involve a Boolean combination of follow-up states.

We will make use of the following well-known theorem.

Theorem 2.5 (König's Lemma). *If in a tree each node has only finitely many children and there are nodes of arbitrary depth, then the tree has an infinite path.*

3   Non-emptiness of Alternating One-Pebble Büchi Automata

In this section, we show that the complexity of non-emptiness for alternating Büchi automata with one pebble is **EXPSPACE**-complete. This result is not too surprising, as it matches the corresponding result on finite strings [11]. Nevertheless, the infinite string case is considerably more involved and the proofs in [10,11,9] cannot be easily adapted to this case.

Recall that a run of an alternating Büchi automata A with one pebble is an infinite tree, the nodes of which are labeled with configurations (q, i, j), where q is the state, i is the position of the head and j is the position of the pebble ($\bot$ if

---

[2] We can assume that every branch is infinite. For an accepting leave, we simply move to an accepting state that is never left again.

the pebble is not present). We are interested in runs of the following particularly simple structure. A run is *homogeneous* if, for every existential configuration (q, i, j), all nodes with configuration (q, i, j) have the same configuration at their child.

Note that the configuration graph of A on an input w can be seen as the arena of a two-player game with a Büchi condition. Thus, from the existence of memoryless winning strategies in such games [4,14] (see also [25]), it follows that if A has an accepting run on input w then it also has a homogeneous accepting run. Thus it is sufficient to check whether, for the given input, A has a homogeneous accepting run.

Theorem 3.1. *Non-emptiness of alternating one-pebble Büchi automata is complete for* **EXPSPACE**.

Proof. Hardness follows immediately from the corresponding result for finite strings [11]. For the upper bound, we show that, for each alternating one-pebble Büchi automaton A, there is an equivalent non-deterministic Büchi automaton B of size $|\Sigma_A| \cdot 2^{2^{O(|Q_A|)}}$, which can be constructed from A in space exponential in $|Q_A|$. The result then follows by Proposition 2.4. As already indicated above, B checks, on input w, whether A has a homogeneous accepting run ρ on w.

A run is *not* accepting if and only if it has a non-accepting path. Thus, B checks that ρ has no non-accepting path. The non-accepting paths can be classified as follows. First, a path can be *bounded*, i.e., there is some m such that all head positions of π are at most m, otherwise, we call it *unbounded*.

There are two kinds of unbounded non-accepting paths:

(1a) At some point, the automaton drops the pebble at some position j and never lift it again. In this case, all further configurations are of the form (q, i, j), for some q, i.

(1b) Otherwise, the path has infinitely many configurations of the form $(q, i, \bot)$, with arbitrarily large i.

Likewise, there are two kinds of bounded non-accepting paths.

(2a) The first kind drops the pebble at some position j and never lifts it again. Thus, there are q and i such that (q, i, j) occurs infinitely often on π. Consequently, there must be a subpath from configuration (q, i, j) to (q, i, j) which does not visit any accepting state, does not lift the pebble, and does not visit any positions larger than i.

(2b) The other kind of bounded paths has infinitely many configurations of the form $(q, i, \bot)$, hence there is again a maximum i and a state q such that $(q, i, \bot)$ occurs infinitely often and only finitely many nodes have a configurations $(p, i', \bot)$ with $i' > i$. Therefore, there is a subpath from configuration $(q, i, \bot)$ to $(q, i, \bot)$ which does not visit any accepting state and does not visit any pebble-free positions larger than i.

In the following we describe the information that B maintains in order to check that ρ has only accepting paths.

For each i, let S_i be the set of states q for which $(q, i, \bot)$ occurs in ρ. We consider two kinds of *left paths* (*right paths* are defined accordingly):

- paths starting from a configuration $(p, i, \bot)$ and ending in a configuration $(q, i, \bot)$ without an intermediate configuration $(p', i', \bot)$ with $i' > i$ (intermediate configurations (p', i', j') with $j' \leq i$ and $i' > i$ are allowed);
- paths starting from a configuration (p, i, j) and ending in a configuration (q, i, j), without any intermediate lifting of the pebble and without any intermediate configurations (p', i', j) with $i' > i$.

For each i, we denote by L_i the subset of $Q \times Q \times \{+, \exists\}$, such that

- $(p, q, +) \in L_i$ if and only if all left paths of ρ from $(p, i, \bot)$ to $(q, i, \bot)$ visit an accepting state, and
- $(p, q, \exists) \in L_i$ if and only if ρ has a left path from $(p, i, \bot)$ to $(q, i, \bot)$,

and by R_i the subset of $Q \times Q \times \{+, \exists\}$, such that

- $(p, q, +) \in R_i$ if and only if all right paths of ρ from $(p, i, 0)$ to $(q, i, 0)$ visit an accepting state, and
- $(p, q, \exists) \in R_i$ if and only if ρ has a right path from $(p, i, 0)$ to $(q, i, 0)$.

It should be noted that in the definition of R_i, the actual position of the pebble does not matter, as long as it is smaller than i. The reader should also observe the asymmetry between the L_i and the R_i. The L_i only concern sub-computations from a configuration without pebble, the R_i only from a configuration with pebble.

Furthermore, B uses the following sets which are parametrized by the current position j of the pebble. Let, for each $i \geq 0$, $j \leq i$, $S_{i,j}$ be the set of states p such that (p, i, j) occurs in ρ. Likewise, let $L_{i,j}$ be the subset of $Q \times Q \times \{+, \exists\}$ such that

- $(p, q, +) \in L_{i,j}$ if and only if all left paths of ρ from (p, i, j) to (q, i, j) visit an accepting state and
- $(p, q, \exists) \in L_{i,j}$ if and only if ρ has a left path from (p, i, j) to (q, i, j).

Recall that left paths from a configuration (p, i, j) never lift the pebble.

Additionally, B uses sets U_i, $U_{i,j}$ and R_i' which will be defined below. For each i, we let X_i be the set $\{(S_{i,j}, L_{i,j}, U_{i,j}) \mid j \leq i\}$. Finally, for each i, let the characteristic vector C_i of position i be $(S_i, L_i, R_i, R_i', U_i, X_i)$. The intended state of B at position i is basically (C_{i-1}, C_i).

The sets of the form $S_i, S_{i,j}, R_i$ and the transitions of A are guessed by B and the remaining information can be determined from it. It is not hard to check that local consistency of these sets can be tested by B. It should be noted that the computation of L_i uses R_i to handle subpaths that drop the pebble at i and lift it sometimes later.

Whether a path of type (2b) exists at position i can be inferred from L_i and the transitions $\delta_{q,i}$ at position i. Likewise, paths of type (2a) can be tested with the help of the sets $L_{i,j}$.

Thus, it remains to describe how to rule out paths of types (1a) and (1b) and how to check that the sets R_i are correct.

To this end, we define an increasing sequence $l_0, l_1, \ldots$ of positions of w as follows. First of all, $l_0 = 0$. Given l_k, l_{k+1} is the minimum $l > l_k$ such that the following conditions hold.

(i) For each state $q \in S_{l_k}$, each subpath starting from a node with configuration $(q, l_k, \bot)$ and reaching a configuration $(p, l, \bot)$ contains an accepting state.

(ii) For each $j \leq l_k$ and each state $q \in S_{l_k, j}$, each subpath starting from a node with configuration (q, l_k, j), reaching a configuration (p, l, j) without lifting the pebble contains an accepting state.

(iii) For each $(p, q, \exists) \in R_{l_k}$, there is a path from $(p, l_k, 0)$ to $(q, l_k, 0)$ on which all nodes have head positions $i \leq l$.

With the help of König's Lemma, it is not hard to see that such an l exists if ρ is accepting.

For each k and each i, $l_k < i \leq l_{k+1}$, let U_i be the set of states q such that there is a node w with configuration $(q, i, \bot)$ and a path from a node v with position l_j to w that does not pass any accepting state and only has positions $\leq i$. Note that by the definition of l_{k+1}, $U_{l_{k+1}} = \emptyset$. Likewise, for each i, j, $j \leq i$, let $U_{i,j}$ be the set of states q such that there is a node w with configuration (q, i, j) and a path from a node v with a configuration (q', l_k, j) to w that does not pass any accepting state and only has positions $\leq i$. Note that by the definition of l_{k+1}, $U_{l_{k+1}} = \emptyset$.

Finally, let R'_i be a set of tuples $(p, q, \exists) \in R_i$, which still have to be fulfilled in order to satisfy condition (iii) for k.

The accepting states of B are those for which $U_i = \emptyset$, for all $(S, L, U) \in X_i$, $U = \emptyset$ and $R'_i = \emptyset$.

It is not hard to see that B can maintain the characteristic vectors C_i and that B accepts w if and only if A has a homogeneous accepting run.

Furthermore, there are at most doubly exponentially many different possible sets X_i and thus the number of possible states of B is at most doubly exponential in the size of Q_A. Using standard space saving techniques, B can be constructed in space $|\Sigma_A| \cdot 2^{O(|Q_A|)}$.

4 Bounded-Variable Fragments over the Natural Numbers

In this section, we turn to the complexity of bounded-variable fragments of hybrid logics. We first show that even the one-variable fragment is expressively complete. Next, we prove that its satisfiability problem is **EXPSPACE**-complete (the main result of this section) and that model checking can be done in polynomial time. Finally, we show that two variables already cause non-elementary complexity for satisfiability.

4.1   Expressivity

As hybrid logics can be embedded into first-order logic by the *Standard Translation* [18], first-order logic is an upper bound for all considered fragments.

The unbounded language $\mathcal{HTL}(\downarrow)$ is expressively complete, even over linear structures [6]. It should be noted that over arbitrary frames $\mathcal{HTL}(\downarrow, @)$ corresponds to the *bounded fragment* and is therefore strictly less expressive than first-order logic [3].

We use the classical result that $\mathcal{LTL}$ is expressively complete [12,8,7] and thus, we obtain expressive completeness of $\mathcal{HL}(\downarrow^2, @)$ and $\mathcal{HTL}(\downarrow^1)$ by the following two semantical equations.[3]

$$\varphi \mathbf{U} \psi = \downarrow x.\mathbf{F} \downarrow y.(\psi \wedge @_x \mathbf{G}(\mathbf{F}y \rightarrow \varphi))$$
$$\varphi \mathbf{U} \psi = \downarrow x.\mathbf{F}(\psi \wedge \mathbf{H}(\mathbf{P}x \rightarrow \varphi))$$

Proposition 4.1. $\mathcal{HL}(\downarrow^2, @)$ *and* $\mathcal{HTL}(\downarrow^1)$ *are expressively complete over the natural numbers.*

In contrast, it can be shown by a bisimulation argument that $\mathcal{HL}(\downarrow^1, @)$ is strictly less expressive. Intuitively, it cannot name a state and then talk about smaller states. To overcome this weakness, it is sufficient to label the smallest state by a special nominal i_0.

Proposition 4.2. *The language* $\mathcal{HL}(\downarrow^1, @)$ *is expressively complete over the natural numbers with zero.*

4.2   Satisfiability for the One-Variable Fragment

Although restricting the number of variables does not cause any loss of expressive power, there is a difference in succinctness of formulas. In fact, as a consequence of the following result there are properties which can be expressed non-elementarily more succinct with an unbounded number of variables than with one variable.

Theorem 4.3. *Satisfiability of* $\mathcal{HL}(\downarrow^1, @)$, $\mathcal{HTL}(\downarrow^1)$, *and* $\mathcal{HTL}(\downarrow^1, @)$ *over the natural numbers is complete for* **EXPSPACE**.

The lower bound can be proved by a reduction from the 2^n-*corridor tiling problem*, known to be **EXPSPACE**-complete (cf. [19]).

We only give the proof of the upper bound, which is by a reduction to non-emptiness of alternating one-pebble Büchi automata, which is in **EXPSPACE** by Theorem 3.1. By Lemma 2.3, we only need to consider $\mathcal{HTL}(\downarrow^1)$.

We start with the observation that nesting of the $\downarrow$-operator can be avoided. This simplifies the simulation of variables by one pebble.

Lemma 4.4. *For every* $\mathcal{HTL}(\downarrow^1)$-*formula* φ *of length* n, *there is an* $\mathcal{HTL}(\downarrow^1)$-*formula* ψ *of length* $O(n)$ *without nested occurrences of the* $\downarrow$-*operator, such that, over the natural numbers,* φ *is satisfiable if and only if* ψ *is satisfiable.*

---

[3] We stress that these equations hold for the frame of natural numbers.

Proof. We add, for each sub-formula $\theta = \downarrow x.\xi$ of φ a new proposition p_θ. In a bottom-up fashion, we replace every occurrence of a formula θ by p_θ and add to φ one conjunct $\mathbf{GH}(p_\theta \leftrightarrow \theta')$, for every θ. Here θ' results from θ by replacing all sub-formulas $\downarrow x.\chi$ by the respective proposition. Note that the resulting formula has indeed linear size. $\square$

Now, the proof of the upper bound is a straightforward extension of a proof in [20], constructing an alternating Büchi automaton for a given $\mathcal{LTL}$-formula.

Proposition 4.5. *Satisfiability of an $\mathcal{HTL}(\downarrow^1)$ formula over the natural numbers can be decided in exponential space.*

Proof. Given an $\mathcal{HTL}(\downarrow^1)$-formula φ without nested occurrences of the $\downarrow$-operator, we build an alternating one-pebble Büchi automaton $A_\varphi = (Q, \Sigma, q^0, \delta, F)$, with $\Sigma = 2^{\mathsf{PROP} \cup \mathsf{NOM}}$, such that φ holds at the initial state of some model over the natural numbers if and only if A_φ accepts the corresponding infinite word.

In the following, we denote the *dual* of a formula ψ by $\overline{\psi}$. It is obtained from ψ by switching $\wedge$ and $\vee$, and by negating all other maximal subformulas, e.g., $\overline{x \vee (\neg x \wedge \mathbf{F}p)} = \neg x \wedge (x \vee \neg \mathbf{F}p)$ (cf. [21]).

The set Q of states is the Fisher-Ladner-closure of φ, consisting of the sub-formulas of φ, the formulas $\psi \vee \mathbf{F}\psi$ or $\psi \vee \mathbf{P}\psi$ for every subformula $\mathbf{F}\psi$ or $\mathbf{P}\psi$ of φ, respectively, and the duals of all these formulas. The initial state q^0 is φ. The set F of accepting states contains $\top$ and all formulas of the form $\neg\mathbf{F}\psi$ from Q. The latter is only needed to cover infinite branches consisting, from some point on, entirely of states $\neg\mathbf{F}\psi$. These branches result from evaluating formulas of the type $\mathbf{F}\psi$. The branches spawned from such a branch verify that $\neg\psi$ holds all over the string.

The transition function δ is defined by induction on the formula structure.

$$\begin{array}{ll}
\delta(\top, \sigma) = (\top, \text{stay}) & \delta(p, \sigma) = (\top, \text{stay}) \quad \text{if } p \in \sigma \\
\delta(x, \sigma) = (\top, \bot, \text{lift}) & \delta(\psi \wedge \xi, \sigma) = (\psi, \xi, \wedge) \\
\delta(\neg\psi, \sigma) = \overline{\delta(\psi, \sigma)} & \delta(\mathbf{F}\psi, \sigma) = (\psi \vee \mathbf{F}\psi, \text{right}) \\
\delta(\mathbf{P}\psi, \sigma) = (\psi \vee \mathbf{P}\psi, \text{left}) & \delta(\downarrow x.\psi, \sigma) = (\psi, \text{drop})
\end{array}$$

where $p \in \mathsf{PROP} \cup \mathsf{NOM}$, $x \in \mathsf{SVAR}$, and the notion of a dual is extended to δ as follows. If $\delta(\psi, \sigma) = (\chi, a)$ then $\overline{\delta(\psi, \sigma)} = (\overline{\chi}, a)$, e.g., $\overline{\delta(\psi \wedge \xi, \sigma)} = (\overline{\psi}, \overline{\xi}, \vee)$, e.g., $\overline{\delta(\mathbf{F}\psi, \sigma)} = (\neg\psi \wedge \neg\mathbf{F}\psi, \text{right})$, and $\overline{\delta(x, \sigma)} = (\bot, \top, \text{stay})$.

The result follows by Theorem 3.1. $\square$

4.3   Model Checking

The model checking problem for hybrid logics is defined as follows: Given a finite hybrid model $\mathcal{M}$, an assignment g, and a hybrid formula φ, is there a state $m \in M$ such that $\mathcal{M}, g, m \models \varphi$? It can be solved in polynomial time for $\mathcal{HTL}(@)$, but is **PSPACE**-complete for $\mathcal{HL}(\downarrow, @)$ [5]. Intuitively, the latter hardness is mainly due to the nesting of variables. In the one variable case, there is no real nesting of variables. Consequently, complexity drops down to polynomial time again.

Theorem 4.6. *Model checking for $\mathcal{HTL}(\downarrow^1, @)$ can be done in polynomial time.*

Proof. The algorithm uses a straightforward tableau approach. For each subformula, ψ and each pair m, m' of states it computes whether ψ holds at m if x is assigned to m'. $\square$

4.4   The Two-Variable Fragment

As noted before, from the complexity results for $\mathcal{HTL}(\downarrow, @)$ and $\mathcal{HTL}(\downarrow^1, @)$ and the expressive completeness of $\mathcal{HTL}(\downarrow^1, @)$, one can conclude that the unbounded language is non-elementarily more succinct. We show next that this succinctness gap is located between the one-variable and the two-variable fragment.

Theorem 4.7. *The satisfiability problem for $\mathcal{HL}(\downarrow^2, @)$ over the natural numbers has non-elementary complexity.*

Proof. We give a reduction from the emptiness problem for star-free regular expressions built from union, concatenation, and negation. This problem is known to have non-elementary complexity [17]. With a string of length i over an alphabet Σ we associate a structure $(\mathbb{N}, <, p_\sigma$ for all $\sigma \in \Sigma, q)$, as shown in Figure 1.

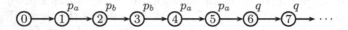

Fig. 1. The model used to represent the string *abbaa* as described in the proof of Theorem 4.7 (edges caused by transitivity are left out)

All states beyond i carry the label q. The following formula ψ holds at state 0 if and only if the structure is an encoding of a string, e.g., every state belonging to the string is labeled by exactly one p_σ.

$$\psi = (\neg q) \wedge \; \downarrow x.\mathbf{F} \downarrow y.((q \wedge \mathbf{G}q) \wedge @_x \mathbf{G}(\mathbf{F}y \rightarrow (\neg q \wedge \bigvee_{\sigma \in \Sigma} (p_\sigma \wedge \bigwedge_{\sigma \neq \sigma' \in \Sigma} \neg p_{\sigma'}))))$$

We map every star-free expression α to a formula φ_α. The idea is that x and y are always used to mark a substring which is matched with respect to a star-free (sub-)expression. More precisely, x marks the left neighbor of the first position of the substring and y marks the last position. We use $\underline{\mathbf{F}}\psi$ as an abbreviation for $\psi \vee \mathbf{F}\psi$:

$$\varphi_\alpha = \psi \wedge \downarrow x.\underline{\mathbf{F}}((\neg q \wedge \mathbf{G}q) \wedge \downarrow y.@_x \alpha')$$

where α' is inductively defined as follows:

$$
\begin{aligned}
\varepsilon' &= y & \sigma' &= \mathbf{F}(y \wedge p_\sigma) \wedge \neg\mathbf{F}\mathbf{F}y \quad, \text{ for all } \sigma \in \Sigma \\
\emptyset' &= \bot & (\alpha \cdot \beta)' &= \underline{\mathbf{F}}(\underline{\mathbf{F}}y \wedge \downarrow y.@_x \alpha' \wedge \downarrow x.\beta') \\
(\neg\alpha)' &= \neg\alpha' & (\alpha \cup \beta)' &= \alpha' \vee \beta'
\end{aligned}
$$

Note that φ_α might be exponentially larger than α, since every $\underline{\mathbf{F}}$ doubles the formula size, but this does not do any harm as we reduce from a problem with non-elementary complexity. □

By Lemma 2.3, this result also applies to the other two-variable fragments.

Corollary 4.8. *The satisfiability problems for $\mathcal{HTL}(\downarrow^2)$ and $\mathcal{HTL}(\downarrow^2, @)$ over the natural numbers have non-elementary complexity.*

5   Conclusion

In this paper, we investigated bounded-variable fragments of hybrid logics containing the $\downarrow$-operator to create names for states. We restricted to the widely used frame of the natural numbers. We identified a fragment of $\mathcal{HTL}(\downarrow, @)$, the one-variable fragment, which has the same expressive power as the unbounded language over such frames, but whose satisfiability problem is **EXPSPACE**-complete (as opposed to non-elementary in the unbounded case) and allows for polynomial time model checking (as opposed to **PSPACE**-complete).

We also showed that there is no benefit from restricting to two variables, since complexity of satisfiability is as bad as in the unbounded case.

To prove these results, we showed that the non-emptiness problem for alternating Büchi automata with one pebble is **EXPSPACE**-complete.

The next natural step is to see how these results translate to branching structures. We conjecture **2EXPTIME**-completeness for $\mathcal{HTL}(\downarrow^1, @)$ over the class of trees with the descendant relation.

References

1. C. Areces, P. Blackburn, and M. Marx. A road-map on complexity for hybrid logics. In *Proc. of 13th Computer Science Logic (CSL '99)*, volume 1683 of *LNCS*, pages 307–321. Springer, 1999.
2. C. Areces, P. Blackburn, and M. Marx. The computational complexity of hybrid temporal logics. *Logic Journal of the IGPL*, 8(5):653–679, 2000.
3. C. Areces, P. Blackburn, and M. Marx. Hybrid logics: Characterization, interpolation and complexity. *Journal of Symbolic Logic*, 66(3):977–1010, 2001.
4. E. A. Emerson and C. S. Jutla. Tree automata, mu-calculus and determinacy. In *Proc. of 32nd IEEE Symposium on Foundations of Computer Science (FOCS)*, pages 368–377. IEEE, 1991.
5. M. Franceschet and M. de Rijke. Model checking hybrid logics (with an application to semistructured data). *Journal of Applied Logic*, 2005.
6. M. Franceschet, M. de Rijke, and B.-H. Schlingloff. Hybrid logics on linear structures: Expressivity and complexity. In *10th TIME / 4th ICTL*, pages 192–202. IEEE Computer Society, 2003.
7. D. M. Gabbay. The declarative past and imperative future: Executable temporal logic for interactive systems. In *Proc. of Temporal Logic in Specification 1987*, volume 398 of *LNCS*, pages 409–448. Springer, 1989.

8. D. M. Gabbay, A. Pnueli, S. Shelah, and J. Stavi. On the temporal basis of fairness. In *Conference Record of the 7th Annual ACM Symposium on Principles of Programming Languages (POPL'80)*, pages 163–173. ACM Press, 1980.

9. N. Globerman and D. Harel. Complexity results for two-way and multi-pebble automata and their logics. *Theoretical Computer Science*, 169(2):161–184, 1996.

10. P. Goralčik, A. Goralčiková, and V. Koubek. Alternation with a pebble. *Information Processing Letters*, 38(1):7–13, 1991.

11. T. Jiang and B. Ravikumar. A note on the space complexity of some desicion problems for finite automata. *Information Processing Letters*, 40:25–31, 1991.

12. H. Kamp. *Tense logic and the Theory of Linear Order*. PhD thesis, University of California Los Angeles, 1968.

13. O. Kupferman, N. Piterman, and M. Y. Vardi. Extended temporal logic revisited. In *CONCUR 2001*, volume 2154 of *LNCS*, pages 519–535. Springer, 2001.

14. A. W. Mostowski. Games with forbidden positions. Technical report, Uniwersytet Gdanski, Instytut Matematyki, 1991.

15. M. Mundhenk, T. Schneider, T. Schwentick, and V. Weber. Complexity of hybrid logics over transitive frames. In *Proc. of M4M-4*, volume 194 of *Informatik-Berichte*, pages 62–78. Humbold-Universität Berlin, 2005.

16. U. Sattler and M. Y. Vardi. The hybrid μ-calculus. In *Proc. of IJCAR 2001*, volume 2083 of *LNCS*, pages 76–91. Springer, 2001.

17. L. J. Stockmeyer. *The complexity of decision problems in automata theory and logic*. PhD thesis, MIT, 1974.

18. B. ten Cate and M. Franceschet. On the complexity of hybrid logics with binders. In *Proc. of 19th Computer Science Logic (CSL 2005)*, volume 3634 of *LNCS*, pages 339–354. Springer, 2005.

19. van Emde Boas. The convenience of tilings. In *Complexity, Logic, and Recursion Theory*, volume 187 of *Lecture Notes in Pure and Applied Mathematics*, pages 331–363. Marcel Dekker, Inc., 1997.

20. M. Y. Vardi. Nontraditional applications of automata theory. In *Proc. of Theoretical Aspects of Computer Software (TACS '94)*, volume 789 of *LNCS*, pages 575–597. Springer, 1994.

21. M. Y. Vardi. An automata-theoretic approach to linear temporal logic. In *Logics for Concurrency: Structure versus Automata*, volume 1043 of *LNCS*, pages 238–266. Springer, 1996.

22. M. Y. Vardi. Reasoning about the past with two-way automata. In *Proc. of ICALP'98*, volume 1443 of *LNCS*, pages 628–641. Springer, 1998.

23. M. Y. Vardi and P. Wolper. Reasoning about infinite computations. *Information and Computation*, 115(1):1–37, 1994.

24. P. Wolper, M. Y. Vardi, and A. P. Sistla. Reasoning about infinite computation paths (extended abstract). In *24th Annual Symposium on Foundations of Computer Science (FOCS)*, pages 185–194. IEEE, 1983.

25. W. Zielonka. Infinite games on finitely coloured graphs with applications to automata and infinite trees. *Theoretical Computer Science*, 200:135–183, 1998.

Rank-1 Modal Logics Are Coalgebraic

Lutz Schröder[1] and Dirk Pattinson[2]

[1] Department of Computer Science, University of Bremen, and DFKI Lab Bremen
[2] Department of Computing, Imperial College London

Abstract. Coalgebras provide a unifying semantic framework for a wide variety of modal logics. It has previously been shown that the class of coalgebras for an endofunctor can always be axiomatised in rank 1. Here we establish the converse, i.e. every rank 1 modal logic has a sound and *strongly* complete coalgebraic semantics. As a consequence, recent results on coalgebraic modal logic, in particular generic decision procedures and upper complexity bounds, become applicable to arbitrary rank 1 modal logics, without regard to their semantic status; we thus obtain purely syntactic versions of these results. As an extended example, we apply our framework to recently defined deontic logics.

1 Introduction

In recent years, coalgebras have received a steadily growing amount of attention as general models of state-based systems [18], encompassing such diverse systems as labelled transition systems, probabilistic systems, game frames, and neighborhood frames [21]. On the logical side, modal logic has emerged as the adequate specification language for coalgebraically modelled systems. A variety of different frameworks have been proposed; here, we work with *coalgebraic modal logic* [15], which allows for a high level of generality while retaining a close relationship to the established syntactic and semantic tradition of modal logic.

In fact, one can reverse the viewpoint that coalgebraic modal logic is a specification language for coalgebras and regard coalgebra as a generic semantics for modal logics of essentially arbitrary nature, including non-normal and non-monotone ones. Under this perspective, coalgebraic modal logic is a generic notion of modal logic that subsumes e.g. Hennessy-Milner logic, graded modal logic [4], majority logic [13], probabilistic modal logic [12, 7], and coalition logic [16], but also modal operators of higher arity as e.g. in conditional logic [3].

It has been shown in [20] that every coalgebraic modal logic can be axiomatized by formulas of rank 1, i.e. with nesting depth of modal operators uniformly equal to 1 (logics of arbitrary rank are obtained by restricting the relevant class of coalgebras, which play the role of generic frames); such axioms may be regarded as concerning precisely the single next transition step. Here, we establish the converse: given a modal logic $\mathcal{L}$ of rank 1, we construct a functor $M_{\mathcal{L}}$ that provides a sound and strongly complete semantics for $\mathcal{L}$; i.e. *coalgebraic modal logic subsumes all rank-1 modal logics*. The functor $M_{\mathcal{L}}$, which can be viewed as a generalization of the neighbourhood frame functor, is moreover a canonical se-

W. Thomas and P. Weil (Eds.): STACS 2007, LNCS 4393, pp. 573–585, 2007.

mantics for $\mathcal{L}$ in a precise categorical sense; a finitary modification of $M_{\mathcal{L}}$ provides a canonical finitely branching semantics.

Besides rounding off the picture in a pleasant way, these results make the rapidly expanding meta-theory of coalgebraic modal logic applicable to arbitrary rank-1 modal logics, even when the latter are given purely syntactically or equipped with a semantics that fails to be, or has not yet been recognized as, coalgebraic. This includes results on the Hennessy-Milner property [19] and bisimulation-somewhere-else [10], and most notably generic decidability and complexity results [20, 21], of which we now obtain purely syntactic versions. As an extended example, we discuss applications of these results to recently defined variants of deontic logic [5].

2   Coalgebraic Modal Logic

We briefly recapitulate the basics of the coalgebraic semantics of modal logic. Coalgebraic modal logic in the form considered here has been introduced in [15], generalising previous results [9, 17, 11, 14]. For the sake of readability, we restrict the exposition to unary modalities. However, we emphasize that all our results extend in a straightforward way to polyadic operators, found e.g. in conditional and default logics [19].

A *modal signature* is just a set Λ of (unary) modal operators. The set $\mathcal{F}(\Lambda)$ of Λ-formulas ϕ is defined by the grammar

$$\phi ::= \bot \mid \phi \wedge \psi \mid \neg\phi \mid L\phi$$

where L ranges over all modalities in Λ. Other boolean operations are defined as usual; propositional atoms can be expressed as constant modalities.

Generally, we denote the set of propositional formulas over a set V by $\mathsf{Prop}(V)$, generated by the basic connectives $\neg$ and $\wedge$, and the set of propositional tautologies by $\mathsf{Taut}(V)$. We use variables ϵ etc. to denote either nothing or $\neg$. Thus, a *literal* over V is a formula of the form ϵa, with $a \in V$. A *clause* is a finite, possibly empty, disjunction of literals. The set of all clauses over V is denoted by $\mathsf{Cl}(V)$. We denote by $\mathsf{Up}_\Lambda(V)$ the set $\{La \mid L \in \Lambda, a \in V\}$. If $V \subseteq \mathcal{F}(\Lambda)$, we also regard propositional formulas over V as Λ-formulas. We sometimes explicitly designate V as consisting of *propositional variables*; these retain their status across further applications of Up_Λ and Prop (e.g. V is also the set of propositional variables for $\mathsf{Up}_\Lambda(\mathsf{Prop}(V))$). An *L-substitution* is a substitution σ of the propositional variables by elements of a set L; for a formula ϕ over V, we call $\phi\sigma$ an *L-instance* of ϕ. If $L \subset \mathcal{P}(X)$ for some X, then we also refer to σ as an *L-valuation*.

Definition 1. A *rank-1 clause* (in Λ) over a set V of propositional variables is an element of $\mathsf{Cl}(\mathsf{Up}_\Lambda(\mathsf{Prop}(V)))$. A *rank-1 (modal) logic* is a pair $\mathcal{L} = (\Lambda, A)$, where A is a set of rank-1 clauses in Λ.

Note that the definition of rank-1 clause rules out axioms involving purely propositional components, such as $\Box a \rightarrow a$ (results covering also such more general axioms are under way); the archetypal rank-1 logic is K.

Given a rank-1 logic $\mathcal{L} = (\Lambda, A)$, we inductively define $\mathcal{L}$-*derivability* $\vdash_{\mathcal{L}}$ from a set $\Phi \subseteq \mathcal{F}(\Lambda)$ as follows:

$$\frac{\phi \in \mathsf{Taut}(\mathcal{F}(\Lambda))}{\Phi \vdash_{\mathcal{L}} \phi} \quad \frac{\phi \in \Phi}{\Phi \vdash_{\mathcal{L}} \phi} \quad \frac{\Phi \vdash_{\mathcal{L}} \phi, \phi \to \psi}{\Phi \vdash_{\mathcal{L}} \psi} \quad \frac{\psi \in A}{\Phi \vdash_{\mathcal{L}} \psi\sigma} \quad \frac{\Phi \vdash_{\mathcal{L}} \phi \leftrightarrow \psi}{\Phi \vdash_{\mathcal{L}} L\phi \leftrightarrow L\psi}$$

where σ is an $\mathcal{F}(\Lambda)$-substitution. The last rule above is referred to as the *congruence rule*. We write $\vdash_{\mathcal{L}} \psi$ instead of $\emptyset \vdash_{\mathcal{L}} \psi$.

It has been shown in [20] that rank-1 clauses may be equivalently replaced by *one-step rules* ϕ/ψ, where $\phi \in \mathsf{Prop}(V)$ and $\psi \in \mathsf{Cl}(\mathsf{Up}_\Lambda(V))$. We shall present rank-1 logics as pairs $\mathcal{L} = (\Lambda, \mathsf{R})$, with R a set of one-step rules, when convenient; in this case, the penultimate clause above is replaced by

$$\frac{\Phi \vdash_{\mathcal{L}} \phi\sigma \quad \phi/\psi \in \mathsf{R}}{\Phi \vdash_{\mathcal{L}} \psi\sigma}.$$

The extension of R by the congruence rule is denoted R_C. Coalgebraic modal logic interprets modal formulas over coalgebras, which abstract from concrete notions of reactive system; here, the interpretation of modalities is given by a choice of predicate liftings. We recall the formal definitions:

Definition 2. Let $T : \mathsf{Set} \to \mathsf{Set}$ be a functor, referred to as the *signature functor*, where Set is the category of sets. A *T-coalgebra* is a pair $C = (X, \xi)$ where X is a set (of *states*) and ξ is a function $X \to TX$ called the *transition function*. A *morphism* $(X_1, \xi_1) \to (X_2, \xi_2)$ of T-coalgebras is a map $f : X_1 \to X_2$ such that $\xi_2 \circ f = Tf \circ \xi_1$. States x, y in coalgebras C, D are *behaviourally equivalent* if there exist coalgebra morphisms $f : C \to E$ and $g : D \to E$ such that $f(x) = g(y)$. A *predicate lifting* for T is a natural transformation $\lambda : Q \to Q \circ T^{\mathrm{op}}$, where Q denotes the contravariant powerset functor $\mathsf{Set}^{\mathrm{op}} \to \mathsf{Set}$.

We view coalgebras as generalised transition systems: the transition function maps states to a structured set of successors

Assumption 3. We can assume w.l.o.g. that T preserves injective maps ([2], proof of Theorem 3.2). For convenience, we will in fact sometimes assume that $TX \subseteq TY$ if $X \subseteq Y$. Moreover, we assume that T is non-trivial, i.e. $TX = \emptyset \implies X = \emptyset$ (otherwise, $TX = \emptyset$ for all X).

Recall that a functor is *ω-accessible* if it preserves directed colimits.

Lemma 4. *([1], Proposition 5.2) For a set functor T, the following are equivalent:*

1. *T is ω-accessible*
2. *T preserves directed unions*
3. *For every set X, $TX = \bigcup_{Y \subseteq X \text{ finite}} TY$ (recall Assumption 3).*

The coalgebraic semantics of modal logics is defined as follows. Given a modal signature Λ, a *Λ-structure* consists of a signature functor T and an assignment of a predicate lifting $[\![L]\!]$ for T to every modal operator $L \in \Lambda$. The satisfaction relation $\models_C$ between states x of a T-coalgebra $C = (X, \xi)$ and Λ-formulas is defined inductively, with the usual clauses for the boolean operations. The clause for a modal operator L is

$$x \models_C L\phi \iff \xi(x) \in [\![L]\!][\![\phi]\!]_C,$$

where $[\![\phi]\!]_C = \{x \in X \mid x \models_C \phi\}$. We drop the subscripts C when C is clear from the context. When we speak of a coalgebraic modal logic informally, we mean a Λ-structure; if the interpretation of modalities is clear from the context, this structure is simply referred to as T.

Satisfaction of Λ-formulas is invariant under behavioural equivalence [15]. Conversely, Λ has the *Hennessy-Milner property* for T, i.e. states that satisfy the same Λ-formulas are behaviourally equivalent, if T is ω-accessible and Λ is *separating* in the sense that $t \in TX$ is determined by the set $\{(L, A) \in \Lambda \times \mathcal{P}(X) \mid t \in [\![L]\!](A)\}$ [19].

Definition 5. Given a Λ-structure T, we write $\Phi \models_T \psi$ for a Λ-formula ψ and a set $\Phi \subseteq \mathcal{F}(\mathcal{L})$ if, for every state x in every T-coalgebra, $x \models \psi$ whenever $x \models \Phi$ (i.e. $x \models \phi$ for all $\phi \in \Phi$). The logic $\mathcal{L}$ is *sound* over T if $\Phi \models_T \psi$ whenever $\Phi \vdash_{\mathcal{L}} \psi$, and *strongly (weakly) complete* if $\Phi \vdash_{\mathcal{L}} \psi$ ($\vdash_{\mathcal{L}} \psi$) whenever $\Phi \models_T \psi$ ($\emptyset \models_T \psi$).

The requirement that axioms are of rank 1 means that every axiom makes assertions precisely about the next transition step. This allows us to capture soundness as a property exhibited in a single transition step as follows. Given a set X and a $\mathcal{P}(X)$-valuation τ, we define interpretations $[\![\phi]\!]\tau \subset X$ and $[\![\psi]\!]\tau \subset TX$ for $\phi \in \mathsf{Prop}(V)$ and $\psi \in \mathsf{Prop}(\mathsf{Up}_\Lambda(\mathsf{Prop}(V)))$ by the usual clauses for boolean operators and by $[\![L\phi]\!]\tau = [\![L]\!][\![\phi]\!]\tau$. We write $X, \tau \models \phi$ if $[\![\phi]\!]\tau = X$, correspondingly for TX.

Definition 6. A rank-1 clause ψ (one-step rule ϕ/ψ) is *one-step sound* for a Λ-structure T if $TX, \tau \models \psi\tau$ for each set X and each $\mathcal{P}(X)$-valuation τ (such that $X, \tau \models \phi$). An *$\mathcal{L}$-structure* for a rank-1 logic $\mathcal{L}$ with signature Λ is a Λ-structure for which all axioms (or rules) of $\mathcal{L}$ are one-step sound.

It is easy to see that one-step soundness impliess soundness, so $\mathcal{L}$ is *sound for all $\mathcal{L}$-structures*. Additional conditions guarantee weak completeness [20]. In general, this is all one can hope for, as many coalgebraic modal logics fail to be compact [20]. However, it will turn out that $\mathcal{L}$ is indeed *strongly* complete for the canonical $\mathcal{L}$-structure constructed below.

Example 7. We give a brief description of some coalgebraic modal logics, illustrating in particular the fact that many interesting modal logics are axiomatised in rank 1. We mostly omit the definition of predicate liftings and the axiomatisations; for these and further examples, cf. [20, 21].

1. The Kripke semantics of the modal logic K, defined in terms of a single operator $\Box$ and the axioms $\Box\top$ and $\Box(a \to b) \to \Box a \to \Box b$, is obtained as the K-structure given by the covariant powerset functor $\mathcal{P}$ and $[\![\Box]\!](A) = \mathcal{P}(A) \subset \mathcal{P}(X)$ for $A \subseteq X$.

2. *Graded modal logic* (GML) [4] has operators $\Diamond_k$ for $k \in \mathbb{N}$ of the nature 'in more than k successor states, it is the case that'. A GML-structure is given by the finite multiset functor, which takes a set X to the set of maps $A : X \to \mathbb{N}$ with finite support, where $A(x) = n$ is read 'multiset A contains x with multiplicity n'. Over this functor, one can also interpret the additional operator W of *majority logic* [13], read 'in at least half of the successor states, it is the case that'.

3. *Probabilistic modal logic* (PML) [12, 7] has modal operators L_p for $p \in [0, 1] \cap \mathbb{Q}$, read 'in the next step, it is with probability at least p the case that'. A PML-structure is given by the finite distribution functor, which takes a set X to the set of finitely supported probability distributions over X.

3   From Rank-1 Logics to Coalgebraic Models

In this section we construct for a given rank-1 modal logic $\mathcal{L}$ a *canonical $\mathcal{L}$-structure* $M_\mathcal{L}$ for which $\mathcal{L}$ is (sound and) *strongly complete*. Moreover, we consider a finitely branching substructure $M_\mathcal{L}^{fin}$ of $M_\mathcal{L}$ which is canonical among the finitely branching $\mathcal{L}$-structures. For $M_\mathcal{L}^{fin}$, $\mathcal{L}$ is (sound and) weakly complete and has the Hennessy-Milner property, i.e. states satisfying the same formulas are behaviourally equivalent. This tradeoff is typical: the Hennessy-Milner property holds only over finitely branching systems, while strong completeness will fail over such systems due to the breakdown of compactness.

The construction of the canonical structure resembles the construction of canonical models using maximally consistent sets, but works, like many concepts explained in the previous section, at the single step level:

Definition 8. Let $\mathcal{L} = (\Lambda, A)$ be a rank-1 logic, and let X be a set. *One-step derivability* $\Phi \vdash_\mathcal{L}^X \psi$ of $\psi \in \mathsf{Prop}(\mathsf{Up}_\Lambda(\mathcal{P}(X)))$ from $\Phi \subseteq \mathsf{Prop}(\mathsf{Up}_\Lambda(\mathcal{P}(X)))$ is defined inductively by

$$\frac{\phi \in \Phi}{\Phi \vdash_\mathcal{L}^X \phi} \qquad \frac{\phi \in \mathsf{Taut}(\mathsf{Up}_\Lambda(\mathcal{P}(X))}{\Phi \vdash_\mathcal{L}^X \phi} \qquad \frac{\Phi \vdash_\mathcal{L}^X \phi \to \psi \quad \Phi \vdash_\mathcal{L}^X \phi}{\Phi \vdash_\mathcal{L}^X \psi} \qquad \frac{\psi \in A}{\Phi \vdash_\mathcal{L}^X \psi\tau}$$

where τ is a $\mathcal{P}(X)$-valuation. (In the last clause, elements of $\mathsf{Prop}(\mathcal{P}(X))$ are implicitly interpreted as elements of $\mathcal{P}(X)$ in the obvious way. If $\mathcal{L}$ is presented by rules ϕ/ψ, the last clause is modified accordingly, with additional premise $X, \tau \models \phi$.) The set Φ is *one-step consistent* if $\Phi \nvdash_\mathcal{L}^X \bot$, and *maximally one-step consistent* if Φ is maximal w.r.t. $\subseteq$ among the one-step consistent subsets of $\mathsf{Prop}(\mathsf{Up}_\Lambda(\mathcal{P}(X)))$.

The canonical $\mathcal{L}$-structure $M_\mathcal{L}$ for $\mathcal{L}$ is now given by the functor $M_\mathcal{L}$ that takes a set X to the set of maximally one-step consistent subsets of $\mathsf{Prop}(\mathsf{Up}_\Lambda(\mathcal{P}(X)))$. For a map $f : X \to Y$, $M_\mathcal{L}(f)$ is defined by

$$M_\mathcal{L}(f)(\Phi) = \{\phi \in \mathsf{Prop}(\mathsf{Up}_\Lambda(\mathcal{P}(Y))) \mid \phi\sigma_f \in \Phi\},$$

where σ_f is the substitution $A \mapsto f^{-1}[A]$. This definition is justified by

Lemma 9. *For $\Phi \in M_\mathcal{L}(X)$, the set $M_\mathcal{L}(f)(\Phi)$ is maximally one-step consistent.*

Remark 10. From the point of view of Stone duality, a rank-1 logic defines a functor $L : \mathsf{BA} \to \mathsf{BA}$ on the category BA of boolean algebras. In this framework, the functor $M_\mathcal{L}$ arises as the composition $M_\mathcal{L} = USL\bar{Q}$ where $\bar{Q} : \mathsf{Set}^{\mathrm{op}} \to \mathsf{BA}$ is the contravariant powerset functor, $S : \mathsf{BA}^{\mathrm{op}} \to \mathsf{Stone}$ is part of the duality between Stone spaces and boolean algebras, and $U : \mathsf{Stone} \to \mathsf{Set}$ is the forgetful functor; see [10] for details.

The interpretation of modal operators by predicate liftings for $M_\mathcal{L}$ is now obvious:

Theorem and Definition 11. *The assignment*

$$[\![L]\!]A = \{\Phi \in M_\mathcal{L}(X) \mid LA \in \Phi\}.$$

defines an $\mathcal{L}$-structure $M_\mathcal{L}$, the canonical $\mathcal{L}$-structure.

Note that this immediately implies soundness of $\mathcal{L}$ over $M_\mathcal{L}$. We now turn to *strong completeness*, which is established by a canonical model construction that generalizes the standard notion of canonical Kripke structure. The carrier of the canonical model is the set C of maximally consistent sets of $\mathcal{L}$-formulas. The key to the construction is the *existence proof* (rather than the explicit construction) of a suitable $M_\mathcal{L}$-coalgebra structure on C, a technique first employed in [20]:

Lemma and Definition 12 (Existence Lemma). *There exists a canonical model, i.e. an $M_\mathcal{L}$-coalgebra structure $\zeta : C \to M_\mathcal{L}C$ such that*

$$\zeta(A) \in [\![L]\!]\hat{\phi} \quad \textit{iff} \quad L\phi \in A$$

for all $L \in \Lambda$, $\phi \in \mathcal{L}$, $A \in C$, where $\hat{\phi} = \{B \in C \mid \phi \in B\}$.

Lemma 13 (Truth Lemma). *For canonical models (C, ζ), $A \models_{(C,\zeta)} \phi$ iff $\phi \in A$.*

Theorem 14 (Strong completeness). *The logic $\mathcal{L}$ is strongly complete for $M_\mathcal{L}$.*

Finally, we consider the Hennessy-Milner property (cf. Section 2). The functor $M_\mathcal{L}$ fails to be ω-accessible for obvious cardinality reasons. Intuitively, $M_\mathcal{L}$-models have unbounded branching, while the Hennessy-Milner property can only be expected for finitely branching systems (as is the case already for standard Kripke models). We thus consider a subfunctor $M_\mathcal{L}^{fin}$ of $M_\mathcal{L}$ that captures precisely the finitely branching models.

In order to construct $M_\mathcal{L}^{fin}$, we can rely on the following general mechanism. We define the *ω-accessible part T^{fin}* of a set functor T by

$$T^{fin}X = \bigcup_{Y \subseteq X \text{ finite}} TY \quad \subseteq TX$$

(recall Assumption 3). It is easy to see that T^{fin} is a subfunctor of T. By Lemma 4, T^{fin} is ω-accessible. Moreover, T^{fin} agrees with T on finite sets. A predicate lifting λ for T restricts to a predicate lifting λ^{fin} for T^{fin} given by $\lambda_X^{fin} A = \lambda_X A \cap T^{fin} X$.

We define the *canonical finitely branching $\mathcal{L}$-structure* $M_{\mathcal{L}}^{fin}$ as the ω-accessible part of $M_{\mathcal{L}}$, with modal operators interpreted by restricted predicate liftings as described above. We then obtain

Theorem 15. *$\mathcal{L}$ is weakly complete and has the Hennessy-Milner property for $M_{\mathcal{L}}^{fin}$.*

Example 16. We give explicit descriptions (up to natural isomorphism) of $M_{\mathcal{L}}$ and $M_{\mathcal{L}}^{fin}$ in some concrete cases.

1. For $\mathcal{L} = (\{\Box\}, \emptyset)$, $M_{\mathcal{L}}$ is the neighbourhood frame functor $Q \circ Q^{op}$.

2. For the standard modal logic K (Example 7.1), M_K^{fin} is the finite powerset functor, while M_K is the filter functor [6].

3. For graded modal logic GML (Example 7.2), M_{GML}^{fin} is a modification of the finite multiset functor where elements of multisets may have infinite multiplicity.

4. For probabilistic modal logic PML (Example 7.3), M_{PML}^{fin} is a modification of the finite distribution functor where events A are assigned 'probabilities' PA which are downclosed subsets of the rational interval $[0,1] \cap \mathbb{Q}$. Thus, the space of 'probabilities' essentially consists of the interval $[0,1]$ and an additional copy of $[0,1] \cap \mathbb{Q}$, where the second copy of $q \in [0,1] \cap \mathbb{Q}$ is infinitesimally greater than the first. The distributions $P \subset M_{\mathcal{L}}^{fin}(X)$ are required to obey the axiomatization of PML [21] w.r.t. the canonical semantics; it is presently unclear whether this requirement can be replaced by a simpler condition.

4   An Adjunction Between Syntax and Semantics

We now set up an adjoint correspondence between rank-1 logics and set functors as their semantic counterparts. This establishes the canonical structure of a rank-1 logic as indeed canonical in a precise sense, i.e. as a universal model capturing all other ones. This situation is analogous (although not in any obvious sense technically related) to similar correspondences in equational logics and type theory: e.g. to a single-sorted equational theory, interpreted over cartesian categories (i.e. categories with finite products) with a distinguished object, one associates a Lawvere theory, which is again a cartesian category with a distinguished object and may simultaneously be regarded as an initial model and as a semantic representation of the given theory. The situation is dual for modal logics: the canonical structure serves as a *final* model of the given rank-1 logic, into which all other models may be mapped.

We make the categorical setting precise by collecting all rank 1 modal logics in a category **ModL** with morphisms $(\Lambda_1, A_1) \to (\Lambda_2, A_2)$ all maps $h : \Lambda_1 \to \Lambda_2$ such that the induced translation of formulas maps axioms in A_1 to derivable formulas in (Λ_2, A_2). The category of semantic structures is the category $\mathbf{Fn} =$ [Set, Set] of set functors and natural transformations. We have a functor Th : $\mathbf{Fn}^{\mathrm{op}} \to \mathbf{ModL}$ which takes a functor T to the logic (Λ_T, A_T), where Λ_T is the set of all predicate liftings for T, and A_T is the set of all rank-1 clauses over Λ_T which are one-step sound for T. Given a natural transformation $\mu : T \to S$, $\mathsf{Th}(\mu) : \mathsf{Th}(S) \to \mathsf{Th}(T)$ is the morphism taking a predicate lifting $\lambda : Q \to Q \circ S^{\mathrm{op}}$ for S to the predicate lifting $Q\mu \circ \lambda$ for T. Note that, in this terminology, an $\mathcal{L}$-structure is just a morphism of the form $h : \mathcal{L} \to \mathsf{Th}(T)$. In particular, the canonical $\mathcal{L}$-structure can be cast as a morphism $\eta_{\mathcal{L}} : \mathcal{L} \to \mathsf{Th}(M_{\mathcal{L}})$. The arrows $\eta_{\mathcal{L}}$ are part of the announced adjunction:

Theorem 17. *The canonical $\mathcal{L}$-structure $\eta_{\mathcal{L}}$ is universal; i.e. for each $\mathcal{L}$-structure $h : \mathcal{L} \to \mathsf{Th}(T)$, there exists a unique natural transformation $h^{\#}$: $T \to M_{\mathcal{L}}$ such that $\mathsf{Th}(h^{\#})\eta_{\mathcal{L}} = h$.*

In other words, the canonical structure is the final $\mathcal{L}$-structure, where a morphism of $\mathcal{L}$-structures is a natural transformation between the associated functors which is compatible with the interpretation of modal operators. A similar result holds for the canonical finitely branching $\mathcal{L}$-structure $M_{\mathcal{L}}^{fin}$, which now becomes a morphism $\eta_{\mathcal{L}}^{fin} : \mathcal{L} \to \mathsf{Th}(M_{\mathcal{L}}^{fin})$.

Theorem 18. *The $\mathcal{L}$-structure $\eta_{\mathcal{L}}^{fin}$ is universal among the finitely branching $\mathcal{L}$-structures; i.e. for each $\mathcal{L}$-structure $h : \mathcal{L} \to \mathsf{Th}(T)$ with T ω-accessible, there exists a unique natural transformation $h^{\#} : T \to M_{\mathcal{L}}^{fin}$ such that $\mathsf{Th}(h^{\#})\eta_{\mathcal{L}}^{fin} = h$.*

Theorems 17 and 18 allow us to replace rank-1 logics by functors in the definition of the coalgebraic semantics: an $\mathcal{L}$-structure may equivalently be regarded as a natural transformation $T \to M_{\mathcal{L}}$; analogously, an $\mathcal{L}$-structure over an ω-accessible functor T may be regarded as a natural transformation $T \to M_{\mathcal{L}}^{fin}$. We have

Proposition 19. *An $\mathcal{L}$-structure T is separating iff the associated natural transformation $T \to M_{\mathcal{L}}$ is injective.*

Thus, we have the following classification result.

Theorem 20. *Up to natural isomorphism, the ω-accessible $\mathcal{L}$-structures for which $\mathcal{L}$ has the Hennessy-Milner property are precisely the subfunctors of the canonical finitely branching $\mathcal{L}$-structure $M_{\mathcal{L}}^{fin}$.*

5   Applications

A benefit of the coalgebraic semantics constructed above is that we can now apply results on coalgebraic modal logic to arbitrary rank-1 modal logics, even when the latter lack a formal semantics. This includes in particular the generic decidability and complexity results of [20, 21], of which we now obtain purely syntactic versions.

In [20], a generic finite model construction was given which yields criteria for decidability and upper complexity bounds for coalgebraic modal logics. The generic complexity bounds generally do not match known bounds in particular examples, typically *PSPACE*. This is remedied in [21], where a generic *PSPACE* decision procedure for coalgebraic modal logics based on a shallow model construction is given, at the price of stronger assumptions on the logic.

A crucial role in the algorithmic methods of [20] is played by the following localised version of the satisfiability problem:

Definition 21. The *one-step satisfiability* problem for a Λ-structure T is to decide, given a finite set X and a conjunctive clause ψ over $\mathsf{Up}_\Lambda(\mathcal{P}(X))$, whether ψ is *one-step satisfiable*, i.e. $[\![\psi]\!] \subset TX$ is non-empty.

The satisfiability problem of a coalgebraic modal logic is

- decidable if its one-step satisfiability problem is decidable
- in *NEXPTIME* if one-step satisfiability is in *NP*
- in *EXPTIME* if one-step satisfiability is in *P*

(cf. [20]). This instantiates to the canonical structure as follows.

Lemma 22. *One-step satisfiability in $M_\mathcal{L}$ is one-step consistency in $\mathcal{L}$.*

Corollary 23. *The consistency problem of a rank-1 logic $\mathcal{L}$ (i.e. deciding whether an $\mathcal{L}$-formula ϕ is consistent) is*

- *decidable if one-step consistency (over finite sets) is decidable*
- *in NEXPTIME if one-step consistency is in NP*
- *in EXPTIME if one-step consistency is in P.*

Corollary 24. *The consistency problem of $\mathcal{L} = (\Lambda, \mathsf{R})$ is decidable if Λ is finite and R is recursive (i.e. it is decidable whether a one-step rule ϕ/ψ is contained in R up to propositional equivalence of premises).*

The generic *PSPACE*-algorithm of [21] relies on a notion of *strictly one-step complete* rule set. Rather than repeating the definition here, we recall that strict one-step completeness follows from one-step completeness (i.e. $TX, \tau \models \psi$ implies $\vdash^X_\mathcal{L} \psi$ for all $\psi \in \mathsf{Prop}(\mathsf{Up}_\Lambda(V))$) in combination with *resolution closedness*. The latter refers to a notion of rule resolution where propositional resolvents of the conclusions of two rules are formed and the premises are combined by conjunction, with possible subsequent elimination of propositional variables; cf. [21] for a formal definition. As an example, consider the rules

$$(N)\ \frac{a}{\Box a} \qquad (RR)\ \frac{a \wedge b \to c}{\Box a \wedge \Box b \to \Box c} \qquad (RK_n)\ \frac{\bigwedge_{i=1}^n a_i \to b}{\bigwedge_{i=1}^n \Box a_i \to \Box b}\ (n \geq 0).$$

The rule set $\{(N), (RR)\}$ presents the modal logic K, and its resolution closure consists of the rules (RK_n). Cf. [21] for further examples.

In [21], a shallow model property is proved based on strictly one-step complete rule sets. The canonical semantics allows us to turn this into a shallow proof property:

Definition 25. A set Σ of formulas is called *closed* if it is closed under subformulas and negation, where $\neg\neg\phi$ is identified with ϕ. The smallest closed set containing a given formula ϕ is denoted $\Sigma(\phi)$. A subset H of Σ is called a Σ-*Hintikka set* if $\bot \notin H$ and, for $\phi \wedge \psi \in \Sigma$, $\phi \wedge \psi \in H$ iff $\phi, \psi \in H$, and, for $\neg\phi \in \Sigma$, $\neg\phi \in H$ iff $\phi \notin H$.

Theorem 26. *Let* $\mathcal{L} = (\Lambda, \mathsf{R})$, *where* R *is resolution closed. Then* $\vdash_{\mathcal{L}} \phi$ *iff for every* $\Sigma(\phi)$-*Hintikka set* H *containing* $\neg\phi$, *there exist a clause* $\bigvee_{i=1}^{n} \epsilon_i L_i \rho_i$ *over* $\Sigma(\phi)$ *and a rule* $\psi/\bigvee_{i=1}^{n}(\epsilon_i L_i a_i)$ *in* R_C *such that* $\vdash_{\mathcal{L}} \psi[\rho_i/a_i]_{i=1,\dots,n}$ *and* $\epsilon_i L_i \rho_i \notin H$ *for all* i.

Theorem 26 implies that for $\mathcal{L}$ as in the statement, every provable formula ϕ has a tableau proof of linear depth which mentions only propositional combinations of subformulas of ϕ, in particular mentions only the modal operators contained in ϕ.

Remark 27. We hope to generalize Theorem 26 to more general classes of logics (i.e. beyond rank 1), possibly using purely proof-theoretic methods. This would also imply wider applicability of the generic *PSPACE* algorithm discussed below.

Corollary 28. *Let* $\mathcal{L} = (\Lambda, \mathsf{R})$ *be a rank-1 logic with* R *resolution closed, and let* $\Lambda_0 \subset \Lambda$. *Let* $\mathcal{L}_0 = (\Lambda_0, \mathsf{R}_0)$ *where* R_0 *consists of all* R-*rules that only mention* Λ_0-*operators. Then* $\mathcal{L}$ *conservatively extends* $\mathcal{L}_0$, *i.e.* $\Phi \vdash_{\mathcal{L}} \phi$ *implies that* $\Phi \vdash_{\mathcal{L}_0} \phi$ *for all* $\phi \in \mathcal{F}(\mathcal{L}_0)$ *and all* $\Phi \subseteq \mathcal{F}(\mathcal{L}_0)$.

Applied to majority logic (Example 7), this immediately leads to a complete axiomatisation of the majority operator alone.

Example 29. In the presentation of [21], a resolution closed set of rules for majority logic (Example 7.2) was given, consisting of the rules

$$(M_m) \quad \frac{\sum_{i=1}^{n} a_i + \sum_{r=1}^{v} c_r + m \leq \sum_{j=1}^{k} b_j + \sum_{s=1}^{w} d_s}{\bigwedge_{i=1}^{n} \Diamond_{k_i} a_i \wedge \bigwedge_{r=1}^{v} W c_r \rightarrow \bigvee_{j=1}^{k} \Diamond_{l_j} b_j \vee \bigvee_{s=1}^{w} W d_s} \quad (m \in \mathbb{Z})$$

with side conditions $\sum_{i=1}^{n}(k_i + 1) - \sum_{j=1}^{k} l_j + w - 1 - \max(m, 0) \geq 0$ and $v - w + 2m \geq 0$ (the sums in the premise refer to the — propositionally expressible — arithmetic of characteristic functions, cf. [21]). By Corollary 28, the rules

$$(W_m) \quad \frac{\sum_{r=1}^{v} c_r + m \leq \sum_{s=1}^{w} d_s}{\bigwedge_{r=1}^{v} W c_r \rightarrow \bigvee_{s=1}^{w} W d_s} \quad (m \in \mathbb{Z})$$

with side conditions $w - 1 - \max(m, 0) \geq 0$ and $v - w + 2m \geq 0$ form a complete axiomatisation of the majority operator W.

Theorem 26 suggests an obvious recursive algorithm for checking provability (or, dually, consistency). In order to ensure that this algorithm is feasible, we need to make sure that we never need to prove 'small' clauses by instantiating propositional variables with identical formulas in 'large' rules. We thus further require *reduction closedness* of the rule set, in the sense that every rule instance where a literal is duplicated in the conclusion can be replaced by an instance of another rule where all literals are distinct; cf. [21] for a formal definition.

The main result of [21] states that the satisfiability problem of a Λ-structure T is in *PSPACE* if T has a strictly one-step complete reduction closed rule set which is *PSPACE-tractable*, which essentially means that the rules applied according to Theorem 26 have representations whose size is polynomial in the matched clause and from which the clauses of the premise are easily extracted (again, cf. [21] for a formal definition). Applying this result to the canonical $\mathcal{L}$-structure, we obtain a purely syntactic criterion for a rank-1 logic to be in *PSPACE*:

Theorem 30. *The consistency (provability) problem of $\mathcal{L} = (\Lambda, \mathsf{R})$ is in PSPACE if R has a resolution closure which has a PSPACE-tractable reduction closure.*

6   Example: Deontic Logic

A typical application area for the above results are modal logics that come from a philosophical background, such as epistemic and deontic logics, which are often defined either without any reference to semantics at all or with a neighbourhood semantics essentially equivalent to the canonical semantics described above. Deontic logics [8], which have received much recent interest in computer science as logics for obligations of agents, are moreover often axiomatised in rank 1.

Standard deontic logic [3] is just the modal logic KD. This has been criticized on the grounds that it entails the *deontic explosion*: if O is the modal obligation operator 'it ought to be the case that', the K-axiom $(Oa \wedge Ob) \leftrightarrow O(a \wedge b)$ implies that in the presence of a single deontic dilemma, everything is obligatory, i.e. $Oa \wedge O \neg a \rightarrow Ob$. Some approaches to this problem are summarized in [5], where the novel solution is advocated to restrict at least one direction of K to the case that $a \wedge b$ is *permitted*, i.e. to $P(a \wedge b)$, where P is the dual $\neg O \neg$ of O. This leads to the axioms

(PM)	$O(a \wedge b) \wedge P(a \wedge b) \rightarrow Oa$
(PAND)	$Oa \wedge Ob \wedge P(a \wedge b) \rightarrow O(a \wedge b)$

(in [5], (PM) is formulated as a rule (RPM)). Two systems are proposed (both including the congruence rule): given the further axioms (N) $O\top$, (P) $\neg O \bot$, and

(ADD) $(Oa \wedge Ob) \rightarrow O(a \wedge b),$

DPM.1 is determined by (PM), (N), and (ADD), while DPM.2 is given by (PM), (PAND), (N), and (P). A further system PA, consisting of (PAND), (P), (N), and the standard monotonicity axiom is rejected, as it still leads to a form of deontic explosion where everything permitted is obligatory in the presence of a dilemma.

It is shown in [5] that DPM.1 and DPM.2 are sound and *weakly* complete w.r.t. the obvious classes of neighbourhood frames, and that both logics are decidable; the proofs are rather involved. In our framework, the situation presents itself as follows. The neighbourhood semantics of [5] is easily seen to be precisely the canonical semantics; the new insight here is that the semantics is coalgebraic. The rest is for free: by Theorem 14, both DPM.1 and DPM.2 are even *strongly* complete (the reason that the strong completeness proof fails in [5] is that an explicit construction of a canonical model is attempted). Decidability is immediate by Corollary 24; the finite model property (proved in [5] using filtrations) follows from the results of [20]. Moreover, the resolution closures of DPM.1 and DPM.2 enjoy the pleasant proof theoretic properties listed in Theorem 26. (The same holds for PA, and in fact for rather arbitrary variations of the axiom system.) A challenge that remains is to establish that DPM.1 and DPM.2 are in *PSPACE* by the method described at the end of the previous section, the main problem being to harness closure under reduction.

7   Conclusion

We have established that every modal logic $\mathcal{L}$ of rank 1 has a canonical coalgebraic semantics for which $\mathcal{L}$ is sound and strongly complete. Moreover, $\mathcal{L}$ has a canonical finitely branching coalgebraic semantics for which $\mathcal{L}$ is sound and weakly complete and has the Hennessy-Milner property, and from which all finitely branching semantics for which $\mathcal{L}$ has the Hennessy-Milner property are obtained as substructures. This is a converse to the previous insight that every coalgebraic modal logic can be axiomatized in rank 1 [20]. It allows us to formulate purely syntactic versions of semantics-based generic decidability and complexity criteria for coalgebraic modal logic [20, 21], including e.g. the result that *every recursively axiomatised rank-1 logic with finitely many modal operators is decidable*. We have applied this framework to recently defined versions of deontic logic which accommodate deontic dilemmas [5]. In particular, we have obtained decidability and strong completeness for these logics as immediate consequences of our generic results, while the original work has rather involved proofs and moreover establishes only decidability and weak completeness. Application of the generic *PSPACE* upper bound [21] to these logics remains an open problem.

We emphasise that the restriction to rank 1 is not an inherent limitation of the coalgebraic approach — the fact that coalgebraic modal logics are of rank 1 is due to the interpretation of these logics over the whole class of coalgebras for the relevant functor (in analogy to the standard modal logic K), and logics outside rank 1 may be modelled by passing to suitable subclasses of coalgebras. Ongoing work is aimed at pushing the generic results beyond strict rank 1; preliminary results have been obtained for axioms that combine rank 1 with rank 0, i.e. a coalgebraic counterpart of KT. A further point of interest is to obtain completeness and decidability results for coalgebraic modal logics with iteration, i.e. the coalgebraic counterpart of CTL.

References

[1] J. Adámek and H.-E. Porst. On tree coalgebras and coalgebra presentations. *Theoret. Comput. Sci.*, 311:257–283, 2004.

[2] M. Barr. Terminal coalgebras in well-founded set theory. *Theoret. Comput. Sci.*, 114:299–315, 1993.

[3] B. Chellas. *Modal Logic*. Cambridge, 1980.

[4] K. Fine. In so many possible worlds. *Notre Dame J. Formal Logic*, 13:516–520, 1972.

[5] L. Goble. A proposal for dealing with deontic dilemmas. In *Deontic Logic in Computer Science*, volume 3065 of *LNAI*, pages 74–113. Springer, 2004.

[6] H.-P. Gumm. Functors for coalgebras. *Algebra Universalis*, 45:135–147, 2001.

[7] A. Heifetz and P. Mongin. Probabilistic logic for type spaces. *Games and Economic Behavior*, 35:31–53, 2001.

[8] R. Hilpinen. Deontic logic. In L. Goble, editor, *The Blackwell Guide to Philosophical Logic*. Blackwell, 2001.

[9] B. Jacobs. Towards a duality result in the modal logic of coalgebras. In *Coalgebraic Methods in Computer Science*, volume 33 of *ENTCS*. Elsevier, 2000.

[10] C. Kupke, A. Kurz, and D. Pattinson. Ultrafilter extensions for coalgebras. In *Algebra and Coalgebra in Computer Science*, volume 3629 of *LNCS*, pages 263–277. Springer, 2005.

[11] A. Kurz. Specifying coalgebras with modal logic. *Theoret. Comput. Sci.*, 260:119–138, 2001.

[12] K. Larsen and A. Skou. Bisimulation through probabilistic testing. *Inform. Comput.*, 94:1–28, 1991.

[13] E. Pacuit and S. Salame. Majority logic. In *Principles of Knowledge Representation and Reasoning, KR 04*, pages 598–605. AAAI Press, 2004.

[14] D. Pattinson. Semantical principles in the modal logic of coalgebras. In *Theoretical Aspects of Computer Science, STACS 01*, volume 2010 of *LNCS*, pages 514–526. Springer, 2001.

[15] D. Pattinson. Expressive logics for coalgebras via terminal sequence induction. *Notre Dame J. Formal Logic*, 45:19–33, 2004.

[16] M. Pauly. A modal logic for coalitional power in games. *J. Logic Comput.*, 12:149–166, 2002.

[17] M. Rößiger. Coalgebras and modal logic. In *Coalgebraic Methods in Computer Science*, volume 33 of *ENTCS*. Elsevier, 2000.

[18] J. Rutten. Universal coalgebra: A theory of systems. *Theoret. Comput. Sci.*, 249:3–80, 2000.

[19] L. Schröder. Expressivity of coalgebraic modal logic: the limits and beyond. In *Foundations of Software Science And Computation Structures*, volume 3441 of *LNCS*, pages 440–454. Springer, 2005. Extended version to appear in *Theoret. Comput. Sci.*

[20] L. Schröder. A finite model construction for coalgebraic modal logic. In *Foundations Of Software Science And Computation Structures*, volume 3921 of *LNCS*, pages 157–171. Springer, 2006. Extended version to appear in *J. Logic Algebraic Programming*.

[21] L. Schröder and D. Pattinson. PSPACE reasoning for rank-1 modal logics. In *Logic in Computer Science*, pages 231–240. IEEE, 2006. Presentation slides available under www.informatik.uni-bremen.de/~lschrode/slides/rank1pspace.pdf.

An Efficient Quantum Algorithm for the Hidden Subgroup Problem in Extraspecial Groups*

Gábor Ivanyos[1], Luc Sanselme[2], and Miklos Santha[2,3]

[1] SZTAKI, Hungarian Academy of Sciences, H-1111 Budapest, Hungary
[2] Univ Paris-Sud, Orsay, F-91405
[3] CNRS, LRI, UMR 8623, Orsay, F-91405

Abstract. Extraspecial groups form a remarkable subclass of p-groups. They are also present in quantum information theory, in particular in quantum error correction. We give here a polynomial time quantum algorithm for finding hidden subgroups in extraspecial groups. Our approach is quite different from the recent algorithms presented in [17] and [2] for the Heisenberg group, the extraspecial p-group of size p^3 and exponent p. Exploiting certain nice automorphisms of the extraspecial groups we define specific group actions which are used to reduce the problem to hidden subgroup instances in abelian groups that can be dealt with directly.

1 Introduction

The most important challenge of quantum computing is to find quantum algorithms that achieve exponential speedup over the best known classical solutions. In this respect, the most extensively studied problem is the paradigmatic hidden subgroup problem. Stated in a group theoretical setting, in $\mathrm{HSP}(G, f)$ we are given explicitly a finite group G and we also have at our disposal a function f that can be queried via an oracle, and which maps G into a finite set. We are promised that for some subgroup H, f is constant on each left coset of H and distinct on different left cosets. We say that f hides the subgroup H. The task is to determine the hidden subgroup H. We measure the time complexity of an algorithm by the overall running time when a query counts as one computational step. An algorithm is called efficient if its time complexity is polynomial in the logarithm of the order of G.

We don't know any classical algorithm of polynomial query complexity for the HSP, even in the restricted case of abelian groups. In this respect, probably the most important result of quantum computing is that the HSP can be solved efficiently for abelian groups by quantum algorithms. We will call this solution, for which one can find an excellent description for example in Mosca's

---

* Research supported by the European Commission IST Integrated Project Qubit Applications (QAP) 015848, the OTKA grants T42559 and T46234, the NWO visitor's grant Algebraic Aspects of Quantum Computing, and by the ANR Blanc AlgoQP grant of the French Research Ministry.

W. Thomas and P. Weil (Eds.): STACS 2007, LNCS 4393, pp. 586–597, 2007.

thesis [15], the standard algorithm for HSP. The main quantum tool used in the standard algorithm is Fourier sampling based on the approximate quantum Fourier transform that can be efficiently implemented by a quantum algorithm in case of abelian groups [11]. Among the important special cases of this general solution one can mention Simon's xor-mask finding [21], Shor's factorization and discrete logarithm finding algorithms [19], and Kitaev's algorithm [11] for the abelian stabilizer problem.

Since the realization of the importance of the abelian HSP, intensive efforts have been made to solve the hidden subgroup problem also in finite non-abelian groups. The intrinsic mathematical interest of this challenge is increased by the fact that several famous classical algorithmic problems can be cast in this framework, like for example the graph isomorphism problem. The successful efforts for solving the problem can roughly be divided into two categories. The standard algorithm has been extended to some non-abelian groups by Rötteler and Beth [18], Hallgren, Russell and Ta-Shma [8], Grigni, Schulman, Vazirani and Vazirani [7] and Moore, Rockmore, Russell and Schulman [14] using efficient implementations of the quantum Fourier transform over these groups. In a different approach, Ivanyos, Magniez and Santha [10] and Friedl, Ivanyos, Magniez, Santha and Sen [5] have efficiently reduced the HSP in some non-abelian groups to HSP instances in abelian groups using classical and quantum group theoretical tools, but not the non-abelian Fourier transform.

All groups where the HSP has been efficiently solved are in some sense "close" to abelian groups. Extraspecial groups, in which we present here an efficient quantum algorithm, are no exception in this respect: they have the property that all their proper factor groups are abelian. They form a subclass of p-groups, where p is a prime number, and play an important role in the theory of this family of groups. Extensive treatment of extraspecial groups can be found for example in the books of Huppert [9] and Aschbacher [1].

Extraspecial 2-groups are heavily present in the theory of quantum error correction. They provide a bridge between quantum error correcting codes and binary orthogonal geometry [3]. They form the real subgroup of the Pauli group [4] which plays a crucial role in the theory of stabilizer codes [6]. For general p, extraspecial p-groups give rise to the simplest examples of Clifford codes, see [12].

Efficient solutions for the HSP have already been given in several specific extraspecial groups. Extraspecial p-groups are of order p^{2k+1} for some integer k. For odd p, they are of exponent p or p^2, and extraspecial 2-groups are of exponent 4. The class of groups for which Ivanyos, Magniez and Santha [10] provide a solution include extraspecial p-groups when p is a fixed constant and the input size grows with k. When p is fixed, the smallest extraspecial groups are of size p^3. Up to isomorphism there are two extraspecial groups of order p^3. Recently two independent works dealt with quantum algorithms for the HSP in the group of exponent p, the Heisenberg group. Radhakrishnan, Rötteler and Sen [17] have followed the standard algorithm with non-abelian Fourier transform, and proved that strong Fourier sampling with a random basis leads to a query efficient quantum solution. In a subsequent work, Bacon, Childs and van Dam [2] devised an efficient quantum algorithm, where a state estimation technique, called the pretty good measurement, is used to reduce the HSP to some matrix sum problem that they could solve classically.

In this paper we provide an efficient quantum algorithm for the HSP in any extraspecial group. Our main contribution is an efficient algorithm in extraspecial p-groups of exponent p when p grows with the input size. A simplified version of this algorithm gives another solution for the groups of constant exponent. The remaining case, groups of exponent p^2 when p is large is easily reducible to the case of groups of exponent p.

Our approach for groups of exponent p is completely different from the above two solutions for the Heisenberg group. In our solution only abelian Fourier transforms and von Neumann measurements are used. In fact, our algorithm is a series of reductions, where we repeatedly use the standard algorithm for abelian groups, or a slight extension of it. In this extension, instead of a classical hiding functions we have an efficient quantum hiding procedure at our disposal. This procedure outputs a quantum state for every group element so that the states corresponding to group elements coming from the same left coset of the hidden subgroup are identical, whereas the states corresponding to group elements from different left cosets are orthogonal. Repeated invocations of the procedure might yield different states for the same group element.

At the end of our reductions we are faced with the problem of creating an efficient hiding procedure in the above sense for the subgroup HG' of G, where G is an extraspecial p-group of exponent p when p is large, $G' = \{z^i : 0 \leq i \leq p - 1\}$ is its commutator, and H is the hidden subgroup. It is easy to see, that if we could create the coset state $|aHG'\rangle$ for some $a \in G$, then the group action multiplication from the right, which on a given group element g would output $|aHG' \cdot g\rangle$, is a hiding procedure. Unfortunately, we can create these states efficiently only when p is constant. In the general case, we can create efficiently only the states $|aHG'_u\rangle$ for a random $0 \leq u \leq p - 1$, where $|G'_u\rangle = \frac{1}{\sqrt{p}} \sum_{i \in \mathbb{Z}_p} \omega^{-ui} |z^i\rangle$. Our main technical contribution is to show that several (in fact four) copies of these states can be combined together so that the disturbing phases cancel each other. To achieve this goal we exploit certain nice automorphisms of the group to define more sophisticated group actions that can be used for our purposes.

The structure of the paper is quite simple. After a discussion on the extension of the standard algorithm and a basic description of extraspecial groups in Section 2, our reduction steps are presented in Section 3. The summary of these reductions is stated in Theorem 1: An efficient hiding procedure for HG' is sufficient to solve the HSP in an extraspecial group G. In Section 4 we establish our main result in Theorem 2, the existence of an efficient solution for the HSP in extraspecial groups. The proof is given according to the three cases discussed above. The most important case of groups of exponent p when p is large is dealt with in Section 4.2, where in Theorem 3 we provide the hiding procedure for HG'.

2 Preliminaries

2.1 Extensions of the Standard Algorithm for the Abelian HSP

We will use standard notions of quantum computing for which one can consult for example [13]. For a finite set X, we denote by $|X\rangle$ the uniform superposition $\frac{1}{\sqrt{|X|}} \sum_{x \in X} |x\rangle$ over X. For a superposition $|\Psi\rangle$, we denote by $\mathsf{supp}(|\Psi\rangle)$ the support of $|\Psi\rangle$, that is the set of basis elements with non-zero amplitude.

The general solution for the abelian HSP consists essentially of Fourier sampling of the hiding function f. More specifically, it involves the creation of the superposition $\sum_{g \in G} |g\rangle |f(g)\rangle$ and the Fourier transform over G. Clearly, for the former part it is essential to have access to a hiding function. In fact, this requirement can be relaxed in some sense, and in this paper we will use such a relaxation. A relaxation was already used by Ivanyos et al. [10] who extended the notion of the hiding function to quantum functions. More precisely, for a finite set X, and a quantum function $f : G \to \mathbb{C}^X$, we say that f hides the subgroup H of G if $|f(g)\rangle$ is a unit vector for every $g \in G$, and f is constant on the left cosets of H, and maps elements from different cosets into orthogonal states. The simple fact is proven in Lemma 1 of [10] that in the standard solution of HSP for abelian groups, one can just as well use a quantum hiding function.

The standard algorithms for the abelian HSP in fact repeats polynomially many times the Fourier sampling involving the same (classical or quantum) hiding function. In fact, in each iteration a random element is obtained from the subgroup orthogonal to H. Our extension is based on the observation, that for the sampling, one doesn't have to use the same hiding function in each iteration, different hiding functions will do just as well the game. For the sake of completeness we formalize this here and state the exact conditions that will be used in our case.

We say that a set of vectors $\{|\Psi_g\rangle : g \in G\}$ from some Hilbert space $\mathcal{H}$ is a *hiding set* for the subgroup H of G if

- $|\Psi_g\rangle$ is a unit vector for every $g \in G$,
- if g and g' are in the same left coset of H then $|\Psi_g\rangle = |\Psi_{g'}\rangle$,
- if g and g' are in different left cosets of H then $|\Psi_g\rangle$ and $|\Psi_{g'}\rangle$ are orthogonal.

A quantum procedure is *hiding* the subgroup H of G if for every $g \in G$, on input $|g\rangle|0\rangle$ it outputs $|g\rangle|\Psi_g\rangle$ where $\{|\Psi_g\rangle : g \in G\}$ is a hiding set for H. Let us underline that we don't require from a quantum hiding procedure to output the same hiding set in different calls. The following fact recasts the existence of the standard algorithm for the abelian HSP in the context of hiding sets.

Fact 1. *Let G be a finite abelian group. If there exists an efficient quantum procedure which hides the subgroup H of G then there is an efficient quantum algorithm for finding H.*

Proof. It is immediate from the proof of Lemma 1 in [10]: indeed, the exact property of the quantum hiding function f which is used there is that $\{|g\rangle|f(g)\rangle : g \in G\}$ forms a hiding set for H. □

2.2 Extraspecial Groups

Let G be a finite group. For two elements g_1 and g_2 of G, we usually denote their product by $g_1 g_2$. If we conceive group multiplication from the right as a group action of G on itself, we will use the notation $g_1 \cdot g_2$ for $g_1 g_2$. For a subset X of G, we will denote by $\langle X \rangle$ the subgroup generated by X. The derived subgroup G' of G is defined as $\langle \{ x^{-1} y^{-1} xy \; : \; x, y \in G \} \rangle$, and its center $Z(G)$ as $\{ z \in G \; : \; gz = zg$ for all $g \in G \}$. The Frattini subgroup $\Phi(G)$ is the intersection of all maximal subgroups of G.

For an integer n, we denote by $\mathbb{Z}_n$ the group of integers modulo n, and for a prime number p, we denote by $\mathbb{Z}_p^*$ the multiplicative group of integers relatively prime with p. A p-group is a finite group whose order is a power of p. A p-group G is *extraspecial* if $G' = Z(G) = \Phi(G)$, and its center is cyclic of prime order p.

If G is an extraspecial p-group then $|G| = p^{2k+1}$ for some integer k. The elements of G can be encoded by binary strings of length $O(k \log p)$, and an efficient algorithm on that input has to be polynomial in both k and $\log p$.

The smallest non-abelian extraspecial groups are of order p^3. For $p = 2$, we have, up to isomorphism, two extraspecial 2-groups of order 8. These are the quaternion group Q, and the dihedral group D_4, the symmetry group of the square in two dimensions. The exponent of both of these groups is $p^2 = 4$.

For $p > 2$, up to isomorphism we have again two extraspecial p-groups of order p^3. The first one is the Heisenberg group H_p, which is the group of upper triangular 3×3 matrices over the field $\mathbb{F}_p$ whose diagonal contains everywhere 1. The exponent of H_p is p. The other one is A_p, the group of applications $t \mapsto at + b$ from $\mathbb{Z}_{p^2}$ to $\mathbb{Z}_{p^2}$, where $a \equiv 1$ modulo p and $b \in \mathbb{Z}_{p^2}$. The exponent of A_p is p^2.

We give now via relations equivalent definitions of the extraspecial p-groups of order p^3. These definitions will be useful for the arguments we will develop in our algorithms. To emphasize the similarities between these groups, we will take three generator elements x, y, z for each of them. The element z will always generate the center of the group. Here are the definitions via relations:

$$Q = \langle x^2 = y^2 = [x, y] = z, \; z^2 = 1 \rangle,$$

$$D_4 = \langle x^2 = y^2 = z^2 = 1, \; [x, y] = z, \; [x, z] = [y, z] = 1 \rangle,$$

$$H_p = \langle x^p = y^p = z^p = 1, \; [x, y] = z, \; [x, z] = [y, z] = 1 \rangle,$$

$$A_p = \langle x^{p^2} = y^p = 1, \; [x, y] = z = x^p, \; [y, z] = 1 \rangle.$$

From these definitions it is clear that every element in an extraspecial group of order p^3 has a unique representation of the form $x^i y^j z^\ell$ where $i, j, \ell \in \mathbb{Z}_p$.

Extraspecial p-groups of order p^{2k+1}, for $k > 1$, can be obtained as the central product of k extraspecial p-groups of order p^3. If $G_1, \ldots, G_k$ are extraspecial p-groups of order p^3 then their *central product* $G_1 \mathbf{Y} \ldots \mathbf{Y} G_k$ is the factor group

$$G_1 \times \ldots \times G_k \bmod z_1 = \cdots = z_k,$$

where z_i is an arbitrary generator of $Z(G_i)$ for $i = 1, \ldots, k$.

Since $D_4 \mathbf{Y} D_4 = Q \mathbf{Y} Q$, up to isomorphism the unique extraspecial 2-groups of order 2^{2k+1} are $\mathbf{Y}_{i=1}^k D_4$ and $(\mathbf{Y}_{i=1}^{k-1} D_4) \mathbf{Y} Q$. All of these groups are of exponent $p^2 = 4$. When $p > 2$, we have $H_p \mathbf{Y} A_p = A_p \mathbf{Y} A_p$. Therefore, up to isomorphism the unique extraspecial p-groups of order p^{2k+1} are $\mathbf{Y}_{i=1}^k H_p$ and $(\mathbf{Y}_{i=1}^{k-1} H_p) \mathbf{Y} A_p$. The former groups are of exponent p, the latter ones are of exponent p^2.

It follows from the above that any extraspecial group of order p^{2k+1} can be generated by $2k+1$ elements $x_1, y_1, \ldots, x_k, y_k$ and z. Any element of the group has a unique representation of the form $x_1^{i_1} y_1^{i_1'} \cdots x_k^{i_k} y_k^{i_k'} z^\ell$, where $i_1, i_1', \ldots, i_k, i_k', \ell \in \mathbb{Z}_p$. Also, $G' = Z(G) = \{z^\ell | \ell \in \mathbb{Z}_p\}$.

3   Reduction Lemmas

Our results leading to our main technical contribution can be the best described via a series of reduction lemmas.

Lemma 1. *Let G be an extraspecial p-group, and let us given an oracle f which hides the subgroup H of G. Then finding H is efficiently reducible to find HG'.*

Proof. Since G' is a cyclic group of prime order, either $G' \subseteq H$ or $G' \cap H = \{1\}$. It is simple to decide which one of this cases holds by checking if $f(z) = f(1)$. If $G' \subseteq H$ then $H = HG'$, and therefore the algorithm which finds HG' yields immediatly H.

If $G' \cap H = \{1\}$ then we claim that HG' is abelian. To see this, it is sufficient to show that H is abelian, since G' is the center of G. Let h_1 and h_2 be two elements of H. Then there exists $\ell \in \mathbb{Z}_p$ such that $h_1 h_2 = h_2 h_1 z^\ell$. This implies that z^ℓ is in $G' \cap H$ and therefore $z^\ell = 1$.

The restriction of the hiding function f to the abelian subgroup HG' of G hides H. Therefore the standard algorithm for solving the HSP in abelian groups applied to HG' with oracle f yields H. $\qquad\square$

We will show that finding HG' can be efficiently reduced to the hidden subgroup problem in an abelian group. For every element $g = x_1^{i_1} y_1^{j_1} \ldots x_k^{i_k} y_k^{j_k} z^\ell$ of G, we denote by $\overline{g}$ the element $x_1^{i_1} y_1^{j_1} \ldots x_k^{i_k} y_k^{j_k}$. We define now the group $\overline{G}$ whose base set is $\{\overline{g} : g \in G\}$. Observe that this set of elements does not form a subgroup in G. To make $\overline{G}$ a group, its law is defined by $\overline{g_1} * \overline{g_2} = \overline{g_1 g_2}$ for all $\overline{g_1}$ and $\overline{g_2}$ in $\overline{G}$. It is easy to check that $*$ is well defined, and is indeed a group multiplication. The group $\overline{G}$ is isomorphic to G/G' and therefore is abelian. For our purposes a nice way to think about $\overline{G}$ as a representation of G/G' with unique encoding. In fact, it is also easy to check that $\overline{G}$ is isomorphic to $\mathbb{Z}_p^{2k}$. Finally let us observe that $HG' \cap \overline{G}$ is a subgroup of $(\overline{G}, *)$ since HG'/G' is a subgroup of G/G',

Lemma 2. *Let G be an extraspecial p-group, and let us given an oracle f which hides the subgroup H of G. Then finding HG' is efficiently reducible to find $HG' \cap \overline{G}$ in $\overline{G}$.*

Proof. Since $HG' = (HG' \cap \overline{G})G'$, a generator set of HG' in G is composed of a generator set of $HG' \cap \overline{G}$ in $\overline{G}$ together with z.   □

The group $\overline{G}$ is abelian but we don't have a hiding function for $HG' \cap \overline{G}$. The main technical result of our paper is that using the hiding function f for H in G, we will be able to implement an efficient quantum *hiding procedure* for HG' in G. Our last reduction lemma just states that this is sufficient for finding $HG' \cap \overline{G}$.

Lemma 3. *Let G be an extraspecial p-group, and let us given an oracle f which hides the subgroup H of G. If we have an efficient quantum procedure (using f) which hides HG' in G then we can find efficiently $HG' \cap \overline{G}$ in $\overline{G}$.*

Proof. The procedure which hides HG' in G hides also $HG' \cap \overline{G}$ in $\overline{G}$. Since $\overline{G}$ is abelian, Fact 1 implies that we can find efficiently $HG' \cap \overline{G}$.   □

Our first theorem is the consequence of these three lemmas. It says that if in an extraspecial group we succeed to transform the oracle hiding the subgroup H into a quantum procedure hiding HG' then we can determine H. This reduction is the basis of our algorithm.

Theorem 1. *Let G be an extraspecial p-group, and let us given an oracle f which hides the subgroup H of G. If we have an efficient quantum procedure (using f) which hides HG' in G then $\mathrm{HSP}(G, f)$ can be solved efficiently.*

Observe that if $G' \subseteq H$ then $HG' = H$, and therefore the following corollary is immediate.

Corollary 1. *Let G be an extraspecial p-group, and let us given an oracle f which hides the subgroup H of G. If $G' \subseteq H$ then we can solve efficiently $\mathrm{HSP}(G, f)$.*

4   The Algorithm

We now describe the quantum algorithm which solves the HSP in extraspecial groups. In fact, we will deal separately with three cases: groups of constant exponent, groups of exponent p when p is large, and groups of exponent p^2 when p is large. The case of constant exponent is actually not new, it follows from a general result in [10]. Nevertheless, for the sake of completeness we show how a simplified version of the algorithm for the second case works here. The algorithm for extraspecial groups of exponent p that goes to infinity is our main result. Finally, the case of groups of exponent p^2 can be easily reduced to the case of groups of exponent p. These results are summarized in our main theorem.

Theorem 2. *Let G be an extraspecial p-group, and let us given an oracle f which hides the subgroup H of G. Then there is an efficient quantum procedure which finds H.*

4.1 Groups of Constant Exponent

In Theorem 9 of [10] it is proven that in general the HSP can be solved by a quantum algorithm in polynomial time in the size of the input and the cardinality of G'. This includes the case of extraspecial groups of constant exponent. Nonetheless, for the sake of completeness we describe here an efficient procedure, similar in spirit to the one used for the next case but much simpler.

First remark that for every $a \in G$, the set $\{|aHG' \cdot g\rangle : g \in G\}$ is hiding for HG' in G. The efficient hiding procedure for HG' computes, for some $a \in G$, the superposition $\frac{1}{\sqrt{p}} \sum_{u \in \mathbb{Z}_p} |u\rangle |aHG'_u\rangle$ which by Lemma 4 of Section 4.2 can be done efficiently. Then the first register is measured. This is repeated until the result of the observation is 0. Since p is constant, after a constant number of iteration the superposition $|0\rangle |aHG'_0\rangle = |0\rangle |aHG'\rangle$ is created and finally $|aHG' \cdot g\rangle$ is computed.

Observe that this simplified approach can not work for large exponents since p, the expected number of iterations, is not polynomial in the size of the input.

4.2 Groups of Exponent p When p Is Large

For every $u \in \mathbb{Z}_p$, let $|G'_u\rangle = \frac{1}{\sqrt{p}} \sum_{i \in \mathbb{Z}_p} \omega^{-ui} |z^i\rangle$ and observe that $|G'_u \cdot z\rangle = \omega^u |G'_u\rangle$.

Lemma 4. *There is an efficient quantum procedure which creates $\frac{1}{\sqrt{p}} \sum_{u \in \mathbb{Z}_p} |u\rangle |aHG'_u\rangle$ where a is a random element from G.*

Proof. We start with $|0\rangle |0\rangle |0\rangle$. Since we have access to the hiding function f, we can create the superposition $\frac{1}{\sqrt{|G|}} \sum_{g \in G} |0\rangle |g\rangle |f(g)\rangle$. Observing and discharging the third register we get $|0\rangle |aH\rangle$ for a random element a. Applying the Fourier transform over $\mathbb{Z}_p$ to the first register gives $|\mathbb{Z}_p\rangle |aH\rangle$. Multiplying the second register by z^{-i} when i is the content of the first one results in $\frac{1}{\sqrt{p}} \sum_{i \in \mathbb{Z}_p} |-i\rangle |aHz^i\rangle$. A final Fourier transform in the first register creates the required superposition. $\square$

For $j = 1, \ldots, p-1$, we define the automorphisms ϕ_j of G mapping x_i to x_i^j, y_i to y_i^j and z to z^{j^2} when $i \in \{1, \ldots, k\}$. These maps (defined on generators) extend in fact to automorphisms of G since the elements $x_1^j, y_1^j, \ldots x_k^j, y_k^j, z^{j^2}$ generate the group G and satisfy the defining relations.

In our next lemma we claim that the states $|aHG'_u\rangle$ are eigenvectors of the group action of multiplication from the right by $\phi_j(g)$, whenever g is from HG'. Moreover, the corresponding eigenvalues are some powers of the root of the unity, the exponent does not depend on a, and the dependence on u and j is relatively simple.

Lemma 5. *We have*

1. $\forall h \in H, \exists \ell \in \mathbb{Z}_p, \forall a \in G, \forall u \in \mathbb{Z}_p, \forall j \in \mathbb{Z}_p^*, \quad |aHG'_u \cdot \phi_j(h)\rangle = \omega^{u(j-j^2)\ell} |aHG'_u\rangle$,
2. $\forall a \in G, \forall u \in \mathbb{Z}_p, \forall j \in \mathbb{Z}_p^*, \quad |aHG'_u \cdot \phi_j(z)\rangle = \omega^{uj^2} |aHG'_u\rangle$.

Proof. To begin with let's remark that for $h \in H$, we have $|aHG'_u \cdot h\rangle = |aHG'_u\rangle$ and that $|aHG'_u \cdot z\rangle = \omega^u|aHG'_u\rangle$.

To prove the first part, let h be an element of H. Then $\phi_j(h) = h^j z^t$ where t depends on h and j. We will show that $t = (j - j^2)\ell$ where ℓ depends only on h. This will imply the claim.

Let j_0 be a fixed primitive element of $\mathbb{Z}_p^*$. Then $\phi_{j_0}(h) = h^{j_0} z^s$, for some $s \in \mathbb{Z}_p$. We set $\ell = s(j_0 - j_0^2)^{-1}$, and $k = hz^\ell$. Then $\phi_{j_0}(k) = h^{j_0} z^{\ell(j_0 - j_0^2)} z^{\ell j_0^2} = k^{j_0}$. Therefore $\phi_j(k) = k^j$ and $\phi_j(h) = \phi_j(k)\phi_j(z^{-\ell}) = h^j z^{\ell(j - j^2)}$. The proof of the second part is immediate. $\qquad\square$

The principal idea now is to take several copies of the states $|a_i HG'_{u_i}\rangle$ and choose j_i so that the product of the corresponding eigenvalues becomes the unity. Therefore the actions $\phi_j(g)$, when g is from HG', will not modify the combined state. It turns out that we can achieve this with four copies.

For $\bar{a} = (a_1, a_2, a_3, a_4) \in G^4$, $\bar{u} = (u_1, u_2, u_3, u_4) \in \mathbb{Z}_p^4$, $\bar{j} = (j_1, j_2, j_3, j_4) \in (\mathbb{Z}_p^*)^4$ and $g \in G$, we define the quantum state $|\Psi_g^{\bar{a}, \bar{u}, \bar{j}}\rangle$ in $\mathbb{C}^{G^4}$ by

$$|\Psi_g^{\bar{a}, \bar{u}, \bar{j}}\rangle = |a_1 HG'_{u_1} \cdot \phi_{j_1}(g), a_2 HG'_{u_2} \cdot \phi_{j_2}(g), a_3 HG'_{u_3} \cdot \phi_{j_3}(g), a_4 HG'_{u_4} \cdot \phi_{j_4}(g)\rangle.$$

Our purpose is to find an efficient procedure to generate triples $(\bar{a}, \bar{u}, \bar{j})$ such that for every $g \in HG'$ we have $|\Psi_g^{\bar{a}, \bar{u}, \bar{j}}\rangle = |a_1 HG'_{u_1}, a_2 HG'_{u_2}, a_3 HG'_{u_3}, a_4 HG'_{u_4}\rangle$. We call such triples *appropriate*. The reason to look for appropriate triples is that they lead to hiding sets for HG' in G as stated in the next lemma.

Lemma 6. *If $(\bar{a}, \bar{u}, \bar{j})$ is an appropriate triple then $\{|\Psi_g^{\bar{a}, \bar{u}, \bar{j}}\rangle : g \in G\}$ is hiding for HG' in G.*

Proof. To see this, first observe that HG' is a normal subgroup of G. If g_1 and g_2 are in different cosets of HG' in G then for every $j \in \mathbb{Z}_p^*$, the elements $\phi_j(g_1)$ and $\phi_j(g_2)$ are in different cosets of HG' in G since ϕ_j is an automorphism of G. Also, for every $a \in G$ and for every $u \in \mathbb{Z}_p$ we have $\mathsf{supp}(|aHG'_u\rangle) = \mathsf{supp}(|aHG'\rangle)$, and therefore $\mathsf{supp}(|aHG'_u \cdot \phi_j(b)\rangle)$ and $\mathsf{supp}(|aHG'_u \cdot \phi_j(b')\rangle)$ are included in different cosets and are disjoint. Thus for every $\bar{a} \in G^4, \bar{u} \in \mathbb{Z}_p^4$ and $\bar{j} \in (\mathbb{Z}_p^*)^4$, the states $|\Psi_{g_1}^{\bar{a}, \bar{u}, \bar{j}}\rangle$ and $|\Psi_{g_2}^{\bar{a}, \bar{u}, \bar{j}}\rangle$ are orthogonal.

If g_1 and g_2 are in the same coset of HG' then $g_1 = gg_2$ for some $g \in HG'$, and $\phi_{j_i}(g_1) = \phi_{j_i}(g)\phi_{j_i}(g_2)$. Thus $|\Psi_{g_1}^{\bar{a}, \bar{u}, \bar{j}}\rangle = |\Psi_{gg_2}^{\bar{a}, \bar{u}, \bar{j}}\rangle = |\Psi_{g_2}^{\bar{a}, \bar{u}, \bar{j}}\rangle$. $\qquad\square$

Let us now address the question of existence of appropriate triples and efficient ways to generate them. Let $(\bar{a}, \bar{u}, \bar{j})$ be an arbitrary element of $G^4 \times \mathbb{Z}_p^4 \times (\mathbb{Z}_p^*)^4$, and let g be an element of HG'. Then $g = hz^t$ for some $h \in H$ and $t \in \mathbb{Z}_p$, and $\phi_{j_i}(g) = \phi_{j_i}(h)\phi_{j_i}(z^t)$ for $i = 1, \ldots, 4$. By Lemma 5 there exists ℓ such that $|a_i HG'_{u_i} \cdot \phi_j(h)\rangle = \omega^{u_i(j_i - j_i^2)\ell}|a_i HG'_{u_i}\rangle$ and $|a_i HG'_{u_i} \cdot \phi_j(z^t)\rangle = \omega^{u_i j_i^2 t}|a_i HG'_{u_i}\rangle$, and therefore

$$|\Psi_g^{\bar{a}, \bar{u}, \bar{j}}\rangle = \omega^{\sum_{i=1}^4 (u_i(j_i - j_i^2)\ell + u_i j_i^2 t)}|a_1 HG'_{u_1}, a_2 HG'_{u_2}, a_3 HG'_{u_3}, a_4 HG'_{u_4}\rangle.$$

We say that $\bar{u} \in \mathbb{Z}_p^4$ is *good* if the following system of quadratic equations has a nonzero solution:

$$\begin{cases} \sum_{i=1}^4 u_i(j_i - j_i^2) = 0 \\ \sum_{i=1}^4 u_i j_i^2 = 0, \end{cases} \tag{1}$$

and we call a solution $\bar{j}$ a *witness* of u being good. It should be clear that for every $\bar{u}$, if $\bar{u}$ is good and $\bar{j}$ witnesses that then $(\bar{a}, \bar{u}, \bar{j})$ is an appropriate triple.

The next lemma states that a random $\bar{u}$ is good with constant probability, and that in this case one can find efficiently $\bar{j}$ witnessing that.

Lemma 7. *For every $\bar{a} \in G^4$, we have*

$$\Pr \bar{u} \in \mathbb{Z}_p^4 \bar{u} \text{ is good} \geq (p - 9)/2p.$$

Moreover, when $\bar{u}$ is good a witness $\bar{j}$ can be found efficiently.

Proof. Let us simplify system (1) to the equivalent system

$$\begin{cases} \sum_{i=1}^4 u_i j_i^2 = 0 \\ \sum_{i=1}^4 u_i j_i = 0. \end{cases} \tag{2}$$

To solve (2), we take $j_3 = 1$ and $j_4 = -1$, and we set $v = u_3 + u_4$ and $w = u_3 - u_4$. We will show that for random $(u_1, u_2, v, w) \in \mathbb{Z}_p^4$, the reduced system (3) has a solution $(j_1, j_2) \in (\mathbb{Z}_p^*)^2$ with probability at least $(p - 9)/2p$, and that the solution is easy to find:

$$\begin{cases} u_1 j_1^2 + u_2 j_2^2 = -v \\ u_1 j_1 + u_2 j_2 = -w. \end{cases} \tag{3}$$

With probability at least $1 - 3p$ we have $u_1 \neq 0$, $u_2 \neq 0$, $u_1 + u_2 \neq 0$. In that case we can substitute $j_2 = -\frac{w + u_1 j_1}{u_2}$ in the first equation and get in j_1 the quadratic equation $(u_1 u_2 + u_1^2) j_1^2 + 2 u_1 w j_1 + (w^2 + v u_2) = 0$. It is a non degenerate quadratic equation whose discriminant $D = -4 u_1 u_2 (w^2 + (u_2 + u_1) v)$ is uniformly distributed in $\mathbb{Z}_p$ since it is linear in v. Therefore D is a quadratic residue with probability $(p - 1)/2p$, and we can efficiently compute a square root of D modulo p (see, for example, subsection 13.3.1 of [20]). We also have to ensure that $j_2 \neq 0$. If j_2 is zero, then $w^2 = -v u_1$, which happens with probability $1/p$. Therefore the probability of finding a solution $(j_1, j_2) \in (\mathbb{Z}_p^*)^2$ is at least $(p - 1)/2p - 4/p$. $\square$

Theorem 3. *Let G be an extraspecial p-group of exponent p, where p grows with the input size, and let us given an oracle f which hides the subgroup H of G. Then there is an efficient quantum procedure which hides HG' in G.*

Proof. We describe the efficient hiding procedure. It computes, for some $\bar{a} \in G^4$, the superposition

$$\frac{1}{p^2} \bigotimes_{i=1}^4 \sum_{u_i \in \mathbb{Z}_p} |u_i\rangle |a_i H G'_{u_i}\rangle,$$

which by Lemma 4 can be done efficiently, and then it measures the registers for the u_i. This is repeated until a good $\bar{u} \in \mathbb{Z}_p^4$ is measured. By Lemma 7, this requires a constant expected number of iterations. Also, when a good $\bar{u}$ is measured, it finds efficiently a solution $\bar{j} \in (\mathbb{Z}_p^*)^4$ for system (1). Such a triple $(\bar{a}, \bar{u}, \bar{j})$ is appropriate, and therefore by Lemma 6 $\{|\Psi_g^{\bar{a},\bar{u},\bar{j}}\rangle : g \in G\}$ is hiding for HG' in G. Using the additional input $|g\rangle$, the procedure finally computes $|\Psi_g^{\bar{a},\bar{u},\bar{j}}\rangle$.   □

The proof of Theorem 2 in that case follows from Theorem 1 and Theorem 3.

4.3 Groups of Exponent p^2 When p Is Large

Here we deal with the group $G = A_p \mathbf{Y}(\mathbf{Y}_{i=1}^{k-1} H_p)$, where we start with a function f hiding some subgroup H. As in Lemma 1, we will distinguish the cases when $G' \subseteq H$ and when $G' \cap H = \{e\}$. The first case is already taken care of by Corollary 1.

If $G' \cap H = \{e\}$ then H contains only elements whose order is at most p. Indeed an element of order p^2 cannot be in H since the pth power of such an element is in G'. Therefore H is a subgroup of $K = \langle y_1, x_2, y_2, \ldots, x_k, y_k, z \rangle$, where x_1 is the unique generator of order p^2 of G. The subgroup K is also (isomorphic to) a subgroup of $\mathbf{Y}_{i=1}^k H_p$. We claim that we can extend the restriction of f to K into a function F defined on the whole group $\mathbf{Y}_{i=1}^k H_p$ that also hides H. Such an extension can be defined for example as $F(x_1^{i_1} y_1^{j_1} \ldots x_k^{i_k} y_k^{j_k} z^\ell) = (i_1, f(y_1^{j_1} \ldots x_k^{i_k} y_k^{j_k} z^\ell))$, and it is easy to see that it is indeed a hiding function. Therefore the problem is reduced to the HSP in extraspecial groups of exponent p.

5 Concluding Remarks

The main technical contribution of the present paper is a quantum procedure which hides HG' in an extrapsecial p-group G where p is a large prime. We remark that it is possible to present the proof of its correctness in terms of irreducible representations of G. However, the present approach is shorter and it does not make use of concepts of noncommutative representation theory. Finally, our method can in turn be extended to finding hidden subgroups efficiently in arbitrary finite two-step nilpotent groups, that is groups G satisfying $G' \le Z(G)$. This extension will be the subject of a subsequent paper.

Acknowledgment. The authors are grateful to Péter Pál Pálfy for his useful remarks and suggestions.

References

1. M. Aschbacher. *Finite Group Theory*. Cambridge University Press, 2000.
2. D. Bacon, A. Childs, and W. van Dam. From optimal measurement to efficient quantum algorithms for the hidden subgroup problem over semidirect product groups. In *Proc. 46th IEEE FOCS*, pages 469–478, 2005.

3. A. Calderbank, E. Rains, P. Shor and N. Sloane. Quantum error correction and orthogonal geometry. *Phys. Rev. Lett.*, 78:405–408, 1997.
4. A. Calderbank, E. Rains, P. Shor and N. Sloane. Quantum error correction via codes over GF(4). *IEEE Transactions on Information Theory*, 44(4):1369–1387, 1998.
5. K. Friedl, G. Ivanyos, F. Magniez , M. Santha and P. Sen. Hidden translation and orbit coset in quantum computing. In *Proc. 35th ACM STOC*, pages 1–9, 2003.
6. D. Gottesman. *Stabilizer Codes and Quantum Error Correction*. PhD Thesis, Caltech, 1997.
7. M. Grigni, L. Schulman, M. Vazirani, and U. Vazirani. Quantum mechanical algorithms for the nonabelian Hidden Subgroup Problem. In *Proc. 33rd ACM STOC*, pages 68–74, 2001.
8. S. Hallgren, A. Russell, and A. Ta-Shma. Normal subgroup reconstruction and quantum computation using group representations. *SIAM J. Comp.*, 32(4):916–934, 2003.
9. B. Huppert. *Endliche Gruppen*. Vol. 1, Springer Verlag, 1983.
10. G. Ivanyos, F. Magniez, and M. Santha. Efficient quantum algorithms for some instances of the non-Abelian hidden subgroup problem. *Int. J. of Foundations of Computer Science*, 14(5):723–739, 2003.
11. A. Kitaev. Quantum measurements and the Abelian Stabilizer Problem. Technical report, Quantum Physics e-Print archive, 1995. http://xxx.lanl.gov/abs/quant-ph/9511026.
12. A. Klappenecker, P. K. Sarvepalli. Clifford Code Constructions of Operator Quantum Error Correcting Codes Technical report, Quantum Physics e-Print archive, 2006. http://xxx.lanl.gov/abs/quant-ph/0604161.
13. M. Nielson and I. Chuang. *Quantum Computation and Quantum Information*. Cambridge University Press, 2000.
14. C. Moore, D. Rockmore, A. Russell, and L. Schulman. The power of basis selection in Fourier sampling: Hidden subgroup problems in affine groups. In *Proc. 15th ACM-SIAM SODA*, pages 1106–1115, 2004.
15. M. Mosca. *Quantum Computer Algorithms*. PhD Thesis, University of Oxford, 1999.
16. M. Püschel, M. Rötteler, and T. Beth. Fast quantum Fourier transforms for a class of non-Abelian groups. In *Proc. 13th AAECC*, volume 1719, pages 148–159. LNCS, 1999.
17. J. Radhakrishnan, M. Rötteler and P. Sen. On the power of random bases in Fourier sampling: hidden subgroup problem in the Heisenberg group. In *Proc. 32nd ICALP*, LNCS vol. 3580, pages 1399–1411, 2005.
18. M. Rötteler and T. Beth. Polynomial-time solution to the Hidden Subgroup Problem for a class of non-abelian groups. Technical report, Quantum Physics e-Print archive, 1998. http://xxx.lanl.gov/abs/quant-ph/9812070.
19. P. Shor. Algorithms for quantum computation: Discrete logarithm and factoring. *SIAM J. Comp.*, 26(5):1484–1509, 1997.
20. V. Shoup. *A Computational Introduction to Number Theory and Algebra*. Cambridge University Press, 2005.
21. D. Simon. On the power of quantum computation. *SIAM J. Comp.*, 26(5):1474–1483, 1997.

Weak Fourier-Schur Sampling, the Hidden Subgroup Problem, and the Quantum Collision Problem

Andrew M. Childs[1], Aram W. Harrow[2], and Paweł Wocjan[3]

[1] Institute for Quantum Information, California Institute of Technology,
Pasadena, CA 91125, USA
amchilds@caltech.edu
[2] Department of Computer Science, University of Bristol,
Bristol, BS8 1UB, UK
a.harrow@bris.ac.uk
[3] School of Electrical Engineering and Computer Science,
University of Central Florida, Orlando, FL 32816, USA
wocjan@cs.ucf.edu

Abstract. Schur duality decomposes many copies of a quantum state into subspaces labeled by partitions, a decomposition with applications throughout quantum information theory. Here we consider applying Schur duality to the problem of distinguishing coset states in the standard approach to the hidden subgroup problem. We observe that simply measuring the partition (a procedure we call *weak Schur sampling*) provides very little information about the hidden subgroup. Furthermore, we show that under quite general assumptions, even a combination of weak Fourier sampling and weak Schur sampling fails to identify the hidden subgroup. We also prove tight bounds on how many coset states are required to solve the hidden subgroup problem by weak Schur sampling, and we relate this question to a quantum version of the collision problem.

1 Introduction

The hidden subgroup problem (HSP) is a central challenge for quantum computation. On the one hand, many of the known fast quantum algorithms are based on the efficient solution of the abelian HSP [21, 22, 38, 41]. On the other hand, the *nonabelian* HSP has potential applications: in particular, the graph isomorphism problem can be reduced to the HSP in the symmetric group [8, 14], and the shortest lattice vector problem can be reduced to a variant of the HSP in the dihedral group [36]. Unfortunately, no efficient algorithms are known for these two instances of the nonabelian HSP. However, some partial progress has been made: there is a subexponential time algorithm for the dihedral HSP [31, 37], and it is known how to solve the HSP efficiently for a variety of other nonabelian groups [2, 16, 17, 19, 25, 28, 33].

In the HSP for a group G, we have black-box access to a function $f : G \to S$, where S is some finite set. We say that f hides a subgroup $H \leq G$ provided

W. Thomas and P. Weil (Eds.): STACS 2007, LNCS 4393, pp. 598–609, 2007.

$f(g) = f(g')$ iff $g^{-1}g' \in H$. The goal is to determine H (say, in terms of a generating set) as quickly as possible. In particular, we say that an algorithm for the HSP in G is efficient if it runs in time poly$(\log |G|)$.

Nearly all quantum algorithms for the HSP use the so-called *standard method*, in which we query f on a uniform superposition of group elements and then discard the function value, giving a *coset state* $|gH\rangle := |H|^{-1/2} \sum_{h \in H} |gh\rangle$ for some unknown, uniformly random $g \in G$. This state is described by the density matrix

$$\rho_H := \frac{1}{|G|} \sum_{g \in G} |gH\rangle\langle gH| = \frac{1}{|G|} \sum_{h \in H} R(h) \tag{1}$$

(called a *hidden subgroup state*), where R is the *right regular representation* of G, satisfying $R(g)|g'\rangle = |g'g^{-1}\rangle$ for all $g, g' \in G$. Now the HSP is reduced to the problem of distinguishing the states ρ_H for the possible $H \leq G$.

The symmetry of ρ_H can be exploited using Fourier analysis. In particular, the group algebra $\mathbb{C}G$ decomposes under the commuting left and right multiplication actions of G as

$$\mathbb{C}G \overset{G \times G}{\cong} \bigoplus_{\sigma \in \hat{G}} V_\sigma \otimes V_\sigma^* \tag{2}$$

where $\hat{G}$ denotes a complete set of irreducible representations (or *irreps*) of G, and V_σ and V_σ^* are the (row and column, respectively) subspaces acted on by $\sigma \in \hat{G}$. The unitary transformation that relates the standard basis for $\mathbb{C}G$ and the basis for the spaces $V_\sigma \otimes V_\sigma^*$ is the Fourier transform, which can be carried out efficiently for most groups of interest [7, 12, 23, 32].

Since ρ_H is invariant under the left multiplication action of G, the decomposition (2) shows that it is block diagonal in the Fourier basis, with blocks labeled by the irreps $\sigma \in \hat{G}$. For each σ, there is a dim $V_\sigma \times$ dim V_σ block that appears dim V_σ times (or in other words, the state is maximally mixed in the row space). Thus, without loss of information, we can measure the irrep name σ and discard the information about which σ-isotypic block occurred.

The process of measuring the irrep name σ is referred to as *weak Fourier sampling*. For most nonabelian groups (including the symmetric group [19, 25] and the dihedral group), weak Fourier sampling alone produces insufficient information to identify the hidden subgroup H. To obtain further information about H, we must perform a refined measurement inside the resulting subspace. This is referred to as *strong Fourier sampling*, and there are many possible ways to do it, especially if G has large irreps.

Of course, with either weak or strong Fourier sampling, a single hidden subgroup state is not sufficient to determine H: we must repeat the sampling procedure to obtain statistics. However, repeating strong Fourier sampling a polynomial number of times is not sufficient for some groups (such as the symmetric group), even if measurements can be chosen adaptively and unlimited classical processing is allowed [34]. To solve the HSP in general, we must perform a joint measurement on $k = \text{poly}(\log |G|)$ copies of $\rho_H^{\otimes k}$. In fact, there are groups (again including the symmetric group) for which the measurement must be entangled across $\Omega(\log|G|)$ copies [24]. Thus the difficulty of the general HSP may be attributed at least in part to that fact that highly entangled measurements are required. While $O(\log|G|)$ copies are always information-theoretically sufficient [15] (so that, in particular, the query complexity of the HSP is polynomial), there are many groups for which it is not known how to efficiently extract the identity of the hidden subgroup.

Although previous work on the HSP has focused almost exclusively on Fourier sampling, there is another measurement that can also be performed without loss of information. The idea is to exploit the symmetry of $\rho_H^{\otimes k}$ under permutations of the k registers. Thus, we should consider the decomposition of $(\mathbb{C}G)^{\otimes k}$ afforded by *Schur duality* [18], which decomposes k copies of a d-dimensional space as

$$(\mathbb{C}^d)^{\otimes k} \overset{\mathcal{S}_k \times \mathcal{U}_d}{\cong} \bigoplus_{\lambda \vdash k} \mathcal{P}_\lambda \otimes \mathcal{Q}_\lambda^d \tag{3}$$

where the symmetric group $\mathcal{S}_k$ acts to permute the k registers and the unitary group $\mathcal{U}_d$ acts identically on each register. The subspaces $\mathcal{P}_\lambda$ and $\mathcal{Q}_\lambda^d$ correspond to irreps of $\mathcal{S}_k$ and $\mathcal{U}_d$, respectively. They are labeled by partitions λ of k (denoted $\lambda \vdash k$), i.e., $\lambda = (\lambda_1, \lambda_2, \ldots)$ where $\lambda_1 \geq \lambda_2 \geq \ldots$ and $\sum_j \lambda_j = k$. (We can restrict our attention to partitions with at most d parts, since $\dim \mathcal{Q}_\lambda^d = 0$ if $\lambda_{d+1} > 0$.)

Since $\rho_H^{\otimes k}$ is invariant under the action of $\mathcal{S}_k$, the decomposition (3) shows that it is block diagonal in the Schur basis with blocks labeled by $\lambda \vdash k$. For each λ, there is a $\dim \mathcal{Q}_\lambda^{|G|} \times \dim \mathcal{Q}_\lambda^{|G|}$ block that appears $\dim \mathcal{P}_\lambda$ times (or in other words, the state is maximally mixed in the permutation space). Thus, no information is lost if we measure the partition λ and discard the permutation register. By analogy to weak Fourier sampling, we refer to the process of measuring λ as *weak Schur sampling*. This is a natural measurement to consider not only because it can be performed without loss of information, but also because it is a joint measurement of all k registers, and we know that some measurement of this kind is required to solve the general HSP. Unfortunately, we will see in Section 2 (and see also Corollary 4 below) that weak Schur sampling with $k = \text{poly}(\log|G|)$ provides insufficient information to solve the HSP unless the hidden subgroup is very large (in which case the problem is easy, even for a classical computer).

In fact, since both weak Fourier sampling and weak Schur sampling can be performed without loss of information, it is possible to perform both measurements simultaneously (with the caveat that we must discard the irrelevant information about the order in which the irreps of G appear). Even though the statistics of the irrep name σ and the partition λ do not provide enough information to identify the hidden subgroup, this does not preclude the possibility that their joint distribution is more informative. However, we will see in Section 3 that unless we are likely to see the same representation more than once under weak Fourier sampling (which is typically not the case), the Fourier and Schur distributions are nearly uncorrelated. Formally, we have

Theorem 1 (Failure of weak Fourier-Schur sampling). *The probability that weak Fourier-Schur sampling (defined in Section 3) applied to $\rho_H^{\otimes k}$ (defined*

in (1)) provides a result that depends on $|H|$ is at most $k^2 d_{\max}^2 |H|/|G|$, where $d_{\max}$ is the largest dimension of an irrep of G.

This implies that k needs to be large for most cases of interest, including the dihedral and symmetric groups.

Corollary 2 (Weak Fourier-Schur sampling on $\mathcal{D}_N$ and $\mathcal{S}_n$). *(a) Weak Fourier-Schur sampling on the dihedral group $\mathcal{D}_N$ cannot distinguish the trivial subgroup from a hidden reflection with constant advantage (i.e., success probability $\frac{1}{2} + \Omega(1)$) unless $k = \Omega(\sqrt{N})$. (b) Weak Fourier-Schur sampling on the symmetric group $\mathcal{S}_n$ or on the wreath product $\mathcal{S}_n \wr \mathbb{Z}_2$ cannot distinguish the trivial subgroup from an order 2 subgroup with constant advantage unless $k = \exp(\Omega(\sqrt{n}))$.*

The proof that weak Schur sampling fails is based on the simple observation that distinguishing the trivial subgroup from a subgroup of order $|H|$ in this way requires us to distinguish 1-to-1 from $|H|$-to-1 functions on G, i.e., to solve the $|H|$-collision problem for a list of size $|G|$. Since there is an $\Omega(\sqrt[3]{|G|/|H|})$ quantum lower bound for this problem [1], poly$(\log |G|)$ registers are insufficient. In fact, the problem resulting from the HSP is potentially harder, since the basis in which the collisions occur is inaccessible to the Schur measurement. This naturally leads to the notion of a *quantum* collision problem, and raises the question of how quickly it can be solved on a quantum computer, which we discuss in Section 4.

We first consider a sampling version of the quantum r-collision problem. Using results on the asymptotics of the Plancherel measure on the symmetric group, we prove that $k = \Theta(d/r)$ registers are necessary and sufficient to solve this problem. In particular, we have

Theorem 3 (Quantum collision sampling problem). *Given $\rho^{\otimes k}$, distinguishing between [case A] $\rho = I/d$ and [case B] $\rho^2 = \rho/\frac{d}{r}$ (i.e., ρ is proportional to a projector of rank d/r) is possible with success probability $1 - \exp(-\Theta(kr/d))/2$. In particular, constant advantage is possible iff $k = \Omega(d/r)$.*

In addition to providing the first results on estimation of the spectrum of a quantum state in the regime where $k \ll d^2$, this gives tight estimates of the effectiveness of weak Schur sampling, which we see requires an exponentially large (in $\log |G|$) number of copies to be successful.

Corollary 4 (Failure of weak Schur sampling). *Applying weak Schur sampling to $\rho_H^{\otimes k}$ (where ρ_H is defined in (1)), one can distinguish the case $|H| \geq r$ from the case $H = \{1\}$ with constant advantage iff $k = \Omega(|G|/r)$.*

The connection between Theorem 3 and Corollary 4 is explained in Section 2.

In Section 4 we also introduce a black box version of the quantum collision problem. We show that it can be solved using $O(\sqrt[3]{d/r} \log d/r)$ queries, nearly matching the query lower bound from the classical problem.

2 Weak Schur Sampling

We begin by considering only the permutation symmetry of $\rho_H^{\otimes k}$, without taking into account symmetry resulting from the group G. In other words, we consider only the Schur decomposition (3), and we perform *weak Schur sampling*, i.e., a measurement of the partition λ.

The projector onto the subspace labeled by a particular $\lambda \vdash k$ is

$$\Pi_\lambda := \frac{\dim \mathcal{P}_\lambda}{k!} \sum_{\pi \in \mathcal{S}_k} \chi_\lambda(\pi) \, P(\pi) \tag{4}$$

(see e.g. [40, Theorem 8]), where χ_λ is the character of the irrep of $\mathcal{S}_k$ labeled by λ and P is the (reducible) representation of $\mathcal{S}_k$ that acts to permute the k registers, i.e., $P(\pi)|i_1\rangle \ldots |i_k\rangle = |i_{\pi^{-1}(1)}\rangle \ldots |i_{\pi^{-1}(k)}\rangle$ for all $i_1, \ldots, i_k \in \{1, \ldots, d\}$. For any d^k-dimensional density matrix γ, the distribution under weak Schur sampling is

$$\Pr(\lambda|\gamma) = \operatorname{tr}(\Pi_\lambda \gamma). \tag{5}$$

To use weak Schur sampling in a quantum algorithm, it is important that the measurement of λ can be done efficiently. The simplest implementation of the complete Schur transform [5], which fully resolves the subspaces $\mathcal{P}_\lambda$ and $\mathcal{Q}_\lambda^d$, runs in time $\operatorname{poly}(k, d)$, and thus is inefficient when d is exponentially large, as in the HSP. It can be modified to run in time $\operatorname{poly}(k, \log d)$ either by a relabeling trick [26, footnote in Section 8.1.2] or by *generalized phase estimation* [4, 26] (which may be viewed as a generalization of the well-known swap test [6, 10]). Generalized phase estimation only allows us to measure λ, but for weak Schur sampling this is all we need. In this procedure, we prepare an ancilla register in the state $\frac{1}{\sqrt{k!}} \sum_{\pi \in \mathcal{S}_k} |\pi\rangle$, use it to perform a conditional permutation $P(\pi)$ on the input state γ, and then perform an inverse Fourier transform over $\mathcal{S}_k$ [7] on the ancilla register. Measurement of the ancilla register will then yield $\lambda \in \hat{\mathcal{S}}_k$, interpreted as a partition of k, distributed according to (5).

The distribution of λ according to weak Schur sampling is invariant under the actions of the permutation and unitary groups, since these groups act only within the subspaces $\mathcal{P}_\lambda$ and $\mathcal{Q}_\lambda^d$, respectively. In other words, for any $U \in \mathcal{U}_d$, any $\pi \in \mathcal{S}_k$, and any d^k-dimensional density matrix γ, we have $\Pr(\lambda|\gamma) = \Pr(\lambda|P(\pi)U^{\otimes k}\gamma U^{\dagger \otimes k}P(\pi)^\dagger)$. In particular, the invariance under $U^{\otimes k}$ implies that for $\gamma = \rho^{\otimes k}$, the distribution according to weak Schur sampling depends only on the spectrum of ρ.

Now it is easy to see that weak Schur sampling on $k = \operatorname{poly}(\log |G|)$ copies of ρ_H provides insufficient information to solve the HSP. The state ρ_H is proportional to a projector of rank $|G|/|H|$, since

$$\rho_H^2 = \frac{1}{|G|^2} \sum_{h,h' \in H} R(hh') = \frac{|H|}{|G|} \rho_H. \tag{6}$$

Because the distribution of measurement outcomes $\Pr(\lambda|\rho_H^{\otimes k})$ depends only on the spectrum of ρ_H, and this spectrum depends only on $|H|$, different subgroups of the same order cannot be distinguished by weak Schur sampling. In fact, even distinguishing the trivial hidden subgroup from a hidden subgroup of order $|H| \geq 2$ (which would suffice for, e.g., graph isomorphism) requires an exponential number of hidden subgroup states.

Suppose that weak Schur sampling could distinguish between hidden subgroup states corresponding to $H = \{1\}$ and some particular H of order $|H| \geq 2$. Since the distribution of λ depends only on the spectrum, this would mean that we could distinguish k copies of the maximally mixed state $I_{|G|}/|G|$, where I_d is the $d \times d$ identity matrix, from k copies of the state $J_{|G|/|H|}/(|G|/|H|)$, where $J_{d'}$ is a projector onto an arbitrary subspace of dimension d'. This in turn would imply that we could distinguish 1-to-1 functions from $|H|$-to-1 functions using k queries of the function. Then the quantum lower bound for the $|H|$-collision problem [1] shows that $k = \Omega(\sqrt[3]{|G|/|H|})$ copies are required.

Of course, this does not mean that $O(\sqrt[3]{|G|/|H|})$ copies are sufficient. In fact, it turns out that a linear number of copies is both necessary and sufficient, as we will show by a more careful analysis in Section 4. There we will sketch the proof of Theorem 3, which by the arguments of this section implies Corollary 4.

3   Weak Fourier-Schur Sampling

In the previous section, we showed that weak Schur sampling provides insufficient information to efficiently solve the HSP. However, even though weak Fourier sampling typically also does not provide enough information, it is conceivable that the joint distribution of the two measurements could be substantially more informative. In this section, we will see that this is not the case: provided weak Fourier sampling fails, so does weak Fourier-Schur sampling.

Since neither measurement constitutes a loss of information, it is in principle possible to perform both weak Fourier sampling and weak Schur sampling simultaneously. If we perform weak Fourier sampling in the usual way, measuring the irrep label for each register, then we will typically obtain a state that is no longer permutation invariant. However, since the irrep labels are identically distributed for each register, the order in which the irreps appear carries no information. Only the *type* of the irreps, i.e., the number of times each irrep appears, is relevant. Thus, it suffices to perform what we might call *weak Fourier type sampling*, in which we only measure the irrep type. Equivalently, we could perform complete weak Fourier sampling and then either randomly permute the k registers, or perform weak Schur sampling and discard the $\mathcal{P}_\lambda$ register.

We begin by performing weak Fourier sampling. The hidden subgroup state ρ_H defined in (1) has the following block structure in the Fourier basis:

$$\rho_H \cong \frac{1}{|G|} \bigoplus_{\sigma \in \hat{G}} I_{\dim \mathcal{V}_\sigma} \otimes \sum_{h \in H} \sigma(h)^* =: \sum_{\sigma \in \hat{G}} \Pr(\sigma) \frac{I_{\dim \mathcal{V}_\sigma}}{\dim \mathcal{V}_\sigma} \otimes \rho_{H,\sigma}. \tag{7}$$

Here the probability of observing the irrep σ under weak Fourier sampling is $\Pr(\sigma) = (\dim \mathcal{V}_\sigma/|G|) \sum_{h \in H} \chi_\sigma(h)^*$ and the state conditioned on this observation is $\rho_{H,\sigma} = \left(\sum_{h \in H} \chi_\sigma(h) \right)^{-1} \sum_{h \in H} |\sigma\rangle\langle\sigma| \otimes \sigma(h)^*$

Repeating weak Fourier sampling k times, we get $\rho_{H,\underline{\sigma}} = \rho_{H,\sigma_1} \otimes \cdots \otimes \rho_{H,\sigma_k}$, where $\underline{\sigma} := (\sigma_1, \sigma_2, \ldots, \sigma_k) \in \hat{G}^k$ may be viewed either as the actual outcome of the k instances of weak Fourier sampling, or merely as a representative of the irrep type, as discussed above. Given this state, the conditional probability of observing the partition λ is

$$\Pr(\lambda|\underline{\sigma}) = \operatorname{tr}(\Pi_\lambda \, \rho_{H,\underline{\sigma}}) = \frac{\dim \mathcal{P}_\lambda}{k!} \sum_{\pi \in \mathcal{S}_k} \chi_\lambda(\pi) \operatorname{tr}[P(\pi) \rho_{H,\underline{\sigma}}]. \tag{8}$$

Note that $\operatorname{tr}[P(\pi) \rho_{H,\underline{\sigma}}] = 0$ if $\pi(\underline{\sigma}) \neq \underline{\sigma}$, where $\pi(\underline{\sigma}) = (\sigma_{\pi^{-1}(1)}, \ldots, \sigma_{\pi^{-1}(k)})$.

Proof (Theorem 1). Assume that $\underline{\sigma}$ is multiplicity-free, i.e., that all the σ_i's are different. In this case the traces are zero for all $\pi \neq 1$ (the identity of $\mathcal{S}_k$). Then $\Pr(\lambda|\underline{\sigma}) = \frac{\dim \mathcal{P}_\lambda}{k!} \chi_\lambda(1) \operatorname{tr} \rho_{H,\underline{\sigma}} = \frac{(\dim \mathcal{P}_\lambda)^2}{k!}$, which is nothing but the Plancherel distribution over $\hat{\mathcal{S}}_k$, and which in particular is independent of the hidden subgroup H. This shows that we cannot extract any information about H provided that we have obtained a multiplicity-free $\underline{\sigma}$.

Finally, we can use $|\chi_\sigma(h)| \leq \dim \mathcal{V}_\sigma$ to show that the probability of any σ is $\leq d_{\max}^2 |H|/|G|$, and then use a union bound to prove that $\underline{\sigma}$ is multiplicity-free with probability $\geq 1 - \binom{k}{2} d_{\max}^2 |H|/|G|$.

In [11] two of us considered an alternative approach to graph isomorphism based on the nonabelian hidden shift problem. It can be shown that weak Fourier-Schur sampling fails for similar reasons when applied to hidden shift states instead of hidden subgroup states.

4   The Quantum Collision Problem

In Section 2, we saw that weak Schur sampling cannot efficiently solve the HSP since this would require solving the collision problem. In fact, the problem faced by weak Schur sampling is considerably harder, since no information is available about the basis in which collisions occur. This motivates quantum generalizations of the usual (i.e., classical) collision problem, which we study in this section.

Let us briefly review the classical problem. The classical r-collision problem is the problem of determining whether a black box function with d inputs (where r divides d) is 1-to-1 or r-to-1. This problem has classical (randomized) query complexity $\Theta(\sqrt{d/r})$—as evidenced by the well-known birthday problem—and quantum query complexity $\Theta(\sqrt[3]{d/r})$ [1,9]. The classical algorithm is quite simple: after querying the function on $O(\sqrt{d/r})$ random inputs, there is a reasonable probability of seeing a collision, provided one exists. The quantum algorithm is slightly more subtle, making use of Grover's algorithm for unstructured search [20]. In particular, while the classical algorithm queries the black box nonadaptively, it is essential for the quantum algorithm to make adaptive queries.

Here we first consider a sampling version of the quantum collision problem, which is closely connected to the weak Schur sampling approach to the HSP, and then study a full-fledged black box version of the problem.

The quantum collision sampling problem. The *quantum r-collision sampling problem* is the problem of deciding whether one has k copies of the d-dimensional maximally mixed state or of a state that is maximally mixed on an unknown subspace of dimension d/r. This is exactly the problem faced by the weak Schur sampling approach to the HSP, so our results on the quantum collision sampling problem give tight bounds on the effectiveness of weak Schur sampling. It turns out that $k = \Theta(d/r)$ copies are necessary and sufficient to distinguish these two cases with constant advantage, as stated by Theorem 3.

Proof sketch (Theorem 3). Weak Schur sampling is the optimal strategy to distinguish states ρ with [case A] $\rho = I/d$ or [case B] $\rho^2 = \rho/\frac{d}{r}$. We call the resulting distribution of $\lambda \vdash k$ arising in case A the *Schur distribution*, Schur(k,d), with

$$\Pr(\lambda) = \frac{\dim \mathcal{P}_\lambda \dim \mathcal{Q}_\lambda^d}{d^k} = \frac{(\dim \mathcal{P}_\lambda)^2}{k!} \prod_{(i,j)\in\lambda} \left(1 + \frac{j-i}{d}\right). \tag{9}$$

The second equality follows from Stanley's formula for $\dim \mathcal{Q}_\lambda^d$ [42], interpreting λ as a Young diagram, where $(i,j) \in \lambda$ iff $1 \le j \le \lambda_i$. The outcomes in case B are also Schur-distributed (by a simple representation-theoretic argument), but here the distribution is Schur$(k, d/r)$.

Our first goal is to show that the distributions Schur(k,d) and Schur$(k, d/r)$ are close when $k \ll d/r$. We do this by showing that when $k \ll d$, Schur(k,d) is close to the *Plancherel distribution* of $\lambda \vdash k$, Planch(k), for which

$$\Pr(\lambda) = \frac{(\dim \mathcal{P}_\lambda)^2}{k!}. \tag{10}$$

Using (9) and (10), the ℓ_1 distance $\Delta_{k,d} := \| \text{Schur}(k,d) - \text{Planch}(k)\|_1$ is

$$\Delta_{k,d} = \mathop{\mathbf{E}}_{\lambda\vdash k} \left| \prod_{(i,j)\in\lambda} \left(1 + \frac{j-i}{d}\right) - 1 \right| \tag{11}$$

where the expectation is over Planch(k). Using Cauchy-Schwartz and the inequality $1 + x \le e^x$, we can upper bound (11) by

$$\Delta_{k,d}^2 \le \mathop{\mathbf{E}}_{\lambda\vdash k} \exp\left(2 \sum_{(i,j)\in\lambda} \frac{j-i}{d}\right) = \sum_{m=1}^{\infty} \frac{2^m}{m!\, d^m} \mathop{\mathbf{E}}_{\lambda\vdash k} v_1(\lambda)^m, \tag{12}$$

where $v_1(\lambda) := \sum_{(i,j)\in\lambda}(j-i)$. Finally, we use calculations of the moments of v_1 obtained by Kerov in the course of describing the asymptotically Gaussian fluctuations about the limiting shape of the typical diagram under the Plancherel distribution [29]. This establishes $\Delta_{k,d} \le \sqrt{2}(k/d)$, and it follows from the triangle inequality that Schur(k,d) and Schur$(k, d/r)$ are close when $k \ll d/r$.

Conversely, we would like to show that if $k \gg d/r$, then Schur(k,d) is far from Schur$(k, d/r)$. We do this by first proving a lower bound on $\Delta_{k,d}$ (using similar techniques as in the upper bound on $\Delta_{k,d}$, as well as a one-sided Chebyshev inequality showing $v_1(\lambda)^2 \ge \Omega(k^2)$ with constant probability). Then we combine this with the upper bound on $\Delta_{k,d}$ and use a monotonicity argument $(\|\mathrm{Schur}(k,d_1) - \mathrm{Schur}(k,d_2)\|_1 \geq \|\mathrm{Schur}(k,rd_1) - \mathrm{Schur}(k,rd_2)\|_1)$ to separate the Schur distributions. This completes the proof sketch.

To put Theorem 3 in context, we can compare it to results on spectrum estimation. When $k \to \infty$ with d fixed, applying the measurement $\{\Pi_\lambda\}_{\lambda \vdash k}$ to $\rho^{\otimes k}$ and outputting $\bar{\lambda} := \lambda/k$ has long been known to be a valid estimator of the spectrum of ρ [30]. Indeed, if $r_1 \geq \ldots \geq r_d$ are the eigenvalues of ρ, then $\mathrm{tr}\, \Pi_\lambda \rho^{\otimes k} \leq (k+1)^{d(d-1)/2} \exp\left(-kD(\bar{\lambda}\|r)\right)$, where $D(p\|q) := \sum_i p_i \log(p_i/q_i)$ is the (classical) relative entropy [13,27]. This inequality is usually only interesting when $k = \Omega(d^2)$, so our Theorem 3 can be viewed as the first positive result for spectrum estimation in the regime where $k = o(d^2)$.

A black box for the quantum collision problem. A complete definition of the quantum collision problem requires us to specify a unitary black box that hides the function, and that allows us to make adaptive queries. We now propose one such definition, and show that the resulting quantum r-collision problem can be solved in $O(\sqrt[3]{d/r} \log d/r)$ queries, nearly matching the $\Omega(\sqrt[3]{d/r})$ lower bound from the classical collision problem.

Consider a quantum oracle that implements the isometry $|i\rangle \mapsto |i\rangle|\psi_{f(i)}\rangle$, where $\mathcal{B} := \{|\psi_1\rangle, \ldots, |\psi_d\rangle\}$ is an arbitrary (unknown) orthonormal basis of $\mathbb{C}^d$ and f is either a 1-to-1 function or an r-to-1 function. The goal is to determine which is the case using as few queries as possible. We assume that the isometry is extended to a unitary operator R acting on $\mathbb{C}^d \otimes \mathbb{C}^d$ by $|i\rangle|y\rangle \mapsto |i\rangle U|y \oplus f(i)\rangle$, where $U := \sum_i |\psi_i\rangle\langle i|$ is the unitary matrix effecting a transformation from the standard basis to $\mathcal{B}$. We also assume we can perform its inverse $R^\dagger$.

By considering the case where the basis $\mathcal{B}$ (or equivalently U) is known, it is clear that the quantum lower bound for the usual collision problem implies an $\Omega(\sqrt[3]{d/r})$ lower bound for the quantum collision problem as well. We present an algorithm for this problem that uses only $O(\sqrt[3]{d/r} \log d/r)$ queries. The basic idea is to adapt the quantum algorithm for the classical collision problem [9]. That algorithm is not directly applicable to the quantum problem since we cannot check equality of quantum states. However, the swap test can determine whether two states are identical or orthogonal with one-sided error of $1/2$. With $O(\log d)$ copies of each state, this error (and the resulting state disturbance) can be reduced to $1/\mathrm{poly}(d)$. We use this *amplified swap test* to prove

Theorem 5. *The query complexity of the quantum r-collision problem for a list of size d is $O(\sqrt[3]{d/r} \log d/r)$.*

Proof. We first outline the quantum algorithm of [9] for the classical collision problem. The algorithm builds a table of a random set of $\sqrt[3]{d/r}$ items and uses Grover's algorithm to search the remaining items for a collision with an entry of the table. The entries of the table are distinct with high probability. If f is r-to-1, there are $(r-1)(d/r)^{1/3}$ solutions among $< d$ items, for a total query complexity of $O(\sqrt{d/[r(d/r)^{1/3}]}) = O((d/r)^{1/3})$.

Now we adapt this algorithm to the quantum problem. Using the amplified swap test, we can effectively test equality using $m := 2 + 2\log d/r$ copies of the quantum states, increasing the query complexity only by a factor of $O(\log d/r)$. For this to work, it is important that we can reuse the states corresponding to the entries in the table, so we will need m copies of each state in the table as well. Iterating this swap test, we find that the error after ℓ Grover iterations is at most $\ell \cdot 2^{1-m/2} \leq \ell r/d$. Since the number of Grover iterations is $\ell = O((d/r)^{1/3})$, the total error is asymptotically negligible, and we obtain nearly the same performance as in the classical collision problem.

5 Discussion

We have shown that weak Fourier-Schur sampling typically provides insufficient information to solve the hidden subgroup problem. Nevertheless, it remains possible that Schur duality could be a useful tool for the HSP. Just as weak Fourier sampling refines the space into smaller subspaces in which we can perform strong Fourier sampling, even when it alone fails to solve the HSP, so we can use weak Fourier-Schur sampling to decompose the space even further. The Schur decomposition has the additional complication that the refined subspaces are no longer simply tensor products of single-copy subspaces, but this may actually be an advantage since entangled measurements are known to be necessary for some groups. Also, Schur sampling may be useful for implementing optimal measurements, which are typically entangled [2, 3].

In principle, strong Fourier-Schur sampling is guaranteed to provide enough information to solve the HSP, simply because the hidden subgroup states are always distinguishable with $k = \text{poly}(\log |G|)$ copies. However, it would be interesting to find a new efficient quantum algorithm for some HSP based on strong Fourier-Schur sampling. Perhaps a first step in this direction would be to analyze the performance of measurement in a random basis, as has been studied extensively in the case of weak Fourier sampling [19, 33, 35, 39].

Moving away from our original motivation of the HSP, the quantum collision problem may be of independent interest. As discussed in Section 4, our results on the quantum collision sampling problem can be viewed as an exploration of spectrum estimation with $k = o(d^2)$ copies, but much remains unknown about that regime. Many open problems also remain regarding variants of the black box version of the quantum collision problem.

Acknowledgments. We thank Scott Aaronson, Andris Ambainis, Masahito Hayashi, Keiji Matsumoto, Pranab Sen, and Umesh Vazirani for helpful discussions. We also thank Patrick Hayden for organizing a Bellairs Research Institute workshop on representation theory in quantum information, at which the seeds for this work were planted. This work was supported in part by the National Science Foundation under grant PHY-456720, by the Army Research Office under grant W911NF-05-1-0294, by the European Commission under Marie Curie grants ASTQIT (FP6-022194) and QAP (IST-2005-15848), and by the U.K. Engineering and Physical Science Research Council through "QIP IRC."

References

[1] S. Aaronson and Y. Shi, *Quantum lower bounds for the collision and the element distinctness problems*, J. ACM **51** (2004), no. 4, 595–605.

[2] D. Bacon, A. M. Childs, and W. van Dam, *From optimal measurement to efficient quantum algorithms for the hidden subgroup problem over semidirect product groups*, Proc. 46th FOCS, 2005, pp. 469–478.

[3] _____, *Optimal measurements for the dihedral hidden subgroup problem*, Chicago J. Th. Comp. Sci. (2006), no. 2.

[4] D. Bacon, I. L. Chuang, and A. W. Harrow, *Efficient quantum circuits for Schur and Clebsch-Gordan transforms*, quant-ph/0407082.

[5] _____, *The quantum Schur transform: I. Efficient qudit circuits*, to appear in Proc. 18th SODA, 2007, available at quant-ph/0601001.

[6] A. Barenco, A. Berthiaume, D. Deutsch, A. Ekert, R. Jozsa, and C. Macchiavello, *Stabilisation of quantum computations by symmetrisation*, SIAM J. Comput. (1997), 1541–1557.

[7] R. Beals, *Quantum computation of Fourier transforms over symmetric groups*, Proc. 29th STOC, 1997, pp. 48–53.

[8] R. Boneh and R. Lipton, *Quantum cryptanalysis of hidden linear functions*, Proc. Advances in Cryptology, LNCS **963**, 1995, pp. 424–437.

[9] G. Brassard, P. Høyer, and A. Tapp, *Quantum cryptanalysis of hash and claw-free functions*, Proc. 3rd Latin American Symposium on Theoretical Informatics, LNCS **1380**, 1998, pp. 163–169.

[10] H. Buhrman, R. Cleve, J. Watrous, and R. de Wolf, *Quantum fingerprinting*, Phys. Rev. Lett. **87** (2001), 167902.

[11] A. M. Childs and P. Wocjan, *On the quantum hardness of solving isomorphism problems as nonabelian hidden shift problems*, quant-ph/0510185.

[12] D. Coppersmith, *An approximate Fourier transform useful in quantum factoring*, Technical Report RC 19642, IBM Research Division, Yorktown Heights, NY, 1994, quant-ph/0201067.

[13] M. Christandl and G. Mitchison, *The spectra of density operators and the Kronecker coefficients of the symmetric group*, Commun. Math. Phys. **261** (2006), no. 3, 789–797.

[14] M. Ettinger and P. Høyer, *A quantum observable for the graph isomorphism problem*, quant-ph/9901029.

[15] M. Ettinger, P. Høyer, and E. Knill, *Hidden subgroup states are almost orthogonal*, quant-ph/9901034.

[16] K. Friedl, G. Ivanyos, F. Magniez, M. Santha, and P. Sen, *Hidden translation and orbit coset in quantum computing*, Proc. 35th STOC, 2003, pp. 1–9.

[17] D. Gavinsky, *Quantum solution to the hidden subgroup problem for poly-near-Hamiltonian groups*, Quant. Inf. Comp. **4** (2004), 229–235.

[18] R. Goodman and N. R. Wallach, *Representations and Invariants of the Classical Groups*, Cambridge University Press, Cambridge, 1998.

[19] M. Grigni, L. Schulman, M. Vazirani, and U. Vazirani, *Quantum mechanical algorithms for the nonabelian hidden subgroup problem*, Combinatorica **24** (2004), 137–154.

[20] L. K. Grover, *A fast quantum mechanical algorithm for database search*, Proc. 28th STOC, 1996, pp. 212–219.

[21] S. Hallgren, *Polynomial-time quantum algorithms for Pell's equation and the principal ideal problem*, Proc. 34th STOC, 2002, pp. 653–658.

[22] ———, *Fast quantum algorithms for computing the unit group and class group of a number field*, Proc. 37th STOC, 2005, pp. 468–474.

[23] L. Hales and S. Hallgren, *An improved quantum Fourier transform algorithm and applications*, Proc. 41st FOCS, 2000, pp. 515–525.

[24] S. Hallgren, C. Moore, M. Rötteler, A. Russell, and P. Sen, *Limitations of quantum coset states for graph isomorphism*, Proc. 38th STOC, 2006, pp. 604–617.

[25] S. Hallgren, A. Russell, and A. Ta-Shma, *The hidden subgroup problem and quantum computation using group representations*, Proc. 32nd STOC, 2000, pp. 627–635.

[26] A. W. Harrow, *Applications of coherent classical communication and the Schur transform to quantum information theory*, Ph.D. thesis, MIT, 2005.

[27] M. Hayashi and K. Matsumoto, *Quantum universal variable-length source coding*, Phys. Rev. A **66** (2002), 022311.

[28] G. Ivanyos, F. Magniez, and M. Santha, *Efficient quantum algorithms for some instances of the non-abelian hidden subgroup problem*, Int. J. Found. Comp. Sci. **14** (2003), 723–739.

[29] S. Kerov, *Gaussian limit for the Plancherel measure of the symmetric group*, Comptes Rendus Acad. Sci. Paris, Sér. I **316** (1993), 303–308.

[30] M. Keyl and R. F. Werner, *Estimating the spectrum of a density operator*, Phys. Rev. A **64** (2001), 052311.

[31] G. Kuperberg, *A subexponential-time quantum algorithm for the dihedral hidden subgroup problem*, SIAM J. Comput. **35** (2005), 170–188.

[32] C. Moore, D. N. Rockmore, and A. Russell, *Generic quantum Fourier transforms*, Proc. 15th SODA, 2004, pp. 778–787.

[33] C. Moore, D. N. Rockmore, A. Russell, and L. J. Schulman, *The hidden subgroup problem in affine groups: Basis selection in Fourier sampling*, Proc. 15th SODA, 2004, pp. 1113–1122.

[34] C. Moore, A. Russell, and L. J. Schulman, *The symmetric group defies strong Fourier sampling*, Proc. 46th FOCS, 2005, pp. 479–490.

[35] J. Radhakrishnan, M. Rötteler, and P. Sen, *On the power of random bases in Fourier sampling: Hidden subgroup problem in the Heisenberg group*, Proc. 32nd ICALP, LNCS **3580**, 2005, pp. 1399–1411.

[36] O. Regev, *Quantum computation and lattice problems*, Proc. 43rd FOCS, 2002, pp. 520–529.

[37] ———, *A subexponential time algorithm for the dihedral hidden subgroup problem with polynomial space*, quant-ph/0406151.

[38] A. Schmidt and U. Vollmer, *Polynomial time quantum algorithm for the computation of the unit group of a number field*, Proc. 37th STOC, 2005, pp. 475–480.

[39] P. Sen, *Random measurement bases, quantum state distinction and applications to the hidden subgroup problem*, quant-ph/0512085.

[40] J. P. Serre, *Linear Representations of Finite Groups*, Graduate Texts in Mathematics, vol. 42, Springer, New York, 1977.

[41] P. W. Shor, *Polynomial-time algorithms for prime factorization and discrete logarithms on a quantum computer*, SIAM J. Comput. **26** (1997), 1484–1509.

[42] R. P. Stanley, *Theory and application of plane partitions*, Studies in Appl. Math. **1** (1971), 167–187 and 259–279.

Quantum Network Coding

Masahito Hayashi[1], Kazuo Iwama[2,*], Harumichi Nishimura[3,**],
Rudy Raymond[4], and Shigeru Yamashita[5,***]

[1] Japan Science and Technology Agency, ERATO-SORST Quantum Computation
and Information Project, Tokyo 113-0033, Bunkyo-ku, Hongo 5-28-3, Japan[†]
masahito@qci.jst.go.jp
[2] School of Informatics, Kyoto University, Kyoto 606-8501, Sakyo-ku,
Yoshida-Honmachi, Japan
iwama@kuis.kyoto-u.ac.jp
[3] School of Science, Osaka Prefecture University, Sakai 599-8531, Gakuen-cho, Japan
hnishimura@mi.s.osakafu-u.ac.jp
[4] Tokyo Research Laboratory, IBM Japan, Yamato 242-8502,
Simotsuruma 1623-14, Japan
raymond@jp.ibm.com
[5] Graduate School of Information Science, Nara Institute of Science and Technology
Nara 630-0192, Ikoma, Takayama-cho 8916-5, Japan
ger@is.naist.ac.jp

Abstract. Since quantum information is continuous, its handling is
sometimes surprisingly harder than the classical counterpart. A typical
example is cloning; making a copy of digital information is straightforward but it is not possible exactly for quantum information. The question
in this paper is whether or not *quantum* network coding is possible. Its
classical counterpart is another good example to show that digital information flow can be done much more efficiently than conventional (say,
liquid) flow.

Our answer to the question is similar to the case of cloning, namely,
it is shown that quantum network coding is possible if approximation is
allowed, by using a simple network model called Butterfly. In this network, there are two flow paths, s_1 to t_1 and s_2 to t_2, which shares a single
bottleneck channel of capacity one. In the classical case, we can send two
bits simultaneously, one for each path, in spite of the bottleneck. Our results for quantum network coding include: (i) We can send any quantum
state $|\psi_1\rangle$ from s_1 to t_1 and $|\psi_2\rangle$ from s_2 to t_2 simultaneously with a
fidelity strictly greater than $1/2$. (ii) If one of $|\psi_1\rangle$ and $|\psi_2\rangle$ is classi-
cal, then the fidelity can be improved to $2/3$. (iii) Similar improvement
is also possible if $|\psi_1\rangle$ and $|\psi_2\rangle$ are restricted to only a finite number
of (previously known) states. (iv) Several impossibility results including
the general upper bound of the fidelity are also given.

---

[*] Supported in part by Scientific Research Grant, Ministry of Japan, 16092101.
[**] Supported in part by Scientifis Research Grant, Ministry of Japan, 18244210.
[***] Supported in part by Scientific Research Grant, Ministry of Japan, 16092218.
[†] Also, Superrobust Computation Project, Information Science and Technology
Strategic Core, (21st Century COE by MEXT), Graduate School of Information
Science and Technology, The University of Tokyo, Japan.

W. Thomas and P. Weil (Eds.): STACS 2007, LNCS 4393, pp. 610–621, 2007.

1   Introduction

In [1], Ahlswede, Cai, Li and Yeung showed that the fundamental law for network flow, the max-flow min-cut theorem, no longer applies for "digital information flow." The simple and nice example in [1] is called the Butterfly network as illustrated in Fig. 1. The capacity of each directed link is all one and there are two source-sink pairs: s_1 to t_1 and s_2 to t_2. Notice that both paths have to use the single link from s_0 to t_0 and hence the total amount of (conventional commodity) flow in both paths is bounded by one, say, $1/2$ for each. In the case of digital information flow, however, the protocol shown in Fig. 2 allows us to transmit two bits, x and y, simultaneously. Thus, we can effectively achieve larger channel capacity than what can be achieved by simple routing. This is known as *network coding* since [1] and has been quite popular (see Network coding home page [16] for recent developments).

Network coding obviously exploits the two side links, s_1 to t_2 and s_2 to t_1, which are completely useless graph-topologically. Now the primary question in this paper is whether this is also possible for *quantum* information: Our model is the same butterfly network with (unit-capacity) quantum channels and our goal is to send two qubits from s_1 to t_1 and s_2 to t_2 simultaneously. To this end, one should notice that the protocol in Fig. 2 uses (at least) two tricks. One is the EX-OR (Exclusive-OR) operation at node s_0; one can see that the bit y is encoded by using x as a key which is sent directly from s_1 to t_2, and vise versa. The other is the exact copy of one-bit information at node t_0. Are there any quantum counterparts for these key operations?

Neither seems easy in the quantum case. For the copy operation, there is the famous no-cloning theorem. Also, there is no obvious way of encoding a quantum state by a quantum state at s_0. Consider, for example, a simple extension of the classical operation at node s_0, i.e., a controlled unitary transform U as illustrated in Fig. 3. (Note that classical EX-OR is realized by setting $U = X$ "bit-flip.") Then, for any U, there is a quantum state $|\phi\rangle$ (actually an eigenvector of U) such that $|\phi\rangle$ and $U|\phi\rangle$ are identical (up to a global phase). Namely, if $|\psi_1\rangle = |\phi\rangle$, then the quantum state at the output of U is exactly the same for $|\psi_2\rangle = |0\rangle$ and $|\psi_2\rangle = |1\rangle$. This means their difference is completely lost at that position and hence is completely lost at t_1 also.

Thus it is highly unlikely that we can achieve an exact transmission of two quantum states, which forces us to consider an *approximate* transmission. As an approximation factor, we use a (worst-case) *fidelity* between the input state $|\psi_1\rangle$ at s_1 ($|\psi_2\rangle$ at s_2, resp.) and the output state ρ_1 at t_1 (ρ_2 at t_2, resp.) Recall that the fidelity is at most 1.0 by definition and 0.5 is automatically achieved by outputting a completely mixed state. Thus our question is whether we can achieve a fidelity of strictly greater than 0.5.

Our Contribution. This paper gives a positive answer to this question. We first show that we do need the (topologically useless) side channels for our goal exactly as in the classical case (Theorem 1). Namely, without them, we can prove that for any protocol, there exists a quantum state $|\psi_i\rangle$ ($i = 1$ or 2) and its output state ρ_i such that $F(|\psi_i\rangle, \rho_i) \leq 1/2$. We then give our protocol which

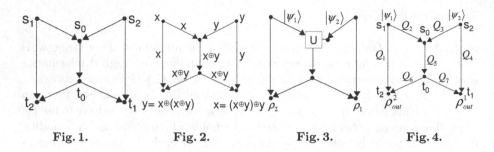

Fig. 1.   **Fig. 2.**   **Fig. 3.**   **Fig. 4.**

achieves a fidelity of strictly greater than $1/2$ for the butterfly network (Theorem 2). The idea is discretization of (continuous) quantum states. Namely, the quantum state from s_2 is changed into classical two bits by using what we call "tetra measurement." Those two bits are then used as a key to encode the state from s_1 at node s_0 ("group operation") and also to decode it at node t_1. Our protocol also depends upon the approximate cloning by Bužek and Hillery [7]. This obviously distorts quantum states, but interestingly, it also has a merit (creating entanglement between cloned states) by which we can handle the second problem on the state distinguishability previously mentioned.

Note that the present general lower bound for the fidelity is only slightly better than $1/2$ (some 0.52). However, if we impose restriction, the value becomes much better. For example, if $|\psi_1\rangle$ is a classical state (i.e. either $|0\rangle$ or $|1\rangle$), then the fidelity becomes $2/3$ (Theorem 4). Similar improvement is also possible if $|\psi_1\rangle$ and $|\psi_2\rangle$ are restricted to only a finite number of (previously known) states, especially if they are the so-called quantum random access coding states [2]. By using those states, we can design an interesting protocol which can send two classical bits from s_1 to t_1 (similarly two bits from s_2 to t_2) but only one of them, determined by adversary, should be recovered. It is shown that the success probability for this protocol is $1/2 + \sqrt{2}/16$ (Theorem 6), but classically the success probability for any protocol is at most $1/2$.

On the negative side, several upper bounds for the fidelity are given. Again, the most general one (Theorem 3) may not seem very impressive (some 0.983), but it is improved under restrictions. In particular, if we impose the BC (bit-copy) assumption, we can prove an upper bound of $11/12$ (Theorem 5). (BC means that whenever we need to copy a classical bit, we use the classical (exact) copy, which seems quite reasonable.) We also give a limit of transmitting random access coding states. Note that Theorem 6 can be extended to the three-bit case (with success probability some 0.525) but that is the limit; no protocol exists for the four-bit transmission with success probability strictly greater than $1/2$ (Theorem 8).

Related Work. We usually allow approximation and/or errors in quantum computation, which seems to be an essence of its power in some occasions. One example is observed in communication complexity: The quantum communication complexity to compute the equality function EQ_n exactly is n [15]. However, even one qubit communication enables us to compute EQ_n with success probability larger than $1/2$. Another example can be seen in locally decodable codes and private information retrievals: Any $2n$-bit Boolean function F can be computed with success probability $> 1/2$ from an $(n+1)$-qubit information [24]. Namely, $n + 1$ qubits can encode $2n$ classical bits for computing *any* Boolean function approximately.

Thus "$1/2 + \epsilon$ for very small ϵ" seems very powerful. Interestingly, this is not the case in some other occasions. the Nayak bound [18] says that there is no way to send two bits by one qubit with success probability $> 1/2$. Moreover, [14] shows that one-qubit random access coding for four bits can only be done with success probability at most $1/2$, although we can enjoy a good success probability up to three bits. In this context, our model in this paper also shows a clear difference depending on whether or not the two side links exist.

The study of coding methods on quantum information and computation has been deeply explored for error correction of quantum computation (since [23]) and data compression of quantum sources (since [21]). Recall that their techniques are duplication of data (error correction) and average-case analysis (data compression). Those standard approaches do not seem to help in the core of our problem. More tricky applications of quantum mechanism are quantum teleportation [4], superdense coding [5], and a variety of quantum cryptosystems including the BB84 key distribution [3]. The random access coding by Ambainis, Nayak, Ta-shma, and Vazirani [2] is probably most related one to this paper, which allows us to encode two or more classical bits into one qubit and decode it to recover any one of the source bits. Our third protocol is a realization of this scheme on the Butterfly network.

The introduction of quantum network coding [13] triggered several new studies: Leung, Oppenheim, and Winter [17] examined the asymptotic relation between the amount of quantum information and channel capacities on the Butterfly network (and more). Shi and Soljanin [22] considered multicasting networks from the viewpoint of lossless compression and decompression of copies of quantum states.

2 The Model

Our model is described as a quantum circuit which corresponds to Fig. 1. The information sources at nodes s_1 and s_2 are pure one-qubit states $|\psi_1\rangle$ and $|\psi_2\rangle$. (It turns out, however, that the result does not change for mixed states because of the joint concavity of the fidelity [19].) Any node does not have prior entanglement with other nodes. At every node, a physically allowable operation, i.e., trace-preserving completely positive map (TP-CP map), is done, and each edge can send only one qubit. They are implemented by unitary operations with additional ancillae and by discarding all qubits except for the output qubits [19].

Our goal is to send $|\psi_1\rangle$ to node t_1 and $|\psi_2\rangle$ to node t_2 as well as possible. The quality of data at node t_j is measured by the fidelity between the original state $|\psi_j\rangle$ and the state ρ_j output at node t_j by the protocol. Here, the fidelity between two quantum states ρ and σ are defined as $F(\sigma, \rho) = \left(\mathrm{Tr}\sqrt{\rho^{1/2}\sigma\rho^{1/2}}\right)^2$ as in [8,6,9]. (The other common definition is $\mathrm{Tr}\sqrt{\rho^{1/2}\sigma\rho^{1/2}}$.) In particular, the fidelity between a pure state $|\psi\rangle$ and a mixed state ρ is $F(|\psi\rangle, \rho) = \langle\psi|\rho|\psi\rangle$. (To simplify the description, for a pure state $|\psi\rangle\langle\psi|$ we often use the vector representation $|\psi\rangle$ and we also use bold fonts for a 2×2 or 4×4 density matrix for exposition.) We call the minimum of $F(|\psi_1\rangle, \rho_1)$ over all one-qubit states $|\psi_1\rangle$ and $|\psi_2\rangle$ the *fidelity at node* t_1 and similarly for *fidelity at node* t_2.

Before presenting our protocols achieving a fidelity of strictly greater than $1/2$, we show that the two side links, which are useless graph-topologically, are indispensable. One might think this is trivial from the Nayak bound [18]. Namely, if the two inputs are classical $0/1$ bits, then they cannot be sent using a single quantum channel (s_0 to t_0) with success probability ($=$ fidelity) greater than $1/2$. This is not true since our definition only requires a fidelity at *each* sink. In fact, we can achieve a fidelity of at least 0.75 in our definition, by simply using the one-qubit random access coding for two bits [2] and the phase-covariant cloning (a kind of approximated cloning) [6,9]. (Note that $0.75^2 > 0.5$ but this does not violate the Nayak bound since the success probabilities at the two sides are not independent.) The proof of the following theorem needs a careful consideration of physical operations on the Bloch ball (see, e.g., [10,20]) and the trace distance. In this paper, the trace distance between two quantum states ρ and ρ' is defined to be $||\rho - \rho'||_{tr}$ without the normalization factor 2 as in [19]. (If two states are qubits, this distance is equal to the geometrical distance of the corresponding points in the Bloch ball.)

Theorem 1. *No quantum protocol can achieve fidelity larger than $1/2$ if both side links are removed from the Butterfly.*

Proof. We show that, for any proper protocol, if the fidelity at t_2 is larger than $1/2$ (say, $1/2 + \epsilon$ with $\epsilon > 0$) then the fidelity at t_1 is strictly less than $1/2$. For our purpose, we consider the case where the sources at s_1 and s_2 are a qubit $|\psi\rangle$ and a classical bit b, respectively. We can assume that they are sent to s_0 without any transformation (since otherwise their operations at s_1 and s_2 can be delayed until s_0). Now, let $\mathcal{E}_b$ be the images of the Bloch ball resulting from operations at s_0 when b is sent from s_2. Let the distance between $\mathcal{E}_0$ and $\mathcal{E}_1$ be the minimum trace distance between any state in $\mathcal{E}_0$ and that in $\mathcal{E}_1$. Then, the following lemma holds from the fidelity requirement at t_2:

Lemma 1. *The distance between $\mathcal{E}_0$ and $\mathcal{E}_1$ is at least 4ϵ.*

Proof. Let C_b be the TP-CP map at s_0 when b is sent from s_2. We can regard the operations at t_0 and t_2 along the path s_2-t_2 as the measurement defined by a POVM (positive operator-valued measure) $\{E_0, E_1\}$. (Recall that any measurement is defined by a POVM $\{E_i\}_i$, that is, each operator E_i is positive and $\sum_i E_i = I$.) Then, to prove the lemma we need to show that for any one-qubit states $|\psi\rangle, |\psi'\rangle$, $||C_0(|\psi\rangle) - C_1(|\psi'\rangle)||_{tr} \geq 4\epsilon$. However, by the fidelity requirement at t_2, for any $|\psi\rangle, |\psi'\rangle$ and any $b = 0, 1$, it must hold that $\text{Tr}(E_b C_b(|\psi\rangle)) \geq 1/2 + \epsilon$ and $\text{Tr}(E_b C_{1-b}(|\psi'\rangle)) \leq 1/2 - \epsilon$. Thus, we have $||C_0(|\psi\rangle) - C_1(|\psi'\rangle)||_{tr} \geq \sum_{b=0,1} |\text{Tr} E_b(C_0(|\psi\rangle) - C_1(|\psi'\rangle))| \geq 4\epsilon$, where the first inequality is obtained from the following fact: For any quantum states ρ, ρ',

$||\rho - \rho'||_{tr}$ equals $\max_{\{F_0, F_1\}} \sum_b |\mathrm{Tr} F_b(\rho - \rho')|$ where the maximization is over all POVMs $\{F_0, F_1\}$ [19].

By Lemma 1, the center of the Bloch ball is outside at least one of $\mathcal{E}_0$ and $\mathcal{E}_1$. Now let $\mathcal{F}_b$ be the final images at t_1 when b is the source at s_2, and let T be the composite TP-CP map of t_0 and t_1 along the path s_1-t_1. Note that $\mathcal{F}_0 = T(\mathcal{E}_0)$ and $\mathcal{F}_1 = T(\mathcal{E}_1)$, and T is linear. Since T transforms the Bloch ball into an ellipsoid within the Bloch ball [10,20], the center of the Bloch ball is outside one of ellipsoids $\mathcal{F}_0$ and $\mathcal{F}_1$, say $\mathcal{F}_0$. This means that there exists some input state $|\psi\rangle$ at s_1 such that $|\psi\rangle$ and its output state ρ_ψ at t_1 are in different half of the Bloch ball, that is, $F(|\psi\rangle, \rho_\psi) < 1/2$. Therefore the fidelity at t_1 is $< 1/2$.

3   Protocol for Crossing Two Qubits

Theorem 2. *There exists a quantum protocol whose fidelities at nodes t_1 and t_2 are $1/2 + 2/81$ and $1/2 + 2\sqrt{3}/243$, respectively.*

3.1   Overview of the Protocol

Fig. 4 illustrates our protocol, Protocol for Crossing Two Qubits (XQQ). As expected, the approximated cloning is used at nodes s_1, s_2 and t_0. At node s_0, we first apply the tetra measurement to the state of one-qubit system $\mathcal{Q}_3$ and obtain two classical bits $r_1 r_2$. Their different four values suggest which part of the Bloch sphere the state of $\mathcal{Q}_3$ sits in. These four values are then used to choose one of four different operations, the group operations, to encode the state of $\mathcal{Q}_2$. These four operations include identity I, bit-flip X, phase-flip Z, and bit+phase-flip Y. At node t_1, we apply the reverse operations of these four operations (actually the same as the original ones) for the decoding purpose.

At node t_2, we recover the two bits $r_1 r_2$ (actually the corresponding quantum state for the output state) by comparing $\mathcal{Q}_1$ and $\mathcal{Q}_6$. This should be possible since $\mathcal{Q}_2$ ($\approx \mathcal{Q}_1$) is encoded into $\mathcal{Q}_5$ ($\approx \mathcal{Q}_6$) by using $r_1 r_2$ as a key but its implementation is not obvious. It is shown that for this purpose, we can use the Bell measurement together with the fact that $\mathcal{Q}_1$ and $\mathcal{Q}_2$ are partially entangled as a result of cloning at node s_1.

Remark. It is not hard to average the fidelities at t_1 and t_2 by mixing the encoding state at t_1 with the Bell state $(|00\rangle + |11\rangle)/\sqrt{2}$, implying $1/2 + 2(2 - \sqrt{3})/27 \approx 0.52$ at both sinks.

3.2   Building Blocks

Universal Cloning (UC). As the first tool of our protocol, we recall the notion of the approximated cloning by Bužek and Hillery [7], called the *universal cloning*. Let $|\Psi^+\rangle = \frac{1}{\sqrt{2}}(|01\rangle + |10\rangle)$. Then, it is given by the TP-CP map UC defined by $UC(|0\rangle\langle 0|) = \frac{2}{3}|00\rangle\langle 00| + \frac{1}{3}|\Psi^+\rangle\langle\Psi^+|$, $UC(|0\rangle\langle 1|) = \frac{\sqrt{2}}{3}|\Psi^+\rangle\langle 11| + \frac{\sqrt{2}}{3}|00\rangle\langle\Psi^+|$, $UC(|1\rangle\langle 0|) = \frac{\sqrt{2}}{3}|11\rangle\langle\Psi^+| + \frac{\sqrt{2}}{3}|\Psi^+\rangle\langle 00|$, $UC(|1\rangle\langle 1|) = \frac{2}{3}|11\rangle\langle 11| + \frac{1}{3}|\Psi^+\rangle\langle\Psi^+|$. This map is intended to clone not only classical states $|0\rangle$ and $|1\rangle$

but also any superposition equally well by mixing the symmetric state $|\Psi^+\rangle$ with $|00\rangle$ and $|11\rangle$ as the output. Let $\boldsymbol{\rho}_1 = \mathrm{Tr}_2 UC(|\psi\rangle)$ and $\boldsymbol{\rho}_2 = \mathrm{Tr}_1 UC(|\psi\rangle)$, where Tr_i is the partial trace over the i-th qubit. Then, easy calculation implies that $\boldsymbol{\rho}_1 = \boldsymbol{\rho}_2 = \frac{2}{3}|\psi\rangle\langle\psi| + \frac{1}{3} \cdot \frac{\boldsymbol{I}}{2}$. We call its induced map $|\psi\rangle \mapsto \boldsymbol{\rho}_1$ (or $|\psi\rangle \mapsto \boldsymbol{\rho}_2$) the *universal copy*.

Tetra Measurement (TTR). Next, we introduce the tetra measurement. We need the following four states $|\chi(00)\rangle = \cos\tilde\theta|0\rangle + e^{i\pi/4}\sin\tilde\theta|1\rangle$, $|\chi(01)\rangle = \cos\tilde\theta|0\rangle + e^{-3i\pi/4}\sin\tilde\theta|1\rangle$, $|\chi(10)\rangle = \sin\tilde\theta|0\rangle + e^{-i\pi/4}\cos\tilde\theta|1\rangle$, and $|\chi(11)\rangle = \sin\tilde\theta|0\rangle + e^{3i\pi/4}\cos\tilde\theta|1\rangle$ with $\cos^2\tilde\theta = 1/2 + \sqrt{3}/6$, which form a tetrahedron in the Bloch sphere representation. The *tetra measurement*, denoted by TTR, is defind by the POVM $\{\frac{1}{2}|\chi(00)\rangle\langle\chi(00)|, \frac{1}{2}|\chi(01)\rangle\langle\chi(01)|, \frac{1}{2}|\chi(10)\rangle\langle\chi(10)|, \frac{1}{2}|\chi(11)\rangle\langle\chi(11)|\}$.

Group Operation (GR). In what follows, let $X = |0\rangle\langle 1| + |1\rangle\langle 0|$ be the bit-flip operation, $Z = |0\rangle\langle 0| - |1\rangle\langle 1|$ be the phase-flip operation, and $Y = XZ$. Notice that the set of unitary maps on one-qubit states $\rho \mapsto W\rho W^\dagger$ ($W = I, Z, X, Y$) is the Klein four group. The *group operation under* a two-bit string $r_1 r_2$, denoted by $GR(\boldsymbol{\rho}, r_1 r_2)$, is a transformation defined by $GR(\boldsymbol{\rho}, 00) = \boldsymbol{\rho}$, $GR(\boldsymbol{\rho}, 01) = Z\boldsymbol{\rho}$, $GR(\boldsymbol{\rho}, 10) = X\boldsymbol{\rho}$, and $GR(\boldsymbol{\rho}, 11) = Y\boldsymbol{\rho}$. Note that we frequently use simplified expressions like $X\boldsymbol{\rho}$ instead of $X\boldsymbol{\rho}X^\dagger$.

3D Bell Measurement (BM). Moreover, for recovering $|\psi_2\rangle$ at node t_2 we introduce another new operation based on the Bell measurement, $BM(\mathcal{Q}, \mathcal{Q}')$ (or $BM(\boldsymbol{\sigma})$), which applies the following three operations (a), (b), and (c) with probability $1/3$ for each, to the state $\boldsymbol{\sigma}$ (a 4×4 density matrix) of the two-qubit system $\mathcal{Q} \otimes \mathcal{Q}'$: (a) Measure $\boldsymbol{\sigma}$ in the Bell basis $\{|\Phi^+\rangle, |\Phi^-\rangle, |\Psi^+\rangle, |\Psi^-\rangle\}$, and output $|0\rangle$ if the measurement result for $|\Phi^+\rangle = \frac{|00\rangle + |11\rangle}{\sqrt{2}}$ or $|\Phi^-\rangle = \frac{|00\rangle - |11\rangle}{\sqrt{2}}$ is obtained, and $|1\rangle$ otherwise. (b) Measure $\boldsymbol{\sigma}$ similarly, and output $|+\rangle$ if the measurement result for $|\Phi^+\rangle$ or $|\Psi^+\rangle$ is obtained, and $|-\rangle$ otherwise. (c) Measure $\boldsymbol{\sigma}$ similarly, and output $|+'\rangle = \frac{1}{\sqrt{2}}(|0\rangle + i|1\rangle)$ if the measurement result for $|\Phi^+\rangle$ or $|\Psi^-\rangle = \frac{|01\rangle - |10\rangle}{\sqrt{2}}$ is obtained, and $|-'\rangle = \frac{1}{\sqrt{2}}(|0\rangle - i|1\rangle)$ otherwise.

3.3   Protocol XQQ and Its Performance Analysis

Protocol XQQ: Input $|\psi_1\rangle$ at s_1, and $|\psi_2\rangle$ at s_2; Output $\boldsymbol{\rho}_{out}^1$ at t_1, and $\boldsymbol{\rho}_{out}^2$ at t_2.

Step 1. $(\mathcal{Q}_1, \mathcal{Q}_2) = UC(|\psi_1\rangle)$ at s_1, and $(\mathcal{Q}_3, \mathcal{Q}_4) = UC(|\psi_2\rangle)$ at s_2.

Step 2. $\mathcal{Q}_5 = GR(\mathcal{Q}_2, TTR(\mathcal{Q}_3))$ at s_0.

Step 3. $(\mathcal{Q}_6, \mathcal{Q}_7) = UC(\mathcal{Q}_5)$ at t_0.

Step 4 (Decoding at node t_1 and t_2). $\boldsymbol{\rho}_{out}^1 = GR(\mathcal{Q}_7, TTR(\mathcal{Q}_4))$, and $\boldsymbol{\rho}_{out}^2 = BM(\mathcal{Q}_1, \mathcal{Q}_6)$.

We give the proof of Theorem 2 by analyzing protocol XQQ (see [13] for details and similarly for the remaining part of the paper). For this purpose, we introduce the notion of shrinking maps (also known as a depolarizing channel [19]), which plays an important role in the following analysis of XQQ: Let ρ be any quantum state. Then, if a map C transforms ρ to $p \cdot \rho + (1 - p)\frac{\boldsymbol{I}}{2}$ for some

$0 \leq p \leq 1$, then C is said to be *p-shrinking*. The following three lemmas are immediate:

Lemma 2. *If C is p-shrinking and C' is p'-shrinking, then $C \circ C'$ is pp'-shrinking.*

Lemma 3. *If C is p-shrinking, $F(\boldsymbol{\rho}, C(\boldsymbol{\rho})) \geq 1/2 + p/2$ for any state $\boldsymbol{\rho}$.*

Lemma 4. *The universal copy is 2/3-shrinking.*

Computing the Fidelity at Node t_1. We first investigate the quality of the path from s_1 to t_1. Fix $\boldsymbol{\rho}_2 = |\psi_2\rangle\langle\psi_2|$ as an arbitrary state at node s_2 and consider four maps $C_1\colon |\psi_1\rangle \to \mathcal{Q}_2$, $C_2[\boldsymbol{\rho}_2]\colon \mathcal{Q}_2 \to \mathcal{Q}_5$, $C_3\colon \mathcal{Q}_5 \to \mathcal{Q}_7$ and $C_4[\boldsymbol{\rho}_2]\colon \mathcal{Q}_7 \to \boldsymbol{\rho}_{out}^1$. We wish to compute the composite map $C_{s_1 t_1} = C_4[\boldsymbol{\rho}_2] \circ C_3 \circ C_2[\boldsymbol{\rho}_2] \circ C_1$ and its fidelity. We need two more lemmas before the final one (Lemma 7).

Lemma 5. $C_3 \circ C_2[\boldsymbol{\rho}_2] = C_2[\boldsymbol{\rho}_2] \circ C_3$.

Lemma 6. *(Main Lemma)* $C_4[\boldsymbol{\rho}_2] \circ C_2[\boldsymbol{\rho}_2]$ *is $\frac{1}{9}$-shrinking.*

Lemma 7. *For any $|\psi_1\rangle$, $F(|\psi_1\rangle, C_{s_1 t_1}(|\psi_1\rangle)) \geq 1/2 + 2/81$.*

Proof. By Lemma 5, $C_{s_1 t_1} = C_4[\boldsymbol{\rho}_2] \circ C_2[\boldsymbol{\rho}_2] \circ C_3 \circ C_1$. C_3 and C_1 are both 2/3-shrinking by Lemma 4 and $C_4[\boldsymbol{\rho}_2] \circ C_2[\boldsymbol{\rho}_2]$ is $\frac{1}{9}$-shrinking by Lemma 6. It then follows that $C_{s_1 t_1}$ is $\frac{4}{81}$-shrinking by Lemma 2 and its fidelity is at least $1/2 + 2/81$ by Lemma 3.

Now we prove Lemma 6. See Fig. 4 again. Since we are discussing $C_4[\boldsymbol{\rho}_2] \circ C_2[\boldsymbol{\rho}_2]$, let $\rho_1 = \begin{pmatrix} a & b \\ c & d \end{pmatrix}$ be the state on $\mathcal{Q}_2$, $\boldsymbol{\rho}_2 = |\psi_2\rangle\langle\psi_2| = \begin{pmatrix} e & f \\ g & h \end{pmatrix}$ be the state at s_2 and assume that $\mathcal{Q}_5 = \mathcal{Q}_7$. We calculate the state on $\mathcal{Q}_2 \otimes \mathcal{Q}_3 \otimes \mathcal{Q}_4$, the state on $\mathcal{Q}_5 \otimes \mathcal{Q}_4$ ($= \mathcal{Q}_7 \otimes \mathcal{Q}_4$) and $\boldsymbol{\rho}_{out}^1$ in this order. For $\mathcal{Q}_2 \otimes \mathcal{Q}_3 \otimes \mathcal{Q}_4$, recall that $\boldsymbol{\rho}_2$ is cloned into $\mathcal{Q}_3$ and $\mathcal{Q}_4$ and so, by the TP-CP map UC in Sec. 3.2, the state on $\mathcal{Q}_2 \otimes \mathcal{Q}_3 \otimes \mathcal{Q}_4$ is written as the tensor product of ρ_1 and

$$|0\rangle\langle 0| \otimes \left(\frac{2e}{3}|0\rangle\langle 0| + \frac{f}{3}|0\rangle\langle 1| + \frac{g}{3}|1\rangle\langle 0| + \frac{1}{6}|1\rangle\langle 1| \right) + |0\rangle\langle 1| \otimes \left(\frac{1}{6}|1\rangle\langle 0| + \frac{f}{3}I \right)$$

$$+ |1\rangle\langle 0| \otimes \left(\frac{1}{6}|0\rangle\langle 1| + \frac{g}{3}I \right) + |1\rangle\langle 1| \otimes \left(\frac{1}{6}|0\rangle\langle 0| + \frac{f}{3}|0\rangle\langle 1| + \frac{g}{3}|1\rangle\langle 0| + \frac{2h}{3}|1\rangle\langle 1| \right).$$

Then, we apply the group operation to the first two bits of $\mathcal{Q}_2 \otimes \mathcal{Q}_3 \otimes \mathcal{Q}_4$. In general, for $\mathcal{Q} \otimes \mathcal{Q}'$, $GR(\mathcal{Q}, TTR(\mathcal{Q}'))$ is given as follows.

Lemma 8. *Let ρ be the state on $\mathcal{Q}$. Then, $GR(\mathcal{Q}, TTR(\mathcal{Q}'))$ is the following TP-CP map:*

$$\rho \otimes |0\rangle\langle 0| \mapsto \frac{1}{\sqrt{3}}V(I, Z)\rho + \frac{\sqrt{3}-1}{\sqrt{3}}\frac{I}{2}, \quad \rho \otimes |1\rangle\langle 1| \mapsto \frac{1}{\sqrt{3}}V(X, Y)\rho + \frac{\sqrt{3}-1}{\sqrt{3}}\frac{I}{2},$$

$$\rho \otimes |0\rangle\langle 1| \mapsto \frac{1}{2\sqrt{3}}(V(I, X)\rho - V(Y, Z)\rho + \imath(V(I, Y)\rho - V(Z, X)\rho)),$$

$$\rho \otimes |1\rangle\langle 0| \mapsto \frac{1}{2\sqrt{3}}(V(I, X)\rho - V(Y, Z)\rho - \imath(V(I, Y)\rho - V(Z, X)\rho)).$$

Here, $V(I,Z)\rho = \frac{1}{2}(I\rho + Z\rho)$, and $V(X,Y)\rho$, $V(I,X)\rho$, $V(Y,Z)\rho$, $V(I,Y)\rho$, and $V(Z,X)\rho$ are similarly defined. Those six operations are I-invariant (meaning it maps I to itself) TP-CP maps.

Now the state on $Q_5 \otimes Q_4$ is obtained by applying Lemma 8 to the state on $Q_2 \otimes Q_3 \otimes Q_4$. From now on, we omit the term for $\frac{I}{2}$. Namely, if the one-qubit state is $\rho + \alpha\frac{I}{2}$, we only describe ρ. This is not harmful since any operation in this section is I-invariant and hence the $\frac{I}{2}$ term can be recovered at the end by using the trace property. Thus, the state on $Q_5 \otimes Q_4$ looks like

$$\frac{1}{\sqrt{3}}V(I,Z)\rho_1 \otimes \left(\frac{2e}{3}|0\rangle\langle 0| + \frac{1}{6}|1\rangle\langle 1|\right) + \frac{1}{\sqrt{3}}V(I,Z)\rho_1 \otimes \left(\frac{f}{3}|0\rangle\langle 1| + \frac{g}{3}|1\rangle\langle 0|\right)$$

$$+ \frac{1}{2\sqrt{3}}V(I,X;I,Y;+)\rho_1 \otimes \frac{1}{6}|1\rangle\langle 0| + \frac{1}{2\sqrt{3}}V(I,X;I,Y;+) \otimes \frac{f}{3}I$$

$$+ \frac{1}{2\sqrt{3}}V(I,X;I,Y;-)\rho_1 \otimes \frac{1}{6}|0\rangle\langle 1| + \frac{1}{2\sqrt{3}}V(I,X;I,Y;-) \otimes \frac{g}{3}I$$

$$+ \frac{1}{\sqrt{3}}V(X,Y)\rho_1 \otimes \left(\frac{1}{6}|0\rangle\langle 0| + \frac{2h}{3}|1\rangle\langle 1|\right) + \frac{1}{\sqrt{3}}V(X,Y)\rho_1 \otimes \left(\frac{f}{3}|0\rangle\langle 1| + \frac{g}{3}|1\rangle\langle 0|\right),$$

where $V(I,X;I,Y;\pm)\rho = V(I,X)\rho - V(Y,Z)\rho \pm \iota(V(I,Y)\rho - V(Z,X)\rho)$, and the terms such that the state of Q_5 is $\frac{I}{2}$ are omitted.

We next transform the state of $Q_5 \otimes Q_4$ to ρ_{out}^1 by using Lemma 8 again. For example, $V(I,Z)\rho_1 \otimes |0\rangle\langle 0|$ is transformed to $\frac{1}{\sqrt{3}}V(I,Z)V(I,Z)\rho_1$. To simplify the resulting formula, the following lemma is used.

Lemma 9. *1)* $V(I,Z)V(I,Z)\rho_1 = V(X,Y)V(X,Y)\rho_1 = \begin{pmatrix} a & 0 \\ 0 & d \end{pmatrix}$.

2) $V(I,Z)V(X,Y)\rho_1 = V(X,Y)V(I,Z)\rho_1 = \begin{pmatrix} d & 0 \\ 0 & a \end{pmatrix}$.

3) $V(I,X)V(I,X)\rho_1 = V(Y,Z)V(Y,Z)\rho_1 = \frac{1}{2}\begin{pmatrix} 1 & b+c \\ b+c & 1 \end{pmatrix}$.

4) $V(I,X)V(Y,Z)\rho_1 = V(Y,Z)V(I,X)\rho_1 = \frac{1}{2}\begin{pmatrix} 1 & -b-c \\ -b-c & 1 \end{pmatrix}$.

5) $V(I,Y)V(I,Y)\rho_1 = V(Z,X)V(Z,X)\rho_1 = \frac{1}{2}\begin{pmatrix} 1 & b-c \\ c-b & 1 \end{pmatrix}$.

6) $V(I,Y)V(Z,X)\rho_1 = V(Z,X)V(I,Y)\rho_1 = \frac{1}{2}\begin{pmatrix} 1 & c-b \\ b-c & 1 \end{pmatrix}$.

7) For any two operators V, V' taken from any different two sets of $\{V(I,Z), V(X,Y)\}$, $\{V(I,X), V(Y,Z)\}$, and $\{V(I,Y), V(Z,X)\}$, $VV'\rho_1 = \frac{I}{2}$.

Now it is a routine calculation to obtain $\rho_{out}^1 = \begin{pmatrix} m_1 & m_2 \\ m_3 & m_4 \end{pmatrix}$ where m_1 through m_4 are equations using a, b, c and d (e, f, g and h disappear). Using the fact that $a + d = 1$, we have $\rho_{out}^1 = \frac{1}{9}\rho_1 + \frac{1}{9}I$. Recovering the completely mixed state omitted in our analysis, we obtain $C_4[\rho_2] \circ C_2[\rho_2](\rho_1) = \frac{1}{9}\rho_1 + \frac{8}{9} \cdot \frac{I}{2}$. Thus, the map is $\frac{1}{9}$-shrinking. This completes the proof of Lemma 6.

Computing the Fidelity at Node t_2. By analyzing the quality of the path from s_2 to t_2, we have $F(|\psi_2\rangle, \rho_{out}^2) \geq 1/2 + 2\sqrt{3}/243$. Its analysis is different from the previous one by the antisymmetry of the protocol. Details are given in the complete version.

3.4 Upper Bounds

The following theorem shows a general upper bound for the fidelity of crossing two qubits over Butterfly. Recall that we showed in Sec. 1 (also Fig. 3) that the operation at s_0 must not resemble a controlled unitary operation. Thus, it must be a more general TP-CP map (unitary operation with some ancillae). The basic idea of the proof is by showing that a good TP-CP map, the one which results in the protocol with fidelity close to 1.0, can be "approximated" by a controlled unitary operation. Hence, the fidelity of sending two qubits over Butterfly must be bounded away from 1.0. Similar to the proof of Theorem 1, we use a geometric view of the TP-CP map on the Bloch ball. However, it is much complicated since we have to consider the side links.

Theorem 3. *Let q be the fidelity of a protocol for crossing two qubits simultaneously. Then, $q < 0.983$.*

4 Protocol for Crossing a Qubit and a Bit

This section deals with the case where one of two sources (say, at s_2) is a classical bit. Under this situation, we can design a protocol, called as XQC (crossing a quantum bit and a classical bit), whose fidelity is much better than XQQ.

Theorem 4. *XQC achieves the fidelities of $13/18$ and $11/18$ at t_1 and t_2. (By averaging the fidelities at both sinks as before, we can also have a protocol whose fidelities are the same $2/3$ at t_1 and t_2.)*

On the contrary, assuming that the copies of the bit at s_2 are sent to s_0 and t_1, we can obtain an upper bound that is significantly better than Theorem 3. In general, this assumption, denoted as the *BC (bit-copy) assumption*, is reasonable since whenever we need to send a bit to multiple nodes in the network, simply sending its (classical) copies does not appear to cause disadvantages.

Theorem 5. *Let p be the fidelity of a protocol for crossing a bit and a qubit under the BC assumption. Then, $p < 11/12$.*

5 Protocols for Crossing Two Multiple Bits

In this section, we consider the case that both sources are restricted to be one of the four $(2, 1, 0.85)$-quantum random access (QRA) coding states [2]. Note that (m, n, p)-QRA coding is the coding of m bits to n qubits such that any one bit chosen from the m bits is recovered with probability at least p. In this case, we can achieve a much better fidelity. As an application, we can consider a more interesting problem where each source node receives two classical bits, namely, $x_1 x_2 \in \{0,1\}^2$ at s_1, and $y_1 y_2 \in \{0,1\}^2$ at s_2. At node t_1, we output one classical bit Out^1 and similarly Out^2 at t_2. Now an adversary chooses two numbers $i_1, i_2 \in \{1,2\}$. Our protocol can use the information of i_1 only at node t_1 and that of i_2 only at t_2. Our goal is to maximize $F(x_{i_1}, \text{Out}^1)$ and $F(y_{i_2}, \text{Out}^2)$, where $F(x_{i_1}, \text{Out}^1)$ turns out to be the probability that $x_{i_1} = \text{Out}^1$ and similarly for $F(y_{i_2}, \text{Out}^2)$. The key of our protocol $X2C2C$ is also on how to encode at s_0: its operation at s_0 combines an optimal measurement MM_2 to estimate which QRA coding state is sent from s_2, with the group operation similar to XQQ.

Theorem 6. $X2C2C$ achieves a fidelity of $1/2 + \sqrt{2}/16$ at both t_1 and t_2.

By contrast, any classical protocol cannot achieve a success probability greater than $1/2$ for the following reason: Let fix $y_1 = y_2 = 0$. Then the path from s_1 to t_1 is obviously equivalent to the $(2,1,p)$-classical random access coding, where the success probability p is at most $1/2$ [2].

Extending $X2C2C$, we can construct the protocol $X3C3C$ which solves the problem with probability $> 1/2$ for the case when each source node receives three bits. The key of $X3C3C$ is to need eight operations instead of four in $X2C2C$. So, we use not only the Pauli operations but an approximation of the universal NOT gate [8,11], which maps a point within the Bloch sphere into its antipodes.

Theorem 7. $X3C3C$ achieves a fidelity of $1/2 + 2/81$ at both sinks.

Interestingly, there is no $X4C4C$, which is an immediate corollary of the nonexistence of $(4,1,p>1/2)$-QRA coding [14].

Theorem 8. If an $X4C4C$ protocol achieves fidelity q, then $q \leq 1/2$.

6   Beyond the Butterfly Network – Concluding Remarks

Obviously a lot of future work remains. First of all, there is a large gap between the current upper and lower bounds for the achievable fidelity, which should be narrowed. Equally important is to consider more general networks. To this direction, it might be interesting to study the network introduced in [12]. It has k source-sink pairs (s_i, t_i) all of which share a single link from s_0 to t_0. For the network, we can design the protocol XQ^k by a simple extension of XQQ. The idea is to decompose the node s_0 (similarly for t_0) into a sequence of nodes of indegree two. At each of those nodes, we do exactly the same thing as before, i.e., encoding one state by the two bits obtained from the other state. It is not hard to see that such a protocol achieves a fidelity strictly better than $1/2$.

References

1. R. Ahlswede, N. Cai, S.-Y. R. Li, and R. W. Yeung. Network information flow. *IEEE Transactions on Information Theory* **46** (2000) 1204–1216.
2. A. Ambainis, A. Nayak, A. Ta-shma, and U. Vazirani. Dense quantum coding and quantum finite automata. *J. ACM* **49** (2002) 496–511.

3. C. H. Bennett and G. Brassard. Quantum cryptography: public key distribution and coin tossing. *Proc. IEEE International Conference on Computers, Systems and Signal Processing*, pp. 175–179, 1984.

4. C. H. Bennett, G. Brassard, C. Crépeau, R. Jozsa, A. Peres, and W. K. Wootters. Teleporting an unknown quantum states via dual classical and Einstein-Podolsky-Rosen channels. *Phys. Rev. Lett.* **70** (1993) 1895–1899.

5. C. H. Bennett and S. J. Wiesner. Communication via one- and two-particle operators on Einstein-Podolsky-Rosen states. *Phys. Rev. Lett.* **69** (1992) 2881–2884.

6. D. Bruß, M. Cinchetti, G. M. D'Ariano, and C. Macchiavello. Phase-covariant quantum cloning. *Phys. Rev. A* **62** (2000) 012302.

7. V. Bužek and M. Hillery. Quantum copying: Beyond the no-cloning theorem. *Phys. Rev. A* **54** (1996) 1844–1852.

8. V. Bužek, M. Hillery, and R. F. Werner. Optimal manipulation with qubits: universal NOT gate. *Phys. Rev. A* **60** (1999) 2626–2629.

9. H. Fan, K. Matsumoto, X.-B. Wang, and H. Imai. Phase-covariant quantum cloning. *J. Phys. A: Math. Gen.* **35** (2002) 7415–7423.

10. A. Fujiwara and P. Algoet. One-to-one parametrization of quantum channels. *Phys. Rev. A* **59** (1999) 3290–3294.

11. N. Gisin and S. Popescu. Spin flips and quantum information for antiparallel spins. *Phys. Rev. Lett.* **83** (1999) 432–435.

12. N. J. Harvey, R. D. Kleinberg, and A. R. Lehman. Comparing network coding with multicommodity flow for the k-pairs communication problem. MIT LCS Technical Report 964, September 2004.

13. M. Hayashi, K. Iwama, H. Nishimura, R. Raymond, and S. Yamashita. Quantum network coding. Talk at *9th QIP*, 2006. quant-ph/0601088.

14. M. Hayashi, K. Iwama, H. Nishimura, R. Raymond, and S. Yamashita. (4, 1)-quantum random access coding does not exist. *New J. Phys.* **8** (2006) 129.

15. P. Høyer and R. de Wolf. Improved quantum communication complexity bounds for disjointness and equality. *Proc. 19th STACS, Lecture Notes in Comput. Sci.* **2285** (2002) 299–310.

16. R. Koetter. Network coding home page. http://tesla.csl.uiuc.edu/~koetter/ NWC/

17. D. Leung, J. Oppenheim, and A. Winter. Quantum network communication –the butterfly and beyond. quant-ph/0608233.

18. A. Nayak. Optimal lower bounds for quantum automata and random access codes. *Proc. 40th IEEE FOCS*, pp. 369–376, 1999.

19. M. A. Nielsen and I. L. Chuang. *Quantum Computation and Quantum Information*, Cambridge, 2000.

20. M. B. Ruskai, S. Szarek, and E. Werner. An analysis of complete-positive trace-preserving maps on 2×2 matrices. *Lin. Alg. Appl.* **347** (2002) 159–187.

21. B. Schumacher. Quantum coding. *Phys. Rev. A* **51** (1995) 2738–2747.

22. Y. Shi and E. Soljanin. On multicast in quantum network. *Proc. 40th Annual Conference on Information Sciences and Systems*, 2006.

23. P. Shor. Scheme for reducing decoherence in quantum computer memory. *Phys. Rev. A* **52** (1995) 2493–2496.

24. S. Wehner and R. de Wolf. Improved lower bounds for locally decodable codes and private information retrieval. *Proc. 32nd ICALP, Lecture Notes in Comput. Sci.* **3580** (2005) 1424–1436.

Reachability in Unions of Commutative Rewriting Systems Is Decidable[*]

Mikołaj Bojańczyk and Piotr Hoffman

Institute of Informatics, Warsaw University, Poland
{bojan,piotrek}@mimuw.edu.pl

Abstract. We consider commutative string rewriting systems (Vector Addition Systems, Petri nets), i.e., string rewriting systems in which all pairs of letters commute. We are interested in reachability: given a rewriting system R and words v and w, can v be rewritten to w by applying rules from R? A famous result states that reachability is decidable for commutative string rewriting systems. We show that reachability is decidable for a union of two such systems as well. We obtain, as a special case, that if $h : U \to S$ and $g : U \to T$ are homomorphisms of commutative monoids, then their pushout has a decidable word problem. Finally, we show that, given commutative monoids U, S and T satisfying $S \cap T = U$, it is decidable whether there exists a monoid M such that $S \cup T \subseteq M$; we also show that the problem remains decidable if we require M to be commutative, too.

Topic classification: Logic in computer science – rewriting.

1 Summary of Results

A *string rewriting system* R over a finite alphabet Σ is simply a finite set of rules of the form $v \mapsto w$, where v and w are words over Σ (string rewriting systems are also called *semi-Thue systems*). Such a system defines a one-step rewriting relation $\to_R$ and a multistep rewriting relation $\to_R^*$ on words over Σ: a word v rewrites in one step to a word w if there exist words $t, v_0, u, w_0 \in \Sigma^*$ such that $v = t v_0 u$, $w = t w_0 u$ and $v_0 \mapsto w_0$ is a rule of R; the multistep rewriting relation is the reflexive-transitive closure of the one-step relation. In the sequel, the statement "v rewrites to w in R" shall mean that $v \to_R^* w$.

The *(uniform) reachability problem* is defined as follows: Given a string rewriting system R and words v and w in the alphabet of that system, answer whether v rewrites to w in R? This problem is one of the most basic undecidable problems. However, for appropriate restrictions on the form of the rewriting system R, the problem may become decidable.

A string rewriting system is said to be *commutative* if for any two letters a and b of the alphabet it contains the rule $ab \mapsto ba$. Commutative string rewriting

---

[*] First author supported by the EC Research Training Network GAMES, second author by EC project SENSORIA (No. 016004).

W. Thomas and P. Weil (Eds.): STACS 2007, LNCS 4393, pp. 622–633, 2007.

systems are also called *Vector Addition Systems* or *Multiset Rewriting Systems*, since they treat words as multisets of letters — or elements of $\mathbb{N}^\Sigma$, where Σ is the alphabet. These systems are equivalent to *Petri nets*.

The following is a famous result [1,2]:

Theorem 1. *Reachability in commutative string rewriting systems is decidable.*

If R_Σ and R_Γ are rewriting systems over alphabets Σ and Γ, which may be distinct and may have a non-empty intersection, then one may consider the *union system* $R_\Sigma \cup R_\Gamma$ over the alphabet $\Sigma \cup \Gamma$. This system is constructed by simply taking both the rules from R_Σ, as well as the rules from R_Γ.

Note that the union of string rewriting systems may be much more complex than its parts. This is shown by the following example.

A string rewriting system is said to be *symmetric* if for any rule $v \mapsto w$ in the system, the system also contains the rule $w \mapsto v$. Such systems are called *Thue systems*. Sapir [3] (for an outline of the proof see [4]) constructed two symmetric string rewriting systems R_1 and R_2 such that the sets

$$\{v \# w : \ v \text{ rewrites to } w \text{ in } R_1\} \qquad \{v \# w : \ v \text{ rewrites to } w \text{ in } R_2\}$$

are both regular languages, but reachability in the (symmetric) union $R_1 \cup R_2$ is undecidable!

In this paper, we consider unions of commutative string rewriting systems. We do not make any assumptions on how the alphabets Σ and Γ of these systems relate to each other, whether they are disjoint or not, etc. Notice that the union $R_\Sigma \cup R_\Gamma$ of commutative systems R_Σ and R_Γ will not be commutative itself; if a is a letter from $\Sigma \setminus \Gamma$ and b a letter from $\Gamma \setminus \Sigma$, then $ab \mapsto ba$ will not be in the union system; moreover, ab will in general not rewrite to ba in the union system.

The main contribution of the paper is the following theorem:

Theorem 2. *Let R_Σ and R_Γ be commutative string rewriting systems. Then the reachability problem in the union $R_\Sigma \cup R_\Gamma$ is decidable.*

This theorem properly extends Th. 1. Its proof is quite complex, and in the next two sections we only outline it. The full proof will be found in the full version of this paper. The same applies to other omitted proofs.

In Sec. 4, we present results related to *amalgamations* [5] of commutative monoids. Some of these results are straightforward consequences of Th. 2, while others do not depend on it. The following is obtained easily from Th. 2:

Corollary 1. *Let $h : U \to S$ and $g : U \to T$ be homomorphisms of commutative monoids, and let $h' : S \to P$ and $g' : T \to P$ form a pushout of h and g (i.e. $h' \circ h = g' \circ g$ and any homomorphisms $h'' : S \to P'$ and $g'' : T \to P'$ with $h'' \circ h = g'' \circ g$ can be factored as $u \circ h' = h''$ and $u \circ g' = g''$ for a unique homomorphism $u : P \to P'$). Then P has a decidable word problem.*

If the homomorphisms h and g above are injective, then without loss of generality one may assume that $S \cap T = U$ and that h and g are inclusions. In this case the pushout P is called the *amalgamated product*. If S and T are given by symmetric rewrite systems, then the amalgamated product is given by the union of these systems.

In algebra, the following natural problem is considered [5,6,7,8,9,3]: Given monoids U, S and T satisfying $S \cap T = U$, answer whether some monoid M jointly extends S and T, that is, such that $M \supseteq S \cup T$. If so, $S \cup T$ is said to *embed* into M, or to be *embeddable*. To see why a union of monoids may not be embeddable, consider two distinct copies $\mathbb{Z}_1$ and $\mathbb{Z}_2$ of the integers with zero and addition, intersecting on the natural numbers with zero and addition: $\mathbb{Z}_1 \cap \mathbb{Z}_2 = \mathbb{N}$. The union $\mathbb{Z}_1 \cup \mathbb{Z}_2$ is not embeddable, because the two copies $-1_1, -1_2$ of -1 would have to be identified:

$$-1_1 = -1_1 + 1 + -1_2 = -1_2 \ .$$

The embeddability problem is in general undecidable. In fact, Sapir [3] proved the following result:

Theorem 3. *It is undecidable, given finite monoids U, S and T that satisfy $S \cap T = U$, whether there exists a monoid jointly extending S and T.*

We prove that in the case of commutative monoids the situation is rather different. More precisely, the following theorems hold:

Theorem 4. *It is decidable, given commutative monoids U, S and T that satisfy $S \cap T = U$, whether there exists a commutative monoid jointly extending S and T.*

Theorem 5. *It is decidable, given commutative monoids U, S and T that satisfy $S \cap T = U$, whether there exists a monoid jointly extending S and T.*

2   Theorem 2: Proof Strategy

This section and the next section are devoted to a proof of Th. 2. We begin by outlining the proof strategy.

When rewriting a word v into a word w in the system $R_\Sigma \cup R_\Gamma$, each intermediate step can be decomposed into a number of blocks, which are words from either Σ^* or Γ^*. Since the system is a union of two systems, one over Σ and the other over Γ, a single rewriting rule can only be applied within such a block. At first glance, in order to rewrite the word v into w, we may need to introduce new blocks along the way; moreover, there is no apparent bound on the number of these introduced blocks. The essence of our proof is that such a bound in fact exists. We show that we need only consider derivations where almost all blocks can be found already in v or w. Then we show that, when the number of introduced blocks is bounded, the problem is decidable by a reduction to reachability in commutative rewriting systems and an application of Th. 1.

We now give a formal definition of derivation, and then state the two key results: Prop. 1, which says that only derivations with a bounded number of new blocks are needed, and Prop. 2, which says that reachability is decidable when restricted to such derivations. The proof of the former is outlined in Sec. 3.

A derivation is a proof that one word can be rewritten into another, annotated with some geometrical structure. We will use this structure when manipulating derivations.

A *derivation* is a sequence of rows. A *row* contains a *global state*, which is simply a word u over $\Sigma \cap \Gamma$, and a sequence of nodes labeled by words over Σ or words over Γ (in particular, labels with words over $\Sigma \cap \Gamma$ are allowed as well). Each row corresponds to a word in the derivation: the concatenation of all the node labels. The first row in a derivation is called the *source* row, while the last row is called the *target* row. The most important information in the derivation is an edge relation. The idea is that an edge connects a node in one row with the corresponding node in the next row. There are several ways – called *rules* – in which nodes in one row can be connected to nodes in the next row. Because the global state and labels are elements of Σ^* or of Γ^*, and because we are interested in commutative string rewriting systems, the order of letters in the global state and in the labels is irrelevant. Therefore, we treat the global state and the labels as multisets, and if v and w are two such multisets, then we consider them equal if each letter appears in v and w the same number of times. Concatenation on such words is really just multiset union, and we denote such a union by $v + w$. The empty multiset is denoted by ϵ.

The rules on how one row may be connected to the next row are the following:

- *Transition* rule. This is the only rule where the underlying rewriting system is invoked. In this case, the label of one of the nodes is rewritten according to the system R_Σ or R_Γ. The global state can also be used in this rule. More formally, if $v + u$ rewrites in one step to $w + u'$ in the system R_Σ or R_Γ, where $u, u' \in (\Sigma \cap \Gamma)^*$, then two rows can be connected as follows (in the first column, we have the global state, in the subsequent columns we have the contents of the rows):

$$
\begin{array}{cccccc}
u & v_1 \ldots v_{i-1} & v & v_{i+1} \ldots v_n \\
\downarrow & \downarrow & \downarrow \;\; \downarrow & \downarrow \\
u' & v_1 \ldots v_{i-1} & w & v_{i+1} \ldots v_n
\end{array}
$$

The remaining rules are structural rules, which account for creating, deleting, separating and merging nodes.

- *Load* rule. In this rule a value u_2 from the global state $u + u'$ is loaded into a node with label v:

$$
\begin{array}{ccccc}
u + u' & v_1 \ldots v_{i-1} & v & v_{i+1} \ldots v_n \\
\downarrow & \downarrow & \downarrow & \downarrow \;\; \downarrow \\
u & v_1 \ldots v_{i-1} & v + u' & v_{i+1} \ldots v_n
\end{array}
$$

This rule has a dual *Store* rule, which works exactly in the opposite direction, taking a value $u' \in (\Sigma \cap \Gamma)^*$ from a node labeled $v + u'$ and storing it into the global state. (These rules could be simulated by transition rules, if both rewriting systems contained the rule $\epsilon \mapsto \epsilon$.)

- *Creation* rule. In this rule, a new node with empty label is created. The new node has indegree 0. The graph looks as follows:

$$u \qquad v_1 \ldots v_{i-1} \; v_i \ldots v_n$$
$$\downarrow \qquad \downarrow \qquad \searrow \qquad \searrow$$
$$u \qquad v_1 \ldots v_{i-1} \; \epsilon \; v_i \; \ldots v_n$$

This rule has a dual *Delete* rule, again working in the exact opposite direction: it removes a node labeled by ϵ.
- *Merge* rule. In this rule, two neighboring nodes with labels v and w are merged into one node with label $v + w$ without affecting the global state. In this case v and w must either both belong to Σ^*, or both belong to Γ^*.

$$u \qquad v_1 \ldots v_{i-1} \quad v \quad w \; v_i \ldots v_n$$
$$\downarrow \qquad \downarrow \qquad \downarrow \swarrow \swarrow \quad \swarrow$$
$$u \qquad v_1 \ldots v_{i-1} \, v + w \, v_i \ldots v_n$$

Again, the merge rule has a dual *Split* rule, where a node with label $v + w$ is split into two nodes with labels v and w.

A derivation is just an annotated way of showing that a word v can be rewritten into another word w in $R_\Sigma \cup R_\Gamma$. This is formally stated in the following lemma:

Lemma 1. *For any words $v = a_1 \ldots a_n$ and $w = b_1 \ldots b_k$ over $\Sigma \cup \Gamma$, v rewrites to w in $R_\Sigma \cup R_\Gamma$ iff there is a derivation with a source row containing a global state ϵ and nodes labeled $a_1, \ldots, a_n$, and a target row containing a global state ϵ and nodes labeled $b_1, \ldots, b_k$.*

Note that the large majority of edges connect nodes with the same labels. A rule is said to *act* on a node if this is not the case. Formally, the transition rule acts on two nodes (with labels v and w), the store and load rules act on two nodes (with labels $v + u'$ and v), the creation and deletion rules act on one node each (with label ϵ), while the merge and split rules act on three nodes each (with labels v, w and $v + w$).

Two nodes in a derivation are considered *connected* if they are connected by an edge (orientation of the edges is irrelevant). A *component* is a maximal set of nodes that can be pairwise connected by a sequence of edges.

In general, a component can contain labels from both Σ^* and Γ^*, since edges can go from Γ^* to $(\Gamma \cap \Sigma)^*$, and then to Σ^*. However, we can absorb the word from $(\Gamma \cap \Sigma)^*$ into the global state using a load and a deletion rule, and then recreate and restore this node (in a new component) using a creation and store rule, which shows:

Lemma 2. *For any derivation, there exists a derivation with the same source and target rows and such that each of its components contains nodes that are either all labeled by words from Σ^*, or all labeled by words from Γ^*.*

From now on we shall assume that all derivations are of the above type.

Th. 2 is an immediate corollary of Lemmas 1 and 2, and the following two propositions:

Proposition 1. *For any derivation, there is a derivation that has the same source and target rows and uses at most $k + 2$ creation rules, where k is the number of nodes in the target row.*

Proposition 2. *Given $k \in \mathbb{N}$ and source and target rows, it is decidable whether there is a derivation containing at most k creation rules with the given source and target rows.*

3 Theorem 2: Eliminating Creation Rules

In this section we outline our proof of Prop. 1.

Our strategy is as follows. First we show in Sec. 3.2 that without loss of generality one may consider only derivations without *islands* (islands are components that intersect neither the source, nor the target row). Then we show in Sec. 3.3 and 3.4 that every derivation is equivalent to one where each component contains at most one creation rule. This is done in two steps. First in Sec. 3.3 we show that a weaker condition – called compactness – can be obtained. Then in Sec. 3.4 we show how compactness implies Prop. 1.

First however, we need to provide some auxiliary definitions.

3.1 Partial Derivations

A partial derivation is a generalized type of derivation that can also use a *silent* rule:

$$
\begin{array}{cc}
u & v_1 \ldots v_n \\
\downarrow & \downarrow \\
u' & v_1 \ldots v_n
\end{array}
$$

Partial derivations are used to decompose non-partial ones into pieces: if we remove part of a derivation, we must still keep track of the changes to the global state that are caused by the removed part. These changes are witnessed by the silent rule.

Two partial derivations D, D' are considered equivalent, if they have the same number of rows, same source and target rows, same global states, and use silent rules in the same rows.

At the risk of confusion, we will omit the word partial from the term partial derivation. The previously defined derivations – ones without silent rules – will be referred to as non-partial.

We now introduce two operations on derivations: one extracts a smaller derivation from a larger one, the other combines several derivations into a single one.

Subderivations. Let X be a union of components. We denote by $D[X]$ the derivation where only nodes coming from X are left, and the other nodes are removed. Moreover, rules that acted on nodes outside X are replaced by silent rules (which may modify the global state). The following lemma proves the correctness of this construction:

Lemma 3. *If X is a union of components in D, then $D[X]$ is a derivation.*

We say that derivations $D_1, \ldots, D_n$ are *compatible* if they have the same number of rows, they have the same global states in each row, and for each row, at most one of the derivations uses a non-silent rule. Compatible derivations $D_1, \ldots, D_n$ can be joined into a bigger derivation $D_1 \cdots D_n$ by concatenation. In each row of the concatenated derivation, we have a concatenation of the appropriate rows in $D_1, \ldots, D_n$.

Lemma 4. *If derivations $D_1, \ldots, D_n$ are compatible, then the concatenation $D_1 \cdots D_n$ is a derivation.*

3.2   Island Removal

Recall that an island in a derivation is a component that has nodes neither in the source, nor in the target row. As a first step, we eliminate islands. This process is rather straightforward: we move all islands to the right side of the derivation. Since all islands are either of type Σ^* or of type Γ^*, they can be squeezed into two components. We will from now on assume that the derivation does not contain any islands.

3.3   Compact Components

Recall that we want to convert a derivation into one where each component has at most one creation rule. In this section we prove a weaker version of this statement, where only the number of "unguarded" creation rules is bounded.

A *neighbor* of x is a node in the same row, which is directly to the left or right of x. A node is *guarded* if it has a neighbor in the same component. A component is *compact* if each created node is either guarded or is the only node of the component in its row. In particular, a compact component has at most one unguarded created node.

The following proposition is the main result of this section:

Proposition 3. *Every derivation is equivalent to one with all components compact.*

The rest of this section is devoted to a proof of Prop. 3. The proof is by induction on the number of components in the derivation. Before we proceed with the proof, we introduce several auxiliary concepts.

Paths and enclosures. A path is a connected set of nodes X such that each node $x \in X$ is connected with at most two nodes from X. Nodes $x \in X$ that are connected to exactly one node in X are called *ends* of the path. A path with at least two nodes has exactly two ends. Note that the path need not be a directed path: for instance, if two nodes x, y in one row are merged into a node $x \cdot y$ in the next row, then the three nodes $\{x, y, x \cdot y\}$ form a path, whose ends are the nodes x and y.

An *enclosure* is a path X, whose ends $x, y \in X$ are either both in the source row, or both in the target row. The nodes z that satisfy $x < z < y$ are called the *base* of the enclosure (the order $<$ and its non-strict version $\leq$ refer to which node comes first in a row). An enclosure is called *tight* if its base does not contain nodes in the same component as X. The *cobase* is the set of nodes in the source and in the target rows that are not in the base and are not x, y. An enclosure X partitions the nodes of a derivation into three parts:

- The enclosure X itself.
- The *interior* $in(X)$ of the enclosure. These are the nodes that can be connected to the base of the enclosure without passing through X.
- The *exterior* $ex(X)$ of the enclosure. These are the remaining nodes. Stated differently, these are the nodes that can be connected to the cobase of the enclosure without passing through X.

Note that both the exterior and interior can contain nodes from the component of X. We extend the notions of interior and exterior to arbitrary sets of nodes X: the interior $in(X)$ is the union of all interiors $in(Y)$ of all enclosures $Y \subseteq X$. The exterior is the intersection of all the exteriors $ex(Y)$.

We say that a set of nodes Y is *enclosed* by a set of nodes X if $Y \subseteq in(X)$.

The height of a set of nodes is the number of rows used by this set. The *inner depth* of an enclosure X is the maximal height of an enclosed component. The *outer depth* is the height of the enclosure.

One outermost component. When there is only one component, the statement is trivial. A component is *outermost* in a derivation if it is not enclosed by any other component. It can be shown that one only needs to consider derivations with one outermost component:

Lemma 5. *Without loss of generality, one can consider only derivations with one outermost component.*

Compacting. By the above lemma, we may assume that the derivation in Prop. 3 has only one outermost component, which we call X. We now proceed to the heart of the proof of Prop. 3: making components compact.

The procedure we are going to use does not create any new nodes, nor does it modify the type of rules used or the global state. It only rearranges the order of nodes in each row. In particular, all the transformed derivations will have the same nodes.

The following straightforward lemma is given without proof:

Lemma 6. *One can find tight enclosures $X_1, \ldots, X_n$ with pairwise disjoint interiors such that all components enclosed by X are enclosed by one of the X_i.*

For each $i = 0, \ldots, n$, we will inductively correct our derivation, so that the following invariant is satisfied:

- All components enclosed by $X_1, \ldots, X_i$ are compact.
- For $j = 1, \ldots, i$, one cannot find nodes $y_1 \leq x \leq y_2$ lying in one row and such that $x \in X$ and the nodes $y_1, y_2 \notin X$ are enclosed by X_j.

It can be shown that at the end of the process all components become compact, and hence Prop. 3 is obtained:

Lemma 7. *If the invariant is satisfied for $i = n$, then all components in the derivation are compact.*

So, we now proceed to prove the invariant. The base case $i = 0$ is immediate. So let us assume that the invariant holds for $i - 1$; our aim is to make it hold for i.

We assume without loss of generality that the base of X_i is in the source row. Let $\mathcal{Y}$ be the components that are enclosed by X_i. Each of these components has nodes in the source row, but no nodes in the target row (since they are enclosed by X_i). Let y be a node of maximal depth k (row number) among all nodes in components from $\mathcal{Y}$. One can see that y is unique, since it must be acted upon in a deletion rule, and in each row only one rule is applied. Let Y be any path with one end in y and the other end in the source row (such a path must exist, since there are no islands). By maximality of k, both the path Y and all components in $\mathcal{Y}$ are contained in the rows up to k.

We define three groups of nodes of the derivation:

- The nodes A (for "above") whose depth is at most k;
- The nodes B (for "below") whose depth is strictly greater than k.
- The nodes C that belong to one of the components $\mathcal{Y}$.

Note that $A \cap B = \emptyset$ and $C \subseteq A$. Our strategy is to partition the set $A \setminus C$ into two parts: A_0 and A_1. The idea is that nodes in A_0 are to the left of the path Y, while nodes in A_1 are to the right. Now as it is, this is not a clear concept, since the path Y may bend and turn many times; hence the need for a more formal definition. The definition we provide is based on the parity of the number of turns in the path Y. Using this definition, we will reorder the nodes in A so that in each row, all nodes in A_0 are to the left of all nodes in A_1. Finally, we will apply the induction assumption to C, and then place it between A_0 and A_1 as in Fig. 1.

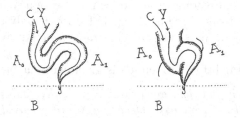

Fig. 1. Reordering the derivation to make it compact

Let x be a node in Y. We say x node is *bending* if it is the target of merge of two nodes from Y or the source of a split into two nodes from Y. Otherwise the node is called *nonbending*. Note that both ends of Y are nonbending. Given a node $x \notin Y$, we write $\#(x)$ for the number of nonbending nodes in Y that are in the same row as x and to the left of x. (This value is 0 when x is outside A.) We define A_0 (resp. A_1) to be the set of nodes $x \in A \setminus C$ where $\#(x)$ is even (resp. odd).

Let $D[C]$ be a derivation obtained from D by only leaving the nodes from C. By the induction assumption, $D[C]$ is equivalent to a compact derivation E. This derivation E only uses rows $1, \ldots, k$. We now construct a derivation D' where the components contained by enclosures $X_1, \ldots, X_i$ are compact. This derivation is obtained from D as follows.

- A row $j = 1, \ldots, k$ of the derivation D' is obtained as follows. We first place all the nodes from row j in D that belong to A_0 (preserving the order from D). Then we insert the j-th row of E. Finally, we place the nodes from row j in D that belong to A_1 (again, preserving the order).
- The rows $> k$ are left unaltered.

The following lemmas show the correctness of this construction; this concludes the proof of Prop. 3.

Lemma 8. D' *is a derivation.*

Lemma 9. *In D' the invariant holds for i.*

3.4   Few Creation Rules

In this section we conclude the proof of Prop. 1. We show that a derivation without islands and with all components compact can be transformed into one with few creation rules. Together with the island removal from Sec. 3.2 and the compacting procedure from Prop. 3, this concludes our proof of Prop. 1.

Let D be a derivation, and x a created node. The node x lies in some component X, which is compact. Since X is compact, x must either be guarded, or be the only node of the X in its row. We show that if x is guarded, then the derivation can be modified so that all nodes remain as in D, and all rules but the one creating x remain as in D as well; the rule creating x will be replaced by a split rule.

The modification of D is straightforward. If x is guarded, then it must have a neighbor x' from X on its left or right side. Suppose x' lies to the right of x and has label v:

$$u \qquad v_1 \ldots v_{i-1} \; v \; v_i \ldots v_n$$
$$\downarrow \qquad \downarrow \quad \searrow \searrow \qquad \searrow$$
$$u \qquad v_1 \ldots v_{i-1} \; \epsilon \; v \; v_i \ldots v_n$$

All we have to do is replace this creation rule by a split rule. This is done by adding an arrow from the node labeled v in the upper row to the node x in the lower row. Since $v = \epsilon + v$, we obtain a legitimate split rule. The same procedure may be used if x' lies to the left of x. Applying this construction iteratively gives us a derivation where all created nodes are the only nodes of their component in their row. Thus, in components that intersect with the source row, no created nodes may appear. In other components, at most one created node may appear per component. Since there are no islands, all the other components must intersect with the target row. Therefore there are at most as many creation rules as there are nodes in the target row.

4   Embeddability of Unions of Commutative Monoids

Any symmetric string rewriting system R over an alphabet Σ naturally defines a monoid M_R: it is the quotient of the free monoid Σ^* by the least congruence containing the rules of R. Elements of the monoid M_R are equivalence classes of the form $[v]$, where v is a word over Σ; classes $[v]$ and $[w]$ are equal iff v rewrites to w in R. The *word problem* for M_R is defined as follows: given words v and w over Σ, answer whether $[v] = [w]$ holds, that is, whether v and w represent the same element of the monoid M_R. Th. 2 implies that the word problem is decidable for monoids M_R, where R is the union of two commutative symmetric string rewriting systems; since pushouts of commutative monoids are of this form, Cor. 1 follows.

We now turn to the embeddability of unions of commutative monoids. Let U, S and T be commutative monoids given by symmetric commutative string rewriting systems R_U, R_S and R_T over the alphabets $\Sigma \cap \Gamma$, Σ and Γ respectively, satisfying $S \cap T = U$. Note that words u, u' over $\Sigma \cap \Gamma$ rewrite one to another in R_U if and only if they rewrite to each other in R_S (resp., R_T). This follows from the fact that U is a submonoid of S (resp., T).

We ask whether a monoid M exists such that $S \cup T \subseteq M$. A second question is whether the monoid M can be commutative. It is well-known [5] that if such an M exists, then as M one may take the pushout of the inclusions of U into S and of U into T (if M is to be commutative, then one takes the pushout in the category of commutative monoids). This is expressed by the slogan: if $S \cup T$ is embeddable, then it is embeddable in its pushout. Let P together with homomorphisms $\sigma : S \to P$, $\tau : T \to P$ be the pushout (or commutative pushout). All that has to be checked is whether σ and τ define an embedding of $S \cup T$ in the pushout, that is, whether they are "jointly injective". Formally,

Lemma 10. $S \cup T$ *is embeddable if and only if:*

1. σ *and* τ *are injective,*
2. *for all* $s \in S$ *and* $t \in T$, *if* $\sigma(s) = \tau(t)$, *then* $s = t \in U$.

The pushout and commutative pushout of $S \cup T$ may be defined easily. The pushout is given by the union $R_{nc} = R_S \cup R_T$ over $\Sigma \cup \Gamma$, while the commutative pushout is given by the union $R_c = R_S \cup R_T \cup \{ab \mapsto ba | a \in \Sigma, b \in \Gamma\}$ over $\Sigma \cup \Gamma$; here σ and τ are the canonical homomorphisms. This together with Lemma 10 leads to the following result:

Lemma 11. $S \cup T$ *is embeddable if and only if:*

1. *for all words v, v' over Σ, if v rewrites to v' in R_{nc}, then the same is true in R_S, and an analogous implication holds for Γ and R_T,*
2. *for all words v over Σ and w over Γ, if v rewrites to w in R_{nc}, then there is a word u over $\Sigma \cap \Gamma$ such that w rewrites to u in R_S and u rewrites to w in R_T.*

An analogous equivalence, with R_{nc} is replaced by R_c, holds for embeddability in a commutative monoid.

It can be shown that in the commutative case the above conditions can be effectively checked, and thus Th. 4 follows. The proof is based on the following powerful result of Taiclin [10]:

Theorem 6. *Given a symmetric commutative string rewriting system over a finite alphabet $\{a_1, \ldots, a_k\}$, one can compute a Presburger formula θ of $2k$ variables, such that:*

$$(n_1, \ldots, n_k)\, \theta\, (m_1, \ldots, m_k)$$

holds in $(\mathbb{N}^k, 0^k, +^k)$ if and only if $a_1^{n_1} \ldots a_k^{n_k}$ rewrites to $a_1^{m_1} \ldots a_k^{m_k}$ in the system.

As for embeddability in a monoid which is not necessarily commutative (Th. 5), this follows from Th. 4 and from the following proposition:

Proposition 4. *If a union of commutative monoids is embeddable, then it is embeddable in a commutative monoid.*

References

1. Mayr, E.W.: An algorithm for the general Petri net reachability problem. SIAM J. Comp. **13** (1984) 441–459
2. Kosaraju, S.R.: Decidability of reachability in vector addition systems (preliminary version). In: STOC'82, ACM (1982) 267–281
3. Sapir, M.V.: Algorithmic problems for amalgams of finite semigroups. J. Algebra **229** (2000) 514–531
4. Hoffman, P.: Unions of equational monadic theories. In: RTA'06. Volume 4098 of LNCS. (2006) 81–95
5. Howie, J.M.: Fundamentals of Semigroup Theory. London Math. Soc. Monogr. (N.S.), No. 12. Oxford Univ. Press (1996)
6. Howie, J.M.: Embedding theorems with amalgamation for semigroups. Proc. London Math. Soc. (3) **12** (1962) 511–534
7. Howie, J.M.: Epimorphisms and amalgamations: A survey of recent progress. Coll. Math. Soc. J. Bolyai **39** (1981) 63–82
8. Hall, T.E.: Representation extension and amalgamation for semigroups. Quart. J. Math. Oxford (2) **29** (1978) 309–334
9. Birget, J.C., Margolis, S., Meakin, J.: On the word problem for tensor products and amalgams of monoids. Intnl. J. Alg. Comp. **9** (1999) 271–294
10. Taiclin, M.A.: Algorithmic problems for commutative semigroups. Soviet Math. Dokl. **9** (1968) 201–204

Associative-Commutative Deducibility Constraints*

Sergiu Bursuc[1], Hubert Comon-Lundh[1], and Stéphanie Delaune[1,2]

[1] Laboratoire Spécification & Vérification, ENS de Cachan & CNRS, France
{bursuc,comon,delaune}@lsv.ens-cachan.fr
[2] School of Computer Science, University of Birmingham, UK

Abstract. We consider deducibility constraints, which are equivalent to particular Diophantine systems, arising in the automatic verification of security protocols, in presence of associative and commutative symbols. We show that deciding such Diophantine systems is, in general, undecidable. Then, we consider a simple subclass, which we show decidable. Though the solutions of these problems are not necessarily semi-linear sets, we show that there are (computable) semi-linear sets whose minimal solutions are not too far from the minimal solutions of the system. Finally, we consider a small variant of the problem, for which there is a much simpler decision algorithm.

1 Introduction

During the past ten years there has been a lot of work devoted to the logical verification of security protocols (as opposed to computational security). In general, the security problem is undecidable. Many authors designed subclasses for which there are decision algorithms (*e.g.* [14,1,5,12]). However, these techniques assume most of the time a *perfect cryptography*: the algebra of messages must be a free algebra. On the other hand, many protocols rely on algebraic properties of some primitives, for instance the Abelian Groups properties of the multiplication of exponents in modular exponentiation or the associativity, commutativity and nilpotence of exclusive or. Sometimes, the protocols cannot be executed when these properties are not considered.

Another research direction consists, instead of considering subclasses of protocols, to bind the search for an attack to a limited number of protocol instances. We get a reasonable confidence in the protocol security if we show that, say, after any 10 plays of the protocol there is no attack. In the free algebra case, the security problem for such a fixed number of sessions is co-NP-complete [15]. This result has then been extended beyond the perfect cryptography assumption: for exclusive or [7,3], for some properties of modular exponentiation [2,13], for properties combining exclusive or and homomorphisms [10] and other combinations [4].

---

* This work was partly supported by the RNTL project PROUVÉ 03V360, ACI-SI Rossignol, and EPSRC project EP/E029833.

W. Thomas and P. Weil (Eds.): STACS 2007, LNCS 4393, pp. 634–645, 2007.
© Springer-Verlag Berlin Heidelberg 2007

However, it seems that every new protocol comes with its own relevant algebraic properties. That is what happened to us when we were faced to a case study of electronic purse submitted to us by France Télécom (see [9]). In [6] two of us gave a result allowing to reduce many equational theories to associativity and commutativity only, at the price of considering many particular instances of the protocol. In particular, the above-mentioned properties of modular exponentiation, the exclusive-or properties, and the properties used in the electronic purse protocol can be reduced to associativity and commutativity alone. Now, this raises the problem of designing an algorithm solving the security problem in an algebra of messages, modulo associativity and commutativity. This were the reasons why we came to the problem, which is studied in this paper.

We consider the simplest instance of the problem (and we hope to be able to reduce many other situations to this one using combination techniques such as those described in [4]). A (AC)-*deducibility constraint* is a conjunction of expressions $T \Vdash u$ where u is a simple term and T is a finite set of simple terms. A simple term is an expression $\lambda_1 x_1 + \ldots + \lambda_k x_k + w$ where $\lambda_1, \ldots, \lambda_k \in \mathbb{N}$ and $w \in \mathbb{N}^m$. A solution of $T \Vdash u$ is an assignment σ of the variables $x_1, \ldots, x_k$ to vectors of $\mathbb{N}^m$ such that there is a linear combination of the simple terms $t\sigma$ of T, which equals $u\sigma$. It is not difficult to see that such problems can be reduced to (non-linear) Diophantine systems. Unfortunately, the converse is also true: AC-deducibility constraints are undecidable. Then, we consider a subclass of such constraints: first we assume a (classical) monotonicity condition between the sets T_i, which corresponds to the increasing of intruder's knowledge. We also assume that every term u in a constraint $T \Vdash u$ contains at most one variable. This ensures the determinacy of protocol executions, but there might be weaker conditions which ensure both determinacy and decidability. The core of our paper is a decision algorithm for this class of Diophantine equations.

Our decidability proof works as follows. We first define a relation between constraints, which is derived from an occurrence relation on variables, and consider the strongly connected components for this relation. In each of such components we show that, if there is a solution, then there is one, which is not far (w.r.t. Euclidian distance) of a solution of some (finitely many) computable semi-linear sets. Then the last step consists in proving that the restrictions of minimal solutions of the whole system to minimal strongly connected components are not far from minimal solutions of the minimal strongly connected components. This allows to derive an algorithm (in NEXPTIME), which solves our constraints.

In a last part of the paper, we consider another interpretation of the constraint system. In this interpretation, the intruder is not only allowed to add messages, but also to substract them. In this interpretation, we show that there is a much simpler decision procedure.

2   AC-Deducibility Constraints and Diophantine Equations

As explained in the introduction, several algebraic properties have been studied recently [7,3,2]. In [6], we gave a result allowing us to reduce many relevant equational theories to associativity and commutativity only. In this section, we focus on this particular equational theory. We consider simple messages built from constants, variables and the symbol + only. Moreover, the only intruder capability consists in adding messages. We believe that many other intruder inference systems can be reduced to this simple one, by combination techniques.

2.1 Basic Definitions

Let $\mathcal{A}$ be a finite set of constants, $\mathcal{X}$ be a set of variable symbols disjoint from $\mathcal{A}$ and $+$ be an associative and commutative (AC) symbol, which will be assumed later to have a neutral element 0. *Terms* are expressions

$$n_1 \cdot X_1 + \ldots + n_k \cdot X_k + m_1 \cdot a_1 + \ldots + m_l \cdot a_l$$

where $n_1, \ldots, n_k, m_1, \ldots, m_l$ are positive (non null) integers, $X_1, \ldots, X_k$ are distinct variable symbols and $a_1, \ldots, a_l$ are distinct constant symbols. Other writings of terms (*e.g.* with repeated variables or constants or with some null coefficients) are normalized into the above canonical form.

Let t be a term and u be a constant or a variable. The *number of occurrences* of u in t, denoted by $|t|_u$, is 0 if u does not occur in t, and the coefficient of u in t otherwise. $|t|_{\max}$ the integer $\max(\{|t|_a \mid a \in \mathcal{A}\})$ and by $t^{\mathcal{X}}$ (resp. t^0) the term such that $|t^{\mathcal{X}}|_a = 0$ for every $a \in \mathcal{A}$ (resp. $|t^0|_X = 0$ for every $X \in \mathcal{X}$) and $t = t^{\mathcal{X}} + t^0$. A *ground term* t is a term such that $t^0 = t$. It can also be viewed as a vector of non-negative integers, whose dimension is $|\mathcal{A}|$. A *substitution* (resp. a *ground substitution*) is a mapping from a finite subset of $\mathcal{X}$, called its *domain* to the set of terms (resp. ground terms). Substitutions are extended, as usual, to endomorphisms of the term algebra. We write $\{X_1 \mapsto t_1, \ldots, X_p \mapsto t_p\}$ the substitution σ whose domain is $\{X_1, \ldots, X_p\}$ and such that, $\forall i = 1, .., p, X_i\sigma = t_i$. A ground substitution $\{X_1 \mapsto t_1, \ldots, X_p \mapsto t_p\}$ can be represented by a p-columns matrix whose i^{th} column is $X_i\sigma$.

Example 1. Let $\mathcal{A} = \{a, b, c, d\}$ and let t be the ground term $2a + b + c$. The representation of t as a vector is described below. We have that $|t|_{\max} = 2$. The substitution $\sigma = \{X_1 \mapsto t, X_2 \mapsto 2d\}$ can be represented as follows.

$$t := \begin{pmatrix} 2 \\ 1 \\ 1 \\ 0 \end{pmatrix} \qquad \sigma := \begin{pmatrix} 2 & 0 \\ 1 & 0 \\ 1 & 0 \\ 0 & 2 \end{pmatrix}$$

$\mathbb{N}^n$ is ordered with the product ordering: if $\Lambda = (\lambda_1, \ldots, \lambda_n)$, $\Lambda' = (\lambda'_1, \ldots, \lambda'_n) \in \mathbb{N}^n$, $\Lambda \leq \Lambda'$ if and only if $\forall i \in \{1..n\}, \lambda_i \leq \lambda'_i$. $\Lambda < \Lambda'$ if and only if $\Lambda \leq \Lambda'$ and $\Lambda \neq \Lambda'$. This ordering is a well-ordering: in any infinite sequence of vectors, there is an infinite increasing subsequence. Following the vector representation of ground terms, this ordering is also used to compare ground terms. For instance $a + b < 2a + b + c$. It can also be extended to ground substitutions: $\sigma \leq \sigma'$ iff $dom(\sigma) = dom(\sigma')$ and $\forall X \in dom(\sigma), X\sigma \leq X\sigma'$. The following definition expresses the intruder deduction capabilities: given the messages $t_1, \ldots, t_n$, he is able to build any combination of them:

Definition 1 (AC-deducibility). *Given terms* $t_1, \ldots, t_n, u$, *we write* $t_1, \ldots,$ $t_n \vdash u$ *if there are non-negative integers* $\lambda_1, \ldots, \lambda_n$ *such that* $\lambda_1 \cdot t_1 + \ldots + \lambda_n \cdot t_n = u$.

Example 2. $2a + x, b + x, a + c \vdash 7a + 2x + 3c$ with $\lambda_1 = 2$, $\lambda_2 = 0$ and $\lambda_3 = 3$.

Definition 2 (AC-deducibility constraint). *An AC-deducibility constraint is an expression* $T \Vdash u$ *where* T *is a finite set of terms and* u *is a term. An AC-deducibility constraint system* $\mathcal{C}$ *is a finite conjunction of such constraints. A ground substitution* σ *is a solution of* $t_1, \ldots, t_n \Vdash u$ *if its domain contains the variables of* $t_1, \ldots, t_n, u$ *and* $t_1\sigma, \ldots, t_n\sigma \vdash u\sigma$. σ *is a solution of a constraint system* $\mathcal{C}$ *if it is a solution of every individual AC-deducibility constraint.*

The previous definition allows to express the ability to mount an attack in a given number of steps: initially, the intruder knows a finite set of messages T_0 and must be able to build an instance of the message u_1 expected by some honest agent. He replies by sending a corresponding message v_1, which increases the intruder knowledge. Again, from T_0 and v_1, the intruder must be able to build an instance of u_2 and gets the corresponding instance of $v_2, \ldots$ and after n such steps the intruder can deduce a message s, which was supposed to be secret. This translates into the constraint system

$$T_0 \Vdash u_1 \ \wedge \ T_0, v_1 \Vdash u_2 \ \wedge \ \ldots \ \wedge \ T_0, v_1, \ldots, v_n \Vdash s$$

The details of this formalism are reported in many papers (see *e.g.* [15]). Variables in the terms represent the pieces of the messages that cannot be analysed by the agent: it could be nonces or cyphertexts whose key is unknown. The agent will accept any message in place of this variable. That is how many classical logical attacks are constructed: the intruder, at some point, replaces the expected message with a message, which only differs from the correct one in the non-analyzable parts. Hence, finding a solution to the above AC-deducibility constraint system amounts to find (constructible) fake instances allowing to retrieve the secret after n steps.

Example 3. Consider the system $a \Vdash X \ \wedge \ a, X + b \Vdash Y$. Typical solutions of this systems are $\{X \mapsto 2a, Y \mapsto 5a + 2b\}, \{X \mapsto k_1 a; Y \mapsto k_2 k_1 a + k_2 b\}$, with $k_1, k_2 \geq 0$.

Putting together Definitions 1 and 2, we get the following problem, whose decision is the subject of this paper:

Given an AC-deducibility constraint system $T_1 \Vdash u_1, \ldots T_n \Vdash u_n$, does there exist a substitution σ such that,

$$\exists (\lambda_{i,t})_{i \in \{1..n\}, t \in T_i} \in \mathbb{N}^{|T_1| + \ldots + |T_n|}. \ \bigwedge_{i=1}^{n} \sum_{t \in T_i} \lambda_{i,t} t\sigma = u_i\sigma$$

Definition 3 (minimal solution). *Let* $\mathcal{C}$ *be an AC-deducibility constraint system and* σ *be a solution to* $\mathcal{C}$. σ *is a minimal solution of* $\mathcal{C}$ *if for every solution* σ' *of* $\mathcal{C}$, $\sigma' \not< \sigma$.

2.2 From AC-Deducibility Constraints to Diophantine Equations ...

In the above problem, if the set of constants is $\{a_1, \ldots, a_m\}$, the equality holds iff the coefficients of every a_i are identical on both sides. Assuming that $X_1, \ldots, X_p$ are the variables of the system $\mathcal{C}$ of n AC-deducibility constraints, $\mathcal{A} = \{a_1, \ldots, a_m\}$ and σ is a solution to $\mathcal{C}$, we consider the variables $x_{i,j}$, representing the coefficient of a_j in $X_i\sigma$ and the coefficients $\lambda_{k,t}$ of the term $t \in T_k$ in the kth constraint $T_k \Vdash u_k$. Then $\mathcal{C}$ has a solution iff there is a solution to the conjunction, for $k = 1..n, j = 1..m$ of the equations

$$\sum_{t \in T_k} \lambda_{k,t}(|t|_{a_j} + \sum_{i=1}^{p} |t|_{X_i} \, x_{i,j}) = |u_k|_{a_j} + \sum_{i=1}^{p} |u_k|_{X_i} \, x_{i,j} \tag{1}$$

This is a system of $n \times m$ quadratic Diophantine equations, whose variables are $x_{i,j}, \lambda_{k,t}$. In addition, we add equations ruling out the solutions $X_i = 0$.

Example 4. Consider the constraint system $2a \Vdash X_1 \wedge 2a, \ X_1 + b \Vdash 3X_2 + a$ and assume that a, b are the only two constants. This constraint can be translated into the equivalent Diophantine system

$$\exists \, \lambda_{1,1}, \lambda_{2,1}, \lambda_{2,2}. \begin{cases} 2\lambda_{1,1} = x_{1,1} \\ 0 = x_{1,2} \\ 2\lambda_{2,1} + \lambda_{2,2}x_{1,1} = 3x_{2,1} + 1 \\ \lambda_{2,2}x_{1,2} + \lambda_{2,2} = 3x_{2,2} \end{cases}$$

which can also be expressed in matricial notation:

$$\exists \, \Lambda. \begin{pmatrix} 2 & 0 & 0 \\ 0 & 0 & 0 \\ 0 & 2 & x_{1,1} \\ 0 & 0 & x_{1,2}+1 \end{pmatrix} \cdot \Lambda = \begin{pmatrix} x_{1,1} \\ x_{1,2} \\ 3x_{2,1}+1 \\ 3x_{2,2} \end{pmatrix}$$

We also ensure that $x_{1,1} \neq 0$ and $x_{2,1}, x_{2,2}$ are not both 0, adding $x_{1,1} = 1 + z_1$ and $x_{2,1} + x_{2,2} = 1 + z_2$.

This shows that we can reduce our problem to some Diophantine systems. Such systems seem to be particular ones. Unfortunately, this is not true, as we show in the next section.

2.3   ... and Back

We show here that we can also go back from Diophantine systems: any Diophantine system can be encoded in an AC-deducibility constraint system. Hence:

Proposition 1. *The problem of deciding whether a system of deducibility constraints has a solution is undecidable.*

To prove this result, we use the following formulation of Hilbert's 10th problem, known to be undecidable [8]. Note that we can simulate the product by using the identity $(u + v)^2 = u^2 + v^2 + 2uv$.

INPUT: a finite set S of Diophantine equations where each equation is of the form: $x_i = m$, $x_i + x_{i'} = x_j$, or $x_j = x_i^2$.
OUTPUT: Does S have a solution in $\mathbb{N}$?

Given an instance S of Hilbert's 10th problem with n variables $x_1, \ldots, x_n$ we built an AC-constraint system $\mathcal{C}(S)$, such that S has a solution iff $\mathcal{C}(S)$ has a solution. We use three constants a, b, c and assume first that variables of $\mathcal{C}$ can be mapped to 0 (neutral element). This is not a restriction as we may then reduce the problem to systems of AC-deducibility constraints by guessing first which variables are assigned to 0.

Our encoding. Let n (resp. p) be the number of equations (resp variables) in S. We describe below how we build the first part $\mathcal{A}(p)$ of our constraint system. For every $i = 1, \ldots, p$, the constraint system $\mathcal{A}(p)$ contains the following five deducibility constraints whose free variables are X_i, Y_i, and Z_i:

$$a \Vdash X_i \quad b \Vdash Y_i \quad a \Vdash Z_i \quad a + b \Vdash X_i + Y_i \quad X_i + b \Vdash Z_i + Y_i$$

Lemma 1. *Let $p \in \mathbb{N}$ and σ a solution of $\mathcal{A}(p)$. For $i = 1, ..p$, $|Z_i\sigma|_a = |X_i\sigma|_a^2$.*

The part $\mathcal{B}(S) = \{d_1, \ldots, d_n\}$ of our coding which depends on $S = \{e_1, \ldots, e_n\}$ and contains one deducibility constraint per equation and is built as follows.

- if e_k is $x_i = m$ then d_k is $X_i + c \Vdash m \cdot a + c$
- if e_k is $x_i + x_{i'} = x_j$ then d_k is $X_i + X_{i'} + c \Vdash X_j + c$,
- if e_k is $x_i = x_j^2$ then d_k is $X_i + c \Vdash Z_j + c$.

Example 5. Let $S_e = \{x_1 = 2, \; x_3 = x_2^2, \; x_2 + x_3 = x_1\}$. We obtain for $\mathcal{B}(S_e)$

$$X_1 + c \Vdash 2a + c \quad X_3 + c \Vdash Z_2 + c \quad X_2 + X_3 + c \Vdash X_1 + c$$

3   A Decidable Class of AC-Deducibility Constraints

AC-deducibility constraints are undecidable. However, fortunately, we may impose relevant restrictions on our constraint system.

3.1   Well-Formed and Simple Constraint System

Given a set of terms T, we let T^0 be the ground terms of T and $T^{\mathcal{X}}$ be the non-ground terms of T, so that $T = T^0 \uplus T^{\mathcal{X}}$. The first restriction we consider is *monotonicity*. As we have seen before when we sketched how the security problem is expressed, the left members of the constraints were increasing, w.r.t. inclusion. This is not by chance: this corresponds to the assumption that the intruder never forgets any information. We add now this assumption:

Definition 4. *A system $\mathcal{C}$ is monotone (resp. monotone w.r.t. ground terms) if its constraints can be ordered $T_1 \Vdash u_1, \ldots, T_n \Vdash u_n$ in such a way that $T_i \subseteq T_{i+1}$ (resp. $T_i^0 \subseteq T_{i+1}^0$) for any i such that $1 \le i < n$.*

The next restriction corresponds to the way in which variables are bounded: messages $u_1, \ldots, u_n$ are sent in this order over the network. When it is sent, the corresponding instance of u_i is determined (and not before). Hence, each time a variable occurs first in some u_i, it must not have occurred before in some T_j, with $j \leq i$. Furthermore, the protocol must be deterministic: upon reception of u_i (or its instance), the agent must not have any choice in sending its message. For instance, a protocol rule, which, upon receiving $X + Y$, states that X must be replied, is ambiguous on many instances, and cannot be implemented in a reasonable way. Determinacy is ensured by introducing the variables one by one:

Definition 5 (well-formed). *Let* $\mathcal{C} = \{T_1 \Vdash u_1, \ldots, T_n \Vdash u_n\}$ *be a monotone constraint system. We say that* $\mathcal{C}$ *is well-formed if it satisfies*

1. *(origination property) for every* $i \leq n$ *for every* $X \in vars(T_i)$, *there exists* $j < i$ *such that* $X \in vars(u_j)$. *We will write* $\min(X)$ *the index of the constraint in which* X *appears for the first time.*
2. *(deterministic) for all* $X, Y \in vars(\mathcal{C})$, *if* $X \neq Y$ *then* $\min(X) \neq \min(Y)$.

The notion of origination and the notation $\min(X)$ are defined in a similar way on constraint systems which are monotone w.r.t. ground terms. The hypotheses introduced so far are not considered as real restriction and have already been used in [3,2]. We will actually require a stronger property, implying determinacy:

Definition 6 (simple). *A deducibility constraint* $T \Vdash u$ *is said simple if* u *is of the form* $\beta X + u_0$ *for some variable* X, *some* $\beta \in \mathbb{N}$ *and some ground term* u_0. *A constraint system* $\mathcal{C}$ *is said simple if all the constraints in* $\mathcal{C}$ *are simple.*

By convention, $\beta = 0$ means that $u = u^0$ and $u^0 = 0$ means that $u = \beta X$.

Example 6. The system $\mathcal{C}$ described below is simple and well-formed.

$$2a \Vdash X_1 + a \ \wedge \ 2a, X_1 + b \Vdash 3X_2 + b \ \wedge \ 2a, X_1 + b, X_2 \Vdash a$$

As in Section 2.2, each ground substitution can be viewed as a $p \times m$ tuple of integers if there are p variables in its domain and m constants. Then, to each AC-deducibility constraint system $\mathcal{C}$, we can associate the set of tuples of integers $S(\mathcal{C})$ corresponding to its set of solutions.

Sets of integers defined by solutions of AC-deducibility constraint systems strictly include semi-linear sets. Using an example similar to Example 3, we can define, using AC-deducibility constraints, the set of triples $\{(u, v, uv + w) \mid u, v, w \in \mathbb{N}\}$, which is not semi-linear and might even not be semi-polynomial [11].

The remainder of this section is devoted to the proof of the following theorem.

Theorem 1. *The problem of deciding whether a simple and well-formed AC-deducibility constraint system has a solution is decidable.*

We will allow assignments to 0, a neutral element for $+$. This is not a restriction, since we can force variables to be distinct of 0 by guessing, for each variable of the system, a constant c_X and replacing X with $c_X + X'$ in the system. This replacement preserves simplicity and well-formedness.

3.2   The Algorithm

From now, by "constraint system" we mean a simple well-formed AC-deducibility constraint system.

First step. In a first phase, given a constraint system $T_i \Vdash u_i$, we guess what are the useful terms $\mathcal{U}_i$ in each $T_i^{\mathcal{X}}$, *i.e.* we guess which coefficients are assigned 0.

Definition 7 (solution compatible with $\mathcal{U}$). *Let $\mathcal{C} = \{T_1 \Vdash u_1, \ldots, T_n \Vdash u_n\}$ be a constraint system. Let $\mathcal{U}$ be the sequence $(\mathcal{U}_1, \ldots, \mathcal{U}_n)$ with $\mathcal{U}_i \subseteq T_i^{\mathcal{X}}$. Let σ be a solution of $\mathcal{C}$. We say that σ is* compatible with $\mathcal{U}$ *if there exists a tuple of $\lambda_{k,t} \in \mathbb{N}$, one for each $k \in \{1, \ldots, n\}, t \in T_k$ such that:*

$$\forall k \leq n. \begin{cases} \sum_{t \in T_k} \lambda_{k,t} t\sigma = u_k \sigma \\ \forall t \in T_k^{\mathcal{X}}. \ \lambda_{k,t} \neq 0 \ \Leftrightarrow t \in \mathcal{U}_k \end{cases}$$

Example 7. Consider the constraint system $\mathcal{C}$ described in Example 6. Let $\mathcal{U}$ be the sequence $(\emptyset, \{X_1 + b\}, \{X_2\})$. Consider the substitution $\sigma = \{X_1 \mapsto a, X_2 \mapsto a\}$. We claim that σ is a solution of $\mathcal{C}$ compatible with $\mathcal{U}$. Indeed, we may choose $\lambda_{1,2a} = \lambda_{2,2a} = \lambda_{2,X_1+b} = \lambda_{3,X_2} = 1$ and $\lambda_{i,t} = 0$ otherwise.

Second step. This step consists in constructing a dependency graph on variables:

Definition 8. *Let $\mathcal{C} = \{T_1 \Vdash u_1, \ldots, T_n \Vdash u_n\}$ be a constraint system. Let $\mathcal{U}$ be a sequence $(\mathcal{U}_1, \ldots, \mathcal{U}_n)$ with $\mathcal{U}_i \subseteq T_i^{\mathcal{X}}$. The relation $\mathcal{R}_{occ}^{\mathcal{U}}$ on $vars(\mathcal{C})$ is defined by:*

$$X \ \mathcal{R}_{occ}^{\mathcal{U}} \ Y \Leftrightarrow \exists i. \begin{cases} Y \in vars(u_i), \ and \\ X \in vars(t) \ for \ some \ term \ t \in \mathcal{U}_i. \end{cases}$$

We consider the equivalence relation $=_{occ}^{\mathcal{U}}$. We have $X =_{occ}^{\mathcal{U}} Y$ if, and only if, $X \prec_{occ}^{\mathcal{U}} Y$ and $Y \prec_{occ}^{\mathcal{U}} X$ where $\prec_{occ}^{\mathcal{U}}$ is the transitive closure of $\mathcal{R}_{occ}^{\mathcal{U}}$. We denote by $[=_{occ}^{\mathcal{U}}]$ the equivalence classes induced by $=_{occ}^{\mathcal{U}}$. $\prec_{occ}^{\mathcal{U}}$ is then an ordering on $[=_{occ}^{\mathcal{U}}]$. In the last example, $X_1 \prec_{occ}^{\mathcal{U}} X_2$ and $[=_{occ}^{\mathcal{U}}] = \{\{X_1\}, \{X_2\}\}$.

Third step. Now, we choose one of the minimal classes (minimal strongly connected component in the graph) and solve the subsystem consisting of variables in that class.

Definition 9. *Let $\mathcal{C} = \{T_1 \Vdash \beta_1 X_1 + u_1, \ldots, T_n \Vdash \beta_n X_n + u_n\}$ be a simple constraint system. Let $\mathcal{U}$ be the sequence $(\mathcal{U}_1, \ldots, \mathcal{U}_n)$ with $\mathcal{U}_i \subseteq T_i^{\mathcal{X}}$ and M be a minimal class of $[=_{occ}^{\mathcal{U}}]$. We let $\mathscr{C}_M(\mathcal{C}, \mathcal{U})$ be the constraint system defined as follows.*

$$\mathscr{C}_M(\mathcal{C}, \mathcal{U}) = \{T_i^0 \cup \mathcal{U}_i \Vdash \beta_i X_i + u_i \mid X_i \in M\}.$$

Example 8. Consider the system $\mathcal{C}$ described in Example 6 and the sequence $\mathcal{U}$ described in Example 7. We have $M = \{X_1\}$ and $\mathscr{C}_M(\mathcal{C}, \mathcal{U}) = \{2a \Vdash X_1 + a\}$.

We first show that this subsystem inherits good properties of the original system. However, note that $\mathscr{C}_M(\mathcal{C}, \mathcal{U})$ is not always monotone.

Lemma 2. *Let $\mathcal{C} = \{T_1 \Vdash u_1, \ldots, T_n \Vdash u_n\}$ be a simple and well-formed constraint system. Let $\mathcal{U}$ be the sequence $(\mathcal{U}_1, \ldots, \mathcal{U}_n)$ with $\mathcal{U}_i \subseteq T_i^{\mathcal{X}}$ and M be a minimal class of $[=_{occ}^{\mathcal{U}}]$. The minimal component $\mathscr{C}_\mathsf{M}(\mathcal{C}, \mathcal{U})$ is simple, monotone w.r.t. ground terms and satisfies the origination property.*

Then, we prove that the set of solutions of $\mathscr{C}_\mathsf{M}(\mathcal{C}, \mathcal{U})$ can be represented by a semi-linear set. We also show that we can compute a bound $\delta(\mathscr{C}_\mathsf{M}(\mathcal{C}, \mathcal{U}))$ on minimal solutions of such systems. This is detailed in section 3.3.

Fourth step. We prove (this is the subject of section 3.4) that a minimal solution of the system is "not far" from a minimal solution of $\mathscr{C}_\mathsf{M}(\mathcal{C}, \mathcal{U})$, for which we computed a bound. Then we guess a partial substitution, on the variables of the minimal class, within the computed bound, and replace it in the system. At this point, we eliminated at least one variable, while keeping the set of minimal solutions. We only have to iterate the process, until all variables are eliminated.

Summary of the procedure. Let $\mathcal{C} = \{T_1 \Vdash u_1, \ldots, T_n \Vdash u_n\}$ be a simple and well-formed constraint system.

1. Guess $\mathcal{U}$
2. Compute $[=_{occ}^{\mathcal{U}}]$
3. While $[=_{occ}^{\mathcal{U}}] \neq \emptyset$:
   (a) extract a system $\mathscr{C}_\mathsf{M}(\mathcal{C}, \mathcal{U})$
   (b) Compute the minimal solutions S of this system
   (c) Guess a replacement in $\mathcal{C}$ of the variables of $\mathscr{C}_\mathsf{M}(\mathcal{C}, \mathcal{U})$, which is at a distance bounded by δ from a solution in S.

This procedure yields a finite set of AC-deducibility constraint systems in which every term is ground. The satisfiability of such systems can be decided in non-deterministic polynomial time by reducing it to linear Diophantine equations.

3.3   The Case of a Strongly Connected Variable Graph

In this section, we show that the solutions of $\mathscr{C}_\mathsf{M}(\mathcal{C}, \mathcal{U})$ is a semi-linear set.

Lemma 3. *Let $\mathcal{C}' = \mathscr{C}_\mathsf{M}(\mathcal{C}, \mathcal{U}) = \{T_1 \Vdash \beta_1 X_1 + u_1, \ldots, T_n \Vdash \beta_n X_n + u_n\}$ There exists a bound $\eta(\mathcal{C}') \in \mathbb{N}$, effectively computable from $\mathcal{C}'$, such that for every solution σ of $\mathcal{C}'$ compatible with $(T_1^{\mathcal{X}}, \ldots, T_n^{\mathcal{X}})$, there exist a tuple of $\lambda_{i,t} \in \mathbb{N}$, one for each $k \in \{1, \ldots, n\}, t \in T_i$, such that:*

$$(t \in T_i^{\mathcal{X}} \Rightarrow \lambda_{i,t} \leq \eta(\mathcal{C}')) \wedge \sum_{t \in T_i} \lambda_{i,t} t\sigma = \beta_i X_i \sigma + u_i$$

To prove this lemma, we simply use, for each variable, a non trivial cycle on it in the graph $\mathcal{R}_{occ}^{\mathcal{U}}$. Assuming X occurs in t and putting together all inequalities along the cycle we get $\lambda_{i,t} \leq (\prod_{j \in c} \beta_j)(1 + \sum_{j \in c} |u_j|_{\max})$ where c is the cyclic sequence of indices starting from i.

Now the coefficients of non-ground terms are bounded, we are back to linear Diophantine systems: we can guess a value $r_{i,t}$, within the above-computed bound, for the coefficients $\lambda_{i,t}$ when t is not ground, and get an equivalent (disjunction of) systems

$$\bigwedge_{i=1}^{n} \sum_{t \in T_i^0} \lambda_{i,t}t + \sum_{t \in T_i^{\mathcal{X}}} r_{i,t}t = \beta_i X_i + u_i \tag{2}$$

whose variables are the remaining $\lambda_{i,t}$ and the X_i. We also let the homogeneous system be:

$$\bigwedge_{i=1}^{n} \sum_{t \in T_i^0} \lambda_{i,t}t + \sum_{t \in T_i^{\mathcal{X}}} r_{i,t}t^{\mathcal{X}} = \beta_i X_i \tag{3}$$

Lemma 4. *For the system $\mathcal{C}' = \mathscr{C}_{\mathsf{M}}(\mathcal{C}, \mathcal{U})$, the solutions of (1) form a semi-linear set. Given an assignment θ of the $\lambda_{i,t}$ (t non ground) to $r_{i,t}$, we let $\Sigma_0(\theta)$ be the minimal solutions of (2) and $\Sigma_h(\theta)$ be the minimal non-null solutions of (3). Each solution of $\mathcal{C}'$ assigns the $\lambda_{i,t}$, for t not ground, to some $r_{i,t} \leq \eta(\mathcal{C}')$, which defines a substitution θ. Then the remaining solutions assign the variables to the vectors $V_0 + \sum_{i=1}^{N} \mu_i V_i$ for $V_0 \in \Sigma_0(\theta)$, $\Sigma_h(\theta) = \{V_1, \dots, V_N\}$ and $\mu_1, \dots, \mu_N$ are arbitrary non-negative integers.*

For the next step, we need to compute a distance within which the restriction of the minimal solutions of $\mathcal{C}$ to variables of $\mathscr{C}_{\mathsf{M}}(\mathcal{C}, \mathcal{U})$ lie. Then let

$$\delta(\mathscr{C}_{\mathsf{M}}(\mathcal{C}, \mathcal{U}), \theta) = \sum_{\sigma \in \Sigma_0(\theta)} \sigma + \beta(\mathscr{C}_{\mathsf{M}}(\mathcal{C}, \mathcal{U})) \cdot \sum_{\sigma \in \Sigma_h(\theta)} \sigma$$

where $\beta(\mathcal{C}) = \prod_{X \in vars(\mathcal{C})} \beta_{\min(X)}$. Let $\delta(\mathscr{C}_{\mathsf{M}}(\mathcal{C}, \mathcal{U})) = \max_{\theta \leq \theta^0}(\delta(\mathscr{C}_{\mathsf{M}}(\mathcal{C}, \mathcal{U}), \theta))$ where θ^0 assigns $\eta(\mathscr{C}_{\mathsf{M}}(\mathcal{C}, \mathcal{U}))$ to all variables.

3.4 The Projections of Global Minimal Solutions Are Not Far from Minimal Solutions of the Minimal Classes

In this section, we show that if a simple and well-formed constraint system $\mathcal{C}$ has a solution compatible with a given sequence $\mathcal{U}$, then there is one such σ satisfying $\sigma|_{\mathsf{M}} \leq \delta(\mathscr{C}_{\mathsf{M}}(\mathcal{C}, \mathcal{U}))$. The proof relies on the above bound,

Proposition 2. *Let $\mathcal{C} = \{T_1 \Vdash \beta_1 X_1 + u_1, \dots, T_n \Vdash \beta_n X_n + u_n\}$ be a simple and well-formed constraint system. Let $\mathcal{U}$ be the sequence $(\mathcal{U}_1, \dots, \mathcal{U}_n)$ with $\mathcal{U}_i \subseteq T_i^{\mathcal{X}}$ and M be a a minimal class of $[=_{occ}^{\mathcal{U}}]$. If σ is a minimal solution of $\mathcal{C}$ compatible with $\mathcal{U}$ then $\sigma|_{\mathsf{M}} \leq \delta(\mathscr{C}_{\mathsf{M}}(\mathcal{C}, \mathcal{U}))$.*

This also concludes the proof of the main theorem: the algorithm is roughly described in Section 3.2 and we can now complete the last step of the loop: we guess an assignment $\sigma|_M$ of the variables of $\mathscr{C}_{\mathsf{M}}(\mathcal{C}, \mathcal{U})$, within a finite set, bounded by $\delta(\mathscr{C}_{\mathsf{M}}(\mathcal{C}, \mathcal{U}))$.

4   Another Deducibility System

In this section, we consider again AC-deducibility constraint systems, but with a different interpretation of the deducibility relation. More precisely, we keep the same definitions as in Section 2, except for Definition 1 which becomes:

Definition 10. $t_1, \ldots, t_n \vdash u$ iff $\exists \lambda_1, \ldots, \lambda_n \in \mathbb{Z}$ such that $\sum_{i=1}^{n} \lambda_i t_i = u$.

The main difference is now the ability of using negative coefficients. Note however that we do not have any opposite symbol: variables can only be substituted by positive combinations of constants. This new inference system, denoted by $\mathcal{I}_{\pm}$, allows us to obtain a procedure, which is simpler than the one presented in the previous section and also to deal with a broader class of constraint systems. Moreover, the additional capabilities given to the attacker through this inference system is realistic in most of our applications.

Theorem 2. *The problem of whether a well-formed constraint system has a solution w.r.t. $\mathcal{I}_{\pm}$ is decidable.*

Note that we allow here right hand sides to contain more than one variable. For the proof of this theorem, we perform a variable elimination. Considering a minimal constraint (w.r.t. inclusion of left hand sides), it has the form $T \Vdash \beta X + u_0$: by origination, T can only contain ground terms and, by determinacy, the right hand side contains at most one variable. We eliminate X by showing that there is a bound on the coefficients of $t \in T$ in a solution:

Lemma 5. *Let $\mathcal{C}$ be a well-formed satisfiable (w.r.t. $\mathcal{I}_{\pm}$) constraint system. Let $T \Vdash \beta X + u_0$ be a constraint of $\mathcal{C}$ with a minimal left hand side, with $\beta \in \mathbb{N}$ and u_0 a ground term. Then there exists a solution σ of $\mathcal{C}$ and coefficients $\lambda_{1,t}$ for $t \in T$ such that $\sum_{t \in T} \lambda_{1,t} t = \beta X \sigma + u_0$ and $\forall t \in T. 0 \leq \lambda_{1,t} \leq \beta + |u_0|_{\max}$.*

This lemma heavily relies on the ability to substract. For instance, if the coefficient of some t is negative in a solution, then we increase the coefficient and the corresponding value of X. Then, this is compensated in other constraints by substracting to coefficients what is added by the new contribution of X.

5   Conclusion

We have shown the decidability of two deducibility constraint systems modulo associativity and commutativity. These results are a first step towards a general decision procedure for security protocols in a bounded number of sessions. Our results have several weaknesses. The first one is algorithmic complexity. An analysis of the algorithms show that they are in NEXPTIME. It is not clear whether this would be applicable in practice. There is a hope still, since security protocols are in general very small (up to 6 protocol rules). Only an implementation would prove the usefulness of the method. There is however a long way before implementing the techniques. We need first to establish a combination result, which would allow to handle more complicated constructions and inference systems. The last weakness of our results is the additional condition (right hand side only contain one variable) we have in Theorem 1. It is not clear that it is necessary. Though protocols generally satisfy this condition, it might not be the case for the constraints which are computed using the procedure of [6].

References

1. B. Blanchet and A. Podelski. Verification of Cryptographic Protocols: Tagging Enforces Termination. *Theoretical Computer Science*, 333(1-2):67–90, 2005.
2. Y. Chevalier, R. Küsters, M. Rusinowitch, and M. Turuani. Deciding the security of protocols with Diffie-Hellman exponentiation and product in exponents. In *Proc. 23rd Conf. on Foundations of Software Technology and Theoretical Computer Science (FST&TCS'03)*, vol. 2914 of *LNCS*, pages 124–135. Springer-Verlag, 2003.
3. Y. Chevalier, R. Küsters, M. Rusinowitch, and M. Turuani. An NP decision procedure for protocol insecurity with XOR. In *Proc. 18th IEEE Symp. Logic in Computer Science (LICS'03)*, pages 261–270. IEEE Comp. Soc. Press, 2003.
4. Y. Chevalier and M. Rusinowitch. Hierarchical combination of intruder theories. In *Proc. 17th International Conference on Rewriting Techniques and Applications (RTA'06)*, volume 4098 of *LNCS*, pages 108–122. Springer, 2006.
5. H. Comon and V. Cortier. Tree automata with one memory, set constraints and cryptographic protocols. *Theoretical Computer Science*, 331(1):143–214, 2005.
6. H. Comon-Lundh and S. Delaune. The finite variant property: How to get rid of some algebraic properties. In *Proc. 16th Int. Conf. on Rewriting Techniques and Applications (RTA'05)*, vol. 3467 of *LNCS*, pages 294–307. Springer, 2005.
7. H. Comon-Lundh and V. Shmatikov. Intruder deductions, constraint solving and insecurity decision in presence of exclusive or. In *Proc. 18th IEEE Symp. Logic in Computer Science (LICS'03)*, pages 271–280. IEEE Comp. Soc. Press, 2003.
8. M. Davis, Y. Matijasevich, and J. Robinson. Hilbert's tenth problem, Diophantine equations: positive aspects of a negative solution. In *Proc. of Symposia in Pure Maths*, pages 323–378, 1976.
9. S. Delaune. *Vérification des protocoles cryptographiques et propriétés algébriques*. Thèse de doctorat, ENS Cachan, France, 2006.
10. S. Delaune, P. Lafourcade, D. Lugiez, and R. Treinen. Symbolic protocol analysis in presence of a homomorphism operator and *exclusive or*. In *Proc. 33rd International Colloquium on Automata, Languages and Programming (ICALP'06)*, volume 4052 of *LNCS*, pages 132–141. Springer, 2006.
11. W. Karianto, A. Krieg, and W. Thomas. On intersection problems for polynomially generated sets. In *Proc. 33rd International Colloquium on Automata, Languages and Programming (ICALP'06)*, volume 4052 of *LNCS*. Springer, 2006.
12. G. Lowe. Towards a completeness result for model checking of security protocols. *J. Computer Security*, 7(2–3):89–146, 1999.
13. J. Millen and V. Shmatikov. Symbolic protocol analysis with an abelian group operator or Diffie-Hellman exponentiation. *J. Computer Security*, 13(3):515–564, 2005.
14. R. Ramanujam and S. P. Suresh. Decidability of context-explicit security protocols. *J. Computer Security*, 13(1), 2005.
15. M. Rusinowitch and M. Turuani. Protocol insecurity with finite number of sessions is NP-complete. In *Proc. 14th IEEE Computer Security Foundations Workshop*, 2001.

On the Automatic Analysis of Recursive Security Protocols with XOR[*]

Ralf Küsters[1] and Tomasz Truderung[2]

[1] ETH Zurich
ralf.kuesters@inf.ethz.ch
[2] University of Kiel and Wrocław University
tomasz.truderung@ii.uni.wroc.pl

Abstract. In many security protocols, such as group protocols, principals have to perform iterative or recursive computations. We call such
protocols *recursive protocols*. Recently, first results on the decidability
of the security of such protocols have been obtained. While recursive
protocols often employ operators with algebraic, security relevant properties, such as the exclusive OR (XOR), the existing decision procedures,
however, cannot deal with such operators and their properties. In this
paper, we show that the security of recursive protocols with XOR is decidable (w.r.t. a bounded number of sessions) for a class of protocols in
which recursive computations of principals are modeled by certain Horn
theories. Interestingly, this result can be obtained by a reduction to the
case without XOR. We also show that relaxing certain assumptions of
our model lead to undecidability.

1 Introduction

In group protocols and other classes of security protocols a protocol step performed by a principal (i.e., receiving a message and then sending a message)
typically involves recursive or iterative computation. We will refer to such protocols by *recursive protocols*, in contrast to *non-recursive protocols* where the
computation performed in one protocol step is simple and does not require recursion. Many, in fact, most of the recursive protocols proposed in the literature employ operators, such as Diffie-Hellman exponentiation and exclusive OR
(XOR), which have algebraic, security relevant properties (see, e.g., [12,13,7]).
The present work is concerned with the automatic security analysis of such protocols. While recently first results on the decidability of the security (more precisely, the secrecy property) of recursive protocols have been obtained [8,10,15],
these results do not take into account operators with algebraic properties (see
also the related work).

The attacks on recursive protocols presented in the literature illustrate that
dealing with algebraic properties of operators is security relevant (see, e.g.,
[12,13,7]). One example is the Recursive Authentication (RA) protocol proposed

---

[*] This work was partially supported by the DFG under grant KU 1434/4-1.

W. Thomas and P. Weil (Eds.): STACS 2007, LNCS 4393, pp. 646–657, 2007.
© Springer-Verlag Berlin Heidelberg 2007

by Bull and Otway [1]. In this protocol, a key distribution server receives a list of (arbitrary many) requests of pairs of principals who want to establish session keys among them. The server processes this list iteratively, generates the session keys, and then distributes them. In [11], Paulson proved that the RA protocol is secure under the assumption that session keys are distributed using (ideally) secure encryption. However, Ryan and Schneider [13] showed that there is an attack on the protocol if XOR is used to distribute keys, which in fact was the original proposition by Bull and Otway: In the attack by Ryan and Schneider, the adversary is given one session key generated by the server and using this key he can obtain all other session keys by chaining messages via XOR.

CONTRIBUTION OF THIS WORK. In this paper, we extend the model for recursive protocols proposed in [15], henceforth called the *Horn theory model*, by adding XOR (along with its algebraic properties). In the Horn theory model, recursive/iterative computations performed by principals in one protocol step are modeled by certain Horn theories, hence the name. While in models for non-recursive protocols XOR can be added without losing decidability of security (w.r.t. a bounded number of sessions) [2,6]—security even remains NP-complete just as in the case without XOR [2]—for recursive protocols things are more involved. We show that a naïve extension of the Horn theory model by XOR leads to undecidability of security. (As a byproduct we also obtain undecidability in case complex keys are used in the Horn theory model, a fact that has not been observed before.) More precisely, we obtain undecidability in case principals may conjoin arbitrary messages received from the network by XOR. Conversely, we show decidability in case principals may only conjoin a fixed message, i.e., a message that does not depend on messages received from the network, with a message that depends on messages received from the network. We call protocols which only contain such principals ⊕-linear. From a practical point of view, ⊕-linear protocols are sufficient in many cases, e.g., for the RA protocol and other protocols [13,2,7]. We emphasize that we do not constrain the intruder in its ability to conjoin messages by XOR.

The technique used to obtain decidability is very different to the one in [15]. In fact, the main part of our proof is to reduce the security problem in the Horn theory model with XOR to the one without XOR. More precisely, we first prove certain properties of attacks involving XOR. Based on these properties we then reduce the security problem to the case without XOR, which by [15] is decidable. In the reduction we use the ability of principals to perform recursive computations in order to mimic applications of the XOR operator.

FURTHER RELATED WORK. For non-recursive protocols decidability of security (w.r.t. a bounded number of sessions) was shown for several operators with algebraic properties, e.g., XOR [2,6], Diffie-Hellman Exponentiation [3,14], and commuting public-key encryption [4]. However, the models employed in these works cannot handle recursive computations of principals, such as the computation of the server in the RA protocol. The techniques differ as well: Due to the absence of recursive computations, the reduction technique developed in the present work is not applicable in these models. Conversely, the techniques for bounding the size of attacks and the constraint solving techniques employed in [2,6,3,14,4] cannot immediately be applied to recursive protocols.

In [8,10], transducers were used to model recursive computations of principals. The expressiveness of these transducer-based models is orthogonal to the Horn theory model: While the transducer-based models allow to output messages of complex structure, in the Horn theory model only lists (or sets) of messages of a more simple structure can be produced. The main disadvantage of the transducer-based model is that, unlike the Horn theory model, messages cannot be tested for equality without losing decidability. This, as already observed in [10], immediately implies that security is undecidable in the transducer-based model with XOR (or Diffie-Hellman exponentiation) since these operators allow for (implicit) equality tests between arbitrary messages. In the transducer-based model, even one equality test (or alternatively, one application of the XOR operator) suffices for the undecidability.

Horn theories have also been used for the automatic analysis of *non-recursive* protocols (see, e.g., [5,16] and references therein). The results and techniques employed in these works are very different to the ones presented here: The main goal of these works, which also consider operators with algebraic properties, is automatic protocol analysis w.r.t. an *unbounded* number of sessions, where, however, the intruder knowledge is over-approximated.

STRUCTURE OF THE PAPER. In the following section, we introduce our protocol and intruder model, with an example presented in Section 3. The undecidability and decidability results are stated in Section 4 and 5, respectively. We conclude in Section 6. We refer the reader to our technical report for full proofs [9].

2   The Protocol and Intruder Model

In this section, we introduce our protocol and intruder model, including messages, principals, protocols, and attacks, along the lines of [15] where, unlike the model in [15], here messages may contain the exclusive OR (XOR).

HORN THEORIES. Let Σ be a finite signature, V be a set of variables, and $\mathcal{T}$ denote the set of terms over Σ and V. *Ground terms* are terms without variables. Substitutions are defined as usual. The application of a substitution σ to a term t is denoted by $t\sigma$. Substitutions are defined on sets of terms and atoms (see below) in the obvious way. For a unary predicate q and a (ground) term $t \in \mathcal{T}$ we call $q(t)$ a *(ground) atom*. For a set S of terms we write $q(S)$ for the set $\{q(s) \mid s \in S\}$ of atoms. Let $\sim$ be a congruence relation over $\mathcal{T}$. We write $q(t) \sim q'(t')$ if $q = q'$ and $t \sim t'$. A *(unary) Horn theory* T is a finite set of Horn clauses of the form $a_1, \ldots, a_n \Rightarrow a_0$ with atoms a_i for every i. Given a set of ground atoms A and a ground atom a, we say that a can be derived from A w.r.t. T (written $A \vdash_T a$) if there exists a *derivation* for a from A using T, i.e., there exists a sequence $b_1, \ldots, b_l$ of ground atoms such that $b_l \sim a$ and for every $i \in \{1, \ldots, l\}$ we either have $b_i \in A$ or there exists a substitution σ and a Horn clause $a_1, \ldots, a_n \Rightarrow a_0$ in T such that $a_0\sigma \sim b_i$ and for every $j \in \{1, \ldots, n\}$ there exists $k \in \{1, \ldots, i-1\}$ with $a_j\sigma \sim b_k$.

MESSAGES. Let $\mathcal{A}$ be a finite set of constants (also called *atomic messages*), such as principal names, nonces, and keys, and let $\mathcal{K}$ be a subset of $\mathcal{A}$ (the set of keys). We assume that $0, \mathsf{Sec} \in \mathcal{A}$ and that there is a bijection $\cdot^{-1}$ on $\mathcal{K}$ which maps every public (private) key k to its corresponding private (public) key k^{-1}. Let $\Sigma_{\mathcal{A}}$ (or simply Σ) be a finite signature consisting of all constants from $\mathcal{A}$, the unary function symbol $\mathsf{hash}(\cdot)$ (*hashing*), and the following binary function symbols: $\langle \cdot, \cdot \rangle$ (*pairing*), $\{\cdot\}$. (*symmetric encryption*), $\{\!|\cdot|\!\}$. (*public key encryption*), and $\oplus$ (*exclusive OR*).

The set of terms over Σ and V is defined by the following grammar:

$$\mathcal{T} ::= \mathcal{A} \mid V \mid \mathsf{hash}(\mathcal{T}) \mid \langle \mathcal{T}, \mathcal{T} \rangle \mid \{\mathcal{T}\}_{\mathcal{K}} \mid \{\!|\mathcal{T}|\!\}_{\mathcal{K}} \mid \mathcal{T} \oplus \mathcal{T}.$$

Note that we assume atomic keys, i.e., keys used to encrypt messages are required to be constants. We denote by $Var(t)$ the set of variables occurring in t.

Ground terms, i.e., terms without variables are called *messages*. To model the algebraic properties of XOR, we consider the congruence relation $\sim$ on $\mathcal{T}$ induced by the following equational theory:

$$x \oplus y = y \oplus x$$
$$(x \oplus y) \oplus z = x \oplus (y \oplus z)$$
$$x \oplus x = 0$$
$$x \oplus 0 = x$$

For example, we have that $a \oplus b \oplus \{0\}_k \oplus b \oplus \{c \oplus c\}_k \sim a$. (Due to the associativity of $\oplus$ we often omit brackets and simply write $a \oplus b \oplus c$ instead of $(a \oplus b) \oplus c$ or $a \oplus (b \oplus c)$.)

PRINCIPALS AND PROTOCOLS. A *protocol step* consists of a protocol rule and a send program. A *protocol rule* is of the form $t \to q(s)$ where $t, s \in \mathcal{T}$ and q is some unary predicate symbol. A *send program* Φ is a unary Horn theory where every Horn clause is of one of the following forms:

$$q'(t) \Rightarrow q''(x) \qquad \text{with } x \in Var(t), \qquad (1)$$
$$q'''(s) \Rightarrow I(s') \qquad \text{with } Var(s') \subseteq Var(s), \qquad (2)$$

where I is a distinguished unary predicate symbol, which will model the network, and hence, the intruder, $q', q'', q''' \neq I$ are arbitrary (not necessarily different) unary predicate symbols, t is a linear term (i.e., every variable in t occurs at most once) which does not contain the symbol $\oplus$, and the terms s and s' may be non-linear and may contain $\oplus$. Intuitively, clauses of the form (1), called *push clauses*, allow a principal to recursively traverse a term from top to bottom (e.g., process a list). Clauses of the form (2), called *send clauses*, are used by a principal to perform checks on messages (by matching them against s) and to output messages on the network, as will be clearer from the following definition:

For a ground atom $q(m)$, we define the set of *terms sent using* Φ by

$$[\![q(m)]\!]_\Phi = \{m' : q(m) \vdash_\Phi I(m')\}.$$

Now, the intuition behind a protocol step which consists of a protocol rule $t \to q(s)$ and a send program Φ is that a principal, after having received a term $t\theta$ for some ground substitution θ, sends all the terms from the set $[\![q(s\theta)]\!]_\Phi$ on the network, i.e., to the intruder, by running the send program Φ.

The decidability result in [15] in the Horn theory model without XOR works if t in (1) is flat, i.e., is of the form $t = f(x_1, \ldots, x_n)$ where the variables x_i are not required to be different. We could also allow such terms in (1). However, (complex) linear terms are better suited for modeling protocols. It is easy to see that linear terms in (1) can be turned into flat form by using auxiliary predicate symbols.

A *principal* Π is a finite edge-labeled tree where every edge is labeled by a protocol step. If the protocol rule of a protocol step is of the form $t \to q(s)$, we require that every variable occurring in s also occurs in t or the left-hand side of a protocol rule preceding $t \to q(s)$ in the tree Π. We also assume, w.l.o.g., that the set of predicates used in send programs of different protocol steps are pairwise disjoint, except that I may be used in all of the send programs. The intuition is that if a principal waits at a node of the tree and receives a message, then she can apply one of the protocol steps whose left-hand side (i.e., the left-hand side of the corresponding protocol rule) matches with the incoming message, and after having run the corresponding send program, moves to the next node.

For a principal Π we call a sequence π of protocol steps a *run of* Π if π is a sequence of protocol steps obtained when traversing Π from the root to some node of Π (not necessarily a leaf).

A *protocol* P is a tuple $(\Pi_1, \ldots, \Pi_l)$ of principals Π_i. We assume, w.l.o.g., that the set of variables of protocol rules of different principals are disjoint.

ATTACK. The intruder is the standard Dolev-Yao intruder extended by the ability to apply the XOR operator [6,2]. Formally, the intruder is modeled by the following Horn theory $T_\oplus$ where $k \in \mathcal{K}$ and $x, y \in V$:

$$I(x), I(y) \Rightarrow I(\langle x, y \rangle) \quad I(x), I(k) \Rightarrow I(\{x\}_k) \quad I(\{x\}_k), I(k) \Rightarrow I(x)$$
$$I(\langle x, y \rangle) \Rightarrow I(x) \quad I(x), I(k) \Rightarrow I(\{\!|x|\!\}_k) \quad I(\{\!|x|\!\}_k), I(k^{-1}) \Rightarrow I(x)$$
$$I(\langle x, y \rangle) \Rightarrow I(y) \quad I(x) \Rightarrow I(\mathsf{hash}(x)) \quad I(x), I(y) \Rightarrow I(x \oplus y)$$

Given a protocol $P = (\Pi_1, \ldots, \Pi_l)$, a *protocol execution scheme* of P is a sequence of protocol steps $\pi = \pi_1, \ldots, \pi_n$ such that each π_i can be assigned to one of the principals $\Pi_1, \ldots, \Pi_l$ and such that, for every i, the subsequence of elements of π assigned to Π_i is a run of Π_i, i.e., π is an interleaving of runs of the Π_i.

Now, an *attack* on P is a pair (π, θ) where $\pi = ((t_i \to q_i(s_i), \Phi_i))_{i=1}^n$ is a protocol execution scheme of P and θ is a ground substitution of the variables in $Var(\{t_1, s_1, \ldots, t_n, s_n\})$ such that

$$I(0), I([\![q_1(s_1\theta)]\!]_\Phi), \ldots, I([\![q_{i-1}(s_{i-1}\theta)]\!]_\Phi) \vdash_{T_\oplus} I(t_i\theta), \quad \text{for } i = 1, \ldots, n \quad (3)$$
$$I(0), I([\![q_1(s_1\theta)]\!]_\Phi), \ldots, I([\![q_n(s_n\theta)]\!]_\Phi) \vdash_{T_\oplus} I(\mathsf{Sec}) \quad (4)$$

where $\Phi = \bigcup_{i=1}^{n} \Phi_i$ (recall that different send programs use disjoint sets of predicates, except that they all may use I). Condition (3) says that in every step of the protocol execution the intruder is able to derive the message expected by the respective principal and (4) says that at the end he is able to derive the secret Sec. Note that, w.l.o.g., initially the intruder only knows the constant 0: One can define a designated principal that expects to receive 0 and in return outputs messages the intruder is allowed to know, e.g., public keys. A protocol is called *insecure* if there exists an attack on it. Let $\textsc{Attack}_{general} = \{P \mid P \text{ is an insecure protocol}\}$ denote the corresponding decision problem.

3   An Example Protocol

To illustrate our model, we present a formal description of the Recursive Authentication (RA) Protocol [1]. In what follows, we abbreviate messages of the form $\langle m_0, \ldots, \langle m_{n-1}, m_n \rangle \cdots \rangle$ by $m_0, \ldots, m_n$ and messages of the form $\langle m, \mathsf{hash}(\langle k, m \rangle) \rangle$, i.e., a message m along with a keyed hash on m, by $\mathsf{hash}_k(m)$.

The key distribution server S of the RA protocol shares a long-term (symmetric) key with every principal and performs only one (recursive) protocol step in a protocol run. In this protocol step, S receives an a priori unbounded sequence of requests of pairs of principals who want to obtain session keys for secure communication and then generates so-called certificates which contain the session keys. An example of the kind of message S receives is

$$\mathsf{hash}_{K_c}(C, S, N_c, \mathsf{hash}_{K_b}(B, C, N_b, \mathsf{hash}_{K_a}(A, B, N_a, -))) \tag{5}$$

where N_c, N_b, and N_a are nonces generated by C, B, and A, respectively, and K_c, K_b, and K_a are the long-term keys shared between the server S and the principals C, B, and A, respectively. Recall that, for instance, $\mathsf{hash}_{K_a}(A, B, N_a, -)$ stands for the message $\langle\langle A, \langle B, \langle N_a, - \rangle\rangle\rangle, \mathsf{hash}(\langle K_a, \langle A, \langle B, \langle N_a, - \rangle\rangle\rangle\rangle)\rangle$. Message (5) consists of three requests and indicates that C wants to share a session key with S, B with C, and A with B. The constant "$-$" marks the end of the sequence of requests. We emphasize that messages sent to S may contain an arbitrary number of requests—which must be processed by S recursively. Now, given message (5), S processes the requests starting from the outermost. First, S generates two certificates for C, namely, $\langle C, S, K_{cs} \oplus \mathsf{hash}_{K_c}(N_c), \{C, S, N_c\}_{K_{cs}} \rangle$ and $\langle C, B, K_{bc} \oplus \mathsf{hash}_{K_c}(N_c), \{C, B, N_c\}_{K_{bc}} \rangle$ (from these certificates C can easily deduce K_{cs} and K_{bc} and check whether the encrypted messages have the expected form). In the same way, certificates for B and A are generated, where A only obtains one certificate (containing the session key for communication with B).

Formally, the protocol step performed by S is as follows, where we assume that $P_0, \ldots, P_n$ are the principals that may participate in the RA protocol, with $P_n = S$, and every P_i, $i < n$, shares a long-term key K_i with S: The protocol rule of S is simply $x \to q(x)$ and the send program consists of the following Horn clauses, where $j \leq n$ and $i, i' < n$:

$$q(\langle\langle x_1, \langle x_2, \langle x_3, x_4\rangle\rangle\rangle, x_5\rangle) \Rightarrow q(x_4)$$
$$q(\text{hash}_{K_i}(P_i, P_j, x, -)) \Rightarrow I(M_{i,j})$$
$$q(\text{hash}_{K_i}(P_i, P_j, x, \text{hash}_{K_{i'}}(P_{i'}, P_i, x_1, x_2))) \Rightarrow I(M'_{i,i'})$$
$$q(\text{hash}_{K_i}(P_i, P_j, x, \text{hash}_{K_{i'}}(P_{i'}, P_i, x_1, x_2))) \Rightarrow I(M_{i,j})$$

where $M_{i,j} = \langle P_i, P_j, K_{ij} \oplus \text{hash}_{K_i}(x), \{P_i, P_j, x\}_{K_{ij}}\rangle$ and $M'_{i,i'} = \langle P_i, P_{i'}, K_{i'i} \oplus \text{hash}_{K_i}(x), \{P_i, P_{i'}, x\}_{K_{i'i}}\rangle$. The server would also check whether the first request is addressed to it. This can easily be captured by using another predicate; however, for simplicity of presentation this is not modeled here. The model of the principals $P_0, \ldots, P_{n-1}$ of the RA protocol is rather standard as they do not need to perform recursive computations. We therefore omit their formal specification here.

4   Undecidability of the General Case

We prove the following theorem (see [9] for details):

Theorem 1. *The problem* $\text{ATTACK}_{general}$ *is undecidable.*

The main intuition behind the proof is that, by combining recursive computations and XOR, it can be checked whether a sequence $C_0, \ldots, C_n$ of configurations corresponds to an (accepting) computation of a Turing machine. More precisely, let $M_i = C_i, \ldots, C_n$. The intruder can guess a sequence $C_0, \ldots, C_n$ and then a single principal performing just one protocol step checks whether i) C_0 corresponds to the initial configuration, ii) C_n corresponds to a final configuration, and iii) C_{i+1} is a successor configuration of C_i, for every $i < n$. If i) and ii) are satisfied, the principal outputs $\{M_0\}_k$ and $\{M_n\}_k \oplus \text{Sec}$, respectively, to the intruder. If iii) is satisfied, for i, the principal outputs $\{M_i\}_k \oplus \{M_{i+1}\}_k$ to the intruder. Now, if all checks—i), ii), and iii) for every $i < n$—are successful, and hence, the sequence of configurations is a valid computation, the intruder can XOR all messages obtained from the principal. This yields Sec. If at least one check failed, at least one "link" in the XOR chain would be missing in order to obtain Sec.

A similar reduction as the one sketched above also works if XOR is replaced by symmetric encryption where keys may be arbitrary messages (complex keys). Hence, we also obtain the following theorem, where $\text{ATTACK}_{compkey}$ is the security problem in our model with complex keys (and without XOR).

Theorem 2. *The problem* $\text{ATTACK}_{compkey}$ *is undecidable.*

5   Decidability of ⊕-Linear Protocols

In the proof of undecidability (Theorem 1) we used that a principal may conjoin two messages by XOR where both messages may depend on messages received from the network. In ⊕-linear protocols, defined next, this is forbidden.

In this section, we show that the existence of attacks can be decided for $\oplus$-linear protocols.

A protocol P is $\oplus$-*linear* if for each subterm of the form $t \oplus s$ occurring in P (both in protocol rules and in send programs), t or s is ground. For example, if the term $(x \oplus a) \oplus y$ with $a \in \mathcal{A}$, $x, y \in V$ occurs in P, then P is not $\oplus$-linear. The RA protocol (Section 3) is an example of an $\oplus$-linear protocol; see, e.g., [2] for another example. Let $\text{ATTACK}_{\oplus-linear} = \{P \mid P \text{ is an } \oplus\text{-linear, insecure protocol}\}$.

The main result of this paper is:

Theorem 3. *The problem* $\text{ATTACK}_{\oplus-linear}$ *is decidable.*

Before we provide a proof sketch of this theorem, we note that our result extends the decidability results presented in [6,2] for non-recursive protocols to recursive protocols, in case the protocols are $\oplus$-linear and restricted to atomic keys.

The proof of Theorem 3 consists of two main steps: First, we prove certain properties of derivations in the Horn theory model with XOR (Section 5.1). Based on these properties we then reduce the security problem to the case without XOR, which by [15] is decidable. In the reduction we use the ability of principals to perform recursive computations in order to mimic operations involving XOR. The reduction is sketched in Section 5.2. An initial (minor) step, not further discussed in this extended abstract, is to turn a protocol into simple form. This is used to combine all derivations carried out in (3) and (4) into a single derivation from $I(0)$ to $I(\mathsf{Sec})$. So, we may consider an attack as a single derivation, called *attack derivation* (see [9] for details).

5.1   Good Derivations

In this section, we identify and analyze properties of attack derivations.

First, we need to introduce some notation and terminology. We call a term *standard* if its top-symbol is not $\oplus$; otherwise, it is called *non-standard*. For a protocol P, let $\mathcal{S}_P$ denote the set of all the ground subterms of terms occurring in P and let $\mathcal{C}_P$ be the set consisting of all terms of the form $t_1 \oplus \cdots \oplus t_n$ with $t_i \in \mathcal{S}_P$ modulo $\sim$. Elements of $\mathcal{C}_P$ are referred to by c and decorations thereof. In what follows, non-standard terms will be written as $c \oplus t_1 \oplus \cdots \oplus t_n$ where c stands for a (ground) term in $\mathcal{C}_P$ and $t_1, \ldots, t_n$ are standard terms not in $\mathcal{C}_P$. A term is $\mathcal{C}_P$-*long* (or just *long*, if $\mathcal{C}_P$ is clear from the context) if it is of the form $c \oplus t_1 \oplus \cdots \oplus t_n$, for $n > 1$. Otherwise it is called $\mathcal{C}_P$-*short* (or just *short*).

We now introduce what we call modest and normal derivations and prove properties about them.

A derivation is *modest* if it uses the rules depicted in Figure 1 instead of $I(x), I(y) \rightarrow I(x \oplus y)$ where $c, c_0, \ldots, c_n \in \mathcal{C}_P$ and $t, t', t_1, \ldots, t_n$ are standard ground terms not in $\mathcal{C}_P$; s and s' are arbitrary ground terms. We observe that in a modest derivation long terms may only be used to obtain an element of $\mathcal{C}_P$, by applying rule (6). In all other rules ((7)–(10)), only short terms may be conjoined by XOR. However, (10), which allows to combine an unbounded number of short terms, may produce a long term.

$$I(s), I(s') \rightarrow I(c) \qquad \text{for } s \oplus s' \sim c \qquad (6)$$
$$I(c \oplus t), I(c) \rightarrow I(t) \qquad (7)$$
$$I(c \oplus t), I(c') \rightarrow I(c \oplus c' \oplus t) \quad \text{for } c \not\sim 0 \text{ and } c \oplus c' \not\sim 0 \qquad (8)$$
$$I(t), I(c) \rightarrow I(c \oplus t) \qquad (9)$$
$$I(c_0), I(c_1 \oplus t_1), \dots, I(c_n \oplus t_n) \rightarrow \qquad \text{for } n > 1, \text{ where the terms} \quad (10)$$
$$I(c \oplus t_1 \oplus \cdots \oplus t_n) \qquad t_1, \dots, t_n \text{ are pairwise distinct}$$
$$\text{and } c \sim c_0 \oplus \cdots \oplus c_n$$

Fig. 1. $\oplus$-Rules in Modest Derivations

The next lemma states that it is enough to consider modest derivations. Therefore, in the remainder of this section we will assume derivations to be modest.

Lemma 1. *If there exists an attack on P, then this attack can be proven by a modest derivation.*

We now introduce normal derivations. In a normal derivation, applications of certain classes of rules are grouped into segments and segments occur in a certain order. In this extended abstract, we will only define some aspects of normal derivations (see [9] for a full definition).

If $b_1, \dots, b_l$ is a derivation, then $b_i, b_{i+1}, \dots, b_j$ for $i \leq j$ is a subsequence of the derivation. A *segment* of a derivation is a maximal subsequence which does not contain any atom of the form $I(c)$, for some $c \in \mathcal{C}_P$, or any atom obtained by a protocol rule.

Rule (8) is called *variant rule*. A *variant segment* of a derivation is a maximal subsequence of a segment containing only atoms obtained by variant rules. Among others, a *normal* derivation satisfies the following conditions: (i) it does not contain two atoms a, a' such that $a \sim a'$, (ii) each segment contains at most one variant segment, and (iii) variant rules do not use as a premise an atom obtained from a variant rule. We can show the following:

Lemma 2. *If there exists an attack on P, then there exists a modest and normal derivation for this attack.*

Because the cardinality of the set $\mathcal{C}_P$ is exponentially bounded w.r.t. the size of P, the number of segments in an attack derivation is also exponentially bounded in the size of P. Now, as a result of Lemma 2 and the definition of normal derivations we obtain:

Lemma 3. *In a modest and normal attack derivation the number of variant segments is exponentially bounded in the size of the protocol.*

We now show that the number of long terms can be bounded in attack derivations. The key is the notion of a *profile* of a standard term. A profile α is defined w.r.t. an attack derivation δ and consists of an element c in $\mathcal{C}_P$ and a natural number k. Roughly speaking, two standard ground terms satisfy the same profile if they behave similarly w.r.t. c in the k-th segment of δ. In particular, if two terms have the same profile, each of them can be used instead of the other one when long terms are constructed by Rule (10). So, for a given derivation δ and a profile α, we will fix a term t_α^δ and use it whenever a term of profile α is used to build a long term.

If $c \oplus t_1 \oplus \cdots \oplus t_k$, for $k > 1$, is a long term, the positions where $t_1, \ldots, t_n$ occur are called *unimportant*. We can show the following lemma:

Lemma 4. *If there exists an attack on a protocol, then there exists a normal attack derivation δ for this protocol such that whenever terms t, t' of the same profile α occur in δ at unimportant positions, then $t = t'$.*

We call derivations of the form described in Lemma 4 *good*. Now, from the definition of profiles it immediately follows that the number of different profiles is (exponentially) bounded in the size of the protocol. Together with Lemma 4 we obtain:

Corollary 1. *If a term $c \oplus t_1 \oplus \cdots \oplus t_n$ occurs in a good attack derivation, then n is bounded exponentially in the size of the protocol. Furthermore, in a good attack derivation for a protocol, the number of distinct terms of the form $c \oplus t_1 \oplus \cdots \oplus t_n$, for $n > 1$, is bounded by some (computable) number M in the size of the protocol.*

5.2   Reduction to the $\oplus$-Free Case

We now show how the security problem can be reduced to the $\oplus$-free case, i.e., given a protocol P we construct a protocol P^+ which does not contain $\oplus$ such that there exists an attack on P (in the sense defined in Section 2) iff there exists an attack on P^+ in the $\oplus$-free setting. The main steps are i) to represent terms with $\oplus$ by $\oplus$-free terms and ii) to mimic intruder rules involving $\oplus$ in the $\oplus$-free setting.

For i)—representing terms—we use additional constants: a new constant e and, for each equivalence class $[c]_\sim$, $c \in \mathcal{C}_P$, a new constant denoted by $[c]$. Now, for a term t, we obtain its $\oplus$-free representation, denoted by $\ulcorner t \urcorner$, by recursively applying to each non-standard subterm of t the following transformation: a subterm of the form $c \oplus t$ (recall that, according to our convention, $c \in \mathcal{C}_P$ and t is a standard term not in $\mathcal{C}_P$) is transformed into $\{t\}_{[c]}$, and a subterm of the form $c \oplus t_1 \oplus \cdots \oplus t_n$, for $n > 1$, is transformed into $\{\{t_1, \{\ldots, \{\langle t_{n-1}, t_n \rangle\}_e \cdots\}_e\}_e\}_{[c]}$. We also substitute every $c \in \mathcal{C}_P$ by the constant $[c]$.

Now, we turn to intruder rules involving $\oplus$ and show how they can be mimicked in the $\oplus$-free setting. By the results of Section 5.1, we may assume that attack derivations are modest, normal, and good. In particular, by Lemma 1, it suffices to mimic rules (6) to (10):

- *Rule (7) and (9):* These rules can easily be mimicked by ordinary intruder rules (decryption and encryption). Consider, for instance, rule (7): In the original attack atoms $I(c \oplus t)$ and $I(c)$ are used to obtain $I(t)$. Now, $I(\ulcorner t \urcorner)$ can be derived from $I(\ulcorner c \oplus t \urcorner) = I(\{\ulcorner t \urcorner\}_{[c]})$ and $I(\ulcorner c \urcorner) = I([c])$ by the standard decryption rule.

- *Rule* (6): The result of this rule is of the form $I(c)$ with $c \in \mathcal{C}_P$. Because there is a bounded number, say L, of elements in $\mathcal{C}_P$, we can mimic this rule by adding L principals to P each with a single protocol step of the form $\langle \{x\}_{[c]}, \{x\}_{[c']} \rangle \to I([c \oplus c'])$.

- *Rule* (10): The result of this rule is a long term and we know, by Corollary 1, that the number of such terms is bounded by a constant M which only depends on the size of the protocol, so, again, we can handle this case by adding a bounded number of principals each with a single protocol step of the form

$$\langle [c_0], \{y_1\}_{[c_1]}, \ldots, \{y_n\}_{[c_n]} \rangle \to I(\{\{y_1, \{\ldots, \{y_{n-1}, y_n\}_e \cdots \}_e\}_e\}_{[c]}).$$

- *Rule* (8): By Lemma 3, we know that the number of variant segments (i.e., blocks of atoms obtained by the variant rule) is bounded by a number N depending only on the protocol size and that no element obtained by a variant rule is necessary as a premise of a variant rule in the same variant segment. Hence, each of these variant segments can be handled by a protocol step of the following form: (Note that it performs recursive computation.)

$$z \to p(z) \qquad \text{with the following send program:}$$
$$p(\langle x, y \rangle) \Rightarrow p(y)$$
$$p(\langle x, y \rangle) \Rightarrow p'(x)$$
$$p'(\langle \{x\}_{[c]}, [c'] \rangle) \Rightarrow I(\{x\}_{[c \oplus c']}) \qquad \text{for } c, c' \in \mathcal{C}_P$$

More details on the construction of P^+ can be found in [9]. We can show:

Lemma 5. *For an $\oplus$-linear protocol P there exists an attack on P (in the sense of Section 2) if and only if there exists an attack on P^+ in the $\oplus$-free setting.*

Since the security of P^+ is decidable [15] and P^+ can effectively be computed from P, Theorem 3 follows. A more careful analysis of the complexity of our construction reveals that the size of P^+ is double exponential in the size of P. As the secrecy of P^+ can be decide in NEXPTIME [15], we obtain a 3-NEXPTIME upper bound, which, however, we believe can be reduced to NEXPTIME by a more careful construction and a refinement of the proof in [15].

6   Conclusion

In this work, we have proved that security (w.r.t. a bounded number of sessions) is decidable for the class of $\oplus$-linear protocols. This is the first decidability result for recursive protocols involving algebraic properties of operators. We have also shown that relaxing certain assumptions of our model lead to undecidability of security. Our decidability result was obtained in a modular way by first reducing the problem of deciding security in the Horn theory model with XOR to the one without XOR and then using the existing decidability result for the latter model. We expect that the modular proof technique developed in this paper also helps to deal with other operators, such as Diffie-Hellman exponentiation.

References

1. J.A. Bull and D.J. Otway. The authentication protocol. Technical Report DRA/CIS3/PROJ/CORBA/SC/1/CSM/436-04/03, Defence Research Agency, Malvern, UK, 1997.
2. Y. Chevalier, R. Küsters, M. Rusinowitch, and M. Turuani. An NP Decision Procedure for Protocol Insecurity with XOR. In *LICS 2003*, pages 261–270. IEEE, Computer Society Press, 2003.
3. Y. Chevalier, R. Küsters, M. Rusinowitch, and M. Turuani. Deciding the Security of Protocols with Diffie-Hellman Exponentiation and Products in Exponents. In *FSTTCS 2003*, volume 2914 of *LNCS*, pages 124–135. Springer, 2003.
4. Y. Chevalier, R. Küsters, M. Rusinowitch, and M. Turuani. Deciding the Security of Protocols with Commuting Public Key Encryption. *ENTCS*, 125(1):55–66, 2005.
5. H. Comon-Lundh and V. Cortier. New Decidability Results for Fragments of First-order Logic and Application to Cryptographic Protocols. In *RTA 2003*, volume 2706 of *LNCS*, pages 148–164. Springer, 2003.
6. H. Comon-Lundh and V. Shmatikov. Intruder deductions, constraint solving and insecurity decision in presence of exclusive or. In *LICS 2003*, pages 271–280. IEEE, Computer Society Press, 2003.
7. V. Cortier, S. Delaune, and P. Lafourcade. A survey of algebraic properties used in cryptographic protocols. *Journal of Computer Security*, 14(1):1–43, 2006.
8. R. Küsters. On the Decidability of Cryptographic Protocols with Open-ended Data Structures. *International Journal of Information Security*, 4(1–2):49–70, 2005.
9. R. Küsters and T. Truderung. On the Automatic Analysis of Recursive Security Protocols with XOR. Technial Report, 2007. Available from http://people. inf.ethz.ch/kuestral/publications_html/KuestersTruderung-TR-STACS-2007.pdf.
10. R. Küsters and T. Wilke. Automata-based Analysis of Recursive Cryptographic Protocols. In *STACS 2004*, volume 2996 of *LNCS*, pages 382–393. Springer, 2004.
11. L.C. Paulson. Mechanized Proofs for a Recursive Authentication Protocol. In *CSFW-10*, pages 84–95. IEEE Computer Society Press, 1997.
12. O. Pereira and J.-J. Quisquater. A Security Analysis of the Cliques Protocols Suites. In *CSFW-14*, pages 73–81, IEEE Computer Society Press, 2001.
13. P.Y.A. Ryan and S.A. Schneider. An Attack on a Recursive Authentication Protocol. *Information Processing Letters*, 65(1):7–10, 1998.
14. V. Shmatikov. Decidable Analysis of Cryptographic Protocols with Products and Modular Exponentiation. In *(ESOP 2004)*, volume 2986 of *LNCS*, pages 355–369. Springer, 2004.
15. T. Truderung. Selecting theories and recursive protocols. In *CONCUR 2005*, volume 3653 of *LNCS*, pages 217–232. Springer, 2005.
16. K.N. Verma, H. Seidl, and T. Schwentick. On the complexity of equational horn clauses. In *CADE 2005*, volume 3328 of *LNCS*, pages 337–352. Springer, 2005.

Improved Online Algorithms for the Sorting Buffer Problem[*]

Iftah Gamzu[1],[**] and Danny Segev[2]

[1] School of Computer Science, Tel-Aviv University, Tel-Aviv 69978, Israel
iftgam@post.tau.ac.il
[2] School of Mathematical Sciences, Tel-Aviv University, Tel-Aviv 69978, Israel
segevd@post.tau.ac.il

Abstract. An instance of the *sorting buffer* problem consists of a metric space and a server, equipped with a finite-capacity buffer capable of holding a limited number of requests. An additional ingredient of the input is an online sequence of requests, each of which is characterized by a destination in the given metric; whenever a request arrives, it must be stored in the sorting buffer. At any point in time, a currently pending request can be served by drawing it out of the buffer and moving the server to its corresponding destination. The objective is to serve all input requests in a way that minimizes the total distance traveled by the server.

In this paper, we focus our attention on instances of the problem in which the underlying metric is either an *evenly-spaced* or a *continuous* line metric. Our main findings can be briefly summarized as follows:

1. We present a *deterministic* $O(\log n)$ competitive algorithm for n-point evenly-spaced line metrics. This result improves on a randomized $O(\log^2 n)$ competitive algorithm due to Khandekar and Pandit.
2. We devise a *deterministic* $O(\log N \log \log N)$ competitive algorithm for continuous line metrics, where N is the input sequence length.
3. We establish the first non-trivial lower bound for the evenly-spaced case, by proving that the competitive ratio of any deterministic algorithm is at least $\frac{2+\sqrt{3}}{\sqrt{3}} \approx 2.154$.

1   Introduction

An instance of the *sorting buffer* problem consists of a metric space (V, d), a server initially positioned at $\rho_0 \in V$, and a finite-capacity sorting buffer, capable of holding up to k requests. An additional ingredient of the input is an online sequence $\sigma = \langle \sigma_1, \ldots, \sigma_N \rangle$ of N requests, each of which corresponds to a point in V; whenever a request arrives, it must be stored in the sorting buffer. At any point in time, a currently pending request σ_i can be served by drawing it out

---

[*] Due to space limitations, some proofs are omitted from this extended abstract. We refer the reader to the full version of this paper (currently available online at http://www.math.tau.ac.il/~segevd), in which all missing details are provided.
[**] Supported by the German-Israeli Foundation and by the Israel Science Foundation.

W. Thomas and P. Weil (Eds.): STACS 2007, LNCS 4393, pp. 658–669, 2007.
© Springer-Verlag Berlin Heidelberg 2007

of the buffer and moving the server to σ_i. The objective is to serve all input requests in a way that minimizes the total distance traveled by the server.

The sorting buffer problem models a diverse collection of applications in networking, file server management, computer graphics, and even in the automotive industry. Due to space limitations, we refer the reader to directly related papers [5,8,9] and the references therein for a comprehensive review of these applications. However, to the best of our knowledge, essentially no non-trivial results are known for this problem in its utmost generality, i.e., when the given metric space has no particular structure. In fact, this statement holds even for the seemingly simple offline version, in which the input sequence σ is known in advance.

In light of this state of affairs, we focus our attention on instances of the problem in which the underlying metric is either an *evenly-spaced line metric* or a *continuous line metric*. More formally, in the former case $V = \{1, \ldots, n\}$, whereas in the latter $V = \mathbb{R}$, noting that the distance function in both cases is $d(p, q) = |p - q|$. Although such restricted settings may appear to be very simple at first glance, we proceed by demonstrating that line metrics capture one of the most fundamental problems in the design of storage systems.

In most disk devices, the *seek time*, which is the time it takes the disk arm to move to the proper cylinder, dominates the time it takes to complete a read/write request. Consequently, reducing the mean seek time can dramatically improve the performance of the underlying storage system. Needless to say, when requests are served in the exact same order by which they arrive (i.e., FIFO order), the seek time is a predetermined constant. However, modern disks are capable of handling requests in an out-of-order fashion by maintaining a limited capacity buffer, in which requests can be temporarily stored. Hence, a scheduling policy that utilizes such a buffer to reorder requests may achieve a significant improvement over FIFO scheduling. Efficiently designing and implementing buffer-based scheduling policies has become one of the foremost objectives in the design of storage systems; it is referred to as the *disk arm scheduling* problem (see, for example, [10,11]). This problem can be modeled as a sorting buffer instance on a line metric. Specifically, the disk's cylinders correspond to a set of points on the real line, the disk arm corresponds to the server, and the buffer used to reorder read/write requests corresponds to the sorting buffer.

The evenly-spaced line case has recently been studied by Khandekar and Pandit [7], who proposed a *randomized* online algorithm that obtains an expected competitive ratio of $O(\log^2 n)$ against an oblivious adversary. Their approach is based on probabilistically embedding the given metric into a distribution over *binary hierarchically well-separated trees* [2,3,6]. It is worth noting that even though an embedding of this nature may seem somewhat artificial, the structural properties it guarantees considerably simplify the tasks of suggesting a buffer management policy and analyzing its performance.

1.1 Our Results

Evenly-spaced line metrics. The main result of this paper is a *deterministic* online algorithm for the sorting buffer problem on an evenly-spaced line metric, which yields a competitive ratio of $O(\log n)$. This result improves on the randomized $O(\log^2 n)$ competitive algorithm due to Khandekar and Pandit [7]. It also refutes their conjecture, stating that a deterministic strategy is unlikely to obtain a non-trivial competitive ratio. The specifics of this algorithm are presented in Section 2.

Continuous line metrics. We study the sorting buffer problem on a continuous line metric, and employ the algorithm mentioned in the previous item as a subroutine to devise a deterministic online algorithm. Consequently, we achieve a competitive ratio of $O(\log N \log \log N)$, where N denotes the length of the input sequence. This result appears in Section 3.

A deterministic lower bound. We establish the first non-trivial lower bound for the sorting buffer problem on an evenly-spaced line metric. Specifically, we prove that the competitive ratio of any deterministic online algorithm is at least $\frac{2+\sqrt{3}}{\sqrt{3}} \approx 2.154$. This result settles, to some extent, an open question due to Khandekar and Pandit [7], who posed the task of attaining lower bounds on the achievable competitive ratio as a foundational objective for future research. Further details are provided in Section 4.

1.2 Related Work

Räcke, Sohler and Westermann [9] seem to have been the first to study the sorting buffer problem in online settings, concentrating on the uniform case, in which all pairwise distances are equal. Their main result was a deterministic online algorithm that has a competitive ratio of $O(\log^2 k)$, where k denotes the buffer capacity. They also established a lower bound on the competitive ratio of several well-known heuristics. For example, they proved a lower bound of $\Omega(k)$ on the performance of the Most-Common-First strategy and a lower bound of $\Omega(\sqrt{k})$ on that of FIFO and Least-Recently-Used. Later on, Englert and Westermann [5] improved the main result of Räcke et al. [9], by suggesting a deterministic $O(\log k)$ competitive algorithm. In fact, their algorithm extends to a non-uniform case which is referred to as a star-like metric. They also investigated the possible gain in using a sorting buffer and showed that, for any metric space, a buffer of size k cannot reduce the total distance traveled by a factor of more than $2k - 1$. Very recently, Englert, Röglin and Westermann [4] suggested an alternative way of analyzing the algorithm of Englert and Westermann [5], and experimentally evaluated the performance of several strategies on random input sequences.

A concurrent line of work, initiated by Kohrt and Pruhs [8], studied the offline setting. They considered a maximization version of the sorting buffer problem, in which the objective is to maximize the cost reduction compared to a bufferless schedule, and proposed a polynomial-time 20-approximation on a uniform metric. Subsequently, Bar-Yehuda and Laserson [1] examined a generalized variant, for which they presented a polynomial-time algorithm that achieves an approximation ratio of 9.

2   Evenly-Spaced Line Metrics

In this section, we study the sorting buffer problem on an evenly-spaced line metric, and devise a deterministic online algorithm that achieves a competitive ratio of $O(\log n)$. Prior to describing the finer details of our approach, we introduce the notion of a doubling partition, which will considerably simplify the suggested algorithm and its analysis.

Definition 1. A *doubling partition* with respect to a point $p \in V$, denoted by $\mathrm{DP}(p)$, is a partition of $V \setminus \{p\}$ into $2(\lfloor \log n \rfloor + 1)$ pairwise-disjoint sets of points $L_0(p), \ldots, L_{\lfloor \log n \rfloor}(p), R_0(p), \ldots, R_{\lfloor \log n \rfloor}(p)$, where

$$L_i(p) = \left\{ q < p : 2^i \leq d(q,p) < 2^{i+1} \right\} , \quad R_i(p) = \left\{ q > p : 2^i \leq d(q,p) < 2^{i+1} \right\} .$$

Figure 1 provides a concrete example to a doubling partition in an evenly-spaced line metric.

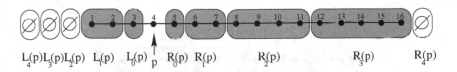

$$L_4(p)\,L_3(p)\,L_2(p) \quad L_1(p) \quad L_0(p) \underset{p}{\uparrow} R_0(p)\,R_1(p) \qquad R_2(p) \qquad\qquad R_3(p) \qquad\qquad R_4(p)$$

Fig. 1. A doubling partition in an evenly-spaced 16-point line metric with respect to the point $p = 4$. Note that empty doubling partition sets are marked with $\emptyset$.

2.1   The Algorithm

Noting that Englert and Westermann [5, Thm. 1] established an upper bound of $O(k)$ on the competitive ratio of the FIFO strategy for any metric space, we may assume in the remainder of this section that $k \geq 2(\lfloor \log n \rfloor + 1)$. Furthermore, for ease of exposition, it would be convenient to denote $m = 2(\lfloor \log n \rfloor + 1)$ and assume that k is an integral multiple of m.

Algorithm Moving Partition works in phases, each of which is logically built from an *accumulation step*, in which newly read requests are stored, followed by a *clearance step*, in which the server travels to clear subsets of pending requests.

Phase initialization: Let p be the current position of the server. Associate a unique $\frac{k}{m}$-sized sub-buffer (of the k-sized sorting buffer) with each of the m point sets in $\mathrm{DP}(p)$.

The accumulation step: Store each arriving request in the sub-buffer corresponding to the doubling partition set this request relates to[1]. If the current request relates to p, it is served immediately. This step ends when one of the sub-buffers becomes full or when the sequence of requests ends.

---

[1] A request *relates to* $S \subseteq V$ when the destination of this request lies in S.

The clearance step:

- If one of the sub-buffers is full, let $0 \leq t \leq \lfloor \log n \rfloor$ be the maximal index for which at least one of $R_t(p)$ and $L_t(p)$ has at least $\frac{k}{2m}$ pending requests in its corresponding sub-buffer. We assume without loss of generality that the latter property is satisfied by $R_t(p)$ (henceforth, the *maximal half-full set*), and designate its leftmost point by q. Move the server $p \rightsquigarrow$ leftmost point of $L_t(p) \rightsquigarrow$ rightmost point of $R_t(p) \rightsquigarrow q$, while clearing all pending requests that relate to $\bigcup_{i=0}^{t}(L_i(p) \cup R_i(p))$ along the way. Then, the phase ends.
- If the sequence of requests ends, move the server $p \rightsquigarrow$ leftmost point in buffer $\rightsquigarrow$ rightmost point in buffer, while clearing all pending requests along the way. Then, the algorithm ends.

Figure 2 illustrates how the server travels during the clearance step when one of the sub-buffers becomes full. We remark that if $L_t(p)$ is the maximal half-full set (instead of $R_t(p)$), the server travels in a completely symmetrical way. That is, the server first travels to the rightmost point of $R_t(p)$, then to the leftmost point of $L_t(p)$, and finally to q, which is the rightmost point of $L_t(p)$ in this case.

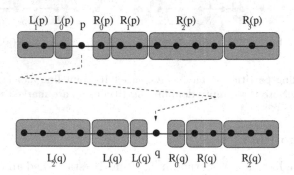

Fig. 2. The server's movement during the clearance step, when its initial position is p and the maximal half-full set is $R_2(p)$

2.2   Analysis

To prove the correctness of Algorithm Moving Partition, it is sufficient to show that, at any point in time, the sorting buffer holds at most k pending requests. However, the following theorem demonstrates that the suggested algorithm satisfies an even stronger property.

Theorem 2. *At any point in time, none of the sub-buffers (associated with the current doubling partition) overflows.*

Proof. We prove, by induction on the number of phases, that every sub-buffer contains strictly less than $\frac{k}{m}$ pending requests at the beginning of any phase. The theorem follows by observing that sub-buffers cannot overflow during a phase (particularly, during the accumulation step).

The induction claim is trivially satisfied at the beginning of the first phase, since the sorting buffer is currently empty. Suppose the claim is satisfied at the beginning of phase ℓ and suppose that in the clearance step of this phase, all pending requests that relate to $\bigcup_{i=0}^{t}(L_i(p) \cup R_i(p))$ are cleared and that the final position of the server is q, which is without loss of generality the leftmost point of $R_t(p)$. We next show that every sub-buffer associated with a set in $\mathrm{DP}(q)$, which is exactly the doubling partition at the beginning of phase $\ell + 1$, contains strictly less than $\frac{k}{m}$ pending requests:

$L_i(q)$ **for** $0 \leq i \leq t$. It is easy to verify that $\bigcup_{j=0}^{t} L_j(q) \subseteq \bigcup_{j=0}^{t}(L_j(p) \cup R_j(p)) \cup \{p\}$. Thus, since all pending requests that relate to $\bigcup_{j=0}^{t}(L_j(p) \cup R_j(p)) \cup \{p\}$ were served during the clearance step, it follows that the sub-buffer associated with $L_i(q)$ is empty.

$L_i(q)$ **for** $t + 1 \leq i \leq \lfloor \log n \rfloor$. Consider a point $v \in L_i(q)$. Notice that $d(v, q) \geq 2^i$, $d(q, p) = 2^t$, and $d(v, p) + d(p, q) = d(v, q)$ since $v < p < q$. Hence, we have

$$d(v, p) = d(v, q) - d(p, q) \geq 2^i - 2^t \geq 2^i - 2^{i-1} = 2^{i-1} .$$

On the other hand, $d(v, p) < d(v, q) < 2^{i+1}$. Consequently, $v \in L_{i-1}(p) \cup L_i(p)$. This implies that any pending request that relates to $L_i(q)$ was previously stored in one of the sub-buffers associated with $L_{i-1}(p)$ and $L_i(p)$. Recall that every sub-buffer associated with a set of $\mathrm{DP}(p)$ holds at most $\frac{k}{2m} - 1$ pending requests at the end of a clearance step. Thus, the sub-buffer associated with $L_i(q)$ holds at most $\frac{k}{m} - 2$ pending requests.

$R_i(q)$ **for** $0 \leq i \leq \lfloor \log n \rfloor$. Now consider a point $v \in R_i(q)$. Clearly, $v \in R_j(p)$ for some $j \geq i$. Accordingly, all the metric points of $R_i(q)$ appear in at most two consecutive sets of $\mathrm{DP}(p)$. Arguments similar to those of the previous item imply that the sub-buffer associated with $R_i(q)$ holds at most $\frac{k}{m} - 2$ pending requests. ∎

In what follows, we prove that the algorithm under consideration achieves a competitive ratio of $O(\log n)$. For ease of presentation, it would be convenient to view the evenly-spaced line metric as an undirected graph $G = (V, E)$ with $V = \{1, \ldots, n\}$ and $E = \{(1, 2), \ldots, (n - 1, n)\}$. In addition, we introduce the following notation:

- Let OPT denote the total distance traveled by the server in an optimal solution, and let ON denote the total distance traveled by the server in Algorithm Moving Partition.
- Let P be the sequence of points $p_0, p_1, \ldots, p_\ell$, where p_i is the position of the server at the end of the i-th phase of Algorithm Moving Partition. Note that p_0 is the initial server position ρ_0 and that p_ℓ is the position of the server just before the final clearance step begins.
- Let $C_P(e)$ be the number of times the edge $e \in E$ is crossed with respect to the walk determined by the points of P (i.e., the walk $p_0 \leadsto p_1 \leadsto \cdots \leadsto p_\ell$), and let $C_{\mathrm{OPT}}(e)$ be the number of times this edge is crossed in the optimal solution. Notice that $\sum_{e \in E} C_P(e) = \sum_{i=1}^{\ell} d(p_{i-1}, p_i)$ whereas $\sum_{e \in E} C_{\mathrm{OPT}}(e) = \mathrm{OPT}$.

Lemma 3. $\mathrm{ON} \le 7\sum_{e \in E} C_P(e) + 2 \cdot \mathrm{OPT}$.

Proof. Consider a phase $1 \le i \le \ell$, in which a full sub-buffer was detected, and let t be the index of the maximal half-full set of that phase. Then, the total distance traveled by the server in this phase, denoted by ON_i, is at most $3(2^{t+1} - 1) + (2^t - 1) \le 7 \cdot 2^t$, while $d(p_{i-1}, p_i) = 2^t$. Thus, $\sum_{i=1}^{\ell} \mathrm{ON}_i \le 7\sum_{i=1}^{\ell} d(p_{i-1}, p_i) = 7\sum_{e \in E} C_P(e)$.

During the clearance step of the final phase (i.e., phase $\ell + 1$), the server clears all pending requests in the buffer. Obviously, the total distance $\mathrm{ON}_{\ell+1}$ traveled by the server in this phase satisfies $\mathrm{ON}_{\ell+1} \le 2 \cdot \mathrm{OPT}$, as the server crosses each edge between the leftmost and the rightmost requests that have ever arrived (including the initial server position) at most twice, and any feasible solution must cross each such edge at least once. Hence, $\mathrm{ON} = \sum_{i=1}^{\ell+1} \mathrm{ON}_i \le 7\sum_{e \in E} C_P(e) + 2 \cdot \mathrm{OPT}$. ∎

Lemma 4. $C_P(e) \le (12m + 4)C_{\mathrm{OPT}}(e)$ *for every* $e \in E$.

Proof. Let $e = (i, i + 1)$. We first prove the following two claims.

Claim I: $C_{\mathrm{OPT}}(e) \ge 1$ whenever $C_P(e) \ge 1$. Assume without loss of generality that the first time e is crossed in the walk determined by P is from left to right. Accordingly, the initial position of the server must reside left of e (i.e., $p_0 \in \{1, \ldots, i\}$), and there must be at least one request that resides right of e (i.e., in $\{i + 1, \ldots, n\}$). Thus, in any feasible solution, the server must cross e.

Claim II: $C_{\mathrm{OPT}}(e) \ge \lfloor \frac{C_P(e)}{6m+2} \rfloor$. In every clearance step of Algorithm Moving Partition, each of the m sub-buffers that has at least $\frac{k}{2m}$ pending requests is cleared. Thus, at the beginning of each phase, the overall number of pending requests is at most $\frac{k}{2}$. Also notice that each time P crosses e from left to right, the server clears at least $\frac{k}{2m}$ requests that reside right of e. Consequently, in $3m + 1$ times P crosses e from left to right, at least $(3m+1)\frac{k}{2m} - \frac{k}{2} > k$ requests must have arrived to the right of e. Since similar arguments are applicable to the opposite case (i.e., when e is crossed from right to left), and since e is alternately crossed by P from different directions, it follows that during $6m + 2$ times P crosses e, any algorithm must cross it at least once.

The lemma clearly holds when $C_P(e) = 0$. When $C_P(e) \ge 1$, the claims stated above imply that $\frac{C_P(e)}{6m+2} \le \lfloor \frac{C_P(e)}{6m+2} \rfloor + 1 \le 2C_{\mathrm{OPT}}(e)$, or equivalently $C_P(e) \le (12m + 4)C_{\mathrm{OPT}}(e)$. ∎

Theorem 5. *Algorithm* Moving Partition *is* $O(\log n)$ *competitive.*

Proof. Using the previously stated results, we have

$$\mathrm{ON} \le 7\sum_{e \in E} C_P(e) + 2 \cdot \mathrm{OPT} \le 7(12m+4)\sum_{e \in E} C_{\mathrm{OPT}}(e) + 2 \cdot \mathrm{OPT} = (84m+30)\mathrm{OPT},$$

where the first inequality follows from Lemma 3, and the second is due to Lemma 4. Since $m = 2(\lfloor \log n \rfloor + 1)$, it follows that $\mathrm{ON} = O(\log n)\mathrm{OPT}$. ∎

3   Continuous Line Metrics

In this section, we present a deterministic online algorithm that attains a competitive ratio of $O(\log N \log \log N)$ for continuous line metrics. We begin by considering an inherently simpler setting, in which certain properties of the input sequence are known in advance. Later on, we show that the dependency on these properties can be eliminated by utilizing online "guessing" techniques.

3.1   A Semi-online Algorithm

In the following, we deal with a restricted special case of the problem under consideration, in which we have a prior knowledge of two input-related characteristics: $\tilde{N}$, an upper bound on the number of requests (i.e., $N \leq \tilde{N}$), and $\tilde{D}$, an upper bound on the maximal distance between the initial server position and any input request (i.e., $\sigma_i \in [\rho_0 - \tilde{D}, \rho_0 + \tilde{D}]$, for every $1 \leq i \leq N$). We now propose Discretized Simulation, a deterministic online algorithm for these particular settings.

Discretization: Let V be the set of $\tilde{N}+1$ points equally dividing $[\rho_0 - \tilde{D}, \rho_0 + \tilde{D}]$ into $\tilde{N}$ disjoint intervals, each of length $\frac{2\tilde{D}}{\tilde{N}}$. In addition, let $\tilde{\sigma} = \langle \tilde{\sigma}_1, \ldots, \tilde{\sigma}_N \rangle$ be the discretized input sequence, in which $\tilde{\sigma}_i$ is the point in V nearest to σ_i, where ties are broken arbitrarily.

Simulation: Apply Algorithm Moving Partition to the input sequence $\tilde{\sigma}$. Move the server to clear requests in the exact same order by which they are cleared in Moving Partition.

Analysis. Since all algorithms described in this section are assumed to have identical sorting buffer sizes k and initial server positions ρ_0, as far as notation is concerned – we may focus on their input sequences. Consequently, we use OPT_σ to denote the total distance traveled by the server in an optimal algorithm when the input sequence is σ, DS_σ to denote the total distance traveled in Algorithm Discretized Simulation when the input sequence is σ, and $\text{MP}_{\tilde{\sigma}}$ to denote the total distance traveled in Algorithm Moving Partition when the input sequence is $\tilde{\sigma}$.

Lemma 6. $\text{OPT}_{\tilde{\sigma}} \leq \text{OPT}_\sigma + 2\tilde{D}$ and $\text{DS}_\sigma \leq \text{MP}_{\tilde{\sigma}} + 2\tilde{D}$.

Proof. In what follows, we prove the first inequality, noting that the second inequality can be easily established by using nearly identical arguments. To prove $\text{OPT}_{\tilde{\sigma}} \leq \text{OPT}_\sigma + 2\tilde{D}$, it is sufficient to show that the entire sequence $\tilde{\sigma}$ can be processed within a traveling distance of at most $\text{OPT}_\sigma + 2\tilde{D}$. For this purpose, let $\text{ALG}(\tilde{\sigma})$ denote the algorithm that serves requests from $\tilde{\sigma}$ in exactly the same order by which the corresponding requests of σ are served in an optimal algorithm whose input sequence is σ. In other words, if the j-th request ρ_j served by the latter algorithm is σ_i, then the j-th request $\tilde{\rho}_j$ served by $\text{ALG}(\tilde{\sigma})$ is $\tilde{\sigma}_i$. Notice that

$$d(\tilde{\rho}_j, \tilde{\rho}_{j+1}) \leq d(\tilde{\rho}_j, \rho_j) + d(\rho_j, \rho_{j+1}) + d(\rho_{j+1}, \tilde{\rho}_{j+1}) \leq d(\rho_j, \rho_{j+1}) + \frac{2\tilde{D}}{\tilde{N}} \, ,$$

where the second inequality holds since $d(\rho_j, \tilde{\rho}_j) \leq \frac{\tilde{D}}{N}$, for every $0 \leq j \leq N$. It follows that the total distance traveled by the server in $\mathrm{ALG}(\tilde{\sigma})$ is

$$\sum_{j=0}^{N-1} d(\tilde{\rho}_j, \tilde{\rho}_{j+1}) \leq \sum_{j=0}^{N-1} d(\rho_j, \rho_{j+1}) + N \cdot \frac{2\tilde{D}}{\tilde{N}} \leq \mathrm{OPT}_\sigma + 2\tilde{D} \ . \qquad \blacksquare$$

Theorem 7. $\mathrm{DS}_\sigma = O(\log \tilde{N}) \cdot (\mathrm{OPT}_\sigma + \tilde{D})$.

Proof. Using the previously stated results, we have

$$\mathrm{DS}_\sigma \leq \mathrm{MP}_{\tilde{\sigma}} + 2\tilde{D} \leq c \log \tilde{N} \cdot \mathrm{OPT}_{\tilde{\sigma}} + 2\tilde{D} \leq c \log \tilde{N} \cdot (\mathrm{OPT}_\sigma + 2\tilde{D}) + 2\tilde{D} \ .$$

The first inequality follows from the second claim in Lemma 6. The second inequality follows from Theorem 5, stating that there exists a constant $c > 0$ such that $\mathrm{MP}_{\tilde{\sigma}} \leq c \log \tilde{N} \cdot \mathrm{OPT}_{\tilde{\sigma}}$. Finally, the last inequality is due to the first claim in Lemma 6. $\qquad \blacksquare$

3.2   A Fully-Online Algorithm

In what follows, we show that the dependency on knowing $\tilde{N}$ and $\tilde{D}$ in advance, exhibited by Algorithm Discretized Simulation, can be eliminated by guessing these parameter in online fashion. The specifics of our approach are formally presented in Algorithm Doubling Simulation, which works in phases, each of which is logically built from a *simulation step* and a *doubling step*. We initially set $\tilde{N} = 4$ and $\tilde{D} = 0$.

The simulation step: Simulate the execution of Algorithm Discretized Simulation, assuming that $\tilde{N}$ and $\tilde{D}$ are upper bounds on the number of requests and the maximal distance between ρ_0 and any input request, respectively. Move the server to clear requests in the exact same order by which they are cleared in Discretized Simulation. This step ends when the next input point $\tilde{\sigma}$ is the $(\tilde{N}+1)$-th request arrived so far or when $\tilde{\sigma} \notin [\rho_0 - \tilde{D}, \rho_0 + \tilde{D}]$.

The doubling step: Let p be the current position of the server. Move the server $p \rightsquigarrow \rho_0 - \tilde{D} \rightsquigarrow \rho_0 + \tilde{D} \rightsquigarrow \rho_0$, while clearing all pending requests in the sorting buffer along the way. If $\tilde{\sigma}$ is the $(\tilde{N}+1)$-th request arrived so far, set $\tilde{N} = \tilde{N}^2$. If $\tilde{\sigma} \notin [\rho_0 - \tilde{D}, \rho_0 + \tilde{D}]$, set $\tilde{D} = 2d(\rho_0, \tilde{\sigma})$. Then, the phase ends.

Analysis. For the purpose of analyzing the performance of Algorithm Doubling Simulation, we introduce the following notation:

- Let T be the number of phases in the algorithm, and let $\tilde{N}_t$ and $\tilde{D}_t$ denote the values of $\tilde{N}$ and $\tilde{D}$ at the beginning of phase t, respectively.
- Let OPT denote the total distance traveled by the server in an optimal algorithm, and let ON denote the total distance traveled in Algorithm Doubling Simulation.
- Let $\mathrm{ON}_t^{\mathrm{sim}}$ and $\mathrm{ON}_t^{\mathrm{dbl}}$ denote the total distance traveled by the server in the simulation and doubling steps of phase t, respectively. Notice that $\mathrm{ON} = \sum_{t=1}^{T}(\mathrm{ON}_t^{\mathrm{sim}} + \mathrm{ON}_t^{\mathrm{dbl}})$.

- Let ϱ_t be the sub-sequence of σ that consists of the requests processed in phase t of the algorithm. Notice that $\sigma = \langle \varrho_1, \ldots, \varrho_T \rangle$. Additionally, let OPT_t denote the total distance traveled by the server in an optimal solution where the initial position of the server is ρ_0 and the input sequence is ϱ_t.

Lemma 8. $\log \tilde{N}_T < 2 \log N$.

Lemma 9. $\text{ON}_t^{\text{dbl}} \leq 5 \tilde{D}_t$ *for every* $1 \leq t \leq T$.

Lemma 10. $\sum_{t=1}^{T} \tilde{D}_t \leq 2(\log \log N + 2)\text{OPT}$.

Lemma 11. $\sum_{t=1}^{T} \text{OPT}_t \leq \text{OPT} + 6 \sum_{t=1}^{T} \tilde{D}_t$.

Proof. Consider the execution of an optimal algorithm, and break it up into T sub-executions such that for every $1 \leq t \leq T - 1$, the t-th sub-execution begins when the first request of ϱ_t arrives and ends just before the first request of ϱ_{t+1} arrives. Specifically, it ends after the algorithm serves a request, whose destination is q_t, that precedes the arrival of the first request of ϱ_{t+1}. In addition, sub-execution T begins when the first request of ϱ_T arrives and ends when the algorithm ends. Now suppose we modify each of these sub-executions in the following way:

- For every $1 \leq t \leq T - 1$, when sub-execution t ends, we move the server $q_t \rightsquigarrow \rho_0 - \tilde{D}_t \rightsquigarrow \rho_0 + \tilde{D}_t \rightsquigarrow \rho_0$, and clear all pending requests in the sorting buffer along the way.
- For every $2 \leq t \leq T$, when sub-execution t begins, we move the server $\rho_0 \rightsquigarrow q_{t-1}$.

It is easy to verify that the movement of the server in this modified execution is valid and that the total distance traveled is at most $\text{OPT} + 6 \sum_{t=1}^{T} \tilde{D}_t$, which follows from the fact that without loss of generality $q_t \in [\rho_0 - \tilde{D}_t, \rho_0 + \tilde{D}_t]$, for every $1 \leq t \leq T - 1$.

We now argue that, for every $1 \leq t \leq T$, the total distance traveled in modified sub-execution t provides an upper bound on OPT_t. This follows from the observation that at the beginning of modified sub-execution t, the server is positioned at ρ_0, and that at the end of this sub-execution, all requests of ϱ_t were served. Hence, $\sum_{t=1}^{T} \text{OPT}_t \leq \text{OPT} + 6 \sum_{t=1}^{T} \tilde{D}_t$. ∎

Theorem 12. *Algorithm* Doubling Simulation *is* $O(\log N \log \log N)$ *competitive.*

Proof. Using the previously stated results, we have

$$\text{ON} = \sum_{t=1}^{T} (\text{ON}_t^{\text{sim}} + \text{ON}_t^{\text{dbl}}) \leq c \sum_{t=1}^{T} \left(\log \tilde{N}_t \cdot (\text{OPT}_t + \tilde{D}_t) \right) + 5 \sum_{t=1}^{T} \tilde{D}_t$$

$$\leq 2c \log N \cdot \text{OPT} + (14c \log N + 5) \sum_{t=1}^{T} \tilde{D}_t$$

$$\leq \left((2c \log N) + 2(\log \log N + 2)(14c \log N + 5) \right) \text{OPT}$$

$$= O(\log N \log \log N)\text{OPT} .$$

The first inequality is obtained by combining Lemma 9 and Theorem 7, stating that there exists a constant $c > 0$ such that $\text{ON}_t^{\text{sim}} \leq c \log \tilde{N}_t \cdot (\text{OPT}_t + \tilde{D}_t)$ for every $1 \leq t \leq T$. The second inequality holds since $\log \tilde{N}_t \leq \log \tilde{N}_T < 2 \log N$ for every $1 \leq t \leq T$, which follows from Lemma 8, in conjunction with Lemma 11. Finally, the last inequality is due to Lemma 10. ∎

4   A Lower Bound for Any Deterministic Algorithm

In this section, we establish a lower bound of 2.154 on the competitive ratio of any deterministic online algorithm for the sorting buffer problem. We begin by introducing the notion of laziness, which reduces the objective of proving a lower bound for any deterministic online algorithm to that of proving a lower bound for the family of deterministic lazy algorithms.

Definition 13. A *lazy* algorithm for the sorting buffer problem is an algorithm that satisfies the following properties:

1. The server stores newly read requests as long as the buffer is not full.
2. When the buffer holds a request that relates to the current server position, the server clears it immediately.

Theorem 14. *The competitive ratio of any deterministic online algorithm is at least $\frac{2+\sqrt{3}}{\sqrt{3}} \approx 2.154$, even for evenly-spaced line metrics.*

Proof. The forthcoming arguments will be based on the fact that every sorting buffer algorithm can be made lazy without increasing the total distance traveled by the server. Having this observation in mind, suppose we are given a line metric in which the left-to-right order of the points is $p, p_0, \ldots, p_{k-1}$, with $d(p, p_0) = \alpha(k-1)$ and $d(p_i, p_{i+1}) = 1$ for every $0 \leq i \leq k-2$, where $\alpha > 0$ is a parameter whose value will be determined later. We assume, for simplicity, that $\alpha(k-1)$ is integral. Hence, by adding dummy points the specified metric can be viewed as an evenly-spaced line metric on $\alpha(k-1) + k$ points.

Let p_0 be the initial position of the server, k be the size of the sorting buffer, and $\sigma_{k-1} = \langle p^{k-1} \, p_1 \, p_2 \cdots p_{k-1} \, p \, p_{k-1} \rangle$ be the input sequence given by the adversary. We identify any lazy deterministic algorithm with the maximal index i for which, given the sequence σ_{k-1}, the server initially travels from p_0 to $p_1, \ldots, p_i$, and then travels to p. For all algorithms identified with $i < k-1$, the adversary changes the input sequence to $\sigma_i = \langle p^{k-1} \, p_1 \, p_2 \cdots p_{i+1}^k \, p \rangle$, that is, the postfix $\langle p_{i+2} \cdots p_{k-1} \, p \, p_{k-1} \rangle$ of σ_{k-1} is replaced by $\langle p_{i+1}^{k-1} \, p \rangle$. We now consider two cases, depending on which sequence was picked by the adversary:

Case I: The input sequence was σ_{k-1}. The total distance traveled by the server is at least $(3+2\alpha)(k-1)$, since it moves $p_0 \rightsquigarrow p_{k-1} \rightsquigarrow p \rightsquigarrow p_{k-1}$. However, the optimal distance is at most $(1+2\alpha)(k-1)$, as all requests can be cleared by traveling $p_0 \rightsquigarrow p \rightsquigarrow p_{k-1}$. Thus, the competitive ratio of any lazy deterministic online algorithm identified with $k-1$ is at least $\frac{3+2\alpha}{1+2\alpha}$.

Case II: The input sequence was σ_i, **for** $i < k - 1$. The total distance traveled by the server is at least $3\alpha(k - 1) + 4i + 2$, since it moves $p_0 \rightsquigarrow p_i \rightsquigarrow p \rightsquigarrow p_{i+1} \rightsquigarrow p$, whereas an optimal solution travels $p_0 \rightsquigarrow p_{i+1} \rightsquigarrow p$, to obtain a total distance of $\alpha(k - 1) + 2i + 2$. Thus, the competitive ratio of any lazy deterministic online algorithm identified with i is at least

$$\frac{3\alpha(k - 1) + 4i + 2}{\alpha(k - 1) + 2i + 2} \geq \frac{3\alpha(k - 1) + 4k - 6}{\alpha(k - 1) + 2k - 2} = \frac{3\alpha + 4}{\alpha + 2} - \frac{2}{(\alpha + 2)(k - 1)},$$

where the inequality holds since the left-hand side is minimized when $i = k - 2$. It follows that for any $\epsilon > 0$ we can pick a sufficiently large value of k so that

$$\frac{3\alpha + 4}{\alpha + 2} - \frac{2}{(\alpha + 2)(k - 1)} \geq \frac{3\alpha + 4}{\alpha + 2} - \epsilon .$$

Therefore, the competitive ratio of any lazy deterministic online algorithm on an evenly-spaced line metric is at least $\max_{\alpha > 0} \min\left\{\frac{3+2\alpha}{1+2\alpha}, \frac{3\alpha+4}{\alpha+2} - \epsilon\right\}$. By optimizing the value of α (i.e., setting $\alpha^* = \frac{\sqrt{3}-1}{2}$), we obtain a lower bound of $\frac{2+\sqrt{3}}{\sqrt{3}} - \epsilon$ for any $\epsilon > 0$. However, recall that we assumed $\alpha(k - 1)$ to be integral. Since α^* is irrational and k is an integer, it follows that this assumption does not hold. Nevertheless, this difficulty can be resolved by standard approximation of an irrational number by a rational number, losing an extra additive factor of ϵ in the lower bound. ∎

References

1. R. Bar-Yehuda and J. Laserson. Exploiting locality: Approximating sorting buffers. In *3rd WAOA*, pages 69–81, 2005.
2. Y. Bartal. Probabilistic approximations of metric spaces and its algorithmic applications. In *37th FOCS*, pages 184–193, 1996.
3. Y. Bartal. On approximating arbitrary metrices by tree metrics. In *30th STOC*, pages 161–168, 1998.
4. M. Englert, H. Röglin, and M. Westermann. Evaluation of online strategies for reordering buffers. In *5th WEA*, pages 183–194, 2006.
5. M. Englert and M. Westermann. Reordering buffer management for non-uniform cost models. In *32nd ICALP*, pages 627–638, 2005.
6. J. Fakcharoenphol, S. Rao, and K. Talwar. A tight bound on approximating arbitrary metrics by tree metrics. *Journal of Computer and System Sciences*, 69(3):485–497, 2004.
7. R. Khandekar and V. Pandit. Online sorting buffers on line. In *23rd STACS*, pages 584–595, 2006.
8. J. S. Kohrt and K. Pruhs. A constant approximation algorithm for sorting buffers. In *6th LATIN*, pages 193–202, 2004.
9. H. Räcke, C. Sohler, and M. Westermann. Online scheduling for sorting buffers. In *10th ESA*, pages 820–832, 2002.
10. A. Silberschatz, P. B. Galvin, and G. Gagne. *Applied operating system concepts*. John Wiley and Sons, Inc., 2000. Disk scheduling is discussed in Section 13.2.
11. A. S. Tanenbaum. *Modern Operating Systems*. Prentice Hall PTR, second edition, 2001. Disk scheduling is discussed in Section 5.4.

Cost Sharing Methods for Makespan and Completion Time Scheduling*

Janina Brenner and Guido Schäfer

Institute of Mathematics, Technical University Berlin, Germany
{brenner,schaefer}@math.tu-berlin.de

Abstract. Roughgarden and Sundararajan recently introduced an alternative measure of efficiency for cost sharing mechanisms. We study cost sharing methods for combinatorial optimization problems using this novel efficiency measure, with a particular focus on scheduling problems. While we prove a lower bound of $\Omega(\log n)$ for a very general class of problems, we give a best possible cost sharing method for minimum makespan scheduling. Finally, we show that no budget balanced cost sharing methods for completion or flow time objectives exist.

Keywords: game theory, mechanism design, cost sharing mechanisms, combinatorial optimization, scheduling problems.

1 Introduction

Many combinatorial optimization problems are concerned with establishing a good or service at a minimum cost. Often, these problems can be viewed as consisting of a set of users that act strategically in order to receive this service. In a scheduling context, we can imagine jobs to be owned by agents wishing their jobs to be executed on a machine. Besides finding a way of providing the service, the problem is then to distribute the resulting cost among the users in a fair manner. Meanwhile, the service provider may have to decide upon a subset of users that are served.

In this paper, we study *cost sharing mechanisms* for combinatorial optimization problems, with a particular focus on scheduling problems. The general setting is as follows. We are given a set U of n players that are interested in a certain service. Every player $i \in U$ has a private *utility* $u_i \geq 0$ for receiving this service and announces a *bid* $b_i \geq 0$ which designates the maximum price she is willing to pay. Associated with the underlying optimization problem, we are given a non-decreasing cost function $C : 2^U \to \mathbb{R}^+$ describing the minimum cost of serving a set of players $S \subseteq U$.

A *cost sharing mechanism* M first solicits all bids $\{b_i\}_{i \in U}$ from players in U, and based on these bids (i) determines a set $S \subseteq U$ of players that receive the

---

* This work was supported by the DFG Research Center MATHEON "Mathematics for key technologies".

W. Thomas and P. Weil (Eds.): STACS 2007, LNCS 4393, pp. 670–681, 2007.

service, and (ii) for every player $i \in S$, fixes a non-negative payment $x_i(S)$ that she has to pay for the service. This payment is usually referred to as the *cost share* of a player $i \in S$. We assume that the mechanism complies with the following three natural assumptions: (a) a player is not charged more than her bid, (b) a player is charged only if she receives service, and (c) a player is guaranteed to receive service if she reports a sufficiently high bid.

Define the *benefit* of a player i as $u_i - x_i$ if i receives service and as zero otherwise. We assume that each player's strategy is to maximize her benefit. Since the outcome computed by the cost sharing mechanism solely depends on the bids $\{b_i\}_{i \in U}$, a player may have an incentive to misreport her actual utility, i.e., to declare a bid $b_i \neq u_i$, if advantageous.

There are several desirable properties of a cost sharing mechanism: A cost sharing mechanism M is *β-budget balanced* if the cost shares charged to the players in S deviates by at most a factor $\beta \geq 1$ from the actual cost $C(S)$, i.e.,

$$C(S)/\beta \leq \sum_{i \in S} x_i(S) \leq C(S). \tag{1}$$

If $\beta = 1$, we simply call the cost sharing mechanism budget balanced.

A mechanism is called *strategyproof* if bidding truthfully, i.e., announcing $b_i = u_i$, is a dominant strategy for every player. If this is true even if players collude, then we call a mechanism *group-strategyproof*. For a set $S \subseteq U$, define $u(S) := \sum_{i \in S} u_i$. A cost sharing mechanism M is called *efficient* if it selects a set of players that maximizes the *social welfare* $u(S) - C(S)$.

Classical results in economics [8,24] state that budget balance and efficiency cannot be achieved simultaneously; even for simple cost functions and if only strategyproofness is required. As a consequence, most of the previous work has concentrated on either achieving budget balance or efficiency.

Very recently, Roughgarden and Sundararajan [25] introduced an alternative efficiency measure that attempts to circumvent the intractability results. They define the *social cost* of a set $S \subseteq U$ as

$$\Pi(S) := u(U \setminus S) + C(S).$$

A mechanism is said to be *α-approximate* if the set of players it determines has social cost at most α times the minimum social cost (over all subsets of U). It is not hard to see that a set S minimizes the social cost iff it maximizes the social welfare.

A large class of group-strategyproof cost sharing mechanisms are based on a framework due to Moulin and Shenker [20]. This framework provides a means to obtain group-strategyproof cost sharing mechanisms from *cross-monotonic cost sharing methods* (definitions are given below). Moreover, Immorlica et al. [13] prove that every group-strategyproof cost sharing mechanism (satisfying some natural conditions) corresponds to a cross-monotonic cost sharing method.

Our Results. In this paper, we study cost sharing methods for optimization problems in light of the new efficiency measure introduced by Roughgarden and Sundararajan [25]. Our contribution is threefold:

1. Lower Bound on Approximability of Cost Sharing Methods. We present a general inapproximability result for cost sharing methods of combinatorial optimization problems. In particular, we prove that there is no cost sharing method that is α-summable and satisfies cost recovery for any $\alpha < \log n$, where n denotes the number of players. Our proof holds if the underlying cost function satisfies a certain "stability" property.

As a consequence, our result implies a lower bound of $\log n$ on the approximability of cost sharing mechanisms for various optimization problems, such as, for instance, facility location, minimum spanning tree (and thus also minimum Steiner tree and forest), single-source rent-or-buy, minimum makespan scheduling, etc. Despite its generality, our lower bound is tight for some specific problems such as facility location and minimum makespan scheduling.

2. An Optimal Cost Sharing Method for Makespan Scheduling. We study the *minimum makespan scheduling problem*, one of the most fundamental problems in scheduling theory, in a cost sharing context. In this problem, we are given a set of jobs N that have to be executed on m parallel machines. The goal is to assign all jobs to the machines such that the maximum completion time is minimized. We assume that jobs act strategically and attempt to get processed at a low cost. We develop a cross-monotonic cost sharing method for this problem that is $(2 - 1/m)$-budget balanced and $\log n$-approximate; this is tight with respect to both budget balance and approximability.

3. Budget Balance of Cost Sharing Methods for other Scheduling Problems. There are several other scheduling problems that can be considered in a cost sharing context. We show that for scheduling problems in which we aim at minimizing the total (weighted) completion (or flow) time, there is no cross-monotonic cost sharing method that is β-budget balanced for any $\beta < n/2$.

Previous and Related Work. The development of cost sharing mechanisms for combinatorial optimization problems has recently attracted a lot of attention in the theoretical computer science literature.

The framework of Moulin and Shenker [20] has been applied to game-theoretic variants of classical optimization problems such as fixed multicast [1,5,6], submodular cost sharing [20], Steiner trees [14,15], facility location, single-source rent-or-buy network design [22,19,10] and Steiner forests [16]. Lower bounds on the budget balance factor that is achievable by a cross-monotonic cost sharing mechanism are given in [13,17]. Very recently, researchers started to investigate cost sharing mechanisms in light of the novel efficiency measure of Roughgarden and Sundararajan; see [9,25,26,4].

Very notably, although network design problems have been studied extensively in a cost sharing context, very little attention has been given to scheduling problems; in particular if jobs are assumed to act strategically, and group-strategyproofness is a desirable objective. In most of the previous works, authors have either concentrated on scheduling problems where machines act selfishly [21, 2,18], or strategyproofness (but not group-strategyproofness) is an issue [23,11].

Related to our work is the recent work of Bleischwitz and Monien [3]. The authors present a cross-monotonic cost sharing method for the minimum makespan scheduling problem. However, as we argue below, their cost sharing mechanism does not approximate social cost.

2   Preliminaries

Moulin Mechanisms. A *cost sharing method* ξ is a function $\xi : U \times 2^U \to \mathbb{R}^+$ that assigns to each user $i \in U$ and subset $S \subseteq U$ a non-negative cost share $\xi(i, S)$. We define $\xi(i, S) := 0$ for all $i \in U \setminus S$, for all $S \subseteq U$. ξ is *cross-monotonic* if the cost share of a player does not increase as the player set grows; more formally, for all $S' \subseteq S \subseteq U$ and for every $i \in S'$, it holds that $\xi(i, S') \geq \xi(i, S)$.

Similar to the definition in (1), ξ is *β-budget balanced* if

$$\forall S \subseteq U : \quad C(S)/\beta \leq \sum_{i \in S} \xi(i, S) \leq C(S).$$

We say that ξ satisfies *β-cost recovery* if the first inequality holds; it is *competitive* if the latter inequality is fulfilled.

Moulin and Shenker [20] showed that, given a budget balanced and cross-monotonic cost sharing method ξ, the following cost sharing mechanism $M(\xi)$ satisfies budget balance and group-strategyproofness: Initially, let $S := U$. If for each player $i \in S$, the cost share $\xi(i, S)$ is at most her bid b_i, we stop. Otherwise, remove from S all players whose cost shares are larger than their bids, and repeat. Eventually, let S be the final player set and define the payments as $x_i(S) := \xi(i, S)$ for all $i \in S$. Jain and Vazirani [14] later observed that the result of Moulin and Shenker also holds if one considers approximately budget balanced and cross-monotonic cost sharing methods.

Yet another fairness concept in cooperative game theory that we use in this paper is the *β-core*. A cost sharing method ξ is in the *β-core* iff it is β-budget balanced and

$$\forall S' \subseteq S \subseteq U : \quad \sum_{i \in S'} \xi(i, S) \leq C(S').$$

Social Welfare vs. Social Cost. A mechanism M is said to be *α-approximate* if it computes a final set S^M of social cost at most α times the minimum over all sets $S \subseteq U$, i.e., $\Pi(S^M) \leq \alpha \cdot \Pi(S)$ for all $S \subseteq U$. Since $u(U) - \Pi(S) = u(S) - C(S)$, the traditional definition of efficiency, and $u(U)$ is a constant, a set S has minimum social cost iff it has maximum efficiency.

Roughgarden and Sundararajan [25] revealed a relation between the approximability of a Moulin mechanism $M(\xi)$ and a property of the cost sharing method ξ: Assume we are given an arbitrary order σ on a subset $S \subseteq U$ of players, i.e., $S = \{i_1, \ldots, i_{|S|}\}$, where $i_j \prec_\sigma i_k$ if and only if $1 \leq j < k \leq |S|$. We define $S_j \subseteq S$ as the (ordered) set of the first j players of S according to the order σ. A cost sharing method ξ is *α-summable* if for every ordering σ and every subset $S \subseteq U$:

$$\sum_{j=1}^{|S|} \xi(i_j, S_j) \leq \alpha \cdot C(S). \tag{2}$$

Roughgarden and Sundararajan [25] proved that the Moulin mechanism $M(\xi)$ is $(\alpha + \beta)$-approximate and β-budget balanced if the underlying cost sharing method ξ is α-summable and β-budget balanced. Moreover, the authors argue that $\max\{\alpha, \beta\}$ is a lower bound on the approximability of $M(\xi)$.

In this paper, we use $[n]$ to denote the set $\{1, \ldots, n\}$. Moreover, we define H_n to be the n-th harmonic number, i.e., $H_n := \sum_{i=1}^{n} 1/i$. As n grows to infinity, $H_n \approx \log n$, and we use both values interchangeably.

3   A General Lower Bound on Summability

In this section, we prove a lower bound of $\Omega(\log n)$ on the summability of cost sharing methods. Our lower bound holds if the underlying cost function C satisfies a certain "stability" property, which is fulfilled by a variety of combinatorial optimization problems such as facility location, Steiner tree, parallel machine scheduling, etc. Together with the recent result of Roughgarden and Sundararajan [25], this shows that for several problems, the approximability of Moulin mechanisms cannot be better than $\Omega(\log n)$.

Theorem 1. *Let ξ be a cost sharing method on a universe U that satisfies the β-cost recovery condition with respect to a cost function C. Suppose that there is a set $S \subseteq U$ with $|S| \geq |U|/\gamma$ for some constant $\gamma \geq 1$ such that $C(S') \geq C(S)/\delta$ for all $S' \subseteq S$ and some constant $\delta \geq 1$. Then ξ is not α-summable for any $\alpha < H_{\lceil n/\gamma \rceil}/(\beta \cdot \delta)$, where n is the number of players in U.*

Proof. It is sufficient to prove that there exists an order σ on U such that

$$\sum_{j=1}^{|S|} \xi(i_j, S_j) \geq \frac{H_{\lceil n/\gamma \rceil}}{\beta \cdot \delta} \cdot C(S),$$

where S_j is the set of the first j players in S and i_j is the jth player of S (ordered according to σ).

We construct σ by determining the sets S_j and users i_j inductively as follows. Initially, set $j = |S|$ and assign $S_j = S$. Now, suppose we have determined sets $S_{|S|}, \ldots, S_j$. By an average argument, there must exist a user $i \in S_j$ such that

$$\xi(i, S_j) \geq \frac{C(S_j)}{\beta \cdot |S_j|} = \frac{C(S_j)}{\beta \cdot j} \geq \frac{C(S)}{\beta \delta \cdot j},$$

since ξ satisfies the β-cost recovery condition. The last inequality holds because $S_j \subseteq S$. Assign $i_j := i$ and $S_{j-1} := S_j \setminus \{i_j\}$.

Let $S = \{i_1, \ldots, i_{|S|}\}$ be the set of players in S ordered according to the order σ constructed above. We have

$$\sum_{j=1}^{|S|} \xi(i_j, S_j) \geq \left(1 + \frac{1}{2} + \cdots + \frac{1}{|S|}\right) \cdot \frac{C(S)}{\beta \delta} \geq \frac{H_{\lceil n/\gamma \rceil}}{\beta \delta} \cdot C(S),$$

where we exploit that $|S| \geq n/\gamma$ and $|S| \in \mathbb{N}$. $\square$

This lower bound applies to many problems, as e.g. to the following ones:

Example 1 (Fixed-tree Multicast Problem). Users are located at vertices of an undirected graph and wish to receive a broadcasting service which is produced in a root vertex. The cost of serving a set of users U is the cost of a minimum spanning tree containing U and the root. An instance fulfilling the conditions of the above theorem is the one in which all users are located on the same vertex which is connected to the root by an edge of length 1. There are better lower bounds for this problem.

Example 2 (Facility Location Problem). Users are located at vertices and wish to be connected to an open facility. Facilities can be opened at a given subset of vertices. Here, a sample instance is the one in which there is only one vertex v at which a facility may be opened, and all users are located directly on v. Then, the cost of a solution is independent of the number of users and equal to the opening cost of the facility. This lower bound is tight, as has been shown in [26].

Another example for which Theorem 1 applies is the makespan machine scheduling problem that we define in Section 4. There, we show that the bound on summability is tight for this problem.

4 Minimum Makespan Scheduling

We consider the classical *minimum makespan scheduling problem*. We are given a set of n jobs N that have to be scheduled on m identical machines. Each job $i \in N$ has a non-negative *processing time* p_i, which is the time needed to execute i on one of the machines. We denote the completion time of job i by C_i. Every machine can execute at most one job at a time; preemption of jobs is not allowed. The objective is to schedule all jobs in N on the m machines such that the maximum completion time $\max_{i \in N} C_i$, also called *makespan*, is minimized. Following the naming scheme introduced by Graham et al. [7], this problem is referred to as $P||C_{\max}$.

In a game-theoretic variant of the machine scheduling problem, each job is associated with a player, who wants her job to be processed on one of the m machines. We therefore identify the universe of players U with the set of jobs N. The cost $C(S)$ incurred to schedule all jobs in S is the minimum makespan. We are interested in designing a cost sharing mechanism for the minimum makespan scheduling problem that is β-budget balanced and α-approximate for every possible instance.

Let $p_{\max}(S)$ denote the maximum processing time over all jobs in S. Define $\mu(S)$ as the average machine load, i.e., $\mu(S) := \sum_{i \in S} p_i/m$. The following fact is folklore (see, e.g., [12]).

Fact 1. *For a given set $S \subseteq U$ of jobs, let $C(S)$ be the makespan of an optimal schedule for S. The following two inequalities hold:*

1. $C(S) \leq \mu(S) + (1 - \frac{1}{m}) \cdot p_{\max}(S)$;
2. $C(S) \geq \max\{\mu(S), p_{\max}(S)\}$.

4.1   Cross-Monotonic Cost Shares

Bleischwitz and Monien [3] describe a cross-monotonic cost sharing method ξ^{BM} for the above machine scheduling problem. We briefly review their cost sharing method.[1]

We call a job i *large* with respect to S if $p_i = p_{\max}(S)$ and *small* otherwise. Let $\ell(S)$ be the number of large jobs in S. Given a subset $S \subseteq U$ of the jobs, we define the cost share of $i \in S$ as:

$$
\xi^{\mathrm{BM}}(i, S) := \begin{cases} \dfrac{p_i}{m} + \dfrac{p_i - \mu(S)}{\ell(S)} & \text{if } p_i = p_{\max}(S) \text{ and } p_i > \mu(S), \\[2ex] \dfrac{p_i}{m} & \text{otherwise.} \end{cases} \tag{3}
$$

The intuition is as follows: Every job gets a cost share of p_i/m. If the average machine load $\mu(S)$ is less than the maximum processing time $p_{\max}(S)$, every large job additionally obtains an equal share of the cost $p_{\max}(S) - \mu(S)$. We summarize one of the main results of Bleischwitz and Monien [3] in the following theorem.

Theorem 2. ξ^{BM} *is a $(2m/(m+1))$-budget balanced cross-monotonic cost sharing method for the minimum makespan scheduling problem. Moreover, there is no β-budget balanced cross-monotonic cost sharing method ξ for this problem, for any $\beta < 2m/(m+1)$.*

Albeit Theorem 2 proves that the Moulin mechanism $M(\xi^{\mathrm{BM}})$, driven by the cost sharing method ξ^{BM} by Bleischwitz and Monien, is optimal with respect to budget balance, we show below that it is far from being optimal with respect to social cost. In fact, the social cost of the final set S^M output by $M(\xi^{\mathrm{BM}})$ can be as large as $n/2$ times the optimal social cost, where n is the number of jobs in the universe U.

Lemma 1. *For every $n \in \mathbb{N}$, there exists an instance of the minimum makespan scheduling problem such that the cost sharing method ξ^{BM} is not α-summable for any $\alpha < n/2$.*

Proof. It is sufficient to define an instance of the minimum makespan scheduling problem on n jobs and a permutation σ for which the cost share sum in (2) with respect to ξ^{BM} is at least $n/2$ times the minimum makespan.

Let $U := \{i_1, \ldots, i_m\}$ be an (ordered) set of m jobs, where $m = n$ is the number of machines. Define the processing time of job i_j to be $p_{i_j} := 1 + (j-1)\epsilon$ for all $j \in [m]$ and some small $\epsilon > 0$. Since the number of jobs equals the number of machines, the makespan of an optimal assignment for U is $C(U) = 1 + (m-1)\epsilon$.

---

[1] At first sight, the cost shares that we state here differ from the ones defined by Bleischwitz and Monien in [3]. However, it can easily be verified that both definitions are in fact equivalent; we feel that the definition we present here is more intuitive.

Observe that the processing time of job i_j, $j \in [m]$, is maximum among all jobs in the set $S_j = \{i_1, \ldots, i_j\}$, i.e., i_j is large. Furthermore, i_j is the only large job in S_j and thus $\ell(S_j) = 1$. The average machine workload of S_j is

$$\mu(S_j) = \frac{1}{m} \sum_{l=1}^{j} p_{i_l} = \frac{1}{m} \left(j + \frac{j(j-1)\epsilon}{2} \right) \leq 1 + (j-1)\epsilon = p_{\max}(S_j).$$

Hence, the cost share that job i_j obtains with respect to S_j is

$$\xi^{\mathrm{BM}}(i_j, S_j) = \frac{p_{i_j}}{m} + p_{i_j} - \mu(S_j) = p_{i_j} - \mu(S_{j-1}),$$

where we define $S_0 := \emptyset$. We obtain

$$\xi^{\mathrm{BM}}(i_j, S_j) = (1 + (j-1)\epsilon) - \frac{1}{m} \left((j-1) + \frac{(j-1)(j-2)\epsilon}{2} \right) \geq 1 - \frac{j-1}{m}.$$

Therefore,

$$\sum_{j=1}^{m} \xi^{\mathrm{BM}}(i_j, S_j) \geq m - \frac{m(m-1)}{2m} = \frac{m}{2} + \frac{1}{2} \geq \frac{m}{2}(1 + (m-1)\epsilon) = \frac{m}{2} \cdot C(U),$$

where the last inequality holds if we choose ϵ sufficiently small.   □

Intuitively, this high summability gives voice to the fact that processing times exceeding the average workload $\mu(S)$ are punished in an unfair manner: Instead of sharing the additional cost of $p_{\max}(S) - \mu(S)$ among all jobs for which $p_i > \mu(S)$, only those jobs attaining the maximum processing time come up for it. We tackle this problem in the next section.

4.2 Approximate Cost Shares

We continue by proposing new cost shares ξ^{BS} for the minimum makespan scheduling problem that are still $(2-1/m)$-budget balanced and cross-monotonic, but concurrently $\log n$-summable. This is tight in terms of both budget balance and summability.

We use a different definition of *small* and *large* jobs here: A job i is *large* with respect to S iff $p_i > \mu(S)$ and *small* otherwise. The cost share of a job $i \in S$ with respect to S is defined as

$$\xi^{\mathrm{BS}}(i, S) := \begin{cases} \dfrac{p_i}{m} + \displaystyle\int_{\mu(S)}^{p_i} \dfrac{1}{|\{j \in S : p_j \geq t\}|} \, dt & \text{if } p_i > \mu(S), \\[2ex] \dfrac{p_i}{m} & \text{otherwise.} \end{cases} \qquad (4)$$

Intuitively, every job receives a cost share of p_i/m. A large job i obtains some additional cost share: for every time instant $t \in [\mu(S), p_i]$, i shares the cost of $1dt$ evenly with all other jobs in S whose processing time is at least t.

We show that ξ^{BS} is a cost sharing method that satisfies cross-monotonicity and approximate budget balance and summability.

Theorem 3. ξ^{BS} *is a cross-monotonic, $(2-1/m)$-budget balanced and (H_n+1)-summable cost sharing method for the minimum makespan scheduling problem.*

The proof of Theorem 3 follows from Lemmas 2, 3 and 4 that are given below.

Lemma 2. ξ^{BS} *is cross-monotonic.*

Proof. Consider some set $S \subseteq U$ and a job $i \in S$. We prove that if a new job $j \notin S$ is added to S, the cost share of i does not increase.

If i was small in S, then it remains small, and hence i's cost share stays p_i/m. If i was large in S and becomes small in $S \cup \{j\}$, then i's cost share decreases to p_i/m. It remains to show that the cost share of i does not increase if i stays large. Note that by adding job j, the number of jobs whose processing time is at least t for some $t \geq 0$ does not decrease. Moreover, we have

$$\int_{\mu(S)}^{p_i} \frac{1}{|\{j \in S : p_j \geq t\}|} \, dt \geq \int_{\mu(S\cup\{j\})}^{p_i} \frac{1}{|\{j \in S \cup \{j\} : p_j \geq t\}|} \, dt,$$

since $\mu(S) \leq \mu(S \cup \{j\})$. This concludes the proof. $\square$

We show next that the budget balance condition is satisfied.

Lemma 3. ξ^{BS} *is $(2-1/m)$-budget balanced.*

Proof. It is easy to verify that with the cost share definition in (4) we have

$$\sum_{i \in S} \xi(i,S) = \max\{\mu(S), p_{\max}(S)\}.$$

By Fact 1, $C(S) \geq \max\{\mu(S), p_{\max}(S)\}$, which proves competitiveness. Moreover, the cost shares satisfy $(2-1/m)$-cost recovery because

$$\left(2 - \frac{1}{m}\right) \cdot \max\{\mu(S), p_{\max}(S)\} \geq \mu(S) + \left(1 - \frac{1}{m}\right) p_{\max}(S) \geq C(S),$$

where the last inequality follows from Fact 1. $\square$

Finally, we prove that the cost shares fulfill $O(\log n)$-summability.

Lemma 4. ξ^{BS} *is (H_n+1)-summable.*

Proof. Let σ be an arbitrary order on the jobs in U, and let $S := \{i_1, \ldots, i_{|S|}\} \subseteq U$ be a subset of U ordered according to σ. First, observe that

$$\sum_{j=1}^{|S|} \xi^{\mathrm{BS}}(i_j, S_j) \leq \sum_{j=1}^{|S|} \left(\frac{p_{i_j}}{m} + \int_{\mu(S)}^{p_{i_j}} \frac{1}{|\{k \in S_j : p_k \geq t\}|} \, dt \right)$$

$$\leq \sum_{j=1}^{|S|} \left(\frac{p_{i_j}}{m} + \int_{0}^{p_{i_j}} \frac{1}{|\{k \in S_j : p_k \geq t\}|} \, dt \right)$$

$$\leq \mu(S) + \sum_{j=1}^{|S|} \int_{0}^{p_{i_j}} \frac{1}{|\{k \in S_j : p_k \geq t\}|} \, dt.$$

Fix a point in time $t \in [0, p_{\max}(S)]$. Define $r(t)$ as the number of jobs in S whose processing time is at least t. Using this definition, we obtain

$$\sum_{j=1}^{|S|} \int_0^{p_{ij}} \frac{1}{|\{k \in S_j : p_k \geq t\}|} \, dt = \int_0^{p_{\max}(S)} \sum_{r=1}^{r(t)} \frac{1}{r} \, dt = \int_0^{p_{\max}(S)} H_{r(t)} \, dt \leq p_{\max}(S) \cdot H_{|S|}.$$

Thus,

$$\sum_{j=1}^{|S|} \xi^{\mathrm{BS}}(i_j, S_j) \leq \mu(S) + p_{\max}(S) \cdot H_{|S|} \leq (H_n + 1) \cdot C(S). \qquad \square$$

Lemma 4 is tight, as the following corollary shows.

Corollary 1. *Let ξ be a cost sharing method for the minimum makespan scheduling problem that satisfies the β-cost recovery condition. Then the summability of ξ is no better than H_n/β.*

Proof. Consider an instance that consists of n jobs with unit processing times and $m := n$ machines. Clearly, $C(S) = 1 = C(U)$ for all $S \subseteq U$. Theorem 1 now gives a lower bound of H_n/β. $\qquad \square$

5 Minimum Weighted Completion Time Scheduling

In the *minimum weighted completion time scheduling problem*, we are given a set of n jobs N and m identical machines. Each job $i \in N$ has a processing time p_i and a weight w_i. The objective is to assign all n jobs to the m machines such that the total weighted completion time $\sum_{i \in N} w_i C_i$ is minimized.

In the cost sharing context, we define $U := N$ as before, and let C be the total weighted completion time of an optimal schedule. We show that the β-core of this scheduling problem is empty for $\beta < (n+1)/2$.

Theorem 4. *Consider the 1-machine minimum completion time scheduling problem $1||\sum_i C_i$. There is no cost sharing method ξ that is in the β-core for any $\beta < (n+1)/2$.*

Proof. Let U be a set of n jobs and define $p_i := 1$ for each $i \in U$. Clearly, the optimal cost for every singleton set $\{i\}$, $i \in U$, is $C(\{i\}) = 1$. The β-core property therefore implies that the cost share of i is at most 1, i.e., $\xi(i, S) \leq 1$ for all $i \in S$ and for all $S \subseteq U$. On the other hand, $C(S) = |S|(|S|+1)/2$ for all $S \subseteq U$.

The condition of β-cost recovery now implies that for every $S \subseteq U$

$$\beta \geq \frac{C(S)}{\sum_{i \in S} \xi(i, S)} \geq \frac{\frac{|S|(|S|+1)}{2}}{|S|} = \frac{|S|+1}{2}. \qquad \square$$

Since every β-budget balanced cross-monotonic cost sharing method is in the β-core, this theorem implies the same lower bound for the budget balance factor of *cross-monotonic* cost sharing methods for the 1-machine minimum completion time scheduling problem. Remind that cross-monotonic and n-budget balanced cost sharing methods trivially exist for these problems.

This result also carries over to all scheduling problems that are generalizations of the 1-machine minimum completion time scheduling problem, as e.g. the *minimum weighted flow time scheduling problem*, and problems with additional constraints such as release or due dates.

6   Conclusion

We proved that in many cases, efficiency is not approximable within less than logarithmic factors even with the new approach of social cost. This reduces the hope to find truly efficient cost sharing mechanisms, while on the other hand allowing us to evaluate social cost approximation factors in terms of their highest polylogarithmic power.

We studied cost sharing methods for the two cases of minimum makespan and minimum completion time scheduling. Our results demonstrate that different scheduling problems can behave very differently. While the completion time setting raises the question of how to handle problems for which the here examined framework does not allow for any (reasonable) solutions, there are many more scheduling problems that deserve to be studied.

References

1. A. Archer, J. Feigenbaum, A. Krishnamurthy, R. Sami, and S. Shenker. Approximation and collusion in multicast cost sharing. *Games and Economic Behavior*, 47(1):36–71, 2004.
2. A. Archer and E. Tardos. Truthful mechanisms for one-parameter agents. In *Proc. of the 42nd Annual Sympos. on Foundations of Computer Science*, pages 482–491. IEEE Computer Society, 2001.
3. Y. Bleischwitz and B. Monien. Fair cost-sharing methods for scheduling jobs on parallel machines. In *Proc. of the 6th Int. Conf. on Algorithms and Complexity*, volume 3998 of *Lecture Notes in Comput. Sci.*, pages 175–186, Berlin, 2006. Springer.
4. S. Chawla, T. Roughgarden, and M. Sundararajan. Optimal cost-sharing mechanisms for steiner forest problems. submitted to WINE.
5. J. Feigenbaum, A. Krishnamurthy, R. Sami, and S. Shenker. Hardness results for multicast cost-sharing. *Theoretical Computer Science*, 304:215–236, 2003.
6. J. Feigenbaum, C. Papadimitriou, and S. Shenker. Sharing the cost of multicast transmissions. *J. Comput. System Sci.*, 63(1):21–41, 2001. Special issue on internet algorithms.
7. R. Graham, E. Lawler, J. Lenstra, and A. Rinnooy Kan. Optimization and approximation in deterministic sequencing and scheduling: a survey. *Annals of Discrete Mathematics*, 5:287–326, 1979.

8. J. Green, E. Kohlberg, and J. J. Laffont. Partial equilibrium approach to the free rider problem. *Journal of Public Economics*, 6:375–394, 1976.
9. A. Gupta, J. Könemann, S. Leonardi, R. Ravi, and G. Schäfer. An efficient cost-sharing mechanism for the prize-collecting steiner forest problem. In *ACM-SIAM Sympos. on Discrete Algorithms*. ACM Press, 2007. to appear.
10. A. Gupta, A. Srinivasan, and É. Tardos. Cost-sharing mechanisms for network design. In *Proc. of the Seventh Int. Workshop on Approximation Algorithms for Combinatorial Optimization Problems*, 2004.
11. B. Heydenreich, R. Müller, and M. Uetz. Decentralization and mechanism design for online machine scheduling. unpublished manuscript.
12. D. Hochbaum, editor. *Approximation Algorithms for NP-hard Problems*. PWS Publishing Company, 1997.
13. N. Immorlica, M. Mahdian, and V. S. Mirrokni. Limitations of cross-monotonic cost sharing schemes. In *Proc. of the Sixteenth Annual ACM-SIAM Sympos. on Discrete Algorithms*, pages 602–611. ACM Press, 2005.
14. K. Jain and V. Vazirani. Applications of approximation algorithms to cooperative games. In *Proc. of the 33rd Annual ACM Sympos. on the Theory of Computing (STOC)*, pages 364–372, 2001.
15. K. Kent and D. Skorin-Kapov. Population monotonic cost allocations on MSTs. In *Proc. of the 6th Int. Conf. on Operational Research (Rovinj, 1996)*, pages 43–48. Croatian Oper. Res. Soc., Zagreb, 1996.
16. J. Könemann, S. Leonardi, and G. Schäfer. A group-strategyproof mechanism for Steiner forests. In *Proc. of the Sixteenth Annual ACM-SIAM Sympos. on Discrete Algorithms*, pages 612–619. ACM Press, 2005.
17. J. Könemann, S. Leonardi, G. Schäfer, and S. van Zwam. From primal-dual to cost shares and back: a stronger LP relaxation for the Steiner forest problem. In *Automata, Languages and Programming*, volume 3580 of *Lecture Notes in Comput. Sci.*, pages 930–942. Springer, Berlin, 2005.
18. A. Kovacs. Fast monotone 3-approximation algorithm for scheduling related machines. In *Proc. of the 13th Annual European Sympos. on Algorithms*, Lecture Notes in Comput. Sci. Springer, 2005.
19. S. Leonardi and G. Schäfer. Cross-monotonic cost sharing methods for connected facility location games. *Theor. Comput. Sci.*, 326(1-3):431–442, 2004.
20. H. Moulin and S. Shenker. Strategyproof sharing of submodular costs: budget balance versus efficiency. *Econom. Theory*, 18(3):511–533, 2001.
21. N. Nisan and A. Ronen. Algorithmic mechanism design. *Games and Economic Behavior*, pages 166–196, 2001.
22. M. Pál and É. Tardos. Group strategyproof mechanisms via primal-dual algorithms. In *Proc. of the 44th Sympos. on the Foundations of Computer Science (FOCS)*, pages 584–593, 2003.
23. R. Porter. Mechanism design for online real-time scheduling. In *Proc. of the ACM Conference on Electronic Commerce*. ACM Press, 2004.
24. K. Roberts. The characterization of implementable choice rules. In J. J. Laffont, editor, *Aggregation and Revelation of Preferences*. North-Holland, 1979.
25. T. Roughgarden and M. Sundararajan. New trade-offs in cost-sharing mechanisms. In *STOC*, 2006.
26. T. Roughgarden and M. Sundararajan. Approximately efficient cost-sharing mechanisms. arXiv report, http://www.arxiv.org/pdf/cs.GT/0606127, June 2006.

Planar Graphs: Logical Complexity and Parallel Isomorphism Tests

Oleg Verbitsky[*]

Institut für Informatik
Humboldt Universität zu Berlin, D-10099 Berlin
verbitsk@informatik.hu-berlin.de

Abstract. We prove that every triconnected planar graph on n vertices is definable by a first order sentence that uses at most 15 variables and has quantifier depth at most $11 \log_2 n + 45$. As a consequence, a canonic form of such graphs is computable in AC^1 by the 14-dimensional Weisfeiler-Lehman algorithm. This gives us another AC^1 algorithm for the planar graph isomorphism.

1   Introduction

Let Φ be a first order sentence about graphs in terms of the adjacency and the equality relations. We say that Φ *distinguishes* a graph G from a graph H if Φ is true on G but false on H. We say that Φ *defines* G if it distinguishes G from every H non-isomorphic to G. The *logical depth* of a graph G, denoted by $D(G)$, is the minimum quantifier depth of a Φ defining G.

The *k-variable logic* consists of those first order sentences which use at most k variables (each of the k variables can occur a number of times). The *logical width* of a graph G, denoted by $W(G)$, is the minimum k such that G is definable by a Φ in the k-variable logic. If $k \geq W(G)$, let $D^k(G)$ denote the logical depth of G in the k-variable logic. Similarly, for non-isomorphic graphs G and H we let $D^k(G, H)$ denote the minimum quantifier depth of a k-variable sentence Φ distinguishing G from H.

The latter parameter is relevant to the Graph Isomorphism problem, namely, to the *k-dimensional Weisfeiler-Lehman algorithm* (see [1,5] for the description and history). Cai, Fürer, and Immerman [1] prove that, if $k \geq W(G) - 1$, then the output of this algorithm is correct for all input pairs (G, H). Furthermore, this condition on k is necessary if we consider the width of G in the logic with *counting quantifiers*. The latter parameter of G, as shown in [1], can be linear in the number of vertices.

Note that the k-dimensional Weisfeiler-Lehman algorithm is polynomial-time only if k is constant. Thus, the algorithm can be successful only for classes of graphs whose width in the logic with counting quantifiers is bounded by a constant. Cai, Fürer, and Immerman ask if this is the case for planar graphs. An affirmative answer is given by Grohe [3].

---

[*] Supported by an Alexander von Humboldt fellowship.

W. Thomas and P. Weil (Eds.): STACS 2007, LNCS 4393, pp. 682–693, 2007.
© Springer-Verlag Berlin Heidelberg 2007

In [5] we extend the approach to Graph Isomorphism suggested in [1] by taking into consideration not only the dimension but also the number of rounds performed by the Weisfeiler-Lehman algorithm. It turns out that the logarithmic-round k-dimensional Weisfeiler-Lehman algorithm is implementable in TC^1 and its count-free version even in AC^1. We apply this fact in [5] to show that the isomorphism problem for graphs of bounded treewidth is in TC^1 (earlier Grohe and Marino [4] proved that such graphs have bounded width in the logic with counting).

According to [5], to put the isomorphism problem for a class of graphs C in AC^1, it suffices to prove that, for a constant k, we have $D^k(G, G') = O(\log n)$ for all G and G' in C. We now apply this approach to planar graphs. Due to the efficient decomposability of graphs into triconnected components [8], it is enough to treat the class of triconnected planar graphs.[1]

Theorem 1. *Let G and G' be non-isomorphic triconnected planar graphs and let G have n vertices. Then $D^{15}(G, G') < 11 \log_2 n + 45$.*

Corollary 2. *The isomorphism problem for triconnected planar graphs is solvable in AC^1 by the logarithmic-round 14-dimensional Weisfeiler-Lehman algorithm.*

The seminal polynomial-time algorithm for this problem is designed by Hopcroft and Tarjan [6,7]. The first AC^1 algorithm follows from a work of Miller and Reif [11]. Another AC^1 algorithm is suggested in [5]. Both [11] and [5] start with AC^1 embedding of input graphs (as in [14]) and then use different methods to test isomorphism of the plane drawings. The new algorithm of Corollary 2 is combinatorially much simpler and more direct. In particular, we now do not need any embedding procedure. Curiously, the Weisfeiler-Lehman approach to Graph Isomorphism appeared a bit earlier even than [6,7] (cf. [15]), but only now we are able to establish that this method, and even its parallel version, works correctly for triconnected planar graphs.

With not so much extra work, we are able to strengthen Theorem 1.

Theorem 3. *For a triconnected planar graph G on n vertices we have $D^{15}(G) < 11 \log_2 n + 45$.*

In the framework of [5], this means that an appropriate modification of the logarithmic-round 14-dimensional Weisfeiler-Lehman algorithm computes a canonic form of a triconnected planar input graph, putting this problem in the class AC^1. Miller and Reif [11] show that the canonization of planar graphs AC^1-reduces to the triconnected case. Using this reduction, we hence obtain a new AC^1-algorithm for the planar graph isomorphism problem.

---

[1] Theorem 1 cannot be extended to biconnected planar graphs. For example, to distinguish between two complete bipartite graphs $K_{2,n-1}$ and $K_{2,n}$, we need to use n first order variables. We could try to extend Theorem 1 to all planar graphs by allowing counting quantifiers but this would require a further delicate analysis (and anyway would not lead us to Corollary 4 directly, since introducing counting quantifiers weakens an AC^1 bound to a TC^1 bound).

Corollary 4. *The canonization problem for planar graphs is solvable in* AC^1.

Theorem 3 is also a contribution in a recent line of research [10,12,13] devoted to a general study of the logical depth $D(G)$ as a mysterious graph invariant.

Sections 2 and 3 contain the necessary preliminaries. The proof of Theorem 1 takes Sections 4 and 5. Theorem 3 is proved in Section 6.

2   Ehrenfeucht-Fraïssé Games

Here we introduce the main technical tool for establishing first order definability properties of finite structures. Let G and G' be graphs with disjoint vertex sets. The *r-round k-pebble Ehrenfeucht-Fraïssé game on G and G'*, denoted by $\mathrm{Ehr}_r^k(G, G')$, is played by two players, Spoiler and Duplicator, with k pairwise distinct pebbles $p_1, \ldots, p_k$, each given in duplicate. Spoiler starts the game. A *round* consists of a move of Spoiler followed by a move of Duplicator. At each move Spoiler takes a pebble, say p_i, selects one of the graphs G or G', and places p_i on a vertex of this graph. In response Duplicator should place the other copy of p_i on a vertex of the other graph. It is allowed to move previously placed pebbles to another vertex and place more than one pebble on the same vertex.

After each round of the game, for $1 \le i \le k$ let x_i (resp. x_i') denote the vertex of G (resp. G') occupied by p_i, irrespectively of who of the players placed the pebble on this vertex. If p_i is off the board at the moment, x_i and x_i' are undefined. If after each of r rounds the component-wise correspondence $(x_1, \ldots, x_k)$ to $(x_1', \ldots, x_k')$ is a partial isomorphism from G to G', this is a win for Duplicator; Otherwise the winner is Spoiler.

Let $\bar{v} = (v_1, \ldots, v_m)$ and $\bar{v}' = (v_1', \ldots, v_m')$ be sequences of vertices in, respectively, G and G' and let $m \le k$. We write $\mathrm{Ehr}_r^k(G, \bar{v}, G', \bar{v}')$ to denote the game that begins from the position where, for every $i \le m$, the vertices v_i and v_i' are already pebbled by p_i.

Proposition 5. (Immerman, Poizat, see [9, Theorem 6.10]) $D^k(G, G')$ *equals the minimum r such that Spoiler has a winning strategy in* $\mathrm{Ehr}_r^k(G, G')$.

All the above definitions and statements have a perfect sense for any kind of structures. Say, in Section 5 we deal with structures having ternary and quaternary relations. The notion of a partial isomorphism for such structures should be understood appropriately.

For our convenience, everywhere below it is assumed that vertex names correspond to pebbling; for example, vertices v in G and v' in G' are always under the same pebbles. Furthermore, we will write *Spoiler wins* with meaning that *Spoiler has a strategy winning against any Duplicator's strategy*.

3   Graph-Theoretic Notation and Definitions

The vertex set of a graph G is denoted by $V(G)$. The distance between vertices u and v is denoted by $d(u, v)$. If u and v are in different connected components, we set $d(u, v) = \infty$. The set $\Gamma(v) = \{ u : d(u, v) = 1 \}$ is called the *neighborhood* of a vertex v in G and $\deg v = |\Gamma(v)|$ is the *degree* of v.

A graph is k-*connected* if it has at least $k + 1$ vertices and remains connected after removal of any $k - 1$ vertices. *Biconnected* and *triconnected* graphs correspond to $k = 2, 3$.

A *sphere graph* is a graph drawn in a sphere with no edge crossing. A *spherical embedding* of a graph G is an isomorphism from G to a sphere graph $\tilde{G}$. As very well known, a graph G is planar iff it has a spherical embedding. Two spherical embeddings $\sigma : G \to \tilde{G}$ and $\tau : G \to \hat{G}$ are equivalent if the isomorphism $\tau \circ \sigma^{-1}$ is induced by a homeomorphism of a sphere taking $\tilde{G}$ onto $\hat{G}$. A classical theorem of Whitney says that all spherical embeddings of a triconnected planar graph G are equivalent (see, e.g., [2]).

Throughout the paper $\log n$ denotes the binary logarithm. Unless stated otherwise, n will denote the number of vertices in a graph G.

4 Capturing Unique Embeddability by First Order Formalism

To prove Theorem 1, we have to design a strategy allowing Spoiler to win the Ehrenfeucht-Fraïssé game on non-isomorphic triconnected planar graphs G and G' with 15 pebbles in less than $11 \log n + 45$ rounds. A crucial fact on which the strategy will be based is the rigidity of triconnected planar graphs as stated in the Whitney theorem. In this section we aim at developing an important ingredient of the strategy forcing Duplicator to respect this rigidity at least locally.

A *configuration* C in a graph G is a set of labeled vertices of G. In fact, labels will be the pebbles in an Ehrenfeucht-Fraïssé game. At the same time we will often use a label as a name of a vertex. By an X-*configuration* we mean 5 pairwise distinct vertices labeled by x, y, u, v, and w such that $x, y, u, v \in \Gamma(w)$. By an H-*configuration* we mean 6 pairwise distinct vertices labeled by x, y, z, u, v, and w such that z and w are adjacent, $x, y \in \Gamma(z)$, and $u, v \in \Gamma(w)$. Thus, contraction of the edge $\{z, w\}$ makes an H-configuration an X-configuration. Suppose that G is a triconnected planar graph and consider its unique spherical embedding. We call an X-configuration C *collocated* if u, x, y, v occur around w exactly in this order (up to cyclic shifts and the direction of a roundabout way). We call an H-configuration C *collocated* if $xzwu$ and $yzwv$ are segments of the two facial cycles containing the edge $\{z, w\}$. A configuration obtained from a collocated X- or H-configuration by interchanging the labels x and y will be called a *twisted* configuration.

We will treat X- and H-configurations uniformly, setting $z = w$ for X-configurations. Whenever we use the term *configuration* alone, it will refer to any X- or H-configuration.

Lemma 6. *Let G and G' be triconnected planar graphs, G having n vertices. Let $C = \{x, y, z, u, v, w\}$ and $C' = \{x', y', z', u', v', w'\}$ be sets of pebbled vertices in, respectively, G and G' such that C is a collocated configuration and C' is a* *twisted configuration. Starting with this position, Spoiler wins the Ehrenfeucht-Fraïssé game on G and G' with 15 pebbles in less than $6 \log n + 26$ moves.*

The proof of Lemma 6 is omitted due to space limitation and can be found in [16].

5   Proof of Theorem 1

Lemma 6 allows us to reduce the Ehrenfeucht-Fraïssé game on G and G' to the game on their spherical embeddings (which are unique by the Whitney theorem). We use two combinatorial specifications for the concept of an embedding. One is a standard notion of a *rotation system*. The other is a related, but in a sense "poorer", notion of a *layout system* (see Subsections 5.1 and 5.3 for the definitions). Denote the rotation and the layout systems for G and G' by R and R' and by L and L' respectively. As we proved in [5], every rotation system is succinctly definable, in particular, Spoiler has an efficient winning strategy in the Ehrenfeucht-Fraïssé game on R and R'. In Subsection 5.2 we will see that Spoiler can win the game on L and L' by emulating the game on R and R'. In its turn, Lemma 6 allows Spoiler to win the game on G and G' by emulating the game on L and L'. This emulation is presented in Subsection 5.4. After all these steps are made, the proof of Theorem 1 in Subsection 5.5 follows easily.

5.1   Two Specifications of a Graph Embedding

The following definitions are introduced for a connected graph G with minimum vertex degree at least 3.

A *rotation system* $R = \langle G, T \rangle$ is a structure consisting of a graph G and a ternary relation T on $V(G)$ satisfying the following conditions:

(1) If $T(a, b, c)$, then b and c are in $\Gamma(a)$, the neighborhood of a in G.

(2) For every a the binary relation $T_a(b, c) = T(a, b, c)$ is a directed cycle on $\Gamma(a)$ (i.e., for every b there is exactly one c such that $T_a(b, c)$, for every c there is exactly one b such that $T_a(b, c)$, and the digraph T_a is connected).

If G is embedded in a surface, it is supposed that T_a describes the circular order in which the edges of G incident to a occur if we go around a clockwise.

Given a rotation system $R = \langle G, T \rangle$, we define another rotation system $R^* = \langle G, T^* \rangle$ by $T_a^*(b, c) = T_a(c, b)$ and call it the *conjugate* of R. Geometrically, R^* is a variant of R if we look at R from the other side of the surface. Obviously, $(R^*)^* = R$.

A *layout system* $L = \langle G, T, Q \rangle$ is a structure consisting of a graph G and two relations on $V(G)$, ternary T and quaternary Q, satisfying the following conditions:

(1) If $T(a, b, c)$, then b and c are in $\Gamma(a)$. Furthermore, for every a the binary relation $T_a(b, c) = T(a, b, c)$ is an undirected cycle on $\Gamma(a)$ (that is, T_a is symmetric, irreflexive, and connected).

(2) If $Q(b_1, a_1, a_2, b_2)$, then b_1, a_1, a_2, b_2 is a path in G or, if $b_1 = b_2$, it is a cycle. Every pair (a_1, a_2) with a_1 and a_2 adjacent in G extends to exactly two

quadruples (b_1, a_1, a_2, b_2) and (c_1, a_1, a_2, c_2) satisfying Q. Moreover, for both $i = 1, 2$, the b_i and c_i are the neighbors of a_{3-i} in the cycle T_{a_i}, that is, $T(a_i, a_{3-i}, b_i)$ and $T(a_i, a_{3-i}, c_i)$ are both true.

Relations T and Q also have clear geometric meaning. Namely, T_a determines the (undirected) circular order in which the edges of G incident to a are embedded. Note that now we specify no clockwise (or counter-clockwise) direction around a. This is the point where a layout system deviates from a rotation system. Thus, if a vertex a_1 and its neighborhood are already embedded and a_2 is adjacent to a_1, we have still two different ways to embed the neighborhood of a_2. The proper choice is determined by Q. Namely, it is supposed that the facial cycle going via b_1, a_1, a_2 goes further via b_2 and the facial cycle going via c_1, a_1, a_2 goes further via c_2.

Given a rotation system $R = \langle G, T_R \rangle$, we associate with it a layout system $\mathsf{L}(R) = \langle G, T_L, Q \rangle$ according to the geometric meaning. Namely, T_L is defined by $T_L(a, b, c) = T_R(a, b, c) \vee T_R(a, c, b)$. To define Q, we first introduce the successor and the predecessor functions on $\Gamma(a)$, s_a and p_a, by the equalities $c = s_a(b)$ and $b = p_a(c)$ if $T_R(a, b, c) = 1$. Now we set the following two relations true: $Q(p_{a_1}(a_2), a_1, a_2, s_{a_2}(a_1))$ and $Q(s_{a_1}(a_2), a_1, a_2, p_{a_2}(a_1))$. As easily seen, $\mathsf{L}(R) = \mathsf{L}(R^*)$.

Let $L = \mathsf{L}(R)$. The following simple lemma says that the pair $\{R, R^*\}$ is reconstructible from L.

Lemma 7. *If* $\mathsf{L}(R') = \mathsf{L}(R)$*, then either* $R' = R$ *or* $R' = R^*$.

In fact, Lemma 7 is essentially strengthened below, see Lemma 10. The following result is obtained in [5, Theorem 10].

Theorem 8. *For a rotation system* $R = \langle G, T \rangle$*, we have* $D^5(R) < 3 \log n + 8$.

5.2   Reducing the Play on Layout Systems to the Play on Rotation Systems

Lemma 9. *Let* $R = \langle G, T \rangle$ *and* $R' = \langle G, T' \rangle$ *be rotation systems. Let* $L = \mathsf{L}(R)$ *and* $L' = \mathsf{L}(R')$*. Suppose that, while* $T(a_1, b_1, c_1) = T(a_2, b_2, c_2) = 1$ *in* R*, in* R' *we have* $T'(a'_1, b'_1, c'_1) = T'(a'_2, c'_2, b'_2) = 1$*. Then Spoiler wins* $\mathrm{Ehr}^9_{2 \log n + 4}(L, a_1, b_1, c_1, a_2, b_2, c_2, L', a'_1, b'_1, c'_1, a'_2, b'_2, c'_2)$.

Proof. Case 1: $a_1 = a_2 = a$. Correspondingly, suppose that $a'_1 = a'_2 = a'$. The case that $\{b_1, c_1\}$ and $\{b_2, c_2\}$ intersect is simple; we hence suppose that all these vertices are pairwise distinct. Spoiler restricts play to the graphs $T_a \setminus \{b_1, b_2\}$ and $T'_{a'} \setminus \{b'_1, b'_2\}$, where T_a and $T'_{a'}$ denote undirected cycles in the structures L and L'. In these graphs $d(c_1, c_2) = \infty$ while $d(c'_1, c'_2) < \infty$ and hence Spoiler wins in less than $\log \deg a + 1$ moves using the standard halving strategy.

Case 2: a_1 *and* a_2 *are adjacent.* It suffices to consider a special subcase where $b_1 = a_2$ and $b_2 = a_1$. Spoiler can force either this subcase or Case 1 in 2 extra moves. By the definition of $\mathsf{L}(R)$, we have $Q(c_1, a_1, a_2, c_2) = 0$ whereas $Q'(c'_1, a'_1, a'_2, c'_2) = 1$, which is a win for Spoiler.

Case 3: $d(a_1, a_2) \geq 2$. Spoiler reduces this case to Case 2 in $\lceil \log d(a_1, a_2) \rceil$ moves. He first pebbles a vertex a_3 on the midway between a_1 and a_2 and then two more vertices b_3, c_3 so that $T(a_3, b_3, c_3) = T(a_i, b_i, c_i)$, $i = 1, 2$. For Duplicator's response a_3', b_3', c_3', assume that one of the relations $T'(a_3', b_3', c_3')$ or $T'(a_3', c_3', b_3')$ is true for else Spoiler has already won. We have either $T'(a_3', b_3', c_3') \neq T'(a_1', b_1', c_1')$ or $T'(a_3', b_3', c_3') \neq T'(a_2', b_2', c_2')$. In either case, one of the tuples $(a_i, b_i, c_i, a_3, b_3, c_3)$, for $i = 1$ or $i = 2$, is similar to the initial position, while the distance between the two a-vertices has decreased. Spoiler just iterates this trick sufficiently many times.

Let $W(S, S')$ denote the minimum k such that non-isomorphic structures S and S' are distinguishable in the k-variable logic.

Lemma 10. *Let $R = \langle G, T' \rangle$ and $R' = \langle G, T \rangle$ be rotation systems such that neither $R' \cong R$ nor $R' \cong R^*$. Suppose that $m \geq \max\{W(R, R'), W(R^*, R')\}$ and set $k = 3 + \max\{m, 6\}$. Let $L = \mathsf{L}(R)$ and $L' = \mathsf{L}(R')$. Then*

$$D^k(L, L') \leq \max\{D^m(R, R'), D^m(R^*, R')\} + 2 \log n + 7.$$

Proof. We design a strategy for Spoiler in $\text{Ehr}^k(L, L')$. In the first three rounds he pebbles vertices a_0, b_0, c_0 in $V(G)$ so that $T(a_0, b_0, c_0) = 1$. Denote Duplicator's responses by a_0', b_0', c_0' and suppose that either $T'(a_0', b_0', c_0') = 1$ or $T'(a_0', c_0', b_0') = 1$ (otherwise Spoiler has won). Without loss of generality, suppose the former (otherwise just interchange b_0 and c_0 and consider R^* and T^* instead of R and T). Starting from the 4-th round, Spoiler emulates $\text{Ehr}^m(R, R')$ keeping the pebbles on a_0, b_0, c_0. His win in this game means that either the equality, or the adjacency in G, or the ternary relation is violated. The former two cases imply also Spoiler's win in $\text{Ehr}^k(L, L')$. In the latter case we arrive at the conditions of Lemma 9 and Spoiler needs no more than $2 \log n + 4$ extra moves to win.

5.3 The Layout and the Rotation System of a Triconnected Planar Graph

Let σ be an embedding of a connected graph G with minimum degree at least 3 in a sphere. Recall that, by definition, σ is an isomorphism from G to a sphere graph $\tilde{G}$. We define the rotation system $R_\sigma = \langle G, T_\sigma \rangle$ according to a natural geometric meaning. Namely, for $a \in V(G)$ and $b, c \in \Gamma(a)$ we have $T_\sigma(a, b, c) = 1$ if, looking at the neighborhood of $\sigma(a)$ in $\tilde{G}$ from the standpoint at the sphere center, $\sigma(b)$ is followed by $\sigma(c)$ in the clockwise order. Note that R_σ^* corresponds to the view on $\tilde{G}$ from the outside. We can define the layout system L_σ also geometrically, as described in Subsection 5.1. Equivalently, we set $L_\sigma = \mathsf{L}(R_\sigma)$.

Let $\sigma : G \to \tilde{G}$ and $\tau : G \to \hat{G}$ be two spherical embeddings of G. Suppose that they are equivalent, that is, $\tau \circ \sigma^{-1}$ is induced by a homeomorphism from the sphere where $\tilde{G}$ is drawn onto the sphere where $\hat{G}$ is drawn. Since $\tau \circ \sigma^{-1}$ takes a facial cycle to a facial cycle, we have $L_\sigma = L_\tau$. By Lemma 7, we also have $\{R_\sigma, R_\sigma^*\} = \{R_\tau, R_\tau^*\}$.

Given a triconnected planar graph G, we define $L_G = L_\sigma$ and $R_G = R_\sigma$ for σ being an arbitrary embedding of G in a sphere. By the Whitney theorem, the definition does not depend on a particular choice of σ if we agree that R_G is defined up to taking the conjugate.

5.4   Reducing the Play on Graphs to the Play on Layout Systems

Lemma 11. *Suppose that G and G' are non-isomorphic triconnected planar graphs. Let $L_G = \langle G, T, Q \rangle$ and $L_{G'} = \langle G', T', Q' \rangle$.*

1. *If $T(a, b, c) \neq T'(a', b', c')$, then Spoiler wins $\text{Ehr}_{6\log n + 28}^{15}(G, a, b, c, G', a', b', c')$.*
2. *If $Q(b_1, a_1, a_2, b_2) \neq Q'(b_1', a_1', a_2', b_2')$, then Spoiler wins $\text{Ehr}_{6\log n + 30}^{15}(G, b_1, a_1, a_2, b_2, G', b_1', a_1', a_2', b_2')$.*

Proof. 1. Let $b, c \in \Gamma(a)$ and $b', c' \in \Gamma(a')$. Suppose that $T(a, b, c) = 0$ while $T'(a', b', c') = 1$ (the other case is symmetric). The former condition implies that $\deg a \geq 4$ and in the embedding of G the vertices b and c are separated by vertices $s, t \in \Gamma(a) \setminus \{b, c\}$. Spoiler pebbles such s and t. Let Duplicator respond with $s', t' \in \Gamma(a') \setminus \{b', c'\}$. Without loss of generality, suppose that, if in the embedding of G' we go around a' in the order b', c' and so on, then we meet s' before t' (otherwise just change the notation by transposing s and t).

Consider X-configurations $C = \begin{smallmatrix} u & x & y & v & w \\ s & b & t & c & a \end{smallmatrix}$ and $C' = \begin{smallmatrix} u' & x' & y' & v' & w' \\ s' & b' & t' & c' & a' \end{smallmatrix}$. Here the bottom row consists of vertices and the top row of their labels. Clearly, C is collocated. Since the configuration $\tilde{C}' = \begin{smallmatrix} u' & x' & y' & v' & w' \\ s' & t' & b' & c' & u' \end{smallmatrix}$ is collocated, the C' is twisted. By Lemma 6, Spoiler wins having made at most $6 \log n + 28$ moves in total.

2. Let, say, $Q(b_1, a_1, a_2, b_2) = 0$ and $Q'(b_1', a_1', a_2', b_2') = 1$. Assume that we are not in the conditions of Item 1 and that the equality relation is always respected by Duplicator. In particular, $T(a_2, a_1, b_2) = T(a_1, a_2, b_1) = 1$. It easily follows that $b_1' \neq b_2'$ and that neither of the facial cycles going through $a_1 a_2$ is a triangle. Spoiler pebbles the vertices c_1 and c_2 in G such that $C = \begin{smallmatrix} x & y & z & u & v & w \\ c_2 & b_2 & a_2 & b_1 & c_1 & a_1 \end{smallmatrix}$ is a collocated H-configuration. Denote Duplicator's responses by c_1' and c_2'. Unless we arrive at the conditions of Item 1, the configuration $C' = \begin{smallmatrix} x' & y' & z' & u' & v' & w' \\ c_2' & b_2' & a_2' & b_1' & c_1' & a_1' \end{smallmatrix}$ is twisted and Spoiler wins by Lemma 6.

Lemma 12. *Suppose that G and G' are non-isomorphic triconnected planar graphs. Denote $L = L_G$ and $L' = L_{G'}$. Let $m \geq W(L, L')$ and $k = \max\{m, 15\}$. Then*

$$D^k(G, G') \leq D^m(L, L') + 6 \log n + 30.$$

Proof. We have to design a strategy for Spoiler in $\text{Ehr}^k(G, G')$. He emulates $\text{Ehr}^m(L, L')$ following an optimal strategy for this game. His victory in $\text{Ehr}^m(L, L')$ means that one of the conditions of Lemma 11 is met and hence Spoiler needs $6 \log n + 30$ extra moves to win $\text{Ehr}^k(G, G')$.

5.5 Finishing the Proof of Theorem 1

Let $L = L_G$ and $L' = L_{G'}$. Let $R = R_G$ and $R' = R_{G'}$ (any of the two conjugated variants can be taken). Applying successively Lemmas 12, 10, and 8, we get

$$D^{15}(G, G') \leq D^{15}(L, L') + 6 \log n + 30$$
$$\leq \max\{D^5(R, R'), D^5(R^*, R')\} + 8 \log n + 37$$
$$< 11 \log n + 45.$$

6 Defining a Triconnected Planar Graph (Proof of Theorem 3)

We now prove Theorem 3. It differs from Theorem 1, which we already proved, by allowing G' to be an *arbitrary* graph non-isomorphic to G. Luckily, the proof techniques we used for Theorem 1 are still applicable. The idea is to show that for every G' one of two possibilities must be the case: Either G' even locally is far from being triconnected planar and Spoiler can efficiently exploit this difference or G' is locally indistinguishable from a triconnected planar graph, in particular, with G' we can naturally associate a rotation system, and hence Spoiler can apply the strategy of Theorem 1 designed for triconnected planar graphs.

Let G be a triconnected planar graph on n vertices. We use the tight connection between logical distinguishability of two structures and the Ehrenfeucht-Fraïssé game on these structures. Lemma 6 for X-configurations can be rephrased as follows: For every collocated X-configuration C in G and every twisted X-configuration T in a triconnected planar graph H (a possibility that $H \cong G$ is not excluded), there is a first order formula $\Phi_{C,T}(w, x, y, v, u)$ of quantifier depth less than $6 \log n + 26$ with 15 variables, of which the variables w, x, y, v, u are free, such that $G, C \models \Phi_{C,T}$ and $H, T \not\models \Phi_{C,T}$. Similar formulas $\Psi_{C,T}(z, w, x, y, v, u)$ exist for H-configurations.

Given a collocated X-configuration C in G, define Φ_C to be the conjunction of $\Phi_{C,T}$ over all twisted configurations T. A problem with this definition is that there are infinitely many triconnected planar graphs H and twisted X-configurations T in them. However, every $\Phi_{C,T}$ has quantifier depth at most $6 \log n + 26$ and, as well known, over a finite vocabulary there are only finitely many inequivalent first order formulas of a bounded quantifier depth. If Φ_{C,T_1} and Φ_{C,T_2} are logically equivalent, then we put in Φ_C only one of these formulas thereby making Φ_C well-defined. Furthermore, we define $\Phi(w, x, y, v, u)$ to be the disjunction of Φ_C over all collocated X-configurations C in G. We also suppose that Φ explicitly says that x, y, v, u are pairwise distinct and all adjacent to w.

Similarly, for H-configurations we define a formula $\Psi(z, w, x, y, v, u)$ by $\Psi = \bigvee_C(\bigwedge_T \Psi_{C,T})$.

Notice that the order of variables we have chosen for $\Phi(w, x, y, v, u)$ plays some role. Namely, if the 5-tuple (w, x, y, v, u) is a collocated X-configuration as defined in Section 4, then in the embedding of G the vertices x, y, v, u occur around w in the order as written. Introduce two permutations $\sigma = (xyvu)$ and $\tau = (xu)(yv)$. The former corresponds to the cyclic shift of the four vertices around w, the latter corresponds to a reflection (changing the direction around w). Define

$$\hat{\Phi}(w, x, y, v, u) = \bigwedge_{i=0}^{1} \bigwedge_{j=0}^{3} \Phi(w, \tau^i \sigma^j(x), \tau^i \sigma^j(y), \tau^i \sigma^j(v), \tau^i \sigma^j(u)).$$

We now make an important observation: $\hat{\Phi}$ has a clear geometric meaning for 5-tuples of vertices of G.

Lemma 13. Let $a \in V(G)$ and $b_j \in \Gamma(a)$ for all $j \leq 4$. In the embedding of G, the vertices b_1, b_2, b_3, b_4 occur around a in the order as written if and only if $G, a, b_1, b_2, b_3, b_4 \models \hat{\Phi}$.

Proof. Indeed, suppose that b_1, b_2, b_3, b_4 is a right order around a. Then the X-configuration $C = \begin{smallmatrix} x & y & v & u & w \\ b_1 & b_2 & b_3 & b_4 & a \end{smallmatrix}$ is collocated and remains so after reassigning the labels x, y, v, u with respect to the permutation $\tau^i \sigma^j$ for any i and j. It remains to notice that Φ is true for any collocated X-configuration by construction.

For the opposite direction, suppose that b_1, b_2, b_3, b_4 is a wrong order around a. Consistently with the previous notation, let $\sigma = (1234)$ and $\tau = (14)(23)$. A key observation here is that, for some permutation $\pi = \tau^i \sigma^j$, the X-configuration $T = \begin{smallmatrix} x & y & v & u & w \\ b_{\pi(1)} & b_{\pi(2)} & b_{\pi(3)} & b_{\pi(4)} & a \end{smallmatrix}$ is twisted. By the definition of $\Phi_{C,T}$, we have $G, a, b_{\pi(1)}, b_{\pi(2)}, b_{\pi(3)}, b_{\pi(4)} \models \neg \Phi_{C,T}$ for every collocated X-configuration C in G. It follows that $G, a, b_{\pi(1)}, b_{\pi(2)}, b_{\pi(3)}, b_{\pi(4)} \models \neg \Phi_C$ for every C and hence $G, a, b_{\pi(1)}, b_{\pi(2)}, b_{\pi(3)}, b_{\pi(4)} \models \neg \Phi$. Equivalently, we have $G, a, b_1, b_2, b_3, b_4 \models \neg \Phi(w, \pi(x), \pi(y), \pi(v), \pi(u))$. Thus, $G, a, b_1, b_2, b_3, b_4 \models \neg \hat{\Phi}(w, x, y, v, u)$, as required.

Let $\sim$ denote the adjacency relation. Define a first order statement

$$A_G = \forall x, y_1, y_2, y_3, y_4 \left(\bigwedge_{i=1}^{4} y_i \sim x \wedge \bigwedge_{i \neq j} \neg(y_i = y_j) \to \right.$$

$$\left(\hat{\Phi}(x, y_1, y_2, y_3, y_4) \vee \hat{\Phi}(x, y_2, y_1, y_3, y_4) \vee \hat{\Phi}(x, y_1, y_3, y_2, y_4) \right) \wedge$$

$$\left. \left(\hat{\Phi}(x, y_1, y_2, y_3, y_4) \to \neg \hat{\Phi}(x, y_2, y_1, y_3, y_4) \wedge \neg \hat{\Phi}(x, y_1, y_3, y_2, y_4) \right) \right),$$

The quantifier depth of A_G is at most $6 \log n + 31$. Note that $y_1 y_2 y_3 y_4$, $y_2 y_1 y_3 y_4$, and $y_1 y_3 y_2 y_4$ are the three possible arrangements of four vertices up to the action of the dihedral group $D_4 = \{\tau^i \sigma^j\}_{i,j}$. Saying that exactly one of these arrangements corresponds to the geometric order around x, the A_G is true on G.

Suppose now that G' is an arbitrary graph non-isomorphic to G. We have to bound $D^{15}(G, G')$ from above. We assume that G' is connected and has minimum degree at least 3; otherwise Spoiler wins fast. If $G' \not\models A_G$, then G and G' are distinguished by A_G and hence $D^{15}(G, G') \leq 6 \log n + 31$.

Suppose that $G' \models A_G$. The A_G ensures that, for every vertex a in G' and $b_1, b_2, b_3, b_4 \in \Gamma(a)$, we have a unique (up to shifting and redirecting) ordering of b_1, b_2, b_3, b_4 satisfying $\hat{\Phi}(x, y_1, y_2, y_3, y_4)$. We use it to associate with G' a layout system $L' = \langle G', T', Q' \rangle$ (as if this ordering corresponds to some embedding of G'). Given $a \in V(G')$ of degree at least 4, we first want to define pairs $b, c \in \Gamma(a)$ such that b and c are neighboring in this "pseudo-embedding" of G'. We let $N(a, b, c) = \neg \exists s, t \, \hat{\Phi}(a, b, s, c, t)$. Consider a first order sentence

$$B_G = \forall a, b \Big(\deg a \geq 4 \wedge b \sim a \to \exists_{=2} c \, N(a, b, c) \Big)$$

(written with harmless shorthands). This sentence has a clear geometric meaning and is true on G. If $G' \not\models B_G$, then G and G' are distinguished by B_G and we are done.

Suppose that $G' \models B_G$. We are now able to define a ternary relation T' on $V(G')$. Suppose that $b', c' \in \Gamma(a')$ and $b' \neq c'$. If $\deg a' = 3$, we set $T'(a', b', c') = 1$. Let $\deg a' \geq 4$. In this case we set $T'(a', b', c') = 1$ iff $N(a', b', c')$ is true.

The B_G ensures that, for every a', $T'_{a'}$ is a union of cycles. If $T'_{a'}$ is disconnected for some a', Spoiler wins fast. He first pebbles the a'. Denote Duplicator's response in G by a. Spoiler restricts further play to $\Gamma(a)$ and $\Gamma(a')$ and follows his winning strategy in the game on graphs $(T_G)_a$ and $T'_{a'}$, one of which is connected and the other is not. Spoiler's win in this game entails disagreement $N(a, b, c) \neq N(a', b', c')$ for some pebbled b, c in G and the corresponding b', c' in G'. In the next two moves Spoiler forces disagreement between the truth values of $\hat{\Phi}$ on some 5-tuples and wins in $6 \log n + 26$ extra moves.

Suppose hence that $T'_{a'}$ is connected for every a', i.e, is a cycle on $\Gamma(a')$. Similarly to the above, we can use the formula Ψ to construct a sentence Λ_G of quantifier depth at most $6 \log n + 32$ providing us with the following dichotomy. If $G' \not\models \Lambda_G$, the G and G' are distinguished by Λ_G and we are done. Otherwise Ψ in a natural way determines a quaternary relation Q' such that $L' = \langle G', T', Q' \rangle$ is a layout system.

We have to consider the latter possibility. In its turn, it splits into two cases. If $L' = \mathsf{L}(R')$ for no rotation system R', this means that, if we fix a triple a_1', b_1', c_1' with $T'(a_1', b_1', c_1') = 1$ and set $T'_{R'}(a_1', b_1', c_1') = 1$, then there are a triple a_2', b_2', c_2' and two a_1'-a_2'-paths P_1 and P_2 such that propagation of the truth value of $T'_{R'}(a_1', b_1', c_1')$ along P_1 and P_2 gives different results, say, $T'_{R'}(a_2', b_2', c_2') = 1$ for P_1 and $T'_{R'}(a_2', c_2', b_2') = 1$ for P_2. Spoiler pebbles $a_1', b_1', c_1', a_2', b_2', c_2'$. Let Duplicator respond with $a_1, b_1, c_1, a_2, b_2, c_2$ in G. Suppose that $T_R(a_1, b_1, c_1) = 1$ for $R \in \{R_G, R_G^*\}$. Spoiler wins similarly to the proof of Lemma 9, using P_1 if $T_R(a_2, c_2, b_2) = 1$ and P_2 if $T_R(a_2, b_2, c_2) = 1$. This argument works only if P_1 and P_2 are not too long. It is not hard to show that, if the diameter of G' is smaller than n, then we have a choice of such paths with P_1 of length less than

n and P_2 of length less than $2n$. The case of G and G' having different diameters is easy for Spoiler.

If $L' = \mathsf{L}(R')$ for some rotation system R', then Spoiler plays as if G' was a triconnected planar graph. Namely, he follows the strategy of Section 5 using L' for $L_{G'}$ and R' for $R_{G'}$. Spoiler's win in this simulation means that he forces pebbling some tuples of vertices in G and G' on which the formula Φ or the formula Ψ disagree, and hence logarithmically many extra moves suffice for Spoiler to have a win in $\mathrm{Ehr}^{15}(G, G')$. The proof is complete.

Acknowledgment. I acknowledge valuable discussions with Martin Grohe on the topic and am grateful to Hans-Jürgen Prömel for his kind hospitality during my two-year research stay at the Humboldt-University of Berlin.

References

1. Cai, J.-Y., Fürer, M., Immerman, N.: An optimal lower bound on the number of variables for graph identification. Combinatorica **12** (1992) 389–410
2. Diestel, R.: Graph theory. Springer-Verlag (2006)
3. Grohe, M.: Fixed-point logics on planar graphs. In: Proc. of the Ann. Conf. on Logic in Computer Science (1998) 6–15
4. Grohe, M., Marino, J.: Definability and descriptive complexity on databases of bounded tree-width. In: Proc. of the 7th Int. Conf. on Database Theory. Lecture Notes in Computer Science, Vol. 1540. Springer-Verlag (1999) 70–82
5. Grohe, M., Verbitsky, O.: Testing graph isomorphism in parallel by playing a game. In: Automata, Languages and Programming (ICALP 2006). Lecture Notes in Computer Science, Vol. 4051. Springer-Verlag (2006) 3–14
6. Hopcroft J.E.: An $n \log n$ algorithm for isomorphism of planar triply connected graphs. Technical Report CS-192. Stanford University (1971)
7. Hopcroft, J.E., Tarjan, R.E.: Isomorphism of planar graphs (working paper). In: Complexity of computer computations. Plenum Press (1972) 131–152
8. Hopcroft, J.E., Tarjan, R.E.: Dividing a graph into triconnected components. SIAM Journal on Computing **2** (1973) 135–158
9. Immerman, N.: Descriptive complexity. Springer-Verlag (1999)
10. Kim, J.-H., Pikhurko, O., Spencer, J., Verbitsky, O.: How complex are random graphs in first order logic? Random Structures and Algorithms **26** (2005) 119–145
11. Miller, G.L., Reif, J.H.: Parallel tree contraction. Part 2: further applications. SIAM J. Comput. **20** 1128–1147
12. Pikhurko, O., Spencer, J., Verbitsky, O.: Succinct definitions in first order graph theory. Annals of Pure and Applied Logic **139** (2006) 74–109
13. Pikhurko, O., Veith, H., Verbitsky, O.: First order definability of graphs: tight bounds on quantifier rank. Discrete Applied Mathematics **154** (2006) 2511–2529
14. Ramachandran, V., Reif, J.: Planarity testing in parallel. J. Comput. Syst. Sci. **49** (1994) 517–561
15. Weisfeiler, B.Yu., Lehman, A.A.: A reduction of a graph to a canonical form and an algebra arising during this reduction (in Russian). Nauchno-Technicheskaya Informatsia, Seriya 2. **9** (1968) 12–16
16. Verbitsky, O.: Planar graphs: Logical complexity and parallel isomorphism tests. E-print (2006) *http://arxiv.org/abs/cs.CC/0607033*

Enumerating All Solutions for Constraint Satisfaction Problems*

Henning Schnoor and Ilka Schnoor

Institut für Theoretische Informatik, Universität Hannover, Appelstr. 4, 30167
Hannover, Germany
{henning, ilka}.schnoor@thi.uni-hannover.de

Abstract. We contribute to the study of efficient enumeration algorithms for all solutions of constraint satisfaction problems. The only algorithm known so far, presented by Creignou and Hébrard [CH97] and generalized by Cohen [Coh04], reduces the enumeration problem for a constraint language Γ to the decision problem for a slightly enlarged constraint language Γ^+, i.e., it yields an efficient enumeration algorithm for the case where $\mathsf{CSP}(\Gamma^+)$ is tractable. We develop a new class of algorithms, yielding efficient enumeration algorithms for a broad class of constraint languages. For the three-element domain, we achieve a first step towards a dichotomy theorem for the enumeration problem.

Keywords: computational complexity, constraints, enumeration.

1 Introduction

Constraint satisfaction problems (CSPs) have attracted considerable attention in complexity theory. Especially the non-uniform version of the problem, $\mathsf{CSP}(\Gamma)$ has been studied. Here, we fix a constraint language Γ, which is a set of finitary relations over an arbitrary domain. The problem $\mathsf{CSP}(\Gamma)$ is the satisfiability problem for propositional formulas, where the form of the clauses appearing is restricted by Γ, so-called Γ-formulas. If the domain is Boolean, then these problems generalize many common restrictions of the satisfiability problem (2SAT, 3SAT, Horn-SAT, etc). In the non-Boolean case, $\mathsf{CSP}(\Gamma)$ can generalize problems as colorability in graphs, scheduling problems, database queries, and others. In fact, most combinatorial problems where the goal is to find some assignment to variables which needs to satisfy a collection of "local" conditions can be seen as a CSP. Due to this property, CSPs can be seen as the "combinatorial core of complexity theory" [CKS01], and are of interest for theoretical reasons as well.

The complexity of $\mathsf{CSP}(\Gamma)$ was first studied by Thomas Schaefer. In his seminal paper [Sch78], he showed that in the Boolean case, this problem is always solvable either in polynomial time, or is NP-complete, and he gave easy criteria for Γ which allow for a polynomial time decision procedure. The study of constraint satisfaction problems becomes much more challenging when considering non-Boolean domains. For example, Bulatov proved that an analog of Schaefer's

---

* Supported in part by grant DFG VO 630/5-2.

W. Thomas and P. Weil (Eds.): STACS 2007, LNCS 4393, pp. 694–705, 2007.

dichotomy holds for the case where the domain is of cardinality three [Bul06], but the proof is much more involved. It is conjectured that dichotomy results hold for arbitrary finite domains. In fact, CSP is in a certain context the largest class of problems for which such results are possible [FV98].

Besides satisfiability of formulas, other computational goals have been studied, as for example optimal satisfiability [RV00], counting the number of solutions for constraint formulas [CH96], and equivalence and isomorphism [BHRV02] for a fixed constraint language Γ. In many of these cases, dichotomy theorems have been proven for Boolean domains. A lot of research has been done for the case where the domain is a non-Boolean finite set, see e.g. [JCG97], [Dal05], [DK06], and [Bul06].

A problem which is very relevant in practice is the enumeration problem for constraint formulas, which we study in this paper. Here the task is to enumerate, for a given Γ-formula, the set of its solutions. Roughly speaking, an "efficient" algorithm requires only polynomial time for each solution it generates. Such an algorithm can only exist if the satisfiability problem for Γ-formulas can be solved in polynomial time. For the Boolean domain, the question in which cases efficient enumeration algorithms exist has been studied by Creignou and Hébrard in [CH97]. In [Coh04], it was shown that their algorithm can be applied to arbitrary finite domains. The algorithm reduces the enumeration problem to the decision problem as follows: for the constraint language Γ, let Γ^+ be the constraint language containing the relations from Γ and relations representing literals over the domain D, i.e., it lets us express clauses like $x = \alpha$ for variables x and values α from D. If the satisfiability problem for Γ^+ can be solved in polynomial time, then a search-reduces-to-decision algorithm can be used to generate all solutions to a Γ-formula. This is the only enumeration algorithm for constraint formulas known so far, and in [CH97], it was shown that it is indeed the only one for the Boolean domain. It has been conceivable that this is also true for arbitrary domains, i.e., that Γ-formulas can be efficiently enumerated if and only if the constraint satisfaction problem for Γ^+ can be solved in polynomial time. In exhibiting a new class of enumeration algorithms, we prove that this is not the case, unless $P = NP$. The contribution of this paper is as follows:

1. We consider refinements of the notion of efficient enumeration, demanding that the solutions can be generated not only efficiently, but also in highly customizable order. We show that for a constraint language Γ, this can be done efficiently if and only if the above-mentioned criterion is met, i.e., $\mathsf{CSP}(\Gamma^+)$ can be solved in polynomial time.

2. We develop efficient enumeration algorithms for broad classes of constraint languages Γ for which $\mathsf{CSP}(\Gamma^+)$ cannot be solved in polynomial time (unless $P = NP$). All of these cannot be enumerated by the known search-reduces-to-decision algorithm.

3. For the three-element case, we obtain a first step towards a full classification. We show that in the case where the constraint language satisfies an algebraic condition, our algorithms cover all cases that exist. Hence, we obtain a dichotomy theorem for enumeration in this case.

The structure of the paper is as follows: In Section 2, we state the necessary definitions and known results from the literature. In Section 3, we present the above-mentioned refinement of enumeration algorithms to deal with orderings, and show that such an algorithm exists if and only if $\mathsf{CSP}(\Gamma^+)$ is tractable. Then we present our new enumeration algorithms, and show that there is a broad class of constraint languages for which these give an efficient enumeration procedure. The technically most involved result of the paper is Theorem 3.8, which gives an easily verifiable criterion that a constraint language Γ needs to fullfill for our algorithms to be applicable. Section 4 contains the mentioned dichotomy theorem for a subclass of constraint languages over the three-element domain.

All proofs can be found in the extended version of the paper [SS06a].

2   Preliminaries

For a domain D and a number n, an *n-ary relation over* D is a subset of D^n. In this paper, all domains are finite. A *constraint language* Γ *over* D is a finite set of relations over D. We say that a relation or a constraint language is *Boolean*, if the domain has cardinality 2. A Γ-*formula* is a conjunction of the form

$$\varphi = R_1(x_1^1, \ldots, x_{n_1}^1) \wedge \cdots \wedge R_k(x_1^k, \ldots, x_{n_k}^k),$$

where the R_i are relations from Γ of arity n_i (we use the same symbol for the relation and its predicate). The set of occurring variables is denoted with $\mathrm{VAR}\,(\varphi)$. An assignment $I\colon \mathrm{VAR}\,(\varphi) \to D$ *satisfies* φ, or is a *solution of* φ, if for every $1 \leq i \leq k$, $(I(x_1^i), \ldots, I(x_{k_i}^i)) \in R_i$ holds (we write $I \models \varphi$). The formula φ is *satisfiable* if there exists a solution of φ. The set of solutions of φ is denoted with $\mathrm{SOL}\,(\varphi)$. The problem $\mathsf{CSP}(\Gamma)$ is to decide whether a given Γ-formula is satisfiable. A constraint language Γ is *tractable* if $\mathsf{CSP}(\Gamma)$ can be solved in polynomial time. For Boolean constraint languages Γ, Schaefer showed that $\mathsf{CSP}(\Gamma)$ is solvable in P or is NP-complete [Sch78]. This dichotomy also holds for the three-element case [Bul06].

For $\mathbf{v} \in D^n$, we write $\mathbf{v}[i]$ for the i-th component of $\mathbf{v}$. For a formula φ and strings t_1 and t_2, $\varphi[t_1/t_2]$ is obtained from φ by simultaneously replacing every occurrence of t_1 with t_2. For a set D and values $a, b \in D$, the function $f_{a \to b}\colon D \to D$ is defined as $f(a) = b$, and $f(\alpha) = \alpha$ for all $\alpha \in D \setminus \{a\}$. For $f\colon D \to D$ and $\mathbf{v} \in D^n$, let $f(\mathbf{v}) := (f(\mathbf{v}[1]), \ldots, f(\mathbf{v}[n]))$. For a relation $R \subseteq D^n$ let $f(R) := \{f(\mathbf{v}) \mid \mathbf{v} \in R\}$. For a formula $\varphi(x_1, \ldots, x_n) = \bigwedge_{i=1}^l R_i(x_1^i, \ldots, x_{k_i}^i)$ let $f(\varphi)(x_1, \ldots, x_n) = \bigwedge_{i=1}^l f(R_i)(x_1^i, \ldots, x_{k_i}^i)$, and finally for an assignment $I\colon \mathrm{VAR}\,(\varphi) \to D$, let $f(I)$ be the assignment defined as $f(I)(x) := f(I(x))$.

Definition 2.1. *Let* $f\colon D^k \to D$, *and let* R *be an* n-*ary relation over* D. *We say* R *is* closed under f, *or* f *is a* polymorphism *of* R, *if for all* $\mathbf{v_1}, \ldots, \mathbf{v_k} \in R$, *it holds that*

$$\Big(f(\mathbf{v_1}[1], \ldots, \mathbf{v_k}[1]), \ f(\mathbf{v_1}[2], \ldots, \mathbf{v_k}[2]), \ \ldots, \ f(\mathbf{v_1}[n], \ldots, \mathbf{v_k}[n])\Big) \in R,$$

i.e., the tuple obtained from applying f *coordinate-wise to* $\mathbf{v_1}, \ldots, \mathbf{v_k}$ *is in* R.

We denote the set of polymorphisms of R with $\mathrm{Pol}(R)$. For a constraint language Γ, $\mathrm{Pol}(\Gamma)$ is the set of functions which are polymorphisms of all relations in Γ. It is known that the set $\mathrm{Pol}(\Gamma)$ determines the complexity of $\mathrm{CSP}(\Gamma)$ up to logspace reductions [ABI+05]. In the enumeration context, this can be shown not to be the case. A counter-example is omitted for space reasons.

We define a Boolean relation or a Boolean constraint language to be *Schaefer*, if it has a polymorphism depending on at least two of its variables.

In general a formula has an exponential number of solutions. Therefore for an enumeration algorithm to be considered efficient, we do not require it to give all solutions in polynomial time, but to generate the solutions with *polynomial delay* [JPY88]: the algorithm has to enumerate all solutions of φ in such a way that the time between each pair of assignments, between the start of the algorithm and the first solution, and between the last solution and the termination of the algorithm is polynomial in the input size. We also require each solution to be printed exactly once. A constraint language Γ has an *efficient enumeration algorithm*, if there is a polynomial delay algorithm which, when given a Γ-formula φ as input, enumerates the set $\mathrm{SOL}\,(\varphi)$ with polynomial delay.

Let us consider one of the simplest types of enumeration algorithms conceivable, suggested in [Val79]. For a formula φ with $\mathrm{VAR}\,(\varphi) = \{x_1, \ldots, x_n\}$, and for each $\alpha \in D$, we check if $\varphi \wedge (x_1 = \alpha)$ is satisfiable. If yes, we recursively enumerate the solutions of $\varphi[x_1/\alpha]$ augmented with the assignment $x_1 = \alpha$. If the satisfiability tests in this approach can be performed in polynomial time, then this is a polynomial-delay enumeration algorithm for the solutions of φ. Obviously, if $\mathrm{P} = \mathrm{NP}$, then all satisfiability tests of this nature can be done in polynomial time, and we always have an efficient enumeration algorithm. Therefore, for this paper we assume $\mathrm{P} \neq \mathrm{NP}$. Also note that, if Γ has an efficient enumeration algorithm, then $\mathrm{CSP}(\Gamma) \in \mathrm{P}$. For a constraint language Γ over D, let $\Gamma^+ := \Gamma \cup \{\{(\alpha)\} \mid \alpha \in D\}$. The unary relations $\{(\alpha)\}$ can be used to force a variable to the value $\alpha \in D$, and hence in Γ^+ we have the power to express literals. The algorithm outlined above yields the following theorem.

Theorem 2.2 ([CH96, Coh04]). *If* $\mathrm{CSP}(\Gamma^+) \in \mathrm{P}$, *then* Γ *has an efficient enumeration algorithm.*

There is a large class of constraint languages Γ which are tractable, but for which tests of the form above are NP-complete. However, in the Boolean case it turns out that if some constraint language Γ has any efficient enumeration algorithm, then the algorithm outlined above works [CH97].

To summarize the above, for a constraint language Γ to have a polynomial-delay algorithm it is required that $\mathrm{CSP}(\Gamma) \in \mathrm{P}$. Furthermore, if $\mathrm{CSP}(\Gamma^+) \in \mathrm{P}$, such an algorithm is guaranteed to exist. Therefore we are only interested in constraint languages Γ such that $\mathrm{CSP}(\Gamma) \in \mathrm{P}$, and $\mathrm{CSP}(\Gamma^+) \notin \mathrm{P}$. We show that there is a rich class of these languages which still have a polynomial-delay enumeration algorithm. The following proposition can easily be proven using results on the algebraic structure of constraint satisfaction problems from e.g. [BKJ00], [BJK05]. For the three-element case, this implies that in the cases we consider, we have a constant polymorphism or a polymorphism of the form $f_{a \to b}$.

Proposition 2.3. *Let Γ be a constraint language such that* $\mathsf{CSP}(\Gamma) \in \mathsf{P}$, *and* $\mathsf{CSP}(\Gamma^+) \notin \mathsf{P}$. *Then Γ has a non-injective unary polymorphism f which, restricted to its range, is the identity.*

3   Efficient Enumeration Algorithms

For more readability we restrict ourselves to one-element constraint languages $\{R\}$ from now on. It can easily be shown that this is not a real restriction. By abuse of notation we refer to such a constraint language $\{R\}$ simply as R.

3.1   Lexicographical Orderings

We extend the algorithm given above: The input is a formula φ with VAR $(\varphi) = \{x_1, \ldots, x_n\}$ and n orderings $<_1, \ldots, <_n$ on D. Let $D = \alpha_1, \ldots, \alpha_k$ such that $\alpha_1 <_n \cdots <_n \alpha_k$. For each i from 1 to k we check if $\varphi \wedge (x_n = \alpha_i)$ is satisfiable and in this case enumerate the solutions of $\varphi[x_n/\alpha_i]$, by applying the algorithm recursively to $\varphi[x_n/\alpha_i]$ and $<_1, \ldots, <_{n-1}$, and augment the solutions with the assignment $x_n = \alpha_i$. This algorithm prints the solutions of φ in the following order: $I_1 \in \mathrm{SOL}(\varphi)$ is printed earlier than $I_2 \in \mathrm{SOL}(\varphi)$ if and only if there is an i such that $I_1(x_i) <_i I_2(x_i)$ and $j > i$ implies that $I_1(x_j) = I_2(x_j)$.

We call an enumeration algorithm with this property a *variable lexicographical enumeration algorithm* for Γ. Boolean constraint languages are efficiently enumerable if and only if they have efficient variable lexicographical enumeration algorithms, i.e., if we can print the solutions with polynomial delay in every possible variable lexicographical order. This follows from [CH97].

The next theorem says, that in the general case as well all constraint languages Γ which have efficient variable lexicographical order enumeration algorithms are those for which $\mathsf{CSP}(\Gamma^+)$ is tractable. Hence, if there is an efficient variable lexicographical order enumeration algorithm, then the one explained above works. In the Boolean case, this is true as soon as there is any efficient enumeration algorithm for Γ. Later we will see that this is not true if we leave the Boolean domain: here there are constraint languages Γ which have an efficient enumeration algorithm, but Γ^+ is not tractable. Hence, they cannot be efficiently enumerated in variable lexicographical order.

Theorem 3.1. *Let Γ be a constraint language over D. There exists an efficient variable lexicographical enumeration algorithm for Γ if and only if $\mathsf{CSP}(\Gamma^+)$ is tractable.*

3.2   Partial Enumerability

We give an example for a relation R which has a polynomial-delay enumeration algorithm, and where R^+ is not tractable—i.e., we show that there are more efficiently enumerable relations than the ones covered by Theorem 2.2. Due to Theorem 3.1, this implies that for non-Boolean domains, there are constraint languages which can be enumerated efficiently, but not with a variable lexi-cographical order algorithm. We then show how the ideas highlighted in this example can be generalized.

Example 3.2. *Let* $R := \{(2,0,0,2),(2,0,2,0),(2,2,0,0),(1,0,0,1),(1,0,1,0),$ $(1,1,0,0),(1,0,0,0)\}$. *Then* R *is efficiently enumerable, and* R^+ *is not tractable.*

Proof Sketch. $\mathsf{CSP}(R^+)$ is NP-complete: CSP(1-in-3) is NP-complete (this follows from [Sch78]), where 1-in-3 $= \{(1,0,0),(0,1,0),(0,0,1)\}$. CSP(1-in-3) reduces to $\mathsf{CSP}(R^+)$ by forcing one additional variable to 2.

To see that R has an efficient enumeration algorithm, consider the following approach: it can be verified that $f_{2\to1} \in \mathrm{Pol}(R)$, and that $f_{2\to1}(R)$ is closed under the Boolean AND operator. Thus, $f_{2\to1}(R)$ is Schaefer, and has an efficient enumeration algorithm due to [CH97]. It can be seen that $f_{2\to1}(R) = R\cap\{0,1\}^4$. Therefore enumerating, for a given R-formula φ, the solutions of $f_{2\to1}(\varphi)$, is the same as enumerating all solutions of φ which assign each of the variables $x \in \mathrm{VAR}\,(\varphi)$ one of the values 0 and 1.

If we can efficiently enumerate, for each solution I as above, all "compatible" solutions J for which $f_{2\to1}(J) = I$, then we can enumerate all solutions of φ. This is because for an arbitrary solution J of φ, $f_{2\to1}(J)$ is a solution of φ as well, since $f_{2\to1} \in \mathrm{Pol}(R)$. Hence the solution J appears in this enumeration scheme.

It remains to prove that for each solution $I \models \varphi$, $I\colon \mathrm{VAR}\,(\varphi) \to \{0,1\}$, we can enumerate the set of all J fulfilling the above conditions efficiently. This is, in essence, a Boolean problem: given such an assignment I, we want to exchange some of the occurring 1s with 2s, such that the assignment J obtained this way satisfies φ. Variables x such that $I(x) = 0$ are left unmodified. Therefore, this is a Boolean problem involving the values 1 and 2. It is natural that there is a Boolean constraint language, which we will later introduce as $\Gamma_R^{E_1\to E_2}$, that can be used to express the "possibilities of changing 1s into 2s." Intuitively, $\Gamma_R^{E_1\to E_2}$ is obtained as follows: for each $\mathbf{v} \in \{0,1\}^4$, consider the relation $R_{\mathbf{v}}$, containing all tuples $\mathbf{v}' \in R$ such that $f_{2\to1}(\mathbf{v}') = \mathbf{v}$. $R_{\mathbf{v}}$ describes the combinations of 2s and 1s that are "allowed." Since we are not interested in the occurring 0s here—they are fixed and we do not change these assignments—we only look at those components of $R_{\mathbf{v}}$ in which 1s and 2s appear. We will introduce the constraint language $\Gamma_R^{E_1\to E_2}$ arising here formally later in this section.   □

Our approach applied in the example is to enumerate solutions in two steps: First we look for all solutions that map to $\{0,1\}$. For each of these, we then enumerate all "fitting" solutions mapping to $\{0,1,2\}$. These are obtained by changing some of the appearing 1s into 2s. Hence, we can see the 1 as a "placeholder" for a value which is either 1 or 2. We could therefore identify the value 1 with the set $\{1,2\}$, since this gives all possibilities for the "fitting" solutions. This is a central idea in our algorithms and we formalize it with *partial assignments*. These assign, to each variable, not a single value but a set of possible values i.e. a subset of D. The assigned subsets must form a partition of the domain. This generalization of the ideas from Example 3.2 is relevant for two reasons: In this more general case, we do not rely on the presence of a special polymorphism anymore, as in the example. Further, this generalizations allows nesting of algorithms, and enables us to state the dichotomy theorem in Section 4.

We introduce some notation on partitions and equivalence relations. Let D be a domain, and E a partition of D. We often identify E with its corresponding equivalence relation, denoted by $\sim_E$. The *discrete partition of D*, D^{disc}, corresponding to the equality predicate on D, is defined as $D^{\text{disc}} = \{\{\alpha\} \mid \alpha \in D\}$. We often identify a partition E and the set of unary relations representing the classes in E. With f^E we denote the function assigning each $\alpha \in D$ its equivalence class. For a relation R, R/E is defined as $f^E(R)$, and for partitions E_1 and E_2 of a domain D we say E_2 is a refinement of E_1 ($E_2 \leq E_1$) if $\alpha \sim_{E_2} \beta$ implies $\alpha \sim_{E_1} \beta$.

Let Γ be a constraint language over D, E_1 a partition of D, and φ a Γ-formula. We say $I : \text{VAR}(\varphi) \to E_1$ is a *partial E_1-assignment*. If E_2 is a refinement of E_1 and J is a partial E_2-assignment, then we say J is *compatible with I* if for all $x \in \text{VAR}(\varphi)$, $J(x) \subseteq I(x)$. We also apply this notion to tuples, i.e., if $\mathbf{v_1} \in E_1^n$, $\mathbf{v_2} \in E_2^n$, then we say $\mathbf{v_2}$ is compatible with $\mathbf{v_1}$ if for all $i \in \{1, \ldots, n\}$, $\mathbf{v_2}[i] \subseteq \mathbf{v_1}[i]$. We identify partial D^{disc}-assignments J for φ and assignments $J : \text{VAR}(\varphi) \to D$, i.e., for such an assignment we say J is compatible with I if $J(x) \in I(x)$ for all $x \in \text{VAR}(\varphi)$. A partial assignment I is a *partial E_1-solution of φ* if there exists some $J : \text{VAR}(\varphi) \to D, J \models \varphi$ such that J is compatible with I. We denote the set of partial E_1-solutions of φ with $\text{SOL}^{E_1}(\varphi)$.

Definition 3.3. *Let E_1 and E_2 be partitions of D, such that E_2 is a refinement of E_1, and R a relation over D.*

- *R is efficiently E_1-enumerable, if there is a polynomial delay algorithm which, given an R-formula φ, enumerates $\text{SOL}^{E_1}(\varphi)$.*
- *R is efficiently $E_1 \to E_2$-enumerable, if there exists a polynomial-delay algorithm which, given an R-formula φ and an assignment $I : \text{VAR}(\varphi) \to E_1$, enumerates all partial solutions $J \in \text{SOL}^{E_2}(\varphi)$ which are compatible with I.*
- *R is efficiently $E_1 \to D$-enumerable, if R is efficiently $E_1 \to D^{\text{disc}}$-enumerable.*

The following theorem is one of our main results, and shows how our approach can be used to obtain enumeration algorithms. In Sect. 3.3, we will show that the prerequisites for this theorem are met by a large class of relations.

Theorem 3.4. *Let E_1 and E_2 partitions of D such that E_2 is a refinement of E_1, and let R be a relation over D.*

1. *If R is efficiently E_1-enumerable and efficiently $E_1 \to E_2$-enumerable, then R is efficiently E_2-enumerable.*
2. *If $\text{CSP}(\{R\} \cup E_1) \in \text{P}$ then R is efficiently E_1-enumerable.*
3. *If R is efficiently E_1-enumerable and efficiently $E_1 \to D$-enumerable, then R has an efficient enumeration algorithm.*

This theorem applies to Example 3.2 with $E_1 = \{\{0\}, \{1, 2\}\}$ and $E_2 = D^{\text{disc}} = \{\{0\}, \{1\}, \{2\}\}$. R is efficiently E_1-enumerable: if we consider the relation $f_{2 \to 1}(R) = R \cap \{0, 1\}^4$, then this enables us, for a given R-formula φ, to enumerate all solutions $I \colon \text{VAR}(\varphi) \to \{0, 1\}$. Now for any solution $J \models \varphi$, the "Boolean solution" $f_{2 \to 1}(J)$ is also a solution of φ, and it can easily be seen that $f_{2 \to 1}(J) \sim_{E_1} J$. Since we can, for every E_1-solution, find all compatible solutions of φ (see proof sketch of Example 3.2), R is efficiently $E_1 \to D^{\text{disc}}$-enumerable.

It follows directly from Theorem 3.4 that if we have partitions $E_k \leq \cdots \leq E_1$ of D, such that $\text{CSP}\{R\} \cup E_1 \in \text{P}$, R is efficiently $E_i \to E_{i+1}$-enumerable for each $1 \leq i < k$, and $E_k = D^{\text{disc}}$, then R has an efficient enumeration algorithm. Note that this result allows to combine different types of algorithms to build an enumeration algorithm for R.

The previous theorem generalizes Theorem 2.2: R^+ is tractable if and only if $\{R\} \cup D^{\text{disc}}$ is, therefore, due to Theorem 3.4, in this case R is efficiently D^{disc}-enumerable. Further, every relation is trivially efficiently $D^{\text{disc}} \to D$ enumerable.

3.3 Enumerability Criteria

In this section we present conditions for partial enumerability, i.e. conditions which guarantee that some relation is efficiently E-enumerable or efficiently $E_1 \to E_2$-enumerable. We show here that there is a rich class of relations meeting the conditions required in Theorem 3.4. The conditions we give can be verified by looking at a constraint language over a smaller domain, thus giving an inductive criterion. The result for partial E-enumerability is quite easy, but needs special prerequisites, which we define now.

Definition 3.5. *Let R be a relation over D, and E a partition of D. We say that E' is a representation system of E compatible with R, if E' contains exactly one element of each equivalence class in E, and $f^{E'} \circ f^E \colon D \to E' \in \text{Pol}(R)$, where $f^{E'} \colon E \to E'$ is the function assigning each equivalence class its corresponding value in E'.*

This definition can be illustrated at the relation R given in Example 3.2. Recall that R has the polymorphism $f_{2 \to 1}$. This gives a canonical partition of the domain $D = \{0, 1, 2\}$: Let $E := \{\{0\}, \{1, 2\}\}$. Since $f_{2 \to 1}$ is a polymorphism of R, $E' := \{0, 1\}$ is a representation system of E compatible with $R \colon f^{E'} \circ f^E$ is just the function $f_{2 \to 1}$. Note that $f^{E'} \circ f^E$ is the canonical function assigning each $\alpha \in D$ its representative in E'. If this function is a polymorphism, then for each partial E-solution I of an R-formula φ, $f^{E'}(I)$ is a solution of φ. This is used in the proof for the following Theorem:

Theorem 3.6. *Let R be a relation over D, and let E be a partition of D such that there is a representation system of E compatible with R. Then R is efficiently E-enumerable if and only if R/E is efficiently enumerable.*

We showed that $f_{2 \to 1}(R)$ from Example 3.2 is Schaefer. With the above definitions, this is the same relation as R/E. Therefore, R/E has an efficient enumeration algorithm due to [CH97], and since E' is a representation system of E compatible with R, we know that R is efficiently E-enumerable by Theorem 3.6.

The corresponding criterion for $E_1 \to E_2$-enumerability is more technical, but holds without prerequisites: to decide whether a relation R is efficiently $E_1 \to E_2$ enumerable, it suffices to consider a constraint language $\Gamma_R^{E_1 \to E_2}$, which we define now. This is the language Γ mentioned in the proof sketch for Example 3.2, allowing us, for each "Boolean solution" I, to enumerate all solutions J such that $f_{2 \to 1}(J) = I$. The definition is more general: we want to enumerate, for a given partial solution I, all "fitting" E_2-solutions, where E_2 is a refinement of E_1. Remember that in Example 3.2, we were not interested in those parts of the relation which are set to 0, we only wanted to get all possible combinations of 1 and 2. The natural generalization is that we are not interested in classes from E_1 which are not partitioned further in E_2. For partial E_1-solutions I and partial E_2-solutions J compatible with I, and variables x such that $I(x) = D_i \in E_1$, if $D_i \in E_2$, then $J(x) = D_i$ has to hold as well. Therefore, these aspects of the relation R are not interesting when determining possible E_2 solutions compatible with a given E_1 solution. Hence, the corresponding components of the relation R are disregarded in the following definition:

Definition 3.7. *1. Let R be an n-ary relation, and let $I \subseteq \{1, \ldots, n\}$, such that $I = \{i_1, \ldots, i_k\}$. Then $R_I(x_{i_1}, \ldots, x_{i_k})$ is the relation obtained from $R(x_1, \ldots, x_n)$ by existentially quantifying all of the variables x_j such that $j \notin I$, i.e.*

$$R_I(x_{i_1}, \ldots, x_{i_k}) \Leftrightarrow \exists j_1 \ldots \exists j_{n-k} R(x_1, \ldots, x_n),$$

where $\{1, \ldots, n\} \setminus I = \{j_1, \ldots, j_{n-k}\}$.

2. Let R be an n-ary relation over D. Let E_1 and E_2 be partitions of D such that E_2 is a refinement of E_1. For $\mathbf{v} \in E_1^n$, we define

$$\mathbf{v}^{E_1 \to E_2} := \{ \mathbf{t} \in E_2^n \mid \mathbf{t} \text{ compatible with } \mathbf{v}, \text{ there is a } \mathbf{u} \in R \text{ comp. with } \mathbf{t} \},$$

$$I_\mathbf{v} = \{ i \in \{1, \ldots, n\} \mid \mathbf{v}[i] \notin E_2 \}, \qquad R_\mathbf{v}^{E_1 \to E_2} := \mathbf{v}_{I_\mathbf{v}}^{E_1 \to E_2},$$

and finally, let $\Gamma_R^{E_1 \to E_2} := \{ R_\mathbf{v}^{E_1 \to E_2} \mid \mathbf{v} \in E_1^n \}$.

The relation $\mathbf{v}_{I_\mathbf{v}}^{E_1 \to E_2}$ describes sets of solutions compatible with a given partial solution: for a constraint application $R(x_1, \ldots, x_n)$ and a tuple $v \in E_1^n$, the set $\mathbf{v}^{E_1 \to E_2}$ contains the partial solutions $J \colon \{x_1, \ldots, x_n\} \to E_2$ compatible with $\mathbf{v}$. As explained above, in those cases where the equivalence classes from E_2 also appear in E_1, the corresponding values are disregarded by existentially quantifying over the corresponding parts of the relation $\mathbf{v}^{E_1 \to E_2}$. Observe that $\Gamma_R^{E_1 \to E_2}$ is a constraint language over the domain $\{ D_2 \in E_2 \mid D_2 \notin E_1 \}$, i.e. the domain containing those equivalence classes from E_2 which are proper refinements of classes in E_1.

An important case is when $E_2 = D^{\mathrm{disc}}$. Then the relation $R_\mathbf{v}^{E_1 \to E_2}$ describes the possible "real" solutions which are compatible with a given partial E_1 assignment. Here, equivalence classes which only contain one element play a crucial role. Since D^{disc} cannot refine these, elements in such classes "disappear," and hence the language $\Gamma_R^{E_1 \to E_2}$ is over a smaller domain. Therefore we can use our knowledge of the cases with smaller domains to solve the question if an efficient enumeration algorithm exists for $\Gamma_R^{E_1 \to E_2}$.

We take another look at the relation R from Example 3.2, and construct the constraint language $\Gamma_R^{E \to D}$. Remember that $D = \{0, 1, 2\}$, and we chose the partition $E = \{\{0\}, \{1, 2\}\}$. We denote the equivalence class $\{0\}$ with $\overline{0}$, and the class $\{1, 2\}$ with $\overline{1}$. Let $\mathbf{v_1} := (\overline{1}, \overline{0}, \overline{0}, \overline{1})$, $\mathbf{v_2} := (\overline{1}, \overline{0}, \overline{1}, \overline{0})$, $\mathbf{v_3} := (\overline{1}, \overline{1}, \overline{0}, \overline{0})$, $\mathbf{v_4} := (\overline{1}, \overline{0}, \overline{0}, \overline{0})$. Every tuple in R is E-equivalent to one of these four tuples. Therefore, for any $\mathbf{v} \notin \{\mathbf{v_1}, \mathbf{v_2}, \mathbf{v_3}, \mathbf{v_4}\}$, the relation $\mathbf{v}^{E \to D}$ is empty. By definition, the following equations hold:

$$\mathbf{v_1}^{E \to D} = \{(2, 0, 0, 2), (1, 0, 0, 1)\} \qquad R_{\mathbf{v_1}}^{E \to D} = \{(2, 2), (1, 1)\}$$
$$\mathbf{v_2}^{E \to D} = \{(2, 0, 2, 0), (1, 0, 1, 0)\} \qquad R_{\mathbf{v_2}}^{E \to D} = \{(2, 2), (1, 1)\}$$
$$\mathbf{v_3}^{E \to D} = \{(2, 2, 0, 0), (1, 1, 0, 0)\} \qquad R_{\mathbf{v_3}}^{E \to D} = \{(2, 2), (1, 1)\}$$
$$\mathbf{v_4}^{E \to D} = \{(1, 0, 0, 0)\} \qquad\qquad R_{\mathbf{v_4}}^{E \to D} = \{(1)\}$$

Hence $\Gamma_R^{E \to D}$ only contains the relations $\{(2, 2), (1, 1)\}$ and $\{(1)\}$. If we view these as relations over the Boolean domain by e.g. identifying the occurring 2s with the Boolean 0, then this language is closed under the Boolean AND. Therefore, $\Gamma_R^{E \to D}$ is Schaefer, thus this language has an efficient enumeration algorithm. This implies that R is $E \to D$-enumerable: for a relation R it holds that $\Gamma_R^{E_1 \to E_2}$ is enumerable if and only if R is $E_1 \to E_2$ enumerable, as shown by the following Theorem 3.8, which is our main technical result. The characterization it gives can be used, with Theorem 3.4, to prove the existence of efficient enumeration algorithms inductively. The proof relies on the ideas explained in the proof sketch for Example 3.2, and in the discussion above.

Theorem 3.8. *Let R be an n-ary relation over a domain D, and let E_1, E_2 be partitions of D such that E_2 is a refinement of E_1. Then R is efficiently $E_1 \to E_2$-enumerable if and only if $\Gamma_R^{E_1 \to E_2}$ is efficiently enumerable.*

4   Towards a Dichotomy for Three-Element Domains

We obtain a complete classification of the case where all polymorphisms are conservative on some partition $E = \{\{a, b\}, \{c\}\}$, in the three-element case. This is proven using implementation results: for the negative cases, we show that the relation R can "express" some other relation in a way preserving enumerability. Note that this result is not an algebraic characterization in the usual sense, since $\Gamma_R^{E \to D}$ being Schaefer does not only depend on the set of polymorphisms of R. For a set $C \subseteq D$ and a function $f : D^n \to D$, we say that f is *conservative on C* if $\alpha_1, \ldots, \alpha_n \in C$ implies $f(\alpha_1, \ldots, \alpha_n) \in C$.

Theorem 4.1. *Let D be a 3-element domain, let $R \subseteq D^n$, and let there be some partition $E = \{\{a, b\}, \{c\}\}$ of D, such that all polymorphisms of R are conservative on the classes in E.*

- If $f_{a\to b} \notin \mathrm{Pol}(R)$ and $f_{b\to a} \notin \mathrm{Pol}(R)$, then R has an efficient enumeration algorithm if and only if R is tractable.
- Otherwise, R has an efficient enumeration algorithm if and only if $\Gamma_R^{E\to D}$ is Schaefer and R/E is Schaefer (or $\mathrm{P} = \mathrm{NP}$).

The proof uses a "canonical way" to express relations, which only needs a limited number of existentially quantified variables. The key method is to find representations which can "re-use" existential variables, so that when transforming a formula over one constraint language to another, we only need to add a constant number of them. This multiplies the number of satisfying solutions by a constant only, and this implementation can be used for enumeration problems after sorting out a few technical issues.

5   Conclusion and Future Research

We have exhibited new enumeration algorithms for constraint languages, and shown that these cover more cases than previously known from [CH97] and [Coh04]. In [SS06a] we present more algorithms that work for cases not covered by algorithms in this paper. These algorithms can be nested and combined with others by using Theorem 3.4. Moreover for three-element domains we present conditions for non-enumerability besides the conservative case.

We believe that the next step to obtain broader negative results than the ones we have is to apply algebraic methods to the enumeration problem. The application of such methods has been very successful for the complexity classification of the decision problem. In [SS06a], we show that the standard algebraic approach to CSPs does not work with enumeration. In [SS06b], we present a refinement of the usual algebraic methods, which hopefully will lead to further results for the enumeration problem.

Acknowledgment

We thank Nadia Creignou and Heribert Vollmer for very helpful discussions and advice on the presentation of this paper. We also thank the anonymous referees for their suggestions.

References

[ABI⁺05]   E. Allender, M. Bauland, N. Immerman, H. Schnoor, and H. Vollmer. The complexity of satisfiability problems: Refining Schaefer's Theorem. In *Proceedings of the 30th International Symposium on Mathematical Foundations of Computer Science*, pages 71–82, 2005.

[BHRV02]   E. Böhler, E. Hemaspaandra, S. Reith, and H. Vollmer. Equivalence and isomorphism for Boolean constraint satisfaction. In *Computer Science Logic*, volume 2471 of *Lecture Notes in Computer Science*, pages 412–426, Berlin Heidelberg, 2002. Springer Verlag.

[BJK05]   A. Bulatov, P. Jeavons, and A. Krokhin. Classifying the complexity of constraints using finite algebras. *SIAM J. Comput.*, 34(3):720–742, 2005.

[BKJ00]   A. Bulatov, A. Krokhin, and P. Jeavons. Constraint satisfaction problems and finite algebras. In *27th International Colloquium on Automata, Languages and Programming*, pages 272–282, 2000.

[Bul06]   A. Bulatov. A dichotomy theorem for constraint satisfaction problems on a 3-element set. *Journal of the ACM*, 53(1):66–120, 2006.

[CH96]   N. Creignou and M. Hermann. Complexity of generalized satisfiability counting problems. *Information and Computation*, 125:1–12, 1996.

[CH97]   N. Creignou and J.-J. Hébrard. On generating all solutions of generalized satisfiability problems. *Informatique Théorique et Applications/Theoretical Informatics and Applications*, 31(6):499–511, 1997.

[CKS01]   N. Creignou, S. Khanna, and M. Sudan. *Complexity Classifications of Boolean Constraint Satisfaction Problems*. Monographs on Discrete Applied Mathematics. SIAM, 2001.

[Coh04]   D. Cohen. Tractable decision for a constraint language implies tractable search. *Constraints*, 9(3):219–229, 2004.

[Dal05]   V. Dalmau. Generalized majority-minority operations are tractable. In Prakash Panangaden, editor, *Proceedings of the Twentieth Annual IEEE Symp. on Logic in Computer Science, LICS 2005*, pages 438–447. IEEE Computer Society Press, June 2005.

[DK06]   V. Dalmau and A. Krokhin. Majority constraints have bounded pathwidth duality. Technical Report NI06017-LAA, Isaac Newton Institute for Mathematical Sciences, 2006.

[FV98]   T. Feder and M. Y. Vardi. The computational structure of monotone monadis SNP and constraint satisfaction: a study through Datalog and group theory. *SIAM Journal on Computing*, 28(1):57–104, 1998.

[JCG97]   P. Jeavons, D. Cohen, and M. Gyssens. Closure properties of constraints. *Journal of the ACM*, 44(4):527–548, 1997.

[JPY88]   D. Johnson, C. Papadimitriou, and M. Yannakakis. On generating all maximal independent sets. *Inf. Process. Lett.*, 27(3):119–123, 1988.

[RV00]   S. Reith and H. Vollmer. Optimal satisfiability for propositional calculi and constraint satisfaction problems. In *Proceedings of the 25th International Symposium on Mathematical Foundations of Computer Science*, volume 1893 of *Lecture Notes in Computer Science*, pages 640–649. Springer Verlag, 2000.

[Sch78]   T. J. Schaefer. The complexity of satisfiability problems. In *Proceedings 10th Symposium on Theory of Computing*, pages 216–226. ACM Press, 1978.

[SS06a]   H. Schnoor and I. Schnoor. Enumerating all solutions for constraint satisfaction problems. In *Complexity of Constraints*, no. 06401 in Dagstuhl Seminar Proceedings, 2006. <http://drops.dagstuhl.de/opus/volltexte/2006/804>

[SS06b]   H. Schnoor and I. Schnoor. New algebraic tools for constraint satisfaction. In *Complexity of Constraints*, no. 06401 in Dagstuhl Seminar Proceedings, 2006. <http://drops.dagstuhl.de/opus/volltexte/2006/805>

[Val79]   L. G. Valiant. The complexity of enumeration and reliability problems. *SIAM Journal of Computing*, 8(3):411–421, 1979.

Author Index

Lecture Notes in Computer Science

For information about Vols. 1–4291

please contact your bookseller or Springer

Vol. 4340: R. Prodan, T. Fahringer, Grid Computing. XXIII, 317 pages. 2007.

Vol. 4339: E. Ayguadé, G. Baumgartner, J. Ramanujam, P. Sadayappan (Eds.), Languages and Compilers for Parallel Computing. XI, 476 pages. 2006.

Vol. 4338: P. Kalra, S. Peleg (Eds.), Computer Vision, Graphics and Image Processing. XV, 965 pages. 2006.

Vol. 4337: S. Arun-Kumar, N. Garg (Eds.), FSTTCS 2006: Foundations of Software Technology and Theoretical Computer Science. XIII, 430 pages. 2006.

Vol. 4335: S.A. Brueckner, S. Hassas, M. Jelasity, D. Yamins (Eds.), Engineering Self-Organising Systems. XII, 212 pages. 2007. (Sublibrary LNAI).

Vol. 4334: B. Beckert, R. Hähnle, P.H. Schmitt (Eds.), Verification of Object-Oriented Software. XXIX, 658 pages. 2007. (Sublibrary LNAI).

Vol. 4333: U. Reimer, D. Karagiannis (Eds.), Practical Aspects of Knowledge Management. XII, 338 pages. 2006. (Sublibrary LNAI).

Vol. 4332: A. Bagchi, V. Atluri (Eds.), Information Systems Security. XV, 382 pages. 2006.

Vol. 4331: G. Min, B. Di Martino, L.T. Yang, M. Guo, G. Ruenger (Eds.), Frontiers of High Performance Computing and Networking – ISPA 2006 Workshops. XXXVII, 1141 pages. 2006.

Vol. 4330: M. Guo, L.T. Yang, B. Di Martino, H.P. Zima, J. Dongarra, F. Tang (Eds.), Parallel and Distributed Processing and Applications. XVIII, 953 pages. 2006.

Vol. 4329: R. Barua, T. Lange (Eds.), Progress in Cryptology - INDOCRYPT 2006. X, 454 pages. 2006.

Vol. 4328: D. Penkler, M. Reitenspiess, F. Tam (Eds.), Service Availability. X, 289 pages. 2006.

Vol. 4327: M. Baldoni, U. Endriss (Eds.), Declarative Agent Languages and Technologies IV. VIII, 257 pages. 2006. (Sublibrary LNAI).

Vol. 4326: S. Göbel, R. Malkewitz, I. Iurgel (Eds.), Technologies for Interactive Digital Storytelling and Entertainment. X, 384 pages. 2006.

Vol. 4325: J. Cao, I. Stojmenovic, X. Jia, S.K. Das (Eds.), Mobile Ad-hoc and Sensor Networks. XIX, 887 pages. 2006.

Vol. 4323: G. Doherty, A. Blandford (Eds.), Interactive Systems. XI, 269 pages. 2007.

Vol. 4320: R. Gotzhein, R. Reed (Eds.), System Analysis and Modeling: Language Profiles. X, 229 pages. 2006.

Vol. 4319: L.-W. Chang, W.-N. Lie (Eds.), Advances in Image and Video Technology. XXVI, 1347 pages. 2006.

Vol. 4318: H. Lipmaa, M. Yung, D. Lin (Eds.), Information Security and Cryptology. XI, 305 pages. 2006.

Vol. 4317: S.K. Madria, K.T. Claypool, R. Kannan, P. Uppuluri, M.M. Gore (Eds.), Distributed Computing and Internet Technology. XIX, 466 pages. 2006.

Vol. 4316: M.M. Dalkilic, S. Kim, J. Yang (Eds.), Data Mining and Bioinformatics. VIII, 197 pages. 2006. (Sublibrary LNBI).

Vol. 4314: C. Freksa, M. Kohlhase, K. Schill (Eds.), KI 2006: Advances in Artificial Intelligence. XII, 458 pages. 2007. (Sublibrary LNAI).

Vol. 4313: T. Margaria, B. Steffen (Eds.), Leveraging Applications of Formal Methods. IX, 197 pages. 2006.

Vol. 4312: S. Sugimoto, J. Hunter, A. Rauber, A. Morishima (Eds.), Digital Libraries: Achievements, Challenges and Opportunities. XVIII, 571 pages. 2006.

Vol. 4311: K. Cho, P. Jacquet (Eds.), Technologies for Advanced Heterogeneous Networks II. XI, 253 pages. 2006.

Vol. 4309: P. Inverardi, M. Jazayeri (Eds.), Software Engineering Education in the Modern Age. VIII, 207 pages. 2006.

Vol. 4308: S. Chaudhuri, S.R. Das, H.S. Paul, S. Tirthapura (Eds.), Distributed Computing and Networking. XIX, 608 pages. 2006.

Vol. 4307: P. Ning, S. Qing, N. Li (Eds.), Information and Communications Security. XIV, 558 pages. 2006.

Vol. 4306: Y. Avrithis, Y. Kompatsiaris, S. Staab, N.E. O'Connor (Eds.), Semantic Multimedia. XII, 241 pages. 2006.

Vol. 4305: A.A. Shvartsman (Ed.), Principles of Distributed Systems. XIII, 441 pages. 2006.

Vol. 4304: A. Sattar, B.-H. Kang (Eds.), AI 2006: Advances in Artificial Intelligence. XXVII, 1303 pages. 2006. (Sublibrary LNAI).

Vol. 4303: A. Hoffmann, B.-H. Kang, D. Richards, S. Tsumoto (Eds.), Advances in Knowledge Acquisition and Management. XI, 259 pages. 2006. (Sublibrary LNAI).

Vol. 4302: J. Domingo-Ferrer, L. Franconi (Eds.), Privacy in Statistical Databases. XI, 383 pages. 2006.

Vol. 4301: D. Pointcheval, Y. Mu, K. Chen (Eds.), Cryptology and Network Security. XIII, 381 pages. 2006.

Vol. 4300: Y.Q. Shi (Ed.), Transactions on Data Hiding and Multimedia Security I. IX, 139 pages. 2006.

Vol. 4299: S. Renals, S. Bengio, J.G. Fiscus (Eds.), Machine Learning for Multimodal Interaction. XII, 470 pages. 2006.

Vol. 4297: Y. Robert, M. Parashar, R. Badrinath, V.K. Prasanna (Eds.), High Performance Computing - HiPC 2006. XXIV, 642 pages. 2006.

Vol. 4296: M.S. Rhee, B. Lee (Eds.), Information Security and Cryptology – ICISC 2006. XIII, 358 pages. 2006.

Vol. 4295: J.D. Carswell, T. Tezuka (Eds.), Web and Wireless Geographical Information Systems. XI, 269 pages. 2006.

Vol. 4294: A. Dan, W. Lamersdorf (Eds.), Service-Oriented Computing – ICSOC 2006. XIX, 653 pages. 2006.

Vol. 4293: A. Gelbukh, C.A. Reyes-Garcia (Eds.), MICAI 2006: Advances in Artificial Intelligence. XXVIII, 1232 pages. 2006. (Sublibrary LNAI).

Vol. 4292: G. Bebis, R. Boyle, B. Parvin, D. Koracin, P. Remagnino, A. Nefian, G. Meenakshisundaram, V. Pascucci, J. Zara, J. Molineros, H. Theisel, T. Malzbender (Eds.), Advances in Visual Computing, Part II. XXXII, 906 pages. 2006.